THE

MUSLIM LAW OF DIVORCE

THE
Muslim Law of Divorce

BY

K. N. AHMED

WITH A FOREWORD BY

Mr. Justice, S. Anwar-ul-Haq

KITAB BHAVAN
New Delhi-110002

Kitab Bhavan
Publishers, Distributors, Exporters & Importers
1784, Kalan Mahal, Darya Ganj
New Delhi - 1100 02 [India]

Phone : (91-11) 23277392 / 93, 23274686, 30906494
Mobile : (91-11) 9910114484
website : www.kitabbhavan.com
Email : nasri@vsnl.com, nusrat@bol.net.in
Fax : (91-11) 23263383

Ist Edition 1978
3rd Edition 2006

ISBN : 81-7151-058-2
Book Code No. : M00061

Published in India by :
Nusrat Ali Nasri for Kitab Bhavan
1784, Kalan Mahal, Darya Ganj
New Delhi - 1100 02 [India]

Printed in India at :
Nice Printing Press
Khureji Khas, Delhi-110051

FOREWORD

The institution of marriage is the foundation of all civilized communities and it is. therefore, only but natural that considerable attention has been paid by all religions and systems of law to the principles and rules regulating the contract of marriage and its dissolution. Although a Muslim marriage is essentially a matter of contract, creating rights and obligations for the parties, yet it is considered to be a virtuous act being commended by religion. Thus a Muslim marriage partakes of the nature of both a sacrament and a civil contract. There is considerable divergence of opinion, in several matters touching marriage and its dissolution, between the Shia and the Sunni doctrines and between the various schools of the Sunni sect itself. Mr. K. N. Ahmed has taken great pains in bringing out the rules applicable to each of these schools of thought. He has drawn extensively upon basic authorities and texts of Muhammadan Law, thus enriching this treatise and enhancing its value and interest to all those concerned with the subject.

This book is perhaps the first comprehensive compilation of Muslim Law on the dissolution of marriage to be published in Pakistan. Mr. Ahmed's style is simple and clear. His approach is analytical, and the comparative study of the different systems of law has been undertaken without bias and any preconceived notions. There is no attempt to show one system as being superior to the others. Such objectivity in presentation of this difficult subject is indeed commendable.

Mr. Ahmed's treatment of the effect of conversion of the husband or wife on a Muslim marriage, and his discussion of the conflict of laws in this behalf, will be found to be of particular interest by students of law, lawyers and judges alike. The subject is, of course, stimulating and offers a vast field of study, having international ramifications. Mr. Ahmed has dealt exhaustively with the subject in the light of original

Muslim texts as well as leading judgments of the Superior Courts of a number of countries. The changes introduced by the Dissolution of Muslim Marriages Act, 1939, have also been appropriately noticed.

The development of Muslim Law has considerably suffered in the past owing to a rigid adoption of the doctrine of Taqlid. There is no doubt that the views of the earlier Imams and Jurists are entitled to the utmost respect, and no Court or Commentator will differ from them, except for very compelling or sound reasons, nor can the difference of interpretation mean a departure from a clear injunction of law as contained in the Qur'an or Sunnah, or even Ijma, on any grounds of equity, good conscience or public policy. But the right to understand and interpret the law in the context of the present-day conditions must be recognised and conceded, if the dynamic and universal character of the religion and laws of Islam is to be preserved. I am confident that Mr. Ahmed's book will be found extremely useful for the purpose of promoting an intelligent understanding of Muslim law relating to dissolution of marriage. It is bound to prove indispensable for the legal profession.

S. ANWARUL HAQ
Chief Justice, High Court of Lahore

Lahore,
November 13, 1971

PREFACE

There are several valuable and authentic books on Muslim Law available to us and books by authorities like Ameer Ali and Sir Abdur Rahim command the same respect now as they did nearly a century ago. Many other useful books on Muslim Law have been written by such eminent writers as Tyebji, Nawab Abdur Rahman, Sircar, Wilson, Macnaghten, Saksena and others. These books had been written when India was governed by the English and we were subject to English Law. No doubt, the Muslims were governed by the Muslim Law but even then encroachment was made in the personal laws like those of marriage, divorce etc. Moreover, the English Law used to be applied where so enacted, or where there was a conflict between it and the Muslim Law, while the Anglo-Indian Courts were greatly influenced by the English Law. The result is that the Anglo-Muslim Law differs in several important respects from the Muslim Law, as has been pointed out in the book at relevant places. Another draw-back was that those books covered the entire field of Muslim personal law in one or two volumes with the result that no single aspect of Muslim Law could be given exhaustive treat-ment. Still another difficulty was sometimes felt by the fact that these books dealt with only the Hanafi Law and to some small extent with the Shiah Law. The laws of the other schools of the Sunnis were practically ignored because these books were mainly meant for India, the vast majority of the population of which consists of the Hanafis. The Hanafi Law allows the adoption of the law of another Sunni sect whenever the rigid adoption of Hanafi rule involves hardship to its followers. Unfortunately, this very important principle was either not noticed or was ignored by the Anglo-Indian Courts. Great need has, therefore, been felt for a book overcoming these difficulties.

In this book I have discussed at length in the chapter on Conversion, the conflict between the Muslim, the Hindu and the English laws and the law in force in the U.S.A. It was not possible for me to give the entire Maliki, Shafi'i, Hanbali and Shiah Laws in the book. It would have involved unnecessary repetitions and would have made the book unwieldy and difficult to refer to. I have, therefore, confined myself to discussing the Hanafi Law at length and to giving the laws of the other sects where they differed with the Hanafi law.

I have given and discussed the case-law on various aspects of the law of divorce, but I have not hesitated to differ with the views taken therein where some important provisions of the Muslim Law have been overlooked. All subjects have been discussed exhaustively, and I have relied in my discussion on authoritative books on Muslim Law. I have also endeavoured to give and discuss the basic ideas underlying the rules laid down by the Imams and other Muslim Jurists. The book will not be found to be lacking in authority on these aspects.

The Muslim writers have followed the same order of treatment in their books throughout the ages as was adopted in the second year of the Hijrah. It is rather arbitrary and not very convenient to readers. In this book I have adopted my own order of treatment and it is hoped that it will be found to be more methodical and convenient.

In the end I must confess that the many handicaps under which I worked and wrote this book and which are usually experienced in most developing countries have not allowed me to write the book as I really wanted to. I only hope that the indulgent reader will tolerate any defects that may be found in the work and that future writers will find it helpful as a stepping-stone.

It may be added that different law journals and books have given different spelling of names. In case of difficulty it will be useful to have recourse to the Index of Cases.

Before concluding the Preface, I must fulfil the pleasant task of expressing my gratitude to some persons who rendered me great help in writing the book. I am thankful to Mufti Amjad Ali Sahib for his selfless and kind assistance. I would have experienced great difficulty in writing the book in the absence of the same. I am especially grateful to Mr. Khalid M. Ishaque, former Advocate-General of West Pakistan, for his ready and unstinted help and encouragement. He read through many chapters of the manuscript and offered valuable advice on several points. He also put his entire library including a collection of rare books on Oriental and foreign laws, at my disposal, and helped me similarly in a number of other ways. In short, Mr. Khalid M. Ishaque's kindness and generosity have been unlimited and I owe a heavy debt of gratitude to him. I must also thank Dr. Fazlur Rahman, former Director, Islamic Research Institute, for his great encouragement to me and the keen interest he took in the book. Dr. Ahmad Hasan also deserves my thanks for his valuable help in proof-reading, checking references etc. and for completing the index of Arabic, Persian and Urdu books. My thanks are also due to Hakim Mohammed Said, S.I. for his kind cooperation in connection with the chapter on Defects in Spouses. I must express my thanks to Aqa Mohammad Shaikh Shariat for his guidance on various Shi'i problems. Lastly, I must express my gratitude to my wife, Masuda Khatun, and my daughters, Miss Rehana Ahmed and Miss Fauzia Ahmed, for their painstaking help and encouragement. They read the greater portion of the book and made many useful suggestions.

My thanks are due to the following for their assistance: Dr. Miss Mahmooda Said, Dr. Mrs. Sadika Naeem A. Jafery, Maulana Abu Talib Jauhary; Mr. A. A. Zuberi, Secretary, Islamic Research Institute; and Khwaja Salamuddin of Ripon Press, Lahore.

Karachi
January, 1972

K. N. AHMED

NOTE ON TRANSLITERATION

The system of transliteration of Arabic words adopted in this series is the same as has been employed by the editors of the Encyclopaedia of Islam, new edition, with the following exceptions : q has been used for k and j for dj, as these are more convenient to follow for English-knowing readers than the international signs. The use of ch, dh, gh, kh, sh, th, and zh with a subscript dash, although it may appear pedantic, has been considered necessary for the sake of accuracy and clearer pronunciation of letters peculiar to Arabic and Persian. As against the Encyclopaedia, tā marbūṭah has throughout been retained and shown by the ending h or t, as the case may be. This was also found necessary in order to avoid any confusion. In words of Persian origin the retention of the final h is essential as it stands for hā-yi mukhtafī, which should not be dispensed with.

References in the text to Qur'ānic verses are from the English translation of the Qur'ān by Maulana Muhammad Ali Lahore.

ACKNOWLEDGEMENTS

I desire to express my thanks to the following publishers of books and law journals for their kind permission to quote from their works :—

BOOKS

1.	The Ahmadiyya Anjuman, Isha'at-i-Islam, Lahore	English translation of Quran by Maulana Mohammad Ali.
2.	The Bobbs Merrill, Indianapolis.	1. Keezer on Marriage and Divorce. 2. Harper, Problems of the Family.
3.	Champman and Hall Ltd., London,	Morals in Evolution by L. T. Hobhouse.
4.	The Calarendon Press, Oxford.	Private International Law: G. C. Cheshire.
5.	Ernest Benn Ltd. London	The Mischief of Marriage, J. T. W. Baden Worsley.
6.	Methuen & Co. Ltd., London.	Divorce & Its Problems. E. S. P. Haynes and D. Walker Smith.
7.	Woking Muslim Mission, London.	Mishkat-al-Masabih, English Translation by Al-Haj Maulana Fazal al-Karim.
8.	William Heineman, London	Ideal Marriage, Van. de Velde

LAW JOURNALS

1.	All England Law Reports, London.	The All-England Law Reports.
	Pakistan Law Decision, Lahore.	The Pakistan Law Decisions.
2.	The Canadian Bar Association, Otawa, Canada.	The Canadian Bar Review.
3.	The Incorporated Council of Law Reporting for England, London.	Law Reports
4.	Stevens Sons Ltd., London.	The Law Quarterly Review.

(1) W. E. Beckett : The Recognition of Polygamous Marriages under English Law.

(2) E. J. Cohn, The Nullity of Marriage.

(3) G. C. Cheshire, Nullity jurisdiction and Remarriage during voidable Marriage.

(4) Prof. J. D. Huges, Judicious method and the problem in Ogden vs. Ogden.

(5) H. C. Morris, Nullity of Marriage.

(6) M. Schmithoff, Validity of Marriage and the Conflict of Laws.

(7) Nullity Jurisdiction and Marriage (Notes).

5.	W. Green and Sons Ltd. Edinburough, Scotland.	Scots Law Times.

6. Many other Law Journals have also been consulted in the preparation of this book and this is gratefully acknowledged.

TABLE OF STATUTES

ABBREVIATIONS

A.C. preceded by date e.g., (1900) A.C.	Law Reports, Appeal Cases, House of Lords. since 1890 (Eng.).
Add.	Adams Ecclesiastical Reports, 3 vols. 1822-1826 (Eng.).
Agra H.C.R.	Agra High Court Reports (India).
A.I.R. Preceded by the number of year, name of H.C. and followed by the number of page. Thus A.I.R. 1950 Lah. 236. The High Courts referred are : Allahabad (All.) ; Bombay (Bom.); Calcutta (Cal.), Lahore (Lah.); Madras (Mad.); Nagpur (Nag.); Oudh; Patna (Pat.); Peshawar (Pesh.); Rangoon (Rang.); Sind.	All India Reporter.
Ala.	Alabama Reports (U.S.A.).
Alaska.	Alaska Reports (U.S.A.).
A.L.J.	Allahabad Law Journal (India).
All.	Indian Law Reports, Allahabad.
A.L.R.	Annotated Law Reports series (Eng.).
All. E.R.	All England Law Reports, Since 1936 (Eng.).
Am. Dec.	American Decisions (U.S.A.).
Am. Rep.	American Reports (U.S.A.).
Am. St.	American State Reports (U.S.A.).
App. Cas.	Law Reports, Appeal Cases, House of Lords, 15 vols., 1875-1890 (Eng.).
App. Div.	South Africa Reports, Appellate Division.
Ariz.	Arizona (U.S.A.).
Arks.	Arkinsas Reports (U.S.A.).
Atl.	Atlantic Reporter (U.S.A.).
A.W.R.	Allahabad Weekly Reporter.
B. Mon.	B. Monroe's Reports (Kentucky).
Beng. L.R.	Bengal Law Reports (India).
Bom. H.C.R.	Bombay High Court Reports, 12 vols. 1861-1875 (India).
Bom. L.R.	Bombay Law Reports (India).

Bom. L.J.	Bombay Law Journal (India).
Bur. L.J.	Burma Law Journal (Burma).
Bur. L.T.	Burma Law Times (Burma).
Cal.	California Reports (U.S.A.).
Cal. App.	California Appellate Reports (U.S.A.).
Can B.R.	Canadian Bar Review (Canada).
Car.	Carolina Reports (U.S.A.).
Ch. preceded by date.	Law Reports, Chancery Division, since 1890.
Ch. App.	Law Reports, Chancery Appeals 10 vols., 1865-1875 (England).
Ch.D.	Law Reports, Chancery Division 45 vols., 1875-1890 (England).
Cl. & Fin.	Clark & Finnelly's Reports, House of Lords, 12 vols., 1831-1846 (England).
C.L.J.	Calcutta Law Journal (Indian).
C.L.R.	Calcutta Law Reporter (Indian).
Colo.	Colorado Reports (U.S.A.).
Conn.	Connecticut Reports (U.S.A.).
Cr. L.J.	Criminal Law Journal.
Curt.	Curtei's Ecclesiastical Reports, 3 vols. 1834-1844 (England).
C.W.N.	Calcutta Weekly Notes (India).
D.L.R.	Dacca Law Reports (Pakistan).
Dec. (Deccan) L.R.	Deccan Law Reports, Hyderabad Deccan.
Drew.	Drewry's Reports, Chancery, 4 vols. 1852-1859 (Eng.).
E.A.L. Reports	East Africa Law Reports.
Ecc. & Ad.	Spink's Ecclesiastical and Admiralty Reports, 2 vols. 1853-1855.
Ga.	Georgia Reports (U.S.A.).
Hag. Con.	Haggards Consistorial Reports, 2 vols., 1789-1821 (England).
Hag. Ecc.	Haggards Ecclesiastical Reports, 4 vols. 1827-1833 (England).
H.L.Cas.	Clark's Reports, House of Lords, 11 vols., 1847-1866. (England).
I.A.	Law Reports, Indian Appeals Privy Council, 1873.
I.C.	Indian Cases.
Ill.	Illinois Reports (U.S.A.).
Ill. App.	Illinois Appellate Reports (U.S.A.).
I.L.R.	Indian Law Reports.
Ind.	Indiana Reports.

Ind. App.	Indiana Appeals Reports.
Iowa.	Iowa Reports (U.S.A.).
J.P.	Justice of the Peace, since 1837 (Eng.).
Jur.	Jurist Reports, 18 vols. 1837-1854 (Eng.).
Kans.	Kansas Reports (U.S.A.).
K. B : preceded by date and number of vol. follwed by page, e.g. 1905 2 KB 3.	Law Reports, King's Bench Division, 1900-1952-53 vols.
Kyi	Kentucky Reports (U.S.A.).
Ky.L.	Kentucky Law Reports, U.S.A.
L. (Lah).	Law Reports, Lahore Series (Pakistan).
L.B.R.	Lower Burma Rulings.
L.J. (Ch)	Law Journal, Chancery 1831-1946 (Eng.).
L.J. (o.s.)	Law Journal, Old Series, 10 vols. 1823-1831 (Eng.).
L.J.P.	Law Journal, Probate, Divorce and Admiralty, 1875-1946. (Eng.).
L.J. (P.C.).	Law Journal, Privy Council, 1865-1946 (Eng.).
L.J. (P. & M).	Law Journal, Probate and Matrimonial Cases. 1858-1859; 1866-1875 (Eng.).
L.J. (P. M. & A.)	Law Journal Probate, Matrimonial and Admiralty. 1860-1865 (Eng.).
L.J. Q.B. or K.B.	Law Journal, Queens' Bench, or Kings Bench 1822-1946 (Eng.).
L.L.J. preceded by date	Lahore Law Journal (Pakistan).
L.J.R preceded by date.	Law Journal Reports, 1947-1949 (Eng.).
L.Q.R.	Law Quarterly Review (Eng.).
L.R.A	Lawyer's Reports, Annotated. (Eng.).
L.R.A.C.	Law Reports. Appeal Cases (Eng).
L.R. Ch.D.	Law Reporter, Chancery Division (Eng.).
L.R.H.L.	Law Reports, English and Irish Appeals and Peerage Claims, House of Lords, 7 vols. 1866-1875 (Eng.).
L.R.(K.B.) .	Law Reports, Kings Bench, 10 vols., 1865-1875 (Eng.).
L.R.P.C.	Law Reports, Privy Council, 6 vols., 1865-1875 (Eng.).
L.R.P. &. D.	Law Reports, Probate and Divorce, 3 vols., 1865-1875 (Eng.).
L.R. (Q.B.).	Law Reports, Queens' Bench, 10 vols., 1865-1875 (Eng.).

L.R. (Sc. & Div.).	Law Reports, Scotch and Divorce Appeals, House of Lords, 2 vols. 1866-1875 (Eng.).
L.T.	Law Times Reports, 1859-1947 (Eng.).
Lucknow.	Indian Law Reports, Lucknow series.
M. (Mad).	Indian Law Reports, Madras Series. All India Reporter, Madras Series.
Mass.	Massachusetts Reports (U.S.A.).
Md.	Maryland Reports (U.S.A.).
M.H.C.R.	Madras High Court Reports.
M.I.A.	Moore's Indian Appeal Cases, Privy Council, 15 vols. 1836-1863.
Mich.	Michigan Reports (U.S.A.).
Minn.	Mineсotta Reports (U.S.A.).
Misc.	Miscellaneous Reports (U.S.A.) (N. Y.)
M.L.J	Madras Law Journal (India).
M.L.T.	Madras Law Times (India).
M.L.W.	Madras Law Weekly (India).
M.O.App.	Missourie Appeal Reports U.S.A.
Mont.	Montana Reports U.S.A.
M.W.N.	Madras Weekly Notes.
Nag.	India Law Report, Nagpur.
Nag.L.J.	Nagpur Law Journal (India).
Nag.L.R.	Nagpur Law Reporter (India).
N.Car.	North Carolina Reports (U.S.A.).
N.Dak.	North Dakota Reports (U.S.A.).
N.E.	North Eastern Reports (U.S.A.).
N.H.	New Hampshire Reports (U.S.A.).
N. L. J.	Nagpur Law Journal.
N.Mex.	New Mexico Reports (U.S.A.).
N.W.	North Western Reports (U.S.A.)
N.Y.	New York Reports (U.S.A.).
N.Y.S.	New York Supplement (U.S.A.).
O. C.	Oudh Cases (India).
Okla.	Okla Reports.
O.L.J.	Oudh Law Journal (India).
Ore.	Oregone Reports (U.S.A.)
Oudh.	All India Reporter, Oudh Series.
O.W.N.	Oudh Weekly Notes (India).
Preceded by date.	Law Reports, Propbate, Divorce and Admiralty Division, since, 1890 (Eng.).
Pa.	Pensylvania Reports (U.S.A.).
Pa.Sup.Ct.	Pennsylvania Supreme Court Reports (U.S.A.).
Paige.	Paige Chancery (N.Y.) (U.S.A.).

Pat.	Indian Law Reports, Patna Series.
Pat.L.J.	Patna Law Journal (India).
Pat.L.R.	Patna Law Reporter (India).
Pat. L.T.	Patna Law Times (India).
P.D.	Law Reports, Probate, Divorce and Admiralty Division, 15 vols., 1875-1890
Pak. Case.	Pakistan Cases (Pakistan).
Phila.	Philadelphia Reports, U.S.A.
P.L.D.	Pakistan Law Decisions (Pakistan).
P.L.R.	Punjab Law Reporter (Pakistan).
P.R.	Punjab Record (Pakistan).
P.W.R.	Punjab Weekly Reporter (Pakistan).
Pesh. L.J.	Peshawar Law Journal (Pakistan).
Q.B.	Queens Bench Reports. (Eng.) Adolphus and Ellis, New Series, 18 vols. 1841-1852 (Eng.).
Q.B.D.	Law Reports Queen's Bench Division, 25 vols., 1875-1890 (Eng.).
Rangoon.	Indian Law Reports, Rangoon Series.
Rob.Eccl.	Robertson's Ecclesiastical Reports, 2 vols., 1844-1853 (Eng.).
R.R.	Revised Reports (Eng.).
Russ.	Russel's Reports Chancery, 5 vols., 1824-1829 (Eng.).
S.Car.	South Carolina Reports (U.S.A.).
S.E.	South Eastern Reports (U.S.A.).
Sind.	All India Reporter, Sind Series.
S.L.R.	Sind Law Reporter.
S.L.T.	Scot's Law Times, since 1893 (Scotland).
So.	Southern Reporter (U.S.A.).
Sol.Jo.	Solicitors Journal, since 1856 (Eng.).
Stark.	Starkie's Reports, Nisi Prius, 3 vols., 1814-1823 (Eng.).
Sup.Ct.	Supreme Court Law Reports.
S.W.	South West Reports.[(U.S.A.)
S.W.R.	Sutherlands Weekly Reporter, 25 vols., 1864-1876 (Eng).
Sw. and Tr.	Swabey and Tristrams Reports, Probate and Divorce, 4 vols., 1858-1865 (Eng.).
Tex.	Texas Reports (U.S.A.).
T.L.R.	The Times Law Reports, 1884-1952 (Eng)..
U.B.R.	Upper Burma Rulings.
U.S.	United States Reports (U.S.A.).
Utah.	Utah Reports (U.S.A.).

Ves.	Vessey Jun's Reports, Chancery, 19 vols. 1789-1817 (Eng).
Wash.	Washington State Reports, U.S.A.
Win.	Winch's Reports, Common Pleas Fol. I, vol. 1621 1625 (Eng.).
Wis.	Wisconsin Reports (U.S.A.).
W.L.R.	Western Law Reports (U.S.A.).
W.R.	Weekly Reporter (Sutherlands) 54 vols., 1852-1906 (Eng.).

REFERENCES

I.—ARABIC, PERSIAN AND URDU SOURCES

'Abd al-'Alī al-Birjandī, See al-Birjandī.
'Abd al-Ḥayy, *Majmū' al-Fatāwā*, Lucknow, n. d.
'Ābid Ḥusayn, *al-Jāmi' al-'Abbāsī*, (Urdu tr.) Delhi, 1305 A.H.
Abū Ja'far Muḥammad b. al-Ḥasan, See al-Ṭūsī.
Abū Bakr al-Bakrī *I'ānat al-Ṭālibīn*, Cairo, 1938.
Abū Bakr al-Jaṣṣaṣ, *Aḥkām al-Qur'ān*, Constantinople, 1335 A.H.
Abu'l-Ḥasan al-Mūsawī, *Wasīlat al-Najāt*, Najaf, 1364 A H.
Abū Dā'ūd, *Sunan*, Kanpur, n. d.
Aḥmad b. Ḥanbal, *Musnad*, Cairo, 1313 A.H.
Akmal al-Dīn, *al-'Ināyah 'ala'l-Hidāyah* (on the margin of *al-Fath al-Qadir*), Cairo, 1356 A.H.
'Alā al-Dīn Abu'l-Ḥasan, *Mu'īn al-Ḥukkām*, Cairo, 1300 A.H.
'Alī al-Muttaqī, *Kanz al-'Ummal*, Hyderabad, Deccan, 1313 A.H.
Amīr 'Alī, *Tafsīr Mawāhib al-Raḥmān*, Lucknow, 1926.
Anwar Shāh, *Hindūstān āwr Dār al-Ḥarb*, Monghyr, 1382, A.H.
Ashraf 'Alī Thānawī, *Bayān al-Qur'ān*. Delhi, n. d.
Ashraf 'Alī Thānawī, *al-Ḥīlat al-Nājizah*, Karachi, 1955.
Al-Awzjandī, See Qāḍī Khān.
Al-'Aynī, Badr al-Dīn, *'Umdat al-Qārī*, Damuscus, n. d.
Al-Bayhaqi, *al-Sunan al-Kubrā*, Hyderabad, Deccan, 1353 A H.
Al-Bukhārī, *al-Jāmi' al-Ṣaḥīḥ*, Delhi, 1938.
Burhān al-Dīn, See al-Marghīnānī.
Burhān (Urdu monthly), Delhi, July, August, September 1966.
Al-Birjandī, *Sharḥ al-Wiqāyah*, Lucknow, 1301 A.H.
Al-Fatāwā al-Hindiyah, Kanpur, 1349 A.H.
Fatāwā 'Ālamgīrī, (Urdu tr. by Syed Amīr 'Alī), Lucknow, 1899.
Al-Ghazālī, *al-Wajīz*, Cairo, 1317 A.H.
Al-Ghazālī, *Iḥyā 'Ulūm al-Dīn*, Cairo, 1358.
Al-Ḥaṣkafī, *al-Durr al-Mukhtār*, Cairo, 1318 A.H.
Al-Ḥillī, See Ja'far b. al-Ḥasan.
Ibn 'Ābidīn al-Shāmī. *Radd al-Muḥtār*, Cairo, 1318 A.H.
Ibn al-'Arabī, *Aḥkām al-Qur'ān*, Cairo, 1957.
Ibn Ḥajar al-'Asqalānī, *al-Dirāyah* (published on the margin of *al-Hidāyah*)
Ibn Ḥajar al-'Asqalānī, *Fatḥ al-Bārī*, Cairo, 1325 A.H.

Ibn Ḥazm, *al-Muḥallā*, Cairo, n. d.
Ibn al-Humām, *Fatḥ al-Qādir*, Cairo, 1356 A.H.
Ibn Mājah, *Sunan*, Lucknow, 1315 A H.
Ibn Nujaym, *al-Baḥr al-Rā'iq*, Cairo, 1311 A.H.
Ibn Nujaym, *Al-Ashbāh wa'l Naẓā'ir*, Cairo, 1322 A.H.
Ibn Qayyim, *Aḥkām ahl al-Zimmah*, Cairo, n. d.
Ibn Qayyim, *Zād al-Ma'ād*, Cairo, 1369 A.H.
Ibn Qudāmah, *al-Mughnī*, Cairo, 1307 A.H.
Ibn Rushd, *Bidāyat al-Mujtahid*, Cairo, n. d.
Ibn Rushd, *Bidāyat al-Mujtahid*, (Urdu tr.), Rabwah, 1958.
Ibn Taymiyah, *Fatāwa Ibn Taymiyah*, Cairo, 1328 A.H.
Al-Iṣfahānī, Muḥammad Ḥasan, *Kashf al-Lithām*, Tehran, n. d.
Ja'far b. al-Ḥasan al-Ḥillī, *Sharā'i' al-Islām*, Tehran, 1377 A.H.
Al-Jazīrī, Abd Raḥmān, *al-Fiqh. 'ala'l-madhāhib al-arba'ah*, Cairo, n. d.
Al-Kasānī, 'Alā' al-Dīn, *Badā'i' al-Ṣanā'i'*, Cairo, 1324 A H.
Khalīl b. Isḥāq, *Mukhtaṣar*, Paris, 1318 A.H.
Khurram 'Alī, *Ghāyat al-Awṭār*, Lucknow, 1925.
Al-Khawārizmī, *al-Kifāyah*, (on the margin of *al-Hidāyah*) Delhi, n. d.
Makhdūm Muḥammad Ja'far, *al-Matūnah*, Karachi, 1962.
Mālik, *al-Muwaṭṭa*, Cairo, 1951.
Manāẓir Aḥsan Gīlānī, *Ḥaḍrat Abū Ḥanīfah kī Siyāsī Zindagī*, Karachi, 1966.
Al-Maqdisi, *al-Iqnā'*, Cairo, n. d.
Al-Maqdisī, 'Abd al-Rahmān, *al-Uddah*, Cairo, 1382 A.H.
Al-Marghīnānī, 'Alī b. Alī Bakr, *al-Hidāyah*, Delhi, n. d.
Al-Mardāwī, *al-Insāfs*, Cairo, n. d.
Mawdūdī, Abū'l-A'lā, *Ḥuqūq al-Zawjayn*, Lahore, 1961.
Mawdūdī, Abu'l-A'lā, *Rasā'il wa Masā'il*, Lahore, n. d.
Mīr Syed Alī, *Tawḍiḥ al-Msā'il*, Najaf, 1382 A.H.
Muḥammad al-Ālūsī, *Rūḥ al-Ma'ānī*, Cairo, n. d.
Muḥammad b. Abi'l-'Abbās, See al-Ramlī.
Muḥammad Abū'l-Sa'īd, *Fatḥ Allah al-Mu'īn*, Cairo, 1287 A.H.
Muḥammad b. 'Abd al-Raḥmān, *Raḥmat al-Ummah fi ikhtilāf al-a'immah*, Cairo, 1300 A.H.
Muḥammad b. Aḥmad, *Jawāhir al-'Uqūd*, Cairo, 1355 A.H.
Muḥsin al-Ḥakīm, *Muntakhab al-Rasā'il*, Najaf, 1380 A.H.
Mullā Khusraw, See Munlā Khusraw.
Munlā Khusraw, *Durar al-Ḥukkām*, Canstantinople, 1329 A.H.
Al-Nasa'ī, *Sunan*, Delhi, 1335 A.H.
Al-Nasafi, *Kanz al-Daqā'iq*, Deoband, 1368 A.H.
Al-Nawawī, *'Minhāj al-Ṭalibīn*, (Eng. tr. by Van den Berg.), London, 1914.
Qāḍī Khān al-Awzjandī, *Fatāwā Qāḍī Khān*, Kanpur, 1310 A.H.
Qawm (daily newspaper) 24 March 1919.
Qur'ān

Al-Ramlī, *Nihāyat al-Muḥtāj*, Cairo, 1357 A H.

Al-Rāzī, Fakhr al-Dīn, *Mafatīḥ al-Ghayb*, Cairo, 1308 A.H.

Rūḥ Allah al-Mūsawī, Mukhtaṣar, *Tawḍiḥ al-Ma'sāil*, Najaf, 1390 A.H.

Saḥnūn b. Sa'īd, *al-Mudawwant al-Kuhrā*, Cairo, 1323 A.H.

Al-Sarakhsī, *al-Mabsūṭ*, Cairo, 1324 A.H.

Al-Shāf'ī, *Kitāb al-Umm*, Cairo, 1325 A.H.

Shāh 'Abd al-'Azīz, *Fatāwā 'Azīziyah*, Hyderabad, Deccan, 1313 A.H.

Shāh Walī Allah, *Fiqh 'Umar* (Urdu tr.), Lahore, 1952.

Shaltūt, Tanzim Nasl (Urdu tr.), *Fikr-wa-Nazar*, July, August, 1963.

Shaykhzādah, 'Abd al-Raḥmān b. Muḥammad, *Majma' al-Anhur*, Constantinople, 1327 A H.

Al-Sha'rānī, *al-Mīzān al-Kubrā*, Cairo, 1279 A H.

Al-Shaykh al-Ṣadūq, *man lā Yaḥḍurah al-Faqīh*, Tehran, n. d.

Shiblī Nu'mānī, *Sīrat al-Nabī*, Azamgarh, n. d.

Shiblī Nu'mānī, *al-Fārūq*, Azamgarh, 1892.

Al-Shīrāzī, *al-Muhadhdhab*, Cairo, 1296 A H.

Al-Suyūṭī, *al-Durr al-Manthūr*, Baghdad, 1377 A.H.

Syed Muḥammad Sadiq, *Rawā'i' al-Aḥkām* (Urdu tr. of *Sharā'i' al-Islām*), Hyderabad, 1897.

Syed Husayn Brujardī, *al-Badr al-Ẓāhir fī Ṣalāt al-Jumu'ah wa'l-Musāfir*, Qumm, 1378 A.H.

Al-Tirmidhī, *Jāmi'*, Kanpur, n. d.

Al-Ṭūsī, *al-Khilāf*, Tehran, n. d.

Al-Ṭūsī, *al-Istibṣār*, Najaf, 1956.

'Ubayd Allah b. Mas'ūd, *Sharḥ al-Wiqāyah*, Delhi, 1345 A.H.

Waḥīd al-Zamān, *Nūr al-Hidāyah*, (Urdu tr. of *Sharḥ al-Wiqāyah*), Kanpur, 1293 A.H.

Walī al-Dīn al-Khaṭīb, *Mishkāt al-Maṣābīḥ*, Delhi, 1350 A.H.

II.—ENGLISH SOURCES

A

Act, XXXI, 1850, ...545.

Act, 1870, ...561.

Alaska Compiled Laws, 609, 682.

Al-Mukhtasar, Shaikh Khalīl b. Isḥāk, English tr. Ruxton, London, 1916

Anglo Muhammadan Law, Sir Ronald, Knyvet Wilson, Calcutta, ...1930, 164, 233, 885.

Arbitration Act, X of 1940, 289, 294.

Artha Shastra, Chanakya 549.

St. Augustine, 538.

B

C

D

E

F

G

H

I

J

L

M

Marriage of Lunatics Act, 1811, ...357.
Married Women's Property Act, 1870 (33 and 34 Vict. C. 93) ......561, 754.
Married Women's Property Act, 1882, (45 and 46 Vict. C. 75) ......561, 754.
Matrimonial Causes Act, 1857, (20 and 21 Vict. C. 85) ......567.
Matrimonial Causes Act, 1937, (1 Edw. 8 and 1 Geo. 6, C. 57) 380, 392, 409, 432, 447, 450, 777.
Matrimonial Causes Act, 1950, (14 Geo. 6 C. 25) ......357, 365, 381, 428, 431, 432, 447, 450, 521, 579, 581, 661, 731.
Matrimonial Causes Act, 1952, ...410.
Matrimonial Causes Act, 1953, ...410.
Matrimonial Causes Act, 1955, ...578.
Matrimonial Causes Act, 1956, (4 and 5 Eliz. 2. C. 46) ......582.
Matrimonial Causes Act, 1965, (1965 C. 72) 660, 661, 663, 664, 753, 754, 777.
Matrimonial Causes (War Marriage) Act, 1944, ...582, 583.
Matrimonial Proceedings (Magistrates Court) Act, (8 and 9 Eliz. 2 C., 48 Courts) 1960, ...720, 731, 735, 753, 754.
Menu, Laws of, Jones, ...533.
Minhaj al-Talibin, English tr. by Van Den Berg and Howard London, 1911, 368, 412.
Mischief of the Marriage Laws, J. T. W. Baden Worsley, London, 1932, 557, 559, 561, 562, 583, 683.
Mishkat al-Masabih, English tr. by al-Haj Maulana Fazl al-Karim.
Moohummudan Law, Digest of, Neil B. E. Baillie, London, Morals in Evolution, L. T. Hobhouse, London 1951, ...558, 561.
Muhammadan Jurisprudence, Principles of, Abdur Rahim, Lahore, 1958, 2, 307, 918.
Muhammadan Law, Principles of, Faiz Badruddin Tyebji, Calcutta, 1919, ...882, 883,
Muslim Family Laws Ordinance, 1961, ...11, 12, 17, 30-33, 37, 39, 76, 78, 82, 83, 87, 135, 138, 143, 146, 280, 293, 684, 914.
Muslim Personal Law (Shariah) Application Act, 1937, ...106, 117, 436, 484.

N

National Assistance Act, 1948, 635, (11 and 12 Geo. 6, C. 29) ......635, 637.
National Insurance Act, 1955, (1965 C. 51) 638.
National Insurance (Industrial) Act, 1965, ...638.
Native Converts' Marriage Dissolution Act, Act XXI of 1866, ...553, 699, 700, 775.
New Mexico Statutes, 1941, ...609, 682.
Nortons Leading Cases on Hindu Law, Madras ......A selection of Hon'ble John Bruce, ...551.

TABLE OF CONTENTS

CHAPTER 1

GENERAL DISCUSSION

CHAPTER 2

DIVORCE (GENERAL DISCUSSION)

CHAPTER 3

CAPACITY TO DIVORCE

CHAPTER 8

RAJ'AH OR REVOCATION OF DIVORCE

CHAPTER 9

CHAPTER 10

KHIYĀR AL-BULŪGH OR OPTION OF PUBERTY

CHAPTER 11

TAFWĪḌ OR DELEGATION OF THE POWER OF DIVORCE

CHAPTER 12

KHUL'

CHAPTER 13

ARBITRATION

CHAPTER 14

ILL-ASSORTED MARRIAGES

CHAPTER 15

DEFECTS IN SPOUSES

CHAPTER 16

IMPOTENCY

CHAPTER 17

OTHER DEFECTS

CHAPTER 18

LI'ĀN

CHAPTER 19

MAFQŪD AL-KHABAR OR MISSING HUSBAND

CHAPTER 20

CONVERSION

CHAPTER 21

NAFQAH OR MAINTENANCE

CHAPTER 26

TABĀYUN DĀR OR DIFFERENCE OF DOMICILE

CHAPTER 27

'IDDAH OR WAITING PERIOD

CHAPTER 28

NASAB OR PATERNITY

CORRIGENDA

Wherever these Arabic words occur in this book please correct them as follows :

Incorrect	*Correct*
al-Durr al-Mukhtār	*al-Durr al-Mukhtār*
Ashbab wan Nazair	*al-Ashbah wa'l-Naẓāi'r*
Tahtavi	al-Ṭahṭawī
al-Radd al-Muḥtār	*Radd al-Muḥtār*
al-ṭalaq al-sunnah	*ṭalaq al sunnah*
al-Bada'i 'wa'l-Ṣanā'i'	*Bada'i' al-Ṣanā'i'*
Abū Qāsim Ṣaffār	Abu'l-Qāsim al-Ṣaffār
Fatawā al-'Alamgīriyah	*Fatāwā 'Ālamgīriyah*
ulama	*'ulāmā'*
shariah	*sharī'ah*
Hidāyat al-Murtasid	*Hidāyat al-Mustarshid*
Ta'sīs un-Nazā'ir	*Ta'sīs al-Naẓar*
Al-Hilat al-Najizah	*al-Ḥīlat al-Nājizah*
rajah	*raj'ah*
talaq	*ṭalāq*
Ila'	*'Īlā*
Khiyar ul-Balugh	*Khiyār al-Bulūgh*
Tufwid	*Tafwīḍ*
Ibn Taimiyah	Ibn Taymiyah
Shī'i	Shī'ī
Ibn al-Hummām	Ibn al-Humām
Sharā'i al-Islām	*Sharā'i' al-Islām*
Sunni	Sunnī
al-Mutānah	*al-Matānah fī marammat al-Khizānah*
makṣubah	*maksūbah*
Ibn 'Ābidīn	Ibn 'Ābidīn
Ṭaḥāwi	al-Ṭaḥāwī
Karkhi	al-Karkhī
al-Muḥit	*al-Muḥīṭ*
al-Khilāl	al-Khallāl
Futwā	*fatwā*
Tatārkhaniah	*Tātārkhāniyah*
Bazaziah	*al-Bazzāziyah*
Ībn 'Abbās	Ibn 'Abbās
al-Qinyah	*al-Qunyah*
raja'i	*raj'ī*

Incorrect	orrect
Ba'in	*Bā'in*
Sareeh	*Ṣarīḥ*
Kinayah	*Kināyah*
Ṭalāq al-Bid'ī	*al-Ṭalāq al-Bid'ī*
al-Baqarāh	*al-Baqarah*
al Hidayah	*al-Hidāyah*
al-Khilwah al-Sahibah	*al-Khalwah al-Ṣaḥīḥah*
Qadi	*Qāḍī*
al-Baḥr al-Rai'q	*al-Baḥr al-Rā'iq*
Māliki	Mālikī
Ḥanbali	Ḥanbalī
Bid'i	Bid'ī
Khul'	*Khul'*
Mubārah	*Mubārāh*
mughallazah	*mughallaẓah*
Wasilat al-Najat	*Wasīlat al-Najāt*
al-Marghīnanī	al-Marghīnānī
Zāhiriah	*Ẓāhiriyah*
Khafiah	*Khafiyah*
al-Ṭalāq al-Kināyah	*Ṭalāq Kināyah*
Ṭalāq al-Mu'llaq	*Ṭalāq mu'allaq*
Ghair	*Ghayr*
Ṭalāq al-Ahṣan	*Ṭalāq Aḥsan*
Ṭalāq al-Bā'in	*Ṭalāq Bā'in*
al-Kasani	al-Kāsānī
Akramah	'Ikrimah
Rukanah	Rukānah
Shāfi'i	Shāfi'ī
Minhaj al-Talibīn	*Minhāj al-Ṭālibīn*
Hanafi	Ḥanafī
Majma' al-unhur	*Majma' al-Anhur*
Shahab-ud-Dīn	Shihāb al-Dīn
Tohfat al-Mohtaj	*Tuḥfat al-Muḥtāj*
fi	*fī*
Khulfā'	Khulafā'
al-Maṣābih	*al-Maṣābīḥ*
Sa'ūd	Sa'ūd
al-Mu'īn	al-Mu'īn
Ja'maa-ush-Shittat	*Jāmi' al-Shatāt*
al-Mabsūt	*al-Mabsūṭ*
thabt	*thabt* —

Incorrect	*Correct*
Ibn Najaym	Ibn Nujaym
Vakīl	*Wakīl*
Fatḥ al-Qadir	*Fatḥ al-Qadīr*
qat'i	*qaṭ'ī*
Wali al-Din al-Khatib *Mishkat al-Masabih*	Wali al-Dīn al-Khaṭib *Mishkāt al-Maṣābīh*
Abu Hanifa	Abū Hanīfah
Shah Wali ullah	Shāh Walī Allāh
Aḥādith al-Muatta	*Aḥādith al-Muwaṭṭa*
tatliqaha	*taṭlīqah*
Al-Suyūti	Al-Suyūṭī
Ghayat al-Autar	*Ghāyat al-Awṭār*
al-Ramlī	al-Ramlī
Qādi Khān	Qāḍī Khān
makruh	*makrūh*
maraḍ al-maut	*maraḍ al-mawt*
Tahrīr-al-Ahkām	*Taḥrīr al-Aḥkām*
Tafsir Muwahib-ur-Rahman	*Tafsīr Mawāhib al-Raḥman*
Mujahid	Mujāhid
Al-Awzā'ī'	al-Awzā'i
Fatimah b. Atbah	Faṭimah b. 'Utbah
Umdat al-Qārī	*'Umdat al-Qarī*
Bayan al-Qur'ān	*Bayān al-Qur'ān*
Sahih al-Bukharī	*Ṣaḥīḥ al-Bukhārī*
Ibn al-Arabi	Ibn al-'Arabī
Ishāq	Isḥāq
Ibn Majushān	Ibn al-Mājishūn
Asbagh	Aṣbagh
Ibn Nāwāz	Ibn al-Mawwāz
Khurram Ali	Khurram 'Alī
Sufyan al-Thari	Sufyān al-Thawrī
al-Hasan	al-Ḥasan
al-Iqnā'	*al-Iqnā'*
Shī'ah	Shī'ah
fasik	*fāsiq*
Sharaf al-Dīn al-Maqdisi	Sharaf al-Dīn al-Maqdisī
al-Mughni	*al-Mughnī*
shakkaz	shakkāz
Bakhr	*Bakhar*
Ifdah	*Ifḍa*
Istahadah	*Istiḥāḍah*

Incorrect	*Correct*
Adhita	al-Adhṭ (Adhyūṭ)
Afal	*'Afal*
Shaykhzadah	Shaykhzādah
Bidayat al-Mujtāhid	*Bidāyat al-Mujtahid*
Basur	Bāsūr
Nasur	Nāsūr
Mahi al-Din Abu Zakaria	Muḥī al-Dīn Abū Zakariyā
Yahya Ibn Sharifen Nawawi	Yaḥyā ibn Sharaf al-Dīn al-Nawawī
Al-Maqdisi	Al-Maqdisī
Jamai Abbasi	*Jami' Abbāsī*
Baha-ud-Din Amli	Bahā' al-Dīn Āmilī
Khussee	*Khaṣiyy*
Ja'far b. Hasan	Ja'far b. al-Ḥasan
Ibn Rushd	Ibn Rushd
mashota	*al-mathn* (*or mathana*)
Janūn	*Junūn*
ineen	*'innīn*
Shareh vikaya	*Sharḥ al-Wiqāyah*
Nur al-Hedayah	*Nūr al-Hidāyah*
Wahid as-Zaman	Waḥīd al-Zamān
Sahnun	Saḥnūn
Ibn Qudamah	Ibn Qudāmah
Zaa'd al-Maa'd	*Zād al-Ma'ād*
Rawūi al-Aḥkam	*Rawa'i' al-Aḥkam*
al-Nawawi	al-Nawawī
Nusuv	*Nasab*
Shaltūt	Shaltūt
Tanzim	*Tanzīm*
ibn Majah	*Ibn Mājah*
Akhrin	*Akhirayn*
al-Muwatta'	*al-Muwaṭṭa'*
Mishkat	*Mishkāt*
Li'ān	*Li'ān*
muḥsanah	*muḥṣanah*
Hakim	Ḥakīm
Abbas	'Abbās
Dahhak	Ḍaḥḥāk
Al-Maidah	*Al-Mā'idah*
Uthman	'Uthmān
Hudhayfah	Ḥudhayfah

Incorrect	*Correct*
Talhab b. Ubayd	Ṭalḥah b. ʻUbayd
Dar al-Islam	*Dār al-Islam*
Dar al-Harb	*Dār al-Ḥarb*
al-Badr uz-Zahir fi Salat al-Juma wa'l-musafir	*al-Badr al-Ẓāhir fī ṣalāt al-Jumu'ah wa'l-musāfir*
Muntakhib	*muntakhab*
nashizah	*nāshizah*
al-Jazari	al-Jazīrī
Ibn Qayyum	Ibn Qayyim
Mulla Khusraw	Munlā Khusraw
Abd al-Aziz	ʻAbd al-ʻAzīz
al-Awṭū	*al-Awṭār*
iddah	*ʻiddah*

Chapter 1

DISSOLUTION OF MARRIAGE

GENERAL DISCUSSION

DIVORCE is a controversial subject. On one hand, it cannot be denied that dissolution of marriage brings about the disintegration of family life with consequent uncertainty and unhappiness for children born of the marriage, but, on the other hand, it must be equally conceded that dissolution of marriage is evidently desirable when the spouses can no longer live in harmony and have lost all mutual regard. The continuance of an unhappy marriage breeds hate and disgust, and is likely to ruin the lives of the parties involved or at least of one of them.

Islam takes a realistic and sympathetic view of human affairs and therefore it attaches great importance to the happiness of both the spouses. It provides that every attempt should be made to maintain a marriage, but once it is established that a marriage has proved a failure, Muslim law does not scruple to allow the parties to separate from each other. In Islam marriage in the ordinary course is to last till one of the spouses dies. But if a husband and wife cannot live happily together so that the very objects of marriage are defeated and it becomes a mere farce, then its continuance is no longer considered desirable. Under such circumstances, divorce and dissolution of marriage are allowed under Islamic law.

Marriage is regarded by some religions as a sacred tie, and its dissolution is either disallowed or is permitted under conditions so exacting that the happiness of the spouses is sacrificed in following the rigours of the law. A Christian marriage was regarded a sacrament and hence indissoluble at one time in Europe, but many European countries have changed this view on account of the hardships that resulted from that conception and now regard it as a civil contract. The same view prevails in several States of the United States of America.

A Muslim marriage, unlike marriages in certain other religions, is not a sacrament. It has been stated by some writers and also held in some cases that it is a civil contract. But this view is equally incorrect and a Muslim marriage is not a mere civil contract. Great importance has been given to marriage by Islam and *al-Durr-al-Mukhtar* and *Ashbah wan Nazair* and other books have called it an act of devotion. The former has stated it to be incumbent on a person whose passion is ungovernable. The Prophet (peace be on him) has said, "Marriage is my Sunnah." But in spite of the above it is not to be considered a sacred and indissoluble tie and *al-Durr-al-Mukhtar* goes so far as to state that when there is any fear of injustice, marriage becomes abominable. Similarly, it is stated in *Tahtavi* that marriage when injustice is certain is unlawful. A sacrament cannot be violated but Muslim Law unquestionably allows divorce. On the other hand, there is no virtue attached to a civil contract but marriage in Islam is considered a virtuous act. Hence to say that it is a sacrament or to describe it as a mere civil contract is not correct. As pointed out by Abdur Rahim in his well-known book, *Muhammadan Jurisprudence*, marriage under Muslim Law partakes of the nature of both a sacrament and a civil contract.[1] Being commended by religion it tends to be treated as a holy injunction. It holds a position midway between the two. But so far as the rights and obligations of the parties in relation to each other are concerned, they are governed by the ordinary law of contracts. It is open to the spouses to specify and restrict each other's rights and obligations arising out of the marriage and fix the conditions for its termination by mutual consent. Muslim writers treat it as something between religious matters and worldly affairs. The Muslims have been enjoined to contract marriage as a safeguard against loose living. A marriage also unites two different individuals by love and affection and two

1. Abdur Rahim, *Muhammadan Jurisprudence*, 1958, Lahore, p. 327.

different families by a bond of kinship. When these objects, amongst others, fail, the continuance of a marriage may not be in the interest of the spouses and so its dissolution is permitted. Divorce is not regarded as a disgrace in Islam nor necessarily a sequel that follows misconduct by either the husband or the wife or by both.

Muslim law does not compel the spouses to lead a miserable life when their marriage has proved a failure, but grants them the right to separate. At the same time it does not contemplate separation on frivolous and trivial grounds, such as are now recognized sufficient in some parts of the world.

In Arabia itself divorce, prior to Islam, was a frequent occurrence without any regard to marital obligations and every individual took as many wives as he could afford and then divorced them at his sweet will.

II. Religious Sanction

In Islam divorce, when not absolutely necessary, is strongly disapproved of and discouraged. This has been done in two ways, namely, condemning divorce except in certain circumstances and commending forbearance and the continuation of marital relationship even in the case of disagreement and some suffering. The Prophet (peace be on him) has said, "Of all the permitted things divorce is the most abominable with God."[2] Even when a man is not satisfied with his wife, the Qur'ān enjoins forbearance. It says, "And retain them (the wives) kindly. Then if you hate them, it may be that you dislike a thing while God has put abundant good in it."[3] The Prophet (peace be on him) has said, "That man is better amongst you who is better to his wife."[4] On another occasion he said, "The most perfect amongst the faithful in respect of faith is he who is best in disposition among them (women) and better among you are those who

2. Abū Dāwūd, *Sunan*, Kānpūr, I : 296.
3. Qur'ān, IV : 19.
4. Walī al-Dīn al-Khaṭīb, *Mishkāt al-Maṣābīḥ*, Delhi, 1350 A.H., p. 181

are better towards their wives."[5]

Abū Hurayrah reports that the Prophet (peace be on him) said, "Let not the faithful man hate the faithful woman; if he dislikes some of her habits, he may like others."[6] He is also reported to have said, "Marry, do not divorce, for God does not like men and women who relish variety in sex matters."[7] In short, the husbands have been enjoined not to divorce their wives except in the case of their being unfaithful.[8]

III. Divorce, When Permitted

If it is established that a husband and wife cannot live together in peace and harmony, they are given the option to separate. Divorce is also permitted when the wife's conduct is undesirable as when she does injury to her husband or is not chaste. Divorce is obligatory on a husband when he is incapable of matrimonial intimacy or cannot maintain his wife, and the like.[9] This rule is based on a Qur'ānic text wherein the husbands have been enjoined "to keep the wives with kindness."[10]

Divorce is permitted as a matter of necessity for the avoidance of greater evil which may result from the continuance of a marriage. But even in such cases an attempt is first to be made for reconciliation by referring the matter to arbitration. Thus it is laid down in the Qur'ān, "And if you fear a breach between the two (husband and wife), then appoint an arbiter from his (husband's) people and an arbiter from her (wife's) people. If they desire agreement, Allāh will effect harmony between them."[11] According to the spirit of the law, it is only when disagreement continues and efforts to bring about a reconciliation prove unavailing that the parties

5. Walī al-Dīn al-Khaṭīb, *Mishkāt al-Maṣābiḥ*, Delhi, 1350 A.H., p. 282.
6. *Ibid.*, 280.
7. 'Alī al-Muttaqī, *Kanz al-'Ummāl*, Hyderabad Deccan, 1313 A H., V : 159.
8. *Ibid.*, 'Ibn 'Ābidīn, *Al-Radd al-Muḥtār*, Cairo, 1318 A.H., II : 426-7.
9. *Ibid.*
10. Qur'ān, II : 231.
11. *Ibid*, IV : 35.

may dissolve the marriage. Judicial separation in which the aggrieved spouse is allowed to live separate from the other without the marriage being dissolved is an institution not recognized by the Muslim law. The reason for this is that the objects of marriage are not restored by a judicial separation, while it may result in immorality which in Islam is an evil far greater than divorce. The Muslim law, while it permits divorce, insists that there shall be some guarantee that the husband or the wife is not acting from caprice or frivolity or on the impulse of a momentary provocation. For this purpose certain restrictions are imposed by the law upon the spouses' right to dissolve their marriage. The object of these restrictions, as stated above, is to ensure that the spouses should not act in haste such as under the influence of wine, anger, excitement, and the like, and that an opportunity is provided to the parties for *rapprochement*. This cautious attitude towards divorce forms the basis of the *al-ṭalāq al-sunnah* under which marriage is terminated only after a minimum period of three terms of the wife's menstrual courses from the time of the pronouncement of divorce. During this period the husband has the option to take the wife back.

The above discussion will make it clear that a Muslim husband cannot justly divorce his wife in the absence of reasonable grounds and without having recourse to an attempt at reconciliation. It is unfortunate that this basic principle regarding divorce has been lost sight of and divorce given capriciously and without any justification, whatsoever, is considered good in law, though it is strongly discouraged in religion. This conception of law ignores the strong condemnation and disapproval of divorce in Islam and has led many a husband to make an unscrupulous use of his power to divorce. This often results in great misery and unhappiness for the wife and has made marriage insecure and the wife's position very precarious.

Muslim jurists have held different views regarding divorce in Islam. According to some, divorce is prohibited but is permissible in case of necessity. It is stated in *al-Radd al-Muḥtār*, dealing with Ḥanafī law, that no doubt it (divorce) is forbidden, but it becomes *mubāḥ* (permitted) for certain outside reasons. Its *ibāḥah* (permission) arises from the necessity for release (from the marital tie) in certain cases. Therefore, when there is no cause for separation whatsoever, there is no necessity for release, and if there is no legal ground for *ṭalāq*, or release, then it must be considered unlawful, for the Qur'ān says, "So if they (your women) obey you, seek not a way against them."[12] The Ḥanafī jurists also assert that divorce in itself is a pernicious thing and is a disapproved procedure, as it dissolves marriage, a tie or relationship which involves many considerations of temporal as well as spiritual nature—nor is its propriety at all admitted except on the ground of urgency of release from an undesirable wife.[13] They further add that the propriety of divorce rests upon the cause of the urgency. The urgency itself being a matter concealed and unascertainable (but by virtual proof) and the act of proceeding to divorce is proof of the urgency.[14] The explanation of the Ḥanafi jurists is based on too technical a ground. The underlying principle is, however, clear. Most of the Muslim jurists, while discussing *ṭalāq*, say that '*ṭalāq* . . . being in itself a pernicious and disapproved procedure, it is only the urgency of release that can give sanction to it.[15] It is a very reasonable and sound view of the matter and it is not clear why it was not adopted by all the jurists who, however, agree that divorce is pernicious and should be discouraged. Hence, if a person divorces his wife without there being an urgent need for release, he shall be guilty of sin. Abū Ḥanīfah is of the opinion that if there is no urgent need for release from the marriage-tie, the divorce is '*ḥarām*' (forbidden).[16]

12. Qur'ān, IV : 34.
13. Al-Marghīnānī, 'Alī b. Abī Bakr, *al-Hidāyah*, Delhi, n.d., II : 335; Ibn 'Ābidīn. *op. cit.*, II : 426-7.
14. Al-Marghīnānī, *op. cit.*, II : 335; Ibn al-Humām, *Fatḥ al-Qadīr*, Cairo, 1356 A.H., III : 24.
15. Ibn 'Ābidīn, *op. cit.*, II : 426-7.
16. *Ibid.*

The author of *al-Badā'i' wa 'l-Ṣanā'i'* has discussed the matter at length. He says, "Marriage is a beneficial union which becomes the means for obtaining benefits in the hereafter and in this world and divorce destroys it and the destruction of a good thing is reprehensible. God has said, 'And verily Allāh does not like mischief.' And this means that in law it (divorce) is undesirable, for God does not love it. It can happen that sometimes on account of disparity in temperament and nature or due to disputes the advantage of marriage is lost; the husband knows that the benefits bypass him because of his marriage with a particular woman and on account of his living with her, and that in such cases advantage would lie in divorce so that the objectives of marriage might be fulfilled by marriage with another woman. However, there is constant likelihood that he may not have thought over the matter as carefully as its gravity requires and he might not have visualized all the possible consequences, so the *Sharī'ah* and reason both require that he should reconsider the matter and for this reason he is expected to give her one revocable divorce so that the woman may repent her misconduct and dislike (for him) and might return to the path of rectitude. But when she has tasted the bitterness of separation and does not repent, the husband will consider his own situation whether he can stay away from her. And if he feels he will not be able to bear a separation, he might bring her back, but if he feels that he will be able to bear the separation, he may divorce her again in the second *tuhr*.."[17]

It is unfortunate that some later jurists have overlooked this basic concept regarding divorce, nor have they taken into consideration the hardship caused to a wife as a result thereof. It cannot be gainsaid that the present practice which allows a husband to divorce his wife unscrupulously, does not only contravene the basic principle of the Muslim law of marriage and divorce but also very often ruins the life of the wife and even leaves her absolutely destitute. There is no *Bayt al-Māl* (Public Treasury) to support her now, and it is, therefore,

17. Al-Kāsānī, 'Alā' al-Dīn, *Badā'i' al-Ṣanā'i'*, Cairo, 1324 A.H., III : 95.

necessary that this outlook should be changed and a reasonable view in keeping with the basic principle of Muslim law be adopted.

IV. *Modifications in Muslim Law*

Many Muslim jurists of the past did not hesitate to modify the law to make it suit the needs of their own times and we should also do the same. These jurists considered themselves bound only by express injunctions of the Qur'ān and the Traditions regarding obligations to do a thing or to abstain from doing a certain thing. But, where the law was not obligatory and was merely permissive, they allowed its modification whenever necessary. Muslim law is very elastic. The Muslim jurists in later times, however, considered themselves absolutely bound by the law laid down by the early jurists, without caring to see if it suited the needs and conditions of their times, and so they made the law very rigid.

Muslim law, however, is full of instances where necessary modifications, to meet the requirements of their own times had been made by the jurists. To quote a few instances, drinking was punishable with forty stripes during the caliphate of Abū Bakr, but 'Umar increased the number to eighty in order to put a stop to the evil habit.[18] Pronouncement of three divorces at one and the same time was considered tantamount to one divorce in the time of the Prophet (peace be on him) and Abū Bakr, and during the first two or three years of the caliphate of 'Umar. People, however, used to wantonly repeat the pronouncement many times simultaneously thereby ignoring the seriousness of divorce. 'Umar considered it necessary to discourage this practice and held that repetition of three pronouncements at the same time would amount to three divorces. To give another example, conquered lands were distributed amongst the Muslim warriors by the Prophet (peace be on him), but 'Umar stopped this practice in the public interest. Again, marriage with a *Kitābīyah* (Christian or Jewish woman) was permitted by the Prophet (peace be on him) and the first three Caliphs, though

18. Abū Dāwūd, *op. cit.*, II : 259-60.

the second Caliph discouraged it, and when a Governor had married a Jewess, the Caliph ordered him to divorce her.[19] But 'Alī, the fourth Caliph, took up a very strong attitude and according to the majority of Shī'ī *'ulamā'* such a marriage is absolutely forbidden. According to some other Shī'ī jurists, the marriage is not forbidden though it is considered highly undesirable. The Supreme Court of Pakistan has accepted the latter view. For a learned and interesting discussion of the subject, see *Syed Ali Nawaz Shah Gardezi* v. *Lt.-Col. Muhammad Yusuf Khan*, P.L.D. 1962 (W.P.), Lahore 558; *Lt.-Col. Muhammad Yusuf* v. *Syed Ali Nawaz Gardezi*, P.L.D. 1963 (W.P.), Lahore 141, and *Syed Ali Nawaz Gardezi* v. *Lt.-Col. Muhammad Yusuf*, P.L.D. 1963 S.C. 51.

This practice of modifying rules of law continued even after the orthodox Caliphs as can be seen from the following instances :

(*a*) Formerly, if a husband wanted to take his wife to another place and she refused to accompany him, then, according to Abū Ḥanīfah, Abū Yūsuf, and Muḥammad, she was considered disobedient and lost her right to maintenance. But later, Abū Qāsim Ṣaffār held that the rule was applicable in the times of those *Imāms*, but in Ṣaffār's time the husband could not take her to another city (against her wishes).[20] The modification in the rule is probably due to the fact that travelling had become dangerous in later times. Also, because the Muslims had then spread out to very distant lands and means of communication were difficult and it was not considered desirable to force a wife to leave her relations and country in such circumstances.

(*b*) In the '*Ālamgīrīyah* it is stated, "If a person divorces his wife while under the influence of hemp or *bhang*,

19. Shāh Walīy Allāh, *Fiqh 'Umar* (Urdu Translation), Lahore, 1952 A.D., pp. 65-6.

20. *Al-Fatāwā al-Hindiyah*, Urdu (Translation), *Fatāwā al-'Ālamgīriyah*, Lucknow, 1899 A.D., II : 406.

then, according to *Tahdhīb*, divorce would not be effected. But a divorce under such circumstances would now be given effect to and the husband would also be liable to punishment because of the prevalence of the vice (of the taking) of *bhang* or hemp amongst the people in our times and the *Fatwā* in our time is in accordance with this view."[21]

To give instances of our own times, we may quote some important changes introduced in the Muslim law of divorce by the Dissolution of Muslim Marriages Act of 1939. The Bill was introduced in the Central Legislative Assembly by the late Muḥammad Aḥmad Kāẓimī, a member of the Working Committee of the Jam'iyyat al-'Ulamā'-i Hind, because it was considered necessary to bring about certain important modifications in the then prevalent provisions of Muslim law. The following will show the extent to which modifications were made :

(*i*) A Muslim girl could not formerly exercise her option of puberty on attaining majority if she had been given away in marriage, while a minor, by her father or paternal grandfather. This rule was based on the reasoning that they were so closely related to the girl that it could be presumed that they must have acted in the best interests of the girl and must have given her away in marriage to the most suitable person. But, in course of time, it was found that a father or a grandfather gave away his daughter or granddaughter in marriage to a very undesirable person or even to a man of depraved character either through carelessness or simply for the sake of some monetary or other gain and thus sacrificed the girl's future happiness. The law was, therefore, amended to meet this situation and a girl can now exercise her option of puberty even when she is given away in marriage by her father or grandfather during her

21. *Al-Fatāwā al-Hindīyah* (Urdu Translation), *Fatāwā al-'Ālamgīriyah*, Lucknow, 1899 A.D., II : 145.

minority.

(*ii*) The Ḥanafī law did not allow the dissolution of a marriage on the basis of the husband's cruelty to the wife or for his failure to maintain her, which was found to result in great hardship to her. The Act now allows the dissolution of a marriage on these grounds.

(*iii*) Under the Ḥanafī law, the wife of a missing husband had to wait for at least sixty years before contracting a second marriage.[22] Under the Mālikī law the period of waiting is four years only. The Act has adopted the latter rule with some modifications in order to save the wife from obvious hardship.

(*iv*) There was a great difference of opinion amongst the Muslim jurists about the effect of the conversion of a Muslim wife to a revealed religion. The majority of Muslim jurists held the view that the marriage would get dissolved on the renunciation of Islam by the wife, but the *'ulamā'* of Mā-warā' al-Nahr (Transoxiana) held a different opinion and stated that the marriage would not be dissolved under these circumstances.[23] The Act has adopted the latter opinion.

The Government of Pakistan has enacted an Ordinance, namely, the Muslim Family Laws Ordinance, 1961, to further ameliorate the conditions of wives. According to the Ordinance, a husband who has divorced his wife shall promptly inform in writing the Chairman of the Union Council of this fact and the Arbitration Council shall do its best to bring about a reconciliation.[24] Nor can the husband enter into another marriage if he has got one or more wives living without first convincing the Arbitration Council that circumstances justify his proposed marriage. Realization of maintenance

22. Ibn 'Ābidīn, *op. cit.*, II : 338.
23. *Ibid.*, II : 402-3.
24. Section 7 (1) of the Muslim Family Laws Ordinance, 1961.

allowance has also been made easy.[25] These provisions, however, still fall short of fully meeting the needs of the time, and more protection should be provided to wives.

Both the Dissolution of Muslim Marriages Act, 1939, and the Muslim Family Laws Ordinance, 1961 have greatly curtailed the absolute power given to the husband under the then existing law and have helped to bring the existing law in conformity with the spirit of Muslim law.

It can be seen from the above discussion that the Muslim jurists have often modified provisions of Muslim law when a change was considered necessary to meet the particular conditions or requirements of their own times.

V. *Reasons for Differences of Opinion*

We sometimes find that the Muslim jurists have expressed different views on a particular point. It may be mentioned here that the difference is often due to a difference in the mode of interpretation as explained below :

(*a*) One group of Muslim jurists considers that a verse of the Qur'ān or a Tradition is to be interpreted literally, but the other group prefers to look into the underlying idea and to apply the basic principle according to the changed conditions and to meet the requirements of their own times. They consider that the spirit of a rule cannot be changed, but its application changes with time, environment, circumstances, conditions, etc. It is obvious that these two modes of interpretation will result in a difference in the application of the rule though there is no difference in the basic rule applied by them.

(*b*) The other ground for difference lies in the application of a certain rule of law. Thus, some jurists hold that a rule should be followed and applied strictly so that people should not take undue advantage in any way and may not lightly ignore

25. Section 6 of the Muslim Family Laws Ordinance, 1961.

it and commit a breach of it. But there are other jurists who are of the opinion that Allāh wants to be merciful and does not want to be hard on mankind and so we should be lenient in applying the rule of law in order to avoid the infliction of hardship on the people.

It can thus be seen that often there is no real difference in the basic rule applied by the jurists, but the difference arises out of the process of application of a rule.

As the basic rule in each case is generally the same, it is open to us to adopt such interpretation of law as meets the needs and requirements of our own times.

Some one has aptly stated that all kindness and leniency is due to the injunctions of Allah and the Prophet (peace be on him) while all hardships and difficulties arise out of the rules laid down by Ulama. Ibn Qayyim has nicely explained that the *Shariah* (Muslim law) is based on wisdom and is meant for the worldly and spiritual benefit of the people, and means complete justice for all and absolute kindness and wisdom. Hence we cannot consider that Code of Law a Law of the *Shariah* in which there is cruelty instead of justice, hardship in place of leniency, loss instead of advantage and foolishness in place of reason. He stresses that law changes with the change of environment, time, place, financial conditions, and customs of the people and that misunderstanding has arisen among people due to their ignorance of the relation between human society and the law, which has constricted the scope of *Islamic Shariah*. They do not realise that such narrow-mindedness can have no place in a system which has given most consideration to the welfare of the people.[26]

VI. *Wife's Right to Dissolve Marriage*

Under the provisions of Muslim law, the right to the dissolution of marriage does not rest with the husband alone, but the wife has also been given this right,

26. *Hidayat-al-Murtasid* (Urdu tr. of *Bidyat-ul-Mujtahid*) Idarat al-Musannifin, Rabwah, 1958 A.D., p. 35.

though it is not as absolute as that of the husband. She can herself terminate her marriage under certain conditions or get it dissolved through a *qāḍī* if there are genuine grounds for such a step. But, generally speaking, the right of the wife is not coextensive with that of the husband. The difference lies in the fact that whereas the husband can himself divorce his wife, the wife can, except under special circumstances or conditions, obtain the dissolution of her marriage only through the intervention of a *qāḍī* or an Arbitrator.

VII. *Difference in Powers of Husband and Wife*

There are two verses in the Qur'ān which deal with this matter. It is stated in the first verse, "They (the women) have rights similar to those (of men) over them in kindness and men are a degree above them."[27] The other says, "Men are the maintainers of women with what Allāh has made some of them to excel others and with what they spend out of their wealth."[28]

VIII. *Reasons for the above-mentioned Difference*

The superiority of men over women has been explained in the second verse to be due to two reasons, namely,

(*a*) because they spend of their property (for the support of women), and

(*b*) because Allāh has made one of them to excel the other.

This shows that superiority has been given to man because of his responsibility to support and his capacity to protect his wife. He has to bear a greater burden of domestic life than the wife and so, consequently, enjoys greater rights in some matters than she does. As regards the second ground, it is generally accepted that men are physically superior to women. There is a very interesting judgment of the Supreme Court of the U.S.A. in which the position of women as against men has been discussed. Their Lordships in the course of their judgment stated, "Yet they [certain legislation and opinions]

27. Qur'ān, II: 228.
28. *Ibid.*, IV: 34.

are significant of a widespread belief that woman's physical structure, and the functions she performs in consequence thereof, justify special legislation restricting or qualifying the conditions under which she should be permitted to toil."[29] Their Lordships then referred to extracts from over ninety reports of Committees, Bureaus of Statistics, Commissioners of Hygiene, Inspectors of Factories, both in their own country and also in Europe, to the effect that "long hours of labour are dangerous for women, primarily because of their special physical organization" and then observed, "A woman's physical structure and the performance of maternal functions place her at a disadvantage in the struggle for subsistence is obvious. History discloses the fact that woman has always been dependent upon man. He established his control at the outset by superior physical strength, and this control in various forms, with diminishing intensity, has continued to the present. It is still true that in the struggle for subsistence she is not an equal competitor with her brother. Though limitations upon her personal and contractual rights may be removed by legislation, there is that in her disposition and habits of life which will still operate against a full assertion of those rights. She will still be where some legislation to protect her seems necessary to secure a real equality of right. Doubtless, there are individual exceptions, and there are many respects in which she has an advantage over him, but looking at it from the viewpoint of the effort to maintain an independent position in life, she is not upon an equality . . . It is impossible to close one's eyes to the fact that she still looks to her brother and depends upon him. Even though all restrictions on political, personal, and contractual rights were taken away, and she stood, so far as Statutes are concerned, upon an absolutely equal plane with him, it would still be true that she is so constituted that she will rest upon and look to him for protection." Their Lordships then referred to the denial of elective franchise that may disclose a lack of political equality in all things with her

29. *Curt Muller* v. *State of Oregon*, 208 U.S., p. 412.

brother and remarked that "the reason runs deeper and rests in the inherent difference between the two sexes, and in the different functions in life which they perform."[30] This discussion will show that there can be no doubt that woman is placed at a disadvantage on account of her physical structure. It is considered that man is physically superior to woman and, therefore, enjoys greater rights than she does. From time immemorial man has been protecting woman and, though in a way, she enjoys the same rights as man, yet due to her structure and nature she stands in need of some protection by man who thus gets an authority over her. It seems that this is what is meant by the above-quoted verse of the Qur'ān. But the partial superiority of men, as stated in the Qur'ān, is by no means prejudicial to the ultimate equality of the sexes. It only indicates authority of man over woman to a small degree and is not to be used in a way which may be prejudicial to the interests of the other sex. The Prophet (peace be no him) has emphasized the fact that real superiority consists in character.[31]

IX. *Dissolution of Marriage*

The Muslim jurists and *qāḍīs* used to follow faithfully the following injunction laid down in the Qur'ān, "To keep them (the wives) with kindness or separate (from them) with humanity."[32] Muḥammad has stated a very useful rule in this connection. He says that if a marriage causes injury to the wife on account of any defect in the husband then let the marriage be dissolved.[33] The *qāḍīs* in earlier times used to follow this rule of law. They used to be realistic in considering the wife's complaint and scrupulously guarded her happiness. They would free a wife from the marriage-tie if they were satisfied that it was impossible for her to live happily with her husband owing to some defect in him. Thus in a case a wife was granted divorce when her husband was found suffering from halitosis (foul breath) to such a degree that the wife

30. *Curt Muller* v. *State of Oregon*. 208 U.S, p. 412.
31. Walī al-Dīn al-Khaṭīb, *op. cit.*, p. 431.
32. Qur'ān, II : 231.
33. Ibn al-Humām, *op. cit.*, III : 268.

could not tolerate it.[34]

In course of time, however, the wives' right to get their marriages dissolved became greatly restricted due to incorrect and sometimes adverse interpretation of law. Many of their rights have, however, been restored to them during the last decade. The Dissolution of Muslim Marriages Act, 1939 (now in force in Pakistan and India), and the Muslim Family Laws Ordinance, 1961, in force in Pakistan, are instances of this. Certain reforms have been made in many other Muslim countries.

X. *Adoption of other Laws by the Ḥanafīs*

The Ḥanafī law is favourable to women in many respects, but in some matters it is very hard (in its application), as Abū Ḥanīfah was prone to be over-cautious, and a wife is sometimes put to great hardship on this account. Later Ḥanafī jurists have tried to overcome the difficulty in several cases. Thus *al-Radd al-Muḥtār* has stated that the Ḥanafīs have adopted the Mālikī law in some cases and it states that Abu'l-Layth has written in his book *Ta'sīs-un-Naẓā'ir* that in case no authority of Abū Ḥanīfah can be found in any particular case then recourse may be had to the law of Mālik because his law is more akin to the Ḥanafī law.[35] It is also stated in *al-Radd al-Muḥtār* that when a wife is put to hardship for not being maintained by her husband, it is open to a Ḥanfaī *qāḍī* to have recourse to the Shāfi'ī law. He cannot, however, decide the case himself according to the Shāfi'ī law, but he can appoint a Shāfi'ī *qāḍī* as his agent (deputy) to decide the case according to the Shāfi'ī law. The decision of the latter shall be binding on the parties.[36] Again, in the case of a missing husband the Ḥanafīs have adopted the Mālikī law.[37] These

34. Dr. Hussain Himmet, *Sexual Diseases and Marriage in Islam*, cited by Th. H. Van De Velde in *Ideal Marriage*, London, 1935 A.D., p. 27.
35. Ibn 'Ābidin, *op. cit.*, II : 552-674.
36. *Ibid.*
37. *Ibid.*, II : 552, Maulana Ashraf Ali, *Al-Hilat al-Najizah*, pp. 115, 116. Karachi, 1955 A.D.

cases seem to lay down the rule of law that it is open to a Ḥanafī *qāḍī* to have recourse to the law enunciated by another *Imām* of the Sunnī sect whose law may be more equitable in a particular case. This is borne out by some cases discussed by them. This rule was made use of by the Ḥanafī *qāḍīs* of old when they would refer a wife to a Shāfi'ī, Mālikī or Ḥanbalī *qāḍī* for the decision of her case. Unfortunately the Courts during the British rule in India ignored this very useful rule and decided the cases according to the law of the particular sect to which the parties belonged. They ought to have followed the rule to decide a case according to the law laid down by any one of the *Imāms* as necessary in the interest of justice, equity and good conscience. Besides, a Court should take a broad view in cases of separation and should not lose sight of the spirit of the law. Such a view can be supported by many Traditions of the Prophet (peace be on him) who repeatedly commanded that women should be treated with kindness.

XI. *Reasons of Difference in Sunnī and Shī'ī Law.*

There is a difference in some rules applicable to marriage and divorce under the Sunnī and the Shi'i laws. It is important to understand the basic principles underlying these differences. The Sunnī jurists seem to consider that a marriage brings about a new and a very important change in the status of the spouses. They consider it essential that all necessary safeguards should be taken so that the newly acquired status is not jeopardized in any way. They, therefore, make it a condition for the validity of a marriage that all necessary precautions should be taken to establish the creation of the new status. Hence, they want full publicity of a marriage and insist on the presence of at least two witnesses at the time of its celebration as necessary under a Tradition of the Prophet (peace be on him). They, however, seem to think that a divorce merely restores the spouses to their original status, and so, while greatly approving of the presence of witnesses at the time of divorce, they do not consider the presence of witnesses at that time an essential condition for its validity. They also consider that the presence of witnesses at the time of marriage is necessary to discourage immorality for, in the absence of such a condition, it can always be open to a man and woman charged with adultery, which is a very serious offence under Muslim law, to plead that they had been secretly married in the absence of witnesses and so escape the consequences of their immoral conduct.

The Shī'ī jurists, on the other hand, relying on their interpretation of a verse of Sūrah *al-Ṭalāq*, insist that the Qur'ān commands the presence of two witnesses for a valid divorce. The verse reads: "So when they have reached their prescribed time-limit, retain them with kindness, and call to witness two just ones from among you, and give upright testimony for Allāh."[38] As pointed out at another place, the Sunnīs consider that the injunction about calling of witnesses relates to retraction or rajah.[39]

They further seem to think that it is not necessary for the *qāḍī* to probe into the conduct of the parties and he must accept the statements of a man and a woman charged with adultery that they have been married secretly as correct—particularly when they shall have to live in future as husband and wife in view of their explanation.

XII. *Failure of Marriage*

The failure of marriage can be due to certain circumstances. It may also be due to certain defects or faults in one or both of the spouses. The spouse at fault is held responsible for failure of the marriage and the other spouse becomes entitled, under certain conditions, to the dissolution of the marriage on that account.

XIII. *Marriage when to be Dissolved*

As already stated, the Muslim jurists are guided in the matters of marriage and divorce by the injunctions of the

38. Qur'ān LXV : 2.
39. See Chapter on Rajah (retraction).

Qur'ān, "Retain them (the wives) in kindness or separate (from them) with kindness."[40] The Muslim jurists state that a husband cannot be said to be keeping his wife in a becoming or kindly manner when the wife cannot live happily with him because of a defect or fault in him and that under such circumstances the husband becomes a transgressor of this injunction of the Qur'ān. The *qāḍī* can, therefore, dissolve such a marriage in order to remove the husband's transgression and to give relief to the aggrieved party.

There is another verse in the Qur'ān, which is equally important in this connection and defines the rights of the spouses. It states, "And women have rights similar to those against them in a just manner."[41] This verse shows that men and women have similar rights and obligations against one another. A party failing to discharge his or her obligations will be failing in his or her duty towards the other and will thus be a transgressor of this injunction of the Qur'ān. In such a case a marriage shall be liable to be dissolved on the complaint of the aggrieved party.

It is not an essential condition for the dissolution of marriage that the party at fault should have actually committed some act which results in misery for the other party. It is quite possible that the husband or the wife may be the victim of causes beyond his or her control. What has to be seen in such a case is whether the aggrieved party can live with the other spouse in a manner whereby the objectives of marriage are not defeated. If that is not possible then the dissolution of marriage becomes desirable.

XIV. *Marital Obligations*

It is also to be seen for the dissolution of a marriage whether the spouses are faithfully and sincerely fulfilling the marital obligations incumbent on them.

The following are some of the important obligations of a husband according to the Muslim jurists :

40. Qur'ān, II : 231.
41. *Ibid.*, II : 228.

(*a*) to protect the wife ;
(*b*) to maintain her ;
(*c*) to pay her dower to her ;
(*d*) to make himself attractive and to be sexually fit so that she (the wife) should not feel completely neglected or be dissatisfied with the marriage on that ground ;
(*e*) to treat the wife with affection and kindness. This includes permission to her to visit her parents and relatives ;
(*f*) not to obstruct her in the performance of her religious duties and
(*g*) to grant her freedom from the bond of marriage when he has no inclination towards her.

The important marital obligations of the wife are :
(*a*) to look after the domestic comforts of her husband ;
(*b*) to be respectful, obedient and faithful to him ;
(*c*) to make herself available to him at all reasonable times ;
(*d*) to make herself attractive to him ;
(*e*) to suckle the children during the prescribed or usual period of time, if so desired by the husband, and to bring up the children properly.

Some of these obligations cast a legal duty on the husband or the wife, as the case may be, while others are in the nature of moral obligations only.

It is not every failure of the marital obligations on the part of one party that entitles the other party to the dissolution of the marriage and such right can be exercised only when the failure is of a serious nature.

A marriage can be dissolved when a wife has an 'invincible' repugnance or aversion for her husband. The dissolution of marriage at the instance of the wife will be discussed in the chapter on *Khul'*.

As already stated, a marriage can also be dissolved when one of the spouses suffers from some serious defect-physical, social, cultural or moral. It may, however, be stated that when one or more of the objects of a marriage are lost due to a defect in one of the spouses, the marriage does not *ipso facto* cease to exist but that it gives option to the other party who may or may not like to continue such a marriage. Thus, a man may marry a woman who may be beyond the age at which she can bear children simply to escape from loneliness or to have someone to attend to his domestic requirements. Similarly, a woman may, for the sake of financial support and material comforts or companionship, marry a man who she knows is suffering from incapacity.

XV. *Right to Dissolve Marriage*

A Muslim marriage is ordinarily a relationship for life based on mutual consent of the parties. But under the Muslim law, unlike some other systems of law, marriage is a special type of civil contract. It follows that the parties to it have a right, as in other contracts, to continue the contract of marriage or to discontinue it on reasonable grounds.

XVI. *Who can Dissolve Marriage*

A marriage can be dissolved by either the husband or the wife or by their mutual consent or by the Qādi or the Arbitrator. It can also get terminated automatically on the happening of certain contingencies. The cause that constitutes a ground for dissolution of marriage can be the conduct or the physical or mental condition of the husband or of the wife. The marriage can also be dissolved when it is ill-assorted.

XVII. *Dissolution of Marriage by the Husband*

A marriage can be dissolved by the husband through divorce, *īlā'* or *ẓihār*.

(*a*) *Divorce* : The present Muslim practice allows the husband full powers to dissolve the marriage at his sweet will without assigning any reason or without even there being a reasonable ground for the divorce. All the Muslim sects, with the exception of the Mu'tazilites, concede this absolute power to the husband. Some of them do admit that marriage being commended, it can be terminated only in case of urgency for its dissolution and that when there is no valid necessity for its termination then the husband is not justified in dissolving it. But, in spite of it, they do not hold a divorce without justification to be legally invalid; they only consider it to be sinful. The view of the vast majority of the *fuqahā'* may, for all practical purposes, be taken in the present times to be the Muslim law on the point. The matter is fully discussed in a subsequent chapter.

(*b*) *Īlā' and Ẓihār*: These are two other methods of dissolving the marriage by the husband, that will be discussed in subsequent chapters.

XVIII. *Dissolution of Marriage by the Wife*

A wife can herself dissolve her marriage by the exercise of *k͟hiyār al-bulūg͟h* (option of puberty) or under *tafwīḍ*, that is, when the power of divorce has been delegated to her by the husband. She can also have recourse to *k͟hul'*.

XIX. *Dissolution of Marriage by Mutual Consent*

It is always open to the spouses to mutually agree to the termination of their marriage for a consideration or without it. This they can do by *k͟hul'*, *mubārāh*, or *ṭalāq bi 'iwaḍ al-māl*.

XX. *Dissolution of Marriage by the Qāḍī*

At the instance of the husband: A husband can get his marriage dissolved by the *qāḍī* without usually becoming liable for the payment of the dower in the following cases:

(*a*) If the wife or the guardian of a minor wife has been guilty of fraud in certain respects;

(*b*) When the husband was married during his minority by his guardian for a dower unreasonably high;

(*c*) When the spouses are non-Muslims and the husband embraces Islam but the wife refuses to do so;

(*d*) When the wife is suffering from some serious defects: physical, social or mental.

The Mālikīs, the Shāfi'īs and the Ḥanbalīs among the Sunnīs, and the Shi'īs hold that a marriage can be dissolved by the *qāḍī* at the instance of the husband on the ground of a serious blemish in the wife. The Ḥanafīs do not agree with this view and do not allow the termination of marriage on this ground as it deprives the wife of a portion of her dower in some cases.

XXI. *At the Instance of the Wife*

A marriage can be dissolved by the *qāḍī* at the instance of the wife on the following grounds :

(*a*) When the husband's conduct is such as has been specifically disapproved of by Islam ;

(*b*) When the husband is suffering from a serious mental or physical defect which renders the continuation of the marriage unsafe or undesirable for the wife ;

(*c*) When she was a minor at the time of her marriage ;

(*d*) When she was given in marriage by her guardian and her dower is unreasonably low, that is, is lower than the customary dower ;

(*e*) When the spouses are non-Muslims and the wife embraces Islam but the husband refuses to do so ;

(*f*) When she embraces Islam and chooses a Muslim State for her domicile but her husband remains behind in a non-Muslim State.[40] (Applicable to non-Muslims).

(*g*) When the husband accuses her of unchastity.

The above grounds are briefly discussed below :—

Undesirable conduct of the husband: The conduct or behaviour of the husband that gives cause for the dissolution of marriage must be such as injuriously affects the wife, such as when the husband :

(1) attributes unchastity to the wife ;

(2) takes a vow not to be intimate with his wife for a period of four months or more and this constitutes *īlā'*;

(3) makes it unlawful for himself to be intimate with his wife by *ẓihār* ;

(4) absents himself from the conjugal domicile for a period of four years or longer, and his whereabouts, are not known or

(5) is guilty of inequality between two or more wives, etc.

XXII. *Automatic Dissolution of Marriage*

Under Muslim law marriage becomes automatically dissolved on

(1) the death of one of the spouses ;

(2) apostasy of one of the spouses ;

(3) under the Sunnī law, on the fufilment of a condition in the case of a conditional divorce or

(4) change of domicile in case of non-Muslims.

The various methods of dissolution of marriage shall be discussed in detail in the subsequent chapters.

If a marriage is dissolved for a cause imputable to the husband then it has, generally speaking, the effect of *ṭalāq* or divorce on the ground that the dissolution of the marriage has been brought about on account of the husband and so he should be deemed to have divorced his wife. Thus, if the marriage is dissolved on the ground that the husband is impotent or insane and the like, then the dissolution of the marriage will have the effect of *ṭalāq* (divorce) even though the marriage is dissolved by the *qāḍī* at the instance of the wife. The dissolution of marriage by or at the instance of a wife is called *fasḵh* (termination). If the marriage is dissolved due to a cause attributable to the wife then also it shall have the effect of *fasḵh* or termination of the marriage by the wife. Thus, if it is dissolved by the wife in the exercise of the option of puberty or by the *qāḍī* on the ground of some serious blemish in her, then it shall be deemed to be *fasḵh* by the wife.[42] It may be added here that the above is not an invariable rule of law and there are certain exceptions to it. Thus, if a marriage is dissolved on account of the apostasy or conversion to Islam of the husband or his adoption of a domicile

42. Ibn 'Ābidīn, *op. cit.*, II : 315.

in *dār al-ḥarb* when the wife resides in *dār al-Islām*, then the dissolution shall be considered to be *faskh*, although the marriage is dissolved for a cause attributable to the husband.

The effect of both these methods, namely, *ṭalāq* and *faskh* is the same as far as dissolution of marriage is concerned. The difference lies in the extent of the husband's liability for payment of dower and the number of divorces effected.

The termination of marriage by the *qāḍī* either on his own initiative or at the instance of the wife or a third person is called *faskh*.

The automatic termination of marriage is called a *furqah* (separation).

XXIII. *At the Instance of a Third Party*

A marriage can be dissolved at the instance of certain near relations of the wife if she contracts a marriage for a dower which is less than the customary dower in her family or if the husband is otherwise unequal to the girl's family.[43]

XXIV. *By the Qāḍī on his own Initiative*

It is the duty of the *qāḍī* to dissolve a marriage if he comes to know that it is *fāsid* or irregular.

The chart facing this page will show at a glance the classification of the dissolution of marriage as mentioned in these pages.

43. For discussion, see chapter on 'Inequality' in Marriages.

Dissolution of Marriage in Muslim Law

- By the husband
  - Talaq or Divorce
  - Ila'
  - Zihar
- By the wife
  - Khiyar ul-Balugh or Option of Puberty
  - Tufwīd
- By mutual consent
  - Khul'
  - Arbitration
- By the Qādi
  - At the instance of the husband
    - When the marriage is unequal
    - When the wife suffers from certain defects
    - When the husband embraces Islam but the wife refuses to do so
  - At the instance of the wife
    - When the marriage is unequal
    - When the husband suffers from certain defects
    - When the husband accuses the wife of unchastity
    - When the husband is missing
    - When the wife embraces Islam but the husband refuses to do so
    - When the husband is incapable of maintaining the wife (under the Maliki, Shaf'i and Hanbali Laws)
    - When the husband illtreats the wife (under the Maliki and Hanbali Laws)
    - When the husband fails to perform his marital obligations (according to Taimiyah and Ibn Qayyim)
    - When the husband does not or refuses to comply with the Qādi's order to divorce his wife
    - When the husband is guilty of inequality between two or more wives
  - At his own initiative
    - When the marriage is Fasid or irregular
- Automatic dissolution of marriage
  - Apostasy of one spouse
  - Change of domicile by one spouse (applicable to non-Muslims)
  - Fulfilment of condition in conditional divorce

Chapter 2

DIVORCE

GENERAL DISCUSSION

I. *Ṭalāq or Divorce*: The most common method of dissolving a marriage is to divorce the wife.

II. *Definition*: *Ṭalāq* (Divorce) may be defined as the release from the marriage-tie either immediately or eventually, by the use of certain words, whether spoken or written, by the husband.[1]

III. *Ṭalāq, how given*: No particular formula or words have been prescribed by the Sunnī law for pronouncing a divorce and any words can serve the purpose so long as they clearly denote the husband's intention to divorce his wife. Divorce may be pronounced before or after the consummation of marriage. According to the Sunnî law, it may be given verbally or in writing.

Shī'i Law: Under the Shi'i law, divorce has to be given by the husband in certain specified words in Arabic. If he is not capable of pronouncing them, he can appoint an agent if one is available, otherwise he can pronounce divorce in any other language known to him as is done in the case of marriage.[2] But it cannot be given in writing except in the case of a person who cannot speak.[3]

IV. *Wife's Consent*: The wife's consent or want of consent to the husband's exercise of the right to dissolve the marriage is immaterial. She cannot object to a divorce by her husband.

V. *Wife's Presence at the Time of Divorce*: The wife's

1. *Al-Fatāwā al-Hindiyah*, Urdu trans., *Fatāwā 'Ālamgīrīyah*, Lucknow, 1899, II : 137, Ibn al-Hummām, Kamāl al-Dīn, *Fatḥ al-Qadīr*, Cairo, 1356 A.H., III : 20.
2. Ja'far b. al-Ḥasan, *Sharā'i al-Islām*, Tehran, 1377 A.H., p. 207.
3. *Ibid.*

presence or absence at the time of pronouncement of divorce is, so far as the validity of divorce is concerned, immaterial. Her presence is not at all an essential condition for the validity of divorce which can be lawfully given in her absence. All that is necessary is that there should be a clear reference to the wife in the pronouncement of divorce so that there may be no uncertainty as to the woman who is being divorced.

Both the Sunni and the Shī'i laws have prescribed certain essentials for the validity of divorce, but the presence of the wife is not one of them. A husband who is absent can lawfully divorce his wife. Again, while discussing divorce both the Sunni and the Shī'i jurists have stated that if a person asks a husband if he has divorced such and such wife of his and he replies "yes" then a divorce would be effected. The above establishes the fact that it is not at all necessary that the wife should be present at the time of divorce. The Supreme Court of Pakistan happens to have stated to the contrary in Syed Ali Nawaz Gardezi Vs. Lt. Col. Muhammad Yusuf, PLD 1963 S. C. 51, and has observed that a divorce should be given in the presence of the wife. This is only an *obita dicta.* It is submitted that neither the Sunni nor the Shī'i law makes it an essential condition for the validity of divorce that the wife should be present at the time when it is pronounced and the view requires reconsideration.

VI. *Whether Divorce is to be Addressed to the Wife or other Person*: It is not necessary that the repudiation should be addressed to the wife, or to any person whosoever. This finds support from a passage in *al-Fatāwā al-'Ālamgīrīyah* and a similar one in *Sharā'i' al-Islām.* The passage reads: "A person asks a man: Have you divorced your wife?' And he answers: 'Yes'. She is divorced."[4]

This shows very clearly that it is not at all essential that the repudiation should be addressed to the wife or to any other

4. *Al-Fatāwā al-Hindīyah, op. cit.,* II: 151; Ja'far b. al-Hasan *op, cit.,* II, p 206.

person. It was held in a case by the Calcutta High Court that the mere pronouncing of the word "*Ṭalāq*" three times without addressing it to any person does not constitute a valid divorce.[5] But it should be noted that it is certainly not a condition of divorce that it should be addressed to the wife or uttered in her presence or addressed to any other person. All that the law requires is that there should be an unmistakable reference to the wife in the pronouncement of the divorce. It seems probable that the Court was referring to an essential condition of divorce, viz., that when it is not addressed to the wife, there must be a clear reference to her so that the identity of the woman who is being divorced should be disclosed or established. The words used in the case violate this condition, but the established facts of the case leave no doubt about the identity of the woman who was being divorced. It is submitted that the view of the Court on this point has been worded too broadly and cannot be justified by any provision of the Muslim law on the point. In another case, this ruling was cited before the Bombay High Court, but that Court did not agree with the view taken by the Calcutta High Court.[6]

VII. *Information to Wife*: It is not essential for the validity of a divorce that information of it should be given by the husband to his divorced wife. The divorce shall be effected as soon as it is pronounced. The only consequence of the husband's failure to give her information about it is that his liability in respect of his wife in certain matters continues till she gets information of the same. Thus, a wife shall be entitled to her maintenance up to the time when she receives such information and also during the period of her *'iddah*, if any be incumbent. Her claim to her deferred dower shall not be affected as long as she does not receive information of the divorce. But in Pakistan, Section 7 of the Muslim Family

5. *Farzand Hussain*. v. *Jaru Bibi*, I.L.R. 4 Cal. 588.
6. *Sarabai* v. Rabia Bai, I.L.R. 30 Bombay 537; *Rashid Ahmad* v. *Anisa Khatun*, A.I.R. (1932) P.C. 25.

Laws Ordinance, 1961, has made it incumbent on the husband to give information of the divorce to the Chairman of the Union Council and to supply a copy thereof to the wife.

VIII. *Intention: General Discussion*: Both the Sunni and Shī'i jurists hold that it is not possible to know what is in a man's heart. The Sunni jurists seem to be of the opinion that as it is not possible to know what is in the mind of a person, effect must be given to what he expressly says or has said without inquiring what was in his mind when he made the statement. They, therefore, do not allow any opportunity to a husband to explain his meaning or intention but rely wholly and solely on what was actually said. The Shī'i jurists, on the other hand, seem to consider that as it is not possible to find what was in the mind of a person, we have to rely on him to tell us what he meant by making a certain statement.[7] Thus, it is stated in the *Sharā'i' al-Islām* that if a person pronounces the *ṣīghah* (formula of divorce) and should he explain that he did not intend *ṭalāq* by that expression, his explanation shall be accepted.[8] The difference in the deductions has given rise to the enunciation of many different rules by each sect.

Sunnī Law: The Sunni jurists hold that a divorce would be effected even when it is pronounced without any intention to severe the marital tie.[9] They seem to have been influenced by the fact that in the absence of such a rule, the husband can be in a position to undo the effect of his divorce whenever he may so want, by explaining that he had pronounced the divorce without any intention to separate from his wife.

As observed before, Islam disapproves of divorce, but considers it lawful. The Sunni jurists have strongly discouraged the careless and wanton use of words purporting to signify a divorce. They rely on two Traditions of the Prophet (peace be on him) for their view. According to one, he has said that in three things, namely, marriage, divorce, and the manumission

7. Ja'far b. al-Ḥasan, *op. cit.*, p. 206-7.
8. *Ibid.*
9. Al-Marghīnānī, Ali b. Abi Bakr, *al-Hidāyah*, Delhi, n.d., II : 339 ; *Fatḥ al-Qadīr*, *op. cit.*, III : 445.

of a slave, jesting is not allowed.[10] In another Tradition he is reported to have said that there are three things of which the serious is serious and the frivolous is serious, namely, marriage, divorce and freeing a slave.[11] The Sunnī jurists have gone so far as to lay down that a marriage would be dissolved on a divorce being pronounced even when it is pronounced without any intention to terminate the marriage and is given only in jest or without understanding the meaning of the words or by a slip of the tongue and even under fraud. They hold that under such circumstances the divorce would be given effect to by the *qāḍī* but the divorce will not be effected in religion so that the spouses can continue to live as husband and wife without being guilty of committing a sin. The *qāḍī* cannot take cognisance of such a case until and unless he is approached by one of the parties.

Ma<u>kh</u>dūm Muḥammad Ja'far has stated that a divorce shall not be effective if a husband has pronounced it without understanding the meaning of the words or has been made to pronounce the words under duress or by deceit.[12] This view is more suitable to be followed in the present time and a divorce given under fraud and pronounced without any intention to severe the marital connection, should not be held binding on the husband. The basic idea that the husband should not be allowed to undo the pronouncement of his divorce lightly has no reference to such a case.

The Pakistan Family Laws Ordinance, 1961, has helped the parties where the husband has pronounced a divorce without an intention to that effect. Under Section 7 of the Ordinance, the divorce shall remain ineffective for ninety days from the date of communication of the information regarding divorce to the Chairman of the Union Council. The Arbitration Council shall try in the meantime to bring about a reconciliation between the parties so that they can continue the marital relationship, if they so decide. If a husband has

10. Walī al-Dīn al-<u>Kh</u>aṭīb, *Mi<u>sh</u>kāt al-Maṣābīḥ*, *op. cit.*, p. 284.
11. *Ibid.*
12. Ma<u>kh</u>dūm Muḥammad Ja'far, *al-Mutanah*, Karachi, 1962, p. 465.

pronounced divorce to his wife without an intention to that effect then he may, within a period of ninety days, take her back.

Shī'i Law : Under the Shī'i law, the husband's intention to divorce his wife is an essential condition of divorce and in the absence of such an intention divorce is not effected.[13] If a husband divorced his wife but he subsequently explained that he had not intended or meant to terminate the marriage-tie, his words shall be accepted and the wife shall not stand divorced. The Shī'i jurists do not attach much importance to the words actually used by the husband and allow him to explain the pronouncement of his divorce and to assert that while pronouncing the divorce, he had no intention to dissolve the marriage.

IX. *Presence of Witnesses* : Under the Sunnī law, the presence of witnesses at the time of divorce is highly approved of, but is not an essential condition of divorce. The absence of witnesses at the time of divorce often leads to great complications because sometimes it is very difficult to prove that a certain woman had or had not been divorced. To meet this difficulty, Section 7 of the Muslim Family Laws Ordinance, 1961, (Pakistan) has made it compulsory for a husband, who divorces his wife, to inform the Chairman of the Union Council about the divorce and also to send a copy of it to the wife.

Shī'i Law: Presence of two trustworthy male witnesses at the time of divorce is an essential condition under the Shī'i law.[14] They should be present together at that time. A full Bench of the Lahore High Court has expressed the view that "the rule regarding the presence of two witnesses is a rule of evidence which stands replaced by the Evidence Act."[15] The Supreme Court of Pakistan did not approve of the view and stated in its judgment that "the law, however, being laid

13. Ja'far b. al-Ḥasan, *op. cit.*, p. 206.

14. *Ibid.*, p. 208; Abu'l-Ḥasan al-Mūsawī, *Wasīlat al-Najāt*, Najaf, 1364 A.H., p. 370.

15. Lt. Col. Muhammad Yusuf, Vs. Syed Ali Nawaz Gardezi, 1963 P.L.D, Lahore 141.

down in categorical terms, it is open to question whether the view taken by the Appellate Bench can be sustained."[16] It may be noted that the view expressed by the High Court requires reconsideration. The rule regarding presence of witnesses is certainly not a rule of evidence, but belongs to the substantive Shī'i law of divorce and is an essential part of the same. Under the Shī'i law, a divorce pronounced in the absence of witnesses shall be invalid. It is stated in *Sharā'i' al-Islām* that the hearing of the pronouncement of divorce is an essential condition for the validity of the divorce. The Shī'i law is so strict in the matter that it has laid down that in the absence of witnesses no divorce shall be effected even if all the other conditions are satisfied, nor shall a divorce be effected if only one witness be present or the two witnesses present are not just and reliable.[17] The Shī'i jurists rely on their interpretation of the verse of Sūrah *al-Ṭalāq* (LXV : 2) which enjoins the presence of two witnesses at the time of divorce. Thus, the Shī'i law is more strict in the matter of divorce than the Sunnī law.

X. *Safeguards for Wife*: To provide against an unjustified divorce by the husband, it is usual for the parents or guardians of a girl to get a big amount of money fixed for her dower so that the husband may not act rashly in divorcing his wife as he would have to pay the amount of the dower which would become due on the pronouncement of the divorce. To provide against an unhappy life a wife can also lawfully enter into an agreement with the husband to the effect that she herself would be competent to pronounce a divorce on his behalf under certain specified conditions.[18] It can also be made a condition of marriage that on separation the wife shall be maintained by the husband till her remarriage or even for her life and that the husband shall pay her a specified amount of money per month. Such a stipulation does not offend

16. Syed Ali Nawaz Gardezi Vs. Lt. Col. Muhammad Yusuf, 1963 P.L.D S. C. 51.
17. Ja'far b. Hasan, *op. cit.*, p. 208 ; Abu Hasan al-Mūsawī, *op. cit.*, p. 370.
18. For discussion, See chapter on '*Tafwīḍ*', (delegation).

against the rule of public policy.[19] Neither does such a stipulation encourage their living separate from each other any more than their living together. The chapter on *Tafwīḍ* gives an idea of the conditions that may be stipulated by a wife for her safeguard.

XI. *Burden of Proof*: Where a particular relationship, such as marriage, has been shown to exist between two persons, there is a presumption in favour of its continuance and the burden of proving that they no longer stand in that relationship to one another lies on the person who alleges it. The Muslim jurists, therefore, hold that the burden of proof lies on the plaintiff.[20]

Where a party relies on the statement of a witness who is alleged to have asked the husband about the divorce and the matter depends upon the question whether the latter had said, "Yes" or "True" in answer, then it is of vital importance that the witness should give the exact words of the husband's reply.[21]

19. For discussion, see chapter on '*Tafwiḍ*'. (delegation).
20. 'Abd Allāh b. Aḥmad al-Nasafī, *Kanz al-Daqā'iq*, Deoband, 1368 A.H., p. 280.
21. Ghulam Muhiudin Khan Vs. Khizar Hussain, A.I.R. 1929 Lahore 6.

Chapter 3

CAPACITY TO DIVORCE

I. Preliminary

As stated before, the legal rights and obligations of the parties against each other in a Muslim marriage are governed by the Law of Contracts. A husband has got the right to terminate the marriage by divorce. The wife can also exercise this power under certain conditions. It is, therefore, necessary, as in other civil contracts, that they must possess the capacity to act in the matter.

The Muslim jurists classify the circumstances which affect the capacity or incapacity of a person to act into two categories, namely, *Samāwī* and *Makṣubah*. The former means what may be called an act of God, that is, circumstances beyond one's control; and the latter are the circumstances created or brought about by one himself. Some instances of the conditions belonging to the former category are lunacy, sleep, fainting, fit etc. Such conditions as ignorance of law or facts, jest, voluntary drunkenness, mistake etc. are instances of the second category.[1] A person can generally have no hand in bringing about the conditions of the former class, but the bringing about of circumstances of the latter class is attributed to him or her. Hence a divorce pronounced under the former condition is not considered effective while a divorce pronounced in the latter condition is considered effective

II. Religious Sanction

The Traditions given below deal with a man's capacity to exercise the power of divorce :—

1. 'Ā'ishah reported, "I heard the Propnet (peace be on him) say: 'There is no divorce and no emancipation by force'."[2]

1. Ibn Qudāmah, Al-Mughnī, Cairo, 1307 A.H. VII : 114.
2. Walī al-Dīn al-Khaṭīb, *Mishkāt al-Maṣābih,* Delhi, 1350 A.H. p. 284.

2. 'Alī reported that the Prophet (peace be on him) said: 'Pen has been lifted from the three: the sleeping man till he is awake; a boy till he attains maturity; and an insane person till he recovers his senses."[3]

3. Abū Hurayrah reported that the Prophet (peace be on him) said: "Every divorce is lawful except the divorce of the lunatic and of one who is demented."[4]

4. Abū Hurayrah has also reported that the Prophet (peace be on him) said: "There are three things of which the serious is serious and the frivolous is serious, namely, marriage, divorce and *raj'ah*".[5]

III. Capacity

Under Muslim law two conditions must be satisfied before a person can lawfully dissolve a marriage. He or she must be major and should possess understanding.[6] If one of these conditions is not fulfilled, he or she shall not be competent to dissolve a marriage. In case of divorce by the husband, intention is not considered a necessary condition for a valid pronouncement by the Sunnis, if the husband uses the word *Ṭalāq*. If, however, the pronouncement of divorce is ambiguous then it will be necessary to ascertain the husband's intention. But there is a difference of opinion amongst the Sunnī jurists in respect of several matters as has been discussed at relevant places in this book. Some of them are such as involve hardship to the parties or at least to one of them. The provisions of the Pakistan Muslim Family Laws Ordinance, 1961, provide against the undesirable aspects of divorce given in certain special circumstances. Thus Section 7 (*i*) of the Ordinance makes it incumbent on a husband who divorces his wife to give information of his action to the

3. Walī al-Dīn al-Khaṭib, *Mishkāt al-Maṣābih*, Delhi, 1350 A.H. p. 284.
4. *Ibid.*
5. *Ibid.*
6. Ibn 'Ābidīn, *Al-Radd al-Muḥtār*, Cairo, 1318 A.H., II; 428; *Al-Fatāwā al-Hindīyah* (Urdu Translation), *'Ālamgiriyah*, Lucknow, 1899 A.D II: 144.

Chairman of the Union Council of his ward and to send a copy of it to his wife. It reads as follows: "Any man who wishes to divorce his wife shall, as soon as may be after the pronouncement of *ṭalāq* in any form whatsoever, give the Chairman notice in writing of his having done so, and shall supply a copy thereof to the wife". Sub-section (3) states, "Save as provided in Sub-section (5), a *ṭalāq*, unless revoked earlier, expressly or otherwise, shall not be effective until the expiration of ninety days from the day on which notice under Sub-section (1) is delivered to the Chairman".

IV. Choice or Free Will

As has been stated in the beginning of this Chapter, the Prophet (peace be on him) has not sanctioned the validity of divorce by force. But in course of time the Ḥanafī jurists have held that a divorce under compulsion is valid.[7]

Mālikī, Sh̲āfi'ī and Ḥanbalī Laws

Under the Mālikī, Sh̲āfi'ī and Ḥanbalī laws choice is an essential condition for pronouncing a divorce. A marriage, therefore, cannot be dissolved by a divorce pronounced under coercion.[8]

Sh̲ī'ī Law

Under Sh̲ī'ī Law majority, understanding, intention and free will are essential conditions for the valid pronouncement of a divorce by a person. A divorce shall not be deemed valid if even one of these four conditions is not fulfilled.[9] Hence, a divorce under the influence of drink or sleep or under compulsion or when pronounced without understanding the meaning of the words pronounced, or under fraud and the like will be absolutely ineffective. In view of this basic principle

7. Ibn 'Ābidīn, *Al-Radd al-Muḥtār*, Cairo, 1318 A.H., II: 428: *Al-Fatāwā al-Hindiyah*, Urdu translation; *'Ālamgīriyah*, *op. cit.*, II: 144.
8. Ibn Qudāmah, *op. cit.*, VII: 114-15.
9. Ja'far b. al-Ḥasan, *Sh̲arā'i' al-Islām*, Tehran, 1377 A.H., pp. 205-6

of law, it has not been considered necessary to discuss the Shī'i Law under the various Sunnī rules.

V. *Wife's Capacity to Receive Divorce*

A divorce is considered to be the sole act and right of the husband and generally speaking the wife has no hand in a divorce by the husband. It can be pronounced even against her wishes and so the wife's capacity is of no consequence. It is not, therefore, necessary that she should be major or should possess understanding.

Ameer Ali has stated, "Both schools insist that the formula or *sighèh*, by which the *talâk* is pronounced, should in every case be understood by the wife. It would seem to follow, therefore, that when she is of such tender age as to be unable to comprehend the legal consequences flowing from the act of repudiation, or does not possess discretion (*rushd*), a valid *talâk* cannot be effected against her. The Shī'ah *Nail-ul-Marām* requires *akl* (sound understanding) on both sides for the effectuation of proper repudiation."[10] It is submitted that as far as the Sunnīs are concerned, this view does not apply to them and there is no such provision under the Sunnī law. But the point of view expressed by Ameer Ali is a sound one and it should have been the duty of our law-givers to give due consideration to it. It is, however, no longer necessary to do so as the Child Marriage Restraint Act prohibits the marriage of a girl below fourteen years of age.[11] The Muslim Family Laws Ordinance, 1961, in force in Pakistan, has increased the age to sixteen years.

VI. *General Discussion of*

The question of capacity is a very important one and some important aspects relating to it are, therefore, discussed below :—

(*a*) *Majority :* Majority is a necessary condition under Muslim law in respect of a man's capacity to divorce his wife.

10. Ameer Ali, *Muhammadan Law*, Calcutta, 1908 A.D., Vol. II, p. 533.
11. Sections 2 (*a*), 4 and 5 of the Child Marriage Restraint Act, 1929.

A minor is not competent to exercise that power even if he may be possessed of understanding.[12] Hence, a divorce by him would be ineffectual even when he confirms it on attaining majority.[13] If, therefore, on attaining majority he wants to persist in the divorce, given by him when he was a minor, he must give a fresh divorce to his wife.[14] A divorce by a boy or a minor is not considered valid for two reasons. Firstly, because the Prophet (peace be on him) has said, "Every divorce is lawful except that of a boy, that is, a minor or lunatic."[15] Secondly, because a man's capacity to act depends on his possession of a sound judgment, which is presumed lacking in the case of minor. The guardian of a minor also cannot divorce a minor's wife on his behalf.[16] If he does so, the divorce will be ineffective and the invalidity cannot be cured even if the minor assents to it on attaining majority.[17]

Majority, age of : Majority of a boy or a girl with regard to his or her capacity in the matter of dissolution of marriage shall be determined according to the age fixed under the Muslim law and not according to the Majority Act.[18]

Shī'ī Law : Shī'ī law is the same as the Sunnī law with regard to the condition of puberty or majority. But under that law the guardian of a minor can divorce the minor's wife on his behalf if the minor is deficient in understanding and the divorce is in the interest of the minor.[19]

(*b*) *Understanding* : It has been seen above that it is an essential condition of divorce that the husband should possess

12. Al-Marghīnānī, 'Alī b. Abī Bakr, *Al-Hidāyah*, Delhi, n.d. II : 338. Ibn Nujaym, *al-Baḥr al-Rā'iq*, Cairo, 1311 A.H., III : 263; Ibn 'Ābidīn, *op. cit.*, II ; 428.
13. *Al-Fatāwā al-Hindīyah* ; Urdu trans., *op. cit.*, II : 145 ; Ibn 'Ābidīn, *op. cit.*, II : 437.
14. *Ibid.*
15. Al-Marghīnānī, *op. cit.*, II : 338.
16. *Al-Fatāwā al-Hindīyah* (Urdu trans.), *op. cit.*, II : 145 ; Ibn 'Ābidīn, *op. cit.*, II : 428.
17. *Ibid.*
18. Section 2 of the Majority Act.
19. Ja'far b. al-Ḥasan, *op. cit.*, p. 205.

understanding. If he is devoid of it as when he is insane then he is not held responsible for his acts and so a divorce pronounced by him shall be ineffective.[20] Want of understanding, however, means complete loss of intellect so that the person cannot understand the nature of his acts. But the mere fact that he cannot fully appreciate the consequences of his acts is not sufficient to bring a person within the exception.[21]

The effect of understanding on the dissolution of marriage can be considered from three aspects, namely, when the husband is (*i*) completely devoid of understanding, or (*ii*) is suffering from a temporary loss of understanding or (*iii*) when he possesses a weak intellect.

(*i*) *Lunatic*: A divorce by a lunatic is not effective. Two reasons are given for this rule. The first is that the Prophet (peace be on him) has said, "Every divorce is lawful except that of a boy or a lunatic."[22] The second is that a man's competency to divorce depends on his possession of a sound judgment which is wanting in the case of a lunatic.[23]

Idiot: The word "Lunatic" is used here in a general sense and includes an "Idiot".

(*ii*) *Temporary loss*: By want or loss of understanding is not meant only a permanent loss of that faculty but even a temporary condition of insanity can bring a case within the exception to the general rule that every person can divorce his wife. This exception, however, shall hold good only during the period the condition lasts.[24] A divorce by a person having lost his understanding for the time being due to some cause such as shock shall also not be effective because in Muslim law possession of understanding is an essential condition

20. Ibn 'Ābidīn, *op. cit.*, II : 437.
21. *Ibid.*
22. Walī al-Dīn al-Khaṭīb, *Mishkāt*, *op. cit.*, p. 284.
23. Al-Marghīnānī, *op. cit.*, II : 338.
24. Ibn 'Ābidīn, *op. cit.*, II : 437-38.

for competency to divorce.[25] This rule holds good both when the husband is a lunatic or has temporarily lost his understanding.

Lucid interval: A person given to fits of lunacy shall be considered a lunatic for the purpose of this rule during the time when a fit is on.[26] But he shall be considered to be sane when he is free of a fit so that a divorce pronounced during the period of lucidity shall be effective.[27] Hence, if a person, while in a lucid interval, pronounces a conditional divorce to be effective on the happening of a certain event and he then becomes insane, the divorce would become effective under the Sunnī Law on the happening of that event whatever be his condition at the time of the happening of the event.[28]

(*iii*) *Person of weak understanding*: The mere fact that a person cannot fully appreciate the consequences of his acts is not sufficient to bring a case within the exception and a divorce pronounced by a person of weak intellect is not invalid but is binding on him.[29] Such a person is not completely devoid of understanding and so his case differs from that of a lunatic. If a person is of weak intellect then it is to be seen if the majority of his acts are normal or not. In the former case he shall be considered to be a normal man and his acts to be binding on him, but in the latter case he shall be considered to be insane and so not bound by his acts. The result is that a divorce pronounced in the former case shall be binding on him but not in the latter case.[30]

25. Ibn 'Ābidīn, *op. cit.*, II: 437-38.
26. *Al-Fatāwā al-Hindīyah*, (Urdu trans.) *op. cit.*, II: 144.
27. Ibn 'Ābidīn, *op. cit.*, II: 437-38.
28. *Ibid.*
29. *Ibid.*
30. *Ibid.*

(c) *Divorce under influence of sleep*: It has already been seen that sleep is a condition which is not brought about by man himself. He is, therefore, not held responsible for an act done by him while under the influence of that condition because the act is done without any volition on his part. A divorce uttered by a person under the influence of sleep shall not be effective.[31] A person cannot be aware of the words uttered by him in his sleep and they are not the result of volition.[32] This rule of law is based on the Tradition that the Prophet (peace be on him) has stated that three classes of persons are not responsible for their acts, namely, a minor till he attains puberty, a lunatic till his recovery and a person who is asleep till he wakes up.[33] A divorce shall not be effected even if he confirms it on awakening.[34] The divorce would be ineffective even if he says, on waking up, to his wife, I divorced you in my sleep.[35]

(d) *Divorce under the influence of drink*: If a person gets intoxicated by drinking some fermented liquor, the question arises whether a divorce pronounced by him while in that condition would be effective or not. A general rule of law is that if a person gets drunk by the use of any liquor, prohibited by Muslim law, then any act done by him, while under the influence of that drink, shall not be excused but shall be held to be effective. Thus, if he divorces his wife while drunk, or sells something, enters into an agreement, borrows or lends money, all these acts shall be held valid and binding on him. This rule is based on the ground that as the cessation of his reason is due to the

31. Ibn 'Ābidīn *op. cit.*, II: 437-38.
32. *Ibid.*
33. Walī al-Dīn al-Khaṭib, *Mishkāt, op. cit.*, p. 284.
34. *Al-Fatāwā al-Hindiyah*, Urdu trans., *op. cit.*, II ; 144 ; Ibn 'Ābidīn *op. cit.*, II : 438.
35. *Ibid.*

committal of a sinful act, namely, drinking of an intoxicant liquor, it shall be presumed that he is still possessed of his reason. The *qāḍī's* order shall be held effective on the above ground.[36]

Al-Radd al-Muḥtār has stated another general rule of law in respect of the effect of pronouncement of divorce while under the influence of drink. It is laid down that what is to be seen in such a case is whether the drink has assumed a form the use of which is forbidden by Muslim law. If it has reached that stage then a divorce pronounced under its influence is effective. But if it has not reached that degree then a divorce pronounced under its influence shall not be effected.[37] The underlying idea is that a drink that has undergone a certain amount of fermentation but has not yet become intoxicating would not come within the prohibition. If a person drinks such a liquor and happens to get intoxicated and divorces his wife under the influence of the intoxication then the pronouncement of the divorce shall not be given effect to. If the liquor has, however, reached a high degree of intoxication, so much so that its use is not permitted by Muslim law, and should a person drink it and then get intoxicated and should he divorce his wife while in that condition, then the pronouncement of the divorce shall be given effect to. It must be noted here that in the first instance he was not guilty of the breach of any provision of Muslim law while in the other case he does commit a breach of the provisions of Muslim law. Hence, a divorce pronounced under the influence of grape-juice, if it has not become wine, shall not be effected. But a divorce shall be effected if the juice has become wine. It may be noted here that the basic principle is that a divorce pronounced when a man is not possessed of under-

36. Ibn 'Ābidīn, *op. cit.*, II ; 435.
37. *Ibid.*

standing is not held to be effective. Thus, a divorce given by a husband while suffering from insanity is absolutely ineffective. But a divorce given while a person is devoid of understanding under the influence of drink is held to be effective simply by way of punishment for the breach of the law restraining the use of strong liquors in order to discourage its use.

The matter may be considered from two aspects : (*i*) when a person gets intoxicated involuntarily and (*ii*) when he gets drunk voluntarily.

Involuntary Drinking : If a person is made drunk against his will or takes liquor from necessity as under medical advice and then gets intoxicated and repudiates his wife while under its influence then the divorce shall not be effective. This rule is based on the principle that his act was not voluntary and he cannot be held responsible for it and so cannot be punished for the act of drinking in such a case. It follows that the pronouncement of the divorce by him too would not be effective.[38] Some jurists hold otherwise but the former opinion is generally accepted as correct and is more reasonable.[39]

Voluntary Drinking: Ḥanafī view : There is a difference of opinion about the effect of the pronouncement of divorce when the husband is in a state of inebriety from voluntary drinking. Some jurists are of the opinion that the matter should be considered with regard to two distinct stages of intoxication. If the husband pronounces a divorce when slightly intoxicated so that he can realize the effect of his acts then it would be effected.[40] But if he prononces it while dead drunk so that he cannot distinguish between right and wrong, then the divorce would not be effected.[41]

It is stated in *al-Hidāyah* and other books that if a person were to drink wine or some other fermented liquor

38. *Ibid.*, Ibn Nujaym, *op. cit.*, III : 266.
39. *Al-Fatāwā al-Hindīyah*, Urdu trans., *op. cit.*, II : 145.
40 *Ibid* , Ibn Nujaym, *op. cit.*, III : 266.
41. *Ibid.*

in such a large quantity as to produce delirium or inflammation of the brain, thereby suspending his reason, and while in that condition he pronounces a divorce then it shall not take effect.[42] 'U<u>th</u>mān b. 'Affān holds that the pronouncement of a divorce by a person under the influence of drink is not effective. The same is the view expressed by Ibn 'Abbās.[43]

Opinions differ amongst the Ḥanafī jurists about the degree of intoxication which would absolve a person from responsibility for his acts while in that condition. According to Abū Ḥanīfah the person should be drunk to such a degree as to lose all understanding so much as to be unable to differentiate between the sky and the earth.[44] Abu Yūsuf and Muḥammad are less exacting in the matter. They consider that a person shall not be held responsible for his acts if he is drunk so much as to bring about a suspension of his reason so that he is not able to have control over his speech as in a delirium.[45]

According to *al-Baḥr al-Rā'iq* the rule laid down by Muḥammad and Abu Yūsuf is to be followed.[46] Ibn al-Humām holds that the opinion of Abū Ḥanīfah shall be applicable for awarding punishment while the opinion of the latter will hold good in cases of divorce.[47] He explains in *al-Taḥrīr* that the drink referred to by Abū Ḥanīfah is the drink the use of which will make the person liable to punishment while the drink referred to by Muḥammad and Abū Yūsuf is the drink the use of which will not subject the person to punishment but to other liabilities and means only the drink under the influence of which the person shall lose control of his speech and may talk wildly. Of course it is not necessary that the whole speech should be meaningless

42. *Ibid.*, Al-Mar<u>gh</u>īnānī, *op. cit.*, II : 338.
43. Al-Bu<u>kh</u>ārī, *al-Jāmi' al-Ṣaḥiḥ*, Delhi, 1938, II : 739 ; Ibn Nujaym *op. cit.*, III : 266,
44. Ibn Nujaym, *op. cit.*, III : 265; Ibn 'Ābidīn, *op. cit.*, II : 434.
45. *Ibid.*
46. *Ibid.*, III : 266.
47. Ibn 'Ābidīn, *op. cit.*, II : 434-35.

or irrational. In his commentary of *al-Taḥrīr*, Ibn Amīr al-Ḥājj explains that what Ibn al-Humām meant is that the greater portion of the speech should be meaningless and only a small portion should be rational. If, on the other hand, the greater portion of the speech should be rational and only a small portion wild and meaningless, he shall be considered to be possessed of understanding. A pronouncement of divorce by him shall, therefore, be effective.[48] Their reasoning is that the reality of intention is connected with the exercise of reason which is suspended during such intoxication and so divorce pronounced under such a condition would be ineffective.[49] Ṭaḥāwi and Karkhi are of the opinion that a divorce given while a man is drunk is wholly ineffective. It is stated in the *Tātar Khāniyah* that this is the generally accepted view. But *Al-Radd al-Muḥtār* opposes this view regarding voluntary drinking.[50] It states that it shall be presumed that the speaker is still possessed of reason and so his pronouncement of divorce shall take effect in order to deter him from drinking liquor which is forbidden. It is clear from this line of reasoning that the divorce is held valid to discourage drinking rather than on account of his capacity to pronounce a valid divorce while in that condition.

The majority of Ḥanafī jurists follow the rule stated by Abū Yusuf and Muḥammad. It is also the view of the other three Imāms, namely, Mālik, Shāfi'ī and Ibn Ḥanbal. It finds full support in a dictum of 'Alī that a drunkard is one who begins to talk irrationally and wildly. It is the view which is generally accepted as correct.[51] But the *Fatāwā al-'Ālamgīriyah* makes no distinction between the stages when a husband is only slightly drunk and when he is drunk to such an extent as to lose his understanding and the divorce pronounced

48. Ibn 'Ābidīn, *op. cit.*, II ; 434-35.

49. *Ibid.*, Al-Marghīnānī, *op. cit.*, II : 338-39.

50. *Ibid.*

51. *Ibid.*

by a person under the influence of wine or other fermented liquor is held to be effective.[52]

It is stated in *Al-Baḥr al-Rā'iq* that a divorce given under the influence of drink shall be effected irrespective of the fact whether the drink was taken voluntarily or under compulsion.[53] A different view has, however, been expressed in the *Fatāwā Qāḍī Khān* where it is stated that the divorce given under the influence of drink, taken under compulsion or from any necessity, shall not be effected.[54] The *Tuḥfah* supported by *Fatḥ al-Qadīr* also preferred the opinion stated in *Tuḥfat al-Fuqahā'*[55] given in *al-Muḥīt*.

Mālikī Law: The Mālikīs do not consider a divorce pronounced under the influence of drink to be effective if the husband is drunk to such an extent as not to distinguish between right and wrong.[56]

Ḥanbalī Law: Aḥmad b. Ḥanbal at one time held the same opinion as expressed by Mālik and considered that a divorce by a husband when he is drunk to such an extent as not to understand what he is talking is not effective.[57] He expressed a different opinion at other times, but finally he left the matter open on the basis that the matter was not clear as there was a difference of opinion on this point amongst the Companions themselves, and that every case has to be decided on its merits. His disciples too are not agreed in this matter. Thus Abū Bakr al-Khilāl, a very well-known Ḥanbalī jurist, holds a divorce, pronounced under such a condition, to be effective while Abū Bakr 'Abd al-'Azīz, an equally famous Ḥanbalī jurist, holds otherwise.[58]

Shāfi'ī Law: Shāfi'ī expressed different views at different times. At first he held that a divorce pro-

52. *Al-Fatāwā al-Hindīyah*, Urdu trans., *op. cit.*, II : 145.
53. Ibn Nujaym, *op. cit.*, III : 267.
54. Qāḍī Khān, *Fatāwā Qāḍī Khān*, Kānpur, 1310 A.H., p. 219.
55. Ibn al-Humām, Kamāl al-Dīn, *Fatḥ al-Qadīr*, Cairo, 1356 A.H., III : 41.
56. Ibn Qudāmah, *op. cit.*, VII : 113.
57. *Ibid.*
58. *Ibid.*, VII : 114-15.

nounced when one has temporarily lost one's reason under the influence of liquor is not valid and is ineffective.[59] He based this view on the ground that the drink might have produced delirium or inflammation of the brain to such an extent as to make him devoid of reasoning faculties. He justifies this opinion on the ground that the divorce pronounced by a minor is not effective because he does not possess understanding and the same rule shall apply here. His second ground is that divorce under the influence of *bhang* (hemp) is not effective and there is no difference in the use of *bhang* and of a fermented liquor as both produce the same result, namely, temporary loss of reason. The third reason is that apostasy under the influence of drink is not permitted and the same rule shall apply here. The Ḥanafīs have explained that Allāh has permitted divorce and there is no exception in the case of a divorce given under the influence of drink. In case a divorce by a minor or a lunatic, it is not effective for want of understading. They have not violated any rule of Muslim law, but in case of drinking the husband has been guilty of an offence and so his divorce shall be held effective by way of punishment. The use of *bhang* is not an offence and so it has no application here. The case of apostasy is also inapplicable because there an attempt is made to save him from renunciation of Islām while here the husband has to be punished to discourage drinking.[60] Without entering into the merits of these statements, it may be stated that S̲h̲āfi'ī subsequently changed his opinion and held divorce given under the influence of wine to be effective.[61] If a drink is prepared from honey or fruits and is allowed to stand then fermentation sets in after some time. If a person consumes it in that condition or when it has fully become an intoxicant, gets drunk and pronounces a divorce

59. Ibn 'Ābidīn, *op. cit.*, II : 435.

60. *Ibid*., Al-Kasānī, 'Alā' al-Dīn Abū Bakr, *Badā'i' al-Ṣanā'i'*, Cairo, 1324 A.H., III : 99.

61. *Ibid.*, III : 99-100.

then there is a difference of opinion about the matter. Muḥammad al-Shaybānī holds that divorce in such a case shall be effected while Abū Yūsuf has expressed the view that it shall not be effected.[62] *Fatāwā Qāḍī Khān* has followed the latter view while *al-Baḥr-al-Rā'iq* has adopted the former view.[63] *Al-Bazzāziyah* has stated, "in our times it is necessary to penalise the consumption of such drinks and so divorce should be held to be effected."[64]

Influence of Bhang (Hemp): The divorce of a person intoxicated with *bhang* (hemp) is held to be ineffective by various Muslim jurists as also in the *Fatāwā Qāḍī Khān* and *al-Taḥrīr*. It is stated in *al-Baḥr al-Rā'iq* that a divorce given by a husband while he is under the influence of *bhang* (hemp) shall not be effected. The author, however, suggests that it would be proper to differentiate between the two cases, namely:

(*a*) when it is taken for pleasure, and

(*b*) when it is taken as medicine.[65]

A divorce shall be effected if *bhang* or opium is taken for pleasure, but it shall not be effected if either is taken by way of medicine.[66] It is stated in *Al-Radd al-Muḥtār* referring to al-Jawāhir that in these times a divorce given by a husband while in a state of intoxication of *bhang* (hemp) or opium shall be held effective in order to discourage the use of these intoxicants.[67] *Fatāwā 'Ālamgīriyah* also holds it to be effected, "on account of the frequency of this act among people, and on this is the *futwā* (dictum) in our times."[68] Ameer Ali remarks, "Just before this rule the contrary was stated from the *Tahzīb*, showing clearly the change in the interpretation and application of the law according to the change of times and social conditions. This conception of the law

62. Ibn Nujaym, *op. cit.* III : 266.
63. *Ibid.*
64. *Ibid.*
65. *Ibid.*
66. *Ibid.*
67. Ibn 'Ābidīn, *op. cit.*, II : 435.
68. *Al-Fatāwā al-Hindiyah*, Urdu trans., *op. cit.*, II : 145.

is lost sight of in the British Indian Courts."[69] A different view has been expressed in *al-Mutānah Fī Marramah al-Khazānah*, where it is given that a divorce pronounced under the influence of *bhang* (hemp) shall not be effected. This view is based on the reasoning that a divorce pronounced when a man is not possessed of understanding is not held to be effective. Thus a divorce given by a husband while suffering from insanity is absolutely ineffective. But a divorce given while a person is devoid of understanding under the influence of drink is held to be effective simply by way of punishment for the breach of the law restraining the use of strong liquors in order to discourage their use. This view is based on the reasoning that a person loses his understanding under the influence of *bhang* but the use of drink or fermented liquor does not necessarily produce this effect.[70]

By Agent when drunk: There is a difference of opinion about the effect of a divorce pronounced by an agent, appointed to pronounce a divorce on behalf of the husband against his wife when the agent is drunk. It is given in *Al-Fatāwā al-Hindiyah* from *Tatārkhāniah* that some jurists hold it to be ineffective while many others hold it to be effective.[71] The compilers of *'Alamgīriyah* have not expressed any opinion of their own. It is stated in Ashbah that such a divorce would not be given effect to while Bazaziah makes a distinction between divorce given by the agent for consideration or without it. It shall not be effective in the former case but shall be effective in the latter case.[2] This view seems to be based on the reasoning that in the former case he has to judge the propriety of the consideration which, being intoxicated, he may not be able to do. But he has not to make any such decision in the latter case and so his pronouncement will be effective as in the case of a divorce by the husband. This view leads to the result that a divorce by the agent will be effective if his authority

69. Ameer Ali, *Muhammadan Law*, Calcutta, 1908 A.D., II : 520, f. n. 3.
70. Makhdūm Muḥammad Ja'far, *al-Mutānah*, Karachi, 1962, A.D., p. 463.
71. *Al-Fatāwā al-Hindiyah*, Kānpur, 1349, A H. II : 48-49.
72. Ibn 'Ābidīn, *op. cit.*, II : 435.

is unconditional but will not be effective if it is subject to certain conditions. But if the agent has to pronounce the divorce under certain conditions then he may not be able to judge about the effectiveness of the conditions, that is, if they have been fulfilled and so a divorce by him while drunk should not be held effective.

Shī'ī Law : Under Shi'i law a divorce given by an agent under the influence of drink will not be held valid for want of intention.

VII. Divorce under Compulsion

There is a great difference of opinion about the effectiveness of a *Ṭalāq* (divorce) pronounced under compulsion not only amongst the various schools of Muslim Law but also amongst the Sunnī jurists themselves. Abū Ḥanīfah, Abū Yūsuf and Muḥammad hold a divorce given under compulsion to be effective. They justify this opinion on two grounds. First, that divorce is the result of necessity. In the case of a person not under compulsion, it is the necessity to separate from a wife who may be odious or disagreeable to him, while in the case of compulsion the necessity is to save himself from the apprehension of that with which he is threatened. Hence, according to them, there is no difference between the two cases and so a divorce under compulsion is effective. The second ground advanced is that the husband who is coerced into pronouncing a divorce cannot be held to have no option for he does possess a choice. He has a choice between two evils, one, the thing with which he is threatened and the other the divorce under compulsion and viewing both he makes a choice and this proves that he has an option.[73] Hence, according to them, there is no difference on principle between a divorce pronounced of free will and one given under compulsion and so the latter is as effective as the former. They further rely on a Tradition that a person approached the Prophet (peace be on him) and stated that he was sleeping when his wife sat on his chest and threatened to cut his throat unless he pronounced the divorce three times which he

73. Al-Marghīnānī, *op. cit.*, II : 338.

did for fear of his life. The Prophet (peace be on him) said that a divorce had been effected and the husband could not revoke it.[74]

Compulsion has been defined by Ḥanafī jurists to mean the act or speech of a person that affects another person so much as to force him to do the act demanded of him against his will. The threat may be caused by speech or conduct.[75] It usurps the free will of the person threatened but not his capacity to do the act demanded of him. The essentials of a threat are:

(*a*) The person who threatens should be in a position to carry it out;

(*b*) The person threatened should be under the conviction that the threat would be carried out unless he complies with the demand;

(*c*) The threat should relate to something serious such as loss of life, limb, grievous hurt or blows or imprisonment either of himself or of a person closely related to him. But if the threat is directed against a person who is not closely related to the husband and the latter repudiates his wife in order to avert the danger from the said stranger then the repudiation shall take effect.[76]

(*d*) The person threatened would not do the act in the absence of the threat;[77]

(*e*) The husband be not in a position to save himself from the threatened act.

The other sects of Sunnī jurists, namely, Mālik, Shafi'ī and Aḥmad b. Ḥanbal rely upon a precept of the Prophet (peace be on him) that God will not hold a person responsible for acts and omissions done through forgetfulness or under compulsion.[78] 'Āi'shah, the wife of the Prophet (peace be on him), has also reported, "I heard the Messengar of Allāh say: 'There is no

74. Ibn al-Humām, *op. cit.*, III : 39.
75. Ibn 'Ābidīn, *op. cit.*, V : 83-84.
76. *Ibid.*
77. *Ibid.*
78. Ibn Qudāmah, *op. cit.*, VII : 118.

divorce and no emancipation by force.[79] There are several other Traditions to the same effect. Thus, it is reported by Ībn 'Abbās that the Prophet (peace be on him) said that God forgives a person for an act done by him under compulsion.[80] Abū Dharr al-Ghifārī and Abū Hurayrah have reported that the Prophet (peace be on him) said that Allāh forgives the acts and deeds done by a Muslim by mistake or through forgetfulness or under compulsion.[81]

The Tradition relied upon by Abū Ḥanīfah and others in this connection relates to a particular incident and does not lay down a general rule of law. The Prophet's interest in the well-being of women is well known and he must have concluded that it must have been a very unhappy marriage or that the husband must have been very cruel to his wife that forced her to take such a serious step to gain her freedom and so he must have declared that particular marriage to have been dissolved under the peculiar circumstances of the case. The Traditions relied upon by the other group of jurists lay down a general rule of law and must be followed in preference to the other Tradition relating to a particular incident. Moreover, the opinion that such a divorce is effective is opposed to public policy, equity and good conscience. It has been laid down by Sulaimān, J. (as he then was) that where there are two opinions on a point of Muslim law, the rule of equity, justice and good conscience should be the guiding principle.[82] This principle of law applies with equal force to the case of a divorce under compulsion. The Courts have generally applied the rule laid down by Abū Ḥanīfah and others to the Ḥanafīs and have held that the pronouncement of a divorce is effective although it has been given under coercion. Thus it was held in an early case that according to Muhammadan Law, as laid down in *Al-Hidāyah*, the divorce of

79. Ibn Mājah, *Sunan*, Lucknow, 1315 A.H., p. 148.
80. *Ibid.*
81. *Ibid.*
82. Aziz Bano Vs. Muhammad Ibrahim Husain, I.L.R. 47 All. 823.

one acting upon compulsion from threats is effective.[83] The Privy Council has expressed the same view.[84] The Calcutta High Court has also taken the same view and has stated that, according to the Ḥanafī School of Law, a pronouncement of divorce is effectual although it has been made under compulsion.[85] The matter again came up for decision before the Allahabad High Court in 1945. Sulaimān, J. pointed out that the Ḥanafī jurists are not unanimous in holding such a divorce to be effective, and such a divorce is against public policy.[86] It is time that the Courts should reconsider the matter as there is no reasonable ground for accepting the validity of such a divorce.

As stated before, when there is a difference of opinion amongst the Sunnī jurists, it is open to a *qāḍī*, if he is possessed of certain qualifications, to adopt any one of the opinions which he considers proper in a particular case. The Courts now hold the same position as held by the *qāḍīs* in former times and can, therefore, take advantage of this rule to decide a case.[87]

Sh̲āfiʻī Law

Under the Sh̲āfiʻī law, a divorce extorted by violence is absolutely ineffective.[88] Sh̲āfiʻī maintains that a divorce given under compulsion is not effective because the husband who has been compelled to do so has no option, and no normal act of law is worthy of consideration unless it is purely optional.[89] Ameer Ali has suggested an interesting proposition regarding the pronouncement of divorce under compulsion by a Ḥanafī. He says, "Supposing a Ḥanafī, under the

83. Ibrahim Moolah Vs. Enayat-ur-Rahman, 12, W. R. 460; al-Marg̲h̲īnānī, *op. cit.*, II : 338.
84. Rashid Ahmad Vs. Anisa Khatun, I.L.R. 54 All. 46 (PC).
85. Jarina Akhtar Khatun Vs. Hafeez Uddin Khan, A.I.R. 1926 Cal. 242 ; 30 C.W.N. 178.
86. Nur Bibi Vs. Ahmad Ali, A.I.R. 1945 All. 550; 88 I.C. 408.
87. *Ibid.*
88. Al-Marg̲h̲īnānī, *op. cit.* II : 337-38 ; Ibn Qudāmah, *op. cit.*, VII : 118.
89. *Ibid.*, 338.

influence of threats and strong coercion, pronounces a *talâk* against his wife, and on recovering his freedom of action, disavows the validity of his act, and places himself under the Shàfe'ī rules to escape from the results of the *talâk*, there can be little doubt that he would be justified in doing so, and the repudiation he had pronounced would be invalidated.''[90]

Mālikī and Ḥanbalī laws: Both Mālik and Aḥmad b. Ḥanbal hold the same opinion as expressed by Shāfi'ī and are of the opinion that a divorce under compulsion is ineffective.[91] Mālik, however, further adds that the husband should not have actually intended to divorce his wife while pronouncing the divorce under compulsion. This intention can refer only to his mental attitude over which there can be no compulsion and his intention to divorce will be independent of compulsion and so shall result in a divorce if he so intended.

Acknowledgement under Compulsion

The jurists are unanimous in that an acknowledgement obtained under compulsion to the effect that a person had divorced his wife is not effective.[92] This is based on the ground that in fact he has not divorced his wife but merely makes an incorrect statement to that effect, hence there having been no divorce, the wife would not be repudiated. The Courts have also followed this rule of the Muslim Law.[93]

Conditional Divorce under Compulsion

Ḥanafī Law: If a person is compelled to take an oath to the effect that his wife would stand irrevocably divorced if he does or omits to do a certain act, a divorce would be effected if he does commit or omits to do that act.[94] This

90. Ameer Ali, *op. cit.*, II : 522.

91. Ibn Nujaym, *op. cit*, III : 264 ; Ibn Qudāmah, *op. cit.*, VII : 118.

92. *Ibid.*

93. Jarina Akhtar Khatun Vs. Hafeez Uddin Khan, A.I.R. 1926 Cal. 242.

94. Ibn Nujaym, *op. cit.*, III : 264.

rule seems to be based on the reasoning that the oath, no doubt, was taken under compulsion, but there was no compulsion when the act was done or the omission made.

There is a curious historical background to the practice of a conditional divorce under compulsion. It is stated that the 'Abbasid Caliphs discovered that people were not sincere in their oaths of allegiance to them and they, therefore, introduced a clause in the oath of allegiance to the effect, "If I am not sincere in my oath or if I violate my oath then my wife shall stand divorced." This put the people in a very difficult position. There were many people who did not like the Caliphs and took the oath merely under the fear of punishment without any intention of being loyal to the Caliphs. They felt very uneasy when the new clause was added to the oath because they were not honestly loyal to the Caliphs and they feared that their wives would be automatically divorced on that ground. The matter of conditional divorce under compulsion was taken to Mālik who gave his *futwā* that a divorce under compulsion is ineffective and a conditional divorce under compulsion can also not be effective. This dictum led to the conclusion that a person could safely take the oath and his wife would not be divorced on his having no real intention of being loyal to the Caliphs or on violating his oath of allegiance since it was under compulsion that he had taken that oath. The Governor of Madinah asked Mālik to withdraw his *futwā* and he was even flogged, but the *Imām* refused to change his opinion.[95]

Appointment of an Agent under Compulsion

The appointment of an agent under compulsion by a person for divorcing his wife is considered to be valid and a divorce pronounced by the agent to be effective.[96]

95. Ibn Rushd, *Bidāyat al-Mujtahid* (*Hidāyat al-Mu'taqid*). Urdu trans., Rabwah, 1958 A.D., II : 191.

96. Ibn Nujaym, *op. cit.*, III : 261 ; Ibn 'Abidīn, *op. cit.*, II ; 432.

Divorce written under Compulsion: A divorce written under compulsion is not considered effective by all the Imāms including Abū Ḥanīfah, Abū Yūsuf and Muḥammad.[97] According to them writing takes the place of speech only under necessity. Here there was no necessity to write, hence no divorce shall be effected.[98]

Shī'ī Law: Under Shī'ī law the divorce will be ineffective because a divorce in writing is not, as a rule, permissible under that law; moreover, it will not be valid for want of intention and free-will.

Divorce under undue Influence

There is not much difference between compulsion and undue influence if it is exerted to such an extent as to divest the person of the exercise of his free-will and in that case the same rule shall apply as to a divorce given under compulsion. But whether undue influence has been exercised is a question of fact to be determined in each case. An adult cannot be presumed to be acting under the influence of his relations, with whom he is living, in the absence of any evidence to that effect. Hence, in the absence of proof to the contrary, divorce given by him shall be considered effective.

Divorce in Jest or given non-seriously

It is considered by Sunnī jurists that the pronouncement of divorce is a serious thing and not a fit subject for jest. It has, therefore, been laid down that a divorce pronounced in jest would take effect even against the wishes of the husband and even when he never meant it.[99] The authority for this rule is a precept of the Prophet (peace be on him) in which he stated, "There are three things in which it makes no difference whether a man is in earnest or in jest, namely, marriage, divorce and *raj'ah*."[100] It means that effect would be given to a man's

97. Ibn 'Nujaym, *op. cit.*, III: 264; Ibn 'Ābidīn, *op. cit.*, II: 432.
98. *Ibid.*
99. *Ibid.*
100. Ibn Mājah, *op. cit.*, p. 148.

words even when spoken inadvertently or as a joke. It is obvious that these are serious matters and a person cannot be allowed to undo the effect of his words by saying that he was not in earnest but had uttered the words by way of a joke. The Privy Council has followed this rule of law and has held that a *Ṭalāq* pronounced in jest is valid and effective.[101]

But a different view has been expressed in *al-Fatāwā al-Bazzāziah* and *al-Qiniyah* and such a divorce has not been considered effective if the pronouncement refers to a past act. But if the pronouncement refers to the present time, the divorce shall be effected.[102]

VIII. Divorce under Fraud

A divorce pronounced by the husband as a result of fraud is deemed by the Sunnīs to be binding on him. This rule is a necessary corollary of the law that intention does not form an essential condition of divorce under the Sunnī law. This rule is justified on the ground that though the husband acted under fraud in pronouncing the divorce, yet the decision to divorce was taken by him voluntarily and deliberately and need not have been taken had not the man considered some alternative such as getting some advantage as higher and more important than the divorce. If he was deceived by a false promise of some material gain or by offer of some compensation he nevertheless allowed himself to be influenced by such offer which he obviously put above the consideration of a broken marriage. The husband has no escape from the effect thereof except by the way provided by the Book, that is, *raj'ah* if possible in the circumstances.

But there can also be cases in which the fraud is of such a nature that the man under the instigation of some mischief-maker or an interested party, pronounced the divorce without understanding the significance of the words or knowing that

101. Rashid Ahmad Vs. Mst. Anisa Khatun, I.L.R. 54, All. 46 ; I.L.R. 1932, P.C. 25.

102. Ibn 'Ābidīn, *op. cit.*, II : 434.

he was thereby divorcing his wife. Thus, there is an example given in *al-Radd al-Muḥtār*, "If some one teaches an illiterate person to pronounce '*Ṭalāq*' and he speaks it while addressing his wife, a divorce would be effected in law according to some jurists but others hold otherwise and have stated that no divorce would be effected so as to save people from loss under fraud."[103]

Here again the Ḥanafīs insist that intention does not form an essential condition of divorce, since no one save God can know the secrets of a man's heart and his words and actions can be the only indication of his intention. However, this argument is not very convincing, as the establishment of the fact that a fraud had been committed on the husband coupled with the husband's statement on oath that he had no intention of divorcing his wife and would not have pronounced the divorce in the absence of the fraud ought to be deemed sufficient by the Court to hold the divorce ineffective. The Courts should not allow the wrongdoing party, that is, the party who has actually committed the fraud or was privy to the same, to take advantage of his fraud.

A good deal of light is thrown on the matter by Ibn Nujaym in al-Qiniyah. It is stated therein on page 181 of the Lucknow edition on the strength of al-Ashbah wan Nazair that if a person admits that he had divorced his wife relying on the futwa of a Mufti, but it transpires subsequently that the futwa was incorrect and the act of pronouncement of the husband had not amounted to a divorce then no divorce would be effected.

IX. Divorce in Ignorance of Meaning

Ḥanafī Law: Under Ḥanafī law, a divorce would be effected even when the husband pronounces it in ignorance of the meaning of the words he utters.[104]

103. Ibn 'Ābidīn *op. cit.*, II : 436.
104. *Ibid.*

Ḥanblī Law: According to Aḥmad b. Ḥanbal, if a husband pronounces a divorce without understanding the meaning of the words the divorce shall not be effected.[105]

Shāfi'ī Law: Shāfi'ī does not recognize the validity of a divorce given in words the meaning of which the husband does not know.[106]

X. *Dumb Person*

The Ḥanafīs hold that a divorce by a dumb man expressed by signs is effective when his defect is of long standing and his signs have become well-understood because signs of dumb persons are recognized in practice and, therefore, admitted to stand in place of speech.[107] It is stated in *Al-Radd al-Muḥtār* and *Al-Fatāwā al-'Ālamgīriyah* that in case the dumb person is literate, his repudiation would be effected by writing only and not by signs.[108] This, as a matter of fact, is the doctrine of Shāfi'ī, but the Ḥanafīs have adopted it and is now considered to be the established law.[109] Divorce by a husband who is capable of speaking cannot be effected by signs.

Shāfi'ī Law: Shāfi'ī considers a divorce given by a dumb person by signs to be valid. But such divorce by a person capable of speech is held invalid and ineffective.[110]

Mālikī Law: If the signs of a dumb person are well understood, a divorce by him by signs shall be effective.[111]

Ḥanbalī Law: The Ḥanbalī law holds a divorce given by a dumb person by signs to be effective provided his signs are well understood. If they are such that some people understand them while others do not, it shall amount to a *kināyah* (ambiguous) divorce. In such a case he shall be asked if he really intended to pronounce divorce.[112]

105. Sharaf al-Dīn al-Maqdisī, *al-Iqnā'*, Cairo, n. d. IV ; 10-11.
106. Al-Ghazzālī, Abū Ḥāmid *al-Wajīz*, Cairo, 1317 A.H., II : 56.
107. *Al-Fatāwa al-Hindīyah*, Urdu trans., *op. cit.*, II : 339 , Ibn 'Ābidīn, *op. cit.*, II : 339.
108. *Ibid.*
109. *Ibid,*
110. Ibn Nujaym, *op. cit.*, III : 267.
111. Sharaf al-Dīn al-Maqdisī, *op. cit.*, IV : 10.
112. *Ibid.*

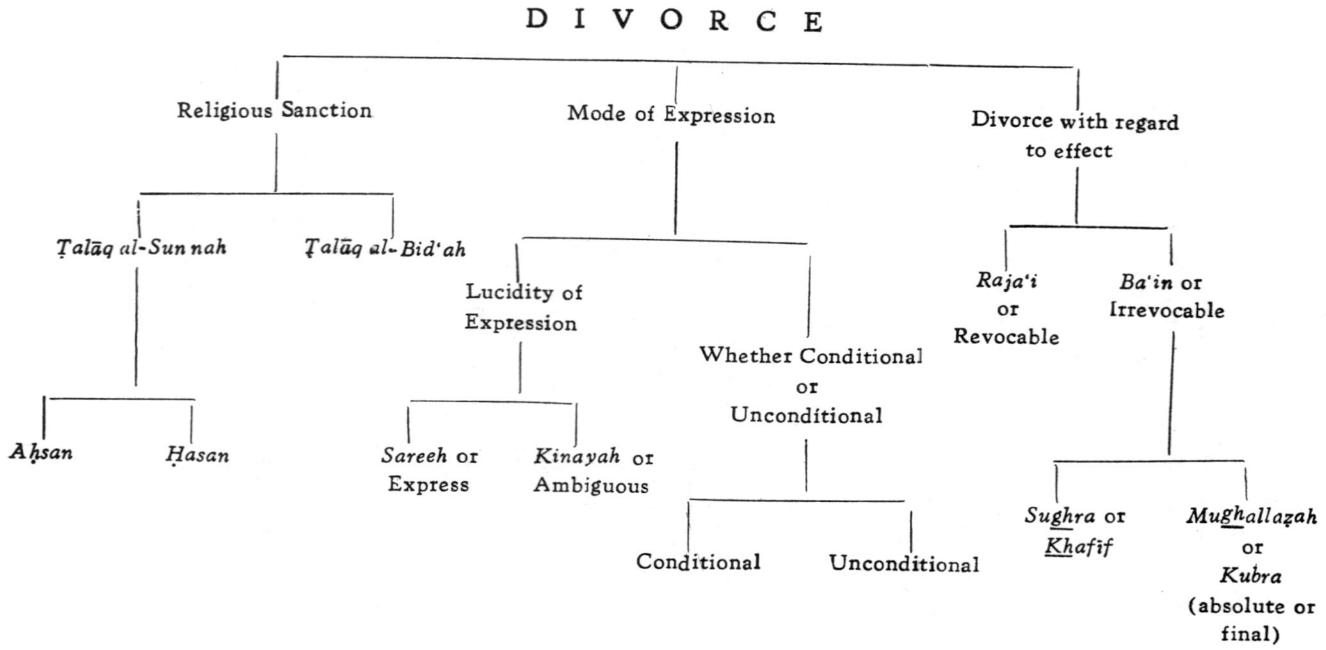
DIVORCE
Religious Sanction
Mode of Expression
Divorce with regard to effect
Ṭalāq al-Sunnah
Ṭalāq al-Bid'ah
Lucidity of Expression
Whether Conditional or Unconditional
Raja'i or Revocable
Ba'in or Irrevocable
Aḥsan
Ḥasan
Sareeh or Express
Kinayah or Ambiguous
Conditional
Unconditional
Sughra or Khafif
Mughallazah or Kubra (absolute or final)

Chapter 4

DIVORCE--CLASSIFICATION

I. Preliminary

Ṭalāq or (divorce) is an Arabic word which means "undoing of or a release from a knot." It is used by Muslim jurists to denote the release of a woman from the marriage-tie, and means a divorce.[1]

II. Classification of Divorce

Ṭalāq (divorce) or dissolution of marriage by the husband may conveniently be discussed under the following main heads :—

(*i*) Religious sanction,
(*ii*) Mode of expression, and
(*iii*) Effect of divorce.

III. Religious Sanction

Divorce under this head is divided under the Sunnī law into two classes :—

(*i*) *Ṭalāq al-Sunnah* and
(*ii*) *Ṭalāq al-Bid'ah* or *Ṭalāq al-Bid'i.*

Description : *Ṭalāq al-Sunnah* is regarded as the regular or orthodox form and *Ṭalaq al-Bid'ah* as the irregular or unorthodox form of *Ṭalāq.* The latter has now become the more common and prevalent method of dissolving a marriage.

(*i*) *Ṭalāq al-Sunnah* : *Ṭalāq al-Sunnah* is again subdivided into two classes, namely :—

(*a*) *Aḥsan* meaning very proper, and
(*b*) *Ḥasan* meaning proper[2].

1. Ibn Qudāmah, *al-Mughnī*, Cairo, 1376 A.H., Vol. VII, p. 96; Ibn 'Ābidīn, *Al-Radd al-Muḥtār*, Cairo, 1318 A.H., Vol. II, pp. 425-26.
2. *Al-Fatāwā al-Hindiyah*, Kānpur, 1349 A.H., Vol. II, p. 45; Ibn 'Ābidīn, *op. cit.*, Vol. II, p. 429.

IV. Description : These two forms of *Ṭalāq al-Sunnah* are described below :

(*a*) *Ṭalāq al-Aḥsan*

Ṭalāq al-Aḥsan means the more proper divorce. The words "more proper" do not denote any intrinsic merit of this kind of divorce. What is meant is that this kind of divorce is the least disapproved of its various forms. The reason for the preference of this form of divorce over others is that it does not immediately sever the marital relationship but allows an opportunity to the spouses to continue the marriage if they so choose and, in pursuing this method, the husband can still exercise his right without the necessity of an intermediary marriage to retain his wife by a reversal of the divorce during the period of her *'iddah*, if he be so inclined. This rule is based on an injunction in the Qur'ān which says : "Divorce may be pronounced twice, then keep them in good fellowship or let (them) go in kindness."[3] It is laid down at another place, "So, if he (the husband) divorces her (the third time) she shall not be lawful to him afterwards until she marries another person."[4] Also because this method is the one lawful method of divorce unanimously agreed upon.

How effected : The method for this kind of divorce is to repudiate an enjoyed wife by a single sentence within a *Ṭuhr*, or term of purity, that is, the period of time which intervenes between two successive menstrual discharges, during which he has not had sexual intercourse with her, and then leave her to the observance of her *'iddah*, unless revoked in the meantime. The repudiation becomes final on the expiry of the prescribed period of *'iddah*, which in case of divorce consists of three periods of purity, or if it cannot be ascertained. then on the expiry of three months. The rule is clearly laid down in the Qur'ān wherein it is stated : "And the divorced women should keep themselves in waiting for three courses."[5] Should the husband be intimate with his

3. Qur'ān, II : 229, Surah al-Baqarāh.
4. *Ibid.*, 230.
5. *Ibid.*, 228.

wife during this period then the divorce is cancelled and the relationship of husband and wife is maintained.[6]

(*b*) *Ṭalāq al-Ḥasan*

Ṭalāq al-Ḥasan means proper divorce. It is not unanimously accepted as a lawful divorce by all the Sunni Schools of law. Mālik considers it to be *Bid'ah* or an innovation.[7] He says that divorce is meant to serve as a prohibition and it is secured by one pronouncement and so, according to him, a divorce would no doubt be effected in this way but the husband would be guilty of sin in pronouncing it. Other Sunnī Jurists accept it as a lawful divorce in the form of *Ṭalāq al-Sunnah.*

How effected : The method for this kind of divorce consists in the husband's giving his enjoyed wife one repudiation in a *Ṭuhr*, or period of purity, in which he has had no sexual intercourse with her, and then to give her another repudiation in the next *Ṭuhr* and a third repudiation in the *Ṭuhr* after the second *Ṭuhr* in the same way as adopted before.[8] It can thus be seen that in this form of divorce it is necessary to repeat the declaration of divorce three times and to abstain from sexual enjoyment with the wife during the whole of this period. The divorce becomes absolute and irrevocable on the pronouncement of the third divorce unless revoked in the meantime.[9]

V. Time of pronouncement of Ṭalāq al-Sunnah when wife is not subject to menstrual course

In the case of a woman who is not subject to menstrual courses whether on account of old age or tender age or otherwise, the husband gives her one repudiation and then another on the expiry of one month after the first pronouncement

6. See chapter on *Raj'ah*.
7. Al-Marghīnānī, 'Alī b. Abi Bakr, *al-Hidayah*, Dehli, n.d., Vol. II, p. 334.
8. *Ibid.*
9. *Al-Fatāwā al-Hindiyah, op. cit.*, Vol. II, p. 45 ; Ibn 'Abidin, *op. cit.* Vol. II, p. 429.

and the third after the lapse of another month.[10] This rule will also apply when the wife is pregnant.[11]

This rule is based on a verse in the Qur'ān wherein it is stated, "And those of your women who despair of menstruation, if you have a doubt, their prescribed time is three months, and of those, too, who have not had their courses."[12] It is not necessary for a person to declare what form of divorce he was using. The marriage will be dissolved by that particular form of divorce which may be applicable in the light of the facts of the case.

VI. Time of pronouncement when marriage not consummated :

The condition that the divorce should be pronounced only during the period of purity applies only in the case of a marriage that has been consummated either actually or under the Ḥanafi, Māliki and Ḥanbali laws by implication, that is, on al-Khilwah al-Sahīhah or valid retirement.[13] In the case of a marriage that has not been consummated, the divorce may be pronounced at any time either during the period of purity or during the period of menstrual discharge and it will amount to a *Ṭalāq al-Ḥasan.*[14]

VII. Time of pronouncement when marriage dissolved by wife :

The condition relating to time, namely, the pronouncement of divorce only during the period of purity does not apply to the dissolution of a marriage by the wife as in the case of *Tafwīd* (delegation), *Khiyār al-Bulūgh* (Option of puberty) and the like.[15]

10. *Al-Fatāwā al-Hindiyah, op. cit.,* Vol. II, p. 45 ; Ibn 'Ābidīn *op. cit.,* Vol. II, p. 429, al-Marghīnānī, *op. cit.,* Vol. II, p. 336 ; Ibn al-Humām, *Fatḥ al-Qadīr,* Cairo, n. d., Vol. III, p. 29.
11. Al-Marghīnānī, *op. cit.,* Vol. II, p. 336 ; Ibn al-Humām, *op. cit.,* p. 32 ; Ibn 'Ābidīn, *op. cit.,* Vol. II, pp. 329-30.
12. Qur'ān, XXVIII : 4, Surah al-Mujādilah.
13. For valid retirement see chapter under that head.
14. *Al-Fatāwā al-Hindiyah, op. cit.,* Vol. II, p. 45 ; Ibn 'Ābidīn, *op. cit.,* Vol. II, p. 429.
15. *Ibid.,* Vol. II, p. 46 ; *ibid.,* Vol. II, p. 429.

VIII. Time of dissolution by the Qadi : The same rule as given above for the pronouncement of divorce by a wife applies in the case of dissolution of marriage by the Qāḍi. The Qāḍi can dissolve a marriage at any time whether during purity or otherwise.[16]

IX. Ṭalāq al-Sunnah provides against hasty action

Both these forms of divorce, namely, Aḥsan and Ḥasan, provide against the effect of hasty action by the husband and allow him an opportunity to undo the harm caused by his act of divorcing the wife by cancelling the same and to continue his marriage as of before.

X. Ṭalāq al-Bid'ah or Ṭalāq al-Bid'i

(*i*) *Preliminary*: The other method of divorce considered from a religious point of view is *Ṭalāq al-Bid'i* or *Ṭalāq al-Bid'ah*, unorthodox divorce. It is so called because it is not approved by Muslim Jurists and is considered an undesirable innovation. Any divorce which does not conform to *Ṭalāq al-Ṣunnah* is deemed to be an innovation or *bid'ah* and is called *Ṭalāq al-Bid'ah*. It is the most disapproved form of divorce. It is highly condemned and even declared sinful, but nevertheless it is considered legally effective. Ameer Ali is not exactly correct when he says, "..........which (*Ṭalāq al-Bid'ah*) was introduced in the second century of the Muhammadan era. It was then that the Ommayad monarchs, finding the checks, imposed by the Prophet (peace be on him) on the facility of repudiation galling, looked about for some escape from the strictness of law and found in the pliability of the Jurists a loophole to effect their purpose."[17] *Ṭalāq al-Bid'i* was sometimes resorted to even in the time of the Prophet (peace be on him). Thus there is the well known case of Ibn 'Umar who had divorced his wife during the period of menstruation. The Prophet (peace be on him) on being informed of this told him that he had acted wrongly and advised him to cancel the divorce by

16. *Al-Fatāwā al-Hindiyah*, *op. cit.*, Vol. II, p. 45 : Ibn Ābidīn, *op. cit.*, Vol. II, p. 429."

17. Ameer Ali, *Muhammadan Law*, Calcutta, 1908, Vol, II, p. 514.

raj'ah (cancellation) and then to proceed in the proper manner if he still persisted in his desire to divorce the wife.[18] The fact is that the Prophet (peace be on him) strongly condemned it and did not sanction it. But in the course of time it came to be considered a valid and legal form of divorce. Moreover, it assumed many other forms in the second century and came to be recognised as an effective divorce.

(*ii*) *How effected* :

Ṭalāq al-Bid'i is effected in one of the following ways:—

(*a*) Repetition of three pronouncements of divorce either at the same time or in the same meeting or on different occasions in the same period of *Ṭuhr*.[19]

(*b*) Pronouncement of divorce in a period of purity in which the husband has had sexual intercourse with his wife.[20]

(*c*) Pronouncement of divorce during the period of menstrual course provided the marriage has been consummated actually or under the Ḥanafi, Māliki and Ḥanbali laws impliedly, that is, when there has been a valid retirement.[21] If the marriage has not been consummated and there has not even been a valid retirement, under the Ḥanafi, Māliki and Ḥanbali laws, then such a pronouncement of divorce shall take effect as *Ṭalāq al-Ḥasan.*

(*d*) Pronouncement of divorce in one single sentence.[22]

The above points relating to *Ṭalāq al-Bid'ah* are fully discussed below :—

(*a*) *Repetition of Pronouncement* : The most prevalent method of exercising *Ṭalāq al-Bid'ah* under the Sunnī law now-a-days is to pronounce three divorces at the same time.[23]

18. Abū Bakr al-Jaṣṣāṣ, *Aḥkām al-Qur'ān*, Constantinople, 1335 A.H., Vol. I, p. 380; Walī al-Dīn al-Khaṭīb, *Mishkāt al-Maṣābiḥ*, Dehli, 1932 A.D., p. 283.

19. Al-Marghīnānī, *op. cit.*, Vol, II, p. 335 ; al-Nasafī, *Kanz al-Daqā'iq*, Deoband, 1368 A.H., Vol. II, p. 120; *al-Fatāwā al-Hindiyah*, *op. cit.*, Vol. II, p. 46 ; Ibn 'Abidin, *op. cit.*, Vol. II, p. 430.

20. *Ibid.* 21. *Ibid.* 22. *Ibid.*

23. For discussion see "*Mughallaẓah* divorce."

It is not necessary that the husband should repeat the pronouncement three times in order to constitute an irrevocable divorce. The triple repetition is merely one of the many forms by which such a divorce can be effected and the same result can be obtained by any other method recognized for the purpose. A husband can effect such a *Ṭalāq* even by only one pronouncement if he makes it clear that he was pronouncing a *Ṭalāq al-Bain*, that is, an irrevocable divorce. Thus, to effect such *Ṭalāq* the husband may say, "You are repudiated thrice."[24] He can also convey his intention of pronouncing three divorces by saying, "You are divorced so many times" and showing three fingers at the same time which will result in a *Ṭalāq al-Bid'i*.[25]

(*b*) *Divorce in period of purity in which there has been intimacy*: It is not permissible to divorce the wife in a *Ṭuhr* (period of purity) in which the husband has been intimate with her. If he does so, then according to the Sunnīs a *Ṭalāq al-Bid'i* shall be effected. The reasoning of the Jurists for this rule is that a divorce is to be given only when there is necessity and in the absence of necessity a divorce is not to be given. The fact that the husband was intimate with the wife during the period of purity shows that he does stand in need of her and so there is no necessity for divorce in such a case and a divorce cannot be properly given under such circumstances.[26] The prohibition does not apply when the wife is incapable of pregnancy whether on account of tender or old age.[27] A girl below nine years and a woman fifty-five years of age or older is supposed to be incapable of pregnancy and so a *Ṭalāq* is permissible in such a case in a period of purity in which there has been intimacy between her

24. *Al-Fatāwā al-Hindiyah, op. cit.*, Vol. II, p. 46; Ibn 'Ābidīn, *op. cit.*, Vol. II, p. 431.
25. *Ibid.* Ibn Nujaym, *al-Baḥr al-Rā'iq*, Cairo, 1311 A.H., Vol. III, p. 259.
26. Ibn 'Ābidīn, *op. cit.*, Vol. II, p. 429; Ibn Nujaym, *op. cit.*, Vol, III, p. 259.
27. Al-Marghīnānī, *op. cit.*, Vol. II, p. 335; *al-Fatāwā al-Hindiyah, op. cit.*, Vol. II, p. 46.

and her husband.[28] Such a *Ṭalāq* would be considered to be a *Ṭalāq al-Ṣunnah*.

(c) *Divorce during the period of impurity*: A divorce given while the wife is in her monthly course is considered *Bid'i* or innovation, because it is against the prescribed method of divorce. Thus there is a Tradition to the effect that Ibn 'Umar divorced his wife during the period of impurity (menstruation). The Prophet (peace be on him) was told of this and he said to Ibn 'Umar, "O Ibn 'Umar ! God has not allowed you to act like that. You have gone against the Sunnah (*i.e.* against the approved religious law). The correct method is to wait till she is pure and then to pronounce the divorce in the period of purity, "and he further asked him to revoke the divorce by *raj'ah* (retraction).[29] The Ḥanafi law holds such divorce to be effective, but it is considered proper for the husband to revoke it and to pronounce a fresh divorce in a period of purity in order to escape from sin.[30] According to some Jurists, the revocation of divorce is incumbent on the husband. It is stated in some books that this view is the better view.[31] It is explained in *al-Hidāyah* that revocation of divorce is incumbent on the husband for three reasons, namely :—

(a) The order of the Prophet (peace be on him) to Ibn 'Umar as cited above.

(b) The pronouncement of divorce during the period of impurity is sinful, and it is the duty of every man to redress the wrong by every means within his power, and

(c) The protraction of the *'iddah* places an extra burden on the wife, which transgresses the limits prescribed by the Book.[32]

28. Al-Marghīnānī, *op. cit.*, Vol. II, p. 336 ; Ibn Nujaym, *op. cit.*, Vol, III, p. 258 ; Ibn 'Ābidīn, *op. cit.*, Vol. II, p. 430.

29. Abū Bakr al-Jaṣṣāṣ, *op. cit.*, Vol. I, 369 ; Walī al-Dīn al-Khaṭīb, (*Mishkāt*), *op. cit.*, p. 283.

30. Al-Marghīnānī, *op. cit.*, Vol. II, p. 337; *al-Fatāwā al-Hindiyah*, *op. cit.* Vol. II, p. 46 ; Ibn 'Ābidīn, *op. cit.*, Vol. II, p. 430.

31. *Ibid.* Ibn Nujaym, *op. cit.*, Vol. III, p. 260.

32. Al-Marghīnānī, *op. cit.*, Vol. II, p. 337.

Māliki Law : Mālik holds that a *Ṭalāq al-Bid'i* shall effect a separation, but considers it to be disapproved of. He makes it an essential condition of a valid divorce that it should fulfil the following conditions and a *Bid'i* divorce is one which does not fulfil them :—

(*a*) It must be given when the wife is in a state of purity, that is, not during the period of menstrual flow nor during the *Nifās* (the term after childbirth). The maximum period of *Nifās* is fixed at forty days or according to a woman's usual period in such cases.[33]

(*b*) The husband should not have been intimate with the wife in the period of purity in which the divorce is pronounced.

(*c*) After pronouncing a divorce no fresh divorce be given during the period of *'iddah*.

(*d*) Not more than one divorce should be pronounced at the same time.[34]

If the husband contravenes the conditions given above he shall be forced to take back his wife.[35] This is, however, subject to the condition that the marriage has been consummated. If there has been no intimacy then compulsion shall not be used and wife shall become separated on the pronouncement of divorce.[36]

Shāfi'ī Law : Shāfi'ī has expressed the opinion that a *Ṭalāq al-Bid'ai* is forbidden but nevertheless it effects a separation between the spouses.[37] He considers it to be sinful.[38]

Ḥanbali Law : Aḥmad ibn Ḥanbal agrees with Abū Ḥanifah and holds that a *Ṭalāq al-Bid'i* would be effective, though sinful.[39]

33. Saḥnūn, *al-Mudawwanat al-Kubrā*, Cairo, 1323 A.H., Vol. V, pp. 101-5 ; Ibn Qudāmah, *op. cit.*, Vol. VII, p. 98.

34. *Ibid.* 35. *Ibid.* 36. *Ibid.*

37. Ibn Qudāmah, *op cit.*, Vol. VII, pp. 99-100.

38. *Ibid.* 39. *Ibid.*

Shī'i Law: Under the Shī'i law *Ṭalāq* (divorce) is divided in two main classes, namely :

(*a*) Bid'i (irregular or heretical), and

(*b*) Sunnī (regular)

(*a*) *Bid'i Ṭalāq* is considered irregular. It is constituted in the following three ways :

I. Divorce against an enjoyed wife who is not pregnant and who is in her courses, or *Nifās* (puerperal discharge) when her husband is present with her or absent from her for a period less than the prescribed period. It is the discharge after childbirth and, according to the Shi'i jurists, its maximum period can be ten days while according to the Sunnīs it can last for forty days.

II. Pronouncement of divorce against a wife, who is not pregnant, in that period of the wife's purity in which the husband has been intimate with her. Period of purity means the period when the wife is free of her menstrual courses.

III. Pronouncement of three divorces whether by one sentence or one after another when there has been no intermediate revocation.[40]

The first two forms of divorce are considered void and absolutely ineffective under the Shi'i law.[41] This also holds good in respect of three pronouncements at the same time. But if they are pronounced at different times then the first pronouncement may be given effect to.

The second class of *Ṭalāq* is called Sunnī. The word Sunnī is used in contradistinction to Bid'i.

Ṭalāq al-Sunnah is divided by Shi'i jurists into three classes, namely :

(*a*) *Bain*,

(*b*) *Raja'i*, and

(*c*) *Ṭalāq al-'iddah*.

40. Ja'far b. al-Ḥasan, *Kitāb Sharā'i' al-Islām*, Tehran, 1377 A.H., p. 209 ; Abu'l-Ḥasan al-Mūsawī, *Wasīlat al-Najat*, Najaf, 1364, p. 371.

41. *Ibid.*

(*a*) *Ṭalāq Bain* is that divorce which cannot be revoked. It is constituted in the following six ways :

I. Divorce against a wife with whom there has been no intimacy.

II. Divorce against a wife who is past child-bearing age.

III. Divorce against a wife of such a tender age that she is not subject to menstrual courses This age is fixed at nine years.

IV. Divorce against a wife who has obtained a *Khul'* divorce for consideration.

V. Divorce against a wife who has secured a divorce under the doctrine of Mubārah.

It is necessary in the case of the fourth and fifth class of divorce that the consideration for Khul' or Mubārāh has not been revoked. If it has been revoked then the divorce shall be a *Raja'i* divorce and not a *Bain Ṭalāq*.

VI. Divorce against a wife who has been thrice repudiated with two intermediate revocations.

(*b*) *Talāq Raj'i* : *Ṭalāq Raj'i* is that kind of divorce in which the husband has got a right to cancel it. This he can do before the expiry of the wife's *'iddah.* If the period of the wife's *'iddah* expires then a revocable divorce is effected. But if the spouses want to unite then they can remarry without the necessity of there being an intermediary marriage.

(*c*) *Ṭalāq al-'Iddah* : In this form of divorce, the husband divorces his wife under the requisite conditions ; he then recalls her and cohabits with her before the expiration or completion of her *'iddah*. He again divorces her a second time in another *ṭuhr*, that is, other than that in which he was intimate with her. He recalls her again and cohabits with her and then divorces her in a subsequent *ṭuhr.* This kind of divorce effects what is called a *mughallaẓah* divorce in which the wife becomes forbidden to the husband. She can become lawful to him only if after the divorce she marries another person and that marriage is dissolved after consummation.[42] It is only then that she can marry the former husband. It is a necessary condition of such *Ṭalāq* that there must be intercourse after each revocation. If the husband divorces his wife before such intercourse, the divorce would be effected, but it would not be *Ṭalāq al-'iddah.*

XI. Divorce Considered with Regard to the Mode of Expression

A divorce can be considered with respect to the mode of expression from two aspects, namely, (*a*) Lucidity of expression and (*b*) Whether it is conditional or unconditional.

XII. Divorce Considered with Regard to Lucidity of Expression

The language used by a husband to divorce his wife may or may not be clear enough to denote his intention of divorcing her. The pronouncement of divorce considered with regard to lucidity of expression is divided into two kinds, namely :—

1. *Ṣarīḥ* or express or plain and
2. *Kināyah* or implied or ambiguous.[43]

(1) *Ṣarīḥ or Clear Expression*: A *ṣarīḥ* or clear pronouncement of divorce is one which is given in such spoken words the meaning of which is unmistakable, as for example, when a husband says to his wife, "I have divorced you" or "You are divorced."[44] Such a pronouncement of divorce includes the use of expressions that have acquired a particular significance by long usage and are not used in any other sense than of divorce.[45] As the expressions are not used in any sense other than that of divorce and are well understood

42. Ja'far b. al-Ḥasan, *Kitāb Sharā'i' al-Islām*, Tehran, 1377, p. 209; Abu'l-Ḥasan al-Mūsawī, *Wasilat al-Najat*, Najaf, 1364, p. 371.
43. Al-Marghīnānī, *op. cit.*, Vol. II, p. 339; *al-Fatāwā al-Hindiyah*, *op. cit.*, Vol. II, p. 49; Ibn 'Ābidīn, *op. cit.*, Vol. II, p. 440.
44. *Ibid.*, Ibn Nujaym, *op. cit.*, Vol. III, p. 269.
45. Al-Marghīnanī, *op. cit.*, Vol. II, p. 340; Ibn 'Ābidīn, *op. cit.*, Vol. II p. 441.

as implying divorce, no proof of intention to divorce is required under the Sunnī law.[46] In divorces given by *Ṣarīḥ* or clear pronouncements the law will hold that the husband meant what the actual words used by him conveyed without permitting him to explain that he meant something else.[47] In *Ṣarīḥ* expressions the actual intention of a husband who divorces his wife is immaterial and a *Raj'i* divorce shall be effected. It is the intention conveyed by his words in repudiating his wife that shall be taken into consideration, and the validity and effectiveness of the divorce would not be governed by any mental reservation on the part of the husband to the effect that the divorce pronounced by him was not a genuine divorce.[48]

The word *Ṭalāq* is used in Pakistan and India in the same sense as in Arabic and is well understood by every one and even by illiterate persons. The word *Ṭalāq* has acquired in Urdu the technical meaning by reason of usage and so must be given its technical import. The sentences in which the word is used form *ṣarīḥ* or clear expressions and so no explanation or evidence can be given to denote a contrary intention under the general rule of the Sunnī law.

If a husband is asked whether he has divorced his wife and he replies in the affirmative it would amount to *Ṣarīḥ* divorce.[49] If a wife says to her husband, "Am I a divorcee?" and should he reply, "Yes", then too it would amount to a *Ṣarīḥ* divorce.[50]

A number of such expressions as constitute express divorce have been given in *al-Hidāyah* and other books, but the expressions given as the form of *Ṣarīḥ* divorce are not

46. Al-Marghinānī, *op. cit.*, Vol. II, p. 340 ; Ibn 'Ābidīn, *op. cit.*, Vol. II, p. 441.
47. *Ibid.*, Vol. II, pp. 442, 497 ; Ibn 'Ābidīn. *op. cit.*, Vol. II, p. 339 ; *al-Fatāwā al-Hindiyah*, *op. cit.*, Vol. II, p. 49.
48. *Ibid.*
49. Ibn 'Ābidīn, *op. cit.*, Vol. II, p. 442 ; *al-Fatāwa al-Hindiyah*, *op. cit.*, Vol. II, p. 50 ; Ibn Nujaym, *op. cit.*, Vol. III, pp. 274-75.
50. *Ibid.*

exhaustive and serve as merely illustrative expressions.

Māliki Law: According to Mālik, *Ṣarīḥ* expressions are *four* in number and can only be denoted by the word *Ṭalāq*.[51] They are such as given below:

(*a*) I divorce you,

(*b*) You are divorced as regards myself etc.

Shāfi'ī Law: According to Shāfi'ī law, expressions which clearly indicate severance of the marriage relationship are termed *Ṣarīḥ* (clear) expressions. They denote repudiation, separation, dismissal.[52] Such expressions are as "I repudiate you," "You are repudiated," "You are free," etc. The expression may be explicitly pronounced in any language provided the expressions employed correspond to the above terms.[53]

Ḥanbali Law: According to Ahmad ibn Ḥanbal *Ṣarīḥ Ṭalāq* is that expression which is not used for any other purpose than *Ṭalāq*. The husband can say, "I divorce you" or "You are a divorcee."[54]

Effect of: In the absence of words to denote an intention to the contrary the pronouncement of a *Ṭalāq* by *Ṣarīḥ* expression shall effect a *Ṭalāq al-Raj'i* or a revocable divorce, that is, a divorce that leaves it in the power of the husband lawfully to take back his wife at any time before the expiration of the period of *'iddah*.[56] But if the marriage has not been consummated then the very first pronouncement of divorce shall effect an irrevocable divorce.[56] Section 7 of the Muslim Family Laws Ordinance, 1961, has done away with the difference between a *raj'i* (revocable) and a *bā'in* (irrevocable) divorce.

51. Ibn Qudāmah, *op. cit.*, Vol. VII, p. 121.
52. Ibn Rushd, *Bidāyat al-Mujtahid*, Cairo, n.d., Vol. II, p. 61.
53. Ibn Qudāmah, *op. cit.*, Vol. VII, p. 121 ; Ibn Rushd, *op. cit.*, Vol. II, p. 61.
54. *Ibid.*
55. Al-Marghīnānī, *op. cit.*, Vol. II, p. 339 ; *al-Fatāwā al-Hindiyah*, *op. cit.*, Vol. II, p. 50.
56. Al-Marghīnānī, *op. cit.*, Vol. II, p. 351 ; Ibn al-Humān, *op. cit.*, Vol. III, p. 88 ; Ibn 'Ābidīn, *op. cit.*, Vol, II, p. 447.

Kināyah or implied expressions of divorce: *Kināyah* or implied expression of divorce means an expression which is ambiguous as opposed to a clear expression. The ambiguous expressions are such as can mean a divorce as well as something else and in which the real purpose of the speaker is not clear but is concealed.[57] A divorce is not effected by a *kināyah* expression unless there is intention of which there is proof or it can be gathered from the surrounding circumstances or there is a mention of divorce. As a *kināyah* expression does not denote divorce alone but may also mean something else, hence intention is requisite in such cases to determine the meaning of the pronouncement.[58]

The Sunnī Jurists have given a very large number of examples of expressions of *kināyah* or implied divorce which would or would not effect a divorce according to the intention of the husband. A few are given below :—

"You are not to me as a wife,"
"I have no need of you,"
"Leave me" or "Leave me alone,"
"Go back to your family,"
"You are of no use to me,"
"I do not desire you,"
"I am unlawful to you,"
"I give up all relations with you and will have no connection of any sort with you,"
"You are nobody to me,"
"Go to your own relations,"
"Go out."

If the wife should say to her husband, "You are not a husband to me" and he should say, "I believe you," intending divorce, it would take effect and she would be divorced. When a man intending to divorce his wife says to her, "You

57. Al-Marghīnānī, *op. cit.*, Vol. II : 354 ; Ibn Nujaym, *op. cit.*, Vol. III, pp. 321-22; *al-Fatāwā al-Hindiyah*, *op. cit.*, Vol. II, p. 61 ; Ibn 'Ābidīn, *op. cit.*, Vol. II, pp. 474-75.
58. *Ibid.*

are not to me as a wife" or "I am not to you as a husband,' it takes effect according to Abū Ḥanīfah. But Muḥammad and Abū Yūsuf do not agree with him.[59]

As a general rule a divorce by *Kināyah* expression amounts to an irrevocable divorce.[60] But under the provisions of the Muslim Family Laws Ordinance, 1961, the divorce shall be *Raj'i* (revocable) only.

Shāfi'ī Law: Shāfi'ī agrees with the Ḥanafis in the matter of divorce by *kināyah* expressions. But he holds that divorce by *kināyah* or ambiguous expressions amounts to such a divorce as the husband intended. According to him the nature and number of *kināyah* divorce shall depend on the husband's intention as stated by him. In the absence of any intention only one revocable divorce shall be effected.[61] All *kināyah* divorces, according to him, amount to a revocable divorce unless the expression used indicates three divorces when it shall amount to an irrevocable divorce.[62] He has given his own examples of *kināyah* or ambiguous expressions.[63]

Māliki Law: Mālik also agrees -- with the Ḥanafīs about divorce by *kināyah* or ambiguous expressions.[64] He divides *kināyah* (ambiguous) expressions into two classes, namely,

(*a*) *Kināyah Zāhiriah*

(*b*) *Kināyah Khafiah*

(*a*) *Kināyah Zāhiriah*: The expression indicates the use of language which refers to divorce but only indirectly. In such a case the intention of the husband is immaterial and the husband shall be taken to have divorced his wife by a revocable divorce unless there is proof or the circumstantial evidence points otherwise.[65]

59. *Ibid.*, Ibn Nujaym, *op. cit.*, Vol. III, pp. 324-26.
60. *Ibid.*
61. Ibn Qudāmah, *op. cit.*, Vol. VII, pp. 127-28.
62. *Ibid.*
63. *Ibid.*, Vol. VII, pp. 128-32 ; Ibn Rushd, *op. cit.*, Vol. II, p. 63.
64. *Ibid.* 65. *Ibid.*

(*b*) *Kināyah Khafiah*: *Kināyah Khafiah* means an expression which does not clearly indicate a divorce. Divorce shall be effected only when the husband so intended and not otherwise.[66]

Ḥanbali Law: According to Aḥmad b. Hanbal the nature and number of divorce shall depend on the husband's intention.[67]

Shī'i Law: The Shī'ahs do not recognise *al-Ṭalāq al-Kināyah.*

XIII. Divorce considered with regard to conditions

Divorce under the Sunnī law may be *Ṭalāq al-Mu'allaq* or *Ṭa'līq al-Ṭalāq*, that is, conditional or it may be *Ghair-Mu'allaq*, that is, unconditional. A condition can be attached while pronouncing a divorce so that the divorce takes effect only upon the fulfilment of the condition to which it is subject.[68] The condition may refer to the occurrence or non-occurrence of a certain specified future event or it may refer to a certain place or time.[69] A conditional divorce remains in suspense and the marriage subsists till the condition, subject to which it was pronounced, is fulfilled. A divorce is effected as soon as the condition is fulfilled. If, however, the condition becomes impossible of fulfilment then the declaration of the husband, that is, the conditional divorce becomes ineffective, and the marriage continues to subsist as before.[70]

If the divorce is made contingent on a default on the part of the husband in the performance of certain condition or conditions agreed upon between the parties, a divorce would be effected on the occurrence of the breach of the condition.[71] If the divorce is given subject to the fulfilment of two or more conditions, the divorce would be effected

66. Ibn Qudāmah, *op. cit.*, Vol. VII, pp. 128-32; Ibn Rushd, *op. cit.*, Vol. II, p. 63.
67. Ibn Nujaym, *op. cit*,, Vol. IV. p. 2.
68. *Ibid.*, Ibn 'Ābidīn, *op. cit.*, Vol. II. pp. 505-7.
69. *Ibid.*, *al-Fatāwā al-Hindiyah*, *op. cit.*, Vol. II, p. 82.
70. *Ibid.*
71. *Al-Fatāwā al-Hindiyah*, *op. cit.*, Vol. II, p. 82.

only when all the conditions are fulfilled.[72]

The condition subject to which a divorce is pronounced may relate to a specified place and the husband may say that divorce shall take effect only at a certain place. Thus he may say, "You are divorced when you enter Mecca," and in such a case the wife would not be divorced till she actually enters Mecca.[73] Similarly, he may say to his wife, "If you enter your father's house or the house of 'A' then you are divorced." A divorce shall take effect in that case only when she enters her father's house or A's house but till then the divorce remains in suspense.[74]

A conditional divorce is to be distinguished from a mere statement of divorce. Thus should the husband say to his wife, "You are divorced in Mecca" or "in such a house" then a divorce shall be effected immediately and shall not be suspended till the wife enters Mecca or the specified house.[75] This rule is based on the reasoning that there is no condition attached to the divorce and the word "In Mecca", or "In such a house" are merely redundant and carry no significance.[76]

A divorce may be so pronounced as not to come into effect immediately but to remain in suspense till some future specified time. In that case it shall take effect only on the arrival of the time to which it has been referred.[77] Thus, if a man says to his wife, "You are divorced tomorrow", divorce shall take place on the morning of the next day.[78] Similarly, if he says, "You are divorced after a month", a divorce shall be effected immediately on the expiry of the month, but not before.[79]

72. *Ibid.* Vol. II, p. 82 ; al-Marghīnānī, *op. cit.*, Vol, II, pp. 343-44 ; Ibn 'Ābidīn, *op. cit.*, Vol. II, pp. 449-53.
73. *Ibid.*
74. *Ibid.*
75. *Ibid.*
76. *Ibid.*
77. Al-Marghīnānī, *op. cit.*, Vol. II, pp. 343, 365 ; Ibn Nujaym, *op. cit.*, Vol. III, pp. 286-88 ; Ibn 'Ābidīn, *op. cit.*, Vol. II, pp. 449-53.
78. *Ibid.*
79. *Ibid.*

Conditions : It is essential that the conditions should be definite, certain and possible.[80] If the declaration is ambiguous or relates to something that is uncertain or impossible then not only the condition but the declaration of divorce itself shall be void.[81] Thus if a husband were to say to his wife, "If you do not immediately return the purse you have removed from my pocket then you are divorced" and it should happen that the purse is in his own pocket then the wife shall not be divorced for it is not possible for the wife to restore the purse.[82]

Cancellation of conditional divorce : It has been laid down by the Ḥanafi Jurists that once the husband has pronounced a divorce contingent on a condition he cannot cancel the pronouncement.[83] It is a very hard rule and sometimes involves great hardship. Conditional divorce is generally pronounced only in anger or excitement as when a husband asks his wife to do or to abstain from doing a certain act and to emphasise his demand he pronounces a conditional divorce. It is obvious that his pronouncement is not the result of cool deliberation nor, as a general practice, intended to be effected and it is very hard on him and often on his wife also if he is not allowed to revoke the pronouncement of divorce. No doubt the strict view adopted by the Ḥanafi jurists is to discourage the wanton pronouncement of divorce and also because the jurists consider that a wife should not be deprived of a chance to get rid of an undesirable husband. The very fact that he has divorced the wife shows that he is not a desirable person. But even then an opportunity must be given to a husband to rectify the hasty action, particularly in view of the fact that Islam discourages divorce and provides an opportunity for reconciliation. Strict enforcement of a divorce pronounced under excitement often causes hardship to the spouses and there is no reason to enforce

80. Ibn 'Ābidīn, op. cit., Vol. II, p. 506.
81. *Ibid.*
82. *Ibid*, Vol. II, p. 507.
83. *Ibid.*, Vol. II, p. 573.

it rigorously, particularly if the wife also wants the continuation of the marriage. To escape from hardship the Ḥanafis suggest that the husband should divorce his wife by a revocable divorce. Let the wife, after the expiry of the period of *'iddah*, when the marriage stands dissolved, do the act which she was forbidden to do. The husband may afterwards remarry her. It is explained that on the expiry of the *'iddah* the marriage becomes dissolved when the woman is no longer the wife of that person and so she can commit the act that was forbidden and to which the divorce was subjected. She will not be affected by the commission of the act as on being divorced she becomes a stranger. The husband can then marry her.[84] In Pakistan, such a divorce shall not bring about an immediate dissolution of marriage and under the provisions of section 7 of the Muslim Family Laws Ordinance, 1961, the marriage shall be dissolved only on the expiry of ninety days from the time when information of the divorce is received by the Chairman of the Union Council from the divorcing party.

Shī'i Law : There is no conditional divorce under the Shī'i law.

XII. Divorce Considered with Regard to Effect

Divorce with regard to its effect can be divided into the following two main classes :

(*a*) *Raj'i* (revocable),

(*b*) *Bā'in* (irrevocable).

(*a*) *Raj'i* or revocable divorce is such as does not immediately dissolve the marriage but leaves it within the power of the husband to revoke it within the prescribed period of *'iddah* and thus to maintain the marriage.[85] *Ṭalāq al-Aḥsan* amounts to a revocable divorce.[86] It is only on the expiry of the period of *'iddah* that such a divorce becomes

84. Ibn Nujaym, *op. cit.*, Vol. IV, p. 33. Ibn 'Ābidīn, *op. cit.*, Vol. II, p. 510.

85. Ibn 'Ābidīn, *op. cit.*, Vol. II, p. 442.

86. *Ibid.*, Vol. II, pp. 426-28 ; al-Kāsānī, *Badā'i' al-Ṣanā'i'*, Cairo, 1327 A.H., Vol. III, pp. 88-89.

an irrevocable divorce.[87] This is subject to the condition that the marriage has been consummated, otherwise the divorce would amount to an irrevocable divorce. This rule is based on the fact that a husband can revoke his divorce only during the period of *'iddah*. But there is no *'iddah* incumbent on a wife whose marriage has not been consummated because, as a general rule, *'iddah* is incumbent to ascertain if the wife is pregnant or not. But in this case there can be no question of pregnancy hence no *'iddah* is prescribed for a woman who is divorced by her husband before cohabitation. Thus, it is stated in the Qur'an, "O you who believe, when you marry believing women, then divorce them before you touch them, you have in their case no term which you should reckon...."[88]

(*b*) *Bā'in* literally means separation as it separates the parties and leaves no right to resume conjugal relations except by renewing the marriage. *Bā'in* or irrevocable divorce is such as immediately dissolves the marriage on the very pronouncement of the divorce.[89] It does not leave any discretion to the husband to cancel it. In Pakistan, the Muslim Family Laws Ordinance, 1961, has done away with *Bā'in* divorce. The marriage is no longer considered to be dissolved absolutely on the pronouncement of a *Ṭalāq al-Bid'ah*, but the *Bā'in* or unorthodox divorce shall not be considered to be effective until the expiry of ninety days from the date when information of the divorce is given to the Chairman of the Union Council.[90]

Ṭalāq al-Bā'in or irrevocable divorce is divided into two classes, namely,

(*a*) *al-Ṭalāq al-Mughallaẓah* and

(*b*) *al-Ṭalāq al-Khafif* or *Ghair-Mughllaẓah*.

87. *Ibid.*, Vol. II. pp. 426-28; al-Kasani, *Bada'i al-Sana'i* Cairo, 1327 A.H., Vol. III, pp, 88-89.

88. Qur'ān, XXII: 49, Surah al-Ahzāb.

89. Al-Kāsānī, *op. cit.*, Vol. II, p. 180f.

90. See Section 7 of the Muslim Family Laws Ordinance, 1961.

The word *Mughallazah* means "very hard", but here it conveys the idea of finality and we may call it a final or absolute divorce. Under the Muslim law, a husband can remarry his wife if he had divorced her revocably only once or twice and the period of her *'iddah* has expired, but she becomes absolutely forbidden to him after the pronouncement of three divorces so that he cannot remarry her until and unless she marries another person and that other marriage is dissolved after consummation. This rule is based on a verse in the Qur'ān wherein it is stated, "So if he (the husband) divorces her (the third time) she shall not be lawful to him afterwards until she marries another husband."[91] The further stipulation about the consummation of the second marriage is based on a direction to this effect given in a Tradition the trustworthiness of which is accepted by all Muslim jurists. Rifā'ah's wife approached the Prophet (peace be on him) and said that her husband had given her three divorces. He told her that nothing could be done in the matter and an intermediary marriage was necessary before renewal of the marriage.[92]

The three divorces may be pronounced either on three different occasions or on two different occasions or at the same time. The *Mughallaẓah* divorce shall become effected as soon as the third pronouncement of divorce is made. The husband can remarry his divorced wife without the necessity of an intermediary marriage only if he has divorced her once or twice. The object of this rule is to impress upon the husband the necessity of proceeding with caution, sound judgement and patience, and also to keep men away from this form of divorce. It serves as a check against hasty and undesirable repetition of pronouncement of divorce by the husband. The passion of jealousy in a man will stop him from carelessly divorcing his wife or from wantonly repeating the pronouncements of divorce because he knows that after the third pronouncement he cannot remarry her until and unless

91. Qur'ān, II, 230, Surah al-Baqarāh.
92. Walī al-Dīn al-Khaṭīb, *Mishkāt, op. cit.*, p. 284.

she marries someone else and that marriage is dissolved after consummation.

XIV. Triple Pronouncement

There is a great controversy regarding the effect of triple pronouncement of divorce at one and the same time. The difference in the opinions of the Muslim jurists is due to the difference in their interpretation and application of the law. One set of jurists is of the opinion that no leniency is to be shown in the application of the laws so that people should not take undue advantage on that account. Abū Ḥanīfah and Mālik, therefore, hold three repetitions of divorce to be final. The other set of jurists explain that Allah wants that people should be dealt with leniently so that they may not be put to hardship, and also to minimise the chances of separation. Hence, they hold the three repetitions to amount to one divorce only.[93] Ibn Rus͟hd has explained that Islām believes in the golden mean. Thus, it has not allowed the husband to revoke his divorce on indefinite occasions. Had it done, so the husband could harass his wife by every time revoking the divorce before the expiry of the period of the *'iddah*. Similarly, if every divorce amounted to an irrevocable divorce then it would have involved hardship to the husband as he would get no opportunity of revoking the divorce. He then concludes that to hold three repetitions of divorce at one and the same time to amount to three divorces is to lose sight of the policy of the Muslim law.[94] Some Sunnī jurists hold that if the second and the third pronouncements were made merely to emphasise the first pronouncement then only a *G͟hair-Mug͟hallaẓah* or revocable divorce shall be effected. They apply the same rule when the second or even the third pronouncement was made under a momentary excitement without the *intention* to pronounce a *Mug͟hallaẓah* divorce. Others hold that a *Mughallaẓah*, final divorce, shall be effected as soon as the third pronouncement is made irre-

93. Ibn Rus͟hd, *op. cit.*, Vol. II, pp. 50-51.
94. *Ibid.*

spective of the fact whether it was made intentionally, unintentionally or merely to emphasise the first pronouncement. Abū Ḥanīfah has stated that the three pronouncements shall amount to three separate divorces so that they shall result in a *Mughallaẓah* or final divorce. The explanation that the husband had used the three pronouncements simply for the sake of emphasis cannot change the nature of the divorce and a *Mughallaẓah* divorce shall be effected.[95] This is also the view held by the majority of Ḥanafi jurists who hold that in such a case a *Mughallaẓah* divorce would be effected and would be good in law though it may be bad in religion.[96] The expression "good in law" means that it will be given effect to by a Qāḍi or the Court. Ibn Taymiah holds that if a husband does not repeat the divorce three times, but says "I divorce you three times or thrice" or uses some similar expression then the pronouncement shall amount to only one pronouncement of divorce and so shall be a non-*Mughallaẓah* divorce.[97] Ibn Isḥāq, Tāwūs, 'Akramah and Ibn 'Abbās hold that the three pronouncements of divorce at one and the same time constitute only one divorce.[98] Ibn 'Abbās has reported that the pronouncement of three divorces at one and the same time was treated as one divorce during the time of the Prophet peace be on him), the first Caliph and during the first two or three years of regime of the second Caliph.[99] But the second Caliph found that people used to pronounce divorces wantonly many times and in order to discourage this undersirable practice he introduced the rule that pronouncement of three divorces at one and the same time shall be treated as three divorces or a final or *Mughallaẓah* divorce. It is also reported that 'Umar used to punish people who pronounced three divorces at the

95. Al-Sha'rānī, *al-Mīzān al-Kubrā*, Cairo, 1279 A,H,, Vol. II, p. 138; Ibn 'Ābidīn, *op. cit.*, Vol. II, p. 430.
96. Ibn al-Humām, *op. cit.*, Vol. III, p. 25; Ibn 'Ābidīn, *op. cit.*, Vol. II, pp. 466-67.
97. Ibn Taymīyah, *Fatāwā*, Cairo, 1328 A.H., Vol. III, p. 14f.
98. Ibn Rushd, *op. cit.*, Vol. II, p. 51; Ibn 'Abidīn, *op. cit.*, Vol. II. p. 430.
99. *Ibid.*, Abū Da'ūd, *Sunan*, Kānpur, n.d., Vol. II, p. 299.

same time.[100] This also supports the view that he wanted to discourage people from wantonly repeating divorces. The Sunnī jurists who consider three pronouncements to amount to three or a final divorce have explained that in those times the people did not actually mean three divorces but meant only one divorce and the other two pronouncements were meant merely to emphasise the first pronouncement.

It is stated in *Radd al-Muḥtār* that it is now settled law that a triple pronouncement of divorce shall amount to a *Mughallaẓah* or final divorce as supported by the following reasons :—

(*a*) At the time when 'Umar modified the law, there were living a very large number of the Companions of the Prophet (peace be on him) but they did not object to this modification. We can, therefore, presume that there might have been a Tradition known to them, but which has not reached us on the basis of which the modification must have been made.

(*b*) In any case the Companions accepted the modified law and so the modified law becomes binding on the basis of *Ijmā'*.

(*c*) The fact that the modification was accepted by the Successors of the Companions and the early jurists also gives the modification the force of law by the principle of *Ijmā'*.[101]

As regards the first two grounds, it may be explained that the very words of Caliph 'Umar show that he was introducing a change in the law to meet the exigencies of his time. The third ground is quite correct, but it also establishes the fact that we can change the law if it is not suitable for a particular period of time. This is exactly what has been done by many Muslim countries. Thus under section 7 of the Muslim Family Laws Ordinance, 1961, a divorce by triple pronounce-

100. Abū Dā'ūd, *op. cit.*, Vol. II, p. 299 ; Ibn Qudāmah, *op. cit.*, Vol. VIII, p. 104.

101. Ibn 'Ābidīn, *op. cit.*, Vol. II, p. 430.

ment is no longer considered *Mughallazah* or final and it is open to the spouses to continue the marriage if reconciliation is brought about between them within the prescribed period. The law was amended even earlier in Egypt, Sudan, Jordan, Syria, Morocco and Tunisia.

The view that mere repetitions of the divorces without an intention to give a *Mughallaẓah* or final divorce and simply by way of emphasis or in momentary excitement does not amount to a *Mughallaẓah* or final divorce finds full support from two Traditions. It is reported that the Prophet (peace be on him) was told of a Muslim who had pronounced three divorces against his wife at the same time whereupon the Prophet (peace be on him) stood up in anger and exclaimed that the man was making a plaything of the Book of Allah even while he (the Prophet) was in their midst.[102] He was so angry that, according to one report, one of his Companions wanted to kill the offender (the husband).[103] If the repetitions were permissible then it is not clear as to why the Prophet (peace be on him) should have been so angry. There is another Tradition reported by Rukanah Ibn 'Abd al-Yazīd that he divorced his wife thrice and informed the Prophet (peace be on him) about it and said, "I call Allah to witness that I intended only a single divorce." The Messenger of Allah said, "Dost thou call Allah to witness that thou didst not intend but single divorce ?" I said, "Yes, I call Allah to witness that I did not intend but a single divorce." So the Messenger of Allah returned her (the wife) back to me."[104] This Tradition leaves no doubt that if a person pronounces one divorce against his wife and then repeats the divorce a second or even a third time simply to emphasise the first pronouncement and not with a view to effect a *Mughallaẓah* or final divorce, it shall be open to him to explain his intention and to take back his wife ; otherwise how could the wife have been asked by the Prophet (peace be on

102. Walī al-Dīn al-Khaṭīb, *Mishkāt*, *op. cit.*, p. 283.
103. Aḥmad b. 'Alī al-Nasā'ī, *Sunan*, Dehli, n.d., Vol. II, p. 98.
104. Walī al-Dīn al-Khaṭīb, *Mishkāt*, *op. cit.* p. 283.

him) to return to her husband. It is clear from the above discussion that a triple pronouncement of divorce on one occasion was originally considered to amount to only one divorce. But the Ḥanafi jurists consider it to amount to a *Mughallazah* divorce even though they call it *Bid'i* or innovation. This interpretation goes against the very spirit of divorce as laid down in the Qur'an which enjoins that in the cases of a breach between the husband and the wife it should be referred to arbitration and, failing an amicable settlement, a divorce is allowed subject to a period of waiting or *'iddah* during which a reconciliation is possible and the husband can take back his wife. Islam has permitted the dissolution of marriage in case of necessity, but dissolution has been strongly disapproved of and discouraged. A divorce in the proper form, laid down in the Qur'an, becomes final and absolute only after the observance of *'iddah* and so ample time is given to a husband to think over the matter coolly and to retrieve his action if he so decides. The main idea in the procedure for divorce, as laid down by Islām, is to give the parties an opportunity for reconciliation. If the three pronouncements are treated as a *Mughallaẓah* divorce, then no opportunity is given to the spouses or the husband to retrieve a hasty divorce. This rule was introduced long after the time of the Prophet (peace be on him) and it renders ineffective the measures provided in the Qur'ān against hasty action thereby depriving people of a chance to change their minds, retrieve their mistakes and retain their wives. The object of Caliph 'Umar in treating it as a *Mughallaẓah* divorce was clearly to stop people from wanton repetitions of divorce and from treating the matter of divorce in a light and non-serious way. It must have suited the needs of his own time, but the practice in the modern times has resulted in a great deal of harm. People in the excitement of the moment give three divorces to the wife at one and the same time without the least intention to pronounce a *Mughallaẓah* divorce but simply to emphasise the first pronouncement, a step which they grievously repent afterwards when they find that the mischief cannot be undone.

Ameer Ali suggest that in the case of a divorce pronounced under the influence of threats and strong coercion, the husband can, if he wants to retain his wife, adopt the Shāfi'i doctrine when he shall be validly entitled to keep his wife.[105] This can also apply in the case under discussion. The well-known Muslim jurist, Maulana 'Abd al-Ḥayy of Lucknow, has expressed the view that a person who has pronounced (in anger) three divorces can, in case of urgency, when separation from the woman be difficult and there should be an apprehension of greater improper acts, validly follow the view of another (Sunnī) Imām.[106]

Māliki Law : Mālik makes a distinction between various expressions used in the pronouncement of divorce. A husband may use the word "and" in the pronouncement of the divorce as when he says, "I divorce you and divorce you and divorce you." He may, on the other hand, not use it as when he says, "I divorce you, divorce you, divorce you." In the former case the pronouncements shall amount to three divorces or to *Mughallaẓah* divorce.[107] In the latter case the matter can, according to the Imām, be considered from three aspects.

I. When the husband merely repeats the words "you are divorced" three times or as when he says, "You are divorced, divorced, divorced." In such a case if the husband explains that he had repeated the words three times merely to emphasise the divorce then his explanation that he had repeated the divorce to make it more emphatic would not be accepted.[108] This is irrespective of the fact whether the marriage has been consummated or not.[109]

II. If the husband did not repeat the divorce to lay emphasis but intended three divorces or repeated the divorce without any intention at all then three divorces shall be

105. Ameer Ali, *Muhammadan Law*, Calcutta, 1908, Vol. II, p. 522.
106. 'Abd al-Ḥayy, *Majmū' al-Fatāwā*, Lucknow, n.d., Vol. I, p. 349.
107. Muḥammad b. Aḥmad, *Jawāhir al-'Uqūd*, Cairo, 1955 A.D., Vol. II, p. 134, Al-Sha'ranī, *op. cit.*, Vol. II, p. 138.
108. *Ibid*,
109, Al-Sha'rānī, *op. cit.*, Vol. II, p. 137.

effected.[110] If the husband pronounces three divorces on different occasions but in the same *Ṭuhr* then the same result shall follow.

III. If the husband repeats the divorce while giving a conditional divorce concerning only one thing as when he says, "If you speak to A then you are divorced, divorced, divorced," in such a case his explanation shall be accepted. If the repetitions relate to different things as when he says, "If you go out of this house then you are divorced, if you speak to *A* then you are divorced, if you do not take your meals then you are divorced" then in such a case three divorces shall be effected only on the fulfilment of all the conditions.[111]

Ḥanbali Law: Aḥmad ibn Ḥanbal has laid down the following rules :—

(*a*) If the husband does not use the word "and" in the repetitions as when he says, "You are divorced, divorced, divorced" or "I divorce you, divorce you, divorce you," and the second and the third pronouncements are used simply for emphasis then only one divorce shall be effected if the marriage has not been consummated. If it has been consummated then three divorces shall be effected.[112]

(*b*) If the husband does not use the three pronouncements to lay emphasis then three divorces shall be effected.

(*c*) If the husband uses the word "and" as when he says, "You are divorced, and divorced and divorced" then if he used the second and the third repetitions to emphasise the first pronouncement then only one divorce shall be effected irrespective of the fact whether the marriage has or has not been consummated. But if he used the three pronouncements without the

110. Al-Sha'rānī, *op. cit.*, Vol. II, p. 137.
111. Ibn Qudāmah, *op. cit.*, Vol, VII, p. 198.
112. Muḥammad b. Aḥmad, *op. cit.*, Vol. II, p. 134; al-Sha'rānī, *op. cit.*, Vol. II, p. 138.

intention to emphasise the first pronouncement, one *Mughallaẓah* divorce shall be effected.[113]

Shāfi'i Law : Shāfi'i holds that if a marriage has been consummated and the husband repeats three pronouncements of divorce against his wife whether using or without using a conjunctive word like "and" but without intending three divorces and merely to lay emphasis on the first pronouncement, a single divorce shall be effected. If he pronounces the three pronouncements intending or without any definite intention, three divorces shall be effected.[114] If the marriage has not been consummated then only one divorce shall be effected under such circumstances.[115]

XIV. Concealment of Divorce

If the husband pronounces three divorces but conceals the fact even from the wife and continues to be intimate with her then in such a case he alone may be guilty of adultery. No blame may attach to the wife, and the children born after such divorce shall be considered legitimate. If a husband pronounces three divorces with the intention of effecting a final divorce or without an intention to pronounce a final divorce and he continues the marital relationship, but the wife comes to know of the three pronouncements or the matter is brought before the Qāḍī, then an irrevocable or *Mughallazah* divorce shall be effected. The marriage shall continue as long as it is not set aside by the Qāḍī or the wife remains ignorant of the divorce.

113. Muḥammad b. Aḥmad *op. cit.*, Vol. II, p. 134 ; al-Sha'ānī, *op. cit.*, Vol. II, p. 138. Minhāj al-Tālibīn, Eng. Tr. E. G. Howard, London 1914, A.D.

114. *Ibid.*

115. *Ibid.*

DIVORCE IN WRITING

- *Marsūm* (Customary)
- *Ghayr Marsūm* (Not Customary)
  - *Mustabīn* (Manifest)
  - *Ghayr Mustabīn* (Not Manifest)

Chapter 5

DIVORCE IN WRITING

I. *Preliminary*: The Sunnī jurists recognise the validity of a divorce in writing. They hold that divorce can be given orally as well as in writing and both are equally binding on the spouses. It is true that writing is not necessary to the legal validity of a divorce under the Muslim law, but when valuable rights depend upon the marriage and are affected by the divorce, the parties should in their own interest execute some documents which should afford satisfactory evidence of what they have done. The effect of a divorce in writing is just the same as that of a divorce given orally. The jurists, however, differ on some small details.

II. *Essentials*: There are certain conditions which must be fulfilled before a divorce in writing can be considered to be valid. They relate to certain aspects that have been discussed below under the following heads :—

(*a*) Husband's capacity,
(*b*) Wife,
(*c*) Freedom of choice, and
(*d*) Writing.

(*a*) *Husband's Capacity*: A person who gives a divorce in writing should possess the same capacity as is necessary in the case of a person pronouncing a divorce. He must be adult, that is, major under the provisions of the Muslim law, and should possess understanding.

(*b*) *Wife*: As in the case of an oral divorce, a divorce in writing can be given only in respect of the wife. If the woman is not the wife of the man then naturally he can have no authority over her and so cannot exercise the power of divorce in respect of her. It can, however, be written in respect of a woman who is not yet the wife of the divorcer if it is to take effect at a time when the woman becomes his wife.[1]

Shī'ī law: Under Shī'ī law a divorce in writing, when permissible, can be given only in respect of the wife permanently married to the husband. Hence it cannot be given in respect of a *Mut'ah* wife. However, Shī'ī law does not allow a conditional divorce and so a divorce cannot be given in respect of a woman not yet the wife of the divorcer but is to take effect at some future time when she becomes his wife.

(c) *Freedom of choice*: The husband should have freedom of choice. He must be acting, that is, giving the divorce in writing of his free-will without any compulsion being brought on him in the matter. A divorce written under compulsion is not valid or binding on the husband.[2] It is explained in *Fatāwā Qaḍī Khān* and *Radd al-Muḥtār* that a divorce written under compulsion would not be effective because writing takes the place of speech only when necessary, but there is no necessity in this case and so the divorce is ineffective.[3] The explanation is not very convincing but it seems that the Sunnī jurists, having held an oral divorce under compulsion to be valid, were anxious to restrict its application, hence this rule. (For a discussion on the effect of compulsion see discussion under the heading "Divorce (oral) under compulsion.") It has been held by the Calcutta High Court that a divorce written under compulsion is valid.[4] It is submitted that this ruling requires reconsideration. As stated above, such a divorce is not valid.

Written acknowledgment under compulsion: An acknowledgment or a declaration in writing under compulsion by the

1. Al-Marghīnānī, 'Alī b. Abī Bakr, *al-Hidāyah*, Delhi, n. d., Vol. II, p. 365.
2. Ibn, 'Ābidīn, *Radd al-Muḥtār 'ala'l-Durr al-Mukhtār*, Cairo, 1318 A.H., Vol. II, p. 432.
3. *Ibid.*, Ibn Nujaym, *al-Baḥr al-Rā'iq*, Cairo, 1311 A.H., Vol. III, p. 264.
4. Jarina Akhtar Khatun Vs. Hafeez-ud-Din Khan, A.I.R. 1926, Cal. 242.

husband that he had divorced his wife is wholly ineffective.[5] Thus when a person writes under compulsion that his wife is a divorcee, that is, that she had been divorced but as a matter of fact she had not been divorced then his wife would not be separated.[6] The Courts have followed this view. It seems to be based on the reasoning that the writing does not contain a pronouncement of divorce but merely a declaration, namely, that the wife had been divorced, which declaration is incorrect and so no divorce would be effected.

Shī'ī law: As intention is an essential condition of divorce under Shī'ī law, a divorce or its acknowledgment written under compulsion is ineffective even if it is otherwise permissible. Acknowledgment under compulsion of a divorce having been given would also be quite ineffective for want of intention.

(*d*) *Form of writing*:

(*i*) *General*: No particular form or language is prescribed for a divorce in writing. Any form or language can be used for the purpose. But there should be no uncertainty in the writing about the divorce being given, otherwise it would not be effected.[7] Thus if a husband writes to his wife, "you are divorced if it pleases God", then no divorce shall be effected on account of uncertainty.[8] The words, "if it pleases God" must, however, be used in a continuation with the clause effecting a divorce.

When the language of document clearly indicates that the intention was to give an irrevocable divorce then it is not necessary that the divorce should be repeated three times or that the writing should contain three pronouncements of divorce.

5. Ibn 'Ābidīn, *op. cit.*, Vol. II, p. 432; al-Sarakhsī, *Kitāb al-Mabsūṭ*, Cairo, 1324 A.H., Vol. XXIV, p. 83.
6. *Ibid*.
7. Ibn 'Ābidīn, *op. cit.*, Vol. II, p. 439; Qāḍī Khān al-Awzjandī, *Fātāwā Qāḍī Khān*, Kānpur, 1310 A.H., Vol. II, p. 219.
8. *Ibid.*, p. 222.

Shī'ī law : Under Shī'ī law a divorce cannot validly be given in writing except under certain specified conditions as when the husband is unable to speak.[9] Some jurists maintain that a husband can lawfully divorce his wife in writing if he is absent from her.[10] This view, however, is not held to be reliable. But the fact that a husband has actually pronounced divorce in the presence of witnesses can be reduced to writing which may be forwarded to the wife to establish the divorce.

(*ii*) *Classification of* : The Hanafi jurists have classified writings into two classes, namely *Marsūm*, that is, customary and *Ghayr-Marsūm* or unusual or not customary.[11] The former are those which are properly superscribed and addressed, while the latter are those which are not so superscribed and addressed.[12] The latter are further sub-divided into "*Mustabīn*" or manifest and "*Ghayr Mustabīn*" or not manifest.[13] The *Mustabīn* or manifest are such as can be read and comprehended such as written on a paper, wall, etc. Writings which are not manifest are such as cannot be read and comprehended. Thus if a person writes something in the air or on the surface of water, the writing would not be capable of being read and comprehended and so would be termed *Ghayr Mustabīn* or non-manifest.[14]

(*iii*) *Intention: Ḥanafī law*: Under the Ḥanafī law if the writing is *Marsūm* and *Mustabīn* then a divorce shall be effected irrespective of the husband's intention.[15] If it is *Ghayr Mustabīn* then no divorce shall be effected, even if the husband intends to do so. If it is *Mustabīn* but *Ghayr Marsūm* divorce shall

9. Ja'far b. al-Ḥasan, *Kitāb Sharā'i' al-Islām*, Tehran, 1377 A.H., p. 207.
10. *Ibid.*
11. Qāḍī Khān al-Awzjandī, *op. cit.*, Vol. II, p. 219.
12. *Ibid.*
13. *Ibid.*
14. *Ibid.*
15. *Ibid.*

be effected, provided the husband intends it.[16]

There are two reports about the opinion of Aḥmad ibn Ḥanbal respecting intention of the husband to divorce his wife by a divorce in writing. According to one report such intention is not necessary. But according to the other report intention to divorce the wife is an essential condition for its validity. The latter report is generally accepted as correct. The same view is reported to have been held by Abū Ḥanīfah, Mālik, and al-Shāfi'ī. It is explained that it is possible that he did not intend a divorce but wrote the divorce merely to try his pen or merely by way of exercise to improve his writing or even to frighten his wife.[17]

(*iv*) *Wife's presence at the time of writing the divorce:* It is not necessary that the wife should be present at the time when her husband orally divorces her. On an analogy the same rule shall apply in the case of divorce in writing and it is not necessary for the validity of such a divorce that the wife should be present at the time when the divorce is being written. The various illustrations given in *Fatāwāi Qāḍī Khān*, *'Alamgīrīyah*, etc., fully support this view. The Courts have followed this view.[18] It is also not necessary that it should be signed in her presence.

(*v*) *Whether to be addressed to wife*: It is not necessary that the writing should be addressed to the wife herself; it can be addressed to any other person. The only condition for the validity of a divorce in writing addressed to a person other than the wife is that there must be a clear indication in it about the wife so that the identity of the person intended to be divorced and an intention to divorce her are clearly

16. Qāḍī Khān al-Awzjandī, *op. cit.*, Vol. II, p. 219.
17. Ibn Qudāmah, al-Mughnī, Cairo, 1367 A.H., Vol. VII, p. 239.
18. Asha Bibi Vs. Kadir Ibrahim Rowther (I.L.R.) 33 Mad. 22; Nur Bibi Vs. Ahmed Ali, 88 I.C, 408, A.I.R. 1925, All. 550; Raja Sahib Rasul Sahib, (I.L.R.) 44 Bom. 44; Sarabai Vs. Rabiabai (I.L.R.) 30 Bom. 537; Abdul Qadir Vs. Aziza Bee, A.I.R. 1944 Mad. 227; Ahmed Kasim Mulla Vs Khatun Bibi, A.I.R. 1933 Cal. 27.

indicated by the writing.

The opinion was expressed by the Calcutta High Court at one time that according to Ḥanafī law, a written divorce is valid only if it is addressed to any pers on.[19] This view of the Calcutta High Court was considered in some later cases but was not followed. A different view was taken in these later cases by the same Court when it was held that it is not necessary that the writing should be addressed to the wife.[20]

(*vi*) *Information to the wife*: It is not necessary for the validity of a deed of divorce that information of its execution should be sent to the wife. The Courts have expressed the same view.[21] Thus the Calcutta High Court has stated that a divorce is valid where it is made by a written instrument in customary (*marsūm*) form notwithstanding that it is not brought to the knowledge of the wife.[22] The Lahore High Court has taken the same view and has laid down that if a divorce is in writing and in the customary form then no notice of it to the wife is legally necessary.[23] It has been held in a case by the Bombay High Court that a *bā'in ṭalāq* reduced to manifest and customary writing even when not communicated to the wife takes effect immediately on the mere writing of divorce as from the date of the document.[24]

(*vii*) *Receipt of a conditional divorce in writing*: In a case where a divorce is to be effected only when it is received by the wife, it becomes necessary sometimes to determine when it can be deemed to have been received by her. According to

19. Jarina Khatun Vs. Hafeez-ud-Din Khan, (I.L.R.) 4 Cal. 588; A.I.R. 1926 Cal. 242.
20. Muhammad Ishaq Vs. Mst. Sairan, A.I.R. 1936, Lah. 611; Mst. Lalàn Bibi Vs. Muhammad Ashraf Ali, P.L.D. 1951, Lah. 467; Asha Bibi Vs. Muhammad Ibrahim Rowther, I.L.R. 33 Mad. 22.
21. Mst. Lalan Bibi Vs. Muhammad Ashfaq Ali, 1951 P.L.D. Lah, 467; Aesha Bibi Vs. Ibrahim Kadir Rowther, (I.L.R.) 33 Mad. 32.
22. Ahmed Kasim Molla Vs. Khatun Bibi, A.I.R. 1933 Cal. 27; Sarabai Vs. Rabiabai, I.L.R. 30 Bom. 537.
23. Muhammad Ishaq Khan Vs. Mst. Sairan, A.I.R. 1936 Lah. 611; Mst. Lalan Bibi Vs. Muhammad Ashfaq Ali, P.L.D. 1951, Lah. 467.
24. Sarabai Vs. Rabiabai, I.L.R. 30, Bom. 537.

Muslim jurists, receipt means actual receipt. The Ḥanafī jurists have laid down certain rules to determine if a writing can be deemed to have been received by the wife. According to them there are three cases in which the writing may be said not to have been received by the wife. Firstly, if the paper on which the writing is written is not at all received by her. Secondly, if the paper is received by her but it contains nothing which can be called "writing". Thirdly, when the letter is delivered to another person and she does not receive it.[25] The second class of contingency can arise if the husband were to write a letter which contains other matters in the beginning, and he writes the words, "when you receive this writing of mine, then you are divorced," after the other matters, and he were subsequently to strike out the other contents, written in the beginning, leaving only the above mentioned sentence and the wife receives the paper, there would be no divorce. The explanation given is that the writing received by her merely contains a divorce clause and that there should have been some additional writing to fulfil the condition. As she has not received any writing apart from the divorce clause itself, the condition precedent is not fulfilled. Therefore no divorce takes effect. If he were to strike out the words "when you receive this writing of mine" and leaves the other contents written in the beginning of the letter, and she receives the letter, divorce will be effected.[26] If he tears a small portion of the letter containing other matters and leaves the clause containing divorce, and the letter is received by his wife, a divorce shall be effected, because a portion of the writing still remains. But if the portion containing the sentence of divorce is torn out, and the remaining portion is received by her, no divorce will take effect.[27]

Receipt of writing by Agent: According to the jurists, the receipt of letter by the father acting as an agent of the

25. Qāḍī Khān al-Awzjandī, *op. cit.*, Vol. II, p. 219.
26. *Ibid.*
27. Ibn Qudāmah, *op. cit.*, Vol. VII, p. 241.

wife is tantamount to a receipt by her if he has authority of the disposal of her affairs generally, and receives the letter in the town where she is living. Hence, a divorce would be effected if the agent receives the letter addressed to the wife in which the husband has conditionally divorced her.[28]

The principle of agency has been introduced in the matter of divorce in writing to this extent by the jurists that if the writing should go to her father or agent, who takes it and tears it without delivering it to her then in such case if the father or the agent has the disposal of her affairs generally, and the letter reaches him in the town where she is living, repudiation does take effect, but not otherwise unless it reaches the wife herself. Hence it shall not be effected if the father is not her agent for all purposes.[29] It is explained that in such a case the receipt of the letter by her agent whilst he is transacting all her affairs is tantamount to its receipt by herself and knowledge of the contents of the letter would be imputed to her as when she receives the letter but does not care to read it and tears without reading it.[30] But it is necessary in such a case that she must be in a position to read it. If her father does not fulfil the above conditions and so cannot be considered to be her agent or he tears the letter and then informs her of the receipt of the letter, and delivers it to her torn as it is, then if it can be read and understood, only then would the repudiation be effective, but not otherwise.[31]

The above rules, however, pertain to the Muslim law of Evidence which has been superseded and shall not be followed now in India or Pakistan. A case shall now be decided according to the present law. The receipt of such conditional writing by an agent shall not effect a divorce merely because the agent holds a general power-of-attorney unless he has been specifically empowered to receive such a letter on

28. Ibn Qudāmah, *op. cit.*, Vol. VII, p. 220.
29. *Ibid.*
30. *Ibid.*
31. *Ibid.*

behalf of the wife.

(*viii*) *Presence of witnesses*: According to Aḥmad ibn Ḥanbal the presence of two witnesses to the writing is an essential condition for the validity of the divorce.[32] But the other Sunnī Imāms do not agree with this view. According to them, it is not necessary that any witnesses should be present at the time when the divorce is being written.

Shī'ī Law: Under Shī'ī law, it is an essential condition of divorce that two trustworthy witnesses should be present at the time when divorce is being written.[33] They must be males and should understand that a divorce is being given.[34] The Supreme Court of Pakistan has followed this rule of Shī'ī law.[35]

(*ix*) *Acknowledgment of Divorce*: An acknowledgment in writing by a husband that he has divorced his wife shall effect a divorce. Thus where a husband in a suit for maintenance by the wife took in his written statement the plea that he had divorced his wife long ago and followed it by a statement on oath to this effect then a divorce was held to have become operative, even when the husband's statement was not believed in.[36] It was explained in another case that an acknowledgment will operate as a divorce since it is an expression of his intention to divorce his wife.[37] Similarly, where a husband made such an endorsement on a notice issued by a Court in proceedings for maintenance, it was held that the endorsement operates as a divorce.[38]

(*x*) *Divorce by Dumb Person*: If a person is unable to pronounce a divorce as when he is dumb then he can lawfully effect a divorce by writing the same. But there are two

32. Ibn Qudāmah, *op. cit.*, Vol. VII, p. 241.
33. Muḥammad b. al-Ḥasan, *al-Istibṣār*, Najaf. 1956 A.D., Vol. III, p. 301.
34. Ja'far b. al-Ḥasan *op. cit.*, p. 209.
35. Syed Ali Nawaz Gardezi Vs. Lt.-Col. Muhammad Yusuf, 1963 P.L.D. S.C. 51.
36. Khatija Bi Vs. Wilayat Ali, 1943 A.L.W. 276.
37. Muhammad Hussain Vs. Rasul Bi, 14 Deccan L.R. 37; Wahab Ali Vs. Qamra Bibi, A.I.R. 1951, Hyd. 117.
38. Abdul Aziz Vs. Kabira Bi, 32 Deccan L.R. 192.

reports regarding this matter. According to one, he can give a divorce by writing only if he knows writing and not by signs. But according to the other report he can give a divorce either in writing or by signs if the signs are well understood.[39] The former view is generally accepted as correct.

Māliki Law: Mālik holds that divorce by a dumb person can be effected by writing as well as by signs.[40]

Shāfi'ī Law: According to the usually accepted view Shāfi'ī held that a dumb person can give a divorce by writing as well as by signs.[41] Some of the Shāfi'ī jurists hold that if a dumb person is literate, he can give divorce only in writing.[42]

Ḥanbalī Law: According to Aḥmad ibn Ḥanbal divorce by a literate dumb person can be effected by writing as well as by signs.[43]

Shī'ī Law: According to Shī'ī law, repudiation cannot be effected by writing by a husband who is present and is able to pronounce the proper words. If a husband is unable to speak and writes a divorce, fully intending repudiation, it takes effect and is quite valid.[44] Thus where he is dumb, he may give the repudiation in writing.

(*xi*) *Effect of*: When a husband writes a divorce which can be read and comprehended but which is not addressed to the wife or to any one else as when he writes "my wife is divorced" without addressing the writing to any one, then divorce would be effected only if it is proved that the intention of the husband was to divorce his wife but not otherwise.

A divorce would not be effected in any way by a writing which cannot be read and comprehended, that is, when it is *ghayr-marsūm ghayr mustabīn*, that is, "not customary" and

39. Qāḍī Khān, *op. cit.*, Vol. II, p. 220; Ibn Ābidīn, *op. cit.*, Vol. II, p. 436.
40. Saḥnūn b. Sa'īd, *al-Müdawwanat al-Kubrā*, Cairo, 1323 A.H., Vol. VI, p. 24.
41. Abū Bakr al-Bakrī, *I'ānat al-Ṭālibīn*, Cairo, 1938 A.D., p. 16.
42. Ibn al-*Humām Fatḥ al-Qadīr*, Cairo, n.d., Vol. III, p. 42.
43. Ibn Qudāmah, *op. cit.*, Vol. VII, p. 239.
44. Ja'far b. al-Ḥasan, *op. cit.*, p. 207.

"not manifest" even though there be an intention to divorce.[45]

(*xii*) *When to take effect*: Divorce by writing may be so expressed as to take effect immediately or at a future time. In the absence of a different condition, a divorce in writing shall be effected immediately when written and not with effect from the time when information regarding it is received by the wife. Thus when a person, having prefaced his letter with the usual compliments, says, "But after these, you are repudiated", repudiation would take effect immediately when the sentence is written.[46]

(*xiii*) *Nature of divorce*: A divorce in writing effects a revocable or irrevocable divorce as be the intention of the husband.

45. Qāḍī Khān, *op. cit.*, Vol. II, p. 219.
46. *Ibid.*

Chapter 6

ĪLĀ'

(*i*) *Preliminary* : *Īlā'* is not exactly a divorce, but has been treated as a form of the same by the Muslim jurists. It was a common practice in pre-Islamic days and is one of the expressions for divorce used by the uncivilised Arabs of that period to harass their wives. By *Īlā'* the marriage was not completely dissolved ; it meant only a cessation of sexual relations between the husband and the wife. The wife was thus deprived of the sexual intimacy but she remained tied down to her husband and could not contract another marriage.[1] Islam has put a check to the evil effects of this practice. It has discouraged the use of such expressions by imposing a penalty on a husband who wants to retain his wife after the use of the expression while if he does not repent and cancel his declaration within the prescribed period, he stands to lose his wife.

It has also restricted the maximum period for the cancellation of *Īlā'* to four months.

(*ii*) *Definition* : The word in its literal sense means a vow and the maker of the vow is called a *mūlī*, who is defined as a person who cannot approach his wife for a period of four months without incurring some penalty or some very troublesome, serious or difficult liability. In Muslim law it implies a husband's swearing by God or making a declaration to abstain from sexual intercourse with his wife for a period of four months or a longer period or that he shall undergo some specified hardship by way of penalty if he is intimate with the wife within the specified period of time or make some specified expiation that shall involve some hardship to him.[2]

1. Al-Marghīnānī 'Alī b. Abī Bakr, *al-Hidāyah*, Delhi, n.d., Vol. II, p. 381.
2. Ibn Ābidīn, *Radd al-Muḥtār 'ala'l-Durr al-Mukhtār*, Cairo, 1318 A.H., Vol. II, p. 560.

But according to Mālik and Aḥmad b. Ḥanbal, it is necessary to invoke the name of God but not necessary according to Abu Ḥanīfah and Shāfi'ī for the validity of *Īlā'*. It is stated in *al-Mughnī* that all the Sunnī Jurists hold that a vow in the name of Allah or one of His attributes whereby the husband makes it unlawful for himself to be intimate with his wife constitutes an *Īlā'*.[3] But there is a difference of opinion whether a vow of other classes to abstain from intimacy will constitute an *Īlā'*. The correct view is that what-so-ever be the vow by which intimacy is made unlawful, an *Īlā'* shall be effected provided the vow incurs some hardship. The above opinion has been expressed by Abū Ḥanīfah, Mālik, Shāfi'ī and all Imāms of Ḥijāz and 'Irāq.[4]

(*iii*) *Religious Sanction :* The Muslim law of *Īlā'* is founded on the following verses of the Qur'ān :

"Those who swear that they will not go in to their wives should wait four months ; then if they go back, Allah is surely Forgiving, Merciful."

And if they resolve on a divorce, Allah is surely Hearing, Knowing."[5]

(*iv*) *Applicability*: *Īlā'* is very uncommon, but is still extant and enforceable in Pakistan and India. It was clearly mentioned in section 2 of the Muslim Personal Law (*Sharī'ah*) Application Act, 1937, as applicable to Muslims. Clause ix of section 2 of the Dissolution of Muslim Marriages Act, 1939, lays down that a wife can seek the dissolution of her marriage on any ground which is recognised as valid for the dissolution of a marriage under Muslim law. A remark in Sayeeda Khanum Vs. Mohammad Sami also supports this view.[6]

3. Muḥammad b. 'Abd al-Raḥmān, *Raḥmat al-Ummah fī Ikhtilāf al-A'immah*, Cairo, 1300 A.H., p. 115.
4. Ibn Qudāmah, al-Mughnī, Cairo, 1367 A.H., Vol. VII. p. 298 f.
5. Qur'ān II : 226, 227, Surah Al-Baqarah.
6. Sayeeda Khanum Vs. Muhammad Sami, P.L.D. 1952, Lah. p. 113, at p. 138.

(*v*) *Essentials* : The essentials of *Īlā'* relate to the following subjects :

(*a*) Husband,
(*b*) Wife,
(*c*) Vow,
(*d*) Cancellation, and
(*e*) Effect.

(*a*) *Husband* : The person competent to pronounce an *Īlā'* is one who is competent to repudiate the marriage, that is, he should be adult and sane.[7]

(*b*) *Wife* : The woman in respect of whom an *Īlā'* vow can be made should be the wife of the person making the vow at the time when *Īlā'* is to take effect.[8] But an *Īlā'* can be made in respect of a woman not yet the wife of the speaker provided it is to take effect in future at a time when the marriage has actually taken place and she becomes his wife.[9] Thus a man may say to a woman, "By God, I shall have no sexual intercourse with you when I marry you", then *Īlā'* shall be effected if he marries her because his vow makes *Īlā'* applicable when the woman acquires the status of being his wife.[10] But if *Īlā'* is made in respect of a woman other than the wife without reference to her status at the time when *Īlā'* is to take effect then the *Īlā'* shall be ineffective.[11] Thus if a person says to a woman who is not his wife, "By God I will never have sexual intercourse with you," and he afterwards marries her then *Īlā'* shall not be established.[12] Here there is no reference to her status at the time when *Īlā'* is to take effect. There is a Tradition to the effect that the Prophet (peace be on him) has stated that there is no vow for the son of Ādam in what he does not own, and no divorce in what he

7. *Al-Fatāwā al-Hindiyah* (*'Ālamgīrī*), Kānpur, 1349 A.H., Vol. II, p. 113 ; Ibn 'Ābidīn, *op. cit.*, Vol. II, p. 560.
8. Ibn 'Ābidīn, *op. cit.*, Vol. II, p. 560.
9. *Ibid.*
10. *Ibid.*
11. *Ibid.*, pp. 559, 560, 566 ; al-Marghīnānī, *op. cit.*, Vol. II, p. 383.
12. *Ibid.*

does not own.[13]

(c) *Vow*: The vow must be for four months or for a longer period or for an indefinite time.[14] But if it relates to a period less than four months then the vow does not constitute *Īlā'*.[15] This is so even though the accumulated period of two or more consecutive *Īlā'* vows may amount to four months or a longer period of time.[16] Thus if a man makes a vow, saying to his wife, 'By God, I will not have sexual connection with you for two months, nor for two months after that, *Īlā'* is established. But if a man swears that he will not have sexual connection with his wife for two months", and then remains silent for a day, and the next day again swears that he will not have carnal connection with her for two months after the other two month, *Īlā'* is not established because the second vow is distinct and separate from the former.[17]

A husband shall not be held to have pronounced *Īlā'* except when he takes an oath against having sexual intercourse with his wife. If the husband's oath refers to something else than sexual intercourse then he shall not be held to have made *Īlā'*. Thus if a man says to his wife. "By God, my skin shall not touch thy skin", he shall not be deemed to have made an *Īlā'* because the vow refers to a breach of something other than sexual intercourse and touching of their skins is possible without there being intimacy between them.[18] It is also a necessary condition of *Īlā'* that it should not be possible for the husband to violate the vow, that is, to have sexual intercourse with his wife, without being guilty of the breach of his vow. Thus if a husband being in Karachi and his wife being in Delhi swears that he will not go to Delhi then *Īla'* is not established because there is no reference to intimacy while he can still be intimate with his wife without incurring any

13. Walī al-Dīn *al-Khāṭib, Mishkāt al-Maṣābīh*, Delhi, 1932 A.D., p. 284.
14. Ibn 'Ābidīn. *op. cit.*, Vol. II, p. 561.
15. *Ibid.*
16. *Ibid.*, Vol. II, p. 564 ; *al-Fatāwā al-Hindīyah, op. cit.*, Vol. II, p. 115.
17. *Al-Fatāwā al-Hindīyah, op. cit.*, Vol. II, p. 115.
18. *Ibid.*, p. 113.

penalty as by sending for her at Karachi and being intimate with her there[19].

(*vi*) *Expression*: The words by which *Īlā'* is effected may be either *Ṣarīḥ* (express) or *Kināyah* (ambiguous).[20] In the former case an *Īlā'* shall be established without proof of intention, but in the latter case an *Īlā'* shall be constituted only when such is the intention of the speaker.[21] Thus the expression. "By God I shall not sleep with you" is not clear. It can mean a vow of *Īlā'* as well as a mere statement and so no *Īlā'* shall be effected unless such be the intention of the speaker.[22] Similarly, the expression, "I shall not touch you", "I will not approach you", "I will not sleep near you" are examples of *Kināyah* expressions of *Īlā'*.[23] It is also a necessary condition of *Ilā'* that there should be no uncertainty or vagueness in the expression used. The expression may be conditional or unconditional. But a vow depending on a condition which is uncertain or which may or may not happen within four months does not constitute an *Īlā'*.[24] Thus the expression, "By God I will have no sexual intercourse with you until such a person arrives or such a thing happens when it is possible for the person to come within four months or for the thing to happen within that period of time, does not amount to an *Īlā'*.[25]

(*vii*) *Particular Penalty*: A husband can take a vow that he will not be intimate with his wife and that on breach of the vow he shall be liable to a particular penalty involving some great hardship and in such a case, that is, if he commits

19. Al-Marghīnānī, *op cit.*, Vol. II, p. 382; Ibn 'Ābidīn, *op. cit.*, Vol. II, p. 565.
20. *Al-Fatāwā al-Hindīyah*, *op cit*, Vol. II, p. 112; Ibn 'Ābidīn, *op. cit.*, Vol. II, pp. 561-62.
21. Ibn 'Ābidīn, *op. cit.*, Vol. II, pp. 561-62.
22. *Al-Fatāwā al-Hindīyah*, *op. cit.*, Vol. II, p. 113; Ibn 'Ābidīn, *op. cit.*, Vol. II, p. 563.
23. *Ibid.*
24. *Al-Fatāwā al-Hindīyah*, *op. cit.*, Vol. II, p. 116.
25. *Ibid.*

a breach of his vow he shall incur only the particular penalty specified by him; if the penalty involved is light and something of everyday practice then there shall be no *Īlā'*. Thus if he says, "By God, I shall not be intimate with you for four months, if I commit a breach of my vow then it shall be incumbent on me to read the Qur'ān, or to offer prayers", etc., then no *Īlā'* shall be constituted.[26] But if he says that he will recite the Qur'ān one hundred times or offer prayers hundred times then *Īlā'* shall be constituted because these acts do involve hardship.[27] Similarly, if he swears by God that he will have no sexual connection with his wife for a period of four months and that if he should commit a breach of the vow within that time then he shall perform a *Ḥajj* or fast for a specified time, etc., then on a breach of the vow he shall have to perform the particular penalty specified by him, as for example, the performance of the *Ḥajj* or fasting for the specified number of days or whatever other penalty he had declared in his vow.[28]

A declaration by the husband that his wife would be a wife in name only was not held to amount to an *Īlā'* vow.[29] This can be based on the fact that here the husband had merely made a statement and had not taken a vow and does not undertake any penalty on being guilty of its breach.

(*viii*) *Cancellation of*: The only way to render the vow ineffective is by having sexual intercourse with the wife within the period of four months from the time of taking the vow.[30] If the husband should be intimate with his wife during the prescribed period of four months then he shall be forsworn in his vow and the *Īlā'* would cease after cohabita-

26. Ibn 'Ābidīn, *op. cit.*, Vol. II, pp. 562-63.
27. *Ibid.*
28. *Al-Fatāwā al-Hindīyah, op. cit.*, Vol. II, p. 113; Ibn 'Ābidīn, *op. cit.*, Vol. II, pp. 562-63.
29. Bibi Rehana Khatoon Vs. Iqtịdar-ud-Din Hussain, A.I.R. 1943, All, 84.
30. *Al-Fatāwā al-Hindīyah, op. cit.*, Vol. II. p. 112; Ibn 'Ābidīn, *op. cit.*, Vol. II, p. 563.

tion.[31] An expiation shall, however, be incumbent upon the husband as a penalty for the breach of his vow.[32] The vow cannot be cancelled by speech but only by conduct, that is, by having sexual intercourse with the wife except under certain special circumstances.[33] Thus, if during the time in which an *Īlā'* can be revoked there should be any natural or accidental impediment to sexual intercourse on the part of either the man or the woman, such as serious illness or wife's tender age, or being at such a distance from one another as does not admit of their meeting during the term of the *Īlā'* then in such a case it shall be lawful for the man to rescind his *Īlā'* by speech, as, for example, by saying "I have returned to my wife", upon which the *Ilā'* drops.[34] But this holds good only so long as the impediment lasts. If it should become possible to have sexual intercourse before the expiration of four months then this right of return by speech would be cancelled and another cancellation must be made by intercourse.[35] If *Īlā'* has been constituted by a vow in the name of Allāh then expiation shall be incumbent for the breach of the vow. But it shall not be incumbent in other cases.[36]

(ix) Expiation: If the husband has intercourse during the period of *Īlā'* he will violate his vow. He should, therefore, make the expiation for the infringement of his vow.[37] It consists of manumission of a slave, or clothing or feeding ten poor persons. If he has not the ability to do either of them, he

31. *Al-Fatāwā al-Hindīyah, op. cit.*, Vol. II. p. 112, Ibn 'Ābidīn, *op. cit.*, Vol. II, p. 563.
32. *Ibid.*
33. *Al-Fatāwā al-Hindīyah, op. cit.*, Vol. II, p. 117 ; Ibn 'Ābidīn, Vol. II, pp. 566-67.
34. *Ibid.*
35. Al-Marghīnānī, *op. cit.*, Vol. II, p. 383 ; Ibn 'Ābidīn *op. cit.*, Vol. II, p. 567.
36. Al-Marghīnānī, *op. cit.*, Vol. II, pp. 381-82; Ibn 'Ābidīn, *op. cit.* Vol. II, p. 563.
37. Al-Marghīnānī, *op. cit.*, Vol. II, pp. 381-82.

should keep fast for three days consecutively. This expiation is based on the Qur'ānic verse V : 89.[38] If he has mentioned any particular penalty in his vow, then the expiation is the performance of the same. Thus, for instance, if he had stated that on breach of his vow, that is, on cohabitation, he shall perform *Ḥajj*, or shall fast or will give something in charity, then he shall have to discharge the *Īlā'* by performing the specified expiation.[39] The husband's declaration that he has made the expiation shall be considered sufficient without any proof of the same.

(*x*) *Effect* : If the vow is kept, that is, if the husband abstains from sexual intimacy with his wife or does not cancel the *Īlā'* within four months then under the Ḥanafī law there shall be effected an automatic divorce on the expiry of that period.[40] If he is intimate with his wife during the period of four months then he *is forsworn* in his vow.[41]

According to Mālik, Shāfi'ī and Aḥmad, b. Hanbal there can be no automatic divorce, but the matter shall remain suspended till the husband either revokes his *Īlā'* or divorces his wife. If he does neither then the wife can have recourse to the *Qāḍī*.[42]

(*xi*) *Qāḍī's Decree* : Under the Ḥanafī law no decree of separation by the *Qāḍī* is necessary but the wife is divorced automatically on the expiry of four months.[43]

Māliki Law : Under the Māliki law, the *Qāḍī* shall ask the husband to resume his sexual connection with his wife or to divorce her. If the husband refuses or fails to comply with the *Qāḍī's* order, the *Qāḍī* shall himself dissolve the marriage.[44]

38. Surah Al-Māidah Al-Marghinānī, *op. cit.*, Vol. II, p. 461.
39. *Ibid.*, Vol. II, p. 383 Ibn 'Ābidīn, *op. cit.*. Vol. II, pp. 562-63.
40. Ibn Rushd, *Bidāyat al-Mujtahid wa Nihāyat al-Muqtaṣid*, Cairo, 1329 A.H., Vol. II, p. 83 ; Ibn 'Ābidīn, *op. cit.*, Vol. II, p. 563.
41. *Al-Fatāwā al-Hindīyah*, *op. cit.*, Vol. II, p. 112.
42. Ibn Rushd, *op. cit.*, Vol. II, p. 83.
43. Ibn 'Ābidīn, *op. cit.*, Vol. II, p. 563.
44. Ibn Qudāmah, *op. cit.*, Vol. VII. pp. 318-19.

Shāfi'ī and Ḥanbalī Laws: Shāfi'ī and Aḥmad ibn Ḥanbal have expressed the same view as is given by Mālik.[45]

The difference between the Ḥanafi and the other Sunnī schools arises due to different interpretations of the Qurānic verse II : 227 surah al Baqarah about *Īlā'*, given before.

The Ḥanafi school argues that the husband's not breaking the vow for four months is proof of his intention to divorce the wife. They also assert that *Īlā'* was a form of divorce in pre-Islamic days and Sharī'ah has only placed conditions and limitations on it without changing its nature.

The opposite view, on the other hand, is justified on the plain reading of the verse, referred to above, which speaks of formation of intention of divorce after the expiry of the period of the vow and not divorce itself. The other reason in support of this view is, that *Īlā'* is a wrong caused to the wife by the husband, who denies her the right of marital life and as such he is punished by the dissolution of the marriage at her instance.[46]

(*xii*) *Nature of Divorce*: Under the Ḥanafī law, the divorce that is effected by *Īlā'* amounts to an irrevocable divorce.[47] But according to Mālik and Shāfi'ī and Aḥmad ibn Ḥanbal it would amount only to a *Raj'ī* or revocable divorce.[48] A divorce by the *Qāḍī* shall also amount to one revocable divorce. According to Aḥmad b. Ḥanbal, as certain reports say, it would amount to an irrevocable divorce.[49]

(*xiii*) *Shī'ī Law*: The Shī'ī law can be discussed under three main heads, namely,

(*a*) The husband pronouncing *Īlā'* called ***mūlī***,

(*b*) The wife, and

(*c*) The vow.

(*a*) *Husband*: The husband who takes an *Īlā'* vow should

45. Ibn Qudāmah, *op. cit.*, Vol. VII, pp. 318-19.
46. Ibn al-'Arabī, *Aḥkām al-Qur'ān*, Cairo, 1957 A.D., Vol. I, pp. 180-81.
47. Al-Marghīnānī, *op. cit.*, Vol. II, p. 381 ; *al-Fatāwā al-Hindīyah*, *op. cit.*, Vol. II, p. 112.
48. Ibn Rushd, *op. cit.*, Vol. II, p. 84 ; Ibn Qudāmah, *op. cit.*, Vol. II, p. 331.
49. *Ibid.*

be major, sane and should possess understanding. He should be acting under his free will and should pronounce the vow with an intention to exercise *Īlā'*.[50]

(*b*) *The wife*: The woman must be the lawfully married wife of the person taking the vow at the time of the *Īlā'*. There can be no *Īlā'* in respect of a woman married in *mut'ah* form, that is, by a temporary marriage. Further, the marriage must have been consummated.[51]

(*c*) *The vow*: The vow of *Īlā'* must be in the name of God and cannot be made merely by a declaration. It cannot be made for four months but the period should exceed it.[52] It must be absolute and either for an indefinite period or for a period exceeding four months.[53] The vow cannot be made to depend on a condition or to take effect at a future time. If a person who is ill takes an *Īlā'* vow with the intention to avoid cohabitation with his wife during the period of his or her illness then it shall not amount to *Īlā'*. It is not necessary that the vow should be taken in Arabic.[54]

(*xiv*) *Cancellation*: Under Shī'ī law if the vow relates to a definite period then it abates on the expiry of the specified period when the husband can approach his wife without incurring any penalty. The vow cannot be cancelled by speech but can be cancelled only by cohabitation.[55] If a person is temporarily unfit for cohabitation then he can cancel *Īlā'* by speech, but he should declare that he will cancel the *Īlā'* by cohabitation when he is able to do so.[56]

(*xv*) *Effect*: A divorce is not effected by the mere expiry of the time of four months, but the wife shall have to seek

50. Ja'far b al-Ḥasan, *Kitāb Sharā'i' al-Islām*, Tehran, 1377 A,H., p. 228.
51. *Ibid.*
52. *Ibid.*, pp. 227-28 Abu'l-Ḥasan al-Mūsawī, *Wasīlat al-Najāt*, Najaf, 1364 A.H., p. 390.
53. *Ibid.*
54. *Ibid.*
55. Ja'far b. al-Ḥasan, *op. cit.*, p. 229; Abū Ja'far Muḥammad b. al-Ḥasan, *Man la Yaḥḍuruh al-Faqih*, Tehran, n.d., p. 449.
56. Ja'far b, al-Ḥasan, *op. cit.*, p. 229.

the aid of the Judge.[57]

(*xvi*) *Judge's Order* : The Judge cannot dissolve the marriage but shall order the husband either to take back his wife or to divorce her. On the husband's failure or refusal to do so, the Judge can imprison and punish him to force him to choose one of the above two alternatives.[58]

(*xvii*) *Nature of Separation*: The separation effected by a divorce given on an *Īlā'* shall amount to a *Raj'ī* (revocable) divorce unless the husband gives a *Bā'in* (irrevocable) divorce.[59]

The S̲h̲ī'i law wants the continuation of marriage and to discourage its termination as far as possible. Hence, if the husband alleges that he has cancelled the *Īlā'* by being intimate with the wife during the period of four months or says that the period of four months has not expired but the wife denies such an allegation then the husband's version would be accepted in preference to her denial so that the marriage may not be dissolved.[60]

57. Ja'far b. al-Ḥasan, *op. cit.*, p. 228.
58. *Ibid.*. p. 228; Abū Ja'far b. al-Ḥasan, *op. cit.*, p. 449.
59. *Ibid.*, p. 228.
60. *Ibid.*, pp. 228-29.

Chapter 7

ẒIHĀR

I. *Preliminary*

In pre-Islamic times the half civilised Arabs used to deprive their wives of sexual enjoyment and to tie them down to a miserable life in a number of ways. *Ẓihār* is one of them. It is an unusual form of temporary prohibition in which the husband compares his wife to his mother. In *Ẓihār* the marriage is not dissolved and the woman still remains the wife of the person, but the husband cannot be intimate with her and she is deprived of all sexual intimacy. Islam has freed the wife from this hard lot and has also discouraged the use of such expressions. It has made it clear that a wife does not become the mother or other relation by the idle and foolish talk of a person while a penalty has been imposed on the husband who has expressed *Ẓihār* but wants to retain his wife. The wife has been empowered to force the husband either to divorce her or re-establish the matrimonial connection on paying the prescribed penalty.

In pre-Islamic times *Ẓihār* was considered to be a sort of divorce. Muslim law, while preserving its nature which is prohibition from intimacy with the wife, has altered its effect to a temporary prohibition only which does not dissolve the marriage, and so *Ẓihār* does not exactly amount to a divorce and is distinct from it.

II. *Religious Sanction*

The law about *Ẓihār* is based on the injunctions in the Qur'ān given below :—

> "Allah has not made for any man two hearts within him; nor has He made your wives whom you desert by *Ẓihār*, your mothers, nor has He made those whom you assert (to be your sons) your sons. These are the words

of your mouths. And Allah speaks the truth and He shows the way".[1]

"Those of you who put away their wives by calling them their mothers—they are not their mothers : None are their mothers save those who gave them birth, and they utter indeed a hateful word and a lie. And surely Allah is Pardoning, Forgiving and those who put away their wives by calling them their mothers, then go back on that which they said, must free a captive before they touch one another. To this you are exhorted ; and Allah is Aware of what you do."

"But he who has not the means, should fast for two months successively before they touch one another, and he who is unable to do so should feed sixty needy ones. That is in order that you may have faith in Allah and His Messenger. And these are Allah's limits. And for the disbelievers is a painful chastisement."[2]

III. Description

The word *Ẓihār* is derived from "*Ẓahr*" (back), *Ẓihār* means "To oppose back to back". It is explained that when there is discord between the husband and the wife, they instead of remaining face to face towards each other turn their backs against each other. In the language of law it signifies a man comparing his wife to any of his female relations within such prohibited degrees of relationship, whether by blood, fosterage or by marriage, as renders marriage with her invariably unlawful.[3]

IV Applicability

Ẓihār is very rarely used in India and Pakistan as is clear from the fact that there is practically no case-law on the subject. But the doctrine of *Ẓihār* is still applicable to Muslims in India and Pakistan. Section 2 of the Muslim Personal Law (*Sharī'at*) Application Act, 1937, and sub-

1. Qur'ān, XXXIII: 4, Surah Al-Aḥzab.
2. Qur'ān, LVIII: 2-4, Surah Al-Mujādilah.
3. *Al-Fatāwā al-Hindīyah*, Kanpur, 1349 A.H., Vol, II, p. 126.

section IX of Section 2 of the Dissolution of Muslim Marriages Act, 1939, make this clear. A remark in Saeeda Khanam Vs. Muhammad Salim also supports this view.[4]

V. Essentials

Certain conditions have to be satisfied for the validity of *Zihār*. They relate to the following aspects :

(*a*) Expression.
(*b*) Comparison.
(*c*) Husband.
(*d*) Wife, and
(*e*) Expiation.

(*a*) *Expression or Language*: There is no fixed formula for *Ẓihār* and any expression can be used for the purpose. But the language should be clear, unambiguous and certain. There should be no uncertainty attached to *Ẓihār* and an uncertain expression of *Ẓihār* is invalid. Thus if a husband says to his wife, "God willing you are to me . , . " then no *Ẓihār* will be established.[5] *Ẓihār* can be given orally or in writing and even by signs by a dumb person if they are well-understood and denote his intention in this respect.[6]

In many cases an expression can amount to a divorce by implication as well as to *Zihār*. It becomes necessary in such a case to find the effect of the expression. According to Muslim jurists, such an expression takes effect according to the husband's intention as explained by him. Thus, if he were to say, "you are to me like my mother", it is necessary to ascertain his intention. The expression may be used merely to show respect or appreciation or to denote a divorce or a *Ẓihār* or without any definite intention at all. In the first and the last cases the expression would neither establish a

4. Saeeda Khanum Vs. Mohd Sami, P.L.D., 1952, Lahore, 113, at p. 138.
5. *Al-Fatāwā al-Hindīyah, op. cit.*, Vol. II, p. 126, Ibn 'Ābidīn, *Radd al-Muḥtār 'al-Durr al-Mukhtār*, Cairo, 1318 A.H. Vol. II, p. 589.
6. *Al-Fatāwā al-Hindīyah, op. cit.*, Vol. II, p. 127; Ibn 'Ābidīn, *op. cit.*, Vol. II, p. 589.

Zihār nor a divorce.[7] But in the second and the third cases a divorce or a *Zihār* would be established according to the intention of the speaker.[8] Hence, if he declares that he had no particular intention, *Ẓihār* will not be established. But if he intended divorce, divorce will be established.[9]

When the expression used consists of a comparison of the wife to a part of the body of his mother or other prohibited women as when he says, "you are to me like the back of my mother", *Ẓihār* only will be established because the expression is used only for *Ẓihār* and cannot be used for divorce and so no divorce would be effected by such an expression even when such be the intention of the husband.[10]

Under the present law, however, the bare statement of the husband will not suffice and the Court will give its finding on the evidence produced before it and will be guided by the circumstances of a particular case.

(*b*) *Comparison.* Comparison is a necessary condition of *Ẓihār*, and so there will be no *Ẓihār* if there is no comparison as when a husband calls his wife as his daughter, mother etc.; without comparison the expression may amount to a divorce if he so intends but cannot amount to *Ẓihār*.[11] Further, the comparison should be to a woman permanently prohibited to him. If the wife be compared to a woman, only temporarily prohibited, there is no *Ẓihār*.[12] Thus, a comparison to one's sister-in-law will not amount to *Ẓihār* as marriage with her is possible on the dissolution of the present marriage by divorce or the wife's death.[13] When the comparison relates to a part of the body of a woman, the part must

7. *Al-Fatāwā al-Hindīyah, op. cit.*, Vol. II, p. 126; Ibn 'Ābidīn, *op. cit.*, Vol. II, p. 591-92.
8. *Ibid.*
9. *Ibid.*
10. *Ibid.*
11. *Ibid.*
12. Al-Marghīnānī, *al-Hidāyah*, Delhi, n.d., Vol. II, p. 390; *al-Fatāwā al-Hindīyah*, *op. cit.*, Vol. II, p. 126.
13. Ibn 'Ābidīn, *op. cit.*, Vol. II, p. 590.

be such as is not proper for him to see. Hence, when the comparison is to what can be seen in decency by him as the face, hands, hair, etc., there is no *Ẓihār*.[14]

(*c*) *Husband.* It is a condition of *Ẓihār* that the husband should be a person capable of making expiation, that is, he must be sane and adult.[15] Hence, the *Ẓihār* of a minor or an insane person is not valid. Further, the husband should not be in a faint or under the influence of sleep; *Ẓihār* by anyone in one of these conditions is not valid.[16] But it is not necessary under the Ḥanafī law that the husband should be in earnest so that *Ẓihār* by one in jest or in mistake is valid.[17] *Ẓihār* under compulsion is valid and effective according to the Ḥanafis.[18] But Shāfi'ī and Aḥmad ibn Ḥanbal do not agree with this view and according to them *Ẓihār* under compulsion is invalid.[19] *Ẓihār* by a dumb husband is valid when made in writing or by intelligible signs and with intention.[20] *Ẓihār* by a drunken man is valid according to the Ḥanafis.[21]

(*d*) *Wife.* *Ẓihār* can only be made in respect of the lawfully married wife of the speaker.[22] Hence, if a person says to a woman who is not his wife, "you are to me like the back of my mother" and afterwards marries her, *Ẓihār* shall not be established because the woman was not his wife when he used the expression of *Ẓihār*.[23] But if he says to a woman, "if I marry you then you are to me as the back of my mother" and afterwards marries her then *Ẓihār* shall be established and

14. Ibn 'Ābidīn, *op. cit.*, Vol. II, p. 591.
15. *Al-Fatāwā al-Hindīyah*, *op. cit.*, Vol. II, p. 126.
16. *Ibid.*, Ibn 'Ābidīn, *op. cit.*, Vol. II, p. 589.
17. *Al-Fatāwā al-Hindīyah*, *op. cit.*, Vol. II, p. 126.
18. *Ibid.*, Ibn 'Ābidīn, *op. cit.*, Vol. II, p. 589.
19. Ibn Qudāmah, *al-Mughnī*, Cairo, 1376 A.H., Vol. VII, p. 339.
20. *Al-Fatāwā al-Hindīyah*, *op. cit.*, Vol. II. p. 127; Ibn 'Ābidīn, *op. cit.*, Vol. II, p. 589.
21. Ibn 'Ābidīn, *op. cit.*, Vol. II, p. 589.
22. *Ibid.*, p. 589.
23. *Ibid.*

expiation shall become incumbent on him.[24] It is not necessary that the wife should be major, sane or Muslimah as *Ẓihār* like divorce, is valid even when the wife is a minor, lunatic or *kitābiyah*.[25]

Zihār by the wife. It is not open to the wife to use the expression of *Ẓihār* against her husband.[26]

Wife's right. A wife is entitled to call her *Muẓāhir* (i.e. one who has expressed a *Ẓihār*) husband to return to his matrimonial duties.[27] She can also prevent him from intimacy with her till he has made the necessary expiation.[28] If he does not make it, then according to the Muslim law the *Qāḍī*, on her complaint, is to imprison and punish him till he does so or repudiates her.[29] The *Qāḍī* can also order the beating of the husband in such a case.[30] Islam has thus forbidden a husband to keep a wife in suspense by giving up intimacy with her and at the same time not divorcing her. Thus, there is an injunction in the Qur'ān, namely,

> "But turn not away (from a woman) altogether so as to leave her (as it were) hanging (in the air).[31] (i.e. in suspense)."

If the husband declares that he has performed the expiation, his declaration is deemed sufficient and the *Qāḍī* is not required to inquire if the allegation is true or not and the husband's version will be accepted as correct until it is proved to be incorrect.[32]

Expiation. It is obligatory on a *Muẓāhir* (i.e. a husband who has declared *Ẓihār*) to make an expiation if he intends to have intercourse with his wife after the *Ẓihār*.[33] But if he

24. Ibn 'Ābidīn, *op. cit.*, Vol. II, p. 590.
25. *Ibid.*, p. 589.
26. *Ibid.*, p. 590.
27. *Ibid.*, p. 592.
28. *Ibid.*
29. *Ibid.*
30. *Ibid.*
31. Qur'ān, IV: 129, Surah Al-Nisā.
32. Ibn 'Ābidīn *op. cit.*, Vol. II, p. 592.
33. *Ibid.*, p. 591.

is determined that she should remain unlawful to him, and has no intention of returning to matrimonial intercourse with her, he is not liable to expiation.[34]

VI. Conditional

Under the Ḥanafi law *Ẓihār* can be made conditional. Thus a husband may say, "If thou entereth that house or speaketh to such a person, thou art to me like my mother."[35]

VII. Limited in Time

Ẓihār can be limited in point of time. Thus, where a husband says to his wife, "You are to me like my mother's back for one year", *Ẓihār* will be effective for the period of one year only and will become ineffective after that period, and he can renew his sexual relations with her on the expiry of the period without incurring expiation.[36] But according to Mālik, an expression of *Ẓihār* limited in time shall amount to an absolute *Ẓihār* and shall not become ineffective with the expiry of the specified time. Expiation would, however, be incumbent on him if he is intimate with the wife before the expiry of the period.[37] Shāfi'ī and Aḥmad ibn Ḥanbal agree with Abū Ḥanīfah.[38]

VIII. The Māliki, Shāfi'ī and Ḥanbalı Laws

The Māliki, Shāfi'ī and Ḥanbali laws are the same as the Ḥanafi law discussed above at various places.

IX. Breach of

If a man, having pronounced *Ẓihār* upon his wife, has matrimonial connection with her, he is not liable to any penalty other than the expiation for *Ẓihār*.[39]

34. Ibn 'Ābidīn, *op. cit.*, Vol. II, pp. 59, 92.
35. *Al-Fatāwā al-Hindiyah*, *op. cit.*, Vol. II, p. 127.
36. *Ibid.*, p. 126.
37. Ibn Qudāmah, *op. cit.*, Vol. VII, p. 349.
38. *Ibid.*
39. *Al-Fatāwā al-Hindiyah*, *op. cit.*, Vol. II, p. 126.

X. *Effect of*

The effect of *Ẓihār* is to prohibit the person who pronounces it, from sexual connection with his wife as well as from kissing, embracing or touching her and similar acts until he shall have made an expiation.[40] A marriage is not, however, dissolved by mere *Ẓihār*,

XI. Shī'i Law

(*a*) *Capacity.* Under the Shī'i law the husband must be adult, sane, and must have freedom of choice and intention.[41] Hence, the *Ẓihār* of a minor, an insane person, or one acting under compulsion or temporarily incapable of intention through stupor, drunkenness or paroxysm of passion is invalid.[42]

(*b*) *Wife.* With regard to the "*muẓaharah*" or the woman who is the subject of *Ẓihār* it is necessary that she should be the duly and permanently married wife of the *Muẓāhir*. She must be in purity, i.e., free from her monthly course, at the time when *Ẓihār* is pronounced unless the husband is away from his wife and no intercourse has taken place between them since the last menstruation.[43] But in order to minimise the risk involved in such a case the Shī'i jurists recommend that the husband should pronounce the *Ẓihār* twice at the interval of twelve days; she is bound to be free of menstrual courses at the time of one pronouncement.[44]

(*c*) *Witnesses. Ẓihār* must be pronounced in the presence of two just and reliable witnesses who must hear the words constituting the *Ẓihār*.[45]

(*d*) *Effect of Ẓihār.* The husband cannot be intimate

40. *Al-Fatāwā al-Hindīyah, op. cit.*, Vol. II, p. 126, *Ibid.*, Ibn 'Ābidīn. *op. cit.*, Vol. II, p. 591.
41. Ja'far b. al-Ḥasan, *Kitab Sharā'i 'al-Islām*, Tehran, 1377, p. 222.
42. *Ibid.*
43. *Ibid.*
44. Abu' l-Ḥasan al-Mūsawī, *Wasīlat al-Najāt*, Najaf, 1364, p. 389.
45. Abū Ja'far Muhammad b. al-Ḥasan, *al-Istibṣār*, Najaf, 1956, Vol. III, p. 258.

with his wife till he makes the expiation.[46] But if he divorces her by a rajai' divorce, he can approach her within the period of her *'iddah* provided he makes an expiation when it shall amount to Raj'ah and expiation shall be incumbent on him.[47]

(*e*) *Wife's right*. The wife is entitled to call her *muẓāhir* husband to return to his matrimonial duties and on his failure to do so, she can approach the Judge. The Judge shall force the *Muẓāhir* (one who has pronounced a *Ẓihār*) husband either to perform the necessary expiation or on his failure to do so, to divorce his wife. He should give the husband three months' time either to make expiation and to return to his wife or to divorce her. If the husband fails to do either, the Judge can restrict his food and water, starve him and even beat him to compel him to do one of the two alternatives.[48] The Judge can also imprison the husband till he either makes the expiation or divorces his wife. But the Judge cannot himself pronounce a divorce on behalf of the husband.

In other respects the Shī'i law is the same as the Sunnī law discussed above.

46. Ja'far b. al-Ḥasan, *op. cit.*, p. 222.
47. *Ibid.*, p. 222.
48. *Ibid.*, p. 223; Abu' l-Ḥasan al-Mūsawī, *op. cit.*, p. 389.

Chapter 8

RAJ'AH OR REVOCATION OF DIVORCE

I. Preliminary

A husband who has repudiated his wife by a revocable divorce has the right to take her back without the necessity of remarrying her under certain conditions. This right can be exercised only during the period of *'iddah* because the marital relationship terminates on the expiry of the prescribed period of *'iddah*. It follows that such right cannot be exercised when *'iddah* is not prescribed. There can be no retraction in the case of an irrevocable divorce because the relationship of husband and wife is completely severed on the very pronouncement of it.

II. Definition

Raj'ah literally means "Restitution." In law it signifies a husband's returning to or receiving back his wife after divorce and restoring her to her former position, that is, her position as his wife before the divorce.[1]

It is defined as maintaining of a marriage in its former condition while the wife is still in her *'iddah*.[2]

III. Religious Sanction

It is laid down in the Qur'ān:

> "And when you divorce women and they reach their prescribed time, then retain them in kindness or set them free with kindness and retain them not for injury."[3]
>
> "And the divorced women should keep themselves in waiting for three courses. And their husbands have a better right to take them back in the meantime if they

1. *Al-Fatāwā al-Hindiyah*, Kanpur, 1349 A.H., Vol. II, p. 109.
2. *Ibid.*
3. Qur'ān, II : 231, Surah Al-Baqarah.

wish for reconciliation."[4]

IV. How Effected

Revocation can be effected (*a*) by speech or (*b*) by conduct.[5] All the Sunnī jurists hold that *raj'ah* may be effected by speech, but they differ about *raj'ah* by conduct.

(*a*) *Raj'ah by Speech.*—A husband can take back his wife, whom he has divorced by a revocable divorce, by expressing his desire in words. Thus, he may tell the wife that he is exercising his right of *raj'ah* and taking her back or that he is restoring her to her former position of being his wife or that he is cancelling his divorce and is keeping her as his wife. There is no fixed formula or expression prescribed for the purpose. All that is required is the clear expression of his intention to retain her as his wife and he can use for this purpose any words he likes.[6]

The revocation of the divorce or retention of the wife by speech is of two kinds, namely,

(*a*) *Sunnī* or regular, that is, expressed in the prescribed manner, and

(*b*) *Bidi'* or irregular, that is, against the prescribed manner.

Sunnī and Bidi' Forms.—The *Sunnī* form is when a man retains his wife by speech, calls two witnesses to attest to the fact and gives intimation to her about her retention. In the other, namely, the *Bidi'* form, the husband may retain her by speech without calling upon witnesses to attest to the fact or in the presence of witnesses but without giving any intimation to her.[7] The difference in the two forms is that whereas the observance of the three conditions is necessary in the first form, the observance of the first and one of the second or the third condition is considered sufficient in the *Bidi'* form. The

4. Qur'ān, II : 228, Surah Al-Baqarah.
5. *Al-Fatāwā al-Hindīyah, op. cit.*, Vol. II, p. 109.
6. Shaykhzādah 'Abd al-Raḥmān b. Muḥammad, *Majma' al-Unhur*, Constantinople, 1327 A.H., Vol. I, pp. 432-33.
7. *Al-Fatāwā al-Hindīyah, op. cit.*, Vol. II, p. 109.

latter form is irregular but valid.[8]

Classification of Expressions.—The expressions used for *Raj'ah* or retention by speech may be (1) *Ṣarīḥ* or express and (2) *Kināyāh*, that is, ambiguous or implied.[9]

(1) *Express.*—An expression is considered *ṣarīḥ* or express when the words denoting the retention or taking back of the wife are clear and direct.[10] Thus, the expressions, "I have retained you" or "I have restored you to the position of my wife" or "I have taken you back as my wife" are *ṣarīḥ* or direct and clear expressions.

(2) *Kināyah or Ambiguous.*—The *Kināyah* or ambiguous expressions are such as imply the sense that the husband wants to retain the wife but does not mention that fact clearly.[11] Thus, the following expression illustrates the ambiguous expression : "You are to me as you were before."[12]

It can be gathered from various books on *Fiqh* that according to Mālik and Shāfi'ī, *raj'ah* can be express (*ṣarīḥ*) or ambiguous (*kināyah*).[13] There are two versions attributed to Aḥmad bin Ḥanbal. According to one, *raj ah* should be expressed (*ṣarīḥ*), and according to the other it can also be ambiguous (*kināyah*).[14]

(*b*) *Raj'ah by Conduct.*—Raj'ah can also be effected by the conduct of the husband or the wife. Thus, if the husband cohabits with his wife after a revocable divorce during the period of *'iddah*, it is clear that he wants to maintain the relationship of husband and wife. The conduct must, however, consist of such acts as clearly establish the husband's intention to retain the woman as his wife, e.g., cohabitation, kissing with desire, etc.[15]

8. *Al-Fatāwā al-Hindīyah, op. cit.,* Vol. II, p. 109.
9. *Ibid.*
10. *Ibid.*, Shaykhzādah, *op. cit.*, p. 433.
11. *Al-Fatāwā al-Hindīyah, op. cit.*, Vol. II, p. 109.
12. Shaykhzādah, *op. cit.*, p. 433.
13. Shahab-ud-Dīn Aḥmad, *Tohfat al-Mohtaj*, Vol. VIII, pp. 47, 48, Cairo.
14. Ibn Qudāmah, *al-Mughnī* Cairo, 1367 A.H., Vol. VII, p. 284.
15. *Al-Fatāwā al-Hindīyah, op. cit.*, Vol. II, p. 109; Ibn 'Abidīn, *Radd al-Muḥtār*, Cairo, 1318 A.H., Vol. II, p. 544.

Mālik holds that *Raj'ah* can be effected by conduct as well as by speech but the husband must have an intention to take back his wife in the former case.[16]

Under Shāfi'ī law, revocation or *Raj'ah* can be effected only by express declaration and not by conduct.[17] This difference between the Ḥanafīs and the Shāfi'īs is due to the fact that the former regard a marriage to be subsisting till the third divorce is pronounced and the marital rights are merely suspended till then. The latter, however, hold that the marriage tie is dissolved by the first pronouncement and that *Raj'ah* is virtually a remarriage.[18]

There are two versions attributed to Shāfi'ī and Aḥmad b. Ḥanbal. According to one, they held that the presence of witnesses is essential for the validity of *Raj'ah*, while according to the other version, the presence of witnesses is approved of but is not essential.[19] What is considered more correct and followed by the followers of Shāfi'ī is the view that the presence of witnesses is approved of (*mustaḥabb*) and not essential.[20] Mālik holds the same view as held by Abū Ḥanīfah.[21] According to Aḥmad b. Ḥanbal, *Raj'ah* can be effected by speech as well as by conduct. The conduct can consist of cohabitation only in which case intention is not necessary.[22]

V. *Wife's Conduct*

Raj'ah may also be effected by the wife's conduct as by kissing with desire or touching with desire provided it is done to the husband's knowledge and without his prohibition or

16. Ibn Qudāmah, *op. cit.*, Vol. VII, p. 283.
17. *Ibid.*, p. 283.
18. Al-Marghīnānī, *al-Hidāyah*, Delhi, n.d., Vol. II, p. 375.
19. *Ibid.*, p. 375; Ibn Rushd, *Bidāyat al-Mujtahid*, Cairo, 1329 A.H., Vol. II, p. 70; Ibn Qudāmah, *op. cit.*, Vol. VII, pp. 282-83.
20. Muḥammad b. 'Abd al-Raḥmān, *Raḥmat al-Ummah fi Ikhtilāf al-A'immah*, Cairo, 1300 A.H., p. 114; Ibn al-Humām, *Fatḥ al-Qadīr* Cairo, n.d. Vol. III, p. 163.
21. *Ibid.*, Ibn Rushd, *op. cit.*, Vol. II. p. 70.
22. Ibn Qudāmah, *op. cit.*. Vol. VII, p. 283.

objection.[23] It is stated in *al-Durr al-Mukhtār* and *Fatāwā al-Hindīyah* that a *Raj'ah* can be effected or established by the wife's conduct without the husband's consent or even by force provided she does it with desire, that is, in sexual excitement and this fact is admitted by the husband.[24] But a *Raj'ah* by the wife shall be effected only by conduct and not by speech. Thus she cannot effect it by saying "I have returned to thee".[25]

Under the Ḥanāfī law, the following conditions are essential for the exercise of *Raj'ah* by the wife :

(*a*) The wife should have been divorced by a *Raj'ī* (revocable) divorce.

(*b*) The wife's period of *'iddah* should not have expired.

(*c*) The marriage should have been consummated.[26]

According to Mālik, the following conditions should be satisfied in order that *Raj'ah* can be effected by a wife :

(*a*) The wife should not have been divorced by an irrevocable divorce,

(*b*) The wife should be observing *'iddah* of a valid marriage,

(*c*) The marriage must have been consummated.[27]

According to Shafi'ī, the following conditions are necessary for *Raj'ah* by the wife :

(*a*) The marriage should he valid.

(*b*) The wife should be still lawful to the husband, that is, the marriage should be still subsisting. Thus, if the wife has apostatized then he cannot have recourse to *Raj'ah* as the marriage is dissolved immediately on her apostasy.[28]

23. Ibn 'Ābidīn, *op. cit.*, Vol. II, p. 544 ; Shaykhzādah, *op. cit.*, Vol. I. p. 433.
24. *Al-Fatāwā al-Hindīyah*, *op. cit.*, Vol. II, p. 109 ; Ibn 'Ābiddīn, *op. cit.*, Vol. II, p. 544.
25. *Ibid.*
26. Ibn Qudāmah, *op. cit.*, Vol. VII, p. 278.
27. *Ibid.*
28. *Ibid.*

According to Aḥmad b. Ḥanbal the same conditions are necessary for *Raj'ah* as have been laid down by Mālik.[29]

VI. Wife's Consent

According to the *Sunnī* jurists a husband's exercise of this right does not depend on the wife's consent so that he can take her back even when she does not desire or consent to it.[30] It is stated in *al-Hidāyah*[31] that this rule is based on the sacred text in the Qur'ān, 'Retain them in kindness'[32] in which there is no distinction between the wife's willingness or the absence of it. *Bidāyat al-Mujtahid*[33] has supported this view on the basis of another verse of the Qur'ān namely, "And their husbands have a better right to take them back".[34]

It is difficult to understand how a husband can be considered to be keeping his wife with humanity or in kindness when he keeps her against her wishes. On the contrary, the husband in such a case will be transgressing the injunction of the Qur'ān and will certainly not be keeping her with humanity.

There is yet another reason. If the divorce—through *Raj'i* form—is the result of a dispute then all the verses which cast a duty on the husband to keep his wife with kindness would seem to imply that in such cases she should at least have a right to get the disputes settled through arbitration or otherwise. If a wife who is afraid of likely oppression or neglect has a right to arbitration, it would appear still more necessary where a man almost wrecks her life by a unilateral act and then wants to take her back, against her wishes.

29. Ibn Qudāmah, *op. cit.*, Vol. VII, p. 278.
30. Ibn 'Ābidīn, *op. cit.*, Vol. II, p. 545; Ibn Qudāmah, *op. cit.*, Vol. VII, p. 282.
31. Al-Marghīnānī, *op. cit.*, Vol. II, p. 374.
32. Qur'ān, II : 220, Surah Al-Baqarah.
33. Ibn Rushd, *op. cit.*, Vol. II, p. 70.
34. Qur'ān, II : 228, Surah Al-Baqarah.

VII. Essentials

(*a*) *'Iddah-Raj'ah* presupposes that the wife is observing *'iddah.*[35] Right of *Raj'ah* can be exercised only during the subsistence of marriage and once the period of *'iddah* is over or is not required to be observed the marriage ceases to subsist. When the relationship of husband and wife comes to an end, there can be no question of taking her back. *Raj'ah* is exercisable when there is no *Ṭalāq-Bā'in* and only a *Ṭalāq-Raj'ī* has been pronounced. In the latter case the right of marriage subsists till such time as the woman completes the *'iddah.* The observance of *'iddah* is a necessary condition only in marriages which have been consummated. A divorce pronounced before actual consummation of marriage amounts to an irrevocable divorce. Hence, there can be no *Raj'ah* in such a case even after a valid retirement because the marriage is terminated on the very pronouncement of divorce unless the husband alleges consummation of the marriage.[36] Shāfi'ī does not accept valid retirement to amount to consummation of marriage in any way hence, according to him, there can be no *Raj'ah* after mere valid retirement.[37]

(*b*) *Unconditional.* To be valid, *Raj'ah* must be immediate and unconditional. Any *Raj'ah* expressed to take place in future or subject to a condition is not valid.[38]

(*c*) *Intention. Ḥanafi law.* According to the Ḥanafīs, intention is not a necessary condition of *Raj'ah* in case of cohabitation or by *ṣarīḥ* (express) expression. It shall be effected even when it is not the intention of the husband to take back his wife. Hence, it is valid when made under compulsion or in jest or even by mistake.[39]

But in *kināyah* (ambiguous) expression, intention to take back the wife is an essential condition.

35. *Al-Fatāwā al-Hindiyah, op. cit.,* Vol. II, p. 109.
36. Ibn Nujaym : *al-Bahar al-Ra'iq,* Vol. III, p. 54, Cairo, 1311 A.H.
37. Ibn Rushd, Vol. II, p. 22. Cairo.
38. *Al-Fatāwā al-Hindiyah, op. cit.,* Vol, II, p. 109.
39. *Ibid.*

Māliki law. Under the Māliki law, intention is an essential condition of *Raj'ah* when a *kinayah* or ambiguous expression is used, but intention is not necessary when the expression is *ṣarīḥ* or express.[40] Mālik holds that there will be *Raj'ah* by conduct only if the husband so intended, but there can be no *Raj'ah* without such intention.[41] Hence there can be no *Raj'ah* under compulsion.

Shāfi'ī law. Under the Shāfi'ī law *Raj'ah* can be effected only by speech and not otherwise.[42]

Ḥanbali law. According to Aḥmad b. Ḥanbal, *Raj'ah* can be effected by speech as well as by conduct. In case of conduct intention is not necessary.[43] Conditional *Raj'ah* is not valid.[44]

Witnesses. The presence of witnesses to *Raj'ah* by speech is approved of under the Ḥanafi law, but it is not considered an essential condition of *Raj'ah.*[45]

The presence of witnesses is an essential condition of *Raj'ah* under the Mālikī law according to *al-Hidāyah.*[46] But this view does not seem to be correct. The author of *al-Mughnī* states that under the Mālikī law the presence of witnesses at the time of *Raj'ah* by speech is not an essential condition.[47] According to *al-Mizān al-Kubrā* the correct version is that he did not hold the presence of witnesses necessary but only approved of it.[48]

There are two versions attributed to Shāfi'ī. According to one, witnesses are not necessary; according to the other,

40. Ibn Hammam : *Fatḥ al-Qadīr*, Vol, III, p. 161, Cairo, 1316 A.H.
41. Ibn Rushd, *op. cit.*, Vol. II, p. 70.
42. *Ibid.*
43. Ibn Qudāmah, *op. cit.*, Vol. VII, p. 283; al-Shar'ānī 'Abd al-Wahhāb, *Kitāb al-Mīzān al-Kubrā*, Cairo, 1279 A.H., Vol. II, p. 140.
44. Ibn Qudāmah, *op. cit.*, Vol. VII, p. 285.
45. Al-Marghīnānī, *op. cit.*, Vol. II, p. 375.
46. *Ibid.*
47. Ibn Qudāmah, *op. cit.*, Vol. VII, p. 283.
48. Al-Sha'rānī, *op. cit.*, Vol. II, p. 140.

witnesses are necessary for the validity of *Raj'ah.*[49] But the correct view is that the presence of witnesses is merely approved of.[50]

There are contradictory reports about the opinion of Aḥmad b. Ḥanbal with regard to the presence of witnesses to *Raj'ah*. According to one report he considered the presence of witnesses at the time of *Raj'ah* by speech to be essential for its validity while according to a second report the presence of witnesses was not considered necessary by him. The generally accepted view is that the presence of witnesses is not an essential condition to the validity of *Raj'ah.*[51]

VIII. Proof

If the spouses agree that the period of *'iddah* has expired, but disagree as to the fact of *Raj'ah*, that is, when the husband alleges that he had during the period of the woman's *'iddah* exercised his power of revocation but the wife denies this fact then her statement shall be believed.[52] But if the husband produces witnesses in support of his allegation that he had during the period of *'iddah* retained her then his statement will be accepted.[53] It is stated in *Fatāwā-i 'Ālamgīrīyah* that if on the expiry of the *'iddah* the husband produces witnesses to prove that he had retained her or that he alleged cohabitation (that is revocation by conduct) then this is *Raj'ah*. The words "this is *Raj'ah*" do not mean that the allegation made even after the expiry of the *'iddah* would effect a *Raj'ah* ; all that is meant is that the husband's allegation supported by witnesses would prove *Raj'ah* under the Muslim law of Evidence but the same having been superseded

49. Ibn Qudāmah, *op, cit.*, Vol. VII, p. 282, al-Marghīnānī, *op. cit.*, Vol. II, p. 375.

50. Al-Sha'rānī, *op. cit.*, Vol. II, p. 140.

51. Ibn Qudāmah, *op. cit.*, Vol. VII, pp. 282-83 ; al-Sha'rānī, *op. cit.*, Vol. II, p. 140.

52, *Al-Fatāwā al-Hindīyah*, *op, cit.*, Vol. II, p. 109 ; Ibn 'Ābidīn, *op. cit.*, Vol. II, p. 546.

53. *Ibid.*

in India and Pakistan, a case of this nature would now be decided according to the provisions of the present law of Evidence.

IX. Effect of

Retraction of a revocable divorce restores the parties to their original position and the relationship of husband and wife continues between them.

X. Raj'ah by acquiescence

If an unauthorized person pronounces some expression to denote *Raj'ah*, on behalf of the husband and should the husband accept his act then *Raj'ah* shall be established.[54]

XI. Husband's Waiver

The right of *Raj'ah* is a legal right of the husband. It will not be lost even if he declares that he gives up this right.[55]

XII. Shī'i Law

The Shi'i law is practically the same as the Ḥanafi law, but under the Shī'i law, a mere denial of divorce by the husband within the period of the wife's *'iddah* would be tantamount to revocation, and it amounts to a retention of the woman.[56]

54. *Al-Fatāwā al-Hindīyah, op. cit.,* Vol. II, p. 109.

55. Al-Marghīnānī, *op. cit.,* Vol. II, p. 374.

56. Ja'far b. al-Ḥasan, *Kitāb Sharā'i al-Islām,* Tehran, 1377 A.H., p. 211.

Chapter 9

EFFECT OF DISSOLUTION OF MARRIAGE

The dissolution of marriage either by *ṭalaq* (divorce) or otherwise gives to the following results :

I. The marriage becomes dissolved immediately in the case of an irrevocable divorce and in the case of a revocable divorce on the expiry of the wife's *'iddah.*

II. The parties become absolutely prohibited to each other on the pronouncement of triple divorce and cannot even remarry until and unless the wife marries another person and that marriage is dissolved after consummation. Section 7 of the Muslim Family Laws Ordinance, 1961, in force in Pakistan, has modified this rule to some extent. Thus it is laid down as under :

Talaq. (1) Any man who wishes to divorce his wife, shall, as soon as may be after the pronouncement of *ṭalaq* in any form whatsoever, give the Chairman notice in writing of his having done so, and shall supply a copy thereof to the wife.

(3) " . . . . a *ṭalaq*, unless revoked earlier, expressly or otherwise, shall not be effective until the expiration of ninety days from the day on which notice under sub-Section (1) is delivered to the Chairman (of the Union Council).

(5) If the wife be pregnant at the time *ṭalaq* is pronounced, *ṭalaq* shall not be effective until the period mentioned in sub-Section (3) or the pregnancy, whichever be later, ends.

(6) Nothing shall debar a wife whose marriage has been terminated by *ṭalaq* effective under this section from re-marrying the same husband, without an intervening marriage with a third person, unless such termination is for the third

time so effective." Under the general Muslim law the parties can remarry without the necessity of an intervening marriage only if the divorce has been pronounced once or twice.

III. Cohabitation between the parties becomes unlawful from the time of the pronouncement of an irrevocable divorce and in the case of a revocable divorce from the time of expiry of the wife's *'iddah.*

IV. The wife shall be entitled to contract another marriage on the expiry of her *'iddah.*

V. The husband cannot marry after divorce, certain women, prohibited to him on account of his marriage. He also cannot marry another woman during this period if the divorced wife was one of four living wives.

VI. The wife has to observe *'iddah* for the prescribed period unless she is exempt for its observance.[1]

VII. The husband's liability for maintenance of the wife terminates on the expiry of the period of the wife's *'iddah.*

VIII. The wife's prompt dower becomes due in the case of revocable divorce on the expiry of the wife's *'iddah* and immediately in the case of irrevocable divorce[2] without any demand being made by the wife.

IX. The parties' right to inherit to each other ceases immediately an irrevocable divorce is pronounced. In the case of a revocable divorce the right shall cease on the expiry of the period of the prescribed *'iddah.*

X. *Nasab* or legitimacy of a child shall be established only if it is born within a certain period from the time of dissolution of marriage.[3]

1. For details see Chapter on *'Iddah.*
2. *Ibid.*
3. For details see Chapter on *Nasab.*

Chapter 10

<u>KH</u>IYĀR AL-BULŪ<u>GH</u> OR OPTION OF PUBERTY

I. *Preliminary*

A minor cannot legally enter into a binding contract nor is a contract entered into by a guardian on his or her behalf always binding on the minor. The minor can, on attaining majority, ratify such a contract if he or she so chooses. A Muslim marriage is normally governed by the same principle of law as applies to contracts entered into on behalf of minors. Hence, when a marriage is contracted for a minor by a guardian he or she, on attaining, majority, has a right under certain conditions to choose whether he or she wishes to submit to the marriage or wants it to be dissolved. This right of dissolution of marriage on attaining majority is called *<u>Kh</u>iyār al-Bulū<u>gh</u>* or option of puberty.

In Muslim law an adult husband is considered to have an absolute legal right to the dissolution of his marriage, hence it is the wife who stands mostly in need of help for the dissolution of marriage and the doctrine of option of puberty comes to her aid. The only aspect of the doctrine in which a husband derives advantage from it is with regard to dower as is discussed under that head. Hence, the discussion respecting other matters relates mostly to the wife alone.

II. *Option of Puberty Provides Safeguard*

The option of puberty is one of the safeguards which the Muslim law provides against an undesirable marriage. This safeguard like so many others has suffered by later developments that had their origin long after the time of the Prophet (peace be on him) and the <u>Kh</u>ulfā' Rā<u>sh</u>idūn (the immediate four successors of the Prophet (peace be on him) and having a tendency to minimise the beneficence of the original laws by restrictions and limitations. The basic idea underlying the doctrine of option of puberty is to protect a minor from an unscrupulous or undesirable exercise of authority by his or her guardian for marriage. The right has been given to the minors to dissolve a marriage on attaining majority where the guardian showed a want of affection and discretion by contracting the minor in an undesirable marriage.

III. Religious Sanction

Ibn 'Abbās reported that a virgin girl came to the Prophet (peace be on him) and said that her father had given her in marriage, which was not to her liking. The Messenger of Allah (peace be on him) then gave her option.[1] Abū Dāwūd reported that the father of Khansā' gave her in marriage while she was not a virgin. She did not like the match and so she came to the Prophet (peace be on him). He annulled her marriage.[2]

IV. Discussion

The following matters have to be taken into consideration in respect of the exercise of option of puberty:

(1) Capacity,
(2) Subsistence of marriage,
(3) Right of the minor,
(4) Waiver, and
(5) Time of exercise.

(1) *Capacity.*—The capacity to exercise this right occurs only when a minor attains puberty or majority. As discussed fully in another chapter, a minor is deemed to have attained puberty or majority when he or she has completed the age of fifteen years.[3] The age of fifteen years has been increased in Pakistan to sixteen years by Section 12 of the Muslim Family Laws Ordinance, 1961.

1. Walī al-Dīn al-Khaṭib, *Mishkāt al-Maṣābih,* Delhi, 1932 A.D., p. 271, Abū Dā'ūd, *Sunan,* Kanpur, n.d., Vol. I, pp. 285-86.
2. Walī al-Dīn al-Khaṭīb, *op. cit.*, p. 270 ; Abū Dā'ūd, *op. cit.*, p. 286.
3. For discussion see chapter on majority.

(2) *Subsistence of Marriage.*—The option of puberty can be exercised only when a valid marriage is subsisting between the parties. It is necessary that there should be a marriage which is binding on the husband and the wife when such option is exercised and for this purpose the marriage must be valid ab origine. It is obvious that there would be no need for the exercise of this right in respect of a marriage if the same is *bāṭil* (void) or *fāsid* (irregular) and is therefore not binding on the parties to it.

(3) *Right of Minor* : (*a*) *Preliminary.*—The minor can, on attaining majority, exercise the option of puberty as a matter of right. It has been held in a case that the right can be exercised even when a girl had herself contracted the marriage during her minority with the consent of her father but the father had not actually contracted the same.[4]

(*b*) *Marriage by Guārdian.*—The *Sunnīs* have made a distinction between marriages contracted for a minor by his or her father and paternal grandfather on the one hand and those by any other guardian for marriage on the other as discussed below.

ḤANAFĪ LAW :

(*i*) *Marriage by Guardian other than Father or Paternal Grandfather.*—Under the Ḥanafī law a minor can, on attainment of puberty, dissolve a marriage contracted for her by a guardian for marriage other than the father or the grandfather.[5] This she can do as a matter of right.

(*ii*) *Marriage by Father or Paternal Grandfather.*—A marriage contracted for a minor by the father or the paternal grandfather was generally considered binding on the minor, both under the *Sunnī* and the Shi'ī laws.[6] Mālik confines this rule to the father alone and does not extend it to the grandfather.

4. Joygun Nessa Bibi Vs. Muhammad Ali Biswas, A.I.R., 1938, Cal. 71 ; 174 I.C. 612.

5. *Al-Fatāwā al-Hindiyah*, Kanpur, 1349 A.H., Vol. II, p. 10 ; Ibn 'Ābidīn, *Al-Radd al-Muḥtār*, Cairo, 1318 A.H., Vol. II, pp. 313-14.

6. *Ibid.*, Ja'far b. al-Ḥasan. *Kitāb Sharā'i al-Islām*, Tehran, 1377 A.H., p. 173.

The Mu'tazilites, however, do not make any such distinction and according to them a marriage contracted by a father or grandfather for the minor stands on no higher level than a marriage contracted by any other guardian and can also be dissolved by the minor on attaining puberty.

This distinction observed by the jurists in the right to exercise the option when a marriage is contracted for the minor by the father or the paternal grandfather on the one hand and a marriage contracted by any other guardian on the other hand is based on the presumption that a father or a grandfather cannot, on account of his natural love for the minor, act against his or her interests and contract for the minor a marriage that may not be desirable. But if it is established that he had ignored the interests of the minor or that the marriage is to the minor's manifest disadvantage, then the minor is entitled to exercise this option.[7]

(iii) Dissolution of Marriage contracted by Father or Grandfather.—The Ḥanafīs consider a marriage disadvantageous to a girl and allow the exercise of this right to her in the cases given below even when it is the father or the paternal grandfather who had contracted the marriage :—

(*a*) If the father or the grandfather has ignored the interests of the minor or has acted fraudulently or negligently and the marriage is to the manifest disadvantage of the minor as when a girl has been married to a lunatic or the husband is suffering from some serious disease or has a grave physical deformity.[8] But a mere disparity in the ages of the husband and the wife, if not glaring, does not constitute a manifest disadvantage.[9]

(*b*) If the husband's worldly position is such that the change from the father's house to that of the bridegroom would be one attended by material discomfort to her.[10]

7. Ibn 'Ābidīn, *op. cit.*, Vol. II, p. 312; Muḥammad Abu'l-Sa'ūd, *Fatḥ Allah al-Mu'īn*, Cairo, 1287 A.H., Vol. II, p. 32.
8. *Ibid.*
9. For discussion see Chapter on Equality (*Kufw*); Fatima Bibi Vs. Mian Eusoof Sulaiman, A.I.R., 1937, Rangoon, p. 361.
10. *Ibid.*

(*c*) If the father or grandfather marries his minor boy to a girl belonging to a very low family such as the daughter of a slave then the marriage shall be binding on the boy according to the opinion of Abū Ḥanīfah. Abū Yūsuf and Muḥammad, however, held that the boy shall be entitled to exercise his option of puberty on attaining puberty or majority.[11]

(*d*) If the father or grandfather gives the boy or the girl in marriage for a dower which is highly excessive in the case of the boy or grossly inadequate in the case of the girl. Dower is considered to be highly excessive or grossly inadequate when it is more than the customary dower or less than half of the dower usually fixed in the boy's or girl's family, that is, the customary dower prevalent in the family.[12]

(*e*) When the father or the grandfather is known to have a bad or depraved character, and is notorious for his greed or is a profligate or is notorious for lack of worldly discretion. It is even stated that such a marriage is not valid.[13]

(*f*) If the father or the grandfather was drunk at the time of the marriage to such an extent as not to understand what was going on there. As a point of law such a marriage is not considered to be valid so that the minor shall have a right to get it dissolved on attaining puberty.[14]

Marriage Disadvantageous to a Girl.—The Muslim jurists have held that a marriage is disadvantageous to a girl as when the dower has been fixed at a grossly low figure. The Courts have held that a girl has an option of repudiating her marriage on attainment of majority when:

(*a*) The marriage is to the total disregard of her interests.[15]

11. Ibn 'Ābidīn, *op. cit.*, Vol. II, pp. 312-313; Muḥammad Abu'l-Sa'ūd, *op. cit.*, p. 32.
12. *Ibid.*
13. *Ibid.*
14. *Ibid.*
15. Hasan Bibi Vs. Fazl Elahi, A.I.R., 1929, Lahore, 804.

(*b*) When the bridegroom is diseased or of weak intellect or has some gross deformity.[16]

(*a*) *Mālikī and Shāfi'ī Laws.*—According to the generally accepted view, Mālik has laid down that it is only the father of a minor girl who can give her in marriage and that no one else can exercise that power.[17] According to Shāfi'ī, the power to give a minor in marriage can be exercised by the father as well as by the paternal grandfather. Both the Imāms hold that the marriage shall be binding on the minor and cannot be dissolved by the exercise of the option of puberty or otherwise.[18]

(*b*) *Ḥanbalī Law.*—Aḥmad ibn Ḥanbal agrees with Malīk in the matter of option of puberty.[19]

Shī'i law.—The Shī'i law is practically the same as the Sunnī law discussed above.[19a]

Modification of the Rule.—The indigenous Muslim law does not give the right to a girl to dissolve her marriage by the exercise of option of puberty when the same has been contracted for her by her father or paternal grandfather, unless under special circumstances as fully discussed above. The distinction introduced by the Muslim jurists of old does not suit the present times. In Pakistan and India the Dissolution of Muslim Marriages Act, 1939, has done away the distinction between the marriages contracted by the father or the paternal grandfather on the one hand and by other guardians on the other hand.

Clause VII of Section 2 of the Act reads as under:

"That she, having been given in marriage by her father or other guardian. . ."

16. Fatima Bibi Vs. Mian Eusoof Sulaiman, A.I.R., 1937, Rangoon, 361.
17. Ali b. Abi Bakr, Al-Marghīnānī, *al-Hidāyah*, Delhi, n.d., Vol. II, p. 296; Muḥammad Abu'l-Sa'ūd, *op. cit.*, Vol. II, p. 33.
18. *Ibid.*
19. Al-Sha'rānī, *al-Mīzān al-Kubrā*, Cairo, 1279 A.H., Vol. II, p. 124.
19a. Ja'far b. al-Hasan *op. cit.*, Vol. I, p. 231, Urdu Translation 1897 A.D.; Ja'maa-ush-Shittat cited by Ameer Ali: Mohammadan Law, Vol. II, p. 411, Calcuta, 1908 A.D.

In Pakistan the age of fifteen years has been raised to sixteen years.[20]

(4) *Waiver.*—A minor can on attaining puberty waive her right and submit to the marriage. But anything done by the minor during the period of minority would not destroy the right which accrues to her only on the attainment of puberty.

Consummation of Marriage

(*a*) Cohabitation during the period of minority with or without the girl's consent does not destroy her right because a minor is not capable of giving her consent to any act as long as she is a minor; and secondly, because the right to exercise the option arises only after she has become a major and so is not lost by anything done or happening before that period of time.[21] The option of puberty shall be considered to have been waived by allowing the marriage to be consummated only if it is done (*i*) after the girl has attained majority; (*ii*) she consented to it of her free will.

(*b*) *Consummation, Proof of.*—The consummation of the marriage must be proved as a fact and the mere refusal of the girl to have herself examined by a lady doctor cannot be taken as a proof of the consummation of marriage.[22]

(5) *Time of Exercise.*—The next point for consideration is the time when the dissent to a marriage is to be expressed by the wife or the husband on the attainment of puberty. The law in respect of the time when the option is to be exercised by a boy and by a *thayyibah*, that is, a girl who is not a virgin, is different from that applicable to the case of a girl who is a virgin and so these two aspects are discussed below separately.

(*a*) *Confirmation by a Boy or a Girl who is not Virgin.*—In the case of a boy or a *thayyibah*, that is, a girl who is not a virgin, the ratification of the marriage must be express and

20. Clause (*b*) of Section 13 of the Muslim Family Laws Ordinance, 1961.
21. Al-Marghīnānī, *op. cit*,, Vol. II, pp. 297-98.
22. Ratan Moni Debi Vs. Nagandra Narain Singh, A.I.R., 1949, Cal. 404 at p. 407.

they retain the right to dissolve the marriage till they assent to it by express declaration or conduct.[23] They can express their assent or dissent at any time after attaining puberty ; the right shall not be lost simply on account of a delay in expressing it.[24] It shall subsist until the boy or the girl dissents or submits to the marriage as by allowing consummation of the marriage or demanding dower or maintenance by a girl after attaining puberty.[25] It is also not necessary that the declaration should be made in the presence of witnesses.

(*b*) *Option, Exercise by Virgin.*—In the case of a virgin girl the rule is very stringent. She has to make her option before witnesses as soon as puberty is developed and on a failure to do so she loses her right to cancel the marriage.[26] Thus, if she was sitting somewhere when the signs of puberty become apparent she must express her disapprobation then and there and the time for the exercise of the right would not be extended to the time when she leaves the place or the sitting is terminated.[27] Her mere silence in respect of the marriage on attaining puberty is sufficient to deprive her of this right because her silence is presumed to imply her consent.[28] This is based on the analogy of a Tradition that the Prophet (peace be on him) said, "A virgin shall not be married till her consent is sought." They (the people) asked, "How shall be her permission ?" He said, "If she remains silent."[29] The presence of witness is not essential for the validity of the declaration, but is meant to provide proof of her declaration because should the husband deny her allegation, her bare statement cannot suffice to discharge the burden that lies on her.

(*c*) *Virgin, Definition of.*—A girl shall be considered to be

23. Ibn ʻĀbidīn, *op. cit.*, Vol. II, pp. 318-19.
24. *Ibid.*
25. *Ibid.*
26, *Ibid.* ; *al-Fatāwā al-Hindiyah*, *op. cit.*, Vol. II, p. 10,
27. *Ibid.*
28. ʻAlī b. Abī Bakr, *op, cit.*, Vol. II, p. 297.
29. Walī al-Dīn al-Khaṭīb, *op. cit.*, Vol, II, p. 270.

a virgin for the purpose of this provision even if she loses her hymen due to accident, disease, operation, rape or adultery.[30] The same result will follow if she had been married but the marriage was dissolved before consummation though after valid retirement under the Ḥanafī, Mālikī and the Ḥanbalī laws.[31]

(*d*) *Status of Minor Wife on Intimacy during Minority.*—If the husband of a minor girl should be intimate with her during her minority then the option of the minor shall not be lost. But for the purpose of expressing her dissent she shall be treated as non-virgin so that her mere silence at the time when she attains puberty shall not be considered tantamount to consent. She shall retain her option until she consents to the marriage expressly or by conduct such as by demanding maintenance or allowing intimacy.[32]

(*e*) *Rule not Suitable for Modern Time.*—The rule laid down by the Ḥanafī jurists that a virgin must express her dissent the moment the signs of puberty appear does not find support from any verse of the Qur'ān or any Tradition, but was subsequently introduced by Muslim jurists to suit the requirements of their own time. It is not at all suitable for modern times. She would naturally require some time to consider the matter and then to decide her future course of conduct. It was pointed out in a case that the right to repudiate a marriage is unknown to many girls, and in such cases a girl can exercise the right when she becomes aware of her right to repudiate the marriage.[33] But the right would be lost if, after attaining puberty and after being informed of the marriage and of her right to repudiate it, she does not repudiate the marriage without unreasonable delay.[34] The option shall be prolonged until she becomes aware of her marriage and of

30. *Al-Fatāwā al-Hindiyah, op. cit.*, Vol. II, p. 12 ; Ibn 'Ābidīn, *op. cit.*, II, p. 310.
31. *Ibid.*
32. *Al-Fatāwā al-Hindiyah, op. cit.*, Vol, II, p. 10.
33. Mst. Ayesha Vs. Muhammad Yunus, A.I.R., 1938 Patna, 604.
34. *Ibid.*

her legal right of repudiation.[35]

(*f*) *Courts' View.*—The rule laid down by Ḥanafī jurists was explicitly followed in some early cases. Thus, the Lahore High Court held in 54 P. R. (1888) and 157 P. R. (1897) that the option must be exercised immediately on attaining puberty. This view was affirmed in a subsequent case in which it was held that the right determines immediately on attaining puberty.[36] The tendency of the Courts, however, changed subsequently and it was held that for a due compliance of this right it would be sufficient if it has been exercised within a reasonable time after attaining puberty.[37] Thus a girl of seventeen years of age was allowed to dissolve her marriage by the exercise of her option of puberty. It was pointed out by the Court that the principle underlying the provision of the Muslim law is that there should be no acquiescence in the marriage.[38]

(*g*) *Modification of Law.*—A provision in the Dissolution of Muslim Marriages Act (Act VIII of 1939) has now removed the hardship. Clause VII of Section 2 of the Act authorises a Muslim girl to get her marriage dissolved in the exercise of this power at any time before attaining the age of eighteen years if she was married while she was a minor, that is, before attaining the age of fifteen years. In Pakistan the age of fifteen years has been raised to sixteen years by the Muslim Family Laws Ordinance, 1961. It is, therefore, no longer necessary that she must exercise the option of puberty immediately on attaining puberty. Her right to exercise this option shall extend up to the time when she attains the age of eighteen years, provided she has not in the meantime submitted to or acquiesced in the marriage after attaining puberty.

35. Mst. Aishah Vs. Jodh Ram, A.I.R., 1938, Lahore, 719.
36. Mst. Ghulam Fatima Vs. Khaira, A.I.R., 1923, Lahore, 674.
37. Hussain Vs, Mst. Jiwani, A.I.R , 1924, Lahore, 385, 69 I.C. 281, Channo Vs. Bagh Behari, A.I.R., 1925, Lahore, 66, Mst. Mukhan Vs. Haider, A.I.R., 1932, Lahore, 449.
38. Hussain Vs. Mst. Jiwani, A.I.R., 1924, Lahore, 385.

(*h*) *Delay.*—Having once protested against her marriage before witnesses at the proper time any delay in taking judicial action does not result in the loss of the minor's right under the Ḥanafī law unless in the meantime she has assented to the marriage expressly or by conduct.[39] The Dissolution of Muslim Marriages Act, 1939, has not in any way affected this provision of the Muslim law. Clause VII of Section 2 of that Act only requires that the marriage must be repudiated before the attainment of the age of eighteen years, and it is not laid down as to when a suit should be filed. But under the provisions of the Limitation Act such a suit should be filed within six years of the time when the cause of action arises.[40]

Girl's Ignorance: (*i*) *Preliminary.*—The next question to be considered is the effect of a minor's ignorance at the time when she attains puberty of the fact of her marriage or of her legal right to repudiate it. It is obvious that a minor cannot exercise the option of puberty unless she is aware of the marriage and of her legal right to its dissolution. Both these cases are discussed below.

(*j*) *Ignorance of Marriage.*—As regards a minor's ignorance of the fact of her marriage the law is that the minor retains the option of repudiating the same until she becomes aware of the fact.[41] This rule of Ḥanafī law has been followed by the Courts.[42] The Lahore High Court took a contrary view in an early case, namely, in Mst. Ghulam Fatima Vs. Khaira (A. I. R. 1923 Lah. 574) but it has now taken the same view

39. *Al-Fatāwā al-Hindiyah, op. cit.*, Vol. II, p. 10.

40. Section 120 of the Limitation Act ; Muhammad Hamid Ullah Khan Vs. Fakhre Jehan Begum, A.I.R., 1922, Oudh 109 ; 65 I.C. 452.

41. Al-Marghīnanī, *op. cit.*, Vol II, p. 297 ; *al-Fatāwā al-Hindiyah, op. cit.*, Vol. II, p. 10.

42. Mauladad Vs. Mst. Fateh Bibi A.I.R., 1926, Lahore, 545 ; Sardar Ali Vs. Shrimati Ābida Bibi A.I.R., 1928, Cal. 549 ; Sultan Vs. Maryam A.I. R., 1923 ; Lahore, 502 ; Aishah Vs. Johd Ram, A.I.R., 1938, Lahore, 719 ; Rehmat Ali Vs. Mst. Allah Ditta, A.I.R. 1929, Lahore, 827 ; Bismillah Begum Vs. Noor Mohammad, A.I.R., 1922, All., 155.

as that of the other High Courts. The minor must, however exercise the right within a reasonable time from the time when she comes to know of her marriage.[43]

(*k*) *Ignorance of Legal Right.*—As regards the second point, namely, the ignorance of a minor about her legal right to dissolve the marriage on attaining puberty it has been laid down by Abū Ḥanīfah and Abū Yūsuf that the time for the exercise of the right shall not be prolonged on account of the minor's ignorance of her legal right.[44] They have based this opinion on the rule of law that ignorance of law is no excuse. Also on the ground that according to the dictates of the Prophet (peace be on him) it is the duty of every Muslim man and woman to acquire knowledge and that for that reason no Muslim could plead want of knowledge of the provisions of Muslim law.[45] Muḥammad has held that her right to exercise the option of puberty shall be extended up to the time when a girl comes to know that she possesses such a right.[46]

The rule laid down by Abū Ḥanīfah and Abū Yūsuf involves great hardship because the vast majority of women and men of the present day are illiterate and very few persons even amongst the educated class have any knowledge of religious doctrines. The number of girls who have any knowledge of this right is negligible. The view might have suited the time of the *Imāms*, having regard to the particular conditions of their age and the fact that they lived in a Muslim State where acquisition of religious knowledge was comparatively easy and almost compulsory, but it certainly is not suitable for the present time. It is a valuable right and a girl should not be deprived of the benefit of it. We can follow the view expressed by Muḥammad in preference to the view expressed

43. Mst. Mukhan Vs. Haider, A.I.R., 1932 Lahore, 449; Maula Dad Vs. Fazal, A.I.R., 1923, Lahore, 594, 116, I.C.E., 557; Rehmat Vs. Allahditta A.I.R., 1929, Lahore, 827.

44. Al-Marghīnanī, *op. cit.*, Vol. II, p. 297; Ibn 'Ābidīn, *op. cit.*, Vol. II, p. 318.

45. Ibn 'Ābidīn, *op. cit.*, Vol. II, p. 318.

46. *Ibid.*

by Abū Ḥanīfah and Abū Yūsuf on the basis of justice and equity, taking into consideration the conditions prevalent now.

(*l*) *Courts' View.*—The Courts have generally followed the view expressed by Muḥammad. Thus, the Allahabad High Court has followed this view in several cases. It has held that the right is prolonged until a girl becomes acquainted with the fact that she possesses such a right. It is reasonable and equitable.[47] It has been pointed out by the Patna High Court that this right is unknown to many girls and so a girl can exercise it when she becomes aware of her legal right to repudiate the marriage.[48] The Lahore High Court formerly took a different view but has now expressed the same opinion as that of the Allahabad High Court.[49] The Calcutta High Court expressed different views at different times and held that ignorance of the law is no ground for prolongation of the time during which a minor can exercise her option of repudiation.[50] But the Allahabad, Lahore and Patna High Courts have held ignorance of law to be a sufficient ground for prolongation of the time till the minor gets knowledge of the law in this respect. The majority of cases are in favour of the latter view. A wife can take advantage of the rule and her right shall not be lost if she was ignorant of her legal right to repudiate her marriage.[51] Under the provisions of the Dissolution of Muslim Marriages Act, 1939, the wife has to exercise the right before she attains the age of eighteen years. The Act is silent about a girl's right to the extension of time when she was ignorant of the marriage or of her legal right in the matter. The provisions of

47. Ahmad Husain Vs. Amir Bano, A.I.R., 1940 All., 63.
48. Mst. Ayesha Vs. Mohd. Yunus, A.I.R., 1938, Pat., 604.
49. Rahmat Ali Vs. Mst. Allah Ditta A.I.R., 1929, Lahore, 827; Mst. Mukhan Vs. Haider Ali A.I.R., 1923, Lahore, 449; Aishah Vs. Jodh Ram, A.I.R., 1938, Lahore, 719.
50. Sardar Ali Vs. Shrimati Abeda Bibi A.I.R., 1928, Cal, 549.
51. Ahmad Husain Vs. Amir Bano A.I.R., 1940, Allahabad, 63; Aishah Vs. Jodh Ram, A.I.R., 1938, Lahore, 719; Sughra Vs. Muzaffar, 1929, A.L.J., 101; Sultan Vs. Maryam, A.I.R., 1923, Lahore, 502; Mauladad Vs. Mst. Fateh Bibi A.I.R., 1926, Lahore, 545.

the indigenous Muslim law can, therefore, be applied in such a case. But as against this view is the possibility that an unscrupulous girl may take advantage of this rule of law. Thus, she may be fully cognisant of the fact of her marriage and the relevant law, but may plead ignorance of the same, in which case it shall be difficult for a husband to establish the wife's knowledge of the rule. The difficulty has been minimised considerably in India and Pakistan as a girl can no longer be given in marriage in these countries when she is a minor. Sections 5 and 6 of the Child Marriage Restraint Act, 1929, make it an offence to give away in marriage a girl below fifteen years (in Pakistan sixteen years). Some other Muslim countries have increased the age at which a girl can be given away in marriage.

(*m*) *Burden of Proof.*—It has been held by the Lahore High Court that it lies on the husband to prove that the wife had knowledge of her marriage or her right to exercise the option of puberty a considerable time before the institution of the suit.[52] It appears from the trend of the decision of the Court that it formed this opinion because the girl was only sixteen years and eight months old and that a different view might have been held if she had been older. The Allahabad High Court has disagreed with this view and has stated that the fact that a woman has knowledge of her right to exercise the option of puberty at a particular time must be especially within her knowledge and, therefore, the burden of proving such a fact must be on her.[53] It has expressed this opinion on the basis of Section 106 of the Evidence Act wherein it is stated that when any fact is especially within the knowledge of any person then the burden of proving that fact is upon him or her. It is submitted that the latter view is more in consonance with equity than the other view. The burden of proving that the girl attained puberty earlier than at the age of fifteen or sixteen years lies on the person alleging it.

52. Mst. Mukhan Vs. Haider, A.I.R., 1932, Lahore, 449.
53. Ahmad Hussain Vs. Mst. Amir Bano, A.I.R., 1940, Allahabad, 63.

V. Procedure

Under the Ḥanafī law if a virgin girl wants to take advantage of this right on attainment of puberty then she must express her disapproval of her marriage and declare before at least two witnesses that she does not consent to it and this must be done immediately on attaining puberty.[54]

(*a*) *Presence of Witnesses.*—The presence of witnesses is not essential for the validity of the act of cancellation but is meant simply to help in establishing that fact.[55] If the husband denies her allegation then the *Qāḍī* cannot decide the case in her favour merely on the basis of her uncorroborated statement.

(*b*) *Courts' View.*—The Courts have not laid much stress on the presence of witnesses. Thus, it has been laid down by the Allahabad High Court that the repudiation need not be akin to an oral repudiation before witnesses.[56] The Courts have deemed it sufficient if the girl exercises her disapproval of the marriage in some form or other.[57] Thus, the institution of a suit by a girl for the dissolution of her marriage was considered a mode of proclaiming her option.

VI. Expression, Mode of

(*a*) *Preliminary.*—The next question that arises is the manner in which a minor husband or wife should exercise his or her assent or dissent to the marriage on attaining puberty. The law is the same in the case of a husband as in that of a wife who is not a virgin. Their assent or dissent should be expressed in words or by conduct while in the case of a wife who is a virgin the assent may be express or implied.[58]

54. *Al-Fatāwā al-Hindiyah, op. cit.,* Vol. II, p. 10; Ibn 'Ābidīn, *op. cit.,* Vol. II, p. 318.
55. Ibn 'Ābidīn, *op. cit.,* Vol. II, p. 318.
56, Shafi Ullah Vs. E., A.I.R., 1934, All., 589.
57. Mst. Ghulam Sakina Vs. Falak Sher Allah Bux, A.I.R. 1950, Lahore, 45.
58. Inb 'Ābidīn, *op. cit.,* Vol. II, pp. 318-19.

(*b*) *Express Assent or Dissent.*—In the case of express dissent no formula or particular expression is prescribed for use in exercising this option. All that is required is that the minor must express his or her approval or disapproval of the marriage. It has been stated by the Lahore High Court that if a wife is not sure whether she was in fact married or not, there is no bar to her declaring, whether she was married or not, that she does not want the person concerned as a husband. In a case in which the girl was said to have been given away in marriage when she was four years old, in her suit against the alleged husband she said that if it was found that her marriage did take place, the same be dissolved as she had exercised her option of puberty on attaining majority when she came to know of it. The husband contended that the wife should not be allowed to exercise her option of puberty regarding problematic marriage. The Court rejected this plea and held the option to have been rightly exercised.[59] In certain circumstances even mere denial of marriage has been considered to amount to its repudiation. It was stated that the only question is whether she is prepared to accept him (husband) as a husband or not, and if she unequivocally says she is not, the option of puberty is exercised.[60]

(*c*) *Assent or Dissent by Conduct.*—Dissent of a boy or *thayyibah* girl by conduct can consist of such acts as refusal by a girl to allow consummation of the marriage or refusal by the boy to pay dower or maintenance to the wife. Assent of a girl can be inferred from such acts as allowing consummation of the marriage or demand for maintenance or dower by her or its payment by the husband.[61] But if a girl merely wants to know the amount of her dower or the particulars about the husband, her consent shall not be presumed and

59. Ala-ud-Din Vs. Mst. Farkhanda Akhtar, P.L.D., 1953, Lahore, p. 131; Abdul Bari Abdul Aziz Vs. Abeda Khatoon, A.I.R., 1955, Tripura, p. 2.

60. Ala-ud-Din Vs. Mst. Farkhanda Akhtar, P.L.D., 1953 Lah., 131 at p. 136.

61. Ibn al-Humām, *Fatḥ al-Qadīr*, Cairo, n.d., Vol. II, p. 410; Ibn 'Ābidīn, *op. cit.*, Vol. II, p. 319.

her right shall not be lost. This seems to be based on the reasoning that she may want to know these particulars so that she may make up her mind as to whether to agree to the marriage or not to do so.

(*d*) *Illustrative Cases.*—It has been held that a girl's dissent to her marriage can be gathered from her conduct. Thus, it can be inferred from the fact that the girl files a suit for the dissolution of her marriage.[62] Similarly, her refusal to allow consummation of the marriage by the husband would also amount to such dissent.[63] When the husband of a minor girl was convicted and was in prison at the time when she attained puberty and she then contracted a second marriage it was held that this conduct was sufficient indication that she did not ratify her first marriage.[64] The Allahabad High Court has held that there can be no surer repudiation of marriage than the girl's conduct in marrying another person on attaining puberty.[65] The Lahore High Court has considered the mere fact of a girl instituting a suit on attaining puberty for a declaration that she is not the defendant's wife is in itself an exercise of the right.[66] Even the mere denial of her marriage by a girl, on attaining puberty, was deemed sufficient repudiation.[67] Similarly, it was considered sufficient expression of dissent when in the husband's suit for restitution of conjugal rights the wife pleaded the exercise of this right.[68]

(*e*) *Dispute about Assent.*—If there is a dispute about the girl's assent or dissent to the marriage on attainment of puberty, as when the husband alleges her consent while the wife denies

62. Hasan Bibi Vs. Fazal Ilahi, 1929, Lahore, 804, 121, I.C. 381.
63. Ibn 'Ābidin, *op. cit.*, Vol. II, p. 319.
64. Badal Aurat Vs. Q. E., I.L.R., 19, Cal., 79.
65. Shafi-Ullah Vs. E., A.I.R., 1934, All., 589.
66. Hasan Bibi Vs. Fazal Elahi, A.I.R. 1929, Lahore, 804.
67. Ala-ud-Din Vs. Mst. Farkhanda Akhtar, P.L.D., 1953 Lah., 131.
68. Mst. Bhawan Vs. Gaman, A.I.R, 1934, Lahore, 77; Nazimuddin Vs. Hussaini, A.I.R., 1960, Madh Bh., p. 12; Betulan Vs. Zahoor Shah A.I.R., 1952, Madh, Bh. p. 30.

his version, then the wife's statement shall be accepted in preference to the husband's statement under Muslim law.[69]

(*f*) *Implied Assent or Dissent.*—A girl's assent to her marriage may be presumed by implication when on attainment of puberty she keeps silent and does not object to the marriage.[70]

(*g*) *Denial of Marriage.*—The denial of the factum of marriage, however, is an entirely different thing from the exercise of the option of puberty and does not constitute a repudiation of the marriage.[71] But it was held in a later case that under certain conditions even a denial of marriage may amount to repudiation.[72] It is submitted that the first view is the better view. It was stated by the wife that she was not married to the alleged husband and in the alternative that she had repudiated the same. It was contended by the husband that the wife could not be allowed to take inconsistent pleas. The Court held, "If a woman is not sure whether in fact she was married or not, there is no bar to her declaring that whether she was married or not, she does not want the person concerned as a husband." It is submitted that if a woman is not certain of her marriage then it is open to her to repudiate the same, but mere denial of the marriage does not amount to its repudiation. For the exercise of her right of repudiation, her choice must be clearly expressed.

VII. Information to Husband.—A disapproval of marriage by a girl in the presence of witnesses, if she is a virgin, is sufficient and it is not necessary that the husband must be personally informed of it. It is also not necessary for the girl to serve the husband with a notice about the exercise of her option, and the bringing of a suit in this respect has been considered to be sufficient information of the exercise

69. Ibn al-Humām, *op. cit.*, pp. 403-4 ; Ibn Ābidīn, *op. cit.*, pp. 310-11.
70. Sahib Jan Vs. Ghulam Hyder, 15 I C., 560.
71. Ghulam Mohammad Vs. Emperor, 140 I.C., 617.
72. Ala-ud-Din Vs. Farkhanda Akhtar P.L.D., 1953 Lah., p. 131.

of option.[73]

VIII. Qāḍī's Order.—The question whether the order of the *Qāḍī* is an essential condition for a valid separation between the parties on the exercise of option of puberty involves some difficulty on account of the views expressed by some modern writers and the Courts. The Muslim jurists of old and the original authoritative books on Muslim law are unanimous in saying that the *Qāḍī's* order is an essential condition for the dissolution of marriage. Thus, *al-Durr al-Mukhtār*, of which *Radd al-Muḥtār* is a commentary, states that the *Qāḍī's* order is an essential condition for cancellation of the marriage.[74] The author of *al-Radd al-Muḥtār* justifies this view on the ground that the girl's option to repudiate the marriage is a weak right, hence the necessity to obtain the *Qāḍī's* order and that the order is required for proving (establishing) the cancellation of the marriage and not as a corroboration of repudiation by the wife. If the wife chooses to exercise the option of repudiation then the repudiation shall not be proved (be effective) unless there is an order by the *Qāḍī*.[75]

It is stated in the *Hidāyah* that the order of a *Qāḍī* is a condition precedent for the dissolution of marriage under the exercise of the option of puberty as it tends to affect other rights of the parties and so the *Qāḍī's* order is an essential condition to safeguard the rights.[76] In other words, it makes the obtaining of an order of the *Qāḍī* essential for the dissolution of marriage. *Alamgīrīyah* has followed this view and laid down, "if a minor boy and a minor girl are contracted in marriage by any guardian other than the father or paternal grandfather then, on attaining puberty, each of them *shall have a right to submit to the marriage or to cancel it*......if on attaining puberty the boy or girl chooses separa-

73. Hasan Bibi Vs. Fazal Ilahi, A.I.R. 1929 Lahore, 804.

74. Ibn 'Ābidīn, *op. cit.*, Vol. II, pp. 314-15.

75. *Ibid.*

76. Al-Marghīnānī, *op. cit.*, Vol. II, p. 297.

tion and the *Qāḍī* has not separated them then if one of them dies they shall inherit to each other. And until the *Qāḍī* separates them till then it is lawful for the husband to cohabit with the wife.

It is stated in *Majmu' al-Unhar* that "the *Qāḍī's* order is a condition precedent to the cancellation of the marriage by the exercise of the option of puberty, whether the right is exercised by a boy or a girl. Hence a marriage would not become void (cancelled) until the *Qaḍī* gives his order because the marriage had become effective (operative), hence it would not become ineffective (cancelled) by mere dissent (of a party) without the *Qāḍī's* order. The option is a right about the propriety of which there is a difference of opinion. It is further stated that the reason of the cancellation is unknown and is secret, that is, whether there was some want of affection and kindness in the guardian who had given the minor in the marriage. The cancellation of the marriage is to render ineffective the right of another and the party exercising the right is not empowered to do so. It also leads to the result that if the husband be absent, the *Qāḍī's* order of cancellation shall not be valid because it amounts to a decision against an absentee which is not valid."[78]

It is stated in *Kanz al-Daqā'iq* that if one of the spouses happens to die then the survivor shall inherit to him or her if the death happens (*i*) before the exercise of the option of puberty, or (*ii*) before confirmation by the *Qāḍī* of the girl's exercise of her option. This shows that a marriage shall subsist till the *Qāḍī's* order is passed.[79] If the *Qāḍī* has given his decree then the right of inheritance and intimacy shall be lost unless the spouses remarry.

The provisions regarding the *Qāḍī's* order are also justified in *al-Mabsūṭ* on the ground that option of puberty

77. *Al-Fatāwā al Alamīgrīah*, pp. 31, 32.

78. Shaykhzadah 'Abd al-Raḥman b. Muḥammad, *Majma' al-Unhur*, Constantinople, 1327 A.H., Vol. I, pp. 336-37.

79. Ibn Nujaym, *al-Baḥr al-Rā'iq*, Cairo, 1311 A.H., Vol. III, p. 133.

is a weak right and so must be supported by the order of the *Qāḍī*. Another ground given there is that all the Muslim jurists do not agree to the doctrine of the option of puberty and that Abū Yūsuf and some others do not accept it hence the necessity to get the *Qāḍī's* order, that is, to give it a legal sanction so that the dissolution may become valid even if the doctrine be not correct. The justification for this rule given in *Badā'i'-al-Ṣanā'i'* is that when two parties enter into an agreement which subsequently proves to be defective but one of the parties to it does not agree to its cancellation then it can be cancelled only by the order of the *Qāḍī* and that on this analogy the *Qāḍī's* order is also necessary in the case of option of puberty.[80] Abū Ḥanīfah has explained that the cause on the basis of which a marriage is dissolved may be obvious or hidden. The former causes are such as *Īlā'*, apostasy, *fāsid* (irregular) marriage etc. The *Qāḍī's* order to confirm the separation is not necessary in these cases. The cases of the other class are seven in number, namely, impotency, castrated husband, inequality in marriage, *li'ān*, option of puberty, inadequacy of dower, the adoption of Islam by the wife when the husband refuses to do so. The *Qāḍī's* order shall be an essential condition in these cases.[81]

It is stated in *al-Baḥr-al-Rā'iq* that dissolution of marriage may be classified into thirteen classes seven of which require the *Qāḍī's* order for their validity, or, in other words, the *Qāḍī's* order is a condition precedent in these seven cases. The other six classes are such as do not require the *Qāḍī's* order for their validity, but the marriage is dissolved automatically without such order.[82] The first class refers to the following cases :

(*a*) Dissolution of a marriage because the husband is a *majbūb* (eunuch).

80. 'Alā al-Dīn Abī Bakr al-Kāsānī, *Badā'i' al-Ṣanā'i'*, Cairo, 1327 A.H., Vol, II, p. 316.
81. Ibn Nujaym, *op. cit.*, Vol. III, p. 130.
82. *Ibid.*

(*b*) Dissolution of marriage on the ground of the husband's impotency.

(*c*) Dissolution of marriage by the exercise of option of puberty.

(*d*) Dissolution of marriage on the basis that it is unequal;

(*e*) Dissolution of marriage on the ground that the (girl's) dower has been fixed at a grossly low figure;

(*f*) Dissolution of marriage on the ground that the husband had accused the wife of unchastity or *Li'ān;*

(*g*) Dissolution of marriage when the wife embraces Islam but the husband refuses to do so.

The second class of separation relates to the following cases:

(*a*) Dissolution of marriage on the basis of *Īlā'*;

(*b*) When one of the spouses renounces Islam;

(*c*) When the spouses are separated because the marriage is *Fāsid*;

(*d*) When one of the non-Muslim spouses takes up his or her domicile in a Dar ul-Islam or Muslim State while the other settles in a non-Muslim State;

(*e*) If a slave girl, given in marriage by her master to someone, is set free;

(*f*) When one of the spouses becomes the owner of the other.

This can happen when one of them is a slave.[83]

The author of *al-Radd al-Muḥtār* says that the repudiation of marriage is not established until it is done by the *Qāḍī*. It states, *Lā yat͟hbutu al-fask͟h, illa bi sharṭ il-qāḍā'* The word (*t͟habt*) means either to exist or to strengthen, confirm. If the former meaning is accepted then it shall mean that a marriage shall subsist until it is dissolved by the *Qāḍī*. If the other meanings are accepted then it shall mean that the *Qāḍī's* order merely confirms the repudiation already brought about by the girl. The author then proceeds

83. Ibn Nujaym, *op. cit.*, Vol. III, p. 130.

to say that the other books establish the proposition that there can be no dissolution of the marriage without the *Qāḍī's* order and hence on an equitable interpretation we shall adopt the first meaning.[84]

It can thus be seen that under the Ḥanafī law a marriage subsists after the exercise of the option of puberty till the necessary order is obtained from the *Qāḍī*.

Court's View.—There is a difference of opinion amongst the various High Courts about the necessity of the Court's order. The Calcutta High Court has now followed the view expressed in *al-Hidāyah*, *Fatāwā 'Alamgīrī*, *al-Mabsūt*, etc., and has held "It is undoubtedly true that there is need for obtaining a judicial decree and that a repudiation will not be effective unless and until a judicial decree is obtained confirming it."[85] A Division Bench of Sind Chief Court has also held that the marriage subsists until the wife obtains a decree of a court declaring that the marriage had been dissolved.[86] A contrary view was taken by the Lahore High Court which held that it is not necessary for the repudiation of a marriage by the exercise of the option of puberty to get a formal order of a Court.[87] It was held by the Allahabad High Court that the wife's contracting a second marriage was itself evidence of repudiation of the first marriage by her.[88] It was not considered necessary that the Court's decree should be obtained. But the view was expressed in another case that a decree of the Court is necessary.[89]

The trend of modern judgements favours Ameer Ali's interpretation of *al-Radd al-Muḥtār* that a decree of the Court is not esssential for the dissolution of a marriage by the

84. Ibn 'Ābidīn, *op. cit.*, Vol. II, p. 315.
85. Sadar Ali Vs. Shrimati Abeda Bibi, A.I.R., 1928, Cal., 549.
86. Usman Vs. Budha, A.I.R., 1932, Sind, 92.
87. Ghulam Mohd. Vs. E., A.I.R. 1933, Lahore, 88.
88. Shafi-Ullah Vs. E., A.I.R., 1934, All., 549.
89. Pir Mohammad Vs. The State of Madhya Pradesh, A.I.R. 1960 Madhya Pradesh, 24.

exercise of the option of puberty. Section 2 (vii) of the Dissolution of Muslim Marriages Act, 1939, now makes it clear that a wife has to get a decree of a Court for the dissolution of her marriage on the ground of exercise of option of puberty. There are certain conditions which must be satisfied before a girl can validly exercise this right. Thus, she can exercise it only:

(*a*) if she was given in marriage before she obtained puberty;

(*b*) if she repudiated the marriage immediately on attaining puberty. The Courts have laid down in some cases that the right can be exercised within a reasonable time after attaining puberty. The Dissolution of Muslim Marriages Act, 1939, allows a wife to exercise this right up to the time when she attains the age of eighteen years.

Admittedly both these conditions are essential to the exercise of the right of puberty. Who will see if these conditions have been satisfied if the marriage is dissolved by the exercise of the option by the wife? It, therefore, seems that the Court's decree is necessary to give effect to the exercise of the option by the girl. If the wife satisfies the Court that all the conditions had been satisfied when she exercised her option, only then will she be entitled to get a decree.

The correct view is that the wife can exercise the option of puberty as a matter of right, but she has to satisfy the Court that she has complied with all the necessary conditions and till then the marriage subsists. If it is proved to the satisfaction of the Court that the conditions had been satisfied, it cannot say "no" to the girl's suit for dissolution of her marriage and the marriage has to be annulled irrespective of any other consideration.

The Courts have in some instances laid down the law too broadly.[90] The mere fact that the wife has contracted a second marriage cannot by itself amount to the exercise of

90. Shafi-Ullah Vs. E., A.I.R., 1934 All., 549.

the option of puberty. Moreover, it is very necessary that there should be some evidence of the fact that the wife has exercised her right independent of her conduct which may be illegal and so cannot be the basis for a legal presumption that the right has been exercised.

It has been explained by the Lahore High Court that in the case of the exercise of the option of puberty the Court does not dissolve the marriage by its own act, but recognizes the termination of the marriage.[91] Section 2 (vii) of the Dissolution of Musilm Marriages Act, 1939, now makes it clear that a wife has to get a decree of a Court for the dissolution of her marriage on the ground of exercise of the option of puberty. Difference between the views of the Muslim jurists and the Courts: it is submitted that the rulings quoted above do not conform with the law laid down by Muslim jurists wherein it is definitely stated that the *Qāḍī's* order for the dissolution of marriage by the exercise of the option of puberty is an essential condition for separation. The view taken by the Courts no doubt is meant to help the wives, but the provisions of Muslim law cannot be ignored simply for that purpose. Care has to be taken that too much latitude in this respect may not open the door for bigamy. The Courts have in a number of cases expressed the view that the *Qāḍī's* order is not essential for the dissolution of marriage by the exercise of the option of puberty. This view was first expressed by Ameer Ali, the well-known scholar on Muslim law in his valuable book on Mohammadan Law, and also in a judgement delivered by him namely, Badal Aurat Vs. Q.E, I.L.R. 19 Cal. 79. S. A. Rahman *J.*, as he then was, in an elaborate judgement has expressed the same opinion as expressed by Ameer Ali. He has stated, "... I have reached the conclusion that a Court's order is not essential for conferring validity on the exercise of option of puberty. The *Qāḍīs* must be replaced by the civil Court's. The Court's order would seem to be only necessary to invest it

91. Mst. Muni Vs. Habib Khan, P.L.D., 1956, Lahore, 403.

with the judicial *imprimatur* in order to avoid any possible disputes as Mr. Ameer Ali has explained."[92] The majority of the Courts have been greatly influenced by the view expressed by Ameer Ali and have followed it. With respect, it is submitted that the view expressed by Ameer Ali is not in accordance with the view of the Muslim jurists in this respect.

Ameer Ali, while dealing with the matter has stated as under: "... Upon this arise two questions: (*a*) what is the reason for requiring the Kazi decree in such a case, (*b*) what would be the effect if the woman were to remarry without obtaining a judicial declaration? There can be no question regarding the right itself; no decree is required to affirm it. It is also quite clear that the Kazi cannot make any declaration unless the party who claims the right has himself or herself exercised and asserted the right. Then, what does the condition imply? To my mind it means simply this, that in order to cause an effective cancellation or to impress on the act the judicial *imprimatur*, an order of the *Kazi* is necessary. Until that has been obtained the status remains in an inchoate condition, the parties may lawfully cohabit which would amount to a recantation of the "option", or if either of them were to die, a right of inheritance would be established in the survivor."

"... The validity of the recission, it seems to me, does not depend on the *imprimatur* of the Kazi, as the judicial declaration is needed to provide judicial evidence in order to prevent disputes, and judicial confirmation and authentication of the exercise of the right ..."[93]

It is submitted that the above view is not in accord with the law laid down by Muslim jurists as has been stated above and it is necessary to thoroughly discuss the matter. It will be helpful to take into consideration the following aspects of the case:

92. Muhammad Bukhsh Vs. Crown, P L.D., 1956, Lahore, 403.
93. Ameer Ali, Mohammadan Law, Calcutta, 1888 A.D., Vol. II, p. 416.

(*i*) Whether a girl can on attaining puberty dissolve her marriage as a matter of right.

(*ii*) Whether the *Qāḍī's* order is an essential condition for the dissolution of marriage by the exercise of the option of puberty. If so, for what purpose, and what is the nature of the *Qāḍī's* order?

(*iii*) Whether the marriage is terminated immediately on repudiation by the wife.

(*iv*) A girl can on attaining puberty decide whether she wants to submit to the marriage or whether she does not accept it.

(*v*) Whether the Court's decree is essential to the dissolution of marriage by the exercise of the option of puberty.

(I) A girl can on attaining puberty decide whether she wants to submit to the marriage or whether she does not accept it.

It is her absolute right to accept or not to accept the same. Thus '*Alamgīrīyah* states, "if a minor boy and a minor girl are contracted in marriage by any guardian other than the father or paternal grandfather then on attaining puberty each of them *shall have the right to submit to the marriage or to cancel it.*[94] The same view has been expressed in other authoritative books on Muslim law. This statement makes it abundantly clear that it is within the discretion of the girl to submit to the marriage or to dissent to it and it is her absolute right to refuse to submit to the marriage if she so wants. The *Qāḍī* cannot deny her this right. It may be noted here, as stated before, that it seems that the words, "shall have a right to cancel it (marriage)" and similar expressions have been loosely used by the Muslim jurists. This is borne out by the fact that the jurists expressing the above view have at the same time stated that the marriage shall subsist till an order for its dissolution has been passed by the *Qāḍī*. What they seem to mean is that the wife shall have an absolute right to express her dissent to the marriage. The girl's dissent to

94. *Al-Fatāwā al-Hindiyah*, *op. cit.*, Vol. II, p. 10.

the marriage amounts to a declaration of her choice, that she does not want to submit to the marriage. As discussed before, her dissent does not dissolve the marriage and the same continues to subsist till the *Qāḍī* passes his order in the matter. The correct position is that the girl can exercise her option of repudiation and claim the dissolution of her marriage as a matter of right, but she has to satisfy the *Qāḍī* that she has complied with the legal formalities. Once this is done, the *Qāḍī* has no choice in the matter and has to pass a decree in the wife's favour.

(II) The view of the Muslim jurists that the *Qāḍī's* order is essential for the dissolution of a marriage, when the girl dissents to it, by the exercise of her option of puberty has been stated in various authoritative books on Muslim law. They have been discussed in a previous topic and need not be repeated here. It may, however, be stated once again that the Muslim jurists have definitely laid down the rule that the *Qāḍī's* order is essential for dissolution of marriage by a wife by the exercise of her option of puberty. But it has been stated in some books in English dealing with Muslim law that such is not the case and that the *Qāḍī's* order is not an essential condition of the dissolution of marriage in case of its repudiation by the girl on attaining majority. Ameer Ali was the first to express the view which has been followed by other writers and also by the majority of the Courts. He has relied upon and quoted a passage from *al-Radd al-Muḥtār*. It may be stated here that *al-Durr al-Mukhtār* of which *al-Radd al-Muḥtār* is a commentary has stated that the *Qāḍī's* order is an essential condition for the repudiation of a marriage.[95] The author of *al-Radd al-Muḥtār* has justified this rule on the ground that, "the girls option to repudiate the marriage is a weak right, hence the necessity to obtain the *Qāḍī's* order," and that, "the decree is required for establishing the cancellation of the marriage and not as a corroboration of repudiation by the wife. If the minor chooses to exercise

95. Ibn 'Ābidīn, *op. cit.*, Vol. II, p. 314.

the option of repudiation then the repudiation shall not be proved unless there is an order by the *Qāḍī*."[96] Ameer Ali has stated, "In short, when a minor boy and girl are married to each other by any person other than the father or grand-father, then they have an option to cancel the marriage on (attaining) puberty or on becoming cognisant of it (the marriage). If they decide on cancellation such cancellation shall not become confirmed (*lā yathbut al-faskh*) except by the decree of the *Kazi* . . ." The words, "*lā yathbut al-faskh*" are important in order to reach a correct interpretation of the view of *al-Radd al-Muḥtār*. The word "*thabt*" means "to exist, to strengthen, to conform". If the latter meaning are accepted then the expression, "*lā yathbut al-faskh*" shall mean that the *Qāḍī's* order merely confirms the repudiation already brought about by the girl. If the former meaning are accepted then the expression shall mean that the marriage shall subsist until it is dissolved by the *Qāḍī*. The other authors have also expressed the view that a marriage is not dissolved without the *Qāḍī's* decree and the same is an essential condition for the dissolution of marriage.[97] But leaving aside the interpretation of this expression, we find that all the Muslim jurists are agreed on the necessity of obtaining the *Qāḍī's* order and even *al-Radd al-Muḥtār* has accepted this view. It is only in discussing the reason for the necessity of the *Qāḍī's* order that the author has used the expression, "*la yathbut al-faskh*." But what is to be seen in this connection is not to find the justification for the rule but to ascertain the rule itself, namely, whether it is an essential condition for the dissolution of marriage by the exercise of the option of puberty that the *Qāḍī's* order must be obtained.

Al-Durr al-Mukhtār further makes the observation, "and they shall inherit from each other in this, that is, in the marriage, before the confirmation of its cancellation." Ameer Ali then gives his own conclusion and says, ". . . there

96. Ibn 'Ābidīn, *op. cit.*, Vol. II, p. 315.
97. Ibn Najaym, *op, cit.*, Vol. III, p. 128 ; Qāḍī Khān, *Fatāwā Qāḍī Khān*, Calcutta (Mustafa'i Press), Vol. I, p. 166.

can be no question regarding the right itself; no decree is required to affirm it . . . Then what does this condition imply? To my mind it means simply this—that in order to cause an effective cancellation or to impress on the act the judicial *imprimatur*, an order of the *Kazi* is necessary. Until that has been obtained, the *status* remains in an "inchoate" condition, the parties may lawfully cohabit which would amount to a recantation of the "option" or, if either of them were to die, a right of inheritance would be established in the survivor."[98] As observed before, if we translate the word "*thabt*" to mean "exist" then the expression, "*thabt al-faskh*" will mean that the cancellation shall not exist, that is, shall not take effect. Moreover, some important words used in the expression, quoted by him, have escaped the attention of Ameer Ali. The full passage reads as follows:

"*Lā yathbut al-faskh illā bi sharṭ al-qaḍā'*." The passage means, "if they (the minor boy or minor girl) choose cancellation of marriage then this cancellation shall not be established except by the order of the *Qāḍī*." It will be useful to quote from another book in this connection. It is stated in *Majma' al-Unhur*, "the *Qāḍi's* order has been made a condition for cancellation (of marriage) by the exercise of the option of puberty. whether it be exercised by a minor boy or a minor girl. Hence, marriage shall not be rendered void (cancelled) until it is decided by the *Qāḍī* because the marriage has come into existence and so it cannot be rendered void (cancelled) by mere dissent."[99] Further, it is stated, "hence if one of the two (spouses) dies before separation (then) the other shall be his or her heir whether he or she died while a major or not a major because the marriage is valid and ownership (of the marriage) is established by it (the marriage), hence when one of them dies then the marriage comes to an end. Whether he or she died before (attaining) majority or after (attaining) majority

98. Ameer Ali, *op. cit.*, Vol. II. p. 419.
99. Shaykhzādah. *op. cit.*, Vol. I. pp. 336-37.

because separation between them does not occur but where the *Qāḍī* gives his order. Hence, they shall be heirs (to each other) and the whole dower shall become due even when (it becomes due) before consummation of the marriage.[100] It is stated in *al-Muḥīṭ* that, "if one of the two (spouses) dies before cancellation by the *Qāḍī* then the other shall inherit to him or her because the status of marriage still subsists."

The very fact the spouses can cohabit even after the exercise of the option of puberty if they so like and that if one of them dies then the survivor inherits to the deceased, establishes clearly that the marriage has not been dissolved but continues to subsist. We must, therefore, determine the relative position and result of the two distinct steps, namely (*a*) the exercise of the option of puberty and (*b*) the *Qāḍī's* order. It is submitted that the exercise of option by a girl on attaining puberty merely establishes the fact that she does not agree to the marriage contracted for her during her minority by her guardian. It is her absolute right to agree or not to agree to the marriage. The Muslim jurists seem to have used the word "repudiation" in a loose way for their expression "the right to have the marriage repudiated," and this has led to a great deal of confusion amongst the modern writers and the Courts. *Al-Fatāwā al-Hindiyah* states, "if a minor boy and a minor girl are contracted in marriage by any guardian other than the father or the paternal grandfather then on attaining majority (puberty) each of them shall have a right to submit to the marriage or to cancel it."[101]

It is significant that at another place it clearly lays down that the *Qāḍī's* order is necessary for the cancellation of the marriage. As stated before, a girl has to establish the following facts before she becomes entitled to get her marriage dissolved under the indigenous Muslim laws:

(*a*) She was given in marriage while she was a minor,

(*b*) The person who gave her in marriage was some guardian other than her father or paternal grand-

100. Shaykhzādah *op, cit.*, Vol. I, p. 337.

101. *Al-Fatāwā al-Hindiyah, op. cit.*, Vol. II, p. 10.

father.

(*c*) She expressed her choice as soon as the sign of puberty appeared, and

(*d*) She has not acquiesced to the marriage on attaining puberty as by allowing intimacy to the husband, asking for maintenance, dower etc.

Now it is obvious that there must be some one to see and decide, if she has complied with these conditions and naturally it can only be the *Qāḍī* or the Court which can decide the matter. The purpose of obtaining the *Qāḍi's* order is to establish that she has faithfully complied with these requirements. The required order is not meant to confirm or to establish the dissolution of the marriage because the marriage is not dissolved by the declaration of the wife. But once the wife has decided to refuse to accept the marriage by exercising her option of puberty, the matter must be referred to the *Qāḍī* for his order. The wife's right is limited to taking a decision to continue the marriage or to get it dissolved. She, however, cannot by herself dissolve it. The *Qāḍi's* order is a condition precedent in many cases even when a party possesses an absolute right in the matter. Thus, for example, a person has got an absolute right to acquire a house when his immediate neighbour has sold it to a stranger and when that person has complied with certain formalities. He, however, does not become entitled to get physical possession over the same until and unless the *Qāḍī* passes an order in his favour. The *Qāḍī's* order is required not to establish the person's right but to see if he has complied with the necessary legal formalities. In the case of option of puberty the wife has to establish that she was a minor at the time of her marriage, that she has made a declaration of her dissent at the proper time etc. It is obvious that the *Qāḍī* has to see and determine if the wife has complied with these prerequisites. The dissolution of the marriage shall be effected only when the *Qāḍī* is satisfied in the matter and passes his order.

(III) Whether the marriage is dissolved immediately the girl declares her dissent to the marriage. The marriage is not terminated immediately on the repudiation of the wife. This, as stated above, is clear from the fact that it is open to the spouses to lawfully cohabit with each other. Thus it is stated in *Alamgīrīyah* that, if on attaining puberty the minor boy or girl chooses separation and the *Qāḍī* has not separated them then if one of them dies, they shall inherit to each other. And until the *Qāḍī* separates them till then it is lawful for the husband to cohabit with her."[102] If the marriage was terminated on the repudiation being pronounced or announced by the girl then it is obvious that no right to inheritance would be left while intimacy between the spouses would be unlawful and would amount to adultery as the separation amounts to an irrevocable divorce. This situation establishes the fact that the marriage is not terminated on the repudiation of the marriage by the minor. Ameer Ali has stated, "there can be no question regarding the right itself; no decree is required to affirm it . . . To my mind it means this—that in order to cause an effective cancellation or to impress on the act the judicial *imprimatur*, an order of the *Qāḍī* is necessary. Until that has been obtained, the *status* remains in an inchoate condition; the parties may lawfully cohabit which would amount to a recantation of the "option", or if either of them were to die, a right of inheritance would be established in the survivor."[103] It is submitted that there is some confusion in this observation. The expressions, "in order to cause an effective cancellation" and, "the status remains in an inchoate condition" are rather unhappy.

It may be noted here that the *Qāḍī's* order is certainly not meant or is necessary to "cause an effective cancellation." Under Muslim law, there is nothing like an effective cancellation. Either the marriage is cancelled or it is not cancelled. If the marriage was cancelled on the very exercise

102. *Al-Fatāwā al-Hindiyah op. cit.*, Vol. II., p. 10

103. Ameer Ali, *op. cit.*, p. 415.

of the option of puberty, then it cannot be open to the parties to be intimate with each other. Cohabitation under such circumstances would render them liable to punishment for adultery. Moreover, they would not be entitled to inherit to each other.

The status of marriage does not remain in an *inchoate* condition under Muslim law in any case. Either there exists a marriage when the parties hold the position of husband and wife or it does not exist when the spouses cease to hold that position. Even in the case of a revocable divorce, the status is not inchoate and the parties remain husband and wife till the divorce becomes irrevocable on the expiry of the prescribed period of the *'iddah* and the marriage certainly does not remain in an inchoate condition. The revocation of the divorce merely avoids the effect that would follow on the expiry of the *'iddah.*

It can be seen from the above discussion that the marriage is not dissolved by the exercise of the option of puberty by the wife, but continues to subsist till it is terminated by an order of the *Qāḍī.*

(IV) Whether the Court's decree is essential to the dissolution of marriage by the exercise of the option of puberty.

It has been seen above that the *Qāḍī's* order is an essential condition for the dissolution of marriage. The Civil Courts have now taken the place of the *Qāḍī* and so it can be assumed that a decree for the dissolution of marriage by the Court is also an essential condition. The opening clause of Section 2 of the Dissolution of Muslim Marriages Act, 1939, makes the whole position clear. It read as under :

"2. A woman married under Muslim law shall be entitled *to obtain a decree* for the dissolution of her marriage on any one or more of the following grounds, namely."

It can be seen from the above that the section gives a right to a woman to obtain a decree for the dissolution of her marriage; it does not entitle her to dissolve the marriage by herself. This leads to the obvious inference that it shall only be the decree of the Court which shall dissolve the marriage.

But here again, the girl shall have a right to the dissolution of her marriage by the exercise of her option of puberty if certain conditions specified in clause VII have been fulfilled. They are that (*i*) she must have been married before she attained the age of fifteen years in India and sixteen years in Pakistan ; (2) she repudiated the marriage before attaining the age of eighteen years and that (3) the marriage has not been consummated after the attainment of the age of majority. If the woman can establish that these conditions have been fulfilled then the Court cannot refuse to dissolve the marriage. As in the case of Muslim law a marriage subsists till an order is passed for its dissolution by the *Qāḍī*. Similarly the marriage shall subsist till a decree for its dissolution is passed by the Court. The section is explicit on this point. If a girl exercises the option of puberty then under Section 2 of the Act she can become entitled only to get a decree for the dissolution of her marriage. Her exercise of her right shall not dissolve the marriage. If the Legislature had intended to invest her with the power then Section 2 would have read somewhat as under :

"2. A woman married under Muslim law shall be entitled to obtain a declaration that her marriage had been dissolved on the ground that having been given in marriage. . ."

The opinion was expressed by the Sind Chief Court in a case that under the Act a woman cannot contract a second marriage without first obtaining the Court's decree dissolving her marriage and that the marriage subsists till such decree has been obtained. It was also pointed out that a woman is not under the indigenous Mohammadan law competent to repudiate the marriage contracted for her by her father. S. A. Rahman J. (as he then was) in an elaborate judgement did not agree with this view. He stated, "clause VII of Section 2 (of the Act) is really based on the opinion of one school of thought in Islam. It is true that among the Ḥanafīs generally the view prevailed that a marriage arranged by the father was not subject to the right of repudiation. The view of the Muʿtazilah and *Mālikīs* was, however, always different".[104] It is submitted that under the Mālikī law also, a marriage contracted for a girl by her father is held binding on her. It is only with regard to a marriage arranged by the paternal grandfather that is not binding on her. She can, therefore, use her option of puberty in respect of such a marriage. But she cannot use her option in respect of a marriage contracted for her by her father. The Mu'tazilī School has practically ceased to exist. It was also stated in the Lahore ruling, "Section 2 of Act VIII of 1939, therefore, did no more than recognise an existing view of Mohammadan Law, which was obviously considered by the Legislature to be more in accord with the liberal spirit of the age. It would be incorrect to say, therefore, that a new remedy was provided by the Legislature. To my mind, the position, as recognized now, is that a marriage, arranged by the father or the paternal grandfather during a girl's minority stands on the same footing as regards the option of puberty as a marriage arranged by any other guardian. The mere fact that Section 2 gives a right to a girl in this position to a decree for dissolution of marriage does not imply that apart from the provisions of Section 2, she has no right to exercise the option of puberty in such cases." It is true that the Act has done away with the distinction between marriages contracted by the father or the paternal grandfather on the one hand and those contracted by other guardians on the other hand, but then the provisions of the Act are to be fully followed and complied with before relief can be obtained under it. The Act does allow the repudiation of marriage by a girl on attaining majority even when it was contracted by the father or the paternal grandfather, but it does make it a condition of such repudiation that the marriage should be dissolved by the Court by its decree. It only entitles and establishes the right of a girl to get such a decree if the necessary conditions are satisfied. The marriage is not dissolved until and unless such a decree has been passed. The

104. Mohammad Bukhsh Vs. Crown, P.L.D., 1950, Lah., 403.

Act, no doubt, has taken a view which is more in accord with the liberal spirit of the age, but we cannot ignore the definite provisions laid down by the Legislature and have to follow the provisions of the law as they are. The Court has also discussed the Muslim law in this respect and has referred to the opinion of Ameer Ali, but both of these matters have been fully discussed before and need not be repeated here. This view was accepted in a later case by the same High Court.[105] A case involving the same point again came up for decision before the Calcutta High Court. It was held by that Court and, with respect it is submitted, rightly that under the indigenous Mohammadan Law, "the option of puberty" cannot be exercised validly by the girl (wife) to affect the marriage-tie, when she was given in marriage by the father or the paternal grandfather as guardian, except possibly, under very special circumstances.[106] A similar view was expressed by the High Court of Mad. Pradesh when it was held that a decree of the Court is necessary for the dissolution of marriage.[107]

In short, the position now is that the exercise of the option of puberty by a girl makes it clear that she does not accept the marriage, but her dissent alone does not dissolve the marriage. The marriage continues to subsist until she obtains the order of the Court. This is clear from the fact, as pointed out before, that the parties can lawfully cohabit even after the exercise of the option of puberty which could not have been done if the marriage were dissolved on the very exercise of the option of puberty as the separation amounts to an annulment and so intimacy between the spouses would be unlawful and this right will be lost only when the *Qāḍī* passes his order. To hold otherwise would open the door for bigamy for it will always be open to such a girl to contract another marriage on attaining majority and when prosecuted

105. P.L.D., 1956, Lahore, 712.

106. Shaib Ali Biswas Vs. Jinnatan Nahar, A.I.R., 1960, Cal., 717.

107. Pir Mohammad Kukail Vs. the State of Madhya Pradesh, A.I.R., 1960, Madhya Pradesh, 24.

for bigamy to set up the defence that she had already dissolved her former marriage by the exercise of the option of puberty. It is pertinent to note that the Shāfi'ī and Shī'ī laws do allow a wife to dissolve the marriage by herself in certain cases without the intervention of the *Qāḍī*, but repudiation by the exercise of the option of puberty is not one of them. The above discussion would show clearly that the Court's order is an essential condition for the dissolution of marriage by the exercise of the option of puberty.

IX. Bigamy

Another important question that arises in connection with *Khiyār al-Bulūgh* or option of puberty is whether a girl can be considered guilty of bigamy if she contracts another marriage after exercising her option of puberty but without obtaining the Court's decree in that behalf. Before discussing the matter it is necessary to study the provisions relating to bigamy. It is given in Section 494 of the Penal Code and reads as under :

494. Whoever, having *a husband or wife living*, marries in any case in which *such marriage is void by reason of its taking place during the life of such husband or wife*, shall be punished with imprisonment of either description for a term which may extend to seven years, and shall also be liable to fine.

Exception :—

This section does not extend to any person whose marriage with such husband or wife *has been declared void by a court of competent jurisdiction*, nor to any person who contracts a marriage during the life of a former husband or wife, if such husband or wife, at the time of the subsequent marriage, shall have been continuously absent from such person for the space of seven years and shall not have been heard of by such person as being alive within that time, provided the person contracting such subsequent marriage shall, before such marriage takes place, inform the person with whom such marriage is contracted of the real state of facts so far as the same are within his or, knowledge."

There are certain important expressions used in the above section which require careful consideration, important ones being the following :—

I. Having a husband or wife living,

II. Has been declared void by a Court of competent jurisdiction, and

III. Such marriage is void by reason of its taking place during the life of such husband or wife.

I. The first factor provides that the husband or the wife should be living. It means that the first marriage should be subsisting because once it is terminated, the spouses cease to hold that status ; the person who formerly was the husband or the wife may be living, but he or she no longer holds the status of being the husband or wife of the other so that he or she is not living as a husband or wife of the other, but is living in his individual capacity. It has been discussed before that a marriage continues to subsist even after the exercise of the option of puberty so that the spouses continue to hold their respective legal character even after the exercise of the option of puberty. This leads to the conclusion that a girl shall be guilty of bigamy under the provisions of the Act if she contracts a second marriage before the dissolution of the former marriage by the decree of a Court.

II. The second factor envisages that a competent Court has declared the first marriage to be void. In the case of the exercise of option of puberty, the Court does not declare the marriage to be void but merely dissolves it and such a case shall fall under the first factor. The Court may give a declaration that a certain marriage has been dissolved or that the woman is not the wife of the man. Such a declaration shall serve the purpose. No criminal Court will be so technical as to ignore such a declaration. The wife, if she contracts a second marriage after obtaining a decree for the dissolution of her former marriage or a declaration that the marriage does not exist, cannot be considered to be guilty of bigamy.

III. The third factor indicates that such marriage (namely, the second marriage) is void by reason of its taking place during the life of such husband or wife : it may be stated here that under Muslim law *shubhat al-'aqd* or marriage under misapprehension is considered to be *fāsid* or irregular. Ameer Ali has stated in his learned and useful book on Muslim law, that, "The Indian Law Courts have often convicted of bigamy girls who in their infancy had been contracted in marriage by their guardians but who, on attaining their majority, had married other men. In any case, these convictions would be wrong, for supposing even consummation had taken place after the first marriage, the subsequent marriage being *shubhat al-'aqd*, neither the women nor the men marrying them would *under Mohammadan Law* be liable to any punishment though the *Qāḍī* might give back the woman to the first husband."[108]

This view of Ameer Ali has been accepted as correct and has been followed in several cases.[109] But this factor of the offence involves an important aspect which requires careful consideration. *Shubhat al-'aqd* means that the woman under a misapprehension that her first marriage was not subsisting and was dissolved on the exercise of the option of puberty contracts a second marriage sincerely believing that she was doing a lawful act whereas such is not the case. As she had contracted the second marriage under a sincere belief that her second marriage was lawful and had no intention of contravening the law, Muslim law does not hold her to be guilty of adultery and so does not impose any punishment on her. In this interpretation of law, the Muslim jurists followed their legal maxim that punishment should not be inflicted on a person when there is the least ground for doubt of the accused's

108. Ameer Ali, *op. cit.*, Vol. II, pp. 416-418.

109. Bulanda Vs. E., 83 C. 494 ; Ghulam Mohammad Vs. E., A.I.R., 1933, Lahore, 88 ; Mst. Hajul Vs. Palo. A.I.R. 1936. Sind, 189 ; Mohammad Bakhsh Vs. Crown, P.L.D., 1950, Lahore, 133; Mafizuddin Vs. Rahima Bibi, A.I R., 1934, Cal., 104, etc.

guilt. Muslim law, therefore, accepts the wife's explanation as correct and does not punish her for adultery in the case when the second marriage amounts to *shubhat al-'aqd.* The question whether a marriage can be considered to be *shubhat al-'aqd* present considerable difficulty with regard to its application in a criminal case. It may be pointed out that under the existing law, as well as under the Muslim law, ignorance of law, as a general rule, is not considered sufficient to absolve a person from the consequences of his or her act. Under the Muslim law of evidence the wife's statement on oath would be accepted as correct that she was ignorant of the true legal position and had acted *bona fide* under a sincere belief that her first marriage had been dissolved by virtue of the exercise of option of puberty. If her husband were to contradict her on oath then the matter would be decided on its merits. Under the law applicable in Pakistan and India the mere statement of the accused unsupported by any evidence would not be considered sufficient to absolve her of the offence. It would obviously be difficult for the wife to produce convincing evidence in support of her mental state that she was ignorant of the correct legal position. The Muslim laws of evidence, criminal procedure and crimes have been superseded and under the existing law the prosecution would find no difficulty in establishing the wife's guilt by proving the two marriages when the burden would lie on the wife to prove her innocence. Ameer Ali has expressed the view that, "the subsequent marriage being *shubhāt al-'aqd*, neither the women nor the men marrying them would *under the Mohammadan Law* be liable to any punishment.[110] This view is, it is respectfully submitted, quite correct, but it does not solve the difficulty. The problem before us is whether the woman or the man marrying her would be liable to punishment for bigamy under the existing laws which have superseded the Muslim laws of crimes and evidence. Ameer Ali has not discussed the matter from this point of view. It can

110. Ameer Ali, *op. cit.*, p. 416.

be easily realised that in Ameer Ali's time, Muslim women suffered great hardship and naturally he must have felt it necessary to interpret the law within permissible limits in such a way as to be helpful to them. But now the laws have been modified in many cases so as to restore the rights given by Islam to women. Moreover, girls can no longer be given in marriage in their infancy. Under the Child Marriage Restraint Act, a girl cannot be contracted in marriage in Pakistan unless she is sixteen years old and in India unless she is fourteen years of age. It is, therefore, no longer necessary to stretch the law, in order to provide relief to women. We must also remember that due to degeneration and low standard of morality too much faith cannot be placed in the explanation of a woman accused of bigamy. Care has to be taken so as not open the door for immorality and defiance of law. The Courts which have considered *shubhat al-'aqd* to be a good defence have not generally discussed the matter, but have merely quoted Ameer Ali.

The Muslim laws of marriage and divorce are still extant and so a marriage under misapprehension or *shubhat al-'aqd* will give rise to certain civil rights. Thus, the children born of such a marriage shall be considered to be legitimate. But the mere allegation that the second marriage amounted to *shubhat al-'aqd* will not in all probability be considered sufficient by a criminal Court for the acquittal of the woman. The provision to the section provides that a woman shall not be considered guilty of the offence of bigamy if her first marriage *has been declared void by a Court of competent jurisdiction.* It is obvious that it can be only a Civil Court which can give such a declaration. A marriage under misapprehension or *shubhat al-'aqd* is not a void marriage but only a *fāsid* marriage. There is not much difference between the two and a declaration that a marriage is *fāsid* shall be covered by the proviso. This, however, is more or less only an academic matter, because if a woman can get such a declaration then she can equally get a declaration that her first marriage has been dissolved by the exercise of her option of puberty. This proviso gives an indication that the Criminal Court shall not be satisfied by the mere allegation of the woman that she had contracted the second marriage under misapprehension. It may require the wife to produce an order of a Court of competent jurisdiction to show that her first marriage was void and it is suggested that Criminal Court should pass such an order in the interest of justice. An order that her first marriage had been dissolved would be equally effective to establish that the wife was not guilty of bigamy.

It is again a debatable point whether a Muslim woman can get a declaration that there is no relationship of husband and wife between her and the alleged husband, and in the alternative for a decree for dissolution of marriage. These points arose in a case in which the wife filed a suit against her husband for a declaration that the defendant had terminated the marriage . . . by an oral *ṭalāq* and in the alternative for a decree for dissolution of marriage on the ground of adultery. During the pendency of the suit, the husband filed a complaint under Section 498/380 of P.P.C. The wife applied to the High Court for a stay of proceedings in the Criminal Court pending the decision of the civil suit. The Court observed " . . . However, a declaration of non-existence of marriage granted in an ordinary suit by the Court is not a judgement in the exercise of the matrimonial jurisdiction merely because it relates to a marriage. It is just a declaration under Section 42 of the Specific Relief Act. Matrimonial jurisdiction . . . is a special jurisdiction. If a declaration be of a kind which can be granted by an ordinary Civil Court, and it be claimed that it is in fact in exercise of a special jurisdiction, reference has to be made to some law which creates such jurisdiction. In the case of Christians and in respect of marriages under the Special Marriage Act, the *Legislature* has created a special jurisdiction for matrimonial causes which enables the Court to make binding pronouncement as to existence of marriage but there is no similar jurisdiction given to Courts in other cases." The Court also observed, "if the declaration be on account of divorce, it obviously simply recognises the fact of non-existence of a marriage and the position is not different in the case of repudiation on attaining puberty. Such repudiation puts an end to the marriage without the aid of any Court, and when the matter comes to Court, the Court does not dissolve the marriage by its own act, but recognises the termination of marriage." The Court dismissed the application for want of jurisdiction.[111] A case of somewhat the same nature was decided by the Tripura Judicial Commissioner's Court. In that case the husband got the wife arrested under a warrant in a criminal case. The wife filed a suit for a declaration that she was not the wife of A. B. and in case the Court found that the marriage had been performed during her minority, the same be dissolved as she exercised her option of puberty after attaining puberty. The Court observed, "Legal character is the same thing as a man's status." (A.I.R. 1951 Madras 584). According to Holland, the chief varieties of status among natural persons may be referred to the following causes: (1) Sex, . . . (4) coverture, (5) celibacy . . . It will be clear from the above that "Legal character" is the same thing as status and status includes sex, coverture, celibacy etc. . . . the plaintiff's suit for a declaration that she had not been married to the defendant thus involved a question of her status and also a legal character . . . If the defendant without any good reason asserted that the plaintiff-respondent was his legally wedded wife and when it is proved in this case that no marriage actually took place and the defendant got her arrested in execution of a warrant issued by the Criminal Court, I think the circumstances of this case fully justified of the declaration prayed for in the peculiar circumstances of the case. The granting of declaratory relief is discretionary and I think the Courts below exercised their discretion properly in declaring that the defendant was not the husband of the plaintiff and, consequently, he had no right to harass her by obtaining warrant etc. against her through Criminal Court or

111. Mst. Muni Vs. Habib Khan, P.L.D., 1956, Lahore, 403.

in any other manner . . . [112] Husband's suit for restitution of conjugal rights : Another question that sometimes arises is whether in a suit for restitution of conjugal rights by the husband is it open to the wife to set up a defence that she had already dissolved her marriage by the exercise of her option of puberty. It has already been discussed before that the marriage is not dissolved by the wife's exercise of the option of puberty as long as she does not get the *Qāḍī's* order for its dissolution. It has, however, been held by the Calcutta High Court that it is not necessary for the wife to get a decree of the Court in proceedings independent of the husband's suit.[113] The same view has been expressed by the Madha Bharat High Court.[114]

It is respectfully submitted that the above view is correct. As stated above the *Qāḍī's* order is meant only to determine whether the wife has fully complied with the necessary requirements. It is immaterial whether he is satisfied about this matter in a suit for dissolution of marriage or when the wife seeks only a declaration to that effect. It has been stated above that the *Qāḍī* cannot refuse to dissolve the marriage if the wife satisfies him that she has complied with the prescribed conditions. Hence, his declaration that the marriage has been dissolved amounts to his implied dissolution of the same though the order is couched in different language.

X. *Dower*

When a separation takes place by the exercise of the option of puberty and the marriage has not been consummated the wife has no title to dower. But if the marriage had been consummated, she is entitled to her full dower irrespective of the fact whether the separation has taken place by her own option or by the option of her husband.[115]

112. Abdul Barik Vs. Khatoon, A.I.R., 1955, Tripura, 2.

113. Sadar Ali Karikar Vs. Srimati Abeda Bibi, A.I.R., 1928, Cal., 549.

114. Batoolan Vs. Zahoor Shah, A.I.R., 1952, Madha Bharat, 30; Nizamuddin Vs. Hussaini. A.I.R., 1960, Madha Bharat, 12.

115. *Al-Fatāwā al-Hindiyah, op. cit.*, Vol. II. p. 11.

XI. Nature of Separation

A separation between a wife and her husband in consequence of the exercise of the option of puberty does not amount to a divorce if it proceeds from the wife. It is merely an annulment or cancellation of the marriage.[116] If the marriage is annulled on the initiative of the husband then it shall amount to an irrevocable divorce.[117] By the exercise of the option of puberty the marriage ceases to be a marriage and must be deemed as having never taken place.

XII. Limitation

It has been stated above that under the provisions of Section 2 (VII) of the Dissolution of Muslim Marriages Act, a girl shall be entitled to cancel a marriage contracted during her minority up to the time when she attains the age of eighteen years. As discussed before, this period may be extended if she was ignorant of her marriage or of her right to cancel the same. The provision about the enlargement of the time for the exercise of her right is a substantial part of Muslim law and shall be considered to be still extant. It is akin to the provisions of Section 5 of the Limitation Act and is based on equity.

But it is not necessary that she should institute her suit before the attainment of the age of eighteen years. It is only the right that has to be exercised by that time. She can institute a suit within the period of limitation calculated from the time when the cause of action arose which shall be the time when she exercised her option of puberty. Under Article 120 of the Limitation Act the suit must be instituted within six years of the cause of action.

116. *Al-Fatāwā al-Hindiyāh, op. cit,* Vol. II, p. 11, al-Marghīnanī, *op. cit.*, Vol. II, p. 298.

117. *Ibid.*

Chapter 11

TAFWĪḌ OR DELEGATION OF THE POWER OF DIVORCE

I. Preliminary

It has already been stated that a husband can divorce his wife without the intervention of the Court. He can either exercise the right of dissolving the marriage by himself or appoint an agent to exercise this power on his behalf or, in other words, he can delegate his power of divorcing his wife to another person who may be the wife herself. This delegation of power of divorce to the wife is called *Tafwīḍ* and is well recognized in Muslim law.

As already stated elsewhere, marriage in some religions is a sacrament and so indissoluble. This is not so in Islam. Marriage amongst the Muslims is practically a civil contract as far as the parties to it are concerned. This is borne out by the fact that under the Muslim law the husband has the right to divorce his wife. The wife also has, under certain conditions, the right to dissolve the marriage, *e.g.*, by the exercise of the option of puberty, *K͟hul'* etc. A man and woman entering into a contract of marriage may also impose certain conditions upon which their marriage is to take place. The imposed conditions would define their future marital rights and obligations *inter se* so as to modify the rights and obligations that ordinarily flow from a valid marriage. The spouses may, for example, enter into an agreement under which the wife secures from the prospective husband the power to divorce herself on his behalf. Such an agreement amounts to a delegation of his power by the husband and the pronouncing of the divorce by the wife amounts to the husband's pronouncing it. Such delegation of power may be either conditional or unconditional. It is of course obvious that the terms and conditions that may be agreed upon should be such as are valid under the Muslim law.

II. Definition

The Muslim jurists have divided the delegation of the power to divorce by the husband into three classes, namely,

(*a*) *Tafwīḍ*, that is, delegation ;
(*b*) *Tawkīl* or agency and
(*c*) *Risālah* or messengership.

These three classes differ from one another as discussed below :

Tafwīḍ.—The wife to whom the power is delegated exercises it in respect of her own person and has got a right to exercise the power or not to do it.

Tawkīl.—In *Tawkīl*, the husband appoints an agent to divorce his wife on his (the husband's) behalf. The agent exercises the power delegated to him in respect of another, that is, the wife. He has no authority to continue the marriage, as such power has not been given to him, but can only divorce the wife.

Risālah.—In *Risālah* the husband appoints a person, his messenger, to convey his message to the wife that he has delegated the power to her (wife).[1]

The power given by *Tafwīḍ* cannot be revoked, but the other two can be revoked by the husband as long as it has not been exercised.[2] But the case would be different if the husband gives an option to the *vakīl* (agent) to divorce his wife whenever he may like or not to do so as the agent may desire or choose.[3]

III. Religious Sanction

The doctrine of the delegation of the power of divorce is based on an incident mentioned in the Qur'ān wherein

1. Ibn 'Ābidīn, *Radd al-Muḥtār*, Cairo, 1318 A.H., Vol. II, p. 487.
2. *Ibid.*, pp. 488-89.
3. *Ibid.*, p. 489.

the Prophet (peace be upon him) told his wives that they were at liberty to live with him or to get separated from him as they chose. Thus it is stated:

> O Prophet ! say
> To thy consorts,
> If it be that ye desire
> The life of this world
> And its glitter,—then come,
> I will provide for your
> Enjoyment and set you free
> In a handsome manner.[4]

It is explained by the Muslim jurists that the Prophet (peace be on him) had, in obedience to the above injunction of the Qur'ān, empowered his wives to choose either him or a separation, that is, they might either get the marriages dissolved or prefer to choose their continuation. 'Ā'ishah has explained that we (the wives) chose the Prophet (peace be on him), that is, we preferred the continuation of the marriages, and so we were not divorced and the marriages were not dissolved. It is inferred from this Tradition that a husband can lawfully delegate to his wife the power to dissolve the marriage if she so wants.

IV. *Safeguard for Wife*

It is a very important provision of Muslim law of marriage and enables a wife to safeguard her future married life. She can make it a condition of her marriage that the husband should delegate his power of divorce to her so that she can exercise it, that is, divorce herself on his behalf, whenever she is not satisfied with his behaviour or the husband commits a breach of the terms agreed upon. Such a divorce by her will take effect as if a divorce had been pronounced by the husband himself.[5]

4. Qur'an XXI : 28, Surah Al Ahzāb.
5. Mohammad Amin Vs. Amina Bibi, A.I.R. 1931, Lah. 134.

V. Power, how Delegated

A husband can authorise another person to dissolve the marriage in three ways, namely,

(*a*) *Tafwīḍ* or delegation, that is, when he gives the authority or power to his wife to dissolve the marriage. In such a case it depends on the wife to dissolve the marriage or not to do so.

(*b*) *Tawkīl* or appointing an agent to dissolve the marriage on his behalf. The agent has to comply with the husband's desire and can act only within the terms of the authority, but cannot go against it. In other words, it is not open to him not to dissolve the marriage, and

(*c*) *Risālah* or appointing a messenger who merely informs the wife that the husband has delegated the power to dissolve the marriage to her.[6] It is obvious that the messenger cannot dissolve or maintain the marriage.

Delegation of the Power to Divorce.—The delegation of the power of divorce may be unconditional or conditional so that its exercise may be made to depend on the occurrence or non-occurrence of a certain specified contingency. This is clear from the illustrative cases discussed by Muslim jurists in connection with delegation of the power to divorce. Thus the husband may authorise the wife to divorce herself if he marries another woman. In such a case the wife shall be entitled to exercise the power only when he marries another woman.[7] Similarly, he may authorise the wife to divorce herself if he fails to pay her maintenance within a specified period of time. In such a case the wife shall become entitled to divorce herself if he fails to do so.[8]

6. Ibn 'Ābidīn, *op cit.*, Vol. II, p. 487. Cf. *al-Durr al-Mukhtār* on the margin of *Radd al-Muḥtār*, Vol. II, p. 487.
7. *Al-Fatāwā al-Hindiyah*, Kanpur, 1349 A.H., Vol. II, pp. 72-73.
8. Ibn 'Ābidīn, *op. cit.*, Vol. II, p. 493.

It is a necessary condition for the exercise of the power by the wife that she should not have contributed to the breach of the condition by the husband. Thus a husband may authorise the wife to divorce herself on his failure to maintain her for a specified period of time. He fails to do so but his failure is due to the fact that the wife refuses to live with him without any justification. In such circumstances the wife is not entitled to exercise the power as she refused to live with him, and so she becomes disentitled to be maintained by the husband.

The Muslim jurists see no objection in the grant of an absolute power of divorce by the husband to the wife. They have considered the matter from the point of *tamlīk* or transfer of a right and agency. The various acts are divided by Muslim jurists into two classes, namely, *ithbātāt* or such acts as create rights and *isqāṭāt* or such acts as destroy or extinguish certain right or rights. The act of divorcing the wife destroys a right vested in the husband and so falls under the second class, namely, *isqāṭ*. Under Muslim law the transfer of one's right to another is called *tamlīk* and the person who possesses the right is called the *Mumallik* while the transferee is called *Mumallak*. In case of the transfer of a thing or right, the transfer must be absolute so that the transferee becomes the absolute owner of the thing or right transferred while the transferor loses his right in the thing or the right altogether. Morever, *tamlīk* cannot be made conditional so that the transferor may retain some right in the thing or right transferred while the transferee may not become its absolute owner. We have seen that in case of *tafwīḍ* or transfer of the power to divorce both the wife and the husband can exercise it. It means in other words that the husband does not absolutely divest himself of the right transferred to the wife. Moreover, *tafwīḍ* or the transfer of rightto effect a divorce can be made conditional so that the wife can effect a divorce only under certain specified circumstances. Both these incidents attached to *tafwīḍ* show that the conditions prescribed for *tamlīk* have not been fulfilled. It is also a necessary condition of *tamlīk* that it must be accepted in the same *majlis* or sitting in which the right is transferred. But in the case of *isqāṭ* a condition can be attached to the exercise of the act extinguishing the right so that the right can be invested subject to certain conditions. It is also not necessary in the case of *isqāṭ* that it should be accepted in the same *majlis* in which the right is vested in *Mumallak* or transferee and it is not revocable. The above discussion will show that while *tafwīḍ al-ṭalāq* amounts to *tamlīk* yet it differs in some respects from the same. Some Muslim jurists have explained that *tafwīḍ* is a special kind of *tamlīk* as is clear, according to them, from the fact that in case of ordinary *tamlīk*, the original owner loses altogether the ownership of the thing or the right but in the case of *tafwīḍ* he retains his right of divorce while the wife is also invested with it. In other words, both the husband and the wife become owner of the right of divorce which goes against the principle regarding *tamlīk*, stated above. These jurists state that *tafwīḍ* only partially partakes the character of *tamlīk* and so a condition can be attached to the exercise of the right. The husband cannot revoke the power once he has given it to the wife. But other Muslim jurists have pointed out the fallacy in this line of argument. They have explained that the husband no doubt possesses the right of divorcing the wife by himself but that it is not necessary that he should himself exercise the power of divorcing the wife; he can appoint a deputy or agent for the purpose and this deputy or agent may be the wife herself. What he transfers to the wife under the doctrine of *tafwīḍ* is not the right of divorce, but the right to effect a divorce which is different and distinct from the right of divorce.[9] Hence on *tafwīḍ al-ṭalāq* the husband retains his power of divorce as the same has not been transferred to the wife. The wife, on the other hand, becomes an agent merely to effect a divorce. An agent can exercise only such power as has been given to him or her and cannot exceed that limit.

9. Ibn Nujaym, *al-Baḥr al-Rā'iq*, Cairo, 1311 A.H., Vol. III, p. 335 *f*.

The *Ḥanafīs* also state that in the absence of words showing a different intention, the wife must exercise the power immediately in the same *majlis* in which she gets the information that such power has been invested in her. But the husband may make it clear that the wife could exercise the power given to her at any time she may like. Thus the husband may say to his wife, "Divorce yourself whenever you like". In such a case the wife is not bound to exercise the power immediately she is informed of the investment of the power, or even in the same *majlis*, but she can wait and can exercise the power at her own convenience. This discussion will show that there are two classes of *tafwīḍ*, namely,

1. *Tafwīḍ* restricted in time so that it has to be exercised immediately or in the same *majlis* in which the wife gets information of the same,

2. General power to effect a divorce, unrestricted in time.

In the case of the first class, the power must be exercised in the *majlis* or sitting in which information is conveyed to her. The wife's right shall be extinguished once the said time has expired and the sitting comes to an end. In the second case the wife's right shall extend indefinitely. Some jurists state that there may be a third class of expression as when the husband uses such language as does not belong to either of the above expressions. In this case he does not restrict the exercise of the power to a particular time nor indicates that it is to be used whenever the wife may like. But strictly legally such expressions are included in the first class and the power has to be exercised by the wife in the same *majlis*.[10]

As stated above, the delegation may be unconditional when the wife is allowed to divorce herself either immediately

10. For full discussion see Ibn Nujaym, *op. cit.*, Vol. III, pp. 335-37; Ibn al-Humam, *Fatḥ al-Qadir*, Cairo, 1356 A.H., Vol. III, p. 99 *f*; Ibn Àbidīn, *op. cit.*, Vol. II, p. 513 *f*; al-Kāsānī, *Badā'i al-Ṣanāi'*, Cairo, 1910 A.D., Vol. III, p. 113 *f*.

when the power is delegated to her or when she receives the news or whenever she may so desire. A very large number of cases given in *Fatāwā 'Alamgīryah* and other books, while dealing with the subject of *tafwīḍ*, are such as contain an unconditional delegation of the power of divorce to the wife by the husband.

Under the Muslim law the power may be delegated by the husband orally or in writing. It may be delegated prior to, at the time of or subsequent to a marriage.

VI. Language to be used for Delegation

No particular form or expression is prescribed for the delegation of the power of divorce by the husband. All that is necessary is that there must be a definite delegation of the power in unequivocal terms. The Muslim jurists have discussed a large number of expressions of delegation of the power to divorce but they do not constitute an exhaustive list of such expressions and are meant as merely illustrations. This is clear from the fact that the various books such as *al-Hidāyah*, and *al-Durr al-Mukhtār*, *Fatāwā Qāḍī Khān* and others do not contain identical expressions and some have given only a few of them.

Classification of Expressions.—The Muslim jurists have divided the expressions by which the power is delegated to the wife into three classes, namely,

1. *Ikhtiyār* or choice,
2. *Amr bi'l-yad* or liberty, and
3. *Mashīyat* or pleasure.[11]

The expression known as *Ikhtiyār* or choice is such as denotes an offer by the husband to the wife of a choice either to divorce herself or not to do so. It is of the form "choose yourself", "divorce thyself" etc.[12] The second class of expressions called *Amr bi'l-yad* or "thy business in thy hand"

11. Al-Marghīnānī, *al-Hidāyah*, Delhi, *n.d.*, Vol. II, pp. 358-365; Ibn 'Ābidīn, *op. cit.*, Vol. II, p. 487.
12. Ibn 'Ābidīn, *op. cit.*, Vol. II, pp. 487-88.

means that "you are at liberty to do as you please" or in other words, that the husband has entrusted his power of divorce to the wife who can exercise it just like him.[13] The third class of such expressions called *Mas̲h̲īyat* or pleasure or option means that it depends on the pleasure of the wife whether to divorce herself or not to do so. Thus the husband may say to his wife, "Divorce yourself if you desire" meaning that he has given the power to her to divorce herself or not to do so as she may please.[14]

As stated before, the Muslim jurists have stated many Arabic sentences to illustrate these various classes of expressions by which the power to divorce is delegated to the wife. These sentences are very technical and cannot be properly translated in Urdu or English. Moreover, they are not used in India or Pakistan and it will not serve any useful purpose to translate them. It has been, therefore, considered sufficient to state here the general rules of law that may be deduced from them. It will be preferable to follow these general rules than to get involved in the quandary of those uncommon expressions used in the old Arabic books on *Fiqh*. It will be risky to follow them too rigidly as their translation cannot give a clear sense of the original sentences.

VII. Basic Rules

Wife's Exercise of the Power.—The wife has to be careful about the expression she uses to exercise the power delegated to her. The expression must convey the sense of absolute separation between the parties. The Muslim jurists do not infer the intention of the wife from an incomplete expression but make it essential for her that she must declare her intention in clear and unambiguous terms. Thus if the husband says to his wife, "Divorce yourself", and should the wife reply, "I accept myself" (*ik̲h̲tartu nafsī*), then no divorce shall be

13. Al-Marg̲h̲īnānī, *op. cit.*, Vol. II, p. 358; Ibn 'Ābidīn, *op. cit.*, Vol. II, p. 487.

14. Al-Marg̲h̲īnānī, *op. cit.*, Vol. II, p. 360; Ibn 'Ābidīn, *op. cit.*, Vol. II, p. 489.

effected.[15] They also emphasise the use of the correct expression by the wife. Thus if the husband has delegated the power to his wife saying, "Choose" and the wife says, "I have chosen", then no divorce shall be effected because the husband's delegation and the wife's reply do not convey the idea of severance of the marriage-tie.[16] Similarly, if the wife says to her husband, "I want to tell you something or I want to do a certain thing, do you accept it" ? and should the husband say, "Yes, I accept it's". The wife then divorces herself (on his behalf) then no divorce shall be effected for want of intention to divorce which is necessary when the expression is not *ṣarīḥ* (clear). If the husband understands what the wife wants to say or do and he allows the wife to proceed then a divorce shall be effected.[17] A divorce shall be effected when the husband says, "Choose a repudiation" and the wife replies, "I choose". Similarly, a divorce shall result if the husband says, "Choose" and the wife replies, "I have chosen a repudiation". It can be seen that these two sentences taken together make it clear that the wife has exercised her power and has terminated the marriage.[18]

This rule is rather technical and what is necessary is that the wife should make it quite clear that she is divorcing herself under the power delegated to her. But of course there should be no ambiguity in the expression used by her. She must make it fully clear that she was dissolving the marriage and completely severing the relationship of husband and wife. The wife has to address the husband if he is present. If he is absent then she has to inform him that she has divorced herself.[19]

15. Al-Marghīnānī, *op. cit.*, Vol. II, p. 360; Ibn 'Ābidīn, *op. cit.*, Vol. II, p. 491.
16. *Ibid.*
17. *Al-Fatāwā al-Hindīyah*, *op. cit.*, Vol. II, pp. 71-72.
18. Al-Marghīnānī, *op. cit.*, Vol. II, p. 356; Ibn Ābidīn, *op. cit.*, Vol. II, p. 491.
19. Ibn 'Ābidīn, *op. cit.*, Vol. II, p. 488.

When the husband vests this power in his wife, she does not become entitled to act on her own behalf but only as a representative or agent of the husband. Hence if she says to her husband, "I have divorced thee", then this statement will be ineffective for actually she represents the husband. Moreover, divorce is attributed to a woman and not to man.[20] She has, therefore, to use an expression like the following, "I am unlawful on thee", "I am absolutely separated from thee", "I divorce myself on thy behalf" or "I divorce myself under the power delegated to me by thee".[21]

It was remarked in a case that the wife would be at libery to divorce the husband when he committed a breach of the conditions agreed upon.[22] Here, it seems, the expression 'divorce the husband' was somewhat loosely used and she was merely acting as an agent of the husband and she cannot divorce the husband but herself.

VIII. Capacity

Husband's Capacity.—A delegation to be valid must fulfil certain requirements. Thus the husband must possess certain capacity. The husband must possess the same capacity for delegating the power of divorce to his wife as in the case of divorce. He should be major and sane in order to be competent to lawfully delegate his power of divorce to his wife or to another person.

The majority will be determined by the provisions of the Muslim law and not by the Majority Act. Hence a person who is major under the provisions of Muslim law but a minor under the Majority Act can lawfully delegate to his wife or to another person the power to divorce [23] It has been held by a Court that even if the parties are minors, consent on his or her behalf can be expressed by the guardian for marriage who

20. Ibn 'Ābidīn, *op. cit.*, Vol. II, p. 495.
21. *Ibid.*
22. Saifuddin Shaikh Vs. Mst. Soneka Bibi, A.I.R. 1955, Assam, 153.
23. Mst. Fatima Vs. Fazal Karim Mea, A.I R 1926, Cal. 303.

is legally authorised to make a valid contract of marriage.[24]

In the case of *tafwīḍ* the conditions of sanity must exist at the time of delegation of the power and any subsequent change in the mental condition of the husband who delegated the power of divorce to the wife does not affect the validity of the delegation.[25] Thus if a person should delegate the power of divorce to his wife while in a sane condition but should afterwards become insane, his subsequent insanity shall not invalidate the authority.[26]

A minor cannot appoint an agent for delegating his power to divorce his wife.[27]

Wife's Capacity.—It can be gathered from a discussion in *Radd ul-Muḥtār* that the wife to whom the power of divorce is delegated need not be major or sane and the Muslim jurists justify this rule on the ground that a divorce given by a wife under the doctrine of *tafwīḍ* is somewhat akin to a conditional divorce which takes place on the fulfilment of the agreed condition, here the condition being the exercise of the power by the wife. It may also be said that when the wife divorces herself she does not do it in her own right, but only on behalf of the husband, who is major and sane. Under the Ḥanafī law the power can be delegated to a minor or non-Muslim wife.[28]

It is obvious that if the wife herself wants to settle the terms with her husband then she should be major under the Muslim law. If the wife be minor then her guardian can settle such terms with the husband on her behalf and she shall be entitled to the benefit of these conditions, even though she was not a party to the agreement.[29]

Shāfi'i Law.—Under the Shāfi'ī law the power of divorce

24. Marfat Ali Mirja Vs. Jabeedunnessa Bibi, 45, C.W.N. 910.
25. Ibn 'Ābidīn, *op. cit.*, Vol. II, p. 489. For discussion see chapter on Capacity.
26. *Ibid.*
27. *Ibid.*
28. *Ibid.*, p. 494.
29. Marfat Ali Mirja Vs. Jabeedunnessa Bibi, A.I.R. 1941, Cal. 657.

cannot be delegated to a minor wife.[30]

Ḥanbalī Law.—Under the Ḥanbalī law the power to divorce can be delegated to a minor wife if she is possessed of understanding to such an extent that she can understand what is meant by divorce. If she cannot, then the power cannot be delegated to her.[31]

IX. Documents delegating Power to Wife

When the power is to be delegated by a document then it must clearly specify the consequence of a breach of the terms of it. The agreement must in unequivocal words define the right of the wife that will accrue to her in the case of a breach by the husband of the terms agreed upon. The words must be definite enough to put upon the husband the obligation to carry out and fulfil the conditions contained in the agreement.

A divorce pronounced by a wife under the terms of an agreement, "I shall not marry another woman in the presence of my wife and if I do so, she is to be held to have been divorced by me on account of my second marriage, simultaneously with that second marriage she will be "*qaṭ'i ḥarām*" (absolutely forbidden) to my person and this very divorce by me in her favour would be valid and legal", was considered to be equivalent to a divorce by the wife under the power of divorce delegated to her.[32] It should be noted that the language of the agreement does not amount to a delegation of the power of divorce. It would, however, amount to a conditional divorce and would take effect on the fulfilment of the condition, that is, on the committal by the husband of a breach of the condition, namely, the act of marrying a second wife.[33] In another case the relevant clause was as under :—

If I do not give the wife her maintenance for two years

30. Muhammad b. Abi'l-'Abbās, *Nihāyat al-Muḥtāj*, Cairo 1938 A D. Vol. VI, p. 428.
31. Ibn Qudāmah, al-Mughnī, Cairo, 1368 A.H., Vol. VII, p. 145.
32. Muhammad Amin Vs. Amina Bibi, A.I.R. 1931, Lah. 134.
33. See "Conditional Divorce."

three *Ṭalāq-i-bā'in* (irrevocable divorce) will take effect on the wife herself". He failed to maintain her for the agreed period. It was contended by the wife that she was entitled to divorce herself by virtue of the above condition.[34] There is nothing in the para to confer the power of divorce on her and the clause merely amounts to a conditional divorce which would take effect on the fulfilment of the condition.

X. *Difference in Muslim Jurists' View and Courts' View*

It has already been stated that under the Muslims law delegation of the power to divorce by the husband to the wife may be absolute or its exercise may be subject to certain conditions. It is contended sometimes in legal proceedings that absolute or unconditional delegation is not valid and that the delegation of the power of divorce by the husband to the wife must be subject to certain conditions. The difference in the views lies in the fact that the Muslim jurists consider that a husband is the "absolute owner of marriage" and has unrestricted power to dissolve it and that it is immaterial whether he exercises that power by himself or through an agent who may be the wife herself. The wife, according to them, is a representative of the husband and so she can wield the same powers as can be exercised by the husband. The Courts do not agree with this view and consider that the wife cannot exercise an absolute and unrestricted power to dissolve the marriage. In this they have been influenced by the conception of a Christian marriage as well as by the law of Contracts relating to agreements. Notice has not been taken in these cases of the fact that there is a great difference in the conception of the nature of a Christian marriage and that of a Muslim marriage. A Christian marriage is indissoluble at the will of the parties to it. The principle governing it is that a marriage is the voluntary union for life of one man and one woman to the exclusion of all others. A Muslim marriage, on the other hand, is dissoluble by a husband and under certain

34. Ahmad Ali Vs. Selaha Khatun Bibi, 1952, P.L.D., Dacca, p. 385.

conditions by or at the instance of a wife or by the mutual agreement of a husband and his wife. The Muslim law, therefore, allows a provision in an agreement for a future separation and does not look askance at such an agreement. The fact that a provision of Muslim law is opposed to a provision in the Contract Act or of the English law or the English conception of marriage is certainly not a sufficient ground to nullify it, particularly as the Muslims are to be governed by their own personal laws in the matters of marriage and divorce. It may also be noted here that clause IX of the Dissolution of Muslim Marriages Act, 1939, provides that a marriage can be dissolved on any other ground which is recognised as valid for the dissolution of marriages under Muslim law. It is quite clear from the Muslim authorities that a wife can dissolve her marriage regardless of the fact whether a condition is in restraint of marriage or is now considered unreasonable or opposed to the present public policy. Hence no objection should be raised to the delegation to and exercise of such a power by the wife. The Dacca High Court has also held that an unconditional delegation of the power of divorce is valid.[35]

Valid Agreement.—An agreement which serves to ensure peace and domestic happiness should not be disregarded as invalid and opposed to public policy.[36]

Invalid Agreements.—The Courts consider an agreement to be invalid when :—

(*a*) It provides for a future separation between the parties ;

(*b*) It is in restraint of marriage ;

(*c*) The conditions contained in the agreement and subject to which the wife is to exercise the power of divorce are :—

(*i*) Opposed to public policy, or

(*ii*) Unreasonable.

35. Aklima Khatoon Vs. Mahib-ur-Rehman, P.L.D. 1963, Dacca 602.

36. Saifuddin Shaikh Vs. Mst. Soneka Bibi, A.I.R. 1955, Assam, p. 153,

(*a*) *Agreement for Future Separation.*—An agreement which provides for a future separation between the parties has been considered to be invalid by the Courts. It is, however, not disallowed or considered illegal under the Muslim law. As explained before, it is considered axiomatic in Muslim law that the husband has an absolute right to dissolve a marriage without consent of his wife. On this reasoning it is but a corollary of the first principle that he may exercise this right or power and dissolve the marriage in any way he likes and under any conditions he decides. He can delegate the power to someone else to be exercised unconditionally or subject to certain conditions. It is his look out to decide as to what is best for him and it is not for the *Qāḍī* (the Court) to object to the conditions mutually agreed upon between the husband and the wife. In this view the Muslim Jurists rely upon the fact that the Qur'ān enjoins every Muslim to fulfil the covenant he enters into and the Prophet (peace be on him) has also laid great stress on this matter. He has said, "Of all the conditions which you have to fulfil the most entitled to fulfilment are the conditions upon which you enter the union of marriages.[37]

(*b*) *Agreement in Restraint of Marriage.*—This condition is based on section 26 of the Contract Act which reads as under :—

> "Every agreement in restraint of the marriage of any person, other than a minor is void".

An agreement which purports to stop a person from marrying is considered to be in restraint of marriage. Thus a covenant not to marry anyone other than a certain woman who is under no legal liability to marry the man would be in restraint of marriage as the woman is under no obligation to marry him and so may not marry him with the result that the man would not be free to marry at all. Cases which can

37. Wali al-Dīn al-Khatib, *Mishkat al-Masabih*, Delhi 1350, A.H., p. 271.

strictly be governed by the above section do not generally occur amongst the Muslims. The vast majority of cases involve a restraint against a second marriage during the subsistence of the first marriage. Under the Muslim law a Muslim can marry four wives at the same time. The question arises if a condition in an agreement between him and his wife that in effect prevents him from contracting a second marriage during the subsistence of the first marriage can be regarded as an agreement in restraint of marriage. It must be remembered, as explained before, that a husband does not lose his right of marrying another woman during the life-time of the present wife. It is his legal right of which he cannot be deprived. But there is nothing to stop him from authorising his wife to divorce any woman whom he marries subsequently during the subsistence of the present marriage.[38] He can also authorise the wife to divorce a woman married to him by a previous marriage.[39] As explained before, he can divorce these wives whenever he may choose to do so and he can lawfully appoint another person to act on his behalf in the matter. In other words, he can empower a particular wife to do the above act on his behalf as his agent. The result shall be that the wife shall get a right to terminate her own marriage as well as the marriage of her husband with another woman. It has already been seen above, that a wife can stipulate for the delegation of unrestricted power of divorce to her, or that she can divorce herself on the breach of a specified condition such as the husband contracting a second marriage in the life-time of the first wife. The Muslim jurists do not invalidate such an agreement on the ground that it is in restraint of marriage. It, therefore, follows that such an agreement will be perfectly valid under the Muslim law and some Courts have also given effect to such an agreement. Thus it has been laid down that a provision in a

38. *Al-Fatāwā al-Hindīyah, op. cit.*, Vol. II, p. 71 *f* ; Fatawa Alamgīriyah *op. cit.*, Vol. II, pp. 211, 235.

39. *Ibid.*

marriage deed whereby a Muslim husband authorises his wife to divorce herself from him in the event of his marrying a second wife is not void under section 26 of the Contract Act. The Courts have followed this dictum in numerous cases and it may be taken as the settled law that such an agreement is not invalid.[40]

(c) Conditions in Agreements

Preliminary.—It has been seen above that the Muslim law allows full liberty to the spouses to settle such terms as they like relating to their marriage and its dissolution. The Courts, however, considered that if the conditions are opposed to public policy or are unreasonable then they cannot be given effect to and the agreement containing them would be unenforcible. The present tendency of the Courts has been to give more and more latitude to the spouses to settle the terms for governing their future marital relations and they have given effect to the conditions freely agreed upon between the parties as far as possible.[41]

(*i*) *Public Policy.*—It is difficult to lay down exactly as to what conditions are opposed to public policy. The Lahore High Court has followed an English case in which it was held that "Public Policy" is always an unsafe and a treacherous ground for legal decisions and must, therefore, be kept within its reasonable grounds.[42] Besides, public policy under the Muslim law differs from the present notion of public policy. It was stated in a recent case that the term "Public Policy" is very broad and it is not safe to rely upon it in such cases as a ground for legal decision.[43]

40. Mst. Sadiqa Begum Vs. Ataullah, A.I.R. 1933, Lah. 885 ; Muhammad Amin Vs. Mst. Amina Bibi, A.I.R. 1931, Lah 134 ; Khalil-ur-Rahman Vs. Mariam Bibi, 59, I.C. 804.

41. Muhammad Zaman Vs. Irshad Begum, P.L D. 1967, Lah, 1104.

42. Muhammad Ali Akbar Vs, Fatima Begum, A.I.R. 1929, Lah. 660; Driefontain Vs. Consolidated Mines Ltd., (1902), A.C. 484 ; 87 L.T. 372.

43. Muhammad Zaman Vs. Irshad Begum, P.L.D. 1967, Lah. 1104.

(*ii*) *Reasonable Conditions.*—No hard and fast rule can be laid down to determine what are reasonable conditions and what conditions are unreasonable. Some agreements in which the wife is given the power to live separately from her husband under certain conditions such as maltreatment of the wife by the husband have been considered valid and enforcible.[44] Thus agreement providing for payment of maintenance to the wife at her parents' house or when living separate from her husband in case of disagreement, have been held to be valid.[45] It has recently been held by the Lahore High Court that an agreement which allows the wife the right to live separate from her husband in case of disagreement or on his taking a second wife is not within the meaning of Section 23 of the Contract Act.[46] The Calcutta High Court has held an agreement to be valid which provided that if there be divorce between the parties then the husband would be under an obligation to continue to pay to the wife an adequate subsistence allowance or if no sum had been mentioned a reasonable sum during the life-time of the wife or for a specified period.[47]

Valid Conditions.—The following conditions in various agreements have been held to be valid and enforcible by the Courts and it has been held that a wife shall be entitled to divorce herself under them :

(*a*) If the husband marries a second wife during the subsistence of the instant marriage ;[48]

44. Bunney Sahib Vs. Abeda Begum, A.I.R. 1922, Oudh. 251 ; Mst. Sakina Faruq Vs. Shamshad Khan, A.I.R. 1936, Pesh. 195.

45. Syed Abbas Ali Vs. Najmun Nissa Begum, 43, C.W.N. 1059 ; Buffatan Bibi Vs. Sheikh Abdul Salam, A.I.R. 1950, Cal. 304 ; Mst. Hamidan Vs. Muhammad Umar, A.I.R. 1932, Lah. 65 ; Muhammad Moinuddin Vs. Jamal Fatima, A.I.R. 1921, All. 192.

46. Muhammad Zaman Vs. Irshad Begum, P.L.D. 1957, Lah. 1104.

47. For contra see Bai Fatima Vs. Ali Muhammad Aiyub, 37, B.L.R. 280, 47, I.C. 546.

48. Mst. Sadiqa Begum Vs. Ataullah, 144, I.C. 497, A.I.R. (1933), Lah. 885 ; Shrimati Ayetunness Bibi Vs. Karamal i12, C.W.N. 907, 36, Cal. 23; Muhammad Amin Vs. Amina Bibi, A.I.R. 1931, Lah. 134, etc.

(*b*) When the husband by his conduct gives the wife or her parents or relatives mental pain ;[49]

(*c*) If the husband does not lead a respectable life, does not earn his livelihood and does no live in a house approved by the wife and her parents.[50]

(*d*) If the husband fails to live in a house approved by the wife and her parents.[51]

(*e*) If the husband fails to deliver certain ornaments agreed to be given to the wife on a demand by her.[52]

(*f*) If the husband keeps a concubine.[53]

(*g*) If the husband refuses to carry out the wife's most unreasonable wishes and to serve her as a servant.[54]

(*h*) If the husband fails to pay separate specified maintenance to the wife in case of disagreement between the parties.[56]

(*i*) If the husband does not pay the wife an agreed sum of money while she is living with her parents.[56]

(*j*) If the husband does not pay maintenance to the wife even if she does not reside in the house with him and his second wife.[57]

(*k*) If the husband does not continue to pay to the wife an adequate or specified subsistence allowance when

49. Srimati Samserannessa Vs. Abdus Samad, A.I.R. 1926, Cal. 1144 ; 93 I.C. 1018.
50. Muhammad Yasin Vs. Mumtaz Begum, A.I.R. 1936, Lah. 716.
51. *Ibid.*
52. Nuruddin Vs. Mst. Chenuri, 3, C.L.J. 49 ; Tahazzad Hossain Sikdar Vs. Hossenara Begum, P.L.D, 1967, Dacca 42.
53. Meer Ashruf Ali Vs. Meer Ashhad Ali, (1871), 16 W.R. 260.
54, Muhammad Amin Vs. Amina Bibi, A.I.R. 1931, Lah. 134, 194.
55. Mirjan Ali Vs. Mst. Maimuna Bibi, A.I.R. 1949, Assam 14 ; Buffatan Bibi Vs. Sheikh Abdul Salam, A.I.R. 1950, Cal. 304 ; Muhammad Muinuddin Vs. Mst. Jamal Fatima, A.I.R. 1921, All. 152 ; Mst. Hamidan Vs. Muhammad Umar, AI..R. 1932, Lah. 65 ; Syed Abbas Ali Vs. Nazeem-un-Nessa 43, C.W.N. 1059.
56. Mst. Sakina Faruk V. Shamshad Khan, A.I.R. 1936, Pesh. 195.
57. Mansur Vs. Mst. Azizul, A.I.R. 1928, Oudh 303.

the relations between the parties become strained.[58] But a different view has been taken in some other earlier cases.[59] The Calcutta High Court has explained in a later case that there is nothing in Muhammadan Law opposed to an agreement which does not allow the wife to deny her husband's conjugal rights but permits her, when ill-treated, to leave her husband's house or insist on those rights being exercised in her parents' residence.[60]

(*l*) If the husband leaves the wife without making any provision for her maintenance.[61]

(*m*) If the husband treats the wife habitually in a criminal manner.[62]

(*n*) If the husband persistently neglects to visit the wife.[63]

(*o*) If the husband does not pay to the wife her prompt dower on demand.[64] This holds good even when the marriage has been consummated.[65]

(*p*) If the husband fails to perform the marital duties and obligations.[66]

(*q*) If the husband would bring any of his other wives to

58. Muhammad Ali Akbar Vs. Fatima Begum, A.I.R. 1929, Lah. 660; Mst. Bufatan Bibi Vs. Sheikh Abdul Salam, A.I.R. 1950, Cal. 304; Mst. Hamidan Vs. Muhammad Umar, A.I.R. 1932, Lah. 65; Sakina Faruk Vs. Shamshad Khan, A.I.R. 1936, Pesh. 195.
59. Bai Fatima Vs. Ali Mohammad Aiyub, I.L.R. 37, Bom. 280; Imam Ali Patwari Vs. Arfatunnessa, A.I.R. 1914, Cal. 369; A.I.R. 1916, Cal. 223 (D.B. Appeal).
60. Sabed Khan Vs. Bilatunnessa Bibi, A.I.R. 1919, Cal. 825.
61. Khalil-ar-Rahman Vs. Mariam Bibi, 59 I.C. 804.
62. *Ibid.*
63. *Ibid.*
64. Hamidoolah Vs. Mst. Faizunnessa, I.L.R. 8, Cal. 327; Abdul Shakoor Vs. Mst. Machuna Khatoon, 7 D.L.R. 451.
65. Gul Nawaz Khan Vs. Mst. Maherunnessa Begum, P.L.D. 1965, Dacca 274.
66. Khalil-ar-Rahman Vs. Mariam Bibi, 59, I.C. 804.

stay with him without the consent of the wife.[67]

(*r*) If the husband assaults the wife.[68]

(*s*) That the wife, if a minor, shall live with her parents for a specified period of time during her minority.[69]

(*t*) That the husband shall not take his wife outside her permanent place of residence where they were married.[70]

Invalid Conditions.—The following conditions have been held by the Courts to be unreasonable or opposed to public policy and so invalid.

(*a*) The condition that left the wife absolutely free to separate herself from her husband without any reason.[71]

(*b*) The condition that the wife would be entitled to dissolve the marriage on the husband's failure to maintain her during a specified period when the wife is herself responsible for the non-maintenance by the husband.[72] A case of similar nature came up for decision before a Division Bench of the Calcutta High Court and the learned judges gave effect to the agreement.[73]

(*c*) The condition that the husband would live permanently with the parents of the wife and on his failure to

67. Saifuddin Shaikh Vs. Mst. Soneka Bibi, A.I.R. 1955, Assam 153.

68. Muhammad Ali Akbar Vs. Fatima Begum, A.I.R. 1929, Lah. 660; Mst. Bafatan Vs. Abdus Salam, A.I.R. 1950, Cal. 304; Moinuddin Vs. Jamal Fatima, A.I.R. 1921, All. 152; Mst. Hamidan Vs. Muhammad Umar, 1952, Lah. 66; Mst. Sakina Faruq Vs. Shamshad Khan, A.I.R. 1936, Pesh. 195; Mansur Vs. Azizul, A.I.R. 1928, Oudh 303.

69. Mst. Nafeesun Nessa Vs. Bodi Rahman, 20, I.C. 642; Azizullah Chowdhury, Vs. Sakina Bibi, L.B.R. 351; Marifat Ali Mirja Vs. Mst. Jabeedun Nessa Bibi A.I.R. 1944, Cal. 658.

70. Akbarun Nessa Vs. Hussain-uddin, *Deccan Law Reports*, Vol. VI, p. 28.

71. Mehr Ali Mooray Vs. Saker Khanoo Bai, 7 B L.R. 602; Banney Sahib Vs. Abeda Begum. A.I.R. 1922, Oudh 251.

72. Ahmed Ali Vs. Sabha Khatoon, P.L.D. 1952, Dacca 385.

73. Bafatan Bibi Vs. Shaikh Abdus Salam, A.I.R. 1950, Cal. 304.

do so, the wife would be entitled to divorce herself.[74] If in spite of such an agreement she leaves her parents' house to live with her husband in his house then she will be taken to have waived her right, if any, under the agreement.[75]

It may be stated here that Hazrat Shāh 'Abd al-'Azīz has expressed a different view. He has stated that such a condition is absurd but nevertheless if agreed upon between the parents of the wife and the husband then it shall be binding on the husband. He has based this opinion on the ground that the Qur'ān enjoins on the Muslims to abide by their agreements.[76] Moreover, the condition that the husband would not remove the wife during her minority from her parents' house has been held valid as stated above.

XI. Conditions that are held valid under the Muslim law and on the breach of which the wife is entitled to divorce herself.

They are either expressly stated by the Muslim writers or compilers or can be deduced from what they have written, as given under :

1. That the husband shall not absent himself from their place of residence for a specified period of time.[77]
2. It can be gathered from *Fatāwā' Hindiyah* that the wife cannot be forced to prepare food or wash clothes and so this can be made a condition of the marriage.[78]
3. That the husband shall not keep the wife in the same house with his other wife. It is stated in *Fatāwā'*

74. Imam Ali Patwari Vs. Arfatun Nessa; 21, I.C. 87, A.I.R. 1914, Cal. 369; Khatun Bibi Vs. Rajjab, A.I.R. 1926, All. 615, 94, I.C. 224; Hameedun Nessa Bibi Vs. Zahiruddin Sheikh (1890), 17, Cal. 670.
75. Fatima Bibi Vs. Noor Muhammad, A.I.R. 1928, Lah. 328.
76. Shah 'Abd' al-Aziz, *Fatāwā al-Aziziyah*, Hyderabad, Deccan, 1313, A.H., p. 326.
77. *Al-Fatāwā al-Hindīyah*, *op. cit.*, Vol. II, p. 73.
78. *Ibid.*, pp. 75, 144.

Hindiyah that a wife can lawfully refuse to live with another wife of the husband.[79]

4. That the husband shall not stop the wife from going to her parents once a week and other near relations once a month.[80]
5. That the husband shall not indulge in gambling ;[81]
6. That the husband shall not drink forbidden liquor ;[82]
7. That the husband shall not maltreat the wife.[83]
8. That the husband shall not use filthy language for the wife ; [84]
9. That the husband shall pay the wife maintenance every month by a specified date or give her a specified sum of money by a certain date ;[85]
10. That the husband shall not leave the place they are living in without the wife's permission ;[86]
11. That the husband shall not be guilty of immorality.[87]

XII. Interpretation

When the conditions agreed upon are contained in a marriage agreement or *Nikāh Nāmāh*, as it is called, then its terms or conditions are to be looked at and construed in the same way as the terms of any other contract.[88] When an agreement consists of two parts one of which is invalid and the other is valid and the two are separable then the stipulation contained in the portion which is valid can be enforced. But if they are inseparable then the agreement cannot be enforced.[89] It was stated in a case by the Lahore High Court that the words in a document in an oriental language are not to be considered too literally but in a reasonable and

79. *Al-Fatāwā al-Hindīyah, op. cit.*, Vol. II, p. 41.
80. *Ibid.*, p. 148.
81. *Ibid.*, p. 74.
82. *Ibid.* 83. *Ibid.* 84. *Ibid.*
85. *Ibid.* 86. *Ibid.* 87. *Ibid.*
88. Ahmad Kassim Molla Vs. Khatun Bibi, A.I R. 1933 Cal. 27.
89. Section 57. Contract Act ; Mehar Ali Mooraj Vs. Saker Khatoon Bai, 7 B.L.R. 602.

intelligent manner. In that case the agreement provided that the husband would not demur to carry out the wife's most unreasonable wishes and would serve as her servant. The condition was not held to be unreasonable and it was explained that the condition only meant that the husband would try his utmost to study the wishes of his wife as a servant would do in the case of his master.[90]

XIII. *Time of Delegation*

Under the provisions of Sunnī law the power can be delegated at three stages, namely,

(*a*) Prior to the marriage ; [91] or

(*b*) at the time of the marriage ; [92] or

(*c*) subsequent to the marriage.

The Muslim jurists hold that the delegation of the power is perfectly valid at whichever of these stages it may be given.[93] The time of delegation does not, under the Muslim law, affect the validity of the delegation in any way. Most of the authorities on Muslim law have discussed the cases of delegation of the power to the wife after the marriage. They have also given instances when the power was given prior to the marriage.

Courts' View.—All the Courts agree with the Muslim jurists as regards the first and the second contingencies, namely, when the power is delegated before or at the time of the marriage. But in a few early cases they have differed with the Muslim jurists with regard to the third contingency, that is, when the power is delegated to the wife subsequent to the marriage and have held such delegation to be invalid. They have attached great importance to the matter of consideration in some cases. When an agreement has been executed or the terms have been agreed upon before or at the time of marriage, the wife's consenting to the marriage is considered sufficient consideration. But an agreement executed

90 Mst. Sahra Jan Vs. Abdul Raoof, A.I.R. 1921, Lah. 194.

91. Ibn 'Ābidīn, *op. cit.*, Vol. II, p. 497.

92. *Ibid.*

93. *Ibid.*, pp. 487, 497.

after a marriage, in the absence of other consideration, has been held to be without consideration and so invalid. Thus where a person had entered into an agreement with his wife and a quarrel arose between them and the husband entered into a second agreement with his wife's brother undertaking to carry on the terms of his previous agreement, it was held that the latter agreement was nothing more than a promise as it was without consideration.[94] The Courts are not, however, unanimous on this point and have expressed different views in different cases. The Oudh Judicial Commissioner's Court has distinguished the cases when an agreement is entered into at the time of a marriage and when it is entered into subsequent to a marriage. It has been pointed out that the distinction between the agreements is one of consideration. The marriage itself is sufficient consideration in the first case, but after marriage, there would, as a general rule, be no consideration. It implied that as a general rule such an agreement would be invalid.[95] The Calcutta High Court has taken a different view and has held that an agreement under which the wife is given an option to divorce herself on behalf of her husband on breach of certain conditions is valid and not opposed to public policy even when it is entered into subsequent to the marriage.[96] The Lahore High Court has also held such delegation to be valid and not opposed to public policy.[97] It has stated that there is ample authority to the effect that an agreement made before or after the marriage by which it is provided that the wife should be at liberty to divorce herself from her husband under certain specified valid conditions is valid.[98]

94. Abdul Piroj Khan Vs. Hussain Bi, 6 B.L.R. 728; Mst. Saddan Vs. Faiz Bakhsh, A.I.R. 1920, Lah. 211.

95. Banney Sahib Vs. Abeda Begum, A.I.R. 1922, Oudh 251-69, I.C. 778; Abdul Piroj Khan Vs. Hussain Bi, 6 B.L.R. 728.

96. Mst. Fatima Khatun Vs. Fazal Khan, A.I.R. 1928, Cal. 303; Saidud-din Vs. Lateef-un-Nessa Bibi, 46, Cal. 141-48, I.C. 609.

97. Mst. Sadiqa Begum Vs. Ata Ullah, A.I.R. 1933, Lah. 885; Muhammad Yasin Vs. Mumtaz Begum, A.I.R. 1936, Lah. 716; Sayeeda Khanum Vs. Muhammad Sami, 1950, P.L.D. Lah. 113.

98. Muhammad Amin Vs. Amina Bibi, A.I.R. 1931, Lah. 134.

Muslim Jurists' View.—Under the Muslim law the agreement shall not be invalid because it considers such an agreement to be merely the appointment of an agent with authority to do a certain act under certain conditions. It attaches no importance to consideration or to its absence. But what is more important is the fact that before the actual solemnization of the marriage the prospective husband has no control over the prospective wife and it is only when the marriage has been performed that he gets a right to have some control over her. The Muslim jurists are of the opinion that in agreements executed before or at the time of the solemnization of the marriage, it should be made clear that the agreement shall be applicable after the solemnization of the marriage.

Reason for the Difference in the Muslim Jurists' and the Courts' Views.—The difference of opinion between the Muslim jurists and the Courts is due to the difference in the point of view from which the matter is considered. The Muslim jurists hold that the husband possesses the power to divorce his wife at any time he likes. He may exercise the power to dissolve the marriage by himself or he may appoint an agent to exercise the power on his behalf. It makes no difference as to who that person is. He can, therefore, authorise his wife to exercise the power on his behalf. When the wife dissolves the marriage, she does not exercise the power in her own right but merely as an agent of the husband. It is, therefore, immaterial according to them at what stage the power is delegated to her. They hold that it is only after the marriage that the husband can validly delegate the power to the wife. He cannot delegate it before the actual celebration of the marriage. Delegation of a right to the wife necessarily involves the idea that the man is possessed of a right which he is vesting in the wife. The prospective husband has no concern with or control over the prospective wife. He can, therefore, exercise no power over her, and when he is not possessed of the power, he obviously cannot delegate it to the girl. If he executes any agreement before the marriage he has to make it clear that the agreement shall be enforcible only after the celebration of the marriage. Thus he has to state something like this, "When I am married to you then I shall be bound by the conditions specified below", or "When I am married to you then you shall have the power to dissolve the marriage on my behalf whenever you like". If there is no such reference to the forthcoming marriage or if it is not made clear that the agreement shall be enforcible only after the marriage then according to the Muslim jurists it shall be invalid and so ineffective. Thus if he says in the agreement executed before the marriage, "I am being married to you and I delegate to you the power of dissolving the marriage absolutely subject to the terms specified in the agreement," then the agreement shall be invalid because being a stranger he has no right or control over the prospective wife and cannot exercise any control over her and so he cannot delegate any right to her as he himself is not possessed of any. The Muslim jurists do not attach any importance to the question of consideration. The Courts that have differed with the Muslim jurists have based their judgment on the basis of "consideration." They have held that when an agreement delegating the power of divorce is entered into before or at the time of the marriage then the marriage itself forms its consideration, but when such an agreement is made subsequent to the marriage then there is no consideration for the husband's delegation and so the agreement is invalid.[99]

It is submitted that the law of delegation of the power of divorce is an integral part of the Muslim laws of marriage and divorce and the Muslims are governed by their own personal laws in these matters. The cases should, therefore, be decided according to the principles and provisions of the Muslim law. There is no reason why an agreement executed subsequent to a marriage should not be allowed to govern the

99. Banney Sahib Vs. Mst. Abeda Begum, A.I.R. 1922, Oudh 251-69, I.C. 778.

rights and liabilities of the parties. Even under the Contract Act, it may be considered as a gift of his power to the wife on account of love and affection.

XIV. *Agreement settled before but executed after marriage*

An agreement the conditions of which have been settled before the marriage but executed subsequent to the marriage is perfectry valid.[100]

XV. *Pronounceement by Wife*

A marriage does not become dissolved automatically on a breach of the stipulated condition by the husband. The wife must pronounce a divorce for that purpose. It is not necessary for the validity of the divorce that the wife should pronounce it in the presence of the husband or witnesses.[101] This rule is based on the reasoning that it is not necessary that a husband should pronounce a divorce in the prence of witnesses in order to make it valid. It shall be effective even when given in the absence of the wife or witnesses. Here the wife is acting merely as an agent of the husband on his behalf and so the same conditions shall prevail as in the case of the husband.

XVI. *Performance*

The Ḥanafī jurists insist on a literal performance of the conditions. Thus where a husband undertook to send maintenance to his wife from a certain town and stipulated that on his failure to do so, the wife shall be entitled to divorce herself and he did send the maintenance but from a different town then under the Ḥanafī law the wife shall be competent to exercise the power.[102] If the husband says to his wife, "If I do not send your maintenance within such period then you can repudiate yourself and he does send it within

100. Sabed Khan Vs. Bilat-un-Nisa Bibi, 30 C.L.J. 510.
101. Ibn Nujaym, *al-Bahr' al-Rā'iq*, Cairo, 1311 A.H. Vol. III, p. 335.
102. *Al-Fatāwā al-Hindīyah*, *op. cit.*, Vol. II, p. 73.

the specified time, but it does not reach the wife and is lost in transit then the wife shall not become entitled to exercise the power because the husband has complied with his undertaking.[103] But if he had used the expression, "If you do not receive your maintenance within such and such time then you can divorce yourself" and the same does not reach her though he had sent it then she can divorce herself.[104] If the husband undertakes to abstain from doing two things and authorises the wife to divorce herself if he is guilty of a breach of his undertaking then the wife can repudiate herself even if he commits the breach of one condition only. Thus if he says, "If I remain absent for six months or you do not receive your maintenance during this period then you can divorce yourself," and later on he remains absent but sends the maintenance then the wife can exercise the power.[105]

XVII. Time of Exercise

In the absence of a condition the wife must according to the Hanafi law exercise the power immediately she is invested with it or receives the information that she has been so invested with the power.[106] If it be subject to a condition then the wife can exercise the right subject to the condition.[107] It is stated by the Muslim jurists that she must exercise her right in the same sitting and in the same posture in which she was when she received the information.[108] Stress is laid on the condition to such an extent that if she was sitting when the power was given to her or when she receives the information and then lies down or stands up before exercising

103. *Al-Fatāwā al-Hindiyah, op. cit.*, Vol. II, p. 73.
104. *Ibid.*
105. *Ibid.*, p. 74.
106. Ibn 'Ābidīn, *op. cit.*, Vol. II, p. 488.
107. *Ibid.*
108. Al-Marghīnānī, *op. cit.*, Vol. II, p. 356 ; Ibn 'Ābidīn, *op. cit*, Vol. II, p. 488.

her power then her right would be lost.[109] Similarly, if she busies herself in some other occupation such as reading or taking her meals or attending to her toilet, etc., after being invested with the power and before exercising the same, then too she loses her right.[110] It is explained that her attitude shows that she is not keen on exercising her right. But if she wants time to consult her father or to call witnesses then her right shall not be lost on account of the delay.[111] She will not lose her right if she was standing when she received the news of the delegation and then sits down or was sitting and then reclines against a pillow or was reclining and then sits upright.[112] It is explained that these acts do not denote her lack of interest. On the contrary, they indicate her interest and desire to deeply consider over the matter. If the husband raises her upright or is intimate with her even by force then too she shall lose her right because, it is explained, she could have exercised the power to divorce herself immediately it was delegated to her so as to leave no chance to the husband to undo his delegation and her delay shows her lack of keenness in the matter, namely, exercise of the power immediately on being invested with it or on receiving information of the delegation. This rule is obviously very hard and technical and literal compliance with it is often very difficult. A wife does require some time to decide such a a serious matter which shall affect her whole future life. But the exercise of the power, delegated to the wife, as a general rule, is at the present time made to depend on the occurrence or non-occurrence of a specified condition, and so the wife gets sufficient time to think over and decide the matter beforehand. In other cases, the power is so delegated as to give the wife the power to take advantage of it whenever she may so like and it is not obligatory on her to exercise it the

109. Al-Marghīnānī, *op. cit.*, Vol. II, p. 356; Ibn 'Ābidīn, *op. cit.*, Vol. II p. 488.

110. *Ibid.*

111. Ibn 'Ābidīn, *op. cit.*, Vol. II, p. 490.

112. *Ibid.*

moment the husband commits a breach of the specified condition or conditions. It has been held by the Calcutta High Court that when the power is given to the wife by the marriage-contract to divorce herself on her husband marrying again, she is not bound to exercise her option at the very first moment she learns the news. The injury done to her is a continuing one, and it is reasonable that she should have a continuing right to exercise the power.[113]

The power to divorce can be delegated by the husband to his wife for an indefinite period as when he says, "you can divorce yourself whenever you like". The wife can then exercise the power at any time she likes.[114] It will not be necessary for her in such a case to exercise the power immediately on delegation. Her right shall not be lost even if she refuses to exercise it.[115] The husband can also delegate the power to divorce to his wife for a limited period. Thus he may empower the wife to exercise it within ten days or one year when she shall be entitled to exercise it within ten days or one year, as the case may be, and her right shall be lost if she does not exercise the power within the specified time.[116] The time shall be deemed to commence from the time when the power was delegated to her irrespective of the fact whether the wife received the information of the delegation or remained unaware of it.[117]

XVIII. Effect of delegation by the Husband

The effect of delegation of the power of divorce by the husband to his wife is that she becomes authorised to exercise that power as a representative of her husband.

The pronouncement of divorce by the wife amounts to

113. Shrimati Ayat un-Nessa Bibi Vs. Karam Ali, I.L.R. 36 Cal. 23; 12 C.W.N. 997.

114. Al-Marghīnānī, *op. cit.*, Vol. II, p. 361; Ibn 'Ābidīn, *op. cit.*, Vol. II, p. 489.

115. *Ibid.*

116. *Al-Fatāwā al-Hindīyah*, *op. cit.*, Vol. II, p. 72.

117. *Ibid.*

her husband's pronouncing it. There is no difference between a husband agreeing that he shall be held to have divorced his wife when a certain contingency arises and a condition allowing the wife to divorce herself upon a certain contingency arising.[118]

The delegation does not divest the husband of the power of divorce and both he and his wife can exercise the power. This can be inferred from the cases discussed in the various books.[119] *Al-Baḥr al-Rā'iq* has, however, made the matter quite clear. It states, while discussing the subject of Tafwīḍ or delegation of the power of divorce to the wife, that a question arises here as to how can the husband exercise the power of divorce when he has delegated the power to the wife and so made her the owner of the divorce. It then explains on the strength of al-Kāfī that what the husband entrusts to the wife is not the ownership of divorce, but only the right to exercise the power of divorce and so he still remains the owner of the divorce. Hence both the husband and the wife can effect a divorce. The husband is not divested of this power and he can exercise the power as long as the wife does not divorce herself on his behalf.[120]

XIX. Husband's subsequent Ratification

An unauthorised pronouncement of divorce by the wife shall not become effective even if subsequently ratified by the husband. The subsequent ratification will, however, amount to the delegation of the power of divorce to her and she can after that validly exercise the power. Thus should an unauthorised man say to the wife of another person, "I give the power of divorce to you" and should the woman then say, "I have chosen myself" and the husband on learning of this consents to the same even then a divorce shall not be effective. But she can then subsequently exercise the power.[121] Similarly, if a woman say, "I vest myself with the

118. Muhammad Amin Vs. Amina Bai, A.I.R. 1931, Lah. 134.
119. Ibn 'Ābidīn, *op. cit.*, Vol. II, p. 497.
120. Ibn Nujaym, *al-Baḥr al-Rā'iq*, Cairo, 1311, A.H., Vol. III, p. 335.
121. *Al-Fatāwā al-Hindīyah, op. cit.*, Vol. II, p. 73.

power of divorce and I have chosen myself", that is, she has divorced herself and the husband consents to the same even then no divorce shall be effected but she shall then become vested with the power.[122] In the same way, if a woman says, "I vest myself with the power of divorce and *divorce* myself" and the husband then consents to the same then a revocable divorce shall be effected.[123] This is based on the reasoning that here she has explicitly divorced herself and has not merely chosen herself.

XX. *Power not Revocable*

The power once delegated to the wife cannot be revoked or taken away from her.[124] This rule has been justified on the ground that once a person makes another the owner of a certain thing then his power to revoke it is lost and he is no longer competent to cancel it.[125] But if the husband empowers a third person to divorce his wife on his behalf then this power can be revoked at any time before it has been exercised.[126]

Shafi'ī Law.—Shafi'ī has held otherwise. According to him the husband can revoke the power at any time before its exercise by the wife.[127]

Mālikī Law.—According to Mālik, the husband cannot revoke the power delegated to the wife but he can do so in the case of *Tawkīl* or agency.[128]

Ḥanbalī Law.—Under the Ḥanbalī law, the husband can revoke the power whether it is delegated to the wife or to a third person.[129]

122. *Al-Fatāwā al-Hindiyah, op. cit.*, Vol. II, p. 71.
123. *Ibid.*
124. Ibn 'Ābidīn, *op. cit.*, Vol. II, p. 489.
125. Al-Kāsānī, *Badā'i al-Ṣanā'i'* Cairo, 1327 A.H., Vol. III, p. 113.
126. Ibn 'Ābidīn, *op. cit.*, Vol. II, p. 489.
127. Ibn Rushd, *Bidāyat al-Mujtahid*, Cairo, n.d., Vol. II, p. 60.
128. *Ibid.*, p. 59.
129. Ibn Qudāmah, *op. cit.*, Vol. VII, pp. 142-45.

XXI. Burden of Proof

When a wife seeks to exercise the power delegated to her to divorce herself she must establish clearly that the conditions under which she was authorised to exercise the power have been fulfilled.[130]

XXII. Nature of Separation

The nature of separation depends on the expression used by the husband and the wife. If it is *Kināyah* or ambiguous then it shall amount to an irrevocable divorce. Thus if the husband should say, "Choose" and should the wife reply "I have chosen myself", then the expressions are *Kināyah* and so the divorce shall be irrevocable.[131] If the husband should say, "Divorce yourself if you so desire" and should the wife reply, "I divorce myself" then these are *ṣarīḥ* or clear expressions and so a revocable divorce shall be effected in such a case.[132]

There is a difference of opinion about the nature of separation effected under the doctrine of delegation.

Ḥanafi Law.—Abu Ḥanifa lays down that the separation effected by the exercise of the power of divorce shall amount to an irrevocable divorce. He explains that if it be held to be revocable then it can serve no purpose and the wife gains no advantage from the delegation.[133]

Māliki Law.—Mālik holds that when a husband authorises his wife to divorce herself, he shall be deemed to have empowered her to effect an irrevocable divorce. He explains that in such a case the object of the husband's delegation is that the wife should be separated from him. Similarly, her object when she exercises the power, is to be separated from

130. Mirjan Ali Vs. Maimuna Bibi, A.I.R. 1949, Assam 14; Buffatan Bibi Vs. Shaikh Abdul Salam, A.I.R. 1950, Cal. 304-309.

131. Al-Marghīnānī, *op. cit.*, Vol. II, pp. 356-57; Ibn 'Ābidīn, *op. cit.*, Vol. II, pp. 487-88.

132. *Ibid.*

133. Ibn Rushd, *op. cit.*, Vol. II, p. 60.

him. He concludes from this line of argument that the spouses want to be separated irrevocably and so such shall be the effect of the exercise of the power by the wife.[134]

Shafi'ī Law.—According to one report Shafi'ī held that the separation effected in the case of delegation amounts to a cancellation of the marriage. But according to his later opinion the nature of the separation shall be divorce and its nature shall depend on the intention of the husband. If he wanted the separation to be irrevocable, the divorce effected shall be irrevocable. If, on the other hand, he wanted only a revocable divorce then only a revocable divorce shall result.[135]

Shi'ī Law.—The Shi'ahs do not recognise the doctrine of delegation of the power of divorce by the husband to his wife.[136]

134. Ibn Rushd, *op. cit.*, Vol. II, p. 60.
135. *Ibid.*
136. Ameer Ali, *Mohammadan Law*, Vol. II, p. 536, Calcutta, 1908 A.D.

Chapter 12

KHUL'

I. Preliminary

The contract of marriage with the exception of a *Mut'ah* or temporary marriage, permissible under the Shī'i law, is to last for the life-time of the husband and wife. But when relations between the spouses become so strained that a continuation of their union becomes undesirable, the spouses are allowed to terminate it. It can be dissolved either by husband on his own initiative or at the instance of the wife or by mutual agreement. In the first two cases there is breach of the implied contract that the marriage will subsist during the life-time of the parties. If it is the husband who is guilty of this breach, he is penalised by becoming liable for the immediate payment of his wife's deferred dower, while if it is the wife who wants the termination of the marriage, she has, as a rule, to compensate the husband. This termination of the marriage at the instance of the wife is called *Khul'*. It is one of the ways of the dissolution of marriage and has been well recognized and followed from the early period of Islam. It is stated in the Qur'ān: "And women have rights similar to those against them in a just manner, and men are a degree above them. And Allah is Mighty, Wise."[1] This shows that men and women have similar rights. Man has been given the right of divorce but the woman has not been deprived of the right to separation in case of necessity. This right has been given to her by the doctrine of *Khul'*.

II. Definition

(*a*) *Khul'*: The word *Khul'* literally means "to put off", as a man is said to *Khala'a* his garment when he puts it off. In law it is the demission or laying down by the husband of his

1. Qur'ān, II : 228, Surah al-Baqarah

right and authority over his wife at her instance on acceptance of consideration by means of the word "*Khul*' ".[2] It is stated in *Fatāwā Qāḍī Khān* that it signifies a conditional agreement on the part of husband entered into for the purpose of dissolving the marital relationship at the desire of the wife in lieu of a compensation paid by her to the husband out of her property.[3]

The use of the word "Agreement" (*yamīn*) is rather unfortunate and has led to the misconception that it is only on an agreement between the parties that a marriage can be dissolved by *Khul*'. *Al-Fatāwā al-Hindīyah* while referring to *Khul*' has not used the word "Agreement" (*yamīn*) and has stated that *Khul*' means the relinquishment of the ownership of marriage (that is the right to maintain it) at the instance of and on payment of a consideration by the wife. According to Abū Ḥanīfah, *Khul*' is a conditional agreement (*yamīn*) on the part of the husband and compensation on the part of the wife, but according to Abū Yūsuf and Muḥammad b. al-Ḥasan, it is agreement from both of them.[4]

Abū Ḥanīfah has stated that the dissolution of marriage for consideration with the consent of the wife is called *Khul*'.[5]

Mālik has expressed the view that every divorce in lieu of consideration is called *Khul*' irrespective of the fact that the word *Khul*' has or has not been used.

According to Shāfi'ī every word which brings about a separation between the spouses for a consideration is *Khul*'.[6]

Aḥmad b. Ḥanbal says, according to one version, that *Khul*' is a separation of the husband in lieu of some considera-

2. *Al-Fatāwā al-Hindiyah*, Kanpur, 1349 A.H., Vol. II, p. 118 ; Ibn 'Ābidīn, *Radd al-Muḥtār*, Cairo, 1318 A.H., Vol. II, pp. 571-72.
3. Qāḍī Khān, *Fatāwā Qāḍī Khān*, Kanpur 1310 A.H., Vol. II, p. 256 ; *cf.* Ibn 'Ābidīn, *op. cit.*, Vol. II, p. 573.
4. *Al-Fatāwā al-Hindiyah*, *op. cit.*, Vol. II, p. 118 f ; Akmal al-Dīn, *al-'Ināyāh 'ala'l-Hidāyah*, (on the margin of *Fatḥ al-Qadīr*) Cairo, 1356 A.H., Vol. III, p. 199.
5. *Ibid.*
6. Ibn Qudāmah, *al-Mughnī*, Cairo, 1367 A.H., Vol. VII, p. 57.

tion realised by him. According to another version, it is a divorce.[7]

Their Lordships of the Privy Council have stated, "A divorce by Khul' is a divorce with the consent and at the instance of the wife and in which she gives or agrees to give a consideration to the husband for her release from the marriage-tie. In such a case the terms of the agreement are matters of arrangement between the husband and the wife, and the wife may, as consideration, give up her dower and other rights or make any other arrangement for the benefit of the husband."[8] The Lahore High Court has also expressed the same view.[9]

(b) *Mubārāh* : The termination of marriage-tie by mutual consent and as a result of mutual aversion or disagreement is called *Mubārāh*. As the marriage is terminated at the desire of both the husband and the wife, no consideration is to be paid in such a case by the wife to the husband.[10]

(c) *Ṭalāq-bi'iwaḍ al-Māl*: The expression used in *Ṭalāq-bi'iwaḍ al-māl* mentions the word "*Ṭalāq*" as well as words to denote the sale of the ownership of the marriage or the right of divorce by the husband to the wife or the purchase of the same by her.[11] Thus the wife may say, "I have purchased the right of divorce from you for (so much)" or the husband may say, "I have sold the right of divorce to you for (so much)" Khul' and *Ṭalāq-bi'iwaḍ al-māl* differ in another respect also. In the case of Khul' if the consideration is unlawful even then an irrevocable divorce shall be effected, but in the latter case it shall be revocable only.

The Muslim jurists have used the word Khul' rather loosely. Thus they have stated that a stranger can obtain a Khul' from the husband by offering him a consideration. But

7. Ibn Qudāmah, *op. cit.*, Vol. VII, pp. 56-57.
8. Moonshee Buzuloor Rahman Vs. Lateef-un Nissa, 8, M.I.A. 379.
9. Saddan Vs. Faiz Buksh, I.L.R. 21 Lahore : 402.
10. Umar Bibi Vs. Mohammad Din A.I.R. 1945, Lahore : 51.
11. *Al-Fatāwā al-Hindiyah*, *op. cit.*, Vol. II, p. 118 ; Ibn 'Ābidīn, *op. cit.* Vol. II, pp. 575, 580-81.

obviously this will not amount to a *Khul'*. Supposing A wants to marry B's wife and he offers some consideration to A to induce him to divorce his wife, so that she may be compelled to marry him on account of financial difficulty or otherwise but the wife is not agreeable to this arrangement. According to Muslim jurists this will amount to a *Khul'*. It is submitted that the word *Khul'* has been loosely used here and is not the appropriate word. *Khul'*, as stated before, is based on a verse in the Qur'ān which says that when the spouses are apprehensive that they cannot live within the limits of Allah then there is no harm in the wife's giving some consideration to the husband to induce him to divorce her. Under this verse the following conditions must be fulfilled for the due application of the verse, *viz.*

(*a*) Apprehension of the husband and the wife that they cannot live within the limits of Allah.

(*b*) It is the wife who seeks a separation from the husband and it must be she who is to pay the consideration.

When a stranger secures a separation of the wife from the husband, these conditions are not fulfilled. The stranger's action can amount to a *ṭalāq bi'iwaḍ al-māl* or divorce in lieu of some consideration from him without any initiative by the wife. This arrangement is justified on the reasoning that the husband has got a right to divorce his wife irrespective of her desire one way or the other, and the fact that he is doing so in lieu of some consideration is immaterial. If we understand the basic ideas underlying these expressions, there can be no difficulty in the use of the appropriate word. If the parents or other guardian of a major wife secures a separation from the husband for some consideration, this arrangement too would amount to *Ṭalāq ala'l-māl*. But if the wife happens to be a minor then obviously being a minor she cannot enter into an agreement with the husband. In such a case if the father or other guardian for marriage finds that the marriage has proved a failure, or under its peculiar circumstances the ends of marriage cannot be achieved, they can, in the interest of the minor, obtain a *Khul'* for her. When the aversion or disagreement is mutual, the correct word would be *Mubārāh.*

Difference between Khul' and Ṭalāq: There is a difference between *Khul'* and *Ṭalāq* as will be clear from the following points :—

(1) A divorce is pronounced by the husband at his own initiative. A *Khul'* is, however, given at the instance of the wife when she has an invincible aversion for her husband.

(2) In divorce the husband becomes liable for the immediate payment of the wife's dower, but in *Khul'* it is the wife who makes a payment to the husband in order to induce him to release her from the marriage-tie and the consideration may consist of the dower itself.

(3) A divorce can be given only under certain specified conditions. Thus a husband cannot divorce his wife when she is in a state of impurity, that is, when she is having her menstrual course nor in the period of purity in which he has been intimate with her. But a *Khul'* can be validly given in such circumstances.[12]

Difference between Khul' and Ṭalāq ala'l-māl or Ṭalāq bi-'iwaḍ al-māl: The marriage is dissolved in *Ṭalāq bi-'iawḍ al-māl* by the use of the word "*Ṭalāq*", but this word is not used in the case of *Khul'* and the word *Khul'* or some equivalent word is used in the case of *Khul'*.

2. In *Khul'* dower shall generally be extinguished, but not in the case of *Ṭalāq ala'l-māl.*[13]

3. Another difference is that if the consideration be unlawful, the divorce shall be irrevocable in the case of *Khul'*, but revocable in the case of *Ṭalāq bi'iwaḍ al-māl.*

Difference between Ṭalāq and Mubārāh: The difference

12. Ibn Qudāmah, *op. cit.*, Vol. VII, p. 52.

13. Ibn 'Ābidīn, *op. cit.*, Vol. II, pp. 581-82.

between *Ṭalāq* and *Mubārāh* is that in case of *Mubārāh* the marriage is dissolved with the mutual consent of both the husband and the wife. But *Ṭalāq* is given by the husband on his own initiative and desire without any reference to the wife.

III. Religious Sanction

It is laid down in the Qur'ān, "Then if you fear that they (the spouses) cannot keep within the limits of Allah, there is no blame on them for what she gives up to become free thereby."[14] It means, in other words, that when the husband and the wife have reason to apprehend that the ends of marriage are not likely to be achieved by a continuance of their union, the woman need not scruple to release herself by offering such a compensation as may induce the husband to liberate her. There is nothing wrong in the husband's acceptance of such compensation, nor in the wife's giving it when the spouses are not living in harmony. It is stated at another place, "If a woman feareth ill-treatment from her husband or desertion, it is no sin for them twain if they make terms of peace between themselves. Peace is better. And avarice is met with in the minds (of men). If ye do good (to the other) and keep your duty, lo ! surely Allah is Aware of what ye do."[15]

IV. Traditions

There are two well-known Traditions about Khul'. The first relates to the case of Jamīlah, daughter of 'Abd Allah b. Ubyy b. Salūl and wife of Thābit Ibn Qays. One day she appeared before the Prophet (peace be on him) and said, "O Messenger of Allah ! I and Thābit can never live together. I saw him coming from the other side with some men. I found that he had the smallest stature, was the blackest and ugliest amongst them ; I swear by God that I do not dislike him on account of any religious or moral turpitude, but I dislike

14. Qur'ān, II : 229, Surah al-Baqarah.
15. Qur'ān, IV : 128, Surah al-Nisā'.

him on account of his ugliness. I swear by God that if I did not fear God I would spit on his face when he comes to me (meaning that she hated his very sight). O Messenger of Allah! You can see how beautiful I am while Thābit is an ugly person. I do not blame him for any depravity in his religious practices or morality, but I fear that I may be guilty of transgression of the injunctions of Islam." The Prophet (peace be on him) asked her if she would return the orchard given by Thābit to her as dower. She replied, "Yes: and if he demands more, then I am ready to give him more than that". The Messenger of Allah (peace be on him) said, "No: Not more than what he had given to you." He then asked Thābit to take back the orchard and to release her from the marriage-tie by divorcing her which he did.[16]

The other Tradition relates to another wife of Thābit named Ḥabībah, daughter of Suhayl. One early morning, when the Prophet (peace be on him) came out of his house, he saw Ḥabībah waiting outside. He asked her what the matter was and why she was standing there. She said that she could not pull on with Thābit. When Thābit came there, the Prophet (peace be on him) said to him, "Here is Ḥabībah daughter of Suhayl. She has complained against you." Ḥabībah said, "O Messenger of Allah! I have still got all that Thābit had given me for dower." The Prophet (peace be on him) then ordered Thābit to take it and to release her, that is, to divorce her.[17] It may be noted that her grievance was also due to the ugliness of Thābit and she too had used the same words as used by Jamīlah, *viz.*, "I would spit on his face if I did not fear Allah." [18]

Object: The object of *Khul'* is to enable a wife to get a

16. Al-Bayhaqī, *al-Sunan al-Kubrā*, Hyderabad, Deccan, 1353 A.H., Vol. VII, pp. 313-14; al-Suyūṭī, *al-Durr al-Manthūr*, Baghdad, 1377 A.H., Vol. I, p. 280.

17. Abū Dā'ūd, *Sunan*, Kanpur, 1346 A.H., Vol. I, p. 303; al-Suyūṭī, *op. cit.*, Vol. I, p. 280.

18. Ibn Mājah, *Sunan*, Lucknow, 1315 A.H., p. 149; al-Suyūṭī, *op. cit.*, Vol. I, p. 281.

release from the marriage-tie when she finds that the ends of the marriage are not likely to be achieved by a continuance of their union or when she suffers ill-treatment from her husband or when she finds that it is not possible for her to live with her husband in harmony and peace.

Wife's right under Khul'

Preliminary: A very important question relates to the wife's right under the doctrine of Khul'. There is no clear injunction in the Qur'ān or the Traditions about the rights and obligations of the spouses under Khul'. Hence there is a great difference of opinion amongst the Muslim jurists in this matter. It is, therefore, necessary to discuss it here fully. It may be pointed out at the very outset that the Muslim jurists have sometimes described Khul' as an agreement between the busband and the wife by means of which a wife gets a release from the marriage-tie. As stated in the beginning, it is described in *al-Hidāyah* as an agreement, but *al-Durr al-Mukhtār*, *al-Fatāwā al-Hindīyah*, *Fatāwā Qāḍī Khān* have not defined Khul' as an agreement. The word "agreement" has led to the notion that a *Khul'* can be effected only when the husband agrees to it and not otherwise. But this view is not correct as is established by the cases decided by the Prophet (peace be on him) and the Caliphs. Thus the dissolution of a marriage by the *Qāḍī* at the instance of the wife for a consideration to be paid by her to the husband shall amount to a Khul' though there is no agreement in this case between the spouses. The cases of dissolution of marriage under the doctrine of Khul' can arise under the following circumstances:

(1) When both the husband and the wife mutually decide a separation.

(2) When it is only the wife who wants to get a release from the marriage-tie.

(1) *By Mutual Consent*: If both the spouses want separation, there can be no difficulty. They can mutually agree to the termination of the marriage and the hubsand can divorce her

subject to such terms, if any, as may be agreed upon between them. Similarly, if it is the wife who wants a *Khul'* and the husband agrees to dissolve the marriage on certain conditions agreed upon between them then too there will be no difficulty. In these cases it would not be necessary for the parties to have any recourse to the *Qāḍī*.

(2) *Husband unwilling to Khul' or to the Consideration*: It is the second clause that presents a difficulty and which has given rise to much controversy. In this case it is only the wife who is desirous of the termination of the marriage. If the husband refuses to agree to *Khul'* or if the spouses cannot agree to the terms on which the marriage is to be dissolved, the question arises if anything can be done in such a case. Is the wife at all entitled to get a separation and if so, under what circumstances? If she does possess such a right, can she dissolve the marriage by herself or can the marriage be dissolved only by the *Qāḍī* at her instance? Another question that arises is whether she can claim the dissolution of the marriage as a matter of right or does it depend on the husband or the *Qāḍī* to grant her a *Khul'* or to refuse to do so. A further question then arises, namely, whether the *Qāḍī* can dissolve the marriage even when the husband does not agree to it.

Various aspects of Khul': The various aspects of *Khul'* may be discussed as under:

(*a*) Can the wife dissolve the marriage under the doctrine of *Khul'* by herself or can it be done only by the husband or the *Qāḍī*?

(*b*) Can the wife claim a *Khul'* as a matter of right on restoring or agreeing to restore to the husband the dower or other consideration given by the husband to her?

(*c*) Is the consent of the husband a condition precedent to the dissolution of the marriage under *Khul'* or has the *Qāḍī* the power to dissolve the marriage even when the husband does not want or agree to it?

(*a*) *Can the wife dissolve the marriage by herself*: The question to be considered is whether a wife can dissolve her marriage under *Khul'* by herself or has she to seek the aid of the *Qāḍī*. In all the cases decided by the Prophet (peace be on him) or the Caliphs, we do not find a single case in which the wife divorced herself under the doctrine of *Khul'* and then merely informed the Prophet (peace be on him) or the Caliph of what she had done. On the other hand, in all those cases the wives sought the intervention of the Prophet (peace be on him) or the Caliphs. This establishes the law that a wife cannot dissolve her marriage under *Khul'* by herself, but she has to get it done by the *Qāḍī*. Moreover, *Khul'* of necessity involves the payment of a consideration by the wife to the husband. The consideration is not restricted to the dower paid or to be paid by the husband but may be something different or in addition to that. When the husband does not agree to *Khul'* or to the consideration offered by the wife, the question of the amount and the nature of the consideration does arise because the wife cannot herself fix it. Hence it is necessity that there should be a third party who can decide the matter.

(*b*) *Has a wife an absolute right to Khul'*: It is a very important question whether a wife has got an absolute right to the dissolution of her marriage on restoring to the husband the consideration paid to her by him, or does the dissolution of marriage depend on the decision of the *Qāḍī*. We have seen that in all the cases decided by the Prophet (peace be on him) and the Caliphs, the wives were allowed *Khul'* on paying a consideration to the husband. But the matter does not end there; it requires further elucidation. It can be resolved into three questions, namely,

(*i*) Whether the ground on the basis of which the wife seeks a *Khul'* is her sole concern or if it is for the *Qāḍī* to determine if it is an adequate and reasonable ground for *Khul'* or not;

(*ii*) Whether the *Qāḍī* is bound by the allegation of the wife that she cannot tolerate her husband and cannot live with him within the limits of Allah or if he has to satisfy himself about this matter ;

(*iii*) Whether the *Qāḍī* is bound to dissolve the marriage if it is established that a harmonious married life is not possible.

(*i*) *Whether the Qāḍī has to judge the reasonableness of the wife's ground of separation*: We find that in none of the cases decided by the Prophet (peace be on him) or the Caliphs did they try to remonstrate with the wives or even tried to find out if they had got a reasonable ground for separation. This leads to the presumption that the *Qāḍī* has not to make any inquiry to find out if the wife's grievance is based on reasonable grounds or not.

It may, however, be contended that the grounds on the basis of which Jamīlah sought a separation from Thābit must have been known to the Prophet (peace be on him) as she was his cousin and he must have been able to judge its reasonableness as he must have fully known her feelings. Besides the ground for separation, namely, ugliness of Thābit, was so obvious that no inquiry was necessary. The first case served as a guide for the determination of the case of the second wife of Thābit, as in both cases Thābit figured as the husband and the ground on which the wives wanted a separation was the same in both the cases. We do not find anything in these cases which may enable us to decide for or against this contention.

An incident that happened in the time of 'Umar, the second Caliph, throws important light on this question. It is reported that a woman approached him and asked him to get her a release from her marriage-tie. 'Umar asked her to refrain from such a step, but she persisted in her demand whereupon the Caliph kept her in confinement for three days and nights in a dirty stable meant for keeping camels. He then called her and asked her if she had given up her desire for separation. She replied, "I swear by God that I have never slept better than during these three nights." On this the Caliph called the husband and said to him, "Divorce her even though you may take her very ear-rings."[19] A similar case came up for decision before 'Uthmān, the third Caliph. One Rubayyih daughter of Mu'awwadh, wanted to obtain *Khul'* from her husband who did not agree to it. She then sought the intervention of the Caliph who asked the husband to dissolve the marriage for any consideration he wanted.[20] In both the cases the ground on which the wives sought *Khul'* were not explained to the Caliphs nor did they try to find it, but even then they helped the wives to secure a *Khul'*. These cases establish the fact that it is no concern of the *Qāḍī* to see if the ground on which a wife seeks a *Khul'* is reasonable or not.

Again, there may be cases in which a wife may not like to disclose her reason for her disgust or dislike of her husband even though she may feel the reason very strongly. In such a case there can be only two alternatives for the *Qāḍī*, namely, to dissolve the marriage on the wife's request or to force her to live with her husband in spite of her disgust or dislike for him. The latter step, as pointed out by Mawlānā Mawdūdī, is more undesirable than the act of dissolving the marriage and may lead to some very undesirable results.[21] It will be clear from the above discussion that the *Qāḍī* has not to judge the reasonableness or otherwise of the wife's request for dissolution of her marriage. Shah Wali Ullah has gone to the length of holding, "Even if she (the wife) obtains Khula' without any reason it is lawful but not approved."[22]

(*ii*) *Has the Qāḍī to judge if harmony between the spouses is not possible:* The next question that arises is whether the *Qāḍī* has to accept the wife's version that she is unhappy with her husband and that she cannot tolerate him and live with him within the limits of Allah, or if he has to satisfy himself in the matter. We have already seen that the basis for *Khul'* is

19. Al-Suyūṭī, *op. eit.*, Vol. I, p 282.
20. *Ibid.*
21. Abu'l-A'lā Mawdūdī, *Ḥuqūq al-Zawjayn*, Lahore, 1961 A.D., p. 69.
22. *Al-Musawwa min Ahādith al-Muatta*, Vol. II, p. 160; Khurshid Bibi Vs. Muhammad Amin. P.L.D. 1967 s.c. 97.

an injunction in the Qur'ān which allows *Khul'*. It reads as under :

> "Then if you fear that they cannot keep within the limits of Allah, there is no blame on them for what she gives to become free thereby."[23]

The guiding words in the above verse are, "that they cannot keep within the limits of Allah", so that *Khul'* is permissible if it is found that the spouses are not living or cannot live within the limits of Allah. It means, in other words, that they cannot perform the duties and fulfil the obligations incumbent on them on account of their marriage. We have also seen that the second Caliph kept the wife under confinement for three days and nights. The question arises as to why he did so when she had not committed any offence. The only explanation can be that the Caliph wanted to gauge the true feelings of the woman, that is, whether she was seeking a divorce under a passing whim or if she was earnest in her desire for a separation from her husband. A marriage is a serious thing and cannot be dissolved lightly, and its dissolution is ordinarily considered undesirable except under special circumstances. It can be terminated only if the need for its dissolution is greater than to maintain it. It is, therefore, necessary for the *Qāḍī* to see if a harmonious married state subsists or can subsist between the parties. Hence the *Qāḍī* has to judge whether the wife is serious in her desire for a separation or she is acting on a passing whim. In other words, the *Qāḍī* has to determine if the marriage has proved a failure or not.

(*iii*) *Whether the Qāḍī is bound to dissolve marriage :* The question that is to be seen is whether the wife possesses an absolute right to *Khul'* when it is established that the spouses cannot live in harmony for any reason whatsoever. For the determination of this question we have to seek guidance from the Qur'ān. We find that it has repeatedly stressed the husband's duty in several verses. It makes it his duty to keep the wife with kindness. Thus it is laid down in the Qur'ān,

23. Qur'ān, II : 229, Surah al-Baqarāh.

"Then keep them in good fellowship or let (them) go with kindness."[24] This has again been repeated in the following verse which says : "Then retain them in kindness or set them free with kindness."[25] Husbands have been ordered to "retain them not for injury so that you exceed the limits. And whoever does this, he indeed, wrongs his own soul."[26] The husbands have again been told, "To treat them (the wives) kindly."[27] Even in the case of disagreement between the spouses it is stated, "So, if they obey you seek, not a way against them."[28] The husbands have been ordered not to desert their wives as is clear from the injunction, "Not to leave a wife in suspense."[29] The repetition of this injunction in several verses makes it quite clear that a husband is under a solemn obligation to keep his wife with kindness, and failure to comply with these injunctions of the Qur'ān will make him a transgressor of the sacred text. The Prophet (peace be on him) has also greatly stressed kind treatment by the husband towards his wife as has been stated in the introductory chapters. Even in the case of disagreement between the spouses it is laid down in the Qur'ān, "So, if they obey you, seek not a way against them."[30] It is stated in *Badā'i' al-Ṣanā'i'* that God Almighty has made it incumbent on the husbands to treat their wives kindly, but a husband shall not be considered to be keeping his wife kindly when he deprives her of her rights. What is to be seen is whether the spouses can live within the limits of Allah. If the husband is not happy with the wife, he can divorce her and he does not stand in need of the *Qāḍī's* help. *Khul'* has nothing to do with such a case and in *Khul'* we are only concerned with the wife. It has already been discussed before that it is not an essential

24. Qur'ān, II : 229, Surah al-Baqarah.
25. Qur'ān, II : 231, *ibid.*
26. *ibid.*
27. Qur'ān, IV : 19, Surah al-Nisā'.
28. Qur'ān, IV : 34, *ibid.*
29. Qur'ān, IV : 129, *ibid.*
30. Qur'ān, IV : 34, *ibid.*

condition for dissolving a marriage under *Khul'* that the husband should be at fault. The case of Jamīlah fully establishes this view. The wife may not be able to live happily with him. What is to be considered is if she is bound to live with her husband in such a case. Does Islam force her to live a miserable life and provide no relief for her? Can it be said that the unhappiness of the wife is no concern of Muslim law and that it would rather let the wife adopt an undesirable course of conduct than to dissolve the marriage. It would be unreasonable to think that Muslim law prefers that a marriage shall not be dissolved even when the wife cannot live within the limits of Allah and may transgress the limits enjoined on a wife and when the very ends of marriage shall be frustrated. The Qur'ānic duty to keep them with kindness requires that if mutual love cannot work, husband should release the wife from the bond of marriage. If in spite of the wife's unhappiness, the husband refuses to give her a release he shall be guilty of not complying with the injunctions of the Qur'ān. The marriage shall, therefore, become liable to be dissolved on the basis of the husband's defiance of the sacred text. In other words, the wife shall be entitled to the dissolution of her marriage if it is proved to the satisfaction of the *Qāḍī* that harmony is not possible between the spouses. We have not to see if the husband is at fault in any way, but what we have to see is whether harmony is possible between the spouses; the cause which results in the disharmony between the parties is immaterial. The *Qāḍī* shall give a relief to the wife by ordering the husband to divorce her and on his failure or refusal to do so the *Qāḍī* shall become competent to divorce the wife on behalf of the husband.[31] Wilson has pointed out that the very fact that an unscrupulous use of *Khul'* by the wife is strongly condemned by the Prophet (peace be on him) shows that she does possess a legal right to it in appropriate cases.[32] If she did not possess such a right then there could have been no necessity to condemn

31. Al-Kāsānī, *Badā'i' al-Ṣanā'i'*, Cairo, 1327 A.H., Vol. II, p. 323.
32. Wilson, Roland, *Anglo-Mohammadan Law*, Calcutta, p. 154.

its unscrupulous use by her. We cannot lose sight of the fact that possibly the husband may be put to hardship in such a case. There are two general rules of law that shall enable us to decide the case. The first is that the law cannot help the wrong-doer or a transgressor and the second is that that party shall be helped by law which is less at fault of the two.[33] Hence it is necessary for the *Qāḍī* to take these various matters into consideration when deciding a case. Thus if he finds that the husband is not at fault and the marriage has to be dissolved on account of the wife, he shall order the wife to compensate the husband by paying such compensation to him as the *Qāḍī* may deem reasonable. The case of Jamīlah is a precedent for this rule. If the *Qāḍī* finds that the wife is bent on the dissolution of her marriage, on account of the husband's fault, he may compel the husband to divorce the wife in which case the husband shall have to pay the dower of the wife.

The Traditions relating to the cases of Jamīlah and Ḥabībah. given above under 'Religious Sanction' leave no scope for doubt that a wife has got a legal right to get a Khul' and it was exercised by the wives without any objection by or disapproval of the Prophet (peace be on him). Some other cases decided by the Caliphs also support this view.

In an elaborate judgment, a Division Bench of the High Court of West Pakistan, Lahore Bench, has observed that the words, "If you fear...." are addressed to the State or the Judge and he has to find if the spouses cannot live within the limits of Allah. If he finds that such is the case, but can do nothing further and cannot dissolve the marriage, then the determination of this matter by the judge would become meaningless. The Bench, after discussing the matter at length, came to the decision that "The wife is entitled to dissolution of marriage on restoration of the benefit she had received from the husband if the judge apprehends that

33. Mubarak-un-Nisa Begum Vs. Syed Ashraf Ahmed (1341), *Deccan Law Report*, p. 555.

the parties will not observe the limits of God."[34]

The next question is whether the spouses can be said to be living within the limits of Allah in any particular case. For this purpose it is necessary to see if the aims and objects of the marriage are being achieved or if they have been frustrated. It may be stated at the outset that the failure of some of the objects of marriage mentioned in a previous chapter does not necessarily give a cause for its dissolution in some cases while the failure of a single object may be sufficient for a separation in some other cases. Hence every case has to be decided on its particular facts. To determine this question, it is necessary to consider and to state here, even at the cost of repetition, that the following are some of the chief aims and objects of a marriage according to Muslim jurists :—

(1) Legitimate indulgence of sexual passions.
(2) Procreation of children.
(3) Happy companionship between the spouses.
(4) Development of the soul in the upbringing of virtuous children and care of the wife.

I. Human beings have to satisfy their natural cravings and passions. Both religion and morality demand that it should be done in a legitimate manner. It is obvious that the spouses should be allowed to derive full pleasure out of the sexual act but this is possible only when they are not only physically fit but also when the relations between husband and wife are cordial. If this is not the case and they are, on the other hand, on bad terms or are hostile to each other, they cannot be expected to be intimate with each other. If they continue to be intimate or if one of them forces the other to be intimate with him or her, such intimacy will amount even to less than mere animal lust. Under the circumstances, the parties do not and cannot derive full or even reasonable pleasure out of the sexual act and this object of the marriage

34. Bilqis Fatima Vs. Najmul Ikram, P.L.D. 1959, Lahore, p. 566 at page 594.

shall be lost totally or partially under the peculiar circumstances of the case.

II. Procreation of Children

Procreation of children was a very important consideration in old times because this generally meant greater security. Also there is an inherent desire in men and women to have a child or children of their own. Another ground for this desire was a sort of provision for old age when the children were expected to look after their old and infirm parents. The presence of a child or children also provided a common interest and tended to bring the spouses together. The idea that the presence of children forms a link between the spouses, helps to patch up differences and brings them together does not hold good in every case. In the present-day economic life and high standard of living the presence of child or children does not necessarily serve to cement affection between the spouses on account of their common interest in a child or children. On the other hand, it may mar the relationship between them. It will be shutting one's eyes to the realities of life to say that the presence of children shall necessarily secure *sukūn* (peace of mind) to the spouses even when they are on unpleasant terms. When the marital relations between the spouses are unhappy, the mere presence of children is not likely to give *sukūn* or peace of mind to the spouses or at least to one of them. Peace of mind is obtained when there is happy companionship between the spouses, but it is absolutely lacking when the relations are unhappy and the presence of children can have no effect.

The desire to have child or children is as often a ground for disharmony as for harmony. Thus, a wife may be anxious to have a child but the husband may be averse to the idea on account of greater burden and responsibility for additional expenditure or loss of comfort. Similarly, it may be the wife who may object to have a child on account of her delicate health or the greater work and responsibility that will be thrown on her. The presence of a child or children is not an unmixed blessing. The responsibility to meet additional expenditure and the additional burden to rear the child often results in great worry and misery for the spouses. This state is rendered even more trying if the husband finds it hard to earn extra money for the additional expenses of the child. Someone has aptly said, "when poverty enters the door, love flies out of the window." Besides, as stated above, to have a child is no doubt one of the chief objects of marriage, but is certainly not the only object. Even if this object is achieved and the other objects are defeated then it is quite possible that the marriage may prove a failure.

III. Another aim of marriage is to secure happy companionship between two members of the opposite sexes and great stress is laid in the Qur'ān on this aspect of marriage. It is stated therein, "One of His signs is that He has created mates for you from among yourselves that you may find solace (and peace) in them and He has put between you love and compassion.[35] Again, it is stated in another verse, "He it is Who created you from a single soul, and of the same, did He make his mate that he may find comfort (solace) in her."[36] It is laid down at another place, "You are apparel for them and they are apparel for you."[37]

The words, "You may find solace (and peace) in her" and "He has put between you love and compassion" clearly indicate that there should be love between the spouses which results in a happy companionship between them. There can be no solace or peace or love and companionship between them if there is fundamental or constant discord between them. Hence, if it is shown that instead of there being love between them there is mutual hatred, then obviously this object—and it is a very important object of marriage—shall fail. The wife shall, in such a case, certainly have a reasonable

35. Qur'ān, XXI : 21, Surah al-Rūm.
36. Qur'ān, IX : 189, Surah al-Ar'āf.
37. Qur'ān, II : 187, Surah al-Baqarah.

and genuine ground for the dissolution of her marriage.

IV. When there is strife between the spouses the upbringing of children is more often than not marred ; and this important aim of marriage, the most important one from the point of view of the community is lost. Dissolution of marriage in such circumstances is the best solution. It is laid down in the Qur'ān, "And if they separate, Allah will make both independent out of His abundance":[38] and again, "Then, when they are about to reach their (prescribed) term, keep them with kindness or put them away with kindness.."[39]

The above discussion would show that the objects of marriage are lost if the relations between the spouses are very unhappy. Such a condition of life will constitute a reasonable and genuine ground for the dissolution of marriage. But mere differences of temperament, or small differences should be distinguished from serious strife and quarrels. The former are often bound to happen between two individuals, however, much they may love each other. Hence mere slight incompatibility of temperament is not considered sufficient ground for the dissolution of a marriage. It will have to be seen in such a case if the disagreement between the spouses is of such a serious nature as to lead to the presumption that they cannot live in peace together. If it is not of such serious nature, it will not constitute a ground for the termination of the marriage because people are bound to have different dispositions which will result in difference of temperament. For *Khul'* there should exist such a fundamental repugnance for the husband or serious incompatibility as to create a hazard for the parties not being able to live within the boundaries fixed by Allah.

The only condition for the dissolution of a marriage on the desire of the wife is that "they (the spouses) cannot keep within the limits of Allah", that is, that they cannot fulfil the obligations cast on them by their marriage so that the

38. Qur'ān, IV : 131, Surah al-Nisā'.
39. Qur'ān, II : 231, Surah al-Baqarah.

harmonious married state, as envisaged by Islam, is not possible between them.

The Court will also take into consideration the fact that the rift between the parties is so serious that they cannot live happily and that there is risk that one of the spouses may be led astray by this condition of the married life which may be due to serious incompatibility of temperament. Here incompatibility of temperament has been defined as incapacity for harmonious association on account of difference of disposition or frame of mind resulting in lack of mutual adaptation.[40] If the difference in the dispositions of the spouses has reached to such an extent as to engender hatred in both or one of them so that it is not possible for them to live together in peace and harmony then the marriage is liable to be dissolved at the instance of the aggrieved spouse. The Courts have to infer this fact from instances of the behaviour of the spouses.[41]

Unscrupulous Use Condemned: It has been stated in a previous chapter that a husband is not entitled to exercise the power of divorce unless there is some valid ground to do so. Similarly, the wife is not entitled to get her marriage dissolved under the provisions of *Khul'* unless there are some genuine grounds for the same. It is only in cases where it is impossible or very difficult for the wife to live happily with her husband and when there is no scope for reconciliation, that *Khul'* is permissible. An unscrupulous use of *Khul'* has been strongly condemned in Islam. A wife must, therefore, ask her husband for a *Khul'* only when there is justification for it.

Husband's Consent and the Qāḍī's Authority: The next question to be considered is whether the husband's consent is a condition precedent to the dissolution of marriage under the provisions of *Khul'* or has the *Qāḍī* the power to separate the parties even against the wishes of the husband, when he is satisfied that the spouses cannot live "within the limits of Allah."

40. Sayeeda Khanum Vs. Mohd. Sami, 1952 P.L.D., Lahore 113.
41. *Ibid.*

This is a very important rule of Muslim law and greatly affects the rights of Muslim wives. It is, therefore, necessary to discuss the matter in some detail.

The Muslim jurists have generally expressed the view that a *Qāḍī* is not competent to do so. The Courts have followed this view. Thus it was held by the Allahabad High Court that a suit by a Muslim wife to compel her husband to give her a *K͟hul'* divorce is not maintainable. It was held that the divorce by *K͟hul'* is the sole act of the husband, and to exercise such power is wholly a matter within his own discretion and it is not demandable by the wife as a matter of right under the Muslim law.[42] The Lahore High Court has expressed the same view in two elaborate judgements. The first case is that of Mst. Umar Bibi Vs. Mohd Din.[43] It was held that it is only the husband or his agent who can effect a *K͟hul'* divorce, and that it is not possible for a *Qāḍī* or Court to do so by virtue of the powers vested in them. The second case was decided by a Full Bench and the same opinion was expressed.[44]

The cases decided by the Prophet (peace be on him) and the Caliphs strongly lead to the view that the decision of such a case does not depend on the sweet will of the husband. The case of Jamīlah and her husband T͟hābit b. Qays has been fully discussed before. It has been stated there that the Prophet (peace be on him) asked T͟hābit to divorce his wife.

They also establish the fact that in genuine cases *K͟hul'* was freely granted. But in course of time women's rights were greatly curtailed by adverse views, and men placed many restrictions on their rights and the present doctrine of *K͟hul'* is one of such cases. We have to remember that Islam attaches great importance to the happiness of the spouses and does not force them to live a miserable life simply in order to maintain the integrity of marriage.

It was stated in the case of Umar Bibi Vs. Muhammad Din

42. Mariam Bibi Vs. Nur Mohd. (1882) All. 83.
43. Umar Bibi Vs. Mohd Din A.I.R. 1945, Lahore: 51.
44. Sayeeda Khanum Vs. Muhammad Salim, 1952, P.L.D. Lahore: 113.

that in the Traditions relating to the cases of Jamīlah and Ḥabībah, wives of Thābit b. Qays, it was not the Prophet (peace be on him) who pronounced the divorce, but it was Thābit who had divorced his wives which he was bound to do on account of his great reverence for the Prophet (peace be on him) and that the incidents do not establish the view that the *Qāḍī* has the right to dissolve the marriage. According to the Sunnī law, the *Qāḍī* cannot dissolve a marriage himself on his own initiative. The right to divorce the wife belongs under the Sunnī law absolutely to the husband. Where the *Qāḍī* is satisfied that there is a genuine need for separation between the wife and the husband he has to ask the husband to divorce her. If the husband fails or refuses to do so, he becomes a transgressor of the verse in the Qur'ān, namely, "To keep the wives with humanity", and the *Qāḍī* is seized of the power to divorce the wife on behalf of the husband. According to a version, the Prophet (peace be on him) had used the words, "*iqbal al-ḥadīqah wa ṭalliqhā taṭliqah*", meaning (accept the orchard, and divorce her).[45] This amounts to an order.

Further, we have to distinguish between the Prophet's orders, suggestions and recommendations because he never imposed his own will on others. Thus there is a Tradition that there was a person named Mughīth who was madly in love with his wife Barīrah who did not care for him. The reason for the wife's aversion was that Mughīth was an ugly, black slave. He became so much affected by her indifference that he used to roam about weeping in the streets of Madīnah after her. The Prophet (peace be on him) felt pity for Mughīth and one day said to Barīrah, "Would that you would return to him (her husband)!" Barīrah asked if it was an order whereupon the Prophet (peace be on him) said that it was not an order and that he only wanted to intercede on behalf of Mughīth. The woman refused to go back to her husband, and the Prophet (peace be on him) did not order her to return to her husband.[46] His order to Qays in the case of

45. Al-Bukhārī, *al-Jāmi' al-Ṣaḥīḥ*, Delhi, 1937, A.D. Vol. II, p. 794.
46. *Ibid.*, p. 795.

Jamīlah and his non-interference in the case of Barīrah fully establish that he did not interfere in the affairs of others unless a case called for an order by him as a *Qāḍī*. This fact, namely, his non-intervention in the case of Barīrah and his intervention in the cases of Jamīlah and Ḥabībah and his order to Thābit, shows that it is open to a *Qāḍī* to order a husband to divorce his wife if he is satisfied that it is necessary in a particular case to pass such an order.

The interpretation of the verse, "To keep the wives with kindness", by the Muslim jurists is illustrated by the case of an impotent person. It is explained that such a husband cannot be deemed to be keeping his wife with kindness and so it is his duty in obedience to the above injunction of the Qur'ān to release her from the marital-tie. If he fails to do so then it is the duty of the *Qāḍī* to see that the wrong done to the wife is rectified and so he shall order the husband to divorce her. If the husband refuses or fails to comply with this order, he becomes a transgressor and, it being the duty of the *Qāḍī* to redress wrongs, he shall use his power to separate the wife from her husband.[47] The Prophet (peace be on him) acting as a *Qāḍī* had, therefore, to ask the husband to dissolve the marriage. As Thābit readily divorced his wives, there arose no necessity for the Prophet (peace be on him) to use his power as a *Qāḍī*. The *Qāḍī* has, in the first instance, to ask the husband to release the wife from the marriage-tie and it will be only on the husband's failure or refusal to comply with the *Qāḍī's* order that the *Qāḍī* shall become entitled to act on behalf of the husband and to divorce the wife. There is absolutely no reason to restrict the application of the rule to the case of an impotent person alone and not to apply it to other cases of equal importance when the fault lies with the husband or when the wife does not find it possible to live happily with him.

The incident that happened in the time of 'Umar, the second Caliph, and which has been fully described in the

47. Ibn 'Ābidīn, *op. cit.*, Vol. II, p. 611.

previous sub-section throws some light on this question. The Caliph had kept in confinement for three days and nights the wife who wanted a release from her marriage-tie. After being satisfied with the genuineness of the wife's aversion for her husband he told the husband to divorce her.[48] There was a possibility that the husband might have refused to comply with the Caliph's suggestion if it was only a recommendation because people were very free with him. The Caliph must have known that he could dissolve the marriage on the husband's refusal to do so, otherwise where was the necessity to keep the wife in confinement. Supposing the husband had refused to divorce the wife and the Caliph did not possess the right to dissolve the marriage then the confinement of the woman would have been not only meaningless but an infringement of her freedom. 'Umar, therefore, must have felt sure that on the husband's refusal to divorce his wife, he as a Ruler or a *Qāḍī* could dissolve the marriage. This also supports the view that a *Qāḍī* can in case of necessity order the husband to divorce his wife.

A similar case arose before 'Uthmān, the third Caliph. One Rubayyī', daughter of Mu'awwadh, wanted to get a divorce from her husband who did not agree to it. She then sought the intervention of the Caliph who asked the husband to divorce her for any consideration he desired.

If it is within the absolute discretion of the husband to agree to a *Khul'* divorce and if he refuses to free his wife from the marriage-tie even when it is established that he and his wife cannot keep within the limits of Allah and she consents to pay a consideration for getting out of the marriage-tie, then the wife shall have to remain tied to her marriage-bond though she may transgress the limits incumbent on her under Islam and may even lead an immoral life. It would be unreasonable to think that such a wife can be allowed no relief. No one would lay down such a rule of law. Islām does not

48. Al-Suyūtī, *op. cit.*, Vol. I, p. 282.

and cannot tolerate such a condition of the wife and in such a case the very ends of marriage shall be frustrated. Besides, if Khul' is made to depend on the sweet will of the husband then the very purpose of the doctrine of Khul' is rendered infructuous. Even in the absence of Khul' it would be always open to a wife to induce her husband to divorce her by making a payment to him. The laying down of this doctrine shows that it is something independent of the ordinary case of inducing the husband to divorce the wife.

The present-day Courts hold the same position as was held by the *Qāḍīs* in old times. They certainly can dissolve a marriage for reasons for which it could have been dissolved under Muslim law regardless of the fact whether that reason has been recognised by certain Courts or not.[49] This view finds full support by clause IX of sub-section VIII of section 2 of the Dissolution of Muslim Marriages Act, 1939, which allows the dissolution of marriage on any ground which is recognised as valid for its dissolution under Muslim law. The Supreme Court of Pakistan has taken this view.[50]

The *Qāḍī* has to redress a wrong and so if he finds that a marriage has proved a failure on account of the husband, he has to separate the spouses. As a general rule, if the *Qāḍī* finds that the husband is at fault, he shall order the husband to divorce his wife and the husband shall become liable for the payment of her dower if not already paid. If it is the wife who is found to be at fault, the *Qāḍī* shall dissolve the marriage under *Khul'* so that the wife shall have to pay such compensation to the husband as may be fixed by the *Qāḍī*. A person is considered to be at fault when he or the wife does not follow the laws laid down by Allah or when he or she transgresses the limits fixed by Allah.

Who can Secure a Khul'?

A Khul' can be obtained by a wife, by herself or through

49. Umar Bibi Vs. Mohammad Din, A.I.R. 1945, Lahore : 51.
50. Khurshid Bibi Vs. Muhammad Amin, 1967 P.L.D. S.C. 97.

her father or other guardian or through an agent who may be even a stranger. If she happens to be a minor then her father can obtain a *Khul'* on her behalf from her husband.[51]

Mālikī Law. Under the Mālikī law a father or guardian may obtain a release on behalf of and out of the property of his minor daughter who is still under his authority and upon whom he has imposed the marriage, if he thinks it better for her. This may be done even without the woman's consent.[52]

Shāfi'ī Law. Shāfi'ī has expressed the same view as stated by Abū Ḥanīfah.[53]

Ḥanbali Law. Aḥmad ibn Ḥanbal agrees with Mālik in the matter.[54]

Essentials. There are certain conditions which must be fulfilled before a *Khul'* can be effected and they are considered to be essential for a *Khul'*. It will be convenient to discuss the matter under the following heads:—

(*a*) Subsistence of marriage,
(*b*) Proposal and acceptance,
(*c*) Expression or language used,
(*d*) Capacity of the husband and wife,
(*e*) Intention,
(*f*) Consideration, and
(*g*) Time of *Khul'*.

(*a*) *Subsistence of Marriage.* It is an essential condition of *Khul'* that the parties must stand to one another as husband and wife. It means, in other words, that a marriage be subsisting between them at the time of *Khul'*. But it is immaterial whether the marriage has or has not been consummated. Moreover, the marriage must be valid. A wife cannot, therefore, exercise a *Khul'* when the marriage is *bāṭil* (void) or

51. *Al-Fatāwā al-Hindiyah*, *op. cit.*, Vol. II, p. 124.
52. Ibn Qudāmah, *op. cit.*, Vol. VII, p. 83.
53. Ibn Rushd, *Bidā'yat al-Mujtahid*, Cairo, n.d., Vol. II, p. 57.
54. Ibn Qudāmah, *op. cit.*, Vol. VII, p. 83.

fāsid (irregular) because a void or irregular marriage does not create the relationship of husband and wife between a man and a woman. If a wife pays consideration to her husband for obtaining Khul' and it transpires subsequently that the marriage was void or invalid then he is bound to return the consideration received by him from the wife as he was not entitled to it.[55] Hence there can be no Khul' if a man and a woman do not stand to one another as husband and wife at the time when it is exercised. Thus if a wife is divorced by an irrevocable divorce or one of the spouses apostatizes, the marital relationship ceases and Khul' is not then permissible.[56]

(*b*) *Proposal and Acceptance* :

I. Proposal may be made by a Spouse or other Person. It is a necessary condition of Khul' that there must be a proposal by one party and its acceptance by the other party. But it is not necessary that the proposal for Khūl' should emanate from one of the parties to a marriage. It can be made by the guardian of a minor. According to some jurists a third party may persuade the husband to give a Khul' to his wife for a consideration agreed to be paid.[57] Thus, according to them, should a third person say to the husband, "give a Khul' to your wife in consideration of my house or for so much money belonging to me," and should the husband act accordingly, a Khul' shall be effected. In the same way if some persons ask the wife if she was willing to get a Khul' in consideration of a specified return and she agrees and then they ask the husband if he agrees to give a Khul' for the specified consideration and he too agrees then a Khul' shall be effected.[58] A husband's consent to a proposal for Khul' may be express or implied as when he accepts the consideration for a proposed Khul' without expressly giving his consent to it. The marriage shall be dissolved on his acceptance of the consideration even when

55. Ibn 'Ābidīn, *op. cit.*, Vol. II, p. 572.
56. *Ibid.*
57. *Al-Fatāwā al-Hindīyah, op. cit.*, Vol. II, p. 124 ; Ibn 'Ābidīn, *op. cit.*, Vol. II, p. 572.
58. *Al-Fatāwā al-Hindīyah, op. cit,*, Vol. II, p. 124.

he does not divorce the wife.

The proposal must convey the idea of the passing of a consideration for *Khul'* and so there should be a mention in it of words like sale, exchange etc. Thus the wife may say to her husband, "I want to purchase your right of divorce for so much," or "give me a release from the marriage-tie for so much." Similarly the husband may say to his wife, "I sell or exchange the right of divorce to you for so much."

In Urdu language, the words sell, purchase and similar words are generally not used but the idea of payment of consideration is conveyed directly or indirectly to the other party in the proposal and in its acceptance. Thus the wife may say, "I give up my such and such claim as consideration for your divorcing me" or "I give up my claim for my dower while my husband releases me from the marriage-tie."

Acceptance—Requisites of. The acceptance of a proposal for *Khul'* must be expressed in the same terms as the proposal, that is, the acceptance cannot introduce a new or different consideration or a different condition. When a wife delivers the consideration demanded by the husband without expressly giving her consent to the husband's proposal, it shall be deemed to be an implied consent and a *Khul'* would be effected. Similarly, it is not necessary that the husband should expressly give his assent to the wife's proposal. Such assent may be inferred from his conduct. Thus where a wife seeks a *Khul'* for a specified consideration and the husband accepts the same, his consent shall be presumed and a *Khul'* shall be effected as soon as he accepts the same.

Time of Acceptance. The wife must give her reply in the same sitting in which she receives information of the husband's proposal. If she fails to do so, her right shall be lost and the husband's proposal shall cease to have any effect.[59] Similarly, the husband should accept the wife's proposal in the same sitting in which he receives the proposal. If he fails to do so, the proposal shall stand cancelled.[60]

59. Ibn 'Ābidīn, *op. cit.*, Vol. II, p. 573.

60. *Ibid.*, p. 573.

The condition that the wife should declare her acceptance to the husband's proposal for Khul' in the same sitting in which she receives it is very hard. It seems to be based on the Muslim jurists' conception of the law of contracts which has lost much of its importance in modern times. Under the present law, an acceptance of an offer has to be made within a reasonable time and it is not only desirable but necessary that effect should be given to this aspect of *Khul'* also, irrespective of the fact whether it is the wife or the husband who has to express the assent or dissent.

In India and Pakistan, the Muslim Law of Contracts has been superseded by the existing law and the above-mentioned provisions should no longer be held binding on the parties.

II. Option by Wife. The wife can reserve an option in respect of her proposal for *Khul'* that she shall have the right to withdraw or revoke her proposal within a certain specified time.[61]

III. Option by Husband. A husband cannot reserve an option in respect of *Khul'* that he can withdraw or cancel his offer within a specified time.[62] If he makes such a proposal and the wife gives her consent to the same, the option shall be invalid and the divorce shall be effected.[63]

But a husband can give an option to the wife to accept or refuse to accept his proposal for *Khul'* within a certain specified time according to Abū Ḥanīfah.[64] Muḥammad and Abū Yūsuf do not agree with him and hold the option to be invalid.[65] A divorce shall be effected on the acceptance of the husband's proposal by the wife without any regard to the option.

IV. Retraction of Proposal by Wife. If it is the wife who

61. Ibn 'Ābidīn, *op. cit.*, Vol II, p. 574.
62. *Ibid.*
63. *Al-Fatāwā al-Hindiyah*, *op. cit.*, Vol. II, p. 122; Ibn 'Ābidīn, *op. cit.*, Vol. II, p. 574.
64. Al-Marghīnānī, *al-Hidāyah*, Delhi, 1380 A.H., Vol. II, p. 387; Ibn 'Ābidīn, *op. cit.*, Vol. II, p. 574.
65. Al-Marghīnānī, *op. cit.*, Vol. II, p. 387.

makes the proposal for *Khul'*, that is, she asks her husband to divorce her in lieu of a specified consideration, she can retract her proposal at any time before its acceptance by the husband.[66]

V. Retraction by Husband. If the proposal proceeds from the husband, as when he tells his wife that he is prepared to give *Khul'* on receiving a specified consideration by her then he cannot retract it till the wife expresses her consent or dissent to it.[67]

Shāfi'ī Law. According to Shāfi'ī, a husband has the right to withdraw his offer of *Khul'* at any time before its acceptance by the wife. It is explained that the husband's offer is a conditional offer to effect a bilateral agreement so that the contract is not completed till the consent of the wife, and so he can retract his proposal at any time before the contract becomes complete.[68]

Similarly, if it is the wife who has made the offer then she has a right to withdraw it at any time before its acceptance by the husband.[69]

Ḥanbalī Law. Under the Ḥanbalī law, the husband can retract his proposal at any time before its acceptance by the wife.[70]

Conditional Khul'. The wife and the husband can propose a *Khul'* subject to a condition contingent on the occurrence or non-occurrence of certain specified future events.

VI. Sometimes the parties want to make their position safe before the acceptance of *Khul'* lest the other party should back out after dower has been released or divorce has been pronounced. To provide against such a contingency it is usual to propose a *Khul'* subject to a condition. Thus

66. *Al-Fatāwā al-Hindīyah, op. cit.*, Vol. II, p. 122.
67. *Ibid.*
68. Al-Ramlī, Muḥammad b. Abi'l 'Abbās, *Nihā'yat al-Muḥtāj*, Cairo, 1357, A.H., Vol. VI, p. 399.
69. *Ibid.*
70. Sharaf al-Dīn Mūsā al-Ḥijawī, *al-Iqnā'*, Cairo, n.d. Vol. III, p. 260.

the wife may say to her husband, "When you divorce me then you shall stand relieved of the liability for the payment of dower". Similarly, the husband may say, "When you pay me such and such consideration I shall be presumed to have given you a *Khul'* and the marriage then shall stand dissolved."

An offer for *Khul'* by the husband should be distinguished from a conditional divorce. The difference between them is that a *Khul'* pronounced with some such safeguards as mentioned above is effected and the marriage dissolved immediately the proposal for it is accepted irrespective of the payment of the consideration forthwith.[71] In case of a conditional divorce the marriage shall subsist as long as the condition is not satisfied.[72]

VII. Effect of Acceptance of Proposal. It can be gathered from various books on Muslim law that as soon as a proposal for *Khul'* has been accepted by the other party, a *Khul'* shall be effected irrespective of the fact as to whether the consideration agreed upon has been paid or not.[73]

(c) *Expression or Language Used.* Under the Sunnī law it is not an essential condition of *Khul'* that only the Arabic language should be used to obtain or to give a *Khul'*. The spouses can use any language which they know and use. *Fatāwā-i Qāḍi Khān* has given a number of expressions in Persian by which a *Khul'* can be effected. It is also stated in *al-Fatāwā al-'Ālamgīrīyah* that *Khul'* given in Persian language is valid.[74] Hence if a *Khul'* is permissible in Persian, it is obvious that it can be given in any other language also. This view finds support from the fact that the wife should understand the meaning of the expression of *Khul'* because

71. See Failure to pay consideration.
72. For discussion see "conditional divorce."
73. Khurram Ali: *Ghayat al-Autar* (Urdu tr. of *al-Durr al-Mukhtār*). Lucknow, 1925 A.D., Vol. II, pp. 179, 188; *Fatāwā al-'Alamgiriyah,* (Urdu tr, of *Fatāwā al-Hindiyah*), Lucknow, 1899 A.D., Vol. II, pp. 350, 353.
74. *Al-Fatāwā al-Hindiyah, op. cit.*, Vol. II, p. 123.

Khul' amounts to an exchange and there can be no exchange unless the return to be paid is understood by the party concerned, that is, the wife in this case.[75]

Shāfi'ī Law. Under the Shāfi'ī law every divorce in consideration of property constitutes *Khul'* irrespective of the fact whether the word "*Khul'*" has been used or not.[76] It is, however, necessary that the word or expression must refer to a *Khul'* whether expressly or by implication.[77]

Mālikī Law. The Mālikī law is the same as the Shāfi'ī law.[78]

Ḥanbalī Law. The Ḥanbalī law prescribes the use of certain specified words such as *Khul'*, *Faskh* (cancellation) and *Fidyah* (surrender) and describes it as that divorce in which the husband separates from his wife by the use of certain specified words for a consideration accepted by him.[79]

(*d*) *Capacity of the Spouses.* Both the husband and the wife must satisfy the same conditions as are prescribed in the case of divorce.

1. Husband. A minor or insane husband cannot give a *Khul'*. His father or other guardian also cannot give a *Khul'* on his behalf, because the minor is not possessed of the right to divorce his wife, and the father or other guardian cannot possess a better right than that of the minor.[80]

Mālikī Law. The husband should be major and sane. But under the Mālikī law, the guardian of a minor or insane husband can grant a *Khul'* on behalf of a minor husband. The compensation is, however, to be received by the husband himself.[81]

75. Ibn 'Ābidīn, *op. cit.*, Vol. II, p. 574.
76. Ibn Qudāmah, *op. cit.*, Vol. VII, p. 57.
77. *Ibid.*
78. *Ibid.*
79. *Ibid.*
80. *Al-Fatāwā al-Hindīyah, op. cit.*, Vol. II, p. 125.
81. Al-Sha'rānī, *al-Mīzān al-Kubrā*, Cairo, 1279 A.H., Vol. II, p. 135; Ibn Rushd, *op. cit.*, Vol. II, p. 57.

Shāfi'ī Law. Under the Shafi'i law the husband should be major and sane.[82] The guardian of a minor husband cannot give a *Khul'* to the wife on behalf of the husband.[83]

Ḥanbalī Law. The Ḥanbali law also requires that the husband should be major and sane.[84] As regards the guardian's power to give a *Khul'* on behalf of a minor or insane husband, there are two reports in the matter. According to one the guardian can give a *Khul'* in such circumstances, but, according to the other, he is not competent to do so.[85]

II. Wife. Any adult and sane wife can seek a *Khul'*. The wife must possess understanding and reason so that she can understand the significance and consequences of *Khul'*.[86] If she lacks in one or both of these essential conditions then the payment of the consideration stipulated by her shall not be incumbent on her, nor shall her dower be extinguished, but a divorce shall be effected on the husband's acceptance of the offer.[87] But in such a case the divorce shall be revocable and not irrevocable.[88] A wife is not competent to obtain a *Khul'* for consideration even if she is a major but is lacking in worldly wisdom. This rule is based on the ground that she cannot realise the consequences of her act, namely, securing a *Khul'* and what is good or bad for her. In such a case a divorce shall be effected but the payment of the consideration shall not be incumbent on her.[89] If the girl is minor or is insane, her father or other guardian (for marriage) can obtain a *Khul'* for her provided the consideration is paid out of his own property.[90] If he

82. Al-Sha'rānī, *al-Mizān al-Kubrā*, Cairo, 1279 A.H., Vol. II, p. 135; Ibn Rushd, *op. cit.*, Vol. II, p. 57.
83. *Ibid.*
84. Sharf al-Dīn Mūsā al-Ḥijawī. *op. cit.*, Vol. III, p. 252.
85. Al-Sha'rānī, *op. cit.*, Vol. II, p. 135.
86. Ibn Nujaym, *al-Baḥr al-Rā'iq*, Vol. IV, p. 90, Cairo 1311 A.H. Syed Amir Ali, *Al-Fatāwā 'Alamgiriyah op. cit.*, Vol. II, p. 356; Ibn 'Ābidin, *op. cit.*, Vol. II, pp. 583.
87. Ibn 'Ābidīn, *op. cit.*, Vol. II, pp. 583-84.
88. *Ibid.*, p. 583.
89. *Ibid.*
90. Ibn Rushd, *op. cit.*, Vol. II, p. 57; al-Sha'rānī, *op. cit.*, Vol. II, p. 135.

stipulates payment of consideration out of her property and the husband agrees to it, *Khul'* shall be effected, but the consideration shall not be payable.[91] The father too shall not be liable for its payment unless he has taken a personal responsibility for payment of a specified consideration.[92] A wife can validly get a *Khul'* even in *maraḍ al-mawt* or death illness, but the consideration in such a case cannot exceed one-third of her assets.[93]

Mālikī Law. Under the Mālikī law the wife should be major and should possess understanding. A father or guardian may obtain a release on behalf and out of the property of his minor daughter who is still under his authority and upon whom he has imposed the marriage. This may be done even without the woman's consent.[94]

Shāfi'ī Law. Under the Shāfi'ī law the wife should be major and sane. If an insane girl asks her husband for *Khul'* for some consideration and the husband agrees to it, *Khul'* shall be effected but no consideration shall be payable. The separation shall amount to a *ṭalāq raj'ī* (revocable divorce).[95] But if the father or guardian has given consent to the payment of the consideration, the dissolution shall amount to an irrevocable divorce and the consideration shall be payable.[96]

Ḥanbalī Law. The Ḥanbalī law is the same as Ḥanafī law. Under the Ḥanbalī law, a minor wife can obtain a *Khul'* with the consent of her father.[97] The father or other guardian of such a girl can obtain a *Khul'* on her behalf, if he pays the consideration out of his own property.[98]

91. Ibn 'Ābidin, *op. cit.*, Vol. II, pp. 583-84.
92. *Ibid.*
93. *Ibid.* p. 586 ; Shaykhzadah Abdar Rahman b. Muhammad, *Majmal Unhur*, p. 568, Cairo.
94. Al-Sha'rānī, *op. cit.*, Vol. II, p. 135 ; Ibn Rushd, op. cit., Vol. II, p. 57.
95. Al-Ramlī, Muḥammad b. Abi 'l-'Abbās, *Nihāyat al-Muḥtāj, op. cit.*, Vol. VI, p. 389.
96. *Ibid.*, p. 388.
97. Al-Sha'rānī, *op. cit.*, Vol. II, p. 135.
98. *Ibid.*

(e) Intention :

I. Khul' given under Compulsion. Ordinarily intention is a necessary condition of *Khul'* because the amount of consideration of *Khul'* cannot be settled when the husband has no intention of giving a release to the wife in lieu of a specified consideration. But as in the case of divorce the Ḥanafīs hold that a *Khul'* given under compulsion is valid.[99]

Khul' under Compulsion by the Husband. If the husband forces his wife to take a *Khul'* and she does so, a divorce shall be effected, but the payment of the consideration shall not be incumbent on her.[100] It is stated in *Jawāhir al-'Uqūd* that if a husband forces his wife to seek a *Khul'* under coercion as by threatening to kill her or beating her or by starving her then a divorce shall be effected but the payment of any consideration shall not be incumbent on her. The divorce in such a case shall be *Raj'ī* or revocable.[101] The same view has been given in *al-Mughni.*[102]

Mālikī, Shāfi'ī and Ḥanbalī Laws. As stated before, Mālik, Shāfi'i and Aḥmad ibn Ḥanbal do not accept the validity of a divorce under compulsion. The same principle of law will naturally apply in the case of *Khul'*. It is stated in *Nihāyat al-Muḥtāj* that a husband who is competent to give a divorce can also give a *Khul'*, but if he is not competent to give a divorce then he cannot give a *Khul'* also.[103] The author of *Jawāhir al-'Uqūd* has stated that under the Mālikī, Ḥanbalī and Shāfi'ī laws a *Khul'* under compulsion is not valid.[104]

Khul' given under the Influence of Drink. There is a difference of opinion amongst the Sunnī jurists in respect of a *Khul'* given under the influence of drink. According to

99. *Al-Fatāwā al-Hindīyah, op. cit.*, Vol. II, p. 125.
100. Ibn 'Ābidīn, *op. cit.*, Vol. II, p. 576.
101. Muḥammad b. Ahmed, *Jawāhir al-'Uqūd*, Cairo, 1374 A.H., Vol. II, p. 114.
102. Ibn Qudāmah, *op. cit.*, Vol. VII, pp. 55, 56.
103. Al-Ramli, *op. cit.*, Vol. VI, p. 388.
104. Muḥammad b. Ahmed, *op. cit.*, Vol. II, p. 103.

Dāwūd of Isfahan, a *Khul'* by a drunken man is not valid. Ḥasan b. Ziyād and Abu'l-Ḥasan al-Karkhī and Abu'l-Qāsim al-Ṣaffār are also of the same opinion. Shafi'ī expressed different views at different times. Abū Naṣr b. Muḥammad b. Salām says that *Khul'* shall be effected only if his act of drinking is voluntary and without any necessity.[105] Abū Ḥanīfah stated that according to *Istiḥsān* the *Khul'* is not valid, but according to *Qiyās*, it is valid. Abū Yūsuf also holds it to be valid.[106] In the face of this difference of opinion it is open to the *Qāḍī* to accept and follow any one of these views and it is stated in *Fatāwāi Qāḍi Khān* that the *Khul'* shall be valid if so held by the *Qāḍī*.[107] It is stated in *al-Fatāwā al-Hindīyah* that such *Khul'* is valid.[108]

Māliki Law. Mālik holds that a *Khul'* under the influence of drink shall be valid.

Shāfi'ī and Ḥanbalī Laws. Both Shāfi'i and Aḥmad b. Ḥanbal have expressed different views at different times. But the usually accepted view of the *Imāms* is that *Khul'* given under the influence of drink shall be effected.[109]

(f) Consideration. The consideration to be paid for *Khul'* must satisfy certain requirements. It will be convenient to discuss the subject with regard to the following aspects :—

(1) Acceptance of consideration,
(2) Free consent of the wife,
(3) Nature of consideration,
(4) Specification of consideration,
(5) Amount of consideration,
(6) Subsequent change in the amount of consideration,
(7) Liability for payment of consideration,
(8) Non-payment of consideration, effect of,

105. Qāḍī Khān, *Fatāwā Qāḍi Khān*, *op. cit.*, Vol. II, p. 261.
106. *Ibid.*
107. *Ibid.*
108. *Al-Fatāwā al-Hindīyah*, *op. cit.*, Vol. II, p. 125.
109. Muḥammad b. Ahmed, *op. cit.*, Vol. II, p. 134.

These different points are now discussed in some detail below.

1. *Acceptance of Consideration.* In Khul' there must exist an aversion in the wife for her husband and it should not be the husband who should have an aversion for her. If the aversion is on the part of the husband, it would be abominable in him to take anything at all from her.[110] This is based on the principle laid down in the Qur'ān :

> "And if ye wish to have (one) wife in the place of another and you have given one of them a heap of gold, take nothing from it".[111]

It is stated in *al-Radd al-Muḥtār* that if Khul' is due to ill-treatment by the husband, he cannot lawfully take any consideration from the wife because Allah has enjoined on the husbands not to take back anything from the wives on separation as stated in the above verse. If he has realised it, it shall be considered to be *makruh* (abominable) property.[112]

It is stated by Ibn Zayd that another verse of the Qur'ān shall be applicable here, namely, "Then if you fear that they (husband and wife) cannot keep within the limits of Allah there is no blame on them for what she gives to become free thereby."[113] It is, therefore, lawful for the husband, in his opinion, to accept a consideration even when it is he who bears a malice for the wife and is himself the aggressor.

Fatḥ al-Qadīr has explained that the first verse shall be applicable when the husband is at fault and happens to be the aggressor. The second verse shall apply when the husband is not at fault. It has also been stated there that this proposition of law is supported by *Ijmā'* or consensus of opinion of the learned. Besides the above, there is a third verse in the Qur'ān wherein the Muslims have been

110. Al-Marghīnānī, *op. cit.*, Vol. II, p. 384, *Al-Fatāwā al-Hindiyah*, *op. cit.*, Vol. II, p. 118.
111. Qur'ān, IV : 20, Surah al-Nisā'.
112. Ibn 'Ābidīn, *op. cit.*, Vol. II, pp. 575-76.
113. Qur'ān, II : 299 ; Surah al-Baqarāh ; Ibn 'Ābidīn, *op. cit.*, Vol. II, p. 576.

enjoined "to retain them not for injury,"[114] ***Fatḥ al-Qadīr*** then states that it will be doubly unlawful for the husband under the circumstances to take any consideration from the wife.[115] But it has been held by the Muslim jurists that in strict law the husband can take compensation from the wife even when the aversion or cruelty is on his part.[116] They hold the view that it will be good in law though bad in religion. They also hold that it would be lawful for the husband to take more than what he had given to the wife or settled upon her by way of dower.[117] The author of *al-Hidāyah* says that to take more consideration is disapproved of even when the wife is at fault. If it is the husband who is at fault, he should not take any consideration at all, although in strict law he can do so.[118] It is submitted that this opinion goes against the very injunction of the Qur'ān quoted above. In the Tradition relating to Jamīlah wife of Thābit b. Qays, as stated in the beginning, the Prophet (peace be on him) asked Jamīlah if she was willing to return the orchard given to her by Qays by way of dower and she said, "Yes, and even more than that." The Prophet (peace be on him) then said, "No, not more than that." This injunction establishes very clearly that a husband cannot lawfully take from the wife more than what he had given to her by way of dower. We must, therefore, follow these injunctions in preference to the rules laid down by the Muslim jurists.

2. *Free Consent of Wife.* It is an essential condition for *Khul'* that the wife should seek it or agree to it of her own free-will without any compulsion by the husband. Hence it is not lawful for a husband to force his wife to ask for a *Khul'* in order to obtain some consideration from her or to escape his liability for payment of the wife's dower or other

114. Qur'ān, II : 231 ; Surah al-Baqarāh; Ibn al-Humām, *Fatḥ al-Qadīr*, Cairo, 1356 A.H , Vol. III, p. 203.
115. *Fatḥ al-Qadīr, op. cit.*, Vol. III, p. 203.
116. *Ibid., al-Fatāwā al-Hindīyah, op. cit.*, Vol. II, p. 118.
117. *Al-Fatāwā al-Hindīyah, op. cit.*, Vol. II, p. 118.
118. *Ibid.*, p. 118 ; al-Marghīnānī, *op. cit.*, Vol. II, p. 384.

property or rights. Such conduct of the husband is considered most reprehensible and the payment of the consideration by the wife shall not be valid. If the husband makes his wife, under compulsion, to accept a Khul' for a certain consideration or for the surrender by her of some right then an irrevocable divorce shall be effected, but the wife shall not be liable for the payment of the consideration or the surrender of her right.[119]

Validity of Consideration taken by Compulsion, Deceit or Fraud.

Free consent presupposes that the wife's consent to a Khul' has not been obtained by fraud or deceit. If a man proposes a Khul' to his wife in consideration of her dower and the right to maintenance during the *'iddah* and by deceit makes her repeat her assent in Arabic which she does not understand then there is a difference of opinion amongst the jurists. But the generally accepted view is that neither the Khul' nor the release shall be valid because the Khul' as far as the wife is concerned is tantamount to making a return and so Khul' shall not be valid without her knowledge of the meaning of the words.[120]

Privy Council Ruling. The Privy Council has held that when a Khul' is given but the husband fails to establish that the wife did seek or obtain it of her own free-will and after fully understanding the significance of Khul' then a divorce shall be effected, but the abandonment of her dower or payment of other consideration that the wife had agreed to pay shall not be valid or binding on her.[121]

Mālikī Law. Under the Mālikī law a husband has to return the consideration received by him if his wife proves that she was forced to ask for the Khul' on account of her husband's ill-treatment or on account of his being tainted with such a defect as would have entitled her to get a separation from him.[122] The Khul', however, shall be binding on him.

119. Ibn 'Ābidīn, *op. cit.*, Vol. II, p. 576.
120. Qāḍī Khān, *op. cit.*, Vol. II, pp. 258-59.
121. Moonshee Buzuloor Rahman, Vs. Lateef-un Nissa, 8 M.I.A. 379.
122. Ibn Qudāmah, *op. cit.*, Vol. II, p. 55.

Shāfi'ī Law. The Shāfi'ī law with regard to consideration paid under compulsion or fraud is the same as the Ḥanafī law.[123]

Ḥanbalī Law. Under the Ḥanbalī law, if a person ill-treats his wife in order to force her to seek a *Khul'* then no *Khul'* shall be effected and the wife shall be entitled to the return of the consideration paid by her. If the husband is guilty of ill-treatment but without any intention to coerce her to seek a *Khul'* and a *Khul'* is given then a divorce shall be effected but payment of consideration shall not be valid.[124]

Consideration in case of Failure of Khul'. If *Khul'* fails for any reason whatsoever then the wife's right to her dower shall revive. The husband shall be bound to return any compensation already received by him.

Failure to pay Consideration. It can be inferred from the discussion of various cases that the failure of the wife to pay the consideration agreed upon does not cancel the *Khul'* but the husband shall be entitled to recover the same from her under the law. He can also set it off against any claim that she may have against him. If the wife promises to give some consideration which does not exist then no consideration shall be payable ; *Khul'* shall be effected but she shall have to return the dower. But if the wife deliberately deceives him and offers as a consideration for *Khul'* something in or over which she has no right or authority even then the *Khul'* shall be binding on the husband but the wife shall have to pay the consideration.[125] This view has been adopted by the Courts.[126] According to Abū Ḥanīfah, the wife shall have to return the dower if she has realized it. If not, then it shall be extinguished. According to Abū Yūsuf and Muḥammad, she shall have to pay the stipulated consideration or its equivalent.[127]

123. Ibn Qudāmah, *op. cit.*, Vol. II, p. 55.
124. *Ibid.*
125. Ibn Nujaym, *al-Baḥr al-Rā'iq*, Cairo, *op. cit.*, Vol. IV, p. 85.
126. Saddan Vs. Faiz Buksh, 1 Lahore, 402, 55 I.C. 184.
127. Ibn 'Ābidīn, *op. cit.*, Vol. II, p. 576.

3. *Nature of Consideration.* Whatever is lawful to be accepted for dower can also be lawfully accepted as consideration for Khul'.[128] Thus it can consist of such things as immovable property, cash, jewels, etc. But it cannot consist of things which cannot be lawfully possessed by a Muslim.[129] Thus it cannot consist of wine, swine, pork etc. But if the husband agrees to release his wife in consideration of such an unlawful object the Khul' divorce shall be effected, but the payment of such consideration would not be incumbent on the wife.[130] This is due to the fact that the husband cannot lawfully possess such an object and so he cannot ask the wife to give it to him.

Mālikī Law. Under the Mālikī law all things which are lawful can form the consideration for Khul'. If the consideration consists of such things as are forbidden like pork, wine or something which had been obtained by theft or by violent means or by usurpation then the Khul' shall be valid but the husband shall not be entitled to any consideration.[131]

Shāfi'ī Law. Under the Shāfi'ī law all things which can be given for dower can be given for Khul'. It should consist of lawful things. The wife must be capable of delivering it to the husband. If it consists of such things as are not lawful like pork, wine, etc., then the wife shall have to pay the dower of a woman of equal standing (*mithl*).[132]

Ḥanbalī Law. Aḥmad ibn Ḥanbal holds that if Khul' is agreed on for unlawful things it will be effected, but no consideration shall be payable by the wife.[133]

4. *Specification of Consideration.* The amount of the consideration to be paid for Khul' has to be specified. If a husband gives a Khul' to his wife without specifying or fixing any consideration and the wife agrees to the Khul', an irrevoc-

128. Ibn 'Ābidīn, *op. cit.*, Vol. II, p. 573 ; al-Marghīnānī, *op. cit.* Vol. II, p. 385.
129. *Ibid.*, p. 576.
130. *Ibid.*, al-Marghīnānī, *op. cit.*, Vol. II, p. 385.
131. Ibn Rushd, *op. cit.*, Vol. II, p. 56.
132. *Ibid.*, Ibn Qudāmah, *op. cit.*, Vol. II, p. 73.
133. Ibn Qudāmah, *op. cit.*, Vol. II, p. 73.

able divorce shall be effected but no consideration shall be payable by the wife.[134] She shall, however, have to return the dower if she has already realised it. If she has not realised it, it shall be extinguished. Moreover, all the rights of the wife against the husband arising out of the marriage shall also be extinguished.[135] There must be a definite mention of payment of consideration. If there is no mention of any consideration then the expression used by the husband may amount to a divorce, but cannot effect a Khul'. Thus if a husband says to his wife, "I have made Khul' unto you" and the wife agrees to his proposal then a divorce shall be effected, but no consideration shall be due by the wife except the return of the dower and the extinguishment of the other rights of the wife.[136] This is due to the fact that the wife had not undertaken to pay any specified consideration and is therefore not bound to pay any. The same result will follow if it is the wife who seeks a Khul' from her husband who agrees to it while no mention of any consideration has been made.[137] Even her dissent cannot have any effect, because a wife's dissent to a divorce is immaterial. Hence if the husband gives a Khul' to his wife without her proposal or without her consent to pay a consideration to him, then divorce shall be effected but there would be no obligation on the wife to pay any consideration to him because she had not undertaken or consented to pay any. It is, however, open to the husband to suggest to a wife if she would agree to a Khul' divorce for a specified consideration, and it shall be only on the wife's agreeing to it that a Khul' shall be effected. If the husband sues the wife for certain consideration on the allegation that he had given Khul' for consideration to which she had agreed and should the wife deny the husband's allegation, a Khul' shall be established on the husband's own assertion but the matter of payment of the consideration shall be

134. Ibn 'Ābidīn, *op. cit.*, Vol. II, p. 585.
135. *Ibid.*
136. *Ibid.*
137. *Ibid.*

decided on the basis of proof produced in the case.[138] If the case be the reverse, that is when the wife alleges a Khul' by her husband for a specified consideration while the husband denies it then no Khul' shall be established, because the same depends on the husband's acceptance which is wanting here.[139] If a husband gives a Khul' to his wife in consideration of her returning to him whatever he has given to her or for some specified goods given by him to her and it turns out that she has already transferred the same to someone else, then she shall give the husband similar goods if available or their value if they are not available.[140]

Time of Payment. The consideration has to be paid immediately or at an agreed time. If no time has been fixed for the payment of the consideration then it has to be paid immediately when the Khul' is given. This is based on the analogy of sales and mortgages.[141] Hence the postponement of the consideration for a definite period is valid. The postponement would be valid though the period should be unknown if it is capable of being fixed. If the period of time when the payment is to be paid be not known nor be capable of being fixed, then Khul' shall be effected, and customary dower shall become immediately due.

5. *Amount of Consideration.* Under the Hanafi Law, as a general rule, the amount of the consideration paid or to be paid for a Khul' should not exceed the amount of the wife's dower or property given to her by the husband if the Khul' is proposed by the husband. If it does, it is disapproved (*makrūh*) but valid.[142]

The Prophet (peace be on him) did not approve of or even allow payment of a consideration greater than the dower in a Khul' divorce. As stated before, when Jamīlah, wife

138. Ibn 'Ābidīn, *op. cit.*, Vol. II, p. 579.
139. *Ibid.*
140. *Ibid.*, p. 576.
141. *Ibid.*, p. 573 *f.*
142. *Ibid.*, p. 576; *Al-Fatāwā al-Hindīyah*, *op. cit.*, Vol. II, p. 118.

of Thabit b. Qays desired *Khul'* then the Prophet (peace be on him) asked her if she was prepared to return the orchard given to her by her husband by way of dower. She replied that she was prepared not only to return it, but to pay something in addition to it. The Prophet (peace be on him), however, said, "No, not more than that."[143] The Muslim jurists have, however, stated that a higher consideration fixed in contravention of this rule would amount to a moral offence only and the consideration would be valid in law.[144] This rule contravenes the injunction of the Prophet (peace be on him) which is more binding on us than a rule laid down by the Muslim jurists. This matter has already been discussed before under the heading, "Acceptance of Consideration."

If a husband and wife agree to a *Khul'* divorce but leave the settlement of the consideration to the other or to a third person then the *Khul'* shall be valid and the consideration fixed by such person shall be payable. But he cannot fix the consideration for *Khul'* in excess of or less than what has been given by the husband to the wife.[145] If it is the husband who is to settle the consideration, he can fix it for a sum not exceeding what he has given to her unless the wife agrees to it.[146] Similarly, if the fixation of the consideration is left to the wife, she cannot fix it for a sum less than what the husband has given to her unless the husband agrees to it.[147]

The Muslim jurists have generally expressed the opinion that half the amount of dower is the proper consideration when the wife has a justification for seeking a *Khul'* divorce. But if the wife wants a *Khul'* without any reasonable cause then the consideration is the full amount of the dower.[148] They have, however, stated that a consideration higher than that specified above, fixed in contravention of this rule would,

143. Al-Bayhaqī, *op. cit.*, Vol. VII, p. 314.
144. *Al-Fatāwā al-Hindiyah, op. cit.*, Vol. II, p. 118.
145. *Ibid.*, p. 121.
146. *Ibid.*
147. *Ibid.*
148. Al-Syed Amir Ali, *al-Fatāwā Alamgiriyah, ov. cit.*, 1899 A.D., Vol. II, p. 351.

amount to a moral offence only but the consideration would be valid in law.[149] It is submitted that the directive of the Prophet (peace be on him) to Jamīlah was very clear and does not allow the payment of a consideration greater than the dower given to her by the husband. If there is a dispute between the husband and the wife about the amount of the consideration alleged to have been agreed upon, then under the Muslim law, the version of the wife shall be accepted. But if the spouses produce witnesses in support of their versions then the statement of the husband's witnesses shall be preferred. All the Sunnī jurists agree that if the wife is at fault, the husband should take only so much consideration from her as is equal to what he has given to her. If he gives up his claim this will be the better. If it is the husband who is at fault, he should not take anything at all from her.[150]

6. *Subsequent Change in Amount of Consideration.* Once *Khul'* has been entered into for a specified consideration then any subsequent addition to the consideration shall be void.[151] This condition is meant to safeguard the wife's interests so that she may not be forced to add to the consideration already agreed upon to be paid, particularly when a final and binding contract has already been entered into.

7. *Liability for Payment of Consideration.*

Khul' by a Minor Wife. If a minor wife gets a *Khul'* in consideration of her dower or other property and the husband agrees to it, one revocable divorce shall be effected but the payment of the consideration shall not be incumbent on her.[152] The divorce in such a case shall be revocable and not an irrevocable divorce.[153]

Consideration in Khul' at the Instance of Father. If a man obtains a *Khul'* for his major daughter with her consent or if she ratifies it, she shall be responsible for the payment of

149. *Al-Fatāwā al-Hindīyah* (Arabic), *op. cit.*, Vol. II, p. 118.
150. *Ibid.*
151. *Ibid.*, p. 119.
152 *Ibid.*, p. 125.
153. *Ibid.*

the agreed consideration. If the father makes himself liable for its payment, he shall be personally responsible for its payment.[154] If the father secures a *Khul'* for his major daughter in lieu of her dower and the daughter has not accepted or ratified the same, the husband shall be liable for the payment of the dower to her and can recover the same from the wife's father.[155] But if the daughter had not given her consent while the father also did not take any responsibility for its payment then the *Khul'* shall be invalid.[156] But if the father makes himself liable for the paymant of the consideration the *Khul'* shall be valid.[157]

If a person obtains a *Khul'* divorce for his minor daughter in consideration of her property or dower, she shall not be liable to pay the same or to the relinquishment of her dower.[158] This is based on the ground that the father had no right to offer the minor's property and his act regarding the property is unlawful and so the minor does not become bound by her father's act. The father will also not be responsible for the payment of the consideration as he did not make himself responsible for its payment. The *Khul'* divorce, however, shall be effected.[159]

If the father of a minor wife obtains *Khul'* for her from her husband in consideration of a payment for which he makes himself personally responsible, he shall be liable for the payment of the same while the girl shall not be responsible for its payment.[160]

Consideration of Khul' at the Instance of the Mother. If the mother of a minor wife gets a *Khul'* for consideration for which she makes herself responsible, *Khul'* shall be

154. *Al-Fatāwā al-Hindīyah, op. cit.*, Vol. II, p. 124.
155. *Ibid.*
156. *Ibid.*
157. *Ibid.*
158. *Ibid.*, p. 157.
159. Al-Marghīnānī, *op. cit* , Vol. II, p. 389 ; Ibn 'Ābidīn, *op. cit.*, Vol. II, pp. 583-84.
160. *Ibid.*, p. 389 ; *Ibid.*, p. 584.

valid.[161] But if the mother has not made herself responsible for the same, *Khul'* shall not be effected.[162]

Khul' through Agent. If a wife appoints an agent for the purpose of obtaining a *Khul'* divorce from her husband for a specified sum of money, the agent cannot agree to or make payment in excess of the amount specified by her unless he makes himself liable for the payment of this excess.[163]

Rights as Consideration for Khul'. It is not necessary that the consideration for *Khul'* should consist of such tangible property as money, jewellery, etc., only. There can be rights which can form such consideration. Some important cases are discussed below :

Dower. Any lawful object can form the consideration for *Khul'*. Hence, it is open to the spouses to agree to *Khul'* on the condition that the wife surrenders her dower as consideration for *Khul'*. In such a case the marriage shall be dissolved while the wife shall lose her right to her dower. It can, however, be made an express condition of *Khul'* that the wife's dower or a portion thereof shall remain payable by the husband. There is a difference of opinion amongst Ḥanafī jurists about the husband's liability for payment of the wife's dower and the wife's liability for its return if it has already been paid to her.

If the spouses settle consideration other than dower and no mention has been made about the dower, the following results will follow in a *Khul'* divorce with regard to the wife's dower :

(*a*) If the marriage has been consummated and the whole dower has been paid to the wife, she shall be entitled to retain it according to the unanimous view of Abū Ḥanīfah, Muḥammad and Abū Yūsuf. The husband will get only the consideration agreed upon.[164] But if the dower has not been paid to her,

161. Ibn 'Ābidīn, *op. cit.*, Vol. II, p. 584.
162. *Ibid.*
163. *Al-Fatāwā al-Hindīyah, op. cit.*, Vol. II, p. 123.
164. Qāḍī Khān, *op. cit.*, Vol. II, p. 256.

then, according to Abū Ḥanīfah, she is not entitled to claim the dower because, according to him, *Khul*' puts an end to all the rights, which the spouses have against each other except the wife's maintenance and residence during her '*iddah*. But according to Abū Yūsuf and Muḥammad the wife shall be entitled to claim it from her husband because it becomes due if the marriage has been consummated.[165]

(*b*) If the marriage has not been consummated and the whole dower has been paid to her, then according to Abū Ḥanīfah the husband will not be entitled to the return of any portion of the dower. He shall of course take the consideration that may have been agreed upon.[166] But, according to his two disciples, the wife shall have to return half the dower to the husband and will be entitled to keep half of it.[167]

(*c*) If the marriage has not been consummated and dower has not been paid to her, then according to Abū Ḥanīfah no amount of the dower shall be due to her. She shall not be entitled to get her dower or any portion of it from her husband and shall pay to him the consideration agreed upon.[168] According to Abū Yūsuf and Muḥammad, the wife shall be entitled to get half of her dower from the husband.[169] The consideration agreed upon has, of course, to be paid by the wife to the husband in each case.

If the husband divorces his wife by *Khul*' in consideration of her dower and in case the marriage has been consummated and the whole dower has been paid to the wife, then the husband shall be entitled to its return by the wife. If it has not yet been paid to her, the husband's liability for the same shall cease.[170] There are two opinions expressed by Ḥanafī jurists. According to one, the same rules shall apply as held by Abū Ḥanīfah regarding dower in *Khul*'. But,

165. Qāḍī Khān, *op. cit.* Vol. II, p. 256.
166. *Ibid.*
167. *Ibid.*
168. *Ibid.*
169. *Ibid.*
170. *Ibid.*

according to the second opinion which is generally believed to be correct, the same rule shall apply as laid down by Muḥammad and Abū Yūsuf.[171]

Mālikī Law. According to the Mālikī law if the marriage has not been consummated and the parties settle Khul' for a specified consideration, the wife shall have to pay the specified consideration and her right to her dower shall be extinguished. She shall not be entitled to get the whole or any portion of it.[172]

Shāfi'ī Law. According to Shāfi'ī, if the spouses agree to a *Khul'* for a particular consideration and the marriage has not been consummated, the wife shall be entitled to half the dower. If the whole dower has been paid to her, she shall have to return half of it ; while if it has not been paid to her, the husband has to pay half the dower to her.[173]

Ḥanbalī Law. Aḥmad ibn Ḥanbal holds that the right to dower is not lost in consequence of a *Khul'* and the husband remains liable for its payment if the same has not already been paid to the wife.[174]

Right of Maintenance. Ordinarily right to maintenance and residence during the period of *'iddah* is not lost on the pronouncement of a *Khul'* because it arises only on the actual pronouncement of *Khul'* and is not claimable before.[175] If a woman obtains *Khul'* from her husband in consideration of all rights which she has against him even then she does not lose her right to maintenance during the period of her *'iddah* on the ground that the right does not accrue to her before the *Khul'*.[176] In the absence of an egreement to the contrary the wife shall be entitled to maintenance during the period of her *'iddah*. But it is open to the parties to make it a condition of *Khul'* that the wife gives up her right to

171. Qāḍī Khān, *op. cit.*, Vol. II, p. 256.
172. Saḥnūn, *al-Mudawwanat al-Kubrā*, Cairo, 1323, A.H, Vol. V, p. 21.
173. Ibn Qudāmah, *op. cit.*, Vol. VII, p. 56.
174. *Ibid.*
175. Ibn 'Ābidīn, *op. cit*,. Vol. II, p. 581.
176. *Ibid.*, pp. 580-81.

maintenance during the period of her *'iddah*.[177] In the same way the wife's right for claiming maintenance of her minor children shall not be lost unless she gives up her right under an express agreement. The right to maintenance for her minor children can, therefore, be surrendered only under an express agreement to that effect.[178] This is subject to the condition that the time during which the wife gives up her right to the maintenance of the children should be specified. If it is not specified, the right to the maintenance shall not be lost.[179]

Residence. The right to residence cannot be lost even under an agreement.[180] This view is based on the ground that the right of residence has been specifically provided for in the Qur'ān, wherein it is laid down in respect of divorced women : "Expel them not from their houses nor let them go forth unless they commit open immorality."[181] The direction in the Qur'ān cannot be contravened and so the wife's right to residence shall not be lost. It is, however open to a wife to undertake the payment of the rent of a house which does not belong to the husband.[182]

Other Debts, Liabilities and Rights. It is lawful for a wife to give up her claim to a debt or other liability due to her by the husband or surrentder her other rights or give some concession to the husband.[183] Thus if a wife seeks *Khul'* in consideration of grant of time to the husband for paying a debt due from him to her, this consideration shall be deemed to be valid provided that the time has been specified. But if the time has not been specified the consideration is not valid.[184] This rule may be due to want of certainty. In such a case a revocable divorce shall be effected.[185]

177. Ibn 'Ābidīn *op. cit.*, Vol. II, p. 581.
178. *Ibid.*, p. 582.
179. *Ibid.*
180. *Ibid.*, p. 581.
181. Qur'ān, XXVIII : 1. Surah al-Talāq.
182. Ibn 'Ābidīn, *op. cit.*, Vol. II, p. 582,
183. *Ibid.*, pp. 581-82.
184. *Al-Fatāwā al-Hindiyah*, *op. cit.*, Vol. II, p. 120.
185. *Ibid.*

Surrender of the Right to the Custody of Children. Under Muslim law, the mother, in the absence of certain special circumstances, is entitled to keep her minor children with her for a certain period. She can keep her son with her till he is seven years old and a daughter till she attains the age of fifteen years. This rule is meant for the benefit of the children and it is considered that the mother is most suited to look after them till they reach the prescribed ages. It is, therefore, not open to the husband to give *Khul'* on the condition that the wife shall surrender the custody of the children before the attainment of the prescribed ages and she cannot make the surrender of the right to the custody of the children a consideration for *Khul'*. Such an act is considered detrimental to the interests of the children and so is not permissible. Hence if the husband grants her a *Khul'* on the condition that she should surrender the custody of the children to him, this condition shall be void and the children shall remain with their mother but the *Khul'* shall be effected.[186]

Rearing up or Maintaining Children. It is lawful for a husband and wife to agree to *Khul'* on the condition that the wife shall take up the burden of maintaining a child or children born of the marriage during the period when the child is a minor.[187] But it is a necessary condition of such agreement that the period during which the wife shall be responsible for the maintenance of the child or children should be specified. If the period has not been specified, the condition shall not be valid and the wife shall not be bound by it and shall not be responsible for the maintenance of the minors.[188] But in the case of an infant the omission to specify the time shall not make the condition invalid because it can be presumed that she has to suckle the child for the usual period of two years.[189] A condition by a wife undertaking to bring

186. *Al-Fatāwā al-Hindīyah, op. cit.*, Vol. II, p. 119.
187. *Ibid.*
188. *Ibid.*
189. *Ibid.*

up her son after the period when he should be given in the custody of the father shall not be deemed to be valid. This rule is based on the view that it is necessary in the case of a son that he should be trained for his future life by the father and that the mother is not capable of doing so. This cannot be the case with respect to a girl and so an agreement to bring her up even after the prescribed age shall be valid.[190]

Wife's Poverty. If a husband gives his wife *Khul'* on the condition that she shall maintain his minor child for a specified period and should the wife happen to be poor and cannot afford to maintain the child or children then the condition shall not be binding on her. The husband shall have to provide the necessary maintenance which shall amount to debt due from the wife to him.[191] This rule seems to have been made in the interest of the child.

Effect of Khul'. The marriage is dissolved as soon as *Khul'* is given or the proposal is agreed to by the other spouse.[192] As soon as a release has been agreed to by both parties, the wife is completely separated from her husband, even though no compensation has been paid as yet.[193]

Nature of Separation

Ḥanafī Law. The dissolution of marriage by the use of the word *Khul'* or its equivalent words amounts to an irrevocable divorce.[194] If the marriage is dissolved by the use of the word *Ṭalāq* in lieu of consideration, this is *Ṭalāq ala'l māl* and shall amount to an irrevocable divorce.[195] It has been held by the High Court of Azad Jammu and Kashmir that *Khul'* is *Ṭalāq bāin* as reported in PLD 1967 Azad J and K 40. It has been held by the Supreme Court of Pakistan that *Khul'* is separation and not a *Ṭalāq* as the right of the

190. *Al-Fatāwā al Hindīyah, op. cit*, Vol. II, p 119, Ibn 'Ābidīn, *op. cit.*, Vol II, p. 583.
191. Ibn 'Ābidīn, *op. cit.*, Vol. II, p. 583.
192. *Ibid.*, p. 575.
193. *Ibid.*
194. *Ibid.*, *al-Fatāwā al-Hindīyah, op. cit.*, Vol. II, p. 118.
195. *Ibid.*, *Ibid.*, p. 118.

husband to take back the wife after *Khul'* does not exist as it does in the case of *Ṭalāq-i-raja'i* and the period of *'iddat* is different in the two cases.[196]

Mālikī Law. Under the Mālikī law the dissolution of marriage by *Khul'* constitutes an irrevocable divorce.[197]

Shāfi'ī Law. There are two reports about the law laid down by Shāfi'ī. According to one, *Khul'* results in "*Faskh*" or cancellation of the marriage. According to his second and later opinion, *Khul'* amounts to an irrevocable divorce. This is usually regarded as the correct view.[198]

Ḥanbalī Law. According to *Imām* Aḥmad ibn Ḥanbal if the marriage is dissolved by the use of the word *Khul'*, it shall amount to an irrevocable divorce. If it is, however, dissolved by the use of the word "*Ṭalāq*" there are two opinions expressed by him. According to one, it shall amount to a *Faskh* or cancellation of the marriage, but according to the other it shall be deemed an irrevocable divorce.[199]

Agent for Khul'. The parties or one of them can appoint another person to give or receive a *Khul'* divorce in his or her stead. Even a minor can act as an agent for the purpose.[200] But the agent is not personally responsible for the payment of the consideration unless he undertakes to pay it.[201]

Observance of 'Iddah. *Khul'* in its nature is a divorce and brings about the termination of marriage. It is, therefore, incumbent on the wife to observe *'iddah* for the same period of time as in the case of divorce, namely, for three terms of menstrual discharge or for three months if the wife is not subject to them.[202]

Qāḍī's Order. The *Qāḍī's* or the Court's decree to

196. Khurshid Bibi Vs. Muhammad Amin, P.L.D. 1967 S, C. 97.
197. Ibn Qudāmah, *op. cit.*, Vol. VII, p. 59.
198. *Ibid.*, p. 57.
199. *Ibid.*, pp. 56-57.
200. *Al-Fatāwā al-Hindīyah, op. cit.*, Vol. II, p. 118.
201. *Ibid.*
202. Ibn 'Ābidīn, *op. cit.*, Vol. II, p. 573.

confirm a *Khul'* divorce is not necessary just as a divorce by the husband does not require any confirmation by the Court.[203]

(*g*) *Time of Khul'*. A *Khul'* divorce can be given at any time during the subsistence of marriage. It can be given even during the period of the wife's *'iddah*, if it be incumbent, for instance, when she has been divorced by a revocable divorce because in such a case the marriage continues during the period of *'iddah*.[204]

If a wife gets a *Khul'* while the husband is suffering from *Maraḍ al-maut* or illness resulting in death, the wife shall not be entitled to her right of inheritance if the husband happens to die in his illness.[205] Similarly, a wife can obtain a *Khul'* divorce while she is suffering from *Maraḍ al-mawt*.[206]

Mālikī Law. Under the Māliki law the husband shall not inherit her because he has personally divested himself of his rights.

Shī'i Law. The words *Khul'* and *Mubārāh* bear the same meaning under the Shī'i law as under the Sunnī law. The former means the termination of marriage by the husband in lieu of consideration when the wife bears aversion for him.[207] If the aversion is mutual, the termination of the marriage shall be called *Mubārāh*.[208] *Khul'* can be obtained even by a stranger if he takes a personal responsibility for the payment of the consideration agreed upon even when the wife does not want it.[209] The view about a stranger obtaining a *Khul'* on his own initiative has been discussed before. The use of the word, *Khul'* seems to be inappropriate in such a case.

Under Shī'i law the question of *Khul'* is considered in respect of four points. *viz*.,

203. Ibn 'Ābidīn, *op. cit*., Vol. II, p. 573 ; Ibn Qudāmah, *op. cit*., Vol. VII, p. 88.
204. *Ibid*., p. 586 ; *ibid*., pp. 88, 89.
205. *Al-Fatāwā* 'Alamgīriyah, *op. cit*., Vol. II, p. 358.
206. *Ibid*.
207. Ja'far b. al-Ḥasan, *Sharā'i' al-Islām*, Tehran, 1377 A.H., p. 221.
208. *Ibid*.
209. *Ibid*., p, 220.

(*a*) The capacity of the person who grants *Khul'*,

(*b*) The capacity of the woman obtaining her release from marriage by means of *Khul'*,

(*c*) The nature of consideration, and

(*d*) The expression or language used for *Khul'*.[210]

(*a*) As regards the first, the husband who releases his wife by *Khul'* must be adult and sane. According to one opinion, the *Khul'* granted by an idiot is valid but the ransom (consideration) must be given to the guardian of the idiot.[211] The husband must be acting under free will so that there can be no *Khul'* under compulsion. He must also have the intention to release his wife by *Khul'* and there can be no *Khul'* where such was not the intention of the husband, as when he grants it under the influence of drink or through a burst of anger, or when he is raving.[212] A *Khul'* by a minor boy, even with the permission of his guardian, is not valid. But in the case of a person of unsound mind his guardian can enter into an agreement for *Khul'* divorce in lieu of the wife's dower. There is a difference of opinion as to whether the guardian of a minor can give a *Khul'* to the wife on his behalf. The jurists who consider that *Khul'* effects an annulment of the marriage hold that it is open to the guardian of a minor to give a *Khul'* on his behalf. But it is not lawful according to the jurists who consider *Khul'* to amount to a divorce.[213]

(*b*) *Capacity of the Wife.* As regards the second point for obtaining a *Khul'* the wife must also possess the above-mentioned requisites, that is, she must be adult and sane and must possess understanding. It is necessary if her marriage has been consummated that she must be pure, *i.e.*, free from monthly course at the time of *Khul'* and no intercourse must have taken place during that period of purity unless she is a minor or past childbearing age or the husband is away, or

210. Ja'far b. al-Ḥasan, *Sharā'i' al-Islām*, Tehran, 1377 A.H., p. 219.

211. Tahrīr-al-Ahkām.

212. Ja'far b. al-Ḥasan, *op. cit.*, p. 219.

213. *Ibid.*

she is pregnant.[214] Hence the *Khul* of a woman is valid even when intercourse has taken place with her if she is a minor or past the childbearing age or is pregnant. But if the marriage has not been consummated or the husband is absent then *Khul'* can be given even when she is not in a period of purity. *Khul'* of a pregnant woman is valid.[215] It is also necessary that she must have an aversion for her husband. Hence *Khul'* would not be valid if given when there is harmony between the parties.

(*c*) *Consideration.* As regards the third point, it is laid down that the consideration agreed upon must be specific in quantity, description and kind must be such as can lawfully be given to a Muslim. Hence consideration consisting of unlawful things such as wine, pigs, etc., cannot be given. In case the consideration be unspecified the *Khul'* would be invalid.[216] There is no restriction to the amount or quantity of the consideration so that it can exceed the wife's dower. The consideration may be paid by the woman herself or by her agent or by any one who has become a surety for it with her permission.[217] If a woman obtains *Khul'* while she is suffering from death-illness, the consideration cannot exceed the customary dower of the wife.[218] If the consideration is unascertained or unspecified, *Khul'* shall not be effected.[218]

Expression or Language Used for Khul'. As regards the fourth point, the *Khul'* must be expressed unconditionally and the word 'divorce' must be used.

Surrender of dower is a part of the contract of *Khul'* and *Muābārh* and in case of non-payment of the consideration, there would be an option for the husband to revoke the *Khul'*. After the expiry of the period of *'iddah'* the right to

214. Ja'far b. al-Ḥasan, *Sharā'i' al-Islām*, Tehran, 1377 A.H., p. 219.
215. *Ibid.*
216. *Ibid.*, p. 218.
217. *Ibid.*
218. *Ibid.*

reclaim the dower which has been relinquished by her to her husband, cannot be exercised.[219]

It is not lawful for a husband to force his wi.. .o ask for a Khul'. If he does so and repudiates his wife, the repudiation would be valid and revocable but there would be no obligation on her to pay the consideration.[220]

Language for Khul'. Khul' must preferably be made in Arabic. The word *Khul'* must be followed by the word *Ṭalāq* (Divorce).[221]

Witnesses. The agreement of *Khul'* must be made in the presence of two just witnesses.[222]

Time. If the marriage has been consummated, the *Khul'* must be made during the time of the wife's *ṭuhr* (purity).[223]

Nature of Separation. A separation by *Khul'* amounts to an irrevocable divorce. *Khul'* when once given cannot revoked. Once a *Khul'* becomes valid, the husband cannot revoke it. The wife can, however, reclaim ransom (consideration) during the period of her *'iddah*, in which case the husband shall be entitled to revoke the *Khul'*.[224]

Mubārāh. *Mubārāh* is similar to a *Khul'*, the only difference is that in *Khul'* it is only the wife who bears aversion for the husband but in *Mubārāh* the aversion is mutual.[225] In *Mubārāh* it is not lawful for the husband to take from the wife consideration greater than the dower paid by him.[226] It is necessary in case of *Mubārāh* to indicate a separation between the two by the use of some word which indicates divorce. It shall also amount to an irrevocable divorce.[227]

219. Ja'far b. al-Ḥasan, *Sharā'i' al-Islām*, Tehran, 1377 A.H., p. 217.
220. *Ibid.*, p. 218.
221. *Ibid.*, p. 221.
222. *Ibid.*, p. 219.
223. *Ibid.*, p. 217.
224. *Ibid.*, p. 219.
225. *Ibid.*
226. *Ibid.*, pp. 218, 221.
227. *Ibid.*, p. 221.

CHAPTER 13

ARBITRATION

I. Preliminary

One of the aims of marriage, as discussed before, is the happy companionship of husband and wife. If this is not achieved, the marriage can hardly be called a success. Divorce has been discouraged and even condemned in Islam and a Muslim marriage cannot be lightly dissolved. On the other hand, the happiness of the spouses is not to be sacrificed simply to maintain a marriage, and if the couple finds it impossible to live together, then divorce is permissible. However, before the actual dissolution of the marriage, a final effort for reconciliation is always to be made to smooth out any differences between the couple by the appointment of two arbitrators, one representing each spouse. The arbitrators should endeavour to understand the nature and causes of the grievances of the parties and try to bring about a reconciliation between the two. The aim of the arbitration proceedings is to remove ill-feelings and to re-establish, if possible, harmony between the married couple. It happens very often that differences are due to a misunderstanding, or a failure to understand the view-point of the other spouse and a frank discussion of the grievances of both sides before a third party will enable one to understand and realize the cause of complaint of the other. The arbitrators, being relations or friends and well-wishers of the spouses, will, as disinterested persons, help and guide them to come to a possible understanding and better adjustment. If this attempt succeeds then the spouses can continue to live together as husband and wife. This is the procedure now adopted by U.S.A. and many European countries through what are known as Conciliatory Committees.

II. Religious Sanction

The passage in the Qur'ān which deals with disagreement between the spouses reads as follows: "If you fear a *shiqāq* (breach) between the two (spouses) then appoint two arbitrators, one from his family and the other from hers. If they both desire agreement, Allah will effect harmony between them. Surely Allah is Knowing, Aware."[1] This verse provides the procedure to be adopted when there is an apprehension of *shiqāq* or break-up between the spouses. The word *shiqāq* is derived from '*shaqq*' which means breaking asunder, breaking into two. *Shiqāq*, therefore, here means conflict between the couple of such a serious character that the bond of marriage is strained to breakingpoint. It is immaterial as to who is at fault. The crucial point is whether the spouses, or the erring spouse, can be made to listen to reason, and whether there is possibility of restoring harmony; and it is obvious that on failure to achieve this harmony the continuation of the marital relation shipbecomes meaningless.

III. Appointment of Arbitrators

Who can appoint arbitrators: There is a difference of opinion as to whose is the responsibility for the selection and appointment of the arbitrators. The late Maulana Muhammad Ali in his valuable translation of the Qur'an has interpreted the word "You", in the above quoted verse as referring to the "*ulu'l-amr*" or "the *Qāḍī*, or the State." This translation of the word has been accepted in many rulings. It was stated in the case of Mst. Umar Bibi Vs. Din Muhammad that the word contains a direction to the "*ulu'l-amr*" or *Qāḍī* to appoint arbitrators.[2] It was reiterated in a later ruling where it has been definitely claimed that the words "If you fear..." are addressed to 'the State or the judge'.[3] But Justice Abdur Rahman pointed out that in the

1. Qur'ān, IV ; 35, Surah Al-Nisā.
2. Umar Bibi Vs. Muhammad Din, A.I.R., 1945, Lahore 51.
3. Bilqis Fatima Vs. Najmul Ikram Qureshi, 1959, P.L.D. Lahore, p. 566.

present day there are no State-appointed *Qāḍīs* and since they alone could appoint arbitrators, the procedure laid down in the above verse of the Qur'ān cannot be given effect to now. In Sayeeda Khanum Vs. Mohammad Sami Cornelius J. (as he then was) on the other hand, considered the words "*ulu'l-amr*" to have been addressed to the heads of the tribes to which the spouses may belong.[4] But it is submitted that there is no authority to support this interpretation. It is nowhere declared necessary that the arbitrators should be appointed by the heads of tribes of the spouses. Moreover, the verse, as all others in the Qur'ān, is of universal application to all Muslims, and there are many Islamic communities which do not live in tribes.

Similarly, the word "you" does not necessarily mean the State or the *Qāḍīs*. The word has frequently been used in the Qur'ān to address the Muslims at large. Here it would seem that the term is used in the same wide sense, and contains a general directve as to what is to be done in a case when there is fear of '*shiqāq*' between a married couple. This view has been mentioned by several Muslim jurists. Thus it is stated in *Tafsīr Mawāhib al-Raḥmān* that the 'usually accepted' view is that the verse is addressed to the Ruler or his subordinates such as the *Qāḍīs*, but that "some have expressed the view that it is addressed to the Muslims" (in general).

On the whole it seems that the latter view is more appropriate. The parties, their relations, friends or well-wishers can have recourse to arbitration and themselves appoint arbitrators to restore amity and happy conjugal relations between the husband and wife. The Supreme Court of Pakistan has, however, expressed the view that the words, "if you fear" are addressed to the community or those in authority from among you and include the Qazi.[5]

In the light of the verse, quoted in this connection, it

4. Sayeeda Khanum Vs. Mohammad Sami, 1952 P.L D., Lahore 113.
5. Khurshid Bibi Vs. Mohammad Amin, P.L.D., 1967 S.C. 97.

seems to be almost obligatory to appoint arbitrators from amongst the families of the spouses. This may be based upon the fact that the arbitrators thus selected will be fully acquainted with the circumstances of the case and will have full confidence of the parties. They will, therefore, be able to exert their influence on the parties. But the appointment of strangers under certain circumstances is not invalid.[6]

The arbitratots must be appointed in consultation with the spouses unless they are appointed by the *Qāḍī* and even then it will be desirable to appoint them with the approval of the parties to the marriage.

There is a further difference of opinion as to the necessity of the consent of the spouses to the appointment of arbitrators. The generally accepted view is that their consent is necessary.[7] No arbitration would be effective if it is thrust upon the parties against their will.

If one of the spouses does not agree to arbitration or to the appointment of arbitrators, the only recourse left will be that the other should move the *Qāḍī* in the matter, who will then initiate the arbitration proceedings by appointing arbitrators. In Pakistan provision has been made for arbitration by appointing Arbitration Council in case of divorce.[8] It seems desirable to extend the provision in case of *Shiqāq* also, when the relations between the spouses have become strained to the breaking point of the marriage.

Under Muslim law, arbitrators must preferably be appointed with the consent of the parties concerned. But a husband or a wife cannot be allowed to frustrate the case by refusing to appoint an arbitrator or withholding his or her consent to the appointment of one. The verse of the Qur'ān, quoted above, while allowing the *Qāḍī* to appoint arbitrators from amongst the families of the spouses, does not make it a condition that they have to be appointed by the husband

6. Syed Amir Ali, *Tafsîr Mawāhib al-Rahmān* Lucknow, 1926, Vol. V, p. 36.
7. *Ibid.*
8. Section 7 of the Muslim Family Laws Ordinance, 1961.

and the wife or with their consent. Hence, if one of the spouses does not appoint or agree to the appointment of an arbitrator, the *Qāḍī* can certainly appoint an arbitrator from his or her family or even a stranger to represent the husband or the wife as the case may be. It is his duty to redress a wrong. The Courts hold the same position as was held by the *Qāḍīs* in old times and in the matters of marriage and divorce they can follow the provisions of Muslim law.

IV. Verdict of Arbitrators

Preliminary

When there is disharmony between the spouses and the arbitrators appointed to resolve the differences fail in their mission to bring about a reconciliation, it can be concluded that the marriage is a failure and its continuance can no longer serve any useful purpose. The question arises in such a case if the arbitrators have the right to dissolve the marriage or if their work ends when they fail to bring about a reconciliation.

V. Different Aspects for Consideration

It would be convenient to consider the matter having regard to the following aspects that may arise out of the arbitration proceedings:

(*i*) The arbitrators may agree that the differences between the spouses are not serious enough to call for the dissolution of the marriage.

(*ii*) The arbitrators may agree that the dissolution of the marriage is necessary.

(*iii*) The arbitrators may disagree about the necessity for the dissolution of the marriage.

I. *When Dissolution of Marriage not Considered Necessary*

If the arbitrators agree that there is no reasonable cause for the dissolution of the marriage, the wife or the husband shall have no right for its termination, because it is a necessary condition for the dissolution of a marriage that they should have a valid ground for separation and should not be acting on a mere whim or passing fancy. Hence when the arbitrators, one of whom is the husband's or the wife's own representative, come to the conclusion that there is no such reasonable cause for its termination then in such a case the marriage has to be maintained and they can order the husband and the wife to live together.[9] They can ask the spouses to give their marriage another trial. This, however, does not take away their fundamental right to the dissolution of marriage if the efforts at reconciliation prove to be a failure subsequently.

II. If the arbitrators agree that the marriage should be dissolved and the husband or the wife agrees to it or has already given them the power to dissolve the marriage, there can be no difficulty in the matter. A difficulty, however, arises if the parties have not invested the arbitrators with the power to dissolve the marriage. Thus if the arbitrators come to the conclusion that it is desirable to dissolve the marriage, but one of the spouses does not accept their decision, the question arises if the arbitrators can separate the parties in such a case. The matter is not free from doubt and difficulty.

The problem can be considered with reference to two different situations, namely:

(*a*) When the arbitrators are appointed by the parties themselves.

(*b*) When the arbitrators have been appointed by the *Qaḍī*.

(*a*) If the arbitrators have been nominated by the spouses, their position has been considered as that of agents of the spouses and so they cannot exceed the limits of their authority. If the husband has not authorized his nominee to divorce the wife, the agent cannot exercise that power. Similarly, if the wife has not allowed her representative to get a *Khul'* on her behalf, he shall not be competent to do so.

9. Syed Amīr Ali, (*Tafsīr*) *op. cit.*, p. 37.

Hence their order to dissolve the marriage will not be binding on the spouses. Abū Ḥanīfah, his disciples, as well as some other jurists have expressed the same view.[10] As regards Sh̲āfi'ī, there are two reports. According to one, the award shall be binding on the parties. According to the other report, the award shall be binding only if they consent to it, but not otherwise.

Some Muslim jurists of the early period had laid down a general rule of law that if two persons appoint an arbitrator, qualified to decide their case according to the injunctions of the Qur'ān and the Traditions, then he is seized of full authority to pass any order that he thinks proper in the matter and can wield the same power as can be exercised by a *Qāḍī*.[11] They considered that his award or order was binding on the parties and he could decide cases relating to all matters including divorce. But the Muslim jurists of a later period expressed the opinion that it was rather dangerous to invest ordinary people with such wide powers in certain cases, and they made an exception to this general rule so as to exclude cases relating to divorce and emancipation of slaves from its scope. Probably they were influenced into changing their outlook by the degeneration of the people of later days as explained later.

(*b*) If the arbitrators have been appointed by the *Qāḍī* then again there is a difference of opinion as to whether they can dissolve the marriage against the wishes of the husband or maintain it against the desire of the wife.

The matter will be clear from the various views about the different aspects of the matter given below :

10. Syed Amīr Ali (*Tafsīr*), *op. cit.*, p. 37.

11. 'Alā al-Dīn Abu'l-Hasan, *Mu'in al-Hukkām*, Cairo, 1300 A.H., p. 23 : *Al-fatāwā al-Hindiya*, Cawnpore, 1349 A.H., Vol. III, p. 179 ; Shaykhzādah 'Abd al-Rahmān, *Majma' Al-unhur*, Cairo, 1327 A.H., Vol. II p 173 ; Ibn Qudāmah, *al-Mughni*, Cairo, 1376 A.H., Vol. IX, p. 107 ; Ibn 'Ābidīn, Cairo, 1318 A.H., Vol. IV, p. 362.

(*i*) The arbitrators have no right to separate the spouses.

(*ii*) The arbitrators do possess the power to dissolve the marriage.

(*iii*) The arbitrators can separate the spouses only if they have been invested with the power.

(*iv*) When there is a difference between the arbitrators whether to maintain the marriage or to separate the spouses.

The above aspects are now discussed below :

(*i*) It is stated in *Rūh al-Ma'ānī* that the arbitrators have no right to separate the parties, that is, to dissolve the marriage [12]

Abū Dā'ūd. Hasan Basri and some others are also of the opinion that the arbitrators cannot dissolve the marriage. They base this view on the ground that the Qur'ān has mentioned settlement or reconciliation in the verse about arbitration but not a separation so the arbitrators can act in the former matter but not in the latter case.[13]

Justification for the View that the Arbitrators Cannot Separate the Spouses :—It is stated in *Tafsir Muwahib-ur-Rahman* that "the order of the *hakam* is binding in every case according to the Hanafi jurists but they have not applied this rule in all cases to avoid acts of injustice by an ordinary man acting as judge.[14]

(*ii*) *View that Arbitrators can Separate Spouses* :—According to *Tafsir Muwahib-ur-Rahman*, the Ulamā are agreed on the point that the arbitrators have the power either to dissolve the marriage or to maintain it.[15] Ibrāhīm al-Nakha'ī has gone to the extent as to hold that the arbitrators can even pronounce a *mughalazah* divorce.

12. Mahmūd Alūsī, *Rūh al-Mā'ani*, Cairo, n.d., Vol. V, p. 27.
13. Syed Amīr Ali (*Tafsir*), *op. cit.*, Vol. IV, p. 37.
14. *Ibid.*
15. *Ibid.*

Mālik is reported to have held the same opinion.[16] The jurists who are in favour of the proposition that the arbitrators have the authority to separate or not to separate the parties base their views on the reasoning that God Almighty has called the arbitrators as Hakam (judge) and such persons namely, judges, have absolute authority in all matters and here it includes the power to separate the spouses.[17]

It is reported that Caliph 'Alī has expressed the view that it is valid for the arbitrators to maintain the marriage or to terminate it.[18] He has stated that through arbiters Allah brings (spouses) together as well as separates them. It means that arbiters have the power to maintain a marriage or to dissolve it. Shāfi'ī and Mujahid, have stated that the arbiter has got full power to maintain the marriage or to separate the spouses.

It is stated in *Tafsir Muwahib-ur-Rahman* that both the arbiters must try to bring about a reconciliation between the parties. They can order the guilty party to desist from his or her improper or undesirable conduct or they may separate the parties if they consider it proper to do so.[19]

If the arbitrators find that it is the wife who is in the wrong and they consider it desirable to dissolve the marriage then they can separate the parties and shall order the wife to pay such compensation to her husband as they think proper.[20] But if they cannot agree to the amount of compensation then the matter shall remain undecided.[21]

Mālik, al-Awzā'ī and Ishāq are also of the opinion that the arbitrators can exercise this power even without the permission of the spouses and without being specifically authorized in the matter. Mālik has stated "both arbitrators

16. Syed Amīr Ali (*Tafsīr*), *op. cit.*, Vol. II, p. 37.
17. *Ibid.*
18. *Ibid.*
19. *Ibid.*
20. Sahnūn, *al-Mudawwanat al-Kubrā*, Vol. V, p. 50 ; Cairo, 1323 A.H.,
21. *Ibid.*, Vol. V, p. 51.

shall endeavour to reconcile the parties, and if they are unsuccessful, they decide according to the merits of the case. If the husband is in the wrong they pronounce a separation. If they decide themselves in favour of repudiation, their declaration shall have the force of judicial decree, the judgement of the *Qāḍī* is not required."[22] According to another report Shafi'ī also held this view.[23]

Precedents

There are some important cases which are very useful in deciding this matter. The first occurred in the time of 'Uthmān the third Caliph. Fātimah b. Atbah had complained to the Caliph about the undesirable behaviour of her husband and the Caliph appointed two persons, namely, Ibn 'Abbās and Mu'āwiyah bin Abū Sufyān to decide the case. They proceeded to the house of the spouses and ibn 'Abbās remarked that he would separate her (from her husband), but Mu'awiyah said, "I am not such as to cause separation between two descendants of 'Abd Manāf, that is, he would not separate the two members of his own tribe."[24] This incident supports the view that the arbitrators nominated by the State or the *Qāḍī* do have the power to dissolve the marriage if they so decide. Here Mu'āwiyah did not refuse to separate the parties for lack of authority to do so, but because the spouses belonged to his own tribe and so he did not want a separation between them.

It is also reported by Ibn 'Abbās that 'Uthmān, the third Caliph, had directed the arbitrators in a case that they could maintain the marriage or dissolve it as they thought best.[25]

But there is still a much more weighty and clear authority regarding the matter. It is reported that a husband

22. Sahnūn, *op. cit.*, Al-Rāzī, Fakhr al-Dīn, *Mafātih al-Ghayb* (*al-Tafsīr al-Kabīr*), Cairo, 1308 A.H., Vol. III, p. 216.
23. Al-Rāzī, *op. cit.*, p. 216.
24. Syed Amīr Ali (*Tafsīr*), *op. cit*, p. 37.
25. *Ibid.*

and his wife and some other persons approached 'Alī, the fourth Caliph, who enquired of them what the matter was. He was informed that there was a quarrel between the spouses. Caliph 'Alī quoted the verse of the Qur'ān about appointment of arbitrators and asked them if they would abide by the verdict of the arbitrators. The wife said that she would abide by the injunction in the Qur'ān but the husband said that he would not agree to separation if so decided by the arbitrators. Caliph 'Alī thereupon said, "Thou art a liar (that is, at fault in not accepting the injunction of the Qur'ān), thou canst not leave this place until and unless thou also agreest to abide by the decision of the arbitrators as has been done by the woman".[26] This shows very clearly that the *Qāḍī* can force the husband to abide by the decision of the arbitrators.

(*iii*) *The Arbitrators can Separate the Spouses only if They have been Invested with this Power* :—Badr al-Dīn al-'Aynī states in *Umdat al-Qārī* that there is a difference of opinion whether the arbitrators can dissolve the marriage. It was further stated that the Kūfīs (that is Abū Hanīfah, Abū Yūsuf, as well as Muhammad), Shāfi'ī, and Ahmad b. Hanbal have held that the order of the arbiters depends on the authority given to them (by the husband). If he has given them the power to separate then it is good. In the absence of such authority the arbiter cannot give an order (for separation). The arbiter or arbiters will submit their report to the *Qāḍī* who shall base his order on their report.

The Kūfīs, that is, Abū Hanīfah and his disciples, as well as Shāfi'i, and Ahmad b. Hanbal state that the judges (arbitrators) cannot separate the parties unless they have been authorised by the spouses in this behalf.[27] They base their opinion on the ground that divorce lies in the hands of the

26. Al-Rāzī, *op. cit.*, Vol. III, p. 216.
27. *Ibid.*

husband. Hence the marriage can be dissolved only if he gives this power to the arbitrators. If he does not invest the arbitrator or arbitrators with this power then he or they cannot wield it and cannot dissolve the marriage. In the latter case the marriage can be dissolved only by the State or the *Qāḍī*. This is also the opinion expressed in *Bayan al-Qur'an* by Maulana Ashraf Ali Thanvi.[28]

(*iv*) *When the Arbitrators Disagree about Separation* :— It is stated in *Umdat al-Qārī*, the well-known commentary on *Sahīh al-Bukhari*, that if the arbitrators disagree about the desirability of the dissolution of the marriage then their order shall not be implemented, that is, the marriage shall not be dissolved. But this does not seem to be suitable under the present day conditions even if it could have been considered reasonable in early days. It is very likely that the arbitrators chosen from amongst the relations or friends of the husband may be acting under a spirit of partisanship and may not be acting impartially and the husband can then be in a position to defeat the wife's claim even though unjustifiably. Such a state of affairs cannot be conducive to dispensation of justice and will be very undesirable. We should bear in mind that the standard of honesty and justice has undergone a great degeneration since the time of the Imams and we have to guard against injustice as far as we can. The solution stated in *Ahkām al-Qur'ān* as quoted above can apply with equal force here.

VI. Conditions Attached to Appointment

Al-Fatāwā'i al-Alamgīrīyah states that it is open to the parties to attach a condition to the investment of the power in the arbitrator. Thus it can be made a condition of arbitration that the arbitrators shall deliver their award within a certain specified time or that they shall be empowered to exercise such and such powers, but shall not be empowered

28. Ashraf Alī Thānawī, *Bayān al-Qur'ān*, Delhi, n.d., Vol. II, p. 15.

to exercise certain specified powers.[29] The same view has been given in some other books also.

Arbitrators to Report to the Qāḍī

The above discussion will show that there is a difference of opinion amongst the *Imams* and other Muslim jurists about the power of the arbitrators to separate the parties when harmony between them is not possible. Ibn al-Arabi has suggested a very good solution of the difficulty. He states that if the arbitrators find that reconciliation is impossible then they must inform the *Qāḍī* as to which of the parties is at fault. If the *Qāḍī* finds from the arbitrators' report that the fault lies with the husband, he shall force him to divorce his wife and the marriage shall be repudiated. If the *Qāḍi* finds that it is the wife who is at fault then he can force her to take a *Khul'* so that the wife shall be penalised in paying a compensation to the husband for getting a divorce from him. If both of them are at fault, they will be separated in lieu of a part of the dower.[30] This is a very reasonable solution of the difficulty and the procedure is akin to that laid down in the Arbitration Act.

VII. Power of Arbitrators

Mālik, Ishāq, and al-Awzā'ī hold that the arbiters can order a divorce ; it can amount to only one irrevocable divorce and cannot amount to one *mughalazah* divorce, that is, three irrevocable divorces. Ibn Qāsim has stated that the arbiters can order three irrevocable divorces if they are agreed on the point. Mughīrah, Ashhab, Ibn Mājushān and Asbagh and Ibn Nāwāz have stated that if there is disagreement between the arbiters so that one order one irrevocable divorce while the other orders one *mughalazah* divorce then only one divorce shall be effected.[31]

29. *Al-Fatāwā al-Hindiyah, op. cit.*, Vol. III, p. 180.
30. Ibn al-'Arabī, *Ahkām al-Qur'ān*, Cairo, 1957, A.D. Vol, I, pp. 423-25.
31. Badr al-Dīn al-'Aynī, *'Umdat al-Qārī*, Damascus, n.d., Vol. XX, p. 265.

Shī'i View

It is stated in *Bihār al-Anwār*, a book well recognized by *Ithnā'-'Ashrī* sect of the Shī'as that in cases of *nushūz* (disobedience) or *shiqāq* (disharmony), arbitrators may be appointed to settle the dispute or the judge may himself act in the matter and that if no agreement is reached then the marriage ought to be dissolved.[32]

VIII. Courts' View

The Courts on the basis of the authorities produced before them have held that the arbitrators cannot dissolve a marriage for the following reasons :—

(*a*) The power of the arbitrators is confined to bring about a reconciliation but failing that they can do nothing in the matter.

(*b*) The arbitrators can be appointed only by the *Qāḍī* (the Court) when it comes to know of a case of *shiqāq* (disharmony between the spouses). But at present a Court cannot act on his own private information and so the rule is no more applicable.

(*c*) A Court is not competent to appoint arbitrators of its own choice from the families of the spouses.

(*d*) If the verdict of the two arbitrators is not unanimous.[33]

(*a*) This point has been fully discussed above and the discussion need not be repeated here.

(*b*) No doubt it is not possible for the Court to know if a certain marriage has not proved successful, and if a judge happens to know of such a state of affairs even then he cannot take cognisance of the matter. But this difficulty does not render the procedure of arbitration ineffective. It shall be open to the wife to bring the matter to the notice

32. Bihār al-Anwār, cited in Ameer Ali : Mohammedan Law, Calcutta, 1908, pp. 560, 561.

33. Umar Bibi Vs. Mohammad Din, A.I.R., 1945, Lahore, 51 ; Mst. Sayeeda Khanam Vs. Mohammad Sami, 1952. P.L.D., Lahore, 113.

of the Court by a suit when the Court shall be seized of the power to enter into the matter and to appoint arbitrators.

(*c*) The cases decided by the Caliphs establish the fact that the *Qāḍīs* and so the Courts have the power to appoint arbitrators when they find that there is a breach between the husband and the wife so much so that they cannot live happily together. The Caliphs had expressly authorised the arbitrators to dissolve the marriage if such a step was considered necessary. But the Courts, as at present constituted, cannot delegate their power to anyone else to terminate the marriage. It will be necessary for the arbitrators to submit their report or reports to the Court. Under the Muslim Law, the *Qāḍī* is competent to decide the case on the findings of the arbitrators or otherwise. As the Courts hold the same position as the *Qāḍī* in the early days of Islam, there seems to be no reasons why they cannot take the report or reports of the arbitrators into consideration, and decide the case on the basis of the arbitrators' findings or after taking more evidence if necessary.

A case involving the matter came up for decision before the Lahore High Court in 1945.[34] It was pointed out by the learned judge hearing the appeal that a Court is not competent to appoint arbitrators of its own choice from the families of the spouses, that the arbitrators must have been authorised by the parties concerned to dissolve the marriage and they must have agreed to abide by the decision of the arbitrators. The points have been fully discussed before. The difficulty was also pointed out by the Court that it is the State which has to be satisfied about the cause of breach between the parties and that the mere desire of the wife is insufficient. But it is submitted that the wife's suit establishes the fact that there is breach between the husband and the wife. Whether it is so serious as to dissolve the marriage is to be decided by the Court or by the arbitrators and the

34. Umar Bibi Vs. Mohammad Din, A.I.R. 1945, Lahore, 51.

Court has to satisfy itself on the report of the arbitrators, as is done in the case of arbitration proceedings, whether the marriage has to be dissolved. This case was followed by another equally important case that was decided by a full Bench of the same High Court.[35]

The chief grounds on which Cornelius J. (as he then was) accepted the view that the arbitrators cannot separate the parties without the consent of the husband are as given below :

(*a*) "When the husband did not agree, Hazrat 'Alī hesitated, and when Hazrat 'Alī addressed the husband and said that he was wrong, his meaning was that the husband was not right in not doing the same thing as the wife had done."

The learned Judge seems to have concluded from this report that Caliph 'Alī could not decide whether the arbitrators could separate the parties when the husband did not agree to it.

(*b*) Three of the four principal *Imāms* favour the view that the *Ḥakams* cannot grant a divorce unless they be authorised to do so by the husband.

(*a*) It is submitted that the portion omitted in the report before the Court but given in *al-Tafsīr al-Kabīr* is very important. Even in the report before the Court the words "if you decide to separate, separate them" clearly indicate the view of 'Alī. Moreover, if the husband was acting within his rights in refusing a separation, if so ordered by the arbitrators, then how could he be said to be in the wrong. It is unfortunate that the attention of the Court was not drawn to the full report as given in *al-Tafsīr al-Kabīr* or to the reports about 'Uthmān's directions. The full report of the case before Caliph 'Alī and the instructions of Caliph 'Uthman given to arbitrators do not leave any doubt that the arbitrators, appointed by the *Qāḍī*, have full right to dissolve a marriage if they think it necessary to do so.

35. Sayeeda Khanam Vs. Mohammad Sami, 1952, P.L.D., Lahore 113.

(*b*) It is submitted that it is not correct to say that three of the principal *Imāms* were against the power of the arbitrators to separate the parties. The correct position is that at first Imām Shāfi'ī had held the same view as held by Abū Ḥanīfah, but subsequently relying on the instructions of Caliph 'Alī he changed his opinion and held the same view as held by Mālik. Thus there are two *Imāms* on one side, and an equal number hold the opposite view. But the instructions of 'Uthmān and 'Alī carry much more weight than the opinions of any *Imāms.* Hence the opinions of Mālik and Shafi'ī who have followed the view of the Caliphs are more worthy of being followed than the view of the other *Imāms.*

As has already been discussed there is a difference of opinion about this matter but the dictum of Caliph 'Uthmān and Caliph 'Alī makes it clear that the arbitrators can dissolve a marriage even against the wishes of the husband if they are convinced that reconciliation between the parties is impossible. In any case if the arbitrators cannot agree as to what is to be done in the matter then, as they were appointed by the Court, the obvious course for them would be to submit their reports to the Court which can then decide the case after considering the reports and after taking further evidence if it thinks it necessary to do so. Moreover, if the spouses or one of them does not agree to the appointment of arbitrators then it shall be open to the other party to move the Court in the matter and the Court can then initiate the arbitration proceedings by appointing arbitrators. In Pakistan in cases of divorce the parties have to nominate their representatives while the Umpire shall be the Chairman of the Union Council.[36] Section 7 of the Muslim Family Laws Ordinance, 1961, provides that a husband who divorces his wife in any form whatsoever shall give information in writing of the fact to the Chairman of the Union Council. He shall also supply a copy of the same

36. Section 7 of the Muslim Family Laws Ordinance, 1961.

to the wife. The divorce shall remain ineffective for ninety days from the time when information is given to the Chairman who shall constitute an Arbitration Council within thirty days of the receipt of the information and this Council shall take all steps to bring about reconciliation between the parties. It will be only when the Council fails to reconcile the parties within the specified time that the divorce shall become effective on the expiry of ninety days.

IX. Application of the Arbitration Act

It was contended in a case that the Arbitration Act stands excluded by the provisions of the Dissolution of Muslim Marriages Act, 1939. The Court did not accept this view and held, "the Act (Dissolution of Muslim Marriages Act) itself does not prescribe any special procedure which is to be followed in the disposal of suits instituted under the said Act. In the absence of any specific procedure the general procedure which governs all civil suits and actions would be applicable. The Civil Procedure Code and the Arbitration Act and other procedural laws would, therefore, clearly be attracted to suits under Act VIII of 1939...." Following Abdul Kadir Vs. Salima, I.L.R. 8 All. 149, the Court further held, "marriage under Muslim Law is a civil contract. It is not a sacrament but purely a civil contract. Being a civil contract and not a sacrament, it would follow that in the absence of any provision to the contrary in Act VIII of 1939, a suit for dissolution would be a suit to which the provisions of the Arbitration Act would apply.[37]

37. Faqir Mohammad Vs. Amina, A.I.R., 1964 All. 246.

Chapter 14

ILL-ASSORTED MARRIAGES

Preliminary

It is generally recognised now that lawful sexual enjoyment and a happy companionship of the spouses are the primary objects of marriage. A marriage is considered a failure when these objects are not achieved.

The failure of marriage can be due to certain circumstances and also on account of certain defects in one or both of the spouses. The spouse at fault is held responsible for the failure of the marriage and the other spouse becomes entitled under certain conditions to its dissolution on that account.

The English law considered formerly that the primary ends of marriage were :

(1) Procreation of children, and

(2) A restraint against loose-living.

But it was held in a case that the procreation of children was not the principal end of marriage, and that the essence of the Christian doctrine was that children of a marriage, if any, should be born into a family. The Court approved of the statement given in Lord Stair's Institutions that the relevant factor in the matter is "the creation of a situation whereby ariseth that conjugal society, which may have the conjunction of bodies as well as minds, as the general end of marriage is the solace and satisfaction of man."[1]

As has been stated before, the Muslim jurists are guided in the matters of marriage and divorce by an injunction in the Qur'ān, namely, "to keep them (the wives) with kindness or to separate (from them) with humanity."[2] The Muslim jurists state that a husband cannot be said to be keeping his

1. Baxter Vs. Baxter (1947) 2 All. E. R. 886.
2. Qur'ān, II ; 229. Sūrah, Al-Baqarah.

wife with kindness when the wife cannot live happily with him and that under such circumstances he becomes a transgressor of the injunction of the Qur'ān and so the *Qāḍī* can dissolve the marriage in order to remove the transgression and to give relief to the aggrieved party. It is not essential that the party at fault should have actually committed some act which results in the misery of the other party, and he or she may be the victim of causes beyond his or her control. What has to be seen is whether the other party can reasonably be expected to live happily with him or her. If it is not so possible then the dissolution of the marriage becomes desirable. It is also to be seen for the dissolution of marriage if the spouses are faithfully and sincerely fulfilling the obligations incumbent on them on account of the marriage-contract.

The following are some of the important obligations of a husband according to Muslim jurists:—

(*a*) To protect the wife.

(*b*) To maintain the wife.

(*c*) To be sexually fit so that the wife should not be dissatisfied with the marriage or her life on that ground.

(*d*) To treat the wife with affection and kindness including the permission to her to visit her parents and relatives.

(*e*) Not to obstruct her in the performance of her religious duties.

The important marital obligations of the wife are :—

(*a*) To look to the domestic comforts of her husband.

(*b*) To be faithful to her husband.

(*c*) To make herself available to her husband at all reasonable times.

(*d*) To make herself attractive to her husband.

(*e*) To suckle the children during the prescribed period of time if so desired by the husband and to bring them up properly.

Some of these obligations cast a legal duty on the husband or the wife as the case may be while others are in the nature of moral obligations only.

It is not every failure of the marital obligation that entitles the aggrieved party to the dissolution of the marriage and such right can be exercised only when the failure is of a serious nature. It is not, however, necessary that a marriage can be dissolved only when the condition or conduct of one of the spouses is such that the ends of the marriage are not achieved or when he or she fails to perform the marital obligations incumbent on him or her. Thus, a marriage can be dissolved when a wife has got an invincible repugnance or aversion for her husband. This aversion must, however, be based on some reasonable ground and if the *Qāḍī* is satisfied that the wife is sincere in her desire to separate from her husband, he can dissolve the marriage provided that the wife returns the dower and presents received by her from her husband at the time of the marriage or pay some other compensation to her husband. This matter has been fully discussed in the chapter on *Khul'*.

It has been stated before that a marriage can be dissolved under certain circumstances or when one of the spouses suffers from a certain defect or defects. The defects may relate to physical, social, cultural or moral condition of one of the spouses.

The physical defect may consist of incapacity to consummate the marriage or suffering from a loathsome, revolting or injurious disease. This subject has been fully discussed in the chapters on "Defects," "Impotency" and "Other Defects."

The social, cultural or moral adjustment is also very necessary for a happy and successful marriage and the subject has been discussed in this chapter.

It is for the aggrieved party to submit or not to submit to a marriage when one or more of the objects of the marriage are lost due to a defect in the other spouse. Hence such a marriage is not void but only voidable. Thus, a man may marry a woman who may be beyond the age at which a child can be born to her simply to escape from loneliness and to have someone to tend to his domestic requirements. Similarly, a woman may marry a man who, she knows, is suffering from incapacity simply for the sake of financial support and material comforts or companionship.

UNEQUAL MARRIAGES

Preliminary

In Islam and at present in all the civilised countries, one of the chief aims of marriage is considered to be a happy companionship. For this purpose it is necessary that the spouses should be equally matched in certain important matters. It is usually not possible to achieve that degree of equality in which they may be said "to be made for one another." Every prospective husband or wife tries to select the best possible match, but sometimes it does happen that the man or the woman has been misled by some particular glamour in the other spouse, as wealth of the husband or beauty of the wife. The lack of some important characteristics in one spouse often leads to discord, and the other spouse is soon disillusioned in the matter, and then begins a miserable life. If proper care is not taken in the choice of a mate then the marriage may not run a smooth course. Hence, the correct choice of the life-partner is a matter of utmost importance. The Muslim jurists have laid down certain points which they considered necessary for equality in a marriage, so that the marriage might be successful. They have, however, based these points simply on their own experience and have laid different sets of rules for selection of spouse. The most important and sound advice was given by the Prophet (peace be on him) when he stated, "a woman is taken into marriage for four considerations, namely wealth, position of her family, beauty and virtue, but you must give preference to virtue."[3] The aim according to the Muslim jurists is to secure the union of those who are physically and mentally compatible.

It is stated in *al-Durr al-Mukhtār* that marriage shall be

3. Walī al-Dīn al-Khaṭīb, *Mishkāt al-Maṣābiḥ*, Delhi, 1350 A.H., Vol. II, p. 267.

contracted with the intention to remain chaste and a man should marry a woman who is chaste and bears good moral and religious character, and should not marry a woman who belongs to a disreputable family.[4] This last advice can be due to the idea that because of her association and up-bringing she cannot be expected to possess a good character. A man has been advised to marry a woman who is superior to him in morality, character and piety but lower to him in wealth and worldly position. It will be interesting to note the advice given by some jurists regarding marriage. It has been stated by a jurist that a man should not marry a very slim girl of tall stature nor an ugly girl of short stature nor a girl with a bad temper nor a widow having many children, nor a woman notorious for her loose character.[5] The above is a mere advice and does not amount to a rule of law. It is rather unfortunate that the author has not given his reasons for disfavouring marriage with a tall and slim girl and an ugly girl of short stature. He must have attributed some peculiar traits of character to these girls. Manu, the great Hindu law-giver, has given different advice. He states, "Let him (a man) choose for his wife a girl who has an agreeable name, walks gracefully like a pheni-copteros or like a young elephant, whose hair and teeth are moderate respectively in quantity and size; whose body has exquisite softness." He further says, "Let him not marry a girl with reddish hair or with any deformed limbs."

It is necessary for a happy companionship that there should not be a glaring difference between the husband and the wife in respect of education, intelligence, culture, social or financial status, etc. If the spouses are not equally matched or are unequal beyond a reasonable limit then a Court will be justified in dissolving their marriage, if it is established that the ends of the marriage cannot be achieved

4. Al-Haskafi, *Al-Durr al-Mukhtar*. Vol. II, p. 360, Cairo, 1318 A.H.
5. Khurram Ali, *Al-Ghayat al-Autar*, Vol. II, p. 4. Luckhow, 1925 A.D. Urdu translation of *Al-Durr al-Mukhtar*.

in such a case and the marriage has been a failure.

'*Kufw*' means equality. Technically it means equality in marriage. Muslim jurists consider that when a marriage is contracted between spouses who are not equal to each other in certain important respects then, as a general rule, some of the objects of marriage such as happy companionship, harmony etc., are not and cannot be achieved. It is therefore considered very necessary that care should be taken to see that a marriage should be equal and well-assorted and there should not be a marked difference or disparity between the spouses. An unequal marriage may also occasion loss of prestige or even bring disgrace to a family or some substantial injury to one of the spouses. Muslim jurists, therefore, do nöt approve of an ill-assorted marriage and have made equality in certain aspects an essential condition of the validity of marriage.[6] It is stated in *al-Hidāyah* that the desirable ends of marriage, such as cohabitation, society and friendship, cannot be completely achieved except by persons who are each other's equals, as a woman of high rank and family would abhor the society of and cohabitation with a man who is not her equal socially. It is requisite, therefore, that the husband should be the equal of his wife.[7]

Degree of Inequality.—Equality in marriage does not mean absolute equality, but a reasonable degree of it so that a slight difference does not constitute inequality.

Curtailment of Ḥanafi Girl's Rights.—Under the Ḥanafī law, an adult Muslim girl can marry any one she likes and her right in this matter is so absolute that she can exercise it even against the wishes of her parents or other relations and guardians. But it is a well recognised rule of Ḥanafī law that a marriage otherwise lawfully contracted by an adult girl can be set aside by a *Qāḍī* at the

6. Al-Marghīnānī, 'Ali b. Abī Bakr, *Al-Hidayah*, Delhi, n.d., Vol. II, pp. 299-300.

7. *Ibid.*

instance of one of her near relations if he can prove such inferiority or inequality in the husband as injuriously affects the family's credit or prestige. The Ḥanafī jurists have thus curtailed the right of an adult girl to some extent in the case of inequality in marriage. What is to be seen in such a case is not the indiscreet exercise of her right by the girl but the discredit caused or likely to be caused to the family. It would be equally open to a girl to challenge a marriage contracted for her by her guardian if the husband is of an inferior status and the marriage is injurious or disadvantageous to her.

Object of the Rule.—The rule regarding equality is not merely restricted to the safeguard of a family but advantage can be taken of it to save a girl from the consequences of a reckless marriage and to get her release in certain cases from an unhappy marital alliance when she herself cannot get it dissolved. Thus, it happens sometimes that an unsophisticated girl is influenced by an unscrupulous and undesirable person to enter into a runaway marriage with him. Such a marriage often ends in unhappiness and misery to the girl who repents of her blunder afterwards, but finds no way out of it. This rule of law can be applied with advantage in the case of such a marriage and it may be dissolved at the instance of her guardian or any other relation.

Equality in English and American Laws.—There is no such rule in the English and the American laws as the rule relating to equality in marriage in the Muslim law. In some American states, a marriage can be dissolved if one spouse has deceived the other about his or her social position.[8] But the necessity for equality is being realised in America and other countries. Thus an American author has expressed the view that "cultural similarity is essential to happiness in marriage."[9]

8. See Voidable marriages in any book on divorce in U.S.A.
9. Lennon. *Sociology and Social Problems in Nursing*, 1959 A.D., St. Louis Montana.

Unscrupulous Use of the Rule.—Too frequent exercise of the rule by the relations of a girl, however, may amount to an infringement of the freedom of choice by a girl. It must be the unscrupulous use of the rule by the relations of a girl that has led some Muslim countries like Tunisia to abrogate the rule. It is worthy of notice that the vast majority of the Indian and Pakistani Muslims belong to the Ḥanafī sect which is most exacting in the matter of unequal marriages and yet the cases brought by guardians and near relations of a girl on the ground of unequal marriage are rare though unequal marriages do take place in these countries.

Practice in Pre-Partition India.—Cases for dissolution of marriage on the basis of inequality have been very uncommon in pre-partition India. The reason seems to be that marriages were generally arranged by the parents or guardians of girls and they always took care in the interest of the prestige of their own families to see that a husband was in no way unequal to them. Great importance was attached to lineage so much so that a person would refuse to give his daughter in marriage to the son of a millionaire on the ground of inequality in lineage and would gladly marry her to a person of very small means belonging to a Sayyid family. Government service, however low, was considered to be more respectable than trade even though highly flourishing. Of late years this importance attached to lineage has lost much of its importance and wealth has taken its place. In India and Pakistan this is due to some extent to the upheaval that resulted on the partition of the country when families were scattered over distant places. It is also due to the great importance attached to wealth now.

Practice in other Muslim Countries.—In some Muslim countries equality in marriage in certain aspects is still considered of great importance. Thus in Egypt spouses should be equal in lineage, religion, property, piety and profession or social status.

Religious Sanction.—The Prophet (peace be on him) is reported to have said: "Take ye care that none should contract women in marriage but their proper guardians, and that they be not so contracted but with their equals."[10] This authority seems to be rather doubtful in the face of the injunction in the Qur'ān wherein it is stated that the believers are brethren.[11] It is laid down at another place: "Surely the noblest of you with Allah is the most dutiful of you."[12] Here precedence is given to a man solely on account of character so that a non-Arab of the lower class can be superior to the Arab by reason of his character. The Prophet (peace be on him) has also stressed that no one has superiority over others by reason of his nationality or country. Thus he has stated, "the Arabs have no precedence over the non-Arabs, nor the non-Arabs over the Arabs, nor the white man over the black nor the black man over the white one except by excelling in righteousness."[13] He has thus stressed that all human beings are equal, regardless of their individual or racial status, and that no one can claim any preference or superiority over others except by reason of his character. The first Tradition can only mean that the Prophet (peace be on him) stressed that women should not be contracted in disadvantageous marriages.

The law about equality in marriages seems to have been based on practical difficulties experienced in unequal marriages. It is stated in *Badā'i' al-Ṣanā'i'* that many jurists such as Mālik, Karkhī, al-Ḥasan al-Baṣrī, Sufyan al-Tharī do not accept this rule as correct.[14] The above-mentioned jurists hold that equality in marriage is not an essential condition for its validity. They base their opinion on the following grounds

10. Al-Marghīnānī, *op. cit.*, Vol. II, p. 299.
11. Qur'ān, XXVI : 10. Surah Al-Hujurāt.
12. Qur'ān, XXVI : 13. Surah Al-Hujurāt.
13. Aḥmad b. Ḥanbal, *Musnad*, Cairo, 1313 A.H., Vol. V, p. 411.
14. Al-Kasānī, 'Alā al-Dīn Abū Bakr, *Badā'i' al-Ṣana'i'*, Cairo, 1324 A.H., Vol. II, p. 317.

in support of their opinion:

(*a*) Bilāl, a liberated slave, was married to an Arab girl.

(*b*) The Prophet (peace be on him) has said that an Arab has no precedence over a non-Arab.

(*c*) The Prophet (peace be on him) and the Companions did not follow this rule.

But it cannot be denied that some equality in marriage in certain respects is essential to the happiness of the spouses.

Applicability of the Law Relating to Equality in Marriage in Pakistan and India.—The doctrine of equality in marriage is a part of the substantial Muslim law and, therefore, still applies to them. The Punjab Chief Court, however, held in a case that the inferiority in the social status of the husband does not justify the Court in dissolving a marriage.[15] It is submitted that this view contravenes the provisions of the Muslim law. The difficulty has, however, been removed as far as the wife is concerned by clause IX of Section 2 of the Dissolution of Muslim Marriages Act, 1939. The section lays down that a woman married under Muslim law shall be entitled to obtain a decree for the dissolution of her marriage on any ground which is recognised as valid for the dissolution of marriage under Muslim law.

The Muslim law does allow the dissolution of a marriage on the basis of inequality in marriage. A wife can, therefore, take advantage of the above clause to get her marriage dissolved through Court under clause IX on the basis of the husband's inferiority. There seems to be no reason why the guardian or relation of a girl may not take advantage of the law of equality in marriage when a girl contracts such unequal marriage as may bring disgrace to the family or unhappiness to her. A Court can certainly take cognizance of a suit for dissolution of marriage on the basis of inequality. It must, however, take a broad view in the matter and see

15. Jamaat Ali Shah Vs. Mir Mahmud, 38. IC, 10.

if the difference between the spouses is so glaring as to make the marriage unsuccessful and the life of the wife miserable. It is difficult to follow too literally some of the technical rules laid down by Muslim jurists because some of the grounds on which a marriage was considered unequal in the past have now lost their importance. Thus now not much importance is attached to lineage and one comes across a case in which a girl belonging to a Sayyid family has been married to a man belonging to another sect—a thing unheard of fifty years before. An equality in intellectual capacity has become more important now than it was in the past due to the advancement in the education of women. A highly educated woman may not find life very congenial with a man of very ordinary education even though he may be rich. According to some Shi'i jurists, equality in Islam (that is, being Muslims) is not sufficient, but there must also be equality in *Imān* (faith) also. *Imān* (religion) in the Shi'ī textbooks is used in a special sense so as to distinguish the Shī'ahs from the Sunnīs and other sects of Muslims. But it is stated in *Sharāi' al-Islām* that according to the generally accepted view equality in respect of Islam is all that is required. Such a marriage, that is, a marriage between a Sunni and a Shī'ah girl has not been considered "*Ḥarām*" or forbidden but merely "*Makrūh*" or undesirable.[16]

It was held by a Bench of the Calcutta High Court in the case of Syed Ghulam Hossain Chowdhry Vs. Mst. Setabah Begum, 6 WR-88 that they could nowhere find that a Sunni was incapacitated from marrying a Shī'ah girl and held that such a marriage was good. A case of similar nature came up for decision before a Division Bench of the Allahabad High Court.[17] Both Sulaiman J. and Mukerji J. held that the marriage of a Shī'ah girl with a Sunni was valid and legal. The learned judges, however, stated that where a Shī'ah girl

16. Ja'far b. al-Hasan, *Sharā'i' al-Islām*, Urdu translation by Syed Mohd. Sadiq. Vol. I, p. 256. Hyderabad Deccan, 1897 A.D.
17. Aziz Bano Vs. Mohd. Ibrahim Husain, A.I.R., 1925, All. 823.

was given in marriage by her father during her minority then she has a right to repudiate it on attaining majority, because the marriage may affect her religious sentiments and so is to her manifest disadvantage.

The Rule Discussed Under its Two Aspects

The Muslim jurists have dealt with this matter under the heading of *Kufw* or equality. It would be convenient to discuss in this book the mental, social and cultural equality separate from the physical equality. The first section of this chapter deals with the former while the second portion is devoted to a discussion of equality from the other point of view.

What Constitutes Inequality

A marriage is unequal where the status of the husband is inferior to that of the wife's family, or he is inferior to the wife in respect of certain personal qualifications.

Wife's Inferior Status

If a man marries a woman of inferior status, there can be no objection to it. This is based on two considerations. The first is that the inferiority of the wife is not injurious to the husband as she acquires his status. The second is that he can get a release by divorcing her if he so desires. Under Muslim law lineage is counted from the father while a woman on her marriage acquires the status of her husband and so do the children born of the marriage. Hence, if a man marries or is married to a woman of a status inferior to that of his own family, neither family is adversely affected by the marriage and so they cannot object to it on the ground of inequality. Neither husband nor his family can object to the marriage because the wife acquires his or their own status. The woman's family cannot object to such marriage because she is married in a family of a higher status and so they can have no cause for complaint. It can thus be seen that the wife's inferior status does not make the marriage unequal and a man can validly marry a woman of inferior status.[18] If the husband makes equality a condition of the marriage and the wife deceives him in this respect, he cannot seek his relief on the basis of inequality.[19] He can only exercise his right of divorce.

The husband can take advantage of this rule only when his guardian for marriage marries him during his minority for a dower far higher than the dower customary in the girl's family.[20]

Ḥanafī Law

The Muslim jurists differ as to what constitutes inequality. The Ḥanafī jurists are more exacting in this respect than the other jurists. According to Abū Ḥanīfah, equality in marriage pertains to the following matters:

(*a*) Islam, or religion.
(*b*) *Nasab* or family or lineage.
(*c*) *Ḥirfah* or profession.
(*d*) *Ḥurriyah* or freedom (from slavery).
(*e*) *Diyānah* or piety or character.
(*f*) *Māl* or fortune or property, that is, financial condition.[21]

Māliki Law

The Mālikīs differ from the Ḥanafīs in the conception of inequality. According to them the only conditions to constitute equality are Islam, piety and means to maintain the wife. They do not attach any importance to the question of lineage, and profession. But there is a difference of opinion whether Malik made freedom also a condition of equality in marriage. According to another report, Mālik made the

18. *Al-Fatāwā al-Hindiyah, op. cit.*, Vol. II, p. 12.
19. Ibn 'Ābidīn, *Radd al-Muḥtār*, Cairo, 1318 A.H., Vol. II, p. 326.
20. *Ibid.*, pp. 312-14.
21. Al-Marghīnānī, *op. cit.*, Vol. II, pp. 300-301; *al-Fatāwā al-Hindiyah, op. cit.*, Vol. II, pp. 12-13; Ibn 'Abidīn, *op. cit.* Vol. II, pp. 327-30.

following conditions as essential for equality in marriage :

(*a*) Islam or religion.

(*b*) The husband being free of the following defects :

(*i*) Leprosy,

(*ii*) Leucoderma, and

(*iii*) Insanity.[22]

Under the Māliki law an unequal marriage contracted by the father of a girl shall be binding on her even when it is for an inadequate dower, that is, for dower which is less than the customary dower in the family of the girl. She shall have no right to object to the marriage. But she can get a marriage dissolved when the husband is impotent, eunuch or castrated or suffers from leprosy, leucoderma or insanity or is a slave.[23]

Shāfi'ī Law

Shāfi'ī agrees to a great extent with Abū Ḥanīfah about the essentials of equality, the only difference being that he does not make fortune a condition of equality. He adds, however, that the presence of certain defects in the husband is a ground of inequality.[24]

Under the Shāfi'ī law the following conditions are to be taken into consideration for equality in marriage :

(1) Islām or religion.

(2) Piety or character.

(3) *Nasab* or birth or lineage.

(4) Ḥirfah or profession.

(5) *Ḥurriyah*, freedom (from slavery).

(6) Freedom from certain physical defects.[25]

Ḥanbalī Law

There are different opinions expressed by Aḥmad b. Ḥanbal in respect of an unequal marriage. According to one

22. Sidi Khalil, *al-Mukhtasar*, English translation by Ruxton, p. 98, London 1916 A.D.
23. *Ibid.*, pp. 22-23.
24. Ibn Qudāmah, *al-Mughnī*, Cairo, 1367, A. H., Vol. VI, p. 482.
25. *Ibid.*

report he held that an unequal marriage contracted by the father or grandfather of a minor girl shall be perfectly valid. But they cannot marry her to a man suffering from impotency or paralysis. She can exercise her option of puberty if she is contracted in such a marriage. But according to another report if the guardian of a minor girl gives her in marriage to a man of low status or one suffering from a physical defect and he did not know that the husband was unequal to the girl or was suffering from a defect, the marriage shall not be valid, and the girl shall be entiled to exercise her option of puberty.[26] According to another view an unequal marriage shall be invalid and the girl can get it dissolved by her option of puberty. It is explained that Allāh has made the guardian representative or agent of the girl for guarding her interests as she is helpless and unable to conduct her affairs. It is, therefore, not lawful for the guardian to do an act that is prejudicial to the interests of the girl. Hence if he contracts an unequal marriage for the girl, she shall be entitled to exercise her option of puberty.[27]

Discussion About Various Aspects

These matters are discussed in some detail below:

I. *Religion (Islam)*

Sunnī Law

According to all Muslim jurists, both Sunnīs and Shī'ahs, Islam is a necessary condition of equality in marriage. But there is a difference of opinion about the conception of the condition of being a Muslim. It is said that a Muslim by birth shall have a preference over a person who has embraced Islam later. Similarly, one who himself has embraced Islam and whose father was not a Muslim is not the equal of a person whose paternal ancestor was a Muslim. A person who has had only one Muslim ancestor is not the equal of a

26. Ibn Qudāmah, *al-Mughni*, Cairo 1367 A.H., Vol. VI, pp. 488-89; Sharaf al-Dīn Mūsā, *al-Iqnā'*, Cairo, n.d., Vol. III, p. 202.
27. *Ibid.*

person who has two or more Muslim ancestors.[28] But this rule applied only up to three generations after the advent of Islam and a person was considered, under this rule, to be superior to another whose grandfather had embraced Islam later than the grandfather of the other. This rule must have been based on the fact that people who adopted Islam in the beginning were mercilessly persecuted and it required great courage and very firm belief to have adopted Islam in the early days. Such people were, therefore, considered superior to those who adopted Islam in later period when adoption of Islam involved no hardships. Besides, the Companions and the people living in the time of the Prophet (peace be on him) were held in great reverence. The descendants of these people also retained the esteem attached to their ancestors. This rule has lost all importance and no importance is attached to it now, nor is it applicable now. It is stated in *al-Fatāwā al-Hindiyah* that this rule did not apply to Arabs, but only to the non-Arabs "for they pride themselves in this distinction, (*i.e.* freedom and Islam)."[29] Equality in Islam does not mean that the spouses should belong to the same sect. Hence, a marriage between persons belonging to different sects of the Sunnīs shall be considered to be equal. Similarly, a marriage of a Shī'ah to Sunnī is lawful.

Shī'i Law

The Shī'i law also insists on equality in marriage but the only conditions for equality are Islam and the ability to maintain the wife.[30] Under the Shī'i law, the condition regarding Islam has different significance than what it means under the Sunnī law. As discussed above, the condition of Islam under the Sunnī law attaches superiority to a person who or whose ancestor embraced Islam earlier to one who

28. Al-Marghīnānī, *op. cit.*, Vol. II, p. 300; *al-Fatāwā al-Hindiyah, op. cit.*, Vol. II. p. 13, Ibn 'Ābidīn, *op. cit.*, Vol. II, pp. 327-28.

29. *Al-Fatāwā al-Hindiyah, op. cit.*, Vol. II, p. 13. Cf. Ibn 'Ābidīn, *op. cit.*, Vol. II, pp. 327-28.

30. Ja'far b. al-Ḥasan, *op. cit.*, p. 183.

or whose ancestor adopted Islam later. Under the Shī'i law the condition only means that both the spouses should be Muslims.[31] It has no reference to priority in adoption of the faith. It is not, however, an essential condition that they both should be Shī'as and the marriage of a Shī'ah girl with a Sunnī is not invalid. But it has been considered desirable to marry a Shī'ah girl to only a Shī'ah because the wives generally adopt the religion of their husbands.[32] Such a marriage, however, is not invalid in any way but is only disapproved of. But she cannot be given in marriage to a person who openly declares his enmity with the members of the family of the Prophet (peace be on him).[33] There is a difference of opinion in the matter whether a Shī'ah can marry a *Kitābiyah i.e.*, a woman belonging to a revealed religion. According to *Sharā'i' al-Islam*, there are two versions. According to one it is forbidden[34] and according to the other it is valid only in the case of *muta'h* marriage.[35] But the authority of *man lā yaḥḍuruh al-Faqīh* validates it.[36] It is, however, highly disapproved, nevertheless not forbidden. This is the view accepted by the Supreme Court of Pakistan.[37]

II. Nasab or Lineage

Preliminary

Equality in lineage is an essential condition for equality in marriage according to some jurists. The idea that a certain family or tribe or the inhabitants of any particular country

31. Ja'far b. al-Ḥasan, *op. cit.*, p 183; Abū Ja'far Muḥammad b. Abi'l-Ḥasan al-Qummī, *Mahlā Yahḍuruh al-Faqīh*, Tehran, n.d., p. 412.
32. *Ibid.*, pp. 183; 412.
33. Ja'far b. al-Ḥasan, *op. cit.*, p. 183.
34. *Ibid.*, p. 181.
35. *Ibid.*
36. Abū Ja'far Muḥammad b. Abi'l-Ḥasan al-Qummī, *op. cit.*, p. 416.
37. Syed Ali Nawaz Gardezi Vs. Lt. Col. Muhammad Yusuf P.L.D. 1963 S.C. 51.

are superior to any other is alien to Islam which prides itself on removal of all distinctions of caste and colour. The Muslims believe in equality of mankind and there is no distinction of tribe, nation or country in Islam. Thus, it is laid down in the Qur'ān that all tbe faithful are brethren.[38] The Prophet of (peace be on him) has said that an Arab has no precedence over a non-Arab, nor the black man over the white except by excellence in righteousness.[39] The doctrine of equality may be due to the fact that the inhabitants of different countries differ to a great extent from each other in respect of culture, habits etc., with the result that a wife often finds herself unhappy when married to a foreigner.

Ḥanafī Law

The Ḥanafī law insists that there should be equality in lineage in marriage.[40] For this purpose they hold that people belonging to the Quraysh tribe are superior to the other Arabs while all the other Arabs are superior to the non-Arabs.[41] Arabs excepting the Quraysh are considered to be equal to each other, but the Banū Bāhilah tribe (Arabs themselves) are not the equals of the Arabs of other tribes, they being notorious throughout Arabia for every kind of vice.[42] This shows that character not only of an individual, but even of groups to which he belonged was taken into consideration. The Arabs were supposed to be superior to the non-Arabs to such an extent that the marriage of an Arab girl to a non-Arab was considered to be derogatory to the girl's family, however high the worldly

38. Qur'ān XXVI : 10, Surah Al-Hujurāt.
39. Aḥmad b. Ḥanbal, *op. cit.*, Vol. V, p. 411.
40. Al-Marghīnānī, *op. cit.*, Vol. II, p. 300; Ibn 'Ābidīn, *op. cit.*, Vol. II, p. 327.
41. *Al-Fatāwā al-Hindiyah*, *op. cit.*, Vol, II, p. 12; Ibn 'Ābidīn, *op. cit.*, Vol. II, p. 327.
42. Al-Marghīnānī, *op. cit.*, Vol, II, p. 300.

position of the husband might be. Thus, even a non-Arab Ruler is not deemed the equal for marriage with an Arab woman.[43] But great importance is attached to learning so that a non-Arab learned man is entitled to marry any Arab woman, however, high her status may be.[44] As regards the non-Arabs, they are equal to each other irrespective of their caste, nation or country. It is stated in *al-Durr al-Mukhtār* that the condition of equality relates to the Arabs only because the non-Arabs have lost their lineage or racial purity and so equality shall consist in their cases only in being free and in Islam.

Māliki, Ḥanbalī and Shāfi'ī Laws

Māliki, Shāfi'ī and Ḥanbali Laws do not make equality in lineage a condition of equality in marriage.

Whether Equality in Lineage Justifiable

Equality in lineage was not a condition of equality in marriage in the early period of Islam. 'Abdur Raḥmān b. 'Aawf, a prominent Companion, gave his sister in marriage to Bilāl who was a negro emancipated slave. The notion of the superiority of the Arabs over non-Arabs developed later, and it may be the result of their victories over the Persian and Byzantine empires. Besides, the Arabs were very particular about maintaining racial purity and considered themselves superior to the non-Arabs on this account. Thus it is stated in *Sharḥ al-Wiqāyah* that superiority of the Arabs in respect of marriage is due to the fact that the non-Arabs have lost their pedigree (racial purity) by inter-tribal marriages. It also seems likely that non-Arab jurists of later period adopted this view on account of their great reverence for the Prophet (peace be on him) and attached great importance to everything connected with him. Hence they considered the Arabs to be superior to the non-Arabs and

43. Ibn 'Ābidīn, *op. cit.*, Vol. II, p. 327.

44. 'Ubayd Allah b, Mas'ūd, *Sharḥ al-Wiqāyah*, Delhi, 1345 A.H., Vol. II, p. 28.

amongst Arabs they considered the Quraysh tribe, to which the Prophet (peace be on him) belonged, to be superior to other Arabs.[45] Ḥāfiz Ibn Hajar has stated that there is no basis or Tradition for making equality in lineage a condition of marriage.[46] The view described above seems to be correct. The law about equality in lineage seems to have been based on practical difficulties experienced in case of mixed marriages. The translator of *al-Fatāwā al-Alamgiriyah* has given another ground for the adoption of this view. He has explained that Muslim jurists found that the marriages in which husbands and the wives belonged to different races did not prove happy ones and so they introduced this rule of equality in lineage as a safeguard against the unhappiness of the married couple. He has also stated that this rule was not observed then.[47] Thus a non-Arab could act as a minister or governor over the Arabs in an Arab State while a non-Arab Muslim could lead prayers in an Arab congregation.

There is a case which throws a good deal of light in this matter. Zayn al-'Abidīn, great grandson of the Prophet (peace be on him) and a very learned *Imām*, had given his daughter in marriage to a liberated non-Arab slave and had himself taken in marriage an emancipated non-Arab slave girl. The Ruler wrote to him that the *Imām* had brought disgrace on all the Arabs. In reply the *Imām* referred the Ruler to the precedents set up by the Prophet (peace be on him), who had married a liberated Jewess slave girl and had given his own cousin in marriage to Zayd—a liberated non-Arab slave.[48] There is another well-known incident of the early days of Islam. Bilāl, a negro convert. expressed his

45. 'Ubayd Allah b. Mas'ūd, *Sharḥ al-Wiqāyah*, Delhi, 1345 A.H., Vol. II, p. 21.
46. Ibn Hajar al-'Asqalānī, *Fatḥ al-Bārī*, Cairo, 1325 A.H., Vol. IX, p. 104.
47. Sayed Amir Ali, *Al-Fatāwā al-Alamgiriyah*, Urdu translation of *Al-Fatāwā al-Hindiyah*, Vol. II, p. 40. (on margin) Lucknow, 1899 A.D.
48. Manāẓir Aḥsan Gīlānī, *Hadrat Imām Abū Ḥanīfah kī siyāsī zindagī*, p. 177, 1966 A.D., Karachi.

desire to enter into matrimony, and he did get married to an Arab girl.

III. Ḥurriyah (Freedom)

Another aspect relating to equality is being free. A slave cannot be the equal of a free woman.[49] This condition again seems to have been introduced long after the advent of Islam. We have already seen in our discussion on lineage that the Arabs gave their daughters in marriage to slaves after setting them free. No stigma was attached to a slave and there were slaves who even rose to be kings. But the Muslim jurists have laid down that a person whose father was a slave but was freed later cannot be the equal of a free woman.[50] If a father should give his minor son or daughter in marriage to a slave then it shall be valid and binding on the minor because it shall be presumed that the father must have some other more important consideration in view.[51] But if he has acted without any view to a particular advantage, the contract is null.[52] Abū Yusūf and Muḥammad state that the contract is illegal because it involves two-fold disadvantages to the minor, namely, want of equality and his master's consent.[53]

Ḥirfah (Profession)

Another essential condition of equality in marriage, according to the Ḥanafīs, is that the husband should not be carrying on a profession which is inferior to the profession carried on by the members of the wife's family.[54] Abū Yūsuf

49. *Al-Fatāwā al-Hindiyah, op. cit.*, Vol. II, p. 13 ; Ibn 'Ābidīn, *op. cit.*, Vol, II. p. 327.
50. Al-Marghīnānī, *op. cit.*, Vol. II, p. 300; *al-Fatāwā al-Hindiyah op. cit.*, Vol. II, p. 13; Ibn 'Ābidīn, *op. cit.*, Vol. II, p. 327.
51. Al-Marghīnānī, *op. cit*, Vol. II, p. 302 ; Ibn 'Abidīn, *op. cit.*, Vol. II, p. 312.
52. Al-Marghīnānī, *op. cit,*, Vol. II, p. 302.
53. *Ibid.*; Ibn Qudāmah, *op. cit.*, Vol. VI, p. 484; Ibn 'Ābidīn, *op, cit.*, Vol. II, p. 312.
54. Ibn 'Ābidīn, *op. cit.*, Vol. II, p. 330.

and Muḥammad hold equality in profession to be a necessary condition of marriage.[55] Contradictory reports are attributed to Abū Ḥanīfah. According to a report, he does not make equality in profession an essential condition of equality while according to the other report he considers it an enssential condition. According to another report both Abū Yūsuf and Muḥammad hold that profession is not to be taken into consideration unless it is of such a degrading nature as to constitute an insurmountable objection in which case the marriage can be dissolved on this ground as it would be unequal.[56]

Some jurists hold that there can be no condition of equality in profession as a man can change it at any time.[57] But as pointed out elsewhere, the material time when a man's position is to be seen is the time of marriage and a subsequent change in his condition is of no consequence.[58] This condition according to Abū Ḥanīfah did not and does not apply to the Arabs, as reported by al-Karkhī, who were and are considered equals irrespective of their professions.[59] But in countries other than Arabia there was a marked difference in social status and standard of living among various classes of society, and they did not encourage intermarriages between them. Profession, social status and respectability were considered to be so closely associated as to be one and the same thing. This condition was justified on the ground that some prestige and respectability was generally attached to certain professions while a degree of inferiority was annexed to certain other professions on account of their being considered low so that respectability or importance differed with different

55. Al-Marghīnānī, *op. cit.*, Vol. II, p. 301; *Al-Fatāwā al-Hindiyah, op. cit.*, Vol. II, p. 13.
56. Al-Marghīnānī, *op. cit.*, Vol. II, p. 301; Ibn 'Ābidīn, *op. cit.*, Vol. II, p. 330,
57. Al-Marghīnānī, *op. cit.*, Vol. II, p. 301.
58. Ibn 'Ābidīn, *op. cit.*, Vol. II, p. 331.
59. *Ibid.*, p. 330.

professions.[60] The marriage of a girl whose family carried on a more respectable profession to a person whose family carried on a low profession was considered to bring discredit to the girl's family and thus lowered its prestige.[61] There was also a risk that the girl being used to a certain way of living might find it hard to live with people whose standard of living was comparatively very low. Thus, the marriage of the daughter of a merchant to a barber or washerman was looked down upon and was considered to be a disgrace to the girl's family. The distinction of profession was more defined in old times when families carried on and confined themselves to the same business or profession from generation to generation. They came to possess certain particular traits of character. Thus, the members of a family of teachers or *Qāḍīs* would be more advanced in intellect, education, refinement, culture etc. than the members of the merchants families who in their turn would be more advanced than the people carrying on the profession of a barber or washerman etc., and their srandard of living differed a great deal. Experience showed that a marriage between members of different groups resulted in lack of harmony and consequently led to unhappiness. The importance or unimportance attached to a particular profession rested on the general opinion of the public, and sometimes differed in different countries. It was therefore, to be considered with regard to the country of the parties or the country of the wife if the spouses belonged to different countries. In former times, as a general rule, trade was looked down upon and government employees and landlords were considered to be superior to the traders. But great importance was attached to learning so that a teacher was considered the equal of any big landholder and a learned man was regarded as the equal of the most important person. Similarly, a *Qāḍī* or a physician was also considered to be a very important person. The professionals and the traders

60. Al-Marg͟hīnānī, *op. cit.*, Vol. II, p. 301.

61. Ibn 'Ābīdīn, *op. cit.*, Vol. II, p. 331.

were divided into various groups according to the importance or respectability of their work. A physician was regarded superior to a chemist or a druggist. Amongst traders an importer is superior to a merchant who in his turn is superior to a hawker. The profession of a sweeper, shoe-maker, barber or washerman was considered low while that of a teacher, doctor, government servant was considered respectable.[62] A sweeper, cobbler, washerman, or barber was considered lower in respectability than a tailor or a draper. It is stated in *al-Durr al-Mukhtār* that the employees of unscrupulous officials are lower to the lowest professionals even if they are wealthy because their wealth has been earned by corruption.[63]

But this adherence to one profession by a particular family is no longer the rule. The result is that persons carrying on a certain profession can no longer be deemed to possess certain traits of character. Hence, the status attached to various professions has undergone a radical change during recent times and the difference in profession cannot be a safe guide to determine the equality of a marriage unless the difference is so glaring as to leave no doubt in the matter. Moreover, in recent times many professions have assumed a new form. It was considered formerly that a petty shop-keeper or hawker was superior to a washerman, but a dry cleaner may now be considered superior to a petty shop-keeper. Similarly, a manufacturer of shoes is no longer the cobbler of the old times. The importance or want of it, therefore, is to be assessed in the present times according to the present standards. But there can be no doubt that a marriage my be dissolved when the difference between the spouses is very marked in respect of the professions carried on by the husband and the wife's family, and it is established that there is a glaring difference in the intellectual and social conditions and refinement and in the standard of living between the families of the wife and the husband. Thus a runaway marriage between the daughter of a person and his

62. Ibn 'Ābidīn, *op. cit.*, Vol. II, pp. 330-31.

63. *Ibid.*, p. 330.

servant, engaged for menial work, can be considered unequal. Such a marriage will obviously be ill-assorted and is probable to lead to misery and unhappiness of the girl and so may be annulled for that reason on the ground of inequality. It is stated in *al-Radd al-Muḥtār* that the status of professions changes from time to time and so must be decided according to the special conditions of the times.[64]

V. Māl, Property or Wealth

Another condition of equality in marriage, according to the Ḥanafīs, relates to forturne or the financial condition of the husband. According to Ḥanafī jurists, equality must exist in respect of financial position and property also. It is considered that a marriage, ill-assorted with respect to the financial conditions of the spouses, is apt to result in unhappiness. A girl brought up in comfort or luxury may find it hard to live with a husband whose means are very limited so that she shall have to live in a way to which she is not accustomed and may have to experience great hardships on that account. Such a marriage is apt to end in misery and unhappiness. The Ḥanafī jurists also explain that wealth contributes to the prestige of a family while poverty lowers its esteem. As has been pointed out before, an unequal marriage is not void but merely voidable. This condition is meant to help a girl who has been given in marriage by her guardian to a person having a lower standard of living. It can also help a girl who has recklessly married a man of slender means as her marriage can be dissolved at the instance of her relations. But a guardian or relation can also object to the marriage of a girl with a man of poor means on the ground that it shall lower the prestige of the family. By wealth is meant that the husband should be possessed of sufficient means to discharge his dower-debt and provide for the wife's maintenance.[65]

64. Ibn 'Ābidīn, *op. cit.*, Vol. II, p. 331.
65. *Al-Fatāwā al-Hindiyah, op, cit.,* Vol. II, p. 13 ; Ibn 'Ābidīn, *op. cit.*, Vol. II, p. 329.

According to a report, both Abū Ḥanīfah and Muḥammad hold that the fortune of a man is to be considered in general because a man may be capable of paying both the dower and the maintenance of the wife and yet may not be the equal of a wife possessed of large property. They explain that men consider wealth as conferring superiority and poverty as causing loss of prestige. Abū Yūsuf, on the other hand, says that wealth is not to be taken into consideration as it is an unstable thing that may be acquired in the morning and lost before night.[66]

There is a difference of opinion as to whether a husband should be able to meet both the liabilities or if he will be considered to be wife's equal when he is able either to pay the wife's dower or to maintain her. Abū Yūsuf holds that the ability to pay the wife's dower is not a necessary condition of equality. His reasoning is that payment of dower can admit delay, but the payment of maintenance cannot be delayed. He also says that if the father of a minor husband be well-off, it can be presumed that the husband will be able to pay the dower.[67] It is stated in *al-Fatāwā al-'Ālamgiriyah* that if a person gives his minor sister in marriage to a minor husband who is able to maintain the wife but cannot pay her dower and his father who is well-off agrees to the marriage, the marriage shall be considered to be valid because people usually pay the dower of their sons' wives, but do not maintain them.[68] Abū Ḥanīfah and Muḥammad do not agree with the view expressed by Abū Yūsuf and hold otherwise.[69]

Dower

By dower is meant the prompt dower of the wife because there is no present liability for the payment of her deferred dower.

66. Al-Marghīnānī, *op. cit.*, Vol. II, p. 301.
67. *Ibid.*
68. *Al-Fatāwā al-Hindiyah*, *op. cit.*, Vol, II, p. 13.
69. Al-Marghīnānī, *op. cit*,, Vol. II, p. 301.

There is a difference of opinion as to whether the ability to pay the wife's dower is a condition of equality in marriage. Thus, Abū Yūsuf does not hold it to be an essential condition on the ground that payment of dower can admit delay, but the payment of maintenance cannot be delayed.[70] But the generally accepted view is that the husband's ability to pay the wife's dower is an essential condition of equality in marriage.[71]

As already stated, the dower of a girl should not be less than the customary dower prevalent in her family. If the dower fixed is less than the customary dower then the man cannot be considered to be the equal of the girl. This matter may be considered from several aspects, namely,

(*a*) Inadequate dower agreed upon by the wife,

(*b*) Inadequate dower accepted by the wife's guardian,

(*c*) Marriage contracted for inadequate dower by an agent.

(*a*) *Inadequate Dower agreed upon by the Wife*

When a girl contracts a marriage for an inadequate dower then, according to the Ḥanafis, her guardian for marriage or a near collateral can get the marriage dissolved on that ground.[72] This is based on the reason that the interests of the other girls in the family shall be adversely affected by this act of the wife. The fixation of lower dower also affects the prestige of the girl's family.

Abū Yūsuf and Muḥammad hold that the father or guardian or near relations are not possessed of any such authority.[73] They base their opinion on the ground that the dower belongs to the wife and, therefore, she can lawfully relinquish a portion of it by accepting lower amount of dower. They further contend that it is open to a woman after the amount of her dower has been specified to relinquish a portion of it and that there is no difference in the cases

70. Al-Marghīnānī, *op. cit.*, Vol. II, p. 301.

71. *Ibid.*, p. 300 ; *al-Fatāwā Al-Hindiyah op. cit.*, Vol. II, p. 13.

72. Al-Marghīnānī, *op. cit.*, Vol. II. p. 301 ; Ibn 'Ābidīn, *op. cit*, Vol. II, p. 305.

73. Al-Marghīnānī, *op. cit.*, Vol. II, p. 301.

when dower is relinquished before or after the marriage. Abū Ḥanīfah argues that some importance and respectability are attached to a large amount of dower while its smallness may be disgraceful to the wife's family, hence the right of the guardian to object to a small amount of dower.[74] He further says that relinquishment of dower after the marriage does not bring any disgrace to the family as is occasioned by the fixation of a small amount of dower.[75]

Disproportionate Dower fixed by the Father

If a father or paternal grandfather should contract his minor child in marriage for an inadequate or too high a dower the marriage is binding on the minor, but if contracted by any other person, it is liable to be set aside on the suit of the minor.[76] But if the dower is very low or high, them according to Abū Yusūf and Muḥammad, the marriage is not legal and can be set aside. They contend that the binding nature of a marriage by the father or grandfather is based on the presumption that they are acting in the best interest of the child, but where their disregard for the interest of the minor is apparent, this presumption cannot arise, and so the contract of marriage loses its binding force.[77] Abū Ḥanīfah does not agree with this view. He says that the nearness of the relationship establishes the father's tenderness (affection) for the minor and the amount of dower is not the only consideration, but there are many other considerations of still greater importance than the dower, hence the marriage contracted by them shall be binding on the minor.[78] But this rule applies when the father or grandfather's act is *bona fide*; if it is *mala fide* or if he fixes the dower while he is drunk, the marriage would not be binding on the girl.[79]

74. Al-Marghīnānī, *op. cit.*, Vol. II. p, 301.
75. *Ibid.*
76. *Ibid.*
77. *Ibid.*, pp. 301-302.
78. *Ibid.*, p. 302.
79. *Al-Fatāwā al-Hindiyah, op. cit.*, p. 15.

(b) Inadequate dower accepted by Guardian

If the marriage has been contracted for a minor, whether a boy or a girl, and the amount of the dower is lower in the case of a girl or higher in the case of a boy than the customary dower prevalent in the girl's family, the marriage shall be considered unequal. The minor can apply in such a case, on attaining puberty, for the dissolution of the marriage on this ground. This rule seems to be based on the fact that it is against the interests of the boy or girl to agree to a higher or lower dower than the customary dower.

If the marriage for unequal dower is contracted by some one other than the father or the grandfather of the girl then it is an agreed view that the girl possesses a right to get it dissolved.

(c) Marriage by Agent for Inadequate Dower

If a person appoints an agent to contract a marriage for him or her and the agent contracts the marriage for an unreasonably low or high dower then the marriage shall not be binding because the fixation of a reasonable, that is, customary dower was an implied condition of the marriage.[80] This rule, of course, is subject to the condition that the party concerned had not authorised the agent to fix the dower at that amount.

Increment by Husband

The right to the dissolution of a marriage shall be lost if the husband should increase the amount of the dower so as to bring it in conformity with the customary dower.

Subsequent Relinquishment of Dower by Wife

There is a difference of opinion about the relinquishment of the whole or a portion of her dower by the wife subsequent

80. *Al-Fatāwā al-Hindiyah, op. cit.*, Vol. II. p, 16; Ibn 'Ābidīn, *op. cit.*, Vol. II, p. 313.

to the time of the marriage, so that the inequality in the husband may be removed. The father or other guardian have no right to object in such a case.[81] The Ḥanafis justify this opinion on the ground that the dower belongs to the wife and she can deal with it in any way she likes. But it is stated in *al-Fatāwā-al-Ālamgiriyah* that if a woman marries a destitute person (beggar) and then she gives up her claim for her dower even then the man shall not be considered to be the equal of the wife because the ability to pay dower is determined at the time of the marriage.[82]

Maintenance

Different opinions have been expressed as to what constitutes maintenance for the purpose of equality in marriage. Thus, according to one version, maintenance means the ability to maintain the wife for one year, while according to another opinion, the ability relates to maintenance for one month only. According to a third opinion ability to maintain means in case of workers on daily wages the ability of daily maintenance.[83] The second opinion is generally accepted as correct.[84]

Shī'i Law

There are two views as to whether the ability to maintain the wife is a necessary condition of equality in marriage. It is stated in *Sharā'i al-Islām* that the better view is that it is not.[85] It is not clear as to why it should be so. It is obvious that if a husband cannot maintain his wife then she shall be put to great hardship and naturally the father too should not be allowed to give her in such a marriage. A change in the financial condition of the husband when he becomes unable to maintain the wife subsequent to the marriage cannot of course affect the marriage.[86]

81. Al-Marghīnānī, *op. cit.*, Vol. II, p. 300.
82. *Al-Fatāwā al-Hindiyah, op. cit.*, Vol. II, p. 13.
83. *Ibid.*
84. *Ibid.*
85. Ja'far b. al-Ḥasan, *op. cit.*, p. 183.
86. *Ibid.*

PIETY OR VIRTUE

Preliminary

Piety or virtue is another essential condition of equality. The word, "piety" does not merely seem to mean religious devotion but is used in a general sense and may more properly be translated as "character". The ends of marriage are not confined merely to sexual enjoyment and procreation of children, but also include love, friendship, happy companionship and the like. Thus, it is laid down in the Qur'ān, "One of His signs is that He created mates for you from yourselves that you may find quiet of mind in them and He put between you love and compassion."[87] There can be no companionship and the spouses cannot live happily together unless there is parity between them in respect of righteousness (character).

According to Abū Ḥanīfah and Abū Yusūf, equality in piety and virtue is an essential condition of equality.[88] A husband who is dissolute or profligate cannot be the equal of a virtuous girl.[89] He will bring disgrace to her and her family. This is the approved view and accepted by the Ḥanafis. Al-Sara<u>kh</u>si has, however, stated that Abū Ḥanīfah does not consider piety a condition of equality in marriage.[90] Muḥammad differs with this view and holds that positive equality in point of virtue is not to be considered a condition of equality.

Religious Sanction

It is laid down in the Qur'ān, "Vile women are for vile men and impure men for impure women."[91]

According to a Tradition, the Prophet (peace be on him) has said, "A woman is taken into marriage for four considerations, namely, wealth, respectability of her family, beauty and virtue. but you must choose virtue."[92]

87. Qur'ān, XXI: 21, Surah Al-Rūm.
88. Al-Mar<u>gh</u>inānī, *op. cit.*, Vol. II, p. 300; *al-Fatāwā al-Hindiyah, op. cit.*, Vol. II, p. 13.
89. *Al-Fatāwā al-Hindiyah op. cit.*, Vol. II. p. 13.
90. *Ibid.*
91. Qur'ān, XVIII : 4, Surah, Al-Nūr.
92. Walī al-Dīn al-<u>Kh</u>aṭib, *op. cit.*, Vol, II. p. 267.

General Discussion

A husband bearing a loose or depraved character is not considered an equal of a virtuous girl.[93] A depraved husband can, under the Qur'ānic injunction, be the equal only of a woman of loose character and *vice versa* and the marriage of a virtuous girl with a man of depraved character shall be considered unequal.[94] A *fasik* or an immodest person, a profligate is not the equal of a good woman.[95] There is a difference of opinion as to whether equality in intelligence is also an essential condition of equality.[96] But such equality is an important factor for a happy marriage and many marriages prove unsuccessful simply because the spouses have greatly different intellectual levels. A slight difference, however, does not constitute inequality. The difference must be appreciable. A husband guilty of base or degrading misconduct as when under the influence of drink he exposes himself naked, or loses all control over himself, or gets so much intoxicated in public as to indulge in such acts as to invite public ridicule and thus hurt the feelings and self-respect of the wife, cannot in such a case be the equal of a virtuous girl.[97] This view is accepted as correct. A virtuous girl married without her consent to a person of depraved character can, as a matter of right, refuse to submit to the marriage and can get it dissolved.[98]

If a fathergives his daughter in marriage to a man, taking him to be virtuous, but he turns out to be a drunkard, the marriage is considered by some jurists to be void.[99] In any case it can

93. Al-Marghīnānī, *op. cit.*, Vol. II, p. 300 ; *al-Fatāwā al-Hindiyah*, Vol. II. p. 13 ; Ibn 'Ābidīn, *op. cit.*, Vol. II, p. 328.

94. *Ibid.*

95. *Ibid.*

96. *Ibid.*

97. Al-Marghīnānī, *op. cit.*, Vol. II, p. 300 ; Ibn 'Ābidīn, *op. cit.*, Vol II, p. 328.

98. Ibn Rushd, *Bidāyāt al-Mujtahid*, Cairo, n.d., Vol. II, p. 13.

99. *Al-Fatāwā al-Hindiyah*, *op. cit.*, Vol. II, p. 13 ; Ibn 'Ābidīn, *op. cit.* Vol. II, p. 329.

be annulled. All jurists agree on this point. But there is a difference of opinion between Abū Ḥanīfah and his two disciples with regard to a marriage by a father of his daughter to a man whom he knows to be unequal. According to Abū Ḥanīfah, the marriage is lawful because the father is presumed to have acted in the best interest of his daughter.[100] Muḥammad does not agree with this view. He explains the position that positive equality in point of virtue is not to be taken into consideration as that is connected with religion to which rules regarding merely worldly matters do not apply excepting in matters of gross public misconduct, as where the party by any base or degrading misconduct such as a man exposing himself naked and intoxicated in the public street etc. may have incurred derision and contempt.[101]

Miscellaneous Cases

Besides the conditions discussed above, there are some other matters in which equality is stressed. According to some jurists the husband should be free of certain specified diseases.[102] It involves the idea that the husband of a healthy girl should also be healthy because disease is itself a defect. Thus, it is stated by Shāfi'ī that a husband suffering from some loathsome disease such as leprosy, leucoderma etc., cannot be the equal of a girl free of such diseases.[103] According to a report, Mālik also made it a condition of equality that the husband should be free of certain specified defects, namely leprosy, leucoderma and insanity.[104] Ibn Qayyim has stated in *Zād al-Ma'ād* that any such defect in one of the spouses as leads one to feel disgusted with the other is a ground for dissolution of a marriage as the end of marriage, namely, friendship and happy companionship is lost on that account.[105]

100. *Al-Fatāwā al-Hindiyah, op. cit.*, Vol. II, p. 13 ; Ibn 'Ābidīn, *op. cit.*, Vol. II, p. 329.
101. Al-Marghīnānī, *op. cit.*, Vol, II. p. 302.
102. Ibn Rushd, *op. cit.*, Vol. II, p. 42.
103. Ibn Qudāmah, *op. cit.*, Vol. VI, 482.
104. See Chapter on Defects in Spouses.
105. Ibn Qayyim, *Zād al-Ma'ād*, Cairo, 1950 A.D., Vol. IV, p. 31.

Age

Another factor to be taken into consideration for equality of a marriage is the age of the spouses. There is no reference to this condition of equality in Muslim law. The reason appears to be that little importance was attached to parity in ages of the spouses by the Arabs. A man would marry a girl far below him in age or a woman much advanced in age than himself. It is not possible to lay down the exact or even an approximate difference in the ages of the spouses which will render the marriage unequal. But it is obvious that there must be parity to some extent in the ages of the spouses for a happy marriage. A difference of fifteen years in the ages of the spouses was not considered to be so glaring as to lead to the *prima facie* inference that the match was unconscionable.[106] It is, however, explained that equality in this matter is desirable and has been approved of but the *Qāḍī* cannot dissolve a marriage merely on this basis. But such matters as age, health, beauty etc., should be taken into consideration and coupled with other matters may induce a *Qāḍī* to dissolve the marriage.

Beauty

Beauty is also to some extent a condition of equality. In any case such equality has been approved of.[107] It is stated in *al-Fatāwā al-'Ālamgīrīyah* that guardians should observe equality in beauty also.[108] The translator of the *al-Fatāwā al-'Ālamgīrīyah* has stated that equality in the symmetry of the bodies of the spouses must be kept in view.[109] S͟hāh Walī Allah is of the opinion that equality must be considered in the matter of beauty also and that a beautiful girl should not be given in marriage to a man who is ugly or ungainly for, "They (women) too like the same thing as you do, namely, beauty."

106. Shahzada Begum Vs. Abdul Hamid, 1950, P.L.D. Lah : 504.
107. *Al-Fatāwā al-Hindiyah, op. cit.*, Vol. II, p. 13,
108. *Ibid.*, p. 13.
109. Sayed Amir Alī, *Al-Fatāwā al-Alamgīrīyah*, Urdu translation of *Al-Fatāwā al-Hindiyah*, Vol. II, p. 171, Lucknow, 1899 A.D.

Al-Fatāwā al-'Alamgīrīyh has stated on the basis of Tatar Khaniyah that the guardian of a girl should see to equality in the matter of beauty also.[110]

Whether a Court will dissolve a marriage on this ground is doubtful as there is no clear authority on the subject. Muslim jurists too have not laid much emphasis on this point. But a girl may get a separation in such a case by the exercise of her option of puberty. The translator of *al-Fatāwā al-Hindiya* from Arabic into Urdu has expressed the view that considering the low morality of our times, regard should be paid to equality in such matters as the symmetry or general build-up of the bodies of the spouses.[111]

Intelligence.—There is a difference of opinion whether equality in intelligence is an essential condition. *Al-Fatāwā al-'Ālamgīrīyah* here states that some jurists have held that equality in intelligence is not an essential condition for validity of marriage but has not expressed any opinion one way or the other.[112] This may be due to the fact that it may sometimes be difficult to gauge the intelligence of the spouses. If the difference in intellectual capacity be glaring then there should be no objection to dissolve the marriage on the ground because happy companionship and congenial society may not be possible in such a case. There can be no positive criteria to measure intelligence, and it must be judged from such factors as education and general accomplishments.

Ḥanafī Law: Marriage by Father or Grandfather.—As a general rule a minor cannot object to a marriage if it has been contracted by his or her father or paternal grandfather unless they are notorious for their evil ways. This rule is based on the presumption that a father or a grandfather will, on account of his natural affection for the child, find the most suitable match for him or her.[113]

110. Sayed Amir Ali, *Al-Fatāwā al-Alamgiriyah*, Vol. II, p. 41.
111. *Ibid.*, p. 171.
112. *Al-Fatāwā al-Ḥindiyah, op. cit.*, Vol. II, p. 13.
113. *Ibid.*, p. 10.

This provision is, however, subject to the rule that the father or the grandfather should not have acted against the interests of the minor. Where the marriage is clearly prejudicial to the interests of a minor then the presumption does not arise and so the exception to the general rule shall not apply. Thus where a father contracts a marriage for his son for a dower greatly in excess to the customary dower of the girl or marries his daughter for a grossly inadequate dower then the binding character of the marriage is lost.[114] If it is the girl who contracts such a marriage, it shall be liable to be dissolved on the complaint to the *Qāḍī* by the father or other relation.[115] Similarly if it is proved that the father has acted with gross negligence and to the detriment of the minor's interest, the minor has got a right for the dissolution of the marriage. When the father is a noted profligate or a man of depraved character or was drunk at the time of the marriage, the girl has a right to get the marriage annulled.[116] If the marriage has been contracted by a guardian other than the father or grandfather, the girl can exercise her right for its dissolution according to the unanimous opinion of the jurists provided she has not submitted to it.[117]

Neglect to make Enquiry

If a woman marries a person without caring to ascertain his equality, and it is found subsequently that the husband is not the equal of the wife, then it shall not be open to the wife contracting the marriage to object to it, but her guardian can object to it.[118] This view can be based on the ground that the wife is herself to be blamed for the negligence and so the marriage is binding on her. If, however, equality in marriage had been made a condition and the husband had

114. *Al-Fatāwā al-Hindiyah, op. cit.*, Vol. II, p. 15. Al-Marghināni, *op. cit.*, Vol. II, p. 300.
115. Ibn 'Ābidīn, *op. cit.*, Vol. II, p. 312.
116. *Al-Fatāwā al-Hindiyah, op. cit.*, Vol. II, p. 10.
117. *Ibid.*
118. Ibn 'Ābidīn, *op; cit.*, Vol. II, p. 326.

deceived them in the matter, the guardian or the girl, as the case may be, shall have a right to object to the marriage and to get it dissolved. If a person marries his minor daughter to a man without knowing that he is a drunkard but the husband proves to be such while the other members of his family are well-behaved and pious people, the girl shall be entitled on attaining majority to the dissolution of the marriage.[119]

Fraud

If a person deceives the prospective wife about his status and it transpires subsequently that he is not her equal, the marriage shall be liable to be dissolved on the objection of the wife or her relations.[120] Similarly, if equality in marriage has been made a condition of the marriage and the prospective husband deceives in the matter of equality, the marriage shall be liable to be dissolved.[121] But if it is the woman who deceives the prospective husband in the matter of equality, the marriage shall not be liable to be dissolved, because the inferiority of the wife is not derogatory to the husband or his family. Besides, the husband can exercise his power of divorce if he so likes.[122]

Conditions set up by Husband.—If the husband makes it a condition of the proposed marriage that the wife should be free of certain defects or fulfil certain conditions such as that she should not be blind or lame or ugly, should be a virgin, there is a difference of opinion amongst the Muslim jurists about the effect of such conditions as discussed below.

Ḥanafī Law.—Under the Ḥanafī law the conditions shall not be binding on the wife and the marriage shall not be dissolved on a breach of the condition. The marriage shall be considered valid while the condition shall be considered invalid.[123]

119. Ibn 'Ābidīn, *op. cit.*, Vol. II, p. 326.
120. *Ibid.*, *al-Fatāwā al-Hindiyah*, *op. cit.*, Vol. II, p. 10.
121. *Ibid.*, *ibid.*
122. *Ibid.*, *ibid.*
123. *Ibid.*, *ibid.*

Mālikī Law.—Mālik holds the conditions to be valid and binding on the parties. The husband shall have a right to the dissolution of the marriage if the condition is not fulfilled.[124]

Shāfi'ī and Ḥanbalī Laws.—Shāfi'ī and Aḥmad b. Ḥanbal expressed different views in the matter at different times. According to one report, the marriage cannot be dissolved on this ground. According to the other report, the marriage shall be liable to be cancelled on the complaint of the party deceived. The marriage shall, however, be liable to be dissolved if the condition relates to the other party being a Muslim or a free person and it is found afterwards that the other party does not meet this condition.[125]

Unequal Marriage by Agent,—If a person appoints an agent for getting him or her married and the agent contracts an unequal marriage, it shall not be binding and can be dissolved on the basis of inequality.[126] The rule shall apply irrespective of the fact as to whether the party concerned has asked the agent to contract him or her in marriage with a specified person but the agent marries him or her to another person or if no person is specified but the agent contracts the marriage with an unequal person.[127]

Material Time for Determination of Inequality.—The material time for determination of inequality is at the time of marriage. A change in the husband's condition subsequent to the marriage does not make any difference and does not affect the marriage.[128] Thus, if a man was possessed of a good character at the time of the marriage, but subsequently becomes depraved in character, this change in his condition shall not affect the marriage. Similarly, if he was unequal to the wife in social status at the time of the marriage then his subsequent rise in life shall not deprive the wife or her

124. Saḥnūn, *al-Mudawwanat al-Kubrā*, Cairo, 1323 A.H., Vol. IV, p. 48.
125. Ibn Qudāmah, *op. cit*, Vol. VI, p. 526.
126. Ibn 'Ābidīn, *op. cit.*, Vol. II, p. 333.
127. *Ibid.*
128. *Al-Fatāwā al-Hindiyah, op. cit.*, Vol. II, p. 13 ; Ibn 'Ābidīn, *op. cit.*, Vol. II, p. 331.

guardian of the right to the dissolution of the marriage. In the same way if the husband was financially equal to the wife's family at the time of the marriage, but subsequently becomes poor on account of losses then this change shall not affect the marriage.

Who can Object

If the marriage has been contracted by the guardian of a minor girl, it is only she who can object to the unequal marriage. On the other hand, when an unequal marriage has been contracted by an adult woman, it shall be only such paternal relation of the girl who can object to it as would be her guardian for marriage if she were a minor or was of unsound mind.[129] The relations on the mother's side have no such right because a child is affiliated to the father's family and so it will be only that family which will be affected by an unequal marriage. If there is no such guardian or there is a guardian, but he does not object to the marriage, the marriage shall subsist.

Acquiescence

It is now generally accepted that if a marriage is contracted by a guardian with the consent of the girl without caring to know the position of the husband, the marriage cannot be cancelled.[130] But if the husband has deceived them or one of them about his status the marriage is liable to be set aside.[131] If it is the woman who has deceived the husband about herself, the marriage cannot be dissolved.[132]

Consent of Guardian or the Wife

If the guardian or near relation, as the case may be, gives his consent to an unequal marriage, the objection to the marriage shall be waived and it shall be considered to be a

129. *Al-Fatāwā al-Hindiyah, op. cit.*, Vol. II, p. 13,
130. *Ibid.*, p. I4.
131. *Ibid*,
132. *Ibid.*

perfectly valid marriage.[133] If there are several such persons who are equally related to her, the consent to the marriage by one of them shall cancel the right of objection of the others. It shall be considered to be a consent by all who are equal to him or below him.[134] This is based on the analogy that "*amān*" (guarantee for safety) by one Muslim to an enemy is deemed to be binding on all Muslims.[135] But if they are not equally related to her then it shall be the nearest relation only whose assent or dissent shall prevail.[136] A person who is a nearer relation to the wife than the person who has given his consent is not bound by such consent and can still object to the marriage.[137]

Consent Subsequent to an Unequal Marriage

As has been discussed before, if an adult girl contracts an unequal marriage, the Ḥanafi jurists hold different views in the matter. According to one opinion the marriage shall be void while according to the other opinion the marriage shall be voidable. In the former case the guardian's consent expressed subsequent to the marriage can be of no avail and cannot make the marriage valid as it was void *ab initio*. In the latter case the subsequent consent of the guardian can fully validate the marriage which was only voidable till then.

Time for Objection.—There is no limit of time fixed for raising an objection to an unequal marriage. The objection can be raised at any time even after the lapse of a long period and the right to object will not be lost by mere delay, however long it may be. The guardian's right shall be lost only if he does not object till such time that a child is born to the woman or she becomes pregnant. In such a case the dissolution of the marriage shall adversely affect the interests of the child and

133. Ibn Ābidīn, *ov, cit.*. Vol. II, p. 305; *al-Fatāwā al-Hindiyah, op. cit.*, Vol. II, p. 16.
134. *Ibid., Al-Fatāwā al-Hindiyah, op. cit.*, Vol. II, p. 14.
135. Ibn 'Ābidīn, *op. cit.*, Vol. II, p. 305.
136. *Ibid., al-Fatāwā al-Hindiyah, op. cit.*, Vol. II, p. 14.
137. *Ibid.*

so it is not allowed. But till such a contingency occurs, the mere silence of the guardian shall not be considered to amount to his consent.[138]

Qāḍī's Order, if Necessary

A marriage is not dissolved automatically on the discovery of inequality and the wife and her relations are not entitled to dissolve the marriage by themselves. It is only when an order for annulment of the marriage is passed by a *Qāḍī* that the marriage is annulled. The order of a *Qāḍī* is a condition precedent to the annulment of such marriage.[39] Thus it is stated in *al-Hidāyah* that the *Qāḍī's* decree is a necessary condition for the dissolution of a marriage on the basis of inequality. *Al-Fatāwā al-'Ālamgīrīyah* also supports this view.[140] The compilers have justified the necessity of the *Qāḍī's* order on two grounds, namely: (*a*) In the exercise of the option (to get the marriage dissolved) there is an accusation against another, namely, the guardian or the wife for having contracted a disadvantageous marriage, and it is, therefore, necessary to refer the matter to the *Qāḍī* so that the charge be properly adjudged. (*b*) The dissolution of the marriage tends to affect other rights and this also makes it necessary that the matter be investigated and decided by the *Qāḍī*.

Al-Durr al-Mukhtār also makes the *Qāḍī's* order a condition precedent to the dissolution of marriage on the basis of inequality when the husband is a minor. A marriage shall subsist till it is dissolved by an order of the *Qāḍī* so that if one of the spouses dies before the passing of the decree even though during the pendency of the suit, the survivor shall inherit from the deceased.[141]

Effect of Qāḍī's order.—The annulment of a marriage by the *Qāḍī* (Court) on the basis of inequality shall give rise to

138. *Ibid., al-Fatāwā al-Hindiyah, op. cit.*, Vol. II. p. 14.
139. *Ibid.*
140. Al-Marghinānī, *op. cit.*, Vol. II, p. 300 (annotations); *al-Fatāwā al-Hindiyah, op. cit.*, Vol. II, pp. 13-14.
141. Ibn 'Ābidīn, *op. cit.*, Vol. II, pp. 314-15.

the following consequences :

(1) Separation

(2) Dower

(3) *'Iddah.*

1. The marriage shall be terminated and the separation shall amount to an annulment of the marriage and not to a *Ṭālāq* (divorce).

2. If the marriage is dissolved after consummation, the wife shall be entitled to her full dower.[142] The consummation under the Ḥanafī, Mālkī and Ḥanbali laws may be actual or implied as a valid retirement. But no dower is due if it is dissolved before consummation.[143]

3. The wife shall have to observe *'iddah* if the marriage has been consummated, but not otherwise.[144] The *'iddah* shall be for the same period as for divorce.

Nature of Unequal Marriage.—There is a difference of opinion not only amongst the Sunnī jurists but also amongst the Ḥanafī jurists themselves about the nature of an unequal marriage. Besides, there are contradictory reports about their opinions on the subject. The two aspects are therefore discussed below separately;

Unequal Marriage, Valid.—Different and contradictory views have been attributed to Abū Ḥanīfa, Abū Yūsuf and Muḥammad. According to one report an unequal marriage is not illegal, but is valid until it is set aside by the *Qāḍī*, Hence divorce, *ẓihār*, *'īlā* and inheritance are allowed before the marriage is dissolved. Thus. if a woman contracts an unequal marriage, it shall be valid, but the guardian shall have a right to get it dissolved by the *Qāḍī*.[145] According to another version such marriage is void.[146] *Al-Fatāwa al-Hindiyah* has preferred the second opinion. If the guardian contracts an

142. Ibn 'Ābidīn, *op. cit.*, Vol. II, pp. 314-315 ; *al-Fatāwā al-Hindiyah, op. cit.*, Vol. II. p. 14.

143. *Ibid.*

144. *Al-Fatāwā al-Hindiyah, op. cit.*, Vol. II. p. 14.

145. *Ibid.*, p. 13; Ibn, 'Ābidīn, *op. cit.*, Vol. II, pp. 304-5 314-16 and 326.

146. *Ibid.*

unequal marriage with the consent of the woman, but he did not know its inequality, the marriage is valid, and there is no option for the woman and the guardian to get it dissolved.[147] If it is a woman who contracts an unequal marriage without the consent of the guardian and she does not know whether the man she marries is her equal or not, as when he is a slave, she has no option for the dissolution of the marriage, but the guardian has the option to get the marriage dissolved.[148] This gaves rise to the issue whether to object to any unequal marriage is the right of the woman or of her guardian. Al-Ḥaṣkafī, the author of *al-Durr al-Mukhtār*, is of the view that it is the right of the guardian and not of the woman.[149] Ibn 'Ābidīn, the Commentator of *al-Durr al-Mukhtār*, has refuted this view and has expressed the view that it is the right of both. He argues that if a guardian other than father or grandfather contracts an unequal marriage of a minor girl, it is not valid, and the girl has the right to get it dissolved.[150]

Unequal Marriage, Invalid

Al-Ḥasan b. Ziyād (d. 204 A.H.) has reported from Abū Ḥanīfa that an unequal marriage is invalid. It is stated in *Al-Fatāwā al-Hindiyah* that the version stated by al-Ḥasan has been followed by many jurists and that this view is more suitable for being followed in these days. The *fatāwā* have also been given according to this opinion. Further, al-Sarakhsī is reported to have said that this view (as reported by al-Ḥasan) is preferable.[151] The author of *al-Radd al-Muḥtar* also holds the same view, namely, that such marriage is invalid.[152] The reasons for this view, as given in *al-Radd al-Muḥtār*, is that every guardian cannot plead the case in a proper way, nor is every judge just hence it is better to

147. Ibn 'Ābidīn, *op. cit.*, Vol. II, p. 326.
148. Al-Ḥaṣkafī, 'Alā al-Dīn, *al-Durr al-Mukhtar* (on the margin of *al-Radd al-Muḥtar*) Cairo, 1318. A.H., Vol. II, p. 326.
149. *Ibid.*
150. Ibn 'Ābidīn, *op. cit.*, Vol. II, p. 326.
151. *Al-Fatāwā al-Hindiyah*, *op. cit.*, Vol. II, p. 13.
152. Ibn 'Ābidīn, *op. cit.*, Vol., II, pp. 305, 316.

shut the door against such marriages.[153]

Shafi'ī Law.—According to one version Shāfi'ī has expressed the opinion that an unequal marriage is invalid. According to another report, it is valid, but if the guardian disagrees, he can get it dissolved.[154]

Ḥanbalī Law.—There are several reports about the opinion expressed by Aḥmad b. Ḥanbal. According to one report, if the guardian of a minor girl gives her in marriage to an unequal person, the marriage shall be void. According to another report, the marriage shall be valid. Another view of his is that if the guardian knew that the man was unequal to the girl and even then he contracts her in marriage to that person, the marriage shall be invalid. If he, however, did not know of the inequality, the marriage shall be valid but the girl shall have the right to get it annulled on attaining puberty.[155] His views are summed up to the effect that it is not permissible for the guardian to give the girl in marriage to a person who is unequal or suffers from some defect because Allah Almighty has made the guardian her representative for acting in her interest. Hence, it is not open to him to act to the detriment of the girl, for she being a minor, suffers from a disability and so the guardian cannot act in a way that is not in the interest of the girl just as he cannot appropriate her property in a way prejudicial to her. It is considered to be the better view that the girl shall have a right to the annulment of the marriage on attaining puberty.

It will be seen from the above discussion that the Muslim jurists became more strict about the observance of the rule relating to equality as time passed. This seems due to the fact that guardians and relations of girls came to be actuated by selfish motives and would sacrifice the interests of a girl to secure their own ends while the *Qāḍis* became less conscientious in the discharge of their duties as can be seen from the opinion of al-Sarakhsī.

153. Ibn 'Ābidīn, *op. cit.*, Vol. II, pp. 305-316.
154. Ibn Qudāmah, *op. cit.*, Vol. II. p. 481.
155. *Ibid*, pp. 488-89.

Chapter 15

DEFECTS IN SPOUSES

Preliminary

As stated before, two of the important objects of a marriage are happy companionship between the spouses and lawful satisfaction of passions. If one of the spouses suffers from such a defect that his or her condition becomes repulsive or revolting so that the other spouse cannot tolerate his or her company or the condition of one of them is such that the other cannot live with safety with him or her, the first object shall be lost and as a natural consequence the other object may also be lost. Again, the physical or mental condition of one of them may be such that he or she may be unable to perform the various obligations arising out of the contract of marriage when the other spouse may feel very unhappy on account of this aspect of his or her married life and in such cases it will be very hard to bind that spouse to pass his or her whole life in misery and unhappiness. It is considered desirable under Muslim law in such circumstances to dissolve the marriage and free the aggrieved spouse from the marriage-tie. This view is based on a verse of the Qur'ān in which it is stated that, "women have got rights similar to those of men against them in a just manner."[1] This verse very clearly shows that the spouses have reciprocal rights and obligations against each other. If one of them is unable to perform his or her part of the obligations cast on him or her by the express or implied conditions of the marriage contract, he or she shall be deemed to be at fault and the other spouse will become entitled to an adequate relief on this account. Moreover, the husbands have been enjoined by the Qur'ān, "To keep them (the wives) with kindness or let them

1. Qur'ān, Sūrah al-Baqarah, II ; 228.

go in humanity".[2] Hence it is not proper for a husband to keep his wife tied to the marriage when she desires a separation from him on account of a defect in him. When a husband or wife is suffering from a defect which makes a happy companionship between them impossible or renders the discharge of other obligations impracticable, it becomes necessary for the *Qāḍi* to give the aggrieved spouse relief in the matter by dissolving the marriage. Muslim law tries its best not to make marriage insecure but it refuses to sacrifice the happiness of a spouse to the rigidity of law. Once it is satisfied that a wife or a husband cannot live in peace and harmony with the other then it does not scruple to help the aggrieved spouse by dissolving the marriage because under such circumstances the marriage becomes a farce and its continuation undesirable.

There is a risk that the aggrieved spouse may be tempted towards immorality while Islam does not tolerate it. This conception of Muslim law is based on the fact that it does not consider a marriage to be absolutely indissoluble whatever the circumstances be but considers a marriage a civil contract on its practical side, that is, with regard to the rights and obligations arising out of the marriage and the happiness of spouses is its paramount consideration with the result that a marriage is dissolved once it is established that husband and wife cannot live in harmony on account of any defect in the other. Hence, the presence of leucoderma, elephantiasis etc.—harmless diseases in themselves—are considered sufficient grounds for dissolving a marriage if it is found that the husband or the wife would rather shun the company of the partner suffering from a loathsome disease and cannot live happily with the sufferer. Mālik and Aḥmad b. Ḥanbal have stated that a marriage can be dissolved if the husband or the wife emits a very foul smell from his or her body, nose or mouth.[3] Dr. Hussein Himmet has mentioned a case

2. Qur'ān, Sūrah al-Baqarah, II : 228.
3. Sharaf al-Din al-Maqdisi, *Al-Iqna'*, Cairo, n.d. Vol. III, pp. 199, 200, Ibn Qudāmah, *Al-Mughni*, Vol. VI, p. 651, Cairo, 1367 A.H.

in which a wife complained to the *Qāḍi* that she found the foul breath of the husband intolerable and wanted to be freed of the marriage-tie on that ground. The *Qāḍi* found her complaint to be correct and dissolved the marriage.[4]

Defects : Muslim jurists are unanimous on the basic idea to dissolve a marriage when one of the spouses is suffering from certain specified defects. Reference may be made in this connection to two very important rules of law. Muhammad has stated, "Let a marriage be dissolved when it is prejudicial to the interests of the wife".[5] Ibn Qayyim has also laid down the rule that any defect in the husband or the wife which may be revolting to the other spouse so that happiness, sympathy and affection, which are the aims of marriage, are not achieved on that account, it is a ground for dissolution of the marriage.[6] The jurists, however, differ on details. The first point of difference is whether a husband has the right to get his marriage dissolved through the *Qāḍi* on the basis of a defect in the wife. The second point on which the jurists differ relates to the defects on the basis of which a marriage can be dissolved.

As regards the first point, the Ḥanafis do not allow the husband the right to the dissolution of his marriage through the *Qaḍi* on the ground of a defect in the wife.[7] This may be due to the fact that the husband enjoys wide power of divorce and can exercise it when he is not happy with his wife. They deny this right to the husband also because they do not want to deprive the wife of any portion of her dower. They seem to consider that for better or for worse, she is your wife, and you must tolerate her condition. If you are

4. Dr. Hussein Himmet, *Venereal Diseases and Marriage in Islam*, cited by Th. H. Van De Velde : *Ideal Marriage*, p. 23, London, 1933 A.D.
5. Al-Kasani 'Ala' al-Din Abū Bakr, *Bada'i' al-Sana'i'*, Vol II, p. 327, Cairo, 1324 A.H.
6. Ibn Qayyim, *Zad al-Ma'd*, Vol. IV, p. 31, Cairo, 1369 A.H.
7. Al-Marghīnāni, *Al-Hidāyah*, Vol II, p. 402, Delhi, n.d., Al-Kasani, *op. cit.*, Vol. II, p. 32 : *Al-Fatāwā al-Hindiyah*, Vol. II, p. 134, Kanpur, 1349 A.H.

not prepared to do so, you can divorce her and pay her dower.

It may be noted here that the only difference in a divorce by the husband and dissolution of a marriage by the *Qāḍi* on the ground of a defect in the wife lies in the extent of the husband's liability for the payment of dower. If a husband divorces his wife before consummation, he shall have to pay to the wife halt of the dower. If the marriage has not been consummated and is dissolved by the *Qāḍi*, no dower is payable to the wife. If the marriage has been consummated, the whole dower shall be payable.[8]

It will be convenient for a discussion of these defects to divide them in the following classes :—

(*a*) Defects in the husband,

(*b*) Defects in the wife, and

(*c*) Defects common to both the spouses.

The chart on next page will give a clear idea of the defects belonging to these various classes. It may be noted here that the books referred to in this connection do not give all the defects mentioned at relevant places but differ to some extent in this respect. But taken as a whole they establish the various defects referred to--on the basis of which a marriage may be dissolved. Moreover, the Imams have mentioned different defects at various places in relation to some context but have not enumerated all of them at one place when laying down general rules for the dissolution of a marriage on account of them.

8. Ibn Qudāmah, *op. cit.*, Vol. VI, p. 655.

Chart showing Defects in spouses which permit dissolution of marriage.

View of	Defects in husband	Defects in wife	Defects common to both spouses
Abu Ḥanifah Abu Yūsuf	1. Impotency 2. Eunuchism 3. Castration 4. Shakkaz[9]	—Nil—	—Nil—
Muḥammad	1. Impotency 2. Shakkaz 3. Eunuchism 4. Castration 5. Insanity 6. Leprosy 7. Leucoderms[10]	—Nil—	—Nil—
Mālik	1. Impotency 2. Eunuchism 3. Castration 4. Shakkaz 5. Baldness[11]	1. Rataq 2. Qaran 3. Afal 4. Bakhr 5. Ifdah 6. Fataq[15]	1. Insanity 2. Leprosy 3. Leucoderma 4. Elephantiasis 5. Bakhr 6. Adhita 7. Scrufula 8. Baldness.[20]
Shāfi'ī	1. Impotency 2. Eunuchism 3. Castration[12]	1. Rataq 2. Qaran 3. Afal 4. Bakhr.[16]	1. Insanity 2. Leprosy 3. Lucoderma 4. Elephantiasis[21]
Aḥmad b. Ḥanbal.	1. Impotency 2. Eunuchism 3. Castration 4. Shakkaz[13]	1. Rataq 2. Qaran 3. Afal 4. Ifdah or Iftadah 5. Fataq 6. Istahadah[17]	1. Insanity 2. Leprosy 3. Leucoderma 4. Basur 5. Nasur 6. Mashola or incontinence of urine. 7. Incontinence of stool 8. Bakhr 9. Adhita.[22]
Shi'i law	1. Impotency 2. Eunuchism 3. Castration[14]	1. Rataq 2. Qaran 3. Afal 4. Leucoderma 5. Ifdah 6. Fataq 7. Blindness 8. Lameness.[18] 9. Being crippled[19]	1. Insanity 2. Leprosy 3. Leucoderma[23]

9. *Al-Fatāwā al-Hindiyah, op. cit.*, Vol. II, p. 134; Ibn 'Ābidīn, *Radd al-Muḥtar*, Vol. II, p. 613, Cairo. 1018 A.H.

10. Al-Kasani, *op. cit.*, Vol. II, p. 327; Shaykzadah, *Majma'l Unhar*, Vol. I, p. 471, Constantinople, 1327 A.H., Ibn 'Ābidīn, *op. cit.*, Vol. II, p. 613.

11. Ibn Rushd, *Bidayat al-Mujtāhid*, Vol. II, p. 42, Cairo, n.d.; Ibn [*Contd.*

The various defects are discussed below :

Defects in the Husband

There are certain defects which are confined to the husbands alone. There are three diseases which have been mentioned by all the jurists and which, when present in the husband, form a ground for dissolution of marriage on the complaint of the wife. Amongst the Ḥanafis, Muḥammad has added three more diseases, namely insanity, leprosy and leucoderma to the list, but the other Sunnī jurists include them among diseases common to the spouses. Mālik and Aḥmad b. Ḥanbal add "aitarad" (shakkaz) also to the list of the diseases restricted to men as has been shown in the chart. They are described below :

Inneen or Impotent Person: A husband shall be considered under Sunnī law to be inneen or impotent in respect of his wife if he is incapable of intimacy with her.[24]

Qudāmah, *op. cit.*, Vol. VI, p. 651 ; Sidi Khalil, *Al-Mukhtaṣar*, English translation, F. H. Ruxton, p. 104, London, 1916 A.D.

12. Ibn Qudāmah, *op. cit.*, Vol. VI, p 651 ; Mahi al-Din Abu Zakaria Yahya Ibn Sharifen Nawawi, *Minhaj et-Talibīn*, English translation, T. V. Howard, p. 300, London, 1914 A. D.
13. Al-Maqdisi, *op. cit.*, Vol. III, pp. 199, 200.
14. Jafar b. Hasan, *Sharai al-Islam*, p. 190 Tehran, 1377 A.H.
15. Ibn Rushd, *op. cit.*, Vol. II, p. 42 ; Ibn Qudāmah, *op. cit.*, Vol. VI, p. 651.
16. Ibn Qudāmah, *op. cit.*, Vol. VI, p. 651 ; Ibn Rushd, *op. cit.*, Vol. II, p, 42
17. Maqdisi, *op. cit.*, Vol. III, p. 250 ; Ibn Qudāmah, *op. cit.*, Vol. VI, p. 652.
18. Jafar b, Hasan, *op. cit.*, p. 190.
19. Abid Husain, *Jamai Abbasi*, p. 167, Delhi, 1305 A.H., Urdu translation of *Jamai Abbasi*, by Baha-ud-Din Amli.
20. Sahnun, *al-Mudawwanat al-Kubra*, Vol. IV, p. 62 Cairo, 1323 A.H.
21. Ibn Rushd, *op. cit.*, Vol. II, p. 42 ; Ibn Qudāmah, *op. cit.*, Vol. VI, p. 651.
22. Maqdisi, *op. cit.*, Vol. III. pp. 199, 200 ; Ibn Qudāmah, *op. cit.*, Vol. VI, p. 651.
23. Jafar b. Hasan, *op. cit.*, p. 190.
24. Ibn 'Ābidīn, *op. cit.*, Vol. II, p. 613 ; Syed Amir Ali, *Fatāwā Alamgiriyah*, Vol. II, p. 382, Lucknow, 1899 A.D., Urdu translation of *Fatāwā al-Hindiyah.*

Majbūb : A person is called majbūb if the male organ is missing. This condition may be from birth or may be caused by accident or surgery. If the male organ is not absolutely missing but is so short in length as to be unfit for penetrating the wife's body then too he shall be considered to be majbūb.[25]

Khussee : A person is called a khussee when he has no testicles or they are unserviceable either by birth or due to accident, disease or surgical operation. It also applies to a person whose testicles have been so crushed or mutilated as to render them dead and unserviceable.[26] He may not be considered a khussee if he has lost only one testicle because loss of one testicle does not result in impotency.[27]

The above defects have been fully discussed in the next section under the heading 'Impotency'.

Shakkāz or Aitarad : Another defect in the husband which according to the Ḥanafis, Mālik and Aḥmad b. Ḥanbal forms a ground for dissolution of marriage is being shakkāz. Shakkāz is a person who suffers from *ejaculatio ante portas*, that is, the outflow of semen at the man's approach to his wife so that erection collapses just before the commencement of the sexual act and even before penetration[28] so that he cannot be sexually intimate with his wife. A person suffering from the disease does achieve erection, but is sexually so weak that it subsides before penetration and is not regained then. The difference between an impotent person and one who is shakkāz seems to be that in the former, the husband may not achieve erection when approaching his wife but in the latter case he does achieve erection but gets discharged or the erection subsides before penetration. The disease may be

25. Syed Amir Ali, *Fatāwā Alamgiriyah*, *op. cit.*, Vol. IV, p. 382; Ibn 'Ābidīn, *op. cit.*, Vol. II, p. 613.
26. Al-Kasani, *op. cit.*, Vol. II, p. 317 ; Jafar b. Hasan, *op. cit.*, p. 190,
27. Abid Husain, *op. cit.*, p. 167.
28. Khurram Ali, *Ghayat al-Autar*, Urdu translation of *al-Durr al-Mukhtar* Vol. II, p. 269.

due to nervousness or may be an extreme form of premature ejaculation or some other cause.

It may be added here that according to the Ḥanafis, this defect is included in the definition of Impotency as given in *al-Durr al-Mukhtar*, *al-Radd al-Muḥtar* etc.

Defects in the Wife

The Ḥanafi jurists do not allow the dissolution of marriage by the *Qāḍi* when it is the wife who suffers from any disease rendering sexual intimacy impossible or in any case very difficult. Probably they have expressed this opinion on the basis that they do not want to deprive the wife of the dower due to her.

The defects in the case of wives are such (*a*) as do not allow intimacy on account of some obstruction in the vagina or (*b*) render the wife's condition disgusting. There are three diseases which relate to obstruction and are common in the Māliki, Shāfi'ī, Ḥanbali and the Shi'i laws. They are rataq, qaran and afal. There is a difference of opinion about the presence of defects of the second class as can be seen from the chart given above.

Rataq and Qaran: Rataq and qaran have heen described in some books on Muslim Fiqh as bones in the vagina. Some other books, however, consider them to be malformation of tissues. According to *Sharai al-Islam* a woman will be considered to be a rataqa or suffering from rataq when the vagina is so much constricted with flesh as to leave no passage for penetration.[29]

It is true that there can be no bone in the vagina and so the statement of some books on Muslim Fiqh about the presence of a bone in the vagina does not seem to be correct. But it is quite possible that the bony growth of the pelvis protruding towards the vagina might have led people to believe in the existence of a bone. The idea can also be based on the narrowing of pelvic bones due to *osteo malacia*. It is also possible that sometimes the pathological growth of tissues in the

29. Jafar b. Hasan, *op. cit.*, p. 190.

vagina, if very firm, might have led to the idea of there being a bone in the vagina. In such a case penetration in the wife's body will be very difficult if not impossible. When a wife suffers from such a defect, the husband can get his marriage dissolved through a Māliki, Shāfi'i or Ḥanbali *Qāḍi*. The difference between rataq and qaran is this, that is if the bone or rather the malformation of tissues is blunt then it is called rataq, but if it is pointed then it is called qaran (qaran literally means horn). Modern medical science does not accept the views that there can be any bone in the vagina but it seems that the European doctors in the medieval times did believe in the existence of these diseases as is borne out by the fact that they had used their own names for them. Thus rataq is called *vulva impervia coeunti* and qaran is termed *vulva anteriore parte enascens.*[30] But it is very likely that they might have borrowed the idea from the Muslims.

Afal: The third disease usually attributed to women is called afal. Muslim jurists consider it to be an abnormal fleshy growth or tumour at the mouth of the vagina or inside it.[31] Afal or *stresia vaginae* is the narrowing of the vagina. The growth must be to such extent as to leave no passage for penetration. It may be fibrosis that may cause lack of space in the passage. The fleshy growth or tumour can also happen at the mouth of the womb, but then it cannot form a ground for dissolution of marriage. The only result of it will be that no children may be born to the wife but barrenness, as discussed later, is no ground for dissolution of marriage. The disease may be due to injuries, operation, old age, infection or tumour of the vagina.

(*b*) Defects which are filthy :

Ifdah or Iftadah or Recto Vaginal Fistula: It is the rupture of the partition either wholly or partially between vagina and rectum.[32] It can be caused by injury sustained

30. Charles Hamilton, *The Hedaya*, p. 128, London, 1870 A.D.
31. Ibn Qudāmah, *op. cit.*, Vol. VI, p. 651;
32. *Ibid.*

at the time of delivery or as a result of accident or rape on a minor girl. Complete pereneal tear is a very painful and distressing condition for the sufferer who is unable to control the passing out of loose faeces. As the passage from rectum or anus becomes one with vagina, loose faeces may pass through vagina which, if not treated and cured, can be very offensive and the husband may not be able to tolerate the condition.

Fataq : It is the rupture of the partition between vagina and urethera.[33] It is generally due to injury sustained at the time of delivery. It may also be due to accident or rape on a minor girl. Fataq or vesico vaginal fistula if not repaired and cured will lead to continuous soiling of clothes and may lead to its being offensive to the husband and the rest of the family.

Both fataq and ifdah may be due amongst other causes to want of proper care and treatment at the time of delivery or by the husband being intimate with a minor wife. In such cases it is in reality the husband who is responsible for the defect and in justice he should not be allowed to get the marriage dissolved on the basis of such a ground. But if the defect dates back from the time before the marriage, it can be due to accident or rape and it is the duty of the wife or her guardian to disclose this condition of the woman to the prospective husband. The concealment of the defect amounts to an unjustifiable act and may constitute a ground for the dissolution of the marriage in certain cases.

Bakhr : Bakhr in the case of a wife means a very foul and stinking smell in the genital parts.[34] It is usually due to some bad infection causing foul smelling discharge or it may be caused by some disease like ulcer. It can also be due to *recto vaginal fistula* or a very unclean condition of the vulva. The stinking discharge is suggestive of the presence of ulcerative condition. Both Mālik and Aḥmad b. Ḥanbal allow the dissolution of marriage on the ground of bakhr, when it emanates from the genital parts. This view may

33. Ibn Qudāmah, *op. cit.*, Vol. VI, p. 651.
34. *Ibid.*

be based on the idea that in such a case it is not merely the dirty condition of the genital parts, but the fact that it may be due to the presence of ulcer or some other cause. The wife should, however, in justice be given a chance for the cure of her defect as is given to the husband in the case of impotency.

Istahadah : Istahadah or continuous vaginal bleeding is another defect in the wife which constitutes a ground for the dissolution of the marriage.[35] This may be due to the fact that the husband may find the condition of the wife to be filthy and may not feel happy with her.

Shī'i Law: Under the *Shī'i* law the following are the diseases which if present in the wife form a ground for the dissolution of marriage :

1. Rataq,
2. Qaran,
3. Afal,
4. Ifdah,
5. Leprosy,
6. Leucoderma,
7. Blindness and
8. Lameness.[36]

Of the above, the first four diseases have already been discussed before and the last two are discussed below. while insanity, leprosy and leucoderma are being discussed later.

Under *Shī'i* Law, rataq and afal will form a ground for dissolution of marriage only when they form an absolute obstruction to penetration and when the defect cannot be cured or when the wife refuses to be treated.

Blindness : The disease does not stand in the way of sexual enjoyment. But a blind wife cannot attend to the domestic comforts of the husband while her defect may prove a bar to happy companionship. It is obvious that if the husband is of a sympathetic nature, then he will not seek

35. Al-Maqdisi, *op. cit.*, Vol. III, p. 200,
36. Abid Husain, *op. cit.*, p. 169.

a separation from his wife. He will seek such a relief only when he cannot live with her. The *Shī'i* law, therefore, allows dissolution of marriage in such a case. Blindness can mean only absolute and permanent blindness.

Lameness: Lameness or the wife is another ground for dissolution of marriage. Lameness does not seem to mean slight limping but can mean only complete lameness.

Defects Common to the Spouses

There are certain defects which can be present in the husband as well as in the wife and so are common to both. They are being discussed below.

It may be stated at the outset that according to Mālik and Shāfi'ī every defect in the genital parts whether in the husband or the wife, which does not allow sexual intimacy forms a ground for the dissolution of marriage.[37]

Bakhr: Bakhr means a very foul smell from mouth (*Halitosis*), body or vagina.[38] The last belongs to the defects restricted to the wife alone and has been discussed in that connection. Bakhr forms a defect common to both the husband and the wife. If it is very strong so that the other spouse may find it difficult to tolerate it then it forms a ground for dissolution of marriage. Halitosis or foul breath may be due to uncleanliness, severe indigestion ulcer etc. while the others may be due to uncleanliness or some disease. The Imams differ about the various parts from which the bad smell may emanate. that is, whether it emanates from mouth, nose or body to be a ground for dissolution of marriage. But the basic idea underlying the rule is happiness of the parties. It is felt that when a spouse suffers from a very bad smell, the other spouse may not be able to toletate it so that his or her life shall become miserable. It is, therefore, considered necessary to dissolve the marriage under such circumstances. It may be added that there is a difference

37. Ibn Rushd, *op. cit.*, Vol. II, p. 31; Sahun, *op. cit.*, Vol. IV, pp. 62-64.
38. Ibn Rushḍ, *op. cit.*, Vol. II, p, 42; Ibn Qudāmah, *op. cit.*, Vol. VI, p. 651; al-Maqdisi, *op. cit.*, Vol. III,, p. 200.

of opinion amongst the Māliki jurists about Bakhr and the part of the body from which the foul smell should emanate in order to form a ground for dissolution of marriage. A similar difference prevails amongst the Ḥanbali jurists. Ibn Rushd has stated that the generally accepted view holds bakhr a sufficient ground for dissolution of marriage.[39] But bakhr can be a ground for dissolution of marriage only in extreme cases ; foul smell from the mouth is often due to indigestion or bad liver and this defect is not uncommon. Marriage is a serious thing and should not be dissolved unless for something really serious. But if it is established or found that the foul smell is so strong in one spouse that the other spouse cannot in reason be expected to tolerate it, the party not at fault should not be made to pass an unhappy life on that ground. Dr. Hussein Himmet has mentioned, as stated before, that in a case the husband was suffering from highly foul breath, and on the complaint of the wife the *Qāḍi* called the husband and dissolved the marriage.[40] It is obvious that the *Qāḍi* must have been satisfied with the genuineness of the wife's complaint.

Adhita : Adhita is a disease in which the sufferer involuntarily discharges stool at the time of cohabitation.[41] It is a very uncommon disease. It is obvious that such condition of one spouse will divest the act of coitus of all pleasure and will make the other disgusted with the whole thing. It may be due to nervousness or some disease.

Elephantiasis: In elephantiasis, there is an abnormal overgrowth of the skin. It may affect the neck, feet, legs, scrotum, male organ and other part of the body. If the male organ is affected with it, sexual intercourse becomes impossible. Abnormal growth at the scrotum may also make cohabitation very difficult if not impossible. If other parts are affected with it then the objection to the marriage can be the ungainly appearance of that spouse. But where the disease is very

39. Ibn Rushd, *op. cit*,, Vol, II, p. 42.
40. Dr. Hussein Himmet, *op. cit*,. p. 27.
41. Sahnun, *op. cit.*, Vol. IV, pp. 62-64.

prevalent in a certain locality, the persons living there get used to its sight and do not find anything objectionable in the sufferer.

Bāsūr : Basur means piles. It constitutes a ground for the dissolution of marriage under the Ḥanbali law.[42] It is not very clear why this disease has been made a ground for dissolution of marriage.

Nāsūr : Nasur or discharging sinus is considered a ground for dissolution of marriage under the Ḥanbali law.[43]

Māsholā: Mashola means incontinence of urine or the failure of voluntary control of urine.[44] Constant dribbling of urine in the wife causes intense irritation and soreness of the vulva and the surrounding skin. There are four types of the disease. One is true incontinence in which there is dribbling of urine all day and night. It may be due to *vesico vaginal fistula.* The other three types, namely, urgency incontinence, overflow incontinence and stress incontinence are not so severe and in their case escape of urine occurs at specific times or occasions and in between the sufferer is quite dry. Thus in stress incontinence urine may pass involuntarily when the sufferer lifts some heavy weight, coughs or makes a sudden movement. Mashola may be the result of disturbances of nervous mechanism. In men it may be due to stricture of urethra, presence of stone, enlargement of prostate, paralysis, etc. The only reason for considering it a ground for dissolution of marriage can be the filthy condition of the sufferer, which the other spouse may find disgusting. It is doubtful if a Court will apply the rule and dissolve a marriage of non-Ḥanbalis on the ground of this disease. But if it is of a severe type, the constant soiling of clothes will emanate a very foul smell which may be so offensive as to form a reasonable ground for the dissolution of marriage.

Janūn or Madness: Madness means derangement of mental

42. Al-Maqdisi, *op. cit.*, Vol. III, p. 200.
43. *Ibid.*
44. *Ibid.*

faculty and it consists of various types. The Muslim jurists have not differentiated between the different types of mental disorder and have used the word "Janūn" in an exhaustive sense to include a lunatic, an idiot, an imbecile, an insane person or a person of unsound mind. By the word "Majnūn", that is a person suffering from Janūn, they must have meant the persons suffering from all types of mental derangement. But in technical sense and medical language they do differ from each other. The definitions in English law of "mental defectives" are framed in a diminishing scale. They start with "idiots", go on to "imbeciles" whose defectiveness is stated not to amount to idiocy, and then refer to feeble-minded persons whose mental "defectiveness" does not amount to "imbecility" and moral imbeciles.[45] An idiot is a person mentally so defective from birth or from an early age as not to be able to guard himself against common physical danger. He is a fool by birth and has no manner of reason or understanding so that he cannot understand what is for his profit and what is for his disadvantage. The characteristic of idiocy is permanence with very little or no variation.[46] A lunatic is one who has had understanding but by reason of disease, grief, accident or shock has lost the use of his mental faculty. He is incapable of managing his affairs. But he may have lucid intervals when he behaves like a normal person and may manage his affairs with perfect propriety which never occurs in the case of an idiot. An insane person is one who is not of sound mind, suffers from a disordered condition of the mind so that he cannot regulate his actions and conduct. This condition may develop at any time due to disease accident, shock etc. The change from reason to insanity may be gradual. It has been observed in a case that the light of reason may fade gradually and imperceptibly so that people may not know or realise his condition until the darkness becomes obvious.[47] Imbeciles are persons who suffer from

45. Brown Vs. Brown, (1947) 2 All. E. R. 160.

46. *Ibid.*

47. White Vs. White, (1949) 1 All. E. R. 339.

mental derangement but not to such an extent as in the case of idiots. An imbecile person can speak to some extent. A person will be deemed to be of unsound mind whose reason is affected by mental disease. A person was considered to be of unsound mind when the defect of his mind was manifested by total absence of will-power, though he was perfectly sensible in all intellectual matters, and could talk and discuss subjects sensibly.[48] But a person who is temperamental and easily excitable may not be of unsound mind. A person who is mentally abnormal can still be quite capable of preserving a sense of social propriety, and such a person was not considered to be a person of unsound mind.[49] Similarly, a person who was paralytic, had lost the power of speech and was unable to read and write or attend to business was not considered to be a person of unsound mind. But a person who was paralytic and unable through infirmity of mind to manage his affairs was deemed to be of unsound mind.[50]

A person of unsound mind may recover his lost mental power. Persons of unsound mind are incapable of forming any intention. A person who is of unsound mind in the full sense of the word cannot be said to be capable of desertion.[51] Next in the order come feeble-minded persons. They are such persons in whose case there exists a mental defectiveness which, though not amounting to imbecility, is yet so pronounced that they require care, supervision and control for their own protection or for the protection of others.

There are certain other diseases of the mind in which the sufferer is not devoid of complete mental power but suffers from a belief about something which is wrong and without any basis and is the result of his own faulty imagination. They consist of delusion, illusion, hallucination

48. Randall Vs. Randall (1938) 4 All. E. R. 696.
49. White Vs. White, (1949) 2 All. E. R. 338.
50. In re Dewhurst Trust, (1886) 3 Ch.; D. 416,
Re. Martin's Trust, (1807) 34 Ch, D. 618 C.A.
51. Williams Vs. Williams, (1938) 3 All. E. R. 825 ;
Brown Vs. Brown, (1947) 2 All. E. R. 160.

and obsession. In delusion, a person comes to believe in a certain state of affairs which is wrong. Thus, he may come to believe that his wife is unfaithful to him. He becomes so much engrossed with the idea that he continuously but secretly watches his wife's movements and looks with suspicion all her innocent acts and movements. A person suffering from hallucination thinks that he is perceiving something which in reality does not exist. This condition may affect any special sense of the sufferer or all of his senses. Thus he may imagine that he is hearing voices warning him of his wife's infidelity and adulterous connection with other people. A person suffering from illusion mistakes an object for some imaginary thing. Thus he may consider a rope to be a live snake. A person suffering from obsession is one who is constantly under a fixed and morbid, incorrect or aggravated idea which he cannot shake off.

The loss of understanding or reason may be due to natural causes as well as due to one's own conduct. Thus a person may lose his reasoning faculty as a result of excessive drinking.

Muslim Law: As stated before, Muslim jurists have not differentiated between these various classes of mental derangement. They have used the word "Janūn" in an exhaustive sense to include all the above-mentioned mental diseases. They only differentiate between a violent lunatic or insane person and one who is peaceful. There is a difference of opinion about the presence of janūn in one of the spouses. As shown in the chart given in the beginning of the chapter, Abu Ḥanifah and Abu Yūsuf do not consider janūn to be a ground for the dissolution of marriage. Muḥammad differs from them to this extent that he holds that a marriage can be dissolved when it is the husband who suffers from janūn but not when it is the wife who is insane.[52] He makes a distinction between a congenital lunatic and one who is affected by lunacy after the marriage. In the former case, the marriage

52. *Fatāwā Alamgiriyah*, *op. cit.*, Vol. II, p. 383; Mawlana Ashraf Ali Thanvi; *Al-Hilat al-Najiza*, pp. 91-95, Karachi, n.d.

can be dissolved immediately as in the case of a husband who is a majbūb *i.e.* without male organ but in the latter case, the husband shall be allowed one year's time for the cure of his defect, as in the case of an *inneen* (impotent husband).[53] If he is not cured within the specified time, the marriage shall be dissolved by the *Qāḍi*.[54]

Mālikī Law: If one of the parties is affected with insanity before the marriage, the other party is entitled to the dissolution of the marriage and even when the marriage has been consummated. This is, however, subject to the condition that the insane spouse should be violent or causes financial loss. If he or she is harmless, the other party has no cause for dissolution of the marriage. If insanity appears in the husband after the marriage, the wife shall be entitled to the dissolution of her marriage, but if it is the wife who becomes insane, the husband shall have no right to the dissolution of his marriage.[55]

Shāfi'ī Law: A spouse shall have a right to the dissolution of the marriage when the other is insane or has some similar serious disease whether before or after the marriage. Consummation of the marriage shall not affect the right in any way. The spouse may be suffering from permanent insanity or may be subject to fits. The occurrence of the fits should not be negligible as when it occurs only on one or two days in the year. This rule is subject to the condition that the party should be unaware of the condition of the other spouse who suffered from the disease before the marriage. Another condition is that if the wife has submitted to the marriage but her guardian has not agreed to the same then he can get the marriage dissolved provided the husband was afflicted with the disease before the marriage.[56]

53. *Fatāwā Alamgiriyah*, *op. cit.*, Vol. II, p. 383; Mawlana Ashraf Ali Thanvi : *Al-Hilat al-Najiza*, pp. 91-95, Karachi, n.d.
54. *Ibid.*
55. *Sidi Khalid*, English Translation, p. 104.
56. Ibn Rushd, *op. cit.*, Vol. II, pp. 41, 42 ;
Ibn Qudāmah, *op. cit.*, Vol. VI, p. 651.

Ḥanbali Law: Under the Ḥanbali law, a spouse is entitled to the dissolution of his or her marriage when the other suffers from insanity or from similar serious disease irrespective of the fact whether the disease was already present before the marriage or appeared subsequently and irrespective of the fact as to whether the marriage has or has not been consummated. The fact that the husband is a minor makes no difference. The only condition is that the girl, if major, should not have waived her right by expressing her consent to the marriage.[57]

Shī'i Law: Under the Shī'i law a marriage shall be liable to be dissolved when one of the spouses suffers from insanity. It is immaterial whether the spouse was afflicted with the disease before or after the marriage and whether before or after its consummation. It is not necessary that the disease should be permanent and even a temporary condition of one spouse shall entitle the other to the dissolution of the marriage.[58]

English Law: Under the English law insanity is an impediment to marriage because an insane person cannot give that rational consent which is necessary to the validity of a contract. The marriage was, therefore, considered to be void.[59] But the marriage could not be dissolved if one of the spouses became insane after the marriage.[60] Divorce on the basis of insanity was not granted in many cases and the Courts even refused to exercise their discretion. The law has, however, been changed by the Matrimonial Causes Act, 1950, and Section i (c) provides that a divorce can be granted on the ground that the respondent is incurably of unsound mind and has been continuously under care and treatment for a period of at least five years immediately preceding the presentation of the petition. It may be noted here that the Muslim law does not make it a condition that the disease should have subsisted for any specified time.

57. Ibn Qudāmah, *op. cit.*, Vol. VI, p. 653.
58. Jafar b. Ḥasan, *op. cit.*, p. 190.
59. Marriage of Lunatics Act, 1811; Turner Vs. Meyers, (1808) 1 Hag Con., 414.
60. Fisk Vs. Fisk, (1920) 36 T L R 248.

Law in U.S.A.: In many states, in U.S.A. a marriage with a lunatic is considered void on account of want of valid consent and a marriage can be dissolved on this basis provided the defect is permanent or incurable.[61] In the case of insanity visited on a person after the marriage the general attitude of some Courts was against the grant of a divorce.[62] Thus it was observed in the case of Baker Vs. Baker, "Insanity is no reason for dissolving a marriage....surely no principle of justice or morality will justify the severance of the marital ties for any such cause. The judgment and conscience revolt at the thought that such a terrible affliction should be deemed cause for separating the wife from the husband. Divorces are granted not because of misfortune but because of fault. It would be a barbarous code that would allow the wife to put aside the husband because stricken by such an awful calamity as the loss of reason. There is no merit in the argument that the statute requires that a divorce be granted in all cases where the husband fails to provide for the wife. The statute was not meant to apply to cases where the inability to make provision arises from mental or physical disease."[63] It is submitted that these laws ignore the fact that happy companionship, one of the objects of marriage, is not possible in such a case, while intimacy with an insane person can give no pleasure to the other spouse. We should also bear in mind that there may be a dark future for the children born of such a marriage which should not be tolerated in the interest of society. Haynes and Derek Walker-Smith have pertinently stated, "People who are actually certified as incurably insane by the responsible experts are hardly the people who appreciate the significance of the marriage-tie, or of its dissolution: indeed their clouded conscience has in all probability long lost any appreciation of the existence of marriage at all. It is undeniable

61. Keezer, *Marriage and Divorces*, Articles, 445, 451, Indianopolis, 1946 A.D.
62. Keezer, *op. cit.*, Art. 450.
63. Baker Vs. Baker, 82 Ind. 146, Bagley Vs. Jones, 242 Ky. 135.

that if a divorce is given for insanity, a risk is run that pain may be caused to some helpless person whose cup of bitterness is already full....But the risk is perhaps slight compared with the certainty of the unhappiness caused to the sane partner of such unions[64]

It has been stated by Keezer that the Courts did not allow divorce even when discretion was allowed to them in the matter. He has, however, pointed out that there is an increased tendency to allow divorce in such cases now.[65] It may be noted that the law regarding insanity has been charged in Indiana since the decision of Baker Vs. Baker. In State Vs. Brown (213 Indiana 118), the Supreme Court of Indiana observed, "We heartily concur with the sentiments of the foregoing (Baker Vs. Baker)....But since the statute now expressly declares that incurable insanity is a cause for divorce, the holding and reasoning of the foregoing decision is no longer controlling." Many states now provide for divorce on the basis of incurable mental disease subsisting for a specified period ranging from two years to six years.

Under Muslim law it is a general rule of law that the divorce pronounced by a lunatic or insane person is not at all lawful as he is utterly incompetent to act. He will, however, be bound by his pronouncement if he gets lucid intervals and divorces his wife during such a period. It musc be noted here that the rule does not apply to a person of weak intellect. After all, persons differ from one another in the degree of intelligence possessed by them and it cannot be said as a matter of law that a marriage entered into by a person of weak intellect who is neither a lunatic nor an idiot is void simply because he lacks in intelligence although he is able to understand the nature of the bonds of matrimony into which he is entering.[66] But a lunatic can be married to a

64. E. S. P. Haynes and Derek Walker Smith, *Divorce and Its Problems*, p. 124, London, 1953 A.D

65. Keezer, *op. cit.*, Art. 450.

66. Syed Amir Ali, *Fatāwā Alamgiriyah*, *op. cit.*, Vol. II, p. 144.

woman or man by her or his guardian. The question arises as to what will be the effect of insanity on the continuation of the marriage under the Ḥanafi law.

The rule of law laid down by Ibn Qayyim, namely, "If a marriage is prejudicial to the interests of the wife so that she cannot remain with her husband without risk to herself, let it be dissolved", may profitably be applied in such cases.

Delusion, hallucination or eccentricity: The fact that a husband or a wife suffers from delusion, hallucination or eccentricity etc. is not always a ground for divorce. A marriage is liable to be dissolved on the basis of insanity on two grounds, namely, the incapacity of a person to give his consent to the marriage when he is insane, and secondly, the fact that such a person cannot afford happy companionship to the other party. Both these elements are not necessarily present in the case of delusion, eccentricity, hallucination, etc. and so there is no necessity to dissolve a marriage in every case merely on the presence of one of these grounds. But if the delusion takes such a shape as to influence the attitude of one spouse towards the other to such an extent as to make it dangerous and impossible for the other spouse to live in peace with him or her as when one spouse is under the delusion that the other is unfaithful to him or her, constantly watching his or her every act, shadowing his or her every movement thereby making the other nervous and even broken in health, marriage may be dissolved on this account under certain circumstances.[67]

Shī'i Law : The Shī'i law is the same as the Sunni law in this respect.

English Law : The English law holds the same view as the Muslim law.

Law in U.S.A. : Mere eccentricity, delusion or hallucination has been held in the U.S.A. not to be a ground for annulment of marriage.[68]

67. Mst. Titli Vs. Alfred Robert Jones, A.I.R., 1934 All. 625.
68. Meakins Vs. Kinsella, (1912) 162 App. Div. 32; 131 N.Y.

Leprosy : Leprosy is an endemic, chronic, constitutional disease varying in manifestations as the skin, nerves or other tissues are affected. It is infectious as well as contagious and a person can become infected with it either by infection through the breath of the sufferer or by contact. The affected part of the body becomes senseless. If a husband or wife becomes affected by it, it becomes necessary for the other spouse to keep apart from the sufferer and so is deprived of the satisfaction of a married life. Under the Mālikī, Shafi'ī and Ḥanbali laws, as discussed before, the marriage of the sufferer can be dissolved at the instance of the other spouse.[69] Muḥammad holds the same view as held by these jurists when it is the husband who is the sufferer.[70] The opinions of Mālik, Shafi'i and Aḥmad b. Ḥanbal find full support in this matter from a Tradition of the Prophet (peace be on him) that he has said, "Flee from lepers as you would from a a lion".[71] In view of this Tradition, a marriage must be dissolved irrespective of the fact whether it is the husband or the wife who suffers from it. In any case, it is open to a Court in such a case to apply the Mālikī, Shāfi'ī or Ḥanbali law to a Hanafi on the basis of justice, equity and good conscience.

In India and Pakistan a provision has been made in the Dissolution of Muslim Marriages Act, 1939, for the dissolution of a marriage when the husband is suffering from leprosy.[72]

Māliki Law : Under the Māliki law, the wife shall have a right to the dissolution of her marriage irrespective of the fact as to whether the disease appears in the husband before or after the marriage and whether it is slight or has reached an advanced stage. If it is the wife who suffers from the

69. Ibn Rushd, *op. cit.*, Vol. II, p. 42 ; Ibn Qudāmah, *op. cit.*, Vol. VI, p. 351 ; al-Maqdisi, *op. cit.* Vol. III, p. 200.
70. Ibn 'Ābidīn, *op. cit.*. Vol. II, p. 613 ; Shaykzadah, *op. cit* , Vol. I, p. 471; *Shareh Vikaya*, Urdu Translation of *Nur al-Hedayah*, by Wahid az-Zaman, Vol. II, p. 79 ; Kanpur, 1293 A.H.
71. Marghinānī, *op. cit.*, p. 398 ; Ibn Rushd, *op. cit.*, Vol. II. p. 42.
72. Dissolution of Muslim Marriages Act, 1939, Section 2.

disease, the husband shall have a right to the dissolution of the marriage only if the disease dates back from the time before or at the time of the marriage. But he shall have no such right if the wife is affected with the disease after the marriage.[73]

Shāfi'i Law : Under the Shāfi'ī law, a marriage can be dissolved on the ground of leprosy only if it was present before the marriage. But according to his second view the marriage can be dissolved even when the defect appears subsequent to the marriage.[74]

Ḥanbali Law: The Ḥanbali law is the same as the Shāfi'ī's second view.[75]

Shī'i Law : Shī'i law allows the dissolution of a marriage when the wife suffers from leprosy. But the mere appearance of some signs of the disease such as infection of the face or the eyes is not deemed sufficient for this purpose.[76] According to some Shī'i jurists, a marriage can be dissolved irrespective as to who suffers from it.[77]

English Law: There is no clear provision or authority in English law as to whether the presence of leprosy will entitle the other spouse to the dissolution of marriage

Law in U.S.A. : In U.S.A. it is only in Hawaii that leprosy is considered a sufficient ground for divorce.[78]

Leucoderma Leucoderma is considered to be harmless but the appearance of the sufferer may become loathsome and repulsive. Mālik, Shāfi'ī and Aḥmad b. Ḥanbal allow the dissolution of a marriage when one of the spouses suffers from it.[79] This rule can be due to the fact that if a spouse cannot

73. Sidi Khalil, *al-Mukhtaṣar*, English Translation by Ruxton, p. 104, London, 1916 A.D.; Ibn Qudāmah, *op. cit.*, Vol, VI, p. 651; Sahnun, *op. cit.*, Vol. IV, p. 62, 116.
74. Ibn Qudāmah, *op. cit.*, Vol. VI, p. 651,
75. *Ibid.*, al-Maqdisi, *op. cit.*, Vol. III, p. 200.
76. Jafar b. Hasan, *op. cit.*, p. 190.
77. Abid Hussain, *op. cit.*, p. 167.
78. Revised Laws of Hawaii, 1935 A.D.
79. Ibn Qudāmah: *op. cit.*, Vol. VI, p. 651.

tolerate the company of the other spouse, namely, the sufferer, he or she shall be deprived of the pleasures of a happy companionship as well as sexual enjoyment and so should not be forced to live such a life. Deprived of marital happiness, the spouse may seek other ways for his or her relaxation which, in the eye of Muslim law being very undesirable, it is considered proper to dissolve the marriage in such a case. Abu Ḥanifah, and Abu Yūsuf do not allow the dissolution of marriage on this ground.

Muḥammad is of the opinion that a marriage can be dissolved at the instance of the wife when her husband is suffering from leucoderma.[80] But, as stated before, he does not allow the termination of a marriage when it is the wife who is suffering from the disease. But considering the present low standard of morality, it seems desirable to follow the view of the other Sunnī jurists and dissolve a marriage when either spouse suffers from the disease.

Mālıki Law: If one of the spouses is greatly affected with the disease which was already present before the marriage or had started then, the other spouse shall have a right to the dissolution of the marriage through a *Qāḍi*. If it is only slight then only the wife shall have a right to the dissolution of the marriage, but the husband shall not possess such a right in such a case. If the disease appears after the marriage in the wife then the husband shall have no right to the dissolution of the marriage even when the wife is greatly affected with it. He can of course exercise his power of divorce. If it is the husband who is affected with the disease after the marriage, the wife shall have a right to the dissolution of the marriage only if he is greatly affected with the disease.[81]

Shāfi'ī Law: Under Shāfi'ī law, each spouse has a right to the dissolution of the marriage when the other spouse suffers

80. *Shareh Viqayah*, Urdu Translation, *op. cit.*, Vol. II, p. 79; al-Kasani, *op. cit.*, Vol. II, p. 327.

81. Ibn Qudāmah, *op. cit.*, Vol. VI, p. 651; Sahnun, *op. cit.*, Vol, IV, pp. 62-64.

from leucoderma whether it dates back from the time before the marriage or appears subsequently and even after the consummation of the marriage.[82] This is subject to the condition that the aggrieved party did not know of the defect before the marriage.[83]

Ḥanbali Law: Ḥanbali law is the same as the Shāfi'ī law.[84]

Shī'i Law: The Shī'i law does not allow the dissolution of a marriage when it is the husband who suffers from leucoderma. But if it is the wife who suffers from the disease, the husband can get the marriage dissolved on this ground.[85] But according to *Jama'i Abbasi* a marriage can be dissolved even when it is the husband who suffers from it.[86]

English and American Laws: The English and American laws do not allow the dissolution of marriage on the ground that one spouse is suffering from leucoderma.

Venereal Diseases: As stated before, the diseases specified by the jurists do not form an exhaustive list of the same. On the analogy of the Tradition about leprosy we can add other diseases which can form a ground for the dissolution of marriage. The Muslim jurists have not mentioned venereal diseases amongst those that form a basis for the dissolution of a marriage. But such diseases have to be avoided at all costs, and a husband and a wife should not be allowed to communicate them to the other. The rules of law laid down by Muḥammad and Ibn Qayyim to the effect that if a marriage is prejudicial to the interests of the wife so that she cannot remain with her husband without risk to herself, let it be dissolved shall apply in such a case. Mālik and Shāfi'ī have laid down a general rule of law that every defect of genitals whether in the husband or the wife which stands in the way of sexual intimacy is a ground for the dissolution of

82. Ibn Qudāmah, *op. cit.*, Vol. VI, p. 651.
83. *Ibid.*
84. Al-Maqdisi, *op. cit.*, Vol. III, p. 200; Ibn Qudāmah, *op. cit.*, Vol. VI, p. 651.
85. Jafar b. Hasan, *op. cit.*, p. 190.
86. Abid Husain, *op. cit.*, Urdu Translation, *op. cit.*, p. 167.

the marriage.[87] We may take advantage of this rule in the case of venereal diseases and apply it to the Ḥanafis also.

There seems to be no reason as to why a Ḥanafi husband should not be allowed the dissolution of his marriage through Court when it is the wife who suffers from such a disease. The reason for the omission seems to be the fact that such diseases are found in men only and are not found in respectable women but are only confined to women of ill-repute.

Venereal diseases consist of the following diseases:—

(*a*) Syphilis
(*b*) Gonorrhoea
(*c*) Lympho Granuloma Venereum and
(*d*) Soft chancre.

Their presence in the husband is a constant danger to the wife. In India and Pakistan, a wife can get her marriage dissolved when her husband is suffering from a virulent venereal disease under the provisions of section 2 clause VI of the Dissolution of Muslim Marriage Act, 1939.

English Law: The English law allows the dissolution of marriage when the respondent was at the time of the marriage suffering from venereal disease in a communicable form.[88]

The jurists have given their own list of diseases and defects in the spouses on the basis of which a wife or husband can get the marriage dissolved. But the diseases and defects pointed out by them do not and cannot form an exhaustive list of the same; they serve merely as illustrative cases. This has been made clear by reference to Muḥammad. He too has given his own list of diseases in the presence of which a wife can seek the dissolution of her marriage, and they are as given below:—

(1) Impotency,
(2) Eunuchism,
(3) Castration,
(4) Insanity,

87. Ibn Rushd, *op. cit.*, Vol. II, p. 1.
88. Section 8 of Matrimonial Causes Act, 1950.

(5) Leprosy,
(6) Leucoderma.[89]

It is often considered that the *Imām* has restricted the wife's right to the dissolution of her marriage only in the case of the above-mentioned six diseases, but such is not the case. The *Imām* has merely mentioned the diseases to serve as illustrative cases. Al-Kāshānī has made the matter clear as regards the specification of diseases by Muḥammad by treating the specified diseases as illustrative cases as is clear from the use of the word "like" before the above-mentioned six specified diseases. The rule according to him will read as follows :—

"A wife can be granted a divorce when the husband suffers from disease *like* impotency, leprosy, leucoderma or insanity".[90] Besides, Ibn Qayyim has laid down a general and a very important rule of law. According to Ibn Qayyim al-Jawziyah it is necessary for the husband to be free of every defect which may cause injury to the wife.[91] A wife has, therefore, a right to the dissolution of her marriage when her husband suffers from impotency, insanity, leprosy, leucoderma etc., and a wife has an option when her husband suffers from such defect that she cannot live with him without injury to herself. According to another version, Ibn Qayyim has stated, "If a marriage is prejudicial to the interests of the wife so that she cannot live with the husband without an injury to herself let it be dissolved.[92] This is a very useful rule of law and allows the dissolution of a marriage to save the wife from communication by the husband of certain diseases and in certain other circumstances also. It is stated in *al-Durr al-Mukhtār* that when a husband suffers from the specified diseases other than incapacity, the dissolution of the marriage may be obtained through a Māliki, Shāfi'ī, or Ḥanbal *Qāḍīi*.[93] If a

89. Ibn 'Ābidīn, *op. cit.*, Vol. II.
90. Al-Kasani, *op. cit.*, Vol. II, p. 327.
91. Ibn Qayyim, *op. cit.*, Vol. IV, p. 31.
92. *Ibid.*
93. Ibn 'Ābidīn, *op. cit.*, Vol. II, p. 613.

husband is suffering from a contagious disease, a marriage can be dissolved according to the general rules of law laid down by Muḥammad and Ibn Qayyim. This view is also supported by the Tradition already quoted in connection with leprosy. This Tradition establishes very clearly that a person must take precautions against infection from a communicable disease. Shāfi'ī bases his opinion on this Tradition and says that leprosy, madness etc. are causes of natural and insuperable aversion as is confirmed by the Tradition. A wife, therefore, cannot be compelled to live with or to allow intimacy to a husband who is suffering from a certain incurable, contagious or infectious disease. She can seek the dissolution of her marriage when her husband is suffering from an incurable venereal disease, which may be communicated to her.

Ibn Qayyim is opposed to limit the defects to any particular number or specified diseases. He contends that we must bear in mind the basic idea underlying these defects which is to dissolve a marriage on the ground of a defect which stands in the way of a happy companionship, affection and sympathy or creates disgust in the mind of the unafflicted spouse. Thus one spouse may not feel happy to pass his or her whole life when the other happens to be blind, lame, crippled, etc.[94]

The Muslim jurists have laid down certain general rules for guidance in respect of cases relating to defects in the spouses. Some of the important rules are given below :

General Rules for Dissolution of Marriage

1. The husband or the wife should not have been aware of the defect in the other before the time of the marriage.

2. If the husband or the wife came to know of the defect only after the marriage, he or she should not have expressed his or her submission to the marriage—whether expressly or impliedly.

3. After coming to know of the defect in the other, the spouse should not have acquiesced in the marriage through

94. Ibn Qayyim, *op. cit.*, Vol. IV, p. 43.

intimacy, kissing and the like acts.

Ḥanafi Law: The Ḥanafīs do not allow the dissolution of a marriage on the basis of a defect in the wife.[95] There are, therefore, no defects common to the spouses under the Ḥanafī law.

Māliki Law: Under the Māliki law, a marriage can be dissolved on the ground of a defect found only in one of the spouses at the instance of the other if he or she was not aware of the defect at the time of the marriage or if so aware, has not waived his or her right and has not allowed intimacy in spite of the defect or, in other words, has not acquiesced in the marriage.[96] The wife shall have a right to the dissolution of the marriage when the defect appears in the husband after the marriage but before its consummation.[97] If the defect appears in the wife after the marriage or after consummation the husband shall not be entitled to its dissolution.[98]

Shāfi'ī Law: Under the Shafi'ī law the defect may be present at the time of the marriage or may appear subsequently. The wife or the husband is entitled to the dissolution of the marriage even when the other spouse was free of the defect at the time of the marriage and gets afflicted with it only subsequently but before consummation of the marriage. According to the second view of Shāfi'ī the husband has also a right to the dissolution of the marriage in such a case.[99]

Ḥanbalī Law: Under the Ḥanbali law, a marriage is liable to be dissolved on the ground that the other spouse suffers from one of the specified defects provided he or she did not know of it at the time of the marriage. The right shall be lost if the aggrieved party has acquiesced in the marriage, that is, has consented to it expressly or impliedly after becoming cognisant of

95. Syed Amir Ali, *Fatāwā Al-Alamgiriyah, op. cit.*, Vol. II, p. 402.
96. Ibn Qudāmah, *op. cit.*, Vol. VI, p. 654.
97. Sidi Khalil, English Translation, Ruxton. *op. cit.*, p. 104.
98. *Ibid.*
99. Muhiudin Abu Zakaria Yahya ibn Sharif en Nawawi: *Minhaj et Talibin*, English Translation by L. W. E. Van Den Berg and E. C. Howard, London, 1914 A.D., p. 99.

the defect, but in the absence of such acquiescence such right shall not be lost.[100] If the spouse does not object to the defect in the other, but the latter is afflicted with a new defect then the other party shall get a new right for the dissolution of the marriage.[101] A marriage can be dissolved when the defect appears in one of the spouses even after the consummation of the marriage provided the aggrieved party has not expressed his or her assent to marriage after he or she had come to know of the defect.[102] If a minor wife is given in marriage by her guardian to a person suffering from such defects and the guardian was not aware of the same then the marriage shall be void. But if the guardian knew of it, the marriage shall be valid.[103] It will of course be subject to the right of the wife for its dissolution. Under the Ḥanbali Law, the *Qāḍi's* decree for the dissolution of the marriage is an essential condition.[104]

Shī'i Law: Under the Shī'i law, the husband can claim the dissolution of his marriage if the wife was suffering from the specified defects before the marriage, but he cannot claim a divorce if the wife gets afflicted with one or more of the defects after consummation of the marriage.[105] There is a difference of opinion if a defect appears in the wife after the marriage, but before its consummation. The generally accepted view is that he will have no such right. This view seems to be based on the fact that the wife was free of the defect at the time of the marriage and anything that happens subsequently cannot affect the validity of the contract of the marriage.[106] Under the Shī'i law it is open to the spouses to dissolve their marriage by themselves on account of the presence of one or more of the specified defects, the only exception being impotency of

100. Ibn Qudāmah, *op. cit.*, Vol. VI, pp. 653, 655; al-Maqdisi, *op. cit.*, Vol. III, p. 200.
101. *Ibid.*
102. *Ibid.*
103. *Ibid* ; *Ibid.*, p. 203.
104. Ibn Qudameh, *op. cit.*, Vol. VI, p. 851
105. Jafar b. Hasan, *op. cit.*, p. 190.
106. *Ibid.*

the husband in which case it will be necessary for the wife to have recourse to the *Qāḍi*.[107] It is a necessary condition of Shī'i law that the aggrieved spouse must dissolve the marriage promptly on becoming aware of the defect in the other spouse. A delay in so doing amounts to acquiescence in the marriage and he or she will lose the right.[108]

It is possible to draw the conclusion from the various books on Muslim *fiqh* that a marriage is liable to be dissolved on the following grounds :

(1) Defects which preclude sexual intercourse,
(2) Defects which are likely to be communicated to the other spouse,
(3) Defects which may be visited on the children that may be born of the marriage,
(4) Defects which create apprehension of injury to life, limb or property such as violent madness, and
(5) Defects which create disgust in the other spouse.

It is stated in *Zaa'd al-Maa'd* that dissolution of marriage would be incumbent in the case of every defect which gives rise to disgust in the other spouse so that love and affection which are the aims of marriage are not achieved.[109]

The above view seems to be fully justifiable. There seems to be no reason for restricting the dissolution of marriage to certain specified diseases. We must bear in mind the low standard of morality of our time. Besides, as has been stated before happy companionship, sexual relaxation procreation of children are some of the important objects of marriage. Hence, when happy companionship is not possible as and when one spouse suffers from insanity, leucoderma, very strong foul breath, etc., Muslim law allows the dissolution of the marriage. In the same way a marriage can be dissolved when the other spouse suffers from violent madness and there is a likelihood that he or she may cause personal injury

107. Jafar b. Ḥasan, *op. cit.*, p. 190.
108. *Ibid.*
109. Ibn Qayyim, *op. cit.*, Vol. IV, p. 31.

to the other spouse or when there can be no intimacy between the parties due to a defect in the other. No doubt the Muslim jurists have mentioned different diseases on the basis of which a marriage can be dissolved but the basic idea underlying them is the same in all cases.

An important factor to be considered is the view of the Ḥanafi jurists that a marriage cannot be dissolved when it is the wife who suffers from a defect. They do not allow annulment of a marriage in such cases so that the wife may not be deprived of her dower and think that the husband can in such a case exercise his power of divorce. We have to consider how far is this view suitable to the changed conditions of the present day time. In early days it was usual that the husband would pay the dower or a considerable part of it before the marriage. A necessary effect of such a practice was that only such amount was fixed for dower as the husband could afford to pay. This is still the practice in some Muslim countries. But in Pakistan and India the dower is usually fixed so high for ostentation or as a sort of safeguard for the wife as is absolutecy beyond the paying capacity of the husband. If a marriage cannot be dissolved by the Court in such a case, that is when the wife suffers from a defect, or she or her guardian has been guilty of fraud or the wife's illicit pregnancy has been concealed, the husband shall face utter ruin if he divorces his wife or he should continue the marriage when it has become frustrated. Several difficulties have to be taken into consideration in such a case. If the marriage is allowed to be annulled then what is to happen to the wife. These matters require serious consideration of our ulema and Legislature.

Effect of : Under the Sunnī law, the presence of one or more of the specified defects in either spouse shall render the marriage voidable and the other spouse shall have a right to its dissolution through the *Qāḍi* as discussed before.

Under the Shī'i law a husband and wife can dissolve the marriage by themselves when the other spouse suffers from a defect; the *Qāḍi's* order is not required in such a case.[110] This is subject to the exception that if a marriage is dissolved on account of the husband's impotency, it is necessary for the wife to get the *Qāḍi's* order for the annulment of the marriage in the first instance.[111] But in such a case the wife can herself dissolve the marriage on the expiry of the prescribed period of one year if the husband has not been cured of his defect; it shall not be necessary for her to get a second order of the *Qāḍi* in the matter.[112]

Nature of Separation: Under the Ḥanafi, Māliki and Ḥanbli laws, separation due to a defect in a spouse shall amount to one irrevocable divorce.[113] It is not held to be a revocable divorce so as not to leave it in the power of the husband to revoke it but under the Shāfi'i law it amounts to annulment of the marriage.

Under the Shī'i law, the dissolution of marriage on account of a defect in either spouse shall amount to a faskh or annulment of the marriage and it is not held to be a divorce.[114]

Dower: Under Sunnī law a wife shall get the whole of her dower if the marriage has been consummated or under the Ḥanafi, Māliki or Ḥanbli laws if there has been a valid retirement irrespective of the fact whether it is dissolved by the husband or the *Qāḍi*.[115] But in the absence of consummation or valid retirement she shall be entitled to half the dower when marriage is dissolved by the husband.[116] If dissolved by the *Qāḍi* on account of a defect in the wife, she shall not be entitled to get any dower whatsoever.[117]

110. Jafar b. Hasan, *op. cit.*, p. 191.
111. *Ibid.*
112. *Ibid.*
113. Ibn Qudāmah *op. cit.*, Vol. VI. p. 651; al-Maqdisi, *op. cit.*, Vol. III, p. 200.
114. Jafar b. Haaan, *op cit*, p. 192.
115. Ibn Qudāmah, *op. cit.*, Vol. VI. p. 654; al-Maqdisi, *op. cit.*, Vol. III, p. 200.
116. *Ibid.*
117. *Ibid.*

Under the Shī'i law if a marriage is cancelled before consummation either by the husband or the wife on account of the specified defects in the other, no dower shall be payable to her.[118] This is subject to one exception, namely, when the marriage is cancelled by the wife on account of her husband's impotency when she shall be entitled to get half of her dower.[119]

If the marriage is cancelled by either the husband or the wife after its consummation, the wife shall get her full dower.[120]

Maintenance: A wife shall be entitled to maintenance even when she suffers from some physical disability such as rataq, qaran, insanity or has been so old as to become unfit for intimacy.[121]

118. Syed Muhammad Sadiq, *Rawāi al-Ahkam*, p. 277, Hyderabad, 1897, A.D., Urdu translation of *Sharai al-Islam* by Jafar b. Hasan.

119. *Ibid.*

120. *Ibid.*

121. Syed Amir Ali *Fatāwā Alamgiriyah*, *op. cit.*, Vol. II, p. 407.

Chapter 16

IMPOTENCY

Preliminary

Some of the important objects of a marriage, as stated before in a previous chapter, are the procreation of children lawful enjoyment of sexual passions and a happy companionship of two members of the opposite sexes. If some of these objects are lost, the marriage may fail to fulfil its purpose, and sometimes may even be harmful. Thus, when the husband is incapable of consummating the marriage on account of some defect, physical or otherwise, at least the first two of the above-mentioned objects of marriage are lost while it is possible that the third may also be defeated. If coupled with this fact, the wife cannot live happily with him and her life becomes miserable on account of the husband's defect, this state of affairs renders the continuation of the marriage positively undesirable. Muslim law lays great stress on the performance by the husband of the obligation to satisfy the natural desires of his wife, to be intimate with her at reasonable intervals and not to neglect this important obligation. Thus should a husband pass his nights in offering prayers and his days in fastings so that he cannot be intimate with and satisfy the natural demands of his wife then, on her complaint, the *Qāḍi* shall order him to be intimate with her even though he may have to give up worship at night and fasting in the day.[1] Muslim law allows the wife of an impotent person the right of getting her marriage dissolved.

The rule under the English law is the same as the Muslim law. As a matter of fact, dissolution of marriage on the ground of a husband's impotency is now more or less the

1. *Al-Fatāwā al-Hindiyāh*, Kanpur, 1349, A.H., Vol. II, p. 41.

universal rule though there are some States is U.S.A., which do not consider impotency to be sufficient ground for the dissolution of a marriage. But the laws relating to incapacity differ in different countries and the difference lies, as will be seen later, in the notion of impotency and in certain details. The procreation of children, however, is not the sole object of marriage and the spouses may marry simply for companionship and domestic comforts. It is laid down in the Qur'ān :

> "And one of His signs is that He hath created for you from among yourselves mates *so that you may find tranquillity with them and He hath created mutual love and compassion between you*".[2]

This shows how much the idea of a happy companionship has been stressed in Islam.

Under Muslim law a marriage with an impotent person is not void but merely voidable. This is also the view of Hindu law. Thus it is stated by Raghava-Chariar in his book on Hindu law that a marriage does not exist solely for matrimonial intercourse and a marriage with an impotent person cannot be held invalid though one of the chief objects of marriage, namely, begetting of children, is defeated thereby. It was considered in England at one time that the procreation of children was the principal aim of marriage and the avoidance of unlawful sexual relation was the next important object.[3] A different view was, however, expressed later when it was stated in a case that the procreation of children is not the primary end of marriage but that the relevant factor is the creation of a situation, "whereby ariseth that conjugal society, which may have the conjunction of bodies as well as of minds, as the general end of the institution of marriage is the solace and satisfaction of man".[4] Hence, such a marriage is considered to be merely voidable under English law also as

2. Qur'ān, XXX: 21. Surah Al-Rūm.
3. Dickinson Vs. Dickinson (1913), P. 198 ; Cowen Vs. Cowen (1946), P. 36; Weatherley Vs. Weatherley (1947) 1 All, E.R. 563.
4. *Ibid.*

well as under the laws of certain States in the United States of America.

Description

In ordinaty sense, the word "Impotency" means the inability of a man to perform the act of coition and an impotent person is one who is wholly lacking in sexual power.

Definitian

Impotency many be defined as the incapacity of either the husband or the wife to be sexually intimate with the other or to allow or grant sexual gratification to the other. The penetration of glans penis in the wife's body is considered sufficient to constitute intimacy.[5] It is obvious that a person who gets discharged in the preliminary stage, termed "Love play" by some authors, shall be included in the definition of *'Innīn* or Impotent person because then he will not be able of penetration. Such a person is called "*shakkāz*" and is considered to be an impotent person by Muslim jurists.[6] According to Aḥmad b. Hanbal if a person is incapable for intimacy on account of a disease which is expected to be cured, he shall not be considered to be impotent. But if the disease is not expected to be cured, he shall be considered to be *'Innīn* and one year's time shall be given to him for the cure of his defect as discussed later. If the inability is due to old age, the above rule shall be applicable unless the defect is of long standing and the wife has acquiesced to it.[7]

Impotency may be due to congenital constitution, weakness, old age, accident, disease etc. It can also be due to a psychological cause which may have nothing to do with the husband's physical condition. In the former case he will be incapable for all women, but in the latter case his incapacity may extend to some particular woman or women. The Sunni

5. *Al-Fatāwā al-Hindiyah, op. cit.*, Vol. II, p. 133.
6. Ibn 'Ābidīn, *Radd al-Muḥtār*, Cairo, 1318 A.H., Vol .II, p. 608.
7. Sharaf al-Dīn al-Maqdisī, *'al-Iqnā'*, Cairo, n,d. Vol. III, p. 198 ; Ibn Qudāmah, *al-Mughnī*, Cairo, 1307 A H., Vol. VI, p. 670.

jurists have taken a realistic view of the matter and recognise what may be called relative impotency. They consider that it is possible that a man may not be wholly impotent and unfit for all women, but may be incapable for intimacy with a certain woman or women only. Thus he may hold his wife in so much awe on account of her beauty, learning, wealth, youth and the like that he may be unable to be intimate with her though he may be able to have sexual connection with another woman or women. Ugliness or some repulsive defect in the wife may bring about a similar result. In such a case the person shall be regarded, under the Sunnī law, to be impotent with regard to that particular woman or women with whom he cannot be intimate. Hence impotency is not restricted merely to malformation or structural defect in the husband. What the Court has to see in a case involving impotency is whether there is impracticability of consummation of the marriage irrespective of the cause to which it may be due in the husband.

The word, "impotent" has been used here in a general sense and includes a Khusee and a Majbūb. By the word Khusee is meant a person without testicles or whose testicles have been so crushed as to become unserviceable. Majbub means a person without male organ or when it is so short that he cannot penetrate the wife's body.

This rule of law regarding impotency is quite reasonable because the law has to look to the happiness of both the spouses. If the wife leads a miserable life on account of the defect in her husband then the fact that he is sexually fit for women other than herself cannot make her life the less miserable.

The Hindu law also allowed the dissolution of marriage on the ground of the husband's impotency in respect of his wife. Thus there is an interesting passage in *Brihaspati* by Narada wherein it is laid down that "If a man is potent with another woman but impotent with his own wife, his wife shall take another husband. Women have been created for the sake of propagation, the wife being the field and the husband the giver of seed. The field must be given to him who has seed."[8] But at one time impotency of the husband was not regarded as a ground for the dissolution of marriage, under the Hindu law. It was observed by their Lordships of the Andhra High Court, "the Hindu law-givers who regarded impotency as a disqualification for marriage permitted marriage by impotent persons only because the defect caused by their physical debility (incapacity to procreate children), could be made good by recourse to *Niyog* system and thereby borrowing the potency of another for the procreation of children."[9] 'But with the disappearance of *Nitycg* system there can be no valid marriage and the means for the fulfilment of marriage in this vital aspect can no longer be supplied.'[10]

Shī'ī Law: The notion of impotency is rather lenient for the husband under the Shi'ī law as compared with the Sunnī law. The Shi'ī law insists on absolute impotency so that a person shall be considered to be impotent only when he is absolutely incapable of sexual intercourse not only with regard to his wife hut in respect of all women.[11] Hence a husband shall be considered to be impotent only when he cannot be or has not been able to be intimate with any woman whosoever. But the Shi'ī law has taken a more realistic view in another respect. Impotency under it is not confined to mere disability for penetration but includes any cause which renders coition impracticable on account of some cause attributable to the husband. That a husband shall be considered impotent when the male organ is of such an abnormal size as to render coition impossible without severe pain to the wife.[12]

8. Jolly, *Hindu Law*, Calcutta.
9. *Niyog* was system when a person unfit for procreation of children would ask his wife to go or himselfs end her to another person to get a child by him.
10. Malla Reddy and others Vs. Dubbama, A.I.R. 1956, Andhara, p. 237.
11. Ja'far b. al-Ḥasan, *Sharā'i' al-Islām*, Teheran, 1377, pp. 1901-91.
12. *Ibid*., p. 190; Abid Husain, *Jamai' Abbasi*, p. 152, Delhi, 1305, A.H. Urdu translation of *Jamai Abbasi* by Muhammad Baha-ud-din Āmli

English Law : As stated before, marriage under English law was considered a sacrament while under Muslim law it is more of a civil contract in its nature as far as the parties to it are concerned. The result was that its dissolution was much more difficult under English law at one time than it has been under Muslim law. Besides, English law, at one time, insisted on absolute impotency of the husband while under Sunni law it can be relative to the wife only. This notion of impotency led to a curious situation. Thus if a husband was proved impotent, and his marriage was annulled on that account then he could contract another marriage. If he married another woman and a child was born to him by the second wife then it would be considered that a fraud had been played upon the Court in obtaining the annulment of the first marriage and that the husband was not impotent as, it was argued, was clear from the fact that a child was born to him by the second wife. The first marriage could then be reconstituted by setting aside the decree for its annulment. As a result of this, the second marriage would become bigamous and so could be considered, under these circumstances, to be void and the intimacy between the husband and the second wife, therefore, would amount to adultery and the children born of the second wife would be considered illegitimate. This aspect of the law could result in great hardship to the second wife and her children. It was not until the year 1853 that a different interpretation of the law was put on a firm basis by Dr. Lushington and the idea of what may be termed relative impotency was recognised.[13] This difficulty was not experienced under Muslim law. As noted before, it is possible under the conception of the Sunni law that incapacity may be relative only, that is, a man may be impotent with regard to his wife and yet may not be absolutely incapable for cohabitation. Hence the birth of a child to such a person by a second wife does not prove that he was not impotent with regard to his wife. As limited

13. N Vs. M (1853) 2 Rob Ecc 625.

polygamy is allowed by Islam the second marriage shall not be considered invalid under Muslim law. The notion of impotency has since undergone a change under the English law and now it is provided that a person is entitled to a decree of nullity of his or her marriage when the other party, though generally capable of performing the act of coition, is yet incapable of performing it with the petitioner.[14] Hence, a marriage was annulled on the ground of impotency although the evidence showed that it was restricted to the wife and was not a general condition of the husband.[15] The English law now considers a person to be impotent if cohabitation with him or her be not possible for any cause whatsoever.[16] In a case, a wife was held to be impotent when her sexual organs were of insufficient size to permit penetration.[17] Moreover. the English law does not confine impotency only to such defects as render cohabitation impossible but extends it, as under the Shī'ī law, to cases where coition is not practicable, though possible, on account of a defect in the genital organs. The same rule applies to Indian Christians and a husband was held by the Madras High Court under the Indian Christian Marriages Act to be impotent when intimacy with the wife was not possible on account of the abnormal size of the male organ as a result of which ordinary and complete intercourse was physically impossible. It was held that the husband was impotent as far as the wife was concerned. The view was based on the reasoning that impotency includes impracticability of coition.[18] Section 7(*a*) of the Matrimonial Causes Act, 1937, has introduced a new ground for relief. Under this provision it is not necessary that the spouse concerned should be physically incapable of

14. N-r Vs M (1853) 2 Rob Ecc 625.
15. *Ibid.*, G. Vs. M. (1885) 10 App, Cas. 171 ; G. Vs. G. (1908) 25, T.L.R. 328.
16, D-e Vs. A-g (1845) 1 Robberts Ecc 279 ; W Vs H, (1861) 2 Sw. & Tr. 240; G. Vs. G. (1871) L.P. 2 P & D. 287.
17. W Vs. H. (1861) 2, Sw. & Tr. 240.
18. Kanthy Balavendram Vs. Harry, A.I.R. 1954, Mad. 316.

coition but his failure to consummate the marriage for whatsoever person shall suffice for the dissolution of marriage. It reads as under:

> In addition to any other ground on which a marriage is by law void or voidable, a marriage shall be voidable on the ground:—
>
> That the marriage has not been consummated owing to the wilful refusal of the respondent to consummate the marriage.

This provision has been maintained in the Matrimonial Causes Act, 1950, where it has been numerated 8(*a*). Under the provision of this section a marriage shall be liable to be dissolved even when there is no physical incapacity in the husband or the wife but the marriage has not been consummated due to his or her account. Thus a woman or man may be physically quite normal, but she or he may hate the physical act of intimacy and so may not allow the consummation of the marriage. Under the Muslim law, the *Qāḍi* can order him or her to desist from such an abstinence and can force him to give up the practice. He may, if he thinks it necessary, order the husband to divorce the wife or compel the wife to seek a Khul'.

Law in U.S.A.: The law with regard to impotency differs in different States in the United States of America. It forms a ground for divorce is some States and the marriage is considered voidable, while it does not form a ground in others.[19] Again, in some States it can be declared void by sentence of nullity. To form a ground for divorce, the defect must have been present at the time of the marriage and must be incurable according to the law in Connecticut. Illinois, Kansas, Maryland, New Hampshire, and New York. In Colorado, impotency is a ground for divorce even if it was not present at the time of marriage but the husband

19. For particulars see Keezer, Chapter 56 or some other book on Law of Divorce in U.S.A.

acquires it subsequently due to immoral conduct. In Delaware this condition, even if acquired after marriage, will form a ground for the dissolution of a marriage if it is coupled with failure to maintain the family.[20]

Religious Authority: The Muslim jurists allow the dissolutlon of a marriage on account of the husband's impotency on the basis of a verse in the Qur'ān which enjoins on the husbands "To hold them (the wives) with kindness".[21] It is stated by the Muslim jurists that when a person is impotent he is incapable of satisfying the natural desires of the wife and cannot be considered to be holding her with kindness and that the marriage is, therefore, liable to be dissolved on the petition of the wife.[22] The view that a marriage can be dissolved on the ground of the husband's incapacity also finds support from another verse in the Qur'ān wherein it is stated, "They (women) have rights similar to those of (men) over them in a just manner.[23] A busband has got a right to the conjugal society of his wife and so she too has got a similar right against him. Both these rights and duties form an integral though implied part of the marriage-contract. If the husband is incapable of performing his part of the marriage-contract, naturally he is guilty of a breach of this implied term of the marriage contract, and the wife shall be entitled to the cancellation of her marriage in such a case.

Criterion of Potency: The next question that arises is the notion or nature of potency or impotency of a person. The Muslim jurists have laid down the rule that a person shall be considered to be potent with regard to his wife if he is able to penetrate her body and the penetration of only the tip or glans penis is considered sufficient to constitute con-

20. For full particulars see Keezer: *Marriage and Divorce* Indianopolis or some other book.
21. Qur'ān, Surah al-Baqarah, II, 23.
22. Al-Marghīnānī, 'Ali b. Abī Bakr, *al-Hidayah*, Delhi, n.d., Vol. II, p. 400; Ibn 'Ābidīn, *op. cit.*, Vol. II, p. 612; c.f. Qur'ān, II: 231.
23. Qur'ān, Surah, al-Baqarah, II, 228.

summation of marriage.[24] The Muslim jurists do not attach any importance to the duration of coition so that if the husband is capable of only partial penetration or imperfect coition or both as when he discharges immediately on mere penetration then in all these cases he shall not be considered to be impotent. In other words, partial penetration and imperfect coition (from the wife's point of view) is deemed sufficient to constitue consummation of marriage and to establish the potency of the husband.

Coition: The question whether coition is normal or not is a very important matter and vitally affects the happiness of the spouses or at least of one of them. In order to understand this condition of coition it is necessary to understand its nature. Coition consists of several phases and some medical books mention as many as six of them. But from a legal point of view the following are the important phases :

I. Erection,
II. Intromissio or penetration,
III. Orgasm,
IV. Ejaculation.

All of the above phases play an important part in the sexual act and the law takes into consideration some of these various aspects of coition. A healthy and normal functioning of these phases is necessary for the full satisfaction of the sexual urge or passions of the spouses concerned. The phases are closely connected with and interdependent on each other. Thus there can be no penetration when there is no erection and as a general rule there can be no orgasm when there is no penetration.

Erection: Erection is a very important phase and coition is not possible if there can be no erection. The lack of erection can be due to structural or physical defects as well as to psychological causes. It can be due to certain diseases

24. *Al-Fatāwā al-Hindiyah*, *op. cit.*, Vol. II, p. 133, Ibn 'Ābidīn, *op. cit.*, Vol. II, p. 609.

and weakness. A defect in the nervous mechanism is a very common cause of lack of erection. Certain psychological factors can also contribute to this condition. Thus a person may be so much afraid of his failure in the sexual act on the bridal night that he may have no erection at all. Similarly, lack of desire because of repugnance for the physical act of coition or for a particular woman can lead to the same result. In the former case the husband will be unfit for all women, but in the latter case he will be incapable for cohabitation only with the particular woman.

In Muslim law as in other legal systems it is not the lack of erection but the result brought by it, namely, lack of penetration, that materially affects the marital relationship and which is taken into considetation by the law.

Intromissio or *Penetration*: Penetration is an important constituent of coition. The lack of penetration can be due to absolute lack of erection or incomplete erection. It can also be due to malformation of the genital organs in either spouse. This condition in man can happen when the male organ is abnormal in size and also in the presence of certain other defects. In the woman the genital part may be quite undeveloped or there may be unnatural growths and obstructions which may not allow penetration. But whatever the cause for the husband's lack of power to penetrate and obstruction in woman entitle the other spouse, as a general rule, to the dissolution of his or her marriage. Under Shi'i law if the male organ be abnormal in size so that penetration is not possible without severe pain to the wife, the marriage can be dissolved on her complaint.[25]

Muslim Law: As stated before, Muslim jurists hold a person to be potent if he is able even to partially penetrate the wife's body and the penetration of only tip or glans penis is considered sufficient to constitute consummation of marriage[26].

25. Muḥammad Baha'uddin Āmli, *Jāmi' 'Abbāsī* (Urdu tr.), p. 152, Delhi, 1305.

26. *Al-Fatāwā al-Hindiyah*, *op. cit.*, Vol. II, p. 133; Ibn 'Ābidīn, *op. cit.*, Vol. II, p. 609.

It is not at all necessary under the Muslim law that there should be full penetration. Hence, as stated before, partial penetration is considered sufficient for the establishment of potency of a man and he will not be considered to be impotent if he has been able to introduce only the glans penis inside the woman's body.

English Law: The English law is the same as Muslim law in this respect.

Law in U.S.A.: In some States in U.S.A. impotency means complete lack of power of intimacy. It does not include temporary or curable weakness.

Orgasm: Intromissio or penetraticn is immediately followed by copulatory movements. Those movements contribute to the pleasures of coition and constitute an essential part of it. Its duration differs with different ages. It culminates in the discharge of semen in the case of man and in the case of the wife on her complete satisfaction and relaxation which must be simultaneous with that of the husband, so that she may get full satisfaction out of the sexual act. A man generally feels fully relaxed on the discharge of the seminal fluid but such is not the case with a woman.[27] A husband should, therefore, see that there should be no premature ejaculation on his part. It is these effects, namely, miserable life of the wife and injury to her health, with which we are concerned in law. As observed before, two of the objects of marriage are happy companionship and satisfaction of sexual passions and both of these will be lost in such a case as far as the wife is concerned. The question arises how far will the legal position of the spouses be affected by such sexual condition of the husband. It is a very important matter but unfortunately its importance is not generally realised. Harper has mentioned that in an investigation it was found that 115 women out of 442 did not experience any orgasm with their husbands. But what is shocking is the fact that only 49 women

27. Edmund Bergler, *Unhappy Marriages and Divorce*, p. 95, New York. 1949.

out of that number were such as got from coition an agreeable feeling with pleasant after-results and 146 were such as remained unsatisfied.[28] The question arises as to what is a normal orgasm. It is difficult to define it and to determine when the coition begins and when it ends. But it has been nicely described by Van De Velde as "That intercourse which takes place between two sexually mature individuals of opposite sexes; which excludes cruelty and the use of artificial means for producing voluptuous sensations ; which aims directly or indirectly at the consummation of sexual satisfaction, and which, having achieved a certain degree of stimulation, concludes with the ejaculation—or emission—of the semen into the vagina, at the nearly simultaneous culmination of sensation —or orgasm—of both parties."[29]

The important point in above description of normal coition is conveyed by the words ; "nearly simultaneous culmination of sensation or orgasm of both parties." It is very important for a successful marriage that both the spouses should get satisfaction out of the coition and none should be left unsatisfied. If the husband does not obtain full erection or is incapable of full penetration or suffers from premature ejaculation, then it is obvious that the wife shall remain unsatisfied and it is this condition that so often results in the misery of a wife and contributes to make a marriage unhappy and unsuccessful.

Muslim Law : There is no definite provision of Muslim law that governs the case of a dissatisfied wife due to the unsatisfactory sexual condition of the husband as regards orgasm. It does not pay any heed to the condition or nature of coition. Hence, as stated before, partial penetration and imperfect coitus (from the wife's point of view) is deemed sufficient to establish the potency of the husband and for maintenance of the marriage. It seems strange that the Muslim jurists have not made any provision for such a

28. Harper, *Problems of the Family*, p. 304, New York, 1952.
29. Th H Van de Valde, *Ideal Marriage*, London, 1935.

contingency. The case is well covered by the injunction of the Qur'ān, namely "To retain the wives with kindness".[30] It is obvious that a husband cannot be considered to be keeping his wife with kindness when she remains dissatisfied with this aspect of her married life on account of the husband's defective sexual condition. The reason for this position seems to be due to two main grounds, namely:

(*a*) Difficulty in the establishment of the husband's condition and,

(*b*) The fact that in the East such a defect has always been considered to be fully curable.

(*a*) As regards the first point, the matter can generally be decided only on the statements of the spouses in case of premature ejaculation. If the husband fails to appreciate himself or intentionally or unintentionally does not disclose it to the Court it will be very difficult for the Court to decide the cases correctly. It will not consider it justifiable to decree the case against the husband simply on the statement of the wife—particularly as the burden of proof shall lie on her.

(*b*) There can be no doubt that most of the causes that lead to the premature ejaculation are curable. The Muslim jurists must have thought that no man would like to expose himself to the contempt of his wife on account of such a condition and so would get himself cured without any unreasonable delay. But if the husband neglects to get himself cured or if the defect cannot be cured, then the continuation of the marriage would not be desirable.

A Court shall, under these circumsances. be perfectly justified to act on the injunction of the Qur'ān and to hold that the husband was not keeping the wife with kindness and was, therefore, a transgressor of the sacred text and so

30. Qur'ān, Surah al-Baqarah, II. p. 229.

order the dissolution of the marriage on this ground. A Sunnī wife can also rely on the dictum of Ibn Qayyim, 'when a wife cannot remain with her husband without injury to herself, let the marriage be dissolved."[31] A wife whether Sunnī or a Shī'ah can of course claim a separation under the provisions of Khul'.[32]

Ejaculation: The act of intimacy finds its climax in man's ejaculation or emission of semen and the sexual excitement usually terminates in the case of man at this stage.

General Discussion: The ejaculation of semen in the wife's body is an important part of coition. The question of ejaculation can be considered from the following points of view :—

(*a*) Sex side,
(*b*) Procreation of children, and
(*c*) effect on wife's health.

(*a*) As regards the first, it may be stated that the contact of seminal fluid within the female part gives soothing and refreshing sensation to the wife while its lack may result in excessive local irritation and congestion in the wife's body.[33] But its lack by itself is not considered a sufficient ground under any system of law for the dissolution of a marriage.

(*b*) As stated before, procreation of children, is one of the important aims of marriage. If the husband is wanting in ejaculation, there can be no conception and so one of the objects of the marriage is lost. But a marriage cannot be dissolved under the Muslim law on this ground.

(*c*) If the wife's health suffers either on account of the injurious effect of lack of ejaculation or because she is very anxious to have a child then the matter creates a new problem.

31. Ibn Qayyim, *Zād al-Ma'ād*, Cairo, 1950 A.D. Vol. IV, p. 133.
32. For discussion on this subject see chapter on *Khul'*.
33. Van de Velde *op. cit.*, p. 186.

It is now proposed to discuss this matter under the Muslim Law and also under the current English law.

Muslim Law: Under the Muslim law, discharge of semen in the wife's body is not an essential condition of coition and a wife has no cause for the dissolution of her marriage on this account. Thus it is stated in *al-Fatāwā al-Hindiyah* that a wife shall have no right to the dissolution of her marriage if the husband is capable of penetration but lacking in ejaculation.[34] As already discussed, the only essential condition for potency under the Muslim law is penetration. Hence the lack of ejaculation is no ground for dissolution of marriage. No doubt, one of the objects of marriage is the increase of the family and Islam lays great emphasis on procreation of children and the Muslim jurists consider that the upbringing of virtuous children contributes to development of soul yet the husband's inability to ejaculate is not considered a sufficient ground for dissolution of marriage.

Injury to wife's health: The Muslim law does not make a definite provision for a case when the wife's health suffers on account of her unsatisfied desires to have a child. This is probably due to the fact that in the East a man has always been anxious to have children and such a case could not have come to the notice of the Muslim jurists in which a man did not want a child. It is the reverse case that has been greatly in practice, namely, the marriage of a man with another woman on account of the reason that no child was born out of the first marriage. The disinclination of a man to have children is a matter of recent time and cases of this nature are found generally amongst the white nations and such cases are rather infrequent, if any at all, amongst the Muslims, and none has been taken to any Court up till now. But if such a case does occur, a Court can give relief to the wife under the Qur'ānic injunction, namely, "To keep the wives with kindness", and

34. *Al-Fatāwā al-Hindiyah, op. cit.*, Vol. II, p. 134.

can dissolve a marriage if it is satisfied that the husbansd' conduct amounts to cruelty and causes injuries to the wife's health.

English Law: Different and even contradictory opinions have been expressed by English Courts about the nature of complete intercourse and the necessity of ejaculation in the body of the wife. At one time such ejaculation was considered an essential condition of consummation of marriage, and its lack was considered tantamount to impotency in the husband and a sufficient ground for the dissolution of marriage. Thus, it was stated in a case that sexual intercourse in the proper meaning of the term is ordinary and complete intercourse and it does not mean partial and imperfect intercourse.[35] Following the above view it was stated in another case dealing with the practice of coitus interruptus, adopted by the husband in that case, that sexual intercourse cannot be said to be complete when a husband deliberately discontinues the act of intercourse before it has reached its natural termination which is the passage of the male seed into the body of the woman.[36] This view was approved in a later case when the Court held "to establish consummation of marriage, intercourse must be natural and complete. There is no natural and complete intercourse unless there is emission from the one into the body of the other, and the practice of coitus interruptus does not merely prevent the creation of children, it also prevents any real intercourse at all and therefore consummation of marriage..It is difficult to see how coitus interruptus can be said to be complete."[37] These views were not, however, accepted as correct in a case decided only a few days after the decision of Grimes vs. Grimes. It was held in the case, "There is complete conjunction of bodies, vera copula, as soon as full entry and penetration has

35. D-e. Vs. A-g (1845) 1 Rob Ecc 279. Lewis Vs. Hayward (1866) 35. L.J.Pr., MJ 105.
36. Cowen Vs. Cowen, (1945), 2 All. E.R. 197.
37. Grimes Vs. Grimes (1948), 2 All. E. R. 147.

been achieved and in case of coitus interruptus marriage cannot be said not to have been consummated. It is impossible to hold that (in such a case) marriage has not been consummated.[38] In a still later case the view expressed in the last case (White vs. White) was preferred to the view stated in Grimes vs. Grimes.[39]

Law in U.S.A. It was held in an American case that the copulation should be complete and should not be imperfect.

Incapacity subsequent to marriage. A husband may be potent at the time of his marriage but may become incapable for coition subsequently due to accident, disease, old age etc. The matter can be considered from two different aspects, namely,

(*a*) When the marriage has been consummated and the husband becomes incapable for intimacy subsequently, and

(*b*) When the husband has not been able to consummate the marriage at all.

(*a*) If the husband has been able to be intimate with his wife even though only once then the marriage cannot be dissolved under Muslim law on the ground of subsequent incapacity.

(*b*) Under the Sunni law it is an essential condition for dissolution of marriage on the basis of the husband's impotency that the he should be impotent at the time of the marriage. Hence the fact that the husband becomes incapable for intimacy after the marriage is no ground for dissolution of the marriage under the Sunni law.[40]

The rule under the Sunni law is very hard for a wife whose husband might have been potent at the time of his

38. White Vs. White (1948), 2 All. E. R. 151.

39. Cackett Vs. Cackett (1950), 1 All. E. R. 677.

40. Al-Nawavi, *Minhaj al-Talibin*, pp. 299, 300 tr. Van Den Berg, London, 1914,

marriage but becomes impotent subsequently. Impotency may be caused, as explained before, by accident, some surgical operations, disease etc. If the husband of a young wife becomes incapable after his marriage, it may mean a very unhappy and miserable future for her and there will be a great temptation for her to fall in evil ways. It is obvious that a husband cannot be keeping his wife "with humanity" when he becomes sexually unfit her. The principle of law that an impotent husband is considered to be a transgressor of the injunction laid down in the Qur'ān, "To keep the wives with humanity" applies with equal force in such a case also. The wife can also claim divorce on the ground that the Qur'ān specifically lays down, "And women have right similar to those against them in a just manner."[41] The husband shall be contravening this injunction of the Qur'ān when he is not capable of performing this important marital obligation.

Shī'ī Law: The *Shī'ī* law allows the dissolution of a marriage when the husband was not impotent at the time of marriage but becomes incapable subsequently.[42]

English Law : The English law was at one time similar in this respect as the Sunni law and insisted that the husband should have been impotent at the time of the marriage. But section 7(*i*)(*a*) of the Matrimonial Act of 1937 has introduced a new ground of nullity of marriage in the English law. It provides that a marriage can be held voidable when it has not been consummated owing to the wilful refusal of the respondent to consummate the marriage. Under this provision it is no longer necessary that the spouse should have been physically unfit to consummate the marriage but the conduct of the husband or the wife in this respect is considered sufficient for a divorce.

Law in U.S.A.: In U.S.A. also impotency acquired after marriage is not generally considered a ground for dissolution of marriage. But in Colorado, the law provides that incapacity

41. Qur'ān, Surah, al-Baqarah, II, 228.
42. Ja'far b. al-Ḥasan, *op. cit.*, p. 190.

acquired through immoral conduct committed after the marriage is a ground for divorce. In Delaware, incapacity acquired after marriage coupled with failure to support the family constitutes a ground for divorce provided the wife did not or could not know of the husband's defect at the time of the marriage.

Incapacity due to old age: Under Muslim law, impotency acquired after the marriage has been consummated, even though only once, cannot be a ground for divorce. Hence, the fact that the husband loses his potency in old age will not entitle the wife to the dissolution of her marriage. If the husband was impotent at the time of the marriage, whether due to old age or any other cause, the marriage shall be liable to be dissolved on the complaint of the wife. But if the husband loses his power after the consummation of the marriage due to old age while the wife is still young then too she will have no remedy under the law laid down by the early Muslim jurist. But, can she be deprived of all relief in such a case in the present-day conditions when the standard of morality is no longer what it was in the early days ? It will be very hard on a wife to give her no relief and save her from great hardship. At the same time it does not seem equitable that a husband in his advanced age when he has supported the wife all along should be deprived at a late stage of his life of the company of his wife and domestic comforts. But then there is the fact that the law should not compel a wife to live a miserable life if she still stands in need of sexual relaxation. A Court must judge each case on its particular facts. If it finds that there is a great difference between the ages of the husband and the wife who shall have to live a very unhappy life on account of the husband's defect then there is no reason why the Court should not give her relief on the basis of justice, equity and good conscience. Such a case can be decided under Muslim law on the principle that the husband is not keeping the wife with kindness if it be established to the satisfaction of the Court that this condition of the husband does involve hardship to the wife and that she is of an age when she may experience sexual urge and genuine need for its relaxation. The Court can also apply the rule of law laid down by Ibn Qayyim in the case of Sunnis.

English Law: Under the English law there is no provision to meet such a case. No doubt an English marriage can be dissolved on the basis of a wilful refusal of one party to be intimate with the other, but there is no wilful refusal to cohabitation in this case.

Law in U.S.A.: There is no clear provision to meet such cases but there are some cases which can be helpful in the matter. It has been held that incapacity due to advanced age will not usually serve as a ground for divorce. A divorce claimed by a wife on account of the husband's incapacity was refused when both the parties were of an advanced age.[43] But in another case the Court was doubtful to dissolve the marriage on the ground of the husband's incapacity when the husband and the wife were seventy-three years and sixty years old respectively.[44] It seems from the trend of the judgment that if the difference had been more glaring the Court might have dissolved the marriage. This ruling indicates that a divorce may be allowed under such circumstances if there is such a great disparity between the ages of the spouses as to involve hardship to the wife.

Wife's Right:

(*a*) *Sunnī Law*: A wife is entitled under the Sunnī law, under certain conditions, to get her marriage dissolved through the *Qāḍī* when her husband is not able to consummate the marriage even though he may not he absolutely unfit sexually and may be able to cohabit with women other than herself. But if a husband has been able to be intimate with

43. Fulmer Vs. Fulmer, 13 Phila (Pa) 166.

44. Hatch Vs. Hatch, 58 Misc. 54; 110 N.Y.S. 18; Briggs Vs. Morgan 1914. 3 Ph. Ecc 325.

his wife though only once, the marriage cannot be dissolved by subsequent incapacity of the husband due to any cause whatsoever. The wife shall lose her right when the marriage is consummated.[45]

(*b*) *Shī'ī Law*: Under the Shī'ī law a wife cannot claim a separation on the ground of her husband's incapacity when it is confined to her alone and is not general. She shall be entitled to the dissolution of her marriage only if he is absolutely unfit for all women including herself.[46] She can have no such right if her husband has had or can have connection with any woman other than herself.[47] But a Shī'ī marriage can be dissolved in India and Pakistan under the provisions of the Dissolution of Muslim Marriages Act, 1939 on the ground that the husband cannot consummate the marriage even though he may be able to be intimate with a woman other than the wife. The word "Impotent" has not been defined in the Act and is used in the ordinary sense of the word which is now the same as defined under the Sunnī law. The Act applies to all Muslims irrespective of creed and so a Shī'īah wife can take advantage of this provision of the Act. Under the Shī'ī law she can herself dissolve a marriage if the husband is found to be without testicles or whose testicles have been crushed. According to the generally accepted view, she can exercise this right also when the husband's organ had been completely severed before the marriage. But if he becomes afflicted with this defect after consummating the marriage, she cannot exercise this right.[48]

Disability in the Wife. If the wife, who wants her marriage to be dissolved on account of her husband's incapacity, should happen to have herself such a malformation of the genital parts as to render intimacy with her impossible, she

45. *Al-Fatāwā al-Hindiyah*, *op. cit.*, Vol. II, p. 133, Ibn 'Ābidīn, *op. cit.* Vol. II, p. 609.
46. Ja'far b. al-Ḥasan. *op. cit.* p. 190.
47. See discussion under the head "Subsequent Impotency".
48. Ja'far b. al-Ḥasan, *op. cit*, p. 190.

shall not be entitled to any relief on the ground of the husband's incapacity.[49] This rule is based on the reasoning that she herself is at fault as her defect does not and cannot allow consummation of the marriage even if the husband was potent and that in such a case there can be no question of his not keeping her with humanity. But the question arises if the wife has to be given an opportunity to get herself cured. It has been stated by Muslim jurists "..... and the ability to perform the act, where any natural obstruction exists, may be obtained as, for instance, in the case of malformation of the genital parts, which is to be remedied by surgical operations."[50] It appears from this passage that surgical operations are permissible to remove obstructions in the genital part of the wife so that coition may become possible. When such permission is granted, there is no reason why an opportunity should not be given to the wife to voluntarily get her defect cured. Under the Mālikī law, a woman whose genitals are abnormal may undergo a treatment at the hand of a gynaecologist. A husband is allowed one year's time for the cure of incapacity and in equity the same period of time may be given to the wife. The Sunnī jurists, with the exception of the Hanafis, and the Shī'ī jurists hold that in the case of malformation in the wife the husband can get the marriage dissolved. But this rule does not mean that the wife cannot be given a chance to get herself cured. But if the operation should happen to be dangerous and should the wife refuse to undergo it, a marriage may be dissolved immediately in equity and justice.

Shī'ī Law: Under the Shī'ī law, a husband can get the cancellation of his marriage if the wife suffers from a malformation of the genital parts provided the defect is incurable or even when it is curable but the wife refuses medical treatment. Hence her right to the dissolution of her marriage on the ground of her husband's incapacity may not

49. Ibn 'Ābidīn, *op. cit.*, Vol. II, p. 609.
50. *Ibid.*

be lost when she suffered from disability which has been cured.

English Law: Under the English law the obstruction must be permanent and incurable to entitle the husband to get the marriage dissolved.

Essentials: According to the Sunnīs, the wife of an impotent person must establish all of the following facts in order to succeed in her suit against her husband for dissolution of her marriage :—

(*a*) That the husband was impotent at the time of the marriage.

(*b*) That she was ignorant of the above fact at that time, that is, at the time of her marriage.

(*c*) That the husband has not been able to consummate the marriage.

(*d*) That the defect has not been cured and the husband is still (*i.e.*, at the time of the suit) impotent, and

(*e*) That she has not waived her right.[51]

If she fails to establish even one of them, she shall not be entitled to get a decree in her favour. Thus if the husband was not impotent at the time of the marriage, but is subsequently afflicted with that condition through accident, disease or otherwise, the wife cannot claim a separation because her husband was not impotent at the time of the marriage which is a necessary condition. Similarly, the right of a wife to claim dissolution of her marriage on the ground of impotency of her husband depends, amongst other things, on her succeeding to establish that she did not know of his impotency at the time of her marriage. Hence, if she was aware of the husband's defect and in spite of this knowledge enters into the contract of marriage, she cannot raise the

51. Al-Nawavi; *Minhaj al-Ṭalibin*, pp. 299, 300 (Eng. tr. Van Den Berg) London, 1914. *Al-Fatāwā al-Hindiyah, op. cit.*, Vol. II, p. 133f., Ibn 'Abidīn *op cit.*, Vol. II, pp. 609, 10.

question afterwards and cannot claim the dissolution of her marriage.[52] She will be estopped from doing so. This is based on the principle of acquiescence. The husband's disability must continue till the final order of the Court. It was held in a case under the Divorce Act that a Court will be very unwilling to dissolve a marriage if it is proved even on the day of the final hearing that the husband has become potent.

Change in the Law: The provisions of Sunnī law regarding ignorance of the husband's incapacity has been changed by the provisions of the Dissolution of Muslim Marriages Act, 1939, and it is no longer necessary for the wife to prove that she was ignorant of the husband's condition at the time of the marriage. The provision that she has not waived her right has also been changed and omitted by the Act.

Shī'ī Laws: Under the Shī'ī law, a wife can claim the dissolution of her marriage when her husband is (1) impotent, (2) Khusee or without testicles or whose resticles have been crushed, (3) or majbūb or whose male organ has been castrated to such an extent that cohabitation be not possible.[53] But it is not an essential condition under Shī'ī law that the husband should be suffering from impotency at the time of the marriage. A wife can claim a separation even when the husband was potent at the time of the marriage but becomes afflicted with the defect subsequently.[54] This is of course subject to the condition that he has not in the meantime consummated the marriage. The Shī'ī law differs from the Hanafi law on certain points discussed below. But in other respects it is the same as the Hanafi law. In order to get the dissolution of her marriage on the ground of the impotency of her husband, under the Shī'ī law, a wife has to establish the following points :—

(*a*) That the husband has not been able tc consummate the marriage.

52. Ibn 'Ābidin, *op. cit.*, Vol. II, pp. 609, 10.
53. Ja'far b. al-Ḥasan, *op. cit.*, p. 190.
54. *Ibid.*

(*b*) That the husband has not been able to be intimate with any woman whosoever.

The Shī'ī jurists differ as to the wife's right to separation on account of her husband's impotency when he is impotent with regard to her, but not with regard to others.[55] One group of the Shī'ī jurist agrees with the Sunnī lawyers whilst the others disagree with them. The latter view is generally accepted as correct. As observed before, she shall be entitled to the dissolution of her marriage in India and Pakistan under the provisions of the Dissolution of Muslim Marriages Act, 1939. The option of cancellation must be exercised by the wife immediately she becomes aware of it under the Shī'ī law. If a woman comes to know of this defect of her husband but does not hasten to cancel it, the contract becomes binding on her.[56] This rule seems to be based on the principle of acquiescence. But this rule of the Shī'ī law must be considered to have been superseded in Pakistan and India by the Law of Limitation under which the husband's defect forms a continuing breach of the marital obligations.

Eunuchism

Castration: Castration is the loss of testicles, and includes in its meaning their actual destruction by mutilation. It is sufficient cause for cancellation of marriage when it has occurred before the contract of marriage. Should the husband become affected with khisa or jabb after the marriage the wife cannot get it dissolved under the Sunnī law as well as under the Shī'ī law.[57]

Procedure: If a wife wants a separation from her husband on ground that he is suffering from incapacity, she must move the *Qāḍī* for necessary action and he shall ask the husband if he admits the truth of the wife's assertion or if he wants to deny it on oath. If the husband admits the wife's

55. Ja'far b. al-Ḥasan, *op. cit.*, p 109.
56. *Ibid.*, p 191.
57. Burhān al-Dīn al-Marghīnānī, *op. cit.*, Vol. II, p. 397 ; Ibn 'Ābidīn, *op. cit.*, Vol. II, pp. 610-11, Ja'far b. al-Ḥasan, *op. cit.*, p. 191.

charge or refuses to or does not deny it on oath then in either case the *Qāḍī* shall by himself allow the husband one year's time for the cure of his defect. Under the provisions of Muslim law, it is the duty of the *Qāḍī* to allow such time to the husband even when he does not request for or even does not want it.[58] Should the husband deny on oath the wife's assertion, the *Qāḍī* shall get the wife examined by women to find if the marriage has been consummated. If it is established that the husband's denial is correct and that the marriage has been consummated, the *Qāḍī* shall dismiss the wife's claim. If, however, the wife's complaint is found to be correct, the *Qāḍī* shall himself grant one year's time to the husband to get himself cured. But no time shall be given to him if he is majbūb (castrated) for no useful purpose can be served by the grant of time.

If on the expiry of the time given to the husband, the wife should still allege that the marriage has not been consummated. the *Qāḍi* shall again require the husband to state on oath if he has or has not been able to consummate the marriage. If he admits his incapacity or refuses to take the required oath, the *Qāḍi* shall give the wife the option to live with or to separate from her husband.

If the husband denies on oath the wife's assertion, the *Qāḍi* shall again get the wife examined by women. If it is found that the marriage has been consummated, the wife's suit shall be dismissed. But if the examination supports the wife's version then too she shall be given a choice to be separated from her husband or not to do so.

When the *Qāḍi* gives an option to the wife to separate herself from her husband or to continue to live with him, she has to make her choice then and there, that is, in the sitting in which the option is given to her. If she fails to make her choice, she shall lose her right of separation from her husband.[59] If the wife chooses to get her marriage dissolved,

58. Burhān al-Dīn al-Marghīnānī, *op. cit.*, Vol. II, p. 397 ; Ibn 'Ābidīn, *op. cit.*, Vol. II, pp. 610-11, Ja'far b. al-Ḥasan, *op. cit.*, p. 191.
59. Ibn 'Ābidīn, *op. cit.*, Vol. II, pp. G. 11-612.

the *Qāḍi* is to order the husband to divorce her, and if he (the husband) neglects or refuses to do so, the *Qādi* himself is to pronounce the separation.[60]

This rule is explained in the following way. A husband is bound to follow the Qur'ānic injunction to, "Hold them (the wives) with kindness", but being unfit for intimacy he cannot perform his marital obligation and so cannot be considered to be keeping his wife with kindness. It is, therefore, his duty to release her from the marital tie. On his failure to do so he is guilty of an unjust act and it is the duty of a *Qāḍi* to redress a wrong and so the *Qāḍi* can redress the act of injustice by ordering the husband to divorce her and on his failure or refusal to do so, to himself pronounce a divorce on behalf of the husband.[61]

The Courts now-a-days, however, pronounce an order without giving the husband any chance of divorcing his wife.

The Sunnīs consider that it is in the absolute discretion of the husband to divorce his wife or not to do so. They rely on a verse in the Qur'ān wherein it is laid down that "...unless they forgo or he (the husband) forgoes in whose hand is the marriage tie.[62] The *Qāḍi* gets a right to dissolve the marriage only when the husband fails or refuses to comply with the *Qāḍi*'s order, but before then it is not open to the *Qāḍi* to do so and he has no right to dissolve the marriage. An annulment of the marriage by the *Qāḍī* before the issue of such an order or before the husband's failure or refusal to comply is considered to be without jurisdiction and illegal. It is submitted that the Legislature should amend the existing law and bring it in conformity with the Sunnī law in the case of Sunnīs. This can be done by passing a preliminary decree ordering the husband to divorce his wife within a few days, say one week, and then passing a final decree after the time

60. Ibn 'Ābidīn, *op. cit.*, Vol, II, p. 612.
61. *Ibid.*, pp. 611-12.
62. Qur'ān, II ; 237, Surah al-Baqarah.

so fixed. Under the Muslim law, the wife is given an option to separate from her husband or not to do so when her husband's incapacity is established, but at the present time the wife is not allowed an option to separate or not to do so after the case is finished. There seems to be no use in giving her such option when she has, after the expiry of one year, prosecuted her suit and produced evidence to prove that her husband has not been cured of impotency.

Shī'ī Law: The procedure to be observed under the *Shī'ī* law with regard to the husband's impotency is the same as the Sunnī law. The only points of difference are as given below :

1. Under the *Shī'ī* law, impotency is established only by the husband's admission or refusal to swear before the *Qāḍī* about his potency. The denial of impotency on oath by the husband shall be conclusive to destroy the wife's claim for separation. But according to the opinion of some jurists, the matter shall be investigated and decided on the result of the investigation. If the husband refuses to deny on oath the wife's accusation his denial shall not be accepred.[63]

2. If the husband is not cured of his weakness even during the prescribed period of one year, allowed to him under the *Shī'ī* law, it shall not be necessary for the wife to bring the matter again before the *Qāḍi*. It shall be open to her to cancel the marriage by herself.[64]

3. If the wife submits to her marriage after her husband's incapacity has been established as by asking him for maintenance, her right to the dissolution of her marriage shall be lost.[65]

Impotency, Determination of : As discussed before, a person may not be wholly lacking in sexual power and may be potent in respect of certain women and may not be able to have sexual

63. Ja'far b. al-Ḥasan, *op. cit.*, p. 191.
64. *Ibid.*
65. *Ibid.*, p. 171.

intercourse with a particular woman or women, Thus he may not be able to be intimate with his wife in which case he shall be deemed under the Sunnī law to be impotent with regard to her. This condition of the husband can be due to a number of causes some of which may have nothing to do with any structural defect or lack of sexual power but may be due to psychological causes. It will not be possible to determine from his general condition if he is or is not potent in respect of his wife because his general sexual capacity cannot be helpful in determining this fact. What, therefore, has to be seen is whether he has been able to consummate the marriage.

The husband's incapacity can arise under the Sunni law under the following circumstances:

(*a*) When he is absolutely unfit for cohabitation,

(*b*) When the husband is sexually fit in respect of his wife, but is unfit for other women, and

(*c*) When the husband is not absolutely unfit for women, but is alleged to be unfit for his wife alone.

(*a*) The first case, namely, when the husband is absolutely unfit for the coition presents no difficulty. The question of his capacity or incapacity can easily be ascertained by a medical examination.

(*b*) The fact that the husband is unfit for women other than the wife also does not present any difficulty because his obligation arises in respect of his wife alone who has no cause for complaint while the other women have no legal claim on him in the matter.

(*c*) If the husband is not absolutely unfit for women but is alleged to be incapable of intimacy in respect of his wife only, such a case can arise under the following two conditions, namely:

(*i*) When the wife is not a virgin as when she was a widow or a divorcee at the time of her marriage with the present husband and her former marriage had been consummated. It can also happen that she had not been married before but had lost the signs of her virginity due to some cause such as an accident or disease or when she had been raped by some man.

(*ii*) When the wife claims to be virgin.

(*i*) A great difficulty will be experienced when the wife does not claim to be virgin while the husband is not absolutely incapable for coition, but is alleged to be unfit only in respect of the wife. Neither the physical condition of the husband nor that of the wife can help in ascertaining whether the husband is potent or impotent with regard to the wife. There can be no circumstantial evidence to help in deciding the matter. Thus the fact that no children have been born of the marriage does not necessarily mean that the husband is impotent as this fact can be due to other causes as, for example, a defect in the wife herself or sterility of one of the spouses. Generally the birth of a child is considered a proof of the potency of the husband and the birth of a child establishes the fact that the husband is not suffering from incapacity. But the methods to determine the husband's capacity or incapacity as discussed later can be helpful in the matter.

(*ii*) If the wife claims to have been a virgin at the time of her marriage, it will be her physical condition and not that of the husband that will enable the determination of the husband's capacity or incapacity because he may be potent and yet for some reason or other he might not have been able to be intimate with the wife and so shall be deemed to be impotent with regard to her. The fact whether the marriage has or has not been consummated will establish his potency or impotency with regard to his wife and this fact can be determined by a medical examination of the wife and by the surrounding circumstances which may lead to a legal presumption of his impotency. It may be noted that the term virgin used here includes a widow or a divorcee when her first marriage had not been consummated.[66]

Test of Virginity. Muslim jurists have pointed out various methods to determine whether a woman is a virgin or not. Thus they have suggested that the wife should be asked to pass water in front of a wall. If the urine should fall on the wall, she will be considered to be a virgin, but if it does not fall on the wall, but flows down to the ground, she will not be considered to be a virgin. Another method suggested is to pour the yellow of an egg on the genital parts. If it gets in, she cannot be a virgin.[67] It is stated in *al-Fatāwā al-Hindiyah* that another test to determine the wife's virginity is to see if a hen's egg can be introduced in the vagina. If it can enter, she is not a virgin, but if it cannot, she should be considered to be a virgin.[68] Another method that has been suggested by some Muslim jurists to ascertain the husband's capacity or incapacity is to apply a certain coloured matter in the vagina and then after the husband's alleged cohabitation to see if the male organ has become dyed with it.[69]

A method that has been suggested to determine the husband's potency or impotency is to make him stand in cold water. If the male organ does not shrink, he will be presumed to be impotent, but if it does then he cannot be suffering from incapacity.[70] But this method applies in the case of Shi'ahs only who insist on absolute impotency and cannot hold good in case of Sunnīs who believe in relative capacity or incapacity. In modern times a useful method to determine this fact would be to have the discharge in the vagina

66. Sayed Amir Ali, *al-Fatāwā Alamgiriyah*, Urdu Tr. *al-Fatāwā al-Hindiyah*, Vol. II, p. 38, Lucknow 1899.
67. *Al-Fatāwā al-Hindiyah*, *op. cit.*, Vol. II, p. 133; Ibn 'Ābidin, *op. cit.*, Vol. II. p. 133; Ibn Ābidīn. *op. cit.*, Vol. II, p. 612.
68. *Al-Fatāwā al-Hindiyah*, *op. cit.*, Vol. II, p. 133.
69. Ja'far b. al-Ḥasan, *op. cit.*, p. 191.
70. *Ibid.*

examined the first thing in the morning after alleged act of intimacy to see if there are any spermatozoa, dead or alive, present there. Their presence or absence will establish if the husband has or has not been able to cohabit with his wife the previous night. The above two methods can be helpful when the wife is not a virgin. With the advancement of medical science better methods have been discovered and so the methods stated by Muslim jurists have lost their value. No hard and fast rules can, however, be laid down to determine the virginity of a wife. But, generally speaking, it may be said that if the hymen is intact and there is nothing to show that the physical condition of the hymen is of an abnormal character, very strong evidence will be needed to rebut the presumption that arises from this state of things against to the consummation of marriage by the husband in spite of the wife having lived with him for many years.[71] The inference of virginity becomes almost certain if the membrane is normal in position and structure, is unlacerated and its aperture is of small size and undilated and if accompanying this condition of hymen, the other signs of virginity are also present.[72] An intact hymen may be so elastic and stretchable as to have allowed coition without any recognisable sign of injury. A torn hymen may on the other hand be the result of accident or of the introduction of foreign body. But the existence of an apparently intact hymen is strong presumtive evidence of virginity while an obviously torn hymen is, in the absence of any proven history of interference, strongly suggestive of the reverse.[73]

Legal Presumption: Under Muslim law, the husband's impotency has to be proved as a fact. But under certain conditions a legal presumption is drawn by Courts that

71. Ibrahim Vs. Altafan, A I.R. 1925, All. 24.
72. Altafan Vs. Ibrahim, A.I.R. 1924, All. 116, 21, All. II, 75.
73. Ibrahim Vs. Altafan, A.I.R. 1925. All. 24; Altafan Vs. Ibrahim A.I.R. 1924. All. 116. G. Vs. M. (1885) 10 App. Cases 171; Lewis Vs. Hayward (1866) 35 L. J. (P. & M.) 105.

the husband is not potent. Thus if the husband and the wife have lived together for a long time in the same house under conditions when sexual intimacy was possible and it be established that the wife is still a virgin, though a fit subject for sexual intimacy, the Court may presume that the husband is incapable for coition at least with regard to the wife.[74] When the husband and the wife had lived together and occupied the same bed for five months and it was found that the marriage had not been consummated while medical evidence proved that there was no malformation or incapacity in the husband, yet a decree nisi was granted on the petition of the wife.[75] It has also been held in some English cases that where the marriage remains unconsummated while both the husband and the wife appear capable of consummation, the incapacity must be imputed to the man.[76] This will hold with still greater force to cases under Muslim law as the Muslim jurists do not attribute impotency to the wife in any case. If the Court is satisfied that a marriage has not been consummated although no impediment to consummation be apparent in the husband, the Court will be justified in dissolving the marriage.[77]

Medical Examination: The decision of a case involving impotency becomes difficult when it is contested and a spouse denies the allegation made by the other. In such a case medical examination of the spouses becomes very important. An examination of the spouses is provided under the provisions of Muslim law. A *Qāḍi* has got full right to order the examination of the spouses or of one of them.[78] It has not

74. Ibrahim Vs. Altafan. A.I.R. 1925. All. 24 ; Altafan Vs. Ibrahim A.I.R. 1924. All. 116. G. Vs. M. (1885) 10 App. Cases 171 ; Lewis Vs. Hayward (1866) 35 L. J. (P. & M.) 105.
75. F. Vs. P. (1896) 75 L.T. 192.
76. Pollard, Vs. Wybourn (1828) I Hagg. Ecc. 725 ; N-r Vs. M-e (1853) 2 Rob. Ecc. 625 ; Lewis Vs. Hayward (1866) 35 L. J. (P & M) 105.
77. Ranga Swami Vs. Arravind Ammal A.I.R. 1937, Mad.
78. Burhān al-Din al-Marghīnānī, *op. cit.*, Vol. II, p. 401 ; *al-Fatāwā al-Hindiyah. op. cit.*, Vol. II, p. 133.

been definitely stated by Muslim jurists as to what will be the consequences of a refusal to allow such examination by a spouse. But it can reasonably be presumed that the *Qāḍi* will be perfectly justified in drawing an inference against the party refusing medical examination and may decide the case against him or her. The Courts in India and Pakistan have wide discretion in ordering medical examination of the parties subject to such conditions as may be necessary in a particular case. It was held in some cases under the Divorce Act (applicable to Christians) and also uuder the Hindu law that on the refusal of a party to attend for medical examination, the Court may draw an unfavourable inference against the party guilty of refusal.[79] But a different view was taken in a later case when it was held that the mere refusal of the wife to have herself examined by a lady-doctor cannot be taken to be a proof of the consummation of her marriage.[80] The English Courts in some cases drew an inference against the spouse who had refused such an examination and presumed the spouse to be impotent.[81] But such refusal has not been held in other cases to be fatal to a case.[82] Under English law, mandatory orders for medical examination are still made in suits for nullity on the ground of incapacity while in the case of suits for nullity on the ground of the wife's refusal to the consummation of the marriage, medical inspection is permissible only.[83] The difference can be due to the fact that in suits for nullity on the ground of incapacity it is necessary to prove that at the time of the marriage the husband or the wife was incapable of consummating the

79. Brinda Kumar Viswas Vs. Hemlata Biswas A. L. R. 48 Cal. 283 ; Ranga swami Vs. Aravindammal A. I. R. 1937. Mad.

80. Ghulam Sakina Vs. Falak Sher. P.L.D. 1949. Lah. 75.

81. B. Vs. B. (1901). P. 39 ; W. Vs. S. (1905). P. 231; S Vs. S. (1908) 24. T.L.R. 253 ; W. Vs. W. (1912) P. 78.

82. S. Pakow Vs. Harrison (1841) 3 Curt 16, 27 Digest 270, 2383 ; T. Vs M. (1865) L R.I.P. & D. 31; E. Vs. E. (1902) 50 W.R. 607; B. Vs. B. (1901), P. 39 ; W. Vs. S. (1905), P. 231, W. Vs. W. (1912), P. 78 : T. Vs. M. (1865). L.R.I.P.D. 31.

83. Baxter Vs. Baxter (1947) 2 All. E. R. 886.

marriage with the other spouse whereas section 22 of the Matrimonial Causes Act, 1937 has introduced, as a ground of nullity, a cause necessarily arising after the marriage. Such examination may be dispensed with when there are other and sufficient materials available to decide a case.[84] Moreover, a husband alleging consummation must prove it as a fact on the consideration of the entire evidence in the case.

Opinions of Experts: The spouses often rely on a doctor's certificate to prove the capacity or incapacity of the other. Such a certificate must, however, be strictly proved by examining the doctor who has issued it so that it may be ascertained what test he has carried out and how has he arrived at his conclusion.[85] The opinion of doctors are relevant but not conclusive as to the matter to which they relate. When the experts differ the value and sufficiency of their value may legitimately form the subject of consideration and scrutiny even despite their acceptances by one Court or another.[86]

Birth of a Child to the Wife of a Husband alleged to be Impotent.

If a marriage is dissolved on the ground of the husband's impotency and should a child be born to the wife within the maximum period of gestation after the dissolution of the marriage, it shall belong to the husband who was alleged to be impotent and the order of annulment of the marriage shall become ineffectual, provided that the woman's adultery in the meantime has not been established and the husband affirms consummation of marriage.[87] This is also subject to the condition that the woman has not in the meantime contracted a second marriage with another person who could be the

84. Intract Vs. Intract (1933), P. 190.
85. Rangaswami Vs. Aravindammal, A.I.R, 1937, Mad. 237; Gonselves Vs. Iswariah, A.I.R. (1953), Mad. 858.
86. Altafan Vs. Ibrahim, 1924, All. 116
87. *Al-Fatāwā al-Hindiyah*, *op. cit.*, Vol. II, p. 134; Ibn 'Ābidīn, *op. cit.*, Vol. II. p. 610.

father of the child. If the husband who was found to be impotent is a majbub, that is, is lacking the male organ, a child born within the maximum period of gestation of the dissolution of the marriage shall belong to him, but the decree for the dissolution of the marriage shall hold good and the marriage shall remain dissolved.[88] This rule of law must be based on the Muslim jurists' abhorrence to cast stigma on a child and they state that it is possible that seminal discharge might have been the result of friction and might have entered the wife's body.[89]

If the marriage is dissolved on the ground of the husband's impotency and should a child be born to the wife after she contracted a second marriage, the question may arise as to which of the two persons is the father of the child. The matter shall be decided according to the provisions of the law of paternity.[90]

English Law: Under the English law children born to an impotent parent were considered to be bastards on the passing of a decree of annulment of the marriage. But section 7 of the Matrimonial Causes Act, 1952, has changed this position and it provides that such children shall remain legitimate regardless of any decree that may be passed annulling the marriage.

Capacity: The wife who seeks dissolution of her marriage on the ground of her husband's impotency should be sane and major.[91] If she happens to be a minor, the marriage shall not be dissolved till she becomes a major.[92] This rule is due to the Muslim jurists' desire not to dissolve a marriage as far as possible, and is justified on the ground that on becoming a major she may choose to submit to the marriage and to

88. *Al-Fatāwā al-Hindiyah*, *op. cit.*, Vol. II, p. 134 ; Ibn 'Ābidīn, *op. cit.*, Vol. II, p. 610.
89. *Ibid.*
90. See Chapter on *Nusūv* or Paternity.
91. Ibn 'Ābidīn, *op. cit.*, Vol. II, p. 609.
92. *Ibid.*

live with her husband in spite of his defect. The guardian of such a wife also cannot file a suit on her behalf for dissolution of the marriage on account of the husband's impotency.[93] If the wife happens to be insane, her guardian can apply on her behalf for dissolution of the marriage.[94]

Husband's Minority: If the husband of a woman is impotent as well as a minor, the wife shall not be entitled to get a decree for dissolution of her marriage till he becomes a major.[95] This rule seems to be based on the ground that it is possible that his defect may be cured when he becomes a major and becomes physically stronger. But should the minor husband be majbūb that is, without male organ, no time shall be given to her.

Marriage only Voidable : It has been observed before that satisfaction of passions and procreation of children are no doubt amongst the important objects of a marriage, but they are not the only objects. It is open to the husband and the wife to enter into matrimony for the sake of a happy companionship, domestic comforts and the like and there is nothing unlawful in such a contract of marriage. Hence, a marriage where a husband is impotent is not void. But, it is obvious that a wife cannot be forced to pass her life with such a husband and she has been given the right to get the marriage dissolved on the ground of the husband's incapacity. The marriage is therefore voidable. She has of course to establish the incapacity of her husband before the marriage can be dissolved.

Qāḍi's order : Under Muslim law, a marriage does not become dissolved simply on account of the husband's defect, but requires the decree of the *Qāḍi* for its dissolution. The Ḥanafī, Mālikī and the Hanbalī laws envisage two decrees. The first provides the grant of one year's time to the husband for the cure of his defect while the second and final decree is passed when the defect is not cured within the time allowed

93. *Al-Fatāwā al-Hindiyah, op. cit.*, Vol. II, p. 134.

94. Ibn 'Ābidīn, *op. cit.*, Vol. II, p. 609.

95. *Al-Fatāwā al-Hindiyah, op. cit.*, Vol. II, p. 134.

to him. The necessity for the first decree is admitted by all the Muslim jurists. The difference arises only in the case of the *Qāḍi's* second order after the expiry of the year of probation if the wife asserts that her husband has not become cured of his defect. Under the Hanafī, Mālikī and Hanbalī laws it is necessary to obtain the second order by the *Qāḍi.* But under the Shāfi'ī law, the *Qāḍi's* second order is not necessary according to some jurists if the husband admits his impotency on the expiry of the time given to him and the wife may in such a case herself dissolve the marriage. But according to some other jurists the *Qāḍi's* order shall be necessary in such a case also. This is borne out by the view expressed in *Minhaj et Talibin* as given on p. 300, English Tr. by L. W. C. Van Den Berg and E. C. Howard (London, 1914).

Shi'ī Law : Under Shī'ī law it is not necessary for a wife to ask the *Qāḍi* for a second order for the dissolution of her marriage on the expiry of the period allowed to the husband for his cure. She can herself cancel the marriage.[96] But it seems that these rules can apply when the spouses do not disagree about the continuation or removal of the defect. If the husband asserts that he no longer suffers from incapacity it may perhaps be necessary for the wife to seek the help of the *Qāḍi.*

Form of Decree: The decree that is passed in the first instance is more or less a decree *nisi.*[97] It is a conditional decree which becomes operative only on the failure of the prescribed conditions. It does not change the status of parties who continue to be husband and wife till the decree becomes final. The husband continues to be liable for the maintenance of the wife while a spouse can, on the death of the other, inherit to the deceased.

The Bombay High Court had, at one time, passed in such a case an interlocutory order adjourning the further

96. Ja'far b. al-Ḥasan, *op. cit.*, p. 191.
97. Mohd, Ibrahim Vs. Altafan, 47 All 283, A.I.R. 1925, All. 24.

hearing of the suit for one year.[98] But in a later case it was not considered a correct procedure to pass a decree and direct its suspension for one year.[99] It was stated in an other case that a Court should adjourn the proceeding for one year and on the expiry of that period pass a decree dissolving the marriage.[100] An order should be given to the wife to allow full access to her husband during the period of one year at all reasonable times to exercise his marital rights as her husband.[101] This accords with the spirit of the Muslim law under which the wife as long as she continues to hold that status, cannot refuse herself to her husband. The place where the wife has to live during this period of time is a question which has to be decided by the Court according to the peculiar circumstances of each particular case.

Nature of Separation: Under the Ḥanafī, Mālikī, and Ḥanbalī laws, the separation amounts to one irrevocable repudiation, whether pronounced by the husband or by the *Qāḍi* because, the act of the *Qāḍi* is attributed to the husband, hence it is the same thing as if he (the husband) has himself pronounced such a divorce,[102] The separation is held to amount to an irrevocable divorce because the object of it is the wife's relief from hardship, which cannot be effected but by a complete separation ; if it were not so, it would still remain in the husband's power to reverse it which would defeat the very object of the provision. Under the Shāfi'ī law the separation shall amount to *faskh* or an annulment of the marriage so that it shall not count towards a Mughallaza divorce.[103]

Shi'ī law : Under the Shi'ī law the separation shall not

98. A. Vs. B. I.L.R. 21 Bom. 77.
99. Fatima Vs. Jalal Din, A.I.R. 1930. Lahore, 501.
100. Mohd. Ibrahim Vs. Altafan, 47 All. 283, A.I.R. 1925, All. 24.
101. *Ibid.*
102. Ibn Qudamah, *Al-Mughnī*, Cairo, 1376, A.H. Vol. VI, p. 669 ; *al-Fatāwā al-Hindiyah*. op. cit., Vol, II, VI, p. 133.
103. Ibn Qudamah. *op. cit.*, Vol. VI, p. 669. Ibn Rushd, *Bidayat al-Mujtahid*, Cairo, n.d. Vol, II. p. 342.

amount to divorce, but to *faskh* or an annulment of the marriage.[104]

Time : The time that is allowed to the husband for the cure of his incapacity should be one year. It cannot be less nor more than that period of time.[105]

Amongst the Muslims, it is the lunar month that is ordinarily used to calculate time and it is stated in *al-Hedayah* that the year of probation fixed by the *Qāḍi* in the case of impotency is to be counted by the lunar calendar.[106] But *al-Fatāwā al-Hindiyah* has recommended the use of solar year by way of precaution.[107] This is the rule usually followed now.

Allowance of Time : An allowance is to be given to the husband when he cannot avail himself of the full time of one year, given to him, on account of reasons over which he has no control.[108] Thus an allowance is to be made for the time during which the wife was absent and such time is not to be reckoned against him, that is, such time shall not be included in the period of one year allowed to a husband.[109] If the husband or the wife should be in prison so that the other party is prevented from access to him or to her, then time will not be reckoned against him.[110] Similarly, the time during which the husband or the wife may be suffering from some serious illness which prevents cohabitation shall be excluded.[111] But no allowance is to be made for the time during which the husband is absent, for he is responsible for his own acts. The days of the wife's courses and of religious fasts such as the days of Ramaḍān and the time during which the husband is absent on any journey are to be taken as falling within the year.[112]

104. Ja'far b. al-Ḥasan, *op. cit.*, p. 191.
105. *Ibid.*, p. 191 ; Ibn 'Ābidīn, *op. cit.*, Vol. II, p. 610.
106. Burhān al-Dīn al-Marghīnānī, *loc. cit.*, Vol. II p. 401.
107. *Al-Fatāwā al-Hindiyah, op. cit.*, Vol. II, p. 133.
108. *Ibid.*
109. *Ibid.*
110. *Ibid.*
111. *Ibid.*
112. *Ibid.*

If a husband is guilty of *Ẓihār* and wants to expiate for its breach by fasting, he has to observe fasts for sixty days. In such a case the period of one year will be extended by the period of two months if he is not possessed of sufficient means to emancipate a slave.[113] This, however, applies only when it is not after the fixation of the period of one year by the Court that he is guilty of *Ẓihār*.[114]

It is not considered necessary to allow time to the husband under certain circumstance as stated below :

If the husband be a "*Majbūb*", that is, lacking male organ, the *Qāḍi* is to pronounce an immediate separation, where such is the woman's desire, because in this case the waiting for one year can be of no advantage. This rule of law is applicable irrespective of the fact as to whether the husband is major or a minor. If, however, he be only "*Khaṣṣī*" that is, without testicles, decision is to be deferred for one year, "because the yard still remains with which it is possible that he may perform the act."[115]

Extension of time : If the husband should ask the *Qāḍi* to grant him an extension of time, the *Qāḍi* is not competent to do so without the consent of the wife and even then she shall have the option to retract her consent whereupon the grant of extension of time shall be cancelled.[116] The Dissolution of Muslim Marriages Act, 1939, makes no provision for extension of time and so none can be allowed now to the husband.

Waiver : Muslim law does not recognise a waiver by the husband, that is, time shall be given to him even when he does not want it or refuses to have it.[117] The Lahore High Court has, however, held in a case that the condition as to

113. *Al-Fatāwā al-Hindiyah, op. cit.*, Vol. II, p. 133.
114. *Ibid.*
115. *Ibid.*, p. 134.
116. *Ibid.*, p. 133.
117. *Ibid.*

adjournment is imposed for the benefit of the husband and if he does not want to avail himself of it he can certainly waive the right and in such a case the condition of suspension of the Court's order will not be necessary and the marriage shall be dissolved forthwith.[118] The principle of law laid down in this ruling is against the rule of Muslim law mentioned above, but, it is submitted, more in accord with justice, equity and good conscience. It would be hard on the wife to make her wait for one year when the husband, for whose advantage the period of one year is granted, does not want it. If he considers that a grant of time is not necessary there is no reason why he should not waive this right. This difficulty cannot be experienced in India and Pakistan as time is granted to a husband under the provisions of the Dissolution of Muslim Marriages Act, 1939, only when he applies for it. But there is nothing to prevent a husband who does not want time to divorce his wife.

Effect of Impotency: Impotency of the husband can affect the following matters, namely :—

(*a*) Bar to remarriage.
(*b*) Dower and
(*c*) *'Iddah.*

(*a*) *Bar to Remarriage*: Separation on account of impotency creates no prohibition of remarriage and the parties can remarry each other again under a new contract of marriage either during or after the period of *'iddah* without the necessity of having an intermediary marriage.[119]

(*b*) *Dower*: According to Abū Ḥanīfah, the wife shall, on dissolution of her marriage, be entitled to her full dower if there has been valid retirement. If there has been no valid retirement then she shall

118. Badruddin Vs. Mst. Allah Rakhi, A.I.R. 1937, Lah. 383.

119. *Al-Fatāwā al-Hindiyah, op. cit*, Vol. II. p. 133 ; Ibn 'Ābidīn, *op. cit.*, Vol. II. p. 613.

get only half the dower.[120] Abu Yusuf and Muḥammad hold that if the husband be a majbub the wife shall get only half the dower irrespective of the fact as to whether there has or has not been a valid retirement.[121]

Māliki Law: Mālik does not allow any dower to the wife when there has been no consummation of the marriage.[122] Under the Māliki law a wife shall not be entitled to any dower if there has been no consummation of the marriage or even a valid retirement.

Ḥanbali Law: According to Aḥmad, b. Hanbal the husband shall be liable to pay the whole dower to the wife if there has been cohabitation or intimacy of any kind such as kissing, embracing etc. But if he did not get any such opportunity then he has to pay only half the dower.[123]

Shī'ī Law: Under the Shī'ī law the wife shall be entitled to get half the amount of her dower.[124]

(c) *'Iddah*: The wife shall on the dissolution of her marriage observe the same *'iddah* as is prescribed in the case of divorce if there has been a valid retirement. If there has been no valid retirement, *'iddah* shall not be incumbent on her.[125] No *'iddah* shall be necessary under the Shāfi'i law if the marriage has not been consummated.

Shī'ī Law: Under the Shī'ī law no *'iddah* shall be incumbent.[126]

Limitation: Under the Sunnī law, a wife is not bound to exercise her right immediately on becoming aware of the

120. Burhān al-Dīn al-Marghīnānī, *op. cit.*, Vol. II, p. 401 ; *Al-Fatāwā al-Hindiyah*, *op. cit.*, Vol. II, p. 133.
121. Al-Marghīnāni, *op. cit.*, Vol. II, p. 306.
122. 'Ibn Rushd, *Bidayat al-Mujtahid*, Cairo n.d. Vol. II, p. 19.
123. Ibn Qudamah, *op. cit*, Vol. II, p. 726.
124. Ja'far b. al-Ḥasan, *op. cit.*, p. 191.
125. *Al-Fatāwā al-Hindiyah*, *op. cit.*, Vol. II, p. 133.
126. Ja'far b. al-Ḥasan, *op. cit.*, p. 191.

defect in her husband. She can seek the dissolution of her marriage at any time she likes provided her right has not been lost in the meantime. Thus if the husband was suffering from incapacity at the time of the marriage and continues to suffer from it for a very long time the wife can even then seek her redress from the Court and she can do so whenever she likes and however long be the period of time that has elapsed since she became aware of her husband's defect.[127] But if the husband has managed in the meantime to consummate the marriage though only once the wife would lose her right.

Shī'ī Law : Under the Shi'i law the wife shall lose her right of separation if on becoming aware of her husband's impotency she delays in seeking for separation.[128]

Limitation Act : Under the present law, applicable in India and Pakistan, a person can seek a relief in respect of a continuing wrong at any time during its continuation and is not bound to seek his or her remedy at the earliest possible opportunity. In the case of marriage it is considered that the husband is bound to perform his marital obligations faithfully one of which is the satisfaction of passion. When he is impotent, he cannot perform his marital obligation in this important matter and so is guilty of a breach of his marital obligation. His duty in this respect extends throughout the marriage or in other words his incapacity amounts to a continuing wrong. The wife can, therefore, file a suit for the dissolution of her marriage at any time she likes. As the law of limitation applies to all Muslims in India and Pakistan, a Shī'ah wife shall be governed by the provisions of the law of limitation and so can seek her remedy whenever she so likes. Section 23 of the Limitation Act provides that in the case of a continuing breach of contract and in the case of a continuing wrong, independent of a contract, a fresh period of limitation begins to run at every moment of the time during which

127. Ibn Qudamah, *op. cit.*, Vol. II. p. 654 ; *Al-Fatāwā al-Hindiyah, op. cit.*, Vol. II, p. 133.

128. Ja'far b. al-Ḥasan, *op. cit.*, p. 191.

the breach of the contract or the wrong, as the case may be, continues. This section applies in the case of the impotency of a husband.[129]

English Law : Under the English law also, delay in filing a suit for termination of a marriage on the ground of impotency is not fatal to it. It has been held that once the impotency is established, the mere delay on the part of the petitioner will not disentitle him or her to relief.[130] Thus, in a case, a delay of 17 years was not allowed to stand in the way of a decree being passed.[131] In another later case a delay of twenty-seven years was not considered a bar to relief being granted to the wife.[132]

Burden of Proof : Malformation and structural defect is not a common thing. Hence there is a presumption of capacity in every case. But this presumption is rebuttable.[133] It was stated by the Calcutta High Court in a case that impotency as a slur on the husband must be strictly proved. Burden of proof is certainly on the petitioner (the wife) and all reasonable doubt must be removed before passing a decree.[134] Moreover, as a general rule, the burden of proving a certain thing lies on the person who asserts it. Hence, under Muslim law, it is for the wife to establish her allegation that her husband is suffering from incapacity. She has also to prove that he has not been cured of his defect within the time given to him by the Court for this purpose. But this aspect of Muslim law, namely, the burden of proof that the husband has not been cured within the time given to him has been changed in India and Pakistan by the provisions of the Dissolution of Muslim

129. Mst, Sahibzadi Vs. Abdul Ghafoor, A.I.R. 1939, Lah. 454 ; 185 I.c. 744 ; Ghizni Vs. Mst. Mehran (1879) 60 P. R. 1879 ; Binda Vs. Khusalia 13 All. 126: (1892) All. W.N. 18.

130, L. Vs. B. (1895), P. 274.

131. S. Vs. S. 21 (1905) 21 T,L.R. 219.

132. Clifford Vs. Clifford (1948) P. 187 ; (1948) I All. E,R. 304.

133. Hudston Vs. Hudston (1922) 39 T.L.R. 108 ; Kay Vs Kay (1936), P. 152.

134. Pratima Routh Vs, Hinday Banjan Routh, A.I.R. (1964) Cal, 474.

Marriages Act, 1939.[135] Under the Act it is for the husband to prove that he has been cured of his defect within the time given to him. Proviso (*c*) to clause of Section 2 states, "before passing decree on ground (V) (impotency of the husband), the Court shall on application by the husband make an order requiring the husband to satisfy the Court within a period of one year from the date of such order that he has ceased to be impotent, and if the husband so satisfies the Court within such period no decree shall be passed on the said ground."

It is obvious that the only proof that a wife can produce in such a case can consist of medical examination and the statements of the doctors who have made the examination. It may also consist of circumstantial evidence. Under the English law if the spouses have lived for a long time as man and wife in the same house under conditions when matrimonial intercourse was possible and yet the wife is found to be *virgo intacta et apta vire* i.e. a woman who is pure virgin though of a marriageable age or one who is a fit subject for consummation of marriage, a presumption arises against the husband and the onus is thrown on him to disprove the facts or to show by clear and satisfactory evidence that the result was due to a cause other than his impotency.[136] But the presumption is capable of being rebutted.

Under Muslim law as under English law, the bare statement of the wife is not, as a general rule, sufficient for the dissolution of her marriage. This rule is borne out by a provision of Muslim law that where a wife seeks separation from her husband on the ground of his incapacity and the husband denies the wife's charge then the *Qāḍi* shall have the wife examined to ascertain if she is a virgin or not. The statement of the wife supported by the medical evidence may suffice.[137]

135. See topic under the heading "Changes introduced by the Dissolution of Muslim Marriages Act, 1939."

136. N-r Vs M-e, (1853) 2 Rob. Ecc. 625.

137. *Al-Fatāwā al-Hindiyah, op. cit.*, Vol. II, p. 133.

Changes introduced by the Dissolution of Muslim Marriage Act (Act VII 1939):

The provisions of Muslim law tegarding impotency have been greatly modified by the provisions of Dissolution of Muslim Marriages Act (VIII of 1939) applicable in India and Pakistan. Clause V of Section 2 of the Act provides for the dissolution of a marriage under certain conditions. It reads as under :

(2) A woman married under Muslim law shall be entitled to obtain a decree for the dissolution of her marriage on any one or more of the following grounds, namely,

V. That the husband was impotent at the time of marriage and continues to be so, provided that

(C) Before passing a decree on ground V the Court shall, on application by the husband, make an order requiring the husband to satisfy the Court within a period of one year from the date of such order that he has ceased to be impotent and if the husband so satisfies the Court within such period, no decree shall be passed on the said ground.

It can be seen from the above that the section has introduced the following changes in the provisions of Muslim law:—

(*a*) It is no longer necessary that the wife should prove that she was ignorant of her husband's incapacity at the time of her marriage.

(*b*) It is no longer necessary for the wife to establish that she has not waived her right.

(*c*) The wife has not to approach the Court immediately on discovering the husband's defect as is necessary under the Shi'i law but she can bring a suit at any time.[138]

(*d*) Time shall be given to the husband for the cure of his defect only if he applies for it.

(*e*) The burden has been shifted on the husband to prove that he has been cured of his defect.

138. For more particulars please see discussion on Limitation.

Chapter 17

OTHER DEFECTS AND ABNORMALITIES

Besides the diseases discussed in the previous chapter, there are certain other infirmities which cannot be considered to amount to incapacity or defects, but they are more or less of a similar nature. It, therefore, seems desirable to consider them here. They can be due to natural causes as well as to artificial ones, but in either case they influence the act of coitus and affect the satisfaction or dissatisfaction of one of the spouses. There are some other matters which may contribute to the dissatisfaction of one of the spouses or which make penetration difficult but not impossible and so they do not form a ground for the dissolution of marriage. Some of the important ones are discussed below:

Over-indulgence and unreasonable abstinence: It has been observed before that one of the objects of marriage is lawful satisfaction of passions. It is the duty of the husband to satisfy this natural urge of the wife. If he fails to do so without a reasonble ground, he is guilty of a breach of this marital obligation. Stress is laid under Muslim law on this aspect of marriage to such an extent that if a man spends his nights in offering prayers and days in fasting so that he cannot be intimate with his wife then the *Qāḍī* can order him on a complaint by the wife to give up fasting and the prayers at night so that he may be in a position to pass some time and be intimate with her.[1] It is stated in *Radd al-Muḥtār* that a pious man can be ordered to be intimate with his wife now and then.[2]

It becomes necessary sometimes to determine whether the frequency of intimacy is reasonable or otherwise. Thus

1. *Al-Fatāwā al-Hindiyah*, Kanpur, 1349 A.H., Vol. II, p. 41.
2. Ibn 'Ābidīn, *Radd al-Muḥtār*, Cairo, 1318 A.H., Vol. II, p. 409.

a husband may be over-indulgent or may observe unreasonable abstinence. It was remarked in an American case that "the marital obligation includes not only the wife's duty of submission upon reasonable request of the husband but also the husband's duty of forbearance upon reasonable request of the wife."[3] The reasonable limit of intimacy differs in different countries, nations and individuals. It also depends on the constitution, health and age of a person, the culture and grade of society to which he belongs and also on his or her natural inclination. It is obvious that as a general rule no number of copulation or length of interval between two acts of intimacy can be fixed at which a husband can be or should be intimate with his wife. Each case has to be decided on its particular circumstances. But it may be stated that over-indulgence as well as unreasonable abstinence has to be avoided in all cases. The Muslim law stresses that there should be no inordinate demand for intimacy by the husband nor should he abstain to any unreasonable extent. Generally speaking, a husband cannot abstain from intimacy for four months unless the wife agrees to it.[4] This view is probably based on an incident that took place in the time of 'Umar, the Second Caliph. It is reported that while making a round of Madinah at night, as was his practice to do, he heard a woman singing a song the purport of which was that it was only the fear of God which restrained her from enjoying sexual intimacy with some one. The Caliph was greatly perturbed when he heard this and made a secret enquiry the next day about the woman. He found that her husband had been away on active service for a number of years. He then held a consultation to find the maximum period during which a wife can be expected to live without the company of her husband and this period was fixed at four months.[5]

3. Mayhew Vs. Mayhew, 61 Conn. 233.
4. Ibn 'Ābidīn, *op. cit.*, Vol. II, p. 409.
5. *Ibid.*

According to the other report of another case a woman told the Caliph that her husband spent his nights in prayers and days in fasting. Zayd ibn T̲h̲ābit explained to him that she was complaining against her husband. She wanted to convey the idea that her husband did not spare any time for her society. The Caliph directed Zayd to decide the case. The husband was called and Zayd told him to go to his wife twice a week.[6] There is, however, a great difference of opinion amongst the jurists in this matter. The difficulty probably arose from the fact that the jurists were men while they had to consider the feelings of the other sex. The extent of the difference of opinion can be seen from the great difference in the reasonable number of intimacy fixed by the various jurists. It is stated in *Radd al-Muḥtār* on the strength of *Fatḥ al-Qadīr* that abstinence for more than one week involves injury (hardship) unless it is so settled by consent of both the spouses.[7]

The Mālikī law lays down that a husband should be intimate with his wife eight times in a day and night. According to another version, the correct number is not eight but is four.[8] Anas b. Mālik, a Companion of the Prophet (peace be on him), has fixed the reasonable number of intimacy in a day and night at ten times while ibn Farḥū fixes it at twelve times.[9] Al-Ṭaḥāwī has fixed this number at twice a week.[10] Abū Hanīfah at one time expressed the opinion that a wife can claim sexual enjoyment of her husband once in a day and night in the week while a husband could be intimate with his wife as a matter of right three times a week.[11] But subsequently he changed this opinion and held

6. Mubarak-un-Nessa Begum Vs. Syed Ashraf Ahmad 22 Deccan Law Report, p. 555 on p. 572.
7. Ibn 'Ābidīn, *op. cit.*, Vol. II, p. 409.
8. *Ibid.*
9. *Ibid.*
10. *Ibid.*
11. *Al-Fatāwā al-Hindiyah, op. cit.*, Vol. II, p. 41.

that the husband should do his best to be reasonably intimate with his wife and to give her satisfaction and that it was not necessary for this purpose to fix any number of days or nights.[12] This view is generally accepted as the correct law.[13] A husband cannot indulge in cohabitation to such an extent as may injure the health of the wife.[14] Due regard must be taken of the condition, health and constitution of the wife. In case of disagreement about the extent of the husband's liberty with the wife, the case can be referred to the *Qāḍī* who shall decide it after taking into consideration her health and constitution.[15] Unreasonable abstinence is also not allowed. The law in this matter is so strict that if a person has two or more wives and does not pass sufficient time with one wife, the *Qāḍī* can order him to give more time to the aggrieved wife and in case of non-compliance with his order can punish the husband.[16] Neglect of this duty of his marital obligations constitutes a sin according to the Muslim Jurists.[17] There are no rules in Muslim law to govern a case where a wife refused to offer herself to her husband or made inordinate demand on him in this respect. The reason seems to be that such cases did not and do not occur in Muslim society probably because of great modesty of Muslim women in such respects and they would not ordinarily make such demands or seek a relief in this matter. But if such a case should arise, the husband can exercise his power of divorce. In exceptional cases the Court may dissolve the marriage under its inherent powers.

Shī'i Law: Under the *Shī'i* law, the wife can claim the society of her husband on one night out of four nights that is, twice a week while the husband can, as a matter of right,

12. *Al-Fatāwā al-Hindiyah*, *op. cit.*, Vol II, p. 41,
13. *Ibid.*
14. Ibn 'Ābidīn, *op. cit.*, Vol. II, p. 409.
15. *Ibid.*
16. *Ibid.*, 410.
17. *Al-Fatāwā al-Hindiyah*, *op. cit.*, Vol. II, p. 41.

claim the society of his wife on three nights out of four nights.[18]

English Law: It was stated in an English case that where a spouse persists in making sexual demands which are known to be regarded by the other spouse as inordinate or revolting, such persistent lack of consideration may amount to a course of conduct so grave and weighty as to justify the other spouse from withdrawing from cohabitation and there must arise a point of time at which persistent lack of consideration in matters of this sort may amount to a course of conduct to cause injury or to affect the health of the other spouse or to lead to a reasonable apprehension of such injury. There is the greatest diversity of standard between one pair of spouses and another as to what is or is not a normal standrad of sexual intercourse. What will be regarded as grossly excessive demand by one spouse will be regarded as quite normal and reasonable by another wife or husband.[19] In this case the wife's grievance was that her husband was after her day and night, at all times and all seasons demanding sexual intercourse somtimes even as much as five times in the night. The Court referred to a passage in Jackson Vs. Jackson wherein it is stated, "Is it right to say that the conditions imposed on the wife were unreasonable for her or any other wife—conditions which it was not competent for a reasonable husband to set up? Were they such conditions that a reasonable wife being so treated by an unreasonable husband, they could not be expected to proceed with the conjugal life.[20] The Court then found that such persistence in sexual demands may amount to a course of conduct so grave and weighty as to justify the other spouse in withdrawing from cohabitation.[21]

American Law: In some States in U.S.A. as Connecticut,

18. Ja'far b. al-Ḥasan, Sharā'i' *al-Islām*, Tehran, 1377 A.H., p. 197.
19. Holborn Vs. Holborn (1947) 2 All. E.R. 32.
20. Jackson Vs. Jackson (1932) 146, L.T. 406.
21. *Ibid.*

Minnesotta, Oklahoma, excessive indulgence in cohabitation by the husband has been considered to amount to cruelty where the wife's health suffered on that account.[22] But the injury to the wife's health is an essential condition of cruelty so that no divorce can be granted on the ground of excess when the wife's health is neither injured nor there is a danger of such injury.[23] It was stated in an American case, "Humanity demands that such complaints be heard. The wife protecting her life from ungoverned lust of her husband by seeking a divorce, presents as strong a case of relief under the law as when she flees from his intolerable cruelty inflicted by brute force.[24] The Court further remarked, if the wife's health is impaired by the husband's act then there is no difference whether it is done dy brutal gratification of his lustful passions, the continued affliction of physical force, or the administering of slow poison.

It is clear from the above discussion of Muslim and other laws that it cannot be possible to give even a reasonable idea of the frequency of coition because it differs considerably with different nations and in the same nation with different individuals. A young friend attributed his run down condition to over-indulgence and told me that sometimes he indulged in sexual intimacy. to such an extent as to be intimate with his wife once a month and he had indulged in the excess for two or even three consecutive months. Another friend happened to tell me that once there was an argument between him and a girl as to who could carry on longer. They carried on, though with increasing difficulty, for four times and after the fifth act of coitus they got so exhausted that they gave up all teasing, turned their backs towards each other and went to sleep. An English lady once complained to me

22. Mayhew Vs. Mayhew 61 Conn. 233 ; Hines Vs. Hines 192 Iowa 569 ; Grant Vs. Grant 53 Minn. 181 ; Hildebrand Vs. Hildebrand 41 Okla. 306.

23. Mayhew Vs. Mayhew 61 Conn. 233 ; Youngs Vs. Youngs 33 Ill. App. 223.

24. Melvin Vs. Melvin 58 N.H. 569, 42 Ams. Rep. 605.

against her husband and said that day in and day out he was after her and wanted the use of her body at all unearthly hours. She gave five times as his usual number of sexual intimacy in one night. I have been told that husbands in the U.S.A. sometimes are intimate with their wives as many as seven times in a night, while in certain English cases, quoted above, the wife found indulgence in intimacy five times a night to be unreasonable. This shows the great divergence in the frequency of coitus. E. Bergler says, "Common experience shows that when intercourse is practised regularly the sexual act is performed once or twice a week."[25]

Harper has quoted a report which has given the frequency of coitus reported in 526 cases as under :—

Frequency.		*Per cent.*
Daily or oftener	..	16
Two or three times a week	..	24
Once or twice a week	..	20
Once a week or ten days	..	17
Fortnightly or monthly	..	10
Once in two to six months	..	2
Less than once a year	..	11

Wilful refusal to cohabit: A person who is not incapable for intimacy and yet refuses to or wilfully abstains from cohabitation cannot be considered to be impotent under the provisions of Muslim law, because impotency is restricted to physical disability only. Under the Muslim law the matter has to be considered differently in respect of wife and husband.

The words "wilful refusal to cohabit" have not been defined or explained by the Muslim jurists and must be taken to have been used in their ordinary sense. The words used in the Matrimonial Causes Act, 1950 are "Wilful refusal to consummate" which convey almost the same sense. The English law also has not defined the expression, but it has

25. Edmund Berglar, *Unhappy Marriage and Divorce*, p. 75, New York, 1947.

been well explained in an English case wherein it is stated that the words do not mean temporary unwillingness due to a passing phase, or the result of coyness, a feeling of delicacy affected or real, or a nervous ignorance, which may be got rid of by patient forbearance, care and kindness, but a determined and steadfast refusal to perform the obligations and to carry out the duties which the matrimonial contract involves.[26]

Husband: In the case of a husband it is to be seen if his conduct in abstaining from sexual intimacy with the wife is with or without justification. Cohabitation is well understood to be an implied condition in every marriage because satisfaction of passions is one of the most important ends of marriage. If the husband wilfully abstains from intimacy without any reasonable cause, it is conceived that he has committed a sin.[27] He shall be transgressor of the sacred text in the Qur'ān where the husbands have been enjoined to keep (the wives) with kindness.[28] And it is also stated that "women have rights similar to those against them in a just manner."[29]

The Muslim law allows a husband to give up matrimonial connection with his wife if she is disobedient to him or has been guilty of immorality.[30] Another ground can be the illness of the husband. But both of them must have a limit and abstinence cannot be persisted for an indefinite period of time. As observed before, it is not lawful for a husband to abstain from sexual intimacy with the wife for a period longer than four months.[31]

The *Qāḍī* can order a husband to perform his marital obligations in this respect and on his failure to comply, the *Qāḍī* may dissolve the marriage as the husband is a transgressor

26. Dickenson Vs. Dickenson (1913), P. 198.
27. Ibn 'Ābidīn, *op. cit.*, Vol. II, p. 409.
28. Qur'ān, II; 229. Surah al-Baqarah.
29. Qur'an, II: 228. Surah al-Baqarah
30. Qur'ān, IV; 34 Surah al-Nisa.
31. Ibn 'Ābidīn, *op. cit.*, Vol. II, p. 409.

of these injunctions in the Qur'ān. The wife may also claim a divorce on the ground of cruelty because the husband's conduct can amount to it. In India and Pakistan, there is a definite provision to meet such a case. Clause IV of section 2 of the Dissolution of Muslim Marriages Act, 1939 provides that a marriage may be dissolved on the ground that the husband has failed to perform his marital obligations without a reasonable cause for a period of three years. But if he pleads that his conduct is based on a reasonable cause then the question shall arise as to what can be considered a reasonable cause for abstinence.

Men have adopted a very curious though absolutely unjustifiable attitude in the matter. It is obviously done for their own advantage. They consider that morality demands that a respectable and decent woman should have no sexual feelings and she should be ashamed of exhibiting the same, should assume an absolutely passive attitude in the matter. She will be considered a shameless if not an immoral woman, if she by the least signs shows any genital or sexual feelings. But the assumption of this superior attitude cannot change human nature and the repression of such feelings can in no way diminish the wife's dissatisfaction and unhappiness and even disgust for her husband. It is unfortunate that the husbands do not realise this fact which is often the root cause of the failure of so many marriages.

Wife: A wife cannot refuse to offer herself without a reasonable cause and the Prophet (peace be on him) has strongly condemned such a conduct.[32]

This injunction is obviously meant to provide against immorality as the husband being deprived of sexual pleasure in a lawful manner may seek relaxation by unlawful means.

The question arises if this refusal can entitle the husband to get the marriage dissolved through *Qāḍī* or does the

32. Walī al-Dīn al-Khaṭīb, *Mishkāt al-Maṣābīh*, Delhi, 1350 A.H., pp. 280-81.

refusal amount only to a moral offence. The reply depends on the fact as to whether the wife's refusal is based on a reasonable ground or not. In the former case no blame shall attach to her while in the latter case she will be considered to be disobedient and so liable to some penalty. The Muslim jurists hold that a wife cannot be considered to be disobedient if she refuses herself to her husband for some reasonable cause such as tender age, illness or when her husband had not paid her prompt dower.[33] It is stated in *Radd al-Muḥtār* that a wife shall not be considered disobedient on her refusal to submit to her husband if she is living with him at his house. This view has been justified on the ground that every bride is reluctant to submit herself to the husband on account of her coyness and is usually an unwilling party and yet the marriage is not dissolved on that ground. The bride requires some persuasion and some pressure before intimacy is possible with her so that the reluctance or unwillingness of a wife shall not amount to disobedience.[34]

It, therefore, appears that such conduct of the wife shall amount to a moral offence only and the marriage shall not be dissolved on this ground. But if the wife refuses to give any opportunity for intimacy to the husband without any reasonable cause so that he is left without any means for lawful relaxation then a difficulty may arise. The Hanafis do not allow the dissolution of a marriage when the wife suffers from a defect which does not allow intimacy and on this analogy it can be inferred that the husband cannot get his marriage dissolved in this case also. The other sects of the Sunnīs as well as the Shī'ahs allow the dissolution of a marriage when intimacy is not possible due to a defect in the wife and so they may allow a divorce in this case also.

English Law: Under the English law wilful refusal to consummate the marriage was not at one time a ground for its annulment. But section 8 of the Matrimonial Causes Act,

33. Ibn 'Abidīn, *op. cit.*, Vol. II, p. 663.
34. *Ibid.*

1950, makes a marriage voidable on this ground so that the aggrieved party can seek the dissolution of his or her marriage when the other refuses to consummate it or to allow its consummation. The English law attributes incapacity to the spouse who refuses to consummate the marriage and the refusal is regarded as evidence of impotency. It grants relief to the other spouse, whether it be the husband or the wife who is guilty of wilful refusal, by dissolving the marriage.[35] The spouse may not be suffering from any physical incapacity, but the husband or the wife may refuse to consummate the marriage because he or she has a repugnance for the other spouse or for the physical act or because he or she is hyper ; sensitive. The Matrimonial Causes Act of 1937 gives a right to a wife or a husband to a decree of nullity of marriage on the basis that, quite apart from capacity, the other spouse has refused to consummate the marriage.

The Use of Contraceptives: The Muslim jurists have given considerable attention to the question of the use of contraceptives whether internal or external. But they have expressed different opinions in the matter. They, as a rule, accept the view that in the absence of a definite injunction in the Qur'ān or the Traditions, it is open to the Muslims to adopt such rule of law as may be suitable to the needs of the time. They discuss the matter taking into consideration the following aspects:

(*a*) Whether the child born of the marriage belongs only to the father,

(*b*) Whether the child belongs both to the father and the mother, and

(*c*) Whether the State has also a claim on the child.

The above aspects are briefly discussed below:

(*a*) The jurists who consider that the child belongs to the father hold that it is open to him to have or not to have a child. It means, in other words, that in their

35. Section 8 (1) (*b*) of the Matrimonial Causes Act (1950).

opinion the husband has the right to practise birth control if he so wishes or refuse to do so even against the wishes of the wife.

(*b*) The jurists who hold that the child belongs to both the spouses naturally hold that one spouse cannot resort to birth control without the consent of the other.

(*c*) There are jurists who consider that the State has also a claim on a child, even though they admit that the parents have a greater claim on the child than does the State. They presume that the parents as a rule do not possess the right to prevent birth of a child to the detriment of the State except under exceptional circumstances. They discuss the matter from two angles namely,

(*i*) Numerical strength of the nation and

(*ii*) The birth of healthy and strong children.

It is important to note that every State is interested to increase its number. But the fact should not be ignored that it is also necessary in the interest of the State that the children which may be born should be healthy and strong.[36]

The use of rubber-sheaths or other contraceptives cannot be considered to make coition incomplete so as to form a ground for the dissolution of marriage on the basis that the coitus is not normal. It is stated in *al-Fatāwā al-Hindiyah* that if a man does not get seminal discharge during the course of coition but is otherwise able for coition, the wife shall not have a right to the dissolution of her marriage on the basis of this weakness.[37] It means that the flow of semen in the wife's body is not an essential condition of coitus in Muslim law. Hence the use of contraceptives cannot form a ground for the dissolution of a marriage under that law.

As observed before, the procreation of children is one of

36. Cf. Shaltūt, *Tanzim Nasl, Fikr-u-Nazar,* Vol. I, No. 1, July, August, 1963, pp. 35-64.

37. *Al-Fatāwā al-Hindiyah, op. cit.*, Vol, II, p. 134.

the important objects, but is not the sole object of a marriage and so the failure to achieve this object does not amount to a failure of the marriage. But there is no case-law on the subject. If a husband is anxious to have children but the wife is opposed to it and does not allow it then he can exercise his wide power of divorce. The difficulty will arise when the case is the reverse, that is, when the wife is anxious to have children but the husband is averse to it. There is no doubt the Prophet (peace be on him) has stressed the begetting of children, but it is doubtful if the husband's act can entitle the wife to the dissolution of her marriage under the Muslim law. Her only ground can be cruelty of conduct by the husband which materially affects her happiness and makes her life miserable.

It may be added here that the use of contraceptives in whatever form is allowed by law and it is only abortion which is considered an illegal act. In the former, foetus is prevented from coming into existence while in the latter foetus is destroyed after it has come into existence and this is considered illegal.

English Law: It was the view of English law at one time that the use of contraceptives was not permissible and that sexual intercourse cannot be regarded as complete when its natural termination is either artificially prevented or deliberately discontinued.[38] In the case before the Court, the husband at first used contraceptives and subsequently resorted to coitus interruptus. The Court dissolved the marriage on the wife's complaint. But it was held in a later case that the use of contraceptives does not prevent the sexual act from amounting to consummation if it is otherwise normal and complete.[39] It has been pointed out that under the English law *vera copula* or normal coition consists of erection (erectio) and intromissio (introduction). The use of contraceptives does not prevent either of those. Hence a marriage cannot be

38. Baxter Vs. Baxter (1947) 2 All. E.R. 886.
39. G. Vs. G. (1924) A.C 349; White Vs. White (1948).

dissolved simply because the husband or the wife is averse to have children and adopts the use of contraceptives. But in a still later case the husband practised coitus interruptus against the wishes of the wife who was anxious to have a child. It was held by the Court that this conduct of the husband amounted to cruelty and the marriage was dissolved on that ground.[40]

Coitus Interruptus: '*Azl* or coitus interruptus consists of withdrawal by the husband before ejaculation occurs, so that no seminal fluid is deposited in the vagina and thus to prevent insemination of the womb. It is intended to serve as a check against birth of a child. The husbands must remember that this method is not always effective since some seminal fluid may escape before the main ejaculation and many men do in fact have a small emission of semen from which conception may take place before the main emission that follows on the completion of the act.[41] Hence when conception takes place in spite of a husband's practice of coitus interruptus, he should not jump to the conclusion that the wife has not been faithful to him. The method also interferes with the attainment of complete orgasm especially for the wife. It was prevalent amongst the Arabs. It seems that it was allowed in case of urgency but was never encouraged. The jurists who hold that '*azl* is permissible base their view on the ground that the wife has an absolute right to sexual pleasure and not to the discharge of the seminal fluid. But it cannot be denied that sometimes the wife does remain unsatisfied in '*azl* and may not only resent her husband's practice, but may feel disgusted with it and a stage may be reached when her health may get impaired as a result of this practice. In such a case '*azl* cannot be permitted. Indulgence of this practice by a husband against the wishes of his wife particularly when the wife's health suffers on that account may constitute cruelty of conduct.

There is a difference of opinion amongst the Muslim Jurists about the validity of the practice of '*azl* or coitus

40. Fowler Vs. Fowler (1952) 2 T.L.R. 143,
41. White Vs. White (1948) 2 All. E.R. 115.

interruptus. Abū Ḥanifah holds that it is not permssible except with the permission of the wife.[42] Mālik also holds that a husband can have recourse to it but only with the consent of the wife.[43] Ibn Qayyim also considers it permissible on the basis of some Traditions. It is reported by Jābir that they (the Companions) used to practise *'azl* in the time of the Prophet (peace be on him) and when he was informed, he did not forbid them.[44] According to another version, Jābir reported that they practised *'azl* while God's Messenger (peace be on him) was alive and the Qur'ān was being revealed. Both *Musnad* of Aḥmad and the *Sunan* of *ibn Majāh* have given a report from Umar b. al-Khattab that the Prophet (peace be on him) forbade us, the Companions, to practise *'azl* without the wife's consent.[45] Ghazzali has stated that *'azl* is an omission to follow counsel of perfection, but there is no commission of the forbidden, that is, *azl* is not desirable but at the same time it is not forbidden because there is no prohibition in the text (of the Quran) or reasoned analogy from the text. According to him a child is conceived by the arrival of the sperm in the womb, and this happens in four stages; namely,

(*i*) Marriage,
(*ii*) Copulation,
(*iii*) Seminal discharge, and
(*iv*) Lodgement of the sperm in the womb.

Existence (life) begins when the sperm reaches the womb, and mixes with the woman's fluid and develops the capacity to receive life. *'Azl* is not like abortion or infanticide, which are against an existing being and to destroy this, namely, fertilized ovum, would amount to an unjust act. He expressed the opinion that the validity or invalidity of *'azl* depends on the motive with which it is practised. He concludes that *'azl*

42. *Al-Hedayah, Akhrin,* Vol. IV, p. 448; Delhi, 1940 A.D.
43. Mālik, *al-Muwatta'*, Cairo, 1951, Vol. II, p. 596.
44. Ibn Qayyim, *Dad al-Ma'ad,* Cairo (1324), A.H., Vol. II, p. 221.
45. Walī al-Dīn al-Khaṭīb *Mishkat, op cit.*, p 276.

is not prohibited when it is practised to (1) preserve the wife's beauty and vitality and to protect her life from the risk of childbirth, (2) to save a man from additional numerous anxieties when he has already a large number of children and is anxious not to add to his anxieties by the addition of another child. But if the motive for the exercise of *'azl* is to avoid the birth of a daughter or because the wife wants to avoid the travails of childbirth and suckling or on account of exaggerated cleanliness then the exercise of *'azl* would not be permissible.[46] The people who express the opinion that *'azl* is permissible also base their opinion on the ground that the women have an undeniable right to sexual intimacy but not to seminal discharge.

Shī'i Law: According to one opinion of *Shī'i* jurists, the practice of coitus-interruptus is unlawful unless it has been agreed upon between the parties at the time of the marriage or the wife agrees to it, but the generally accepted view is that the practice of coitus-interruptus is only disapproved of which means that it is not forbidden or unlawful.[47] The *Shī'i* jurists make it incumbent on the husband to compensate the wife if he indulges in this practice. The amount of the compensation is fixed at 10 dinars.[48]

English Law: The question of coitus-interruptus has been considered in a number of cases by English Courts. In one case the husband at first used contraceptives and then subsequently resorted to coitus-interruptus. It was held on a petition by the wife that sexual intercourse cannot be regarded as complete when its natural termination is either artificially prevented or deliberately discontinued.[49] The matter has been considered in a number of other cases and may conveniently be discussed with regard to two point:

46. Al-Ghazzāli, *Iḥyā' al-'ulūm al-Dīn*, Cairo, 1358 A.H., Vol. II, pp. 52-54. Cf. Shaltūt, *Tanzim Nasl, Fikr-u-Nazar*, Vol. I, No. 1, July-Aug. 1963, pp. 35-64.
47. Ja'far b. al-Ḥasan, *op. cit.*, p. 171.
48. *Ibid.*
49. Baxter Vs. Baxter; (1948), 2 All. E.R. 886.

(*a*) Whether ejaculation or emission is a necessary requirement of *vera copula* and

(*b*) Whether coitus-interruptus amounts to cruelty.

As regards the first aspect, the Courts are divided on the subject. It has been remarked in some cases that imperfect and unnatural coitus does not amount to consummation.[50] Following this view, it was held in a case that coitus-interruptus does not amount to full and natural intercourse.[51] The view was expressed in a case that even in coitus-interruptus there is a minor preliminary emission which might lead to the birth of a child. It was remarked that it was a curious position that which might very well produce a child or children should at the same time be a reason for obtaining a decree of nullity on the ground of non-consummation.[52] In a still later case the Court preferred to follow the view expressed in White Vs. White rather than Grimes Vs. Grimes on the ground that it is not possible to define what amounts to normal sexual intercourse. The Court observed that it would be driven into an impossible position if it tried to define what amounted to normal sexual intercourse for where a woman alleged that the man had failed to complete the sexual intercourse, the Court would have to enquire exactly at what stage emission took place or what degree of satisfaction was reached by the woman and that it is difficult to draw the line between a complete act and an incomplete act.[53]

(*b*) The insistence on the practice of coitus-interruptus may make a normal married life of one of the spouses impossible.[54] The practice may result in serious injury to

50. Grimes Vs. Grimes ; (1948) 2 All. E.R. 147 ; Snowman Vs. Snowman, 1934. P. 186.
51. *Ibid.*
52. White Vs. White ; (1948) 2 All. E.R. 151.
53. Cackett Vs. Cackett (1950) 1 All. E.R. 677.
54. Rice Vs. Rice Raynold-Spring-Rice (1948) 1 All. E.R. 188 ; White Vs. White (1948) ; 2 All. E.R. 151. Cackett Vs. Cackett (1950) 1 All. E.R. 677.

the health of the wife or the husband in some if not in all cases. In the former case it shall amount to cruelty, but not in the latter case.[55]

In a recent case a third aspect, namely, wife's desire to have a child was considered and it was emphasised that the conduct of a husband who deliberately and without good reason permanently denies his wife, having a normally developed maternal instinct, a fair opportunity of having even a single child is, in itself, cruelty and that permanent and unreasonable starvation of the maternal instinct may be of itself a cruel thing.[56] But a different view had been expressed in White Vs. White when it was pointed out that even in coitus-interruptus there is a minor preliminary discharge which might lead to conception.[57]

Sterility: Impotency must not be confused with sterility, that is, incapacity to procreate children. A person shall not be considered to be impotent merely because he or she is unable to procreate children. This is clear from the rule laid down in *al-Fatāwā al-Hindiyah* that a woman shall not have any right to the dissolution of her marriage if the husband does not have any seminary discharge, but is otherwise able for coition. A husband is deemed potent under Muslim law if he can penetrate the wife's body and so the fact that he is sterile cannot render him impotent under the provisions of Muslim law. No doubt that marriage with a sterile woman has not been approved of. Thus there is a Tradition that a person consulted the Prophet (peace be on him) whether he should marry a certain woman who was beautiful and of a respectable family but was sterile. The Prophet (peace be on him) told him not to marry that woman but to marry a woman who was of affectionate temperament and was not barren.[58] But marriage with such a woman is perfectly valid and this condition of the wife does not come within

55. Walsham Vs. Walsham (1949) All. E.R. 774.
56. Knott. Vs. Knott (1955) 2 All. E.R. 305.
57. White Vs. White (1948) 2 All. E.R. 151.
58. Al-Nasa'iy, *Sunan*, Delhi, 1335 A.H., Vol, II, p. 70.

the defects on the basis of which a marriage can be dissolved by the *Qāḍī*.

English Law: The English law is the same as the Muslim law with regard to sterility. Under the English law, the inability of the wife to become a mother or the husband to procreate children is not a ground for the dissolution of a marriage.[59]

Before 1937 the question whether the emission of semen into the body of the wife was necessary in order to constitute such complete penetration as would amount to a consummation of the marriage could arise only if on account of the husband's organs of generation such emission was rendered impossible. But sterility in man or woman has never been a ground for dissolving a marriage.[60] Where the husband was able to obtain an erection and to penetrate his wife, but during the conjunction of their bodies, he was unable to ejaculate, it was held that the marriage had been consummated by the erection and intromissio, although at no time there was any orgasm on the part of the wife. It was remarked that the general end of the institution of marriage is the solace and satisfaction of man, which can be achieved even when the husband is sterile.[61] It was held in White Vs. White that true conjunction is achieved as soon as full entry and penetration has been achieved; what follows goes merely to the likelihood or otherwise of conception.[62] But conception is not the principal end of marriage.[63]

Law in the U.S.A.: Under the law in the U.S.A. sterility is not a ground for the dissolution of marriage.[64] This rule

59, B-n Vs. B-n (1854) 1 Ecc. and Ad. 248; L. Vs. L, (1922) 36 T.L.R. 697; R. Vs. R. (1925) 1 All. E.R. 94; D-e Vs. A-g (1845) 1 Rob. Ecc. L, 279.

60. Baxter Vs. Baxter (1947) 2 All. E.R. 886.

61. R. Vs. R. (1952) 1 All. E.R. 1194.

62. White Vs. White (1948), 2 All. E.R. 151.

63. Baxter Vs. Baxter (1947) 1 All. E.R. 387 affirmed in (1947) 2 All. E.R. 886.

64. J. G, Vs. H. G. 33 Md. 401; Payne Vs. Payne, 46 Minn 467; Smith Vs. Smith 206 Mo. App. 646.

is based on the ground that an essential condition of impotency is the absolute lack of power of cohabitation.

Concealment of Sterility in Muslim Law: The concealment of the fact that the wife cannot bear children, even when it is intentional, cannot entitle a husband to the dissolution of his marriage through a *Qāḍī* because marriage with such a woman is valid.

English Law: The concealment of the fact that a woman is barren or the man is incapable of reproduction is not a ground for dissolution of marriage.

Law in U.S.A.: Sterility is not a ground for dissolution of marriage in the U.S.A.[65] But concealment by the wife from her husband of the fact that she is incapable of bearing children may be a ground for a decree of nullity of the marriage. Thus, where a wife failed to disclose to her husband the fact that she was sterile and could not bear children, it was stated by the Court that the concealment was a fraud in the contract of the marriage affecting an essential purpose of the marriage-relation, namely, the procreation of children which is the most important object of matrimony for without it the human race itself would perish. The marriage was dissolved on the petition of the husband on the ground of fraud.[66]

Artificial insemination: If a wife is inseminated by the husband's seed and gives birth to a child, the conception or birth of the child does not constitute approbation of the marriage. As observed before, penetration, even though partial, is an essential condition of consummation of marriage under the Muslim law. A person who is unable even for partial penetration in respect of his wife shall be considered impotent with regard to her. This is also the view of the English law.[67] It must be remembered that under the English law, coition means sexual connection in the ordinary and

65. Smith Vs. Smith, 206, Mo. App, 646,
66. Turney Vs. Avery, 92 N.J. Eq. 473.
67, L. Vs. L. (1949) 1 All. E.R. 141.

usual way. It will not amount to consummation of marriage if the wife becomes pregnant in some unusual way. Thus in a case the wife had become pregnant by artificial semination with the husband's seed, it was argued that it was a voluntary act of the wife that led to conception and so the marriage should be treated as approbated. The Court did not accept this plea and remarked, "It would be shutting one's eyes to realities to expect the marriage with its background of failure and neurosis to have become an effective marriage."[68]

(*b*) *Kraurosis*: It is the shrivelling and dryness of vulva which generally appears in women in old age. Penetration becomes difficult on account of this condition, but not impossible. It cannot, therefore, be a ground for dissolution of marriage.

(*c*) *Toughness of Hymen*: It happens sometimes that the hymen is abnormally thick and so tough as not to allow penetration. The defect can be removed by surgical treatment when coition will become normally possible. It cannot form a ground fordis solving a marriage. Muslim law allows such treatment in the interest of the spouses.[69]

Vaginismus: It is a defect due to a psychological condition or abnormal nervous system. It is characterised by an involuntary muscular spasm which contracts the sphincter muscle of the vagina and the vaginal orifice and canal on the approach of the male organ. In this condition any attempt at intercourse produces a violent contraction of the constricting muscles of the vaginal orifice, as a result of which intercourse with the woman in that condition generally becomes impossible. Vaginismus may be due to actual pain on contact or fear of pain or repulsion for a particular individual or for the physical act of intimacy when the wife is affected with this condition involuntarily. The defect may be remedied by treatment or by restoring confidence in the wife, but it is possible that it may not respond to treatment. The birth of

68. L. Vs. L. (1949) 1 All. E.R. 141.
69. Ibn "Ābidīn, *op. cit.*, Vol. II, p. 613.

a child would diminish the defect, but not necessarily remove it. The husband may find it difficult or even painful to penetrate the wife's body, but sometimes it may not be impossible to do so. Vaginismus may not be curable. In the latter case it may be a ground for divorce.

English and American Laws: Vaginismus has been considered a sufficient ground for dissolution of a marriage in an English case on the basis of the wife's incapacity for cohabitation.[70] In an American case it was established that the wife was suffering from vaginismus at all material times and that the defect was incurable. The Court dissolved the marriage on the basis of incapacity of the wife for sexual intimacy.[71]

Frigidity: Just as a man suffers from incapacity, a woman may suffer from frigidity. Frigidity is a neurosis, that is, a disease of the unconscious and means the incapacity of a woman to have vaginal orgasm during intercourse. Such women are loath to allow intimacy to the husband. The wife may be reluctant to allow intimacy or she may refuse to have any sexual relation at all. A frigid woman is wholly without interest and there is no trace of vaginal pleasure in her. On the other hand, even if she allows the use of her body, she will experience and even show feelings of repulsion and disgust and the wish to get it over with in a hurry. There is, however, a great difference between impotency and frigidity. In the former case a husband suffering from incapacity will be absolutely unable for the sexual act and absolutely unable to give any opportunity for relaxation to the wife, but there is no such physical inability in the case of a wife suffering from frigidity due to psychological causes. It will be possible for the husband to get relaxation as the penetration of the wife's body is perfectly possible when frigidity is due to psychological causes, the only effect will be the absence of all response by the wife who may maintain a passive and cold attitude

70. L Vs. L (1882) 7 P.D. 16.
71. Vander Berg Vs. Vander Berg (1922) 197 N.Y.S. 641.

during the act of sexual intercourse. She does not derive any enjoyment out of the sexual intercourse.

Frigidity may be due to psychological or physical causes:

(*a*) Frigidity due to psychological causes maybe,

(*i*) relative, or (*ii*) absolute.

(*i*) In case of relative frigidity the woman is not absolutely frigid. She may be quite passionate with one man and yet cold with her husband on account of his appearance physical, moral, or intellectual condition and the like. It may be the result of a man's maltreatment of her or his defective physical condition. Thus a wife may hold her husband in great contempt when he suffers from premature ejaculation specially when her feelings have been aroused but she remains unsatisfied out of the sexual act while the husband persists in his demand regardless of the wife's lack of enjoyment. Many men are not tender in their sexual activity, ignore all preparatory acts and initial pleasure and have not the least regard for the creation of that necessary but undefinable "accord" in sex which can only be achieved through love and tenderness. This condition of the husband is very common but unfortunately is not realised and the husbands do not realise that in many cases they themselves are responsible for the wife's attitude. On the other hand, many women show that they despise and reject the whole sexual act and they reproach the husband for his "animal desire." They consider it indecent, vulgar or even to savour of immorality. Harper says that frigidity in a woman may be due to ignorance on the part of the husband as to the technique of love, ignorance of the time required to arouse a woman as compared to that required to arouse a man, ignorance of menstrual cycles, ignorance of the various possible coital postures, monotony of the husband's sexual technique etc.[72]

Psychological reasons seem to be the chief cause of frigidity amongst advanced societies.

72. Fouler Harper, *Problems of the Family*, pp. 311, 312, Indianapolis, 1952 A.D.

2. *Physical condition*: Some writers include in frigidity of a woman incapacity for sexual act on account of her physical condition. Thus penetration may not be possible due to toughness of the hymen, ulceration, pelvic inflammation or tumour, abnormally small vagina or its total absence, disproportion of the genitals as a small vagina and a normal or abnormally large male organ. Some of these cases have been discussed before under the topic of the wife's defects.

Test of Frigidity: As a general rule, a frigid woman does not get any glandular lubricating secretion or sensation in vagina or clitoris. The chief test is the absence in the wife of the involuntary contractions of her pelvic and perineal muscles at the end of the sexal act. Vaginismus is the highest degree of frigidity.

Legal aspect: The dissolution of marriage is allowed when the husband is quite impotent and on the analogy of this rule a marriage may be liable to be dissolved when the wife does not allow any opportunity whatsoever to the husband for intimacy. The reluctance of the wife to give such opportunity even at infrequent intervals cannot be a ground for the dissolution of the marriage. It will be the attitude of the wife towards her husband in the case of relative frigidity that shall determine the decision of a case.

Muslim society: Cases of frigidity are rarely met with in Muslim society as is clear from the fact that there is no case-law on this subject in India or Pakistan and they occur only in Western countries where women live and enjoy an independent life. The Muslim wife's attitude and her submission to her husband in all cases was, and is due to two main factors. The first is the great influence exerted by Islam which highly condemns the wife refusing herself to her husband. There are many Traditions to this effect. In a Tradition the Prophet (peace be on him) said that a woman whose husband is pleased with her shall enter the paradise.[73]

73. Al-Tirmidhī, *Jāmi'*, Kanpur, n d., Vol. I, p. 150.

The second reason is the influence of society and a wife would consider it immodest to refuse herself to her husband. She would prefer to suffer pain or remain unsatisfied than be guilty of "audacity" of a refusal which, according to her, would amount to lack of delicacy and even to immodesty. But with changed conditions of culture, women with Western education do sometimes deny intimacy to their husbands or in any case allow it with great difficulty and rather very infrequently. The Muslim jurists have not considered this matter, probably because they were not confronted with such a problem. It may also, for reasons explained above, be due to the fact that then divorces were more easy and common. A dissatisfied husband would divorce such a wife while a wife, on the other hand, could under such circumstances get her release by arbitration, *Khul'* or otherwise.

Muslim Law: There are no rules in Muslim law about frigidity in the wife, probably because the jurists must not have come across any such case, and so we must be guided by the general principles laid down by the jurists.

Ḥanafī Law: The Ḥanafī law does not allow the dissolution of marriage on the basis of such a defect in the wife as does not allow penetration and the same principle of law shall be applicable in the case of frigidity.

Mālikī, Shāfi'ī and Ḥanbali Laws: The Mālikī, Shāfi'ī, and Ḥanbalī laws allow the dissolution of marriage when penetration is not possible for a defect in the wife. The same principle of law may be applicable in the case of frigidity in the wife. The Muslim law allows one year's time to an impotent husband for the cure of his defect and justice and equity demand that the wife should be given the same period of time for the cure of her defect.

Shī'ī Law: The Shī'ī law allows the dissolution of a marriage when penetration is not possible due to a defect in wife. Frigidity, therefore, can be a ground for dissolution of marriage when penetration is not possible. The Shī'ī law also allows one year's time to an impotent husband for his cure and the same time may be given to the wife.

English and American Laws : As explained before, lawful enjoyment of sexual passions is one of the chief objects of marriage. Hence the ability for consummation of the marriage is an implied condition in every marriage contract.[74] If the wife suffers from frigidity, there is a breach of this important condition and the marriage is liable to be dissolved on the suit of the husband in the same way as a marriage can be dissolved on the suit of the wife when the husband is suffering from incapacity. But it is necessary in such a case that the wife should be frigid at the time of her marriage and continue to be such till the time of the suit. Section 7(1) (*b*) of the Matrimonial Causes Act, 1937, made the wilful refusal to consummate the marriage a ground for marriage being voidable so that it can be dissolved on the suit of the other party. This provision of law was retained in the Matrimonial Causes Act, 1950 as Section 8(1) (*b*). It was pointed out in some English cases that wilful and persistent refusal, unless it results from incapacity, necessarily arises after the marriage, while a defect arising subsequently to the marriage is no ground for relief.[75]

Premature ejaculation : We have described above in the discussion of "Imperfect coitus" that the man's coitus consists of several phases, namely, erection, penetration, orgasm and ejaculation. In normal man erection takes place very quickly through psychic stimulation and through contact with the woman. In case of premature ejaculation, erection sinks in a very short time after penetration and hence the frictionary motions which are so essential for sexual pleasure come to an end. Premature ejaculation is by far the most common defect in man with regard to sexual defect. A person afflicted with it cannot have a sustained erection. Sometimes he ejaculates on mere penetration while in other cases the ejaculation occurs very soon after penetration long before the wife gets her relaxation so that she receives little, if any, sexual pleasure.

74. Devanbagh Vs. Devanbagh, 5 Paige (N. Y.) 554.

75. Napier Vs. Napier (1915), P. 184; Robert Vs. Robert (1947) P. 164.

Extreme cases of this nature take the form of ejaculation *ante Bortas*, that is, semen is discharged at the mere approach to the vagina. A man suffering from it is called Shakkaz.

The ardour of the man subsides with ejaculation, but that of woman persists long after her orgasm so that she wishes the continuation of the sexual act. It is, therefore, necessary for the husband to indulge in necessary preparatory acts of love-play to enable the wife to achieve orgasm. But many husbands are either ignorant of this important factor or are careless about it and do not make any attempt to arouse the wife so that their full relaxation may be simultaneous or at least almost simultaneous. In the case of premature ejaculation there is no normal intercourse as far as the husband is concerned.

It has already been discussed above that it is very necessary for a happy marriage that the wife should get full satisfaction out of the sexual act. Premature ejaculation applies to those cases in which semen is discharged after a very few of the frictionary motions when the orgastic release of sexual tension in the woman, brought about by normally protracted intercourse, is here made impossible. The natural result of this condition of the husband is that the wife remains unsatisfied and her tension remains unrelaxed. If the husband does not care to cure his defect and persists in coitus without due regard to the wife's satisfaction then the wife shall not only suffer in health but she will feel disgust for cohabitation and even for her husband.

It is difficult to determine the normal duration of intercourse and it greatly differs in different men and at different stages. Bergher has stated that, generally speaking, it lasts from two to ten minutes. This applies to U.S.A. and it is doubtful if the limit of ten minutes applies to India and Pakistan where the condition of health of the people is not as good as in U.S.A.

The Muslim jurists have laid great stress on the satisfaction of the wife. It is stated in *Al-Durr Al-Mukhtār* that it is one of the marital obligations of the husband not to suffer from premature ejaculation.[76] The Muslim jurists have emphasised the fact that the husband must give every satisfaction to the wife and they have gone to such extent in this matter as to lay down the rule that it is obligatory on the husband to care about his proper appearance. It is stated in the same book that just as it is obligatory for the wife to adorn herself for (attracting) her husband in the same way it is obligatory on the husband to make himself presentable to the wife.[77] But, cannot a marriage be dissolved when the husband suffers from this defect?

There is no provision in Muslim law about such a case. Penetration is deemed sufficient to constitute consummation of marriage, which is achieved even in the case of premature ejaculation and so a marriage may not be dissolved on this ground. But the satisfaction of the wife is also very necessary in the interest of her health. The English and the American laws also have not considered this aspect of married life.

Other Cases: The presence of cyst of vulva, fibroid, prolapse of uterus, a solid tumour of the vagina or uterus, etc. may either completely or partially obstruct penetration. The defect is often cured by an operation. If it does not allow penetration and is not curable the marriage may not be dissolved under Ḥanafī law but may be dissolved on the analogy of *Rataq*, *Qaran* and *'Afal*, under the Maliki, Shafi'i and Ḥanbalī laws.

Absence of Vagina: If the vagina is absent altogether or is ill-developed or is too small or is occluded by intra uterine disease then it will render any attempt at intercourse not only painful but impossible. But if it is not completely absent it has to be seen if intimacy is possible or not. As has been discussed above, a marriage can be dissolved on the basis of an incurable obstruction to penetration. The same rule of law must be applied here and the marriage may be dissolved on the ground of impossibility. But when there is not an absolute bar to consummation and penetration is possible, the marriage is not liable to be dissolved.

76. Ibn Ābidīn, *op. cit.*, Vol. II, p. 663.
77. *Ibid.*

English Law : A marriage can be dissolved if penetration is not possible due to absence of vagina or *vera copula* is not possible because of malformed vagina.[78]

Absence of Uterus : Complete absence of the uterus seldom occurs, but cases of arrested development and malformation of uterus are not uncommon. When the uterus is absent altogether even then coitus shall be possible. A marriage cannot be dissolved under the Muslim law on such a ground as penetration is possible which under the Muslim law constitutes cohabitation.

English Law : A marriage cannot be dissolved if penetration is possible. The absence of uterus can only make the birth of a child impossible.

Epilepsy : Epilepsy is a condition in which a person gets recurring attacks of sudden loss of consciousness accompanied by convulsions in which the arms become fixed and the lower limbs rigidly extended. It is followed by some degree of stupor. It can be hereditary and there is risk that it may be inherited and may be visited on the children born of the marriage. There is no reason why a Muslim marriage should not be allowed to be dissolved when the husband suffers from it. Under the Māliki, Shāfi'ī and Ḥanbalī laws the marriage may also be dissolved on the suit of the husband when it is the wife who suffers from it. It is necessary not only in the interest of the other party but also in the interest of society to dissolve a marriage when either spouse suffers from this disease.

Shī'ī Law : Under Shī'i law epilepsy is not a ground for dissolution of marriage.

English Law : Under the English law, a marriage is voidable when one spouse suffers from recurring fits of epilepsy.[79] The defect forms a ground for the dissolution of marriage.

78. D. Vs. D. (1954) 2 All. E.R. 595.

79. Section 7(1)(*b*) of the Matrimonial Causes Act 1937, Section 8(1)(*b*) of the Matrimonial Causes Act, 1950.

Law in U.S.A. Some States in the U.S,A. prohibit a marriage when one of the spouses suffers from epilepsy.[80] The Supreme Court of Wisconsin, however, held a marriage voidable when one of the spouses did not know that the other spouse was suffering from epilepsy.[81] Some of the States restrict the time of prohibition in the case of wives up to the age when they attain an age of forty-five years.[82]

80. Some of such States are Connecticut, Delaware, Indiana, Kansas, Michigan, Minnesota,. Missouri, Nebraska, New Hampshire, New Jersey, North Dakota, Ohio, Pennsylvania, Utah, Virginia, Washington, Wisconsin.
81. In re. Jansa's Estate, 169 Wis. 220 : 171 N, W. 947.
82. Connecticut, Kansas. New Hampshire, North Dakota, Utah, Virginia. Washington.

Chapter 18

LI'ĀN

I. *Preliminary*

Li'ān literally means to drive away. Here it means to drive away from the mercy of Allah on account of imprecations involving the curse and wrath of Allah. When a husband accuses his lawfully wedded wife of adultery directly or indirectly as when he denies the paternity of a child born of her during wedlock, she has a right to apply to the *Qāḍī* to order the husband either to support his accusation by taking the special prescribed oaths or to admit the falsity of his charge.[1] This procedure of taking oaths, fully described later, is called *li'an* and consists in giving of evidence or testimony in person by the husband as well as by the wife before the *Qāḍī*. The oaths are strengthened by imprecations of the curse and the wrath of God. *Li'ān* becomes due when the husband accuses his wife of adultery under such circumstances that if he had made the accusation against any other woman then he would be liable to prosecution for defamation.[2]

II. *English Law*

There is no provision in the English law equivalent to the Muslim law of *Li'ān*. But imputing unchastity to the wife coupled with desertion was held to amount to cruelty which was considered sufficient ground for dissolution of marriage.[3]

III. *American Law*

Several States in U.S.A. recognise that a false charge of

1. Burhān al-Dīn al-Marghīnānī, *al-Hidāyah*, Delhi, n.d., Vol. II, p. 396; *al-Fatāwā al-Hindiyah*, Kanpur, 1349 A.H., Vol. II, p. 129; Ibn 'Ābidīn, *Radd al-Muḥtār*, Cairo, 1318 A.H., Vol. II, pp. 601-602.
2. Ibn Nujaym, *al-Baḥr al-Rā'iq*, Cairo, 1311 A.H., Vol. IV, p. 122; *al-Fatāwā al-Hindiyah*, *op. cit.*, Vol. II, p. 129; Ibn 'Ābidīn, *op. cit.*, Vol. II, p. 601.
3. Jeapes Vs. Jeapes (1903), 89 L.T. 74.

adultery by one spouse against the other is a ground for dissolution of marriage on the basis that such conduct amounts to cruelty if accompanied by threats of violence. Arizona, California, Connecticut, Columbia, Iowa, Kentucky and Michigan etc. have accepted this view. Even charge of lewd and immoral character falling short of adultery made in a rude and vile manner before others has been held to amount to cruelty.[4] But unlike pure Muslim law, a charge of adultery by the husband against the wife would not constitute a ground for dissolution of marriage if it is made in good faith or on reasonable ground.[5] Muslim law does not make any distinction between good or bad faith in making the accusation and considers every charge of the husband to be a ground for *li'ān* whatever his motive might have been. It is a necessary condition under the American law that the charge should be false, as is held by the Courts in India and Pakistan.

IV. *Object*

Under the provisions of the Muslim law, a person who accuses a woman of adultery has to establish his charge by the testimony of four eye-witnesses to the woman's guilt. This is based on a verse in the Qur'ān wherein it is stated. "And those who accuse free women (of adultery) and bring not four witnesses, flog them with eighty stripes and never accept their evidence and these are the transgressors."[6] It is obvious that such a strict punishment is prescribed in order to stop people from recklessly accusing women of such a serious charge and bringing dishonour to them and to their families.

A very strong proof has been required because to damage the character of a woman is a very serious thing which cannot

4. Wheeller Vs. Wheeller, 53 Iowa 591 ; Pinkard Vs. Pinkard, 14, Tex 356 ; Johnson Vs. Johnson, 183, Ky. 421 ; 209, S.W. 385.
5. Veeder Vs. Veeder, 189 Iowa 912 ; Pearson Vs. Pearson, 104, Misc. 675 ; Parman Vs. Parman, 94, Ore 307 ; 185 Pac 922 ; Sallee Vs. Sallee 213 Ky. 125.
6. Qur'ān, Surah al-Nūr, XXIV : 4.

be dealt with lightly. Moreover, the punishment for adultery, called *Ḥadd al-Zinā*, is very severe.[7]

It is not, as a general rule, possible for a person to produce four eye-witnesses and the husband may be the solitary witness of the wife's guilt. He cannot under such circumstances prove his accusation and so shall be liable to *Ḥadd al-Qadhf* or punishment for slander. On the other hand, adultery is a very serious charge which brings disgrace to the wife and her family. *Li'ān* gives an innocent wife, who might have been wantonly accused by her husband, the right to demand of him to either substantiate his accusation by taking the prescribed oaths, or to admit the falsity of his charge against her. For this purpose she can seek the help of the *Qāḍī* who can force the husband to agree to one of the two courses. *Li'ān* thus helps the wife in retrieving her lost reputation.

The husband, after levelling the serious charge of adultery against his wife, may refuse to release her from the marriage-tie either in a spirit of revenge or simply to harass her. The wife can, in such circumstances, get her marriage dissolved by resorting to *Li'ān*.

It is not possible for the spouses to live happily when the husband accuses his wife of adultery. As long as he is under the impression, rightly or wrongly, that his wife has been guilty of misconduct, he will always harbour suspicion against her. He will try to impute evil motives to many innocent acts and movements of hers. If he is of a jealous nature, this continued suspicion will leave him no peace of mind. The wife, on the other hand, will soon find that she is living under a cloud of suspicion and under this strain is likely to become a nervous wreck and will find such sort of life unbearable. Islam lays great emphasis on a happy companionship between the husband and the wife and it naturally does not tolerate a situation where instead of affection there is hatred between the spouses and the life of one or both becomes unbearable.

7. Burhān al-Dīn al-Marghīnānī, *op. cit.*, Vol. II, p. 489.

It is stated in *al-Hidāyah* that under the circumstances the retaining of the woman with humanity is impossible as is incumbent under the injunction of the Qur'ān and so it is incumbent upon the husband to divorce her on the principle of benevolence, but if he refuses to do so, the *Qāḍī* shall dissolve the marriage.[8]

The procedure of *Li'ān* also comes to the rescue of the husband as when, for example, he was the sole witness of his wife's guilt and is unable to produce eye-witnesses in support of his charge and the wife, therefore, cannot be convicted of adultery. Hence there are two courses open to him, namely, to continue to live with his wife in spite of her unchastity or to divorce her. He may not tolerate the first course while in the latter case he will be confronted with one great difficulty, namely, the fact that the paternity of the child that may be born of the wife will be attributed to him which will not only be inequitable but the very idea may be disgusting to him. In such a case the husband can disown the child without fear of becoming liable to punishment for slander.

It is interesting to note how man hates to live with an erring wife and how he excuses his own immorality. This can be seen from the following two quotations :

"I hold that man worst of the public foes,
Who either for his own or his children's sake,
To save his blood from scandal, lets the wife
Whom he knows false, abide and rule the house."[9]

"The adultery of the wife might be the means of palming spurious offspring upon the husband while the adultery of the husband could have no such effect with regard to the wife, the idea seems to be universal."[10]

V. *Religious Sanction*

The provision of *li'ān* has been laid down in the Qur'ān as under :—

8. Burhān al-Dīn al-Marghīnānī, *op. cit.*, Vol. II, p. 398.
9. Tennyson, *Idylls of Guinevere*, 509-512, London.
10. Lord Cranworth's Speech.

And those who launch
A charge against chaste women,
And produce not four witnesses
(To support their allegations)—
Flog them with eighty stripes;
And reject their evidence
Ever after; for such men
Are wicked transgressors:
And those who launch
A charge agaist their spouses,
And have (in support)
No evidence but their own,
Their solitary evidence
(Can be received) if they
Bear witness four times
(With an oath) by God
That they are solemnly
Telling the truth;
And the fifth (oath)
(Should be) that they solemnly
Invoke the curse of God
On themselves if they
Tell a lie.
But it would avert
The punishment from the wife,
If she bears witness
Four times (with an oath)
By God that (her husband)
Is telling a lie;
And the fifth (oath)
Should be that she solemnly
Invokes the wrath of God
On herself if (her accuser)
Is telling the truth.[11]

The occasion for the revelation of this verse is said to be the case of Hilāl b. Umayyah. Ibn 'Abbās reported that

11. Qur'ān, Surah al-Nūr, XXIV, 4, 6-9.

Hilāl accused his wife of having committed adultery with one Sharīk b. Saḥmā'. The verse of the Qur'ān regarding slander of women had been revealed before then in which it is laid down, "those who accuse women of reputation (of adultery) and produce not four witnesses (of the fact) flog them with eighty stripes and never accept their evidence." The Prophet (peace be on him) thereupon asked Hilāl to produce four eye-witnesses or to undergo the punishment of eighty stripes. Hilāl expressed his inability to produce the witnesses and said "O Messenger of Allah, when one of us sees a man upon his wife, must he gö away to look for witnesses"? The Prophet (peace be on him) again asked him to bring proof or undergo the prescribed punishment. Hilāl then said, "I am certainly a truthful man, let Allah reveal what will prove me not guilty for the prescribed sentence." The above verse was then revealed. Hilāl and his wife then took the prescribed oaths and the Prophet (peace be on him) then separated them.[12] Sa'd b. 'Ubādah and Ibn 'Umar have also reported cases of similar nature.[13]

There are several Traditions regarding *Li'ān.* One of them is quoted below:

Ibn 'Umar reported: "The Prophet (peace be on him) allowed imprecations between a man and his wife. He first admonished the husband and told him that the chastisement of this world is easier than the chastisement of the hereafter. Then he called her (the wife) and gave her similar admonition and warning. After the spouses had taken the prescribed oaths, he separated them.'"[14]

VI. *Dispprobation of*

To have recourse to *Li'ān* is strongly disapproved. Thus the Tradition already quoted above clearly shows that the

12. Walī al-Dīn al-Khaṭīb, *Mishkāt al-Maṣābīh*, Delhi, 1350 A.H. Vol. II p. 286 ; al-Nasa'ī, *Sunan*, Delhi, 1335 A.H., Vol, II, p. 108.
13. Walī al-Dīn al-Khaṭīb *Mishkāt, op. cit.*, Vol, II, p. 286 ; Abu Dāw'ūd *Sunan*, Kanpur, n.d., Vol. I, p. 306.
14. Al-Nasa'ī, *op. cit.*, Vol. II, p. 109.

Prophet (peace be on him) highly discouraged the husband and the wife from having recourse to *Li'ān* and taking the imprecations. The *Qāḍī* is to follow this practice and to discourage the spouses from such a serious step'[15]—though it is not an essential condition of *li'ān*. It is only considered proper for him to do so. It is also considered improper for a husband to accuse his wife of such a serious offence merely on the ground of suspicion. The Shī'i law is more strict in the matter and forbids a husband from accusing the wife of adultery on mere suspicion.[16] The Courts nowadays do not offer any advice to the parties in these matters.

Wife's Right: A wife can demand of her husband, who has accused her of adultery, to substantiate his accusation by taking the prescribed oaths or to admit the falsity of his charge against her.[17] She can seek the help of the *Qāḍī* to achieve this purpose.

Husband's Denial of Accusation: Should the husband deny the fact of having accused his wife of adultery then the wife has to prove it as a fact that her husband did accuse her of unchastity. Under the Muslim law she must produce at least two reliable witnesses in support of her version when her allegation shall be accepted as a fact. But if she cannot produce two witnesses to support her version, she cannot have recourse to *li'ān*.[18] If the husband, on the other hand, produces two witnesses to prove that the wife had admitted her guilt then too *li'ān* shall drop.[19] But now the matter shall be decided by the present law and the Court shall decide the case on its merits after judging the evidence of the parties.

Essentials: There are certain conditions which are essential

15. Abū Dāw'ūd, *op. cit.*, Vol. I, pp. 306-7.
16. Ja'far b. al-Ḥasan, *Sharā'i al-Islām*, Tehran, 1377 A.H., p. 230.
17. Burhān al-Dīn al-Marghīnānī, *op. cit.*, Vol. II, p. 396 ; *al-Fatāwā al-Hindiyah*, *op. cit.*, Vol. II, p. 129 ; Ibn 'Ābidin, *op. cit.*, Vol. II, p. 602.
18. *Al-Fatāwā al-Hindiyah*, *op. cit.*, Vol. II, p. 132.
19. *Ibid.*

for *li'ān* and the law of *li'ān* will not be applicable unless they are satisfied. They relate to the following matters:

1. Accusation,
2. Marriage,
3. Spouses, capacity and status of,
4. Absence of witnesses,
5. Demand by wife,
6. Denial by wife,
7. Procedure.

These various conditions are being fully discussed below :—

1. *Accusation*: It is an essential condition of *li'ān* that there must be an accusation by the husband charging his wife with adultery.

The accusation must be definite, certain and unambiguous. The charge of adultery may be express or implied.

Express Charge: If the husband says, "You adultress," or "you are an adultress," "or you have committed adultery", the allegations made amount to an express charge on which *Li'ān* can be resorted to.[20] Similarly, if the husband says to his wife, "You have committed adultery, your pregnancy is by adultery," then it shall amount to an accusation of adultery and shall give cause for *liā'n*[21]. If, however, the accusation is uncertain or conditional, it does not give rise to *li'ān*. Thus if a man were to say to his wife, "I did not find you virgin," there can be no *li'ān* because the fact that he did not find the wife virgin does not necessarily mean that she had committed adultery.[22]

If a man should attribute adultery to another person's wife and that person should say, "I believe what you have said, the woman is such as you say," the husband would be

20. Burhān al-Dīn al-Marghīnānī, *op. cit.*, Vol. II, p. 396; *al-Fatāwā al-Hindiyah, op. cit.*, Vol. II, p. 129; Ibn 'Ābidīn, *op. cit.*, Vol. II, p. 601.
21. *Ibid.*
22. Burhān al-Dīn al-Marghīnānī, *op. cit.*, Vol. II, p. 396; *al-Fatāwā al-Hindiyah, op. cit.*, Vol. II, p. 131.

deemed to have charged his wife with unchastity so as to give cause fot *li'ān*[23] But if he merely says, "I believe you", he would not be held liable for *li'ān* because he has not made a definite charge of adultery against his wife.[24]

In one case the words "the accused is keeping my wife as his own wife" were held by the Court to constitute a charge of adultery.[25] But in another case the allegation made by a husband in his complaint to the Court that the accused was detaining the complainant's wife fo. adultery, was not considered to amount to a charge of adultery.[26] In the former case there is an implied accusation that adultery was being committed while the latter case does not affirm that any adultery has been committed but the allegation merely mentions the accused's motive in detaining the *complainant's* wife.

Implied Charge of Unchastity: A denial by a husband that a child already born to his wife does not belong to him amounts to an accusation of adultery and the wife shall have a right to *li'ān.*[27] An accusation couched in ambiguous expression and made indirectly may not be considered sufficient for *li'ān*. Thus if a husband were to say to his wife, "Your pregnancy is not of me," the expression does not necessarily amount to a charge of adultery on the ground of uncertainty for it is possible that she may not be pregnant at all.[28] This is according to Abū Ḥanīfah and Zafar. But Abū Yūsuf and Muḥammad hold that this statement shall amount to an accusation if a child is born to her within six months of the time of the accusation.[29] In the case of a second marriage,

23. *Al-Fatāwā al-Hindiyah, op. cit.*, Vol. II, p. 130.
24. *Ibid.*
25. Bano Begum Vs. Inayat Husain, A.I.R. 1948, All. 34.
26. Fakhre Jehan Begum Vs. Hamid Ullah Khan, A.I.R. 1929, Oudh, 16.
27. *Al-Fatāwā al-Hindiyah, op. cit.*, Vol. II, p. 131 ; Ibn 'Ābidīn, *op. cit.*, Vol. II, p. 607.
28. Burhān al-Dīn al-Marghīnānī, *op. cit.*, Vol. II, p. 399 ; *al-Fatāwā al-Hindiyah, op. cit.*, Vol. II, p. 131 ; Ibn 'Ābidīn, *op. cit.*, Vol. II, p. 606.
29. *Ibid.*

it is possible that her pregnancy may be due to her first marriage.

The husband can disown the paternity of the child only within the period during which felicitations are usually offered. This period of time is generally fixed from thιee days to seven days.[30] If the husband happens to be out of station, he can deny the paternity of the child within seven days of receiving the information of the child's birth.[31] According to Muḥammad and Abū Yūsuf he can deny the paternity of the child during the period of the wife's puerperal discharge which in extreme cases may extend to forty days.[32]

2. *Marriage*: It is an essential condition of *li'ān* that there should subsist a valid marriage between the parties at all material times, namely, at the time of the accusation, at the time of the wife's demand, at the time of the imprecations and at the time of the *Qāḍī*'s order.[33] Hence an accusation during the period of *'iddah* in the case of a revocable divorce can give rise to *li'ān*.[34] Marriage means a valid marriage.[35] There can he no *li'ān* when the marriage is *bāṭil* (void) or *fāsid* (irregular), because such a marriage does not constitute the relationship of husband and wife.[36] The provision of *li'ān* is applicable only when the relationship of husband and wife subsists up to the time when the proceedings of *li'ān* are terminated and a decree is passed by the *Qāḍī*.

If a man accuses his wife of unchastity and subsequently divorces her irrevocably, the doctrine of *li'ān* shall not be applicable as the marriage does no longer subsist. She can in such a case seek her remedy under the ordinary law of

30. Ibn 'Ābidīn, *op. cit.*, Vol. II, p. 607.
31. *Ibid.*
32. Burhān al-Dīn al-Marghīnānī, *op. cit.*, Vol. II, p. 400; *al-Fatāwā al-Hindiyah*, *op. cit.*, Vol. II, p. 131, Ibn 'Ābidīn, *op. cit.*, Vol. II, p. 607.
33. Ibn 'Ābidīn, *op. cit.*, Vol. II, p. 601.
34. *Ibid.*, p. 602.
35. *Ibid.*
36. *Ibid.*

defamation.[37] If she has been divorced only revocably, she can have recourse to *li'ān* during the period of her *'iddah* because the marriage continues to subsist till the expiry of the period of *'iddah*.[38] But the marriage shall cease to subsist on the expiry of the period of her *'iddah* and the right to *li'ān* shall also cease. If a man accuses a woman who is not his wife and subsequently marries her, *li'ān* shall not be incumbent on him because the woman was not his wife at the time of the accusation.[39]

3. *Spouses*

I. *Capacity*: As a general rule only those persons are competent to take *li'an* who have the capacity to appear as witnesses in any case. It means that they should be adults and possessed of understanding.[40] Thus if a husband is a minor and has not attained discretion or is a lunatic or is dumb, no *li'ān* is incumbent on him. As a matter of fact he is not liable to conviction even for slander.[41] Similarly, if the wife is a child of tender age or is a lunatic or is dumb, she is not entitled to claim *li'ān*.[42] The disability of a dumb person is due to the fact that he or she cannot repeat the prescribed oaths by speech.[43] Also because such a person is not capable of accusing a woman of adultery in words while his signs may be misunderstood,[44] and imprecations are not incumbent unless the accusation is expressed in words.[45] *Li'ān* is, however applicable when both the spouses or one of them

37. Ibn 'Ābidīn, *op. cit.*, Vol. II, p. 602.
38. *Al-Fatāwā al-Hindiyah, op. cit.*, Vol. II, p. 129.
39. Ibn 'Ābidīn, *op. cit.*, Vol. II, p. 602; Shaykhzādah, *Mjma' al-Anhur*, Constantinople, 1327 A.H., Vol. I, p. 463.
40. Ibn 'Ābidin, *op. cit.*, Vol. II, pp. 603-4.
41. Burhān al-Dīn al-Marghīnānī, *op. cit.*, Vol. II, p. 309; Ibn 'Ābidīn, *op. cit.*, Vol. II, p. 601.
42. *Ibid.*
43. Ibn Nujaym, *op. cit.*, Vol. I, p. 131.
44. Burhān al-Dīn al-Marghīnānī, *op. cit.*, Vol. II, p. 399; Ibn 'Ābidīn, *op. cit.*, Vol. II, p. 606.
45. *Ibid.*

is blind.[46] Further, to have recourse to *li'ān* under the Ḥanafī law, the husband and the wife should be Muslims, adults, and of sound mind. It is also necessary that the wife should not be a slave girl or a Christian or a Jewess even when married to a Muslim. This is based on a Tradition that the Prophet (peace be on him) has said that there are four classes of women on whom *li'ān* is not incumbent, namely, Jews and Christians married to Muslims, and slaves married to Muslims and free women married to slaves.[47] But some jurists hold that *li'ān* can be resorted to even when the wife belongs to a revealed religion because the verse of Qur'ān quoted before does not restrict the word "wife" to Muslims only.[47] It is also necessary that neither of the spouses should have been convicted previously for slander because on being punished for slander the husband or the wife's evidence cannot be admitted afterwards in any case even if he or she repents.[48] According to Shāfi'ī, his credibility shall be restored by retraction or repentance.[49] The same rule applies to the wife also.

The capacity of the parties to the proceedings of *li'ān* should subsist till the time of the order of the *Qāḍī*. If either the husband or the wife should lose the capacity to depose as a witness, *li'ān* cannot be resorted to and the matter shall be decided in the ordinary way for defamation.[50] If one of them loses the capacity after *li'ān* but before the pronouncement of an order by the *Qāḍī*, it will have to be seen if the want of capacity is permanent or temporary. If it is permanent, the provision of *li'ān* would drop and the *Qāḍī* shall not order their separation.[51] If, however, it is temporary and is likely to be cured such as insanity of one of the spouses,

46. Ibn Nujaym, *op. cit.*, Vol. IV, p. 123 ; Ibn 'Ābidīn, *op. cit.*, Vol. II, p. 601.
47. Burhān al-Dīn al-Marghīnāī, *op. cit.*, Vol. II, p. 398.
47a. Ibn Rushd, *Bidayat al-Mujtahid*, Vol. II, p. 98, Cairo, n.d.
48. Ibn 'Ābidīn, *op. cit.*, Vol. II, p. 601.
49. *Ibid.*
50. *Ibid.*, p. 605.
51. *Ibid.*

then the *Qāḍī* shall order a separation between them.[52] If the husband or the wife is punished for slander, his or her evidence cannot be accepted in future and this will constitute a permanent bar,[53] as it is a necessary condition for *li'ān* that neither of the spouses should have been convicted previously for slander. But if one of the spouses becomes insane, it is possible that the insanity may be cured and this condition will amount to a temporary bar and can give cause for *li'ān* and so does not stop the proceedings of *li'ān*.[54] However, some of the above mentioned matters relate to the law of evidence and they are no longer applicable at present in Pakistan and India as the Muslim law of evidence has been superseded in these countries.

Shāfi'ī Mālikī and Ḥanbalī Laws: Shāfi'ī, Mālik and Aḥmad do not debar a woman of a questionable character or a non-Muslim or a slave girl from having recourse to *li'ān*. Under Shāfi'ī law *li'ān* is incumbent even when the husband is dumb because his signs are equivalent to spoken words.[55]

Shāfi'ī holds that a husband may with impunity accuse his wife of unchastity, even though he be unable to furnish legal proof when he knows for certain that she has been guilty of it or when he has grave and well-founded suspicion upon the subject or when the woman's guilt is of public knowledge as when she and the adulterer were surprised by someone in the act of her misconduct.[56]

II. *Husband*

It is a necessary condition of *li'ān* that the accuser should be the husband of the woman accused of unchastity

52. Ibn Ābidīn, *op. cit.*, Vol. II, pp. 605.
53. *Ibid.*
54. *Ibid.*
55. Burhān al-Dīn al-Marghīnānī, *op. cit.*, Vol. II, p. 399. Ibn Rushd, *Bidāyat al-Mujtahid*, Cairo, n.d., Vol. II, p. 98 ; Muḥammad b. Aḥmad, *Jawāhir al-'Uqūd*, Cairo, 1955, A.D., p. 177.
56. Al-Ramlī, Aḥmad b. Hamzah, *Nihāyat al-Muḥtāj*, Cairo, 1357 A.H., Vol. VII, p. 105.

at the time of the accusation as well as at the time of *li'ān*. Hence if the marriage happens to be void or, under the Ḥanafī and the Mālikī laws, even a *fāsid* or irregular marriage, the man shall not be considered to be the lawful husband of the woman and so a charge of adultery made by him against the woman shall not give her a right to *li'ān*.[57] This is based on the rule that the law of *li'ān* is applicable only when the accusation is made by the husband but here he cannot be considered to hold that status and his position is not different from that of a stranger. In the case of an accusation by any person other than the husband, the woman can only bring action for libel.[58] If the accuser ceases to be the husband of the wife as when the marriage be dissolved before the proceedings of *li'ān* are commenced then the woman cannot have recourse to *li'ān* and can seek her remedy only by an action for libel.[59]

III. *Wife*

Another condition for *li'ān* is that the woman accused of unchastity should be the lawful wife of the accuser at the time of the accusation, as well as at the time of *li'ān*.[60] Such an accusation against a woman other than the wife will not constitute a ground for *li'ān* but the matter shall be decided by the ordinary law in respect of defamation. Hence if a man accuses a woman of unchastity and subsequently marries her, she shall not be entitled to have recourse to *li'ān* as she was not the accuser's wife at the time of the accusation.[61] If a man accuses his wife of adultery and then divorces her irrevocably before the proceedings of *li'ān* are finished, the doctrine of *li'ān* shall no longer be applicable and she can have her remedy by an action for slander because she is no longer the wife of the accuser.[62] If, however, she has been divorced only recovably she can have resort to *li'ān* during the period of her *'iddah* because she is still the wife

57. Ibn 'Ābidīn, *op. cit.*, Vol. II, p. 601.
58. *Ibid.*, pp. 603-4.
59. *Ibid.*, p. 604.
60. *Ibid.*, p. 601.
61. *Ibid.*, p. 604.
62. *Ibid.*

of the accuser.[63] Her right to *li'ān* shall cease on the expiry of the period of *'iddah.*

It is a condition of *li'ān* that the wife should be *muḥṣanah* and *'afīfah*, that is, a virtuous woman of untarnished reputation and should have lived a chaste life and should also have the reputation of bearing a virtuous character and not having the reputation of being an adultress or a woman of loose character.[64] But the condition of being chaste and of bearing a good character does not refer to the particular incident which has given rise to *li'ān* in suit. When once she has been guilty of immorality, she will never in her future life become a *muḥsanah* so that this condition is to last her whole life.[65] This rule shall apply even when a non-*Muslimah* who was notorious for her loose living or was accused of even a single act of immorality, embraces Islam and then lives an unblameworthy or, even an exemplary life afterwards.[66] The Muslim jurists explain that adultery has been condemned by all religions so that it makes no difference whether she was a Muslim or a non-Muslim when she fell in error.[67] The rule seems to be very hard but is based on the very strict view of morality and chastity entertained by Muslim jurists. It was considered that such a woman could not take the very solemn imprecations in the name of Allah. She, therefore, becomes incapable for being a party to the proceedings of *li'ān*. But Mālik, Shāfi'ī and Aḥmad b. Ḥanbal differ with this view and according to them such a woman could be considered to be a *muḥsanah.*[68]

It is necessary that a woman should be a Muslim, chaste, major, sane and free before she can be considered to be a *muṣhanah.*[69]

63. Ibn 'Ābidīn, *op. cit.*, Vol. II, p. 602.
64. *Ibid.*, Ibn Nujaym, *op. cit.*, Vol. I or IV, p. 122
65. Ibn 'Ābidīn, *op. cit.*, Vol. II, p. 604.
66. *Ibid.*
67. Shaykhzādah, *op. cit.*, Vol. I, p. 616.
68. *Ibid.*
69. *Ibid.*, pp. 612-613.

A similar idea prevailed in England and perhaps in the Christian world in the nineteenth century when a single act of falling astray on the part of a woman was considered a sufficient ground for divorce though it was not considered a sufficient ground in the case of man. The distinction was based on the view that "feminine psychology did not easily lend itself to isolated acts of adultery committed in a moment of ill-regulated but transitory passion; a wife, it was felt, only committed adultery when she was seized with feeling for the adulteror so strong as to be incompatible with the continued existence of marriage or family life." "Masculine psychology, however, was different; a husband might be swept along in a gust of passion to commit an act of adultery which, however regrettable, was transient in duration and should be in effect. Such an action was not necessarily incompatible with the continuance of marriage, and should not be allowed to founder the precious craft of family integrity. Therefore, to meet this reasoning an act of adultery on the part of the husband did not give the wife grounds for divorce."[70] The above theory could perhaps be justified to some extent when women could not move in society freely nor come in contact with men in the absence of chaperon in England, France and some other countries. But it is doubtful if it can still hold good when women are no longer living in semi-seculsion but meet men on equal terms.

Disability: Under the provisions of Muslim law, when cause for *li'ān* is established, that is to say, when the husband has made an accusation of adultery against his wife, but *li'ān* is not permissible on account of disqualification on the part of the woman as when she is a minor, is insane or unchaste then *li'ān* cannot be resorted to and she has no remedy.[71] If the disqualification exists in the husband as when he has been punished for slander, then too *li'ān* will not be permissible but instead he can be proceeded against for libel.[72] If the

70. E.S.P. Haynes and Derek Walker-Smith, *Divorce and its Problems*, London, 1935, p. 45.
71. Ibn 'Ābidīn, *op. cit.*, Vol. II, pp. 603-4.
72. *Ibid.*, p. 603.

husband's disqualification consists of minority or insanity then under the provisions of Muslim law, he is neither liable to *li'ān* nor to conviction for slander.[73] This is based on the ground that being a minor or insane person he is incompetent to take an oath which is necessary for *li'ān* as well as in an action for having committed an offence. If both the husband and the wife or one of them has been punished for falsely accusing some person of adultery then too the husband can be liable only to punishment for libel.[74]

(*e*) *Absence of Witnesses*: It is absolutely necessary for *li'ān* that the husband should not be in a position to produce the prescribed number of witnesses, namely four, to establish the truth of his accusation. If he can produce witnesses to support his version then under the Muslim law the doctrine of *li'ān* shall have no application.[75] If the husband cannot produce four witnesses, but can produce only three or even a lesser number, the doctrine of *li'ān* can be resorted to.

(*f*) *Demand by Wife* : It is an essential condition for *li'ān* that the wife should demand it. If she should not demand it when accused of adultery by her husband even though both of them are competent for *li'ān*, the marriage shall continue and she will remain his wife as before.[76]

(*f*) *Denial bv Wife*: A denial by the wife of the truth of the husband's accusation is an essential condition for *li'ān*.[77] If she admits the charge or does not deny its truth then there can be no *li'ān*.[78]

XI. Procedure

The special procedure prescribed by Islam for the determination of a charge of adultery by the husband against his wife is by swearing and imprecating the curse and the wrath

73. Ibn 'Ābidīn *op. cit.*, Vol. II, p. 603.
74. *Ibid.*
75. *Ibid.*, p. 601.
76. *Ibid.*, p. 602.
77. *Ibid.*
78. *Ibid.*

of God as is laid down in the Qur'ān (XXIV: 6-8). The procedure according to Muslim law is as follows:

The *Qāḍī* first asks the husband either to take the prescribed oaths or to admit the falsity of his charge against his wife. In the latter case he renders himself liable to punishment for slander but the marriage shall not be dissolved. If the husband refuses to do either, he shall be imprisoned till he either takes the prescribed oaths or admits the falsity of his accusation.[79] If the husband persists in his accusation, the *Qāḍī* shall first administer the oath to him (the husband) four separate times by repeating each time, "I call God to witness to the truth of my testimony concerning the adultery with which I charge this woman," (pointing to his wife). After that the husband will be required to pronounce the imprecations by saying, "May the curse of God fall upon me if I have spoken falsely concerning the adultery with which I charge this woman." After this the *Qāḍī* admonishes the wife and advises her to give up her demand, but if she persists, he would ask her either to take the prescribed oaths or to admit her guilt. If she refuses to take the prescribed oaths or to admit her guilt then under the Ḥanafī law she shall be imprisoned till she complies with the *Qāḍī's* order. Mālik, Shāfi'ī and Ahmad b. Ḥanbal hold otherwise and state that she shall be punished for commission of adultery.[80] If she should admit her guilt (of adultery), the marriage shall not be dissolved. Should she persist that her husband's accusation is false then the *Qāḍī* must administer to her the oaths. She must repeat four separate times saying, "I call to Allah witness that my husband's words respecting this adultery with which he charges me are altogether false", and then pronounce the imprecations by saying a fifth time. "May the wrath of Allah light upon me if my husband is just in bringing a charge of adultery against me".[81]

79. Ibn 'Ābidīn, *op. cit.*, Vol. II, p. 603.

80. Ibn Rushd, *op. cit.*, Vol. II, p. 99.

81. Burhān al-Dīn al-Marghīnānī, *op. cit.*, Vol. II, pp. 398-99.

Denial of paternity of a child born of the wife amounts to accusing her of adultery by implication.[82] The prescribed expression to be used by way of imprecation in such a case is, however, slightly different, though the procedure is the same.

When both the parties have taken the imprecations and invoked the curse and wrath of Allah, the judge is to order the husband to divorce his wife and on his refusal or failure to do so the *Qāḍī* shall himself dissolve the marriage.[83]

Shī'i Law : The Shī'i law is the same as the Sunnī law. The only difference is that no order of the *Qāḍī* is required for dissolution of the marriage after the spouses have taken the oaths and the marriage shall stand dissolved *ipso facto.*

XII. Effect of Accusation

An accusation of adultery by the husband against his wife or even her misconduct does not automatically dissolve the marriage, but it remains subsisting so that the husband can lawfully continue to live with her if he so chooses. This is clear from a Tradition reported by Ibn 'Abbās that a man came to the Prophet (peace be on him) and said, "I have a wife who does not retract the hand of a toucher (meaning that she was of a very loose character)". The Prophet (peace be on him) said, "Divorce her," but the man said, "Verily I love her." The Prophet (peace be on him) said, "Keep her in that case".[84]

The accusation only gives a right to the wife to the dissolution of her marriage if she desires. In other words, the marriage becomes voidable.

Effect of the Husband's Admission of the Falsity of his Accusation

It has been seen above that the *Qāḍī* has in the first instance to ask the husband if he admits the falsity of his

82. Ibn 'Ābidīn, *op. cit.*, Vol. II, p. 602.

83. *Ibid.*, p. 605.

84. Walī al-Dīn al-Khaṭīb, *Mishkāt, op. cit.*, p. 287.

charge or if he would take the prescribed oaths. Should he admit that his charge against his wife was false, the marriage shall not be dissolved but he shall be punished for slander.[85] It is the duty of the *Qāḍī* to himself punish the husband for slander on his admission that his charge was false and it is not necessary that the wife should move the *Qāḍī* in this respect.[86]

XIII. 11. Effect of Wife's Confirmation of her Husband's Charge

As stated above, the *Qāḍī* shall ask the wife, who demands a *li'ān* to desist from her demand. If she persists, the *Qāḍī* shall, after the husband has taken the prescribed oaths, ask the wife if she confirms her husband's charge or if she persists in her denial of its truth. Should she accept her husband's charge as true, the marriage shall continue to subsist, but the wife shall not be liable to punishment for adultery even if she confirms her husband's charge four times.[87] This is based on the reasoning that the confirmation is merely meant to avoid taking the imprecations and does not amount to an admission of adultery. A person can be punished for adultery on his or her own confession only if he or she expressly admits his or her guilt four times in certain, definite and clear terms. In *li'ān* the wife's oath consists of the following words, "I state on oath in the name of God Almighty that this man (pointing to her husband) is certainly amongst the *li'ārs* in respect of the accusation of adultery which he has levelled against me." If the wife merely says that "Allah is my witness that my husband brings this accusation in bad faith", it will not amount to a valid imprecation. It is clear from the form of imprecation that there is no express admission of her guilt by the wife.[88]

85. Ibn 'Ābidīn, *op. cit.*, Vol. II, p. 603.
86. Burhān al-Dīn al-Marghīnānī, *op. cit.*, Vol. II, p. 399.
87. Ibn 'Ābidīn, *op. cit.*, Vol. II, p. 603.
88. *Ibid.*, pp. 601-3.

XIV. Retraction by the Husband

(*a*) *Preliminary*: Retraction means the withdrawal of a statement previously made. As already mentioned, when a wife complains to the *Qāḍī* that her husband has falsely accused her of unchastity, the *Çāḍī* has to ask the husband either to admit that his charge against his wife was false or to take the prescribed oaths. Retraction by the husband of his accusation against his wife is not merely a part of the procedure of *li'ān*, but is the substantive right of the husband who may choose to continue the marital relationship and suffer punishment for slander rather than let the marriage be dissolved through *li'ān*. He can exercise retraction as a matter of right. This right of the husband has also been recognised in a number of cases under the present law.[89]

Object: The object of retraction is to give the husband a chance for a *locus paenitentiae* or a chance for repentance before the marriage is dissolved. If the husband realises the injustice he has done to the wife or if in spite of his suspicion and accusation is anxious to maintain the marriage, he can retract his accusation and the marriage shall not be dissolved. But the maintenance of the marriage is not the only object of retraction. What is equally important is the fact that retraction clears the character of the wife.

Retraction by the Husband: It would be convenient for a consideration of this matter to discuss it with regard to its following aspects:—

(*a*) Applicability of the doctrine of retraction.

(*b*) Essentials.

(*c*) Time of, and

(*d*) Effect of retraction.

(*a*) *Retraction, applicability of*: It is contended sometimes that the doctrine of retraction has been superseded, has become

89. Shams-un-Nessa Khatoon Vs. Mir Abdul Mannaf, A.I.R. 1940, Cal. 95 ; Mst. Bano Begum Vs. Inayat Husain A.I.R. 1948, All. 34 etc.

obsolete and is no longer enforcible now. It was stated by the Oudh Chief Court that in the changed circumstances of the present day it cannot be possible to follow the letter of the original Islamic law, but the spirit of the law should be kept in view and the principles underlying it, should be adhered to as far as possible.[90] The Allahabad High Court has expressed the view that the doctrine of retraction is no more applicable in (pre-partition) India. The Court based this view on the ground that marriages can now be dissolved only on the grounds mentioned in the Dissolution of Muslim Marriages Act, 1939, but the proviso to section 2 does not make any reference to the procedure to be applied to cases under clause IX of the Act. The Court inferred from this omission that a marriage cannot be maintained on a retraction by the husband. The Court relied on a ruling of the Peshawar Judicial Commissioner's Court that the provisions of the Act are not subject to the rules of Muslim law but were complete and self-sufficient.[91] It is submitted that this view does not represent the position correctly. The correct position is that certain clauses of the Act are complete in themselves while the other clauses can be interpreted only with a reference to the general Muslim law. Thus for clauses II, IV and IX of the Act, it is necessary to refer to the general Muslim law. Clause II entitles a wife to the dissolution of her marriage when her husband has failed to provide for her maintenance for a period of two years, clause IV gives this right when the husband has failed to perform without reasonable cause his marital obligations for a period of three years while under clause IX she gets this right on any other ground which is recognised as valid for the dissolution of marriage under Muslim law. A husband is not bound to maintain his wife when she is *nāshizah* or disobedient and the question whether a wife is disobedient or not has to be decided on the basis of the general rules of the Muslim law in this respect. Similarly, whether a

90. Fakhre Jahan Begum Vs. Muhammad Hameed Ullah, A.I.R. 1929, Oudh, 16.
91. Mian Said Ahmad Vs. Mst. Sultan Bibi A.I.R. 1943, Pesh. 73.

person is impotent or not has to be decided according to the general Muslim law in respect of impotency. Clause IX simply says that a marriage can be dissolved on any ground which is recognised as valid for the dissolution of marriage under Muslim law. This again envisages the application of Muslim law in such cases. It is, therefore, not correct to say that the Act is self-sufficient and is independent of the general Muslim law in respect of all the matters.[92] The view expressed in the Peshawar ruling on which the Allahabad High Court relied was not followed by the same (Peshawar) Court in a subsequent ruling.[93] It preferred to follow the view of the Sind Chief Court that the Act was not intended to abrogate the general Muslim law applicable to the Muslims.[94] It is submitted that the Act has not even specified the grounds on which a marriage can be dissolved under clause IX of the Act and so naturally could not give the procedure to be applied under those clauses. No doubt it has been held in a number of cases that the procedure prescribed by the Muslim law for *li'ān* has been superseded, but these cases relate to the procedure only like the administration of the prescribed oaths or the advice to be given by the *Qāḍī* to a husband to retract his accusation etc. They do not relate to the rights given by the doctrine of *li'ān* to the husband and the wife. This right of retraction has been expressly recognised in a number of cases.[95] It is submitted that where the Legislature has merely laid down that the provisions of the Muslim law shall be applicable in certain cases and did not fully specify the law then it can be presumed that it intended that the whole of the substantive portion of the Muslim law was intended to be applied. The Bombay High Court has also expressed the view that it is incorrect that retraction is a pure rule of procedure

92. For full discussion see the author's commentary on the "Dissolution of Muslim Marriages Act, 1939".

93. Fazal Mahmood Vs. Umat-ur-Rahim, A.I.R. 1949, Pesh. 7.

94. Mst. Khatijan Vs. Abdullah, A.I.R. 1943, Sind 65.

95. Shams-un-Nessa Khatoon Vs. Mir Abdul Mannaf, A.I.R. 1940, Cal. 95 ; Bano Begum Vs. Inayat Hussain, A.I.R. 1948, All. 34 etc.

and that it does not apply in the civil Courts in India.[96]

Essentials relating to retraction: Certain conditions must be satisfied before a retraction can be considered to be valid. They may be summarised as under :—

(*a*) The husband must admit that he had made the accusation of adultery against his wife.

(*b*) He must clearly and unconditionally admit in unambiguous language that his accusation was false, and

(*c*) The retraction must be made before the close of the case.[97]

(*a*) If the husband denies the wife's allegation that he had accused her of unchastity, the denial does not and cannot amount to a retraction of the accusation. Retraction of necessity involves the idea that a certain statement had previously been made. If a statement has not been made, it cannot obviously be retracted. Hence it is necessary for retraction that the husband should admit the fact that he had made a charge of unchastity against his wife.

(*b*) The second essential condition is that the husband must frankly and unconditionally admit in a clear language that the accusation he had made against his wife was false.[98] As stated before, one of the objects underlying the doctrine of *li'ān* is to clear the character of the wife and this object can be achieved only when the husband admits the falsity of his accusation. This view is supported by the fact that it is laid down in various authoritative books on Muslim law that on retraction the husband shall be punished for slander.[99]

96. Muhammad Ali Muhammad Ebrahim Quraishi Vs. Mst. Hazra Bai, A.I.R. 1955, Bom. 265.
97. Ibn 'Ābidīn, *op. cit.*, Vol. II, pp. 603-6.
98. Mst. Saju Bibi Vs, Muksad Mulla 45 CWN 122 ; Mst. Fakhre Jahan Begum Vs. Muhammad Hameed Ullah Khan, A.I.R. 1929, Oudh, 16 ; Mst. Rahiman Bibi Vs. Fazal, A.I.R. 1927, All. 56.
99. Ibn 'Ābidīn, *op. cit.*, Vol. II, p. 603.

Expressions used for Retraction

An accusation can be retracted by a direct expression as when the husband says, "My charge against my wife was false" and this is the mode of expression usually inferred from the books on Muslim law.[100] But the same object can be achieved when the husband admits the falsity of his accusation in an indirect way. Thus he may say, "My wife is innocent of the accusation made by me against her," while referring to the accusation he had levelled against his wife. These words clear the reputation of the wife and so can lawfully be used for a valid retraction. Where a husband denies the paternity of a child born of his wife the denial amounts to an implied accusation of unchastity against his wife. If the child dies leaving some property and the husband then claims his share in the assets left by the child on the allegation that the child was his then this amounts to are traction of his accusation by implication and the husband shall be punished for libel by the *Qāḍī* in having previously made a false accusation of unchastity against his wife.[101] The Lahore High Court has followed this rule of Muslim law.

A bare withdrawal of the accusation as when the husband says, "The petitioner withdraws the charge made by him against his wife..." does not constitute a valid retraction. The husband must, if he has once wronged his wife by charging her with adultery, be prepared to take the consequences and the only way he can avoid them and maintain the marriage is by making an honest admission that the accusation was false.[102] Similarly, a conditional retraction does not amount to an honest admission of his fault and so is ineffective.

The Chief Court of Oudh has held a retraction, made in the written statement, to be valid when it was expressed in

100. Ibn 'Ābidīn, *op. cit.*, Vol. II, p. 606.
101. *Ibid.*
102. Shamsunnisa Khatoon Vs. Mir Abdul Mannaf, A.I.R. 1940, Cal. 95.

the following language, "If it be proved that the defendant had brought any false charge against the plaintiff (the wife) then the defendant withdraws such charges and expresses his regret for the same... even if the charge brought against her be true, the defendant (the husband) withdraws those charges unconditionally".[103]

It is clear from the husband's statement that hoth the first and second conditions enumerated above had not been fulfilled in the case. The husband had not frankly admitted that he had made a charge of adultery against his wife nor admitted the falsity of the charge. This is evident from the fact that he could not be punished on the basis of his above statement. His statement, therefore, did not amount to a proper retraction.

A retraction wherein the husband does not admit the falsity of his charge is no retraction and the fact that the husband expressed his regret for having made it does not constitute a retraction. The object of the Muslim law is to discourage the wanton accusation of adultery by a husband against his wife as well as to clear her character. It has, therefore, provided that either the husband must be prepared to lose his wife or be ready to undergo punishment for slander. If he prefers to retain his wife, he is required to admit clearly the falsity of his charge and it is incumbent, under the Muslim law, on the *Qāḍī* to punish the husband for slander.[104] As the *Qāḍī* has to punish the husband for slander after his retraction of the charge against his wife it is necessary that the admission of falsity of the accusation must be definite and clear.

103. Fakhre Jahan Begum Vs. Mohammad Hamid Ullah Khan, A I.R. 1929. Oudh, 16; Rahiman Bibi, Vs. Fazal A.I.R. 1927, All. 56; Abdul Rahman Vs. Shah Bibi, A.I.R. 1929, Nag. 262; Shamsunnesa Khatun Vs. Mir Abdul Mannaf, A.I.R. 1940, Cal. 95, Saleha Khatun Vs. Siddik-Ullah, P.L.D. 1958, Dacca, 62.

104. *Al-Fatāwā al-Hindiyah, op. cit.*, Vol. II, p. 130; Ibn 'Ābidīn, *op. cit.*, Vol. II, p. 606.

A good criterion to determine the validity of a retraction is to see if it fastens criminal liability on the husband.

The Bombay High Court followed this rule of Muslim law when it held that in retraction the husband must admit that the charge made by him against his wife was false so that he would make himself liable to be criminally prosecuted.[105]

It has been stated by a Lahore Bench of the High Court of West Pakistan, in a case, "a true and effective retraction takes place when a husband comes to Court and says, "I brought this charge because I was misled by certain circumstances. The circumstances were such that one would reasonably come to the conclusion that my wife was guilty. I have found now that in fact she is altogether innocent. I am very sorry. I withdraw the charge". In such a case, the Court allows the retraction because the husband has not behaved in an improper manner at all and it is simply a case of *bona fide* misunderstanding."[106]

This involves some important points of law, namely,

(*a*) The husband can withdraw his charge,

(*b*) An implied admission of having falsely accused his wife is sufficient for a valid retraction, and

(*c*) The husband's act of having accused his wife of unchastity should be *bona fide*.

All these points require some discussion.

(*a*) Under the Muslim law, withdrawal of the charge is not at all necessary and is immaterial for the decision of a case. The law only aims at clearing the reputation of the wife and this object is achieved as soon as the husband admits that his charge was false. Hence it is not necessary for the husband to withdraw his charge.

105. Mohammad Ali Mohammad Ebrahim Quraishi Vs. Hazra Bai, A.I.R. 1955, Bom. 265.

106. Abdul Aziz Vs. Mst. Bashiran Bibi 1958, P.L.D. Lahore, 59.

(*b*) It is essential for a proper retraction that the husband should admit the falsity of his charge. This can be done directly as when he says, "My charge against my wife was false," and this is usually the mode of expression as inferred from books on Muslim law. But the same object can be achieved when the husband admits the falsity of his charge in an indirect way. Thus he may say that his wife is innocent of the charge he had made. These words will clear the character of the wife and can lawfully be used for a valid retraction. It is submitted that the Court was justified in treating the indirect retraction by the husband as a valid retraction.

(*c*) This clause introduces a new factor in the law relating to retraction. According to this decision, a retraction can be considered to be valid and an accusation may be allowed to be retracted when it was *bona fide* and made on good and strong grounds, but the retraction may be ineffective and the marriage may be dissolved on the basis of the accusation if it was *mala fide* and made on flimsy grounds even when the retraction is made in sincerity. It is submitted that this rule as expressed by the Court finds no place in Muslim law relating to *li'ān* and is foreign to it. The Muslim jurists do not make it a condition for a retraction to be effectual that the accusation should have been made on good, strong or reasonable grounds and that a retraction would not be deemed valid if the accusation was made on flimsy or inadequate grounds even if the retraction is sincere and fulfils the conditions prescribed by Muslim law with regard to it. Under the Muslim law it is immaterial whether the charge was made on good grounds or was made deliberately to harm the wife. The Muslim jurists do not take into consideration the nature of the grounds on the basis of which the husband had made his accusation. They seem to have considered that a retraction was meant to,

(*i*) Clear the reputation of the wife, and

(*ii*) To discourage a husband from wantonly bringing such a serious charge against his wife because on retraction, the *Qāḍī* shall punish him for slander.

Both the above aims of a retraction shall be achieved irrespective of the fact as to whether the accusation was justifiable or not. The Lahore decision has introduced a new proposition of law and requires careful consideration. There can be no doubt that the first aim is fully achieved by retraction irrespective of the nature of grounds on which the accusation was made. But, can it be said that the second object shall also be achieved when the accusation was recklessly made? Under Muslim law the *Qāḍī* had to punish the husband for slander on his retraction. This he did on his own initiative without being asked by the wife in this behalf. It was possible for the *Qāḍī* to do so because he possessed and exercised both civil and criminal powers. These powers are, however, now vested in different Courts so that a suit for dissolution of marriage on the basis of a false charge of unchastity by the husband against his wife shall be entertained by a civil Court, but the matter relating to slander falls within the jurisdiction of the criminal Courts. A civil Court is not seized of the power to convict the husband for slander on his admission that he was guilty of having falsely defamed his wife. It will merely dismiss the wife's suit for dissolution of marriage instituted under the doctrine of *li'ān*, but cannot punish the husband for slander. She will have to file a complaint in a criminal Court when it will be open to the husband to explain that the admission was made under coercion or under undue influence or plead some other such ground. The criminal Court will not punish the husband on the basis of his admission of the falsity of his accusation, but shall require the wife to prove the case of defamation. Hence the aim that the husbands shall be discouraged from wantonly accusing their wives of unchastity shall be lost. It is, therefore, necessary to see that this object shall be achieved in some way or other. This can be done by vesting the civil Courts with power to punish a husband as provided in *li'ān*. But till such power is given to civil Courts, some other measures have to be taken. It is the duty of the Courts to afford protection to the wives against wanton and reckless acts of defamation and to discourage husbands from such acts. It is submitted that under the changed circumstances the decision provides an equitable and just proposition of law. Hence if it is established that the husband's accusation was *mala fide* or was made recklessly then it shall be established that his conduct was not only undesirable but amounted to cruelty and that the continuation of the marriage under these circumstances was very undesirable. The Courts may not, therefore, accept his retraction so that the marriage shall be dissolved.

Time: The next point for consideration is the stage up to which the retraction can be made. Under the Ḥanafī law, the *Qāḍī* shall ask the husband, on the wife's complaint, either to admit that his accusation of adultery against his wife was false or to take the prescribed oaths.[107] It is clear from this that the husband gets his first opportunity of retracting his charge at the commencement of the proceedings. It appears that the Ḥanafī law allows the husband to make his retraction at any time before the *Qāḍī* passes his order of dissolution of the marriage.[108] The husband can retract his accusation even after the *Qāḍī* has separated the parties when the marriage shall not be restored, but the parties shall become competent to remarry if they like.[109] The Courts have differed on the question of the time when the husband can lawfully retract his accusation. In a case before the Allahabad High Court, Sulaiman J. (as he then was) expressed a doubt as to how far the rule of procedure under the Muslim law permitting

107. Ibn 'Ābidīn, *op. cit.*, Vol. II, p. 603.
108. *Ibid*, p. 604; *al-Fatāwā al-Hindiyah, op. cit.*, Vol. II, p. 130.
109. *Ibid.*

a husband to make his retraction even after the evidence of the parties has closed, can now be applicable to a case where retraction did not come till after the close of the evidence.[110] Mears, C. J. refrained from expressing any definite opinion as to what view he would have expressed if the retractiom might have been made in the written statem ent, but it appears that he might have held it valid. It was not, however, necessary for the Court to decide this point as retraction made in that case was held to be no retraction at all. The Oudh Chief Court has held that a retraction made by the husband in his written statement was sufficient and valid.[111] The Allahabad High Court in another case has also expressed the same view as that stated by the Oudh Chief Court and has held that a retraction made by the husband in his written statement cannot be rejected on the ground of delay. It has been pointed out that the first hearing in a suit commences when the Court looks into the pleadings in order to formulate the points in controversy between the parties.[112]

Under the Muslim law, as stated before, a retraction can be made at any time before or after the passing of the *Qāḍī's* order.[113] The Calcutta High Court has stated that a retraction in the husband's deposition cannot be availed of because it was made after the commencement of the hearing of the suit. But the Allahabad High Court has stated in another case that the Muslim law of evidence has been superseded and so under the present law a party cannot set up a new case after the pleadings have been filed.[114] This decision leads to the result that a retraction made after the filing of the written statement cannot help the husband. The important thing to be seen in a

110. Mst. Rahiman Bibi Vs. Fazal, A.I.R. 1927 All. 56.
111. Mst. Fakhre Jahan Begum Vs. Mohammad Hamid Ullah Khan, A.I.R. 1929, Oudh, 16.
112. Kalloo Vs. Mst. Imaman, A.I.R. 1949, All. 445.
113. *Al-Fatāwā al-Hindiyah, op. cit.*, Vol. II, p. 130 ; Ibn 'Ābidīn, *op. cit.*, Vol. II, pp. 604, 605.
114. Shamsunnessa Khatoon Vs. Mir Abdul Mannaf, A.I.R. 1940, Cal. 95; Kalloo Vs. Mst. Imaman, A.I.R. 1949, All. 445.

case is that neither paaty should be taken by surprise and both parties should get an opportunity to meet the case of the other party. But in retraction there can be no question that the wife shall not be in a position to meet the husband's case and shall be taken by surprise. Moreover, the object of retraction is to clear the wife's character and this object is achieved even if the retraction is made at a late stage. It is, therefore, not necessary that it should be made only at the time of the filing of the written statement or before it. It can be made under the provisions of Muslim law at any time before the *Qāḍī's* decree and there is no reason to change the rule. The Dacca High Court has not followed this view and has held that a retraction to be valid must be made before the commencement of the hearing.[115] The Bombay High Court has, however, held that a retraction can be made at any time before the close of a case.[116] It is submitted that this view is correct.

XV. Oaths or Imprecations when not incumbent

The prescribed oaths cannot be administered under the following circumstances:—

(*a*) When the wife does not demand the same,

(*b*) When the husband establishes the wife's guilt in the ordinary way, that is, by producing four eye-witnesses in support of his statement,

(*c*) When the wife is found pregnant as a result of the adultery of which the husband had accused her,

(*d*) When the wife confesses her guilt, and

(*e*) When the husband or the wife loses his or her capacity for *li'ān* before the administration of the prescribed oaths.

XVI. Applicability of Li'ān

Under the current law the doctrine of *li'ān* is not obsolete

115. Mohammad Shariful Islam Khan Vs. Mst. Suraya Begum, P.L.D. 1963, Dacca 947.

116. Muhammad Ali Muhammad Ebrahim Quraishi Vs. Hazra Bai, A.I.R. 1955, Bom. 265.

but is still enforceable and often resorted to in India and Pakistan according to the procedure adopted by the Courts. The Muslim Personal Law (*Sharī'ah*) Application Act of 1937 and the Dissolution of Muslim Marriages Act, 1939, fully support this view. Section 2 of the former reads as follows:—

"Notwithstanding any custom or usage to the contrary, in all questions (save questions relating to agricultutal land) regarding intestate succession, special property of females, including personal property inherited or obtained under contract or gift or any other provision of Personal Law, marriage, dissolution of marriages, including *ṭalāq*, *'īlā'*, *ẓihār*, *li'ān*, *khul'* and *mubārāt*, maintenance, or dower, guardianship, gifts and trust properties and *waqfs* (other than charities, and charitable institutions and charitable and religious endowments) the rule of decision in cases where the parties are Muslims shall be the Muslim Personal Law (*Sharī'at*)."

Section 2(IX) of the Dissolution of Muslim Marriages Act, 1939, provides for dissolution of marriage on any other ground recognised as valid for the dissolution of marriage under Muslim law." Hence a wife can still claim the dissolution of her marriage under the doctrine of *li'ān*.

It is contended sometimes that after the passing of the Dissolution of Muslim Marriages Act, 1939, a marriage can be dissolved only on the grounds laid down in that Act. As *li'ān* is not a ground under that Act, a marriage cannot be dissolved on the basis of a false charge of adultery having been made by the husband against his wife. This contention is not correct for two reasons, namely,

(*a*) Section 2 of the Act provides that a wife shall be entitled to get a decree for the dissolution of her marriage on any one or more of the following grounds.....Various grounds have then been enumerated and clause IX reads as under:

IX. On any other ground which is recognised as valid for the dissolution of marriage under Muslim law.

It is obvious from the above provision that a marriage which can be dissolved under the provisions of the Muslim law can also be dissolved under the provisions of the Act.

Secondly, the Act has considered it sufficient to state in a general way that a marriage can still be dissolved on any ground recognised as sufficient by Muslim law. The Legislature must have thought it necessary to clear this point so that a doubt be not entertained that after the passing of the Act a marriage could be dissolved only on the basis of the grounds specified in the Act and on no other grounds. The Act has not given the procedure to be adopted as that is clear from any book on Muslim law. Thus the Act has not given the various provisions of Muslim law relating to '*Īlā*' and *ẓihār* which is given in all books on Muslim law. As a matter of fact, the Act has not mentioned all the grounds deemed sufficient for dissolution of marriage by Muslim law nor the procedure to be adopted in those cases. Thus a marriage can be dissolved when only the wife of a person embraces Islam. A marriage can, therefore, be dissolved not only on the basis of *li'ān* but on several other grounds also.

The question now arises whether the doctrine of *li'ān* can still be applied entirely in its old form or whether it has become inapplicable. To determine this question, we have to see that the doctrine of *li'ān* consists of two different and distinct parts, namely, (*i*) the investment of a certain legal right in the wife accused of adultery, and (*ii*) the procedure to be adopted for the enforcement of the wife's legal right. The first part constitutes substantive law while the second part merely amounts to procedure. As the Muslim law of marriage and divorce is still applied to Muslims the substantive portion of the law shall govern them. The Courts have accepted this proposition and have expressed the view in several cases that the substantive law is still applicable to Muslims, but the portion relating to procedure is no longer applicable as Muslim law of Evidence and procedure has been superseded by the Evidence Act.[117] It has now to be determined as to what portion of *li'ān* forms substantive law and what portion relates to procedure. *Li'ān* may be con-

117. Mst. Lelan Vs. Rahim Buksh, P.L.D. 1951, B.J. 91.

sidered with regard to its following aspects :—

(1) Wife's right to demand dissolution of her marriage,

(2) *Qāḍī's* advice to the wife to desist from having recourse to *li'ān*.

(3) Administration of the prescribed oaths.

(4) *Qāḍī's* advice to the husband to retract his accusation, and

(5) Retraction by the husband.

1. *Wife's right*: There is no difference of opinion or uncertainty about the wife's right to demand the dissolution of her marriage when her husband accuses her of unchastity. This provision of *li'ān* has been held to relate to substantive Muslim law and so is still applicable in India and Pakistan.[118]

2. *Qāḍī's advice*: Under the provision of Muslim law, the *Qāḍī* has to advise the wife to desist from resorting to *li'ān*. The rule is based on the Traditions relating to *li'ān* wherein it is stated that the Prophet (peace be on him) admonished the husband and told him that the punishment in the next world was far more serious than the punishment to be awarded in the matter (if he retracts). He gave a similar warning to the wife.[119] It was not an essential condition of *li'ān* that the *Qāḍī* should dissuade the parties from resorting to *li'ān* but was considered proper for him to adopt this step. The Courts have held that it is not their duty to ask the wife to desist from her suit. The *Qāḍī's* admonition to the spouses to desist from resorting to *li'ān* relates to procedure only and so is no longer binding on the Courts, since procedure can and has been changed.

3. *Administration of Oaths*: Adultery is a very serious crime in Islam and a very severe punishment has been prescribed for it. Since, however, under *li'ān* the husband

118. Rahiman Bibi Vs. Fazal, A.I.R. 1927, All. 56; Lelan Vs. Rahim Buksh, P.L.D. 1951, B.J. 91; Mst. Bano Vs. Inayat Husain, A.I.R. 1948, All. 34.

119. Abū Dāw'ūd, *op. cit.*, Vol. I, p. 307.

is not required to produce witnesses, the wife cannot be convicted for adultery as that can only be done if the charge against her is substantiated by four eye-witnesses and so it is not possible to establish whether the allegations made by the husband against his wife were correct or not.

Under the circumstances the spouses resorting to *li'ān* are required to take certain oaths, prescribed by the Muslim law, to substantiate their statements, husband's allegations and wife's denial of the same. The oaths, as explained in the discussion on procedure of *li'ān*, are accompanied by imprecations involving the wrath and curse of Allah.

The Muslim Jurists consider that punishment for various crimes has been prescribed to instil fear in the minds of the people so that they may not commit a crime or offence. The punishment may be corporeal or otherwise. The oaths prescribed for the husband and the wife expose one of them whose oaths are false to the curse or wrath of Allah which is a punishment far more severe than any worldly punishment can be. After the imprecations the matter was left between the spouses and their Creator, and no corporeal punishment was awarded although the marriage was dissolved.

Can it be said that the administration of the oaths is a substantive right of the spouses who can escape the punishment for slander and for adultery by having recourse to *li'ān*? Under the existing law in India and Pakistan a wife is not liable to any punishment for committing adultery and so she does not stand in need of *li'ān* to escape any punishment. The view adopted by the Courts in a number of cases is that it is not now incumbent on the spouses to take the prescribed imprecations on the ground that they relate to the Muslim law of evidence and the Muslim law of evidence having been superseded, the spouses shall be governed by the present law wherein the imprecations do not find any place. Besides, formerly if a husband refused to take the prescribed oaths or to admit the falsity of his accusation, the *Qāḍī* could imprison him till he complied with the order. But there is no provision of law which empowers a Court to take such an action. The Court can take action against the party concerned for contempt of Court for not complying with its order, but such an order would be of quite a different nature from the *Qāḍī's* order under which a party was kept in prison so long as it did not comply with his order and cannot be passed now. It was expressly held by the Lahore High Court that the procedure of *li'ān* was the result of circumstances which no longer exist and would be wholly out of place in the present state of the law.[120]

It was pointed out by the Lahore High Court in the case that this provision does not prescribe that the procedure of *li'ān* was to be followed but that it was meant simply to make certain that a wife could get a divorce on the basis of her husband's accusation of her adultery.[121]

The Courts consider that the procedure prescribed by the Muslim law has been superseded by the present-day law, so that the wife cannot ask the Court to order her husband either to retract his statement or to take the prescribed oaths. It is, however, open to the parties to a suit to agree that it may be decided on one spouse taking the prescribed imprecations. This matter shall be governed by the Oaths Act (Act X of 1872) which provides for giving such special oaths as may be agreed upon between the parties.

4. *Advice by the Qāḍī to the husband to retract his accusation against his wife*: Under the provisions of *li'ān* the *Qāḍī* has to ask the husband either to take the prescribed oaths or to admit the falsity of his accusation.[122] The admission by the husband that his accusation against his wife was false amounts to a retraction by him of the accusation. It has been held by the Courts that it is not necessary for a Court to ask the husband whether he wants to retract his accusation or if he wants to

120. Ghulam Bhik Vs. Hussain Begum, 1957, P.L.D. Lahore, 998.
121. *Ibid.*
122. Burhān al-Dīn al-Marghīnānī, *op. cit.*, Vol. II, p. 398 ; *al-Fatāwā al-Hindiyah, op. cit.*, Vol. II, p. 130.

proceed with the case.[123] It is left to the husband to retract his accusation or not to do so as he may think proper without being expressly asked by the Court for it. It was stated that the offer to retract by the *Qāḍī* to the husband relates to procedure and so it is no longer necessary for the Court to make such an offer and it does not form an essential condition of *li'ān.*[124]

It was stated by the High Court of Bombay that the Indian Courts are not bound to give the husband an opportunity or offer to retract. It has also pointed out in that case that Mulla was not right in stating in his book "*Mohammadan Law*" that the High Court of Bombay had expressed the opinion that retraction has no place in the procedure in British Courts in India and that what was actually held was the view that the Indian Courts are not bound to give the husband an opportunity to retract.[125]

XVIII. Burden of Proof

The burden of proof in suits on the basis of *li'ān* can relate to two things, namely,

(*a*) Whether the husband had accused the wife of adultery, and

(*b*) Whether the accusation was true or false.

(*a*) As regards the first point, if the husband denies the wife's allegation that he had accused her of adultery then she has to establish that fact by producing witnesses. If she fails to do so, her suit shall fail.[126] This establishes the fact that the burden of proving that the husband had accused her of adultery lies on the wife.

123. Ahmad Suleman Vohra Vs. Bai Fatima, A.I R. 1931, Bom. 76; Lelan Vs. Rahim Bux, P.L.D. 1951 B.J. 91

124. *Ibid.*

125. Muhammad Ali Muhmood Ebrahim Quraishi Vs. Hazra Bai, A.I.R 1955, Bom. 265.

126. *Al-Fatāwā al-Hindiyah, op. cit.*, Vol. II, p. 132.

(*b*) As already discussed before, the question of the determination of the wife's guilt or innocence is left undecided under the provision of *li'ān.* Hence the question of burden of proof does not come into the picture at all. It has, however, been held by the various High Courts in different cases that the wife in order to succeed in her case must establish that the husband's accusation was false.[127] This view introduces a new condition foreign to the law of *li'ān.* A Lahore Bench of the High Court of West Pakistan has, however, held that a wife is not bound to prove that the husband's accusation was false and she has merely to assert that it was not true and that it is for the husband to establish that his accusation was true.[128] This opinion introduces a new view-point which is different from that taken in other cases but more in conformity with the Muslim law. The correct position would be as stated in the judgement at another place that the wife would be entitled to get a divorce if her husband's accusation against her is not correct, and throws the burden on the husband to prove that his accusation against his wife was true. As stated before, the question of burden of proof does not arise in *li'ān* under Muslim law and the matter is left out of consideration altogether. But under the present-day law, the question of burden of proof cannot be ignored. It must, however, be realised that the view expressed in various rulings that the wife must establish her innocence places her in a very difficult and embarrassing position. Here the husband makes a serious charge against his wife and it is more

127. Zafar Husain Vs. Mst. Umat-ur-Rahman A.I.R. 1919, All. 182.

128. Ghulam Bux Vs. Husain Begum, P.L.D. 1958, Lah. 998 ; Muḥammad Hussain Vs. Mst. Begum Jan A.I.R. 1927, Lahore, 155 Mst. Fakhre Jahan Begum Vs. Mohammad Hameedullah Khan, A.I R. 1929 Oudh, 16 ; Khatija Bibi Vs. Umar Saheb, Ansar Saheb A.I.R. 1928, Bombay, 285.

appropriate that he should prove the correctness of his charge against his wife.

XIX. Changes introduced by the Anglo-Indian Courts

The Courts have introduced certain changes in the Muslim law of *li'ān*, which may be summarised as under :—

(1) It is no longer considered necessary for the husband and the wife to take the oaths prescribed by the Muslim law of *li'ān.*

(2) The parties are required to produce evidence to prove their version. The wife has to prove her innocence of the accusation levelled by her husband against her while the husband has to establish the guilt of his wife.

(3) The Court does not advise the parties to desist from having recourse to *li'ān.*

(4) The Court does not advise the husband to retract his accusation and the wife to withdraw her case,

(5) The provisions of retraction have not been fully observed in some cases.

It is now proposed to fully discuss the above matter.

1. The provisions of *li'ān* make it obligatory on the husband to take the oaths prescribed by the Qur'ān. The Courts have, however, held that this matter relates to procedure and the Mulim law of evidence having been superseded the matter shall be decided by the present law which makes no provision for the prescribed oaths. This matter has already been discussed with regard to the applicability of *li'ān.*

2. As regards the second point, the fact whether the husband's accusation was correct or false is immaterial under the provision of the Muslim law. It is neither decided nor even taken into consideration. The marriage is dissolved not because the accusation was false, but only on the ground that such an accusation of unchastity was made by the husband against his wife.

It is an essential condition of *li'ān* that the husband should not be in a position to produce four eye-witnesses in support of his accusation against his wife.[129] If he is in a position to do so, the wife shall be punished for adultery and the procedure of *li'ān* shall have no application at all.[130] The wife is not required to produce any evidence to prove her innocence. The provisions of *li'ān*, therefore, require the parties to confirm or deny the truth or falsity of the accusation by the prescribed oaths. The Courts have overlooked this important rule of *li'ān* and they require the husband to prove the wife's guilt while the wife has to prove her innocence. The Courts seem to have been misled by the rule of the Muslim law that the wife should be chaste to be entitled to the proceedings of *li'ān*. To understand the position clearly it is necessary to understand that only such men and women are competent for *li'ān* as are competent for giving evidence. The Evidence Act in force now provides that a person should fulfil certain requirements before he or she can appear as a witness. Thus it is necessary that he should be sane. Muslim law of Evidence requires a person to satisfy certain additional conditions before he or she can be held competent to depose as a witness. Thus it is an essential condition for *li'ān* that the husband or the wife should not have been previously punished for slander. In the case of a woman it is also necessary that she should be *muḥṣanah* and *'afīfah* (*i.e.* chaste). This condition of chastity relates to her general character and has no reference to the accusation in respect of which the proceedings under *li'ān* are being held. But as the Muslim law of Evidence has been superseded by the Evidence Act, it is no longer necessary that a witness should possess these requirements. It can thus be seen that there is no basis for the present-day practice that the wife should prove her innocence of the charge made by her husband against her before a decree for the dissolution of her marriage can be passed; such proof is foreign

129. Ibn 'Ābidīn, *op. cit.*, Vol. II, p. 601.
130. *Al-Fatāwā al-Hindiyah*, *op. cit.*, Vol. II, p. 132.

to the doctrine of *li'ān* under which the accusation is not allowed to be proved or disproved but the matter is left open and undecided. The basis of *li'ān* is that a husband cannot be happy with his wife if he suspects that she has been guilty of unchastity. The fact that he has not been able to substantiate his charge can make no difference in his outlook or attitude towards her. His treatment of his wife under such circumstances will obviously be undesirable and unkind if not exactly inimical. It is not considered desirable to force a wife to live in misery and under a cloud of suspicion under such circumstances. It happens sometimes that a husband while harbouring suspicion of unchastity against his wife does not want to release her simply out of a spirit of revenge. It is also to meet such cases that *li'ān* has been sanctioned. The present-day practice of the Courts is not only against the provisions of the Muslim law, but is definitely harmful as it sometimes condemns a wife to a lifelong misery when her husband contrives to prove that she has been erratic in her conduct. It will be more in consonance with the spirit of the Muslim law to dissolve a marriage if it is proved that the husband had made a charge of unchastity against his wife, unless he retracts his accusation as discussed elsewhere.

XX. Nature of Li'ān

Li'ān does not admit of forgiveness or compromise, so that when the procedure of *li'ān* is over, the *Qāḍī* has to separate them (the spouses) even though they may agree or want to forgive each other and even when the husband wants to condone the adultery.[131] This seems to be rather harsh but is meant to check hasty accusation by a husband. In the present-day time the parties can compromise the case at any time before the passing of the decree.

XXI. Appointment of Agent

Li'ān does not admit of agency. Hence if the parties or one of them should appoint an agent for *li'ān* the appointment

131. *Al-Fatāwā al-Hindiyah, op. cit.*, Vol. II, p. 129 ; Ibn 'Ābidīn, *op. cit.*, Vol. II, p. 603.

would not be valid.[132] This is due to the fact that the parties have to take the prescribed oaths in person.

XXII. Effect of Li'ān

The marriage shall be dissolved only by the *Qāḍī's* order, or in other words, the *Qāḍī's* decree is an essential condition for the dissolution of marriage and the marriage subsists till the *Qāḍī's* decree.[133]

When the *Qāḍī* orders a separation between the parties, on the basis of the husband's denial of his paternity of a child then the child shall not be considered to be his, but shall be affiliated to the wife.[134]

Intimacy between the parties becomes unlawful after they have taken the prescribed oaths. But the marriage shall not be dissolved even then so that if one of the spouses happens to die before the *Qāḍī* has given his decree, the other shall inherit from the deceased.[135] If one of the parties loses his or her capacity for *li'ān* before the *Qāḍī's* order as when he or she is convicted for slandering some one or the wife commits adultery, the proceedings of *li'ān* shall drop.[136] This is based on the reasoning that the capacity should continue till the decree is passed.

XXIII. Legitimacy of Child

If a husband denies his parentage of a child, whether actually born or not yet born, this denial shall amount to implied charge of unchastity of the wife. When the *Qāḍī* dissolves the marriage after imprecations on the basis of *li'ān* then it shall be necessary for him to disaffiliate the child from the husband.[137] If the *Qāḍī* fails to do so, the child shall be considered to belong to the husband of its mother.[138] The

132. *Al-Fatāwā al-Hindiyah, op. cit.*, Vol. II, p. 129.
133. *Ibid.*, p. 130 ; al-Marghīnānī, *op. cit.*, Vol. II, p. 398.
134. *Ibid* , p. 131 ; *Ibid.*, p. 399.
135. *Ibid* , p. 130 ; Ibn 'Ābidīn, *op. cit.*, Vol. II, p. 601.
136. *Ibid.*, *ibid.*, p. 605.
137. *Ibid.*, p. 131 ; *ibid.*
138. *Ibid.*, p. 131.

child's descent from the husband of its mother can be negated by the *Qāḍī* only after the proceedings of *li'ān*. Hence if a person denies his parentage of a child and the wife confirms his allegation, there can be no *li'ān* and so the child cannot be disaffiliated from him and shall be considered to be his lawful child.[139] Similarly, if there can be no *li'ān* for want of capacity in the spouses or in one of them, the child shall be considered to be his lawful child in spite of his denial of the parentage of the child.[140] It is stated in *Radd al-Muḥtār* that six conditions, given below, have to be satisfied before a child can be disaffiliated from the husband:

(*a*) The marriage must have been dissolved by the *Qāḍī*,

(*b*) The accusation must have been made at the time of delivery or within the prescribed time.

(*c*) The husband should not have previously owned the child either expressly or by implication,

(*d*) The child should be alive at the time of the disaffiliation,

(*e*) Twin children should not have been born and

(*f*) The child cannot be considered his legitimate child under the provisions of Muslim law.[141]

XXIII. Nature of Separation

The separation that takes place in *li'ān* after the *Qāḍī's* decree is an irrevocable repudiation and puts an end to marital relationship and establishes the illegality of sexual intercourse and of remarriage.[142]

XXIV. Qāḍī's Decree

There is a difference of opinion on this point. Under the Ḥanafī law the mere accusation by the husband does not affect the marriage and separation shall not be effected thereby or by

139. *Al-Fatāwā al-Hindiyah, op. cit.*, Vol. II, p. 131.
140. *Ibid.*
141. Ibn 'Ābidīn, *op. cit.*, Vol. II, p. 605.
142. Al-Marghīnānī, *op. cit.*, Vol. II, p. 398; *al-Fatāwā al-Hindiyah, op. cit.*, Vol. II, p. 130; Ibn 'Ābidīn, *op. cit.*, Vol. II, p. 605.

mere *li'ān*.[143] The marriage shall continue to subsist till it is dissolve by divorce by the husband or by an order of the *Qāḍī*.[144] This rule is based on the fact that 'Uwaymir divorced his wife after the necessary imprecations in the presence of the Prophet (peace be on him) and was not stopped from doing so by the Prophet (peace be on him) which establishes the fact that the marriage is not dissolved by the imprecations but still continues.[145] Zafar, however, holds otherwise and according to him a separation does take place on the completion of *li ān*, that is, when the imprecations have been taken, independently of a judicial decree.[146] But the generally accepted view is that it is only the decree of the *Qāḍī* that dissolves the marriage so that the marriage subsists till then.[147]

Mālikī Law: Mālik has expressed the opinion that a separation takes place when the husband and the wife have taken the prescribed oaths even before the *Qāḍī's* order.[148]

Shāfi'ī Law: According to Shāfi'i the husband's imprecations result in a separation between the parties without any order of the *Qāḍī*.[149]

XXV. Remarriage

There is a difference of opinion as to whether the husband can remarry the wife after *li'ān*. According to Mālik, Shāfi'i Abū Yūsuf, Zafar and al-Ḥasan ibn Ziyād the wife becomes prohibited to the husband for ever on the dissolution of marriage under the provisions of *li'ān*; so that he cannot remarry her under any circumstances, and even on retraction

143. Al-Marghīnānī, *op. cit.*, Vol. II, p. 398; *al-Fatāwā al-Hindiyah, op. cit.* Vol. II, p. 130; Ibn 'Ābidīn, *op. cit.*, Vol. II, p. 605.

144. *Ibid.*

145. Ibn Hajar al-'Āsqalanī, *al-Dirāyah* published on the margin of *al-Hidāyah, op. cit*, Vol. II, p. 398.

146. Burhān al-Dīn al-Marghīnānī, *op. cit.*, Vol. II, p. 398.

147. Ibn 'Ābidīn, *op. cit.*, Vol. II, p. 605.

148. Muhammad b. Ahmad *Jawāhir al-'Uqūd, op. cit.*, p. 177.

149. *Ibid.*, p. 178.

by him.[150] This opinion is based on a Tradition that the Prophet (peace be an him) said, "The two (the spouses) who make imprecations can never come together."[151] Abū Ḥanīfah and Muḥammad, however, contend that after the husband's retraction, *li'ān* becomes null and ineffective and that the Tradition only meant that the parties cannot come together as long as they both persevere in their imprecations but after the husband's retraction the imprecations no longer remain either in substance or in effect and consequently they may then come together that is, remarry each other.[152] The spouses can thus remarry if after the *Qāḍī's* decree the husband admits the falsity of his accusation or the wife confirms the husband's charge.[153] The same result will follow if after *li'ān* but before the *Qāḍī's* order of separation one of the spouses becomes incapable for *li'ān* as when the husband is punished for defaming any other person or the wife commits adultery even though she is not punished for the same.[154] According to them, the husband and the wife can remarry under the following conditions:

(1) When the husband retracts his accusation irrespective of the fact as to whether he has been cnovicted for slander or not, or

(2) The wife admits her guilt, or

(3) When it is found subsequently that at the time of *li'ān* one of the parties was not competent to take the imprecations, or

(4) When both the husband and the wife or one of them renounces Islam and then again embraces it.

150. Al-Marghīnānī, *op. cit.*, Vol. II, p. 398 ; Ibn 'Ābidīn, *op. cit.*, Vol. II, p. 605.

151. Ibn 'Ābidīn, *op. cit.*, Vol. II, p. 601.

152. Al-Marghīnānī, *op. cit.*, Vol. II, p. 398 ; *al-Fatāwā al-Hindiyah*, *op. cit.*, Vol. II, p. 130 ; Ibn 'Ābidīn, *op. cit.*, Vol. II, p. 601.

153. *Al-Fatāwā al-Hindiyah*, *op. cit.*, Vol. II, p. 130 ; Ibn 'Ābidīn, *op. cit.*, Vol. II, p. 605.

154. *Ibid.*

The spouses can remarry only in the above-mentioned cases.[155]

XXVI. *Death of the Wife*

If the wife who was accused of adultery by her husband happens to die whether before or during the proceedings, the husband shall not be liable to be punished for the slander. Should the wife die before the imprecations are taken by the parties, then obviously the husband cannot be punished for defamation. This can be due to the fact that the right to seek redress was restricted to the wife alone and on her death it shall be extinguished. Shāfi'ī does not agree with this view and according to him the punishment is not to be remitted.[156] If she dies after the imprecations then, as stated before, the husband is not liable to any punishment for slander on account of *li'ān.*

XXVII. *Shī'i Law*

The Shī'i law of *li'ān* is practically the same as the Sunnī law. It differs from the latter only in respect of the following points:

(*i*) There can be no *li'ān* with respect to a woman married by a *Muta'h* or temporary marriage.

(*ii*) The wife should not be deaf or dumb.[157] The husband should not be blind because there he is incapable of witnessing the wife's guilt. But he can validly deny the parentage of a child born of his wife.[158]

(*iii*) In case of denial of parentage of a child, it is an essential condition that the marriage should have been consummated.[159]

155. *Al-Fatāwā al-Hindiyah, op. cit.*, Vol. II, p. 130.

156. Al-Nawawī, *Minhāj al-Tālibīn*, (Eng. tr. by Van Den Berg), London, 1914, p. 363.

157. Ja'far b. al-Ḥasan, *Sharā'i' al-Islām, op. cit.*, p. 231.

158. Abū Ja'far Muḥammad b. al-Ḥasan, *al-Istibṣār*, Najaf, 1956, Vol. III, pp. 372, 374.

159. Ja'far b. al-Ḥasan, *op. cit.*, p. 230.

(*iv*) It is not necessary that the proceedings of *li'ān* should be held before the *Qāḍī*; the parties can agree to follow the proceedings before any particular *mujtahid* (or a duly qualified learned man).[160] There is a difference of opinion as to whether a dumb person is competent for *li'ān*. The generally accepted view is that he is competent if his signs are well-understood.[161]

160. Ja'far b. al-Ḥasan, *op. cit.*, p. 232.
161. *Ibid.*, p. 231.

Chapter 19

MAFQŪD AL-KHABAR OR MISSING HUSBAND

Preliminary

A wife whose husband has been missing for a long time, is deprived of protection, companionship, pleasure of life and financial support. She is naturally put to great hardship on that account. It becomes necessary for her, under such conditions, to marry another person but she cannot enter into a second marriage because her marriage still subsists. It, therefore, becomes necessary not only for her but also in the interest of society to release her from the marriage-tie if she so wishes. Practically every nation provides relief for a wife under such circumstances and under the Muslim law she can seek an order from the *Qāḍī* that the husband may be presumed to be dead. She can then, on such order having been made, legally contract a second marriage. The *Qāḍī* can effect a separation between a missing person and his wife after the lapse of a certain period of time for reasons analogous to those in the case of a husband's impotence. When a husband cannot perform his marital duties, he is in law denying his wife the sexual life to which she has a right by virtue of the contract of marriage.[1]

II. *Religious Sanction*

The Muslim law about a missing person is based on a Tradition in which the Holy Prophet (peace be on him) is reported to have said with respect to the wife of a missing person that she is his wife until such time as his death or divorce shall appear.[2] 'Ali, the fourth Caliph, has followed this Tradition and has stated that a wife, in such circumstances,

1. Al-Marghīnānī, 'Alī b. Abī Bakr, *al-Hidāyah*, Delhi, n.d., Vol. II, p. 602.
2. *Ibid.*

shall wait till she receives news of her husband's death or her divorce. 'Umar, the second Caliph, is said to have subsequently adopted the view of 'Ali.[3]

III. *Definition*

A missing person according to Muslim law is one who has disappeared or has been taken a prisoner in a battle by the enemies, and it is not known whether he is still alive or not and whose whereabouts cannot be ascertained and have not been known and it is uncertain whether he is alive or has died.[4]

IV. *Time*

The principle of *Istiṣḥāb al-ḥāl* (i.e. things continue in the condition in which they are, until a change in them or in their condition is established), requires that the marriage should subsist until and unless the husband's death or a divorce by him is proved. But the principle of *Qiyās* (analogy) demands that the marriage should be dissolved as done in the case of impotency and '*Īlā* because the absence of the husband involves hardship to the wife. Hence the wife has the right to separate from her husband.[5] The Ḥanafīs, however, have followed *Istiṣḥāb* in this case and abandoned *Qiyās*. There is a difference of opinion among the Ḥanafī jurists on this point.

The Ḥanafī Jurists have fixed the period of time on the expiry of which a missing person shall be deemed to be dead on two considerations, namely :

(*a*) Natural age of man, and

(*b*) that a missing person should be presumed to be dead at that time when ordinarily he would have died a natural death.

The Ḥanafī Jurists determine this age of a person accord-

3. *Ibid.*, Shaykhzādah, *Majma' al-Anhur*, Constantinople, 1328 A.H., Vol. I, p. 721.

4. *Al-Fatāwā al-Hindiyah*, Kanpur, 1349 A.H., Vol. II, p. 296 ; Shaykhzādah, *op. cit.*, Vol. I, p. 721.

5. Ibn Rushd, *Bidāyat al-Mujtahid*, Cairo, n.d., Vol. II. p. 45.

ing to the period of time on attaining which people of his age and time and resembling him in constitution, health etc. and living in conditions in which he would have lived, die in the ordinary course of nature. Thus it is stated that according to *Ẓāhir al-Riwāyah*, a missing person should be declared to be dead when none of his coevals remain alive.[6] They also took into consideration the natural age of man of their own times, which differed at different times. There are several versions about the age fixed by Abū Ḥanīfah. Thus al-Ḥasan b. Ziyād has given it as one hundred and twenty years.[7] According to several reports Abū Ḥanīfah is stated to have fixed it at thirty, sixty, seventy and eighty years.[8] But it is generally accepted that he has fixed it at one hundred and twenty years.[9] Muḥammad reduced it to one hundred and ten and Abū Yūsuf to one hundred years. It is stated in *al-Hidāyah* also that he (Abū Yusuf) had fixed it at one hundred years.[10]

Al-Hidāyah and *al-Fatāwā al-Ālamgīriyah* have fixed it at ninety years. *Al-Hidāyah* justifies the reduction to ninety years on the ground that "the benevolence of the law, however, suggests that the term be fixed at ninety years as this is the shortest fixed term mentioned (by any Imām) and it is difficult to ascertain anything respecting the circumstances of the missing person's coevals or equals.[11] A missing person shall be considered under the Ḥanafī law to have died at the time when he would have attained an age of ninety and his wife shall then be entitled to the dissolution of her marriage. It can thus be seen that a missing person would be presumed (under the Ḥanafī law) to have died at the time when he would have attained an age at which he would die in the

6. Al-Marghīnānī, *op. cit.*, Vol. II, p. 602; Shaykhzādah, *op. cit.*, Vol. I, p. 721.
7. Al-Marghīnānī, *op. cit.*, Vol. II, p. 602.
8. Shaykhzādah, *op. cit.*, Vol. I, p. 722.
9. Al-Marghīnānī, *op. cit.*, Vol. II, p. 602.
10. *Ibid.*
11. *Ibid.*

ordinary course of nature. Thus if a person is found missing at a time when he was twenty years old his death would be presumed after one hundred, ninety or eighty years according to the opinion of Abū Ḥanīfah, Muhammad and Abū Yūsuf respectively.

It is apparent from the above that different ages were fixed by the Imams according to the natural ages of men in their own time and place.

The rule that a wife shall be free to remarry only when her husband can be presumed to have died a natural death is due to over-cautiousness of the Imāms. It would have been easy for a destitute wife to get financial aid from Bayt al-Māl (Public Treasury) in the times of the Imāms, but it can no longer be possible for the wife of a missing person to get such aid. The Imāms could have no idea of the financial hardships and low standard of morality now prevalent. They laid down rules suitable for their own times. The Jurists of later period fixed the natutal age of man at sixty years. Thus it is stated in *Fatḥ al-Qadīr* that the "moderns" have adopted the age of sixty years on the ground that it is the probable limit of age.[12] Even this period involves great hardship to a wife in modern times and it was for the Muslim Jurists of still later period to further reduce the period to avoid such hardship—particularly when they are so anxious to save a wife from temptation to fall in evil ways.

Under certain exceptional circumstances, the death of a person can be presumed earlier than the above prescribed periods when circumstances point to an earlier death. Thus when a person takes part in some battle and is missing or when be left his abode while suffering from a serious malady in which his death was apprehended or when he went on a voyage but no trace can be found of his ship reaching the coast, the *Qāḍī* can then declare that the missing person should be deemed to have died.[13]

12. Ibn al-Humām, *Fatḥ al-Qadīr*, Cairo, 1356 A.H., Vol. IV, p. 445
13. Ashraf 'Alī Thānawī, *al-Ḥīlat al-Nājizah*, Karachi, n.d., p. 99.

Some Jurists, however, hold that no definite period can be fixed but the matter should be left to the *Qāḍī* who shall decide every case of this nature according to its particular facts and this is the more generally accepted view.[14] Some other jurists are of the opinion that the matter must be decided by the Ruler.[15]

Māliki Law : Mālik has taken a more realistic view of the matter. Under the Mālikī law a wife can apply to the *Qāḍī* for the dissolution of her marriage when her husband has been missing. The *Qāḍī* thereupon shall himself make a search for the missing husband and if he cannot be traced, the urge shall have to wait for four further years. The husband shall then be presumed to be dead and the wife shall have to observe the '*iddah* prescribed for the husband's death. She can then contract a second marriage[16] Mālik has fixed the period of four years on the basis of an order passed by 'Umar, the second Caliph who fixed such period at four years.[17] A second order of the *Qāḍī* on the expiry of the period of four years is not necessary.

According to Mālik the period of fours years commences from the time when the *Qāḍī* passes his decree.[18] According to *Bidyāt al-Mujtahid* four years will be counted from the time the suit was filed.[19]

The period of four years can still be reduced to one year under the Mālikī law when the wife has already waited for a considerable time for her husband or when it is feared that she may be led astray on account of the absence of her

14. Ibn 'Ābidīn, *Radd al-Muḥtār*, Cairo, 1318 A.H., Vol. IV, p. 341
15. *Al-Fatāwā al-Hindiyah, op. cit.*, Vol. II, p. 296 ; Shaykhzādah, *op. cit.*, Vol. I, p. 721.
16. Ashraf 'Alī Thānawī, *op. cit* , p. 104 ; *Cf.* al-Marghīnānī, *op.cit.*, Vol. II, p, 602.
17. Al-Marghīnānī, *op. cit.*, Vol. II, p. 602.
18. Ibn 'Ābidīn, *op. cit.*, Vol. IV, p. 340 ; Ashraf 'Alī, *op. cit.*, p. 104.
19. Ibn Rushd, *op. cit.*, Vol. II, p. 43.

husband and may commit that which is not lawful.[20]

Shāfi'ī Law: Shāfi'ī at first agreed with Mālik and held that a missing husband would be presumed dead on the expiry of four years, but subsequently he changed his opinion and adopted the same view as expressed by the Ḥanafī Jurists and fixed the requisite period at ninety years.[21] The Shāfi'ī law is, therefore, the same as the Ḥanafī law.

Ḥanbali Law: Aḥmad b. Ḥanbal has also fixed the period of time on the expiry of which a person shall be presumed to be dead at four years if the circumstances point to the early death of the husband. In the absence of such circumstances the matter is to be decided by the Imām or by the Ruler of the country.[22] There are contradictory reports about his opinion in respect of commencement of the time. According to one report, the period of four years shall commence from the time of the *Qāḍī*'s order. But, according to the other report, it shall commence from the time of the husband's disappearance.[23]

V. *Adoption of Mālikī and Hanbali Laws by Hanafis*

The Ḥanafī law involves great hardship to the wife of a missing person. The Ḥanafī Jurists, therefore, allow her in such a case to have recourse to a Mālikī or Hanbali *Qāḍī* and have the matter decided by him according to that law.[24] For all practical purposes the law now applicable to the Ḥanafīs is the law as laid down by Mālik and Ahmad b. Hanbal.

VI. *English Law*

It will be interesting to note that under the English Civil law a person was at one time presumed to be dead at such time when he would have attained an age of one hundred years.[25] But considering the hardship that was caused in

20. Ashraf 'Alī, *op. cit.*, pp. 115, 116.
21. Ibn Qudāmah, al-Mughnī, Cairo, 1367 A.H., Vol. VII, p. 488.
22. Ibn 'Ābidīn, *op. cit.*, Vol. IV, p. 340.
23. Ibn Qudāmah, *op. cit.*, Vol. VII, p. 492.
24. Ibn 'Ābidīn, *op. cit.*, Vol, II, p. 552,
25. Taylor, A Treatise on the Law of Evidence, Vol. I, 1931, London.

some cases an exception was provided in English law to this rule to the effect that a person would be presumed to be dead if he has not been heard of by such persons as would have normally heard from him for a period of seven years. Under certain exceptional circumstances a shorter period could be deemed sufficient for the presumption of death. Thus when a person had sailed in a ship two or three years before and the ship had not been heard of since then his death was presumed.[26]

VII. *Change introduced by the Evidence Act*

The law in the case of a missing person forms part of Muslim law of Evidence which has been superseded in India and Pakistan by the Evidence Act, that follows the English law in this matter. Section 108 of the Act provides for a presumption that a person shall be considered to have died if he has not been heard of for seven years by those who would naturally have heard from him if he had been alive. The matter was discussed at length in the case of Mazhar Ali Vs. Budh Singh which has been followed in other cases.[27] It has been held there that the matter of a missing person pertains to the law of Evidence and the Muslim law of Evidence having been superseded, the case of a missing person shall be governed by the provisions of the Evidence Act. A wife had therefore to wait for seven years for her missing husband when he could be presumed to be dead. The period of seven years commences from the time since when the husband has not been heard of and not from the time of the order of the Court as under the Mālikī law.

VIII. *Changes intoduced by the Dissolution of Muslim Marriages Act, 1939*

The Dissolution of Muslim Marriages Act, 1939, has further reduced this period of seven years to four years as the necessary period for presumption of the death of a missing husband with regard to his wife. Section 2 of the Act

26. Watson Vs. King, I Stark, 121.
27. Mazhar Ali. Vs. Budh Singh, I.L.R. 7 All p, 297.

provides that a woman married under Muslim law shall be entitled to obtain a decree for the dissolution of her marriage on the ground :

(*a*) That the whereabouts of the husband have not been known for a period of four years ;

....

Provided that—

....

(*b*) Provided that a decree passed on ground (*a*) shall not take effect for a period of six months from the date of such decree, and if the husband appears either in person or through an authorised agent within that period and satisfies the Court that he is prepared to perform his conjugal duties, the Court shall set aside the said decree.

This clause based on the Mālikī law is an improvement on it inasmuch as the period of four years does not commence from the time of the *Qāḍī's* order, but begins from the time when the husband disappeared. A wife can file a suit under this clause at any time after the expiry of four years from the time of the husband's disappearance. Moreover, the Court shall not ask her to wait any longer but shall decree her suit if the other conditions are satisfied. But it is submitted that even this period of four years is too long. Clause II of section 2 of the Act provides that a woman shall be entitled to the dissolution of her marriage if the husband fails or neglects to maintain her for a period of two years. The wife of a missing person can take advantage of this clause and seek the dissolution of her marriage after the period of two years. There seems to be no reason to force her to wait for a period of four years when her husband is missing. Communication was not only very difficult but also very slow in old times, but such is no longer the case and the whereabouts of a missing person can now be ascertained much sooner than in old times, if he is really alive. It is, therefore, no longer necessary to wait for four years to see if the husband is alive and to make the wife wait for such a long time.

IX. Qāḍī's Order

Under the Muslim law, the *Qāḍī's* declaration about the death of the missing husband is necessary before the husband can be presumed to be dead. It is only on such order having been made that the wife of the missing person shall be entitled to remarry after the observance of the prescribed *'iddah* for death. Under the Ḥanafī law a second order of the *Qāḍī* is necessary but it is not necessary under the Mālikī law. The Mālikī law is usually followed by the Ḥanafīs in respect of a missing person and so it shall not be necessary for her to secure a second order on the expiry of the prescribed period of *'iddah.*

X. Court's Order

Under the provisions of the Dissolution of Muslim Marriages Act, 1939, it is necessary for the wife to get the marriage dissolved by an order of the Court.

XI. Information respecting Husband's Death

If the husband of a woman has gone on journey to a distant place and should she receive reliable news that he has died she can then contract another marriage after the observance of her *'iddah.* This rule is based on the ground that here the husband is not missing, but the news related to an ordinary incident. It is, therefore, not necessary for her to seek the *Qāḍī's* permission.[28] But under the provisions of the present law it shall not be open to her to do so without getting a declaration from the Court about the husband's death.

Reappearance of the Husband: Should the missing husband reappear at a time when his wife has contracted a second marriage but the same has not been consummated then the wife shall go to the first husband. If, however, the marriage has been consummated the first husband shall be given an option either to have the wife or to take back the dower given by him

28. Ibn 'Ābidīn, *op. cit.*, Vol. II, p. 632.

to the wife.[29] It is stated in *Fatḥ al-Qadīr* that 'Ali held that the wife shall in every case belong to the first husband irrespective of the fact as to whether the second marriage has or has not been consummated.[30] 'Umar is said to have subsequently adopted the view held by 'Ali, though he held otherwise before.[31] The view has been adopted in *al-Fatāwa al-'Alamgīriyah* that if a missing husband should reappear at a time when his wife is observing *'iddah* or before it, then he shall be entitled to her, that is, to keep her as his wife. If he returns after she has married another person he shall not be entitled to recover her and the wife shall belong to the second husband.[32] Ameer Ali has also stated that in such a case "the wife would be for him" (that is the missing husband).[33] The right of the first husband to his wife shall not be lost when he returns after the expiry of the period of her *'iddah*, if she has not in the meantime contracted a second marriage.[34] But under the provision of the Dissolution of Muslim Marriages Act, 1939, the marital-tie shall be terminated on the expiry of six months from the time of the Court's decree, and the husband shall have no claim to her after this period.

XII. Shī'ī Law

The Shī'ī law in this matter is practically the same as the Māliki law. When the husband is missing and nothing is known of him and when there is no one to support his wife, she can approach the *Qāḍī* who shall adjourn the case for four years and make diligent enquiry about the husband within this period. If no information is received about him within this time, the *Qāḍī* shall direct the woman to observe *'iddah* as prescribed for the death of a husband and she can enter into a second marriage on the expiry of the *'iddah*.[35] If on the other

29. Ibn Qudāmah, *op. cit.*, Vol. VII, p. 492, Ashraf Ali Thanawi, *op. cit.*, pp. 111-113.
30. Ibn al-Humām, *op. cit.*, Vol. IV, p. 444.
31. *Ibid.*
32. *Al-Fatāwā al-Hindiyah, op. cit.*, Vol. II, p. 296.
33. Ameer 'Alī, *Muhammadan Law*, Calcutta, 1908, p. 117.
34. *Al-Fatāwā al-Hindiyah, op. cit.*, Vol. II, p. 296.
35. Ja'far b. al-Hasan, *Shārā'i' al-Islām*, Tehran, 1377 A.H., p. 213.

hand some information is received of the husband that he has not died then the *Qāḍī* shall direct her to have patience. In such a case it is the duty of the Imām or the Government to maintain her out of the Public Treasury. If she is being maintained by someone on behalf of the missing husband she is not entitled to the dissolution of her marriage.[36]

If the missing husband happens to return at a time when his wife is observing *'iddah* under the order of the *Qāḍī* then he has a right to get her back. But if she has contracted a second marriage or even when the period of the *'iddah* has expired then his right to his wife is lost and he cannot get her back.[37]

36. Ja'far b. al-Hasan, *Sharā'i' al-Islam*, Tehran, 1377 A.H., p. 213.
37. *Ibid.*

Chapter 20

CONVERSION

Section I.—Muslim Law

Preliminary: By conversion is here meant the adoption of Islam by a non-Muslim. To embrace Islam means to accept the unity of God, reckoning of the day of judgment and the prophethood of Hazrat Muhammad. A conversion presents no difficulty when the convert is unmarried or when both the husband and the wife embrace Islam at the same time. Difficulty often arises when the convert happens to be married and the other spouse prefers to remain in the fold of his or her own religion. The cases that generally arise with regard to conversion, relate to Hindu and Christian marriages. The Muslim law and the laws of these religions with regard to marriage and conversion and the effect of the conversion on an existing marriage are briefly discussed below:

Religious Sanction: It is laid down in the Qur'ān:

"And marry not the idolatresses until they believe; and certainly a believing slave girl is better than an idolatress even though she pleases you. Nor give (believing women) in marriage to idolaters until they believe, and certainly a believing slave is better than an idolater even though he pleases you....".[1]

Another verse of the Qur'ān reads:

> "This day (all) good things are made lawful for you. And the food of those who have been given the Book is lawful for you and your food is lawful for them. And so are the chaste from among believing women, and the chaste from among those who have been given the Book before you....".[2]

1. Qur'ān, Surah Al-Baqarah (The Cow) II : 221.
2. Qur'ān, Surah Al-Maidah (The Food), VI : 5.

There are several Traditions that throw light on the full implication of these verses. Ibn Abbas is reported to have said: "A woman accepted Islam and got married (to a Muslim). Her former husband came to the Prophet (peace be on him) and said, "O Messenger of Allah, I have accepted Islam and she had known my Islam", that is, the fact that he had accepted Islam, The Prophet (peace be on him) then separated her from her second husband and gave her back to her first husband.[3] This Tradition gives rise to the rule that if both the spouses adopt Islam or if on the conversion of one, the other also embraces Islam within the prescribed time, their marriage shall be maintained. Similarly, it is reported that the Prophet (peace be on him) rejected the marriages of some women (against their husbands) when the former had embraced Islam but their husbands had refused to do so.[4]

This Tradition establishes the rule that a marriage shall be dissolved when only one spouse adopts Islam and the other spouse refuses to do so. Ummi Hakim accepted Islam but her husband did not accept Islam. Ummi Hakim followed him to Yemen and she invited him to embrace Islam and he too adopted Islam and so they both remained firm in their marriage.[5] Dahhak is reported to have said: "I asked the Messenger of Allah (peace be on him), O' Prophet of Allah, I have accepted Islam, but I have two sisters (as wives)".—— He said, "Choose any of the two you like".[6] This Tradition gives rise to the principle that marriage before acceptance of Islam would remain valid provided it does not conflict with some express prohibition of Islam.

Marriage with a non-Muslim woman: Non-Muslim women can be divided into two classes, namely,

(*a*) Idolatresses, and

(*b*) Women belonging to a revealed religion.

3. Walī al-Dīn Al-Khaṭīb, *Mishkāt al-Maṣābih*, Delhi, n.d, p. 275 (Bab al-Muḥarramat).
4. *Ibid.*
5. *Ibid.*
6. *Ibid.*, p. 274.

Different rules apply to these two classes of women. They are discussed below separately.

(*a*) *Idolatress*: All Muslim jurists are agreed that marriage with an idolatress is absolutely prohibited and, if so contracted, it shall be a void marriage. Ameer Ali is of the opinion that such a marriage shall be *fasid* (irregular) and not *batil* (void).[7] But it is doubtful if the opinion is correct. The very clear prohibition in the Qur'ān and the unanimous rejection of such a marriage by the Muslim jurists leave no scope for doubting the invalidity of such a marriage.

(*b*) *Kitabiyah or women belonging to a revealed religion*: There is a difference of opinion about the validity of the marriage of a Muslim with a woman belonging to a revealed religion. One group of Muslim jurists considers such a marriage to be prohihited. They rely on the following arguments in support of their view:

(1) The word '*Mushrik*' (infidel) has been used in the Qur'ān in a general sense and applies both to 'Idolaters' and "People of the Book".[8] Where a certain verse is meant to apply only to the People of the Book then this matter has been clearly indicated. Here there is no specification about the word '*Mushrik*' which is used in a general sense, and so the People of the Book are included in the prohibiton.

(2) The People who believe in Trinity and attribute parenthood of Jesus Christ to God cannot be considered to belong to a revealed religion, but only such people can be considered to be People of the Book as are monotheists. They argue on the basis of the verse of the Qur'ān: "Certainly they disbelieve who say: Allah, He is the Messiah, Son of Mary.[9] They contend also that the verse in *Surah Al-Maidah* has been modified by the above verse thereby establishing

7. Ameer 'Alī, *Mohammedan Law*, Calcutta, 1908, p. 321.
8. Ameer 'Alī, *Tafsīr Mawāhib ar-Raḥmān*, Lucknow, 1926.
9. Qur'ān, Surah Al-Maidah (The Food), VI: 72.

the fact that Christians believing in Trinity are not People of the Book and marriage with a woman belonging to such people is prohibited because she is a *Mushrikah.*

Verse 5 of *Surah Al-Maidah* reads as under :

"This day all good things are made lawful for you........ And so are the chaste from among the believing women and the chaste from among those who have been given the Book before you, when you give them their dowries, taking (them) in marriage...."

The other group of jurists who constitute the majority base their view on the following grounds:

(1) The word '*Mushrik*' is not used in the above verse in a general sense but refers only to Idolaters as distinguished from the category of 'People of the Book.

(2) The mere belief in Trinity does not take the Christians out of the fold of 'People of the Book'. The verse does not make any distinction between Christians who believe in Trinity and those who are monotheists.

(3) The former verse 221 of *Surah Al-Baqarah* was revealed earlier ,and verse 5 of *Surah Al-Maidah* was revealedl ater, hence it cannot be modified by a verse that had been revealed earlier.

They, therefore, are of the opinion that the prohibition against the marriage with an idolatress does not apply to women who belong to a revealed religion. Aḥmad bin Ḥanbal has stated that the prohibition refers only to idolatresses. The same view is attributed to Abū Ḥanīfah, Abū Yūsuf. Muhammad, Ibn 'Abbas, Mujahıd, and to other early authorities. But such marriages, that is, marriages with women belonging to a revealed religion have been disapproved of and discouraged so that the Muslims may not ignore Muslim women. It is also contended that the mothers influence the beliefs and morals of the children and contact with their non-Muslim families may affect the husband and is bound to affect the beliefs and morals of the children. Such marriages have, therefore, been disapproved of.[10] Besides, when the spouses belong to different religions, sometimes it may not be possible to maintain cordial relations between them and such marriages are not desirable in the interest of Muslim society as well as of the spouses. These jurists contend that verse 5 of *Surah Al-Maidah* makes it clear that the prohibition in *Surah Al-Baqarah* relates only to Idolatresses and does not apply to women blonging to a revealed religion. It may also be noted that there has been a general practice amongst the Muslims to marry Christian women and Jewesses. Many Companions of the Prophet (peace be on him) had taken Christian women and Jewesses for their wives. '*Uthman*, the third Caliph, had married a Christian. Hudhayfah had contracted a similar marriage while Talhah b. Ubayd Allah had married a Jewess. Such marriages have been contracted in almost all countries in all ages. It can, therefore, be assumed that marriage with a Kitabiyāh has been permitted by Islam.

Basic Principles

1. *Preliminary*: The act of embracing Islam by a married non-Muslim couple or by one of them has a fundamental effect on their marriage. But before discussing various problems arising therefrom, it would be convenient to state a some basic rules of Muslim law relating to it.

2. *Universal Applicability of Muslim Law to Muslims*: Islam aims at establishing universal brotherhood and a common code of law for all Muslims wherever they may be living. In other words, it lays down that all Muslim countries shall be governed by the same laws. Islam does not recognise any barriers between Muslims, whether geographical, cultural or of any other kind or nature. A Muslim living in any Muslim country is in law entitled to enjoy the same rights and privileges as are enjoyed by the local Muslims. This is a natural sequence of Islam's conception of

10. Ibn 'Ābidīn, *Radd al-Muḥtār*, Cairo, 1318 A.H., Vol. II, pp. 488-89.

universal brotherhood of Muslims. A Muslim whether he be so by reason of birth or by subsequent adoption of the faith, is governed only by the provisions of Muslim law wherever he or she may be living and wherever he or she may go and reside. A person cannot be governed under the provisions of Muslim law by *lex-domicilii* that is, the law of the country of which he is a permanent citizen or where he intends to settle permanently as opposed to a temporary residence. Thus, if an Arab Muslim takes up his domicile in a foreign country, say England, then, according to the provisions of Muslim law, he shall still be governed by his personal law and not by the English law because the Prophet (peace be on him) is reported to have said "Islam prevails and is not prevailed upon". The same shall be the result if an English man or woman embraces Islam in England but retains his or her domicile there. Under Muslim law he shall immediately on his conversion become subject to Muslim law. This rule of Muslim law was recognised in an even more extended form in a case where it was held that Punjabi Muslims living in East Africa continued to be governed by their personal law, namely. Muslim Hanafi law in that case, and were not subject to the law of the Muslims of that country which happened to be the law of a different sect of the Muslims.[11] On conversion to Islam, a person automatically becomes subject to the Muslim law without any regard to his domicile or the law of the country of his domicile.

3. *Marriage Permitted*: A Muslim can lawfully marry a *Muslimah* and a *Kitabiyah*, that is, a woman belonging to a revealed religion.

4. *Marriage Forbidden*: A marriage cannot be allowed to subsist in violation of the injunctions of the Qur'ān or the Sunnah. Hence, a Muslim cannot marry an idolatress, atheist or any other non-Muslim woman who does not belong to a revealed religion. A marriage between a Muslim and an

11. Fazalan Vs. Tehran, 8 East African Law Reports (Kenya) 200.

idolatress or a woman belonging to a non-revealed religion is not permissible. Islam does not permit polyandry and permits limited polygamy so that a Muslim can have four wives at one and the same time while a Muslimah cannot have more than one husband at the same time. But she can have another husband on the dissolution of her first marriage even during the lifetime of the other party. A Muslimah, that is, a Muslim woman, cannot marry or be married to a non-Muslim whether belonging to a revealed religion or not. Such a marriage is absolutely forbidden.[12]

5. *Validity of Non-Muslim Marriages Recognised*: Islam recognises the validity of the marriages of non-Muslim solemnised according to the provisions of their own religion so that if a non-Muslim married couple embraces Islam, It shall not be necessary for them to solemnise it again according to the provisions of Muslim law.[13] But this rule is subject to the condition that their marriage should be valid according to their own religion even if it contravenes some minor provisions of Muslim law, such as the absence of witnesses or a marriage solemnised during '*iddah*' that is, the term of waiting.[14] But if the marriage be such as is absolutely prohibited under Muslim law, then it shall not be held valid on the conversion of the spouses. Thus if a non-Muslim had married a woman who would be considered prohibited to him by reason of relationship, fosterage, etc. the marriage shall be dissolved on their conversion to Islam.[15] The recognition of a marriage solemnised according to the laws of non-Muslims is based on the fact that in the Qur'ān, mention has been made of the wife of Abu Lahab, who was an idolater while the word "wife" denotes a lawfully married woman.[16] If the marriage

12. Qur'ān, Surah Al-Baqarah (The Cow) II : 221.
13. *Al-Fatāwā al-Hindiyah*, Kanpur, 1349 A.H. Vol. II, p. 38 ; Ibn 'Ābidīn *op cit.*, Vol. II, p. 401.
14. Burhan al-Dīn al-Marghīnānī, *al-Hidayah*, Delhi n.d., Vol. II, p. 324 ; *al-Fūtāwā al-Hindiyah, op. cit.*, Vol. II, pp. 38-39.
15. *Al-Fatāwā al-Hindiyah, op. cit.*, Vol. II, p. 39.
16. Qur'ān, Surah Al-Lahab (The Flame), XXX : 4

is unlawful, according to their religion, then it shall be held invalid under Muslim law and the *Qāḍī* shall separate them.

The rules with regard to conversion applicable in a Muslim country differ from those that apply in a non-Muslim country. It is, therefore, necessary to discuss some important cases of conversion in these two classes of countries separately. But it would be convenient to understand as to who may be called a Muslim, a Dar al-Harb (non-Muslim country) and who is a *Qāḍī*.

Dar al-Islam—Definition of: Dar al-Islam or a Muslim State means a country in which the Muslims have the power to promulgate any laws that they may like.[17] A country shall also be considered to be Dar al-Islam if the laws of Islam are administered there or if the Muslims are able to fulfil freely the obligations incumbent on them by Islam. One of the tests to determine this condition is to see if prayers on Fridays and Eids can be held there.[18]

Dar āl-Harb—Definition of: Harb means war and this had led people to believe that the expression Dar al-Harb means a country which is at war with a Muslim country or is inimical to Muslims. But this notion is not quite correct and the expression is understood by the Muslim jurists in a special sense. By Dar al-Harb they mean a country where the non-Muslims are in power or enjoy such strength that they are in a position to promulgate any laws they like.[19]

Qāḍī—Definition of: A *Qāḍī* is a person appointed by the Government for administration of justice. He wields the powers of a magistrate as well as of a judge, that is, he exercises powers in criminal matters as well as in civil cases. He also attends to certain purely religious matters. As the

17. Ibn 'Ābidīn, *op. cit.*, Vol. III, p. 261.
18. *Ibid.* This problem has been fully discussed in Chapter on Tabayun Dar. (Difference of Domicile).
19. Ibn 'Ābidīn, *op. cit.*, Vol. III, p. 260.

religion in Dar al-Islam is Islam, the *Qāḍī* administers justice according to the provisions of Muslim law. If there were people belonging to various Muslim sects in a Muslim country, *Qāḍī* used to be appointed from each sect and he decided the cases of the particular sect to which he belonged. But the non-Muslims were governed by their own religious laws adminstered by their own priests or other persons in authority.

The rules governing cases of conversion differ in different classes of countries : It would, therefore, be convenient to discuss them in the following order :

(1) Rules common to Dar al-Islam and Dar al-Harb or Muslim and non-Muslim States,

(2) Rules applicable to Dar al-Islam, and

(3) Rules applicable to Dar al-Harb.

1. Rules common to Dar al-Islam and Dar al-Harb, or Muslim and non-Muslim countries.

Conversion—Effect of :

(a) Simultaneous Conversion of the Spouses: A marriage solemnised according to the provisions of any religion is considered a lawful marriage under Muslim law so that if the husband and the wife embrace Islam simultaneously then their marriage continues and it is not necessary for them to get remarried according to the provisions of Muslim law.[20] The domicile or place of residence, that is, whether they are living in a Muslim State or a non-Muslim country in this case makes no difference.[21]

Marriages Prohibited by Muslim Law: The above rule is subject to one exception. If the marriage between the spouses be such as is prohibited under the provisions of Muslim law, it shall terminate or shall be dissolved as the case may be.[22]

20. *Al-Fatāwā al-Hindiyah, op. cit.*, Vol. II, p. 38.
21. *Ibid.*
22. *Ibid.*, pp. 38-39.

The views of various schools on the point shall be presently noticed.

The guiding rule of law is to suppose that they are not married and then to see if they can contract a valid marriage under the provisions of Muslim law. If they can, their marriage shall be maintained but if the marriage is not permissible under Muslim law, then it shall be dissolved on their conversion.[23] Thus if a non-Muslim husband adopts Islam and should his wife or wives be unlawful under the provisions of Muslim law, then his case shall be governed by the provisions of Muslim law. Hence if a non-Muslim has more wives than four, then on conversion to Islam he shall be entitled to retain any four of them. But according to another opinion he can keep the four wives, who were married to him first, and the others shall become separated from him because under Muslim law he can marry and have only four wives at a time. Similarly, if he had married two sisters, the wife who was married first shall remain his wife while the other shall be separated from him.[24]

If more than four women or two sisters had been married by one single contract of marriage then it shall not be possible to distinguish the wives who can be considered lawful from those who shall be unlawful and so the marriage or marriages shall be void and the wives shall be separated from him.[25]

But the first view seems to be the better view and is supported by a Tradition quoted before, where the Prophet (peace be on him) allowed the husband to choose any one of the two sisters he liked.

Effect of Dissolution of Marriage and Re-marriage of the Spouses: It may be noted that under the provisions of the English law and the laws of certain other European countries if a marriage is dissolved then the husband cannot marry his

23. *Al-Fatāwā al-Hindiyah*, *op. cit.*, Vol II, p. 39.
24. *Ibid.*
25. *Ibid.*

sister-in-law and certain other female relations as long as the former wife is alive. The law is so strict in this matter that a clergyman may refuse to solemnise such a marriage and even refuse the use of the church for the solemisation of such a marriage.[26] But there is no such rule under Muslim law. It considers that on the severance of the marital-tie, they have nothing more to do with each other so that there can be no hinderance to the marriage of the former husband to the unprohibited relations of the wife.[27]

2. *Conversion in Dar al-Islam or Muslim State*: Before discussing the rules applicable to different cases of conversion, it would be useful to understand the basic ideas underlying those rules. The first thing to remember is that a marriage cannot be allowed to subsist in violation of the injunctions of the Qur'ān and the Traditions. Thus a marriage between a Muslim and an idolatress is forbidden while a Muslimah cannot marry any non-Muslim. A Muslim can marry a Kitabiyah but such marriages are discouraged. The primary consideration for the Muslim jurists seems to be that when the spouses belong to different religions, their difference of outlook in religious affairs, traditions and ceremonies and even in worldly affairs often leads to misunderstanding and even disharmony between them. These factors may preclude achievement of some of the ends of marriage. The difference of religions may lead to difficulties and complications in matters such as the upbringing and religious education of the child or children born of such marriages. The parents sometimes come to an understanding not to educate the children in any religion but to leave it to the child to choose any religion he or she likes when it grows up. This arrangement is not conducive to the character-building or good morals of the child. Moreover, when two persons are brought up in different religions, their outlook not only in religious matters but also to the mode of life differs considerably and sooner or later it leads to disharmony

26. Section 13(2) of the Matrimonial Causes Act, 1950
27. *Al-Fatāwā al-Hindiyah, op. cit.*, Vol. II, p. 39.

between them. Hence it is considered desirable that the spouses should belong to the same religion. At the same time it is considered that marriage being a serious thing should not be dissolved lightly, but an effort should be made to maintain it and to see that both the spouses adopt the same religion. The Muslim Jurists have laid down that an attempt be made to induce the other party to embrace Islam. If the marriage cannot be maintained on the conversion of one of them, the convert has to seek the aid of the *Qāḍī* and it has been made the duty of the *Qāḍī* to persuade the other spouse to follow the example of the convert and to embrace Islam. For this purpose he is expected to explain the nature of Islam its good points and beauty to the non-convert.

If the unconverted spouse refuses to accept Islam, then the *Qāḍī* shall dissolve the marriage. But if the non-Muslim spouse cannot make up his or her mind or does not express his or her decision in the matter, the *Qāḍī* shall again make another attempt to persuade him or her to accept Islam and if the spouse is still undecided, then a third attempt is to be made.

It will be only on the husband's or non-Kitabiyah wife's refusal or failure to embrace Islam that the marriage shall be dissolved by the *Qāḍī*. The insistence on the *Qāḍī*'s order is in order to ensure that a marriage shall not be dissolved until and unless full opportunity has been given to the other party to adopt Islam and thus to maintain the marriage.

But it is not absolutely necessary for the *Qāḍī* to repeat his invitation to embrace Islam if he should consider that it will not serve any useful purpose. Should the party concerned refuse to adopt Islam then it shall not at all be necessary for the *Qāḍī* to repeat and press the point. There is no time limit fixed during or after which the repetitions have to be made. The matter is left to the discretion of the *Qāḍī* and he may finish the matter in one day or give more time for consideration to the spouse concerned. But the offer must be made by the *Qāḍī* at the earliest opportunity.

It is obvious that this procedure can be adopted only in a Muslim country because it cannot be followed in a non-Muslim country where there can be no *Qāḍī* to perform such acts and duties. Even if there is a *Qāḍī* he cannot enforce the provisions of Muslim law in a non-Muslim State and so it shall not be possible for the *Qāḍī* to offer Islam to the non-convert spouse. The Ḥanafi jurists are very strict about the rule to invite the unconverted spouse to adopt Islam, and they hold that the marriage shall not be dissolved until and unless the *Qāḍī* invites the unconverted party to embrace Islam.[28] It will be only on the refusal or failure of the party concerned to adopt the faith that the marriage shall be dissolved by the *Qāḍī*.

The dissolution of the marriage by the *Qāḍī* shall become effective only on the expiry of three menstrual courses of the wife or if that cannot be ascertained, on the expiry of three months.

Ḥanafi View : The waiting for the prescribed period is incumbent under the Ḥanafi law irrespective of the fact whether the marriage has or has not been consummated. This period of waiting does not constitute *'iddah*, but is meant to provide further time to the unconverted spouse to embrace Islam so that the marriage be maintained.[29] Hence if the unconverted spouse also embraces Islam within this period then the marriage shall be maintained.[30]

Shāfi'ī View : Under the Shafi'ī law it is not necessary to attempt to persuade the unconverted spouse to accept Islam, but the marriage shall become dissolved automatically, if it cannot continue otherwise, on the conversion of one of the spouses. The *Qāḍī's* order is also not necessary.[31] This rule shall not apply if the wife is a Kitabiyah and it is her

28. *Al-Fatāwā al-Hindiah*, *op. oit.*, Vol. II, p. 39, Ibn 'Ābidīn al-Shāmī, *op. cit* , Vol. II, p. 39.
29. *Al-Durr al-Mukhtār*, Vol. II, p. 399 ; *al-Fatāwā, al-Ālamgiriyah*, Vol. II, p. 39, Lucknow.
30. *Al-Fatāwā al-Hindiyah*, *op. cit.*, Vol. II, p. 39 ; Ibn 'Ābidīn. *op. cit.*, Vol. II, p. 399.
31. Burhān al-Dīn al-Marghīnānī, *op. cit.*, Vol. II, p. 326.

husband who embraces Islam, because the marriage shall continue to subsist in that case.

If the party embracing Islam is not domiciled in a Muslim country, but is only living there temporarily while the unconverted spouse is domiciled in a non- Muslim country, then in such a case also the marriage shall become automatically and immediately dissolved if it has not been consummated. If it has been consummated, it shall get automatically dissolved only on the expiry of three monthly courses or if the wife is not subject to them, after three months' time.[32] If the unconverted spouse embraces Islam before the expiry of the prescribed period the marriage shall not be dissolved.[33]

Muslim Country having no Qāḍī: A curious and difficult position arises under the Ḥanafi law when the spouses are living in a Muslim country where no person has been appointed by the Government to exercise the function of a *Qāḍī*. It is an essential condition under Ḥanafi law for dissolution of marriage when one spouse adopts Islam that the *Qāḍī* shall ask the other party to do the same. Under the Ḥanafi law it is only when such invitation to accept Islam has been extended by the *Qāḍī* to the unconverted party and he or she refuses or fails to adopt the faith that the *Qāḍī* shall dissolve the marriage. The marriage shall continue till such order is passed.[34] This position arose in a case before the Calcutta High Court. In that case a Russian married woman embraced Islam at Calcutta, invited her husband by cable to adopt Islam and on his refusal instituted a suit for the dissolution of her marriage. It was stated by the Court that "even if it be presumed that India is an Islamic country, there can be no lawful dissolution of marriage unless Islam has been actually presented to the unconverted party by the Court *acting as the Kazi*. A mere request by cable by a convert to her husband asking him to embrace Islam is not

32. Burhān al-Dīn al-Marg̲h̲īnānī, *op. cit.*, Vol. II, p. 326.
33. *Ibid.*
34. *Ibid.*

sufficient to constitute a valid offer of the faith to the unconverted party. In any case it is the Kazi and not the converted person who should present Islam to the unconverted party and it is for him in a suitable case to dissolve the marriage.[35] The Court, therefore, declined to dissolve the marriage. The Court's attention was not drawn to a very important rule of Ḥanafi law that where a provision of that law involves hardship to any of its adherents then it is open to him or her to adopt a rule of another Sunnī Imām. The Ḥanafi jurists have frequently adopted this procedure and even a Ḥanafi *Qāḍī* has been advised to act on this rule in proper cases.[36] As stated before, a woman on her conversion to Islam becomes absolutely forbidden to her non-Muslim husband while under the Ḥanafi law the husband in a Muslim country retains his right to become a Muslim and claim his wife till such time when Islam is offered to him by the *Qāḍī*. When no such offer has been made or can be made because there is no *Qāḍī* in that country then, under the Ḥanafi law, the marriage shall not be dissolved. If it is the husband who has accepted Islam then his marriage not having been dissolved he shall still be liable for the maintenance of his non-Muslim wife although he cannot be intimate with her and she shall be unlawful for him, as a Muslim is not allowed to marry or have a non-Muslim wife unless she belongs to a revealed religion. If it is the wife who has become a Muslimah, then she shall not be competent to contract another marriage till her marriage with her non-Muslim husband is dissolved. It is obvious that the convert to Islam shall be put to great hardship in such a case, and so it shall be open, under the Ḥanafi law, to the husband or the wife, as the case may be, to have recourse to the law of any other Sunnī Imām if the latter alleviates his or her hardship. It will, therefore, be open to the Court to apply the Shāfi'ī law to the Ḥanafi's in case of necessity and to save the party from hardship.

35. Noor Jehan Begum Vs. Eugene Tiscenco A.I.R. 1941, Calcutta 582.
36. Maulana Abdul Hai, *Majmu' al-Fiqh*, p. 365, Cawnpur.

The Shāfi'ī law can be applied when there is no *Qāḍī* in the Muslim State where the conversion has taken place. The marriage shall get automatically dissolved either immediately on conversion if it has not been consummated or on the expiry of the prescribed period of three months as the case may be. In the latter case the marriage shall continue if the other spouse also embraces Islam. On his or her failure to do so, the marriage shall be dissolved on the expiry of the prescribed period of three months, though it shall be considered to have been dissolved from the time of the conversion of the other spouse.

Conersion of husband belonging to a non-revealed religion : If the spouses belong to a non-revealed religion and should only the husband embrace Islam then the marriage cannot be maintained. This is based on the rule that a Muslim cannot have as his wife a woman who is neither a Muslimah nor a Kitabiyah. In such a case the *Qāḍī* must ask the woman to embrace Islam. If she does so, the marriage shall be maintained, otherwise it shall be dissolved. If the wife happens to be a Kitabiyah and does not embrace Islam while the husband does so, the marriage shall continue.[37]

Conversion of husband belonging to a revealed religion: If the spouses belong to a revealed religion and should the husband alone embrace Islam then the marriage shall continue even when the wife does not adopt Islam because a Muslim can lawfully marry such a woman, that is, a Kitabiyah.[38] In such a case, it shall not even be necessary for the *Qāḍī* to offer Islam to the wife.[39]

Conversion of the Wife : If it is the wife who embraces Islam, the marriage cannot be maintained or continued unless the husband also adopts Islam because a Muslimah (Muslim woman) cannot be the wife of any non-Muslim even when he belongs to a revealed religion. The same rule as stated

37. *Al-Fatāwā al-'Ālamgīrīyah*, Vol. II, p. 118.
38. *Al-Fatāwā al-Hindiyah, op. cit.*, Vol. II, p. 39.
39. *Ibid.*

above in the case of the husband's conversion shall apply in the case of the conversion of the wife. It shall not be necessary under the Shāfi'ī law to offer Islam to the husband when the wife embraces Islam irrespective of the fact whether they both or the husband is living in Dar al-Islam (Muslim State) or in Dar al-Harb (non-Muslim State). This is due to the fact that, as discussed above, the marriage would get automatically dissolved on the expiry of the prescribed period stated above.

When one Spouse is Minor : If one of a married couple happens to be a minor and should the other spouse embrace Islam then what is to be seen is if the minor possesses understanding. If the minor does possess it then he or she shall be invited to adopt Islam and the marriage shall be maintained or dissolved according to whether the minor embraces Islam or refuses or fails to do so. If the minor does not possess understanding then the matter shall remain in suspense till he or she attains understanding or majority and only then the above procedure shall be adopted.[40]

Conversion in Dar al-Harb : If both the spouses happen to be in a non-Muslim country and should one of them adopt Islam then it shall not be possible to offer Islam to the unconverted party. The marriage in such a case shall stand dissolved on the expiry of the third menstrual course or three months.[41] The marriage is not immediately dissolved so as to give time to the other spouse to adopt Islam if he or she so likes.[42]

Temporary Residence in Dar al-Islam or Muslim Country : If the spouses are not the citizens of a Muslim country, but are staying there only temporarily and are the permanent citizens of a Dar al-Harb or non-Muslim country, they cannot be subject to the laws of the Muslim country. Hence if only one of them embraces Islam then it shall not be open to the *Qāḍī* to ask the unconverted party to embrace Islam.

40. *Al-Fatāwā al-Hindiyah, op. cit.*, Vol. II, p. 39.
41. *Ibid.*, Ibn 'Ābidīn, *op. cit.*, Vol. II, p. 401.
42. Burhān al-Dīn al-Marghinānī, *op. cit.*, Vol. II, p. 327.

In such a case the same law shall apply as is applicable in the case of conversion in Dar al-Harb and the marriage shall stand dissolved on the expiry of three menstrual courses or three months if the wife is not subject to them or the same cannot be ascertained.[43]

Custody of Children on Conversion in Dar al-Islam : It is considered that the interests of a child demand that it should be brought up in the custody of a person who is most fitted to bring him or her up. For this purpose it is necessary that the child should be brought up in a healthy religious atmosphere. As Islam is considered to be the best religion by the Muslim jurists it follows that the child should be given in the custody of the spouse who embraces Islam.[44]

It may be interesting to note that a revealed religion comes next to Islam while a non-revealed religion is not considered desirable.[45] As between the Christian and Jewish religions the former has precedence over the latter so that if one of a married couple is a Christian while the other is a Jew then the custody of the child shall be entrusted to the parent who is a Christian.[46] Similarly, a person belonging to a revealed religion is superior to a Majusi.[47]

If only one of the parents adopts Islam while the other prefers to remain a non-Muslim, then the child or children shall be deemed to be Muslims and shall remain in the custody of that spouse who is a Muslim. If the child of a non-Muslim couple happens to be in a Muslim State and should his father adopt Islam in a non-Muslim country then he shall be entitled to the custody of the child because on embracing

43. Ibn 'Ābidīn, *op. cit.*, Vol. II, p. 401 ; *Al-Fatāwā, al-'Ālamgīrīyah, op. cit.*, Vol. II, p. 40.
44. Ibn 'Ābidīn, *op. cit.*, Vol. II, p. 400 ; Muḥammad Waḥīd az-Zamān, *Nūr al-Hedaya* (Urdu Translation of *Shareh Vikaya*). Vol. II, p. 36.
45. Ibn 'Ābidīn, *op. cit.*, Vol. II, p. 405, *Al-Fatāwā al-'Ālamgīrīyah, op. cit.*, Vol, II, p. 40.
46. Ibn 'Ābidīn, *op. cit.*, Vol. II, p. 400.
47. Muḥammad Waḥīd-uz-Zamān, *op. cit.*, Vol. II, p. 36.

Islam he becomes subject to Muslim law.[48] But if the case should be the reverse as when the child is in a non-Muslim country while the father becomes a Muslim in a Muslim State then he shall not be entitled to the custody of the child because Muslim law cannot be applied in a non-Muslim country.[49]

Motive and intention : As fully discussed in the chapter on Apostasy, it is not possible to test or gauge the sincerity of religious belief.[50] No Court can delve into the undisclosed mind of a man and satisfy itself whether that person has or has not belief in any particular religion. Moreover, it is not necessary for any person that he should be fully acquainted with the religious beliefs and usages of his newly adopted religion. It will suffice for a change of religion that the person should be acquainted with the broad articles of faith of his new religion. The Lahore High Court has consistently taken the view that motive of the person renouncing a faith is immaterial and that the renunciation of faith requires no other proof than the declaration of that person. It has been held in a case that the conversion must be of a *bona fide* character.[51] All that a Court can see is whether the conversion is not a colourable transaction. It was held by a Division Bench of the Punjab Chief Court that the Courts of law have no other means of finding out a person's intention other than indicated by his acts and conduct so that if the conversion was an accomplished fact and was not proved to be a colourable transaction, the Court could not decline to give effect to it because the underlying

48. Ibn 'Ābidīn, *op. cit.*, p.Vol. II, 404 ; *al-Fatāwā al-'Ālamgīriyah, op. cit.*, Vol. II, p. 40.
49. *Ibid.*
50. Abdur Razack Vs. Aga Mohammad Jafar Bindaneem 21 I.A. 56 ; Ayesha Bibi Vs. Subodh Chand Chakravarty A.I.R. 1949. Cal. 436.
51. Mst. Khan Bibi Vs. Pir Shah (1884) 132 P.R. Mst. Roshan Bibi Vs. Khuda Buksh, I.L.R. 19 Lahore 277 ; Ayesha Bibi Vs. Subodh Chakravarty A.I.R. 1949, Cal. 436. Noor Jahan Vs. Eugene Tiscenko, A.I.R. 1941 Cal. 582.

motive was not a proper one.[52] Scott-Smith, J. expressed a similar view and stated that the only question which had to be determined was whether renunciation had taken place.[23]

The Courts have even stated that it was not within the jurisdiction of the Courts to enquire into the genuineness or otherwise of the conversion and that if formal renunciation was accompanied by rites of baptism, it was immaterial whether the motive was a genuine conversion or a mere device (on the part of the wife) to get rid of her husband.[53] It was held in another case that so long as conversion was genuine, ulterior and even sordid motives would not affect it.[54] All that has to be done is to prove the factum of renunciation.[55] Din Mohammad, J. has explained that by the expression that conversion or renunciation is not a colourable transaction is meant that the conversion or renunciation had taken place in fact. It was also laid down that to probe into the matter and to try to ascertain the true nature of one's belief is sheer intermeddling not justifiable on any ground. His Lordship also quoted from two English judgments where it was held, "No Court can test or gauge the sincerity of religious belief", and that "even the devil himself knoweth not the heart of man". The Court emphasised the fact that motive for renunciation is immaterial and that a person may renounce his faith for love or for avarice or to get rid of his present commitments or truly to seek salvation elsewhere.[56] But a contrary view was expressed by the Calcutta High Court when it was stated that it is essential for the plaintiff to satisfy the Court that the conversion is *bona fide*.[57] It seems that the Court considered that this fact could be ascer-

52. Ghaus Vs. Faji A.I.R. 1915 Lahore 1929.
53. Bakho Vs. Lal A.I.R 1924 Lahore 397.
54. Amar Nath Vs. Mst. Ved Kaur, A.I.R. 1928, Lahore 976.
55. Mst. Sadasu Vs. Mst. Maryam Bibi, A.I R. 1936, Lahore, 976.
56. Sardar Mohammad Vs. Mst. Maryam Bibi A.I.R. 1936, Lahore 666
Mst. Sardaran Vs. Sharaf A.I R. 1937, 759.
57. Roshan Bibi Vs. Khuda Baksh A.I.R. 1938, Lahore, 842.
58. Noor Jehan Begum Vs. Eugene Tiscenko, A.I.R. 1941, Calcutta, 582.

tained by the cross-examination of the party concerned. No doubt that suspicious circumstances could be established by the cross-examination, but nothing more beyond that. As stated above it is not possible to read as to what is in the heart of a person, and that a suit for divorce cannot be dismissed merely because the conversion is not genuine and is hased on ulterior purpose. It was stated by Ormond J. in a case, "The evidence that the plaintiff herself considers that she has changed her religion and as to the fact of the process or rites of conversion having been performed is uncontradicted and clear. In my opinion, therefore, on proof of these facts alone I should hold at once that there has been an effective conversion with all the legal consequences that follow from such conversion ; and I should so hold without going at all into the motives for conversion or their relative religious or ethical values ; and in my view it is not open to me to do so."[59]

It can be concluded from a judgment of the Supreme Court of Pakistan that the bare statement of the convert if he or she is obviously interested in making the statement and when it is unsupported by independent evidence, must be accepted with a great deal of reserve.[60]

Nature of Separation : Separation due to conversion amounts to a *faskh* or annulment of marriage.[61]

59. Ayesha Bibi Vs. Subodh Chand Chakravarty, A.I;R. 1949, Cal. 436.
60. Ali Nawaz Gardezi Vs. Col. Mohammad Yusuf, P.L.D. 1963, I.C. 51 at p. 69.
61. *Fatāwāi 'Ālamgiryah*, Vol. II, p. 120.

Section II.—Hindu Law

Preliminary: We have already discussed the rules of Muslim law regarding the effects of conversion on the marriages of converts to Islam. But before discussing the effect of the conversion of one of the spouses of a married Hindu couple, it is necessary to understand the nature of a Hindu marriage. It may be stated at the outset that the Hindus, like the Muslims, are not governed by the *lex loci domicilii* but by their personal law wherever they may be.[1]

There were no marriages in early ancient times in India, as was the case in other countries also. But in order to put a stop to corruption and immorality, the institution of marriage was introduced by Svateketu, son of the Sage Uddalak as is stated in Mahabharata, Adipurana.[2] Even then the conception of marriage was a hazy one and included such connections as cannot appeal to us. In early days a marriage was nothing more than the sale of a girl by her father to a man. But by the time of Rig-Veda it had come to be considered a sacrament and was enjoined on all in the interest of this life as well as for the spiritual benefit of the soul and the souls of one's ancestors.

Marriages were divided into eight classes.

The first class is called Paisacha. It is effected by having sexual intimacy with a woman while she is under the influence of sleep or has been made drunk by the administration of certain drugs or strong intoxicating drinks or when she was disordered in intelligence. The next class of marriage is called Rakshasha marriage and consists of the forcible capture of a woman. The third class of marriage is called Gandharva or what may be called a love marriage in which

1. Budansa Rowther Vs. Fatima Bai, A.I.R, (1914) Mad. 192. Soorendranath Vs. Heermonee, 12 M.I.A. 81; Parbat Vs. Jagdis Chunder I.L.R. 29C 433; Govind Vs. Radha, I.L.R. 31 All. 477; etc.
2. Kali Prasad Saksena, *The Principles of Hindu Jurisprudence*, p. 34, Allahabad, 1941.

a girl under mutual understanding with a man leaves her parent's house and elopes with him, without her parent's knowledge or permission, for sexual gratification. The fourth class of marriage is called Asura and consists of the sale of a girl by her father to a man. The sale consideration consists of as much wealth as the suitor can afford or is prepared to give for the particular girl.[3]

The above four classes of marriage are disapproved of but to some extent are still in vogue. The next four classes are approved of and consist of Prajapatya, Arsha, Daiva and Brahma marriages.

In Arsha marriage, the bridegroom gives one or two pairs of kine to the girl's father. Mayne thinks that it is only a survival of the Asura class of marriage in which the sale consideration has been reduced to a token payment.[4] The next class of marriage is called Prajapatya in which it is the man who seeks the girl and she is gifted to him on the condition that she would join him in the performance of religious and worldly duties. Jones and Mayne, however, do not mention the condition but say that in this form of marriage the father gives away the girl with due honour and says, "May both of you perform together your civil and religious duties".[5] The Daiva marriage is the gift by the father of a girl whom he has gaily attired at the time of sacrifice, to the officiating priest who performs the religious rites.[6] The marriage most approved of is called Brahama and consists of the gift of a girl by her father to a man learned in Veda who has been invited for the purpose.[7]

3. W. Jones, *The Laws of Menu*, pp. 46, 47, Calcutta, 1794 A.D.; Thomas Lumisden Strange. *A Manual of Hindoo Law*, p. 9, Madras, 1863, A.D.; John D. Mayne, *A Treatise on Hindu Law and Usages*, p. 96, Madras. 1906, A.D.; Julius Jolly, *Hindu Law and Custom*, pp. 107, 108, Calcutta; H. T. Colebrook, *A Digest of Hindu Law*, pp. 613, 614, Madras, 1865.
4. Mayne, *op, cit.*, p. 97.
5. Jones, *op. cit.*, p. 47 ; Mayne, *op. cit.*, p. 97.
6. *Ibid.*
7. Jolly, *op. cit.*, p, 116.

Originally, different classes of marriage were designed for different castes. But a Brahman could contract all classes of marriage except the Rakhshasha and Paisacha marriages. A Rakshasha marriage was considered befitting the military class. Thus Mahabharata mentions the forcible capture and abduction of women by many heroes like Arjuna, Bhisma, Daryadhana and others. Similarly, Gandharva marriages even without nuptial ceremonies have also been considered as befitting the warrior class.[8] There are many insta nces of such marriages given in Hindu literature and a well-known case of such a union is the marriage of Sakuntala and Dusyanta. It is a disputed point whether it is necessary to later solemnise the marriage according to the prescribed rites.[9] According to an opinion expressed in the Smritis, Gandharva marriages are open to all castes. The Asura class of marriage is considered appropriate for the merchant class.[10] Probably this view must have been based on the peaceful nature of the people belonging to this class.

We can see from the above that the position of women improved as time passed and new and better classes of marriages were introduced. A girl who was treated as a chattel in the beginning and was sold like an animal, now became the object of an affectionate gift. The Asura and the Brahmana marriages are generally in vogue now, but the original condition that the bride was to be given in marriage to a man well-versed in the religious books is no more observed and a girl's father now takes the worldly position of the prospective husband into consideration. Moreover, it has been adopted by other castes also. Mayne has taken rather a harsh view of Hindu marriages and says that several admitted forms of marriages are only euphemisms for

8. *Ibid.*, Strange, *op. cit.*, p. 9, Mayne, *op. cit.*, p. 97.
9. Saksena, *op. cit.*, p. 31, Mayne, *op. cit.*, pp, 100, 101, Colebrook, *op, cit,.* p. 614,
10. *Ibid.*

seduction and rape.[11] Saksena has taken exception to this observation and explains that such marriages were allowed in the interest of a girl's chastity and not for legalising force or fraud, and also that the basic idea of a Hindu marriage was the creation of a permanent relationship of husband and wife irrespective of its form.[12] Ghose also contends that Mayne and other Western writers are not right in their criticism of Hindu marriages.[13]

Polyandry and polygamy appeared after the institution of marriage was introduced. Naturally, they could have no place amongst the people when there was no relationship of husband and wife. There is a great difference of opinion about them and so they are briefly discussed here:

Polyandry: Polyandry was practised in India as is borne out by the well-known marriage of Darupadi with the five Pandava brothers—the heroes of Mahabharata. Some writers call it an isolated instance and deny its prevalence. Mayne has stated that on the objection of the Princess's father, the Pandava princess explained that polyandry had been practised before, and quoted the cases of Iatala who dwelt with seven saints and that of Varski who cohabited with ten brothers. But he concludes that the above were not cases of marriages but cases of special indulgence allowed to Rishis.[14] Some writers have mentioned that polyandry is still in vogue in India in certain parts and amongst certain castes.[15] Jolly quotes from West that it is much more common than is generally believed. It is considered that polyandry was generally a result of poverty when younger brothers could not bear the expenses of a marriage.[16] Moreover, it would have been less expensive to maintain one woman than to maintain several.

Polygamy: Polygamy is in evidence in the Vedas and

11. Mayne, *op. cit.*, p. 73.
12. Saksena, *op. cit.*, p. 31.
13. Ghose, *op. cit.*, p. 785.
14. Mayne, *op. cit.*, pp. 78, 79.
15. Jolly, *op. cit.*, p. 103; Gour, *op. cit.*, p. XVI.
16. Jolly, *op. cit.*, p. 103.

some of the heroes of Mahabharata had many wives.[17] A man could have as many wives and concubines as he liked. Jolly says that even at the present time polygamy is common because it is permissible.[18] Ghose has also stated that polygamy was not allowed according to the spirit of the law but it was very generally practised.[19] Strange, however, says that though a man could have a number of wives, he could do so only under special circumstances.[20] But it cannot be denied that polygamy has been practised from ancient times up to the modern time and has been greatly stopped only by the Hindu Marriage Act of 1955, though monogamy had been the common practice. But even now, polygamy has not been completely eradicated in India. According to a recent study by the Indian Statistical Institute, polygamy still prevails amongst the Hindus in India's urban areas. The Institute found that polygamy persists universally as a cultural trait among the urbanites.[20-a]

Position of Women : Great uncertainly shrouds the position of women in ancient times in India. It is stated by some writers that it is established from Hindu literature that women were held in great respect in ancient times. But in later times the women lost this position and the respect in which they were held declined to such an extent that they were considered to have been created merely for propagation. Narada, the great law-giver, is also reported to have expressed this opinion.[21] Under Hindu law a woman throughout her life remains dependent on man. Thus before her marriage she is dependent on her father, after marriage on her husband and after widowhood on her sons.[22] Narada has stated that through independence even women born of noble families would swerve from their duty ; hence the Lord

17. Jolly, *op. cit.*, pp. 140, 142.
18. *Ibid.*, p. 146.
19. Jogendra Chunder Ghose, *The Principles of Hindu Law*, p. 776, Calcutta, 1917.
20. Strange, *op. cit.*, p. 12.
20-a. *Morning News*, Karachi, dated 21st December, 1968.
21. Prof. Indra, *Status of Women in Ancient India*, Benares.
22. H. T. Colebrook, *A Digest of Hindu Law*, p. 109. London, 1801 A.D.

of created beings has established perpetual dependence.[23] Authorities are found to support each view. Thus it is stated by Manu that where females are honoured, there the deities are pleased but where they are dishonoured, there all religious acts became fruitless.[24] "Where female relations are made miserable, the family of him who makes them so very soon wholly perishes.[25] "Women must be honoured and adored by their fathers and brethren and by the fathers and brethren of their husband's, if they seek abundant prosperity."[26] But as against the above we have sayings like those given below :

"To women not any man is solely dear, nor is any one hateful ; they embrace every man as a creeper, growing in the forest, clings to every tree within its reach."[27]

It is stated in Mahabharata, "There is nothing more sinful than women ; verily women are the roots of all evil". "Fire is never satiated with wood nor can the ocean be filled with the waters brought by the rivers. The destroyer, the God of death, is not satiated with killing all living creatures. Likewise women are not satiated with men."[28] It is given in the Ramayana : "The faces of women are like flowers, their words are like the drops of honey and their hearts are like sharp razors, the interior of them no one can know. There is none whom a woman sincerely loves."[29]

But in spite of the above contradictory statements it is found from Hindu literature that women were the object of respect in ancient times.

Marriage : It has been stated by Strange that, "by no people is greater importance attached to marriage than by the Hindus".[30] Gour has stated that a father could sell his

23. Colebrook, *op. cit*,, p. 109.
24. Colebrook, *op. cit.*, p. 109; Jones, *op. cit.*, p. 49.
25. The Mahabharata quoted by Colebrook, *op. cit.*, p. 121 ; Jones, *op. cit*., p. 49.
26. *Ibid.*
27. The Ramayana, quoted by Colebrook, *op. cit.*, p. 117.
28. The Mahabharata, quoted by Colebrook, *op. cit.*, p. 117.
29. The Ramayana, quoted by Colebrook, *op. cit.*
30. Sir Thomas Strange, *Hindu Law*, *op. cit.*, p. 23, Madras 1875,

daughter and that there was little difference between this and the sale of chattel. He further explains that the acquisition of a wife by a man amounted to her acquisition by the members of his family who therefore could use her for procreation of children."[31]

In the course of time man usurped the rights of the woman, as has happened in many other systems of law also, so that though a man could indulge in polygamy yet the right of dissolution of marriage was denied to the wife, and second marriage was made impossible for her. Her marriage could not be dissolved even when her husband was guilty of cruelty. No doubt the Hindu Widow's Remarriage Act, 1856, provided for the remarriage of Hindu widows but such was the strong hold of public opinion and men's hold over women that the Act did not prove as helpful as it was expected to be. The number of widows who took advantage of it was very small. Marriage still continued to be considered indissoluble. This conception led to great hardship to women. Hindu society felt the necessity to provide some relief to the wife and provisions were made in different parts of India for this purpose from time to time. But these reforms were restricted to only certain specified areas and the women living in other parts still sometimes suffered from great hardships at the hands of their husbands. Modern Hindu society felt the need for reform and a Bill was introduced in the Indian Parliament which met with great opposition from the orthodox people, but was passed by the majority and was called the Hindu Marriage Act, 1955. It extends to the whole of India and to all Hindus, even when they are living outside India. It provides for judicial separation as well as for divorce and has been of great help to Hindu women.

Child Marriage : In ancient times great importance was attached to giving a girl in marriage while she was still a child. The age when a girl should be married was fixed from six

31. Gour, *op. cit.*, p. XIV.

years to eight years. The marriage at such an early age was emphasised to ensure virginity of the bride.[32] It might also have been due to the parents' anxiety to be free from their responsibility for the safety of the girl. Stress was laid on this aspect of marriage to such an extent as to hold that it was a sin to let a mature girl remain unmarried.

Abandonment of Wife : A husband could desert his wife under the following circumstances :—

(*a*) If he apprehended danger from the wife and there was a danger to his life.

(*b*) By mutual consent when there was aversion between them ;

(*c*) When the wife had been degraded and became an outcaste.

(*d*) When the wife was immoral.

Baudhayana has advised the husbands to forsake a wife who is inattentive to her duties or is barren, immoral or speaks unkindly. Manu adds to the above, a woman given to drinking or who hates her husband or is suffering from an incurable disease or is found not to be a virgin or is blemished or has been given to him in marriage under a fraud or who is self-willed, wasteful or mischievous. Yajnavalkia includes in the category a woman who is quarrelsome.[33]

A husband can also supersede a wife if no child is born to her in ten years, a wife to whom only daughters have been born within twelve years or whose children all die within fifteen years. But he can immediately supersede a wife who speaks harshly. By supersession the marriage is not dissolved and the husband has still to maintain her.[34]

A wife could be expelled from her husband's house or even from the town she was living in, if she was guilty of

32. Jolly, *op. cit.*, p. 119.
33. For full particulars see Colebrook, *op. cit.*, pp. 131-135.
34. *Ibid.*, p. 135.

certain undesirable acts or conduct.[35]

The spouses could separate when the ends of marriage were not achieved as when the husband was impotent or the wife was barren; also when either of them suffered from a loathsome or incurable disease.[36]

It transpires from the Smritis that a woman (wife) can take a second husband in any one of the following cases:

(*a*) On the husband's death or disappearance,

(*b*) On the husband s civil death, as when he enters a religious order or becomes an outcaste and therefore degraded,

(*c*) When the husband is impotent.

It is laid down in Vyavastha Chandrika (Vol. II) that a Hindu wife can desert her husband if he becomes an outcaste and therefore degraded, as on account of conversion to another religion, and it is stated in Parashara (Vyavastha Chandrika, Vol. II) that if a husband is degraded then it is lawful for a woman to have another husband.[37]

It is mentioned in the Artha Shashtra of Chanakya that divorce was allowed to both the husband and the wife under the following circumstances:—

(1) If the husband or the wife apprehended danger from the other. But in such a case the husband had to return the property given by the wife at the time of the marriage. If it was the woman who brought about the dissolution of the marriage, then she had to give up her claim in respect of her property.

(2) By mutual agreement when the spouses hated each other,

35. Jolly, *op. cit.*, pp. 145, 146, Colebrook, *op. cit.*, p. 130
36. Sir Thomas Strange, *op. cit.*, p. 35.
37. For an interesting discussion see *Status of Women in Ancient India* by Prof. Indra.

(3) If there was danger to life by the conduct of the other party.
(4) If the other spouse became an outcaste.
(5) If the other spouse renounced the world.
(6) If the other spouse was of a depraved character.
(7) In addition to the above contingencies, a wife could abandon her husband in the following circumstances:—

(*a*) When the husband was missing, and

(*b*) When the husband was suffering from impotency.

Narada and Manu recognise the re-marriage of widows and wives who had been deserted by their husbands.[38]

It will be seen from the above discussion that a wife could forsake her husband and even contract a second marriage when the husband was missing. Absence for a long time is regarded in the Hindu law as amounting to natural death. The question naturally arose as to when she could do so. It is laid down that a woman belonging to the priestly class should wait for her husband for eight years if she has got children, otherwise for only four years. A woman of the warrior class has to wait for six years if she has got children, but only for three years if she has none. A woman of the commercial class has to wait for four and two years respectively. But no period of waiting has been considered necessary for women of the servile class and they can contract an early second marriage.[39]

The above rules apply in the case of a husband of whom there is no information. But if it is learnt that he is living then the period of waiting shall be doubled.[40]

It is further laid down that whether such a husband be alive or dead the wife can have another husband for the sake of ordaining progeny.[41]

38. Colebrook, *op. cit.*, p. 165.
39. *Ibid.*
40. *Ibid.*
41. *Ibid.*, p. 177.

Colebrook has stated on the authority of Vasishata that a parent can take away his daughter if the husband turns out to be a man of low birth or to be impotent, or outcaste, immoral or vicious or suffering from a shocking disease such as epilepsy; and also when they happen to have a common ancestor.[42]

Abandonment of Husband : Devala states that a wife may forsake her husband who is an abandoned sinner or a heretical mendicant or is impotenr or degraded or afflicted with phthisis or if he has been absent for a long time.[43]

Divorce: It is stated by some writers that divorce is not permissible under Hindu law. It is, however, conceded that it is allowed under custom in certain parts of India and amongst certain castes. It is explained that this custom violates the provisions of Hindu law where the relationship of husband and wife continues even after the death of one spouse.[44] But there are other writers who take the opposite view and hold that divorce is permissible under Hindu law.[45] Divorce, however, has not been in vogue in the higher classes and it was considered that it is not permissible to them. Possibly the exercise of polygamy amongst them did not make divorce very necessary for them. It is in vogue in certain areas and amongst certain castes on the basis of custom.[46] Jolly considers that it was permissible under the law, but the laws made its exercise very difficult. It seems that it was fully allowed in ancient time but the law was changed later and divorce was disallowed. This was the natural result of the change in the conception of the nature of marriage which came to be considered indissoluble in later time.

Dissolution of Marriage : Dissolution of marriage was allowed in early ancient times in India. But under the

42. Colebrook, *op. cit.*, pp. 164, 165.
43. Rishindra Nath Sarkar, *A Treatise on Hindu Law*, p. 180, Calcutta, 1936 ; Gour, *op. cit.*, p. 250 ; Sir Thomas Strange, *op. cit.*, p. 40.
44. Gour, *op. cit*, p. 250 ; Ghose, *op. cit.*, p. 782.
45. Jolly, *op. cit.*, pp. 143, 144 ; Gour, *op. cit.*, p. 277.
46. For more information see Mayne's opinion given in the next topic.

Brahmanic influence marriage came to be considered a sacrament and so indissoluble. Divorce was not in vogue, but a man or a woman could abandon or desert the other.

Remarriage: Remarriage can relate to women who are widows or divorcees, or who have been forsaken by their husbands. As regards remarriage of widows, there is a difference of opinion amongst writers on Hindu law. Thus Saksena discusses the arguments for and against the permissibility of remarriage of widows, but he is against such permissibility. He has concluded his discussion by observing that "in any case it was not practised by the higher classes."[47] Jolly has expressed the view that remarriage of women was not allowed by Hindu law and bases this view on the fact that great emphasis was laid on virginity. He further says that there is no authority in Hindu literature permitting second marriage and it is not practised by higher classes even after it has been legalised by law.[48] But as stated, a woman could contract another marriage for the causes stated above. Gour however, thinks that remarriage was not only customary but was obligatory in ancient times, and that it was given up when marriage was considered indissoluble.[49] Sastri has stated that a woman is allowed to remarry even during the life-time of her husband if he abandons her or for any cause such as when he is missing or renounces the world or is impotent or an outcaste. He relies upon a rule laid down by Narada that "another husband is ordained for a woman in five calamities, namely, if the husband is unheard of or is dead or adopts a religious order or be impotent or becomes outcaste."[50] The matter has been ably discussed at length by Mayne in his learned book on Hindu law. After fully discussing the various authorities he has come to the conclusion that originally divorce and second marriages were allowed by Hindu law and specifically men-

47. Saksena, *op. cit.*, p. 36.
48. Jolly, *op. cit.*, pp. 133, 134.
49. Gour, *op. cit.*, p. 275.
50. Gopal Chandra Sarkar Sastri, *A Treatise on Hindu Law*, p. 169, Calcutta, 1927.

tioned by Narada, Devala, Baudhayana, Vasistha and others. According to him, the change in the law is the result of a changed outlook on the nature of marriage, which under the influence of the Brahmanas came to be considered indissoluble. According to him the passages in early books recognising and permitting second marriage of a widow or an abandoned wife were deliberately omitted from a part of the original text by later writers. He considers that when marriage came to be considered a sacrament, second marriages were not allowed and so the passages permitting second marriages were left out. Relying on passages quoted by Dr. Mayr to show that remarriage of widows was sanctioned by the Vedas, he says that the prohibition against second marriages of divorcees or widows has no foundation in early Hindu law or custom, and that marriages of widows, deserted wives and wives who lawfully forsake their husbands is expressly sanctioned by early writers. In support of his contention he has shown that the marriages among aboriginal races or of such races as have not come within the Brahmanic influence are just what Narada has laid down.[51] Ghose agrees with Mayne about the deliberate omission of part of the original texts which denoted the remarriage of women in certain cases.[51]

Custom: Custom plays an important part in the Hindu law and it can even abrogate the law if its existence is established to the satisfaction of the Court. Some castes have adopted the custom of divorce and a second marriage by the wife under certain circumstances even during the life-time of her husband and these customs have been held valid in many cases by the Courts.[52] It has been stated that divorce is not contemplated by the Hindu law yet if it is allowed by custom at any place or amongst any particular caste then it shall be given effect to even though it may be repugnant to the Hindu law.[53] But these customs were restricted to a few castes only.

51. Mayne, *op. cit.*, pp. 112, 113.
52. Gopi Krishna Kasandhan Vs. Jaggo. I L.R , 58 All 397, Reg Vs. Sambhu Baghu, I.L.R., 1 Bom. 347, Bindia Vs. Kausalia I.L,R., 13 All, 126; Kusunj Sundari Letani Vs. Pitambri Letani. I.L.R,, 32 Cal. 871, Virasangappa Vs. Rudrappa, I LR., 98. Mad. 440.
53. Ghose, *op. cit.*, p. 795.

Section III.—Conflict Between Muslim and Hindu Laws

Preliminary: It has been stated before that both the Hindus and the Muslims are governed by their personal laws wherever they may be living. This rule has received legal recognition.[1] Personal laws of course include the laws relating to marriage and divorce. The East India Company found it necessary to make it clear that in its administration there shall not be any interference in the laws of the Hindus and the Muslims. Thus it was laid down in Regulation II of the 21st August, 1772, that in matters relating to marriage, religious usage or institutions etc. the religious law "shall be invariably adhered to". This Regulation was effective and useful where both the parties to a proceeding were Hindus or Muslims. But difficulty was experienced where only one of them was a Hindu or a Muslim while the other party belonged to a different persuasion, or on adoption of Christianity by a Muslim or Hindu. To meet this difficulty it was provided by Regulation VII of 1832 of the Bengal Code that in such cases the laws of those religions shall not be permitted to operate to deprive such party or parties of any property to which, but for the operation of such laws, they would have been entitled. The operation of this Regulation was further extended on the complaint of missionaries and converts to Christianity by Act XXXI of 1850 by which it was provided: "so much of any law or usage now in force within the territories subject to the Government of the East India Company, as inflicts on any person forfeiture of rights or property or may be held in any way to impair or affect any right of inheritance by reason of his or her renouncing or having been excluded from the community or any religion, or being deprived of caste, shall cease to be enforced as law in the Courts of the East India Company and in the Courts established by Royal Charter within the said territories." It was provided by Regulation

1. Budansa Rowther Vs. Fatima Bai, A.I.R.. 1914 Mad. 192.

VIII of 1795 ,"in cases in which the plaintiff shall be of a different religious persuasion from the defendant, the decision is to be regulated by the law of the religion of the latter, excepting where Europeans or other persons, not being either Mohammadans or Hindus, shall be defendant in which case the law of the plaintiff is to make the rule of decision in all plaints and actions of a civil nature." A very important rule of law was enacted by the Regulation of 5th July, 1781, which provided that "in all cases for which no specific directions are hereby given, the judges *do act according to justice, equity* and *good conscience.*" This rule was clarified in Regulation VII of 1832. Section 9 of the Regulation provided: "It is hereby declared, however, that the above rules are intended and shall be held to apply to such persons only as shall be *bona fide* professors of these religions at the time of the application of the case, and were designed for the protection of such persons, not for the deprivation of the rights of others. Wherever, therefore, in any civil suit the parties to such suit may be of different persuasion or when one or more of the parties to the suit shall not be either of the Mohammadan or the Hindu persuasion, the laws of those religions shall not be permitted to operate to deprive such party or parties of any property to which, but for the operation of these laws, they would have been entitled. In all such cases the decision shall be governed by the principles of justice, equity and good conscience, it being clearly understood, however, that this provision shall not be considered to justify the introduction of any foreign law, or the application to such cases of any rule not sanctioned by those principles." The Courts have followed this provision in various cases.[2] Finally, came the Proclamation of Queen Victoria, a portion of which relevant to the matter under discussion reads :

> "Firmly relying ourselves on the truth of Christianity and acknowledging with gratitude the solace of religion

2. Gobind Dayal Vs. Inayat Khan I.L.R. 7 All. 775; Budansa Rowther Vs. Fatima Bai A.I,R., 1914. Mad. 192.

we disclaim alike the right and desire to impose our convictions on any one of our subjects. We declare it to be our Royal Will and Pleasure that none be in any wise for favoured, none molested or disquieted by reason of their religious faith or observances, but that all are alike and we do strictly charge and enjoin all those who may be in authority under us that they abstain from all interference with the religious belief or worship of any of our subjects on pain of our highest displeasure."

This proclamation made it clear that all persons were to be treated equally irrespective of their religious beliefs. The difficulty of a conflict between the adherents of different religions was still experienced. The Courts in such cases were guided by the principles of *justice, equity* and *good conscience.* Thus it was stated in a case: "When the parties belong to different religions as when the husband is a Muslim while the wife is a Hindu then in the absence of any statutory directions it will make its own choice of law in accordance with the rules of *justice, equity* and *good conscience.*"[3]

Conversion of Hindu

Preliminary : The conversion of a Hindu husband or wife to Islam when the other spouse is alive, presents considerable difficulty, as there is a conflict between the Hindu and the Muslim laws involved in the case. It would be convenient to note the following basic rules of law in respect of such cases :—

(*a*) Islam does not allow a Muslimah (Muslim woman) to be the wife of a non-Muslim.

(*b*) A Hindu marriage has come to be considered a sacrament and so to be indissoluble and is to subsist for the lives of the spouses.[4]

3. Jacob Vs. Jacob, 58 C.W.N. 513; Ayesha Bibi Vs. Subodh Ch. Chakravarty, A.I.R. 1949 Cal. 436.
4. The Hindu Marriage Act. 1955, now allows the dissolution of a Hindu marriage on the basis of a number of grounds.

(*c*) The law allows absolute freedom of thought and religion which includes not only the right of a person to go on thinking as before without interference, but also the right to adopt new or different thoughts.

(*d*) The law does not allow a person to suffer disability merely on the ground of his or her religious belief.

Conversion to Islam by both or by one of a married Hindu couple may be discussed with regard to three aspects, namely,

(*a*) When both the husband and the wife embrace Islam,

(*b*) When it is only the husband who embraces Islam while the wife keeps to her religion, and

(*c*) When it is the wife who changes her religion while the husband remains a Hindu.

(*a*) *Conversion of both spouses* : If both the husband and the wife embrace Islam, there does not arise any difficulty in the case. It will not be necessary for them to contract a new marriage according to Muslim rites and their marriage solemnised according to the Hindu rites shall be deemed to subsist and to be valid.

(*b*) *Conversion of the husband* : If it is only the Hindu husband who changes his religion while the wife does not do so, then his Hindu marriage would not get dissolved according to the former Hindu view. The marriage would continue to subsist and the woman would remain his wife ; she could not contract a second marriage as long as her husband was alive unless the Hindu marriage could be dissolved under certain special circumstances and conditions, such as under custom. The convert husband, however, could contract another marriage with a woman belonging to his new religion and he would not be guilty of bigamy as both the Hindu and the

Muslim laws allow polygamy. This rule of law was applied in a case where a Hindu convert to Christianity had married a Christian woman according to the rites of the Roman Catholic Church which insists on monogamy. Subsequently, he reverted to Hinduism and then married a Hindu woman according to Hindu law during the life-time of his first wife and when that marriage was subsisting. It was held that he was not guilty of bigamy because his religion (Hinduism) allowed polygamy and so he was perfectly within the bounds of his religion in taking a second wife.[5] It has been held in some cases that a Hindu marriage is not dissolved on the Hindu husband's conversion because though he may be rendered an outcaste by his conversion yet he may be readmitted to his former status by expiation.[6] It is submitted that this view requires reconsideration. We have to look to the present position of the parties. We cannot rely or take into consideration a future contingency which may or may not happen. It was stated by the Bombay High Court that a Hindu marriage is not dissolved on the conversion of the Hindu husband to another religion and the wife does not cese to be the wife of the Hindu husband upon such conversion.[7] The Hindu wife, however, could not contract another marriage even with a Hindu as her marriage was not considered to be affected by the conversion of the husband. As Hindu law does not allow polyandry except in certain castes the wife could be held guilty of bigamy if she contracted a second marriage when her convert husband was alive. This involved great hardship to her, but the Hindu Marriage Act, 1955 has solved the difficulty as far as India is concerned. Section 13 (11) of the Act allows a spouse to get his or her marriage dissolved on the ground that the other party has

5. E. Vs. Antony, I.L R. 33, Mad, 371; In re Millard and another, I.L.R. 10 Mad. 318.

6. Budansa Rowther Vs. Fatima Bai A.I.R. 1914 Mad. 192; Advocate-General of Madras Vs, Ananda Chari, I.L.R. 9 Mad. 466.

7. The Government of Bombay Vs. Ganga, I.L.R. 4 Bombay 330.

ceased to be a Hindu by conversion to another religion.

Conversion of Hindu Wife. The adoption of Islam by a married Hindu wife presented greater difficulty than was experienced in the case of the conversion of a Hindu husband. The prohibition against second marriage of women either after divorce or upon widowhood has no foundation either in early Hindu law or custom. Certain passages of the Vedas sanction the second marriage of women who have left their husbands for a justifiable cause. It was held in a case that when a married Hindu woman deserts her husband, becomes a convert to Mohammadanism and adopts the habits, and lives as the wife, of a Mohammadan, then she is altogether out of the pale of the Hindu law and ceases to have any recognised status she had according to that law. She becomes civilly dead and the marriage and her relation as a wife becomes thereby absolutely dissolved.[8]

A similar view was expressed in 3 M. H. C. R. 134 ; (1875) 1 Bom. 113 ; 3 M. H. C. R. App. VII ; 4 M. H. C. R. App. III. But subsequently the Courts changed their view and held a Hindu marriage to be indissoluble.[9]

It was held by the Lahore High Court that a marriage between Hindu spouses will remain subsisting even if one of the spouses becomes a convert to Islam unless a decree for the dissolution of the marriage is passed by a competent Court.[10]

The view was expressed by the Calcutta High Court in a case that there is no authority in the Hindu law for the proposition that a degraded person or an apostate is absolved from all civil obligations incurred before degradation or apostasy and that it would be against the spirit of the Hindu law, which

8. Sinammal Vs. Advocate-General of Madras I.L R. (1894) 8, Mad. 169.
9. In Re. Ramkumari, I.L.R. (1885) 18 Calcutta 364. The Government of Bombay Vs. Ganga, I.L R. 4 Bom. 330, Advocate-General of Madras Vs, Ananda, Chari, I.L.R. 9 Mad. 407.
10. Mst. Nandi Vs. Crown, I.L.R 1 Lahore 440.

regards the matrimonial bond as absolutely indissoluble, to annul a marriage on such ground.[11] The Court referred to the case of Rahmat Bibi Vs. Rukaya Bibi but did not accept as correct the view expressed in that case (to the effect that a Hindu marriage becomes dissolved on the wife's conversion to Islam, as was also held in a case reported in Norton's 'Leading Cases,' p. 12). The Courts also held that a Hindu married woman, who on conversion to Islam marries a Muslim, is guilty of bigamy. This view was justified on the reasoning that the Hindu marriage is indissoluble and so subsists even after her conversion to Islam and she remains the wife of her Hindu husband, while Islam does not permit a Muslim to marry the wife of another person.[12] It is submitted that the view requires reconsideration. No doubt the Muslim law does not allow a Muslim to marry the wife of another man, but then Islam does not permit a Muslim woman to marry *or to remain the wife of a non-Muslim* and her marriage would be automatically dissolved after conversion on the expiry of three menstrual courses or three months. It is, therefore, not correct to say that her Muslim husband could not legally marry her on her conversion to Islam under the provisions of the Muslim law. Another point that has been advanced in such cases is that in a Muslim country it is an essential condition for dissolution of the Hindu marriage that the unconverted party should be given an opportunity by the *Qāḍī* to embrace Islam if he so likes but this cannot be done in India as there are no *Qāḍīs* who can issue such notices and so this rule has become obsolete.[13] It is submitted that it is not correct to say that this rule has become obsolete In the first place, the present Courts have taken the place of the *Qāḍīs* of the early days and on an application being made by the wife, the Court in its inherent power can issue a notice to the Hindu husband to show cause why the marriage

11. In the matter of Ram Kumari, I.L.R. 18 Calcutta 264.
12. Budansa Rowther Vs. Fatima Bai, A.I.R. 1914 Mad. 192.
13. In the matter of Ram Kumari, I.L.R. 18 Cal. 264.

should not be dissolved. In one case, Armond, J. was ready to issue such a notice, but did not deem it necessary as he held that India was not a Dar al-Islam so that the marriage could have been dissolved on the expiry of three months' time without the issue of such a notice. It is unfortunate that his Lordship's attention was not drawn to the fact that even in a non-Muslim country the marriage would be held to have been dissolved on the expiry of three months under Muslim law. His Lordship has stated, "I would only add that even had it been necessary to hold that the procedure for the presentment of Islam as in an Islamic country was obligatory, I should have considered that the direction might have been given by myself, as the Judge hearing the suit, to the Registrar for him to serve the requisite letters (repeated three times) calling on the defendant to embrace Islam and notifying him that otherwise on the petitioner's claim a declaration would be liable to be made by the Court of the marriage having become dissolved under Mohammadan law.[14]

The Court also found that the service of letter by the petitioner on the defendant was sufficient for the purpose. Thus it was stated, "and in such a case as this if satisfied, as I am in the present case, that service of the letter had satisfactorily been effected by the petitioner (the wife) herself (or her attorney) instead of by the Registrar, I should have held such service of the notice to have been lawful and effective as being sufficient to satisfy this Court of the service having been made and as equivalent for the requirements of the Mohammedan law to the stipulated presentment by the Kazi." As discussed before the absence of a *Qāḍī* in a country does not affect the dissolution of the marriage, and advantage shall be taken of the Shafi'i law under which the marriage shall become dissolved automatically on the expiry of three months. Hence under Muslim law as explained before, the marriage shall become dissolved automatically on the expiry of three menstrual courses or

14. Ayesha Bibi Vs, Subodh Ch. Chakravarty A.I.R. 1949 Cal. 436.

three months as the case may be. Even in Pakistan, where there are no *Qāḍīs* appointed for the purpose, the converted wife shall not be forced to stick to her former Hindu marriage on the ground that the husband has not been served by a *Qāḍī* with a notice asking him to embrace Islam, but advantage shall be taken in such a case of the Shafi'i law and the marriage shall be considered to become automatically terminated on the expiry of the above-mentioned prescribed period. This is based on the rule of law laid down by Hanafi Jurists that a Hanafi *Qāḍī* can refer the parties to the *Qāḍī* of another Sunni sect when he finds that the Hanafi law involves hardship in the case. There can, therefore, be no difficulty when such a case arises in a Muslim country. It seems that the Court's attention was not drawn to this rule of the Hanafi law. The difficulty pointed out in various cases, mentioned above, does not constitute a real difficulty if the clear provisions of Muslim law are appreciated. An important factor which has not been generally appreciated is the freedom of religion and thought allowed to all the parties concerned. It includes not only the right of a person to go on thinking as before but also the right to adopt a new or different thought. It was stated in a case, that it is impossible to accept the contention that justice and equity require that we should apply Muslim law in deciding the case..It would be patently contrary to justice and right that one party to a solemn pact should be allowed to repudiate it (the marriage) by a unilateral act. It would be tantamount to permitting the wife to force a divorce upon her husband although he may not want it.[15] It is submitted that this view denies freedom of religion to the wife. This principle regarding freedom of religion has been impliedly given effect to in cases under the Native Christian Dissolution of Marriage Act. The provision regarding dissolution of a marriage on conversion in the Act is based on practically the same principle as under the Muslim law, that is, the freedom of the convert to get his or her

15. Robasa Khanum Vs, Khodadad Bomanji Irani, A.I.R. 1947, Bombay 272.

marriage dissolved on his or her conversion when the other party fails or refuses to do so. The Courts in all cases have given effect to this provision of the said Act. The Hindu Marriage Act, 1955, also allows a husband or a wife to get the marriage dissolved on the basis that the other party has ceased to be a Hindu by conversion to another religion. There are two enactments which have a great bearing on the matter, namely, Regulation VIII of 1794, and the Charter of the Establishment of the Supreme Court.

It is stated in Section 24 of the Charter of the Establishment of the Supreme Court that in case of difference of religion the suit shall be decided by the laws and the usage of the defendant. Section 112 of the Government of India Act, 1915 and Section 223 of the Government of India Act, 1935, give effect to the above-mentioned provision of law by enacting that the law to be administered in the High Court shall be the same as was before the Acts came into force. But a doubt was expressed by the Bombay High Court if section 112 of the Government of India Act, 1915, covers a matrimonial case or serves as a guidance and that it does not seem equitable that a case should be decided in all circumstances by the law of the defendant.[16] The correct position would be to decide it according to justice, equity and good conscience according to the provision of the Regulation of 5th July, 1871. Thus it was held by the Madras High Court that "Where a conflict occurs between persons belonging to different religions, the Courts must apply the rules of justice, equity and good conscience."[17] The Privy Council held in a case that if there was no rule of Indian law which could be applied to a particular case then it should be decided by equity and good conscience.[18] The Courts have also followed

16. Rachal Banjamin Vs. Benjamin Solomon Benjamin, A.I.R. (1926) Bom. 169, Robasa Khanum Vs. Khodadad Bomanji Irani, A I.R. 1947 Bom. 272.
17. Budansa Rowther Vs. Fatima Bai, A.I.R. 1914 Mad. 192.
18. Warghala Rajsanji Vs. Sheikh Moslehuddin, I L.R. 11 Bombay 55.

this rule in several cases.[19] If this rule be accepted then the question naturally arises as to what should be the position according to justice, equity and good conscience. On the wife's conversion, the Hindu husband can marry another Hindu wife as polygamy is allowed by Hindu law, and now he can also get his marriage dissolved on the ground of the wife's renunciation of her Hindu religion under the provision of Section 13 (11) of Act XXV of 1955. The wife. however. shall be put in a very unfortunate position. Her Hindu marriage shall not be considered dissolved according to the decisions of the various High Courts so that in spite of her conversion she shall still be deemed to be the wife of her Hindu husband. Her new religion, however, refuses to recognise her marriage and she is prohibited by Islam to treat her former Hindu husband as her lawful husband and the Muslim law shall deem the marriage to be automatically dissolved on the expiry of three terms of her menstrual courses or at the maximum period of three months. Besides, it forbids her to have anything to do with the Hindu husband. It has been held in a case that if the conversion is legal, if there is no statutory restriction, then the Court is.....free, and not only that but is bound to give legal effect to its consequences, if any......To forbid or penalise conversion (whether generally or for a particular class of citizens, such for example that of married Hindu women) would obviously be a retrograde step inconsistent with the objective of freedom of religious thought.....There are no statutory directions preventing the Court in this case giving effect to this conversion. In view of the clearly proved fact of conversion in this case, this case clearly falls to be decided on the footing that at the time of her petition, and today, the petitioner is and was a Muslim". The Court further stated, "She (the convert) will then (on conversion) be governed by that personal law....."[20] Ghose has summed up the problem, and it is submitted correctly,

19. Robasa Khanum Vs. Khodadad Bomanji Irani, A.I.R. 1947 Bombay 272, Budansa Rowther Vs. Fatima Bai, A.I.R. 1914 Mad. 192.

20. Ayesha Bibi Vs. Subodh Ch. Chakravarty A.I.R. 1949 Cal. 439.

by stating in his learned book on Hindu law, 'When either the husband or the wife, by conversion to another religion goes out of the pale of Hindu society and the law of making the continuance of living together as husband and wife impossible, it would be reasonable to hold that the marriage is dissolved and both the parties are entitled to remarry. It is difficult to understand why she should be debarred from marriage if she becomes a Mohammadan. Prohibition of the marriage is not consonant with reason or natural justice in such a case.[21]

The controversy about the indissolubility of a Hindu marriage has now been set at right by the Hindu Marriage Act, 1955, which allows the dissolution of a marriage under certain circumstances. Section 13 of the Act provides for divorce on the grounds that the other party was living in adultery or was suffering from insanity or venereal disease in a communicable form, or was missing for the last seven years, *or had embraced another religion* or renounced the world.

No case of the nature discussed above has arisen in India or Pakistan after the passing of the Hindu Marriage Act, 1955. It will be interesting to see what view will a Court take now when the Act no longer holds a Hindu marriage to be indissoluble, but allows its dissolution under certain circumstances on the petition of the unconverted spouse. To penalise a party on account of a change in her religious outlook is neither just nor equitable. But the difficulty in all probability will not be experienced now as the view that a Hindu marriage is not indissoluble has now been recognised by the Hindu Marriage Act, 1955.

21. Jogendra Chundra Ghose. *Principles of Hindu Law*, p. 776, Calcutta, 1917.

Section IV.—Christian Marriage

Preliminary : Before discussing the effect of conversion to Islam of one of a Christian married couple, it seems desirable to understand the Christian law of marriage, conception of a Christian marriage, the laws that shall apply in such a case, validity of marriage, husband's right to divorce his wife etc. They are discussed below :—

Christian Marriage : The Christian laws of marriage and divorce are based to a great extent on the Roman law. It may, however, be stated at the outset that while the Church did admit the validity of marriage, yet it strongly discouraged it and encouraged celibacy. Marriage was considered harmful to man's spiritual attainment. Even St. Augustine, whose ideal of asceticism caused him to regret his own marriage, put polygamy and prostitution in category with marriage and described them as being as necessary to man as a sewer to a palace.[1] It was allowed, though very reluctantly, when absolutely necessary to avoid loose living on the reasoning that, "It is better to marry than to burn" (in hell). Even then sexual intimacy was allowed to the minimum and to derive enjoyment out of it was considered to contribute to the defilement of the parties.[2]

For a long period of Christian history, no religious ceremony of any kind was deemed necessary by the Church for the validity of marriage. In the early period of Christianity no formalities were prescribed for marriage. A man and a woman could contract a marriage by their free consent without any rites or ceremonies.[3] According to the doctrine

1. J. F. W., Boden-Worsley, *Mischief of the Marriage Law*, p. 70, London 1932.
2. McGregor Heineman, *Divorce in England*, p. 2. London, 1957.
3. *Ibid*,

of the Church the simple consent of the two parties without any ceremonies constituted a valid marriage.[4] The mere statement of each party that they took one another as spouses was deemed sufficient, providing that the mutual pledge referred to the present.[5] In the Middle Ages a religious ceremony appears to have been made obligatory by law, and marriages without the intervention of a priest were considered clandestine and irregular; but they frequently occurred, and their validity was perfectly undisputed.[6]

Before the Marriage Act of 1753 and in accordance with the Common law marriages contracted by simple consent and followed by co-habitation were deemed valid in England without any religious ceremony though they did not bring with them all the civil consequences of a marriage celebrated in Church, and exposed those who contracted them to some ecclesiastical censure and penalties. Clandestine marriages, however, continued to flourish and to stop them the Marriage Act of 1753 was enacted which made it compulsory that marriages should be solemnised by a priest and that otherwise they could be considered null and void. But even this Act did not stop the practice.

Conditions imposed by Roman Catholic Church : Some important changes were made in the marriage laws by the Council of Trent in the year 1547 when there was an open breach and a division occurred between the Roman Catholic and the Protestant Churches. In order to put an end to the numerous abuses growing out of clandestine marriages the Council of Trent for the first time made it a necessary condition of marriage for the Catholics that it should be solemnised by a priest. It also held marriage to be a sacrament and so indissoluble.

4. William Edward Hartpole Lecky, *Democracy and Liberty*, p. 168, London, 1913.
5. L. T. Hobhouse, *Morals in Evolution*, p. 213, London, 1951.
6. Leeky, *op. cit.*, pp. 168-69.

Interpretation by the Catholics : It appears that the Roman Catholics interpreted the sayings of Jesus Christ relating to marriage and divorce literally.

Marriage considered Indissoluble : Marriage came to be considered absolutely indissoluble by the Catholics as it was considered that on its consummation, the husband and the wife became one flesh and so could not be separated. This rule is based on the text, "on marriage, a man leaves his father and mother and cleaves to his wife. and they twain shall be one flesh, so they are no more twain, but one flesh".[7] It is said that in such a case "there exists a God-made bond of matrimony in which God Himself is the joiner", and so it is not open to the parties to unmake it.[8] This conception of the indissolubility of marriage was further strengthened by the text, "What therefore God hath joined together let not man put asunder." This notion of indissolubility of marriage was followed to such an extent that "even if a husband were a leper and had given his disease to his wife", this was not accounted cruelty to the wife and she had no remedy.[9]

Interpretation by Protestants : The Protestants did not accept the literal interpretation of the sayings of Jesus Christ. Thus it was explained, "It was not in accordance with the method of the teaching of the Founder of Christianity to lay down hard and fast rules admitting of no exception. His practice was to provide large principles of recognisable truth to be interpreted and applied not in the letter but in the spirit."[10]

It was also stated, "the recorded sayings of our Lord show no desire to legislate......on the subject of marriage and divorce".[11] "A striking peculiarity of our Lord's teaching in

7. St. Mark, 10 W 7 and 8.
8. McGregor, *op. cit.*, p. 103.
9. J. F. W., Boden-Worsley, *Mischief of the Marriage Law*, p. 89, London, 1932.
10. *Ibid.*, p. 51,
11. E. S. P. Haynes and Derek Walker-Smith, *Divorce and its Problems*, p. 4, London, 1935.

its original form is that He never once lays down a rule of conduct as a rule".[12]

They, therefore, did not agree with the doctrine that a Christian marriage was indissoluble.

Catholics' View of Protestant Marriages : The Catholics were so much set against the Protestants' notion of marriage that they considered their marriages to be simple concubinage. They held a Protestant marriage invalid so that women who had contracted Protestant marriages were allowed, on adoption of Roman Catholicism, to marry a Catholic on the ground that the first marriage was a nullity. Civil marriage was declared by Pope Pius IX to be a filthy concubinage.[13]

Nature of Marriages in England: Marriage continued to be considered indissoluble in England, which was a Protestant country, up to the Middle Ages. It has been remarked, "It seems almost incredible, but it is none the less true, that Protestant England continued content to remain, even after the Reformation, subject to the Roman Catholic theory of divorce and separation until as lately as the year 1857."[14]

Position of Women : In the Middle Ages the law did not help the wife. The position of woman in the year 1801 is graphically described in "The Question of English Divorce" in these words: "Both at this time, and for long after it, multitudes of women and children were working almost naked for the bare living that was to be obtained by dragging coal trucks along subterranean passages so narrow that they could only be traversed on all fours. The sale of wives by their own husbands at Smithfield Market was then no dim and incredible tradition."[15] Blackstone has depicted a wife's position in England in these words : "The very being or legal existence of the woman is suspended during the marriage........The husband also (by the old law) might give his wife moderate

12. E. S. P., Haynes and Derek Walker-Smith, *Divorce and its Problems*, p. 6, London, 1935.
13. Dr. Sanday's evidence before the Royal Commission.
14. *The Question of English Divorce*, p. 34.
15. *Ibid.*, p. 53.

correction.[16] He is bound to provide her with necessaries, but for anything besides necessaries he is not chargeable. She can bring no action without his concurrence."[17] There was literally no protection for the wife of a drunkard struggling to support her children by the labour of her hands from the husband who should choose to sponge upon what she earned. Such earnings were emancipated from the husband's control by the Act of 1870. In 1882 the same principles were applied to all property".[18] Sweden emancipated the wife's earnings in 1874, Denmark in 1880, Norway in 1888 and so on.

Remarriage : As dissolution of marriage was not permitted by the Church, there would not arise any occasion for remarriage. But in any case remarriage is strongly denounced and this conception is supported by the text "Whosoever shall put away his wife and marry another, committeth adultery against her; and if she herself shall put away her husband, and marry another, she committeth adultery."[19] In Luke the version reads as under:—

> "Every one that putteth away his wife and marrieth another committeth adultery, and he that marrieth one that is put away from a husband committeth adultery."

This version is also given with slight variations in Mathew.[20] The above will show that divorce by either the husband or the wife as well as remarriage were strongly condemned by Christianity if we take the sayings of Jesus Christ literally as is done by the Roman Catholics. St. Jerome described a woman who entered into a second marriage as a dog returning to its vomit or a sow seeking again her wallowing place."[21] But St. Paul allows a marriage to be anulled if one of an unbelieving married couple embraces Christianity while the

16. L. T. Hobhouse, *Morals in Evolution*, pp. 219, 220, London, 1956.
17. *Ibid.*, p. 220.
18. *Ibid.*, p. 223.
19. St. Mark, X : 11, 12,
20. Luke, XVI : 18 ; Mathew V ; 31, 32 and XIX : 3-9,
21. J. F. W. Boden-Worsley, *Mischief of the Marriage Law*, p. 70.

other refuses to live with him or her when remarriage by the convert was permissible. This has been made clear by Boden Worsley in *Mischief of the Marriage Law*, where he has explained and states, "Yet, if the unbelieving departeth (i.e. deserts) let him depart : the brother or the sister is not under bondage in such cases i.e. is free to marry again.[22]

The conception that marriage once consummated became absolutely indissoluble and that remarriage was not to be contracted, resulted in untold hardships for, in spite of the best efforts, marriage sometimes does prove a failure. This also resulted in frequency of prostitution. An English writer has stated, "In consequence of persistent adherence of the Legislature in England to laws that were unsuitable to the needs of the people, a state of morality had been produced long before 1857 that was entirely disgraceful."[23]

So much was this the case that one of the most authoritative writers on the subject of Marriage and Divorce (J. P. Bishop) states, "second marriages without divorce, adultery, and illegitimate children were of everyday occurrence, while polygamy was winked at, though a felony on the statute book.[24] It should be borne in mind that this state of things existed in England not fifty years ago, and as a direct result of an inefficient system of law."[25] The principle of the indissolubility of marriage that existed up to 1857 not only led to frequent and open bigamy and to general and notorious immorality but finally produced also a recognised evasion of the law.[26]

Divorce : In Roman law a marriage could be dissolved by mutual consent. This practice of divorce survived until the sixth century. But Emperor Justinian prohibited divorce by

22. J. F. W. Boden-Worsley, *Mischief of the Marriage Law*, p. 65.
23. Bishop: Marriage and Divorce, cited in the *Question of English Divorce*, p. 35, London, 1903.
24. *Ibid*.
25. *Ibid*., p. 45.
26. *Ibid*.

mutual consent. His nephew and successor, Justin, repealed the prohibition. To quote Gibbon, "He yielded to the prayers of his unhappy subjects and restored the liberty of divorce by mutual consent; the civilians were unanimous, the theologians were divided, and the ambiguous word which contains the precept of Christ is flexible to any interpretation that the wisdom of a legislature can demand."[27]

Divorce was up to now denied by the Church. But it is a fact that from the earliest time the need for divorce was always felt and it was allowed to the parties in some form or other. In course of time the Church had, however, to realise that it was essential to give relief to a party in many cases while it could not dissolve a marriage because it considered a marriage to be indissoluble. It, therefore, adopted the idea of nullity of marriage, that is, that there did not and could not exist any lawful marriage between the parties under certain circumstances. For this purpose, the Church had recourse to many new but complicated innovations which allowed the release of the aggrieved party from the marriage-tie but at the same time made the marriage very insecure. Thus a marriage was not allowed when a man and a woman stood within eight degrees of consanguinity.[28] Such a marriage was considered a nullity so that it could be set aside at the instance of one party and could be declared null and of no effect.

But subsequently the Lateran Council of 1215 reduced the degree of prohibition from the eighth degree to the fourth degree. To this prohibition was added the prohibition of affinity, that is, due to the relationship arising out of marriage and also on the ground that a forbidden affinity has been established between the parties who had committed adultery.[29] This prohibition against marriage was also extended to what may be called the spiritual relationship created by baptism

27. Gibbon, *Decline and Fall of the Roman Empire*, Vol. IV, p. 481.
28. *The Question of English Divorce*, p. 28.
29. *Ibid.*

through relationship of god parents.[30] On the other hand, the law allowed great latitude for contracting a marriage so that children over seven years of age could contract a marriage without the consent of their parents.[31]

Development of the Law of Divorce : The necessity for dissolution of marriage was felt by the Protestant Church also and divorce was allowed though to a very small extent and generally to the advantage of the husband only. Even then a divorce *a vinculo matrimonii* (divorce from the bond of matrimony) that is, a divorce which completely dissolved the marriage, was, as a rule, not allowed on the conception that marriage was indissoluble. All that the Ecclesiastical Court allowed in cases of necessity, such as in case of adultery, cruelty, etc. was that the aggrieved party was allowed a divorce *a mensa et thoro* (divorce from board and bed) or what is now called judicial separation, that is, when the marriage is maintained but the aggrieved party is permitted to live apart from the other party *i.e.* the party at fault.

According to Haynes and Walker-Smith, "History tells us that a complete matrimonial stability has never been attained ; monogamy, in fact, has not been accompanied by indissolubility. Nor is a defection from the highest ideal standards, however conscientiously held, surprising : legislation caters for men and women, not for angels.[32]

7. *Reform in Law* : It was realised in England in course of time that the idea of indissolubility of marriage and the rigidity of the ecclesiastical law led to great hardship in many cases. Attempts were made to reform the matrimonial law from time to time, to provide more facility to the parties to separate in case of hardship and to make the law relating to divorce less rigid.

8. *Way to get Dviorce* : Divorce was denied to the parties which led to great hardship, A way out was, therefore, found

30. MacGregor, *op. cit.*, p. 4.
31. *Ibid.*, p. 2.
32. E. S. P. Haynes and Derek Walker-Smith, *op. cit.*, p. 10.

and a novel practice then set in. It was said that the Courts have to follow the laws as they are and cannot go against them and so could not dissolve a marriage, but Parliament which is the maker of laws is not bound by them. It could, therefore, grant a divorce by passing a Private Act. For this purpose a decree was first obtained for a judicial separation from the Eccelesiastical Court and then an action for damages was brought in the Civil Court against the offending party. Armed with these the petitioner instituted proceedings in the House of Lords which passed the Act dissolving the marriage. The parties could then enter into a new marriage. This practically was the only procedure for divorce from the end of the sixteenth century to the middle of the nineteenth century. But it usually cost £600 to £1,000 and so only the rich could afford to have recourse to it while the vast majority of the people could not take advantage of it.

9. *Dissatisfaction with Divorce Laws* : This position gave rise to dissatisfaction amongst the people. It was in the year 1845 that the memorable and an extremely satirical judgment of Justice Maule (reproduced below) in an appeal in which a man had been convicted for bigamy, fully exposed the defective legal system in respect of divorce then in force in England.

"Prisoner at the bar, you have been convicted before me of what the law regards as a very grave and serious offence, that of going through the marriage ceremony a second time while your wife was still alive. You plead in mitigation of your conduct that she was given to dissipation and drunkenness, that she proved herself a curse to your household while she remained mistress of it, and that she had latterly deserted you; but I am not permitted to recognize any such plea. You had entered into a solemn engagement to take her for better, for worse, and if you got infinitely more of the latter, as you appear to have done, it was your duty patiently to submit. You say you took another person to be your wife because you were left with several young children, who required the care and protection of some one who might act as a substitute for the parent who had deserted them; but the law makes no allowances for bigamists with large families. Had you taken the other female to live with you as your concubine, you would never have been interfered with by the law. But your crime consists in having—to use your own language—preferred to make an honest woman of her. Another of your irrational excuses is that your wife had committed adultery, and so you thought you were relieved from treating her with any further consideration; but you were mistaken. The law in its wisdom points out a means by which you might rid yourself from further association with a woman who had dishonoured you; but you did not think proper to adopt it.

"I will tell you what that process is. You ought first to have brought an action against your wife's seducer if you could discover him; that might have cost you money, and you say you are a poor working man, but that is not the fault of the law. You would then be obliged to prove by evidence your wife's criminality in a court of justice, and thus obtain a verdict with damages against the defendant, who was not unlikely to turn out to be a pauper. But so jealous is the law (which you ought to be aware is the perfection of reason) of the sanctity of the marriage-tie, that in accomplishing all this you would only have fulfilled the lighter portion of your duty. You must then have gone, with your verdict in your hand, and petitioned the House of Lords for a divorce. It would cost you perhaps five or six hundred pounds, and you do not seem to be worth as many pence. But it is the boast of the law that it is impartial, and makes no difference between the rich and the poor. The wealthiest man in the kingdom would have had to pay no less than that sum for the same luxury; so that you would have no reason to complain. You would, of course, have to prove your case over again, and at the end of a year, or possibly two, you might obtain a decree which would enable you legally to do what you have thought proper to do without it. You have thus wilfully rejected the boon the legislature offered you, and it is my duty to pass upon you such sentence as I think your offence deserves, and that sentence is, that you be imprisoned for one day; and inasmuch as the present assizes is three days old, the result is that you will be immediately discharged."[33]

In England, as explained above, there was great dissatisfaction with the rigour of laws relating to marriage and divorce while King Henry VIII was dissatisfied with his marriage and with his failure to persuade the Pope to pronounce the marriage null and void. The King's dissatisfaction was not the root-cause but the occasion of the breach. The reform of the ecclesiastical abuses had long been a conscious and crying national need.

The law had to be reformed because, as observed by Haynes and Walker-Smith, that marriage was made for men and not men for marriage.[34] The memorable judgment of Justice Maule (reproduced above) caused a stir in the public and the government found it necessary to do something in the matter. The government soon after appointed a Royal Commission which recorded the evidence of a large number of leading personalities of the time. The Commission was not unanimous; the majority report made a number of recommendations, but only a few were accepted by the House of Commons.

10. *Law Amended*: The Matrimonial Causes Act, 1857 was then passed. Two important changes introduced by it are that it divested the Church of the jurisdiction regarding matrimonial causes and set up a Court of Divorce and Matrimonial Causes. The second was to place divorce within the reach of the common man as distinguished from the Act of Parliament under which divorce could be obtained only by the rich. Remarriage after divorce is permitted but no clergyman is compelled to solemnise the remarriage of divorced persons. The use of Church for the celebration of the marriage, however, cannot be refused. It cannot be denied that the Act has been, as a rule, very helpful to the public,

33. E. S. P. Haynes and Derek Walker-Smith, *op cit.*, pp. 35-38
34. *Ibid.*, p. 8.

though obviously it is not an exemplary piece of legislation. Much complaint has also been made of the large amount of perjury that has taken place in the Divorce Courts.

11. *Concluding Remarks* : It is interesting to note that the English laws of marriage and divorce were very hard and rigid upto the nineteenth century but were made more humane by modifications and necessary reforms so that now they give almost equal facility to the wife to separate from her husband under certain circumstances by replacing the ecclesiastical law by civil law. In Islam, on the other hand, the happiness of the spouses was considered of paramount importance, but in the course of time the rights of the wife were usurped by man and the laws relating to divorce became very rigid. It is only within the last decade that many Muslim countries came to realise the great hardship that was being caused to the wives who could not get any redress on account of the introduction of undesirable innovations in the law. Necessary changes were then introduced and are still being introduced in the matrimonial laws to remove these innovations and to make the laws of marriage and divorce more in consonance with the original Muslim law.

Section V—Domicile

Preliminary: Before discussing the effect of domicile on marriage, it would be desirable to get an idea of domicile itself. Domicile plays a very important part in the matters of jurisdiction, marriage, divorce, custody of offspring and a number of other important matters, and every country wants to impose its own laws on its citizens, and does not tolerate their evasion in any way.

The great importance of domicile lies in the determination of the system of law that shall govern an individual or group of individuals. There are two main systems of law that may be applicable in various matters, namely, the law of nationality and the law of domicile. Nationality and domicile are quite different and distinct from each other. It was stated by Lord Westbury: "The law of England, and of almost all civilised countries, ascribes to each individual at his birth two distinct legal states or conditions; one by virtue of which he becomes the subject of some particular country, binding him by the tie of natural allegiance, and which may be called his political status; another, by virtue of which he has ascribed to him the character of a citizen of some particular country, and as such is possessed of certain municipal rights, and subject to certain obligations, which latter character is the civil status or condition of the individual, and may be quite different from his political status. The political status may depend on different laws in different countries; whereas the civil status is governed universally by one single principle, namely, that of domicile, which is the criterion established by law for the purpose of determining civil status."[1] Nationality or political status depends, apart from naturalisation, on the place of birth or on parentage; civil status, on the other hand, is constituted by permanent residence in a country with a present intention of remaining there indefinitely. To illustrate

1. Udny Vs. Udny, (1869) L.R.I. Sc. and Div. 441 (H.L.).

the above, let us consider the case of a Pakistani born in Pakistan of Pakistani parents. His nationality will obviously be Pakistani. He goes to England and secures some service there and, finding the country to his liking, decides not to return to Pakistan but to settle in England permanently. His civil status or domicile shall become English.

It can thus be seen that nationality is often a consequence of birth and in the absence of exceptional circumstances, such as naturalisation, depends upon parentage or upon the place of birth. Domicile, on the other hand, depends on permanent residence coupled with intention. It was the law of domicile which was accepted and applied till the eighteenth century. But the conception of nationality gained ground in Europe in the beginning of the nineteenth century. Different countries adopted one or the other of the above-mentioned two systems. Thus France, Australia, Italy, Germany, Spain and some other countries are governed by the law of nationality. England, the United States of America, Denmark, etc. are governed by the law of domicile. India at one time being part of the British Empire was also subject to the law of domicile. On partition of the country into two countries, namely, Pakistan and Bharat (India) they have not changed the position, and are still governed by the law of domicile. Domicile is an idea of law ; it is the relation which the law creates between an individual and a particular locality or country.[2]

As stated before, most of our cases arise out of marriages of Muslims with English and American women and it is, therefore, the *lex loci domicilii* of those countries with which we are generally concerned and it is discussed here in some detail. It will extend the scope of this chapter to an inordinate length, if the law of nationality is also discussed here. Any one interested in that subject may consult some book dealing with that matter.

Definition : Attempts have been made to define domicile, but it is difficult to give an exact definition of the same. Thus

2. Bell Vs. Kennedy, (1868) L.R.I. Sc. and Div. 307.

it was observed by Lord Cranworth, "By domicile we mean home, the permanent home, and if you do not understand your permanent home, I am afraid that no illustration drawn from foreign writers will very much help you to it."[3] It was stated in another case, "That place is properly the domicile of a person in which his habitation is fixed without any present intention of removing therefrom."[4] It has also been described as "The place where one has voluntarily fixed his abode...not for a mere special or temporary purpose but with a present intention of making it his home, either permanently or for an indefinite or unlimited length of time.[5]

Another comprehensive definition has been given as, "That place is properly the domicile of a person in which he has voluntarily fixed the habitation of himself and his family, not for a merely special and temporary purpose but with a present intention of making it his permanent home unless and until something which is unexpected or the happening of which is uncertain shall occur to induce him to adopt some other permanent home."[6] It has been defined in another case as "the place where a person lives or has his home while in a large sense, it is where he has his true, fixed and permanent home to which, when absent from it, he intends to return. and from which he has no present purpose to remove."[7]

Discussion: It will be seen from the above definitions that there are two elements which are essential in the case of domicile, namely:

(*i*) Residence, and

(*ii*) Intention.

In order to constitute domicile it is necessary that both these conditions should be satisfied ; the presence of only one of them cannot constitute domicile. Thus mere residence,

3. Whicker Vs. Hume, (1853) 31 L.T. 319.
4. Attorney-General Vs Yule, (1931) All. E.R. Rep. 400.
5. Williams Vs. North Carolina, 325 U.S. 226.
6. Lord Vs. Colvin, (1859) 32 L.T. 377.
7. Horne Vs. Horne, 31 N. Car. 99,

however long, in a country cannot make it the domicile of a person. Residence must be accompanied by an intention to live there permanently or for an unlimited length of time. Similarly, the mere fact that the residence is brief cannot prevent the acquisition of domicile. It was stated in a case that "the mere fact of a man residing in a place different from that in which he has been before domiciled, even though his residence there may be long and continuous, does not of necessity show that he has elected that place as his permanent and abiding home. He may have taken up and continued his residence there for some special purpose, or he may have elected to make the place his temporary home. But domicile, in some of the cases spoken of as "home", imports an abiding and permanent home, and not a mere temporary one.[8] Although residence may be some *prima facie* proof of domicile, it is by no means to be inferred fromt he fact of residence that domicile results, even though you do not find that the party had any other residence in existence or in contemplation."[9]

II. *Intention* : The second essential element to constitute domicile consists of intention which must not be vague or indecisive. If a person resides at a place without any intention of making it his home his mere stay will not constitute domicile in the absence of a fixed intention to settle therep ermanently.[10] There must be a residence freely chosen, and not prescribed or dictated by any external necessity, such as the duties of office, the demand of creditors, or the relief from illness ; and it must be residence fixed not for a limited period or particular purpose, but general and indefinite in its future contemplation. It is true that residence originally temporary, or intended for a limited period, may afterwards become general and unlimited, and in such a case as soon as the change of purpose, or *animus manendi*,

8. Attorney-General Vs. Yule, (1931) All. E.R. Rep. 400.

9. Bell Vs. Kennedy, (1868) L.R.I. Sc. and Div. 307.

10. *Ibid.*, Winans Vs. Attorney,General, (1904) A.C. 287 ; 90 L.T. 721; Ramsay Vs. Liverpool Royal Infirmary, (1930) A.C. 588; 143 L.T. 388

(intention of remaining) can be inferred the fact of domicile is established.[11] Thus if a Pakistani secures a temporary job in the United Kingdom and resides there during the time his service lasts, then his domicile shall be Pakistani. If during his stay he decides to settle permanently in the U.K. then he shall acquire English domicile. It can be seen here that he intended at first to reside in the U.K. for a limited time, but subsequently changes his intention. It is also necessary that the intention must be given effect to. Thus if a Pakistani wants to settle in England, sells his property in Pakistan, but falls ill and dies then his domicile shall not change. Here he has not settled in England and the intention has not been carried out.

Classes of domicile : There are two main classes of domicile, namely,

(*a*) Domicile of Origin, and

(*b*) Domicile of Choice.

To this may be added a third class, generally included in the second class, which Prof. Cheshire calls "domicile under disability." It is this class with which we are mostly concerned in this chapter. The above classes are briefly discussed below.

(*a*) *Domicile of Origin* : The law attributes to every individual as soon as he is born the domicile of his father, if the child be legitimate, and the domicile of the mother if illegitimate. This (domicile) has been called the domicile of origin, and is involuntary.[12] When another domicile is put on, the domicile of origin is for that purpose relinquished, and remains in abeyance during the continuance of the domicile of choice, but as the domicile of origin is the creature of law, and independent of the will of the party, it would be inconsistent with the principles on which it is by law created and ascribed, to suppose that it is capable of being by the act of the party entirely obliterated and extinguished ; it revives and exists whenever there is no other domicile, and it does not require

11. Udny Vs. Udny, (1869) L.R.I. Sc. and Div. 441.
12. *Ibid.*

to be regained or reconstituted *animo et facto* in the manner which is necessary for the acquisition of a domicile of choice.[13]

(*b*) *Domicile of Choice* : As seen above, domicile of origin is created by operation of law which is ascribed to every person on birth. Under certain conditions a person may abandon his domicile of origin and may adopt another domicile which is called domicile of choice, as it is acquired by the free-will of a person. It differs from domicile of origin inasmuch as the domicile of origin is more enduring, its hold stronger and less easily shaken off.[14] It is obvious that as domicile of choice is acquired by free-will of a person he must be capable of changing his previous domicile and should possess freedom to change his or her domicile. As in the case of domicile of origin, the person must be residing in the domicile of choice and this residence must be accompanied by an intention to reside there permanently. In the domicile of choice there must be residence freely chosen, and not prescribed or dictated by any external necessity, and such residence must be fixed not for a limited period, or particular purpose, but general and indefinite in its future contemplation.[15]

(*c*) *Domicile under Disability* : This is the domicile possessed by persons under disability such as infants, children and married women. The former acquire the domicile of their father on their very birth.[16] The latter acquire the domicile of their husbands immediately on the solemnisation of their marriage for the duration of the coverture.[17]

It was held in a case that the home of a wife is necessarily the home of her husband.[18] Sometimes it was contended that under certain circumstances a wife could acquire a

13. Udny Vs. Udny, (1869) L. R. I. Sc. and Div. 441.
14. Winans Vs. Attorney General, (1904) 90 L. T. 721,
15. Udny Vs. Udny, (1869) L. R. I. Sc. and Div. 441.
16. *Ibid.*
17. A. G. for Alberta Vs. Cook, (1926) A.C. 444; Hopkins Vs. Hopkins, (1950) 2 All. E.R. 1035.
18. Dolphin Vs. Robins, (1859) 7 H.L.C. 390.

domicile different from that of her husband. The matter was fully discussed by the House of Lords which came to the conclusion that a wife cannot during the continuation of her marriage have a domicile different from that of her husband.[19] A case involving this point again came up for decision before the Privy Council. It put the rule on a firm ground and expressed the same opinion as expressed above.[20] This view may now be taken as the settled law of England that during the subsistence of a marriage the wife cannot have a domicile different from that of her husband.[21] Domicile must be distinguished from residence or nationality. Nationality is quite different from domicile. It is possible for a man to have domicile in one country and yet not be a national of that country. Thus a Pakistani taking up his permanent abode in the U.S.A. with an intention to settle there permanently will acquire a domicile there though he will still retain his Pakistani nationality.

It will be useful to understand some of the basic rules regarding domicile before discussing the subject in some detail.

The first rule is that no one can be without a domicile. A domicile shall be assigned to a child on its very birth and that domicile shall be the same as the domicile of its father.[22] Domicile is often described as a person's home. It is possible that a person may be homeless, but no one can be without a domicile. Supposing a person is forced to flee from his home and country and seek refuge in another country where he is kept or lives as a refugee and does not know where to go and settle or whether to return to his old home when conditions improve. In such circumstances he will be considered to be homeless, but he will still have his domicile in his old country.

19. Lord Advocate Vs. Jaffrey, (1921) 124 L.T. 129.
20. Attorney-General for Alberta Vs. Cook, (1926) 134 L.T. 717 (Privy Council).
21. Gray Vs. Formosa (1962) 3 All. E. R. 419.
22 Udny Vs. Udny (1869) L. R. I. .Sc. and Div. 441.

Another rule is that no one can have at the same time two or more domiciles.[23] It is possible that a person may live at two or more places at different times as, for example, he may live in Pakistan in winter and in England in summer. He will not have his domicile both in Pakistan and in England but his domicile will be that country where he has his permanent home, where his family lives.

Thirdly, a person retains his domicile of origin until he changes it. As stated before, the domicile of origin is not completely lost on acquisition of a domicile of choice. It only remains in abeyance, and revives once the domicile of choice is lost and no other domicile has been acquired.[24] This is a necessary result of the first rule that no one can be without a domicile.

Muslim Law : Under Muslim law, as stated before, there is no notion of domicile as far as Muslim countries are concerned and the general conception of a Muslim is that he is a citizen of the entire Muslim world and not of any particular part of it, because Islam does not recognise geographical, cultural or any other barrier, whatsoever, amongst its followers. Thus we find that Ibn Batutah was appointed the Head Qādi by the Emperor of Delhi though he belonged to Tunisia and had no intention of remaining permanently at Delhi, but had come to India only for a short time to see the country. In the same way we find that Muslim travellers were received like brothers by the rulers and citizens in every Muslim country wherever they went and no discrimination was made between them and the local Muslims. One has only to read the books of travellers like Ibn Jubayr and Ibn Batutah to realise this conception.

A Muslim woman, on her marriage with a Muslim of a different country, does not acquire his domicile and so the many complications experienced when a European or an

23. Udny Vs. Udny, (1869) L.R, I Sc. and Div. 441, Garthwaite Vs. Garthwaite, (1964) 1 All E.R. 233.

24. Udny Vs. Udny, (1869) L.R. I. Sc. and Div. 441.

American marries a man or woman of a different country, are not met with under Muslim law. If she happens to be a *Kitabiyah* then she, on her marriage to a Muslim, shall become subject to the provisions of Muslim law which are in no way affected by the law of domicile. But in the nineteenth century and more particularly in the twentieth century as a result of their contact with the Western Powers and more often under political influence, many Muslim countries have adopted the conception of nationality. However, even now such is the hold of the conception of universal Muslim brotherhood that most of these countries do not make, as a general rule, the same discrimination between its citizens and Muslims of a different country as is done by the European countries between their citizens and foreigners even when they belong to Christian countries and are Christians. Usually, a Muslim even now will not find much difficulty in settling in a different Muslim country where he will receive a brotherly treatment unless the political relations between the two countries are strained. Moreover, a Muslim woman would not be put to any hardship if she is not living with her husband, but is living in a different Muslim country. The reason is that the Muslim law in respect of marriage, divorce etc, with the exeption of some changes, recently made in some Muslim countries, is practically the same all over the world. The general rule of Muslim law is that a Muslim shall be bound by Muslim law wherever he or she may be.

If the husband and the wife are living in different countries, one living in a Muslim country and the other in a non-Muslim country then the spouse living in the Muslim State shall be governed by Muslim law. Where it is not possible for the spouses to live together their marriage may get dissolved or be allowed to be dissolved under Muslim law.[25] If the non-Muslim wife of a Muslim comes to and settles in a Muslim country, she shall become subject to Muslim law.

25. See Chapter on Tabayan Dār (Difference of Domicile),

Wife's Domicile : The question of domicile is of great importance in cases of marriage and divorce between a Muslim and a non-Muslim woman of a different country, because on her marriage she automatically acquires the domicile of the husband and loses her domicile of origin.

A Muslim marrying a European or American Woman: It is necessary first to give the law of these countries applicable in matrimonial cases before discussing the subject. The majority of such cases involve the laws of England and the U.S.A. and so these are briefly discussed here. It may be stated at the outset that in these countries a wife, on her marriage, acquires the domicile of her husband if it differs from her own domicile.[26] In many European countries, the laws of marriage and divorce are not regulated by domicile but by nationality.

Law in England and U.S.A. : In England and the U.S.A. it is the domicile that governs matrimonial laws. It was held in a case that a woman when she marries a man, not only by construction of law but absolutely as a matter of fact, does acquire the domicile of her husband if she lives with him in the country of his domicile.[27]

The view was expressed that a wife shall be presumed to be living with her husband even if the husband deserts her and establishes a domicile in a foreign country.[28] The effect of this rule has been modified to some extent by Section 1 of the Matrimonial Causes Act, 1955. Actual residence of the wife signifies nothing and shall not, in ordinary circumstances, be set up against the presumption of law that the wife resides with her husband. Thus if an English woman marries in England a foreigner then she loses her English

26. Dolphin Vs. Robins, (1859) 7 H.L.C. 390, De Reneville Vs. De Reneville (1948) 1 All. E.R. 56; Beaumont, Re (1893) 3 Ch. 490.
27. Turner Vs. Thompson, (1888) 13 P.D. 37, 58 L.T. 387 ; Salvesen (Von Lorang) Vs. Administrator of Austrian Property, (1927) 137 L.T. 571.
28. H. Vs. H., (1928) P. 206; Herd Vs. Herd, (1936) 2 All. E.R. 156. Lord Advocate Vs. Jaffrey, (1921) 1 A.C. 146.

domicile and acquires the domicile of her husband. If the husband returns to his own country while the wife remains behind even then she shall retain the domicile of her husband. Should the husband desert her then too the domicile acquired by her on marriage is retained. Thus, where a husband domiciled in Scotland married a woman there, and then went to a foreign country where he lived for more than twenty years till the time of his death, and acquired a domicile there, it was held that the wife also acquired that domicile.[29] In this case the wife had never gone to the foreign country and remained all along in her own country where she was married and yet the foreign domicile was attributed to her. But the Matrimonial Causes Act, 1950, provides relief to a deserted wife. Her marriage can be dissolved if her husband has deserted her without cause for a period of three years.

The wife retains her acquired domicile on the death of her husband or divorce until she changes it by acquiring another domicile.[30] If she separates from him, settles at another place with an intention to live there permanently even then her domicile shall remain the same as that of her husband. But if the husband dies then effect would be given to her new domicile of choice and it shall not be necessary for her to do any new act to establish her new domicile. Her change of residence with an intention to live there permanently shall be given effect to in such a case. It was explained that the intention of the testatrix formed during her life-time was only prevented by a legal situation, namely, the husband's domicile, from being transformed into a legal fact. No new act was required when she continued her intention of changing her domicile after her husband's death.

Under the English law it is a necessary condition for acquisition of the husband's domicile by a woman on her marriage, that the marriage should not be void. It is con-

29. Lord Advocate Vs. Jaffrey (1921) 1 A.C. 146 (H.L.).
30. Re Scullard Estate, (1956) 3 All. E.R. 898; Wallach Re (1950) 1 All. E.R. 199.

sidered that a void marriage is no marriage at all and will be considered as never having taken place and can be so treated by both the parties to it without the necessity of any decree annulling it.[31] The wife does not acquire the domicile of the purported husband. She, therefore, retains her own domicile in such a case. But a voidable marriage is distinct from a void marriage. It is a good marriage as long as it subsists and is not set aside by a Court. In such a case the wife shall acquire the domicile of her husband and shall retain the same even after the dissolution of her marriage.[32] The Court's decree, dissolving her marriage, shall entitle her to change her domicile if she so likes. It can thus be seen that in a void marriage the wife is not presumed to have acquired the husband's domicile at any time but in the case of a voidable marriage she does acquire the husband's domicile which she shall be presumed to retain until a decree annulling it has been pronounced by a Court of competent jurisdiction and she then acquires another domicile.[33]

Thus it was laid down in a case that in nullity cases the parties will have the same domicile at the date of the institution of the suit in one of two events, namely (i) if the marriage is by the proper law voidable and not void, in which case the wife will have acquired the same domicile as that of the husband by the mere fact of marriage and retains that domicile until the marriage is annulled. (2) If the marriage is void but nevertheless the wife on the facts acquired a domicile of choice in the country contemplated as that of the matrimonial domicile and has not subsequently changed that domicile. This occurred in the Salvesen case, where the wife had acquired in fact the husband's German domicile.[34] If the husband happens to change his domicile the wife shall be presumed to have also changed her domicile.

31. De Reneville Vs. De Reneville, (1948) 1 All. E.R. 56.
32. *Ibid.*
33. *Ibid.*
34. (Salvesen.) Von Lorang Vs. the Administraror of Austrian Property, (1927) All. E.R. Rep. 78. De Reneville Vs. De Reneville, (1948), All. E. R. 56.

The importance of domicile lies in the fact that it determines the jurisdiction of Courts in matrimonial matters such as suits for maintenance, dissolution of marriage etc. If the wife loses her own domicile and acquires that of her husband she cannot. as a general rule, sue her husband in her own country, but must go to the country to which he belongs and sue him there. It is obvious that in many cases such a measure will entail great hardship for the wife as when the husband has his domicile in a far distant country.

The English Courts and English and other writers realised the hardship sometimes caused to the wife on account of this rule, and attempts have been made to find a way out for the wife under certain circumstances. The English law is so strict in this matter that it holds that the wife retains the husband's domicile even when the marriage is terminated. There is great force in the suggestion made by Graveson that on the cessation of the marital relationship, the wife's original domicile should be allowed to revive.

It was stated in a case that the domicile of the wife is founded not only upon the duty of the wife to live with her husband but also upon the presumption that he will be faithful to his marriage-vow. If he disregards that obligation, if he commits an offence which entitles her to a judicial separation or a divorce, her legal duty to live with him must undergo considerable modification, and in some cases entirely ceases.[35] This decision, however, was not followed or approved of in some later cases. In Lord Advocate Vs. Jaffery the Court held that the husband and wife could not have different domicile during the continuance of their marriage. It was pointed out that if it were otherwise, proceedings for dissolving the status of marriage might be carried through in two jurisdictions, ...the very evil the exclusion of which has been said by eminent writers on international law to require the acceptance of the principle unrestrictedly.[36]

35. Le Sueur Vs. Le Sueur (1876) 1 P.D. 139.

36. Lord Advocate Vs. Jaffrey, (1921) 1 A. C. 146 (H.L.).

It is a fact that in many cases the wives were put to great hardship, particularly on account of the wars, and so laws have been enacted in England and elsewhere to help them. It happened during the wars that foreign troops were posted in many friendly countries. The soldiers and officers were living under great strain and so were the inhabitants of the countries. Many soldiers and officers, in order to get some relaxation and to escape the strain, entered into matrimonial alliances with the local women without realising the seriousness of the step they were taking. Some time after, the husbands left the country and their wives without making any arrangement for them, who sometimes were expectant mothers, and experienced great hardship on their desertion by their husbands. Under the law they could not contract another marriage as they were already married. On their marriages they also acquired the domicile of their husbands and so could not file a suit in respect of the marriages in their own country while the country to which their husbands belonged was sometimes so far away that they could not afford to go there to take legal proceedings against their husbands. Special war time laws were enacted in many countries to afford relief to the wives and they were allowed, under certain conditions, to sue their husbands for divorce, separation or annulment of their marriages in the Courts of their own country. Thus the Matrimonial Causes (War Marriages) Act, 1944, modified by the Matrimonial Causes Act, 1956, provided that the English Courts would have jurisdiction to grant a decree of nullity or dissolution of marriage in respect of certain "War Marriages" if the following conditions were met—

(*i*) That the marriage was celebrated on or after September 3rd, 1939 and before June 1st, 1950 ;

(*ii*) That at the time of the marriage, the husband was domiciled outside the United Kingdom.

(*iii*) That the wife was, immediately before the marriage, domiciled in England.

(*iv*) That the parties have not since the marriage resided

together in the country in which the husband was domiciled at the time of the residence ;

(*v*) That three years have passed at the date of the presentation of the petition since the date of the marriage.

(*vi*) That the proceedings commenced not later than five years after June 1st, 1950.[37]

Change of domicile : Domicile is an idea of law. It is the relation which the law creates between an individual and a particular country. It continues until and unless it is changed by that person or by some one on whom that person depends. To every adult person the law ascribes a domicile, and that domicile remains his fixed attribute until a new and different attribute usurps its place.[38] It is open to a person to change his or her domicile. The conditions necessary for such a change are (1) residence in a new place and (2) intention to live there permanently. It will be necessary for this purpose that the person should not only take up residence in a different place, but there should be an intention to make the latter place his or her permanent abode. There must be residence in the new country as well as an intention to live there permanently.[39] If both these conditions are not satisfied, there will be no change of domicile. The intention must be to acquire a new or different domicile and to abandon the old domicile. It is necessary that the intention should be free or voluntary. Hence there will be no change of domicile if the change of residence is due to causes beyond one's control such as illness, employment in a foreign country, education abroad etc. but there is no intention to change the domicile. If the residence was without any intention to acquire domicile there, but subsequently the person decides to reside there permanently, there will be change of domicile. A person posted abroad will not change his or her

37. Section 1 (2), of the Matrimonial Causes (War Marriages) Act, 1944.

38. Bell Vs. Kennedy, (1868) L R. 1 Sc. Div. 307.

39. *Ibid.* (Bowie) Ramsay Vs. Liverpool Royal Infirmary, (1930) All. E.R. Rep. 127.

domicile and acquire a domicile in the country where he or she is posted but if the person decides not to return to his or her home, and to settle there permanently he or she will acquire a domicile there.

It seems reasonable to say that if the choice of a new abode and actual settlement there constitute a change of the original domicile, then the exact converse of such a procedure, viz. the intention to abandon the new domicile and an actual abandonment of it, ought to be equally effective to destroy the new domicile.[40]

Law in U.S.A. : Under the law of the U.S.A. if the intention with regard to change of domicile is not *bona fide* but is *mala fide*, then no change of domicile shall be established. Thus if a person goes from one place to another place simply to evade the law of his own domicile to secure a divorce in the new domicile and then returns to his own domicile, he shall not be deemed to have acquired a domicile at the other place. Hence a marriage solemnised there shall not be recognised by the Courts of his domicile.[41] Similarly, the divorce secured at the other place shall not be recognised by the Courts of his domicile on the basis that the Courts of the other place had no jurisdiction to grant the same.[42] But if the change of domicile is made in good faith, divorce granted by a Court of the new domicile shall be good even if the intention to change the domicile was to secure a divorce on a ground recognised there.[43] It may be noted that the law in the U.S.A. requires much less strict proof of an intention to change one's domicile than English and some other laws do.

Abandonment of acquired Domicile: It is open to a person to abandon his acquired domicile by an unequivocal intention and act. On his abandonment of the acquired

40. Udny Vs. Udny, (1869) L.R.I. Sc. and Div. 441.
41. Cunningham Vs. Cuuningham, 206 N. Y. 341.
42. Bell Vs. Bell, 181 U. S. 175 ; Hoffman Vs. Hoffman, 46 N. Y. 30 ; State Vs. Williams, 224, N. Y. S. 183 ; State Vs. Williams 224 N. Car. 183 325 U.S. 226.
43. Gildersleeve Vs. Gildersleeve, 88 Conn. 689,

domicile, he acquires a new domicile of choice in the place where he settles with an intention to make it his permanent abode. But if he abandons his acquired domicile without acquiring a new domicile he cannot be considered to be a person without a domicile for no one can be without a domicile. In such circumstances, his old domicile of origin revives and continues till he acquires another one. The domicile of origin adheres until a new domicile is acquired.[44] There must be sufficient evidence of a definite intention on the part of a person to abandon his domicile of origin and to acquire a new domicile.[45]

In determining whether there was any change of domicile every circumstance in a man's life, however trivial it may be in itself, should not be left out of consideration.[46] The Court may take into consideration the motive of the person. Thus if the residence is of a long duration, it may serve as evidence that the person did intend to reside there permanently. But obviously it will amount to a presumption and cannot serve to establish domicile. It may be noted that the English Courts apply the English law in determining if certain facts constitute domicile.[47]

American Law : The law in the U.S.A. is not so strict regarding change of domicile as the English law. An American writer has explained that Americans freely migrate from one State to another and so the American Courts are liberal in this matter and do not insist on the element of permanence that is required under the English decisions.[48] Thus it was stated in an American case "domicile exists if there is no present intention of removing from the place.... In this new and enterprising country, it is doubtful whether

44. Udny Vs. Udny, (1869) L.R. I Sc. and Div. 441 ; Bell Vs. Kennedy, (1868) L.R. I. Sc. and Div. 307.
45. (Bowie) Ramsay Vs. Liverpool Royal Infirmary, (1930) All. E.R. 127.
46. Drevon Vs. Drevon, (1864) 10 L.T. 370.
47. Re Marten Loustalan Vs. Loustalan, (1900) 82 L.T. 806, (1900). P. 211.
48. George Wilfred Stumbarg, *Principles of Conflict of Laws*, p. 20, Chicago (1937).

one half of the young men ......fix themselves in any town with an intention of always staying there.[49] In some other cases, the American Courts have found that (for domicile) an intention to remain for an indefinite time suffices.[50] Actual residence is, however, a necessary condition as in English law.

Change of domicile by wife: The English law allows a husband to change his domicile whenever he may so want. The wife cannot object to such change though she too acquires the new domicile. English law does not allow a wife to acquire her own domicile independent of the husband's domicile except under certain special circumstances. During the subsistence of a marriage the wife cannot have a domicile different from that of her husband. This rule may or may not be the last barbarous relic of a wife's servitude.[51] The English law is very strict in the matter. The rule is very hard and sometimes involves great hardship for a wife. It was further remarked in that case that "to alter it might have wide repercussions and I think this matter had better be left to Parliament." Attempts have been made to provide some relief for her.

Law in U.S.A.: Like the English law, the law in the U.S.A also follows the rule that a woman, on her marriage, acquires the domicile of her husband. But the law in the United States of America is more liberal in its application to women than the English law. This attitude is partly due to the changed outlook of the Courts in the U.S.A. with regard to divorce. American law allows divorce in many States on grounds not recognised by the English law. It is stated in the Re-Statement of Conflict of Laws that a wife, living apart from her husband without being guilty of desertion under the law of their domicile at the time of separation, may acquire a

49. Putnam Vs. Johnson, 10 Mass 488.
50. Andrade Vs. Andrade, 14 Ariz 379; Price Vs. Price, 156 Pa 617; Jennison Vs. Hopgood, 27 Mass 77.
51. Formosa Vs. Formosa, (1962) 3 All. E.R. 419.

separate domicile.[52]

What is stressed in such a case is that the wife should not be at fault in living separate from her husband. She can also acquire, in case of necessity, a domicile different from that of her husband's.[53]

The American wife can, however, acquire an independent domicile only with the consent of her husband or when it is necessary or proper for her. Hence she can acquire an independent domicile when her husband deserts her or is otherwise guilty of misconduct.[54] She can seek a divorce in the State of her domicile even when the husband is not living there, and is domiciled in a different State. If the wife is living separate from her husband due to her own fault then she cannot acquire an independent domicile.[55]

Conflict between Muslim and English Laws: It will be seen from the above that the English Courts and also the writers on Private International Law have enunciated the rules that:—

(*a*) On her marriage, the wife automatically acquires the domicile of her husband.

(*b*) The laws of domicile shall apply in respect of the essentials of a marriage.

It follows from the above rules that on her marriage to a foreigner, an English woman shall acquire his domicile and shall become subject to the law of his country with respect to her marriage as far as the essentials are concerned. Hence if the law allows polygamy or differs from the English law in certain other matters then the wife ought to be governed by that law. It should not, therefore, be open to her under strict application of the law to object to another marriage by her husband.

It also leads to the result that the wife can take legal proceedings only in the Court of the country where the

52. Restatement of Conflict of Laws Sec 28.

53. Garner Vs. Garner, 56 Md. 127; Burtis Vs. Burtis, 161 Mass 508.

54. Brown Vs. Brown, 164, Ill. App. 589; Perkins Vs. Perkins, 225 Mass 82: Sneed Vs. Sneed 14, Ariz 17.

55. Williamson Vs. Osenton, 232 U.S. 619.

husband is domiciled. This result would naturally cause her great hardship. She is, however, saved from this difficulty by the fact that the English Courts hold a polygamous marriage to be void and a nullity. They also hold that a void marriage shall be deemed as never having existed so that the wife does not acquire the husband's domicile but retains her own domicile. She can, therefore, institute a suit against the purported husband in the country of her own domicile, namely, England.

It was stated in Mir Anwaruddin's case, "An English woman or a woman domiciled in England who marries in England a person domiciled in Scotland, Ireland or India... acquires by the status of marriage the domicile of the husband, and is subject to the law of that domicile, but she does not acquire his religion or become subject to the laws of his religion except in so far as they are the laws of his domicile, and then to that extent only.[56] It is submitted that in Pâkistan and India the law of domicile is the same thing as the personal and religious law. The wife, therefore, shall become subject to the Muslim law on her marriage to a Muslim. Again in Har Shafi Vs Har Shafi, the wife was domiciled in England before her marriage in Israel, the domicile of the husband. Some time after, he divorced her in England. The Court held that the divorce was a valid divorce according to the law of the parties' domicile, namely. Israel[56a]. Here again, it was held that the wife on her marriage had acquired the domicile of her husband and became subject to the law of his domicile. But it may be noted here that the marriage was solemnised in Israel according to the Jewish religion so that it was not an English marriage. The Supreme Court of Pakistan held in a case that the law of Pakistan—the law of the domicile of the husband—shall apply to determine the character of marriage.[57]

56. R. Vs. Hammersmith, Superintendent Registrar of Marriages, Ex parte, Mir Anwar-ud-din, (1917) 1 K.B. 634.

56a. (1952) 2 All. E R. 821.

57. Mrs. Marina Jatoi Vs. Nuruddin K. Jatoi, P.L.D. (1967) S. C. 580.

It would be clear from the above discussion that under the provisions of Private International Law, the wife shall on her marriage with a Muslim, domiciled in a country other than England, acquire his domicile and shall become subject to its laws. The exceptions laid down to the above rule by English Courts will not appeal to a Court in a Muslim country which shall apply its own law in a particular case on the basis that the wife also has her domicile in that Muslim country and shall be governed by its law.

Conflict between American and Muslim Laws :

As observed before, Muslim law does not recognise domicile. But it may happen that a Muslim may marry an American woman whom he subsequently divorces according to his personal law, which will be the same thing as the law of his domicile. There is no American case-law on this point, but it appears from the decisions in respect of Jewish divorces that an American Court will not recognise Talaq (Muslim unilateral divorce). Thus, the Courts refused to recognise a unilateral divorce given by a Jew to his wife.[58] It seems very likely that the same view may be expressed in the case of a Talaq by a Muslim husband. The American Courts, however, recognise the validity of a divorce validly granted by a foreign Court. But they refuse to recognise a divorce if it is against the public policy of the American States or violates the American procedure. The divorce shall, however, be considered valid by a Muslim country or a country which allows the Muslims to be governed by their own law.

Concluding Remarks :

The rule that the wife automatically acquires, on her marriage, the domicile of her husband sometimes results in great hardship to her. It is respectfully submitted that Lord Denning has aptly called it "the last barbarous relic of a wife's

58. Miller, Vs., Miller, 128 N.Y.S. 787; Saperstone Vs. Saperstone, 131 N.Y.S. 241.

servitude."[59] The difficulty created by this notion of domicile is nicely illustrated by Lady Acland. During the World War an English girl fell in love with a Canadian and married him. Soon after he deserted her, when she was an expectant mother, and went back to his own country. A daughter was born to her and she experienced great pecuniary difficulty and being burdened with a baby and of delicate health she could not earn her living. Her parents who were not rich tried their best to support her. There was a man, however, who liked her and wanted to marry her. This could not be done as she was married and could not marry again without getting a divorce. It was, however, not possible for her to do so because on her marriage to a Canadian her domicile also became the same as that of her husband, namely, Canada and a divorce could only be granted by a Canadian Court. It was not possible for her to go to Canada on account of financial reasons.

Lady Acland graphically sums up the position by saying, "if that girl had done what some others did during the war-fever, dispensed with the marriage ceremony and given birth to an illegitimate child, would not she and the child be in a far better position than they are now? She could then have married and settled down in a permanent home."[60]

The Courts in some cases did try not to apply this rule, as discussed before, but their view was disapproved in subsequent cases. The rule that the wife acquires the domicile of the husband is chiefly based on two considerations, namely:

(*a*) The wife on her marriage shall live with her husband and so her domicile shall be the same as that of her husband's. Besides, it may also form her domicile of choice.

(*b*) The fact that the wife may retain her own domicile after her marriage will result in different Courts having

59. Formosa Vs. Formosa. (1962) 3 All. E.R. 419.

60. E.S.P. Haynes and Derek Walker Smith, *Divorce and its Problems*, pp. 105, 106, London, 1935.

simultaneous jurisdiction, which is likely to cause confusion, and so it is necessary that only one Court should have jurisdiction.

(*a*) If the wife never goes to her husband's domicile and continues to live in her own country then the basis of the rule no longer exists, and loses all its importance. Similarly, when a husband, a foreigner, deserts his wife and leaving her in her own country goes to his own domicile then too there is no question of their living together. It seems equitable in such cases to allow the wife to retain her own independent domicile.

(*b*) A conflict in jurisdiction cannot be avoided even now. Thus a Court of a country where polygamy is allowed may give effect to it (polygamy) even when the husband is but the wife is not domiciled there, on the basis of the above rule. An English Court will, however, not give effect to a polygamous marriage. The confusion that is likely to result may perhaps be avoided to some extent if we decide a case impartially according to justice, equity and good conscience. The view that a country should help its own citizens as expressed in several English cases, is a very unjust notion of justice. Justice has been considered blind and a case should be decided according to it regardless of the fact that the decision may adversely affect the citizens of the country concerned. A case involving conflict of laws came up for decision before A. R. Changez J. of the Lahore High Court[61]. In that case Islam, the religion of the country, allowed divorce while it was not permissible under the provisions of the Divorce Act, 1869. There was a conflict between these two laws; the Court did not decide the case according to its own Islamic law, the law of the husband's domicile (which legally was also the domicile of the wife) but preferred to decide it according to the dictates of

Farooq Lievers Vs. Adelaide Bridget Mary, P.L.D. 1958 Lah 431
It is fully discussed at the end of the succeeding section.

justice, equity and good conscience. Such an attitude and an honest attempt to do full justice in a case may to some extent obviate the difficulty when there is a conflict between the laws of different domiciles of the spouses. But there can be a risk that this idea may make the law uncertain because it will not be possible for the parties to definitely know beforehand what view may be taken by a Court in any particular case. Moreover, the idea of justice, equity and good conscience sometimes differs in certain respects in different communities and different countries. Thus, as discussed in the discussion on "insanity" in the chapter on "Defects in the Spouses", it has been stated that an American judge considered it unjust and even barbarous to dissolve a marriage on the suit of the wife when her husband had become insane. A Muslim judge, however, sees nothing wrong in it but will think it just and equitable to dissolve the marriage in such a case.

It, however, cannot be denied that there is a genuine need for the modification of the present-day law regarding the wife's acquisition of her husband's domicile on her marriage to a foreigner, or when he changes his domicile against her wishes. How will an English woman feel when her husband takes his domicile in an unfriendly country when she is not willing to reside in that country? In any case the husband's domicile should not be imposed on a wife when she has never left her own country at any time. It was observed by an English Court in a case: "The English Courts look to the law of domicile to determine status. The Courts have a discrimination and may in a proper case refuse to recognise a status conferred by or imposed upon a person by the law of his domicile and will reach the decision with due regard to common-sense and some attention to reasonable policy."[62] It is submitted that full scope should be given to this view.

62. Indyka Vs. Indyka, (1967) 2 All. E.R. 689.

Sec. VI.—Conflict between Muslim and Christian Laws

Preliminary: By the expression 'Conflict of Laws' is here meant the difference or inconsistency between laws of different countries or systems of law. It can be seen from the discussion in the previous chapter that there is a great difference between the conception of marriage under the Muslim and Christian laws. Thus, under Muslim law, marriage is a civil contract and so dissoluble while it is a sacrament under the Christian and the English law and so indissoluble. This conflict in the conception of marriage under Muslim and Christian laws leads to important results. As regards matrimonial matters, these differences affect, amongst other things, the following aspects, *viz.*

(*a*) Capacity of the spouses or one of them to contract the marriage.

(*b*) The rights and obligations of the spouses arising out of the marriage.

(*c*) Jurisdiction of the Courts in respect of various matrimonal matters such as the determination of the character, validity or invalidity of marriage.

(*d*) Dissolution of marriage by both or one of the spouses, etc.

When the parties to a marriage belong to the same country or are governed by the same system of law, not much difficulty is experienced in deciding such matters. The difficulty arises when the parties belong to countries having different laws or when they are governed by different systems of law. It is possible and often happens that the laws differ in many material aspects in different countries. The personal law of one party or the system of law in one country may attach a fundamental condition to the validity of marriage which may not exist in the personal law of the other party or the system of law in the other country. What is to be seen in such a case is whether the parties have married or can be considered to have married on the basis of that particular condition. Thus when an English woman marries at a Registry Office in England a foreigner whose law allows polygamy, the validity of the marriage shall depend in England, under the English law, on the provisions of that law and not on the personal law of the husband. In such a case it shall be presumed in England to be a condition of the marriage that it shall be monogamous. Hence if the man takes a second wife, the condition of the marriage being monogamous is broken and the second marriage shall be considered under the English law, to amount to bigamy and so shall be considered invalid. The first marriage with the English woman shall be liable to be dissolved under the English law at the instance of the English woman on the ground that the husband was guilty of bigamy and adultery. It is explained that a man who contracts in a country engages for a complete knowledge of the law of contracts of that country. The husband, it is considered, must know or ought to have known that he could not lawfully contract the second marriage. He, therefore, is guilty of a breach of the implied contract of his marriage in England with the English woman.[1]

But if the English woman, domiciled in England, marries a man of polygamous race in his own country according to its law, intending to live with him there, well knowing that she is entering into a potentially polygamous marriage, the substantial validity of the marriage depends on the personal law of the husband and not on the personal law of the wife. If he contracts there a second marriage, the English wife cannot complain.[2] Both the marriages shall be considered valid there. But in England the marriage of the English woman shall not

1. Chetti Vs. Chetti, (1909) P. 67; R Vs. Naguib, (1917) 1K. B. 359; R Vs. Hammersmith, Superintendent Registrar of Marriages, Ex parte, Mir Anwaruddin, (1917) 1 K.B. 634.

2. Kenward Vs. Kenward, (1951) 2 All. E.R. 297.

be considered to be valid on the ground that the English woman does not possess the capacity to contract a polygamous or even a potentially polygamous marriage unless she takes her domicile in the husband's country before her marriage. The above discussion will show the conflict of laws that can arise when parties are governed by different systems of law. In order to meet the practical difficulties that may be experienced in any such case the English Courts and jurists have laid down certain rules of law.[3] Thus they hold that such matters as the rites and ceremonies of the solemnisation of marriage shall be decided by the law of the place where a marriage has been solemnised, that is, by *lex loci celebrationis*, whereas some other matters which do not relate to the celebration of a marriage but arise out of it, such as its dissolution, have to be decided by the law of the place where the spouses, or rather the husband is domiciled, that is, by *lex loci domicilii* or perhaps by the matrimonial domicile. Some other general rules have been laid down by English writers and the Courts for guidance and application in such matters as discussed later. It would be convenient first to understand the nature of a Christian marriage before entering into a discussion of these matters.

Nature of Christian Marriage :

A Christian marriage now simply means the type of the institution generally accepted as marriage in Western countries, the U.S.A. and some other countries. As stated before, the religious notion of marriage has lost its importance in those countries in the course of time and its place has been taken by the legal concept. An English marriage, as now understood, is something more than a contract, whether civil or religious, for besides creating mutual rights and obligations, as all contracts do, it creates a status also.[4] It is no longer considered a religious doctrine, but has become the ordinary law of England and some other countries. It is defined as "the

3. Kenward Vs. Kenward, (1951) 2 All. E.R 297.
4. Hyde Vs. Hyde (1866) L.R. I.P. and D 130 (Divorce Court).

voluntary union for life of one man and one woman to the exclusion of all others.[5] Marriage was considered indissoluble at one time and continued to be so considered in England, a Protestant country, up to the Middle Ages. It was, however, found necessary to make necessary provisions for its dissolution under certain circumstances in order to save the husband or the wife from great hardship, but even now the parties cannot dissolve a marriage by mutual consent. The English Courts are generally so strict about this matter that they will reject a petition for separation if they find that it is the result of collusion between the parties. But the English law has been changed recently and a Bill passed by the Parliament allows divorce by mutual consent and even unilateral divorce under certain circumstances.

The English matrimonial law does not allow its non-Christian citizens to be governed by their religious laws in respect of marriage and divorce, but insists that they should be governed by the law of the land. Hence it did not and does not recognise polygamy or unilateral divorce, or even divorce by mutual consent.

A difficulty arises when a Muslim, domiciled in a Muslim or other polygamous country, marries a non-Muslim woman domiciled in a Christian country like England, when he has already got a wife or subsequently marries another woman or divorces his wife, who belongs to a Christian country. The laws respecting these matters and the dissolution of such marriages differ in different countries and the validity of a marriage and its dissolution shall depend on the fact whether the country where the marriage has been or is being contracted or dissolved is a Christian country, Muslim country or a country which is not a Muslim country but gives effect to the personal laws of the parties as distinct from the law of domicile. When the husband and wife belong to different countries then it happens sometimes that the matrimonial laws applicable in those countries in respect of any one particular matter may

5. Hyde Vs. Hyde, (1866) L.R. I.P. and D 130 (Divorce Court).

differ from one another and so there is a conflict in these two systems with regard to that particular matter.

It may be stated at the outset that as a Muslim woman is not allowed by her religion to marry or to be the wife of a non-Muslim, therefore the cases involving conflict of laws cannot arise where the husband of a Muslim woman is or becomes a Christian. They can arise only when a married non-Muslim woman embraces Islam while the husband remains a non-Muslim or only the husband of a non-Muslim woman embraces Islam, and also when a Muslim marries a woman domiciled in a Christian country. It may also occur when a non-Muslim embraces Islam but retains his own domicile and then marries a Muslim woman. Great difficulty is experienced in Europe and the U.S.A. in matrimonial cases where the spouses belong to different countries. These countries are no longer governed by their religious law, which could have been common to all of them, but are subject to civil laws which differ in different countries.

As the laws of Christian countries differ in certain respects from those of Muslim and certain other countries, so that the same act may produce different results in different parts of the world, it is necessary to discuss the laws separately. As most of our cases involving conflict in the laws of marriage and divorce arise in England or the U.S.A. the subject is discussed below having particular regard to the laws of those countries. But, generally, the same laws may apply in most other Christian countries also.

When both the husband and wife are domiciled in a Christian country such as England, and should one of them be or become a Muslim or should a Muslim domiciled in a Muslim country contract a marriage with a woman belonging to a foreign non-Muslim country then according to Muslim law he or she shall become subject to Muslim law and only that law. But the English law does not recognise personal laws of Muslims and in England the English law shall be considered to be binding on them irrespective of their religion.

They shall, therefore, be governed in England by the English law in respect of marriage and divorce. The Muslim law cannot be enforced there as the couple shall be beyond the jurisdiction of a Muslim country. If they or one of them should happen to come to a Muslim country then the spouses shall become subject to the Muslim law as they or the spouse will be within the jurisdiction of the Courts of the Muslim country. Their marriage shall be liable to be dissolved on any one or more grounds on which a Muslim marriage can be dissolved. The spouse, that is the one domiciled in the Muslim country or in another country which permits polygamy can contract a valid second marriage in that country. But the second marriage shall not be recognised by the English Courts as valid. Thus there is a conflict between the two laws.

Though the scope of this book is limited to dissolution of marriage under Muslim law, it would be incomplete if the various aspects of dissolution of marriage were not discussed in it. This of necessity involves the consideration of conflict of laws. The adoption of Islam by a married Englishman or Englishwoman will entitle him or her to the dissolution of their marriage under the provisions of Muslim law but they shall not be so entitled under the English law. Similarly, a Muslim husband's power of Talaq (divorce) was not, as a rule, recognised by the English Courts in the case of a marriage solemnised in England between a Muslim and an Englishwoman. Indeed, the English Courts refuse to admit the validity of a marriage between a Muslim and an Englishwoman not only when it is actually polygamous, but also when the law of the husband allows plurality of wives. This makes it necessary to consider the question of the nature and effect of mixed marriages.

In the present-day conditions, it is essential for those interested and even well-versed in Muslim law to know the basic problems of the conflict between Muslim law and English law regarding marriage and its dissolution by divorce, annulment, etc. The conflict between Muslim law and

English law can generally arise and may be considered in respect of certain important aspects as given below :

(1) The law that has to be applied.
(2) Domicile
(3) Validity of marriage.
(4) Jurisdiction.
(5) Husband's right of Talaq or divorce.
(6) Effect of conversion of the spouses or the husband or the wife.

The various aspects that arise in respect of marriage are discussed in this and some succeeding chapters.

(1) *Law applicable* : When a marriage is solemnised in a country other than the country of common domicile of both the parties and a difference arises between them the question naturally arises as to which law shall apply in that case.

As stated before, Muslim law lays down that a Muslim, whether a man or a woman, shall be governed only by that law wherever and in whatever country he or she may be. Hence no difficulty can be experienced by Muslim spouses even if they belong to different Muslim countries. In European countries and in the United States of America the parties are not governed by their religious laws but by the civil laws of those countries. But a woman belonging to a Christian country such as England shall not be considered by the foreign Courts to become subject to Muslim law on her marriage to a Muslim. If the wife either before or after her marriage with a Muslim, adopts Islam in a country where the personal laws relating to marriage and divorce are applicable to its citizens, then her case would be dealt with on a different footing. In such a case she would become subject to the law of her new religion and the husband can validly dissolve the marriage by Talaq.[6] But such would not be the case in

6. Jessie Grant Khambatta Vs. Mancherji Cursetji Khambatta, A.I.R. 1935, Bombay 5.

England. Moreover, where a domiciled English woman embraced Islam before her marriage with a Muslim in England, it was held that her conversion would not by itself enable her to contract there a potentially polygamous marriage even when her husband was not domiciled in that country. The rule was justified on the ground that "at the time of the purported marriage, she would be domiciled in England where that type of marriage would not be available to her."[7]

(2) *General rules respecting marriages* : As stated before, Muslim law does not attach any importance to domicile with regard to the validity or invalidity of marriage. English writers and Courts have enunciated the following rules in respect of the law applicable to marriages :

(*a*) The validity of a marriage with regard to the observance of necessary formalities is determined by the law of the place where it is solemnised.[8]

(*b*) The essentials of a marriage-contract and the rights and obligations arising under the marriage-contract are governed by the *lex loci domicilii*, that is, by the law of the country in which, for the time being, they are domiciled.[9] According to another opinion, it is governed by the law of the matrimonial domicile.[10]

The above rules have been elaborated by English and American writers on Private International Law and the Courts, and the various rules enunciated by them may be summarised as under:

(*a*) *Formalities regarding solemnisation of marriage* : The law of the country where a marriage has been solemnised must alone decide all questions relating to validity of the

7. R. Vs. S A. Rahman, (1949) 2 All. E.R. 165.
8. Simonin Vs. Mallac, (1860) 2 L.T. 327 ; Brook Vs. Brook (1861) 4 L.T. 93 ; Re Paine, (1940) 161 L.T. 266.
9. Brook Vs. Brook, (1861) 4 L. T. 93 ; Re Paine, (1940) 161 L. T. 266 ; De Reneville Vs. De Reneville, (1948), 1 All E.R. 56.
10. Ogden Vs. Ogden, (1908) P. 46. C.A. ; De Reneville Vs. De Reneville (948) 1 All E.R. 56 ; G.E. Cheshire, Private International Law, p. 307, Oxford, 1957.

ceremony by which the marriage is alleged to have been constituted.[11] If a marriage is good by the law of the country where it is effected, it is good all the world over, no matter whether the proceedings or ceremony which constituted marriage according to the law of the place would or would not constitute marriage in the country of the domicile of one or other of the spouses. If the so-called marriage violates the rites or ceremonies, or other provisions essential according to the *lex loci celebrationis* and is no marriage in the place where it is celebrated, there is no marriage anywhere, although the ceremony or proceeding if conducted in the place of the parties' domicile would be considered a good marriage.[12] Hence all the requirements of the local law must be substantially complied with in respect of the forms of the marriage. If the spouses belong to different countries, then it would be the *lex loci celebrationis* that would apply and neither of the parties would be heard to say that he or she intended a marriage of a different character from that which the law of that country permits.[13] When a man and a woman are married in the country of their domicile then a foreign Court has only to judge the validity of the marriage by the laws of their country and not to import additional conditions from its own jurisprudence. If the marriage is valid there, it shall be held valid in the foreign country even if it lacks in some of the essentials of a marriage according to the law of the foreign country.[14] It is essential in such a case that the law of one country should prevail and that it is reasonable that the law of the country where the ceremony of marriage took place and where the parties intended to live together and where in fact they lived together, should be regarded as the

11. Brook Vs. Brook, (1861) 4 L.T. 93; Sottomayor Vs. De Barros, (1877) (No. 1) 3 P.D.I. ; Berthiaume Vs. Dastous, (1930) 142 L.T. 54
12. Berthiaume Vs. Dastous, (1930) 142 L.T. 54.
13. Jessie Grant Khambatta Vs. Mancherji Cursetji Khambatta, A.I.R. 1935 Bombay 5.
14. De Reneville Vs. De Reneville, (1948) 1 All E.R. 56.

law which controls the validity of the marriage.[15] A failure to comply with the essential formality prescribed by *lex loci celebrationis* shall result in rendering the marriage to be a nullity.[16]

(*b*) *Essentials of contract of marriage:* While the forms of entering into the contract of marriage are to be regulated by the *lex loci contractus*, the essentials of the contract depend upon the *lex loci domicilii*, the law of the country in which the parties are domiciled at the time of the marriage and in which the matrimonial residence is contemplated.[17]

If the marriage is good in respect of its essentials in the country of domicile of the spouses, it is good everywhere.[18] Thus a marriage between a widow and her deceased husband's brother, both of Italian domicile, being valid according to the law in Italy was held valid in England as it related to the essentials of marriage although the English law did not allow such a marriage.[19] If, however, the contract of marriage is such in essentials as to be contrary to the law of the country of domicile and it is declared void by that law, it is to be regarded as void in the country of domicile though not contrary to the law of the country in which it was celebrated and may be permissible there.[20] It was stated in a case that the law of the country where a marriage has been solemnised cannot give validity to a marriage prohibited by the law of the country of domicile and allegiance of the contracting

15. De Reneville Vs. De Reneville, (1948) 1 All. E R. 56.
16. Ogden Vs. Ogden, (1908) P. 46 ; Von Lorang (Salvesen) Vs. Administrator of Austrian Property, (1927) All E.R. 78.
17. Scrimshire Vs. Scrimshire, (1752) 2 Hag. Con 395; Ogden Vs. Ogden (1908) P. 46, Berthiaume Vs. Dastous, (1930) 142 L.T. 54.
18. Brook Vs. Brook, (1861). 4 L.T. 93 ; Ogden Vs. Ogden, (1908) P. 46 ; De Reneville Vs. De Reneville, (1948) 1 All E.R. 56.
19. Brook Vs. Brook, (1861). 4 L.T. 93 ; Ogden Vs. Ogden, (1908), P. 46 ; Bozzelli's Settlement Re Husey-Hunt, Vs. Bozzelli, (1902) 86 L.T. 445 ; Berthiaume Vs. Dastous, (1930) 142, L.T. 54.
20. Brook Vs. Brook, (1861) 4 L.T. 93 ; Berthiaume Vs. Dastous, (1930) 142 L.T. 54.

parties.[21] Hence a marriage contracted by the spouses in a country, which is not the country of their domicile, is not to be held valid if by contracting it the laws of their own country are violated.[22] Thus where a naturalised Englishman of German origin married in Germany his deceased wife's sister, which marriage was prohibited by the English law but is permissible in Germany, it was held that the marriage was not valid.[23] Similarly, where an English couple contracted such a marriage in Denmark as is prohibited by the English law but allowed by the law of Denmark, the marriage was held to be invalid on the ground that the English law, that is, the law of the domicile, prohibits it.[24] In the same way where a marriage solemnised in England between a man and a woman both residing in England but domiciled in Portugal was good under the English law but void by the Portuguese law, it was held to be a nullity by an English Court on the basis that it was void under the law of the domicile of the parties.[25] It has, however, been made clear in a case that it would be wrong to say that for all purposes the law of domicile is necessarily conclusive as to the capacity arising from status. There are some things which an English Court will not allow a person in this country (England) to do whatever status with its consequential capacity or incapacity the law of his domicile may give him.[26] The English Courts do not recognise a marriage when the *lex loci celebrationis* violates the precepts of religion or of public morals, as in the case of bigamy, or where the marriages are such as are generally considered as incestuous.[27] By religion is here, of course, meant the Christian religion and public morals refer to the English notion of morality.

But, as in other contracts so in that of marriage personal

21. Bozzelli's Settlement Re Husey Hunt Vs. Bozzelli, (1902) 86 L.T. 445.
22. Brook Vs. Brook, (1861) 4 L.T. 93.
23. Mette Vs. Mette, (1859) 1 SW and Tr. 416.
24. Brook Vs. Brook, (1861) 4 L.T. 193.
25. Sottomayor Vs. De Barros, (1877) 3 P.D.I. (C.A.)
26. Baindail Vs. Baindail, (1946), 1 All. E.R. 342.
27. Ogden Vs. Ogden, (1908) P. 46. (C.A.)

capacity must depend on the law of the domicile.[28] Hence the fact whether a marriage is void as being incestuous ought to be decided by the law of domicile because the matter has nothing to do with the ceremony of solemnisation of the marriage but deals with the essentials of a marriage. It is curious and rather unfortunate that having laid down the above rules the English Courts do not always apply them where the husband belongs to a polygamous country and the law of his domicile conflicts with the English law. The English Courts in such cases have recourse to exceptions to the general rules. They will not recognise the validity of a marriage if it is incestuous accordiug to the English notion though it is valid according to the foreign countries.

The English Courts exercising jurisdiction in matrimonial affairs do not give effect to or dissolve marriages which are not monogamous marriages.[29] This has been fully discussed in the chapter on jurisdiction.

It has been held in some English cases that whether a marriage is monogamous or polygamous shall depend, as a general rule, on the form of the celebration prescribed by the *lex loci contractus* irrespective of the law of *loci domicilii.* It is not affected by the personal law of the spouses or one of them.[30] The following rules can be deduced from some English cases:

(*a*) A marriage entered into in a form considered in England to be polygamous and without any civil ceremony as prescribed by the English law shall be considered there to be invalid whatever the domicile of the spouses.

(*b*) A man or a woman domiciled in a country where monogamy is the rule and polygamy is not permitted

28. Odgen Vs. Odgen, (1908) P. 46 (C.A.)

29. Hyde Vs. Hyde, (1866) L.R.I. P. and D. 130; Srini Vasan Vs. Srini Vasan, (1945) 2 All. E.R. 21; Baindail Vs. Baindail, (1946) 1 All. E.R. 342; Risk Vs. Risk, (1950) 2 All. E.R. 973.

30. Bethell, Re Bethell Vs. Hilyard, (1888) 38 Ch. 220; Lendrum Vs. Chakravarty, (1929) S.L.T. 96; Kenward Vs. Kenward, (1950) 2 All E.R. 297.

> cannot legally enter into a polygamous marriage or in other words, they do not possess the capacity to contract such a marriage. The rule will not be rendered ineffective even by the adoption of a religion which allows polygamy.[31]

It is considered that every nation has a right to impose on its own subjects restrictions and prohibitions as to entering into marriage-contracts either within or without its own territories.[32] The English law does not consider as valid the marriage by any of its nationals if it contravenes any rule of the English law.[33]

As stated before, the essentials of the contract of marriage depend under the Private International Law upon the *lex loci domicilii*, that is, the laws of the country in which the parties are or were domiciled at the time of their marriage and in which the matrimonial residence is contemplated.[34]

The rights and obligations of the parties relating to the dissolution of marriage do not form part of the marriage contract, but arise out of and are incidental to such contract and ought to be governed by *lex loci domicilii*.[35]

The Courts in India before its independence were bound to follow the above-mentioned rules. With the achievement of independence the Courts in India and Pakistan no longer feel bound by the said rules and they will follow the personal laws of their own citizens. The Muslim law does not make

31. R Vs. S. A. Rahman, (1949) 2 All E.R. 165.
32. Ogden Vs. Ogden, (1908) P. 46.
33. Hyde Vs. Hyde, (1866) L.R. 1 P. and D. 130 ; Bethell, Re Bethell Vs. Hildyard, (1887) 58 L.T. 674 ; R. Vs. S. A. Rahman, (1949) 2 All. E.R. 165.
34. Brook Vs. Brook (1861), 4 L.T. 93 ; Ogden Vs. Ogden, (1908) P. 46 ; Paine, Re, (1940) 161 L.T. 266 ; Pugh Vs. Pugh, (1951) 2 All E.R. 680.
35. Niboyet Vs. Niboyet, (1878) 4 P.D.I. (C.A.) ; Le Mesurier Vs. Le Mesurier, (1895) 72 L.T. 873 (P.C.) ; Von Lorang (Salvesen) Vs. Administrator of Austrian Property, (1927) All E.R. 78.

any difference between *lex loci celebrationis* and *lex loci domicilii.* It will determine the validity of a marriage, where-ever contracted, by applying its own law. It will not, therefore, consider a marriage to be invalid simply because it is polygamous even when the wife is a non-Muslim or a foreigner and the law of her domicile does not allow polygamy. Here there is a conflict between the Muslim and the English laws in these matters. It is not certain if the Courts in Pakistan would have explicitly followed the rules of Private International Law, and to what extent, if the English Courts would not have recourse to exceptions to the rules laid down by them under the Private International Law and when they make no secret that they were doing so in order to help their own citizens. The rules and principles of Private International Law have in this way lost much of the respect due to them on account of this attitude of the English Courts and writers. A Court in Pakistan may naturally feel inclined to follow the example of the English Courts and not to follow the said rules of Private International Law when they conflict with its own laws. This is a very unfortunate position and it seems desirable that the English Courts and writers should revise their views, ignore exceptions and give effect to the broad principles of Private International Law. Such a course would infuse confidence in other people and they may pay more attention to the dictates of justice, equity and good conscience than to the personal interest of their own citizens. A very good example of this has been provided in a case decided by the Lahore High Court. In this case an Englishman and his wife, married in India in accordance with the Christian rites, took up their domicile in Pakistan. After some time, relations between them seem to have become strained because the wife got an order for judicial separation and payment of alimony against her husband. The husband subsequently embraced Islam, and asked his wife to join him in his new faith, but she refused to do so. Realising that there was no chance of reconciliation, the husband dissolved the marriage by *talaq*. He then filed a suit for a declaration that the defendant had been divorced, was no longer his wife and that the order regarding payment of alimony had become ineffective. The wife contended that her marriage could not be dissolved by *talaq* in view of the provisions of section 7 of the Divorce Act of 1869 which enjoin the Courts to act and give relief on principles and rules which are as nearly as may be conformable to the principles and rules on which the Courts for Divorce and Matrimonial Causes in England for the time being act and give relief.[37] A. R. Changez, J. held that the husband on conversion to Islam could lawfully divorce his wife who had been married to him before his conversion, but that the *talaq* was not permissible in view of the provisions of the Divorce Act of 1869. It may be noted that the Act applies when both or one of the parties is a Christian and is enforcible in Pakistan. Having taken into consideration these inconsistent legal aspects and the particular circumstances of the case, he held that it would be against the dictates of justice, equity and good conscience to grant a decree in the terms of the relief sought.[36]

36. Farooq Lievers Vs, Adelaide Bridget Mary. P.L.D. 1958 Lahore 431.

Section VII—Validity of Muslim Marriage

Preliminary : Before entering into a discussion of validity or invalidity of the marriage of a Muslim with an English woman it is necessary to understand the nature of an English marriage. An English marriage is in effect the same thing as a Christian marriage, which has been defined as "a voluntary union for life of one man and one woman to the exclusion of all others.[1] It has also been explicitly laid down that "a marriage which is not that of one man and one woman, to the exclusion of all others, though it may pass by the name of a marriage, is not the status which the English law contemplates when dealing with the subject of marriage."[2] It has already been explained that the words "Christian marriage" simply denote the concept of marriage prevalent in Christian countries. Emphasis is laid on the condition that the marriage should be a monogamous marriage. If a marriage satisfies this condition, it shall be held valid in England though the parties to it happen to be non-Christians. A Japanese marriage has been held to be valid by the English Courts because Japanese marriages are monogamous even though they are not solemnised according to the Christian rites or form.[3] Similarly, the marriage of a Sikh with a Sikh woman has been held to be valid because under the Hindu Marriages Act, 1955. a Hindu marriage has assumed 'the nature of a monogamous marriage'.[4] The marriage at the time of its solemnisation was potentially polygamous, but the Hindu law was subsequently modified so that polygamy was stopped from 1955. As discussed earlier, Christianity has not defined marriage or prescribed its essentials. The present English law of marriage is the law originally laid down by the Church but modified

1. Hyde Vs. Hyde, (1866) L. R. I. P. and D. 130.
2. Brinkley Vs, A. G., (1890) 15 P. D. 76.
3. *Ibid.*
4. Parkasho Vs. Singh, (1967) 1 All. E. R 737.

from time to time by the Legislature or through the interpretations of the Courts to meet the requirements of the times. Thus at one time marriage was considered absolutely indissoluble, but subsequently it was found necessary to allow its dissolution in certain cases to save the spouses or at least one of them from great hardship. Divorce and annulment of marriage were therefore allowed though on the basis of only a very few grounds. More grounds for dissolution were added from time to time which have completely changed the old law. The changes introduced have been so great that, were a Christian, living a few centuries back, to see the present marriage laws he would be astounded at what would appear to him the laxity with which a Christian marriage can now be dissolved in England and other Christian countries. Thus incompatibility of temperament is a ground for divorce in New Mexico and Alaska.[5] The French law allows the dissolution of marriage on the basis of "a grievous wrong" which expression is interpreted so liberally as to include the writing of an insulting letter by the husband to the wife, the disagreeable spying upon the wife's movements by a jealous husband, or an accusation of conjugal infidelity.[6] All this goes to show to what extent the rigid Christian law of ancient times has been modified in different Christian countries in order to meet the needs of the times and to avoid unnecessary hardship. Recently a Bill has been passed in England which allows mutual and even unilateral divorce through Court under certain circumstances.

Muslim marriage : A Muslim marriage means the voluntary union of a man and a woman for life. Just as a Christian marriage, though for life, can be terminated earlier by the Court, in the same way a Muslim marriage, too, can be dissolved earlier. The only difference is that it can be dissolved not only by the Qadi (the Court) but also by the parties concerned or even by one of them. Muslim marriage

5. New Mexico Statutes, 1941, Alaska Compiled Laws, 1933,
6. G. C. Cheshire : Nullity jurisdiction and Remarriage during voidable Marriage, *The Law Quarterly Review*, Oct., 1945, vol. 61, p. 341,

law differs from the Christian marriage law in certain respects, the important points of difference being the following :

(*a*) The Muslim law allows limited polygamy, that is, it allows the husband to have four wives at one and the same time, and

(*b*) A Muslim marriage can be dissolved by the husband by his unilateral act, and also by the wife by herself under certain conditions.

Recognition of Muslim marriage refused by English Courts : The English Courts refuse to accept a Muslim marriage as a valid marriage because they consider both the above conditions to be repugnant to their ideas of a valid marriage. In addition to this, an English Court will not accept the validity of a marriage when it is :

(1) polygamous
(2) incestuous
(3) against public policy
(4) positively prohibited by English law and
(5) against public morals

It may be stated at the outset that according to Muslim law a Muslim woman cannot marry a non-Muslim man. A Muslim woman can thus marry a European or American only if he embraces Islam. Such cases are rare and they are discussed at the end of this chapter. The overwhelming majority of all cases involving conflict of laws relate to marriages between Muslim men and European or American women, who may or may not have embraced Islam.

(1) *Polygamy* : The most important objection to the recognition of a Muslim marriage is on the first ground, namely, that it is polygamous. Islam permits limited polygamy to the extent that a husband can have four wives at one and the same time. The Christian countries permit only monogamy under which a husband can have only one wife at one time, and polygamy is thus considered to be an infringement of women's rights. It is difficult to comment as to which system is better. It may perhaps be said that no type of

marriage is ideal. The very institution of marriage has become a debatable matter in some European countries and there is even a section of opinion in the West and in the U.S.A. which now considers it a useless and even an undesirable institution.

Muslim history relates that a large number of Muslims had fallen in a fierce battle against a numerically superior enemy's army in the early days of Islam. There then arose the problem as how to provide for the large number of widows and orphans, The verse regarding polygamy was then revealed and it went a great way towards solving the difficulty. Islam, while allowing polygamy, insists that none of the wives should be treated with injustice and that the husband should mete out absolutely equal treatment to all his wives in all objective matters. Thus he has to provide equal maintenance, servants, presents and accommodation to all his wives; he is also under an obligation to pass equal time with each wife turn by turn. On a failure to do so, the Qadi can, on a complaint by the aggrieved wife, order him not to show partiality for any particular wife and on his failure to comply he can annul the marriage if he deems fit and proper.

A great deal of the points for and against polygamy rest on the importance attached to morality. The weakness of the institution of monogamy was exposed during and after the two World Wars. A very large number of men were killed in several European countries with the result that the number of women far exceeded the number of men in those countries. The result was that extra marital relations between men and women became common and the large number of illegitimate children became a problem to those countries.

It cannot be denied that the right of having tour wives was misused by men but for that it is the practice and not the law that is to blame. Necessary steps can be taken and are now being taken to prevent the practice of polygamy without any justification.

View of English Courts : The English Courts have taken a very harsh view of a polygamous marriage and have pronounced it a nullity. Lord Brougham has stated in a case :

> "It is important to observe that we regard it (marriage) as a wholly different thing, a different status from Turkish or other marriages among infidel nations, because we clearly never should recognise the plurality of wives and consequent validity of second marriages, standing the first, which second marriages the laws of those countries authorise and validate."[7]

In a later case Dr. Lush, L.J. described a polygamous marriage, "a union falsely called a marriage."[8] The English Courts in many cases held a polygamous marriage a nullity, no matter where it was solemnised. Thus it was held by Avory, J. in 1917 that a Muslim form of marriage contracted by an Egyptian in Egypt was a nullity.[9]

The same view has been expressed by the Courts of some other countries which follow the concept of a Christian marriage. Thus in one case a married Indian Muslim migrated to Nataal and became domiciled there. During a temporary visit to India he took another wife and had children by her born in India as well as in Nataal. He died and, according to his will, his assets were to be distributed equally among his wives and children by both the wives according to Muslim law. It was held by the Nataal Court that the husband, being domiciled in Nataal at the time of his second marriage, could not, in accordance with the law of that country, contract the second polygamous marriage. This view was based on the ground of public policy though the marriage was good according to the *lex loci contractus*. The children by the second wife were, therefore, held to be illegitimate.[10] In Bethell Re. the husband, a domiciled Englishman, married a woman of the Baralang tribe according to the tribal

7. Warrender Vs. Warrender, (1835) 2 Cl. and F. 488.
8. Harvey Vs. Farnie, (1880) 5 P. D. 153 : 6 P. D. 35.
9. R. Vs. Naguib, (1917) 1 K. B. 359.
10. P. W. E. Beckett, The Recognition of Polygamous Marriages under English Law, *The Law Quarterly*, vol, XLVIII. No. 191 (July, 1932) p. 341 at p. 344.

customs. The custom of that tribe permitted polygamy. A daughter, born of the marriage, was held to be illegitimate by an English Court after the death of her English father who had never contracted another marriage. The ground given was that the marriage was not a marriage in the Christian sense but only in the Baralang sense because, though not actually polygamous, it was potentially so.[11] Lush J. stated in another case, "if one of the numerous wives of any Mohammadan were to come to this country, and marry in this country, she would not be indicted for bigamy because our laws do not recognise a marriage—solemnized in that country, a marriage taking place in a country where polygamy is allowed—as a marriage to be recognized in our Christian country,"[12] An American Court took a more liberal and reasonable view. It observed : (*a*) "....if an American citizen, having already a wife by a marriage contracted in the United States, were to go to Turkey and contract a further (polygamous) marriage there, the second marriage would be void, and (*b*) if a Turk with two wives were to come to the United States, we would not refuse to administer to them the justice due to the relations contracted by them.[13] It was observed in another case, "if a Turkish or Hindu husband were travelling in this country with his wife or were temporarily resident here, we should, without hesitation, acknowledge the relation of husband and wife between them."[14] The remarks quoted above were no doubt *obiter dicta*, but they truly indicate the position. The wives of so many ambassadors from polygamous countries are treated in England as lawfully wedded wives and invited by the English Royalty in that position. Beckett in his interesting article referred to before says, "to hold that all polygamous marriages must be regarded on the same footing as illicit intercourse and that the issue must be regarded as illegitimate is obviously going much

11. Bethell, Re. (1880) 38 Ch. D. 220.
12. Harvey, Vs. Farnie, (1880) 6 P. D. 35.
13. Williams Vs. Oates, 27 North Carolina Rep. 375.
14. Polydore Vs. Prince, Beale's *Cases on Conflict of Laws*, vol. III, p. 2.

farther than to hold that the matrimonial remedies of the English Courts cannot be extended to them because such remedies are unsuitable.[15] The English Courts, as already stated, at one time absolutely refused to recognise polygamous marriages and treated them as a nullity. Thus, where a married foreigner, whose religion allowed polygamy, contracted a second marriage with an English girl in England and subsequently the English wife brought a suit for nullity of her marriage on the ground of bigamy, the Court would not do so because it refused to recognise the first potentially polygamous marriage and considered it a nullity, as if it never existed at all.[16] It was observed by Lord Penzance in Hyde Vs. Hyde (L. R. I. P. & D. 130): "But I expressed at the hearing a strong doubt whether the union of man and woman as practised and adopted among the Mormons was really a marriage in the sense understood in this, the Matrimonial Court of England, and whether persons so united could be considered husband and wife in the sense in which these words must be interpreted in the Divorce Act. Further reflection has confirmed the doubt, and has satisfied me that this Court cannot properly exercise any jurisdiction over such unions."[17] The reason for this conclusion given by Lord Penzance in his judgment in that case is, however, not that it is contrary to public policy to accord any sort of recognition to a polygamous marriage, but because "the matrimonial law of this country is adopted to the Christian marriage and it is wholly inapplicable to polygamy and it would be impossible to do justice to the parties if the law applicable to one institution (monogamous marriage) were applied to a different institution" (polygamous marriage). Although it cannot be denied that the Court was clearly averse to the idea of polygamous marriages Lord Penzance nevertheless made it clear that: "All that is intended to be here decided is that as between

15. W. E. Beckett, *The Law Quarterly Rev.*, p. 341, at p. 346,
16. R. Vs. Naguib, (1917) I. K. B. 359.
17. L. R. 1 P and M 130.

each other they are not entitled to the remedies, the adjudication or the relief of the matrimonial law of England." No objection, it is submitted, can be taken to this view which merely describes the incompetence of Courts of monogamous countries to try cases dealing with polygamous marriages. But later this ruling was sometimes misconstrued as having laid down that a polygamous marriage is a nullity. Thus it is observed by Beckett in the article referred to before: "Nevertheless, the view that no recognition, whatever, can be given under English law to polygamous marriages, and that the issue of such unions must be always regarded as illegitimate, has certainly been held. Indeed, to judge from the rather meagre statements in standard textbooks it might be supposed to be the generally prevalent view of the law. It seems to be sometimes supposed that this position results from Hyde Vs. Hyde, but, as has already been pointed out above, Hyde Vs. Hyde left the question of the legitimacy of children of polygamous unions completely open." It appears from the judgment in "Re Bethell, (L. T. 674) that Stirling, J. thought the issue of polygamous marriage must in all cases be regarded as illegitimate.[18] The Court based its decision on the authority of Hyde Vs. Hyde but, as shown just now, that decision had in fact left this question open. The drastic consequence of ignoring polygamous marriages has been pointed out by Dennis Fitzpatrick who comments that, "to boycott polygamy would be to ignore all family relations among the great majority of the human race, treating all wives among them as mere concubines, all children as bastards and all property left by an intestate among them as escheating on becoming ownerless.[19] Some English writers have also pointed out the discrimination made by the English Courts between Jewish marriages which are potentially polygamous and other polygamous marriages.[20] Since the English

18. Bethell, Re. (1880) 38 Ch. D. 220.

19. *Journal of the Society of Comparative Legislature*, vol. II, p. 359.

20. Cheshire, *Private International Law*, p 295, Oxford, Beckett, *Law Quarterly Review*, p. 341 at pp. 359, 360.

Courts consider a polygamous marriage a nullity they cannot therefore dissolve it as it was, according to them, non-existent.[21] This concept of the English Courts caused in some cases hardship to English women, who had married men of a polygamous race or religion. Thus if the man happened to be already married, that is, he had a former wife at the time of his marriage with the English woman, or contracted a second polygamous marriage with a woman of his own religion or race after his marriage with an English woman, she could not get relief from the English Courts. The man could not be considered to have committed bigamy as the polygamous marriage was not taken into consideration and was considered never to have existed. Later, the English Courts started realising this unfortunate position of these English women. Moreover, the Privy Council decided appeals from many countries—subject nations of England—whose inhabitants had been given a solemn guarantee that there would be no interference in their religious and personal laws. As the religions of the vast majority of these people allowed polygamy, the Privy Council applied the religious and personal laws of these countries in deciding such cases. It had, therefore, to recognise the validity of polygamous marriages and to give effect to them as well as to incidents flowing out of such marriages such as legitimacy, succession, inheritance etc. It seems that in view of these decisions, the English Courts began to take notice of polygamous marriages for certain incidental purposes like legitimacy, succession etc., though still refusing to recognise the marriage itself.

It was thus stated by an English Judge : "I think it is certainly a matter to bear in mind that the prospect of an English Court saying that it will not regard the status of marriage conferred by a Hindu ceremony (polygamous marriage) would be a curious one when very little more than a mile away the Privy Council might be sitting and coming to precisely opposite conclusion as to the validity of such a

21. R. Vs. Naguib, (1917) 1 K. B. 359.

marriage on an Indian appeal."[22] The Courts subsequently began to accept the married status of the husband while refusing to accept his previous polygamous marriage.

Capacity of Parties: According to the English law, there is another factor which contributes to the validity or invalidity of marriage. It is the capacity of the parties to lawfully contract the same. Most of the nations make it a rule for the validity of marriage that the parties should be sane and must have attained a certain prescribed age etc. The English law prescribes a further condition that each party must possess the capacity to contract the marriage. Accordingly, an English man or woman cannot contract a polygamous marriage because they do not possess the capacity to do so. But while the English Courts and writers accept this view, there is a difference of opinion among them on details.

The following question may be considered in this context:

(*a*) Whether the capacity should be possessed by (*i*) both the parties or (*ii*) only by one of them, and if so by whom and

(*b*) What law shall determine the capacity.

(*a*) There is considerable difference of opinion about the party that must possess the capacity to contract a marriage.

(I) According to one theory the capacity must be possessed only by the husband. This theory is justified on the ground that the husband is the head of the family and so we have to take into account only his capacity. (II) According to the second theory, only the wife needs to possess the capacity. An obvious objection to this theory is that on her marriage, the wife shall pass her whole life with her husband. Her capacity, therefore, is not of much consequence, and it is mainly that of the husband which counts.

The English writers and the Courts now generally maintain that each party must possess the capacity to marry

22. Baindail Vs. Baindail, (1946) 1 All. E. R. 342.

the other according to his or her own law.[23] In other words. they follow what is called the dual capacity. A curious result of the theory is that it shall never be open to a domiciled Englishwoman to lawfully marry a person belonging to a polygamous race or religion because such a marriage shall be void under the English law for want of capacity in the English woman. This difficulty may be removed to some extent by adopting the view expressed in Lendrum Vs. Chakravarti (referred to before), that a man of a polygamous race who marries an Englishwoman in England according to English law, by implication enters into a monogamous marriage for there is no judicial difficulty in the concept that a person by such a contract debars himself from some part of the liberties legally allowed to him by his own system of law."[24] The view, however, does not fully solve the problem because whatever the personal intention or conduct of the husband may be, the law of his domicile shall still remain the same. This implied condition of the contract may allow the Englishwoman to marry that person, but it does not and cannot change the capacity of the husband under the law of his religion and domicile to have a plurality of wives. Moreover, it has been held in certain cases that the potentially polygamous character of a marriage shall not be affected by the intention of the husband not to contract another marriage besides the subsisting marriage. The English law is so strict in this matter that it would attach no importance to the husband's oath that he would not contract another (polygamous) marriage[25] even if he swore on the Bible.[26]

(*b*) What law shall determine capacity : The question naturally arises as to what law has to determine the capacity

23. Bozelli Settlement, (1907) Ch, 751 ; Re Paine, (1940) Ch. 49 ; Cheni Vs. Cheni, (1962) 3 All. E. R. 873.
24. (1929) S. L. I. 96.
25. Hyde Vs. Hyde, (1887) 38 Ch, D. 220, (1866) L. R. 1 P and D. 130 ; Risk Vs. Risk, (1950) 2 All. E. R, 973.
26. Sowa Vs. Sowa, (1961) 1 All. E. R. 687 C. A.

of a person to contract a marriage. Different views have been expressed in the matter. According to one view the matter has to be decided by the law of the place where the marriage has been celebrated. But this view was later given up and it was accepted that it is the law of domicile that shall be applicable and it is now this law that determines capacity.

It is then to be examined what is meant by *lex loci domicilii.* It can mean *lex loci domicilii* of the husband, or the law of the matrimonial domicile, or the law of the domicile of each party. As regards the first view, it is explained that the husband is the head of the family and so it is natural and reasonable that it shall be the law of his domicile that shall determine the capacity or incapacity to contract the marriage. It is objected to this that if the woman is incapable of contracting the marriage and if she suffers from incapacity to contract the same then no marriage is constituted and so there is no husband. Writers like Cheshire favour the second view, that the matrimonial domicile should determine the capacity to marry. His opinion finds some support from certain decisions. But his view is also subject to the same objection as raised in the first case. The third view is generally accepted in England as correct and it is said that the law of the domicile of each party should be taken into consideration. But the result of the rule shall be always to bar the marriage of an Englishwoman with a man of polygamous race or community. The difficulty arises from the fact that English law holds a marriage to be void not only when it is polygamous but also when it is merely potentially polygamous.

Cheshire is opposed to this view and has objected to the doctrine of dual domicile and says: "It, the doctrine of dual domicile, is sociologically unsound, wrong in principle, and in practice ineffectual in the sense that in the majority of cases the object can be frustrated without difficulty. Moreover, in the confused state of the authorities, it is more than doubtful whether it represents the law of England."[27] He makes the reasonable

27. Cheshire, *Private International Law*, p. 307

suggestion that the correct doctrine would be to determine the capacity to marry by the matrimonial domicile where the parties intend to establish their permanent home. In general, their future lives will be governed by the laws of that country and their conduct and behaviour will be weighed by the standard of the local laws and practice. It is, therefore, just that their capacity to marry each other should be governed by the laws of that country and that country alone. This result would be in perfect consonance with the reasoning in Kenward Vs. Kenward.

Without attempting to enter into a general discussion of the matter, it is submitted that Cheshire's view that capacity should be determined by the law of the husband's domicile or if it differs from the matrimonial home then by the latter is very reasonable. His view has the advantage that it maintains the dignity of an Englishwoman who has married a Muslim or any other person of a polygamous religion or country. Her marriage shall be valid and she will be held to possess the capacity to contract the same under the law of her husband's domicile and most likely under the matrimonial domicile. If the rule that each party must possess the capacity to contract the marriage be applied the marriage of an Englishwoman with a man of a polygamous religion or country shall always be void even when it is not actually polygamous; such a situation is, to say the least, very undesirable. The English Courts and writers have not realised the serious effect of this rule. It reduces the position of an Englishwoman to that of a concubine and the children to illegitimate issue. They are no doubt given the status of legitimate issue for the purpose of certain incidental purposes in most cases such as inheritance, but they shall nevertheless be considered from a strictly legal point of view to be illegitimate. If the English law insists on keeping its rigid and harsh view of a potentially polygamous marriage, it would certainly be open to apply a general prohibition against such a marriage and thereby save an Englishwoman from entering into that most degrading position. It is well known that a Muslim has the capacity to contract a polygamous marriage and that his marriage with an Englishwoman shall always be potentially polygamous and so void. Every Registrar of Marriages knows or ought to know this fact. Why should he become instrumental in solemnising a marriage that is void from the very beginning. The view of some English writers that the rule that capacity be decided by the law of the husband's domicile or by the law of the matrimonial domicile "would deprive Englishwomen, marrying Muslims, of English matrimonial relief" gives the Private International Law rather a prejudicial outlook.

It has often been the effort of English Courts and writers to interpret or lay down the law in such a way as to help the English people. Thus it was stated in a case, "No country is bound to recognise the laws of a foreign state when they work injustice to its own subjects."[28] It was stated in another case, "Numerous examples may be suggested of the injustice which might be caused to our subjects if a marriage were declared invalid on the ground that it was forbidden by the law of the domicile of one of the parties."[29] Some of the English writers have also adopted this attitude. But Cheshire has suggested that the validity of a marriage should be determined according to the law of the matrimonial domicile. Dicey has stated the rule that each party must possess the capacity according to the laws of his or her own domicile to contract the marriage. But in deference to certain English judgments he gave an exception to this rule to the effect that a marriage would not be declared invalid by any incapacity existing under the foreign law if it was valid under the English law. Cheshire has expressed the opinion that the character of a marriage, that is, whether it is monogamous or polygamous and its validity should be determined according to law of the matrimonial domicile. Dicey has

28. Sottomayor Vs. De Barros, (No. 1) (1877) 3 P. D. 1 ; (No 2) (1879) 5 P. D. 94.

29. Simonin Vs. Mallac, (1860) 2 Sw. and Tr; 2 L. T, 327, 67 ; Chethi Vs. Chethi, (1909) P. 67.

disagreed with this view and has stated that it would deprive Englishwomen marrying Muslims of English matrimonial relief.[30] The inhabitants of the so-called developing countries feel dismayed at this attitude of English Courts and writers. It appears a basic principle that justice is and should remain impartial oblivious to the consideration that the relevant law might favour a foreigner and causes injury to one's own people. Many Englishwomen do marry Muslims and other persons of polygamous community or religion. In some cases, such marriages may be considered valid in England on the ground that, when solemnized there, it would be presumed that the parties had intended a monogamous marriage. But if such a marriage is dissolved on the basis of polygamy the Courts in a polygamous country may hold such a decision to be without jurisdiction and may not admit its legality. The result will be that the Englishwoman will be considered unmarried in England but will be considered by the Courts in a polygamous country as a married woman and the lawful wife of the Muslim husband. It will hold the marriage to be subsisting because it will be considered that the marriage was dissolved by the English Court on a wrong ground—a ground not recognised by the law of that country. It will not, therefore, feel itself bound by the English decision and may refuse to give effect to it.

Some particular cases : As already stated before, Islam recognises limited polygamy, while in Europe, U. S.A. and in some other countries monogamy is the law. The difficulties that arise in cases of mixed marriage between persons whose religion and civil law allow polygamy and other persons whose law enjoins monogamy can relate to the following cases :—

(*i*) When a Muslim having a living Muslim wife subsequently marries a girl domiciled in a country which recognises only monogamous marriages.

(*ii*) When a Muslim having a living non-Muslim wife

30. Dicey and Morris, Conflict of Laws, p. 277 ; Morris, *Cases on Conflict of Laws*, pp. 105, 106.

domiciled in a country whose law allows only monogamy subsequently marries a Muslim girl.

(iii) When an Englishman marries a *Muslimah*.

In each of the above cases, we have to consider the matters with regard to the following factors :

(*a*) Validity of the first marriage.

(*b*) Effect of the first marriage on the second marriage.

(*c*) Effect of a second marriage on the first marriage.

(*d*) Validity of the second marriage.

(*e*) Validity of the marriage of a spouse converted to Islam.

Muslim Law : As limited polygamy is permitted in Islam, both the marriages shall be considered valid under the Muslim law and neither wife can have any objection to her marriage or to the other marriage. The second marriage will not affect the first marriage nor will the first marriage affect the second marriage and both marriages shall be valid. Ameer Ali had expressed a different view, but he did so when India was a subject country of England, and was subject to English law.[31] After attaining independence, India and Pakistan are no longer governed by English law and so shall apply their own laws.

The marriage of a Muslim with a non-Muslim girl can be solemnised under the provisions of the Muslim law or in the Church or by the Registrar of Marriages. In the first case it will be valid according to the provisions of the Muslim law. If the marriage is solemnised according to the rites and ceremonies of the English law in a Church or before a Registrar of Marriages then too it will be considered to be valid by the Muslim law. According to the Muslim (Sunni) law the following conditions have to be satisfied to render a marriage valid :

(*a*) There must be an offer and its acceptance, that is, proposal for the marriage by one party and its acceptance by the other party,

31 Syed Ameer Ali, *Mohammadan Law*, pp. 200, 201, 207, Calcutta

(*b*) Two adult and sane Muslim males or one Muslim male and two females should be witnesses to the marriage and they must be present at the time and must have heard the proposal and the acceptance.

(*a*) *Ceremony*: As there is no priesthood in Islam, it is not necessary that the marriage should be solemnised by a Qadi or a Mawlavi or any other particular official and the marriage can be solemnised by any person. As a matter of fact the parties can themselves enter into a marriage on proposal by one and its acceptance by the other. All that is necessary is that there should be an expressed proposal and expressed acceptance either by the parties by themselves or through their representatives. No particular expression or formula has been prescribed for the proposal and its acceptance and any expression can serve the purpose as long as it is clear that one party wants to marry the other and the other party agrees to it. This condition will be fully satisfied in the solemnisation of a marriage by a Church or before the Registrar of Marriages. Hence, a marriage solemnised between a Muslim and a Christian girl in the Church or before the Registrar shall be perfectly valid.

(*b*) *Presence of Witnesses*: Under the Sunni Muslim law, two adult and sane male Muslims or one such male and two adult and sane females should witness the marriage. Under the Shiah law the presence of witnesses is not necessary. If the marriage ceremony has been witnessed by the witnesses, it shall be perfectly valid under the Sunni law even if solemnised in the Church or before the Registrar of Marriages. If the witnesses happen to be non-Muslims when a person marries a *Muslimah*, the marriage shall be invalid because it is an essential condition of marriage that the witnesses should be Muslims. But an exception is made to this general rule when a Muslim marries a *Kitabiah* or woman belonging to a revealed religion such as Christianity or the Jewish religion. In such a case it is not necessary that the witnesses should be Muslims; any two male and sane *Kitabis* or men belonging to a revelaed religion can act as witnesses to the marriage.[32] It is not even necessary that they should belong to the same religion as that of the bride ; all that is necessary is that they should belong to a revealed religion.[33] Thus, two Jews can be the witnesses to the marriage of a Muslim with a Christian girl. Hence, a marriage of a Muslim with a Christian girl shall be valid if it is solemnised in the Church according to the Christian rites and ceremonies or before the Registrar and the witnesses happen to be Christian.[34]

English Law : I. When a married Muslim marries an English woman :

(*a*) Validity of the first marriage: As Muslim law allows polygamy, the first marriage shall be potentially polygamous while English law insists on monogamy. The English Courts are so strict in the matter that they consider a marriage a nullity even when it is not actually polygamous but only potentially polygamous.[35] The marriage would be against the provisions and spirit of English law and so would not be recognised as a valid marriage by an English Court.

(*b*) Effect of the first marriage on the second marriage: At one time the English Courts considered a polygamous marriage a nullity, as never having existed at any time.[36] As a result of this view, the Muslim marriage could not be taken into consideration, and the second marriage solemnised in England according to English law was considered to be valid.[37] In course of time the English Courts have changed this view and now they hold that the first marriage, though polygamous and a nullity, can be taken into consideration to the extent of vesting the husband with the status of a married person at

32. Ibn Abidin, *Radd al-Muhtar*, vol. II, pp. 280, 281, Cairo, 1318 A.H. ; *al-Fatawa al-Alamgiriyah*, vol, II, p. 1.
33. *Ibid.*
34. *Ibid.*
35. Bethell, Re. (1880) 38 Ch. D. 220 ; Harvey Vs. Farnie, (1880) 6 P. D. 53 C, A. ; R. Vs. Naguib, (1917) 1 K. B. 359.
36. R. Vs. Naguib, (1917) 1 K. B. 359.
37. *Ibid.*

the time of his marriage with the Englishwoman. The first marriage would therefore render the second marriage polygamous and so void.[38]

(*c*) Effect of the second marriage on the first marriage: A Muslim husband's second marriage with an Englishwoman will not affect the first marriage in any way.

(*d*) Validity of the second marriage: The second marriage being bigamous shall be considered null and void and liable to be so declared in England.[39]

II. Muslim married to an Englishwoman subsequently marrying a *Muslimah* :

(*a*) Validity of the first marriage : The first marriage having been solemnised in England according to English law shall be considered to be monogamous and valid.

(*b*) Effect of the first marriage on the second marriage : The first marriage being valid, the second marriage would be bigamous and void according to English law.

(*c*) Effect of the second marriage on the first marriage : The solemnisation of the second marriage would not affect the validity of the first marriage which shall remain valid in spite of the second marriage. It would, however, entitle the first wife to the dissolution of her marriage on the ground that the husband was guilty of bigamy and was living in adultery with the second wife.[40] The view was expressed in one legal decision that it shall be considered in England that when the Muslim contracted the first marriage according to Christian rites, or according to civil law, as when the marriage is performed by the Registrar of Marriages, and used words showing that he bound himself towards his spouse to live monogamously his taking a second wife is an infringement of the contract of monogamy into which he had entered. He will also be deemed to have infringed the marital rights of his English wife under the contract of the marriage. The

38. Baindail Vs. Baindail, (1946) 1 All. E. R. 342.

39. *Ibid.*

40. *Ibid.*

English wife, therefore, shall be entitled to a remedy in any competent court where such a breach is recognised as a ground for dissolution.[41]

(*d*) Validity of the second marriage : The second marriage having been solemnised when the first marriage was subsisting shall be bigamous and so void under English law.

Law in the U.S.A. : Law in the U.S.A. does not deny the validity of a marriage simply because it is potentially polygamous. Moreover, it accords validity to the first (polygamous) marriage of a Muslim having several wives. But obviously such a person shall not be entitled to marry an American woman.

(2) *Incestuous Marriages* : Marriages between near relations have been discouraged generally and even prohibited by majority of nations at all times. The main reason for this discouragement or prohibition was the conception of indecency, immodesty or even immorality attached to such unions. As the conception of decency or immorality differed with different communities, the degrees of nearness of relationship naturally also differed. Thus marriage by a person with his step-mother was allowed by general practice in Arabia in pre-Islamic period, but this practice was stopped by an injunction in the Qur'ān wherein it is stated as under :

> "And marry not women whom your fathers married, except what has already passed. This surely is indecent and hateful, and it is an evil way.[42]

It can be seen from the above that Muslim law prohibits such marriages upon the ground of indecency. The same can be said about marriage with other near relations such as marriage between a man and his daughter or sister or with his grandmother or granddaughter or paternal or maternal aunts etc. But marriage is also prohibited in some cases between persons who are not such close relations. Keezer has

41. Landrum Vs. Chakravarty, (1929) S. L. T. 96.
42. Qur'an, Surah Al-Nisa', IV, 22.

expressed the opinion that marriage between near relations is disfavoured because such marriages are considered inimical to health and the perpetuation of hardy families.[43] No doubt this idea prevails amongst the Muslims also, but with them the conception of indecency forms the main reason.

Prohibited Degree: Islam has specified the women with whom marriage is forbidden but unlike the law in this connection in Christian countries, the prohibitions hold good for all times and no change can be made in them. It is laid down in the Qur'ān, "Forbidden to you are your mothers, and your daughters, and your sisters, and your paternal aunts, and your maternal aunts, and brother's daughters and sister's daughters, and your mothers that have suckled you, and your foster-sisters, and mothers of your wives, and your step-daughters who are in your guardianship (born) of your wives to whom you have gone in, but if you have not gone in to them there is no blame on you, and the wives of your sons who are of your own loins; and that you should have two sisters together, except what has already passed. Surely, Allah is ever Forgiving, Merciful.[44]

"And all married women except those whom your right hands possess (are forbidden); (this is) Allah's ordinance to you. And lawful for you are (all women) besides those provided that you seek (them) with your property, taking (them) in marriage, not committing fornication."[45]

The above comprises a complete and exhaustive list of relations with whom marriage is prohibited under Muslim law.

Islam, Hinduism and some other religions have similarly exhaustively detailed the list of incestuous marriages. Muslim law allows marriages between a larger number of relations than does English law. But as far as the broad principles are concerned, Muslim law has made similar provisions as the English law. Marriage is not allowed by

43. Keezer, Art. 120, p. 219.
44. Qur'an, Surah Al-Nisa', IV ; 23.
45. *Ibid.*, IV, 24.

either law between a person and his or her

(*a*) mother, grandmother
(*b*) father, grandfather
(*c*) husband's or wife's parents, and grandpatents,
(*d*) sister or brother
(*e*) niece, nephew,
(*f*) son's wife or daughter's husband,
(*g*) father's or mother's sister etc.

It has been stated by an American writer, "The courts uniformly state that polygamous and incestuous marriages are so shocking to the moral sense of Christian nations as not to be entitled to recognition by Anglo-American Courts".[46] The above sweeping remark gives rise to curious results. Thus, in one case two first cousins, domiciled in Portugal, contracted a marriage in England. A marriage between such relations is not allowed in Portugal and is considered incestuous, while English law allows it.[47] Hence the moral sense of Christian Portugal must have been shocked by this law of another Christian country. Similarly, a marriage between a man and his deceased wife's sister was not allowed in England on the basis of affinity but was allowed in Denmark. A domiciled Englishman contracted such a marriage with a domiciled Englishwoman in Denmark.[48] According to the view expressed above, the marriage permitted by Denmark—a Christian country—must have shocked the moral sense of England—another Christian country. Many more examples of similar nature can be cited in this respect, while showing that there can be no set moral rule about such marriages, and that marriages considered incestuous by the law of one country may well be acceptable to another. Stumberg has himself admitted, "There is, however, no general agreement as to what relationships are incestuous".[49] The position of English law

46. George Wilfred Stumberg; *Principles of Conflict of Laws*, p. 258, Chicago, 1937.
47. Sottomayor Vs. De Barros, (1877) 3 P. D. 1.
48. Brook Vs. Brook, (1861) 9 H. L. C. 1953.
49. George Wilfred Stumberg, p. 258.

in respect of incestuous marriages has been clarified to some extent in a case where the Court explained that "I believe the true rule to be that the courts of this country will exceptionally refuse to recognise and give effect to a capacity or incapacity to marry by the law of the domicile on the ground that to give it recognition and effect would be unconscionable".[50] The Court laid down the test for determining whether a marriage is incestuous to see "whether the marriage is so offensive to the conscience of the English court that it should refuse to recognise and give effect to the proper foreign law. In deciding that question the court will seek to exercise commonsense, good manners and reasonable tolerance."

The views about the propriety of marriages between certain relations differ not only in different countries, but sometimes change in the same country during the course of time. A marriage between a person and his deceased wife's sister was at one time considered incestuous in England.[51] The restriction was subsequently removed and such a marriage is now valid there. Originally the English law was so strict that marriages were not allowed between persons related within eight degrees through consanguinity, affinity, fosterage or even baptism. The condition was found to be very hard and was subsequently relaxed from time to time. Muslim law does not differ from English and American laws as far as near relations are concerned. But in case of distant relations there is a difference of opinion even among the European and American States. A more liberal view has been taken in this matter by a Court in the U.S.A. An uncle and his niece both domiciled in Maryland where a marriage between such relations is held incestuous contracted a marriage in Rhode Island where this kind of marriage is permissible. The Maryland Court of Appeal held that the marriage was not such as to be generally regarded as incestuous nor such as to be against public policy in Maryland.[52]

50. Cheni Vs. Cheni, (1962) 3 All. E. R, 873.
51. Brook Vs. Brook, (1861) 9 H. L. C. 193.
52. Fernsterwald Vs. Burk, 129 Md. 131.

An interesting point to note incidentally is that an English Court will refuse to recognise a Muslim marriage only when it is actually incestuous from the English point of view and not on the basis that it is potentially incestuous.

(3) *Against Public Policy* : Public policy is a very vague and uncertain expression ; what may be considered to be against public policy by one country or community may be considered to be perfectly in accordance with the public policy of another country or community. Standards of morality and public welfare differ a great deal in various countries and the values attached to various acts by one country may not appeal to another country or may be even repugnant to the latter. It was stated by Tariq Ameer Ali, J. in his judgrment on an appeal, "I cannot agree that this principle of monogamous marriage is to be introduced into India for the purpose of vitiating any rule of personal law—Hindu, Mohammadan, Buddhist as being inconsistent with public policy......I cannot see why any rule of personal law in India is to be vitiated because it is inconsistent with the English conception of marriage for purposes of divorce....It seems to me, therefore, that having no one personal law or law of the domicile or territorial law, there can be no one public or one good conscience....These problems, judicially no less than politically, can only be solved by applying principles of mutual consideration."[53] It was further stated in that judgment : "What is good conscience of one is the bad conscience of the other." It was laid down in an English case that it is both just and reasonable that the differences of married people should be adjudged in accordance with the laws of the country to which they belong."[54] It was stated in another case: "There can be no doubt as to the power of every country to make laws regulating the marriage of its own subjects."[55] It was held by the House of Lords in deciding a case that public policy is not

53. Noor Jahan Vs. Eugene Tiscenko, A. I. R. 1942 Cal. 325 at p. 328.
54. Wilson Vs. Wilson, (1872) L. R. 1 P. and M. 435, Le Mesurier Vs. Le Mesurier, (1895) A. C. 517 P.,C.
55. Pugh Vs. Pugh, (1961) 2 All. E. R. 680.

a safe or trustworthy ground for legal decisions.[56] Fortunately of late we find a tendency amongst the English writers and Courts to give full recognition to the laws of other peoples.

(4) *Positively prohibited by the laws of a country:* It is open to every country to make laws that it considers suitable to its peculiar conditions. These laws of necessity differ from those of other countries. But no country can claim that its laws are the ideal ones and suitable for all other countries. We have seen that there is a great difference of opinion about the prohibitions relating to incestuous marriages. As pointed out above, the prohibitions have been found to change in the same country from time to time. It therefore cannot be open to any country to insist that its laws should be followed by other countries. Similarly, miscegenation or marriages between whites and coloured persons, which expression is usually used in the United States of America mainly for negroes, were prohibited in some States. The laws of Alabama prescribed that it is miscegenation for a white person to marry, live in adultery or fornication with any negro or descendent of any negro. Is every country bound to follow this rule of law ? It goes against the very spirit of Islam which declares that it has removed all distinctions of race, colour and creed. Many States in the United States of America did not follow this rule so much so that it has now been abrogated. It is thus obviously not correct for any country to insist that its laws should be followed by all other countries.

(5) *Against Public Morals* : The English Courts make it a condition of the validity of marriage that it should not be against public morals. They, however, judge public morals by their own standard. They hold the fact that a Muslim can have a plurality of wives to be obnoxious. It was stated in Hyde Vs. Hyde : "And it may be well doubted whether it would become the tribunals of this country to enforce the duties (even if we know them) which belong to a system so

56. Janson Vs. Drufontein Consolidared Ltd., (1902) A. C. 484.

utterly at variance with the Christian conception of marriage, and so revolting to the ideas we entertain of the social position to be accorded to the weaker sex."[57] As observed above, every country and nation has its own standard of morality. Harper has observed in his valuable book, *Problems of the Family*: "How quickly illegitimacy can be converted into authoritatively approved procedure has recently been demonstrated in Germany where healthy young women are advised by their government that it is their duty to produce babies, married or not."[58]

Conclusion: The English Courts till recently took a very harsh view of Muslim and all polygamous marriages and refused to recognise their validity. They considered a marriage void even when it was not actually polygamous, but the husband's law allowed him to have a plurality of wives. Thus in one legal dispute an Englishman had married a woman of a tribe whose law allowed polygamy and died without contracting any other marriage; his daughter was nonetheless held to be illegitimate as the marriage was considered void, being potentially polygamous.[59] The husband's intention and even solemn undertaking not to contract a second marriage carried no weight with the English Courts and it was stated in a case: "The fact that the marriage happens at the moment to consist of only two formally single spouses is immaterial."[60]

From around 1946 onwards, the English Courts started to give effect to some of the consequences of a polygamous marriage, such as succession, legitimacy, relief by certain organizations, etc., without, however, recognising the marriage itself. Dicey states that in the absence of certain strong reasons or some exceptions (not material here) the English Courts will recognize a polygamous marriage as a valid marriage.[61] The facts, however, do not bear out his statement.

57. (1866) L. R. 1 P and D. 130.
58. Fowler Vs. Harper, *Problems of the Family*, p. 99, Indianopolis, 1952.
59. Bethell, Re. V. Hildyard, (1888) 38 Ch. D. 220.
60. Mehta Vs. Mehta (1945) 2 All E. R. 690.
61. Dicey and Morris, *Conflict of Laws*, Rule 36, p. 285, London, 1968.

There are no decisions, except one discussed below, which have stated the recognition in so many words. As pointed out by Graveson, the new English view does not even now give full credit to a polygamous or potentially polygamous marriage.[62] Dicey himself has not quoted any authority in support of his statement. The examples he has quoted relate only to incidents arising out of such marriages. It is true that in Shahnaz Vs. Rizwan the Court has stated, "......our court has never treated a marriage as unlawful merely because it is potentially, or indeed contemporaneously with its celebration, a polygamous marriage ; provided of course that the marriage is a marriage lawful by the personal law of the parties and the *lex loci celebrationis*."[63] But the same Court had explained previous to this statement that "In approaching the problem, it is essential at the outset to distinguish between an unlawful marriage and a marriage which the courts of this country will not regard as a marriage in the sense in which the English court conceives of marriage, that is to say, tested by comparison with the concept of marriage proper entertained by the English court." Further it is stated : "There are a number of instances.........where the courts of this country have given effect to consequences of a polygamous marriage."

It is clear that the Court has not considered a polygamous marriage lawful from the English point of view. It has also quoted Dicey's view given above and cited instances where effect has been given to some consequences of a polygamous marriage. Another remark of the Court further clarifies the position when it is stated, "......it does seem to me that what the courts have held, and always have held, is that neither a husband nor a wife can be granted by the English court any right which inheres in the person seeking the assistance of the court specifically in the character of the husband or of a wife ; and, by parity of reasoning, neither party coming to the court can enforce against the other any

62. R. H, Graveson, *The Conflict of Laws*, p. 207, London, 1966.

63. (1965) 1 Q B. 390.

obligation which arises from, and specifically from, the capacity of the other party as the wife or husband." The Court has explained the attitude of the English Courts when it says, "It is clear that no order for restitution of conjugal rights, no order for divorce or nullity will be made by the English court in favour of a person who, coming to it for help, has to say, "I seek this assistance as "husband"..as "wife"..by force of the marriage, which is a polygamous marriage. The reason, I think, is one of policy, of morality, as considered first in the mid-19th century but surviving into modern times, that nothing should be done to blur the distinction between Christian marriage..marriage properly understood and the concept of such proper marriage..and, on the other hand, polygamous associations more resembling concubinage or slavery."

It is thus plain that the English Courts do not hold a polygamous marriage a valid marriage, but confine themselves to saying that the (polygamous) marriage is valid for certain purposes. It was explained in Din Vs. National Assistance Board, that when a question arises of recognising a foreign marriage or ot construing the word "wife" in a statute, everything in my opinion depends upon the purpose for which the marriage is to be recognised and the objects of the statute. I ask myself first of all ; is there any good reason why the appellant's wife and children should not be recognised as his wife and children for the purpose of the National Assistance Act, 1948 ?"[64] In the same way the issues of a polygamous marriage have been held to be the legitimate children of a person only for the purpose of succession. But even now they cannot succeed to entailed property or title of honour.

The attitude of the Courts towards an Englishwoman marrying a person of a polygamous race is still more unfortunate. She does not, according to them, possess the capacity to contract the marriage and so the same shall be held void and the position of the English wife will be reduced to that of

64. Din Vs. National Assistance Board, (1967) 1 All. E. R. 750.

a concubine.

The English Courts are perhaps no longer so prejudiced against polygamy but they are bound by the precedents established by some very harsh decisions laid down in the past in connection with polygamous marriages. While their attitude is to be appreciated, their logic becomes difficult to follow. How can a woman be recognised as wife of a person for certain set and limited purposes, but not recognised as his wife in the full sense of the word, and where the marriage itself is concerned ?

The decision in Hyde Vs. Hyde had laid down that "matrimonial law of this country is wholly inapplicable to polygamy... the powers conferred on the courts for enforcing or dissolving a marriage tie are not adapted to any form of union between a man and a woman save a monogamous union." Contemporary English Courts endeavour to avoid this rule whenever possible, in order to take cognizance of matrimonial matters. The Court was confronted with such a difficulty in Shahnaz Vs. Rizwan when the wife sued her husband for her dower. The Court stated that "The English courts could not enforce such a (polygamous) marriage or any right arising specifically by virtue of the marriage relationship between the parties." It, however, escaped from the binding rule laid down in Hyde Vs. Hyde by distinguishing that the right which the plaintiff was seeking to enforce was a right in personam, arising not out of the relationship of husband and wife but from a contract entered into in contemplation and in consideration of the marriage and was therefore not a matrimonial right which the court refused to enforce."[65] The Court further remarked "it is clear that no order for restitution of conjugal rights and no order for divorce or nullity will be made by the English court in favour of a person (in the case of a polygamous marriage).

A happy change has been showing itself in the attitude of English Courts and writers in respect of polygamous

65. Shahnaz Vs. Rizwan, (1965) 1 Q.B. 390.

marriages during the last decade. They now do accept the validity of a polygamous marriage—though to a limited extent only—for the purpose of rendering help to the wives, widows and children of a deceased husband.

It was stated in one case, "for many purposes quite obviously, the status would have to be recognized.........If a Hindu domiciled in India died intestate in England leaving personal property in this country, the succession to the personal property would be governed by the law of his domicile and in applying the law of his domicile effect would have to be given to the right of any children of the Hindu marriage, to the rights of the Hindu widow and for that purpose the courts of this country would be bound to recognise the validity of a Hindu marriage. There are purposes for which a polygamous marriage would be recognised as a valid marriage in this country and the word wife may be construed as a polygamously married wife."[66] It was observed in another decision: "A polygamous marriage recognised as valid by the law of the parties cannot be recognised in these courts as a ceremony which in no way affects the status of the parties to it."[67]

The Courts, obviously, are also influenced by the fact that a large number of Muslims have settled and are settling in England. It was stated by the Court in Shahnaz Vs. Rizwan: "As a matter of policy, in view of the large number of Mohammedans resident in England, the law should rather lend its aid to women who come here as a result of a Mohammedan marriage, by enforcing the husband's contractual promise (re dower) than leave them without recourse to legal assistance." The Court in Din Vs. National Assistance Board, recognised the validity of the polygamous marriage to this extent as to hold the woman whom the appellant (the husband) had married polygamously in Pakistan as his wife for the purpose of the National Assistance Act of 1948.[68]

66. Mehta Vs. Mehta, (1945) 2 All E. R. 690.
67. Kassim Vs. Kassim, (1962) P. 224.
68. Din Vs. National Assistance Board, (1967) 1 All E. R. 760.

It was observed in another decision that : "For the purpose of ascertaining the status of this wife, the courts here will recognise the marriage as a valid marriage giving her that status."[69] The widow of a man who died intestate was held to be entitled to succeed to the property left by the husband although the marriage was polygamous.[70] Section 113 (I) of the National Insurance Act, 1965, section 86 (5) of the National Insurance (Industrial) Act, 1965 and section 17 (9) of the Family Allowances Act, 1965, all recognise the validity of a potentially polygamous marriage for the purposes of those Acts. This is, howevэr, subject to the condition that the marriage should in fact be monogamous.

While all these changes are to be welcomed, it is regretted that in some instances they are the result only of expediency and national interest and owe nothing to the principle of mutual respect by different nations and religions for each others' systems of law.

An English Court even today recognises the consequences of a polygamous marriage of an Englishwoman only with the intent of enabling her to avail of certain reliefs and claims. It still refuses to recognise the marriage as such, implying indirectly that all the marriages contracted every day in the biggest areas of the world are in its eyes no better than a form of concubinage. with the consequent result that the Muslims of the entire world, their ancestors and future issue shall not be considered legitimate.

Be that as it may, the point remains that in the contemporary atmosphere of tolerance and broad mindedness the attitude of the English Courts remains strangely insular and rigid.

It is hoped that the English Parliament, Courts and writers will make an earnest attempt to remove this undesirable bias, and to bridge the gulf between the legal systems of different countries. This can be done to some extent by insisting on a strict adherence to the principles of Private International

69. Mohammad Vs. Knot, (1908) 2 All E. R. 563.
70. Coleman Vs. Shang, (1961) A. C. 481.

Law, and not having recourse to exceptions to the principles of that law in order to help some English women married to foreigners. For cordial international relationship and for all practical purposes the religious and secular laws promulgated by the competent authority of any country should be respected by all countries. Any action in violation of such non-interference can and does lead to very unfortunate results.

Thus, for instance, Muslim law attaches great importance to morality and it has laid down that a child cannot be considered legitimate until and unless it is not only born but also conceived in lawful wedlock. It would be obviously unjust if a Muslim country were to apply this rule of its law to English people domiciled or residing there.

Attention is again drawn to the judgement of A. R. Changez, J quoted in the section on "Conflict between Muslim and Christian laws" where he preferred to decide the case on the basis of justice, equity and good conscience rather than according to the provisions of Muslim law, the law of the country and the husband's domicile.[71] But it is to be appreciated that of late years, the English Courts and writers have adopted a more liberal and reasonable attitude in matrimonial cases.

71. Liever Farooq Vs. Adelaide Bridget Mary, P.L.D. 1958 Lah, 431.

Section VIII: Jurisdiction

It becomes necessary at times to determine the Court which shall have the power to decide a particular case. The matter may become complicated when the parties belong to different countries. The English and other European Courts and those in the U.S.A. are often faced with difficult problems of this nature. The Courts and writers of these countries have laid down laws and rules to be applied in such cases. As far as the scope of this book is concerned, the problems arise when a Muslim marries a woman domiciled in England or a country where monogamy is the rule and polygamy is not allowed. It will arise when the help of a Court is sought to determine the character or nature of a marriage, its validity or the validity of a divorce given by the husband.

In early days of Islam it was very uncommon for a Muslim to marry a foreign Muslim or non-Muslim wife. If such a marriage did take place, there would be no difficulty in the case of a marriage between a Muslim of one country and a woman of a different Muslim country. The Courts of both the countries could exercise jurisdiction. As the parties were governed by the same Muslim law the judgment of the Qāḍī deciding the case would be considered binding on both the parties and could be sent to the Qāḍī of the other Muslim country concerned for execution.

Where the wife was a non-Muslim, the decision of a dispute between her and her Muslim husband would depend on whether both or one of them was residing in a Muslim or non-Muslim country. If both were living in a Muslim country the Qāḍī of the place would exercise jurisdiction.[1]

As the question of jurisdiction did not so often arise in Muslim countries in ancient times, there is not much discussion of such jurisdiction in books on Muslim Fiqh and

1. For discussion of the matter see chapter on *Tabāyun al-Dār*.

only some elementary rules have been stated about the rights and powers of the Qāḍīs to decide cases. These are given below :

(1) Under Muslim law the Qāḍīs of different places are bound to co-operate with each other. The Qāḍī seized of one case is entitled to ask the Qāḍī of another area to serve notice on the defendant when the latter is available in his jurisdiction.[2]

(2) A Qāḍī of one place can record the evidence of the parties and their witnesses, if any, and can decide the case on its merits. He can then pass decree, reduce it to writing and give it to the party concerned. The same shall be binding on the parties. The decree-holder can present it to any Qāḍī for execution and the latter shall give effect to it.[3] The Qāḍī can also himself forward the decree for execution to the Qāḍī within whose jurisdiction the subject matter of the suit happens to be or is situated. It may be noted that no such decree can be passed in the absence of the defendant and such a proceeding shall be considered unlawful.[4] However, the Qāḍī can record the statements of the plaintiff and his witnesses in the absence of the defendant and forward it to the Qāḍī concerned who shall not receive the same as evidence in the absence of the defendant.[5]

(3) In order to save a party from hardship, a Qāḍī can examine its witnesses who may happen to be living or be present in his own jurisdiction, record their statements and forward them to the Qāḍī of another place

2. 'Ubayd Allāh b. Mas'ūd, *Sharḥ al-Wiqāyah*, Delhi 1929, Vol. III, pp. 127-28 f ; 'Alī b. Abī Bakr al-Marghīnānī, *al-Hidāyah*, Delhi, n.d., Vol. III, pp. 138-40 f ; Ibn 'Ābidīn, al-Shāmī, *Radd al-Muḥtār*, Cairo, n.d. Vol. IV, pp. 389-90 f.

3. *Al-Fatāwā al-Hindiyah*, Kanpur, n d. Vol. III, pp. 172-173.

4. 'Ubayd Allāh b. Mas'ūd, *Sharḥ al-Wiqāyah*, ed cit. Vol. III, pp. 129-30 f : Al-Marghīnānī, *al-Hidāyah*, ed. cit., Vol. III, pp. 138-41.

5. *Ibid.*

where the other party is living. The latter, on being satisfied with the genuineness of the proceedings, would accept them, include them in his own record and rely on them.[6]

(4) It is the duty of every Qāḍī of every Muslim country to maintain the decree of another Qāḍī unless it is repugnant to the injunctions of the Qur'ān or of the Sunnah or of the agreed view of the Imams.[7] If there is a difference of opinion amongst the Imams in respect of any matter and the Qāḍī passes his order in accordance with one particular opinion, the order shall be binding on all Qāḍīs provided the first Qāḍī is a Mujtahid.[8] Mujtahid means a person who is qualified to deduce from the law and from Traditions principles for the decision of specific cases.

(5) If there be no express injunctions in the Qur'ān or Sunnah in respect of a particular case and the Qāḍī passes his order on the basis of the unanimous view of the Imams or other jurists the same shall be binding on all Qāḍīs.[9]

(6) If there is a difference of opinion among the Muslim jurists and the first Qāḍī does not know of it but passes his order in spite of this ignorance, it shall be open to another Qāḍī to adopt the view of the other jurist or jurists if he believes it to be the better view and in such a case he can reject the view of the first Qāḍī.[10]

English Law

Preliminary: To fully understand the principles of English law concerning jurisdiction, it is necessary to remem-

6. 'Ubyad Allāh b. Mas'ūd *Sharḥ-al-Wiqāyah*, ed. cit. Vol. III, pp. 129-30 f. *al-Fatāwā al-Hindiyah*, ed. cit. Vol. III, pp. 172-73.

7. Ali b. Abī Bakr al-Marghīnānī, *al-Hidāyah*, ed. cit. Vol. III, p. 141; *Sharḥ al-Wiqāyah*, ed. cit. Vol. III, pp. 130-31.

8. *Al-Hidāyah*, ed. cit. Vol. III, p. 141: *Sharḥ al-Wiqāyah*, ed. cit. Vol. III, pp. 132-33.

9. *Ibid.* 10. *Ibid.*

ber that under the Ecclesiastical law, a person could be sued only in the diocese where he was residing. But on the establishment of Civil Courts for divorce and matrimonial causes jurisdiction was vested in them. As times passed and cases involving conflict of laws came up for decision before these Courts, a difficulty was experienced when parties belonged to different countries. Jurisdiction was then determined according to residence, domicile and nationality. The last was given up in England though it still forms the basis for jurisdiction in many European countries. In England jurisdiction came to be assumed on the basis of residence and domicile. It was, however, found that it was necessary to have a common ground for all the countries and that for this purpose domicile was considered to be the best basic ground for jurisdiction. This rule was based on the ground that the application of the laws of different countries to which the spouses belonged would lead to great confusion, hence the necessity to have recourse to one set of rules. It was also considered that on her marriage, the wife automatically acquires the domicile of the husband. This rule was based on the reasoning that on her marriage to a person the latter was bound to look to her maintenance, protection etc., while the wife was to run the house, to look after his domestic comforts and the like and this gave rise to the idea that the wife would live with the husband wherever he choses to live. Hence, the rule was adopted that on her marriage the wife acquires the domicile of the husband.

Full Discussion: It is now proposed to discuss the question of jurisdiction based on domicile in some details. It has already been seen above that the English Courts make a distinction between the place to which the parties belong, that is, *loci domicilii* and the place where the marriage has actually been solemnised or *loci celebrationis*. It was in the year 1872 that Lord Penzance stated a very important rule of law in this connection, namely, "It is the strongest inclination of my opinion that the only fair and satisfactory rule to adopt on this matter of jurisdiction is to insist upon the parties in all cases referring their matrimonial differences to the Courts of the country in which they are domiciled."[11] He further added, "Different countries have different views and laws respecting matrimonial obligations: a different estimate of the causes which should justify divorce. It is both just and reasonable, therefore, that the differences of the married people should be adjusted in accordance with the laws of the community to which they belong, and dealt with by the tribunals which alone can administer those laws." Lord Penzance further justified this rule on the ground, "an honest adherence to this principle moreover will preclude the scandal which arises when a man and woman are held to be man and wife in one country and strangers in another."

But the Courts of a foreign country have no jurisdiction to dissolve the marriage of aliens. It has been held in several cases that foreign Courts could not dissolve the marriage of parties who were not domiciled within their jurisdiction at the time when the proceedings for divorce were commenced.

It was stated by the Calcutta High Court, while dealing with a suit for dissolution of marriage, "where the Court of a country, *in which the spouses are domiciled*, is bound by the municipal law of that country (as in 1924 A.C. 1007) to acknowledge the validity of divorce good according to the religious law of the person concerned, it is bound to make a declaration that the marriage has been dissolved." It was further stated, "a defendant in a suit may be a citizen, native or naturalised, or a foreigner. In regard to the former, while within the territory of their birth or of their adopted allegiance, the jurisdiction of the sovereignty over them is complete and irresistible. It cannot be controlled and it ought to be respected everywhere."[12]

The English law in respect of jurisdiction may conveniently be discussed with regard to the following aspects

11. Wilson Vs. Wilson, (1866) L. R. 2 P. D. 435.
12. **Noor Jahan Vs. Eugene Tiscenk (KD) A.I.R. 1942 Cal. 532 at p. 329.**

of marriage.

(*a*) (*i*) Character of marriage, that is, whether it is void or voidable.

(*ii*) Nature of marriage, that is, whether it is polygamous or monogamous.

(*b*) The law that shall be applicable in a particular case.

(*a*) I. *Jurisdiction to determine character of marriage* : It sometimes becomes necessary to determine the Courts which under the English law have jurisdiction to determine the character of marriage whether it is void, voidable or valid. It has to be seen whether it is the Courts of the place where the marriage has been solemnised or the Courts of the place where the parties are domiciled that can exercise jurisdiction.

The importance of the character of marriage lies in the fact that a void marriage is considered a nullity—as having never existed at all at any time. It can be so treated by both the parties to it without the necessity of obtaining the decree of a Court annulling it.

It has been discussed before that under the English law a woman on her marriage to a foreigner acquires his domicile. A void marriage is, however, no marriage at all and so the ostensible wife does not acquire the domicile of the purported husband but retains her own domicile. She can, therefore, seek a relief in respect of the supposed marriage in a Court of her own domicile which in the case of an English woman shall be an English Court. In the case of a voidable marriage the wife does acquire the domicile of her husband so that she can, as a general rule, seek a relief in respect of her marriage only in a Court of the husband's domicile which shall constitute her domicile also.

It is not necessary for the parties to a marriage which turns out to be void to get it declared a nullity as they can themselves treat it as such. But sometimes they are uncertain or think it safe to get the Court's order in the matter. It shall be open to an ostensible wife to approach the Court of her own domicile on making it clear in her petition that her marriage is void. The Court shall first decide this matter and if satisfied on this point shall exercise jurisdiction in the case.

Some general rules regarding this subject may be adduced from various English decisions:

I. Whether a marriage is void or voidable, having regard to its essential validity, is to be determined by the law of the husband's domicile at the date of the marriage or preferably by the law of the matrimonial domicile at that date.[13]

II. If the law of the husband's domicile holds the marriage to be void, the ostensible wife shall not acquire the domicile of the purported husband but shall retain her own domicile. If she happens to be an English woman, the English Court will then be seized of jurisdiction in respect of the supposed marriage.[14]

III. If it is found that under the law of the husband's domicile the marriage in dispute is voidable the wife shall be considered to have acquired the domicile of her husband. Hence it shall be Court of the husband's domicile or the Court of the matrimonial domicile which shall have jurisdiction with regard to the marriage.[15]

IV. A wife alleging a void marriage can claim her pre-marriage domicile if there is nothing to show that it has been changed except the fact of the marriage. But in the case of a voidable marriage she cannot do that and must accept until the case has been decided that her domicile is that of her husband.[16]

V. In nullity proceedings if the marriage is void, as distinct from voidable, the ostensible wife at the commencement of the suit may have different domicile from that of the ostensible husband and whether she has or has not the same domicile cannot be determined until the pronouncement of the decision whether the marriage is void or not.[17]

13. De Reneville Vs. De Reneville, (1948) 1 All. E. R. 56.
14. *Ibid.*
15. *Ibid.*
16. Ross Smith Vs. Ross Smith, (1962) 1 All. E. R. 344.
17. Garthwaite Vs. Garthwaite, (1964) 2 All. E. R. 233.

VI. If in the case of a wife's petition claiming that the marriage is void *ab initio* and asserting that she has a certain (*e.g.* English) domicile different from that of her purported husband's, the petition on its face alleges facts, which if correct give the Court of the country of claimed domicile the jurisdiction to entertain it. It cannot decline jurisdiction until it has ascertained whether or not the alleged facts upon which its jurisdiction is claimed are true. If the facts are found true, it has jurisdiction to adjudicate upon the claim to relief. If they are not true, it must decline to proceed in the matter.[18] If the petition on its face alleges facts which, if correct, deprive the Court of jurisdiction to entertain it, there is no issue as to its jurisdiction to adjudicate upon the claim to relief, and the Court must decline *in limine* to entertain the proceedings.[19]

VII. A spouse who alleges a marriage to be void can allege and prove that fact in any Court in any place if a decision on that matter is relevant to an issue properly before that Court.[20]

VIII. The fact that the wife has an English domicile can be established in nullity proceedings themselves on a preliminary issue.[21]

IX. The Court of the country in which the parties are domiciled have jurisdiction to pronounce a decree of nullity whether the parties were or were not married in that country.[22]

Another factor that affects determination of jurisdiction is whether the alleged illegality or irregularity relates to the rites or formalities of marriage or to its essentials. The legal requirements prescribed for the celebration of marriage are

18. Garthwaite Vs. Garthwaite, (1964) 2 All. E. R. 233.

19. *Ibid.*

20. Ross Smith Vs. Rose Smith, (1962) 1 All. E.R. 344.

21. De Reneville Vs. De Reneville, (1948) 1 All. E.R. 56.

22. *Ibid.*, Von Lorang (Salvesen) Vs. Administrator of Austrian Boperty, (1927) A.C. 64, 641.

called formalities of marriage while the other requirements that do not relate to the celebration of the marriage but are concerned with the matters arising out of a marriage are termed the essentials of marriage. Generally speaking, the forms, rites and ceremonies directly concerned with the solemnisation of marriage, such as the presence of the prescribed number of witnesses, consent of the parents of the parties when so prescribed, presence of both the parties at the time of the celebration of the marriage, or of representation of both or one of them by proxy, etc. are considered formalities under the English law. The essentials of marriage are such as are not concerned with the celebration of the marriage itself but relate to the consequences arising on the solemnisation of the marriage involving the rights and responsibilities of each party, etc.

The differentiation between essentials and formalities in respect of a marriage is rather unfortunate and is not quite correct. Thus there may be matters relating to the celebration of a marriage which are essential for its validity such as the free consent of the parties. In the same way there may be some matters arising out of and subsequent to the celebration of a marriage which may not be essential for its validity. Nor can there be any universal agreement as to what conditions are essentials. Thus the parent's consent to a marriage by a person below a certain age is an essential condition for its validity under the French law but the English Courts consider the condition to be among the non-essential formalities of the celebration of marriage so that under the English law the parent's permission or refusal does not affect the character of the marriage.[23]

(*a*) II. Courts that can exercise jurisdiction to determine the nature of marriage : The next and a very important question relates to the Courts which can exercise jurisdiction to determine the nature of marriage, that is, whether it is

23. Simonin Vs. Mallac, (1860) 2 Sw and Tr 67 ; Sotto Mayor Vs. De Barros, (1877) 3 P.D,I (C,A)

monogamous or polygamous.

The determination of the nature and the validity or invalidity of a marriage, that is, whether it is polygamous or monogamous and whether a polygamous marriage is valid or void seems to have nothing to do with its celebration but relates to the essential validity of marriage. It has already been stated that it is only the Court of the domicile of the parties that has jurisdiction over matters relating to the essentials of marriage. Hence, it should be the Court of the husband's domicile that can decide the nature and validity of a marriage. The English Courts, however, assume jurisdiction in all such cases irrespective of the law of the husband's domicile. This assumption of jurisdiction is generally based on the following two grounds :—

(1) A marriage celebrated under the English law either in the Church or by the Registrar of Marriages shall be considered monogamous whatever the law of the husband's domicile or religion.

(2) A person domiciled in England does not possess the capacity to be a party to a marriage which is not monogamous.

It has been contended that when a foreigner marries an English woman in England, he must realise that he is contracting a marriage that has got to be monogamous. It has been stated still more explicitly: "When an English woman marries a man of a polygamous race at a Registry office in England intending to set up home here, the substantial validity of the marriage as well as its formal validity depends on the personal law of the wife and not on the personal law of the husband. It is a condition of the marriage that it should be monogamous."[24] When, however, such a marriage takes place in the husband's country of domicile, it is by the law of that country that the nature of the marriage shall be determined. Thus it has been stated :

24. Kenward Vs. Kenward, (1951) P. 124.

".........When an English woman domiciled here marries a man of a polygamous race in his homeland by the ceremonies of his country, intending to live with him there well knowing she is entering into a marriage that is potentially polygamous the substantial validity of that marriage depends on the personal law of the husband and not on the personal law of the wife. The marriage is valid by the law of that country, and is, I should have thought, valid here.[25] While the above dicta are reasonable and correct, it is submitted with respect, that the Court has not taken into consideration a third and the usual contingency, namely, when, despite the fact of the marriage being solemnised in England, the intention is to set up home in the husband's country. At one time this was and is still the general case with most marriages between Muslims and English women and it is only of late that some immigrants from various member countries of the Commonwealth have started settling in England. Some of them marry English women there and the first contingency discussed above will arise in such cases, that is, as the matrimonial home shall be England, it must be the English law that shall govern the case under the Private International Law. However, as we have seen, this is not so under the Muslim law and the average Muslim immigrant remains under the impression that he shall be governed by Muslim law even when settled in England.

The Supreme Court of Pakistan has not accepted the view that a marriage celebrated in England between an English woman and a citizen of Pakistan shall be a monogamous marriage. After quoting with approval certain passages from Cheshire they expressed the view, "It would not, therefore, be correct that a marriage, performed before a Registrar in England, must necessarily import the essentials of monogamy.

25. Kenward Vs. Kenward, (1951) P. 124.

The point has to be decided in the light of the law of Pakistan which is the law of the domicile of the husband."[26]

In the case discussed above both the husband's domicile as well as the matrimonial domicile shall be of a polygamous country. Such a contingency has been described in the following paragraph:

"When a marriage has been duly solemnised according to the law of the place of solemnisation, the parties become husband and wife. But when they become husband and wife what is the character which the wife assumes? She becomes the wife of the foreign husband in a case where the husband is foreigner in the country in which the marriage is contracted. She no longer retains any other domicile than his, which she acquires. The marriage is contracted with a view to that matrimonial domicile which results from her placing herself by contract in the relation of wife to the husband whom she marries, knowing him to be a foreigner, domiciled and contemplating permanent and settled residence abroad. Therefore, it must be within the meaning of such a contract, if we are to inquire into it, that she is to become subject to her husband's law, subject to it in respect of the consequences of the matrimonial relation, and all other consequences depending upon the law of the husband's domicile."[27] This view was upheld in a later case.[28]

The English Courts and writers hold that when a marriage is solemnised in England, it is on the condition that it complies with certain essential requirements of the English matrimonial law. If it does not satisfy these conditions the marriage shall not be valid and that the Courts of the place of celebration alone can decide this matter. Two of the essential English requirements are that :—

(*i*) Each party must possess the capacity to contract the marriage according to the law of his or her own domicile.

26. Mrs. Marina Jatoi Vs. Nuruddin K. Jatoi, P.L.D. 1967 S.C. 580.
27. Harvey Vs. Farnie, (1882) 8 App. Cas. 43.
28. Russ Vs. Russ, (1964) P. 315.

(*ii*) There must be free consent of each party to the marriage.

(*i*) *Capacity*: It is said that it is necessary for the validity of a marriage that each party to the marriage should possess the capacity to contract it. If either party does not possess it, the marriage shall be void. It is further said that the English law does not allow polygamy so that an English woman does not possess the capacity to contract such a marriage. It is rather strange that having laid down this general rule of law the English Courts and writers do not allow a foreigner to take a similar plea. Thus in a case filed by an English woman against her Hindu husband, the latter took the plea that the marriage was void as his religious law did not allow him to marry a non-Hindu woman. In other words his contention was that his marriage was invalid as he did not possess the capacity to contract the same. The Court did not accept the plea and did not attach any importance to the husband's disability under his religious and personal law and observed that the husband could get rid of the incapacity at his will.[29] It is not clear how the husband could get rid of the disability imposed on him by his religious law as long as he remained a Hindu. Moreover, it is submitted, the mere intention of the husband can have no effect on the nature of the marriage. Thus it was held in certain cases that "intention and even express declaration (or contract) not to marry another woman cannot change a potentially polygamous marriage into a monogamous marriage.[30] How these diametrically opposed views can be held in respect of the same aspect of marriage namely an incapacity to marry, is beyond comprehension. It is regrettable and unfortunate that the adoption of such irreconcilable attitudes shows a bias and prejudice in favour of their own law by the English Courts and writers to the disadvantage and total disregard of the comity of nations.

29. Chetti Vs. Chetti, (1909) P. 67,
30. Sowa Vs. Sowa, (1961) 1 All. E.R. 687; Hyde Vs. Hyde, 12 L. T. 235 Ohochuko Vs. Ohochuko, (1960) 1 All. E.R. 253,

(*ii*) *Consent*: It is emphasised that there must be free consent on the part of the wife to contract a polygamous marriage. Free consent, it is stated, implies that the woman should realise the nature of the marriage that it is not monogamous but polygamous. It is explained that it is a rule of law that there can be no valid agreement when there is a fundamental error involved in it and no valid marriage can result from such an agreement. The wife's ignorance of the nature of the marriage, she was entering into, would render the marriage void. The question of free consent, it is said, is an essential condition of the solemnisation of marriage and so the question whether the marriage is void, being polygamous, must be decided by the *lex loci celebrationis*. It has also been held that it is true in most cases where the marriage is void that the Court of the place of celebration is the most fitting to determine the validity of the marriage.[31]

But a very material point for consideration here is that the English woman knows that her Muslim or Hindu husband shall return to and settle in his own country and she marries him in spite of this knowledge. It was stated in an English case, "All persons are legally bound to take notice of the laws of the country where they are domiciled.[32] It seems reasonable that the English woman should acquaint herself with the nature and consequences of her intended marriage under the law of her prospective husband's domicile. This is very important as it shall become her domicile also where she shall pass her whole life. It cannot and should not form a legal presumption that when an English woman marries a foreigner, she does so under an ignorance of the nature of the marriage under the law of the husband's domicile. If she neglects to ascertain the law which shall govern her whole life she has only to thank herself.

It is not clear that when every Muslim marriage is considered to be polygamous in nature why does the English law at all allow its solemnisation in England. The Registrar of

31. Ogden Vs. Ogden, (1908) P. 46; Chetti Vs. Chetti, (1909) P. 67.
32. Baindail Vs. Baindail, (1946) P. 122 (C.A.).

Marriages, a Government official, should not be allowed to be a party to what in all cases is held to be an illegal act. Nor should an English woman be allowed to live all her life as a concubine because a marriage with a Muslim being always ultimately pronounced void, that is the position to which she is logically and invariably reduced.

The Law applicable in particular cases.

The law that applies in various cases differs and so is being discussed below separately for different cases.

Jurisdiction in respect of polygamous marriages : In the case of a polygamous marriage if the husband was already married at the time of marrying an English woman or after marrying her, he contracted a second (polygamous) marriage the English Courts did not at one time dissolve the English marriage. The reasoning advanced for this refusal was that the Court could not recognise the polygamous marriage, which was a void marriage and so the husband could not be considered to have contracted the same or to have two wives at the same time. But the view that the Court could not recognise a polygamous marriage on the ground that it was void naturally caused hardship to English women in some cases. It was realised, too, that the rule caused great hardship to the children born of such a marriage. The Courts were later also influenced by the decisions of the Privy Council which recognised the validity of polygamous marriages.[33] Thus the English Courts subsequently began to recognise such marriages for the purposes of incidental matters such as legitimacy, succession, maintenance etc. The Courts also began to take cognisance of and to dissolve such marriages. The reason for assumption of jurisdiction in such cases is explained to be that although no doubt the Court could not recognise the polygamous marriage, yet it could recognize the status of the husband as being a married person by reason of his previous polygamous marriage.[34]

The two views described above held by the English Courts respecting a polygamous marriage are obviously incom-

33. Baindail Vs Baindail, (1946) P. 122 (C.A.). 34. *Ibid.*

patible with each other and are, in fact, contradictory. If a polygamous marriage is held to be a legal nullity, it is surely illogical to concede that by contracting a polygamous marriage, a person acquires the legal status of a married person. In the case under discussion, we can see that the polygamous marriage being a nullity according to the English conception, the husband cannot be deemed to have acquired a married status or to be a married person. A married status can be acquired only after a legally recognised marriage. As soon as it is stated that a man has a married status, it follows by implication that he is validly married since if the marriage was a nullity, it could not give rise to any legal effect at all as a void marriage has no legal effect even before it is declared void by a Court. Void marriages are non-existent from the very beginning. If the English Court accepts the view of the husband's domicile that he is a married person, the fact cannot be ignored that the husband's domicile considers him a married person only because he is deemed to meet the essential prerequisite of having a valid marriage. If the marriage was void it could not find that the man had a married status. It is thus submitted that the view is not well founded. We have either to fully accept the view of Court of the husband's domicile in the case of a marriage between a Muslim or Hindu and an English woman or to ignore it altogether. But partial acceptance such as described earlier does have advantages for the English wife in such a marriage. As seen above, the marriage of an English woman could not be dissolved on the basis of bigamy under the concept of the English law when her husband contracted a second (polygamous) marriage during the subsistence of his marriage with her. The new modification of the English law helps the Court in dissolving such a marriage though, it is submitted with respect, on inadequate grounds. Nonetheless it is obvious that a Court in India or Pakistan would prefer to follow its own law and the principles of Private International Law and would not attach any importance to this view of the English Court relating to polygamous marriages. In a case decided in pre-partition India it was stated by Lodge, J., "a

Hindu marriage being potentially polygamous would not be recognised as valid by English Courts. But in India it would normally be recognised as valid marriage. I see no reason why the principle recognised in England in connection with Christian marriages should be applied in India to marriages which are not Christian marriages. To determine whether any particular marriage is valid in India or not an Indian Court will have to consider the personal law of the parties and to determine whether the two individuals can contract a valid marriage. The fact that English Courts might not recognise a particular marriage as valid is not conclusive as to its validity in India."[35] Thus, the Courts of the wife's domicile as well as the husband's domicile would both exercise jurisdiction in respect of the marriage, one holding it to be void while the other considering it to be valid which to say the least would be a very undesirable situation.

The result of the practice is that divergent jurisdictions shall be exercised and the English woman shall be considered an unmarried woman in England but the lawfully married wife of the Muslim husband in a Muslim or polygamous country.

Another criticism made against English Courts is that they assume jurisdiction in some cases, when they would deny similar jurisdiction to foreign Courts. It has been stated by a writer, "where, as in England, such jurisdiction is taken it seems, with respect, entirely indefensible to refuse to others what one has taken for oneself.[36] It was observed by another writer, "it is surely a strange system of law which gives its own country jurisdiction which it denies in similar circumstances to the Courts of other civilized countries."[37] Falconbridge and other writers have also raised this objection. This matter has been discussed at relevant places.

35. Sophy Anaenbach Vs. Shivprasad Agarwalla 49 C.W.N. 570.

36. Joseph Jackson, Nullity of Marriage, *The Canadian Bar Review*, Vol. XXVIII. No. 6, June-July 1950.

37. Garner. (1947) 63 L.Q.R. 486 at p. 489.

It has been stated before at several places that the English Courts do have recourse to exceptions to the general rules of Private International Law in order to help an English citizen. They thus assume jurisdiction in some cases which lie legally outside their control when it seems they could not exercise it and have openly stated their attitude in such matters. Thus it has been stated in a case, "No country is bound to recognise the laws of a foreign state when they work injustice to its own subjects."[38] It was observed in another case, "numerous examples may be suggested of the injustice which might be caused to our own subjects if a marriage were declared invalid on the ground that it is forbidden by the law of the domicile of one of the parties."[39] The assumption of jurisdiction to determine the character of marriage has been so well recognised in England that Dicey gives it as a rule of Private International Law and holds that it is the *lex loci celebrationis* that determines the nature of marriage, whether it is monogamous or polygamous.[40] It is submitted that the assumption of jurisdiction and the application of English law in many cases by having recourse to exceptions does not seem to be desirable. Foreign Courts on their part may try to help their own citizens and this will start a very undesirable conflict between Courts in different countries with the result that justice will be sacrificed in the desire to help one's own citizens.

There are bound to be differences between the laws of different countries in some cases. Thus a polygamous country may see no harm in polygamy but it is considered repugnant by English and many other Courts. Nonetheless, a conflict in laws leads to many complications and questionable dissolution of marriages in some cases. An attempt has, therefore, to be made to harmonise the different systems of law as far as possible.

38. Sotomayor Vs. De Barros, (No. 1) (1877) 3 P.D.I; Chetti Vs. Chetti, (1909), P. 67.
39. Simonin Vs. Mallac, (1860) 2 Sw and Tr 67; Chetti Vs. Chetti, (1909), P. 67.
40. Dicey and Morris, The Conflict of Law, rule 33, p. 275, London, 1967.

A foreign Court will probably not accept the binding force or even the validity of the exceptions to the general rules of Private International Law. After achieving independence the Courts of many countries prefer to exercise their own jurisdiction. In some cases and appeals the High Courts and the Supreme Court of Pakistan did exercise jurisdiction to decide cases where the wives were foreigners.[41] This they could do on the basis of the rule that the wife acquires the domicile of the husband thus placing the matter within their jurisdiction.

In recent years the English Courts and writers have taken a more liberal view in matrimonial matters than they used to do earlier.

We have to remember that in mixed marriages, that is, marriage between an English woman and a foreigner the intention is usually to settle in the husband's domicile. It should therefore be the *lex loci domicilii* or better the matrimonial domicile which should determine the character and other incidents resulting from the marriage.

The various other matters and the conditions under which the English Courts exercise jurisdiction are given below :

Void Marriages : The English Courts exercise jurisdiction to give a decree of nullity of a void marriage under the following circumstances :

(*a*) When both the parties to the marriage are domiciled in England at the time of the commencement of the proceedings.[42]

(*b*) When either party is domiciled in England at the time when the proceedings commence.[43]

41. Syed Ali Nawaz Gardezi, Vs. Lt. Col. Mohammad Yusuf Khan, PLD 1963 SC 51 ; Mrs. Marina Jatoi Vs. Nuruddin K. Jatoi PLD 1967 S.C. 580.
42. Lee Vs. Lau, (1964) 2 All, E.R. 248.
43. Von Lorang (Salvesen) Vs. The Administrator of Austrian Property 137 L.T. 571, (1927) A.C. 641 ; De Reneville Vs. De Reneville, (1948) 1 All. E.R. 56, (C.A) ; Ross Smith Vs. Ross Smith, (1962) 1 All. E. R. 344.

(*c*) When the respondent was residing within the jurisdiction of the English Court at the time when the proceedings were commenced.[44]

(*d*) When the marriage was celebrated in England.[45] It has been explained that the parties by professing to enter into a contract in a certain country mutually give to each other the right to have the force and effect of that contract determined by a tribunal of that country.[46]

(*e*) When the wife has been residing for the last three years in England immediately before the commencement of proceedings, provided that the husband is not domiciled in any other part of the United Kingdom or in certain other areas.[47]

Jurisdiction is assumed in the above cases on the reasoning that a void marriage is no marriage at all and does not create any rights and obligations and may be considered never to have existed and so the wife cannot be considered to have acquired the domicile of the alleged husband or to have lost her domicile at all. She can, therefore, take legal proceedings against her husband in the Courts of her own domicile. It is further explained that the rule that the wife shall have the same domicile as that of her husband takes effect only after

44 White Vs. White, (1937) P. 111 ; Kenward Vs. Kenward, (1950) 2 All. E.R. 297. De Reneville Vs. De Reneville, (1948) 1 All. E.R. 56 C.A. Har Shefi Vs. Har Shefi, (No. 1) (1953) 1 All. E.R. 793 (No. 2) (1953) 2 All. E.R 373 ; Lepre Vs. Lepre, (1965) P. 52.

45. Garthwaite Vs. Garthwaite, (1964) 2 All. E.R. 233 C.A. Russ Vs. Russ, (No. 2) (1964) P. 315.

46. Hussein Vs. Hussein (1938) 2 All. E.R. 344 Ross Smith Vs. Ross Smith, (1962) 1 All. E.R. 344 ; Lendrum Vs. Chakravarti (1929), S.L.T. 96; Corbett Vs. Corbett, (1957) 1 All. E.R. 621; Hill Vs. Hill, (1959) 3 All. E.R. 754 ; Hutter Vs. Hutter, (1944) 2 All. E.R. 368 ; Merker Vs. Merker, (1962) 3 All. E.R. 928.

47. Simonin Vs. Mallac. (1860) 2 Sw and Tr. 67, Ross Smith Vs. Ross Smith, (1962) 1 All. E.R. 344 ; Lendrum Vs. Chakravarty, (1929) S.L.T. 96.

solemnisation of the marriage and that before then the wife shall be considered to have her own domicile.

This rule is also justified on the ground that it is undesirable that the parties should not know at the date of the marriage if it is valid or invalid. This explanation is not very convincing. The question will arise only subsequent to the marriage and may not arise for a very long time. The idea underlying this rule can only be to help the English domiciled spouse by deciding the character of a marriage in accordance with the English law. But this is the function of the *lex domicilii.*

It was explained in a case that as long as the parties are not validly married, it would be begging the question to attribute to them a matrimonial domicile, which is a domicile by operation of law, inasmuch as the mere fact that a ceremony was gone through, would not change the domicile of the wife, and she would not, therefore, necessarily have the same domicile as her intended husband's.[48]

Voidable Marriages: In the case of voidable marriages an English Court exercises jurisdiction when :

(*a*) Both the parties were domiciled in England at the commencement of the proceedings.[49] The fact that the marriage was celebrated in some other country does not affect the Court's jurisdiction.[50] As stated before, a wife on her marriage acquires the domicile of her husband when the marriage is voidable and so in practice it would be the husband's domicile which shall give jurisdiction to the Court. It has been stated in a case that it shall make no difference if the husband does not protest against the exercise of jurisdiction by the English Court.[51]

48. 40 (1) a, b, Matrimonial Causes Act 1965.
49. Har Shefi Vs. Har Shefi, 1953) 1 All. E.R. 783.
50. Von Lorang Vs. Administrator of Austrian Property, (1927) A.C. 641 ; De Reneville Vs. De Reneville (1948) 1 All. E.R. 56.
51. Ramsay Fairfax Vs. Ramsay Fairfax, (1955) 3 All E.R. 695 C.A. Ross Smith Vs. Ross Smith (1962) 1 All. E.R. 344 ; Garthwaite Vs. Garthwaite (1964) 2 All. E.R. 233.

(*b*) Both the parties are residents in England.[52] But the residence of the petitioner alone does not give jurisdiction to a Court.[53]

It was stressed by Lord Greene "that a wife who is resident but exhypothesis not domiciled here can compel her husband who is both domiciled and resident abroad to come to this country, and submit the question of his status to the Courts of this country appears to me to be contrary both to principle and convenience." But this principle resulted in hardship to an English wife as when she was residing in a country far from the country of the husband's domicile or when the Courts of the husband's domicile followed laws not recognised by the English law such as polygamy, *ṭalāq*, that is, the husband's power to dissolve the marriage by his unilateral act, etc. We find that the English Matrimonial law was amended to give relief to the wife.

The mere solemnisation of marriage within the jurisdiction of a Court is not sufficient to confer jurisdiction on it.[54] Similarly the residence of the petitioner has not been considered sufficient to confer jurisdiction on a Court.[55]

(*c*) The English Courts assume jurisdiction also when only the respondent is residing in England at the commencement of the proceeding.[56]

(*d*) When a case falls within the provisions of sections 40 (1) (*a*) and 40 (1) (*b*) of the Matrimonial Causes Act 1965, Section 18 of the Matrimonial Causes Act 1950, range made two important exceptions to the

52. De Reneville Vs. De Reneville, (1948) 1 All. E.R. 56.
53. Ramsay Fairfax Vs. Ramsay Fairfax, (1955) 3 All. E.R. 695 C.A ; De Reneville Vs. De Reneville, (1948), 1 All. E.R. 56.
54. De Reneville Vs. De Reneville, (1948) 1 All. E.R. 56.
55. Ramsay Fairfax Vs. Ramsay Fairfax, (1956) P. 115 C A. ; Ross Smith Vs. Ross Smith/ (1962) 1 All. E.R. 344.
56. De Reneville Vs. De Reneville, (1948) 1 All. E.R. 56

general rule in favour of the wife. It reads as under;

> "18 (1) Without prejudice to any jurisdiction exercisable by the court apart from this section, the court shall by virtue of this section have jurisdiction to entertain proceedings by a wife in any of the following cases, notwithstanding that the husband is not domiciled in England, that is to say :
>
> (*a*) In the case of any proceedings under this Act other than proceedings for presumption of death and dissolution of marriage, if the wife has been deserted by her husband, or the husband has been deported from the United Kingdom under any law for the time being in force, relating to the deportation of aliens, and the husband was immediately before the desertion or deportation domiciled in England ;
>
> (*b*) In the case of proceedings for divorce or nullity of marriage, if the wife is resident in England and has been ordinarily resident there for a period of three years immediately preceding the commencement of the proceedings, and the husband is not domiciled in any other part of the United Kindom or in the Channel Islands or the Isle of Man."

It is provision (*b*) which is important from our point of view. The operation of this section is not restricted by the facts that the husband is not domiciled or resident in England or that the marriage was not solemnised there. It is obvious that the Court did not possess any jurisdiction to entertain a suit for divorce or nullity of marriage in these cases. It is meant merely to enable a wife to get a relief, which ordinarily she could not claim, without any regard to the hardship that may be caused to a husband domiciled and residing in a foreign country and not present in England at any stage of the proceedings. A foreign Court may feel justified in refusing to recognise the decree of an English Court when it violates the provisions of its own law.

Suit for judicial separation : The English Courts exercise jurisdiction in respect of cases for judicial separation under the following conditions :

(*a*) When the parties are domiciled in England at the commencement of the proceedings.[57]

(*b*) When the parties are residing in England at the time when the proceedings commenced.[58]

(*c*) When the respondent was residing in England at the commencement of the proceedings.[59]

This rule will lead to the result that if a Muslim, the husband of an English woman, happens to be temporarily residing in England, the wife shall have a right to sue him there though he may not be domiciled or resident there.

(*d*) When the matrimonial home of the parties is in England at the time when the cause of action arose.[60]

(*e*) When the case falls under the provisions of section 40 (1) (*a*) of the Matrimonial Causes Act, 1965.[61]

Suits for restitution of conjugal rights: The English Courts exercise jurisdiction when :

(*a*) The parties were domiciled in England at the time of commencement of the suit.[62]

(*b*) When the respondent was residing in England when the suit was instituted.[63]

57. Ross Smith Vs. Ross Smith, (1963) 1 All. E.R. 344 ; Garthwaite Vs. Garthwaite, (1964) 2 All E.R. 233.

58. Eustace Vs. Eustace, (1924) P. 45 ; Garthwaite Vs. Garthwaite, (1964) P. 356 (CA),

59. Armytage Vs. Armytage, (1898) P. 178 ; Matalon Vs. Matalon, (1952) P. 233 (C.A.)

60. Garthwaite Vs. Garthwaite, (1964) 2 All. E.R. 233

61. Ward Vs. Ward, (1923) 39 T.L.R, 440 ; Milligan Vs. Milligan, (1941) P. 78.

62. Baterman Vs. Baterman, (1901) P. 136 ; Brown Vs. Brown, (1917) 116 LT. 702 ; Garthwaite Vs. Garthwaite, (1964) 2 All. E.R. 233

63. Matalon Vs. Matalon, (1951) P. 233 ; Garthwaite Vs. Garthwaite, (1964) 2 All. E R. 233

(*c*) The parties had a matrimonial home in England at the time when cohabitation stopped.[64]

(*d*) The case is governed by the provisions of section 40 (1) (*a*) of the Matrimonial Causes Act, 1965.

Relief to parties. The English Courts try to help the parties in certain cases. An English Court may exercise jurisdiction if the respondent submits to its jurisdiction when, in the absence of such submission, the Court could not decide the case. Sometimes the parties or one of them may find it difficult to get the character of the marriage determined by the Court of the domicile. An English Court will then determine the character of the marriage by applying the law of the husband's domicile or the matrimonial domicile.[65] There can be no objection to this rule as jurisdiction is exercised simply to help the party concerned and no violation is done to the law of the domicile. An English Court may give a declaration as to whether the marriage of an English woman has been effectively dissolved by her husband according to his personal foreign law.[66]

The English Courts recognise the decree of divorce of a foreign Court if granted on the basis of such ground as are substantially similar to the provisions of English law. Thus the English law allows jurisdiction to English Courts to dissolve a marriage in certain cases such as desertion of the husband, if the wife has been living in England for at least three years before the presentation of her petition. It would, therefore, recognise the decree of a foreign Court on a similar ground. It has gone so far as to recognise a decree of a foreign Court even when the statutory period there is less than three years, but the wife has actually lived there for three years before presenting her petition.[67]

64 Ward Vs. Ward, (923) 39 TLR 440; Milligan Vs. Milligan, (1941) P. 78.

65. De. Reneville Vs. De. Reneville, (1948) 1 All. E.R. 56.

66. Mitford Vs. Mitford, (1923) P. 130; Har Shefi Vs. Har Shefi, (1957) 1 All. E.R. 621.

67. Arnold Vs. Arnold, (1953) P. 246 ; Manning Vs. Manning, (1958) 1 All. E.R. 291 ; Brown Vs. Brown, (1968) 2 All. E.R. 563,

Another rule that comes to the help of the parties is that a foreign Court within whose jurisdiction the parties are residing though they are not domiciled there can dissolve their marriage if the divorce granted by such Court would be held valid by the foreign Court.[68]

(*b*) *Law in the U.S.A.* : In the U.S.A., each State is considered to have full control over its citizens in respect of matrimonial and some other matters including the alteration of the marital status of the parties domiciled there. No other State can interfere with its sovereign powers over its citizens. This rule is based on the principle of law called Full Faith and Credit Clause contained in Article IV Section I of the Constitution of the United States of Amercia. It provides that Full Faith and Credit shall be given in each State to the Public Acts, Records and Judicial Proceedings of every other State.[69] Every State will recognise the divorce given by a competent Court of another State even when it is granted on the basis of a ground not recognised by it.[70] But the rule applies only in respect of the States of the U.S.A. and does not apply to foreign Courts. A State is bound to respect the decision of the Court of another State and to recognise a divorce given by such Court. This rule is, however, subject to the condition that the first Court had exercised its power properly so that its judgment was not without jurisdiction.[72] It will be perfectly open to a State to see if the other State did not act without jurisdiction. Moreover, the Courts of one State cannot divorce the citizens of another State.[73]

Conflict between the law in the U.S.A. and Muslim law : As observed before, Muslim law does not recognise domicile. It may happen that a Muslim may marry a woman whom he subsequently divorces according to his personal law which will be

68. Tijmica Vs. Tijmica, (1967) 3 All. E.R, 976.
69. Harris Vs. Balk, 198 U.S. 215.
70. Atherton Vs. Atherton, 181 U.S. 155.
71. Harding Vs. Harding, 198 U.S. 317.
72. Michigan Trust Co. Vs. Ferry, 228 US 346.
73. Bell Vs. Bell, 181 U.S. 175.

the same thing as the law of his domicile on this point. It appears from the decisions in respect of Jewish divorces that a Court in the U.S.A. will not recognise *Ṭalāq*. But the Courts in the U.S.A. recognise the validity of a divorce validly granted by a foreign Court. They, however, refuse to recognise a divorce if it is against the public policy of the American States or violates the American procedure. The Courts refused to recognise a unilateral divorce given by a Jew to his wife.[74] It appears that the same view may be expressed in the case of a *Ṭalāq*. The divorce shall, however, be considered valid by a Muslim country or a country which allows the Muslims to be governed by their own law.

74. Miller Vs. Miller, 128 N.Y.S. 782, Saperstone Vs. Saperstone, 131 NYS 241.

Section IX—Conversion of Husband and Wife

Preliminary: If a married person embraces Islam, the change of religion affects his or her marriage in several ways. These effects differ in the case of the husband from those of the wife and so it is necessary to discuss them separately. But before entering into a discussion of the matter it would be convenient to understand the basic principles relating to conversion under Muslim law as given below :

(1) The marriage of non-Muslims solemnised according to the provisions of their own religion shall be considered valid under Muslim law unless it contravenes some essential condition of the Muslim law or is invalid under their own law.[1]

(2) If both the spouses embrace Islam simultaneously or if the unconverted party embraces Islam when called upon to do so, the marriage shall be maintained, and they can continue to live as husband and wife[2].

(3) A Muslim can lawfully marry and remain the husband of a *Kitābiyah*, that is, a woman belonging to a revealed religion.[3]

(4) A Muslim cannot marry or be the husband of a woman who is neither a *Muslimāh* nor belongs to a revealed religion such as an idolatress.[4]

(5) A Muslim cannot marry the wife of another person.[5]

(6) A Muslim woman having a (living) husband, cannot marry another person,[6] and

(7) A Muslim woman cannot marry or be the wife of a non-Muslim.[7]

1. Ibn Abidin, *Radd al-Muḥtār* (along with *Durr al-Mukhtār*), Vol. II, p. 530, Egypt, 1324 A.H.; *Al-Fatawa al-Hindiyāh*, Vol. II, p. 38, Deoband.
2. *Ibid.*, p. 534 ; *ibid.*
3. *Ibid.*, p. 397 ; *ibid* , p. 8.
4. *Ibid.*
5. *Ibid.*, p. 380 ; *ibid.*, p. 7.
6. *Ibid.*, p. 381 ; *ibid.*, p. 8.
7. *Al-Fatawa al-Hindiyāh*, *op. cit.*, Vol. II, p. 8.

Husband's Conversion.—The important questions that may arise on a married Englishman's conversion to Islam can relate to the following matters :—

(1) Effect on the present marriage with an Englishwoman.

(2) The husband's right to contract another (polygamous) marriage,

(3) The husband's right to dissolve his marriage with the English wife by *Ṭalaq.*

The above matters are discussed below.

(1) *Effect on Existing Marriage:*—If a married Englishman embraces Islam while the wife remains a Christian, his marriage shall not be affected in any way. Under the Muslim law the marriage shall be maintained because a Muslim can lawfully marry and remain the husband of a woman belonging to a revealed religion.[8] Under the English law also the husband's change of religion shall not affect the marriage in any way because it is not an essential condition of English law that the husband shall also be a Christian nor is renunciation of Christianity a ground for divorce.

(2) *Whether the husband on his conversion can contract a second (polygamous) marriage.*—The question whether the Englishman will on his conversion to Islam acquire the right to contract a second (polygamous) marriage during the subsistence of the first marriage can be considered with regard to its two aspects, namely,

(*a*) in a Muslim or other polygamous country and

(*b*) in a monogamous country.

(*a*) *Second Marriage in a Muslim Country.*—Under the Muslim law or the law of a polygamous country the husband shall be perfectly free to contract another marriage or marriages up to four. The Muslim law shall hold his second marriage or marriages to be perfectly lawful wherever he may be settled or domiciled. On embracing Islam the husband shall acquire all

8. Ibn Abidin, *op. cit.*, Vol. II, p. 34 ; *Al-Fatawa al-Hindiyāh*, Vol. II, p. 8.

the rights which a Muslim possesses and so shall be competent to lawfully contract two or more (polygamous) marriages even when his first marriage with an Englishwoman is subsisting. The Muslim law shall not attach any importance to the law of his domicile. In a case where a Christian husband embraced Islam and contracted a second (polygamous) marriage, the Privy Council confirmed the order of the lower appellate Court quashing his conviction for bigamy. It observed, "Ceylon is a country of many races, many creeds and has a number of marriage Ordinaces and Acts. Whatever may be the situation in a purely Christian country (as to which their Lordships express no opinion) they cannot agree that in a country such as Ceylon, a Christian monogamous marriage prohibits for all time during the subsistence, of that marriage, a change of faith and of personal law on the part of the husband resident and domiciled there. In such countries there must be an inherent right in the inhabitants, domiciled there, to change their religion and personal law and so to contract a valid polygamous marriage if recognised by the law of the country notwithstanding an earlier marriage. If some inherent right is to be abrogated, it must be done by statute."[9]

It was stated in another case, "as soon as a person embraces Islam, he at once becomes subject to the Muslim personal and religious law and is completely cut off from his past. He accepts a new mode of life and enters a new domain where his deeds, words and actions are governed by the laws of his new religion. So far as his individual personality is concerned, there cannot be any doubt about it that his future in all aspects of life becomes amenable to Muslim law from the moment of his conversion to Islam. Although the act of conversion is unilateral, the legal consequences which flow from it directly affect the rights of others which but for the conversion they are entitled to enforce under their own personal law."[10] The religious laws have a far stronger hold in

9. Attorney-General of Ceylon Vs Reid, (1965) 1 All E. R. 812 (P.C.).
10. Farooq Lievers Vs. Adelaide Bridget Mary, P.L.D., 1958 Lah. 431.

a country governed by religious law than any secular law can have. Hence if the Englishman, after his conversion to Islam, were to come to a Muslim country, the country shall recognise his power of contracting a second (polygamous) marriage, even when he is domiciled in England or other monogamous country. It shall ignore the fact that the English law does not give him such a right and that the exercise of the power shall not be recognised in England.

The above discussion will show that the Muslim law will allow the English husband, converted to Islam, the right to contract another (polygamous) marriage or marriages with a *Muslimah* or a *Kitābiyah*, that is, a woman belonging to a revealed religion such as a Christian woman.

(*b*) *Second Marriage in England* :—The English law will not admit the English husband's right to contract another (polygamous) marriage even on his conversion to Islam because all persons domiciled in England are held there to be governed by the English law whatever their religion or nationality be. As the English law does not allow polygamy it will hold the husband's second marriage to amount to bigamy and so it shall be considered invalid in England. His first marriage will remain subsisting and valid, but the second marriage shall, however, entitle the first wife to claim the dissolution of her own marriage on the ground that her husband was guilty of bigamy and was living in adultery with his second wife.

Change of Nature of Marriage :—It has been held in some English cases that the nature of marriage can change and a polygamous marriage can become a monogamous marriage by a personal volition on the part of the husband by such acts as joining a monogamous sect after contracting a polygamous marriage or by a change of religion or domicile.[11]

Thus it was stated in an English case, ". . . But particularly in these days of wide-spread interpenetration of

11. Sinhas Peerage Claim; (1939) ; Mehta Vs. Mehta, (1945) 2 All. E. R. 690 ; Cheni Vs. Cheni, (1962) 3 All E. R. 873 ; Ali Vs. Ali, (1966) 1 All E, R. 664.

societies in different stages of development, it is not a reasonable presumption that spouses who marry polygamously will not by personal volition or act of state convert their marriages or have them converted into monogamous unions.[12] The question that arises in this connection is whether this rule will be applied also when the case is the reverse as when a man, married according to a monogamous form, embraces Islam or takes up his domicile in a polygamous country. Will his monogamous marriage change its nature and become a polygamous marriage. If we accept the general rule stated above, there seems no reason why its converse should not be held to be applicable in appropriate cases so that a monogamous marriage can change into a polygamous one by an act of personal volition by the husband.

It is most likely that the English law will not accept this position and it will be explained that an Englishman does not possess the capacity to be a party to a polygamous marriage. But this is an arbitrary rule laid down by English Courts and writers. There seems to be no reason why this rule should not apply in a converse case when the English husband takes his domicile in a polygamous country without changing his religion and then contracts a second (polygamous) marriage while his first marriage with the Englishwoman is subsisting. In Pakistan and some other countries the citizens are governed by their personal laws. The second marriage being unlawful under his religious and personal law would have been considered unlawful there. But this new conception of English law that a husband can change the nature of his marriage by personal volition will come to his help in a Muslim or other polygamous country. It is very likely to follow the rule laid down by the English Courts in the instant case. A Court in Pakistan is almost certain to hold the second polygamous marriage of the Englishman to be valid if he takes up his domicile in Pakistan.

12. Ali Vs. Ali, (1966) 1 All E. R. 664.

(3) *Muslim Husband's Right of Ṭalāq*

A Muslim marriage differs in many respects from an English marriage. Thus it can be dissolved by the husband by his unilateral act or *ṭalāq*. Muslim law, as discussed in previous chapters, allows the husband the power to dissolve his marriage at his sweet will without the consent of or even without information to the wife of the same. It has been discussed earlier that the idea of indissolubility of marriage was found to be impracticable by the English Courts and so was given up. Morris has stated, "moreover since 1857, it is no longer true that a marriage must be for ever or never. The policy of the state is to recognise and provide facilities for divorce."[13]

English Courts' Refusal to Recognise Validity of Ṭalāq :

The English Courts at one time refused to accept the husband's power to dissolve his marriage solemnised in England with an Englishwoman by *ṭalāq*, even when the *lex loci domicilii* or the law of the matrimonial domicile allowed it, The first question that arises in this connection is whether the English Courts have a right to deny recognition to it. The legal implications of the *lex loci contractus* and *lex loci domicilii* are well-defined and cannot and should not be mixed up. The validity of the formation of marriage is obviously to be determined by the law of the place where it is solemnised. Similarly, the dissolution of marriage is no part of the formation of marriage, but relates to the incidents arising later out of the contract of marriage. Under the Private International Law it is the *lex loci contractus* that shall determine whether the contract of marriage has been properly entered into. It naturally cannot be affected by what may happen in future, as for example, the dissolution of the marriage. The law relating to the latter is under the Private International Law

13. Morris, J. H. C., Nullity Jurisdiction, and Re-marriage, during voidable marriage, *The Law Quarterly Review*, Oct. 1945, Vol. VI, p. 341 at p. 345.

the law of the domicile. The scope of the *lex loci celebrationis* is only to see whether the marriage has been solemnised according to its law and whether the essential conditions for the valid creation of the married status have been fulfilled. Once this is done the scope of the *lex loci contractus* comes to an end and it is in no way concerned as to what may happen in future. Hence the English Courts have no justification to refuse to recognise *ṭalāq* when it is permissible under the law of the domicile. Some English Courts have considered that they have the power to decide the validity of *ṭalāq* or Muslim unilateral divorce by the husband without the intervention of any Court. This conception of the English law violates the principles of Private International Law that in the matter of essentials which must include the dissolution of marriage, it shall be the law of the husband's domicile that shall decide the matter. As a matter of fact this conception goes against the decisions of the English Courts themselves. Thus it was decided in a case that the status of the spouses and the rights and consequences arising from the marriage are to be determined by the law of the country which by the contract of the marriage becomes the domicile of both the parties.[14] Smilarly it has also been held that the rights and obligations of the parties relating to the dissolution of marriage do not form part of the contract of marriage, but arise out of and are incidental to such contracts and are governed by the *lex loci domicilii.*[15] It is obvious that the *lex loci contractus* cannot impose its own conditions for the incidents that do not form part of the contract of marriage but which may arise in future in consequence of the marriage having taken place. Hence, if a Muslim marries an Englishwoman in England the English Court is only concerned with the fact that the conditions considered by it to be essentials for the formation of marriage have been fully observed. How is the marriage to be regulated in future is the function of the matrimonial domicile. If the

14. Harvey Vs. Farnie, (1882) 8 A. C. 35.
15. *Ibid.*

latter allows the dissolution of a marriage by *ṭalāq*, the English Court is not concerned with the matter.

If we study English decisions, we find a curious thing that the Jewish divorces are accepted as valid even though the husband can dissolve the marriage by his unilateral act by giving a get or bill of divorcement to the wife in the presence of Beth Din. Get has been nicely described by Keezer in his valuable book on the Law of Marriage and Divorce as under :

"The divorce paper is termed a 'get' which is thus defined and described : A bill of divorce among the Jews. Like the Ketulva, or marriage contract, this document is drawn up in the Aramaic language, uniformly worded and carefully written by a proper scribe. The orthodox form must contain twelve full and equal lines (neither more nor less) to agree with the numerical value in Hebrew of the letters G.T. After certain preliminary ceremonies and questioning by the rabbi, particularly as to whether both parties agree to the divorce, the husband hands the "get" to his wife in the presence of ten witnesses. In the "get" is contained the date, the names and surnames of the husband and wife and of their fathers, and also the name of the city and its location (whether near a river or sea). After the first lines, containing the date, it runs : I, N., son of N., of the city of N., situated on the river N., set thee free, my wife, N., daughter of N., of the city of N., etc. Thou art set free and art at liberty to marry any man whom thou mayest choose. This document from me is a letter of divorcement and liberty according to the Law of Moses and Israel."[16]

It may be pointed out here that the English Courts' refusal to admit the validity of the unilateral divorce when the Jewish spouses were domiciled in England.[17] It is submitted that this view is perfectly correct because the law that governed the

16. Keezer, Frank. H., *The Law of Marriage and Divorce*, Art. 70 p. 97 Indianapolis, 1946.

17. Preger Vs. Preger, (1926) 134 L. T. 670 ; Spivack Vs. Spivack, (1930) 142 L. T, 492.

validity of the divorce was the law of the domicile of the parties which in this case was the English law which does not allow dissolution of marriage in this manner. Where, however, the husband was domiciled in Israel the English Court considered the divorce to be effective.[18] This view is based on the ground that the law of domicile permits such a divorce. In another case where the Jewish parties were domiciled in Egypt, the Privy Council held such a divorce to be valid, because the Court felt itself bound to recognise and apply the religious laws and customs of non-Christians.[19]

The objections to *ṭalāq* raised by English Courts in various cases and the grounds for the refusal to accept its validity may be summarised as under:

(*a*) It is against natural justice that one party should dissolve the marriage by his unilateral act without the consent of and even without information to the wife;

(*b*) It is opposed to public policy ; and

(*c*) It is inapplicable to a marriage solemnised in English form.[20]

(*a*) *Ṭalāq opposed to natural justice*: One of the grounds given by English Courts and some writers is that unilateral divorce is against natural justice. Thus it was stated in a case that it was opposed to natural justice to allow a man to determine his marriage at his sweet will or pleasure without the consent of or even communication with the woman concerned. It was observed, "Here it is not suggested that there was any consent on the part of the woman; it is the man seeking to be or purporting to be a judge in his own cause, and dissolving his marriage without any communication with the woman or any consent on her part affecting her rights as well as his own. I think it is contrary to natural justice that a man should be a judge in his own cause and determine his marriage at his sweet

18. Har Shefi Vs, Har Shefi, (1953) 2 All. E. R. 373.
19. Sasson Vs. Sasson, (1924) A. C. 1007; 132 L. T. 162.
20. R. Vs. Hammersmith, Superintendent Registrar of Marriages, Ex-Parte Mir Anwaruddin, (1916, 17) All. E. R, 37.

will and pleasure."[21] It is very difficult to lay down a universal rule of law as to what is and what is not in consonance with natural justice and the concept of natural justice differs with different people, communities and countries. Thus Muslim law considers that it is unjust to tie down a woman to a marriage when her husband is insane but a Judge in the U.S.A. held at one time that justice demanded that a marriage should not be dissolved on the ground of the husband's insanity.[22] An Englishman may impose a new domicile on the wife by his unilateral act and thus subject her to laws and conditions which she may not like. The English husband and the English law see nothing wrong in such an act, but most of the Muslims will consider the law very unfair. When an Englishman takes up his domicile in an unfriendly country, the wife shall automatically acquire the same domicile. Will it be in consonance with justice to force her to become subject to the laws of that country and live in conditions which she may not like at all. The expression and the idea of natural justice are uncertain and different communities do differ in their view of natural justice in respect of a certain matter when one may consider it to be in perfect accord with natural justice while another may hold it to be otherwise. It was nicely stated, it it is submitted, by the Calcutta High Court: "The good conscience of one is the bad conscience of the other".[23] Thus an Englishman finds it against natural justice that the husband should have the right to divorce his wife by his unilateral act at his own sweet will and pleasure without the consent of or without communication with the wife. A Muslim, however, sees nothing wrong in it because he feels that the wife knew of the law and has entered into the contract of marriage in spite of this knowledge so that it can safely be presumed that she has willingly accepted this position. Another ground is that the husband's act of divorcing the wife clearly establishes

21. R. Vs. Hammersmith, Superintendent Registrar of Marriages, Ex-Parte Mir Anwaruddin, (1916, 17) All, E. R. 37; Russ Vs. Russ (1962) 1 All. E. R. 649.

22. Baker Vs. Baker, 82 Ind. 146.

23. Noor Jahan Vs. Eugene Tiscenko, A.I.R. 1941 Cal. 581.

the fact that the wife has lost his love for her so much so that he does not want to maintain any relation with her and that it is futile to continue the marriage in such circumstances and the termination of the marriage is preferable to prolonging the miserable lives of the parties or at least of one of them—particularly when the Muslim law does not see anything wrong in re-marriage and does not attach any restrictions to the parties' re-marriage. It was stated in an American case, "A cause more consonant with the mores of the times and needs of society would be to permit divorce where the marriage end has been frustrated by moral or criminal offense or incapacity".[24] The English Courts have realised the difficulty underlying the problem and that there may be cases in which it would be fully in accord with justice to give recognition to *ṭalāq* in the particular circumstances of a case though in some other cases it may not be just to give effect to it. It was stated in a case, "There may, indeed, be other circumstances in which such a divorce would be recognised by English law, *e.g.*, if the Court was satisfied that in all the circumstances it would be just to grant recognition (to *ṭalāq*)".[25] The Court further observed, "The Court retains a residual discretion not to apply the law of the domicile when it is not proper to do so in the circumstances of a particular case." The Court considered that justice required that *ṭalāq* be recognised in the case before it. It was further observed by the Court that there was no denial of justice where the wife entered into the marriage, intending to follow her husband to Egypt, to go through a Mohammedan ceremony of marriage when she arrived there and to live with him in Egypt. Furthermore, she did all these things, living with him in Egypt for some eighteen years....she seems to have been a consenting party to the *ṭalāq* (divorce) in 1932. She was certainly present when it was pronounced, and, thereafter, she regulated her life affairs in reliance on it...."[25]

24. Potet Vs. Potet, 114 Pac. 91 ; 45 N. Mex. 214.
25. Russ Vs. Russ, (1962) 1 All E. R. 649.

Hence, there can be no question of denial of justice when a Muslim husband dissolves his marriage with an English wife by *ṭalāq*. The Englishwoman, in the case of such a marriage generally intends to pass her whole life in the foreign land, the country of the husband. It will be reasonable to assume that she must acquaint herself with the essentials of the law that shall govern her marriage, namely, the husband's right to contract a second marriage and to dissolve her own marriage by his unilateral act, namely, by *ṭalāq*. Moreover if the English Court did not attach any importance to a Russian divorce or a Jewish divorce, which too were unilateral, there seems to be no reason why recognition should not be given to a *ṭalāq* by a Muslim husband to his English wife.

(*b*) *Ṭalāq is opposed to public policy*: As has been discussed in a previous topic, the expression, "public policy" is very vague and uncertain. Different countries have laid down different rules of public policy and one country may consider a matter to be lawful and proper under its public policy while another country may not hold it so. There can be no object to this ground if we apply the expression "opposed to English public policy". There are things which are allowed under the English public policy but which are considered very undesirable under the Islamic public policy. Every nation has a perfect right to frame its own public policy to meet its particular requirements. The matter of public policy has been fully discussed in the topic of "Validity of Marriage."

(*c*) *Inapplicability of ṭalāq to English marriages*: It has also been stated that a Christian marriage cannot be dissolved by a method of divorce which is appropriate to polygamous marriages.[26] But it is not clear how the nature of marriage, namely, whether it is monogamous or polygamous can affect the justifiability of divorce. If *ṭalāq* is inappropriate it shall remain so irrespective of the fact whether the marriage is

26. R. Vs. Hammersmith, Superintendent Registrar of Marriages, Ex-Parte Mir Anwar--ud-Din, (1916, 17) All E. R. 37.

monogamous or polygamous. How is it appropriate to a polygamous marriage and inappropriate to a monogamous marriage?

A case of this nature came up for decision before the Supreme Court of Pakistan in 1963. The Court discussed some decisions of the English Courts and referred to Dicey and Cheshire and then added, "The trend of modern English authorities, therefore, appears to be that if the law of the domicile permits a dissolution of marriage by the pronouncement of *ṭalāq* the divorce may be recognised as valid under the rules of Private International Law in other courts as well."[27] The Court accordingly gave effect to *ṭalāq*, gives in Pakistan by the Muslim husband, domiciled in Pakistan, against a European woman where the marriage was solemnised in England by the Registrar of Marriages and the wife was living with her husband in Pakistan. It may be noted here that the wife had embraced Islam but even if she had remained a Christian her domicile would have been the same as that of her husband. In another case the wife, domiciled and married in England, retained her Christian faith and did not come to Pakistan but remained all along in England. Even then a Karachi Bench of the High Court of West Pakistan held the *ṭalāq* given by the husband to be effective. The Supreme Court of Pakistan upheld this judgment by a majority of the judges.[28] It observed that the latest judicial trend in England favours the principle that if the law of the domicile permits a dissolution of marriage solemnized in England, by the pronouncement of *ṭalāq*, the divorce may be recognised as valid under the rules of Private International Law. This view is obviously based on the fact that the Courts in India and Pakistan are no longer bound by the English law. It may be added here that the views expressed by Ameer Ali, Tyebji and others to the contrary do no longer hold good as those views were expressed when India

27. Syed Ali Nawaz Gardezi Vs. Col. Muhammad Yusuf Khan, P. L. D. 1963 S. C. 51.

28. Mrs. Marina Jatoi Vs. Nur-ud-Din K. Jatoi, P. L. D., (1967) S. C. 580.

was subject to British rule and to the English matrimonial law. With the achievement of independence these countries are no longer bound by the English law and so will naturally give effect to their own laws.

The power of divorce given to the husband by the laws of his religion and domicile was denied to him by the English Courts on some other grounds also. In R Vs. Hammersmith, Superintendent Registrar of Marriages, Ex parte Mir Anwaruddin, the Court relied mainly on the ground that the husband could not obtain a decree from the courts of his domicile, namely, India. Another ground taken in that and in some other cases is the absence of any judicial proceeding or decree when a marriage is dissolved by *ṭalāq*.[29]

Thus the other grounds for refusing to accept the validity of *ṭalāq* are (*a*) Inability to get a decree of divorce on the basis of *ṭalāq* from the Courts of his domicile and (*b*) Absence of any judicial proceeding.[30]

(*a*) As regards the first ground, it was no doubt true that an Indian Court could not give a decree for divorce on the basis of *ṭalāq* when the wife was a domiciled Englishwoman. The powers of the Indian Courts were defined by the Indian and Colonial Divorce Jurisdiction Act, 1926. Section 1 of the Act provides that,

(1) Subject to the provisions of this Act (a High Court in British India constituted by His Majesty by Letters Patent) shall have jurisdiction to make a decree for the dissolution of a marriage....where the parties to the marriage are British subjects domiciled (in any part of the United Kingdom), in any case (where a court in British India) would have such jurisdiction if the parties to the marriage were domiciled in India:

Provided that—

(*a*) the grounds on which a decree for the dissolution of such a marriage may be granted by any such court

29. (1916, 17) All E. R. 37.
30. *Ibid.*

*shall be those on which a decree might be granted by the High Court in England according to the law for the time being in force in England** ; and

(*b*) any such court in exercising such jurisdiction shall act and give relief on principles and rules as nearly as may be conformable to those on which the High Court in England for the time being acts and gives relief....".

The above provisions make it clear that the Indian High Courts were empowered to give a decree for the dissolution of marriage only on those grounds on which a decree could be given in England. As a decree could not be given on the basis of *ṭalāq* in England, the same could not be given in India also. But this and other similar provisions have become inoperative after the independence of the former India and the creation of the two new independent countries, namely India (Bharat) and Pakistan. The Courts of these countries are no longer subject to the law of England and the Courts in Pakistan did hold otherwise in several cases and it is now open to a husband to get a decree that his marriage with a certain woman has been dissolved by *ṭalāq* even when the wife is a domiciled Englishwoman.

(*b*) Another ground for refusing to recognise a *ṭalāq* is the absence of any judicial proceeding in this method of dissolving a marriage. Thus an English Court did not recognise a divorce given without judicial proceeding and considered it absurd that, "if there were a country in which marriage could be dissolved without any judicial proceeding at all, merely by the parties agreeing *in pais* (that is, without legal proceeding) to separate, every other country ought to sanction a separation had *in pais* there...."[31]. The same view was expressed in a later case where it was held, "English law will not recognise a foreign divorce unless it has been decreed by a court of law."[32] This view may be discussed from its two

*Italics supplied.

31. Warrender Vs. Warrender, (1835) 2 Cl. & F. 488.
32. R. Vs. Hammersmith, Superintendent Registrar of Marriages, Ex-Parte Mir Anwar-ud-Din (1916, 17) All E. R. 37.

aspects, namely,

(*i*) When the wife has her domicile in a Muslim country or a country allowing polygamy ; and

(*ii*) When the wife is an English domiciled woman.

As regards (*i*) there can be no objection to the validity of *ṭalāq* in such a case because the wife shall be subject to the provisions of Muslim or civil law which allows divorce. A large number of Privy Council rulings support this view. *Ṭalāq* as well as the dissolution of Jewish marriages by giving the wife a "get", or letter of divorcement before the Beth Din, without the intervention of the Court has been held valid by the Privy Council. It was stated by that Court in a case, "The Court had no jurisdiction itself to dissolve a marriage. It had, however, jurisdiction to declare rights and, in matters relating to marriage.........it was bound in the case of persons not belonging to Christian countries to recognize and apply the religious law and custom of the persons concerned ....Now, the court of domicile here could not grant divorce, but on the other hand it was bound......to acknowledge the validity of a divorce good according to the religious law of the non-Christian subjects."[33]

(*ii*) When the wife is an English domiciled woman judicial proceedings themselves have no inherent virtue, but are and can be meant to ensure that the marriage should be dissolved on a reasonable ground or in compliance with the local law. But what constitutes reasonable ground is a matter so difficult and even uncertain that its determination is almost impossible ; different countries and different communities have sometimes entertained different views in the same matter. Some States in the U.S.A. hold incompatibility of temperament to be a sufficient ground for the dissolution of a marriage.[34] An English Court will not, however, hold it to be a sufficient ground. A sect of the Jews hold that a Jewish

33. Sasson Vs. Sasson, (1924) A. C. 1007.

34. Alaska, Compiled Laws, 1933 ; New Mexico, Statutes, 1941.

marriage may be dissolved on the ground that the food was not properly cooked by the wife.[35] It would be seen from the above discussion that no definite law can be laid down as to what are sufficient grounds for the dissolution of a marriage.

The Muslim jurists seem to have considered that man is a rational being ; all his acts are based on some reason or other. He may express his reason for his conduct in a certain case or he may not express it. Thus the consent to a contract may be express or implied — to be inferred from his conduct. In the same way a man's reason for doing or failing to do a certain act may be unexpressed, to be inferred only from his subsequent conduct. They, therefore, do not make it a condition of the dissolution of marriage by *ṭalāq* that the husband should state his reason for his act. There is a great difference between the Muslim and the English conception about a marriage. As discussed before, Muslim law attaches great importance to the happiness of the spouses. A husband will not dissolve his marriage, in the opinion of the Muslim jurists, unless he is unhappy with the same. Muslim law, therefore, allows the spouses to dissolve their marriage by mutual consent or its dissolution by the husband by his unilateral act, that is by *ṭalāq*, and by the wife by her unilateral act under the provisions of *Khiyār al-Bulugh* (option of puberty) *tafwid*, that is, when the power of divorce has been delegated to her by the husband and also under the doctrine of *khul'*. The Muslim jurists, therefore, do not make it a condition of marriage that it shall not be dissolved except by an order of the *Qāḍi*. This view is divergently opposed to the view of the English law. The question, however, is whether a divorce given without the intervention of the Court is to be held invalid in every case. As stated before, the English Courts have recognised as valid extra-judicial divorce given according to the Jewish law, and have granted a decla-

35. Boden Worsley, J. F. W , *Mischief of the Marriage Law*, p. 49, London, 1932.

ration on the basis of such divorce that the marriage had been dissolved.[36] In some recent cases, the English Courts have extended their recognition to a divorce by the unilateral act of the husband without the intervention of the Court when there was some judicial record of the divorce.[37] It was pointed out by the appellate Court that validity of a *ṭalāq* (divorce) depended not on the existence of any decree, but on whether such a divorce would be recognised by the court of the domicile.[38] This new trend of the English Courts shows that emphasis is not laid on the judicial intervention in the matter but only on the existence of proof that a divorce has really been given. This condition is satisfied in many Muslim countries where registration of divorce has been made compulsory. In Pakistan, the Muslim Family Laws Ordinance, 1961, has made it obligatory on a husband, who divorces his wife, to give written information of the *ṭalāq* to the Chairman of the Union Council where it shall be entered in the register maintained for the purpose by the Union. He has also to send a copy of the same to his wife. This procedure practically amounts to the registration of the divorce,

This procedure ought to suffice for a Muslim husband to obtain a declaration that his marriage has been dissolved by his exercise of the power of *ṭalāq*. Under the provisions of the Code of Civil Procedure, applicable in India and Pakistan, such a suit can be instituted where the defendant resides or where the cause of action arose. In such a case, the cause of action shall arise where the divorce was pronounced.

It is also to be noted that judicial proceedings can only serve the purpose to see if the husband has acted lawfully on the basis of a genuine ground. But, as stated before, the Muslim husband can divorce his wife without any cause or to be more exact, without disclosing the cause for pronouncing the *ṭalāq*. Moreover, it is not open to the wife of a Muslim to

36. Har Shefi Vs. Har Shefi, (1952) 2 All E. R. 821; (on appal) (1953) 1 All E. R, 783.
37. Russ Vs. Russ, (1962) 1 All E. R. 649.
38. (1964) All E. R.

object to her husband's act (of divorcing her) and so judicial proceeding can serve no purpose.

It was observed by an English Court in a case "In general, the status of a person depends on his personal law, which is the law of his domicile".[39] In that case an Egyptian had married an English woman whom he divorced after some years. In Egypt, *ṭalāq* must be given before an authorised officer of the Court, concerned with questions of personal status, whose duty it is to record the *ṭalāq* in the records of the Court which constitutes the recognition by the Courts of the fact of the divorce.

The Court did not attach any importance to the fact that the Egyptian law would recognise a *ṭalāq* if pronounced in the presence of two witnesses even without any proceeding, and that there was no judicial investigation and no decree, but was satisfied that, "nevertheless the Egyptian Courts make available a procedure of judicial recognition and record appropriate to such an important matter as a change of status". It was held in the case that there was judicial process in the courts of the domicile, of recognition and record. It was not deemed necessary that there should be any decree or judicial investigation in the matter. The Court recognised the validity of a *ṭalāq* when it stated, "If, therefore, English law may recognise as a married person one who has entered into a polygamous marriage how can it be said that English law will never recognize as unmarried one who, being domiciled in a country where polygamy is recognized, by his or her personal law, has been validly divorced under that law". The Court held the *ṭalāq* given by the Muslim husband to his English wife to have been effected. It distinguished the Hammersmith decision on the ground that there was absence of any judicial proceeding about the divorce in the Court of the domicile in that case and that such was not the case of the petitioner before it. The decision was confirmed in appeal. It establishes the validity of a *ṭalāq* given according to the law of the husband's

39 Russ Vs. Russ, (1962) 1 All E. R. 649,

domicile which also becomes the domicile of the wife if there is some judicial record of it. The Court also relied on the following observation made in Harvey Vs. Farnie : [40]

"When a marriage has been duly solemnized according to the law of the place of solemnization, the parties become husband and wife. But when they become husband and wife, what is the character which the wife assumes ? She becomes the wife of the foreign husband in a case where the husband is foreigner in the country in which the marriage is contracted. She no longer retains any other domicile than his, which she acquires. The marriage is contracted with a view to that matrimonial domicile which results from her placing herself by contract in the relation of wife to the husband, whom she marries, knowing him to be a foreigner, domiciled and contemplating permanent and settled residence abroad. Therefore, it must be within the meaning of such a contract, if we are to inquire into it, that she is to become subject to her husband's law in respect of the consequences of the matrimonial relation and other consequences depending upon the law of the husband's domicile. The Court then stated the following propositions :

(1) As a general rule English law looks to the law of the domicile to determine status.

(2) The Courts have a discretion and may in a proper case refuse to recognise a status conferred or imposed on a person by the laws of his domicile and will reach their decision "with due regard to common sense and some attention to reasonable policy."

(3) In the particular matter of *ṭalāq* (divorce) the courts have refused to recognize the status imposed on a woman by the mere pronouncement of *ṭalāq* in her absence and in the absence of any proceeding in the courts of the domicile.

(4) It is in consonance with principle and not inconsistent with the *ratio decidendi* of the Hammersmith case for the Court in a proper case to recognise a change of status effected

40. Russ Vs. Russ, (1964) All, E. R.

by a *ṭalāq* (divorce) if that divorce itself has been recognised and recorded in the Courts of the domicile.

The Court also observed, "There may be other circumstances which would be recognised by English law e.g. if the Court were satisfied that in all the circumstances it would be just to grant recognition."

In a recent case two Chinese, husband and wife, mutually dissolved their marriage in accordance with the local law of Hong Kong where they were domiciled "because of surroundings and difference in temperament."[41] This they did by a written document which was authenticated by the "chop" or seal of the local organisation. There was no evidence that the agreement of divorce was made in the presence of anybody. This distinguished the case from the case of Russ vs. Russ (1962) 1 All. E.R. 649, where the *ṭalāq* had been effected in the presence of a Court official and recorded in the records of that Court. There was no such evidence in the Hong Kong case. Cairns J. posed several questions for answer in the case as given below :

(1) Has this court jurisdiction to declare that a marriage, celebrated abroad, has been dissolved by procedure which would dissolve that marriage according to the law of the domicile of the parties ?

(2) If so, can that jurisdiction be exercised when the divorce procedure was by way of a mere agreement and not by any judicial act ?

(3) (No material here).

(4) Can such jurisdiction be exercised if the marriage was potentially polygamous ? and

(5) Assuming that there was a valid marriage, was it validly dissolved by the contract of divorce according to the law of Hong Kong ?

The Court then decided the above points as under :

(1) Relying on Har Shefi vs. Har Shefi, it held that it had jurisdiction to declare that a marriage celebrated abroad

41. Lee Vs. Lau, (1964) 2 All, E. R. 248.

has been dissolved by a procedure which would dissolve that marriage according to the law of the domicile of the parties when the petitioner was domiciled in England.

(2) The Court relying on Ratanachari vs. Ratanachari and Russ vs. Russ held that it could give the declaration sought when the marriage was dissolved by mutual agreement if it was monogamous and divorce by agreement was possible under the local law. This was held even when there was no evidence that the divorce agreement was made in the presence of anybody but was presented to a local organisation and sealed with the seal or "chop" of that body.

(3) The Court stated that the Court will not adjudicate on a marriage without proof that a valid marriage was celebrated but it could adjudicate on a ceremony of marriage without holding that it was a valid marriage. It could, however, adjudicate on the validity of the divorce when it is merely asked to grant a declaration determining status when the husband only wishes to know if he is at the moment free to marry. The Court can grant such a declaration without determining whether the marriage was valid.

(4) The Court will not adjudicate on a potentially polygamous union. The Court, however, held that the status of the husband should be determined before his intended second marriage and that he ought not to have to go to the Hong Kong Courts to obtain such a determination. The Court relying on Har Shefi Vs. Har Shefi stated that, in recent years the English Courts have leaned strongly in favour of enabling a person, domiciled and resident in England, to obtain a decision about his matrimonial status without having to go to a Court abroad for the purpose.

It will be seen from the above discussion that the English Courts are not justified in refusing to give recognition to *ṭalāq*. But it must be noted that they are now becoming less rigid in the matter and use discretion and take a more realistic view in favour of such recognition in appropriate cases. There are also English writers who have assumed a fair and more liberal attitude in this matter. Moreover, the English people now do realise the necessity for divorce in certain cases. Thus a Bill has been passed by the Parliament which permits divorce by mutual consent as well as unilateral divorce, the only condition being that in the former case the spouses must have lived apart for two years and in the latter case for five years. Moreover, the marriage can be dissolved only by the decree of a Court. This provision differs from *ṭalāq*, in two respects, namely, (1) A decree for divorce must be obtained from a competent Court and (2) the spouses must have lived apart for a specified period of time. We may examine here how far are the English provisions an improvement on the Muslim provisions of *ṭalāq*.

(1) When the parties can exercise the right to the dissolution of marriage, the only purpose served by the Court's decree would be to provide documentary proof of the fact of the divorce. This provision is now provided in many Muslim countries where registration of the divorce has been made compulsory.

(2) Muslim law does not consider it necessary that the parties should live apart for any specified period of time. It only fixes a period of three months time for reconciliation of the parties. It is submitted that in the first place the period is not necessary and in any case it is too long and unreasonable. The only purpose it can serve is to ensure that the parties are not acting in a hasty and irresponsible manner but are sincere in their desire for the dissolution of their marriage.

Law in the U.S.A.: It may happen sometimes that a Muslim may marry a woman in the U.S.A. whom he may subsequently divorce according to his personal law which will be the same thing as the law of his domicile or even the law of the matrimonial domicile. There is no American case-law to indicate the view that will be taken by the Courts in the U.S.A. in such a case. But the refusal to admit the validity of a Jewish divorce gives an indication of the attitude that will be taken in respect of a *ṭalāq*.[42] It has already been stated before

42. Sapperstone Vs. Sapperstone; 131 N. Y. S. 241 : Miller Vs. Miller 128 N. Y. S. 787; Keezer, *Law of Marriage and Divorce*, Art. 71, p. 98.

that the Jewish law, like the Muslim law, allows unilateral divorce by the husband. It is very likely that the same view may be expressed in respect of a *ṭalāq*.

Conclusion : It cannot be denied that hardship is caused sometimes to a woman of a foreign non-Muslim country when her Muslim husband divorces her without making any arrangement for her future financial support. This position is aggravated if children are born to them. As the Courts in Pakistan uphold the *ṭalāq*, the wife is not entitled to future maintenance except for three months after the *ṭalāq*. This position may be inequitable in some cases. But it can be avoided to some extent if it be made the duty of the Registrar of Marriages in different countries to explain to the wife the polygamous nature of her marriage and the husband's right of *ṭalāq*. She may also take advantage of the Muslim doctrine of *Tafwīd* and settle necessary terms for her future safeguard. It should also be the duty of a Court in Pakistan to do full justice in a case and to help a wife who is exposed to great future risk and hardship when her Pakistani husband recklessly terminates the marriage without making any arrangement for her maintenance. We must remember that Islam strongly condemns the attitude of men who relish in variety in sexual relations. The example of the Lahore High Court, discussed before, may be followed in all appropriate cases.[43] We must do full justice in a case without allowing technicalities to stand in the way ofa dministration of justice.

Englishman's marriage with a Muslimah : It has been stated before that a Muslimah (a Muslim woman) cannot marry a non-Muslim even though he may belong to a revealed religion. If in spite of the prohibition she does contract such a marriage, it shall be considered void under the Muslim law. It shall not give rise to any legal effect so that it shall not-even be necessary to dissolve it. Whether the husband re

43. Farooq Lievers, Vs. Adelaide Bridget Mary, P. L. D, 1958, Lah. 431.

tains his own domicile or acquires a domicile in a Muslim country shall be immaterial from the Muslim point of view and shall not affect the marriage under the Muslim law in any way. The marriage shall remain void wherever the person may be domiciled.

English Law : Under the English law, a marriage to be valid must be monogamous. Where a domiciled Englishman marries a woman in a polygamous country according to the local forms, then under the English law, the marriage shall even then be considered monogamous. Thus it was observed in a case "An Englishman, marrying in Turkey, contract a marriage of the English kind, that is, excluding a plurality of wives, because he is an Englishman and only residing in Turkey and under Mohammedan law accidentally and temporarily, and because he marries with a view of being a married man and having a wife in England for English purposes ; consequently, the incidents and effect may by the very nature and essence must be ascertained by the English and not by the Turkish law."[44] In another case, a domiciled Englishman contracted a marriage with a woman of the Baralong tribe in Bachuana land, according to the customs of the tribe which allowed polygamy. He declared himself to be a Baralong, desirous of marrying according to Baralong custom. It was held by an English Court that the marriage being potentially polygamous was not a marriage according to the English law.[45] It was stated in another case that when an Englishwoman marries a man of a polygamous race at a registry office in England intending to set up home here, the substantial validity of the marriage, as well as its formal validity, depends on the personal law of the wife, and not on the personal law of the husband. It is a condition of the marriage that it should be monogamous......Where an English woman domiciled here marries a man of a polygamous race in his homeland by the ceremonies of his country, intending

44. Warrender Vs. Warrender, (1835) 2 Cl. & F. 488.
45. Bethell, In re. (1888) 38 Ch. D. 220.

to live with him there, well-knowing that she is entering into a marriage that is potentially polygamous, the substantial validity of that marriage depends on the personal law of the husband and not on the personal law of the wife.........There was no condition of the marriage that it should be monogamous."[46] It would appear from the above decision that the Court determined the character of the marriage by applying *lex loci celebrationis.* It is now a settled rule of English law that the nature of a marriage shall depend on the *lex loci contractus.* Hence, if the marriage is contracted in a Muslim country according to Muslim rules, it shall be polygamous which is considered to be a nullity by the English Courts. If, however, it is solemnised in England, it shall be considered monogamous and valid by the English Courts. The husband shall not be competent in such a case to contract another (polygamous) marriage nor shall be competent to divorce his English wife.

Change of domicile : If the husband takes up his domicile in a Muslim country he shall no longer be subject to the English law, but shall become subject to the provisions of the Muslim law. The marriage shall still remain void.

Change of Religion

Muslim Law : If an Englishman embraces Islam, he can validly marry a Muslim woman under the Muslim law, and a *Muslimah* can lawfully be his wife. The Englishman shall become subject to all the rights and obligations enjoyed by and incumbent on any Muslim husband. He shall have the capacity to marry four wives at one and the same time and to dissolve his marriage by *ṭalāq.* He shall also become liable to pay the wife's dower. If no dower was fixed at the time of the marriage, the parties can fix the same subsequently. If they fail to fix the dower the Court can fix it. In fixing the dower it shall ascertain the dower customary in the wife's family. Also the wife's personal qualifications such as beauty, educa-

46. Kenward Vs. Kenward, (1950) 2 All E. R. 297.

tion, social status. Also the financial condition of the husband.[47]

English Law : Under the English law, the husband shall be bound by the English law irrespective of his religion. The marriage shall be considered monogamous wherever it may be solemnised because he cannot under the English law be a party to a polygamous marriage. If he, however, changes his domicile also, then obviously the English law shall cease to apply to him and he shall be governed by the law of his new domicile.

Wife's Adoption of Islam : The adoption of Islam by a married Christian woman affects the following aspects of her marriage :

(*a*) The continuation of her present marriage,

(*b*) Her right to contract another marriage and

(*c*) Her right to the dissolution of her present marriage.

The above matters are now briefly discussed.

(*a*) *Continuation of the existing marriage* : When a non-Muslim woman, married to a non-Muslim, embraces Islam then under the Muslim law the marriage cannot be maintained or continued unless the husband also embraces Islam. This is based on the rule of Muslim law that a *Muslimah* (Muslim woman) cannot marry, be or remain the wife of a non-Muslim even when he belongs to a revealed religion. She ceases to hold the status of being the wife of the non-Muslim husband from the time of her adoption of Islam. If there is a difference of domicile, the marriage becomes automatically dissolved under certain conditions under the Muslim law. The matter has been fully discussed in the Chapter on Tabayan Dar (difference of domicile). The wife can also ask her husband to join her in her new faith and on his refusal or failure to do so, she can take legal proceedings against him for the dissolution of her marriage. The marriage can be dissolved by the Court if necessary conditions prescribed in the matter have been complied with. This

47. Mrs. Marina Jatoi Vs, Nur-ud-Din K. Jatoi, P. L. D. (1967) S. C. 580.

obviously could not be done in pre-partition India when it was ruled by England and was subject to English law. The Anglo-Indian Courts refused to give effect to this rule of Muslim law. But after the independence of the country, the Courts in Pakistan are certain to follow it while the Courts in India may also give effect to it on the basis of justice, equity and good conscience in appropriate cases.

Section 2 of the Dissolution of Muslim Marriages Act (Act VIII of 1939) lays down the grounds on the basis of which a marriage can be dissolved by a Court. Clause IX of the section is a residuary clause. Section 2 and clause IX read as under :

2. A woman married under Muslim law shall be entitled to obtain a decree for the dissolution of her marriage on any one or more of the following grounds, namely—

"(IX) On any other ground which is recognised as valid for the dissolution of a marriage under Muslim Law."

The above clause shall be greatly helpful in the case under discussion as the Act shall be applicable to it. The preamble and section of the Act make it quite clear that the section and the provisions of the Act do apply to the case of a woman married under English law. The preamble reads : "An Act to consolidate and clarify the provisions of Muslim law relating to suits for dissolution of marriage by women married under Muslim law.' A marriage solemnised under the English law satisfies the conditions essential under the Muslim law for the validity of a marriage. Hence the English wife shall be entitled to the benefit of the provisions of the Act.

As discussed before, it is necessary under Muslim law and imperative under the Ḥanafī law to offer Islam to the unconverted party before the marriage is dissolved. This can be done where the husband is domiciled or residing in a Muslim country. But a non-Muslim Court will not dissolve a marriage on the husband's refusal or failure to embrace Islam. Under these peculiar circumstances, that is, when the husband cannot be offered Islam while the woman ceases to be his wife, it will be necessary to help her. This will be done by adopting and applying the Sāhfi'ī law to a Ḥanafī woman, that is, if the woman has joined the Ḥanafī sect or has not joined any sect at all. Under the Shāfi'ī law it is not necessary to offer Islam to the unconverted party, irrespective of the fact whether the spouses are or the husband is living in a *Dār al-Islam* (Muslim State) or *Dār al-Ḥarb* (non-Muslim State). This is due to the fact that under the Shāfi'ī law the marriage gets dissolved automatically on the expiry of the prescribed period, namely, three months, after the conversion of one spouse.

If the parties or the wife is domiciled in a non-Muslim State as in England or the U.S.A., the Muslim law shall not be applicable there. No Court there will dissolve the marriage as the change of religion is not a ground for the dissolution of marriage under the laws of those countries. But if the spouses or the wife takes up her domicile in a Muslim country or a country which allows the application of Muslim law or personal law then it shall be the Muslim law or personal law that shall govern the case.

If a married non-Muslim woman of European or American domicile embraces Islam and wants that either her husband should also adopt Islam or on his refusal or failure to do so, the marriage be dissolved, the question arises if her English or foreign marriage can be dissolved by a Qāḍī (Court) on such a ground. The difficulty involved in such a case was realised by the Privy Council in a case when it observed, "whether a change of religion made honestly after marriage with the assent of both spouses without any intention to commit a fraud upon the law, will have the effect of altering rights, incidental to the marriage, such as that of divorce, is a question of importance and it may be of nicety.[48] The English and the Courts in the U.S.A. decide a case on the basis of domicile and under these laws a woman on her marriage, automatically acquires the domicile of the husband

48. Skinner Vs. Skinner, (1897) I.L.R. 25 Cal. 637; I.L.R. 23 All 34.

but her conversion to Islam shall not make any difference in her domicile. which shall still remain the same as that of her husband. The rights and obligations of the parties relating to the dissolution of marriage do not form part of the marriage contract, but arise out of, and are incidental to such contract and are governed by the *lex loci domicilii.*[49] Hence the dissolution of a marriage and the determination of the manner in which it may be dissolved are matters for *lex loci domicilii.* If the husband is domiciled in England or other Christian country, it shall be the law of that country which shall apply to the case and as those laws do not envisage a divorce on the ground of change of religion, the marriage cannot be dissolved there on the wife's suit on the basis of her conversion. If an English or American wife embraces Islam, she shall not under those laws be governed by the provisions of Muslim law but shall be governed by the laws of those countries. It will not be open to her, therefore, to obtain the dissolution of her marriage in consequence of the change of her religion. No such case has come up for decision before any English Court. But they did arise in pre-partition India and it will be interesting and useful to discuss a few of these cases before arriving at a conclusion. Mancherji Cursetji Khambatta Vs. Jessie Grant Khambatta is a case in which the marriage was celebrated between a Muslim domiciled in India and a Christian woman of Scottish domicile at the General Registry office in Edinburgh.[50] The parties came to India and the wife embraced Islam. Subsequently, the husband divorced her according to the Muslim law. It was held by the Bombay High Court, "the marriage was a monogamous marriage, and that a Court in India should, so long as the wife remains a Christian, hold that the grounds upon which such a marriage can be dissolved are laid down in the Indian Divorce Act of 1869, and should refuse to recognise a divorce by *talak*". The

49. Mancherji Cursetji Khambatta Vs. Jessie Grant Khambatta, A.I R. 1935 Bom. 5 ; Noor Jahan Begum Vs. Eugene Tiscenko, A.I.R. 1941 Cal. 582.

50. *Ibid.*

Court then stated, "so far as the law of the husband's domicile is concerned, that governs the marriage status by operation of law, regardless of the intention of the parties, and the status might be altered by a change of domicile." It was further stated, "The rights and obligations of the parties relating to the dissolution of marriage do not form part of the marriage contract but arise out of it, and are incidental to such contract and are governed by the *lex domicilii*." It was stated in another case that the wife on her marriage to a Muslim does not acquire the husband's religion along with his domicile and does not become subject to the laws of his religion except in so far as it is part of the law of domicile.'"[51] It was held in another case, "if the courts of the domicile allow to the husband more than one wife, and the right to divorce any wife at his pleasure, and if the courts of the country where the contract was made do not recognise as marriage any union but that of one man to one woman to the exclusion of all others, then the logical result must be that the contract has conferred upon the parties the status of marriage in their own country, but not in the country where the marriage took place." In another case it was stated, "It may well be that the husband's right of pronouncing *ṭalāq* against a Christian wife was taken away when the principle on which the courts in England would act become applicable in India to a Christian wife, but if a Christian wife renounces Christianity by adopting another religion....these grounds and that procedure cease to apply as between her and her Muhammedan husband and I can see no reason why his personal law should not then apply to the marriage."[52] But the religious law in a Muslim country is the same thing as the law of the domicile, and change of religion does affect legal rights in some respects. Thus it was observed in a case by their Lordships of the

51. R. Vs. Hammersmith, Superintendent Registrar of Marriages, Ex-Parte Mir Anwar-ud-Din (1916, 17) All E. R. 37; Noor Jahan Begum Vs. Eugene Tiscenko, A.I.R. 1941 Cal. 582.

52. Mancherji Cursetji Khambatta Vs. Jessie Grant Khambatta, A.I.R. 1935 Bom. 5.

Privy Council, "in case of spouses resident in India, their personal status, and what is frequently termed the status of the marriage, it is not solely dependent upon domicile, but involves the element of religious creed....."[53] It was stated in another case, "it is recognised that the law of the religion is a part of the law of domicile, and change of religion does affect legal rights in some respects...."[54] In AIR 1939 Cal. 412, the case was converse.[55] There a Christian having married a Christian wife embraced Islam and then contracted a second marriage with a *Muslimah.* It was contended in that case that the Christian marriage was a monogamous marriage, and the second marriage was a nullity, The Court relied on a passage in 41 Bom. 181 to the effect, "On conversion to Mohammedanism, no matter what their previous religion may have been, they must be taken at that moment to have renounced all their former religious and personal law in so far as the latter flowed from and was inextricably bound up with their religion, and to have substituted for it the religion of Mohammad with so much of the personal law as necessarily flows from the religion." The Court further stated, "under Mohammedan law, where a Christian embraces Islam, he acquires all the rights which a Mohammedan possesses and can contract a valid marriage even though the first one with the Christian wife subsists." It is clear from the above discussion that on conversion the convert is governed by his or her religious law. Applying this principle of law, a Christian wife, on her adoption of Islam, shall be governed by the law of her new religion.

A case of this nature came up for decision before the Calcutta High Court.[56] In that case a Polish woman had married a Russian according to the Christian rites. The wife

53. John Jiban Chandra Dutta Vs. Abinash Chandra Sen, A.I.R. 1939 Cal. 417.
54. Noor Jahan Begum Vs. Eugene Tiscenko, A,I.R. 1941 Cal. 581.
55. John Jiban Chandra Dutta Vs. Abinash Chandra Sen. A.I.R. 1939 Cal. 417.
56. Noor Jahan Begum Vs. Eugene Tiscenko, A.I.R. 1941 Cal. 582.

embraced Islam in India, asked her husband to adopt the faith and on his refusal sought the dissolution of her marriage under the provisions of the Muslim law. The Court stated, "It is not the policy of the State in the twentieth century to act as a proselytising agency or to promote the interest of one form of religion to the detriment of another....The rule (of Muslim law) is obsolete and opposed to equity, justice and good conscience and is opposed to public policy." It was also stated "....it cannot be the law that a convert to another faith by reason of such conversion should be placed in a position to impose her newly acquired personal religious law upon a person who prefers to retain his own original faith."

It is unfortunate that the attention of his Lordship was not drawn to the provisions of the Native Converts Marriage Dissolution Act, 1866 which read as under:—

"Section 4: If a Native husband change his religion for Christianity, and if in consequence of such change his Native wife, for the space of six continuous months, desert or repudiate him, he may sue her for conjugal society.

Section 5: If a Native wife change her religion for Christianity, and if in consequence of such change her Native husband, for the space of six continuous months, desert or repudiate her she may sue him for conjugal society. Sections 15 and 16 provide that if the respondent, be a female (section 15) or be a male (section 17) and in answer to the interrogatories of the Judge or Commissioners shall refuse to cohabit with the petitioner, the Judge, if upon consideration of the respondent's answers and of the facts which may have been proved by the petitioner, he shall be of opinion that the ground for such refusal is the petitioner's change of religion, shall adjourn the case for a year. At the expiration of such adjournment the petitioner shall again appear in Court and shall prove that the said desertion or repudiation had continued up to the time last herein before referred to: and if the points mentioned in Section 12 and this section of the Act shall be proved to the satisfaction of the judge, and if the respondent on being interrogated by the Judge or Commissioners again refuse to cohabit with the petitioner the respondent shall be taken to have finally deserted or repudiated the petitioner and the Judge shall, by a decree declare that the marriage between the parties is dissolved.

There is an interesting provision not followed in the case of a Muslim marriage. Section 14 lays down that :

14. Every interrogation mentioned in the Act and made by the Judge may, at the discretion of the Judge, take place in open court or in his private room. If any such interrogation takes place in open court, the Judge may so long as it shall continue. exclude from the court all such persons as he shall think fit to exclude.

It is obvious that these provisions are meant to exclude the parents, relatives or friends of the petitioner so that he or she may not be influenced or feel embarrassed by their presence.

The proviso to section 17 provides a similar concession to the husband provided he shall so desire, and reads as under :

Provided that, if the petitioner shall so desire (but not otherwise), the proceedings in the suit shall, *mutatis mutandis* be the same as in the case of a female respondent.

The adove section shows very clearly and in unambiguous words that it is not correct to say, "It is not the policy of the State in the twentieth century to act as a proselytising agency or to promote the interest of one form of religion to the detriment of another." The provisions clearly prove that the British Government did act in the *twentieth century* as *a proselytising agency to promote the interest of Christianity to the detriment of the other Indian religions.* The provisions with some unimportant modifications are practically the same as the Muslim law in the matter. No doubt these provisions do not provide for divorce on refusal or failure of the wife to change her religion but restrict the dissolution of the marriage to the refusal of the unconverted party to live with the Christian spouse. The framers of the rule must have, however, fully known that no Hindu or Muslim wife could live with and perform the duties and obligations of a wife to her Christian husband. The difference of the phraseology is immaterial and the result of the provision of the Act is the same as that of the Muslim law. The Court was also pleased to call this provision of the Muslim law as "obsolete, opposed to equity, justice and good conscience and also opposed to public policy." But the provisions of the sections quoted above have not been held in many cases that arose under the Act to amount to such a description, and the fact that the cases were decided according to those sections shows that such provisions have not been considered obsolete, inequitable, unjust or opposed to public policy even in the twentieth century. The other points on which the Court relied for refusing to decree the suit of the wife converted to Islam are :

a. Islam was not presented to the husband according to the prescribed manner.

b. The authorities, that is, treatises on Muhammedan law, do not appear to contemplate a case of conversion of the wife to Islam in an Islamic country while her husband is a foreigner domiciled in a foreign country.

c. There can be no lawful dissolution of the marital-tie unless Islam has actually been presented to the unconverted party by the Court acting as Kazi.

d. The authorities envisage the actual physical presence of the parties before the Kazi, and in the absence of the unconverted party, it is difficult to see how Islam can be effectively presented to him.

e. The procedure which has been prescribed by the jurists is designed to ensure that the unconverted party fully understands the implications of a refusal to embrace Islam and it does not appear to be applicable when it is impossible to bring that party before the Kazi.

f. A mere cable from a convert to her husband asking him to embrace Islam is not sufficient to constitute a valid offer of the faith to the unconverted party.

g. It is the Kazi and not the convert who should present Islam to the unconverted party.

h. The rule on which the plaintiff relies is obsolete and opposed to public policy.

As the Court seems to have attached great importance to the above points, it is necessary to consider them carefully. Points *a*, *b*, *c*, and *d* can be conveniently considered together, while points *f* and *g* may be discussed at the same time.

It may be stated here that the Muslim jurists divide various countries into two different classes, namely, *Dār al-Ḥarb* (non-Muslim State) and *Dār al-Islām* (Muslim State). In the countries belonging to the former class, presentation of Islam was not possible in the early days as there was no universal system of communication. In the case of different Muslim countries, the Qāḍī of one country could serve his letter or notice. calling upon the unconverted party to embrace Islam, through the Qāḍī of the other Muslim country. But the case would differ when the unconverted party happened to be in a non-Muslim country because there would be no reciprocal agreement between the two countries under which the processes of one country could be served on a certain person by the authorities of the other country. Even if there were such an agreement, no Christian official would have served a notice on a Christian asking him to renounce Christianity and embrace Islam. To meet the difficulty the Muslim jurists laid down the law that in the case of difference of domicile it is not necessary to offer Islam to the unconverted party when he happens to be in a non-Muslim country and the marriage would be considered to be dissolved automatically on the expiry of three terms of the wife's menstrual course, but if it cannot be ascertained then on the expiry of three months.[57] In the light of the above discussion. the difficulty pointed out above does not arise. Moreover, the place of the Qāḍīs has now been taken by the present-day judges and a Muslim convert can have the unconverted party served with

57. See Chapter on Ṭabāyan Dār (Difference of Domicile).

the prescribed notice through the judge. As stated in section I. Ormond J. was prepared to himself serve the other party with a notice to show cause why the wife's suit be not decreed, but under the particular circumstances of the case before him, it was not necessary to do so as the party had already been served. Even if there is no Qāḍī nor a Judge who is ready to make the service, the Ḥanafīs will adopt the Shāfi'ī law and the marriage in dispute shall be considered to be dissolved automatically on the expiry of three months without any notice to the unconverted party.

e. The unconverted party does not get a chance to understand the implications of refusal to accept Islam : It is correct that an attempt has to be made to make the other party to realise the implications of his refusal to embrace Islam. When, however, it is not possible to comply with this rule, the Muslim jurists shall be confronted with two contingencies, namely :

I. Want of an attempt to induce the other party to embrace Islam, and

II. To let the Muslim wife remain the wife of a non-Muslim.

As stated before, a Muslim woman cannot be or continue to remain the wife of a non-Muslim. Compliance with this rule is imperative as this rule has been laid down in the Qur'ān and fully explained in the Traditions. It is obvious that the Muslim jurists will choose the lesser evil, that is, they will not insist on the provision to offer Islam to the unconverted party and to explain the consequences arising on his refusal to do so. The Shāfi'ī law does not make it an essential condition for the dissolution of a marriage that Islam shall be offered to the unconverted party—much less that the consequences of his failure to do so be explained to him. Hence, advantage shall be taken of this rule by the Ḥanafīs also, and the marriage shall be considered to have been automatically dissolved on the expiry of the prescribed period of time.

f, g. The aim of the service of notice on the other party is to give him a chance to maintain his marriage by embracing the faith. Notice was issued and served by the Qāḍī as he was in a better position to do so and also to ensure that the service has, as a matter of fact, been made on the other party. There is no inherent virtue attached to a service by the Qāḍī and it can be made by the party concerned or her attorney provided that the Qāḍī is assured of the same. In the present-day changed conditions, service by registered post can serve the purpose and it will be still preferable if acknowledgement of the addressee is obtained. Ormond J. was, it is submitted, perfectly justified in considering such service as sufficient to comply with the provisions of Muslim law.

h. The rule has become obsolete and is opposed to public policy. The question whether the rule has become obsolete or is opposed to public policy has been fully discussed before.

As India was subject to England, the Indian Courts considered themselves bound by the provisions of the English law as well and the Indian Christian Acts. It is important to remember in this connection that every country wants not only to adhere to its own laws but also wants to give preference to them over the laws of other countries. Thus it has been stressed in an English case "no country is bound to recognise the laws of a foreign state when they work injustice to its own subjects."[58] Hence, where a Hindu domiciled in India married in England an English woman and subsequently denied the validity of the marriage on the ground that his religion did not allow marriage with a non-Hindu girl, the Court in England did not accept the plea.[59] It might be said that the marriage having taken place in England, the validity or invalidity of the same shall be determined according to the *lex loci contractus.* But the dissolution of marriage is governed by the *lex loci domicilii.* The question arises as what is to be done in the case under discussion. It was stated in an English case "it is both just and reasonable that the differences of married people should be adjudged in accordance with the laws of the country

58. Sottomayor Vs. De Barros. (No. 1) (1877) 3 P. D. I. (C. A.)
59. Chetti Vs. Chetti. (1909) P. 67.

to which they belong, and dealt with by the tribunals which alone can administer those laws."[60] It was stated in another English case, "there can be no doubt as to the power of every country to make laws regularising the marriage of its own subjects, declaring who may marry, how they marry, and what shall be the legal consequences of their marriage."[61] Sir, Shadi Lal, C.J, (as he then was) expressed the same opinion when he stated, "It is the duty of the Court before which an action of this description is brought to decide, in accordance with the rules of its own municipal law, whether it has jurisdiction to entertain the action. If the *lex loci* contains definite rule governing jurisdiction over the case, that rule must be followed irrespective of the question whether it is in accordance with the corresponding rule of other countries or not, and whether the decree granted by the Court would or would not be recognised by the tribunals of a foreign country."[62] The Muslim law, which shall be the law of the domicile of the wife if she comes to and settles in Pakistan, allows the dissolution of the marriage on the wife's adoption of Islam and the same law shall be applicable in all the Muslim countries and in India also. If the wife of a Christian embraces Islam, there arises a conflict of laws. The laws of the husband's domicile do not allow dissolution of the marriage on the ground of the wife's conversion to Islam while her religion does not permit her to remain the wife of a non-Muslim. As Islam does not recognise the law regarding domicile, it will ignore the fact that the husband is domiciled in a country which decides matrimonial cases according to the domicile of the spouses. It will bind the wife by her personal and religious law and a Muslim State shall help her in the matter. It was stated in Noor Jehan Begum Vs, Eugene Tiscenko that it cannot be the law that a convert to another faith by reason of such conversion should be placed in a position to impose her newly acquired personal religious law

60. Wilson Vs. Wilson, (1872) L. R. 2 P. & M. 435.
61. Pugh Vs Pugh, (1951) 2 All E. R, 680.
62. Lee Vs, Lee, A.I.R. 1924 Lah. 513.

upon a person who prefers to retain his own original faith.... The plaintiff's case conflicts with the most fundamental principles of English law which are followed in India in matrimonial cases.[63] In appeal, Ameer Ali Tariq remarked, "I cannot see why any rule of personal law in India is to be vitiated because it is inconsistent with the English legal conception of marriage for purposes of divorce.''[64] Nasim Ali, J. another member of the Bench, stated, "It is true that nations assert a claim to regulate the rights and duties and obligations and acts of their own citizens, wherever they may be domiciled. But when such rights, duties, obligations and acts come under the consideration of other countries, and especially of the foreign country where such citizens are domiciled, the duty of recognising and enforcing such a claim of sovereignty is neither clear nor generally admitted. It is a reasonable rule of law that if any effect of a marriage created by the law of one State is deemed by the Courts of another State sufficiently offensive to the policy of the latter State, the latter State will refuse to give that effect to the marriage. The above does not deny the validity of the marriage, but precludes the enjoyment within the State of some particular right or other interest incidental to the marriage." It is to be remembered that all the cases, referred to above, were decided when India was subject to England and the English law was followed in India. With the achievement of independence both India and Pakistan are independent countries and are no longer bound by the English law. The Pakistanis and Indians whether Hindus, Muslims or of any other religion, shall be governed by their personal laws or religious laws in preference to foreign laws. If, therefore, a married woman of foreign non-Muslim country embraces Islam and takes up her domicile in Pakistan or any other Muslim country, her marriage shall automatically become dissolved on the expiry of three months.

In any case Pakistan and many other countries where people are governed by their religious law shall recognise

63. A. I. R. 1941 Cal. 582.
64. A. I. R. 1942 Cal. 325.

the dissolution of her marriage.

The above discussion will show the difficulties to be experienced when a married English, European or American woman embraces Islam while the husband prefers to remain a Christian. Before trying to come to a conclusion, let us summarise these difficulties as under :

(*a*) The greatest difficulty relates to the freedom of religion. Every individual is entitled not only to continue to believe as he or she likes, but also to change his or her religious beliefs whenever he or she honestly takes a preference for any other religion.

Thus it was stated in a case, "This freedom of thought and religion must, as a moment's reflection will show, include not only the right of a person to go on thinking as before without interference but also to adopt new or different thoughts to the extent of becoming converted to a new or different religion, if a person so desires, without interference."[65] It has already been discussed before that no Court can test or gauge the sincerity of religious belief.[66] It has also been held that in arriving at a decision, whether there has or has not been a conversion, the motives of the convert are immaterial.[67] In case of conversion we have to be satisfied with the convert's declaration of the change of religion. If a married non-Muslim woman embraces Islam, she cannot under the provisions of her new religion remain the wife of a non-Muslim. Nothing is more important to a person than the injunctions of his or her religion.

It must be remembered that in India, Pakistan and in most Muslim countries, the religious laws and the secular laws in matters of personal law are one and the same thing, This fact was recognised in a case when it was observed : "In England it is possible for the view of the law-courts to differ in particular respects from the view of the Church on

65. Abdul Razack Vs. Aga Mohammad Bindnee 21 I. A. 56.
66. Mst. Roshan Bibi Vs. Khuda Bakhsh, (1937) I L.R. 19 Lah. 277.
67. Aiyasha Bibi Vs. Subodh Ch. Chakravarty 49 C. W. N. 439.

matters of marriage. In India the legal system and the religious system of Hinduism are largely the same thing. ....So also with the religious system and legal system of Islam ; the two are inextricably interwoven and operate substantially as one. It becomes thus extremely difficult in India on matters of personal law or personal religion in many cases to say where the religious principles end and where legal principles begin."[68] In such circumstances, a Muslim country or a country which applies religious laws to the case of marriage and divorce cannot force the woman to act against the positive injunction of the Qur'ān in this respect. There will be no option for it, but to disregard the English law and the provisions of the Private International Law where they conflict with its religious law and to give effect to the latter.

(*b*) The second difficulty to be experienced is the conflict between the religious law and the Private International Law. We find that the English law has in some cases given preference to expediency than to the abstract rules of Private International Law. Thus, the English Courts refuse to recognise a Muslim or Hindu's marriage with an English woman on the ground that being polygamous, it goes against the conception of an English or rather Christian marriage, that is, a union between one man and one woman for life to the exclusion of all others and so is a nullity. It will be void even when it is not actually polygamous, but the religion of the husband allows polygamy or, in other words, when the marriage is potentially polygamous. In a case a Hindu took up the plea that his marriage with an English woman was a nullity because the marriage was potentially polygamous. But the Court did not accept the plea and held, that the disability could be discarded by the Hindu husband. It considered in other words that he was not bound to contract another (polygamous) marriage.[69] It is submitted that the husband's conduct could not change the provisions of

68. Aiysha Bibi Vs. Subodh Ch. Chakravarty 49 C, W. N. 439.

the Hindu law under which the marriage was void. Such inconsistent views are likely to confuse a Muslim or a Hindu. This attitude of the English Court is unfortunate but the fact remains that in a Muslim country or a country applying the religious or personal laws of the parties, the English woman, on her conversion to Islam, shall cease to be the wife of her former Christian husband. The English Courts will not recognise the cessation of the marital relationship. Hence in a Muslim country she shall be considered to be an unmarried person and so shall be free to contract a second marriage. In England, however, she shall still be considered to be the wife of her English husband and so her second marriage shall not be recognised as valid. This shall be an unfortunate position. It can be avoided—to some extent at least—by strictly adhering to the rules of Private International Law and not having recourse to exceptions in order to meet certain exigencies.

Chapter 21

NAFQAH OR MAINTENANCE

Preliminary : It has already been stated that the Muslim law considers a marriage so far as the duties and obligations of the parties to it are concerned to be a civil contract. On marriage certain obligations are imposed on the parties and certain rights are vested in them. The rights and obligations arising out of a marriage are reciprocal so that if either the husband or the wife fails to perform his or her part of the express or implied conditions of the contract of marriage, he or she shall no longer be entitled to the enjoyment of the rights vested in him or her. Thus one of the rights of the wife is that her husband should support her while she is under an obligation to look after the domestic comforts of the husband and to make herself available to him. This obligation of the wife makes it necessary that she should live with the husband. Hence if the husband fails to provide an adequate amount of money for maintenance or lodging for the wife, she can on her part lawfully refuse to live with him. Similarly, if the wife refuses or fails to live with the husband, the latter is no longer under an obligation to support her.[1]

Description : The term "*Nafqah*", that is, maintenance is often described with regard to a wife what a husband has to spend on the support of the wife. It has been described in *al-Hidāyah* to signify all those things which are necessary to the support of life such as food, clothes and lodging.[2] It also includes such articles as are necessary according to the custom of a country and particular class of people such as cosmetics, cleansing soap, hair oil, articles of domestic use such as cooking utensils, mats, carpets, blankets, furniture.[3] In

1. Ibn 'Ābidīn, *Radd al-Muḥtār*, Cairo, 1324 A.H. Vol. II, p. 888,
2. Al-Marghīnānī *al-Hidāydh*, Karachi, n.d, Vol. II, p. 437.
3. Ibn 'Ābidīn, *op. cit.*, Vol. II, p. 893.

most books on Muslim Fiqh, stress is laid on food, clothes and residence while dealing with the question of maintenance. This gives the impression that maintenance is restricted to only these three items. But such is not the case and it would be wrong to hold that maintenance consists only of the above as is clear from the use of the words "such as" in the description given in *al-Hidāyah*. The items considered to constitute necessaries of life must naturally differ with a country, social status, and way of life of different people and would also change with the change of times.[4] Thus a millstone was included among the articles held to be necessary for the maintenance of a wife in early days of Islam but with the advent of flour mills no one would think of giving a millstone to his wife. Similarly, some Muslim jurists have stated that it is incumbent on a husband to give to his wife every year one suit of clothes for summer and one for winter.[5] But with the present-day higher standard of life, no wife can be expected to wear one suit of clothes all summer or winter. Abū Hanīfah and Mālik have made the position clear when they state, "No amount of maintenance has been fixed in the Qur'ān or by Sharī'ah and it depends on the financial condition of the husband and wife and the country (of their abode) and it changes under different conditions, times and standard of life in a particular country.[6] Is it possible that the word "amount" has been used here in a comprehensive sense to include the word kind as well as amount. In any case, the Qur'ān enjoins Muslims : "And provide for them (the wives) the wealthy according to his means and the straitened, according to his means."[7] This would naturally mean that the maintenance must be supplied according to the standard prevalent amongst a certain class of people in a particular country or age.

The question of the standard to be met by a husband in

4. Ibn Rushd, *Bidāyal al-Mujtahid*, Cairo, 1960, Vol. II, p. 54.
5. Ibn 'Ābidīn, *op. cit.*, Vol. II, p. 893.
6. Ibn Rushd, *op. cit.*, Vol. II, p. 54, Al-Marghīnānī, *op. cit.*, Vol. II. p. 437.
7. Qur'ān, Sūrah al-Baqarah, II, 236.

maintaining his wife is discussed in greater detail elsewhere in this chapter. If this interpretation is not accepted and the word "amount" is taken in its literal sense, it would lead to some absurd results. Supposing a husband was poor at the time of the marriage, but subsequently becomes rich, is the wife to be given more food than formerly or two mill-stones in place of one? If the husband becomes still richer, will the quantity of her food and the number of millstones be also increased? Here obviously it can only mean that the food will improve in quality with the husband's improved financial circumstances and the wife may also be given other articles for her use. This interpretation has been accepted by Muslim Jurists of a later period, and the word 'amount' with reference to maintenance is considered to include both kind and quality.

Shī'ī Law: As under the Sunnī law, the Shī'ī law makes it the duty of the husband to provide maintenance for the wife. Maintenance consists mainly of food, clothes and lodging as under the Sunnī law.

The Shī'ī law is more liberal in the matter of maintenance than the Sunnī law. Can this attitude be possible to the fact that the Shī'ah creed took its firm hold in the beginning in Iran where the inhabitants were more liberal towards women than the Arabs of early Islam. Thus maintenance under the Shī'i law consists not only of food, clothes and lodging but of other articles also while the above three items are given a more exhaustive meaning than is given under the Sunnī law as will be seen from the following discussion:

Food: According to one opinion, the wife is entitled to one *mud* of food, that is to two and a quarter ratal which amounts to a little more than one quarter of a seer.[8] She is entitled to get this prescribed amount of food in every case without any regard to her or her husband's status.[9] But according

8. Syed Muḥammad Sadiq, *Rawa-i-al-Ahkam*, Hyderabad Deccan, 1897 Vol. II, p. 310 Urdu tr. of *Sharū'i al-Islam*. Ja'far b. al-Ḥasan,

9. Syed Mohd. Sadiq *op. cit.*, Vol. II, p. 310.

to another view, no amount of food is fixed and the wife shall be given so much of it as she may require.[10] This latter view is considered to be the better view.[11] It is stated in *Wasīlatal-Najāt* that the wife must be given such food as is taken by women of her status of her city. Moreover, she must be given the food which she is used to and which agrees with her. She must not be given such food as injuriously affects her health.[12] She must also be supplied with such articles as fruit, tea, coffee, tobacco etc. if she is used to them.[13]

Clothes: According to one opinion, the wife must be given four suits of clothes, a pair of shoes and a veil (Burqa).[14] According to another opinion, she shall be supplied with such and so many clothes as are worn by women of her status of her city.[15] She shall be entitled in addition to warm clothes in winter.[16] She must also be given a bedding consisting of mat, duree, carpet, quilt, etc.[17]

Lodging: The wife is entitled to an independent house which she can share only with her husband. Failing the above, she must be given an independent apartment. She can prevent a co-wife and other people from sharing the same with her.[18] The house or the apartment must be such as befits her status.[19]

English law: Maintenance under the English law consists mainly of food, clothes and lodging. It, however, includes

10. *Ibid.*, Shaykh Abū Ja'far al-Ṭūsī, *op. cit.*, Vol, III, p. 74; Syed Muḥammad Ḥasan al-Iṣfahānī, *Kashf al-Lithām*, Tehran, n.d. Vol. II.
11. Syed Muḥammad Sadiq *op cit*. Vol. II. p. 310.
12 Syed Abu'l Ḥasan Mūsawī Isfahānī, *Wasī'at al-Najāt*, Vol. II, p. 359, Syed Husain Brujardi, *al-Badr uz-Zahir fi Salat al-Juma wa al-Musafir*, Qum, 1378 A.H, p. 57.
13. *Ibid.*
14. Syed Muḥammad Ḥasan Isfahaīn, *Kashf al-Lithām*, chapter on Maintanence, Tehran, n d.
15. Syed Abu'l Ḥasan Mūsawī, Iṣfahanī, *op. cit.*, Vol. II, pp. 359, 60.
16. *Ibid.*, Syed Muḥammad Ḥasan Iṣfahānī, *op. cit.*, chapter on Maintenance.
17. *Ibid.*
18. Syed Abu'l Ḥasan Musawī Iṣfahanī, *op. cit.*, Vol. II, pp. 359, 60.
19. *Ibid.*, Syed Muḥammad Ḥasan Iṣfahānī, *op. cit.*, chapter on Maintenance.

other things also as medicines, medical and legal service. The tendency of the English Courts has been to give wider meaning to maintenance. Thus it was stated in Acworth Vs. Acworth, "Maintenance is a very wide word, and, in my view, it should be read as covering everything which a wife may in reason want to do with the income which she enjoys. It includes much more than food, lodging, clothes, travelling and so on. It includes, for instance, charity and making arrangements for the future, thus incurring various liabilities in her discretion, and it is wrong to limit it to any particular form of expenditure.[20]

When the wife purchases expensive goods, the husband's responsibility to pay for them shall depend on whether they are such as are commensurate with the husband's ostensible standard of living.[21]

Law in U.S.A.: The nature and scope of maintenance generally differs in different States in the U.S.A. Thus at one time it was considered in the U.S.A. to consist of food, drink, clothes, lodging and aids to cleanliness as in Muslim law. It also includes medicines, medical, legal and dental fees. In later years it has been considered also to include such articles of utility as are suitable to maintain the wife according to the rank and condition of her husband, or, in other words, according to the social and financial condition of the parties.[22] It was stated in a case that in a general way it may be said that whatever naturally and reasonably tends to relieve distress, or materially and in some essential particular to promote comfort, either of body or mind, may be deemed to be necessary for life for which a wife, under proper circumstances, may pledge her husband's credit.

It would be reasonable if the Courts in Pakistan and India should also take note of the present-day changed social and

20. (1942) 2 All E.R. 704 C.A.
21. Harrison Vs. Grady, (1865) 13 LT 369, Seymour V. Kingscote (1922) 38 TLR 586,
22. Cooper Vs. Cooper, 160 Ill. App. 449; Younge Vs. Younge, 78 Mo. App. 225.

economic conditions of the people in fixing the maintenance payable by the husband to his wife.

Religious Authority: It is laid down in the Qur'ān, "Let him who has abundance spend out of his abundance, and whoever has his means of subsistence straitened to him, let him spend out of that which Allāh has given him."[23] It is stated at another place, as quoted before, "And provide for them (the wives) the wealthy according to his means and the straitened according to his means a provision according to usage."[24] It is enjoined at another place, "Lodge them where you live according to your means and injure them not to straiten them."[25]

The Prophet (peace be on him) emphasised in his sermon at the time of his last pilgrimage the maintenance of the wives and said, "The customary maintenance of your wives is incumbent on you".

IV. The Husband's Duty: It is the bounden duty of the husband to maintain his wife during the subsistence of the marriage and also during the period of the wife's 'iddah in certain cases. He is bound to maintain her regardless of his physical or financial condition. Thus he has to maintain the wife even when he is ill or undergoing imprisonment or even when he is destitute while the wife is rich. It makes no difference whether the wife is a Muslimah or Kitabiyah, such as a Jewess or a Christian woman, rich or poor, young or old, and virgin or otherwise.[26] It shall be due even when intimacy is not possible with the wife due to her old age or some physical defect as when she suffers from ratq, qarn etc.[27]

By his marriage, the husband gets no control over or right in the wife's property. She remains the full owner of the

23. Qur'ān, Sūrah al-Ṭalāq, XXVIII : 7.
24. *Ibid.*, Sūrah al-Baqarah, II : 336.
25. *Ibid*., Sūrah al-Ṭalāq, XXVIII : 6
26. *Al-Fatāwā al-Hindiyah*, Deoband, n.d, Vol. II, p. 142.
27. Ibn 'Ābidīn, *op. cit.*, Vol. II, pp. 887, 88, *Fatāwā Hindiyah*, *op. cit.*, Vol. II, pp. 142, 43.

property belonging to her so that its income is usually not taken into consideration when fixing the maintenance payable by the husband to her. This has been made clear in the Qur'ān wherein it is stated, "Men shall have the benefit of what they earn and women shall have the benefit of what they earn."[28]

The Shī'ī law also makes it the duty of the husband to maintain his wife irrespective of the fact whether she is a Muslimah, a Zimmiyah or a slave girl.[29] Also during the period of the wife's *'iddah* in the case of a revocable divorce.[30] The husband, however, shall not be liable for the maintenance of the wife when either the wife or the husband or both of them are of such a tender age that intimacy is not possible between them.[31] This holds good even when the wife is a major or old enough to be a fit subject for intimacy while the husband is so young as to be unfit for intimacy.[32] The author of *Sharā'i' al-Islam*, however casts a doubt about the correctness of this rule. He considers that maintenance shall be due in such a case.[33]

No maintenance shall be due in the case of a Muta' marriage.[34]

English Law : Under the English law, it is the duty of the husband to provide necessaries to the wife or pay her the necessary amount of money for the same. On his failure to do so, she can purchase the same by pledging her husband's credit.[35] The husband shall be liable for the payment of the same to the tradesman who has supplied them to his wife whom the husband had deserted or turned out without reason-

28. Qur'ān. Sūrah al-Nisā', V : 32.
29. Syed Abu'l Ḥasan Mūsawī Iṣfāhanī, *op. cit.*, Vol. II, pp. 358, 59.
30. *Ibid.*
31. Shaykh Abū Ja'far al-Ṭūsī, *al-Khilāf*, Tehran, n.d. Vol. III, p. 75, Syed Abu'l Ḥasan Mūswī Isfahāni, *op. cit.*, 1364 A.H. Chapter II, pp. 359-61.
32. *Ibid.*
33. Syed Muḥammad Sadiq *op. cit.*, p. 309.
34. *Ibid.*, Syed Rūh Allāh, *op.cit.*, p. 492, Syed Abu'l Ḥasan Mūsawī Isfahāni, *op. cit.*, Vol. II, p. 59.
35. Sandilands Vs. Carus, (1945) 1 All ER. 374 CA.

able grounds.[36] Desertion here includes constructive desertion.

Law in the U.S.A.: The duty which the law in the U.S.A. imposes upon a husband to support his wife is absolute, and not dependent upon her ability to support herself by her own labour or out of her own property.[37] It was said in another case, "The duty of the husband to support his wife is continuous and is not dependent upon his prosperity."[38] Moreover, the fact that the husband is without estate or is not earning any money does not absolve him of his duty to support the wife when he is physically fit and is capable of earning money.[39]

Defect in Husband: If consummation of marriage is not possible solely on account of some defect in the husband, maintenance is incumbent on him. Thus the wife shall be entitled to get her maintenance when the husband is a minor or impotent or too ill to be intimate with her.[40] If the husband is a minor then maintenance shall be realised from his property if he has any or from his father if he has undertaken the liability for the payment of the same.[41]

Shī'ī Law: As seen above, a wife is not entitled to maintenance under the Shi'ī law when intimacy is not possible with her on account of the tender age of the husband even when she is a fit subject for the same.[42] Such a case cannot arise in India and Pakistan as a boy under eighteen years of age cannot be a party to a marriage.

English Law: Under the English law a defect in the husband cannot deprive the wife of her right to maintenance.

Law in the U.S.A. The law in the U.S.A. is the same as the English law.

Wife's Right: It can be seen from the various rules of

36. Biberfeld Vs. Berens, (1952) 2 All. E R. 237 C.A.
37. Stephen Vs. Stephen, 102 Minn 301.
38. Furth Vs. Furth, 39 Atl 128.
39. Masservy Vs. Masservy, 86S. Car. 90; Canine Vs. Canine, 13 Ky L. 124
40. Ibn 'Ābidīn, *op. cit.*, Vol. II, p. 887; *Fatāwā Hindiyah op. cit*, Vol. II, p. 143.
41. Ibn 'Ābidīn, *op. cit.*, Vol II, p. 887.
42. Syed Abu'l Ḥasan Mūsawī Iṣfahānī, *op. cit.*, Vol. II. pp. 359-62.

Muslim Fiqh that it is the absolute right of the wife that the husband should maintain her even when he is destitute while she is wealthy.[43] But in order to be entitled to maintenance, the wife must faithfully perform the obligations devolving on her by her marriage or be ready or be in a position to perform the same. As stated, some of the important objects of marriage are a safeguard against loose living, domestic comfort of the husband, procreation of children, and a happy companionship. Hence a wife may not be entitled to maintenance when these objects cannot be achieved on her account. Thus she shall not be entitled to any maintenance when she is of a very tender age.[44] Maintenance shall be due, however, when sexual intimacy is not possible with her on account of her tender age if she is old enough for the husband to derive sexual enjoyment from her company as by embracing, kissing and the like.[45] Maintenance shall not be due when the wife is *nāshizab*, that is, refractory or unsubmissive.[46] Refraction is usually considered to consist of two things, namely the wife's refusal to live with her husband without any valid cause and unjustifiably refusing herself to her husband.[47]

Shī'ī Law : Under the Shī'ī law, a husband shall be liable for the maintenance of the wife even when intimacy is not possible with her due to a physical defect in her as when she suffers from ratq, qarn etc.[48] Maintenance shall also be due when intimacy is not possible without great pain to the wife on account of the abnormal size of the husband's male organ.[49]

When maintenance is due : A wife shall be entitled to be maintained by her husband only when she has been lawfully married to him. If the marriage is *bāṭil* (void) or *fāsid* (irregular), then she shall not be entitled to receive any

43. *Fatāwā Hindiyah op. cit.*, Vol. II, p. 147.
44. *Ibid.*, p. 142.
45. Ibn 'Ābidīn, *op. cit.*, Vol. II, p. 888.
46. *Fatāwā Hindiyah, op. cit.*, Vol. II, p. 143.
47. *Ibid.*
48. Syed Muḥammad Sadiq, *op. cit.*, p. 309.
49. *Ibid.*

maintenance from him.[50] She shall not, however, lose her right to maintenance if the irregularity consists merely of the absence of witnesses at the time of her marriage.[51] She shall be entitled to maintenance. The following classes of women are entitled to maintenance from the husband :

I. Women lawfully married to a man. Hence a woman shall not be entitled to maintenance when the marriage is *bāṭil* or *fāsid*.[52]

II. A divorcee, during the period of her *'iddah* irrespective of the fact whether the divorce is revocable or irrevocable."[53]

III. An expectant mother till the time of delivery.[54]

Shī'ī Law : Under the Shī'i law, maintenance becomes due subject to the following two conditions :

(*a*) There must be a permanent contract of marriage so that maintenance shall not be due in the case of a *mut'ah* or temporary marriage :

(*b*) There must be *Tamkīn Kāmil*, which means that there must be such retirement that sexual intimacy between the parties may be possible.[55]

As pointed out by Ameer Ali, *Tamkīn Kāmil* is analogous to Khalwat Ṣaḥīḥah (valid retirement) of the Sunnī law in some of its consequences.[56]

English Law : Under the English law, a wife shall be entitled to maintenance when the husband :

(*a*) has deserted her,

(*b*) has been guilty of persistent cruelty to her,

(*c*) has committed adultery,

(*d*) insists on having sexual intercourse with her while suffering from a venereal disease,

50. *Fatūwā Hindiyah, op. cit.*, Vol. II, p. 143.
51. *Ibid.*
52. *Ibid.*
53. *Ibid.*
54. *Ibid.*, p. 148.
55. Syed Muḥammad Sadiq *op. cit.*, p. 308.
56. Ameer Ali, *Mohammadan Law*, Calcutta, 1908, Vol. II, p. 447.

(*e*) when he is an habitual drunkard or drug addict.
(*f*) has compelled her to submit to prostitution,
(*g*) has neglected to provide maintenance to her,
(*h*) has been convicted of an offence against her,[57]

Maintenance when not due : A wife shall not be entitled to maintenance, under the following circumstances :

(*a*) When intimacy with her is not possible on account of her :

(*i*) tender age,[58]
(*ii*) illness.[59]

(*b*) When the wife apostatises, if she has been sent to jail.[60] If she is living with her husband then she shall be entitled to maintenance even on apostasy.[61]

(*c*) When the wife is refractory or unsubmissive, and,

(*d*) When the wife becomes a widow.[62] The above matters are discussed below :

(*a*) (*i*) *Tender age of the wife* : It is the duty of the father to maintain his minor children. His duty continues until a girl attains puberty. If the wife is of such a tender age that sexual enjoyment is not possible with her, it shall be the duty of her father to maintain her and no maintenance shall be due to her from her husband. The husband shall become liable for her maintenance only when she becomes capable of affording sexual intimacy or enjoyment irrespective of the fact as to whether the marriage has or has not been consummated. By the expression "sexual enjoyment" is here meant not only sexual intimacy but such acts as embracing, kissing etc.[63] If she is old enough for this sort of enjoyment though not fit for sexual cohabitation even then maintenance shall be due to her under the Sunni law though not under the Shīʻi law.

57. Matrimonial Proceedings (Magistrates, Courts) Act, 1960.
58. *Fatāwā Hindiyah*, *op. cit.*, Vol. II, p. 142.
59. *Ibid.*
60. *Ibid.*, p. 148.
61. *Ibid.*
62. *Ibid.*
63. Ibn ʻĀbidīn, *op. cit.*, Vol. II, p 888.

(*ii*) *Wife's illness*: If a wife has been living at her father's house and has been so ill, dating from a time before her marriage, as not to be in a position to come to her husband's house, she shall not be entitled to get any maintenance from her husband even when she has not refused to come to his house.[64] According to *Al-Fatawā al-Hindiyah*, she shall be entitled to maintenance in the above case if she asked her husband for the same but he did not pay it provided she has not refused to go to his house.[65] If a wife is ill while living at her father's house so that sexual intimacy is not possible with her and yet goes to the husband's house in that condition, she shall be entitled to maintenance from him.[66] If a wife, while living with her husband at his house, falls ill and comes to her parents' house to live there with her husband's permission, she shall be entitled to get maintenance from him.[67] But if the husband then wants her to return to his house and she fails to do so, her right of maintenance shall depend on whether she is able to undertake the journey. If she is able to do so physically, she shall not be entitled to maintenance, but if her condition does not permit her to travel she shall be entitled to her maintenance.[68]

(*b*) *Apostasy of the wife*: A wife loses her right to maintenance when she renounces Islam until and unless she again reverts to it.[69] Apostasy implies that she must have been a Muslimah before adopting another religion and before renouncing Islam. If she was not a Muslimah, then she cannot be considered an apostate. Hence, if a Muslim marries an Englishwoman who is a Christian, she shall be entitled to maintenance unless she is refractory or unsubmissive. If she becomes an atheist or adopts an unrevealed religion, then her very marriage shall become unlawful and she shall no longer

64. Ibn 'Ābidīn, *op. cit.*, Vol. II, p. 888.
65. *Ibid.*, *Fatāwā Hindiyah*, *op. cit.*, Vol. II, p. 142.
66. Ibn 'Ābidīn, *op. cit.*, Vol, II, p. 889.
67. *Ibid.*
68. *Ibid.*
69. *Ibid.*, 922.

be entitled to maintenance.

(c) *When wife is Nāshizah (refractory)* : A husband is not bound to maintain his wife, if she is *nāshizah*, that is, refractory or unsubmissive. A wife is deemed to be *nāshizah* when she leaves her husband's house against his wishes and when she does not allow him access to herself.[70] But she shall not be deemed to be *nāshizah* or unsubmissive if she does not allow him to be intimate with her while she is living with him at his house.[71] It is considered that she shall be in his power and he can be intimate with her by using some pressure.[72] The idea is explained to be based on the facts that in many countries a bride generally does not allow matrimonial intercourse on account of her coyness until and unless the bridegroom exerts some pressure on her. If the wife leaves her husband's house against his wishes, then she shall not be entitled to get any maintenance from him.[73]

Whether a wife is refractory or not is a question of fact to be determined on the facts of each particular case. The general principle of law that can be deduced is that a wife shall not be considered to be *nāshizah* or refractory if her act (of alleged refraction) does not in fact amount to refraction or is due to causes over which she has no control or is due to a justifiable cause.[74] The matter will be clear from the following instances.

(*i*) If a wife has been living at her father's house since before her marriage and has not yet gone to her husband's house then she shall be entitled to get maintenance from the husband unless he wanted her to come to his house and she failed or refused to do so without any reasonable cause.[75]

(*ii*) There is an aspect relating to the wife leaving her husband and living apart from him, namely, constructive deser-

70. Ibn 'Ābidīn *op. cit.*, Vol. II. p. 890.
71. *Ibid.*
72. *Ibid.*
73. *Ibid.*, *Fatāwā Hindiyah*, *op. cit.*, Vol. II. p. 143.
74. *Ibid.*
75. Ibn 'Ābidīn *op. cit.*, Vol. II, p. 889, *ibid.*

tion which has not been discussed by the Muslim jurists. Such omission can be due either to the fact that such cases did not arise in those times or because their significance was not then appreciated or recognised. But in our present-day complex society, they do arise and the Courts must take them into consideration. There is not much case law on the subject in Pakistan and India, but we can be guided by the decisions of the English Courts in such cases.

Constructive Desertion: A wife who leaves her husband shall not necessarily be considered to be refractory in each and every case, because it is possible that she might have been forced to leave his house on account of his conduct. There is no difference between the case of a husband who leaves his wife and that of one who by his conduct forces her to leave him. In the latter case, the wife's act of living apart from her husband shall be attributed to him.[76] Hence a wife shall not become disentitled to maintenance when it is the conduct of the husband that forces her to leave him and live apart from him. Thus acts of cruelty by the husband may compel the wife to leave him particularly when she is exposed to personal danger. It must be remembered that in a state of personal danger no duties can be discharged and the wife can not live with the husband because the duty of self preservation must take precedence over the duties of marriage which are secondary both in commencement and obligation.[77] Hence in such a case she shall not be considered to be refractory when she does not live with her husband in such circumstances.

The conduct of the husband which entitles the wife to live apart from him is not restricted merely to physical cruelty but may also consist of mental cruelty. Thus a wife can lawfully refuse to live with another wife of the husband as discussed before.[78] The test to determine whether the

76. Sickert Vs. Sickert, (1899) P. 278; Edwards Vs. Edwards, (1948) 1 All E.R. 157.

77. Evans Vs. Evans, (1870), 1 Hag. Con. 35.

78. Ibn 'Ābidīn, *op. cit.*, Vol. II, pp. 913, 14.

husband's conduct is such as may be considered unbearable to his wife is to see if the husband's conduct is such as a reasonable man may not be expected to mete to his wife, and whether the wife's conduct is such that a reasonable wife being so treated by an unreasonable husband, could not be expected to proceed with the conjugal rights.[79] Under such circumstances, she shall be entitled to separate maintenance and to the dissolution of her marriage if the husband fails to provide it to her. A husband shall be presumed to intend the natural consequences of his acts, and if it is the natural consequence of the behaviour of the husband that the wife leaves the marital home, the offending husband must be presumed to intend that the wife should do so.[80]

When a wife goes to her parents' house, with her husband's permission, then in respectable families in India and Pakistan and probably in other Muslim countries also, it is for the husband to send for her and to make necessary arrangements for her return. A wife does not ordinarily come back to her husband's house without being called back by him as it is considered to be immodest and humiliating for her to do so[81]. The husband must make an attempt to induce her to come back and live with him and to fetch her or to send some one to bring her or to make some other arrangement for her coming.[82] Hence a wife shall not be considered disobedient if she does not come back to her husband's house when he does not ask her to return or does not make necessary arrangements for her return. There is no such rule laid down by the Muslim jurists, but it is submitted, that taking into consideration the special conditions prevailing in Pakistan and India, the views of the Court are equitable and must be accepted.[83]

79. Jackson Vs. Jackson, (1932) 146 LT 406, Holborn Vs Holborn, (1947) 1 All E.R. 32 ; Gowan Vs. Gowan, (1948) 2 All. E.R. 1032.
80. Squire Vs. Squire, (1948) 2 All E R. 51 ; Jamieson Vs. Jamieson, (1952) 1 All ER 875 (HL).
81. Fakhruddin Vs. Mst. Hamida, AIR 1953 All 37.
82. Najmun Nessa Begum Vs. Sirajuddin Ahmad Khan, AIR 19:6 Pat. 467.
83. For discussion, see authori's commentary on the Dissolution of Muslim Marriages Act, 1939.

III. *Visits to Parents and Relations*: A wife can as a matter of right visit her parents or receive them at her husband's place once a week.[84] A husband cannot lawfully stop her from the exercise of this right. She shall not be considered to be *nāshizah* when she does so against the wishes of her husband.[85] If the wife's father be invalid so as to require the services of another person but has no attendant, she can attend on him even against the wishes of her husband and she shall not be considered to be disobedient so as to lose her right to maintenance.[86] It is also stated in *al-Hidāyah* that according to another report the husband cannot prohibit his wife's parents from seeing and conversing with his wife wherever they please.[87] She can also visit and receive her relations within the prohibited degree once a month, but the generally accepted view fixes it at once a year.[88] The interval of one year when a woman can meet her brothers and sisters and other close relations seems to be unnecessarily long.

Shī'ī Law: It appears from books on Shī'ī *fiqh* that a wife cannot visit her parents even when they are ill as a matter of right.[89] There can be no question of her visiting her other relations.[90]

IV. *Wife carrying on Profession or Business*: If a wife carries on some profession or business and spends her time on attending to the same the question arises whether she is entitled to be maintained by her husband. It has been stated by Muslim jurists that her right shall depend on the fact as to whether she does the work with his permission or without it. In the former case, she shall be entitled to get her maintenance from him. But if she does so against his permission or wishes, she shall become disentitled to her maintenance.[91]

84. Ibn 'Ābidīn, *op. cit.*, Vol. II, p. 915.
85. *Ibid.*
86. *Ibid.*, pp. 914, 915.
87. *Ibid.*
88. *Ibid.*, p. 915.
89. Syed Abu'l Ḥasan Mūsawī al- Iṣfahānī, *op. cit.* Vol. II, pp. 359-62.
90. *Ibid.*
91. Ibn 'Ābidīn, *op. cit.*, Vol. II, p. 915.

The Muslim jurists base this rule on two grounds namely :—

(*a*) The husband is entitled to the services of his wife at all times she is living with him. But he is deprived of her services during that time which she spends on carrying on her business or profession. Hence he is not liable for her maintenance.[92]

(*b*) The maintenance of a wife is required of the husband because her movements are restricted within the house of her husband and she cannot freely leave the house, and so is not able to earn her own living. This disability is removed when she carries on a profession or business.[93]

It is no doubt correct that if a husband is prepared to maintain and does in fact maintain the wife, it shall not be at all necessary for her to earn any money. Moreover, she will obviously do so by neglecting some, if not all, of the household work. Hence, she is on the one hand not attending to her household work while on the other hand, she does not stand in need of any monetary help from the husband. This reasoning lends support to the view expressed by the Muslim jurists. But it may be pointed out that such cases are rather uncommon nowadays. In the present-day time the husband's income often does not suffice to meet their expenses and the wife makes a sacrifice of her comfort and convenience in undertaking some job to supplement their funds. There can, therefore be no question of her being disentitled to maintenance from her husband.

(*c*) When the wife becomes a widow :

A widow is not entitled to any maintenance from the time of her husband's death.

It is explained that this rule is based on two grounds, namely :

(*i*) Whereas maintenance is allowed to a divorcee because she cannot leave her husband's house

92. Ibn 'Ābidīn *op. cit.*, Vol. II, p. 915.

93. *Ibid.*

during the period of her *'iddah*, the waiting period which is prescribed to ascertain if she is *enceinte* but the residence of a widow at the house of her husband during her *'iddah* is merely to serve as a mark of sorrow and respect for his memory.

(*ii*) Maintenance is paid out of the husband's property during his lifetime; but on the death of a husband his ownership ceases and becomes immediately vested in his heirs including the widow herself and they are in no way responsible for the maintenance of the widow.[94] There is a difference of opinion about her right to maintenance if she is expecting a child. According to one opinion she shall be entitled to maintenance in such a case.[95]

Shī'ī Law: Under Shī'ī law, maintenance shall not be due to a wife when she is of such a tender age that intimacy is not possible with her or when she does not suffer from any such disability but the husband is not capable of intimacy due to his own minority or tender age.[96] As pointed out before, the author of *Shara'i' al-Islam* does not accept the correctness of this view.[97] Maintenance shall also not be due when the wife is *nāshizah* or refractory or unsubmissive. The wife's unsubmissiveness under the Shī'ī law consists in her denial of intimacy to her husband.[98] But she will not be considered to be refractory if her denial is based on some religious or some other valid ground. Thus there shall be no unsubmissiveness when the refusal is due to the fact that the wife has already undertaken a pilgrimage or is having menstrual course when intimacy is not permissible. She can also lawfully refuse intimacy when

94. Ibn 'Ābidīn *op. cit.*, Vol. II, p. 922.
95. *Ibid.*
96. Syed Muḥammad Sadiq *op. cit.*, pp. 308-309; Shaykh Abū Ja'far al-Tūsī, *op. cit.*, Vol. III p. 75, Syed Abu'l Ḥasan Mūsawī, *op. cit.*, Vol. II, pp. 359-62.
97. Syed Muḥammad Sadiq *op. cit.*, Vol. II, p. 309; also see topic, "Husband's duty."
98. Syed Abu'l Ḥasan Mūsawī, *op. cit.*, Vol. II, pp. 359-60.

she is too ill for the same.[99] She will also be considered to be refractory when she does not abstain from such things as produce repulsion and stand in the way of enjoyment of intimacy, as when she remains dirty against the wishes of her husband or refuses to adorn herself when so desired by the husband.[100] She shall also be considered to be refractory when she goes out of her husband's house without his permission.[101] But *nushūz* or unsubmissiveness relates to the commission or omission of only such acts as are incumbent on her. The commission or omission of such acts as are not incumbent on her does not constitute refraction. Thus she will not be considered to be *nāshizah* when she does not or refuses to sweep the house, to cook food, to sew or mend clothes and the like.

Divorcee :[102] A wife is not entitled to maintenance when she has been divorced irrevocably. Her right to maintenance shall cease from the time of the divorce and she shall not be entitled even to lodging.[103]

Widow : A widow is not entitled to any maintenance from the time of her husband's death. But if she happens to be pregnant, she shall be entitled to maintenance till the time of her delivery.[104]

Carrying on Profession or Business : Shī'ī law does not allow the wife to leave her husband's house or do or omit to do such acts as are incumbent on her against the wishes of her husband. Hence she will be considered to be refractory if she is guilty of such conduct.[105] She cannot, therefore, carry on any profession or business against the wishes of her husband and shall become disentitled to maintenance if she does so.

Apostate Wife : Under the Shī'ī law a wife loses her right to maintenance if she renounces Islam and becomes an

99. Syed Abu'l Ḥasan Mūsawī, *op. cit.*, Vol II, pp. 359-60.
100. *Ibid.*
101. *Ibid.*
102. *Ibid.*
103. *Ibid.*
104. *Ibid.*, Mīr Syed 'Alī Allāmah Fāni, Tauzīh al-Mūsawī, *op. cit.*, p. 382.
105. *Ibid*., Shaykh Abū Ja'far al-Ṭūsī, *op. cit.*, Vol. III, p. 75.

apostate. Her right to maintenance shall, however, revive if she embraces Islam.[106] If some time elapses between her apostasy and return to Islam, she shall not be entitled to maintenance for the intervening period.[107]

English Law : Under the English law, the husband is under an obligation to maintain the wife. But his duty in this respect ceases when the wife commits adultery or is guilty of desertion as discussed below :

(*a*) *Wife's adultery* : A husband is not bound to maintain his wife if she commits adultery. The law is so strict in this matter that even a single act of immorality has been held sufficient to disentitle the wife to maintenance.[108] This is, however, subject to the condition that the husband should not have connived at or condoned the adultery. Even a reasonable though mistaken belief about the wife's guilt shall relieve the husband of his obligation to maintain the wife if it has been induced by the conduct of the wife.[109] But if he subsequently becomes aware that his belief was incorrect, his obligation to maintain her revives.[110]

(*b*) *Desertion* : A wife loses her right to maintenance when she deserts her husband. This loss of her right shall last only during the period of desertion.[111] If she becomes insane during this period she shall become entitled to maintenance as under the Muslim law.[112]

Wife earning money : When a wife was earning money or was possessed of means, her husband was not held responsible for the debt incurred by her in respect of necessaries. This view was taken even when she was compelled to leave him on account of his cruel conduct. It was stated that if she had

106. Shaykh Abū Ja'far al-Ṭūsī, *op. cit.*, Vol. III, p. 76.
107. *Ibid.*
108. Wright and Webb Vs. Anandale, (1930) 2 K.B. 8 C.A.
109. Chilton Vs. Chilton, (1952) 1 All. E.R. 1322.
110. West Vs. West, (1954) 2 All. E.R. 505 C.A.
111. Jones Vs, Newtown and Llanidloes Guardians, (1920) 3 K.B. 381 ; Dyson Vs. Dyson, (1953) 2 All E.R. 1511 ; Naylor Vs. Naylor, (1961) 2 All. E.R. 129.
112. *Ibid.*

assets which she could have been reasonably expected to use to pay for her necessaries, she was not her husband's agent of necessity.[113]

If a husband is committed to jail for non-payment of maintenance, his liability for maintenance shall cease in the absence of an order to the contrary for the period during which he remains in jail.[114]

Law in the U.S.A. : A wife is not entitled to maintenance when she herself is at fault in causing separation.[115] Thus if she abandons a suitable home and when the husband is in no way at fault she is not entitled to maintenance.[116] When a wife is refractory as when she persists in dancing with and associating with persons of questionable character against her husband's wishes she cannot claim maintenance from him.[117] A wife who leaves her husband on account of any ground which is not valid as when the husband excludes from his house such relatives of the wife as are distasteful to him, shall be considered to be at fault and so cannot claim maintenance.[118] Adultery of the wife will result in the loss of her right to maintenance.[119]

Wife's duty to support the husband : Under the Muslim law it is never the duty of a wife to support the husband, even when she is rich and he is destitute, If he was well-off at the time of his marriage but subsequently becomes poor for any reason whatsoever even then his wife, though wealthy, shall not be liable to support him.

113. Biberfeld Vs. Berens, (1952) 1 All. E.R. 237.
114. R. Vs. Miskin, Lower Justices, (1953) All. E.R. 495.
115. Bushnell Vs. Cooper, 289, Ill 260 ; Hodgen Vs. Hodgen, 160 Ky 267 ; Loeper Vs. Loeper. 81 Wash 454.
116. Brindley Vs. Brindley, 121 Ala. 429 ; Mattson Vs. Mattson, 181 Cal. 44 ; Reischfield Vs. Reischfield, 166 N.Y.S. 898.
117. Jenny Vs. Jenny, 178 Cal. 604 ; Powers Vs. Powers, 33 App. Div. 126 ; 53 N.Y.S. 346.
118. Davis Vs. Davis, 145 Ga 56 ; Napier Vs. Napier (wife's nephew and nieces) 187 Ky 722.
119. Bickley Vs. Bickley, 136 Ala. 548 ; Elliot Vs. Elliot, 34 Colo. 298.

English Law : Under the English law, a wife is held liable for the support of her husband if she is able to do so while her husband is needy. She must support her destitute husband when she is earning more than is necessary for her support and the support of her children or has substantial private means.[120]

A husband can be given or claim maintenance from his wife when :

(*a*) she files a petition for divorce or judicial separation on the ground of her husband's incurable insanity ;[121]

(*b*) he obtains a decree of divorce or for judicial separation on the ground of the wife's adultery, cruelty or desertion and the wife has property either in possession or reversion. In such a case the Court may make such order as it thinks fit for the settlement of such property for the benefit of the husband.[122]

(*c*) he obtains a decree for restitution of conjugal rights and the wife is entitled to any property either in possession or reversion, the Court may order a settlement of the property or part thereof for the benefit of the husband.[123]

Law in the U.S.A. : It has been stated that inasmuch as alimony could not be granted to the husband at common law, he could not be granted the same in the absence of statutory authority to allow it. Many States in the U.S.A. have allowed alimony and maintenance to the husband. But it was allowed to him even in the absence of statutory authority when the wife had independent means while the husband was destitute and invalid. This was done in view of equity.[124]

Wife's Lodging: The wife is entitled to lodging for her residence. By lodging is meant an independent house for her exclusive use.[125] If the husband happens to be poor so that he

120. Matrimonial Causes Act, 1950, section 16(3) and 20(*b* ; Matrimonial Proceedings (Magistrates Courts) Act, 1960.
121. *Ibid.*, sections 15 (6), 16 (3), 20 (1) (*b*).
122. *Ibid.*, sections 17 (2), and 19.
123. *Ibid.*, section 21 (3).
124. Hagert Vs. Hagert, 22 N. Dak. 290.
125. Ibn 'Ābidīn, *op. cit.*, Vol. II, pp. 912, 913.

cannot afford to give an independent house to the wife, he shall provide at least an independent apartment.[126] If the husband is in affluent circumstances, she must be given an independent bath, toilet and kitchen for her exclusive use.[127] The husband cannot force the wife to share her house or apartment with his parents, brothers, sisters or other relatives.[128] Similarly, he cannot ask her to share her house or apartment with another wife of his.[129] Such an act will not only contravene the provisions relating to maintenance, but will amount to infliction of mental cruelty on the wife. She can refuse to live in a house or apartment with other persons including the relatives of the husband and a co-wife and will not be considered to be *nāshizah* or refractory, because of her refusal, and shall continue to be entitled to her maintenance. The wife on her part cannot accommodate her own relations in the house provided to her by her husband against his wishes.[130]

Shī'ī Law: This matter has been discussed under general discussion of Shi'ī law in respect of maintenance.

English Law: Under the English law, maintenance includes lodging and it is the duty of the husband to provide it for the wife. It must be such as is in consonance with the standard of life chosen by the husband.

Suspension of Maintenance: When a wife is *nāshizah* or refractory, the husband's obligation to support her does not come to an end, but is merely suspended for the time during which she remains refractory or unsubmissive. When a refractory wife returns to her husband's house, she shall become entitled to be maintained by her husband because the cause for the loss of the right to maintenance has been removed.[131]

If the wife is ready to return to her duty and perform her marital obligations but the husband is not ready or refuses to

126. Ibn 'Ābidīn *op. cit.*, Vol. II, pp. 212, 213.
127. *Ibid.*
128. *Ibid.*, p. 913.
129. *Ibid.*
130. *Ibid.*
131. *Ibid.*, p. 890.

receive her even then she shall be entitled to get maintenance from him.[132] If a refractory wife becomes insane, she can no longer exercise her volition and her continued absence or unsubmissiveness shall not be due to her volition. She shall, therefore, become entitled to be maintained by her husband.[133]

Shī'ī Law: Under the Shī'ī law also the loss of the wife's right to maintenance on account of her *nushūz* or unsubmissiveness, is not absolute. Under that law a wife who loses her right to maintenance on account of her *nushūz* becomes entitled to it when she gives up her conduct of refraction. The maintenance shall however become due only from such time when she returns to duty and the husband becomes aware of it.[134]

English Law: Under the English law the husband's liability for the maintenance of the wife ceases when she deserts him. His liability is, however, merely suspended during such time as the desertion continues.[135] It revives when she returns to him or is ready to return but the husband refuses to receive her.[136]

Law in U.S.A.: If a wife offers in good faith to return to her husband but he refuses to receive her, she shall become entitled to maintenance.[137] Similarly, where a husband whose conduct had compelled the wife to leave him sincerely requests her to resume their marital relations but the wife refuses to return to him she shall no longer be entitled to separate maintenance.[138]

Variation of Order for Maintenance: The amount of maintenance after it has been fixed by the *Qāḍī* is open to variation under special circumstances in the interest of justice

132. *Fatāwā Hindiyah, op. cit.*, Vol. II, p. 143.
133. Ibn 'Ābidīn, *op. cit.*, Vol. II, p. 888.
134. Syed Abul Ḥasan Mūsawī, *op. cit.*, Vol. II, pp. 59, 63.
135. Pratt Vs. Pratt, (1939) 3 All. E.R. 437 ; Dyson Vs. Dyson, (1953) 2 All. E.R. 1511.
136. Allen Vs. Allen, (1951) 1 All. E.R. 424.
137. Alderson Vs. Alderson, 113 Ky 830.
138. Johnson Vs. Johnson, 125 Ill 510 ; Hilton Vs. Hilton, 88 Miss 510; Levin Vs. Levin, 68S Car 123.

and equity. Thus if the wife's maintenance was fixed by the *Qāḍī* when the husband was poor but he subsequently becomes rich, the wife can claim an increment in her allowance. The *Qāḍī* can accede to her request in respect of her future maintenance.[139] He cannot, however, give his order with retrospective effect.[140] In the same way if the wife's maintenance was fixed when the spouses were well-off, but subsequently the husband becomes poor, then on his request the *Qāḍī* may reduce the amount of the maintenance.[141] Again, if the wife enteres into an agreement with her husband for the payment of her maintenance in the form of a certain specified sum of money but subsequently she finds that it is inadequate for her requirements and that she cannot live on it, she can apply to the *Qāḍī* to revise the amount and the latter shall accept her demand if satisfied on that score.[142] But the husband cannot claim a reduction of the agreed amount of maintenance on the ground that he cannot afford it.[143] If the *Qāḍī* is, however, satisfied on enquiry that the agreed amount of maintenance is beyond the paying capacity of the husband he can vary the amount of the maintenance and fix it at such amount as may appear to be suitable and proper with regard to the social position of the wife.[141] The last two provisions seem to be similar and it appears at first sight, that there is some confusion in respect of them. But there seems to be a difference between the cases. The first case indicates that the husband cannot claim the reduction as a matter of right but it is within the power of the *Qāḍī* to make a reduction when he is satisfied by making a private enquiry that the husband is in fact unable to pay the same. It is not open to a Court now to make a private enquiry and so the case shall be decided on merits. The *Qāḍī* can also vary the amount of the maintenance

139. Ibn 'Ābidīn, *op. cit.*, Vol. II, p. 905.
140. *Ibid.*
141. *Ibid.*
142. *Ibid.*
143. *Ibid.*
144. *Ibid.*

fixed in a case according to the fall or rise in the prices of commodities.[145]

Shī'ī Law: Under the Shī'ī law it is only the wife's financial and social position that is taken into consideration. The husband's financial position is not taken into consideration so that a change in his financial condition does not affect the amount of her maintenance.[146] The rule has not been stated in so many words, but it will be clear from the discussion of standard of the wife's maintenance in Shi'ī books.

English Law: English law also allows the variation of maintenance order under changed circumstances. Thus the amount of the maintenance fixed by the Court can be varied when the husband's income changes.[147] A change in the price of commodities can also be taken into consideration.

Law in the U.S.A.: An award in respect of alimony can be modified on account of a change in the circumstances of one or both of the spouses. Thus it was changed on account of the helpless condition of the wife[148] and decreased earning power of the husband.[149] Similarly the decree for separate maintenance may be varied on a change in the condition of the husband or wife.[150]

Standard of Maintenance: The next question that needs to be examined is the standard of the maintenance incumbent on a husband. The generally accepted view of Ḥanafī jurists is that the *Qāḍī* must take into consideration the status of both the parties in fixing maintenance. If the husband as well as the wife are rich, the maintenance will be such as befits their standard of living.[151] If both are poor then the main-

145. Ibn Ābidīn *op. cit.*, Vol. II, p. 906.
146. Syed Abu'l Ḥasan Mūsawī Isfahani, *op cit.*, Vol. II, pp. 359-62.
147. Le Roy Lewis Vs. Le Roy Lewis, (1954) 3 All E.R. 57 ; Matrimonial Causes Act, 1965, section 31,
148. Case Vs. Case, 205 Ill. App. 507.
149. Parsons Vs. Parsons, 36 Ky L. 256 ; Davis Vs. Davis, 78 App. Div. 500 ; Karmany Vs. Karmany, 71 Pennsylvania Super, Court 308.
150. Lane Vs. Lane, 211 Ill. App 511 ; Decker Vs. Decker, 56 Mont. 338; Crews Vs. Crews, 175 N. Car 168.
151. Ibn 'Ābidīn, *op. cit.*, Vol. II, p. 888.

tenance must be suitable regard being taken of their position. It is held by some Ḥanafī jurists that the position of the husband alone is to be considered in fixing the maintenance. This is the view expressed in *Ẓāhir al-Riwāyah*, *Toḥfah* and *Fatḥ al-Qadīr* and has been accepted by a large number of Muslim jurists.[152] But the view more generally accepted is that if one of the spouses belongs to a rich family and the other to a poor family then the maintenance will be such as is greater than the maintenance of a poor couple and less than that of a rich one.[153] In other words, the maintenance will be the mean between the two standards.

Household Work: If a woman belongs to a well-to-do family and she did not have to do such household work as cooking prior to her marriage she cannot be compelled to do the same in her husband's house and he shall have to arrange for her food or to maintain her servant or servants. The maintenance of the wife's servants is incumbent on the husband if he is in affluent circumstances as they are essential for her ease and comforts. According to Abū Yūsuf, he must provide maintenance for two servants, as one is required for service within the house, and the other out of doors. But Abū Ḥanīfah and Muhammad hold that one servant is sufficient for the wife.[154] Muhammad has also held that if the husband is poor even then he must maintain one servant for the wife.[155] The same rule applies when she does not belong to a rich family, but cannot do such work on account of her illness.[156]

Shī'ī Law : Under the Shī'ī law, the husband is bound to provide such food, clothes and lodging for the wife as is customary amongst women of her own status living in the city where she is residing. The food must be so much as may be required by her.[157] In the same way the clothes to be given

152. Ibn 'Ābidīn *op. cit.*, Vol. II, p. 888
153. *Ibid.*
154. *Ibid.*, pp. 901, 902.
155. *Ibid.*, p. 902.
156. *Ibid.*
157. Syed Muḥammad Ḥasan Iṣfahānī, *op. cit.*, chapter on Maintenance; Syed Abul Ḥasan Mūsawī, *op. cit.*, Vol. II, pp. 359-63.

to her must be such as are worn by women belonging to her class of her own city. If she belongs to a rich family, she must be supplied with more clothes in addition to the clothes supplied according to the local custom. Thus, if she is used to wear silken clothes, the same shall be provided for her.[158] If she is used to wear costly clothes, the same shall be given to her. The same rule holds good in respect of lodging. The house to be given to her for residence must be such as befits her status and of the standard common to women of her class and her city.[159]

Household Work: A husband shall be bound to provide servant or servants to his wife if she belongs to a well-off family when women of her status are served by servants. If she does not belong to such a family, she must herself attend to the domestic work.[160]

English Law: As a general rule, the English Courts take only the husband's income and status into consideration while fixing the wife's maintenance, and the order is usually based on the amount of money required for necessaries for the wife according to the status of the husband. But it is not necessary that the wife should be allowed such maintenance as may appear reasonable in view of his income according to the standard to which she is expected to live or must live in view of the husband's income and status. It has been held that it is not for the Court but for the husband to choose the scale on which he shall live.[161] Should the husband decide to live a simple life the wife cannot object to it or claim that she must live in a better way in view of her position. The only factor that the Court takes into consideration is if the goods or service supplied by the husband satisfy the standard of life set up by him.[162] The wife's ability to earn

158. Syed Muḥammad Ḥasan Iṣfahāni, *op. cit.*, chapter on Maintenance; Syed Abu'l Ḥasan Mūsawī, *op. cit.*, Vol. II, pp. 59-63.

159. *Ibid.*

160. *Ibid.*

161. Jolly Vs. Rees, (1864) 10 L.T. 298; Phillipson Vs. Hayter, (1870) 23 L.T. 536.

162. Harrison Vs. Grady, (1865) 13 L.T. 369.

may affect the amount of maintenance awarded to her. But this is usually only when she has been voluntarily earning money prior to the time of the fixation of the maintenance. She is not obliged to work simply so that she may reduce the husband's liability[163] for maintenance if she had not worked before[163].

Law in the U.S.A. : Under the law in the U.S.A., the amount of support should be such as may enable the wife to live in decency and comfort.[164] The support must be reasonable.[165] In fixing it, the husband's estate and earning power must be taken into consideration. Also the ages, physical and social conditions, habits and social status of the parties.[166] The separate property or income of the wife may also be taken into consideration.[167] It has also been held that in fixing the amount of temporary alimony, the Court must take into consideration the current needs of the wife, her ability to support herself and the means of the husband.[168] The Court should also consider the manner of living and family conditions[169]: If the husband is in good health and is capable of work and earning money he shall have to pay alimony even if he has no resources.[170] But on the other hand if the wife has independent means or if she can maintain herself by her own earning in the social position she has been accustomed to, she shall not be considered entitled to alimony.[171]

163. Rose Vs. Rose, (1950) 2 All. E.R. 311.
164. Logen Vs. Logen, 2 B. Mon. (Ky) 142, Hires Vs. Hires, 110 All. 513.
165. Belden Vs. Belden, 82 Conn. 611; Harding Vs. Harding, 79 Ill. App. 590; Younge Vs. Younge 78 Mo App. 225.
166. Cooper Vs. Cooper, 160 Ill. App. 449, Younge Vs. Younge, 78 Mo. App. 255.
167. Austin Vs. Austin, 42 Colo. 130; Rawson Vs. Rawson, 37 Ill. App. 491.
168. Coleman Vs. Coleman, 198 Ala 225; Tromper Vs. Tromper, 39 Cal. App. 62; Percival Vs. Percival, 124 N.Y. 637; Keenan Vs. Keenan, 219 Mass 107.
169. Spatz Vs. Spatz, 178 NYS 567; Fitzpatrick Vs. Fitzpatrick 127 Minn 96.
170. Ressor Vs. Ressor, 82 Ill. 442; Bankston Vs. Bankston, 27 Miss 692.
171. Brown Vs, Brown, 22 Mich 242; McCarthy Vs. McCarthy, 137 N.Y. 500; Wright Vs. Wright, G. Tor 29.

Consequences of husband's failure to maintain wife : There is a difference of opinion amongst the Muslim jurists about the effect of the husband's inability, failure or refusal to maintain his wife and the steps that have to be taken in the matter. It is necessary to discuss their views before coming to a conclusion in this matter.

Ḥanafī Law : Under the Ḥanafī law, a marriage is not to be dissolved on the husband's failure to maintain his wife, but the *Qāḍī* can authorise the wife to raise a loan on the husband's credit for her support.[172] In such a case, that is, when she borrows money on her husband's credit with the *Qāḍī's* order, the husband shall be responsible for its payment and the creditor gets a right to recover the same from him.[173] If, however, she borrows money for her expenses, without the *Qāḍī's* order, the husband shall not be liable for payment of the same.[174] It shall also be open to the wife to use such portion of her husband's propeity as may be necessary, even without an order by the *Qāḍī*.[175] Under the Ḥanafī law the *Qāḍī* can commit a husband to jail if he does not comply with his order to maintain the wife.[176] But if the husband is so poor that he is incapable of maintaining the wife, the *Qāḍī* shall not imprison him.[177] If the fact of the husband's poverty is not established yet he does not maintain his wife who insists on her right to maintenance, the *Qāḍī* can commit the husband to jail and keep him there for a few months, or till such time as the *Qāḍī* deems sufficient to test the husband's ability or inability to support his wife. If the *Qāḍī* is satisfied that the husband cannot maintain the wife he may release the husband from the jail.[178] If the husband is rich and can provide maintenance to the wife but neglects or refuses to do so, he is not

172. *Fatāwā Hindiyah, op. cit.*, Vol. II, p. 145.
173. Ibn 'Ābidīn, *op. cit.*, Vol. II, pp. 903, 904.
174. *Ibid.*, p. 904.
175. *Ibid.*
176. *Ibid.*, p. 894 ; *Fatāwā Hindiyah, op. cit.*, Vol. II, p. 144.
177. *Ibid.*, *Fatāwā Hindiyah, op. cit.*, Vol. II, p, 145.
178. *Ibid.*

to be released until he pays the maintenance.[179] The wife shall be entitled to get maintenance from her husband or can be authorised to borrow money on the husband's credit even while he is undergoing imprisonment for non-payment of maintenance.[180] The *Qāḍī* can also give relief to the wife of an absent husband by transferring the husband's such property as can be given to her or by its sale.[181]

A marriage however cannot be dissolved under the Ḥanafī law on the husband's failure to maintain the wife. The Ḥanafī jurists rely on the following grounds in support of their view :

(1) It is laid down in the Qur'ān : "Allah lays not on any soul a burden beyond that which He has given him."[182]

(2) Allah brings about ease after difficulty.[183]

(3) There were many Companions of the Prophet (peace be on him) who were destitute but even then there is no precedent of any marriage having been dissolved on that account.[184]

The above grounds, however, do not seem to be very sound as explained below :

(1) The first ground can apply with equal force in the case of the wife. In view of the injunction of the Qur'ān, she cannot be deprived of her means of maintenance and undergo great hardship. It shall, therefore, be necessary to release her from the marriage bond in such a case.

(2) As regards the second ground, it is no doubt correct that Allah has promised ease after difficulty but no time-limit has been fixed for the same. It may be very hard for a wife to wait indefinitely for the betterment of her husband's financial condition. The dissolution of the marriage may be necessary in such a case to save the wife from great hardship.

(3) As regards the third ground, namely, the absence of

179. *Fatāwā Hindiyah op. cit.*, Vol. II, p. 144 ; Ibn 'Ābidīn, *op. cit.*, Vol. II, p. 891.

180. *Fatāwā Hindiyah, op. cit* , Vol. II, p. 145.

181. *Ibid.*

182. Qur'ān, Sūrah al-Ṭalāq, XXVIII ; 7.

183. *Ibid.*

184. Ibn Qayyim, V*ad al-Ma'ād*, Vol. II, IV, pp. 347, 48.

precedent, this does not establish that the wife of a Companion did demand maintenance and that the Prophet (peace be on him) refused to dissolve the marriage even when he was satisfied that the husband could not or would not maintain his wife. This ground could hold good only if these facts were proved. If the wives of the Companions willingly submitted to their condition and did not seek the aid of the Messenger of Allah (peace be on him), there was no necessity for his intervention in the matters.

It is explained in *Sharḥ al-Wiqāyah* that the Ḥanafī jurists found that the wife could not live without maintenance and that to get a loan was difficult while the betterment of the husband's financial condition was very uncertain. They therefore thought it proper that the Ḥanafī *Qāḍī* should entrust such a case to a *Qāḍī* of a Shāfi'ī sect so that the latter would separate the parties.[185] The same view has been expressed in *Radd-al-Muhtar*.[186]

Shāfi'ī Law : Under the Shāfi'ī law a marriage can be dissolved if the husband cannot or does not maintain his wife. Shāfi'ī supports this view by an injunction in the Qur'ān : "To keep them (the wives) in kindness or to separate (from them) with humanity."[187] He contends that a husband who does not maintain his wife cannot be said to be keeping her with kindness. He must, therefore, under the Quranic injunction separate from her, that is, divorce her. On his failure to do so, he must be separated from her. Two other grounds are given by Shāfi'ī in support of this view. The first is based on a Tradition that Abū Hurayrah asked the Prophet (peace be on him) about a person who could maintain his wife and he was told that the two should get separated. The second ground advanced by him is that dissolution of marriage is allowed when the husband is incapable of coition whereas the injury caused to the wife by the husband's inability to

185. *Sharḥ al-Wiqāyah*, Vol. II, p. 174, Delhi, 1940.
186. Ibn 'Ābidīn, *op. cit.*, Vol. II, p. 903.
187. Qur'ān, Sūrah al-Baqarah, II : 229; *al-Muhazzab*, Cairo, 1296 A.H. Vol. II, p. 134.

maintain her is far greater than in the first case and so the wife should also be entitled to the dissolution of her marriage in this situation.[188] According to Shāfi'ī a husband must supply the necessary number of servants to the wife, at least when the social position of the wife is such that she must have the services of servants. The husband is under an obligation to do so irrespective of the fact whether he is solvent or poor.[189]

The Ḥanafī jurists do not accept the reasoning and contend that if the marriage is dissolved the right of the husband is lost *in toto* which is a grievous injury to him while if the wife is allowed to obtain maintenance on his credit, his right is preserved with the smallest possible degree of injury. Hence they should not be separated.[190] This view, however, overlooks the great hardships that may be caused to the wife. It may also be very difficult if not impossible for her to get a loan on the husband's credit. Hence it is imperative in such a case to follow the injunction of the Qur'ān.

Ibn Qayyim after discussing this matter has arrived at the following conclusions :

(*a*) A wife shall be entitled to the dissolution of her marriage under the following conditions :—

(*i*) If the husband had deceived the wife about his financial condition and made her believe that he was well off but he is found subsequently to be destitute.

(*ii*) If the husband is well off but does not or refuses to maintain the wife ;

(*b*) A wife shall not be entitled to the dissolution of her marriage when :—

(*i*) The wife knew that the husband was poor, yet contracted the marriage, or

(*ii*) If the husband was well-off at the time of the marriage, but became poor subsequently on account of adverse circumstances.

188. Ibn Rushd, *Bidāyat al-Mujtahid*, Vol. II, p. 53, Egypt, 1960 ; *al-Muhazzab*, *op. cit* Cairo, 1959, Vol. II, p. 164.

189. Sidi Khalīl b. Isḥāq, *Mukhtaṣar*, Paris, 1318 A.H. pp. 128, 120

190. Ibn Rushd, *op. cit.*, Vol. II, p, 53.

He justifies the last contingency on the ground that it often happens that a rich man may become poor or a poor man may become rich and people sometimes do suffer from adverse circumstances yet their wives do not rush to the judge or *Qaḍī* for separation.[191]

As regards contingency *b(i)*, it is submitted that it does sometimes happen that a woman has no idea at the time of her marriage of the strained and miserable life she would have to lead when the husband happens to be poor. Very often she is influenced by her parents to contract the marriage. Under these conditions she should not be made to pass her whole life in misery. The Muslim jurists have recognised this situation when they allow a wife who has entered into an agreement about the amount of her maintenance to ask the *Qāḍī* to increase it on the ground that she cannot live on it. There seems to be no difference between these two cases as far as the principle of equitable estoppel is involved.

As regards *b(ii)* it is submitted that if a wife realises that her husband has been the victim of circumstances and is ready on account of her love and affection for the husband or her sense of duty to pass her life with him, her conduct is commendable. But if she is not agreeable to bear patiently her lot (for which the husband may not be responsible in any way), it will not be proper or even just to force her to pass a life of discontent and unhappiness. Indeed, it is likely to be in the husband's own interest to save him from a nagging and disgruntling wife who may merely add to the misery to an already unhappy life. It would be better in such a case to have recourse to the principle of *Khul'a* and disentitling the wife from claiming her dower from the unfortunate husband while releasing her from the marriage tie.

Mālikī Law: Under the Mālikī law if the husband is so poor as to be unable to maintain the wife, the marriage can be dissolved provided the wife was not aware of his financial condition at the time of the marriage.[192] The *Qaḍī* may give

191. Ibn Qayyim, *op. cit.*, Vol. IV, pp. 312, 313.
192. Ibn Rushd, *op. cit.*, Vol. II, p. 52.

him one or two months' time to arrange for the wife's maintenance and on his failure to do so, the *Qāḍī* can order him to divorce his wife.[193] If the husband cannot establish his poverty or being capable of maintaining the wife, neglects or refuses to do so, the *Qāḍī* can order him either to provide maintenance to his wife or to divorce her.[194] In any case if the husband fails to comply with the *Qāḍī's* order the latter can himself dissolve the marriage.[195]

Ḥanbalī Law: When a husband is incapable to maintain the wife, the marriage shall be dissolved by a decree of the *Qāḍī* provided the wife makes a demand for the same because maintenance is her right. If she does not make any such demand, the marriage shall continue. In support of this rule of law the Ḥanbalī jurists contend that dissolution of marriage on account of the husband's failure to maintain the wife is just like its dissolution on the ground of the husband's impotency. The dissolution of the marriage by the *Qāḍī* shall amount to an irrevocable divorce so that the marriage cannot be continued and the divorce cannot be revoked even if the *Qāḍī* or the husband so desire. In this matter the Ḥanbalī law differs from the Mālikī law which considers the dissolution of the marriage to amount to a single (revocable) divorce so that the husband can retract it during the wife's *'iddah* if he becomes in the meantime capable to provide maintenance to the wife.[196]

Adoption of the law of another Sunnī Imām by the Ḥanafi's: The grounds given by the Ḥanafī jurists in support of their view that a marriage cannot be dissolved on the husband's inability or failure to maintain the wife seem to be too technical and do not appear to take the realities of life into consideration. If a husband fails to support his wife then there seems to be no reason why relief should be given to her. It is necessary in such a case to adopt the law of another

193. Ibn Rushd *op. cit.*, Vol. II, p 52.
194. *Al-Muhazzab*, *op. cit.*, Vol. II, p. 163.
195. Sidi Khalīl Iṣhāq, *op. cit.*, 128, 129.
196. Ibn Qudāmah, *al-Mughnī* Cairo, 1376 A.H., Vol. VII, p. 577.

Sunnī sect and to release the neglected wife from the marriage tie by dissolving it. It must be remembered that a wife who was not being supported by her husband could, in early period of Islam, receive financial help from the *Bayt al-Māl* or Public Treasury and so did not experience such hardships as befalls a wife in modern times. To get a loan by pledging the husband's credit would not be possible at the present time, nor do the Courts now issue such decrees. Moreover, there is a possibility that a wife deprived of financial support may succumb to immorality rather than face starvation. These circumstances were generally not faced by wives in old times and so the Ḥanafī jurists could not take them into consideration. The Ulama of the modern times do recognise the critical nature of this situation and have recommended the adoption of the law of another Imam of the Sunnī sect.[197]

The Shāfi'ī, Mālikī and Ḥanbalī laws provide for the dissolution of marriage when the husband is so poor as to be unable to maintain the wife or when he is capable of maintaining the wife, but fails or refuses to do so.

It has been stated above that the Ḥanafī law confines itself to imprisonment of a husband who does not support his wife. It does not allow for the dissolution of the marriage. But, as stated before, the Ḥanafīs can adopt the law of any other Sunnī sect when their own law involves hardship. Hence a Ḥanafī marriage can be dissolved by adopting the provisions of the Shāfi'ī, Mālikī or Ḥanbalī laws.

Shī'ī Law : Under the Shīa law, if the husband refuses or fails to pay such maintenance to the wife as is incumbent on him, the *Qāḍī* shall exert pressure on him. If this does not prove effective and it appears likely that imprisonment may have the effect of making the husband agree to pay the wife her maintenance, he shall be committed to jail.[198] If the husband is in possession of property, then it shall be open to the

197. Mawlānā Ashraf 'Alī Thānwī, Karachi, n.d. *al-Ḥīlat al-Nājizah* p. 118.
198. Syed Abul Ḥasan Mūsawī, *op. cit.*, Vol. II, chapter on Maintenance.

authority concerned to sell the same to provide maintenance to the wife. Ameer Ali has suggested the adoption of the same procedure in respect of wife's maintenance as adopted in the case of discord between the parties, namely, to refer the matter to arbitrators.[199] The marriage, however, cannot be dissolved on the husband's failure or refusal to maintain the wife.

Way to help Shī'ah wife: A Ḥanafī wife is sometimes put to hardship in a case where the Ḥanafī law does not provide adequate relief for her, in a particular matter. To meet this difficulty the Ḥanafī jurists allow the adoption of the law laid down by another Imam of the Sunni sect. A similar problem sometimes arises under the Shī'i law. Thus a marriage cannot ordinarily be dissolved under that law when a husband does not maintain his wife. The Shīah jurists have recourse to a rule of their law in order to alleviate the hardship of the wife in appropriate cases. It is necessary to understand an important and basic principle of Shī'i law in this connection. It provides that the power to decide disputes vests in the Imam or in his nominee or if the Imam has delegated his power in this matter to a particular person to appoint a *Qāḍī*, the *Qāḍī* so appointed by that person.[200] It is only the Imam or the above, mentioned persons who can decide disputes. The question naturally arises as to who is to decide disputes in the present-day in the absence of the Imam or his nominee or other person. To meet this difficulty advantage is taken of certain directions of Imam Ja'far al-Ṣādiq. According to a report cited by Omar b. Hanzalah, the Imam has held the fuqaha (jurists) to be Ḥākim while a Ḥākim is that person to whom disputes are referred to for decision.[201] The disputes mentioned here are such cases the decision of which does not depend on particular individuals but relates to the society in general and the Shiah law-givers do not approve of the

199. Ameer Ali, *op. cit.*, Vol. II, p. 457.
200. Syed Ḥusyan Brujardi, *al-Badr al-Zūhir fi Ṣalāt al-Jum'ah wa'l-Musāfir*, p. 57, Qumm. 1378 A.H.
201. *Ibid.*

suspension of the exercise of such power. These matters include the functions of the *Qāḍī* as well as the decisions of disputes.[202] The Imam has directed the appointment as *Qāḍī* of "such persons who fully know what things are permitted and what things are prohibited by us and who have a full grasp of our laws. The appointment of such persons will be considered to have been made by us.[203] These instructions are obviously addressed to the jurists in general and only the person so appointed by the jurists shall be competent to decide disputes. It may be noted there that all qualified jurists can possess the status of Hākim Shar' under certain conditions. But in order to overcome practical difficulties and for convenience's sake they can and do choose one or more persons from amongst themselves to carry on the functions of Ḥākim Shar'. Now, when the Shiah religion has spread throughout the world, it is no longer practicable that the Shī'ah jurists of the entire world may unanimously choose some particular person or persons to act as Ḥākim Shar'. Hence, advantage is taken of the assemblage at Najaf in Iraq and Qum in Iran of the Ahli Khibrah or such highly qualified jurists who can make a correct discrimination between the right type of jurists who can act as a Ḥākim Shar' and others not so learned or not possessing the required status and character. Whenever a Ḥākim Shar' dies or becomes incapable of discharging his functions, the jurists forming the group of Ahli Khibrah at the above mentioned two places choose one or more persons to fill up the vacancy. The person so chosen cannot lawfully refuse to act as Ḥākim Shar'.[204] It is obvious that the person so chosen should be well-versed and fully qualified in Shī'i law and competent to interpret a rule of law according to his own judgment. He is not bound by the interpretations of a predecessor Ḥākim Shar'. It is explained that the interpretations of a Ḥākim Shar' die with him, that is, lose their binding force on his

202. Syed Ḥusain Brujardi, Qum, 1378 A.H. *al-Badr al-Zāhir fi Ṣalāt al-Juma' w'al Musāfir*, p. 57,

203. *Ibid.*

204. Syed Muḥammad Sadiq *op. cit.*, p. 95

death, and it shall be perfectly open to the new Ḥākim Shar' to accept or reject such interpretations. This rule of law is fully illustrated by the view recently expressed by the late Syed Muhsin al-Ḥākim. He stated that the marriage of a Shī'ah with a Kitābiyah is valid though disapproved of.[205] As a matter of fact, this view had been expressed by some Shī'ah jurists earlier but either it was not generally accepted or was not well-recognised at least in pre-partition India and even after that till 1958 when the view of the late Syed Muhsin al-Ḥākim was quoted before and accepted by a Lahore Bench of the High Court of West Pakistan and subsequently by the Supreme Court of Pakistan.[206]

As stated, the view had been expressed before by various Sh'īah jurists. Thus Syed Abul Ḥusain of Ispahan has stated "different views have been expressed about the validity of the marriage of a Shiah with a Kitābiyah but the view most prevalent is that a permanent marriage with them is forbidden but a *Mut'ah* (temporary) marriage is allowed. Some other jurists are of the opinion that both permanent and temporary marriages are prohibited while others hold both kinds of such marriages to be valid. This is not devoid of support, but is *Makrūh* (disapproved of) particularly in the case of a permanent marriage. It is, however, better to be cautious in the matter and to give preference to a Muslimah over her (Kitābiyah).[207]

Shaykh Abū Ja'far al-Ṭūsī who died in 460 A.H. has stated: "the views expressed by our 'Ulamā lead to the conclusion that marriage with a person belonging to a religion opposed to Islam such as a Jewess or a Christian woman is not valid. But a number of our 'Ulamā have held such a marriage to be valid".[208] It has been stated in another book, "Certain 'Ulamā definitely hold a marriage with a woman belonging to a revealed religion

205. *Muntakhib al-Rasāil*, Najaf, 1380 A.H. p. 107.

206. Syed Ali Nawaz Gardezi Vs. Lt.-Col. Muhammad Yusuf Khan, PLD 1963 S. C. 51.

207. Syed Abul Ḥasan Mūsawī, *op. cit.*, Vol. II, pp. 59, 63.

208. Shaykh Abū Ja'far al-Ṭūsi, *op. cit.*, Vol II, p. 382.

to be absolutely void. But some consider a temporary as well as a permanent marriage with such woman or with such a slave girl (that is, belonging to a revealed religion) to be valid while others hold a *Mut'ah* (temporary) marriage with such women or with such a slave girl to be valid while they hold a permanent marriage with a Kitābiyah to be void.[209] It has been stated in another book, "some of our 'Ulamā have held a permanent marriage with a woman belonging to a revealed religion to be valid."[210] The author of *Masālik al-Afhām*, a well known commentary of *Sharā'i' al-Islām* while discussing this problem, namely, marriage with a Kitābiyah, has stated, "there is a difference of opinion amongst our 'Ulamā. Some of them consider marriage with a Kitābiyah to be perfectly valid while others hold such a marriage to be absolutely void."

The matter has been discussed at great length in *Masālik al-Afhām*. It states that the 'Ulamā have differed in respect of the validity of a marriage of a Shī'ah with a woman belonging to a revealed religion. Syed Murtaza relies on the Quranic verse not to marry a *Mushrikah* until and unless she embraces Islam and says that the verse indicates the unlawfulness of such a marriage. The ground for the inclusion of the Christians in the category of *Mushrikāt* is that the Christians believe in trinity while the Jews believe Ḥaḍrat Aziz to be the son of Allah, and there are also certain verses of the Qurān which establish the Jews and the Christians to be *Mushrik*. Zurārah has reported that Imam Muḥammad Bāqir had said that one should not marry a Kitābiyah. I begged him to enlighten me about the authority of its being valid. He referred me to the Quranic verse : "And hold not to the marriages with disbelieving women.[210a]"

The author then explains that the people who consider such a marriage to be valid rely on verse 5 of Sūrah al Mā'idah. Muḥammad Bin Muslim asked Imam Muḥammad Bāqir about

209. Alī b. 'Abdul 'Ali, *Jām'i al-Maqāṣid fi Sharḥ al-Qawā'id*, chapter on Marriage.

210. 'Allāma Ḥilli, *Tazkir'ah al-Fuqahā*, chapter on Marriage.

210-*a*. Qur'ān, Sūrah al-Mumtaḥanah, XXXIII :-10.

the validity of the marriage (of a Shi'ah) with a Jewess or a Christian woman. The Imam said that there could be no objection to such a marriage and said, "Don't you know Talha b. 'Abdullah had married a Jewess in the life time of the Prophet (peace be on him). Mu'āwiyah b. Wahab has reported that Imām Ja'far al-Ṣādiq was asked if a Muslim could validly marry a Jewess or a Christian woman. He remarked why should he marry such a woman if a Muslimah was available. The man replied that it could be that the man was in love with her. The Imam then said that if the man does marry such a woman, he should stop her from the use of fermented liquor and bacon."

The author has summed the position by saying that if we compare the reasoning of both the groups, it will be established that marriage with a Kitābiyah was disapproved of. In other words he has come to the conclusion that the marriage would be valid, only it would not be approved of.[211]

It can be seen from the above discussion that there has been a difference of opinion about the validity or invalidity of the marriage of a Shi'ah with a woman belonging to a revealed religion from an early period.

But the view generally accepted in pre-partition India and even in Pakistan till the year 1958 was that a Shi'ah cannot lawfully marry a woman belonging to a revealed religion. No doubt, attention was drawn by Ameer Ali, Tyabji and some other writers to the other view also but their discussions show that they were referring to the opinion of the minority and that the view generally accepted by the majority of the Shiahs was that a marriage with a Kitābiyah was not allowed[212] It was for the first time that the view expressed by the late Syed Muhsin al Ḥakīm that put the validity of a marriage of a Shīah with a Kitabiyah on a firm basis.

The above discussion will show the power exercised by Ḥākim Shar' as by the late Syed Muhsin al Hakīm to give

211. Zainuddin, *Masālik al-afhām*, Vol, p.

212. Ameer Ali, *op. cit.*, Vol. II, pp. 320-21 ; *Tyabji, Muhammadan Law*, Calcutta, 1919. p. 138.

one's own interpretation to a legal problem. It will, therefore, be perfectly open to an aggrieved wife to present her case to the Ḥākim Shar' and seek his help in her trouble. The Hākim can dissolve the marriage or authorise some local 'Ālim (jurist) to pronounce a divorce in appropriate cases. A Shī'ah wife can, therefore, seek the help of the Ḥākim Shar' where the rigour of the law exposes her to great hardship as when her marriage cannot be dissolved on the ground of the husband's failure or refusal to maintain her.

It is stated in *Wasīlat al-Najāt* that if there is discord between the spouses to such an extent that they may bear hatred and even enmity for each other and the matter is placed before the Ḥākim Shar' the latter shall appoint two arbitrators, one to represent each spouse. They may take such measures as they may consider proper and they may bring about a reconciliation or effect a separation between the two. Their decision shall be binding on the parties.[213] As discussed before, it is always open to the Ḥākim Shar' to dissolve a marriage under the particular circumstances of a case when the wife is suffering great hardship. The Ḥākim Shar' can, therefore, dissolve a marriage when the husband fails or refuses to support the wife. He will be guided in such a case by equity and good conscience.

A wife shall not be allowed in all probability to get a Court's decree on the strength of the order of the Ḥākim Shar'. Even if he differs from the current view, his order will not be devoid of authority; only the authority might not have been generally accepted. There seems to be no reason why a Court should not do the same when justice and good conscience so demand.

Concluding Remarks : Law in force in Pakistan and India ; Clause II of section 2 of the Dissolution of Muslim Marriages Act, 1939 provides for the dissolution of marriage on the following amongst other grounds :—

"That the husband has neglected or has failed to provide for her (his wife's) maintenance for a period of two years."

213. Syed Abul Ḥasan Mūsawī, *op. cit.*, Vol. II, pp. 59-63.

The application of the clause is subject to the general provisions of the Muslim law so that a wife is not entitled to the benefit of this clause when she herself is at fault and is not entitled to any maintenance under the Muslim law. Thus a wife who is *nashizah* or refractory under the Muslim law is not entitled to maintenance and so her marriage cannot be dissolved on the ground that the husband has failed to maintain her for the prescribed period. It has been held in a case that a wife who refuses to return to her husband without sufficient cause is not entitled to maintenance.[214]

English Law : Under the English law, it is the duty of the husband to support his wife. Maintenance includes food, lodging and clothes. The husband must pay to the wife sufficient money to run the house according to their standard of life or in the alternative supply her with the necessities of life. On his failure to do so, she can purchase the same by pledging the husband's credit as she is considered to be her husband's agent for purchasing necessaries. The husband shall be responsible for the payment of the same. What are necessaries is a question that has to be decided with regard to the living standard of the husband.

Necessaries must be suitable to the wife's status in life as the wife of a particular person and the husband's financial position. If the wife happens to be possessed of independent means, she is not entitled to pledge her husband's credit for necessaries.[215] A wife can purchase expensive goods only if they are conformable to the standard which the husband has set up and authorised the wife to assume.[216] In such a case the wife may not be entitled to pledge the husband's credit for luxury goods. Realisation of maintenance : As stated, the wife can pledge her husband's credit to meet her expenses. The wife can also apply to the magistrate's Court for the realisation of her maintenance which can enforce the realisation

214. Majida Khatoon Vs. Paghalo Mohammad, PLD 1963 Dacca 583 ; Sardar Muhammad Vs. Nasima Bibi, PLD 1966 Lah. 7.

215. Biberfed Vs. Berens, (1952) 2 All. E.R. 227 CD.

216. Harrison Vs. Grady, (1865) 38 L.T. 369.

of the maintenance by attachment and sale of the husband's goods[217] or the attachment of the husband's earnings.[218] The Court can also commit the husband to jail for a period ranging from five days to six weeks if the Court finds that the default was due to his wilful refusal or neglect to maintain the wife.[219] The husband shall not be liable for the wife's maintenance for the period during which he remains in jail.[220] There is no such provision under the Muslim law and the husband shall usually be liable for this period also. A wife who is possessed of means to purchase necessaries is not entitled to obtain the same by pledging her husband's credit.

Points of difference between Muslim and English Laws: The English law differs from the Muslim law in several aspects. Thus under the Muslim law, the husband's responsibility for the maintenance of the wife ceases, in the absence of a contract to the contrary when the wife's *'iddah* expires after the termination of the marriage. An English Court, however, generally orders the husband on the dissolution of marriage to provide to the wife such gross or annual sum of money for her life for such period as the Court may deem fit under the peculiar conditions of a case.[221] For this purpose it will take into consideration the financial condition of the wife. It can also order the husband to make weekly or monthly payments to the wife for her life or such lump sum as the Court may deem reasonable.[222] The English law also differs from the Muslim law in several other aspects. Under the English law, the wife's financial position is also taken into consideration when fixing maintenance whereas Muslim law, as pointed before, does not take into account the wife's personal wealth when fixing the requisite amount of maintenance and the fact that the wife is wealthy

217. Magistrates' Courts Rules, 1952 r. 43; Matrimonial Proceedings (Magistrates' Courts) Act, 1960, section 5.
218. Maintenance Orders Act, 1958, section 6(1).
219. Magistrates' Courts Act, 1952, sections 64(2), (3), 107 (1).
220. Magistrates' Court Act, 1952 section 75
221. Section 16, Matrimonial Causes Act, 1965.
222. *Ibid.*

does not in any way affect her right of maintenance, under Muslim law. Under the English law a wife who wants a separation from her husband on the ground of his insanity may be ordered by the Court to make provision for the maintenance of her husband.[223] A Muslim wife is never responsible for the husband's maintenance in any way.

Again, a wife may be ordered to pay maintenance to the husband when a decree for divorce or judicial separation is passed against her on the ground of her adultery, desertion or cruelty.[224] As also when the husband's earning power diminishes on account of his old age or impaired health and the like.[225] As stated above, such responsibility does not devolve on a Muslim wife in any circumstances. Another point of difference between the English and Muslim laws is that an English wife was not considered entitled to save anything out of the maintenance paid to her by her husband. If she saved any amount and purchased anything with it, it was held to belong to the husband.[226] This involved hardship to the wife and to save her from it section 1 of the Married Women's Property Act provided that the savings shall belong to both the husband and wife in equal shares. Muslim law considers that the maintenance paid to the wife becomes hera bsolute property and she can do whatever she may like with it.[227] Hence the savings out of her maintenance shall belong to her. The only restriction on her right to save anything out of the maintenance paid to her is that she cannot resort to such saving at the cost of her health or decency. Thus if she does not take sufficient food in order to save money or does not dress properly with the same object in view, the husband can complain to the *Qāḍī*

223. Matrimonial Causes Act, 1965, sections 15 (1) (*b*), 16 (3) and 20 (1) (*b*)
224. Matrimonial Causes Act, 1965, sections, 17 (2) and 20 (2).
225. Matrimonial Proceedings (Magistrates' Courts) Act, 1960, section 2 (1)(*c*).
226. Blackwell Vs. Blackwell, (1943) 2 All. E.R. 579 ; Hoddinott Vs. Hoddinott, (1949) 2 KB 406 CA.
227. Ibn 'Ābidīn, *op. cit.*, Vol. II, p. 905.

who shall direct the wife to refrain from such conduct.[228]

Law in the U.S.A.: According to the law in the U.S.A., the husband has to support the wife. But the law in certain States in the U.S.A. differs from the Muslim law in so far as a husband who leaves his wife without any reasonable cause and without making any arrangement for her support if she is destitute is considered to be guilty of desertion. He is liable to a fine as well as imprisonment. But this matter differs in different States in the U.S.A. and there is considerable difference in the amount of fine and the term of the imprisonment.[229] Muslim law does not prescribe any such punishment for the husband.

The law in some States in the U.S.A. is similar to the English law. If differs from the Muslim law with regard to its provision that the wife is liable to maintain the husband if she is rich and possessed of means but the husband is destitute or invalid and unable to earn his living while both are jointly liable to meet the expenses of the family.[230] The law in these States makes it obligatory for the wife in such circumstances to support the husband. There is no such provision under the Muslims law. The Muslim law does not make it the duty of the wife to support the husband even when she is rich and possessed of means while the husband is destitute, invalid[231] and unable to earn his living for any reason whatsoever.

As Muslim law does not allow maintenance to a wife who is *nashizah* or refractory, in the same way the law in the U.S.A. does not require maintenance to be paid to a wife who is herself at fault. Thus a wife may become disentitled to her maintenance when she is guilty of adultery or abandons the matrimonial home without any justifiable cause or associates against her husband's wishes with persons of questionable

228. Ibn 'Ābidīn *op. cit.*, Vol. II, p. 897.

229. Frances W. H. Kuchter, *The Law of Support*, New York, 1949, p. 1.

230. *Ibid.*, p. 5.

231. Hagert Vs. Hagert, 22 N. Dak. 290; Keezer, *op. cit.*, Art 573.

character.[232]

Place where a wife can sue for maintenance: Under the Muslim law, a wife can sue her husband at the place where the parties live. If the husband lives at a different place from that where she lives, she can seek the aid of the *Qāḍī* of the place where she lives and the latter can serve his notice on the husband to appear before him at the appointed date through the *Qāḍī* within whose jurisdiction the husband lives. If the husband lives in a distant province or different Muslim countries, the *Qāḍī* can record the statements of the wife and her witnesses and send the same to the *Qāḍī* of the other province or Muslim country. If the husband has got his property within the jurisdiction of a different *Qāḍī*, the first *Qāḍī* can send his decree for execution to the latter *Qāḍī*.[233]

Law in Pakistan and India: A wife, entitled to maintenance, can sue the husband for the same at the place where she resides. This rule is based on the general principle of law that a debtor must seek the creditor and pay him the money due provided he is living within the realm unless there is a special contract between the parties providing to the contrary.[233a]

Arrears of Maintenance: An interesting and rather important question is if a wife can legally claim the arrears of the maintenance due to her from her husband. There is a difference of opinion amongst the Sunnī jurists in this matter as will be seen from the following discussion.

Ḥanafī Law: Under the Ḥanafī law, a wife is not entitled to claim any arrears of maintenance unless the same had been decreed by the *Qāḍī* or she had entered into a composition with her husband in this respect.[234] If the wife has contracted

232. Buchan Vs. Buchan, 201 Ill. App. 349 ; Keezer, Marriage and Divorce, Indianapolis, 1946. Art 279.

233. See jurisdiction, Muslim Law.

233-*a*. Mst. Kāniz Zohra Vs. Raza Husain, AIR 1937 Nag 39, Tusliman Bibi Vs. Abdul Latif Mia, AIR 1936 Cal 97 ; Fazlan Bibi Vs. Mohammad Azam PLD 1952...227.

234. *Fatāwā Hindiyah*, *op. cit.*, Vol, II, p. 145.

a debt in connection with her maintenance with the sanction of the *Qāḍī*, the same shall be recoverable from the husband.[235] A divorcee is entitled to maintenance for the period of her *'iddah*.[236] If she does not claim it or does not recover it from her husband during the period of her *'iddah* and the period has expired, she cannot recover it from her husband.[237]

Mālikī, Shāfi'ī and Ḥanbalī Laws: Under the Mālikī, Shāfi'ī and Ḥanbalī laws a wife can lawfully claim arrears of maintenance from her husband and the same shall not be lost.[238]

Shī'ī Law: Under the Shī'ī law the wife does not receive maintence as money to be spent by her in the capacity of the husband's agent but in her own right. It is due by the husband to her for services rendered by her and is her absolute property. The arrears of maintenance are in the nature of a debt due by the husband to his wife. Hence they are not lost in any case but are recoverable from him like any other debt, even when the husband has been or becomes unable to pay them.[239] They are not lost irrespective of the fact whether they have been fixed by the Qāḍī or have not been so fixed.[240a]

Court's View: A case involving a claim for arrears of maintenance came up for decision before the Lahore High Court. The Court pointed out that the Hanafis are definitely in favour of the forfeiture of arrears of maintenance while Shāfi'ī. Ḥanbal and Mālik hold otherwise. It observed: "The argument in favour of forfeiture of arrears of maintenance for the past seems to have been based on the assumption that maintenance is an obligation in the manner of a gratuity i.e., an *ex gracia* grant which is paid by way of sympathy and charity which cannot be claimed as of

235. *Fatāwa Hindīyah, op. cit.*, Vol. II, p. 145.

236. *Ibid.* 237. *Ibid.*

238. Ibn Qayyum, *op. cit.*, Vol. IV, p. 343 Cairo n.d.

239. Syed Muḥammad Sadiq *op. cit.*, pp. 311, 312, Syed Abul Ḥasan Mūsawī Isfahani, *op. cit.*,

240. Syed Muḥammad Sadiq *op, cit.*, p. 311 ; Zainuddin, *Masālik al-Afhām*, chapter on Maintenance.

right. The Court differed with this view and stated that the other three (Sunni) jurists hold the view that the arrears of maintenance being a just charge could be realised from the husband. It held, "The courts have thus the jurisdiction to grant such maintenance (arrears) subject of course to consideration of limitation. Muslim law does not allow limitation. But it is enforcible in Pakistan as well as India. There seems to be no reason why an unfortunate wife should be debarred from realising her just dues from a husband who is clearly at fault in not making the payment. We may in the interest of justice adopt the law laid down by Mālik, Shāfi'ī and Aḥmad b. Ḥanbal.[241]

Death of husband or wife: Any arrears of maintenance cease to be reimburseable on the death of either party; a widow is not entitled to the same.[242]

Release from maintenance: If a wife releases her husband from his liability for payment of maintenance, the release is effective if the maintenance had not been decreed by the *Qādī*.[243] If it hns been decreed by the *Qādī*, the release will be effective for one month only.[244] If after the expiry of one month she releases him from the payment of past arrears and future obligations, the former shall hold good but not the latter. The release for the future shall be effective for only the next one month.[245]

English Law: Under the English law, arrears of alimony do not constitute a legal debt and so no action can be taken in the Queen's Bench Division for their recovery.[246] But the wife is not left without any remedy in respect of the same. Thus, she can take advantage of the provisions of the Debtors Act of 1869, under which the Court can order the husband to

241. Sardar Mohammad Vs. Nasima Bibi, PLD 1966 Lah. 723.
242. *Fatāwa Hindiyah, op. cit*, Vol. II, p. 145.
243. *Ibid*,
244. *Ibid*.
245. *Ibid*.
246. Bailley Vs. Bailley, (1884) 13 QBD. 855, CA.

pay the same by instalments. On the husband's failure to comply with the Court's order he can be committed for contempt. It is within the discretion of the Court to determine the amount of the arrears to be paid by the husband. It can remit a part or even the whole of it.[247] But, as a general practice, the Courts enforce arrears for twelve months only.

If a husband is committed to jail, his imprisonment shall discharge him from the liability for further arrears that may accrue while he is in custody.[248] Such shall not be the case under the Muslim law where he shall be liable for the maintenance also for the period during which he remains in jail.

Law in the U.S.A.: Arrears of alimony have been held to be a debt and arrears due in respect of instalments were considered recoverable.[249]

247. Luscombe Vs. Luscombe, (1962) 1 All E.R. 668 ; C.V. ; MacDonald Vs. MacDonald, (1963) 2 All. ER. 857 CA.

248. Section 75, Maintenance Orders Act, 1952, 16, R Vs Miskin. Lower Justices (1953) 1 QB 533.

249. Stella Barber Vs. B. George Barber, 223 US 771.

Chapter 22

FAILURE TO OBSERVE *QASM* OR EQUALITY BETWEEN WIVES

A Muslim is allowed to marry and have up to four wives at one and the same time. But there is a very strict condition attached to the permission, namely, to mete out absolutely equal treatment to the wives. The only exception to this condition is in the matter of the affection which a person may feel in a greater or lesser degree for a particular wife.[1] It is explained that a person can have no control over his inner feelings and he cannot be held responsible for something in which his volition plays no part.[2]

Religious Sanction : It is laid down in the Qur'ān : "And if you fear that you cannot do justice to orphans, marry such women as seem good to you, two, or three, or four ; but if you fear that you will not do justice, then (marry) only one or that which your right hand possesses. This is more proper that you may not do injustice."[3]

It is stated at another place, "And you cannot do justice between wives, even though you wish (it) but be not disinclined (from one) with total disinclination, so that you leave her in suspense.........".[4]

The Prophet (peace be on him) has greatly stressed the observance of equality between several wives and has condemned a man's partiality for one wife.[5]

Description : *Qasm* or equality between several wives applies among other things to the time passed in the society

1. 'Alī b. Abī Bakr al-Marghīnānī, *al-Hidāyah*, Delhi, 1380 A.H., Vol. II, pp. 291, 329 ; Ibn 'Ābidīn, *Radd al-Muhtār*, Cairo, n.d., Vol. II, pp. 431-32 f.
2. *Ibid.*
3. Qur'ān, Sūrah al-Nisā, IV: 3.
4. *Ibid.*, V : 129.
5. Al-Marghīnānī, *op. cit.*, Vol. II, p. 329.

of each wife and the food, clothes and lodging supplied to them.[6]

Husband's Duty: It is incumbent on a husband to maintain absolute equality amongst his wives. He can make no discrimination between his wives irrespective of the fact whether some are virgin or otherwise, young or old, healthy or ill, or even invalid, Muslimah or followers of a revealed religion.[7] In short, he is not to be influenced by any good point in one of them. He has to pass equal time with every wife by turns even when cohabitation is not possible with her on account of a physical defect in her. The condition imposed to pass equal time with each wife is imposed so that none of them may feel lonely or neglected, and not necessarily for sexual intimacy.[8] The law is so strict in this matter that if a husband in order to induce a woman to marry him, promises to spend more time with her than with his other wife or wives, or contracts to give her more property or other compensation, these promises and conditions shall be legally void.[9]

Similarly, if a wife induces her husband by giving him some property or making a reduction in her dower to pass more time with her then too the agreement shall be void.[10] He must spend equal time with his wives even when he is incapable of intimacy on account of impotency, old age etc.[11] Muslim jurists are so strict in this matter that if a husband goes to one wife after Maghrib (dusk) and to another after 'Ishā' (early night), he shall be considered to be guilty of partiality for the first wife.[12]

By the term "time spent" is meant time at night, because a man is generally busy in his occupation in the day time. But if he works at night, the condition shall refer to the

6. Al-Marghīnānī, *op. cit.*, Vol. II, p. 329.
7. *Ibid.*, *Al-Fatāwā al-Hindiyah*, Kanpur, 1349 A.H., Vol. II, pp. 40-41. Ibn 'Ābidīn, *op. cit.*, Vol. II, p. 434.
8. *Ibid.*, pp. 42, 433.
9. *Al-Fatāwā al-Hindiyah, op. cit.*, Vol II, p. 41.
10. *Ibid.*
11. Ibn 'Ābidīn, *op. cit.*, Vol. II, p. 433.
12. *Ibid.*, p. 435.

day time.[13]

As stated before, the injunction of equal treatment of the wives does not apply to the inner feelings over which one has no control, so that a man shall not be considered guilty of inequality if he bears greater love for one wife than for another.[14] The husband may not be able to love his wives equally and may not feel equally interested in all of them, yet he must strive to maintain conjugal relations with all of them and must not leave a wife neglected.

An exception to the rule to give equal time to each wife by fixed turns is when a husband has to attend out of turn, on a wife who is seriously ill, and if there is no one else to nurse her. In such a case the husband can attend to her till her recovery.[15] But, subsequently, he will have to make up the time of which the other wife or wives was or were deprived.[16]

If the husband has to go on a journey and can take only one wife with him, he should draw lots to decide which one should accompany him.[17] But he is not bound to take any wife with him on a journey at all.[18]

Infringement of the condition : A wife who is aggrieved by her husband's unequal treatment towards her can make a complaint to the *Qāḍī* who shall severely admonish the husband and direct him to observe equality amongst his wives and not to deprive the aggrieved wife of her right. If the husband persists in his unlawful conduct the *Qāḍī* shall order his chastisement.[19] According to the Ḥanafī law he can neither imprison him nor can the marriage be dissolved on this ground.[20]

13. Ibn 'Ābidīn, *op. cit.*, Vol. II, p. 435.
14. Al-Marghīnānī, *op. cit.*, Vol. II, p. 329 ; Ibn 'Ābidīn, *op. cit.*, Vol. II, p. 432.
15. Ibn 'Ābidīn, *op. cit.*, Vol. II, p. 435.
16. *Ibid.*
17. *Ibid.*
18. *Ibid.*
19. *Ibid.*, p. 434.
20. *Ibid.*

Mālikī Law : The Mālikī law is similar to the Ḥanafī law described above. But according to a general Mālikī rule, if it is found that the admonition and the chastisement of the husband have proved ineffective, while the wife continues to complain of his conduct to the *Qāḍī*, the latter shall refer the matter to arbitrators. He shall appoint one arbitrator to represent each party. If the arbitrators are in favour of divorce, their declaration shall have the force of a judicial decree and no order of the *Qāḍī* shall be necessary.[21]

Shāfi'ī law : The Shāfi'ī law is practically the same as the Mālikī laws in the matter of inequality between the wives. But it differs from the latter in one respect. The arbitrators appointed by the *Qāḍī* shall be considered under the Shāfi'ī law to be the agents of the two parties and so their nomination must be approved by the parties. Also, the husband's agent must be authorised by the husband to pronounce divorce, or to accept compensation for divorce on his behalf. The arbitrator for the wife should be authorised by her to offer compensation for a divorce, or to accept a divorce on her behalf.[22]

Shī'ī law.—Under the Shī'ī law, equality to be observed between two or more wives is in respect of intimacy only.[23] But for a general rule of law, see discussion of Shī'ī law in the preceding chapter on failure of husband to maintain his wife.

The law in force in Pakistan and India.—It will be seen from the above discussion that the Qur'ān has expressly laid down that a wife should not be neglected, yet the Ḥanafī and the Shī'ī jurists have held that a marriage cannot be dissolved on this ground. It became the practice in pre-partition India for men to contract polygamous marriages while completely ignoring the injunction of the Qur'ān about the observance of

21. Sidi Khalīl, *al-Mukhtāṣar*, English tr. by Ruxton, London, 1916, p. 120.
22. Abū Yahyā Zakariyā al-Anṣarī, *Sharḥ Minhāj al-Ṭālibīn*, Cairo, 1950, Vol. III, p. 443.
23. Ja'far b. al-Ḥasan, *Sharā'i' al-Islām*, Tehran, 1377 A.H., pp. 197-199; Syed Abul Ḥasan Mūsawī, *Wasīlat al-Najāt*, Najaf, 1356 A.H. Vol. II, p. 269.

equality amongst the wives. They would pass their whole time with and shower all their gifts on the latest addition to their harem and the other wife or wives passed a most miserable existence. The enlightened opinion found it necessary to eradicate this evil and to provide necessary relief to the unfortunate wife or wives and a provision was, therefore, made in the law by which a wife, subject to such unlawful and undesirable conduct of a husband, could have her marriage dissolved. Clause VIII (*f*) of section 2 of the Dissolution of Muslim Marriages Act, 1939, reads as under :—

> (2) "A woman married under Muslim law shall be entitled to obtain a decree for the dissolution of her marriage on any one or more of the following grounds, namely : VIII (*f*) if he (the husband) has more wives than one, does not treat her equitably in accordance with the injunction of the Qur'ān."

The above provision has proved of great assistance to unfairly treated and neglected wives who were not meted out fair treatment. It must, however, be noted that the rights and obligations prescribed by Muslim law are reciprocal. Where a wife is herself at fault so that the husband finds it impossible to maintain equal treatment between her and his other wife or wives, she cannot hold her husband at fault, nor can she under this provision be entitled to the dissolution of her marriage on the basis of unequal treatment meted out to her by her husband.[24] The husband, moreover, must be allowed an opportunity of maintaining equal treatment among his wives. Thus if a husband marries a second wife in the absence of his first wife and she does not come to his house at all, it cannot be said that she has not been treated equally with the other wife because the husband has not been given any opportunity of treating her either equally or unequally, and the marriage is not to be dissolved in such a case.[25] But when a husband did not provide any money to one wife while

24. Badr-un-Nessa Bibi Vs. Muhammad Yusuf, A.I.R. 1944, All. 23.
25. *Ibid.*

maintaining his other wife, it was held that he had not treated the two wives equally.[26]

The opening words of section 2, namely, "a woman married under Muslim law" are very wide. If a Muslim marries an English or Christian woman before the Registrar of Marriages, or even in the Church she shall be deemed to have been married to her Muslim husband under the Muslim law. She will, therefore, be entitled to claim the dissolution of her marriage under the provisions of section 2 of the Act. She can also seek relief under the provisions of general Muslim law.

26. Zubaida Begum Vs. Sardar Shah, A.I.R. 1943, Lah. 310,

Chapter 23

OTHER GROUNDS

Husband's Failure to perform Marital Obligations

Preliminary: Marriage vests some rights in the spouses and devolves some obligations on them. As stated, husbands and wives have reciprocal rights and obligations towards each other. There is of necessity a division of labour between them because they specialise in their own sphere of life. It has been pointed out in the Qur'ān, "Allah has made some of them to excel others".[1] The failure by the husband to perform the marital obligations which devolve on him may in some cases constitute grounds for dissolution of marriage. Some of them have not been dealt with and discussed by Muslim jurists as main grounds for divorce but they may be as effective for dissolution of marriage as the other grounds and so attention is drawn to them hereunder.

Religious Sanction: The guiding principle in the matter of the husband's duty towards his wife is provided by the verse of the Qur'ān wherein it is laid down, "To keep them (the wives) with kindness or separate (from them) with humanity".[2] It is stated at another place, "And they (the wives) have rights similar to those against them in a just manner".[3] The Prophet (peace be on him) said in his sermon at the last pilgrimage, "O, my people, you have certain rights over your wives and so have your wives over you". At another time he stressed this matter when he told a person "thy body has a right over thee and thy soul has a right over thee and thy wife has a right over thee"

General Discussion: As stated, one of the important objects of marriage is a happy companionship of the parties.

1. Qur'ān, Surah al-Nisa, V : 34.
2. Qur'ān, Surah al-Baqarah, II : 231.
3. Qur'ān, Surah al-Baqarah, II : 228.

and with this end in view the husband has to perform certain marital obligations. But the failure to perform marital obligations by a husband does not necessarily constitute a cause for the dissolution of marriage. In some cases it may amount to a moral offence only, but in the case of the breach of some important obligations the wife gets a right to the dissolution of her marriage.

In Pakistan and India, a wife can also get her marriage dissolved under the provisions of Act VIII of 1939, if the husband fails to perform his marital obligations. Section 2 and clause IV read as under :

2. A woman married under Muslim law shall be entitled to obtain a decree for the dissolution of her marriage on any one or more of the following grounds namely :—

(*iv*) that the husband has failed to perform, without reasonable cause, his marital obligations for a period of three years.

The section has not described or mentioned the marital obligations of a husband and so we have to rely on Muslim law to find them.

Marital Obligations : Some important marital obligations of the husband under Muslim law are given below :

(*i*) To maintain the wife.

(*ii*) (*a*) to be fit for sexual intimacy,

(*b*) to give sexual relaxation to the wife.

(*c*) Not to indulge in *'azl* (coitus interruptus) without the wife's consent.

(*iii*) To observe equality between his wives if he has more than one.

(*iv*) To mete out kind treatment to the wife.

(*v*) To pay the wife's prompt dower when demanded by her.

(*vi*) To allow the wife to perform her religious obligations without any hinderance.

(*vii*) To divorce the wife in obedience to the *Qāḍī's* order when he is not favourably inclined towards her or otherwise.

(*viii*) To pass a reasonable time in the wife's society.

(*ix*) To make himself attractive to the wife.[4]

The matter is briefly discussed below :—

1. To maintain the wife. The maintenance of the wife is a religious as well as a legal duty of the husband not only in Islam but in many other religions and systems of law. This aspect has been fully discussed in a previous chapter on *Nafqah* or maintenance.
2. To be capable of sexual intimacy.
   (*a*) This matter has been discussed in the chapter on *'Innīn* or Impotency.
   (*b*) To give sexual relaxation to the wives.
   (*c*) Not to indulge in coitus interruptus without the wife's consent.
   These marital obligations of the husband mentioned in clauses (*b*), (*c*) above have been discussed in the chapter on "Other Defects."
3. To observe equality between his wives. Islam while allowing limited polygamy has made it the foremost duty of the husband that he should not neglect one wife and favour another. He must mete out absolute equal treatment to all his wives without any regard that one is younger or beautiful or educated while the other is old or ugly or illiterate. This aspect has been discussed in the preceding chapter on Qasm or equality between wives.
4. *Kind treatment of the wife.* In order that the spouses should lead a happy life, it is absolutely necessary that they should treat each other with kindness and affection. If the husband is not kind to his wife, the marriage may fail to achieve its object, but this conduct of the husband shall not form a ground for the dissolution of the marriage. It is the negation of this obligation, namely, unkindness towards the wife that

4. *Al-Fatāwa al-Hindiyah*, Kanpur, 1349, A.H., Vol. II, p. 148.—

> may in extreme cases entitle a wife to separation. Unkindness when it reaches such a degree as to amount to cruelty is a ground for divorce under Muslim law, as in many other systems of law. The Muslim law gives the notion of kindness a wide and realistic meaning. Thus it includes the husband's implied permission to the wife to visit or receive her parents once a week. According to one report the parents and her children by a former husband can visit her at any time.[5]

If the wife's father is a cripple, or an invalid and there is no one to attend on him, the wife can go to look after him even against the wishes of her husband and she will not be considered to be refractory in such a case.[6] It is obvious that she will feel very miserable on account of her anxiety for her helpless father and kindness demands that in such circumstances she should be allowed to attend on him.

The wife can see her relations within the prohibited degree as a matter of right. According to one report she can do so once a month. According to another report she can do so only once a year and this is considered to be the more approved report.[7] This later opinion may perhaps be based on the difficulties that were experienced formerly in travelling. But in modern times travelling has become easy and safe and there is no reason to deny the right to the wife to see her brother or sister more often than once a year. In any case the period of one year is unreasonably long and it seems equitable to adopt the other view.

The matter of ill-treatment is of vital importance and is fully discussed here.

Ill-treatment of the wife by the husband

Preliminary : One of the primary ends of marriage is a happy companionship of the husband and wife. The only

5. *Al-Fatāwā al-Hindīyah, op. cit.*, Vol. II, p. 148; Ibn 'Ābidīn, *Radd al-Muḥtār*, Cairo, Vol. II, p. 682.
6. Ibn 'Ābidīn, *op. cit.*, Vol. II, p. 682.
7. *Al-Fatāwā al-Hindiyah, op. cit.*, Vol. II, p. 148.

security for a marriage is the reality of the marriage.[8] There can be no happiness when the husband makes the wife's life miserable and even intolerable by his cruel conduct. It involves great hardship to a wife if she is tied for her life to a marriage that has proved a failure. The spirit of Muslim law does not approve of a marriage where instead of love and affection, which are the necessary objects of marriage, there is hatred and ill feeling. Islam allows the severance of the relationship of husband and wife in such cases. As observed earlier, some of the objects of marriage are to serve as a check against immorality, producing a happy union of two members of the opposite sexes and performance of a charitable and desirable act of the upbringing of children in the righteous mode of life, etc. All of these shall be lost when the wife is subjected to ill-treatment.

Religious sanction: The guiding principle in respect of wives is laid down in the Qur'ān in a verse wherein it is enjoined, "Retain them (the wives) in kindness or set them free with kindness."[9] It is stated at another place, "Treat them (the wives) kindly."[10] It is also stated, "And one of His signs is that He created mates for you from yourselves that you might find quiet of mind in them and He put between you love and compassion."[11] Again, it has been said, "It is He Who created you from a single soul, and of the same did He make his mate, that he might find comfort in her."[12]

The Prophet (peace be on him) greatly emphasised kind treatment of the wives. Thus he exhorted the people in his sermon at the last pilgrimage and said, "You have taken them (your wives) only as a trust from God, and you have the enjoyment of their persons by the word of God. So be fearful of Allah in regard to woman and enjoin that they be

8. L. Vs. L. (1949), 1 All. E.R. 141.
9. Qur'ān, Surah al-Baqarah, II : 231.
10. Qur'ān, Surah al-Nisā', IV: 19.
11. Qur'ān, Surah al-Rūm, XXI : 21.
12. Qur'ān, Surah al-A'rāf, IX : 189.

treated well."

General Discussion: It is clear from the verses and the Tradition quoted above that Islam lays great emphasis on kind treatment of the wives and strongly condemns a husband's keeping his wife for injury or harming her. If the husband does not comply with the injunction of the Qur'ān, it is obvious that he shall be guilty of transgressing the sacred text. It shall, therefore, be the duty of the *Qāḍī*, when he is satisfied with the merits of the case, to order the husband in the interest of justice to divorce the wife. If the husband fails or refuses to do so, the *Qāḍī* must himself dissolve the marriage to save a wife from hardship.

It is stated in *al-Fatāwā al-Hindiyah* that marriage enjoins on the husband to be kind to his wife and to associate with her with courtesy and kindness.[13] It is stated at another place that a husband should be directed to be attentive to his wife.[14] Ameer Ali has mentioned a case in which a Court of Algiers held that when a husband habitually uses vile expressions toward his wife it is sufficient cause for divorce.[15] He has also opined that a wife has a right to apply for and obtain a decree for divorce when the husband habitually insults her parents or her relations or makes her life miserable by cruelty of conduct, even when it does not amount to physical ill-treatment.[16] It is stated in *Radd al-Muḥtār*, "The husband is to be kind to the wife in his conduct".[17]

Ḥanafī Law. There is no provision in the Ḥanafī law to dissolve a marriage on the basis of the wife's ill-treatment by the husband. This resulted in great hardship to the wives in many cases and it was found necessary in many cases to give them adequate relief. The Ḥanafī jurists have, as stated earlier, formulated the rule to adopt the law of another Imam of the Sunni sect when circumstances so require. This rule was

13. *Al-Fatāwā al-Hindiyah, op. cit.*, Vol. II, p. 23.
14. *Ibid.*, p. 41.
15. Ameer Ali, *Mohammadan Law*, Calcutta, 1908, Vol. II, p. 563.
16. *Ibid.*, p. 564.
17. Ibn 'Ābidīn, *op. cit.*, Vol. II, p. 682.

adopted by the Indian Muslims (Ḥanafīs) long before the partition of India into Pakistan and India (Bharat) when they adopted the view of the other Sunni Imam. Section 2 (VIII) of the Dissolution of Muslim Marriages Act, 1939, provides that a woman married under Muslim law shall be entitled to obtain a decree for the dissolution of her marriage on the ground that her husband treats her with cruelty.

Mālikī Law. The Mālikī law provides that when a husband is guilty of ill-treating his wife, she can complain to the *Qāḍī*, who shall investigate the matter. If the wife's complaint is found to be correct, the *Qāḍī* shall severely admonish the husband and may even order his chastisement.[18] If the wife is still subjected to ill-treatment by the husband and she makes repeated complaints to the *Qāḍī* but has no proof in support of her allegations, the *Qāḍī* shall appoint two arbitrators one representing each party to look into and decide the case. If they deem it proper to separate the parties they may make a declaration to that effect. This declaration shall amount to a judicial decree for the dissolution of the marriage. This dissolution, however, will be a revocable one in order to give the parties a chance for reconciliation.[19] If the wife complains of the cruelty of her husband to the *Qāḍī* and he is satisfied of the genuineness of her charge, he can dissolve the marriage even in cases where the husband's misconduct is not of long standing. This divorce shall be an irrevocable divorce.[20]

Sh̲āfi'ī Law. If a Sh̲āfi'ī wife complains to the *Qāḍī* that her husband is of an irritable temperament or that he ill-treats her without a cause, the *Qāḍī* should admonish him. If the admonition proves ineffective, the *Qāḍī* may take such measures against the husband as he may deem proper and necessary in order to make the husband give up his undesir-

18. Mālik, *al-Muwaṭṭa* (with commentary by al-Zurqānī), Cairo, 1954, Vol. III, pp. 213-214 ; Saḥnūn, *al-Mudawwanat al-Kubrā*, Cairo, 1323 A.H. Vol. V, pp. 50-51 f ; Ibn Ḥazm, *al-Muḥallā*, Cairo, n.d. Vol. X, pp. 87-88.
19. *Ibid.*
20. *Ibid.*

able and unlawful conduct. If the discord between the parties is of a grave nature, the *Qāḍī* shall appoint two arbitrators, one to represent each party. They will proceed in the matter as if they were the agents of the parties. According to another view they shall be considered to have been appointed agents by the *Qāḍī*. In the former case it is necessary that the husband should authorise his agent to pronounce a divorce or to accept a compensation for dissolution of the marriage on his behalf as may be decided by the arbitrators. The wife on her side should authorise her representative to offer compensation in order to get a divorce, or to accept a divorce on her behalf for a compensation.[21]

Ḥanbalī Law. Under the Ḥanbalī law if the wife complains to the *Qāḍī* against her husband's ill-treatment and the *Qāḍī* is satisfied about the genuineness of her charge, he will appoint two arbitrators with the consent of the parties. The arbitrators should be free men and Muslims of integrity. The arbitrators will investigate the case and will try to bring about a reconciliation between the parties. If they find that no compromise is possible, they can dissolve the marriage. Their decision shall be binding on both the parties.[22]

Shī'ī Law: Under Shī'ī law when the husband is at fault, as when he deprives the wife of any of her rights, she can complain to the judge for redress. The judge shall admonish the husband and ask him to fulfil his responsibilities but he cannot chastise the husband or dissolve the marriage.[23] If the parties cannot live together in peace and there is discord between them they can have recourse to the procedure adopted for *shiqāq*. The judge shall appoint two arbitrators, one to represent each side. If they can bring about a reconciliation the matter ends there. But if they decide to separate the parties, a divorce shall not be valid unless the husband agrees to it. If they decide in favour of a *khul'* the same shall not

21. Al-Ramlī, *Nihāyat al-Muḥtāj ilā Sharḥ al-Minhāj*, Cairo, 1938. Vol. VI, pp. 384-85.

22. 'Abd al-Raḥmān al-Maqdisī, *al-'Uddah*, Cairo, 1382 A.H., pp. 405-406.

23. Abu'l Ḥasan al-Mūsawī, *Wasīlat al-Najāt*, Najaf, 1385 A.H., Vol. II, pp. 296-70.

be valid until and unless the wife is prepared for the same.[24] This aspect of law shall result in great hardship to a wife. Advantage can be taken in such a case of the power of Ḥākim Shar' to give adequate relief in various cases. The law has been fully discussed in the preceding chapter on Nafqah (maintenance) under Shī'ī law and may be consulted there. It may, however, be added here that the Hākim Shar' can exercise the power to dissolve a marriage in appropriate cases. Thus if he is satisfied from the facts of a particular case that the husband is guilty of cruelty to such an extent as no wife can be expected to bear, he may in the interest of justice, equity and good conscience dissolve it. It is unfortunate that the above-mentioned principle of law was not appreciated in Pakistan and India with the result that the Shī'āh wives like the Ḥanafī wives were sometimes put to great hardship on this account. A recourse to the above rule of law can alleviate the hardships of Shī'ah wives to a great extent. But much relief has been provided to them by the provisions of the Dissolution of Muslim Marriages Act of 1939 as discussed below :

The law in force in Pakistan and India: The vast majority of the Muslims in Pakistan and India belong to the Ḥanafī sect. The Ḥanafī law does not allow the dissolution of marriage on the ground of ill-treatment of a wife by the husband, and the Courts of pre-partition India followed this rule. What the Courts do not seem to be aware of is that the Ḥanafī jurists adopt and follow the law laid down by some other Imam of the Sunni sect when necessary. The Courts could have followed this practice and followed the Mālikī, Shafi'ī and Ḥanbalī laws in this matter. The result of the then existing practice proved very injurious to the Ḥanafī wives whose husbands were guilty of cruelty. These women were forced to live miserable lives and they suffered to such an extent that some actually renounced Islam and turned Christian to get rid of their cruel husbands. It is a fact that nearly all of

24. *Ibid.*, Ja'far b. al-Ḥasan, *Sharā'i' al-Islām*, Tehran, 1377 A.H., Vol. II, p. 199.

them embraced Islam again after the dissolution of their marriages under the provisions of the Native Converts Marriage Dissolution Act, 1866. But in a few cases they were induced by the Missionaries to retain their new faith. It was then that the Ulamā were aroused to a sense of duty towards the injured women. The late Mawlānā Ashraf 'Alī Thānawī obtained Fatwās (dictums) of the Māliki 'Ulamā in Medina to meet certain important contingencies and advised people to adopt them when absolutely necessary.[25] The late Maulvi Muhammad Aḥmad Kazmi, Advocate, Allahabad High Court, M.L.A. and a member of the Working Committee of the Jamiat al-Ulama-i-Hind introduced a Bill in the Indian Assembly in 1938 which was passed in 1939 and is known as the Dissolution of Muslim Marriages Act (Act VIII of 1939). The provisions of this Act are mainly based on the decisions of the Algerian Courts mentioned by Ameer Ali.[26] This Act brought a revolution in the lives of Muslim women, Sunnīs as well as Shī'āhs. Some important provisions of the Act read as under:

2. A woman married under Muslim law shall be entitled to obtain a decree for the dissolution of her marriage on any one or more of the following grounds, namely :

VIII—That the husband treats her with cruelty, that is to say :

(*a*) habitually assaults her or makes her life miserable by cruelty of conduct even when such conduct does not amount to physical ill-treatment or,

(*b*) associates with women of evil repute or leads an infamous life,

(*c*) attempts to force her to lead an immoral life,

(*d*) disposes of her property, or prevents her exercising her legal rights over it,

(*e*) obstructs her in the performance of her religious profession or practices, etc.

It will be seen that sub-clause (*a*) provides against mental

25. Ashraf 'Alī Thanawī, *Al-Ḥīlah al-Nājizah*, Karachi n.d. pp. 37, 38.
26. Ameer Ali, *op. cit.*, Vol. II, pp. 561, 62.

cruelty as well as physical cruelty. It has been held by the High Court of East Pakistan, "the conduct on the part of the husband which renders her (the wife's) life miserable is sufficient to attract this provision of the law (section 2 (VIII (*a*) of the Dissolution of Muslim Marriages Act, 1939) and it is not necessary that the treatment has to be accompanied by some assault on her....The entire bundle of circumstances and the background of such occurrences as well as the effect on the life and the physical and mental well-being of the wife has to be considered in arriving at a finding whether the wife's life was rendered miserable thereby or not."[27] If a wife seeks the dissolution of her marriage on the commission or omission of an act by her husband, it is necessary that she should not herself have forced the husband to resort to the conduct complained of. Muslim law has stressed the reciprocal goodwill and kindness in marriage. A wife who is herself guilty of cruelty and harshness towards her husband cannot reasonably complain if the husband fails to show affection or care for her.

The Courts as a rule did not before the passing of Act VIII of 1939 take into consideration the infliction of mental or legal cruelty by the husband on the wife. The clause quoted above has provided a much needed clarification of the attitude of Muslim law towards a husband's cruelty to his wife. A Muslim wife can now sue for dissolution of her marriage even when the husband's conduct does not amount to physical cruelty but constitutes only mental cruelty. But while giving every facility to a wife for the dissolution of her marriage, care must be taken not to make marriages insecure by dissolving them on inadequate grounds. Only when the circumstances are such that it is almost impossible for a wife to live with her husband should she be given relief under the provision of this clause.

English Law : Until well into the 20th century, cruelty was not considered a sufficient ground for the dissolution of

27. Ghoas Ali Vs. Firoza Khatoon, PLD 1969 Dacca, 548.

marriage under the English law but only a ground for judicial separation. It was in 1937 that cruelty was made a ground on the basis of which a husband or wife could seek the dissolution of his or her marriage. Muslim law does not make it necessary that a husband should get his marriage dissolved through a *Qāḍī* on the basis of the wife's cruelty to him. He can himself pronounce a divorce whenever he is not happy with his marriage without the intervention of the *Qāḍī*. As English law does not confer such a power on the husband, it is necessary that the Court should come to his help when he is subjected to cruelty by the wife. The Act of 1937 was repealed and replaced by the Matrimonial Causes Act of 1965. Sec. I of the Act provides for the presentation of a petition of divorce by the husband or wife as given below :

(*a*) By the husband or wife on the ground that the respondent has since the celebration of the marriage treated the petitioner with cruelty.

Cruelty has been defined by the English Courts as conduct of such character as has caused danger to life, limb and health or when there is a reasonable apprehension of the same. It may be physical or mental.[28] Actual danger to health or a reasonable apprehension of the same is a material condition of cruelty.[29] In determining cruelty the English Courts take into consideration both the physical as well as mental cruelty when deciding a case for divorce.

In English law emphasis is laid on the effect of an act i.e., whether it has injuriously affected the petitioner's health or well-being or there is an apprehension of the same. No act will amount to cruelty unless it injuriously affects the petitioner's physical or mental health or there is a reasonable apprehension of the same.[30] A course of conduct creating mental distress and anxiety and thereby injuring bodily health amounts to cruelty.[31] Hence a long continued series of minor acts, no

28. Russell Vs. Russell, (1897) A.C. 395 (H.L.).
29. Jamieson Vs. Jamieson, (1952), 1, All. E.R. 878.
30. Moss Vs. Moss, (1916), P. 155.
31. Jamieson Vs. Jamieson, (1952) 1 All. E.R. 878.

one of which could in isolation be regarded as serious may be more effective than obvious acts of cruelty.[32] Some acts taken by themselves may not constitute cruelty but they will amount to cruelty if their accumulated effect is such as actually causes injury to health or a reasonable apprehension of the same.[33] It has been held that in cruelty there should be wilful and unjustifiable conduct on the part of one spouse which causes pain and misery to the other.[34] Hence prolonged nagging has been held to amount to cruelty.[35] But care should be taken not to take an exaggerated view of such matters as may be considered part of the ordinary wear and tear of married life. The English Courts dissolve a marriage when it is not possible for the wife to live with her husband with safety of life and limb.[36] In determining cruelty the physical, mental and social conditions of the parties are taken into consideration. Whether an act amounts to cruelty in law depends on the circumstances of a particular case and the same act may constitute cruelty in one case but not so in another. Thus it was pointed out in a case that certain acts of indignity, short of physical injury, may constitute cruelty in the case of a sensitive and refined woman belonging to a respectable family of a high standard of culture, but may not be so construed in the case of an uneducated woman of a low social status.[37]

It may be stated here that the Muslim law does not attach any importance to the effect of an act of alleged cruelty. An injurious effect on the wife's health, caused by the husband's conduct may be taken into consideration, but its absence shall not be material to the determination of cruelty.

Law in U.S.A. : Law in the U.S.A. allows the dissolution

32. Watt (Thomas) Vs. Thomas, (1947) 1 All. E.R. 582.
33. Russell Vs. Russell, (1897) A.C. 395; Squire Vs. Squire, (1948) 2 All. E.R. 52; Cooper Vs. Cooper, 1955, P. 99.
34. Horton Vs. Horton, (1940) P. 187.
35. King Vs. King, (1953) A.C. 124.
36. Atkins Vs. Atkins, (1942) 2 All. E.R. 637; King Vs. King (1952) 2 All. E.R. 584.
37. Lissack Vs. Lissack, (1950) 2 All. E.R. 233.

of marriage on the basis of mental cruelty as well as physical cruelty. It is, as we have seen earlier, difficult to define "cruelty" as a ground of divorce. But the Courts in the U.S.A. have expressed the same view as expressed by English Courts that it is legal cruelty if it is such conduct towards the plaintiff by the defendant as will cause him or her injury by actual personal violence, or reasonable apprehension of it, or such course of treatment as endangers his or her life or health and renders cohabitation unsafe.[38] Cruelty has been described as "any unwarranted and unjustifiable conduct on the part of either the husband or the wife which causes the other spouse to endure suffering and distress to such a degree as to wholly destroy peace of mind, and make life with such a spouse unbearable, and which completely destroys the real purpose and objects of matrimony although no physical act of cruelty may have been inflicted.[39]

Physical cruelty does not require much elaboration and each case may be decided upon its simple medical testimony. Even a single act of violence under little or no provocation may sometimes amount to such cruelty as may entitle the wife to divorce if it was she who was subjected to it.[40]

It is more difficult to lay down what acts of mental cruelty will form a ground sufficient under American law for the dissolution of marriage. It was stated in a case, "marriage implies companionship, and is supposed to be based upon mutual regard and affection. For a husband and wife to live and sleep in the same house, and eat at the same table food prepared by the wife, without the husband speaking to the wife, except in anger, for a period of three months at a time must have been, at least very disagreeable if not unbearable. . . The effect of such conduct upon a nervous, sensitive woman can better be imagined than described and may have seriously impaired the plaintiff's health . . . "

The Court found such conduct to be a sufficient ground

38. Morris Vs. Morris, 14 Cal. 76 ; Brown Vs. Brown, 129 Ga. 246 ; Rowe Vs. Rowe, 84 Kans 696.

39. Dickinson Vs. Dickinson, 54 Ind. App. 53.

40. Crabtree Vs, Crabtree, 154 Ark. 401, MacDonald Vs. MacDonald 155 Cal. 655 ; Linnell Vs. Linnell, 249 Mass 51,

for divorce.[41] But what may be cruelty causing great mental distress in one case may not be in another. Each case must depend upon its own facts and circumstances.[42] Inasmuch as the effect of acts done is an important element in the offence of cruelty, the character of the parties, their positions in society, their sensibilities and actual physical reactions to external stimuli, mental make-up and the like are all a part of the facts and circumstances to be presented to the tribunal passing on the ultimate question of cruelty.[43]

Any unjustifiable conduct on the part of either the husband or wife which so grievously wounds the feelings of the other or so utterly destroys the peace of mind of the other as to seriously impair the health . . . constitutes cruelty.[44] It may, however, be pointed out that cruelty and ill-treatment are not to be confused with simple quarrels and differences that are a normal part of an ordinary marriage. Thus it was explained in a case, "As man at best is but human, a nagging, abusive and exasperating wife may cause him to lose control of his temper 'for husbands are men, not angels."[45] Similarly mère family difficulties existing between a husband and wife are not sufficient cause for divorce where they show no grave or insuperable cause which renders cohabitation unbearable.[46] It was explained in one case, "Acts inflicted upon or treatment administered to certain individuals might, because of social standing or peculiar mental make-up, drive such persons to actual insanity; yet the same acts or treatments might be the cause of only hilarious amusement to others. Obviously there is no legal cruelty in the latter case".[47] The term, "cruel and inhuman treatment" is a relative term and depends upon the

41. Reinhard Vs. Reinhard, 96 Wis, 955,
42. Doe Vs. Doe, 48 Utah, 200 ; 158 Pac 781.
43. Fleming Vs. Fleming, 95 Cal. 430 ; Marks Vs. Marks, 56 Minn 264.
44. Carpenter Vs. Carpenter, 30 Kans. 712 ; Barnes Vs. Barnes, 95 Cal. 171 ; Humber Vs. Humber, 109 Mirs 216.
45. Barngrover Vs. Barngrover, 57 Cal. App. 43.
46. Bowen Vs. Bowen, 179 Mich 574.
47. Nye's Appeal, 126 Pa. 341.

circumstances of each particular case."[47-a] Cruel treatment may be accentuated by circumstances as when a husband is guilty of personal violence to the wife in the presence of other people.[48]

Conclusion : It will be seen from the above discussion that Muslim law has laid some general but important principles of law dealing with cases of husband's cruelty to his wife. Although actual examples are not discussed we can deduce rules for our guidance from those general principles to meet particular cases. A further difficulty is the absence of case-law on the subject in Pakistan and India due to the fact that Muslim women were taught to consider it their duty to bear patiently all kinds of cruelty at the hands of their husbands without seeking assistance from a Court of law. Under Muslim law there is no stigma attached to a wife seeking or obtaining a divorce but the Indian Muslims were greatly influenced by the thought and practice of their neighbours, the Hindus. Hindu law did not at one time allow divorce or dissolution of marriage to the wife and Muslim wives, belonging to respectable families, likewise started considering it abhorent to seek a divorce. They preferred to bear all sorts of hardships rather than bear what they considered the shame and disgrace of a divorce.

The attitude of the Courts was also responsible to some extent for this hesitation to seek dissolution because they generally applied Ḥanafī law to the Ḥanafīs even when it involved unnecessary hardship. It seems their attention was not drawn to the practice of the Ḥanafī jurists who allow the adoption of the law of another sect of the Sunnis whenever necessary or desirable in the interest of justice.[49] The Dissolution of Muslim Marriages Act, 1939 has solved the difficulty in Pakistan and India. Many other Muslim countries have also made the husband's cruelty to the wife a ground on the basis of which a marriage can now be dissolved by a Court on the basis of ill-treatment.

47-*a*. Barngrower Vs. Barngrower, 57 Cal. App. 43.

48. Milner Vs. Milner, 4 Swab & T 240 ; Keezer, *Marriage and Divorce*, Indianopolis, 1946 Art 257.

49. Mawlānā Ashraf 'Alī, *op. cit.*, see also Maintenance—Husbands, failure to maintain wife—Ḥanafī law.

V. *Non-payment of dower*: Dower is a necessary requirement of marriage. Stress has been laid on the husband's duty to pay the wife's dower in the Qur'ān wherein it is stated:

"And give women their dower as a free gift."[50]

If the husband does not pay the wife's prompt dower when demanded by her, he shall be guilty of the breach of this condition of the marriage contract. But this breach shall not entitle the wife to the dissolution of her marriage. All that she can do in such a case is to refuse to live with the husband until and unless he pays the dower. She shall not lose her right of receiving maintenance from her husband in such a case.[51] She can also initiate legal proceedings against her husband for the realisation of her dower.

VI. Obstruction to the performance of her religious observances by the wife: It is quite uncommon that a husband should obstruct the wife in the performance of her religious observances when they belong to the same sect of Muslims. A husband may not sometimes on account of religious fanaticism or narrow-mindedness allow the wife such observances of her sect and creed as he dislikes and may try to obstruct her in the observance of the doctrines of her own faith. As stated earlier, a Muslim can lawfully marry a Jewess or a Christian woman. He may feel inclined to forbid her from observing such religious duties as are not performed by Muslims.

There is a difference of opinion amongst the Sunnī jurists on the question whether a husband can stop his Kitābiyah wife from visiting a synagogue or church. The Ḥanafīs are of the view that a husband can stop her from visiting the synagogue or church,[52] and one of the reasons advanced is that the husband has the right over his wife to enjoy her company and in so far as her visiting the synagogue to that extent renders his right inoperative, he can prohibit her from visiting

50. Qur'ān, Sūrah al-Nisā, IV : 4.
51. See Maintenance, Disobedient wife.
52. Al-Jazarī, al-Fiqh 'ala'l-Mazāhib al-Arba'ah, Vol. IV, p. 76.

the church or synagogue.[53] Ibn Qayyim criticises this reason by saying that the same situation would arise in relation to a Muslim female and it is obvious that he cannot stop a Muslim female from visiting mosques on account of a Tradition related from the Prophet,[54] which is to the effect that the Prophet (peace be on him) said:

> "Do not prohibit the female slaves of Allah from visiting His mosques."[55]

This line of reasoning finds support in *al-Mughnī* wherein Ibn Qudāmah after quoting this Ḥadīth relates that al-Zubayr was married to 'Ātikah, daughter of Zayd, son of 'Amr, son of Nufayl, and she used to visit mosques and he did not like this. So he asked her, "Why don't you perform your prayers inside your house?" She said, "I will continue to visit the mosques till you prohibit me therefrom" and he disliked prohibiting her on account of the afore-related Tradition from the Prophet[56] (peace be on him). The other argument offered by Kāsānī in *Badā'i' al-Ṣanā'i'* is that a husband has a right to detain his wife in his house and her going out destroys this right and hence he has a right to stop her.[57] On principle this argument also does not appear to be strong because a wife's staying in her house is *per se* not an act superior to visiting for prayer—a divine place of worship. Qur'ān itself upholds the religious sanctity of synagogues and churches[58]. It also speaks of good Jews and of good Christians, who are promised Allah's mercies for their good conduct.[59] Allah describes as satanic conduct the stopping of a person from "Ṣalāt"[60] while it describes the prayers of Moses and Christ as Ṣalāt.[60-a] In fact even the permission to marry Kitābiyah women is for the chaste ones

53. Ibn Qayyim, *Aḥkām ahl-al-Zimmah*, Cairo, n.d., Vol. II, p. 438.
54. *Ibid.*, pp. 438, 39.
55. Ibn Qudāmah, *al-Mughnī*, Vol. VII, p. 226.
56. *Ibid.*
57. Al-Kāsānī, *Badā'i' al-Ṣanā'i'*, Vol. II, p. 311.
58. Qur'ān, Surah al-Hajj, XVII : 40.
59. Qur'ān, Surah al-Baqarah, I : 62; Surah al-Mā'idah, VI : 69.
60. Qur'ān, Surah al-Baqarah, I : 114; Surah al-Mā'idah, VII : 91.
60-*a*. Qur'ān, Surah al-A'rāf, IX : 170.

among them;[61] and the word "Muhṣanāt" in its larger context would imply a woman given to prayer.

The Mālikīs are of the view that it is not open to a husband to stop his Kitābiyah wife from visiting the synagogue or church or from drinking wine or eating ham. Mālik, however, says that marrying such a woman is not prohibited on account of the express words of Qur'ān but in so far as eating of pork, drinking of wine and visiting synagogue would have effect on the children, marrying such women is not desirable.[62]

Ahmad b. Ḥanbal is credited with two views, that is (*i*) that the husband has a right to stop his wife from visiting the church or synagogue and (*ii*) the contrary view that he cannot stop her.[63] The argument of this school seems to be that the husband can stop her from that which totally destroys his right, but he cannot stop her from that which interferes with the ideal exercise thereof. For instance, according to one view, he can stop her from using garlic, onion as they take away something from enjoyment of her company, but in so far as her use of such things does not render impossible the enjoyment of her company, he cannot command her not to take garlic and onion.

Generally, S͟hāfi'ī is of the view that a Kitābiyah wife has the same rights and privileges as a Muslim wife except in some matters which do not pertain to the present issue.[64] However, as S͟hāfi'ī is of the view that a Muslim can prohibit his Muslim wife from visiting a mosque, on the same reasoning he would appear also to have such a right in relation to a Kitābiyah wife.[65]

One further reason, maintained by Ibn Qayyim, is that by allowing a Kitābiyah wife to visit a church or a synagogue,

61. Qur'ān, Surah al-Mā'idah, VI ; 5.
62. Al-Jazarī, *op. cit.*, Vol. IV, p. 76 ; Saḥnūn, *al-Mudawwanah*, Vol. II, p. 216.
63. Ibn Qayyim, *op. cit.*, Vol. II, p. 438 ; al-Mardāwī, *al-Inṣāf*, Vol. VIII, pp. 351-53.
64. Al-S͟hāfi'ī, *al-Umm*, Vol. V. p. 157.
65. Ibn Qudāmah, *op. cit.*, p. 226.

a Muslim husband might be guilty of acting in aid of *kufr*. But on the very basis that Ibn Qayyim uses for criticising the Ḥanafī views, this reason would appear unsound since by the very fact of marrying a Kitābiyah a Muslim would be aiding *kufr* if being a Christian or a Jew is *per se* kufr. It would be illogical to affirm that Allāh sees no harm in the chaste ones among the Kitābiyah women to be the mothers of Muslim children yet the Muslims could prevent them from visiting churches and synagogues for prayers, when prayer is the very pillar on which good character is built.

Shī'ī Law: The Shī'ah Jurists have expressed the same view as stated by the Ḥanafī, Shāfi'ī and Ḥanbalī jurists. They have said that a husband has got the right to disallow his Kitābiyah wife from going to the church and from drinking intoxicating liquor or cooking or eating pork, bacon and other piggery produce in his house. Mawlānā 'Alī ibn 'Abd al-'Alī says that the husband can also disallow his Kitābiyah wife from going to visit her (Kitābiyah) relations and as a matter of fact from going out of his house altogether.[66] The reason advanced is that due to the wife's absence, the husband cannot avail of her services if he may desire or stand in need of them. 'Allāmah Ḥillī gives still more extensive right to the husband and says that the husband can stop his Kitābiyah wife from going to the church and even on the occasions of festivals. He further states that a husband possesses the right to disallow his wife from going out of his house irrespective of the fact whether she is a Kitābiyah or Muslimah. He bases this view on the same ground as given above.[67] It is stated in *Sharā'i-al-Islām* that the husband can prevent his Kitābiyah wife from going to the church or synagogue in the same way as he can stop her from going out of his house. He can also prevent her from drinking intoxicating liquor or eating pork, bacon etc. eating foods producing offensive odour and from remaining in a state of uncleanliness. She will be considered to be

66. 'Alī ibn 'Abd-al 'Alī, *Jāmi' al-Maqāsid fi Sharḥ al-Qawā'id*, chapter on Marriage.

67. Allamah Al-Ḥilli, *Tazkirah al-Fuqahā*, chapter on Marriage.

refractory if she does not abstain from whatever spoils the pleasure of intimacy such as eating food producing offensive odour. Similarly, she will be held to be refractory if she does not cleanse or adorn herself when so desired by the husband. He can stop such conduct.[68]

To obstruct the wife from the observance or performance of the essential obligations of her religion goes against the very fundamental concept of freedom of religion of every man and woman and may create an undesirable and even an intolerable situation for the wife. But if a matter falls short of religious obligation and consists merely of the exercise of certain rights or performance of certain acts permitted by her religion but not obligatory while they are obnoxious to a Muslim, the husband may stop the wife from the same. Thus he can stop the wife from cooking bacon, ham or other piggery produce in his house. Similarly, he may not allow her to distil intoxicating liquor in his house.[69] But he cannot force her not to do such acts as relate to the essential observances of religious obligations. Thus he cannot force her to give up prayers according to her own religion or prevent her from doing such other acts as are incumbent on her under her religion as fasting on particular occasions. Similarly, he cannot force her to perform such acts as Muslim women have to perform, such as taking a bath under certain conditions.[70]

VII. *To pass reasonable time with the wife*: As stated, one of the important objects of marriage is a happy companionship of the parties who must live together and enjoy each other's company. A husband is usually engaged in outdoor work and so mixes with people, but the wife in most cases remains at home. She, therefore, stands in need of diversion and the husband's company. The Muslim jurists have realised the importance of this aspect of married life. Thus it is stated in *Al-Fatāwā al-Hindiyah*, "When a man has only one wife he

68. Ja'far bin al-Ḥasan, *op. cit.*, Vol. II, p. 181.
69. *Ibid.*, *Al-Fatāwā al-Hindiyah*, *op. cit.*, Vol. II, p. 8.
70. *Ibid.*

may be directed to be attentive to her, and to occupy the same apartment with her at times, though no exact time has been fixed by Zahir Riwāyah."[71] If a husband neglects to perform this marital obligation, the wife can complain to the *Qāḍī* who shall admonish the husband, but the marriage can not be dissolved on this basis.[72] It is universally recognised that companionship, consideration for each other, kindness etc. are highly desirable for a successful marriage, yet the law cannot help the aggrieved wife when the husband fails to perform these obligations. These matters can be resolved only by mutual love and regard, and cannot be enforced by law. A Scottish proverb aptly explains this matter. It says, "A pennyweight of love is worth a pound of law." Again, it was observed in a case that the wife does not occupy the position of a servant. She makes his home cheerful and inviting and ministers to his happiness in a multitude of ways outside of the drudgery of household labours. The husband must also on his part try to make the wife's life cheerful by passing reasonable time with her to give her some relief from her drudgery work. Nonetheless, breach of this marital obligation by the husband amounts only to a moral offence. It is in extreme cases alone, as when the husband deserts the wife, that a *Qāḍī* may give relief to the wife by dissolving the marriage.

VIII. *Non-compliance with the Qāḍī's order to divorce the wife*: Under the Sunnī law it is only the husband who can divorce the wife and no one else can exercise this power. This view is based on a verse in the Qur'ān wherein it is stated "or he foregoes in whose hand is the marriage tie."[73] The Sunnis consider that the verse refers to the husband so that it is only the husband who is empowered to divorce his wife. But there is another equally important verse of the Qur'ān which enjoins on the husbands to keep them (the wives) with

71. *Al-Fatāwā al-Hindiyah, op. cit.*, Vol. II, p. 41.
72. *Ibid.*
73. Qur'ān, Surah al-Baqarah II : 237.

kindness or separate from them with humanity [74] Cases do occur where the husband fails to obey the above injunction. A difficult problem arises here. The husband transgressing the above injunction is guilty of breach of an injunction of the sacred text but the marriage cannot be dissolved when he fails or refuses to divorce the wife since no one else—not even the *Qāḍī*—can dissolve the marriage. This position may result in great hardship to the wife. In order to resolve the problem and to give necessary relief to the wife, the Sunnī jurists have recourse to a chain of reasoning which may be summed up as follows: Allāh is the Ruler of the universe. He made man His vicegerent on the earth. The world is divided into countries which are governed by kings. A country is divided into different parts and the same are governed by such persons as are appointed to perform various functions by the Ruler. It is the duty of the *Qāḍī* to administer justice and to remove wrongs and transgressions in his jurisdiction. If a *Qāḍī* is satisfied that a husband is not keeping his wife with kindness as is incumbent on him under the verse of the Qur'ān cited above, it is the duty of the *Qāḍī* to ask him to separate from the wife as directed by the above verse. If the husband fails or refuses to do so he clearly becomes a transgressor of the above sacred text. The *Qāḍī* must therefore step in and order the husband to divorce the wife in order to remove the transgression. If the husband does not comply with the *Qāḍī's* order, it becomes the duty of the *Qāḍī* himself to remove the transgression and he in this way becomes empowered to divorce the wife on behalf of the husband.

To illustrate the above matter, we may quote the example of a husband who is incapable of sexual intimacy with his wife. In such a case he cannot be considered to be keeping her with kindness and so becomes a transgressor of the above verse in this matter. The *Qāḍī* when satisfied of the husband's incapacity, must order him to divorce the wife. If the husband fails or refuses to comply with the *Qāḍī's* order, he

74. Qur'ān, Surah al-Baqarah II: 231.

is clearly a transgressor and the *Qāḍī*, to be able to remove the transgression, becomes empowered to divorce the wife on behalf of the husband.[75] Another example of a case of this nature is provided when a husband does not mete out equal treatment to all of his wives. The *Qāḍī* can, in such a case, as fully discussed in another chapter, divorce the wife on behalf of the husband.[76] Even where the Ḥanafī law does not provide a remedy, or falls short of providing an adequate remedy, the *Qāḍī* can, in order to have full justice done in a particular matter, send the case to the *Qāḍī* of a Mālikī, Shāfi'ī or Ḥanbalī school whose law provides full relief in the particular case. This has been discussed at several places such as under a husband's failure to maintain the wife.[77]

75. *Al-Fatāwā al-Hindiyah, op. cit.*, Vol, II, p. 133.
76. See chapter on Inequality between Wives (chapter 22).
77. See Maintenance, Husband's failure to maintain wife (chapter 21).

Chapter 24

DISSOLUTION OF MARRIAGE BY THE QĀḌI ON HIS OWN INITIATIVE

In Muslim countries, the function of administration of justice is entrusted to the *Qāḍī*. A *Qāḍī* has been defined in the *Majallat al-Aḥkām* as the person who is appointed by the Sultan to adjudicate upon and determine disputes and claims between contestants according to *Sharī'ah*. The *Qāḍī* differs from a civil judge inasmuch as he wields power not only in civil and criminal matters but also in religious affairs.

Under Muslim law it is the *Qāḍī*'s duty to stop people from transgressing the injunctions laid down by Islam and the Muslim law. If he finds that a person or persons are acting against a clear injunction of Muslim law it shall be his duty to stop such an act on his own initiative. Thus a man and a woman can live together as husband and wife only when they are lawfully married. If they are not so married, their intimacy shall be unlawful and they shall be considered to be living in sin and it shall be the duty of the *Qaḍı* to separate them. The marriage may be *bāṭil* (void) or *fāsid* (irregular).

Bāṭil and Fāsid Marriages: A *Bāṭil* (void) marriage is no marriage at all and the parties to it shall be considered to be living in adultery and shall be liable to punishment for *zinā* or illicit intercourse. It does not require the *Qāḍi's* order for its termination.

A *Fāsid* (irregular) marriage is such as is defective in some way or other. It is presumed under certain circumstances that when one of the prescribed conditions has not been observed, probably the spouses did not know of the legal position or the existence of certain fact or facts and that they had contracted the marriage under a misconception. They, therefore, shall not be liable to punishment for adultery and the children born of the marriage, if any, shall be considered to be legitimate, but in other respects the marriage shall be considered to be unlawful. A *fāsid* marriage is no marriage so that the spouses cannot be considered to be husband and wife but shall be considered to be strangers from a legal point of view. Under such circumstances all intimacy between them shall be regarded to be prohibited from a religious point of view as well as repugnant to the interest of society and they shall be considered to be living in sin. It shall, therefore, be the duty of the *Qāḍī* to separate them on his own initiative when he comes to know of it. It shall not be necessary in such a case that a complaint should be lodged before him by any person. In practice, however, his personal knowledge shall be very restricted and he may have to depend on the information given to him by someone. If the *Qāḍī* is satisfied from his own knowledge or on his enquiry of the truth of the information given to him, he shall immediately order their separation, and he shall ensure that his order is carried out. For this purpose he shall take such measures as he may consider necessary.

Shī'ī Law : The Shī'i view is the same as the Sunnī view in respect of invalidity of *bāṭil* marriages. But under that law it shall also be the duty of the Ḥākim Sharī'ah or Religious head to separate the parties to a *mut'ah* marriage when the parties continue to live as husband and wife although the period of time for which the marriage was agreed upon has expired and they have not entered into a fresh agreement in respect of the same.

English Law : As discussed earlier, the English law also considers a void marriage to be a nullity from the very beginning. It is considered as if no marriage has taken place between the parties to the alleged marriage. The English law will also consider the parties to be living in sin. Unlike Muslim law, however, it shall not be the duty of the Court to take the initiative in the matter, but it will take notice of the matter only when its attention is drawn to it. According to Swiss law, if the marriage is void, anybody may bring a petition (for nullity) and the public prosecutor is under a duty to draw the attention of the Court to the same. The same rule applies to many other European countries, where the public prosecutor is charged with bringing petitions for nullity. But nothing of the sort is done by the King's Proctor in England. There is no such marriage as *fāsid* marriage in English law.

Law in the U.S.A. : The law in respect of the cognisance of a void marriage differs in different States in the U.S.A. The law of some States provides that a petition for the annulment of marriage can be presented by one of the parties to a void marriage. Where the party concerned suffers from a disability such as when he or she is a minor or insane, the petition can be presented by his or her guardian. In some States the law requires that certain public officer or attorney shall appear, represent and guard the interests of the State or one of the parties concerned. It can be seen from the above that a Court in the U.S.A. does not and cannot take cognisance of a case on its own initiative.

Chapter 25

IRTIDĀD OR APOSTASY

Perliminary : The word *Irtidād* is derived from *radd* which means turning back and the word is used to mean going back to unbelief from Islam. It thus means renunciation of Islam by a Muslim who is called *Murtadd*, that is, one who has given up his faith in Islam.

Muslim : Before discussing apostasy it is desirable to understand as to who is a Muslim. A Muslim is one who believes in :—

1. The existence and unity of God, and
2. In the messengership of Muḥammad (peace be on him.)

A belief in the Prophethood of the Prophet (peace be on him) means a belief in his message and that the teachings contained in the Qur'ān are the messages of God conveyed through him and possess an absolute and final authority.

The Qur'ān has laid down five points of belief as essential for a true Muslim. Thus it is laid down, "This Book, there is no doubt in it, is a guide to those who keep their duty, who believe in the Unseen, and keep up prayer and spend out of what We have given them. And who believe in that which has been revealed to thee, and that which was revealed before thee, and of the Hereafter they are sure".[1] To be more explicit, the essential articles of belief are a belief in God, the Great Unseen, in Angels, Prophets,[2] the Divine revelations revealed through different Prophets[2a] and the day of Resurrection.[2b] As regards the devotional acts, a Muslim is enjoined to believe in the obligatory nature of the five daily prayers,[2c] the payment of the prescribed amount of

1. Qur'ān, Surah al-Baqarah, I : 2-4 ; II : 177.
2. Qur'ān, Surah al-Baqarah, II : 177.

2a. Qur'ān, Surah al-Baqarah, II : 136.

2b. Qur'ān, Surah al-Baqarah, II : 177 ; Surah al-Nisā', IV : 162.

2c. Qur'ān, Surah Hūd, XII : 114 ; Surah Banī Isrā'īl, XV : 78; Surah al-Baqarah, II : 238 ; Surah al-Nisā', VI : 162.

Zakāt,[2d] fasting during the month of Ramaḍān[2e] and making a pilgrimage to Mecca if his financial condition allows it.[2f]

A person shall be considered to be a Muslim even if he does not accept the interpretation of the Muslim Jurists on any point or does not perform the religious rituals as long as he believes in the essential articles of the faith, and does not neglect them out of disbelief. This view is supported by a Tradition that the Prophet (peace be on him) has said, "Do not call a person who utters the *Kalimah* a *Kāfir* (unbeliever) simply if he commits a sin".[3] The Courts have held, "a person shall be deemed to be a Muslim if he believes in the Unity of God, and in the messengership of the Holy Phrophet (peace be on him)".[4] A belief in the messengership of the Prophet (peace be upon him) means a belief in the message of God conveyed through him. Applying this criterion it has been held that a person who fulfils the above conditions shall be considered to be a Muslim and even his pronounced dissent from some interpretations of various doctrines does not take him out of the fold of Islam. The Muslims are strictly prohibited from disbelieving the assertion of a person that he is a Muslim. Thus it is laid down in the Qur'ān :

> O, ye who believe:
> When ye go abroad
> In the cause of God,
> Investigate carefully,
> And say not to any one
> Who offers you a salutation :
> "Thou art none of a Believer"
> Coveting the perishable goods
> Of this life : With God
> Are profits and spoils abundant

2*d*. Qur'ān, Surah al-Baqarah, II ; 110, 177, 195 ; Surah al-Nisā', VI : 162 ; Surah al-Mā'idah, VI : 55.

2*e*. Qur'ān, Surah al-Baqarah, II : 183, 185.

2*f*. Qur'ān, Surah al-Baqarah, II ; 196.

3. Walī al-Dīn al-Khaṭīb, *Mishkāt al-Maṣābīḥ*. Delhi, 1932, pp. 17-18.

4 Khalil Ahmad Vs. Israfil, AIR 1916, Pat 87; Jiwan Khan Vs. Habib and others, AIR 1933 Lah. 759

Even thus were ye yourselves
Before, till God conferred
On you His favours; therefore
Carefully investigate,
For God is ever aware
Of all that ye do[5].

They must believe the declaration of a person that he is a Muslim. Thus it is laid down in the Qurān: "And say not to any one who offers you salutation, "thou art not a believer."[6] It may be noted here that the Muslims use their own form of salutation, namely, 'As-Salām 'Alaykum' which means "peace be on you". The use of this form of salutation by a person clearly indicates that he is a Muslim. The above injunction of the Qur'ān makes it clear that no Muslim can disbelieve this indirect declaration by a person that he is a Muslim. The Muslims must believe this indirect assertion of a person that he is a Muslim. The injunction of the Qur'ān, as quoted above, is not restricted merely to wars or battles, but it is a general direction to the Muslims. It is, however, subject to the condition that he should not openly declare his belief in something which is against the essential articles of the faith or express disbelief in these articles of the faith. There is a Tradition that after a certain battle, one of his Companions related to the Prophet (peace be on him), that he had wounded a *Kāfir* (non-believer in Islam) and was about to kill him when he declared that he was a Muslim and recited the *Kalimah* (Muslim's declaration of Faith) in support of his statement, whereupon he left him. The Prophet (peace be on him) approved of this action. Another Companion narrated a similar occurrence and stated that he had not spared his adversary since it was obvious that his sudden assertion of the Faith was only a trick to save his life. The Prophet (peace be on him) was displeased on hearing this and disapproved of his conduct and reprimanded him saying, "How

5. Qur'ān, Surah al-Nisā', V : 94 (Allama Yusuf Ali).
6. *Ibid.*

could you presume to know what was in the heart of your foe?"[7] It must have been on this account that in most cases involving the decision whether the members of a particular sect were Muslim or not only a half-hearted attempt was made to impugn their religious status. The Courts found no difficulty in holding that the Muḥammadīs (or Wahābīs as they are sometimes called) are Muslims.[8]

It is a well settled rule of law, and one of the fundamental principles of law itself, that no Court can test or gauge the sincerity of religious belief in order to hold whether a person is a Muslim and not a *Zikrī* (infidel). It cannot be possible for any Court to delve into the undisclosed mind of a man and satisfying itself whether that person has or has not belief in any particular religion. It is, therefore, sufficient for a Court to be satisfied that a person professes to be a Muslim and it is not permissible for any Court to enquire further into the state of the mind and belief of a person who professes to belong to a particular faith and enquire whether or not his actual beliefs conform to the orthodox tenets of that particular faith.[9]

(*a*) *Apostate, Description of*: A person shall be considered to be an apostate from Islam only if he renounces Islam for another faith or ceases to believe in one or more of the essential articles of the faith.

It is essential in apostasy that a person should have believed in Islam at one time and should have given up his belief in it at some later stage. If he did not believe in Islam from the very beginning, he may be considered to be a non-Muslim but he cannot be called an apostate.

(*b*) *Criterion of* : The important factor to be considered in the determination of the question of apostasy is if there has actually been a renunciation of Islam. This fact can be established by the evidence of the adoption of another religion or by a declaration or conduct of a person showing that he or

7. Walī al-Dīn al-Khaṭīb, *Mishkāt*, *op. cit.*, p. 299.
8. Q. E. Vs. Ramzan, I. L. R. 7, All. 461; Ataullah Vs. Azizullah I.L.R. 12, All. 494; Jangu Vs. Ahmad Ullah, I.L.R. 13, All. 419; Maula Baksh Vs. Amiruddin, 57 I.C. 1000.
9. Maula Bux Vs. Charuk, P.L.D. 1952, Sind 54.

she has given up his or her belief in the faith of Islam.

(*c*) *Rites of Conversion*: The fact whether the apostate has or has not fully observed the rites prescribed for conversion by the new religion adopted by him or her does not affect the question of apostasy. The real question to be determined in such a case is not whether the ceremonies for the adoption of the new religion have been fully and efficaciously observed by the alleged apostate or not, but whether or not he has renounced Islam.[10] Hence if, on conversion to Christianity, it was proved that the baptism was wholly inefficacious, even then the question of apostasy was not considered to be affected by it.[11]

Essentials: The following are the essential points to be considered in the case of apostasy :—

(*a*) Majority,

(*b*) Understanding, and

(*c*) Free-will.

Majority: It is not necessary under the Muslim law that the apostate should be major.[12] According to Abū Ḥanīfah and Muḥammad, he may be a minor and all that is necessary is that he should be able to comprehend the consequences and effect of his act. But S̲h̲āfi'ī does not agree with this view and he holds that a minor's apostasy shall not be considered valid.[13] The same view as stated by Abū Ḥanīfah and Muḥammad has been expressed by the Chief Court of Sind. It held that if a minor willingly and with understanding changes his or her religion then the conversion is not invalid simply on account of his or her minority.[14] The minor should not, however, be of such a tender age as not to possess understanding.[15]

Understanding: It is an essential condition for apostasy

10. Mst. Bakho Vs. Lal, 71 I.C. 830 ; A.I.R, 1924, Lah. 397.
11. Allah Bakhsh Vs. Amir Begum, 61, P.R. 1800.
12. Al-Marg̲h̲īnānī, *al-Hidāyah*, Delhi, n.d., Vol. II, p. 586.
13. *Ibid.*
14. In re. Muhammad Alam, A.I.R. 1939, Sind, 311.
15. *Al-Fatāwā al-Hindiyah*, Kanpur, 1349 A.H., Vol. II, p.279.

that the apostate should possess understanding.[16] There can be no valid renunciation of Islam if the apostate is insane or drunk or has lost his power of understanding due to some similar cause.[17] The use of disrespectful language towards the Prophet (peace be on him) by a Muslim in a paroxysm of anger, without any intention of renouncing Islam, was held by the jurists to amount to apostasy.[18] Stress has been laid on this to such an extent as to hold that a person shall not be absolved of the penalty for apostasy even if he uses such language under the influence of drink.[19] It is, however, stated that apostasy under compulsion with threat of murder or amputation of limb shall not be punishable. But if the threat relates to something less serious than the above then the person shall be punished for apostasy.[20] Shāfi'ī, Mālik and Aḥmad b. Ḥanbal hold that he cannot be pardoned even if he repents of his act but must be dealt with as an apostate.[21] The Ḥanafīs consider that though he becomes an apostate, yet he can be pardoned if he repents.[22]

Free-will: Another essntial condition in the matter of apostasy is that a person should have free-will in his renunciation of Islam. Hence apostasy under compulsion is not considered to have been effected.[23]

Effect: *Marriage*: On renunciation of Islam by either the husband or the wife an immediate separation takes place between the parties without the decree of the *Qāḍī* and their marriage becomes null and void on the apostasy of either the husband or the wife.[24] Every sort of intimacy between them such as kissing or embracing, becomes unlawful. It is immaterial whether the marriage has or has not been consummated.

16. Al-Marghīnānī, *op. cit.*, Vol. II., p. 586.
17. *Al-Fatāwā al-Hindiyah*, *op. cit.*, Vol. II, p. 279.
18. Ibn 'Ābidīn, *Radd-al-Muḥtār*, Cairo, 1318 A.H., Vol. III, pp. 292, 299.
19. *Ibid.*, p. 300.
20. *Ibid.*, p. 292.
21. *Ibid.*, p. 299.
22. *Ibid.*
23. Ibn 'Ābidīn, *op. cit.*, Vol. III, p. 294.
24. *Ibid.*, p. 292.

Ameer Ali relying on *Radd al-Muḥtār* has expressed the opinion that the marriage is not dissolved immediately on apostasy but subsists during the wife's *'iddah* as is proved by the law that the husband has got a right on return to Islam to divorce her during the period of *'iddah*. He concludes that if the marriage had become dissolved on apostasy, his divorce on return to Islam would have been ineffective.[25] It is submitted that this view is not quite correct. No doubt it appears anomalous that the marriage is annulled immediately on apostasy and yet the husband has a right to divorce her during the period of her *'iddah* ; but the Muslim jurists explain it by saying that a husband has a right of pronouncing three divorces, and before the pronouncement of the third divorce he can lawfully remarry the wife without the necessity of there being an intermediary marriage. The wife becomes absolutely unlawful to him only on the pronouncement of the third divorce. They explain that though the marriage is immediately dissolved on apostasy, yet the right to remarry her, without the necessity of an intermediary marriage, remains to him. He can on his return to Islam remarry her. But it is open to him to make the divorce absolute by pronouncing three divorces during the period of *'iddah* in which case it will not be permissible to him to remarry her until and unless she marries another person and that marriage is dissolved after consummation. The Muslim jurists explain that there is nothing to prevent him from exercising his right to divorce, and he can divorce her during *'iddah*.[26]

In some respects the effects of the husband's apostasy differ from those of the wife's and so it is necessary to consider them separately.

Husband's Apostasy : On the husband's apostasy, the relationship of husband and wife is severed and the man ceases to be the husband of his Muslim wife from the time of his re-

25. Ameer Ali, *Mohammadan Law*, Calcutta, 1908, pp. 431-32.

26. Ibn 'Ābidīn, *op. cit.*, Vol. III, p. 310 ; Abdul Ghani Vs. Aziz-ul-Haq, I.L.R. 39 Cal. 409 ; 14, I.C. 641.

nunciation of Islam.[27] It is immaterial what new religion he has adopted, because a Muslim woman is not allowed to marry a non-Muslim to whatever religion or creed he may belong. Ameer Ali has stated that the marriage of a Muslim woman with a non-Muslim is merely *fāsid* or irregular.[28] He terms a *fāsid* marriage as an invalid marriage, but this view is not accepted by other Muslim jurists. According to them the marriage shall be void for there is a clear prohibition against such a marriage in the Qur'ān wherein it is laid down, "Nor give (believing women) in marriage to idolaters until they believe, and certainly a believing slave is better than an idolater, even though he please you".[29] The Muslim jurists have naturally followed this injunction. The word 'idolater' here includes people belonging to a revealed religion.[30] It is explained that the word "Idolater" has been used in the Qur'ān in a general sense to include all non-Muslims but, where necessary, specification has been made of this matter.

If a person renounces Islam under compulsion, his wife shall not be separated from him because apostasy is concerned with belief. As at heart he still believes in Islam, the compelled person does not become an unbeliever by the verbal renunciation. As his apostasy is doubtful his wife shall not be separated from him.[31] According to the Ḥanafīs, if the husband renounces Islam under the threat of loss of life or limb, the marriage shall not be dissolved. But if he renounces Islam under threat relating to something less serious, his marriage shall be dissolved.[32]

II. (*b*) *Wife's Apostasy*: The apostasy of a married Muslim woman can be considered from two different points, namely:

(1) Motive, and

27. Abdul Ghani Vs. Aziz-ul-Haq, I.L.R. 39 Cal. 409 ; 14 I.C. 641.
28. Ameer Ali, *op. cit.*, p. 321.
29. Qur'ān, Surah Al-Baqarāh, II : 221.
30. Ibn 'Ābidīn, *op. cit.*, Vol. III, p. 309.
31. *Ibid.*, p. 492.
32. Qāḍī Khān, *Fatāwā Qāḍi Khān*, Kanpur, 1310 A.H., Vol. IV, p. 420.

(2) The new religion adopted by her.

Regarding the first, there is a difference of opinion amongst the Muslim jurists as to the effect of apostasy on the subsisting marriage in view of the wife's motive. According to one opinion the marriage shall become dissolved automatically without any regard to the wife's motive for renouncing Islam.[33] Most of the jurists of Balkh, Samarqand and Bukhārāh have, however, held the opinion that a woman sometimes apostatises in order to get rid of her husband and so under no circumstances shall the marriage be dissolved, as a check against such devices.[34]

A similar view has been expressed by the Ḥanafī Jurists, Abū Naṣr and Abu'l-Qāsim al-Ṣaffār. According to them, if a Muslim wife shall become an apostate with a view that by renouncing Islam she may get separated from her husband, no separation shall be caused between them so that the woman may not attain her end.[35] The Muslim Jurists of undivided India held the view that a marriage would be dissolved immediately on apostasy but subsequently they changed this view and adopted the view that the marriage would not get dissolved due to apostasy and did not even consider it necessary to see her motive for the act.[36]

Courts' View : The matter came up before the Courts in several cases. It was held in the case of Mst. Bakho Vs. Lal that the only question which has to be determined is whether renunciation has really taken place.[37] The point has been stressed in some cases that it is not within the province of the Court to enquire into the genuineness or otherwise of the renunciation of the religion and that if a formal renunciation has been accompanied by the rites of the new religion such as baptism then it is immaterial whether her motive is a genuine

33. Ibn 'Ābidīn, *op. cit.*, Vol. III, p. 403.
34. *Ibid.*, p. 403 ; Shaykhzādah, *Majma' al-Anhur*, Constantinople, 1327 A.H., Vol. I, p. 372.
35. Qāḍī Khān, *op. cit.*, Vol. II, p. 267.
36. Ashraf 'Alī Thānawī, *al-Hilat al-Nājizah*, Deoband, n.d., pp. 98-99
37. Bakho Vs. Lal, A.I.R. 1924, Lah. 397 ; 71 I.C. 830.

conversion or a mere device to get rid of her husband.[38] A large number of cases on this point were considered by a Division Bench of the Lahore High Court when it was held that renunciation of a religion or faith requires no other proof than a person's declaration, the only condition being that the declaration is not casual of which the declarer may repent afterwards, but it should be such as to which the declarer adheres and in which he persists and that the motive of a declarer is immaterial.[39] The attention of the Court was drawn in a case to the opinion of the '*Ulamā*' of Samarqand and Balkh, butw as not accepted. It was held that if the conversion is an accomplished fact and is not a colourable transaction then the Court cannot decline to give effect to it simply because the underlying motive is not a proper one but is a device to get rid of the husband.[40]

Modification of Law : The matter has been set at rest in India and Pakistan by section 4 of the Dissolution of the Muslim Marriages Act, 1939, which reads as under :—

> "The renunciation of Islam by a married Muslim woman or her conversion to a faith other than Islam shall not in itself operate to dissolve the marriage."

As already stated, this section has given effect to the view expressed by the Jurists of Samarqand and Balkh and makes it clear that the renunciation of Islam by a Muslim wife shall not effect a separation between the spouses. The only exception is that the marriage of a convert to Islam who subsequently renounces Islam and returns to her former religion shall be liable to be dissolved on her apostasy.

(2) *Adoption of another Religion* : As regards the second point, namely, the effect of the new religion adopted, if the wife on her apostasy adopts a religion which is not considered

38. Mst. Rahmat Vs. Nikka, A.I.R. 1928, Lah. 954 ; Mst. Sardaran Vs. Allah Bakhsh, A.I.R. 1934, Lah. 976 ; Sardar Mohammad Vs. Mst. Maryam Bibi, A.I.R. 1936, Lah. 666 ; 165 I.C. 383 ; Mst. Saidan Vs. Sharaf, A.I.R. 1937 Lah. 759.
39. Mst. Resham Bibi Vs. Khuda Bakhsh, A.I.R. 1938, Lah. 482.
40. Ghaus Vs. Fajji, 29 I.C. 857.

to be a revealed religion, the marriage shall stand cancelled from the moment of her apostasy.[41] But this view no longer holds good in India and Pakistan in view of section 4 of the Dissolution of Muslim Marriages Act, 1939, quoted above.

Revealed Religion : By "Revealed Religion" is meant a religion which possesses a Book or Scripture accepted by Muslims as a Book revealed by God and the followers of the Book are called people belonging to a revealed religion. It is ordinarily the Christians and the Jews who are considered to belong to such category of people. But there seems to be no reason to limit the description of the "People of the Book or Scripture" to Christians and Jews only. It is laid down in the Qur'ān :—

> "To every people (was sent)
> An apostle[42].............
> We did aforetime send
> Apostles before thee : of them
> There are some whose story
> We have related to thee,
> And some whose story
> We have not related
> To thee.............[43]

This shows clearly that there can be other people who may be "People of the Scripture." Ameer Ali has held the view that Parsis and Brahmo Samajists are "ahl-e-Kitāb" or People of the Book and belong to a revealed religion.[44] But it is stated in *al-Baḥr al-Rā'iq* and *al-Hidāyah* that fire-worshippers are not Peop.e of the Book.[45] It is stated in *al-Mughnī* that only the Christians and the Jews are People of the Book.[46]

41. Sardar Muhammad Vs. Mst. Maryam Bibi, A.I.R. 1936, Lah. 666.
42. Qur'ān, Surah Yūnus, XI : 47.
43. Qur'ān, Surah Al-Mu'min, XXIV : 78 (Allamah Yusuf Ali's Translation).
44. Ameer Ali, *op. cit.*, p. 183.
45. Qur'ān, Surah Al-Nisa', VI : 164 (Allamah Yusuf Ali's Translation).
46. Ibn Qudāmah, *al-Mughnī*, Cairo, 1367 A.H., Vol. VI, p. 590.

But it is stated in *al-Fatāwā al-Hindīyah* that the expression "People of the Book" is not confined merely to Christians and Jews, but applies to every person who (whose religion) has a revealed Book and who believes in the same. Thus followers of the Book revealed to Abraham and Psalms of David are included in the expression.[47]

Al-Fatāwā al-Hindiyah was compiled at a much later period than the books mentioned above and has taken a more realistic view in the matter. As discussed in the chapter on "Conversion", Muslim jurists have not hesitated to consider Christians as "People of the Book" even when these Christians believed in Trinity. We can see from the opinion expressed in *al-Fatāwā al-Hindiyah* that there can be people other than Jews and Christians who can be included in the expression, "People of the Book". It seems that the only criterion to be applied in the matter is to see if the followers of a certain religion possess a "Book" and believe in the existence of God. Ameer Ali says, "Nor does there seem to be any reason why a marriage with a Hindu woman whose idolatry is merely nominal and who really believes in God should be unlawful." He supports this view by the fact that, "The Moghul Emperors of India frequently intermarried with Rajput (Hindu) ladies and the issue of such marriages were regarded as legitimate and often succeeded to the Imperial throne."[48] It may be noted here that there were a great many *'ulamā'* of outstanding merits, and quite independent in expressing their views in those days, but none objected to these intermarriages. It is stated in Ghāyat-al-Awṭār that by the term "*Kitābiyah*" is meant a woman who believes in a Messenger of God and also in a revealed Book. It also states that marriage with a Christian woman is valid even though she believes Jesus Christ to be the son of God. It adds that such belief makes her a polytheist, but the Muslim law differentiates between "People of the Book" and the Idolaters.[49] Maulānā Muḥammad

47. *Al-Fatāwā al-Hindīyah, op. cit.*, Vol. II, p. 8.
48. Ameer Ali, *op. cit.*, p. 183.
49. Khurram Ali, *Ghāyat al-Awṭār*, Vol. II, p. 8 (Urdu translation of *ad-Durr al-Mukhtār*, Lucknow, 1925).

Alī has stated in his "Commentary of the Holy Qur'ān" that the law given here (namely permission to marry women belonging to a revealed religion) is not limited to the Jews and Christians, but includes the followers of all religions based on revelation. Hence, the law was extended to the Persians by the Companions of the Prophet."[50]

In the case of a wife's conversion to a revealed religion opinions again differ. The majority of the jurists hold that the marriage shall be annulled in such cases also.[51] They base their opinion on the ground that on renouncing Islam she becomes an apostate and the marriage gets dissolved immediately on her apostasy. But the jurists of Balkh and Samarqand hold otherwise. They state that under the provisions of Muslim law a Muslim can lawfully marry a woman belonging to a revealed religion, and so can contract a valid marriage with a Christian woman or a Jewess.[52] Hence the adoption of such a religion by a Muslim wife cannot make any difference in her marital status. She being the follower of a revealed religion can lawfully be married by a Muslim and so on adoption of a revealed religion she can still continue to be his wife. They also state that a woman could be forced in former times to return to Islam, but it cannot be done now and that to hold that the marriage would be dissolved on apostasy would be to further the very object for which she apostatises, namely, to secure a separation from the marriage tie.[52] Their view is based on sound grounds and there is no reason to draw any difference between the case of a woman who belonged to a revealed religion before her marriage to a Muslim and one who adopts a revealed religion subsequent to her marriage. Ameer Ali holds marriage with a Parsi or Brahmosamaj woman as valid.[53]

50. Muḥammad 'Alī, English translation of the Qur'ān, footnote 667, Lahore, 1963, p. 242.
51. Ibn 'Ābidīn, Deoband n.d., Vol. II, p. 398,
52. Ibn 'Ābidīn, *op. cit.*, Vol. III, p. 403.
53. Ameer Ali, *op. cit.*, p. 183.

This view is supported by an analogy of a case similar in nature. If the husband of a *Kitābiyah* woman, that is, a woman belonging to a revealed religion, becomes a Muslim, the marriage shall still subsist on the ground that the marriage of a Muslim with a *Kitābīyah* being lawful *ab initio*, its continuance is also legal "*a fortiori*".[54] In such a case it is not even necessary to offer Islam to the wife, but the marriage will still remain subsisting as before.[55]

The Courts before the passing of the Dissolution of Muslim Marriages Act, 1939, followed the first opinion and held that the marriage was dissolved if the wife adopts Christianity. In a case Agha Haider, J. seems to have been inclined to adopt the view expressed by the jurists of Balkh and Samarqand but felt himself bound to follow the decisions of his own High Court and other Courts. Thus his Lordship has stated, "The marriage of a Muhammadan with a *Kitābiyah* is valid. On first impression the fact that a Muslim embraces Christianity during wedlock ought not to make any difference for the obvious reason that she has gone over from a religion which believes in a *Kitāb*, namely. the Muhammadan religion to another similar religion. This view has been entertained by a very eminent jurist of Balkh and Samarqand and the distinguished commentator of Muhammadan Law, the late Ameer Ali, seemed to be inclined to the same view. But the concurrent judicial opinion in this country seems to be uniform and it has been held in numerous cases that if the wife of a Muhammadan who had married her husband when both of them professed the Muhammadan faith during the subsistence of the marriage abjures Islam and becomes Christian, the marriage is *ipso facto* dissolved."[56]

It is submitted that the view that adoption of a revealed religion by the wife does not result in the cancellation of the marriage is sound and correct and worthy of being followed.[57]

54. Shaykhzādah, *op. cit.*, Vol. I, p. 371,
55. *Ibid.*, al-Marghīnānī, *op. cit.*, Vol. II, p. 327.
56. Sardar Muhammad Vs. Mst. Maryam Bibi, A.I.R. 1936, Lah. 666.
57. Ashraf 'Alī, *op. cit.*, pp. 98-99.

Bigamy : If the marriage is considered to subsist and not to have been dissolved, as discussed above, then naturally the wife who marries again after apostasy shall, along with the second husband, be guilty of bigamy. A woman can be guilty of bigamy only when she marries a man while her first marriage is still subsisting, but there can be no question of bigamy when the first marriage does not subsist. If the marriage is considered to subsist and not to have been dissolved, as discussed above, obviously the wife shall be guilty of bigamy and her second husband may also be held guilty of the offence. It has been mentioned above that the marriage of a Muslim woman was considered to have been cancelled from the time of her apostasy and that she ceased to be the wife of her Muslim husband from the moment of her apostasy according to the trend of opinion of the Courts before the passing of the Dissolution of Muslim Marriages Act, 1939. Her second marriage even during the period of her *'iddah*, therefore, was held not to have resulted in an offence of bigamy.[58] But the Dissolution of Muslim Marriages Act, 1939, has changed this aspect of law. Section 4 of the Act makes it clear that the marriage of a Muslim woman shall not be dissolved on her apostasy. Hence such a wife cannot enter into a second marriage on her apostasy. If she does so, she shall be guilty of the offence of bigamy.

'Iddah : When a marriage is dissolved by the apostasy of the husband or the wife, then the observance of *'iddah* is not necessary if the marriage has not been consummated or under the Ḥanafī, Mālikī and Ḥanbalī laws there has not even been a valid retirement.[59] But if apostasy should take place after consummation of the marriage or valid retirement then *'iddah* is incumbent.[60] The *'iddah* shall be the same as prescribed for dissolution of marriage by divorce. *'Iddah* shall be incumbent irrespective of the fact as to whether it is the husband or

58. Karan Singh Vs. Crown, AIR, 1933, All. 433.
59. Ibn 'Ābidīn, *op. cit.*, Vol. III, p. 402.
60. *Ibid.*

the wife who has apostatised and whether the wife is a *Muslimah* or a *Kitābiyāh.*[61]

Dower : If a marriage has been consummated or if under the Ḥanafī, Mālikī and Ḥanbalī laws there has been a valid retirement the wife shall be entitled to her whole dower irrespective of the fact whether it is the husband or the wife who has left the fold of Islam.[62]

If a marriage has not been consummated or under the Ḥanafī, Mālikī and Ḥanbalī laws there has not been a valid retirement the wife shall get half the dower if it is the husband who has renounced Islam but she shall not be entitled to get any dower if it is she herself who has renounced the faith.[63]

Maintenance : On the apostasy of the husband, the wife shall be entitled to maintenance during the period of her *'iddah* if its observance be necessary. If it is the wife who apostatises from Islam, she shall lose the right of maintenance during the period of *'iddah*, if any be incumbent. But she shall be entitled to the right of residence during the period of *'iddah.*[64]

Nature of Separation : The separation that takes place on account of apostasy of either the wife or the husband does not amount to a divorce but merely to cancellation of the marriage. It is only a provisional prohibition which ceases with the cessation of the cause which produced it, that is, cessation of the apostasy and return to Islam. According to Muḥammad separation that results on the apostasy of the husband shall amount to a divorce.[65]

Return to Islam : It has already been seen that on apostasy, an immediate separation takes place, but it does not create a permanent bar to marriage between them so that on the return to Islam by the party which had renounced the faith

61. Ibn 'Ābidīn, *op. cit.*, Vol. III, p. 402.
62. *Ibid.*
63. *Ibid.*
64. *Ibid.*
65. Al-Marghīnānī, *op. cit.*, Vol. II, p. 328 ; Shaykhzādah, *op. cit.* Vol. I p. 327.

they can remarry without the necessity of an intervening marriage. If both the husband and wife had renounced Islam and again return to the faith together, their marriage shall subsist and a renewal of the same shall not be necessary and the principle, above mentioned, shall apply according to Abū Ḥanīfah and Abū Yūsuf.[66] Muḥammad b. al-Ḥasan, however, holds that if it is the husband who apostatises, the separation shall amount to a divorce.[67] If, however, only one of them returns to Islam, the marriage shall stand dissolved, and in such a case, a renewal of marriage shall be necessary if the other spouse embraces Islam subsequently.[68] Some Ḥanafī jurists have laid down the rule that the renewal of the marriage contract is not necessary if the act of apostasy is due to a mistake on the part of the husband or the act which caused the apostasy is such that the jurists differ on its nature or, in other words, when the act constituting apostasy is a technical one and the jurists differ whether the act does amount to apostasy or not.[69] If, however, there is no uncertainty about the nature of the act and it is recognised to be an act of apostasy, it shall be necessary to renew the contract of marriage. This view is justified by an instance that happened in the time of the Companions. The tribe of Banū Ḥanīfāh apostatised and subsequently returned to Islam, but the Companions did not direct them to renew their marriages.[70] Hence, it shall not be necessary in such a case to have an intermediary marriage. If the husband embraces Islam earlier than his wife, the marriage will not be dissolved according to Mālik, Shāfi'ī and Aḥmad b. Ḥanbal. But if it is the wife who embraces Islam first, the marriage will be dissolved according to them.[71]

66. Al-Marghīnānī, *op. cit.*, Vol, II, p. 328 ; Ibn 'Ābidīn, *op. cit.*, Vol. III, pp. 403-4.
67. Mullā Khusraw, *Durar al-Ḥukkām*, Constantinople, 1329 A.H., Vol. I, p. 354.
68. Ibn 'Ābidīn, *op. cit.*, Vol. III, p. 404.
69. *Ibid.*, p. 403.
70. Al-Marghīnānī *op. cit.*, Vol. II, p. 328.
71. Shaykhzādah, *op. cit.*, Vol. I, p. 373.

Qāḍi's Order: Apostasy from Islam by one of the married parties results in an immediate cancellation of their marriage.[72] A decree of a *Qāḍī* is not required to bring about a separation between them.[73] But the factum of renunciation has, however, to be proved and on a denial of apostasy by the party concerned the marriage shall be presumed to subsist. The party alleging renunciation of Islam by the other shall have to establish the fact and failure to do so shall be fatal to his or her case.[74]

When an apostate wife instituted a suit for a declaration that her marriage with her husband had been dissolved on account of her apostasy, it was held that it was not within the discretion of the Court to withhold a declaratory decree for such relief unless there is absence of sufficient ground to do so.[75] But it may be noted that the suit was instituted before the Dissolution of Muslim Marriages Act 1939, had come into force.

Children: *(a) Religion of*: According to Muslim law, if one of a married couple renounces Islam, the children of the couple shall be considered to be Muslims.[76] In non-Muslim countries, however, a child shall decide his or her own religion if he or she possesses discretion. But if the child is not of such a tender age as not to understand the nature of his or her act, though under the age of eighteen years, he or she shall be entitled to change his or her religion in spite of the father's power of general control over his or her education, religious or otherwise. It is not necessary that it should be proved that the minor is capable to exercise an intelligent preference because religion is more of a matter of faith than of reason. But it must be shown that he or she understood the nature of his or her acts and his or her profession of faith.

72. Ibn 'Ābidīn, *op. cit.*, Vol. III, p. 402.
73. *Ibid.*
74. Mst. Saidan Vs. Sharaf Ali Mohd., A.I.R. 1937, Lah. 759.
75. Mst. Rashid Bibi Vs, Tufail Mohd. A.I.R. 1941, Lah. 291.
76. Ibn 'Abidīn, *op. cit.*, Vol. III, p. 404.

Religion is a matter of conscience, a matter personal to a minor of age to understand.[77]

Renunciation of Islam by Parents of a Minor Girl : A minor girl of tender age is considered to belong to the same religion as that of her parents.[78] Hence if the parents of a married minor girl of tender age adopt a revealed religion on renunciation of Islam, the marriage shall subsist, because the girl shall be considered to belong to a revealed religion and so still remains a fit object of marriage with a Muslin. But if the parents adopt a non-revealed religion, the marriage shall be dissolved because the girl shall be considered to belong to the religion of her parents while the marriage of a Muslim with a woman who is neither a *Muslimah* nor belongs to a revealed religion is forbidden.[79] But this rule is subject to the exception that if the parents are living in a Muslim country the marriage shall not be dissolved because the parents can be persuaded to re-embrace Islam and there is a chance that they may do so.[80] There is, therefore, no necessity to dissolve the marriage. If only one of the parents of a minor wife adopts a non-revealed religion, the marriage shall subsist. If the parents leave a Muslim State and take up their domicile in a non-Muslim State but the girl remains behind then too the marriage shall not be dissolved as the girl being in a Muslim country shall be governed by its laws.[81] If the parents, however, take the girl with them, the marriage shall be dissolved as the girl will no longer be subject to Muslim law.[82] But if one of the parents happens to die in Muslim State whether before or after renunciation of Islam and the survivor renounces Islam and takes the minor wife to a non-Muslim State, the marriage shall not be dissolved.

Custody of Children : If one of the spouses renounces

77. In re Mohammad Alam, Mohammad Ibrahim, A.I.R. 1939, Sind 311,
78. Ibn 'Ābidīn, *op. cit.*, Vol. III, p. 405.
79. *Ibid.*
80. *Ibid.*, p. 404.
81. *Ibid.*, p. 405.
82. *Ibid.*, p. 405, 406,

Islam, the question arises as to which of them is entitled to the custody of a child or children born of the marriage. The Muslim jurists lay great stress on the proper upbringing of children. They consider that the child should be brought up in a healthy religious atmosphere and imparting of religious instructions is considered very important by them. They have expressed the view that the interest of the child demands that it should be brought up in the traditions of the best religion which they hold to be Islam. Hence the child shall be given in the custody of that spouse who is a Muslim.[83] It will be interesting to note that amongst various religions, Islam is considered the best, while a revealed religion comes next and a non-revealed religion is not liked. As between revealed religions, Christianity is given a preference over Jewish religion, so that if one spouse is a Christian while the other is a Jew, the child shall be given in the custody of the Christian spouse in preference to the spouse who is a Jew.[84]

If a mother belongs to a revealed religion then a child born of her shall remain with her on a separation between the spouses according to the Ḥanafīs. They state that her natural love and affection cannot be affected by her belonging to a different religion. But if there is a risk that the child's religious beliefs may be adversely affected by living with her so that there is an apprehension that it may become a non-Muslim, it shall be given in the custody of the Muslim father.[85]

According to Mālik, S͟hāfi'ī and Aḥmad b. Ḥanbal the child shall remain with the Muslim father in every case.[86]

If the Muslim mother of the child apostatises, the child shall be given in the custody of the Muslim father according to all the Sunni schools of law.

S͟hī'ī Law : S͟hī'ī Law is the same as the Sunnī law in respect of apostasy.

83. Ibn 'Ābidīn, *op. cit.*, Vol. III, p. 405; *Fatāwā 'Ālamgiriyah, op. cit.*, Vol. II, p. 121.
84. *Ibid.*, p. 405.
85. *Ibid.*
86. S͟hayk͟hzādah, *op. cit.*, Vol I, p. 491.

Chapter 26

TABĀYUN DĀR (DIFFERENCE OF DOMICILE)

Preliminary: The notion and the nature of *Dār al-Islām* (Muslim State) and *Dār al-Ḥarb* (non-Muslim State) were briefly touched upon in the previous chapter on Apostasy. They now need to be discussed in some great detail.

In the early days of Islam, there were continuous wars between the Muslims and the followers of other religions, for the people burning with religious frenzy often lacked in tolerance. It was, therefore, very difficult, if not impossible, for the followers of different religions to live side by side in the same country. At that time there was a sharp distinction between countries following different religions, but later the cessation of religious wars reduced the spirit of animosity and prejudice. Moreover, the frequent contact of people, generally in carrying on trade, further reduced animosity and increased tolerance for one another.

In most of the countries the place of religious laws was gradually taken by civil laws. No doubt, the latter are often found to be based on religious laws in such personal matters as marriage and divorce, but they show comparatively less intolerance for other people than was formerly the case, though we may still find examples of bias for one's own laws. Modern states, as a rule, claim to make no discrimination between their citizens on the basis of religion. Although, unfortunately, in actual fact there do exist certain countries where minorities do not live on equal footing with the majority people.

The Muslim Jurists of the early period divided countries into two categories, namely, *Dār al-Islām* or Muslim States and *Dār al-Ḥarb* or Non-Muslim States, just as the English Courts at one time divided countries into Christian countries and the countries of the 'Infidels.' *Harb* means war and *Dār al-Ḥarb* means a country at war with the Muslims, or an enemy country, but it was not necessary that a war should be actually going on between it and a Muslim country.

Definition : "*Dār al-Islām* has been defined as a country where the Muslims possess so much power as to be capable of promulgating and enforcing any laws that they wish. *Dār al-Ḥarb*, on the other hand, was defined as the country where the non-Muslims possess so much power that they can promulgate and enforce their own laws or any laws they like.[1] *Dār al-Islām* has been defined in *al-Kifāyah* as that town (country) where the Muslim ruler can promulgate the laws of the *sharī'ah* and (to do) the same may be in his power and the country may be under his rule and administration. *Dār al-Ḥarb* has been defined as that town (country) where the laws of the *sharī'ah* cannot be enforced and it is under the rule of *Kuffār* (non-Believers).[2]

Dār al-Ḥarb or non-Muslim countries may be divided into two classes. The first consists of such countries as do not indulge in war with the Muslims and allow their Muslim citizens full liberty in the exercise and performance of their religious observances and obligations, and guarantee full protection of Muslim lives and property not only in words but in fact. Such countries may rather be called *Dār al-Amān* or countries of security than actual *Dār al-Ḥarb.* The Muslims living there are required by *sharī'ah* to be law-abiding and loyal to such a country. It is stated in the Qurān, "Allah forbids you not respecting those who fight you not for religion, nor drive you forth from your homes, that you show them kindness and deal with them justly. Surely Allah loves the doers of justice."[3] Thus the Ruler of Abyssinia had given protection to some of the early Muslims and they felt it their duty to be loyal to him so much so that they freely and voluntarily offered their services to

1. Ibn 'Ābidīn Al-Shāmī, *Radd al-Muḥtār*. Cairo, 1318 A.H. Vol IV, p. 401.
2. Shah 'Abd al-'Azīz, *Fatāwā 'Aziziyah*, Hyderabad Deccan, 1313 A.H. p. 186,
3. Qur'ān, Surah Al-Mumtaḥanah LX : 8.

the Ruler when that country was invaded by an enemy.[3a] The other class of countries actually constitutes, in its strictest sense, *Dār al-Ḥarb*. These countries are such as are inimical to the Muslims, where the latter cannot openly and adequately fulfil their religious duties and obligations or where they cannot live in peace and perfect security, so that their lives and properties are in constant danger. The Muslims are not to be friendly with such countries and their people, but are enjoined to migrate from there. It is stated in the Qurān, "(As for) those whom the angels cause to die while they are unjust to themselves, (the angels) will say : What were you doing ? They will say : We were weak in tne earth. (They will) say : Was not Allāh's earth spacious so that you could have migrated therein ? So these it is whose refuge is hell—and it is an evil resort."[4] It is stated at another plaće, "Except the weak from among the men and the women and the children who have not the means, nor can they find a way (to escape)."[5] We find another injunction : "And whoever flees in Allāh's way he will find in the earth many a place of escape and abundant resources. And whoever goes forth from his home fleeing to Allah and His Messenger, then death overtakes him, his reward is indeed with Allāh. And Allāh is ever Forgiving, Merciful."[6]

It is again laid down, "And those who believed and migrated and struggled hard in Allah's way, and those who gave shelter and helped—these are the believers truly. For them is forgiveness and an honourable provision."[7] And it is also stressed : "Allah forbids you only respecting those who fight you for religion, and drive you forth from your homes and help (others) in your expulsion, that you make friends of them, and whoever makes friends of them, these are the

3a. Shibli Nawmānī, *Sīrat al-Nabī*, Azamgarh, Vol. I, p. 240. *Burhān* (monthly), Delhi, August, 1966, p. 79.

4. Qur'ān, Surah al-Nisā V : 97.

5. *Ibid.*, V : 98.

6. *Ibid.*, V : 100.

7. Qur'ān, Surah al-Anfāl VIII : 74.

wrong-doers."[8] It can thus be seen that migration becomes due or obligatory when Muslims are not allowed to fulfil their religious obligations.

This obligation to migrate from such a country seems to be based on the apprehension that the Muslims living there may feel compelled by actual force or fear of the same to change their religion. It is obvious that under such circumstances they are almost certain to give up their way of life and to adopt the way of life of the non-Muslims, and this condition is most undesirable and reprehensible.

Discussion. In the definitions of *Dār al-Islām* and *Dār al-Ḥarb* given above emphasis has been laid on the power to promulgate and enforce laws, and no importance is given to the religion of the majority of the inhabitants of a certain country or to the actual promulgation of laws. Thus Muslim armies at one time conquered and occupied countries the inhabitants and even the armies of which far exceeded the number of the Muslim armies. Similarly, European (Christian) countries of later periods conquered and occupied Muslim countries when their armies were much less in number than the population and sometimes even the armies of the conquered lands. Yet the former countries were considered by the Muslim Jurists to be *Dār al-Islām* and the latter to be *Dār al-Ḥarb.* The basis of distinguishing *Dār al-Islām* from *Dār al-Ḥarb* is to see whether it is the Muslims or the non-Muslims who wield power[9] The absence of actual warfare between a Muslim and a non-Muslim country would not change the nature of the latter country, and it would still remain a *Dār al-Ḥarb.* Similarly, mere tolerance in certain matters of the Muslim subjects by a non-Muslim country at war with the Muslims would not turn it into *Dār al-Islām.* Ibn Jubayr, the famous Muslim traveller of the 12th century, has mentioned a political phenomenon that greatly surprised him. A

8. Qur'ān, Snrah al-Mumtaḥanah LX : 9.
9. Mawlāna Muhammad Anwar Shah Al-Kashmīrī, *Hindustan awr Dār al-Ḥarb,* Monghyr. 1382 A.H., p. 5.

fierce war was going on between Sultan Ṣalāḥ al-Dīn (Saladin) and the Crusaders. The Sultan had besieged Kerak, an important stronghold of the Christians, and the siege lasted for several months causing great hardship to the Christians, and feelings between the Muslims and the Christians ran very high, yet Ibn Jubayr was amazed to find that merchants belonging to one country could safely visit the other country without any interference by either army. They had only to pay some tax to the country which they visited with their merchandise. He was greatly impressed by this fact that while the armies were engaged in a fierce war yet the people of these countries were at peace.[10] But a Christian country would not become *Dār al-Islām* simply by this perfunctory tolerance, and would still remain *Dār al-Ḥarb.* Similarly, full liberty given to the non-Muslim subjects in a *Dār al-Islām* to observe and practise non-Islamic laws and obligations—even such as are forbidden by Muslim law, — would not change it into a *Dār al-Ḥarb.* Thus worship of idols was freely practised by the Indian Hindus, who formed the majority of the population in the Moghul period, yet India was then considered a *Dār al-Islām* and no Muslim jurist ever said or considered it was *Dār al-Ḥarb.*

With the passage of time religious feelings were replaced by political feelings (though even today in some countries religious bias has not completely disappeared) and definitions of *Dār al-Islām* and *Dār al-Ḥarb* which were applicable in the conditions prevalent in the early period of Islam when there were constant wars between the Muslims and the non-Muslims, gradually lost their significance.

The decline in the power of the Muslims and the conquest of Muslim countries by Christians further necessitated the modification of the two definitions, particularly of *Dār al-Ḥarb,* since, as already discussed, it sometimes becomes incumbent on Muslims to migrate from a *Dār al-Ḥarb.* To save Muslims

10. Ibn Jubayr, *Riḥlah Ibn Jubayr*, English by R. J. C. Broadhurst, London 1952, p. 300.

from the hardships of unnecessary migrations, it was felt necessary to take a more restricted view of the conditions under which a *Dār al-Islām* became a *Dār al-Ḥarb*.

There is thus found a considerable difference of opinion amongst the Muslim jurists on this question. According to the earlier opinion, as expressed by Muhammad and Abū Yūsuf, the only condition necessary to change a *Dār al-Islām* into a *Dār al-Ḥarb* is the promulgation and enforcement of the laws of the Kuffār (non-believers) in that country, the *Dār al-Islam*.[11] But Abu Hanifah, probably to limit the scope of change of *Dār al-Islām* into *Dār al-Ḥarb*, stated that not only this condition but two others have also to be satisfied before a *Dār al-Islām* shall cease to be such. The additional conditions are :—

(1) Its being situated adjacent to a *Dār al-Ḥarb* so that there is no Muslim country situated between the *Dār al-Ḥarb* and *Dār al-Islam*.

(2) It should not be possible for the Muslims to live in the former *Dār al-Islām with that assurance of security for life and property which they had enjoyed before its conquest* by the Kuffār[12].

The first condition that there shall be no Muslim State between the former *Dār al-Islām* and *Dār al-Ḥarb* is based on the presumption that as it is the duty of every Muslim country to come to the aid of a *Dār al-Islām* in case of distress, such help would be available. This view is based on the injunction in the Qur'an wherein it is stated, "And what reason have you not to fight in the way of Allah and of the weak among the men and the women and the children, who say : Our Lord, take us out of this town, whose people are oppressors, and grant us from Thee a friend and grant us from Thee a helper!"[13] It is thus the duty of every Muslim country to come to the aid of an oppressed Muslim country, or which is

11. Ibn 'Ābidīn, *op. cit.*, Vol. II, p. 401.
12. *Ibid.*
13. Qur'ān Surah al-Nisā' IV : 75,

at war with a non-Muslim country, or is in distress on that account, or has been defeated by the Kuffār. It shall be the duty of the Muslim country situated between a *Dār al-Islām* and a *Dār al-Ḥarb* to shield the Muslim country from the aggression of the *Dār al-Ḥarb.* If no Muslim country is situated between a certain *Dār al-Islām* and a *Dār al-Ḥarb* or enemy country then it cannot reasonably expect any help from a distant Muslim country and so the Kuffār will be in such position and power that it will not be possible for the *Dār al-Islām* in distress to regain its freedom. Mawlana Abdul Bārī has relied on this view to hold India a *Dār al-Islām.* He has explained that this second condition has not been satisfied, because there are Muslim countries situated between India and England. This condition shall be satisfied only when Iraq which is at present occupied by the English government becomes their permanent possession. Hejaz, which is ruled by Sharif who is under the direct tutelage of the English, and Egypt, Palestine, Malta and Dardanelles happen to become the domain of the English government. If such a situation occurs only then there will be no Muslim country separating India from England and only then will India clearly become a *Dār al-Ḥarb.*[14] But this explanation is more technical than actually applicable, and is hardly relevant to the present political circumstances.

The idea underlying the condition presupposed that every Muslim country was strong enough to defeat the Kuffār but with the degeneration of the Muslims this supposition has no force in fact. As pointed out by Mawlana Muḥammad Anwar Shāh, "no Muslim country (for example Afghanistan or Turkey) could oust the English people from India" and the same applies to all other Muslim countries. Shah Sahib concluded from this that British India was not a *Dār al-Islām* but a *Dār al-Ḥarb.*[15]

The second condition to determine if a Muslim country after its conquest by non-Muslims still retains its nature or

14. Syed Rais Ahmed Ja'ffry, *Awrāq-i-Gumgashta*, Lahore 1968, p. 1462.
15. Muhammad Anwar Shāh, *op. cit.*, p. 7.

has changed into a *Dār al-Ḥarb* is to see whether or not the Muslims still enjoy perfect freedom in the performance of their religious duties and obligations without interference from the government and whether they live in perfect peace and security Freedom of religion was generally determined by the permission or prohibition to offer Friday and Eid prayers. As regards the condition relating to security of life and property it may be stated here that it was usual in old times for an alien to obtain *amān* or guarantee of security from a foreign government. On the grant of the *amān*, he could enter and reside in that country without any fear of molestation. The grant of *amān* played an important part in old times as it facilitated commerce between Muslim and non-Muslim countries.

A *Ḥarbī*, that is, a citizen of a *Dār al-Ḥarb*, could enter and reside in *Dār al-Islām* for a period up to one year on obtaining necessary permission from the Muslims or the authority concerned of that country. He had to pay a tax if he wanted to prolong his stay. Similarly, a Muslim could enter and temporarily live in *Dār al-Ḥarb* on securing *amān* from the government of that country. Such persons were called *Musta'min* (or secured) persons.[16]

The Muslim jurists attached great importance to the grant of *amān* or guarantee of security and its effect. Much light is thrown in the matter by an event that happened in the time of the second Caliph. The Muslim army had besieged the city of Irdisabur. They were surprised one day to see that the citizens of the place had opened the gates of the city and were occupied in their daily business. On enquiry they were told that the citizens had been given *amān* and so they did not have any apprehension for themselves. After much investigation it was found that it was a Muslim slave who had given the *amān*. The Muslim Commander refused to be bound by the act of a slave, but finally the matter was referred to the Caliph who upheld the contention of the *Ḥarbīs* and said that once the

16. Ibn 'Ābidīn, *op. cit.*, Vol. III, p. 256 ff.

amān was given it could not be violated on any ground.[17] The Muslim jurists naturally attach great importance to the security enjoyed by Muslims in a certain country and deem the country *Dār al-Ḥarb* if the Muslims do not enjoy absolute security for their lives and property.

The Muslim jurists of later period found it necessary to modify the definitions of *Dār al-Islām* and *Dār al-Ḥarb* and the notion relating to the change of *Dār al-Islām* into a *Dār al-Ḥarb* in view of the changed conditions when many Muslim countries had been conquered by Christian countries. It is stated in *Radd al-Muḥtār* that if the laws of both the Muslims and the non-Muslims are in force in a country then it shall not be declared to be a *Dār al-Ḥarb.*[18] Probably following this opinion some Muslim jurists held that a *Dār al-Islām* shall not cease to be such and shall not change its nature when ruled by non-Muslims if the Muslims are governed by Muslim laws in religious matters and the Muslim inhabitants can freely offer Friday and *'Eid* prayers.[19] This was the view generally expressed in India when it was under British rule and it was stated to be *Dār al-Islām.* It is possible that some *'Ulamā'* might have been influenced by their apprehension that to hold otherwise and declare India to be *Dār al-Ḥarb* might be considered seditious by the then government. But many of the Indian Muslim jurists must have held this view in all sincerity. Even then there were Muslim jurists who expressed a different view. Thus, Mawlānā Shāh 'Abd al-'Azīz while discussing this matter, namely, the nature of India which had been conquered by the English people from the Muslim Ruler, has stated that the laws of *Sharī'ah* are not in force in this country, but the laws of the English Government are enforced here." He has explained that by the enforcement of the laws of *Kufr*, that is, laws of the non-believers is meant the government and administration, realisation of taxes, land revenue, laws applicable to cases of thieves

17. Shiblī Nawmānī, Al-Fārūq, Azamgarh, 1892, pp. 172, 173.
18. Ibn 'Ābidīn, *op. cit.*, Vol. III, p. 261.
19. *Ibid.*

and dacoits and decision of cases by the non-Muslim Rulers according to their own laws. He held non-interference with such acts as to offer Friday and 'Eid prayers, calling of *azān*, sacrifice of cows, to be immaterial because this was being done in the interest of administration while the government did not hasitate to demolish mosques in obedience to their laws. He has further stated that no (Muslim) traveller can come to this country (India) without obtaining the permission of the (then) government.[19a]

In support of this view, he relied on some Traditions and the practice of the Companions. The first Caliph held the town Yarbu to be a *Dār al-Ḥārb* simply on the refusal of the people of that place to pay zakāt even though many *Sharī'ah* laws, offering of Friday and 'Eid prayers, call of the Mu'azzin etc. were in force there. The Caliph also declared the neighbouring towns to be *Dār al-Ḥarb* even though Muslims were also living there. The Prophet (peace be on him) also held Fidak and Khyber to be *Dār al-Ḥarb* even when Muslims were (peacefully) living there.[20] Mawlānā Abdul Aziz Sahib has thus established that the observance of only a few rules of laws of Islam in a certain country does not make it a *Dār al-Islām* and that the denial of even a single injunction of Islam at a place shall change it into *Dār al-Ḥarb.* It can be seen from the above that the Mawlana Sahib was of the opinion that a country can be considered to be *Dār al-Islām* only when the Muslim law in its entirety is or can be enforced and followed there while the permission to follow only some of the Muslim laws and obligations shall not, according to him, serve the purpose.

Mawlānā Muḥammad Anwar Shāh while discussing the question of *Dār* has observed that the point of differentiation between *Dār al-Islām* and *Dār al-Ḥarb* is based on the fact as to who wields power—the Muslims or non-Muslims. According to him every town under the rule of the Muslims shall be

19*a*. *Burhān*, July, 1966, pp. 11, 12.
20. Mawlānā Shāh 'Abd al 'Āzīz, *op. cit.*, p. 106.

considered to be *Dār al-Islām*, while a place under the rule of the non-Muslims shall be called *Dār al-Ḥarb*. He observes that a place shall not be considered a *Dār al-Islām* simply because Muslims live there nor by the fact that certain rules of Muslim law may be followed there *with the permission* of *Kuffār* (non-believers) as the observance of some rules of *Kufr* (non-Islamic rules) in *Dār al-Islām* with the permission of or through the negligence of the Muslims does not affect the nature of the country because the *Kuffār* (non-believers) in the last two cases are not in power there, while the determination of the nature of a country depends solely on the capacity to exercise power. Hence, according to him, the mere fact that Muslims observe certain Islamic practices in a certain locality does not change *Dār al-Kufr* into *Dār al-Islām*. The Prophet (peace be on him) at one time proceeded towards Mecca with a large army and offered prayers and performed certain other religious observances and the number of the Muslims was so large that they could easily overpower the *Kuffār*, but Mecca did not become *Dār al-Islām* on that account because all this was done with the permission of the *Kuffār* and not by virtue of their power by the Muslims. The nature of *Dār al-Ḥarb* shall not change and it shall not become *Dār al-Islām* unless and until it is conquered (by the Muslims). He further remarks that otherwise Germany, Russia, France and other Christian countries shall all be called *Dār al-Islām*. The promulgation of the laws of the *Kuffār* and the incapacity of the Muslims to promulgate and enforce their own laws, but to do so with the permission of the *Kuffār* establishes a lack of supremacy of the Muslims. The nature of a country can be ascertained by the supremacy of the *Kuffār* that they may be so placed as to openly promulgate laws of *Kufr* while the Muslims may hold such subordinate position that they may not be able to promulgate their own laws and may not possess the power to reject the laws of *Kufr* (non-Islamic) as may bring disgrace to Islam. He further states that Abū Ḥanīfah has laid down on the basis of *Istiḥsān* that one should be cautious in declaring a *Dār al-Islām* to be a *Dār al-Ḥarb.* It means, in other words, that should the *Kuffār* be so powerful that it may not be possible for the country to regain its freedom or for another Muslim country to liberate it from the *Kuffār* it shall be considered to be a *Dār al-Ḥarb.* Hence according to him the determining factor is the wielding of power and not the offering of Friday and 'Eid prayers and the like. The observance of certain practices of Islam in *Dār al-Kuffār* with the permission of *Kuffār* whether express or implied, shall never convert the country into *Dār al-Islām.* Now considering the question of India (during British rule) the enforcement of the laws of the Christians is due to their power. If a Collector (usually an Englishman at that time) prohibits offering of prayers in mosques no one, rich or poor, can contravene the order. The security formerly provided by Muslim Rulers is no longer found. The other condition also is no longer applicable now, because no Muslim country (*e.g.* Afghanistan or Turkey), can oust the English people from India." Mawlānā Muhammad Anwar Shah thus concludes that British India was not *Dār al-Islām* but was *Dār al-Ḥarb.*[21]

This *Fatwā* has been attributed to the late Allama Muḥammad Anwar S͟hāh in a work named "*Hindustan awr Dār al-Ḥarb,*" published by Dār al-Is͟hā'at Rahmāni, Monghyr, (Bihar, India) in 1382 A.H. But Sa'īd Ahmad Akbarabadi has stated in an article on the nature of India, from a Muslim point of view, that the *Fatwā* was not actually given by Mawlānā Anwar S͟hāh but that it was given by Mawlana Ras͟hīd Ahmad Ṣāḥib of Gangoh. The mistake according to him, arose out of the fact that the *Fatwā* was found in the papers of the former after his death and was in his own handwriting. It is explained by Mawlānā Sa'īd Ahmad that the *Fatwā* of Mawlānā Ras͟hid Ahmad Ṣāḥib must have been copied by Mawlānā Anwar S͟hāh hence it was found after his death in his papers and in his handwriting.

21. Mawlana Muhammad Anwar S͟hāh, *op. cit.*, pp. 5-7.

22. *Burhān* (Urdu magazine), Vol. 57. Issue No. 1, July 1966. pp. 6, 7,

As time passed on many countries were no longer governed by religious laws, but by civil laws, while Muslim countries often entered into agreements with non-Muslim countries. Hence two more categories of countries were added to the categories discussed above and a country may fall into one of the four categories, namely :

a. *Dār al-Islām* or Muslim State,

b. *Dār al-Ḥarb*, or non-Muslim State,

c. *Dār al-'Ahd*, and

d. *Dār al-Amān.*[23]

The first two categories have already been discussed above. The countries of the third category are those which have entered into an agreement with Muslim countries under the provisions of which the Muslims live in peace with those non-Muslim countries without any molestation and without any interference in their religious and cultural affairs. It may be noted that at one time some non-Muslim countries sought friendship and even the protection of Muslim countries when the latter were at the zenith of their power. S̲h̲āfi'ī called such a country a *Dār al-Ṣulḥ* (country at peace) or *Dār al-'Ahd* or a country which had entered into an agreement. The Ḥanafis and some other jurists did not accept this notion as correct because according to them a country paying a tribute or having sought the protection of or having entered into an agreement with a *Dār al-Islām* became, so to say, a part of the same. But with passage of time, the Muslims became degenerate and weak and then it were they who sought peace with and friendship of a *Dār al-Ḥarb* and entered into agreements with them with reciprocal guarantee of peace and help. The concept of the Ḥanafīs has ceased to be applicable under the changed circumstances and such countries may be called *Dār al-'Ahd* as held by the S̲h̲āfi'īs or *Dār al-Mīt̲h̲āq.*

The fourth category consists of those countries which are *Dār al-Ḥarb* but where Muslims are allowed to follow freely the obligations of their religion and live there in such peace

23. *Burhān*, Issue No. 3, September, 1966 p. 135,

and security of life and property as they enjoyed before their subjugation. The qualifying words, "*as they enjoyed before*" are important and mean that the Muslims should be living in absolute peace and security for their lives and property, and should not be living in fear for the same.

The question of the religious status of India during British rule received serious attention of the Indian Muslim jurists in those days. Some Muslim jurists held India to be *Dar al-'Ahd.* But the late Mawlana 'Abd al-Bārī did not accept this view and said that there was no agreement of any sort between the British Government and the Indian Muslims nor any such agreement is provided in the Qur'ān or Sunnah or Muslim Fiqh. He explained that the Indian Muslims are not living in India under any agreement but merely as a subject nation.[24] He further explained that since Islam holds a position superior to other religions it is easier for a *Dār al-Kufr* to become a *Dār al-Islām* than the conversion of a *Dār al-Islām* into a *Dār al-Kufr* and that for this reason a *Dār al-Islām* will not become a *Dār al-Kufr* as long as even a single law of Islam is enforcible there. It is necessary for the conversion of *Dār al-Islām* into a *Dār al-Kufr* that the entire Muslim law be not enforcible there.[25]

It would be more appropriate to have called India *Dār al-Amān* on the ground that the Muslims were allowed full protection and security of life and property under the proclamation of Queen Victoria issued in 1857.

It seems that many Muslim jurists were influenced by the conditions prevalent in India at a certain time and changed their views with the change in the conditions. Thus Mawlānā Rashīd Aḥmad of Gangoh at first held India to be *Dār al-Ḥarb* but subsequently he felt uncertain in the matter though he appears to favour his earlier opinion. At a still later period he did not hold India[26] to be *Dār al-Ḥarb.* He must have been influenced by the fact that peace prevailed in the country at a later stage and the Muslims

24. *Burhān*, Issue No. 1, July, 1966, pp. 8, 9, 16.
25. *Burhān*, July, 1966, pp. 18, 19 ; August, 1966, pp. 69-72.
26. *Burhān*, July, 1966, pp. 21, 22.

were allowed full liberty in the performance of their religious duties and obligations. But there were other 'Ulama' who held India to be *Dār al-Islām*.[27] Some 'Ulama' held India to be *Dār al-'Ahd* probably on the basis of an implied contract whereby the English Government guaranteed security and liberty in religious affairs.[28]

Courts' View : The question whether India was *Dār al-Islām* or *Dār al-Kufr* came up for decision before different High Courts in several cases. It was observed in the matter of Ram Kumari, "We cannot hold that British India is a foreign country (*Dārul Ḥarb*) within the meaning and intention of the above rules, that is, the rules of Muslim (Law) so that a Hindu marriage would have become dissolved by the conversion of the wife to Islam, on the expiration of a certain period without any notice to the husband."[29] The same High Court did not agree with this view in a subsequent case when it stated, "There appears to have been no detailed argument on the point nor any reason, given for that conclusion. It is to be noticed also that the Court there did-not come to any opposite finding that India is an Islamic country. As a matter of mere illustration, I may be permitted to refer to the current constitutional controversy about the proposals of the Muslim League, a political party, which they have put forward under the heading of a proposed establishment of an independent sovereign State in India to be known as Pakistan. If British India or any part of it were already *Dārul Islām*, there could be no room for any such controversy or proposal. The mere fact of the non-existence at present of any area fulfilling the conditions of the suggested Pakistan is in itself a clear illustration of the extent to which the present British Government is not a government of Islamic rule." The Court then proceeded to decide the case on the basis that British India was not

27. Rais Ahmad Ja'farī, *op. cit.*, pp. 143, 144, *Qawm* (newspaper). March 24, 1919.
28. *Burhān*, August 1966. pp. 80, 81,
29. *Re.* Ram Kumari, (1891) I.L.R. 18 Cal. 264

a *Dārul Islām.*[30]

In another case before the same High Court this question again came up for decision, but the Court did not expressly decide the question.[31] It merely observed, "Even if it be assumed that India is an Islamic country, it appears that there can be no lawful dissolution of the marital tie unless Islam has actually been presented to the unconverted party by the Court acting as *Kazi.*" In a still later case of a similar nature, the Bombay High Court observed, "It is not possible to take the view that India is a country subject to the laws of Islam. It is true that the courts in British India administer the Muslim law as altered and amended by statute law to Muslim parties. But the courts of law do so pursuant to the directions contained in the laws of India. Complete religious neutrality obtains in our country and our Courts administer laws irrespective of the creed of the parties who appear before them. The Courts do not administer the laws of any particular community, but they administer such laws as are valid in British India. Muslim law is administered only in those cases where it happens to be the law of British India in cases where the parties are Muslims."[32] The Court then came to the conclusion that British India was not an Islamic country (*Dār al-Islām*).

A case involving the decision of such a nature came up again before the High Court of Jammu and Kashmir. Abdul Majid, C.J., stated, "By no stretch of reasoning, it can be said that British India was a country subject to the laws of Islam. The rules of Muhammadan law detailed in such treatises as the *Hidāyah* and *Fatāwā al-Hindiyāh* presuppose the existence of Muhammadan law as the law of the State and Islam as the State religion. One has to admit that in British India, the State religion was not Islam. The laws prevailing in British India were quite different from Islamic

30. Ayesha Bibi Vs. Subodh Ch. Chakravarty, A.I.R. 1949. Cal. 436
31. Noor Jehan Vs, Eugene Tiscenko A.I.R. 1941 Cal. 582.
32. Robasa Khanum Vs, Khodad Bomanji Irani, A.I R 1947 Bom. 272.

Laws on several questions. Even now in Pakistan it cannot be said that the law of the State is pure Muhammadan Law. British India could not be considered as *Dār al-Islām* as observed by Abdur Rauf, the Judge in the case reported as ILR. 1, Lah. 440..... In the circumstances, the British India had to be treated as a foreign country........."[33]

It will be seen from the above discussion that there is a difference of opinion amongst the Courts as to whether India was a *Dār al-Islām* (Muslim State) a *Dār al-Ḥarb* (non-Muslim State. It is, however, clear that the general view was to hold British India to be a non-Muslim State. As stated before, the most prevailing view in determining the status of a country in this respect is to see if it is the Muslims or non-Muslims who wield the power to promulgate whatever law or laws they like in the country. Judged by this criterion it is clear that British India was not a *Dār al-Islām* but was a *Dār al-Ḥarb.*

A very interesting point for consideration is whether the present-day European countries are *Dār al-Ḥarb* or *Dār al-Islām*. Obviously they cannot be considered to be *Dār al-Islām* because they do not satisfy the essential condition that the Muslims should be wielding so much power there as to promulgate and enforce their own laws. Some countries bind their citizens, Muslim or others, by their civil laws and do not allow the Muslims to follow Muslim law in some matters. Thus, a Muslim cannot legally marry in England an English woman, even if she is a *Muslimah*, according to the rites and ceremonies observed by Muslims. He can marry her only in the Church or before the Registrar of Marriages or some place registered for the purpose. Muslims have been prosecuted and convicted there for performing such marriages at places other than the above. Similarly, a Muslim cannot marry there two English women, even if *Muslimah*, but will be convicted for bigamy. The same result will follow if being married in his own country he subsequently marries an English woman.

33. Syed Faiz Ali Shah Vs. Ghulam Abbas Shah, P.L.D. 1952 Azad Jammu and Kashmir, 32.

There may be other similar matters. But at the same time, a Muslim is given perfect liberty to offer congregational prayers, and to perform and fulfil many of the obligations which are incumbent on him under Muslim law. The lives and properties of the Muslims are perfectly safe there and there they hold the same status as is held by the English citizens. Mawlānā Muḥammad Anwar S͟hāh has definitely held Germany, Russia, France and other Christian countries to be *Dār al-Ḥarb*.[34] But under the present-day changed conditions, it would be proper to reconsider the matter. Perhaps it may be appropriate to call England and other Christian countries *Dār al-Ṣulḥ* or *Dār al-'Ahd* (Mīt͟hāq) as the case may be on the basis of the agreement express or implied to protect life and property among various members of the United Nations Organisation.

Effect of status of Country: The fact of a country being *Dār al-Ḥarb* affects mainly two aspects, namely :

(*a*) Allegiance by the Muslims to that country; and

(*b*) Marriage.

(*a*) *Allegiance*: As regards the first aspect, it has been explained that *Dār al-Ḥarb* is of two kinds, namely :

I. *Dār al-Ḥarb* in which Muslims are stopped by the people or the government of that country from openly declaring their religion, offering Friday and other prayers in congregations, call of *Mu'azzin*, circumcision and performance of other religious obligations. It becomes incumbent on the Muslims to migrate from that country. Under an injunction of the Qur'ān wherein it is laid down that, "(As for) those whom the angels cause to die while they are unjust to themselves, (the angels) will say : What were you doing? They will say : We were weak in the earth. (They will) say : Was not Allah's earth spacious, so that you could have migrated therein? So these it

34. Mawlānā Muḥammad Anwar S͟hāh, *op. cit.*, p. 5.

is whose refuge is hell—and it is an evil resort.[35] It is laid down at another place, "O you who believe, take not My enemy and your enemy for friends. Would you offer them love, while they deny the Truth that has come to you, driving out the Messenger and yourselves because you believe in Allāh, your Lord?"[36] But if such be not the case or if the Muslims of that country cannot, immediately, find an asylum or place of refuge then immediate migration is not necessary and they can continue to live there till they find a place of security. Mawlānā Shāh Abd al-Aziz has expressed this view and has supported it by the precedent of the Prophet (peace be on him) who remained in Mecca for thirteen years in spite of the fact that the *Kuffār* did not allow him to propagate the religion of Islam and assaulted and injured him and obstructed him from offering prayers, in the sacred place of Ka'bah.[37]

II. *Dār al-Ḥarb* in which Muslims can openly declare their religion, perform their religious obligations as openly offering their prayers. It is not incumbent on the Muslims to migrate from such a country. This view is based on an injunction in the Qur'ān wherein it is stated, 'Allah forbids you not respecting those who fight you not for religion, nor drive you forth from your homes, that you show them kindness and deal with them justly, surely Allah loves the doers of justice."[38] Here there is no apprehension that they may be forced to change their faith and adopt the culture of the non-believers.

35. Qur'ān, Surah al-Nisa V : 97.
36. Qur'ān, Surah al-Mumtaḥana LX : 1.
37. Mawlānā Shāh Abd al-Aziz, *op. cit.*, p. 58.
38. Qur'ān, Surah al-Mumtaḥana LX : 8.

Marriage: As regards the second aspect, namely, marriage, it may be mentioned here that the Muslim jurists divide *Tabāyun Dār* (difference of country or domicile) into two classes, namely, *Tabāyun Ḥaqīqī* (actual difference) and *Tabāyun Ḥukmī* which may be called legal difference as explained below :

(*a*) The husband has his abode in a Muslim State while the wife has her permanent residence in a non-Muslim State; this constitutes a *Tabāyun Ḥaqīqī* or actual difference of domicile.

(*b*) The husband, domiciled in a non-Muslim State, comes to reside in a Muslim State with the *amān* (guarantee of security) of the Muslims leaving behind his wife. This shall constitute *Ḥukmī* (legal) *Tabāyun*, because he still belongs to the non-Muslim State. If he, however, takes up his permanent residence in the Muslim State, leaving his wife behind, this will become *Tabāyun Ḥaqīqī* or actual difference.[39]

The Muslim jurists have laid down certain general rules to govern cases of difference of domicile. But the general rule of law seems to be that there will be no annulment of marriage in the case of *Tabāyun Ḥukmī* or legal difference of domicile but the marriage may be dissolved in the case of *Tabāyun Ḥaqīqī* or actual difference of domicile.

Abode of spouses in different countries: Muslim law lays great stress on companionship of the spouses and to provide against loose living. Both these objects can be achieved only when the parties are living or can live together. The Muslim law relating to *Tabāyun Dār*, or difference of countries, is mainly based on the practical difficulties involved. It is considered necessary that the spouses should live together or at least should be in a position to do so. Moreover, if one of the spouses takes up his or her permanent residence in a non-

39. Shaykhzādah, *Majma' al-Anhur*, Constantinople, 1327, A.H. Vol. I, p. 37, Ibn 'Ābidīn, *op. cit.*, Vol. II, p. 401. Khurram Ali, *Ghāyat al-Awṭā*, (Urdu Tr. of *Al-Durr al-Mukhtār* Lukhnow, 1925, Vol. II, pp. 73, 74, 76.

Muslim country while the other chooses to live in a Muslim country, they become subject to different laws. Muslim law shall apply to the party living in *Dār al-Islām* while the other party shall not be subject to Muslim law and shall be governed by the laws of the non-Muslim country and the *Qāḍī* shall have no control over him or her. The result will be that the husband or the wife living in the non-Muslim country cannot be made to follow the order of the *Qāḍī* of the place where the other spouse is living. Further, there may be restrictions on the free ingress and outgress of the spouses in and from the countries in which they have taken their residence and it may not be possible for them to live together. What is still more important is the fact that by their living separate from each other, the objects of the marriage shall be lost and so its continuation shall become infructuous, and it will be in the interest of the parties that the marriage be dissolved. But as the parties shall be under the control of different Courts in different countries, one of which shall be a non-Muslim country, it is obvious that the dissolution of the marriage shall become a complicated matter. The law of one country may allow the dissolution of the marriage under its own law while the dissolution of the marriage may not be allowed by the law of the other country. To obviate such a difficulty, the Muslim jurists have laid down certain general rules of law.

But it may be noted that these rules are mainly applicable to non-Muslims only and are generally given in books on Fiqh in the chapter on "The Marriages of the *Kuffār*" (unbelievers). The Muslim jurists have stated rules about the effect of such difference of domicile on the marriage of non-Muslim married couples. It seems rather strange that with the exception of a few rules they have not made all the rules applicable to Muslims even when the consideration on the basis of which the rules have been made for non-Muslims apply with equal force to Muslims. The only reason for this omission seems to be that the Muslim jurists of early days could not have imagined the position that when one of the Muslim spouses would come from a non-Muslim country to a Muslim country the other would not do the same or that the spouses would not live together. This idea finds support by the fact that the Muslim jurists did take into consideration the position when a Muslim was married to a *Kitābiyah* in a *Dār al-Ḥarb* and a difference of domicile did occur. They must have considered that in such a case it could be possible that the *Kitābiyah* wife might not leave her own country and accordingly they have made rules to govern such cases and they are practically the same as are applicable in the case of non-Muslims.

The rules governing cases of difference in the domicile of the husband and the wife applicable to non-Muslims and Muslims are given below :—

(*a*) *Rules applicable to Non-Muslims*:

I. As a general rule if one of the non-Muslim spouses retains his or her domicile in a *Dār al-Ḥarb* or non-Muslim country while the other takes up his or her domicile in a Muslim country, then the marriage shall become automatically dissolved on the expiry of three months when the spouse living in the non-Muslim country has no intention of migrating to the Muslim country.[40] It is immaterial whether it is the husband or the wife who takes up his or her domicile in a non-Muslim country.[41] It is also immaterial whether it was a Muslim or non-Muslim country where they were living formerly. These matters will be fully borne out by the following illustrative cases.

II. If the wife comes from a non-Muslim country to a Muslim country and settles there while her husband remains behind, domiciled in the non-Muslim country, then the marriage shall become automatically dissolved on the expiry of the prescribed period.[42]

40. Ibn 'Ābidīn, *op. cit.*, Vol. II, pp. 400-401: al-Marghīnānī, *op. cit.*, p. 327.
41. *Ibid.*, *al-Fatāwā al-Hindiyāh*, Deoband n.d, Vol. II, p. 39.
42. *Ibid.*

Similarly, if it is the husband who takes up his domicile in a Muslim country while the wife remains behind settled in the non-Muslim country then too the marriage shall become automatically dissolved[43].

III. It can be gathered from various books on Muslim Fiqh that if both the spouses come to a Muslim country from a non-Muslim country, their marriage shall not become dissolved but shall continue. This is based on the fact that in this case there is no difference of domicile.[44]

IV. If both the spouses are taken prisoner in a war and are brought together to a *Dār al-Islām* then under the Ḥanafi law the marriage shall not be dissolved as there is no difference of domicile in the case.[45] Under the Shāfa'ī law the marriage shall be dissolved because the Imam considered it a sufficient ground for the dissolution of marriage if a person was made a prisoner of war.[46] But if only one of the spouses is taken a prisoner in a war then according to the unanimous opinion of all the Muslim jurists, the marriage shall be automatically dissolved on the expiry of the prescribed period.[47] These rules can be due to the fact that in old times there used to be no repatriation of prisoners of war who were treated as slaves or sold as such and so their marriages became infructuous and there was no use in maintaining them.

Rules applicable to Muslims: The rules governing cases of difference in the domicile of husband and wife applicable to Muslims are as follows:—

(*b*) I. Should a Muslim marry a *Kitābiyah* in a *Dār al-*

43. Ibn Ābidīn, *op. cit.*, Vol. II, pp. 400-401; al-Marghīnānī, *op.. cit.*, *Fatāwā al-Hindiyāh*, *op. cit.*, Vol. II, p. 39.
44. *Ibid.*
45. *Ibid.*
46. *Ibid.*
47. *Ibid.*

Ḥarb (non-Muslim country) and should he alone migrate to a Muslim country while the wife remains behind, settled in the non-Muslim country, the marriage would be automatically dissolved on account of difference of domicile and the consequent cessation of marital relations.[48]

II. If the Kitābiyah wife of a Muslim comes from a non-Muslim country and settles in a Muslim country while the husband remains behind settled in the non-Muslim country with no intention to change his domicile then the marriage shall be automatically dissolved.[49] The conduct of the husband shows that he has severed his connection with the Muslim country by settling down in a non-Muslim country. The continuation of the marriage in such a case shall become useless.

Mawlānā Abul A'lā Mawdūdī has expressed a different view and has stated that the marriage shall not get automatically dissolved, but it shall be liable to dissolution on the suit of the person who has taken his or her domicile in a Muslim country. He has further stated that if a woman is domiciled in or has taken her domicile in a Muslim country while her husband is domiciled in a non-Muslim country (*Dār al-Kufr*) and is not agreeable to migrate (to the Muslim country), then we can not get her any maintenance nor shall he be subject to the jurisdiction of our Courts. The wife shall be deprived of her rights in such a case unless we send her to the *Dār al-Kufr*. If the woman is not possessed of means of maintenance or there may be a great risk of her being led astray then her marriage should be dissolved without

48. *Ibid. Majma' al-Anhur.*
49. *Ibid.*

any delay.[50]

III. If the *Kitābiyah* wife of a Muslim takes up her domiciled in a Muslim country while the husband, domiciled in a Muslim country, remains behind in a non-Muslim country, the marriage shall not be dissolved because the Muslim husband can come to the Muslim State at any time without any hinderance and settle there. He can claim the woman as his wife as a matter of right and there can be no difficulty in their living as husband and wife and so there is no necessity to dissolve the marriage.[51]

Temporary Residence: Emphasis is laid on the rules about difference of domicile to a complete separation between the parties. Hence if one of the spouses comes to a Muslim country or goes to a non-Muslim country only temporarily then the marriage shall not be dissolved and shall subsist because there is no difference of domicile.[52] It is immaterial if one spouse goes to *Dār al-Ḥarb* from a Muslim country or the case is reverse, that is, when one spouse comes to a Muslim country only temporarily.

Re-Marriage: When a marriage is dissolved because the wife takes up her domicile in a Muslim country then she can at once contract a marriage in the Muslim State in spite of the fact that she is a married woman and has a husband living in the *Dār al-Ḥarb*[53]. Should she be pregnant, then she can contract a marriage only after delivery.[54]

The above rules are based on the fact that in ancient times it was very difficult for one spouse, residing permanently in one country, to get or to bring the other spouse domiciled in a

50. Mawlānā Abul A'lā Mawdūdī, *Rasāil wa Mas'āil*, Lahore, Vol. II, p. 162.
51. Shaykhzādah, *op. cit.*, Vol. I, p. 371; Ibn 'Ābidīn, *op. cit.*, Vol. II, p. 401, *Fatāwa al-Hindiyāh op. cit.*, Vol. II, p. 39, Al-Marghinānī, *op. cit.*, Vol. II, p. 327.
52. *Ibid.*
53. *Ibid.*
54. *bid.*

different country. It was against the policy of the countries in those times to allow one of their subjects to leave his or her country in order to live in another country. But in the modern times in most of the countries this situation will not arise. It cannot, however, be denied that there are still some countries which do not allow their inhabitants to leave their countries while some countries may not like to allow a person from a Muslim country to settle there. This difficulty on which the rules are based will not be experienced in the countries of the first category and it does not seem proper or reasonable to apply the rules of *tabāyun dār* to those countries to the extent that a marriage may get dissolved automatically on account of a difference in the domicile of the spouses. It will not be impossible or even difficult for the spouses to take up their permanent residence in the same country. The above rules of Muslim law can, therefore, have no application in such a case. The rules envisage a different position as when it shall not be possible for the spouses to live together and when the end of the marriage itself shall be frustrated on that account. In the case of the countries of the second category the rules may still apply. It is, however, difficult to lay down any rule of general application in the present changed conditions and every case will have to be decided on its own merits. But a marriage may not be considered to be dissolved automatically on account of a difference of domicile and the Court's decree may be considered necessary.

Observance of 'iddah: There is difference of opinion about the necessity of observing *'iddah* when marriage is dissolved on the wife's adoption of domicile in a Muslim State. According to Abū Ḥanīfah, no *'iddah* shall be incumbent in such a case unless the wife happens to be pregnant. But, according to another report, *'iddah* shall not be incumbent on her even in such a case. She shall not, however, contract another marriage until the delivery of child. Muḥammad and Abū Yūsuf hold that *'iddah* shall be incumbent on the wife.[55] A practical result

55. Al-Marghīnānī, *op. cit.*, Vol. II, p. 327 ; Ibn 'Ābidīn, *op. cit.*, Vol. II, p. 401.

of this difference of opinion is that according to the opinion of *Imām* Abū Ḥanīfah a child born to the woman within six months of the dissolution of marriage shall belong to her non-Muslim husband while a child born after such period shall belong to the second husband. The opinion expressed by Abū Yūsuf and Muḥammad will lead to the result that a child born within two years of the dissolution of marriage shall be considered to belong to the non-Muslim husband. This is, of course, subject to the condition that she has not contracted a second marriage and when the child can belong to the second husband.

Conclusion: Several points will be clear from the above discussion. The first is that the Muslim jurists have greatly emphasised the fact that in order that a country could be deemed to be a *Dār al-Islām* it is necessary that the Muslims should be in a position to enforce Muslim law in that country. The law enforced in a country greatly affects the morality and culture of the people. Thus if adultery by a person or homosexuality is not made a crime in any country then obviously people take a lax view of such conduct of a person. Their mentality, morality and even culture is greatly affected by the laws prevailing in their country. Secondly, the Muslim jurists considered that when the husband and wife took their permanent residence in different countries, the continuation of the marriage became infructuous and it was considered desirable that the marriage be allowed to be dissolved in such a case. As the countries where the spouses would take their abode would be governed by different laws while the spouses would be subject to the jurisdiction of different Courts, the dissolution of the marriage would become rather complicated as there was no International Law or Private International Law in force in those days. It was, therefore, held that where there was a difference of domicile so that one spouse would live in a *Dār al-Islām* while the other lived in a *Dār al-Ḥarb*, the marriage would get dissolved automatically. The Muslim jurists modified their definitions and notions of *Dār* from time to time to meet the needs of their own times in order to reduce the rigidity of the rules and thereby reducing hardship to the Muslims. Thus, as discussed above, many Muslim jurists held India after its conquest by the English to be *Dār al-Ḥarb*, but many of them changed their opinion when conditions became settled and peace and order prevailed while the British government assured the people of its non-interference in religious matters and full liberty in the performance of their religious observances and obligations. But the mere fact that the Muslims are allowed full freedom in religious matters or can live with full security of life and property in a certain country cannot make it a *Dār al-Islām*. At present most European countries and States in the U. S. A. fulfil both these conditions but by no stretch of imaginations can they be said to be *Dār al-Islām*. Hence to determine the nature of a country, that is, whether it is *Dār al-Islām* or *Dār al-Ḥarb*, we have to rely on the unanimously agreed condition as to who is in a position to impose its laws on the inhabitants—the Muslims or the non-Muslims. Formerly, it was the Ruler of a country who promulgated or could promulgate laws but now very few Rulers enjoy such a power and many of them are mere figure-heads and the real power is enjoyed by the representatives of the people through chosen ministers who on their part are responsible to the House of Representatives. The presence of the representatives of the Muslims in the Assemblies or Houses in a certain country cannot affect the nature of the country if they are in such a minority as to be unable to impose laws of their own choice in that country while the non-Muslims can on account of their majority be in a position to impose their own laws on the Muslims.

As stated before, we can consider the European and other countries to be *Dār al-Amān* at the most and a very important question is whether the law regarding difference of domicile has become obsolete or is still extant. There is nothing to show that it has become obsolete. Section 2 (IX) of the Dissolution of Muslim Marriages Act, 1939, makes it clear that it is still applicable. It provides that a marriage can be dissolved on any ground which is regarded as valid for the dissolution of marriage under Muslim Law. Besides, it is necessary to apply it under certain circumstances to save a Muslim from hardship. Thus if a wife on adoption of Islam settles in a Muslim country while her husband prefers to live in a non-Muslim country, it is obvious that the continuation of the marriage shall become infructuous and there is no reason why we should apply the law of the husband's country in preference to our own law. It is an important matter and perhaps our Courts may thoroughly discuss it in some cases of this nature that may come before them.

Chapter 27

'IDDAH OR WAITING PERIOD

Preliminary.—When a marriage is dissolved either by the death of the husband, divorce, or by the decree of a Court or in any other way and a child is born subsequently, the question arises whether it can be affiliated to the person who was the husband of the child's mother before its birth. The question becomes complicated if the woman enters into another marriage and a child is born to her subsequent to such marriage at such a period of time that it may belong to either husband.

To provide against such a difficulty different nations have formulated various rules of law. Thus the Romans forbade a widow to marry until after the expiry of ten months from her husband's death. Some other nations have also adopted some such period of time as ten months, as the necessary period of waiting. Amongst the ancient Arabs, it was the custom for a widow after the death of her husband to withdraw to a small tent, where she spent a whole year during which she was not allowed to cleanse herself. *'Iddah* after divorce was unknown to the Arabs before the advent of Islam. Whosoever married a divorcee, who was pregnant was considered to be the father of the child born after the marriage even though the previous husband was really the father. In Islam, however, the actual father was and is considered the father of the child.

Islam considers that it is not at all necessary to force a woman to wait for a very long time as it may involve hardship and may even lead to immorality. It is considered that such signs appear after a certain time which serve as sure indications of pregnancy and that it is not necessary for a woman to wait any longer. If the signs do not appear within that time then this establishes the fact that the woman is not *en-ceinte.*

Religious Sanction.—The following passages in the Qur'ān provide for the observance of *'iddah* :

"O Prophet, when you divorce women divorce them for their prescribed period, and calculate the period : and keep your duty to Allah, your Lord. Turn them not out of their houses—nor should they themselves go forth—unless they commit an open indecency...."[1]

"And divorced women should keep themselves in waiting for three courses. And it is not lawful for them to conceal that which Allah has created in their wombs...."[2]

"O you who believe, when you marry believing women, then divorce them before you touch them, you have in their case no term which you should reckon. But make provision for them and set them free in goodly manner".[3]

"And those of your women who despair of menstruation, if you have a doubt, their prescribed time is three months, and of those, too, who have not had their courses. And the pregnant women, their prescribed time is that they lay down their burden. And whoever keeps his duty to Allah, He makes his affair easy for him".[4]

"Lodge them where you like according to your means, and injure them not to straiten them. And if they are pregnant, spend on them until they lay down their burden. Then if they suckle for you, give them their recompense, and enjoin one another to do good ; and if you disagree, another will suckle for him".[5]

Description.—When a marriage is dissolved either by divorce or under a dercee of a Court after consummation or death of the husband or in any other way the woman cannot contract a second marriage under the Muslim law till the expiry of a certain period of time. This period of time is called "*'iddah*". *'Iddah* literally means to count. But the Muslim jurists use it technically to mean the period of waiting by a woman on dissolution of her marriage after consummation

1. Qur'ān, surah al-Talāq, XXVIII : 1.
2. Qur'ān, surah al-Baqarah, II : 228.
3. Qur'ān, surah al-Aḥzāb, XXII : 49.
4. Qur'ān, surah al-Talāq, XXVIII : 4.
5. Qur'ān, surah al-Talāq, XXVIII : 6.

or on the demise of her husband or under the Ḥanafī, Mālikī, and Ḥanbalī laws also on a valid retirement.[6] The author of *Radd al-Muḥtār*, on the strength of *Badā'i al-Ṣanā'i'* describes it as the period fixed for the complete cessation of all effects of the marriage.[7]

Definition.—It is defined in *al-Hidāyah* as "The term of probation (or waiting) incumbent upon a woman in consequence of the dissolution of her marriage after carnal connection ; it is the term by the completion of which a new marriage is rendered lawful."[8] It is described in *al-Fatāwā al-Hindiyah* as the waiting for a definite period which is incumbent upon a woman on the death of her husband or after the dissolution of a rightful or semblance marriage that has been confirmed by consummation.[9]

Object.—'*Iddah* is primarily imposed with a view to ascertain whether the woman is pregnant so that the paternity of the child that may be born to her after the death of her husband or the dissolution of her marriage may be determined.[10]

A secondary but less important object is to serve as a mark of respect for the deceased husband or as a mark of sorrow for the dissolved marriage.[11]

On whom incumbent.—Generally speaking, observance of '*iddah* is incumbent under certain conditions on every wife of a Muslim whether she be a Muslimah or a Kitābiyah, that is, woman belonging to revealed religion such as a Christian woman or a Jewess.[12] But no '*iddah* shall be incumbent on a woman whose connection with a man is merely adulterous.

6. Ibn 'Ābidīn, *Radd al-Muḥtār*, Cairo, 1318 A.H., Vol. II, pp. 614-15.
7. *Ibid*., p. 614.
8. Burhān al-Dīn al-Marghīnānī, *al-Hidāyah*, Delhi, n.d., Vol. II, p. 402 (annotations).
9. *Al-Fatāwā al-Hindiyah*, Kanpur, 1349 A.H., Vol. II, p. 134.
10. Burhān al-Dīn al-Marghīnānī, *op. cit.*, Vol. II, p. 402 ; Ibn 'Ābidīn, *op. cit.*, Vol. II, p. 616.
11. *Ibid*., p. 407 ; *ibid*., p. 616.
12. *Al-Fatāwā al-Hindiyāh*, *op. cit.*, Vol. II, p. 134 ; Ibn 'Ābidīn, *op. cit.*, Vol. II, p. 616.

When observed.—Observance of *'iddah* becomes due on divorce after actual cohabitation or on the husband's death. To be more particular, it becomes incumbent after one of the following incidents :

(*a*) Death of the husband,

(*b*) Pronouncement of divorce,

(*c*) Separation by order of Court,

(*d*) Sexual intercourse with a woman under misapprehension.

(*e*) Dissolution of marriage in any other way after consummation or on valid retirement under the Ḥanafi, Mālikī, and Ḥanbalī laws in certain cases.[13]

'Iddah commences for the prescribed period immediately from the time of divorce, husband's death or other cause and is not in any way affected by the wife's ignorance of the fact that it has been effected. Hence, if she does not receive any information about the divorce or the husband's death till such time as when the prescribed period of *'iddah* has already expired then it shall not be necessary for her to observe any *'iddah* at all.

Rules for observance of 'iddah :

(*a*) *Death of the husband.* In a valid marriage *'iddah* is incumbent on a wife on the death of her husband irrespective of the fact whether the marriage has or has not been consummated.[14] The fact that the wife is major or minor makes no difference. The *'iddah* is imposed as a mark of respect for the deceased husband as well as to ascertain if the wife is *en-ceinte.* If the marriage is irregular (*fāsid*) no *'iddah* is incumbent on the wife on the death of her husband if the marriage has not been consummated even when under the Ḥanafī, Mālikī and Ḥanbalī laws there has been a valid retirement.[15] This is due to the fact that such a marriage is not treated as a marriage at all except for legitimacy of the children born of such a marriage

13. Ibn 'Ābidīn, *op. cit*, Vol. II, p. 615 f.

14. *Ibid.*, p. 615 ; *al-Fatāwā al-Hindiyah, op. cit.*, Vol. II, p. 134.

15. Burhān al-Dīn al-Maghīnānī, *op. cit.*, Vol. II, p. 408 ; Ibn 'Ābidīn, *op. cit.*, Vol. II, p. 615.

and the wife is not expected to bear any love for the deceased who was not her husband. If the marriage is irregular (*fāsid*) *'iddah* would be incumbent only when there has been an actual consummation of the marriage so that it is not incumbent after a valid retirement.[16]

(*b*) *Pronouncement of divorce.*—In the case of a divorce whether revocable or irrevocable *'iddah* is incumbent if the marriage is valid and there has been consummation of it, and, under the Ḥanafī, Mālikī, and Ḥanbalī law, also if there has been a valid retirement.[17]

If the marriage is *bāṭil* or void no *'iddah* is necessary in any case whatsoever even when the marriage has been consummated.[18] The necessity for observing *'iddah* does not arise when there is no lawful marriage between the parties. A void marriage is no marriage at all and the relationship of wife and husband does not exist in the case of such a marriage. It has already been stated that the primary object of observance of *'iddah* is to ascertain the parentage of a child that may be born to her. In the case of a void marriage the child is not affiliated to the adulterer and so observance of *'iddah* is not necessary. Hence it is also not necessary for a woman to observe *'iddah* when her connection with a man is merely illicit.[19]

(*c*) *Dissolution of marriage by Court.*—If a valid marriage is annulled by a Court for any reason such as the husband's impotency, exercise of option of puberty by the wife etc., *'iddah* is incumbent only when the marriage has been consummated or, under the Ḥanafī, Mālikī and Ḥanbalī laws, when there has been a valid retirement.[20]

(*d*) *Intercourse under misapprehension.*—*'Iddah* is incumbent on a woman with whom a person had sexual intercourse under a doubt or misapprehension, that is, under the wrong impression that the woman was his wife.[21] If there was no

16. *Al-Fatāwā al-Hindiyāh, op. cit.*, Vol. II p. 134.
17. *Ibid.*, Ibn 'Ābidīn, *op. cit.* Vol. II, p. 615 f.
18. Ibn 'Ābidīn, *op. cit.*, Vol. II, p. 623.
19. *Ibid.*, p. 615 ; *al-Fatāwā al-Hindiyah, op. cit.*, Vol. II, p. 134.
20. Ibn 'Ābidīn, *op. cit.*, Vol. II, p. 616.
21. *Ibid*., p. 615.

doubt and he knew that the woman was not his wife, the act amounts to adultery for which no *'iddah* has been prescribed.

(*e*) *Marriage dissolved automatically.*—If a marriage is dissolved automatically as on account of the apostasy of either the husband or the wife, the observance of *'iddah* is incumbent on the wife.[22]

(*f*) *Women on whom 'iddah is not incumbent.*—*'Iddah* is not incumbent on such women as are described below :—

(*a*) A woman who has been divorced before consummation of marriage and under the Ḥanafī, Mālikī and Ḥanbalī laws also before valid retirement. This rule holds good in case of a valid marriage.[23]

(*b*) A woman whose marriage is dissolved before actual consummation and under the Ḥanafī, Mālikī and Ḥanbalī laws also before valid retirement.[24]

(*c*) A woman whose connection with a man amounts merely to adultery.[25]

(*d*) Two sisters married to a person by one contract and the same has been cancelled.[26]

(*e*) More than four women married to a person by one contract which has been cancelled.[27]

(*f*) A non-Muslim woman who comes to a Muslim country from a non-Muslim country leaving her husband behind and settles in the Muslim country either on adoption of Islam or on securing protection.[28] As explained in the chapter on "Difference of Domicile," the marriage would become dissolved on account of difference of domicile.

(*g*) A woman who is afflicted with the malformation of her genital parts rendering consummation of marriage impossible on the dissolution of her marriage.[28a]

22. Ibn 'Ābidīn, *op. cit.*, p. 616.
23. *Ibid.*, p. 617 ; *al-Fatāwā al-Hindiyah, op. cit.*, Vol. II, p. 134.
24. *Ibid.*, p. 616.
25. *Ibid.*, p. 615 ; *al-Fatāwā al-Hindiyah, op. cit.*, Vol. II, p. 134.
26. *Ibid.*
27. Ibn 'Ābidīn, *op. cit.*, Vol. II, p. 615.
28. *Ibid.*, p. 616.
28*a*. *Ibid.*

Incidents of 'Iddah.—In the case of revocable divorce a marriage is not dissolved immediately in consequence of the pronouncement of the divorce, but is considered to subsist during the period of *'iddah* for certain purposes as a result of which certain restrictions and duties are imposed on the parties and some mutual rights are created between them. It is only on the expiry of the period of *'iddah* that these restrictions are removed and the rights are lost. In case of an irrevocable divoce also there are some incidents which give rise to certain effects during *'iddah.* It may be added here that a breach of some of such incidents shall be considered to be a moral offence only and shall not give rise to any legal consequences.

The following are the important incidents of *'iddah* :—

(*a*) Prohibition against marriage,
(*b*) Observance of mourning,
(*c*) Right of maintenance,
(*d*) Right of dower,
(*e*) Right of inheritance,
(*f*) Status.

(*a*) *Prohibition against marriage.*—The husband cannot contract a marriage with certain women till the period of *'iddah* of his divorced or separated wife has expired.

The Ḥanafī jurists have enumerated twenty cases in which a man has to wait for the termination of the *'iddah.* Important cases are as given below :—

I. Marriage with women who are unlawful to the husband on account of his wife but whom he can marry on the completion of the *'iddah* such as the wife's sister, daughter of the wife's sister or brother etc.[29]

II. Marriage with a woman who happens to be the fifth wife, that is, if the husband has four wives, one of whom he has divorced or she has separated from him then he cannot marry another wife till the period of *'iddah* has expired.[30]

29. Ibn 'Ābidīn, *op. cit.*, Vol. II, pp. 614, 615.
30. *Ibid.*

(*b*) *Mourning in 'Iddah.*—A woman has to observe mourning during the period of her *'iddah* in the case of an irrevocable divorce and on the husband's death. Thus she should not adorn herself, that is, she should not put on silken or fine or even coloured clothes nor wear ornaments nor use scents or perfumes. Mourning is not incumbent on seven classes of women such as are (*a*) physically unfit for intimacy, (*b*) minors (*c*) idolatresses, (*d*) insane women, (*e*) women whose marriages are *fāsid* (irregular), (*f*) women with whom intimacy was committed under misapprehension and (*g*) women under revocable divorce or under manumission.[31] In the case of a revocable divorce mourning is not only disapproved of but the wife is advised to adorn herself nicely in order to attract her husband so that he may revoke the divorce.[32]

S͟hī'i Law.—A husband can marry his divorced wife's sister or a fifth wife (that is including the divorced wife) during the period of her *'iddah* if the divorce is irrevocable but such marriage has been disapproved of. If the divorce is revocable then he cannot contract such a marriage till after the expiry of the *'iddah.*[33]

(*c*) *Maintenance during 'Iddah.*—It has been seen that a marriage is dissolved absolutely on the pronouncement of an irrevocable divorce. But the wife retains her status of being a wife during the period of her *'iddah* for certain purposes. A wife cannot contract a second marriage during this period. Hence the liability of the husband to maintain his wife continues during the period of *'iddah* irrespective of the fact whether the divorce is revocable or irrevocable.[34] This may be due to the fact that the wife is not free to remarry during that period or even to leave his house, and so the husband has been made responsible to maintain her during this period. The rule holds good only as long as she passes her *'iddah* at the

31. Ibn 'Ābidīn, *op. cit.*, Vol. II, pp. 634, 635; Burhān al-Dīn al-Marg͟hīnānī, *op. cit.*, Vol. II, p. 408.
32. *Ibid.*, p. 635.
33. Ja'far b. al Hasan, *S͟harā'i' al-Islām*, Tehran, 1377 A.H., Vol. I, p. 248.
34. Burhān al-Dīn al-Marg͟hīnānī, *op. cit.*, Vol. II, p. 407.

house of her husband. If she leaves his house voluntarily against his wishes no maintenance shall be incumbent on him[35]. An order passed under section 488 of the Code of Criminal Procedure in force in Pakistan and India remains operative during this period, wherever she may be living.[36]

If a divorcee is pregnant maintenance is due till the time of delivery as it is only then that the *'iddah* expires.[37] In the case of the husband's death the widow shall not be entitled to any maintenance for the period of her *'iddah* even if she is *en-ceint.*[37] This rule seems to be based on the fact that on the husband's death his property immediately vests in his heirs and the widow is one of them. Morever the liability for maintenance lies only on the husband and the heirs are not responsible for the same.

Shāfi'ī Law.—Shāfi'ī holds that no maintenance is due to a woman repudiated by an irrevocable divorce, unless she is pregnant.[38]

Qādi's Order.—Order for maintenance can be passed only in respect of a wife and should she cease to be a wife then she is no longer entitled to get the same except for the period of her *'iddah.*[39] In the case of a void marriage, no *'iddah* is prescribed and so the wife is not entitled to any maintenance on the dissolution, annulment or termination of her marriage.

(d) Dower.—The only effect of *'iddah* on dower arises in the case of a deferred dower on the pronouncement of a revocable divorce. There is a difference of opinion about the time when the deferred dower becomes payable. According to one version the deferred dower becomes payable on the pronouncement of the divorce while according to another version it does not become payable till the expiry of the period of *'iddah.*[40] An important result of this difference is that in

35. Burhān al-Dīn al-Marghīnānī, *op. cit.*, Vol. II, p. 407.
36. Shah Abu Ilyas Vs. Ulfat Bibi, I.L.R. 12, All. 50; Mst. Mariam Vs. Kadir Bakhsh, A.I.R. 1929, Oudh 527 ; Syed Sahib Vs. Meeran Bibi, 6, O.W.N. 242.
37. Ibn 'Ābidīn, *op. cit.*, Vol. II, p. 688.
38. Burhān al-Dīn al-Marghīnānī, *op. cit.*, Vol. II, p. 423.
39. Ibn 'Ābidīn, *op. cit.*, Vol. II, p. 664.
40. *Ibid.*, p. 668.

former case the payment of dower having become due on pronouncement of the divorce, revocation of the divorce will not restore the nature of the dower, that is, the dower will not become deferred but shall remain immediately payable. In the other case the dower being not due till after the expiry of *'iddah*, a revocation of the divorce will not affect its payment and it will still remain deferred.

The second view is generally considered to be the correct view. It is stated in *Radd al-Muḥtār* that the dower shall remain deferred till the expiry of the period of *'iddah* and shall become prompt only on the expiry of that period. It is also stated therein that it is the usually accepted view.[41] In case of irrevocable divorce, the dower becomes immediately payable on pronouncement of the divorce as an irrevocable divorce puts an immediate end to the marriage.[42]

(*e*) *Inheritance* :

(*a*) *Revocable divorce.*—In case one of the married couple dies during the period of *'iddah* following a revocable divorce, the survivor inherits from the deceased. It is immaterial whether the husband was in good health or on his death-bed when he pronounced the divorce.[43] Similarly, the fact whether the divorce was pronounced at the desire of the wife or by the free-will of the husband against the wishes of the wife would not affect the matter of inheritance.[44]

(*b*) *Irrevocable divorce.*—In case of irrevocable divorce, if the husband divorces the wife when he is in good health but dies while she is observing her *'iddah* then she does not inherit from him.[45]

If the irrevocable divorce is pronounced when he is in his death illness (*maraḍ al-mawt*) and dies during the period of *'iddah* she shall inherit from him unless the divorce was given at her instance in which case she shall not get any inheritance from him.[46]

41. Ibn Ābidīn, *op. cit.*, Vol. II, p. 368.
42. *Ibid.*, p. 368.
43. *Ibid.*, p. 536-37.
44. *Ibid.*
45. *Ibid.*, p. 537.
46. *Ibid.*, pp. 536-37.

Should the husband die after the expiry of the *'iddah* then she shall not inherit from him in any case.[47]

(*c*) *Apostasy.*—If a marriage is dissolved on account of the apostasy of the husband who dies during the period of the wife's *'iddah*, she shall not inherit from him irrespective of the fact whether he was in health or in death-illness at the time of his apostasy. If it is the wife who apostatises and she was in good health at the time of her apostasy but dies during the term of the *'iddah* the husband does not inherit from her.[48] If she apostatises in death-illness he does inherit from her.[49] If both apostatise and then one of them re-embraces Islam and subsequently dies then the apostate shall not inherit from him. If an apostate husband dies then the Muslim wife shall inherit from him. If it is the apostate wife who dies the husband shall inherit from her only if she apostatised in death-illness. If she was i. good health at the time of apostasy then the husband shali not inherit from her.[50]

Period of 'Iddah :

The period of time prescribed for *'iddah* varies in different cases. Important cases are discussed below :

Death.—A woman has to observe *'iddah* for four months and ten days on the death of her husband irrespective of the fact whether she is major or a minor and whether the marriage has not been consummated.[51] If the marriage be irregular (*fāsid*) and has not been consummated no *'iddah* is necessary. But if it has actually been consummated, she has to observe *'iddah* for three menstrual courses or three months if she is not subject to them. The period of *'iddah* shall begin from the time of the death of her husband.[52]

If a person should give a revocable divorce ands hould he

47. Ibn 'Ābidīn, *op. cit.*, Vol. II, p. 537.
48. *Ibid.*, p. 542.
49. *Ibid.*
50. *Ibid.*
51. *Ibid.*, p. 619 ; *al-Fatāwā al-Hindiyah*, *op. cit.*, Vol. II, p. 134.
52. *Ibid.*, p. 623; *Ibid.*

then die while the divorcee is observing *'iddah* she shall have to observe *'iddah* for four months and ten days from the time of the husband's death and the remaining period of *'iddah* due on account of the divorce shall not subsist any longer.[53] This is due to the fact that a marriage remains subsisting during the period of *'iddah* and so she has to observe *'iddah* on account of her husband's death. If the divorce should be irrevocable then it is to be seen if the divorce was pronounced while he was in health or in death-illness. If given in health, no *'iddah* for death would be incumbent on the wife.[54] If the irrevocable divorce is pronounced in death-illness then she has to observe *'iddah* for either death or divorce whichever period be longer.[55]

Divorce.—When a man divorces his wife either by a revocable or irrevocable divorce, her *'iddah* consists of three full courses (of menstruation).[56] If she is not subject to monthly courses on account of extreme youth or old age, or for any other cause then her *'iddah* shall consist of three months.[57] This is irrespective of the fact whether she is a Muslimah or a *Kitābiyah*.[58] By an old woman is meant a woman who is past child-bearing age and a woman is generally considered to be past child-bearing age when she attains the age of fifty years.[59] But this age may differ with different nations. If her courses happen to start before the expiry of the three months, which are incumbent on her, she must commence a fresh *'iddah* counted by her courses.[60] But if the courses do not start till after the expiry of the three months then she shall not be required to observe her *'iddah* afresh.[61]

53. Ibn 'Ābidīn, *op. cit.*, Vol. II, p. 621 ; *al-Fatāwā al-Hindiyah, op. cit.*, Vol. II, p. 136.
54. *Ibid.*
55. *Ibid.*
56. *Ibid.*, p. 616, Burhān al-Dīn al-Marghīnānī, *op. cit.*, Vol. II, p. 402.
57. *Ibid.* p. 617 ; *ibid.*. p. 403.
58. *Al-Fatāwā al-Hindiyah, op. cit.*, Vol. II, p. 134.
59. Burhān al-Dīn al-Marghīnānī, *op. cit.*, Vol. II, p. 404, Ibn 'Ābidīn, *op. cit.*, Vol. II, p. 618.
60. Ibn 'Ābidīn, *op. cit.*, Vol. II, p. 622.
61. *Ibid.*

If a man divorces his wife while she is in her courses that term is not to be counted.[62] The explanation is that a divorcee has to observe *'iddah* for full three courses but the present one is not a full and complete one and so is not to be taken into consideration.

Fāsid marriage.—If the marriage is *fāsid* or irregular, *iddah* shall be incumbent only when there has been an actual consummation of the marriage, but it shall not be incumbent on her after a mere valid retirement.[63] The *'iddah* of divorce in case of an irregular (*fāsid*) marriage is also three full courses.[64] The period of *'iddah* shall commence from the date of divorce.[65]

Void marriage.—If the marriage is *bāṭil* or void no *'iddah* shall be necessary in any case whatsoever, even when the marriage has been consummated.[66] The necessity for observance of *'iddah* does not arise when there is no lawful marriage between the parties. A void marriage is no marriage at all, and the relationship of husband and wife does not subsist in such a case. It has already been stated that the primary object of *'iddah* is to ascertain the parentage of a child that may be born to the woman. In the case of a void marriage, the child cannot be affiliated to the adulterer, but shall be given to its mother. Hence it shall not be necessary for the woman to observe *'iddah* when her connection with the man is illicit.[67]

Dissolution of marriage.—If a marriage is dissolved by the order of a *Qāḍī* the woman has to observe *'iddah* for the same period as in the case of divorce, namely, three full courses or if she is not subject to them then three months.[68]

If the marriage is annulled automatically as on the apostasy of the husband she has to observe *'iddah* for the same

62. Ibn 'Ābidīn, *op. cit.*, Vol. II, p. 625.
63. *Ibid.*, pp. 617, 619.
64. *Ibid.*
65. *Ibid.* pp. 616-17
66. *Ibid.*, p. 623.
67. *Ibid.*, p. 615.
68. *Ibid.*, p. 627.

period as in the case of divorce.[69]

The period of *'iddah* shall be counted from the time of the decree of the *Qāḍī* or date of the apostasy as the case may be.

Intimacy under misapprehension.—If a man has sexual intercourse with a woman under misapprehension or the mistaken belief that the woman was his wife then the woman has to observe *'iddah* for the same period of time as in the case of divorce, that is three full courses.[70] But no *'iddah* shall be necessary if the man does not separate from her but marries her.[71]

Pregnant woman.—The *'iddah* of a pregnant woman is to be observed up to the time of delivery or miscarriage whether *'iddah* is caused by divorce, judicial decree, death or any other mode of separation.[72] Hence if she is divorced while expecting a child, her *'iddah* will expire only on delivery.[73]

If a man marries a woman who is pregnant as a result of adultery, is intimate with her, should he then die or divorce, her *'iddah* shall be accomplished by delivery.[74] The law does not in such a case take into consideration the pregnancy caused by adultery and so the period of adultery is not observed.

If the death occurs of the husband of a woman who is expecting a child, the question arises whether she must observe *'iddah* till the time of her delivery or the period required to be observed in the case of a husband's death. There is a difference of opinion on this question. According to one opinion the woman must observe *'iddah* for whichever is the longer period of the two. According to another view she must observe *'iddah* only for such period as is enjoined in case of pregnancy.[75]

69. Ibn 'Ābidīn, *op. cit.*, Vol. II, p. 616.
70. *Ibid.*, p. 624.
71. *Ibid.*
72. Burhān al-Dīn al-Marghīnānī, *op. cit.*, Vol. II, p. 403.
73. *Ibid.*
74. Ibn 'Ābidīn, *op. cit.*, Vol. II, p. 620
75. Ibn al-Humām, *Fatḥ al-Qadīr*, Cairo, 1356 A.H., Vol. III, pp. 274-75.

There are two verses in the Quran concerning this matter, namely,

(*a*) "And (as for) those of you who die and leave wives behind, such women should keep themselve in waiting for four months and ten days."[76]

(*b*) "And the pregnant women, their prescribed time is that they lay down their burden."[77]

The second verse is the later of the two and so it shall apply in the matter.[78] Besides, there is a Tradition that the Prophet (peace be on him) has declared that the *'iddah* of pregnant women terminates with delivery.[79] The second view is thus generally accepted and held to be valid.[80]

Missing husband.—'Iddah is to be observed when a marriage is annulled by a *Qāḍi* on the ground that the husband is missing, that is, has not been heard of for the prescribed period. It is the same as for death. This is based on the ground that the marriage is dissolved on the presumption that the husband is dead. The period shall commence from the time of the order of the *Qāḍi*[81].

'Iddah for Apostasy.—A woman has to observe *'iddah* when her husband apostatises and the marriage becomes automatically dissolved on that account provided the marriage has been consummated or under the Ḥanafī, Mālikī or Ḥanbalī law if there has been a valid retirement. The period of *'iddah* is the same as in the case of divorce. She shall observe *'iddah* for full three courses from the time of the husband's apostasy.[82]

'Iddah of Convert.—If a non-Muslim married woman embraces Islam and comes to Dār al-Islām her marriage shall stand dissolved. There is a difference of opinion amongst Abū Ḥanīfah on the one hand and Abū Yūsuf and Muḥammad on

76. Qur'ān, surah al-Baqarah, II : 234.
77. Qur'ān, surah al-Talaq, XXVIII : 4.
78. Ibn Qayyim, Zād al-Ma'ād, Cairo, 1950, Vol. IV, pp. 183-84.
79. *Ibid.*, Ibn al-Humām, *Fatḥ al-Qadir*, Cairo, 1365 A.H. Vol. III, pp. 273-75.
80. *Ibid.*
81. Ibn al-Humām, *op. cit.*, Vol. III, pp. 280, 287.
82. *Ibid.*, p. 276.

the other hand regarding *'iddah*. The former holds that no *'iddah* shall be incumbent on her because the effect of the first marriage is lost. Abū Yūsuf and Muḥammad hold that *'iddah* shall be incubment on her because separation between her and her former husband takes place when she enters Dār al-Islām where she becomes subject to the Muslim law.[83]

Commencement of 'iddah.—The period of *'iddah* commences from the time of divorce, husband's death or other cause. It is not in any way affected by the wife's ignorance of the fact that it had become due. Hence if she does not receive any information about the divorce or the husband's death till such time when the prescribed period of *'iddah* has already expired, no *'iddah* shall be incumbent on her.[84]

Place of iddaḥ.—It is incumbent upon a woman under *'iddah* to observe it in the house where she was residing at the time of dissolution of marriage.[85] If, however, the apartment allotted to her in the house of her deceased husband be not sufficiently spacious for her accommodation, and it should happen that the heirs of the deceased husband exclude her from other parts of the house, then it is lawful for her to shift elsewhere.[86] If the husband dies in a rented house and the wife cannot afford to pay the rent she is allowed to shift elsewhere.[87] If the house where she is residing is in a dilapidated condition and there is a risk that it may fall down or when it is insecure, she can shift to another house.[88]

If *'iddah* becomes incumbent on a wife while on journey with her husband, either on account of a divorce or death of her husband she may return to her own city to observe her *'iddah*.[89] It is, therefore, not an inflexible rule of law that a widow should observe her *'iddah* only in the house of her husband and she can under certain circumstances observe it

83. Al-Marghīnānī, *op. cit.*, Vol. II, pp. 327-28.
84. Ibn 'Ābidīn, *op. cit.*, Vol. II, p. 626.
85. *Ibid.*, p. 636 ; Burhān al-Dīn, al-Marghīnānī, *op. cit.*, Vol. II, p. 408.
86. *Ibid.*, p. 637 ; *ibid.*, p, 409.
87. *Ibid.*
88. *Ibid.*, p. 637.
89. *Ibid.*, al-Marghīnānī, *op. cit.*, Vol. II, p. 409.

elsewhere. Where a wife is repudiated irrevocably, it is requisite that there should be a curtain or partition between them, that is, between the husband and the wife, but there is no objection to their continuing to live in the same house.[90] But if the husband be a dissolute person and there may be an apprehension that he will commit with her what is unlawful she can remove to another place.

The above rules are meant to remove all doubts about the paternity of a child that may be born to the woman after separation from her husband. The fact that she does not get the monthly discharge for three consecutive periods shall establish that she is *en-ceinte*. Similarly, the fact that she gets the discharge will prove that she is not bearing any child.

Marriage during 'iddah.—The wife who is observing *'iddah* cannot lawfully contract a marriage during the period of her *'iddah* except with the husband, who had divorced her or on whose account the marriage had been dissolved, under certain conditions. If contracted otherwise, it would be unlawful.

It has already been stated that a woman has, on the dissolution of her marriage, to wait for a certain period so that the paternity of a child that may be born to her may be ascertained. This object would be lost if she contracts a second marriage during the *'iddah*. Further, as seen before, a husband has got a right to take back his wife during the period of *'iddah* in the case of a revocable divorce. If she contracts a second marriage during this period the second marriage shall give rise to complications. Hence a second marriage during the period of *'iddah* is not allowed.

There is a difference of opinion amongst the Muslim jurists on the nature of a marriage contracted during the period of a woman's *'iddah*. It is stated in *Fatāwā Qāḍī Khān* that such a marriage is *fāsid* (irregular).[91] The same opinion has been stated in *Radd al-Muḥtār*. But a different view has been expressed by other jurists. *Radd al-Muḥtār*[92] and *al-Fatāwā*

90. Ibn 'Ābidīn, *op. cit.*, Vol. II, p. 638; al-Marghīnānī, *op. cit.*, Vol. II, p. 409.
91. Qāḍī Khān, *Fatāwā Qāḍi Khān*, Kanpur, 1310, A.H., Vol. I, p. 162.
92. Ibn 'Ābidīn, *op. cit.*, Vol. II, p. 623.

al-Hindiyah[93] have tried to meet the difficulty by laying down that if a man married a woman knowing that she was observing *'iddah* then his marriage with her shall be void, but if he was ignorant of this fact the marriage shall be irregular (*fāsid*).

It must be remembered that the incidents in consequence of an irregular (*fāsid*) marriage are very nearly the same as that of a void (*bāṭil*) marriage. A void marriage is no marriage at all and it shall not give rise to the incidents of a marriage. Its consummation shall amount to adultery. Hence a child born of such a marriage shall be considered to be illegitimate. An irregular marriage is also unlawful and it is the duty of the *Qāḍī* to separate the parties when he comes to know of a *fāsid* marriage. But the parties shall not be liable to conviction for adultery in the case of a *fāsid* marriage whereas they are so liable when the marriage is void. This is based on the presumption that the parties might have made an honest mistake in contracting an irregular marriage and so are given the benefit of doubt. A child born of an irregular marriage shall therefore be considered to be legitimate. It seems that the creation of the class of *fāsid* or irregular marriage by the Ḥanafīs is meant chiefly to save a child from the stigma of illegitimacy.

It is stated in *Majmū' al-Fatāwā*[94] that marriage during *'iddah* is not lawful and that to solemnise it and even to participate in it is a *kabīrah* (cardinal) sin. It seems that the Muslim jurists considered such marriage to be *fāsid* because they wanted to save the child from the stigma of illegitimacy on the one hand and wanted to discourage marriage during *'iddah* on the other hand. It is stated in *Radd al-Muḥtār* that *fāsid* (irregular) and *bāṭil* (void) marriages are one and the same thing as far as *'iddah* is concerned, but they are different in other matters.[95]

It would be correct to say that a marriage contracted during the period of *'iddah* of a woman ought to be considered to be void and not merely irregular. The Muslim jurists who

93. *Al-Fatāwā al-Hindiyāh*, Lucknow, 1899, Vol. II, p. 397 (Urdu tr.)
94. 'Abd al-Ḥayy, *Majmū'ah Fatāwā*, Lucknow, 1330 A.H. Vol. I, p, 309.
95. Ibn 'Ābidīn, *op. cit.*, Vol. II, p. 623.

hold such a marriage to be merely irregular as discussed above seem to have been influenced by the effect of the marriage on an innocent child that may be born of such a marriage. The Qur'ān prohibits even a direct proposal of marriage to a woman observing *'iddah* and a man is allowed to give only a veiled hint to her of his desire to marry her. Thus it is laid down "and there is no blame on you respecting that which you speak indirectly in the asking of (such) women in marriage or keep (the proposal) concealed within your minds. Allāh knows that you will have them in your minds, but give them not a promise in secret unless you speak in a lawful manner. And confirm not the marriage tie until the prescribed period reaches its end."[96] In another verse it is laid down, "and when you divorce women and they end their term, prevent them not from marrying their husbands if they agree among themselves in a lawful manner."[97] This verse also supports the idea that it is only after the expiry of her *'iddah* that a woman can contract a second marriage. These injunctions of the Qur'ān make it clear that no marriage can be contracted while the woman is observing her *'iddah* and so a marriage contracted during that period shall be void.

Court's view.—The decisions of the various Indian High Courts on this point are not unanimous. It was stated in a case that the practice in the Punjab was to treat such a marriage that is, a marriage during the period of *'iddah* as entirely devoid of any legal consequences so far as the parties themselves are concerned.[98] A different view was taken in a later case when it was laid down that such a marriage is irregular and not void.[99] The same view has been expressed by the Bombay High Court and the Oudh Chief Court.[100] The Calcutta High

96. Qur'ān, surah al-Baqarāh, II : 235.
97. Qur'ān, surah al-Baqarāh, II : 232.
98. Mt. Ruro Vs. Bagh Singh, A.I.R. 1935, Lah, 23.
99. Muḥammad Hayat and others Vs. Muḥammad Nawaz and others A.I.R. 1935, Lah. 622, 17 Lah. 48, 156 I.C. 640, 38 P.L.R. 138.
100. Tajbi Vs. Mowla Khan, 41 Bom. 485 ; 19 Bom. L.R. 300 ; A.I.R. 1917 Bom. 211 ; 39 I.C. 603 ; Md. Shafi Vs. Raunaq Ali, A.I.R. 1928 Oudh, 231 ; 107 I.C. 882 : 5 O.W.N. 20 ; Kaniza Vs. Hasan Ahmad Khan A.I.R. 1926, Oudh, 211 ; 92 I.C. 82. 3 O.W.N. 114.

Court has taken a different view and has held that such a marriage is void.[101] The Allahabad High Court has held that a marriage contracted before the expiry of a woman's period of probation (*'iddah*) would be a mere irregularity which would be perfectly cured by long cohabitation and the treatment of the woman as wife.[102] It is submitted that an illegality cannot be cured by continued cohabitation and treatment of the woman as wife. The Peshawar Judicial Commissioner's Court following 63 Cal. 415 and 1935 Lah. 23 has held that a subsequent consummation of an invalid marriage does not validate it.[103] Under the Muslim law an irregular marriage cannot become validated by subsequent consummation and the treatment of the woman as wife.

Bigamy.—A void or *bāṭil* marriage is no marriage at all and does not create the relationship of husband and wife and *'iddah* is not incumbent on the wife. A second marriage contracted by the wife at any time after a void marriage does not and cannot amount to bigamy. An irregular *fāsid* marriage does not create any marital rights or obligations so that no *'iddah* is incumbent if the marriage has not been consummated. Each of the spouses can terminate it even in the absence of the other. But if the marriage has been consummated *'iddah* becomes incumbent for the ascertainment of legitimacy. The wife is entitled to get maintenance from the husband during the period of *'iddah*. A woman observing *'iddah* for a *fāsid* marriage cannot contract another marriage till after the expiry of her *'iddah*. A marriage is dissolved automatically on the apostasy of the husband and the relationship of husband and wife does not subsist any longer between them. A marriage contracted during the period of *'iddah*, if any be incumbent, cannot therefore amount to bigamy. The Calcutta High Court

101. Aziz-un-Nessa Khatoon Vs. Karim-un-Nessa Khatoon. I.L.R. (1895) 23, Cal. 130.
102. Mst. Mahtab-un-Nessa Vs. Rifaqatullah and others A.I.R. 1925, All. 474, 85 I.C. 459 ; 6 L.R.D. Civ. 145.
103. Mst. Bibi Ahmed-un-Nessa Begum Vs. Ali Akbar Shah, A.I.R, 1942, Pesh. 19; 1942 Pesh. L.J. 19; 199, I.C. 531

has also expressed this view.[104]

Shī'ī law.—Under the Shī'ī law, no *'iddah* is incumbent on a woman on a divorce or separation unless there has been actual consummation of marriage.[105] A valid retirement is not considered by the Shī'ahs to amount to a consummation of marriage, and so no *'iddah* would be incumbent on a woman on a mere valid retirement.[106] A widow has to observe *'iddah* on the death of her husband irrespective of the fact whether the marriage has or has not been consummated. This appears to have been ordained as part of Ḥidād or the act of mourning, which is incumbent on a widow.[107] According to the generally accepted view, *'iddah* would not be incumbent for divorce on a woman who is past child-bearing age or has not yet attained puberty till she becomes nine years old.[108]

If a man marries a woman at a time when the observance of *'iddah* was incumbent on her in ignorance of this fact, the marriage shall be void.[109] The fact whether the woman knew of the necessity of the observance of *'iddah* or was ignorant of it, is immaterial and does not affect the case.[110] The marriage shall be void in both the cases.

104. Abdul Ghani Vs. Azizul Huqq, 14 I.C. 641, I.L.R. 39 Cal. 489, 16 C.W.N. 451, 15 C.L.J. 263, 13 Cr. L J. 257.

105. Ja'far b. al-Hasan, *Shara'i' al-Islām*, Tehran, 1377 A.H., p. 212.

106. *Ibid.*

107. *Ibid.*

108. *Ibid* , Syed Muḥsin al-Ḥakīm, *Muntakhab al-Rasāil*, Najaf, 1380, A.H., p. 110 ; Rūḥ Allah al-Mūsawī, *Mukhtaṣar Tawḍīḥ al-Masāil*, Najaf, 1390 A.H., p. 362.

109. Mīr Syed Ali Allamāh Fāni Isfahani, *Tawḍīḥ al-Masā'il*, Najaf, 1382 A.H. pp. 380, 387.

110. *Ibid.*

Chapter 28

NASAB OR PATERNITY

Preliminary: It is necessary for various purposes such as guardianship, maintenance, inheritance etc. to ascertain the person who can be considered to be the father of a certain child. Different nations have made their own rules to determine this fact. Thus in one system parenthood of a child is attributed to that person who is actually responsible for its conception after his marriage with the child's mother. This is the view adopted by Muslim law under which stress is laid on the time of the conception of a child and it is an essential condition that it should be conceived by the purported father after his marriage with the child's mother. Under a second system, as under strict English law, a child shall be deemed to be the lawful issue of that person who marries the child's mother before its birth regardless of the fact as to whether he is actually responsible for the conception of the child and whether the conception occurred before or after the marriage. All that is necessary is that the child must have been born after the man's marriage with the child's mother, however short the time between the marriage and the child's birth may be. Under a third system that person shall be deemed to be the father of a child who marries its mother even after its birth. This system does not take any notice of the fact as to who was actually responsible for the conception of the child nor to the time of its birth. Paternity under this system may be the result of artificial relationship created by law.

Under some systems the relationship of parenthood can be created artificially, that is, by adoption of a child belonging to another man and also by legitimation, as now in England. As mentioned above, in Muslim law the parenthood of a child is attributed to that person who is actually responsible for its conception after his marriage with the child's mother. It does not accept the relationship recognised under the other systems nor the artificial relationship created by legitimation and adoption.

There is a difference between legitimacy and legitimation. The former is a status which results from certain circumstances while the latter is a proceeding which creates a status which did not exist before.[1]

The doctrine of legitimation per subsequence matrimonium (that is, legitimation of a bastard by the subsequent marriage of its mother) is not recognised at all by the Muslim law.

Adoption is not recognised by Islam though it was common among the Arabs in the pre-Islamic times. This rule is based on the following verses in the Qur'ān :

> "Nor has He made your adopted sons your real sons."[1a] Call them by their fathers' name ; that is, more just in God's sight ; but if ye know not their fathers, then they are your brethren in religion and your clients."[1b]

Muslim Conception : Under Muslim law the presumption of paternity from marriage follows the bed, that is, the paternity of a child born in lawful wedlock is presumed to be in the husband of its mother if certain conditions are satisfied. No doubt the conditions attached to legitimacy are more strict under Muslim law than under other systems, but it is very reluctant to stigmatise a child and no presumption is drawn against its legitimacy as far as possible. It refuses to declare a child a bastard except on the clearest and most positive proof of illegitimacy and refuses to admit illegitimacy when legitimacy can be inferred. Muslim law considers a child to be the legitimate offspring of a person in every case when it is humanly possible that the man can be the father of the child in fact and that there might have been a marriage between him and the mother of the child.

It can be inferred from a number of the problems stated in *Radd al-Muḥtār* that even the slightest ground is worthy of

1. Syed Habibur Rahman Chowdhury Vs. Syed Altaf Ali Chowdhury, A.I.R. 1922 P.C. 159.

1*a*. Qur'ān, Surah al-Ahzab, XXI : 4.

1*b*. *Ibid*., XXI : 5.

consideration, that is, is sufficient to establish the legitimacy of a child.[2]

This explains for a large number of cases in which a child is considered to be legitimate even when the surrounding circumstances point out against its legitimacy on the ground that adultery cannot be presumed.

Determination of Paternity: To determine the legitimacy of a child the following matters have to be taken into consideration :—

(*a*) The status of parents of the child,
(*b*) the conduct of the alleged father,
(*c*) the nature of the marriage, and
(*d*) the period of gestation.

(*a*) *Status of Parents*: The first thing to be considered to determine the legitimacy of a child is to see if it was at all possible that it could have been conceived during the subsistence of a valid marriage of the child's mother with the person alleged to be its father. It is an essential condition of legitimacy under the Muslim law that the child must have been conceived in wedlock or, in other words, the person who is responsible for its conception should be the lawful husband of the child's mother at the time of its conception.

The disinclination of the Muslim jurists to bastardise a child has sanctioned the presumption of legitimacy from even slight evidence of marriage or lawful consort. The presumption of legitimacy is so strong that it is only when a man has no right or even the semblance of a right in a woman that their offspring is considered a bastard.

The Muslim law presumes legitimacy of a child from circumstances without a proof or at least without any direct proof of marriage. When a child is born there is a presumption in favour of a marriage having taken place between its mother and her husband if there has not been a mere casual

2. Ibn 'Ābidīn al-Shāmī, *Radd al-Muḥtār*, Cairo, 1318 A.H. Vol. II, p. 640 f. Cf. Burhān al-Dīn al-Marghīnāni, *al-Hidāyah*, Delhi, n.d., Vol. II, p. 410.

concubinage but a more permanent connection and when there is no insurmountable obstacle to such a marriage.

When it is proved that a man and a woman lived together for a long time as man and wife there is a strong presumption in favour of marriage having taken place between them.[3] This rule holds good with still greater force when the alleged marriage took place so long back that it is difficult to obtain trustworthy account of what really occurred and when the conduct of the parties is shown to be compatible with the existence of the relationship of husband and wife.[4]

If there is a dispute between a man and his wife about the legitimacy of a child when the husband alleges that he was married to her only a month back while the wife says the marriage took place one year or six months before, then her statement shall be accepted and the child shall be held to be legitimate.[5] It is obvious that there should not be any impediment to a lawful marriage which negates the idea of a lawful marriage. Thus the subsistence of a former marriage between the woman and another man at the time of the child's conception or the fact that the woman was prohibited to the man on account of some reason or other will negate the legitimacy of a child alleged to be born of that man.

If the parties to a marriage believe in good faith that there is no impediment to their marriage, it shall be deemed valid for all purposes under Muslim law so far as the parties are concerned. If it be found subsequently that there was such an impediment, the marriage shall be null and void, but the children born of such a marriage shall be held to be legitimate.[6] Moreover, divorce cannot be presumed from long separation between the parties to a marriage. Hence where

3. Bashir-un-Nissa Vs. Bunyad Ali 50 I.C. 677; Abdul Aziz Vs. Ameer Begum 66 I.C. 404.
4. Iftikhar Nazir Ahmad Khan Vs. Ghulam Kibria, P.L.D. 1968 Lah. 582; Aga Mohammed Jaffer Bindanim Vs. Koolsoom Bibi, I.L.R. 21 Cal. 666.
5. Ibn 'Ābidīn al-Shāmī, *op. cit.*, Vol. II, p. 644. Lt.-Col. Mohammad Yusuf Vs. Syed Ali Nawaz Gardezi P.L.D. 1963 Lah. 141.
6. Lt.-Col. Mohammad Yusuf Vs. Syed Ali Nawaz Gardezi, P.L.D. 1963 Lah. 141.

a wife was proved to have resided a few times with her husband while there was no proof of absence of opportunity of access to each other, legitimacy of a child born during such separation cannot be doubted.[7] But mere continued cohabitation for a long period in the absence of proof of marriage is not sufficient to prove marriage, particularly when the woman was a prostitute before the alleged marriage.[8] It was stated in a case that "evidence of intimacy and very close intimacy alone cannot establish a marriage between the parties. There are cases where marriage was presumed from prolonged and continued cohabitation. But in this case the duration of cohabitation is only for a period less than a year." Presumption of there being a valid marriage was not drawn under the circumstances.[9]

Child born of a woman who is not a wife: Under Muslim law the sexual intercourse of a man with a woman who is not his wife is unlawful and is absolutely prohibited. When there is neither the validity nor the semblance of such a relationship between the parties, their intercourse is termed Zinā (adultery) and the offspring of such a union is termed *walad al-zinā* or child of fornication who shall be deemed to be illegitimate. If it be established that there did not subsist at the time of the child's conception a valid or under the Ḥanafi, Māliki or Ḥanbali laws even an irregular or fāsid marriage between its mother and the alleged father then the child cannot be considered to be legitimate. Similarly, if a person is proved not to be the husband of the child's mother at the time of its conception then the child shall be deemed illegitimate unless it be possible that the child might have been conceived after their marriage when under certain circumstances it may be presumed to be legitimate. The descent of an illegitimate child is not established in the husband of its mother in any case. If a woman should become pregnant by illicit intercourse and the seducer subsequently marries her then a child

7. Asad Ullah Khan Vs. Abdul Hamid, P.L.D. 1967 B.J.L.
8. Iftikhar Nazir Ahmad Khan Vs. Ghulam Kibria, P.L.D. 1968 Lah. 587; Ghazanfar Ali Khan Vs. Kaniz Fatima, I.L R. 23 All. 345 P.C.
9. Dr. A. L. M. Abdullah Vs. Rokeya Khatoon, P.L.D. 1969, Dacca-47.

born to her in less than six months of the marriage shall not be considered legitimate.[10] But if that person should acknowledge it to be his lawful child and he does not make any mention of his adultery or the illegitimacy of the child, and nothing is known to hold the child to be illegitimate, it may be held to be legitimate under certain conditions. This rule is based on the idea that nothing being known against the legitimacy of the child, a presumption would be drawn in favour of its legitimacy.[11] This is only, as pointed out by Muslim jurists, to help the child and it is obvious that if it is known that he is not legitimate then such presumption cannot be drawn.

If a husband accuses his wife of unchastity by denying a child born of her, the *Qāḍī* has, after the proceedings of Li'ān, to annul the marriage and he shall in such a case declare the child to be illegitimate and order it to be left in the custody of the child's mother.[12]

(*b*) *Conduct of the alleged father*: The second thing to be considered is the conduct of the alleged father as to whether he has admitted expressly or impliedly that the child is his. The conduct of the alleged father is important in the determination of legitimacy. The failure to deny his parentage of the child when it is legally open to him to disown it constitutes an implied admission that the child belongs to him[13]. It is open to a person to disown a child born to his wife at the time of its birth or within the time a father usually and customarily receives felicitations. This period of time is considered to extend up to forty days according to Abū Yūsuf and Muḥammad. Abū Ḥanīfah says that such period extends to seven days.[14] According to *Radd al-Muḥtār* this period extends from three days to one week.[15]

10. *Al-Fatāwā al-Hindiyah*, Kanpur, 1349 A.H., Vol. II, p. 140.
11. See chapter on *Iqrār* (acknowledgement).
12. Ibn 'Ābidīn al-Shāmī, *op. cit.*, Vol. II, p. 606.
13. *Ibid.*
14. *Ibid.*
15. *Ibid.*

(c) *Nature of Marriage* : *Fāsid Marriage*: As stated before, one of the conditions necessary to establish legitimacy is that the child must be the result of a lawful marriage, that is, it must have been conceived in wedlock. The Muslim law generally draws a presumption of legitimacy in favour of a child born to a man and a woman lawfully married. The Muslim jurists, particularly the Ḥanafī jurists, have tried their best not to consider a child illegitimate as far as possible. The Ḥanafī jurists, therefore, hold that every child born of a valid or even irregular (*fāsid*) marriage is legitimate.[16] A *fāsid* or irregular marriage is not to be tolerated and the *Qāḍī* must separate the spouses when he comes to know of it, but a child born of such a marriage is considered legitimate by the Ḥanafīs.[17] As a matter of fact it appears that this class of marriage was established merely in the interest of the children born under such circumstances.

It was stated in a case that a *fāsid* marriage is one where a man marries a woman under a genuine misapprehension of the fact that the woman was not permissible to him and when she is not absolutely forbidden to him. *Nasab* (legitimacy) is established in a case where a child is born of such a marriage.

The following passage from a learned judgement of a Division Bench of the Calcutta High Court will be found interesting in this connection :

"The punishment for adultery and fornication under the Muhammadan Law—death by stoning—was so severe and the natural objection to bastartadize offspring was so strong, that it was probably a desire to mitigate the vigour of the law in these respects that led to the distinction in the Muhammadan Law between void and invalid marriages. Abū Ḥanīfah, as is well-known, went so far as to hold that consummation was sufficient to legalise any marriage so as to dispense with the necessity of inflicting the punishment or *ḥadd* for adultery and to establish the legitimacy of the children. He was of the opini-

16. Ibn 'Ābidīn al-Shāmī *op. cit.*, Vol. II, pp. 623, 644 ; al-Marghīnanī *op. cit.*, Vol. II, p. 410.

17. *Ibid.*, p. 640.

on that woman was always a fitting subject, inasmuch as all the daughters of Adam were qualified for procreation, which is the primary object of marriage. This broad doctrine, however, was not accepted by his disciples, Abū Yūsuf and Muḥammad, who held that a marriage with a prohibited woman was void and the fruit of it illegitimate and that a person contracting such a marriage was liable to *ḥadd* if he were aware of the illegality. The severity of the punishment of *ḥadd* also doubtless led to the doctrine of semblance or doubtful marriages which is discussed in many of the Muhammadan Law books."[18]

When the connection between a man and a woman was unlawful in its inception it is very difficult to infer subsequent marriage from the fact of mere exclusive cohabitation for a long time.[19]

(*d*) *Period of Gestation* : To determine the legitimacy of a child the Muslim jurists have laid down some general rules for guidance. They have given the periods of time both minimum and maximum during which a fully developed child can be born. These rules are mostly based on their experience. But it is important to note that the Muslim jurists have not based these periods on probability but on possibility. Their aim is to save a child from the stigma of illegitimacy and so they have tried to bestow legitimacy on every child when it is physically possible though not probable that the child could have been the result of lawful union between a man and his wife. They thus apply the rule to every conceivable case including rare and abnormal cases.

(I) *Minimum Period :* The Muslim jurists of all the sects hold that a fully developed child cannot be born before six months. They have based this rule on two grounds, namely, experience and upon an inference drawn from two verses of the Qur'ān. In one verse the combined period of gestation and weaning is given at two years and a half while in the other the period of suckling is mentioned at two years.[20] From

18. Azizun-Nisa Khatun Vs. Karimunnisa Khatoon, I.L.R. 23 Cal. 130.
19. Ghazanfar Ali Khan Vs. Kaniz Fatima, I.L.R. 32, All. 345.
20. Qur'ān, Surah al-Ahqāf, XXVI : 15 Surah al-Baqarah, II : 233.

these two verses they have arrived at the figure of six months for the shortest period of gestation. Hence a child shall be considered legitimate if it is born at or beyond six months of a marriage.[21] But if a fully developed child be born within six months of a marriage it will not be considered legitimate on the ground that the minimum period of gestation being six months, the child must have been conceived before the marriage and so is not legitimate.[22] It can be rendered legitimate under the doctrine of acknowledgement.[23]

Commencement of time: The period of six months shall be counted from the date of a valid marriage. In the case of a *fāsid* (irregular) marriage there is a difference of opinion amongst the Ḥanafī Jurists. Thus Abū Ḥanīfah and Abū Yūsuf are of the opinion that it commences from the date of the marriage while Muḥammad holds the view that it commences from the time of consummation, actual or implied, of the marriage. This is generally accepted as the correct law.[24]

Under the Shī'ah law the period of six months shall commence from the time of coition.[25]

(II) *Maximum Period of Gestation*: There is a difference of opinion amongst the different sects of the Sunnis and the Shī'ahs about the maximum period of gestation. The Ḥanafīs fix it at two years. They consider that it cannot exceed this limit and in this they have been influenced by a Tradition that 'Ā'ishah the wife of the Prophet (peace be on him) said that a child cannot be retained in the body of its mother for a longer period than two years[26] Mālik has fixed it at four years on the basis of an allegation that one Ḍahḥāk b. Muzāḥim was born within four years of its conception. Shāfi'ī and also

21. Burhān al-Dīn al-Marghīnānī, *op. cit.*, Vol. II, p. 410, 413. Ibn 'Ābidīn al-Shāmī, *op. cit.*, Vol. II, pp, 639-40
22. Burhān al-Dīn al-Marghīnānī, *op. cit.*, Vol. II, p. 410.
23. See chapter on Acknowledgment.
24. Mohammad Allahdad Khan Vs. Mohammad Ismail Khan I.L.R. 10 All. 289, at p. 315.
25. Ja'far b. al-Hasan, *Sharā'i' al-Islām*, Tehran, 1377 A.H. p. 19.
26. Ibn 'Ābidīn al Shāmī, *op. cit.*, Vol. II, p. 639.

Aḥmad b. Ḥanbal have fixed the period at four years on the strength of the case of one Muḥammad b. 'Ajlān whose wife was delivered of children every time at an interval of four years.[27] The author of *Sharīfiyah* has not accepted the idea.[28] The author of *Radd al-Muḥtār* has explained that certain diseases produce the same symptoms as are indicated in pregnancy and that a tumour or even wind inside the belly may be mistaken for pregnancy and so he has not accepted the period fixed by Mālik and others.[29] It is obvious that the case of Muḥammad b. 'Ajlān even if correct can only be an abnormal case and cannot be the basis of a rule of law. Delivery may be delayed in exceptional cases.

Cases of Illegitimacy: Cases of illegitimacy may be divided under the following heads:

(*a*) Child of a prostitute conceived or born of intercourse in a brothel,
(*b*) child of incest,
(*c*) child of adultery,
(*d*) child of an idolatress,
(*e*) child of fifth wife,
(*f*) Ante-nuptial child, when there was no legal bar to marriage before conception and birth,
(*g*) child born out of wedlock where there is no legal bar to the marriage.

In case of (*a*), the child, strictly speaking, was of spurious birth. In case of (*b*), (*c*), (*d*), and (*e*) there was a legal bar to a valid marriage and therefore even if marriage did take place, it would be illegal. In case of (*f*) and (*g*) there could be no cogent disproof of marriage except evidence bearing on the probabilities of the case. In the case of concubinage with regard to the birth of children there was a strong semblance of marriage. In the present case mere disproof of marriage

27. Ibn 'Ābidīn al-Shāmī, *op. cit.*, Vol. II, p. 639.
28. 'Alī b. Muḥammad, *Sharīfiyah*, Cairo, n.d. pp. 314-15 f.
29. Ibn 'Ābidīn al-Shāmī, *op. cit.*, Vol. II, pp. 639-40; Ibn al-Humām, *Fatḥ al-Qadīr*, Cairo, 1356 A.H. Vol. III, p. 310.

was not by itself sufficient to establish illegitimacy. It was necessary for the respondent to have proved that there was no semblance of marriage.[30] To the above list may be added another class, namely, children born of a void marriage. A marriage is void when the spouses are within prohibited degree whether on account of birth, fosterage, or when the wife is the wife of another person, or is the fifth wife when marriage with the other four wives are subsisting or the wife is an idolatress, etc.

English and American Laws: English and American laws fix the period of gestation on probability and not on possibility. Moreover, no minimum period of gestation is fixed under those laws, but medical expert stated in a case that an actual foetal life of 28 weeks seems to be the minimum period of gestation.[31] The usual maximum period of gestation is fixed at two hundred and seventy-five to two hundred and eighty days. It is, however, realised that the period of gestation may exceed this limit in some cases.[32]

Medical science now affirms that it is possible though not probable that a child may be born beyond the period of nine months and ten days. It was stated in a case that to prove that a period of so many days between fruitful coition and the time of delivery is in a scientific sense an impossibility.[33] The utmost that a Court of law can demand is that it would be established beyond all reasonable doubt that a child conceived so many days after a particular coition cannot be the result of that coition.[34] It was stated in Williamson Vs. M'Clelland 1913 S.C. 678 ; I. S. L. T. 289 that "It is absolutely clear that neither in law nor in medical science it is possible to fix an actual number of days as the extreme period of gestation." It was remarked in another case that there is no

30. Syed Habibur Rahman Chowdhury Vs. Syed Altaf Ali Chowdhury, I L.R. 46 Cal. 259.
31. Clark Vs. Clark, (1939) P. 228 (1939) 2 All. E.R. 59.
32. Gaskill Vs. Gaskill, (1921) P. 425 ; (1921) 2 All. E.R. 415.
33. Preston-Jones Vs. Preston-Jones (1951) 1 All. E.R. 124,
34. *Ibid.*

inherent impossibility of gestation of 310 or even 330 days, after cohabitation but the matter is suspicious.[35]

The following table will show the number of days considered to be the possible period of gestation :—

270-275 days :	Bosvile Vs. A. G. (1887) 12 P. D. 183 ; 57 L. T. 88
273-280 days :	Burnaby Vs. Baillie, (1889) 42 Ch. D. 282 ; 61 L. T. 634.
331 days :	Gaskill Vs. Gaskill, (1921) P. 425 ; (1921) 3 All. E.R. 365.
346 days :	Wood Vs. Wood, (1947) 2 All. E. R. 95.
349 days :	Hadlum Vs. Hadlum, (1948) 2 All. E.R. 412.
360 days :	Preston-Jones Vs. Preston-Jones, (1951) 1 All. E. R. 124.

The minimum period of gestation has been considered to be 174 days.[36]

Separation by Qāḍī: The annulment or dissolution of marriage by the *Qāḍi* amounts to an irrevocable divorce.[37] A child shall be considered to be the legitimate issue of the former husband only if it is born within two years of the order of the *Qāḍī*.

Commencement of Time: The period of two or four years as the case may be is counted from the time of the marriage.[38]

Shī'ah Law: (*a*) Period of gestation: Under the Shī'ah law there are two opinions about the period of gestation. According to one, the longest period of gestation is nine months but according to the other report which is generally accepted to be correct the period extends to ten months.[39]

(*b*) *Commencement of Time*: Under the Shī'ah law, according to the generally accepted view, the period of ten months is counted from the time of coition and not from the

35. Gaskill Vs. Gaskill (1921) 2 All. E.R. 415.
36. Wood Vs. Wood (1957) 2 All. E.R. 14 : (1957) P. 254.
37. Ibn 'Ābidīn al-Shāmī, *op. cit.*, Vol. II, p. 605.
38. *Ibid.*, p. 610.
39. Ja'far b. al-Ḥasan, *op. cit.*, p. 199.

time of a marriage as under the Sunnī law.[40]

Discussion of Special Cases: The application of the minimum and maximum periods of gestation varies in different cases of the termination of marriage and so these cases have been separately discussed below.

Revocable Divorce: In the case of a revocable divorce it is lawful for the husband to be intimate with his divorced wife during the period of her *'iddah*, namely three courses, and so the maximum period of gestation, namely, two years, is increased by that period, on the ground that the husband might have been intimate with the wife during the period of *'iddah* or waiting as he lawfully could.[41] This rule is subject to the condition that the wife should not have stated or admitted that her period of *'iddah* had passed.[42] A child born within two years and the period of *'iddah* of three courses which is ordinarily considered to consist of a maximum period of three months shall be deemed to be the lawful issue of that person and it shall be presumed that he must have cohabited with her during the period of her *'iddah*.

Irrevocable Divorce: If a child is born within two years of the dissolution of a marriage under the Ḥanafī law it shall be presumed to be the legitimate child of the man who had divorced the child's mother.[43] But if born beyond two years it shall not be presumed to be the legitimate child of its mother's husband, because the longest period of gestation under the Ḥanafī law being two years of the dissolution of the marriage, it is clear that it could not have been conceived during the subsistence of the marriage, because in such a case it is not possible for the husband to approach his wife after the pronouncement of the irrevocable divorce even during the period of her *'iddah* and so the period of two years is to be considered as the longest period of time.[44]

40. Ja'far b. al-Ḥasan, *op. cit.*, p. 199.
41. Ibn 'Ābidīn, *op. cit.*, Vol. II, p. 639.
42. *Ibid.*, p. 639.
43. *Ibid.*, p. 639 ; Burhān al-Dīn al-Marghīnānī, *op. cit.*, Vol. II, p. 410.
44. *Ibid.*, p. 639 ; *Ibid.*, p. 410.

Other cases: The Muslim Jurists have been very anxious to save a child from the stigma of illegitimacy. This will be fully borne out by some cases discussed below that will show to what extent the Muslim jurists have gone for the sake of a child.

Child born after divorce: If a child is born after its mother has been divorced then the legitimacy of the child shall be presumed if it can be possible that it could have been begotten by the alleged father. If it is born within six months of the dissolution of the marriage there can be no doubt of its legitimacy. If the marriage is dissolved by a revocable divorce then it is open to a husband to be intimate with the wife within the period of the woman's *'iddah*, namely three months, according to Abū Yūsuf and Muḥammad and so a child born within nine months of the divorce can also be presumed to be the lawful child of its mother's husband. This rule seems to be based on the ground that adultery of the wife cannot be presumed and it will be deemed that the husband must have had access to the wife. But a child born within two years and three months of a revocable divorce shall be presumed to be the legitimate child of the husband according to Abū Ḥanīfah. This rule is, however, subject to the condition that there is no apparent impediment to the legitimacy of the child.[45] Moreover, this rule will not apply if access to the wife was absolutely impossible as when she was never sent to the husband. In the case of an irrevocable divorce the period of *'iddah* cannot be taken into consideration as intimacy is not allowed during the period of *'iddah* in such a case[46] and so the maximum period shall be only two years.[47] If a marriage has not been consummated and the husband divorces his wife who has not attained puberty but can admit carnal connection then a child born of the wife shall be considered legitimate if it is born within six months of the divorce.

45. Ibn 'Ābidīn *op. cit.*, Vol. II, p. 641.
46. *Ibid.*, pp. 641, 642.
47. Burhān al-Din al-Marghīnānī, *op. cit.*, Vol. II, p. 410.

It is immaterial whether the divorce is revocable or irrevocable because every divorce before consummation amounts to an irrevocable divorce. The husband cannot be intimate with the wife after an irrevocable divorce while no *'iddah* is incumbent on the wife, and so no more time shall be taken into consideration and only the period of six months is taken into account. Hence a child shall be considered legitimate only if it is born within six months of the divorce.[48]

Illicit Intercourse: If a man has illicit intercourse with a woman who then becomes pregnant, and afterwards marries her and she then gives birth to a child, if such child is born after expiration of six months or more, his descent is established. But if she gives birth within less than six months, descent is not established, unless he claims it and does not say that the child is the result of illicit intercourse. But if he says that the child is born of her by illicit intercourse, the descent is not established and it will not inherit from him.[49] If a man marries a woman within prohibited degree, and a child is born to her, then according to Abū Ḥanīfah it would be considered to be the lawful issue of that person. Abū Yūsuf and Muḥammad differ with him and hold that the child shall be considered to be illegitimate. This difference of opinion is due to the fact that Abū Ḥanīfah considers a marriage of a person with a woman within prohibited degree to be *fāsid* (irregular) while the other two Imāms hold that it is *baṭil* (void). The latter opinion is considered to be correct.[50]

The marriage of a Muslim with a non-Muslim [non-Kitabiyah] woman who is not the lawful wife of another is merely *fāsid* and so the children born of such a marriage are legitimate.[51]

Minor husband—death of: If a minor husband, who is capable of intimacy, should happen to die and should a child be born of the marriage within six months of the death of the

48. Qāḍī Khān, *Fatāwā Qāḍī Khān*, Kanpur, 1310 A.H. Vol. II, p. 274; Ibn 'Ābidīn al-Shāmī, *op. cit.*, Vol. II, p. 641.
49. *Al-Fatāwā al-Hindiyah*, *op. cit.*, Vol. II, p. 140.
50. *Ibid.*, pp. 140-41.
51. Zakir Ali Vs. Soghra Bi A.I.R. 1918, Nag. 32; 43 I.C. 883.

husband then it shall be presumed to belong to him.[52] This rule is based on the reasoning that adultery of a wife cannot be presumed and the period of six months is fixed on the ground that the husband must have been intimate with her before his death and that he must be the father of the child. This rule is, however, subject to the condition that the husband must be capable of intimacy.[53] If he is of such a tender age that intimacy is not possible then legitimacy of the child born of the wife shall not be established in him.[54]

Child born to eunuch: If a husband of a woman is a eunuch (*majbūb*) and she gives birth to a child, the child shall belong to him when he acknowledges it to be his child or does not disclaim it.[55] This rule seems to be based on the principle that an acknowledgment or the absence of a *disclaimer* obviates any investigation about his physical condition.[56] If the marriage is dissolved after valid retirement and a child is born to her then according to Abū Yūsuf the child shall belong to him if born within six months of the dissolution of the marriage. According to Abū Ḥanīfah the child shall belong to him if born within two years of the separation. This is subject to the condition that in both the cases he should claim the child to be his.[57]

Child born to an impotent husband: If the husband be impotent then the same rule as applied to eunuchs shall govern the case.

Time in case of husband's death: Under the Ḥanafī law if a child is botn within two years of the death of the husband of the child's mother it shall be presumed to be the legitimate child of that man. But if it is born beyond two years of the alleged father's death, then it shall not be presumed to be the legitimate cnild of that husband[58] because the longest period of gestation

52. Ibn 'Ābidīn al-Shāmī, *op. cit.*, Vol. II, p. 621.
53. *Ibid.*, p. 621.
54. *Ibid.*
55. *Ibid.*, p. 610.
56. Muhammad Allahdad Khan Vs. Muhammad Ismail Khan I.L.R. 10 All., 289 at pp. 333, 336.
57. Ibn 'Ābidīn al-Shāmī, *op. cit.*, Vol. II, p. 610.
58. *Ibid.*, p.642.

being two years and the child having been born after two years of the person's death, it is clear that it could not have been conceived during the subsistence of the marriage.[59] In the case of Mālikīs, Shāfi'īs and Ḥanbalīs, the period shall be four years instead of two years.

If a child is born after the period of two years of the husband's death and should the heirs of the (deceased) husband deny the legitimacy of the child then its legitimacy shall have to be proved by evidence like any other fact unless it can be presumed by an admission of the husband that the woman was *enceinte* by him or if the woman's pregnancy was apparent at the time of his death.[60]

If the husband of a minor wife dies and she declares during the period of her *'iddah* that she is *enceinte*, the child born to her shall be presumed to be legitimate provided it is born within two years of the husband's death in case of Ḥanafīs, because the maximum period of gestation is two years and her declaration that she is *enceinte* established the fact that her deceased husband had been responsible for the conception.[61] But in the absence of any such declaration the legitimacy of the child shall be presumed only if it is born within ten months and ten days of the husband's death because her failure to declare her pregnancy shows that she was cognisant of her not being pregnant at the time of the husband's death.[62] But if a child is born to her within six months of the husband's death then it shall be presumed that the deceased person was responsible for the conception of the child. The rule is based on the reasoning that the minimum period of gestation is six months while a widow cannot marry another person during the period of her *'iddah* which in case of the husband's death is four months and ten days, hence it is presumed that the child must have been begotten by the deceased.[63]

59. Ibn 'Ābidīn al-Shāmī, *op. cit.*, Vol II, p. 642.
60. *Ibid.*, pp. 88, 643, 644.
61. *Ibid.*, 642.
62. *Ibid*
63. *Ibid.*

Applicability of the law of Legitimacy in India and Pakistan: It has been held in a large number of cases that the rules of Muslim law regarding gestation is a rule of evid ence and belongs to the law of evidence and so must be deemed to have been superseded by the Evidence Act.

In India and Pakistan a case is decided according to the provisions of the Muslim law if it is connected with marriage, succession etc., and by the present Evidence Act if it relates to the law of evidence as the Muslim law of evidence has been superseded.

The Muslim law of legitimacy is an integral part of the Muslim personal law and as such ought to have been applied in cases regarding legitimacy where the parties were Muslims. But such has not been the practice and the reason for the same is the adverse rulings of the Courts which lay down that the Muslim law on the subject has been superseded by the Anglo-Indian law, namely, the Evidence Act. The Evidence Act has introduced a principle which is not only foreign to the Islamic conception of legitimacy, but is absolutely opposed to it. The Muslim law makes it imperative that a child must be conceived in lawful wedlock to be considered legitimate. They determine the legitimacy of a child by the time of its conception, and they have fixed the minimum period of gestation at six months.

The Evidence Act follows the English doctrine of legitimacy and holds the time of birth as the main factor which determines legitimacy.

> Section 12 of the Evidence Act reads as under: "The fact that any person was born during the continuance of a valid marriage between his mother and any man, or within two hundred and eighty days after its dissolution, the mother remaining unmarried, shall be conclusive proof that he is the legitimate son of that man unless it can be shown that the parents to the marriage had no access to each other at any time when he could have been begotten."

It can be seen from the above provision that (*a*) child born at any time, however short, after marriage shall be considered legitimate, and (*b*) a child born beyond two hundred and eighty days of the dissolution of a marriage shall not be considered to be legitimate.

The question as to whether the determination of legitimacy is to be decided by the provisions of Muslim law or by section 112 of the Evidence Act depends on the decision as to whether this matter forms part of the substantive Muslim law or the Muslim law of evidence. If it is connected with and forms part of the substantive law, then it shall be governed by the provisions of Muslim law as the matters of marriage, succession, religious usage are determined and decided according to the provisions of Muslim law. But if it forms part of the law of evidence then the Muslim law of evidence having been superseded, cases of legitimacy shall be decided according to the provisions of section 112 of the Evidence Act.

This matter came up for decision in an appeal before the Allahabad High Court in 1888, but it was decided on another point and this point was left undecided by the Court. Mahmud J, the well-known authority on Muslim law, confined himself by saying, "It may some day be a question of great difficulty to determine how far the provisions of that section (section 112 of the Evidence Act) are to be taken as trenching upon the Muhammadan Law of marriage, parentage, legitimacy and inheritance, which departments of law under other statutory provisions are to be adopted as the rules of decision by the Courts in British India. Fortunately the difficulty does not arise in this case."[64]

In a case the Punjab Chief Court expressed the view that section 112 of the Evidence Act was applicable in place of the provisions of Muslim law of Legitimacy.[65] The Nagpur Judicial Commissioner's Court took the opposite view and held that the provisions of Muslim law relating to legitimacy

64. Muhammad Allahdad Vs. Muhammad Ismail Khan, ILR 10 All. p. 289 at p. 339.
65. Warras Muhammad Vs. Ali Baksh, 76 P.R. 1891.

being part of the substantive law of the Muhammadans, the rule laid down in section 112 is not applicable to them.[66] The matter again came up for decision before the Allahabad High Court in several cases. In Sibt Muhammad Vs. Muhammad Hameed (ILR 48 All. 625) the Court held at the very outset that under section 37 of the Bengal, Agra, and Assam Civil Court Act, 1887, questions regarding marriage or inheritance are to be decided according to the Muhammadan Law where the parties are Muhammadans "except so far as such law has, by legislative enactment, been altered or abolished." The Court then said, "Sir Roland Wilson in his treatise on Anglo-Muhammadan Law expressed the opinion that section 112 of the Indian Evidence Act is really, notwithstanding its place in the Statute book, a rule of substantive marriage law rather than of evidence, and as such has no application to Muhammadans in so far as it conflicts with the Mohammadan rule that a child born within six months after the marriage of its parents is not legitimate." It was further pointed out that this view was dissented from by Mr. Mulla and Mr. Tyabji who held that this rule of the Muslim law is superseded by section 112 of the Evidence Act. The Court agreed with the latter view and held that section 112 is applicable to Mohammadans and that it has superseded the provisions of Mohammadan law relating to legitimacy. This ruling was followed by the same High Court in subsequent cases. The Lahore High Court also held the same view in a similar case.[67]

It is submitted that this view is not correct.

In Sibt Mohammad Vs. Mohammad Hameed, the Court preferred to follow the opinion of Mulla and Tyabji in preference to Wilson. Now it is to be noted that Mulla has not expressed any opinion nor discussed the matter at all. He has merely quoted section 112 of the Evidence Act. He has then given several rulings of the various High Courts, but the ruling of the Nagpur Judicial Commissioner's Court has escaped

66. Zakir Ali Vs. Soghra Bi, 43 I.C. 883 ; AIR 1918 Nag. 32.
67. Mst. Rahim Bibi Vs. Chiragh Din and another, AIR 1930 Lah. 97.

him. He has taken it for granted that the view expressed in the rulings quoted by him lay the correct law on the point. It is obvious that he could not have come to any other decision as all the rulings quoted by him are in support of the view stated by him, while the opposite view expressed by the Nagpur Judicial Commissioner's Court was not considered by him. He has not therefore thought it necessary to discuss the point at all. The fact cannot be overlooked that he has not made any attempt to support his view. Tyabji, it appears, has not been definite in his opinion. His conclusion supports the view expressed in Sibt Mohammad Vs. Mohammad Hameed but the trend of his discussion seems to favour the other view.

The attention of the Court was not drawn to the opinion of Ameer Ali, the well-known authority on Muslim law, who has stated, "Section 112 of the Evidence Act embodies the English rule of law and cannot be held to vary or supersede by implication the rules of Mohammadan law."[68]

In Hajira Khatun Vs. Amina Khatun 73 I. C. 983 the Allahabad High Court stated that there is no direct authority on the point, but a similar controversy had been raised as to the presumption contained in section 108 of the Evidence Act (that is, about a missing person) and it was held by a Full Bench of this Court in Mazhar Ali Vs. Budh Singh (ILR 7 All. 297) that this was a provision of the law of Evidence, and was applicable to Muhammadans.

The case of Mazhar Ali Vs. Budh Singh (ILR 7 All. 297) has been referred to in several cases to support the view that section 112 has superseded the Islamic rule of legitimacy and it, therefore, seems necessary to examine that case fully. The question in that case was whether the law about a missing person was governed by the Evidence Act or by the provisions of Muslim law and the Full Bench unanimously decided in favour of the former view. Mahmud, J. based his view on the following grounds in support of his decision:

68. Ameer Ali, Mohammadan Law, Calcutta, 1908, p. 234.

Firstly, the rule of the Mohammadan Law as to missing persons has arisen from a maxim relating to the subject of evidence and the rule of *istiṣḥāb* which is the outcome of that maxim cannot be regarded as a rule of succession, inheritance or marriage.

Secondly, that amongst the great Doctors of the Mohammadan Law there is a great difference of opinion as to the exact manner in which the rule of *istiṣḥāb* is to be applied to missing persons.

Thirdly, that as to the period necessary to elapse before the presumption of death can be applied to missing persons, Mohammadan jurists are far from being unanimous.

Fourthly, while some of the great doctors of the law would leave the fixation of the period to the discretion of the judge in each individual case, others consider the preferable course to be that the matter should be determined by the Imam, that is, by the ruling authority as distinguished from the Qazi or judge.

The concluding part of his judgement is important. He has stated, "these conclusions convince me that the rule of Mohammadan Law as to missing persons is a rule belonging purely to the domain of legal presumption falling under the head of the law of evidence." He therefore came to the conclusion that the provisions of Muslim law relating to missing persons form part of the law of evidence which has been superseded by the Indian Evidence Act, and so the case of a missing person would be governed by section 108 of the Evidence Act and not by the provisions of the Muslim law on the subject.

Duthoit, J. agreed with Mahmud, J. but added:

"The rule...is not a rule of succession, inheritance, caste or any religious usage or institution." Oldfield and Brodhurst, JJ. concurred.

Peterham, C. J. also expressed the same opinion but he was obviously influenced by another aspect of the case as can be seen from the concluding portion of his judgement wherein he has added, "The rule of Mohammadan Law in regard to missing persons dates from ancient times and from social conditions to which it may well have been adopted. But to apply to the totally different conditions of the present day, when the means of communication between distant places have been so extended and improved, and when no man can hide his existence from others in the manner which was formerly possible, and to presume that a man was living for ninety years from the date of his birth, though his death was practically certain, would be a piece of gross injustice. It was to the benefit of the people of this country that section 108 of the Evidence Act was passed."

As stated, other two judges agreed with Mahmud, J.

It can thus be seen that the ruling was based mainly on the grounds that (1) the Muslim jurists themselves considered the rule to belong to the law of evidence, (2) the Muslim rule about a missing person is uncertain as regards the period of time on the expiry of which a person shall be presumed to be dead and also as regards the person by whom the matter is to be decided. Peterham, C. J. considered the Muslim rule to be inappropriate for the present-day time in view of the improved conditions of communication.

Now none of the above reasons can be advanced in the case of the Muslim rule of legitimacy and so the ruling cannot govern or even have any bearing on that law.

The Court did not accept Wilson's opinion that : "Enactments which provide that in matters of status Mohammadans shall be governed by the Mohammadan Law are later in date than the Evidence Act and so section 112 of the Evidence Act is not applicable to Muhammadans," on the ground "if it had been intended in these enactments to repeal a provision of the Evidence Act as applicable to Muhammadans this would have been done directly and not left to be inferred by a remote and precarious inference."

With due respect to the learned Judges it is submitted that this view is not correct. In the first place, the law relating to a missing person has no bearing on the law of legitimacy. As a matter of fact the Bench in that case based its finding on the ground that the law relating to a missing person is a part of Muslim law of evidence and has been so treated by the Muslim Jurists themselves. The fact that the provisions of the Evidence Act have been held to have superseded the provisions of Muslim law relating to a missing person does not lead to the inference that the provisions of Muslim law relating to legitimacy have also been superseded. These two matters, namely, the question of a missing person and that of legitimacy are entirely different. Moreover, it was not at all necessary to expressly lay down in the later enactment that section 112 of the Evidence Act was not applicable to Muslims. It is a well-known rule of the law of interpretation that "Later law abrogates prior contrary one" which is based on the maxim, "*Leges posteriores priores contrarias abrogant.*" It may be noted that the doctrine of acknowldgement is a part of the Muslim law of legitimacy and yet the Courts have held that it is part of the substantive law of the Muslims and is still applicable to them.[69]

A case involving the decision of this question came up for hearing before a Division Bench of the Lahore Bench of the High Court of West Pakistan. His lordship Masud Ahmed, J. after discussing the scope of section 2 of the Evidence Act and the result of the Repealing Act, 1938 observed that "Section 2 of the Evidence Act . . . repealed (1) all rules of evidence not contained in any Statute etc, (2) rules and laws in force under the Indian Council Act, and (3) all enactments mentioned in the Schedule to the Evidence Act. The rule of Muhammadan Law regarding legitimacy, being part of rules not contained in any Statute, it fell within the purview of the first clause of this section, and therefore was repealed by it. This section was repealed by the Repealing Act, 1938. The question that requires decision now is whether by repeal of section 2 of the Evidence Act, the rule of Muhammadan

69. Muhammad Allahdad Khan Vs. Muhammad Ismail Khan, ILR 10 All. 289 at pp. 307, 328.

Law on this subject has been revived, or whether it continues to stand repealed."

"Section 6-A of the General Clauses Act... was on the Statute book when the Repealing Act, 1938, was passed and therefore repeal of section 2 did not affect the continuance of any amendment made by that section, so far as it repealed statute law. The repeal of rules of Muhammadan Law by section 2 of the Act, however, stands on a different footing, because those rules of Muhammadan Law were not part of a Central Act or Regulation and hence their repeal by section 2 of the Evidence Act was not saved by section 6-A of the General Clauses Act. What this section lays down is that where any "Central Act or Regulation" made after the commencement of the General Clauses Act, repealed any "enactment", by which the text of any Central Act or Regulation was amended, then unless a different intention appears, the repeal shall not affect the continuance of any amendments made by the enactments so repealed. The expression "Central Act or Regulation" occurring in the first part of this section would be the Repealing Act 1938, the expression "enactment" would be section 2 of the Evidence Act and the expression "Central Act or Regulation" occurring in this section for the second time, would be the rules, laws, regulations and enactments mentioned in clauses (2) and (3) of section 2 of fhe Evidence Act which had been repealed by that section. As a result of repeal of section 2 by virtue of section 6-A of the General Clauses Act, the rules, laws, regulations and enactments in clauses (2) and (3) of section 2, would not be revived, but the rules of evidence mentioned in clause (1) of section 2 of the Evidence Act, being not part of a Central Act or regulation, the same would not stand repealed after the Repealing Act, namely, section 2 of Evidence Act, had itself been repealed. On this view of the matter I am of the opinion that, after the repeal of section 2 of the Evidence Act, the rules of Muhammadan Law, which has been repealed by clause (1), have been revived and are now part of the law of Evidence. "........I am, therefore, of opinion that it was not the intention of the legislature that those rules, which were not contained in any statutes, and which had been repealed by section 2 of the Evidence Act were not to be revived after that section itself was repealed."[70]

It can be seen from the above that the Court held that the rule of Muhammadan Law, regarding legitimacy, is a rule of substantive law and that by the repeal of section 2 of the Evidence Act this rule of Muhammadan Law has been revived. It seems however desirable to clarify the matter and to remove all uncertainty.

The provisions of Muslim law are such that an application of section 112 of the Evidence Act will lead to great confusion. Some of the difficulties in the matter are pointed out below:

(*a*) A child born within a few days or within a few hours after the marriage is legitimate under the provisions of section 112, but the very idea is abhorent to a Muslim and a Muslim still wants to stick to his conception of legitimacy as based on Muslim law under which a child born within six months of a marriage is not considered legitimate and the Muslim jurists insist that not only should the child be born but must be conceived within wedlock.

(*b*) According to Shī'ah law if a person cohabits with a woman under a mistake, thinking that she was his wife, as a result of which she gives birth to a child then the parentage would be established in him and it would be considered to be a legitimate child of the person. But under section 112 the child shall not be deemed either to be legitimate or the offspring of that person as there has been no marriage.

(*c*) If a child is born under conditions satisfying the requirements of section 112 then it shall be deemed to be legitimate and it cannot be deprived of the attribute of its

70. Abdul Ghani and another Vs. Mst. Taleh Bibi and another, P.L.D. 1962 Lah. 531.

legitimacy. But under Muslim law the child can be proved to be illegitimate under the provisions relating to li'ān even when it is born within two hundred and eighty days after the marriage of its mother and her husband and the law of *Li'ān* is still applicable to Muslims.

(*d*) Section 112 of the Evidence Act contemplates marriages of two kinds, namely, void or valid. But the Hanafi law divides marriages into three classes, namely, valid (*ṣaḥīḥ*), irregular (*fāsid*) and void (*bāṭil*). A child born of a *fasid* or irregular marriage is legitimate though the marriage itself is not valid and is quite distinct from it. There is no provision for such a marriage in section 112 though the Courts have held the children of such a marriage to be legitimate under the provisions of Muslim law.

It seems that the attention of the Legislature was not drawn to the provisions of the Muslim law regarding legitimacy when the Indian Evidence Act was passed. The Muslim jurists have treated the law regarding legitimacy as part of their substantive law and not as that of the Law of Evidence. Thus they have discussed it along with the laws relating to marriage and divorce generally given in the second volume of certain leading books. The law of evidence has been given in another volume of these books. It is in the second volume and just after divorce that *Nasab* (Legitimacy) has been dealt with. Legitimacy is closely and directly connected with marriage and succession which are still decided according to Muslim law and there is no reason why it should not be governed by the provisions of Muslim law particularly when the doctrine of acknowledgement which is a part of the law of legitimacy has been held to be still extant.

It is time that this mistake should be rectified and it be made clear that section 112 of the Evidence Act shall not apply to the question of legitimacy where the parties or the father is a Muslim. The matter can be easily set right by adding a proviso to the section to the following effect: "Provided that where the parties or the father of the child is a Muslim, in which case the child shall be presumed to be legitimate only if it is so held by Muslim law."

Burden of Proof: It is for the claimant to prove that he is the lawful offspring of a certain person. This will be held with still greater force in the case of gestation within the maximum period prescribed by the Muslim law. The different varying maximum periods of pregnancy given in the books of medical jurisprudence and by Muslim law relate to abnormal cases and in such cases it is for the plaintiff who alleges that there were abnormal circumstances attending his birth to show that they existed. But when it is possible to infer a marriage to have taken place between a man and a woman, the Court will always lean more strongly in favour of the conclusion that a marriage has taken place.

It was observed in an English case that when a child is born then sexual intercourse between the husband and the wife must be presumed, and nothing except evidence that the husband did not have sexual intercourse at the period of conception can render illegitimate a child born in wedlock.[71]

71. W Vs. W (1953) 2 All. E.R. 1013.

Chapter 29

IQRĀR—ACKNOWLEDGEMENT

Preliminary : *Iqrār* means acknowledgement. It is derived either from *qarār* or from *qurrat al-'ayn.* The former means rest and confirmation, as if the acknowledger established by his acknowledgement a right against himself. The latter means comfort of the eyes, because the person in whose favour an acknowledgement is made receives thereby comfort in his eyes, and thus the acknowledger comforts the eyes of the person in whose favour the acknowledgement is made.[1] An acknowledgement is giving information as to the right of a person enforcible against the acknowledger, that is, the person who gives such information.[2]

Religious Sanction : *Al-Kifāyah*, the commentary of *al-Hidāyah*, points out that the rule as to the acknowledgement of parentage is based upon the words of the Qur'ān "Call them by (the names of) their fathers."[3]

Muslim jurists state that maternity admits of positive proof because the separation of the child from its mother can be seen but paternity does not admit of a positive proof because the connection of a child to its father is secret. But the absence of direct evidence to establish paternity of a child can be cured by an admission or acknowledgement (*Iqrār*) of paternity by the husband of its mother, or by a subsisting "*Firāsh*" (bed), that is, legally constituted relationship between him and the mother of the child.[4] It is stated in *al-Kifāyah* that the acknowledgement of paternity by a person is con-

1. 'Abd al-Alī al-Birjandī, *Sharḥ al-Wiqāyah*, Lucknow 1301 A.H., Vol. IV, pp. 31, 32.
2. *Ibid.*
3. Qur'ān Surah Al-Ahzāb, XXI : 5.
4. Al-Marghīnānī, *al-Hidāyah*, Delhi, n.d., Vol. II, p. 410 ; Shaykhzādah, *Majma' al-Anhur*, Constantinople, 1327 A.H., Vol. II, p. 484.

sidered sufficient because the burden of the obligations in respect of the child rests especially on the father, and the latter's acknowledgement affects him personally and so is accepted without any confirmation by the mother.[5] This is also the view given in other books. The Muslim law refuses to declare a person a bastard, except on the clearest and most positive proof of his illegitimacy.[6]

Description: Generally speaking, acknowledgement means "to give information by a person as to a right enforcible against his own self.[7] In the absence of a direct proof of marriage between its parents, a child may be affiliated to a man by his admission that the child is his.[8] This admission is technically called *Iqrār* or acknowledgement. It is based on the notion that the burden of obligations in respect of a child rests particularly on the father and his acknowledgement affects him personally and it must be so accepted without any verification.

Applicability: The Muslim law of acknowledgement is still extant in India and Pakistan and has been followed by various Courts.

Nature of : The doctrine of acknowledgement is not a rule of evidence, but a rule of substantive Muslim law.[9] Hence the conditions under which it will take effect must be determined with reference to Muslim law and not in accordance with the law of evidence.

The effect of acknowledgement of paternity, validly made as establishing marriage between the parents of the acknow-

5. Al-Khawārizmī, *al-Kifāyah* on the margin of *al-Hidāyah*, Delhi, n.d. Vol. III, p. 58.
6. Ibrahim Ali Khan Vs. Mubarak Begum, A.I.R. 19:0, Lah. 419 ; 56 I.C. 923.
7. Shaykhzādah, *op. cit.*, Vol. II, p. 289 ; Mullā Khusraw, Muhammad b. Farāmūz, *Durar al-Ḥukkām*, Constantinople 1330 A.H., Vol. II, p. 357.
8. Ibn 'Ābidīn, *Radd al-Muḥtār*, Cairo, 1318 A.H., Vol. II, p. 643.
9. Mst. Hajira Khatun Vs. Mst Amina Khatun, I.L.R. 1923, All. 570 ; Muhammad Allahdad Khan Vs. Muhammad Ismail Khan, I.L.R. 10 All. 289 at pp. 307 ; 328.

ledged child, may be a matter of substantive Muslim law, but the effect of an admission of marriage as proof of such marriage is a question of adjective law governed by the Evidence Act. Its probative value must depend upon surrounding circumstances.[10] The acknowledgement by a father that a child is his, establishes the legitimacy of the child unless the marriage was not possible.[11] Legitimacy may be proved without direct proof of a marriage under certain circumstances.[12]

Marriage is not the only method of establishing legitimacy according to Muslim law; an admission by a person that a certain child is his child is an acknowledgement which is sufficient under the Muslim law to confer legitimacy on the child acknowledged unless there are circumstances and conditions under which the acknowledgement is not considered effective. The doctrine of acknowledgement applies only to cases of uncertainty as to legitimacy, and in such cases acknowledgement has its effect but the effect always proceeds upon the assumption of a lawful union between the parents of the acknowledged child. It proceeds entirely upon the assumption of the possibility of legitimate descent of an acknowledged child from the acknowledger, and the rule as to the effect of such acknowledgement does not extend to a case when such legitimate descent was impossible owing either to the impossibility of a valid marriage between the parents of the child or owing to the existence of such a marriage being disproved by trustworthy evidence. But it is only when direct proof of marriage is not available that indirect proof of marriage by way of acknowledgement of legitimacy in favour of a child is allowed to take the place of direct proof of marriage. Where direct proof is available to establish that marriage was impossible or a marriage would be invalid, no question of

10. Mst. Hajira Khatun Vs. Mst. Amina Khatun, I.L.R. 1923, All. 570; Muhammad Allahdad Khan Vs. Muhammad Ismail Khan, I.L.R. 10 All. 289 at pp. 307; 328.

11. Syed Habibur Rahman Chowdhury Vs. Syed Altaf Ali Chowdhury, I.L.R. 48 AIR 1922 Cal. 856; Ibrahim Ali Khan Vs. Mubarak Begum, AIR 1920 Lah. 419.

12. *Ibid.*

presumption of marriage on account of an alleged acknowledgment can arise.[13]

It is stated in the chapter on manumission of slaves in the *Fatāwā Qāḍī Khān* that some jurists have held that sonship is not established unless it is verified by the person in whose favour it is made. But the correct doctrine is that such a condition is not essential as stated above, and this is in conformity with the doctrine of *al-Hidāyah* and many other books.[14] According to the Ḥanafīs the descent is established without any such verification of the acknowledged below the age of discretion.[15] When the person in whose favour an acknowledgement is made falsifies the acknowledger, the acknowledgement is nullified.[16]

The rule of Muslim law as to acknowledgement is quite different from adoption as understood under other laws. Under Muslim law, acknowledgement of parentage proceeds upon the theory of actual descent of the acknowledged child from the person who acknowledges it, such descent being the result of legitimate intercourse between the child's parents. Adoption under other laws has no reference to the natural descent of the adopted child from the adoptive father, but is established by a gift from the real parents of the child to the adoptive parents. It is, therefore, distinct from the establishment of paternity under the doctrine of acknowledgement.

Similarly, acknowledgement differs from the law of legitimation as understood under other laws. These other laws proceed upon the principle of legitimating children, whose illegitimacy is proved and admitted, while the doctrine of acknowledgement proceeds upon the assumption that the

13. Mohammad Shafiqullah Vs. Nuhullah Khan and others A.I.R. 1926, All. 48 ; I.L.R. 48 All. 58.

14. Qāḍī Khān, *Fatāwā Qāḍi Khān*, Kanpur, 1310 A.H., Vol. II, p. 285 · 'Abd al-'Alī al-Birjandī, *op. cit.*, Vol. IV, p. 37.

15. Ibn 'Ābidīn, *op. cit.*, Vol. IV, p. 485 ; al-Birjandi, *op. cit.*, p. 37.

16. Ibn Nujaym, *al-Ashbāh wa'l-Nazā'ir*, Cairo, 1322 A.H., p. 100.

acknowledged child is not only the offspring of the acknowledger but also a lawful issue of a valid union between him and the child's mother. No acknowledgement by a person that a child, proved to be illegitimate, is his child, can make that child his legitimate issue.[17] There is another difference between legitimacy and legitimation. The former is a status which results from certain facts while the latter is a proceeding which creates a status which did not exist before. In the proper sense there is no legitimation under Muslim law.[18] An acknowledgement of the legitimacy of a child is an indirect proof of the marriage.[19] Hence when a man acknowledges that a certain child is his son or daughter, this acknowledgement amounts *prima facie* to an acknowledgement that the child is his legitimate child.[20] This acknowledgement must not be merely of sonship or of daughterhood but also of legitimate descent.[21] An acknowledgement does not establish of anything for the first time, but merely indicates something which is already in existence and only provides a proof of the same.

According to Muslim law, a valid acknowledgement does not merely provide *prima facie* evidence, but establishes the fact acknowledged.[22] A mere recognition of paternity, however, is not equivalent to a recognition of legitimacy. Hence an acknowledgement by a person of the paternity of a child who is proved to be born of adultery cannot make the

17. Mahaboob Nisa Begum Vs. Mahomed Yusuf, A.I.R. 1950, Hyd. 41.
18. Agha Muhammad Ibn Ali Vs. Zohra Begum, A.I.R., 1927 Oudh, 562.
19. Syed Habibur Rahman Chowdhury Vs. Syed Altaf Ali Chowdhury, I.L.R., 48, Cal. 856; A.I.R. 1922 P.C. 159 Mst. Imam Bandi Vs. Sheikh Haji Mutsaddi, 16 A.L.J. 800.
20. Fuzeelun Bibee Vs. Omdah Bibee 10 W.R. 469; Roshan Bai Vs. Haji Ahmad Umar, A.I.R. 1944 Bom. 213.
21. Mulla Khusraw, *op. cit.*, Vol. II, p. 357; Roshan Bai Vs. Haji Ahmad Umar, A.I.R. 1944 Bom. 213.
22. Mullā Khusraw *op. cit.*, Vol. II, p. 357.

child legitimate.[23]

In the absence of proof of marriage, the mere admission of paternity is not enough to establish legitimacy ; the acknowledgement must not be merely of paternity but of legitimate descent.[24] Once, however, marriage is established, an acknowledgement of paternity is enough.

Form of : No particular form or expression is prescribed for an acknowledgement. It can be made in any form or by any words as long as the intention of the speaker to make the acknowledgment is clear and can be gathered from his speech.

Who can make an Acknowledgement: It is not only the father who can make an acknowledgement of the legitimacy of a cbild but such an acknowledgement can be made by any relation with regard to himself but not as regards others so that he is personally affected by such acknowledgement, but it will not affect the interests of other persons.[25] Thus if he is the heir of a deceased person and acknowledges that a certain child is the issue of the deceased then his own share in the assets shall be affected by the inclusion of the child amongst the heirs on his acknowledgement. But the shares of the other heirs who deny the descent of the child from the deceased shall not be affected by the acknowledgement and so the child shall get a share only from the share of the former, but not from the shares of the latter. This is of course subject to the condition that he has not been proved to be the offspring of the deceased.

Mode of : An acknowledgment can be made expressly or by implication. Express acknowledgment is when a man says: "This is my child." An implied acknowledgment is such as when a man remains silent when he is being congratulated upon the birth of a child. A continuous and consistent course of treatment of a child as a legitimate child amounts to an

23. Feroz Din Khan Vs. Nawab Khan, A.I.R. 1929, Lah. 55 ; Mahaboob Nisa Begum Vs. Mahomed Yusuf, A.I.R. 1950, Hyd. 41.
24. Syed Habibur Rahman Chowdhury Vs. Syed Altaf Ali Chowdhury I.L.R. 48, Cal. 856, A.I.R. 1922 PC 159.
25. Ibn 'Ābidīn, *Radd al-Muḥtār*, Cairo, 1318 A.H., Vol. II, p. 644.

implied acknowledgment. It can be presumed from the conduct of the putative or supposed father and also from circumstances without direct proof of the marriage of its parents. Thus the facts that a child was brought up by a person and treated by him as his son are sufficient to give rise to a presumption that it is the legitimate child of that person.[26]

Under Muslim law, the legitimacy of a child may properly be presumed or inferred from circumstances without direct proof of the marriage of the parties.[26a] If a child is born to a *majbūb* (person without penis) and the husband acknowledges it to be his son, the child shall be considered to be his legitimate son. This rule proceeds from the general principle of Muslim law against bastardising children. The rule is based on the theory that the acknowledgement of parentage by the father obviates any investigation as to the physical condition of the acknowledger's potency or impotency for procreating the offspring of a valid marriage. This rule shall apply even if the child is born within two years of the husband's death or dissolution of his marriage. But the marriage shall stand dissolved in the latter case.[27] The wife can seek the dissolution of her marriage on the basis of her husband's defect even after the birth of a child, because the child becomes his even without proof of sexual intercourse.[28] It must be noted that in the case of an impotent person, paternity of the child shall be established in him, and the marriage shall be restored.[29] This must be on the ground that the birth of the child proves that the husband is not impotent and that the marriage was wrongly dissolved.

26. Suraiya Qadr Vs. Qudsia Begum, 8 A.I.R. 1914, Oudh 1.

26*a*. Mahomed Bauker Hossain Khan Bahadoor Vs. Shurfoon Nisa Begum, 8 MIA 136 ; Ashrufood-Daula Ahmed Hossain Khan Bahadoor Vs. Hyder Hossain Khan, 11 MIA 94.

27. *Ibid.*, Ibn 'Ābidīn, *op. cit.*, Vol. II, p. 610 ; Qāḍī Khān *Fatāwā Qāḍī Khān*, Kanpur, 1310, A.H., Vol. I, p. 172, Suraiya Qadr Vs. Qudsia Begum, 8 A.I.R. 1914, Oudh 1.

28. *Al-Fatāwā al-Hindiyah*, Kanpur, 1349 A.H. Vol. II, p. 134.

29. Ibn 'Ābidīn *op. cit.*, Vol. II, p. 610.

Presumption: Long cohabitation raises a presumption of marriage. But the mere cohabitation of a man with a woman for some years prior to his death without recognising her as his wife does not confer the status of legitimacy on a child born to them.[30] In the case of uncertainty of legitimate descent, an acknowledgement by a person that the child is his legitimate offspring or that he had been married to the child's mother raises a presumption of legitimacy in favour of the child. But the presumption in favour of the legitimacy must rest on sufficient grounds and cannot be permitted to override overbalancing proof of illegitimacy. If a marriage is proved, other conditions being satisfied, no question of acknowledgement remains to be considered while if a marriage is disproved, no amount of acknowledegment can make the presumption override the fact and legitimacy cannot be presumed. It is only when a marriage is unproved by reason of time or circumstances that an acknowledgement by a person, that the woman is his wife or that the child is his legitimate offspring, will raise the presumption of marriage or legitimacy of the child.[31] The presumption of legitimacy cannot be made antedated and so an antenuptial child is considered to be illegitimate.[32] An acknowledgement by a person cannot confer the status of a legitimate child on one who is proved to be the offspring of fornication.[33] or also whose parentage is known to belong to somebody else.[34] Similarly, an acknowledgement of

30. Fateh Muhammad Vs. Abdur Rahman A.I.R. 1931, Lah. 223.
31. Man Mahan Saw Vs. Muhammad Husain Khan, A.I.R. 1924, Pat.191 : 72 I.C. 152; Roshan Bibi Vs. Sulaiman Haji Ahmad Umar, A.I.R. 1944, Bom. 213 ; Syed Habibur Rahman Chowdhury Vs. Syed Altaf Ali Chowdhury, I.L R. 48, Cal. 856 ; A.I.R. 1922 PC 159 ; Abdul Aziz Vs. Ameer Begum, 66 I.C. 404; Mohammad Sadiq Vs. Mohammad Hossain, A.I.R. 1943 Lah. 225.
32. Ashrafood-Daula Ahmad Hussain Khan Bahadur Vs. Hyder Hussain Khan 11 M.I.A. 94.
33. *Al-Fatawa al-Hindiyah*, Deoband, n.d., Vol. III, p. 398 ; Mohammad Sadiq Vs. Mohammad Hossain, A.I.R. 1943, Lah. 225.
34. Ibrahim Ali Khan Vs. Mubarak Begum 56 I.C. 923 ; Syed Habibur Rahman Chowdhury Vs Altaf Ali Chowdhury, I.L.R. 48 Cal. 856, A.I.R, 1922 P.C. 59.

legitimacy is of no avail when it is established that there was no marriage between the acknowledger and the child's mother.[35] Where a child has been born to an acknowledger and a woman between whom there has not been a mere casual concubinage, but a more permanent connection and where there is no insurmountable obstacle to such a marriage then a presumption in favour of marriage having taken place between the person and the mother of the child can be presumed. The presumption of legitimacy raised by an acknowledgement of a person is not a strong one.[36] Thus it would not arise when the mother of a child was a prostitute before she was brought to the house of the alleged father of the child.

From the treatment accorded to a child, acknowledgement might be presumed. But no amount of acknowledgement can make a person the legitimate son of another when he could not have been proved to be legitimate. It is upon the person whose legitimacy is in doubt to prove by substantial irrebutable evidence that he was treated by the alleged father as a legitimate son.

When can acknowledgement be made: An acknowledgement of paternity of a child can be made under the following circumstances:

I. When there is no direct proof of the alleged marriage between a person and the mother of the child,

II. When the legitimacy of a child is uncertain or,

III. When the parentage of the child is not definitely known.

Essentials: An admission of paternity is admissible only when it is in conformity with law and common-sense. An acknowledgement is ineffective when the alleged paternity cannot be possible. The Muslim jurists have stated certain propositions to determine if the alleged paternity is at all possible

35. Fatimah Binti Hafidh Vs. Administrator-General, Zanzibar Protectorate, A.I.R 1949 P.C. 254.

36. Usman Miya Abdulla Miya Vs. Vali Mahomed Husain Bhai, 17 B.L.R. 693.

and so effective. Hence the following conditions must be satisfied before an acknowledgement can be considered valid.[37]

(*a*) The acknowledgment should clearly indicate the child in respect of whom it is made so that there should be no doubt about the identity of the child in respect of whom acknowledgement is being made. It must clearly describe the child and should not merely make an allusion to him which may make the identity of the acknowledged child uncertain.[38]

(*b*) The acknowledgement must be definite, clear and reliable and there must be an intention to acknowledge the child as lawful offspring.[39]

(*c*) The relationship between the acknowledger and the acknowledged child should be immediate and direct without an intermediary link. Thus an acknowledgement that a certain child is the acknowledger's son's son shall not establish a descent of the child from the acknowledger's son.[40]

(*d*) The descent of the child who is being acknowledged should be unknown.[41] If the child is known to be born of a person other than the acknowledger or is known to be the result of adultery then no acknowlegement by a person can make it the lawful child of the acknowledger.[41a]

(*e*) An acknowledgement can be effective only when the descent of the child is unknown for an acknowledgement serves as a proof of parentage or descent only when there is some doubt about it. A child cannot be affiliated to a person by his acknowledgement as when the child has been proved to belong to

37. 'Abd al-'Alī al-Birjandī, *op. cit.*, Vol. IV, pp. 31-38.
38. *Ibid.*, pp. 36-37.
39. *Ibid.*
40. *Ibid.*, p. 36.
41. *Ibid*
41*a*. *Ibid.*

another.[42]

The principle of acknowledgement serves as a proof of parentage only when there is some doubt about it but does not allow the affiliation of a child who cannot belong to him as when it has been proved to be illegitimate.[43]

A passage in a judgment of their Lordships of the Privy Council leads to one think that the contrary is correct. It reads as follows :—

"A child born out of wedlock is illegitimate ; if acknowledged acquires the status of legitimacy."[44] This passage, if taken as an abstract enunciation of law could lead to the result that a child who is proved to be illegitimate may be legitimated under certain circumstances. But it is submitted with respect that such is not the law. The above and other rulings were discussed by the Allahabad High Court when it considered this matter and stated that their Lordships of the Privy Council never intended to go to the length of laying down the rule that a child who is proved to be illegitimate could be legitimated by acknowledgement.[45] Their Lordsiphs of the Privy Council themselves explained the matter to clear the point in a subsequent case wherein they stated :

"......These observations must be taken with a reference to the facts of that case......"[46] It is obvious that if a marriage between a man and a woman is not possible then an

42. 'Abd al-'Alī al-Birjandī, *op. cit.*, Vol. IV, pp. 31-38, *al-Fatāwā al-Hindiyah, op. cit.*, Vol. III, p. 395, Ibn al-Humām, *Fatḥ al-Qadīr*, Cairo, 1356 A.H., Vol. VII, p. 14, Akmal al-Dīn Muḥammad b. Maḥmūd, *al-'Ināyah*, on the margin of *Fatḥ al-Qadīr, op. cit.*, Vol. VII, p. 14.

43. Ashrufood-Dawlah Ahmed Hossein Khan Vs. Hyder Hossein Khan, 11 M.I.A. 94 ; Muhammad Allahdad Khan Vs. Muhammad Ismail Khan, I.L.R. 10 All. 289 at pp. 327, 334, 335.

44. Ashrufood-Dawlah Ahmed Hossein Khan Vs. Hyder Hossein Khan, 11 M.I.A. 94.

45. Muhammad Allahdad Khan Vs. Muhammad Ismail Khan, I.L.R. 10 All. 289, at p. 332.

46. Mohamad Azmat Ali Khan Vs. Lalli Begum, 1881, I.L.R. 8 Cal. 422, L.R. 9, I.A. 8.

acknowledgement of paternity by a man would be ineffective.

(*e*) The marriage between the acknowledger and the mother of the child should be merely uncertain. It should not be disproved or be impossible.[47] A marriage can be impossible on the basis of facts or law. Thus a marriage between a woman and the acknowledger would be impossible when a marriage is proved to be subsisting between her and a third person.[48] Similarly, a marriage would not be possible when the woman was within prohibited degree from the acknowledger at the time when the child could have been conceived.[49] Where the acknowledger had irrevocably divorced the mother of the child, but continued to live with her without a remarriage after an intervening marriage and continued to treat her as his wife and the children born of her as his lawful children, it was held that under such circumstances the status of legitimacy cannot be conferred on the children.[50] This is based on the fact that on an irrevocable divorce the woman became absolutely forbidden to him. He could marry her only after she had married another person and the second marriage had been dissolved after consummation. As this was not done their relationship was not lawful. A void marriage is no marriage at all and the children born of such a marriage shall be considered illegitimate.

(*f*) The ages of the acknowledger and the acknowledged child should be such that parentage of the acknowledger should be possible.[51]

(*g*) The acknowledged child should not repudiate the acknowledgement provided it is of an age when it can understand the significance of the acknowledgement.[52]

47. Mohammad Sadiq Vs. Mohammad Hassan, A.I.R. 1943, Lah. 225.
48. Mubarak Ali Vs. Sahib Jan, A.I.R. 1929, Lah. 372, Syed Habib-ur-Rahman Chowdhury Vs. Syed Altaf Ali Chowdhury.
49. Agha Mahommad Ibn Ali Vs. Zohra Begum, A.I.R. 1927, Oudh 562.
50. Saiyid Rashid Ahmad Vs. Anisa Khatun, A.I.R. 1932, P.C. 25.
51. *Al-Fatāwā al-Hindiyah*, *op.cit.*, Vol. III, p. 398; al-Birjandī, *op. cit.*, Vol. IV, p. 37.
52. *Ibid.*

(*h*) The acknowledgment by a man of a woman as his wife is valid when confirmed by her and when the marriage is possible.[53]

(*i*) The acknowledged child should not be proved to have been born of adultery. When no marriage is proved between the acknowledger and a prostitute, no presumption can be drawn by an acknowledgement that the child belongs to the acknowledger.[54] But continued treatment of a child born of a concubine as a legitimate child of a person was held to furnish evidence of acknowledgement.[55]

Admissibility: A statement by a deceased person that there was a marriage between him and a certain woman is admissible in evidence to prove the legitimacy of his children under Section 32 (5) of the Evidence Act as a statement as to the marriage.[56]

An acknowledgement is like every other presumption of fact and is capable of being set aside by contrary proof.

Revocation of Acknowledgement: A status of sonship once conferred by acknowledgement cannot be destroyed by any subsequent act of the acknowledger or those who claim through him.[57] The Privy Council has held the same opinion and has held that the denial of a son ofter an established acknowledgement, though supported by a deed of repudiation and disclaimer by the father is untenable.[58] Descent, when once established, cannot be dissolved or cancelled, neither can

53. Ibn 'Ābidīn, *Radd al-Muḥtār*, Cairo, 1324 A.H., Vol. II, p. 865 Birjandī, cited in I.L.R. 10 All. 289 ; at pp. 310, 327, Muhammad Ali Khan Vs. Ghazanfar Ali Khan 60 IC 147.
54. Muhammad Ali Khan Vs. Ghazanfar Ali 60, I.C. 147.
55. Ashrufood-Dawlah Ahmed Hossein Khan Vs. Hyder Hossein Khan 11 M.I A. 94 ; Muhammad Allahdad Khan Vs. Muhammad Ismail Khan, ILR 10 All. 289, at p. 332.
56. Zamin Ali Vs. Mst. Azizunnissa, A.I.R. 1933, All. 329, I.L.R. 55, All. 144 ; 144 I.C. 433.
57. Muhammad Allahdad Khan Vs. Muhammad Ismail Khan, I.L.R. 10 All. 289, at pp. 317, 318, 328 ; Abd al-'Alī al-Birjandī, *op. cit.*, Vol. II, p. 65.
58. Ashrafood-Daulah Ahmad Hossein Khan Vs. Hyder Hossein Khan 11 M.I.A. 94.

it be transferred from one person to another.[59]

Effect: When the legitimacy of a child is not certain or the act of the marriage of its mother with the child's alleged father is uncertain, an acknowledgement by that person that the child is his, raises a presumption of the legitimacy of the child. Such an acknowledgement establishes the parentage of the child and renders him or her a legitimate child and heir of that person unless it is impossible that such relationship should exist between them. The acknowledgement if assented to or confirmed by the acknowledger, or after his death establishes a valid relationship, in so far as the parties themselves are concerned and with regard to such rights as affect them. Where either party has acknowledged that he or she was married to the other and the other party has acquiesced in or confirmed the acknowledgement it will be presumed that they are validly married unless prohibition to marry is established between them. In the absence of an absolute bar or impediment to a valid marriage an acknowledgement has also the effect of establishing the marriage when either the fact of the marriage or its exact time with reference to the legitimacy of the child's birth is a matter of uncertainty.[60] The acknowledgement also amounts to *prima facie* proof that the mother of the child is the wife of that man.[61] Hence an acknowledgement of marriage invests the acknowledged wife with the status of a married wife and her subsequently born children with the status of legitimacy unless the marriage was impossible. It also amounts to an acknowledgement that the child is his legitimate child unless the contrary appears. By an acknowledgement a child or a wife becomes one of the acknowledger's heirs to the same extent as one of his other heirs.

Burden of Proof: Under the Muslim law the presumption is in favour of marriage and legitimacy. Hence if a person attributes illegitimacy to another person, it is for him

59. *Al-Fatāwā al-Hindiyah*, Kanpur, 1349 A.H., Vol. II, p. 139.

60. Syed Habibur Rahman Chowdhury Vs. Altaf Ali Chowdhury, I.L.R. 48, Cal. 856, A.I.R. 1922 P.C. 159.

61. *Al-Fatāwā al-Hindiyah*, *op. cit.*, Vol. II, p. 140.

to prove the allegation of illegitimacy. But where a person relies on acknowledgement in his favour then the burden of proof lies on him to establish such acknowledgement.

Once the acknowledgement by a father that a certain child is his child is established, the burden shifts on the other party who denies the legitimacy of the child to establish the fact by proving that marriage between the child's mother and the alleged father was impossible or in fact did not take place or in some such other way. It is for the claimant to establish an acknowledgement in his favour.[62] The onus lies on him to prove a marriage between its mother and the alleged father. When doubt is thrown on the legitimacy of a person, it is upon him to prove by substantial irrebutable evidence that he was treated by the alleged father as a legitimate son.[63]

The effect of an acknowledgment by a man that a certain child is his child raises so strong a presumption of legitimacy as to throw a heavy onus on the person denying it.[64] He must establish his allegation and show that marriage between the acknowledger and the mother of the acknowledged child was impossible or some such other grounds.

62. Mahaboob Nissa Begum Vs. Mahomed Yusuf ; A.I.R. 1950 Hyd. 41, Mohammad Sadiq Vs. Mohammad Hassan, AIR 1943 Lah. 225.

63. *Ibid.*

64. Zakir Ali Vs. Sograbibi, A.I.R. 1918, Nag. 32.

Chapter 30

KHALWAT ṢAḤĪḤAH OR VALID RETIREMENT

I. Definition: The married couples' retiring by themselves to a secluded place where they are safe from observation by other people and where matrimonial intercourse in privacy is possible is called *Khalwat ṣaḥīḥah*, that is, Valid Retirement.[1]

II. Presumption: In case of valid retirement the Hanafis, Mālikīs and the Ḥanbalīs draw a presumption that the marriage has been consummated even when there is no proof of actual cohabitation between the parties.[2] But this presumption is rebuttable and it is always open to a party to prove that there has been no actual consummation of the marriage. The Shāfi'īs and the Shī'ahs do not draw any such presumption from mere valid retirement.

Shafi'ī Law: The Shāfi'īs do not agree with the Ḥanafīs, the Mālikīs and the Ḥanbalīs in the matter of valid retirement and do not accept the doctrine. Shāfi'ī at first agreed with Abū Ḥanīfah but subsequently he changed his opinion and did not attach any validity to valid retirement.[3]

III. Shī'ī Law: Under the Shī'ī law mere valid retirement does not amount to cohabitation.[4] But if there has been a valid retirement and should the wife assert consummation of the marriage, then the mere denial of the fact by the husband will not suffice to disprove the wife's allegation. According to another report, the statement of the husband will be accepted.[5]

IV. Impediments: A presumption of consummation of marriage cannot naturally arise when there is some such

1. *Al-Fatāwā al-Hindiyah*, Kanpur, 1349 A.H., Vol. II, p. 20; al-Marghīnānī, *al-Hidāyah*, Delhi, n. d., Vol. II, pp. 305-6.
2. Ibn Qudāmah, *al-Mughni*, Cairo, 1376 A.H., Vol. VI, p. 724; al-Sha'rāni, *al-Māzān al-Kubrā*, Cairo, 1279 A.H., Vol. II, p. 133.
3. *Ibid.*
4. Ja'far b. al-Ḥasan, *Sharā'i' al-Islām*, Tehran, 1377 A.H., p. 194.
5. *Ibid.*, p. 197.

impediment present that actual consummation of the marriage is not possible.[6] The impediment may be due to one or more of the following causes :—

(*a*) Physical obstacle,
(*b*) Religious restriction,
(*c*) Moral restriction,
(*d*) Legal bar or,
(*e*) Risk to husband.

(*a*) *Physical obstacles* : Physical obstacles can be such as serious illness of one or both the spouses, impotency of the husband, some defect in the woman which does not allow sexual intercourse, tender age of one or both the spouses.[7]

(*b*) *Religious Restrictions* : Religious restrictions may be such as the performance of *Ḥajj* by the husband or the wife or by the both of them when sexual intercourse is forbidden, fasting during the month of Ramaḍān when intimacy is prohibited during the time of actual fasting.[8] Similarly, when the wife is in her menstrual courses because cohabitation is not allowed at such a time.[9]

(*c*) *Moral restrictions* : Instances of moral restrictions are such as the presence of a third person or the exposure of the place to outsiders.[10]

Privacy: It is essential for valid retirement that there should be privacy and there can be no valid retirement when there is no privacy or seclusion because the parties cannot in decency in such a case be intimate with each other. The fact that the third person is asleep or is blind or deaf or dumb does not make any difference.[11] There can be a valid retirement, however, if the third person is insane or happens to be in a faint so that he cannot describe to others what he has seen.[12]

6. *Al-Fatāwā al-Hindiyah, op. cit.*, Vol. II. p. 20.
7. *Ibid.*, p. 20 f ; Ibn 'Ābidīn, *Radd al-Muḥtār*, Cairo, 1318 A.H., Vol. II, p. 347.
8. Ibn 'Ābidīn, *op. cit.*, Vol. II, p. 347.
9. *Ibid.*
10. *Ibid.*
11. *Ibid.*, p. 348 ; *al-Fatāwā al-Hindiyah, op. cit.*, Vol. II, p. 20 .
12. *Ibid.*

If that other person gets intervals of lucidity, valid retirement shall not be presumed if he is possessed of understanding at the time when the spouses meet, but not otherwise.[13] If the stranger is a child then it is to be seen whether he has gained discretion so that he can describe to others what he has seen. If he can do so, a valid retirement cannot be presumed. But if the child is of a tender age so that he cannot describe what he has seen then a valid retirement can be presumed.[14]

Exposure : It is necessary for valid retirement that the place where the spouses meet should not be exposed to view by others and so a valid retirement will not be presumed if it is possible that the parties may be seen by outsiders.[15] It is considered that the parties cannot in decency indulge in matrimonial connection under such circumstances. Hence there cannot be a valid retirement if the married couple meet on an open roof exposed to view or in a house having no door or even if there are doors but they are open or the walls are so low that the inmates are exposed to the view of the people outside.[16] The same will be the result if they meet in a garden having no walls or having walls with no doors fixed or with low walls.[17] If there is privacy of any sort, valid retirement can be presumed. Thus if the parties meet in a tent or in a portion of a house screened off from the other portion by a thick curtain then there is privacy and valid retirement can be presumed.[18] If, however, the curtain is so thin that they can be seen by people on the other side, there can be no privacy and consequently no valid retirement.[19]

(*d*) *Legal bar* : Legal bar may arise when the husband goes to his wife but does not recognise her or the wife goes to her husband and stays there for some time but the husband

13. *Al-Fatāwā al-Hindiyah, op. cit.*, Vol. II, p. 20.
14. *Ibid.*, p. 20.
15. *Ibid.*
16. *Ibid.*, Ibn 'Ābidīn, *op. cit.*, Vol. II, p. 348.
17. *Ibid.*, p. 21 ; Ibn 'Ābidīn, *op. cit.*, Vol. II, p. 349.
18. *Idid.*
19. *Ibid.*

does not know her. In such cases there can be no valid retirement, for he cannot consummate the marriage when he does not know that she is his wife.[20] But if he knows her and she goes to him when he is alone, valid retirement will be presumed even though he may be asleep.[21]

(*e*) *Risk to husband* : Muslim jurists have stated that consummation of marriage will not be possible if it is attended with certain risks to the husband. Thus the presence of a dog given to biting will not allow intimacy. The same result will follow if the dog is not given to biting but belongs to the wife for it is likely to misunderstand the act of the husband and may attack him in the defence of its owner, namely, the wife.[22] In such circumstances a valid retirement may not be presumed.

V. Effect of valid retirement : For certain purposes valid retirement is tantamount to consummation of marriage according to the Ḥanifīs, the Mālikīs and the Ḥanbalīs, provided the marriage is valid. In such cases the legal consequences which follow actual consummation of marriage also arise on valid retirement. Thus valid retirement establishes the legitimacy of a child born of the wife. These consequences occur in respect of the following matters :—

(*a*) Legitimacy,
(*b*) Dower,
(*c*) *'Iddah,*
(*d*) Maintenance, including residence, and
(*e*) Prohibition in respect of certain marriages.[23]

(*a*) *Legitimacy* : According to the Ḥanafīs, the Mālikīs and the Ḥanbalīs, if there has been a valid retirement and should a child be born to the wife at or beyond six months from that time then it shall be deemed to be the lawful issue of that

20. *Al-Fatāwā al-Hindiyah, op. cit.,* Vol, II, p. 21 ; Ibn 'Ābidīn, *op. cit.,* Vol. II, p: 349.
21. *Ibid.,* p. 21 ; *Ibid.,* p; 348.
22. *Ibid.,* p. 20 : *Ibid.*
23. *Ibid. Ibid.,* p. 350.

person. This is based on the idea that there was no obstacle in the way of the husband from being intimate with the wife and it is most likely that intimacy might have taken place between the spouses and it resulted in the birth of the child. It is considered much preferable to make the presumption than to hold a child a bastard.[24]

(*b*) *Dower* : The whole dower of the wife becomes due after valid retirement, even when the husband is impotent.[25] This is based on the reasoning that it is not due to any fault of the wife that the marriage has not been consummated and so she cannot be deprived of her dower. But if the marriage be '*fāsid*' (irregular) and is dissolved before actual consummation then valid retirement does not entitle the wife to claim her dower.[26] In case of dissolution of marriage, however, at the instance of the wife before actual consummation, the wife shall not be entitled to half her dower even when there has been a valid retirement.

(*c*) '*Iddah* : '*Iddah* becomes incumbent on a wife on the dissolution of her marriage after valid retirement.[27]

(*d*) *Maintenance* : The husband would be liable for the wife's maintenance during '*iddah* on dissolution of the marriage after valid retirement.[28]

(*e*) *Bar against marriage* : The husband cannot, during the period of the wife's '*iddah* after valid retirement, marry his divorced wife's sister or such other relatives whom the husband cannot marry in the presence of his wife. He also cannot marry, according to the said three schools, four other women so that the number of his wives including the divorced wife should not exceed four.[29]

24. For discussion see chapter on 'Legitimacy'.
25. Al-Marghīnānī, *op. cit.*, Vol. II, p. 306 ; Ibn 'Ābidīn, *op. cit.*, Vol. II, p. 350.
26. *Al-Fatāwā al-Hindiyah, op. cit.*, Vol. II. p. 21 ; Ibn 'Ābidīn, *op. cit.*, Vol. II, pp. 359-60.
27. *Ibid.*, p. 21 ; *Ibid.*, p. 363.
28. *Ibid.*
29. *Ibid.* For full discussion see chapter on '*Iddah*.

VI. Virginity : If the wife was a virgin at the time of the marriage and the marriage is dissolved before actual consummation but after valid retirement then she would still be regarded a virgin.[30]

VII. Points of difference in the effect of consummation of marriage and valid retirement : Valid retirement differs from consummation of marriage in certain cases such as given below :

(*a*) If a husband divorces his wife after consummation, he can take her back during the period of *'iddah* by *Raj'ah* ; if, however, he divorces her when the marriage has not been consummated but there has been a valid retirement, then he cannot take her back.[31] This is due to the fact that a divorce before consummation of marriage amounts to an irrevocable divorce and mere valid retirement does not amount to a consummation of the marriage in such a case.[32]

(*b*) There can be no cancellation of '*Īlā*' by valid retirement but only by actual cohabitation.[33]

(*c*) On actual consummation of marriage the wife's daughter by a former husband becomes unlawful to the present husband, but such is not the result of a valid retirement.[34]

(*d*) Another difference is that if a husband divorces his wife after consummation of marriage and then dies during the period of *'iddah*, the wife shall inherit from him but she shall not inherit from him after mere valid retirement.[35]

30. *Al-Fatāwā al-Hindiyah op. cit.*, Vol. II, p. 21. For full discussion see chapter on *'Iddah*, p. 21.
31. *Ibid.*, p. 21, Ibn 'Ābidīn, *op. cit.*, Vol. II, p. 351.
32. Ibn 'Ābidīn, *op. cit.*, Vol. II, p, 352.
33. *Al-Fatāwā al-Hindiyah, op. cit.*, Vol. II, p 21.
34. *Ibid.*, p. 21 ; *al-Mīzān al-Kubrā*, p. 118.
35. Ibn 'Ābidīn, *op. cit.*, Vol. II, p. 351.

Chapter 31

BULŪGH or MAJORITY

Preliminary: The various systems of law fix a particular age on the attainment of which the mental capacity of a child is supposed to have developed to such an extent as to give rise to the presumption that he or she can then arrive at a proper and reasonable decision on any matter. This particular age is called the age of majority and a person is considered to have become a major when he or she attains that age. It is only then that he or she can independently enter into a binding civil contract. Section II of the Contract Act lays down, "Every person is competent to contract who is of the age of majority according to the law to which he is subject." A child does not usually possess sufficient understanding to realise the consequences of his acts and so as a general rule is not held responsible for them. His contracts are not held binding on him in order to avoid the possibility that an unscrupulous person may take advantage of his position or of the undeveloped mental capacity of the child to enter into contracts with him, which may be disadvantageous to the child.

Age of Majority: *Bulūgh* or puberty and majority are one and the same thing under Muslim law, and a minor becomes major when he or she attains puberty. A boy or a girl can under the provisions of the Muslim law enter into binding contracts on reaching this age. A child is considered to gain puberty or majority when he or she becomes a fit subject for marriage. The puberty of a boy is established by his becoming subject to nocturnal emission or emission in the act of coition while the puberty of a girl is established by the commencment of menstruation.[1] The Muslim jurists, however, differ on the age of puberty or majority. Some jurists have

1. Shaykhzādah, *Majma' al-Anhur*, Constantinople, 1327 A.H., Vol. II, p. 444; Munlā Khusraw, *Durar al-Ḥukkam*, Constantinople, 1329 A.H., Vol. II, p. 275.

fixed this age at twelve years for a boy and nine years for a girl.[2] According to a report, Abū Ḥanīfah has fixed the age of puberty at eighteen years for a boy and seventeen years for a girl.[3] Abū Yūsuf and Muḥammad have laid down that a boy or a girl attains puberty on the completion of fifteen years and according to a report, Abū Ḥanīfah also agreed with this view.[4] The Ḥanafīs do not attach any importance to the growth of pubic hair.[5]

Shāfi'ī Law: Shāfi'ī holds the same view. He holds that puberty shall be presumed when a boy gets nocturnal emission or gets pubic hair or attains an age of fifteen years. A girl shall be considered to have attained majority when she gets menstruation or attains the age of fifteen years.[6]

Mālikī Law: Mālik has stated that a child attains his majority at puberty, when a boy gets nocturnal emission or gets pubic hair and a girl gets menstrual discharge or hair grown on the pubic. As regrds age, there are two reports attributed to him. According to one, ne holds a boy or a girl to attain puberty or majority on attaining an age of fifteen years while according to the other report, he fixed the age at eighteen years.[7]

Ḥanbalī Law: Nocturnal emission is a sign of puberty in a boy and another sign is the growth of pubic hair. As regards age, a boy or girl shall be presumed to become major on attaining fifteen years. A girl shall be deemed to become a major when she gets menstruation.[8]

It is now the generally accepted view that a child gains puberty or majority on the completion of fifteen years. But this rule is subject to the condition that signs of puberty have

2. Shaykhzādah, *Majma' al-Anhur*, Constantinople, 1327 A.H., Vol. II, p. 444; Munlā Khusraw, *Durar al-Ḥukkām*, Constantinople, 1329 A.H., Vol. II p. 275.
3. *Ibid.*
4. Al-Marghīnānī, *al-Hidāyah*, Delhi, n. d., Vol. III, p. 358.
5. Ibn Qudāmah, *al-Mughnī*, Cairo, 1367 A.H., Vol. IV, pp. 459-60.
6. *Ibid.*, p. 459.
7. *Ibid.*
8. *Ibid.*, pp. 459-460.

not appeared earlier. The rule that a child attains puberty on the completion of fifteen years amounts to a legal presumption. It is really the appearance of the signs of puberty that constitute the determining factor and it is only in the absence of evidence to the contrary that the presumption of law has to be given effect to. Hence it is open to a person to contend that a boy or a girl had attained puberty before completing the age of fifteen years.[9] It may be noted here that in Pakistan, Section 12 of the Muslim Family Laws Ordinance, 1961, has fixed the minimum age at which a boy or a girl can contract a marriage at eighteen and sixteen years respectively.

Custody: Muslim Jurists make a distinction in the age of *tamīz* (understanding) and that of *bulūgh* or puberty. By the former is meant the age when a child can look after itself, that is, can take his or her food, attend to his or her toilet, can dress himself or herself and do such other acts without the help of any one else. It is considered that on attaining this age the child must be trained for future life. Before the attainment of this age the mother is considered to be the fittest person to take care of the child. But after the attainment of this age it is felt that the father is more suitable of the parents to prepare a boy for his future life and a mother to train a girl for her future life. The mother is, therefore, entitled to the custody of the children only till they attain the age of understanding but after reaching that age a boy must be given in the custody of the father and a girl must remain in the custody of her mother till she reaches the marriageable age when she must be given in the custody of the father. He is under an obligation to defray the expenses of his daughter's marriage and is in a better position to arrange for the same and to look after her protection. He is, therefore, entitled to the custody of the girl when she attains puberty.[10]

IV. Age of Understanding: A child is considered to attain understanding when he is seven years old.

9. Munlā Khusraw, *op. cit.*, Vol. II, p. 275.
10. *Ibid.*, Vol. I, p. 411 : Shaykhzādah, *op. cit.*, Vol. II, p. 489.

V. Age of Majority: Religious Sanction: The Muslim jurists seem to have been influenced in fixing the age of majority at fifteen years by the following agreed Tradition :—

Ibn 'Umar reported, "I offered myself to the Prophet (peace be on him) in the year of Uḥud (a well-known battle) while I was a boy of 14 years. He turned me back. Afterwards I appeared before him in the year of the battle of Trench while I was a boy of 15 years. Then he gave me permission (to participate in the battle).[11]

Shī'ī Law: Under the Shī'ī law a child is deemed to become a major when he attains puberty. In the absence of earlier signs of puberty it is considered that a boy attains majority or puberty on the completion of fifteen years and a girl on the completion of nine years.

Age under the Majority Act: The Majority Act has provided that a minor shall be deemed to have attained majority when he shall have completed the age of eighteen years.

VI. Capacity of Minor: It can be seen from what has been stated above that the age of majority fixed under the Majority Act differs from that recognised by the Muslim law. But in passing the Majority Act the Legislature was desirous to provide as much as it could, against interfering with the personal law of Muslims as, for example, the laws of marriages, and majority.[12] In section 2 of the Act, express provision is made to the effect that the enactment shall not affect the capacity of any person to act in matters of marriage, dower, divorce and adoption. As ragards these matters, the capacity of minors is left untouched by the Majority Act. It is as if the Act has never been passed.

Interpretation. To act in the matter of marriage: The Bombay High Court held that the expression, "To act in the matter of marriage" within the meaning of section 2 of the Majority Act means not only to enter into a contract of

11. Walī al-Dīn al-Khaṭīb, *Mishkāt al-Maṣābiḥ*, Delhi, 1932, Vol. I, p. 292.
12. Sarat Chandra Chakrabarti Vs. Forman, I.L.R. 12 All. 213.

marriage, but it also includes the acts arising out of a marriage. The expression includes such acts of the parties as change their status.[13] The same view was expressed by the Calcutta High Court where it stated that no doubt betrothal is generally the first stage towards the solemnisation of a marriage but it is not an essential part of the marriage and is entirely independent of it. The expression, "capacity to act in the matter of marriage" means the capacity to be a party to a valid marriage and relates to the acts of the parties by which their status is changed but does not refer to a prenuptial agreement to contract a marriage in the future.[14]

The Rangoon High Court expressed the same opinion and stated that capacity to act in the matter of marriage means the capacity to be a party to a valid marriage, and that the expression does not refer and is not applicable to a prenuptial agreement to contract a marriage in future.[15] The Bombay High Court again expressed the view to the same effect when it said that a promise to marry is not strictly speaking an act in the matter of marriage within the meaning of section 2 of the Majority Act, and that the capacity to act in the matter of marriage must be confined to the marriage itself and acts arising out of the marriage but not to bethrothal which precedes it.[16] It was held by the Calcutta High Court that a boy who is a major under his personal law though minor under the Majority Act is competent to execute a Kabinnamah (deed of marriage) regularising his conduct towards his wife in a number of ways and vesting some powers and rights in his wife. Similarly, the filing of a suit by the wife that her marriage is not binding on her, but is null and void amounts to acting in the matter of marriage.[17] A boy major under the provisions of Muslim law but minor under the Majority Act was held competent under

13. Bai Shirin Bai Vs. Kharshedji Nusservanji Massalawala I.L.R. 22, Bom. 430.
14. Maung Tun Aung Vs. Ma E. Kye, A.I.R. 1936 Rang. 212.
15. *Ibid.*
16. Frenny Barjorji Engineer Vs. Shahpurji Kekobad Modi, A.I.R. 1937, Bom. 392.
17. Fatma Khatoon Vs. Fazlul Karim Mea, A.I.R. 1928 Cal. 303.

section 2 of the Majority Act to give his sister in marriage as he would be acting in the matter of marriage.[18]

To act in the matter of dower: It was stated by the Madras High Court, "When the Legislature permitted a person to act in the matter of dower, it only intended to allow that person who was not otherwise competent under the ordinary law to act in the matter to initiate the religious acts and ceremony which under the personal law he or she was capable of initiating. The legal consequences flowing from this primary act were not intended to be controlled by section 2 of the Majority Act. It was then held that to act in the matter of dower means to do all acts in relation thereto including entering into a contract for payment of a dower and fixing its amount and nature.[19] The Calcutta High Court expressed the opinion that the expression, "To act in the matter of dower" means to act or do such acts as may relate to dower.[20] The Allahabad High Court has expressed the view that settlement of dower comes within the exceptions contained in section 2 of the Majority Act. It further stated that the agreement to pay a certain amount of dower is a part of the contract of marriage and that there is no reason to suppose that a person who is minor under the Majority Act but is major under his personal law although he is capable of entering into a contract of marriage, he is incapable of fixing the amount of dower.[21]

It can be concluded from the above discussion that a person who is major under his or her personal law as when he or she has attained the age of fifteen years but is minor under the Majority Act being under 18 years of age is competent to enter into an agreement for payment of dower. He or she can also fix its amount and nature.

(c) *Relinquishment of dower*: There is a great difference amongst several High Courts as to whether a girl who is under

18. Mst. Sat Bharai Vs. Nur Elahi, P.L.D. 1951, Lah. 408.
19. Abi Dhunimsa Bibi Vs. Mohammad Fathiudini Sahib, A.I.R. 1918, Mad. 319.
20. Mazhar-ul-Islam Vs. Abdul Gani Ala, A.I.R. 1925, Cal. 322.
21. Qasim Husain Beg Vs. Bibi Kaniz Sakina, A.I.R. 1932, All. 649.

18 years of age but is major under her personal law is capable of relinquishing or entering into a contract to relinquish her dower or a portion of the same. A case involving the decision of this matter came up for decision before the Madras High Court. In this case the wife had relinquished her dower in favour of her husband as a gratuitous gift. It was justified by the husband on the ground that the wife was competent to do so as she was "acting in the matter of dower." The Court did not accept this submission and observed "the construction set upon the word "act" seems far-fetched ... The word "act" has been used here as a comprehensive verb to control the steps to be taken in the four specified classes of cases ... The legal consequences flowing from the primary act were not intended to be controlled by section 2 of the Act." It further stated that "the Act should not be so construed as to deprive a person of rights which he is otherwise entitled to." The Court then quoted Sir Abdur Rahim's Muhammadan Jurisprudence that "generally speaking only such acts and transactions of a minor will be upheld as are of benefit to him and whatever is injurious to his interests will be disallowed." The Court then held that the wife being a minor under the Act was not competent to relinquish her dower.[22] It is submitted that this view requires reconsideration. If a girl is competent to settle her dower there seems to be no reason why she cannot relinquish it. In the first place, the rule of Muslim law referred to by Sir Abdur Rahim is no longer applicable in India and Pakistan as the Muslim Law of Contract has been superseded. A person can now take advantage of the provisions of the Contract Act, but if his case does not fall within the scope of its provisions then we cannot restrict the scope of section 2 of the Majority Act simply to save a minor from loss by taking advantage of a provision of the Muslim law, but have to give effect to the plain words of section 2 of the Act. Moreover, relinquishment of dower does not necessarily involve loss to a girl and in some cases it may be to her advantage to do so.

22. Abi Dhunimsa Bibi Vs. Muhammad Fathiudini Sahib, A.I.R. 1918 Mad. 319.

Thus she may like to give up her dower as a consideration for Khul' to get her release from an undesirable and unhappy marriage. Another case of this nature came up for decision before the Calcutta High Court which pointed out that Wilson in his book on Mohammadan law had differed with the view expressed by the Madras High Court. The general trend of the judgement shows that the Calcutta High Court did not agree with the view of the Madras High Court.[23] A case of similar nature was decided by the Allahabad High Court in 1932. It held that the settlement of dower and its relinquishment would come within the exceptions contained in section 2 of the Majority Act. Referring to the Madras view, the Court said that it has not been followed by a Bench of the Calcutta High Court (reported in AIR 1925 Cal. 323) and the Court agreed with the view of the Calcutta High Court. It further stated that a person is capable of relinquishing the dower as consideration for obtaining a Khul'. If the Act had applied and the girl would have been a minor incapable of relinquishing her dower then the father as her guardian would have to relinquish her dower debt on her behalf as a consideration for the Khul'. But when the Majority Act does not apply the father could not by his own relinquishment have bound her unless she had agreed to such relinquishment.[24] The Patna High Court agreed with the view expressed by the Madras High Court and stated that the relinquishment of a part of dower fixed at the time of the marriage or changing its character from prompt into deferred does not fall within the exception of section 2 of the Majority Act. It distinguished the Allahabad case on the ground that in that case the surrender was a consideration for obtaining the divorce, and divorce is specifically excepted by the Act while the surrender of the dower in the case before it was not a consideration for any divorce but was a gratuitous surrender. The Calcutta view was distinguished on the ground that marriage being

23. Mazhar-ul-Islam Vs. Abdul Gani Ala, A.I.R. 1925, Cal, 322.
24. Qasim Husain Beg Vs. Mst. Kaniz Sakina, A.I.R. 1932 All. 649.

excepted by the Act it could not be performed under Muhammadan law without there being a promise of dower and therefore as a necessary element of the performance of the marriage he could fix the amount of the dower.[25]

The Madras and the Patna High Courts also expressed the view that once a marriage has been performed, dower has been sattled, the dower becomes a property of the wife like her any other property. The dower is a debt payable to the wife and any transfer of this debt, or foregoing it altogether or portion of it are not matters in any way connected with marriage and such acts must be governed by the ordinary law of the land.

It is submitted that both the Madras and the Patna High Courts seem to have considered that marriage has been excepted from the operation of the Majority Act by section 2 and a dower being an essential element of marriage comes under the exception. It is submitted with respect that this view overlooks the fact that dower itself has been excepted by section 2 quite independent of marriage. Moreover the view that on celebration of marriage, dower becomes ordinary property of the wife requires reconsideration. The dower does not lose its peculiar characteristic and does differ and is distinct from an ordinary loan. Thus the period of limitation does not commence in the case of promp dower until and unless a demand for it is made by the wife. A still more important factor is that before celebration of marriage dower has no value while on the performance of the marriage, dower becomes, according to the above view, ordinary property or loan. Why then did the Legislature include dower amongst the exceptions ? It would have been quite sufficient to mention amongst the exceptions only marriage, divorce and adoption. The fact that the Legislature did include it amongst the exceptions shows quite clearly that it did not attach to dower the notion attributed to it by the Madras and the Patna High Courts.

To act in the matter of divorce : The expression "to act

25. Najmunnissa Vs. Siraj-ud-din Ahmad Khan, A.I.R. 1939 Patna 133.

in the matter of divorce" includes the husband's power to delegate the power to divorce.[26] The expression is wide enough to include in it the institution of a suit for divorce by a wife.[27] A girl who is major under her personal law though minor under the Majority Act can sue for dissolution of her marriage on the ground of exercise of option of puberty.[28]

To sue without a next friend : There is great difference of opinion as to whether a person who is minor under the Majority Act but is major under his or her personal law can sue without a next friend. It is a very important matter as it greatly affects the right to sue by persons who are minors under the Act but major under the Muslim law.

This difference of opinion in due to the fact that some High Courts give a restricted meaning to the expression, "to act in the matter of . . ." while others interpret it in a broad way. As seen above the High Courts of Allahabad, Bombay and Calcutta have stated that the expression means to do all acts in relation to the specified acts so that a person major under his or her personal law but minor under the Majority Act is competent to sue in respect of the specified acts without a next friend. In an early case the Madras High Court expressed the view that section 2 of the Act refers only to capacity to contract and not to capacity to sue. It therefore held that a girl major under the Muslim law but minor under the Act was not competent to sue without a next friend.[29] The Bombay High Court held otherwise and stated that such a girl could sue for divorce without a next friend, as she would be acting in the matter of divorce. It distinguished the Madras view on the ground that in that case the suit was for recovery of dowery or stridhan which was not covered by section 2 of the Act.[30]

26. Fatima Khatun Vs. Fazlul Karim Mea, A.I.R. 1928, Cal. 303.
27. Ahmad Suleman Vohra Vs. Bai Fatima, A,I.R. 1931. Bom. 76; Naksetan Bibi Vs. Habibar Rahman, Mandal A.I.R. 1948 Cal. 66 ; Achia Khatoon Vs. Abdul Hai, A.I.R. 1952, Cal. 361.
28. Mst. Sat Bharai Vs. Nur Elahi, P.L.D. 1951, Lah. 408.
29. Puyikuth Ithayi Umah Vs. Khairhiropokil Momud, I.L.R. 3 Mad. 248.
30. Bai Shirin Bai Vs. Kharshedji Nusservanji Massalawala I.L.R. 22 Bom. 430.

The Calcutta High Court expressed the view that a girl who has attained majority under the provision of Muslim law though she was a minor under the Majority Act could sue for recovery of dower by herself without a next friend as the expression "to act in the matter of dower" means to do such acts as may relate to dower.[31] In a case decided in 1932, the Allahabad High Court followed the view expressed in 1925 Calcutta 323 and did not agree with the view stated in AIR 1918 Madras 319.[32] The Calcutta High Court again following the view of the Bombay High Court, held that the words, "to act" are wide enough to include in it the institution of a suit.[33] The Oudh High Court took the same view as taken by the Madras High Court and stated that section 2(*a*) of the Majority Act does not mean that to bring a suit for dower is to act in the matter of dower. It held that in the institution of suits, such a wife will have to act through a next friend.[34] The Calcutta High Court again reiterated in a case decided in 1951 its former opinion and stated that a suit in the matters of marriage, dower and divorce was maintainable by a girl, major under the Muslim law though minor under the Majority Act without the necessity of a next friend.[35] The same view was expressed by the Lahore High Court in a case decided in the same year.[36] In 1955 the Madras High Court did not agree with the view expressed by the Bombay and Calcutta High Courts and followed the view taken by it previously.[37] The Lahore High Court in 1956 followed its own opinion stated in 1951 Lahore 408 and held that a girl major under the Majority Act must file an appeal herself and not through a next friend.[38] In 1961, the Calcutta High Court

31. Mazhar-ul-Islam Vs. Abdul Gani Ala, A.I.R. 1925, Cal. 322.
32. Qasim Husain Beg Vs. Bibi Kaniz Sakina, A.I.R. 1932 All. 649.
33. Naksetan Bibi Vs. Habibur Rahman, A.I.R. 1948 Cal. 66.
34. Usman Ali Khan Vs. Mst. Khatun Bibi, A.I.R. 1942, Oudh 243.
35. Mst. Achia Khatoon Vs. Abdul Hai, A.I.R. 1952, Cal. 1381.
36. Mst. Sat Bharai Vs. Nur Elahi, P.L.D 1951, Lah. 308.
37. Abdul Azeez Vs, Pathumma Bi, A.I R. 1955 Mad. 754.
38. Mst. Daulan Vs. Dosa, P.L D. 1956, Lah. 712

again decided that a Muslim girl, major under her personal law though below 18 years of age can sue for dissolution of her marriage by herself. It seems that the Court's attention was not drawn to the view expressed by the Madras and Oudh High Courts as there is no reference to the same in the judgement of the Court.[39]

Concluding Remarks : It can be seen from the above discussion that the Madras, Patna and the Oudh Courts have given a restricted right to a person who is a minor under the Majority Act though a major under his or her personal law. The Allahabad, Bombay, Calcutta, and Lahore High Courts have, on the other hand, taken a different view and have held that such a person is competent to institute a suit without a next friend. It is submitted that when the Legislature permitted a person to act in the matters of marriage, dower etc. it only intended that a person who was not otherwise competent under the ordinary law to act in these matters but was capable of doing so under his own personal law should be competent to act and initiate in these matters. The legal consequences arising from this primary act were not intended to be curtailed by section 2 of the Act. The Act should not be so curtailed as to deprive a person of rights which he is otherwise entitled to.[40] It is submitted that the views expressed by the Allahabad, Bombay, Calcutta and Lahore High Courts are more in consonance with the spirit of section 2 of the Majority Act than the views restricting the application of the section. The section or the Act was not meant to restrict the exercise of a legal right by a minor but was only intended to safeguard the interest of the minor. If a girl is not happy with her marriage and wants to get a release from the same, there is no reason why she should be forced to seek her remedy through another person. A liberal interpretation of the section is necessary in order to give the

39. Hanufa Bibi Vs. Mokshed Ali Mondal, A.I.R. 1961, Cal. 59.
40. Fatima Khatun Vs. Fazlul Karim Mea, A.I.R. 1948, Cal. 303 ; Achia Khatoon Vs. Abdul Hai, A.I.R. 1952, Cal. 351.

greatest benefit to a minor.

English law : English law like Muslim law also prescribes the ages on attaining which a boy or a girl can contract a marriage. At one time this age was fixed at seven years, but subsequently it was raised to fourteen years for a boy and twelve for a girl. In 1929, the age was raised to sixteen years in the case of a boy and a girl.[41] This age was maintained by the Marriage Act, 1949. Section 2 of the Act provides that a marriage solemnized between persons either of whom is under the age of sixteen years shall be void. A person remains a minor till he attains the age of twenty-one years; such a person is required to obtain the consent of his parents before he can lawfully contract a marriage.[42] The superintendent registrar of marriages may dispense with the necessity of obtaining any consent when it cannot be obtained by reason of absence or inaccessibility of the person whose consent is required or by reason of his being under disability.[43] The Court is also authorised to give consent to a marriage.[44] If the person whose consent is required refuses his consent, the Court may grant such consent which shall be sufficient for the solemnisation of the marriage.[45]

The consent is to be given by both the parents if they are living together, or if one has died, by the survivor. It they are divorced or separated by an order of any Court or by agreement, consent is to be given by the parent having the custody of the minor.[46]

Law in the U.S.A.: The law in the U.S.A. provides that the marriage of a boy or a girl below the age of seven years shall be void. It is necessary that the boy or the girl must have attained the age of consent which varies in different States. It is generally fixed at eighteen years for a boy and

41. See Halsbury's Statutes (2nd edition), p. 776.
42. The Marriage Act, 1949, section 3 (1).
43. *Ibid*, section 3(1) *a*.
44. *Ibid*., section 3(1) *b*.
45. *Ibid*.
46. *Ibid*., second schedule.

sixteen years for a girl. In some States it is fixed at sixteen years for both a boy and a girl.[47] The maximum age of consent usually fixed is twenty-one years for a boy and eighteen years for a girl while the minimum age for a boy and a girl has been fixed at fourteen and twelve years respectively in some States.[48] In Washington the minimum age of consent is fixed at fourteen years for a boy and fifteen years for a girl.[48a] At Common law, a boy is considered to attain puberty when he becomes fourteen years old and a girl shall be so considered when she becomes twelve years old.

The marriage of a person before he or she has attained this age shall be considered to be voidable and it shall be open to such a person on attaining the age of consent even during a reasonable time afterwards to disaffirm the marriage and get it annulled by the Court concerned.[49] But if on reaching the age of consent he or she continues the cohabitation of the marriage it shall be considered to be validated. The Courts generally take a sympathetic view and give consent to a marriage if the girl is pregnant even when she has not reached the age of consent.

A person is considered an infant till he or she is twenty-one years old and such a person has to obtain the consent of his parents or other guardian to his or her marriage. But a marriage solemnized in contravention of this rule is not considered void and shall be considered lawful.[50] In any case it shall be deemed valid until it is set aside by the decree of a competent Court.[51]

47. For full particulars, see Keezer, Art. 145, p. 203.
48. Fixed in Kansas, Massachusette Mississippi.
48*a*. Keezer: Marriage and Divorce Indianapolis 1946, Art 155, p. 213,
49 Radford Vs. Radford, 214 Mich 545, People Vs. Slack 15 Mich 193, Macri Vs. Macri, 177 App. Div. 292.
50. Milford Vs. Milford, 7 Mass, 48.
51. Owen Vs. Coffey, 201 Ala. 531 ; Wolf Vs. Wolf, 194 App. Div. 33 ; Levy Vs. Downing, 213 Mass. 334.

INDEX OF CASES

A

B

C

D

E

F

G

H

I

M

N

S

INDEX OF NAMES

GENERAL INDEX

A

B

C

D

I

K

N

Q

R

V

APPENDICES

Appendix I

THE EVIDENCE ACT

Act 1 *of* 1872

Section 107. When the question is whether a man is alive or dead, and it is shown he was alive within the last thirty years, the burden of proving that he is dead is on the person who affirms it.

Section 108. (Provided that when) the question is whether a man is alive or dead, and it is proved that he has not been heard of for seven years by those who would naturally have heard of him if he had been alive, the burden of proving that he is alive is shifted to the person who affirms it.

The above two sections apply in the case of a missing husband. At one time a Muslim Hanafi woman could take advantage of these two sections and her marriage would be dissolved if her husband had been missing for seven years preceding the institution of her suit. This period was unnecessarily long, taking into consideration the present conditions of life. The Dissolution of Muslim Marriages Act has adopted the Maliki law and has fixed the period of four years as sufficient for presumption of the death of a missing husband. The period of four years is still very very long and it seems advisable to reduce it to two years. For discussion of the subject see the Chapter on Mafqood al-Khabar or Missing Husband.

Section 112. The fact that any person was born *during the continuance** of a valid marriage between his mother and any man or within two hundred and eighty days after its dissolution, the mother remaining unmarried, shall be conclusive proof that he is the legitimate son of that man, unless it can

*Italics supplied.

be shown that the parties to the marriage had no access to each other at any time when he could have been begotten.

This section is based on the English Law of Evidence and differs from the provisions of Muslim Law relating to this matter in several respects. People often do not appreciate the significance of the word "during". All that is necessary for the legitimacy of child under this section is that it must have been born at a time when its parents had been married; however short the time may be from time of the marriage. There is no provision that it must have been conceived in valid wedlock. Under Muslim law it is an essential condition that the child must be born at a minimum period of six months from the time of the marriage establishing that it was conceived after the marriage. Another important difference is that under Muslim law a child may be considered legitimate even if it is born at a period longer than two hundred and eighty days after the dissolution of the marriage. For discussion, see Chapter on Legitimacy.

Appendix II

THE MAJORITY ACT

Act IX of 1875

"2. Nothing herein contained shall affect :—

(*a*) The capacity of any person to act in the following matters (namely), Marriage, Dower, Divorce and Adoption."

There is a great deal of difference of opinion among various courts about the interpretation of the expression "to act". The matter has been fully discussed in Chapter 31 on Balūgh or Majority.

3. Subject as aforesaid, every minor of whose person or property, or both, a guardian, other than a guardian for suit within the meaning of Chapter XXXI of the Code of Civil Procedure, has been or shall be appointed or declared by any court of justice before the minor has attained the age of eighteen years, and every minor of whose property the superintendence has been or shall be assumed by any Court of Wards before the minor has attained that age, shall, notwithstanding anything contained in the Succession Act (X of 1865) or in any other enactment, be deemed to have attained his majority when he shall have completed his age of twenty-one years, and not before.

Subject, as aforesaid, every other person domiciled in British India (Pakistan) shall be deemed to have attained his majority, when he shall have completed his age of eighteen years and not before.

This section lays down the general rule of law that a person shall be deemed to have attained majority when he becomes eighteen years old. Section 2, however, provides an exception to the above rule in order that the personal laws of the Muslims and Hindus be not interfered with. It lays down that the provisions of the Act shall not apply in matters relating to the four specified matters, namely, marriage, dower, divorce and adoption. In the above-mentioned matters, a person shall be deemed to have attained majority when he or she becomes a major under the provisions of his or her personal law. In the case of Muslims, a person is deemed to have attained majority when he attains puberty. It is usually held that a boy or a girl reaches that age when he or she attain the age of fifteen years. This leads to the conclusion that a boy or a girl shall be entitled to act in the matters of marriage, dower and divorce when he or she becomes fifteen years old. For full discussion of the subject see Chapter on Balūgh.

Appendix III

CHILD MARRIAGE RESTRAINT ACT, 1929

Act XIX of 1929

1. The Bill was introduced in the Indian Assembly to stop child-marriages. Amongst the Hindus, child-marriage was very much in vogue because of religious injunctions. Amongst the Muslims, such marriages were generally prevalent only amongst the lower uneducated classes. There was great opposition to the Bill by Hindus as well as by some Muslims, but was passed by the majority. It was adopted by Pakistan in 1947.

Section 3 :

Definitions : In this Act, unless there is anything repugnant in the subject or context,

(*a*) "Child" means a person who if a male is under eighteen years of age and if a female, is under sixteen years (fifteen years in India) of age,

(*b*) "Child Marriage" means a marriage to which either of the contracting parties is a child ;

(*c*) "Contracting Party" to a marriage means either of the parties whose marriage is or is about to be thereby solemnised ;

(*d*) "Minor" means a person of either sex who is under eighteen years of age ;

(*e*) "Union Council" means the Union Council or the Town or the Union Committee constituted under the Basic Democracies Order, 1959 (P.O. No. 18 of 1959) within whose jurisdiction a child marriage is *or about to* be solemnised.

2. The ages originally prescribed were increased to eighteen years in the case of a male and fifteen years in the case of a female. In Pakistan the age of fifteen years has been increased to sixteen years by Section 12 of the Muslim Family Laws Ordinance 1961. The Act is intended to put a stop to

the marriages of children by making it an offence to marry or give in marriage a boy or girl below the prescribed age. The cases can be tried only by a magistrate of first class on the complaint of the Union Council or other authority authorised for this purpose. The complaint must be made within one year from the date of the marriage as the court cannot try a case if the complaint is made after the expiry of one year. The Court shall hold or get a preliminary enquiry made in the case. The Court can prevent such a marriage being solemnised by issuing an injunction prohibiting such a marriage after giving it an opportunity to satisfy the Court that no such action is necessary.

The relevant sections are given below :

4. *Punishment for male adult above eighteen years of age marrying a child.*—Whoever, being a male above eighteen years of age, contracts a child marriage shall be punishable with simple imprisonment which may extend to one month, or with fine which may extend to one thousand rupees, or with both.

5. *Punishment for solemnising a child marriage.*—Whoever performs, conducts or directs any child marriage shall be punishable with simple imprisonment which may extend to one month, or with fine which may extend to one thousand rupees, or with both, unless he proves that he had reason to believe that the marriage was not a child marriage.

6. *Punishment of parent or guardian concerned in a child marriage.*—(1) Where a minor contracts a child marriage, any person having charge of the minor, whether as parent or guardian or in any other capacity, lawful or unlawful, who does any act to promote the marriage or permits it to be solemnised, or negligently fails to prevent it from being solemnised, shall be punishable with simple imprisonment which may extend to one month, or with fine which may extend to one thousand rupees, or with both :

Provided that no woman shall be punishable with imprisonment.

(2) For the purpose of this section, it shall be presumed, unless and until the contrary is proved, that where a minor has contracted a child marriage, the person having charge of such minor has negligently failed to prevent the marriage from being solemnised.

7. *Imprisonment not to be awarded for offences under section* 3.—Notwithstanding anything contained in section 25 of the General Clauses Act, 1897, or section 64 of the Pakistan Penal Code, a Court sentencing an offender under section 3 shall not be competent to direct that, in default of payment of the fine imposed, he shall undergo any term of imprisonment.

8. *Jurisdiction under this Act.*—Notwithstanding anything contained in section 190 of the Code of Criminal Procedure, 1898, no Court other than that of a Magistrate of the first class shall take cognizance of, or try, any offence under this Act.

9. *Mode of taking cognizance of offences.*—No Court shall take cognizance of any offence under this Act except on a complaint made by the Union Council, or if there is no Union Council in the area, by such authority as the Provincial Government may in this behalf prescribe, and such cognizance shall in no case be taken after the expiry of one year from the date on which the offence is alleged to have been committed.

10. *Preliminary inquiries into offences under this Act.*—The Court taking cognizance of an offence under this Act shall, unless it dismisses the complaint under section 203 of the Code of Criminal Procedure, 1898, either itself make an inquiry under section 202 of that Code, or direct a Magistrate of the first class subordinate to it to make such inquiry.

11. [*Omitted by Muslim Family Laws Ordinance,* 1961]

12. *Power to issue injunction prohibiting marriage in contravention of this Act.*—(1) Notwithstanding anything to the contrary contained in this Act, the Court may, if satisfied from information laid before it through a complaint or otherwise that a child marriage in contravention of this Act has been arranged or is about to be solemnised, issues an

injunction against any of the persons mentioned in sections 3, 4, 5 and 6 of this Act prohibiting such marriage.

(2) No injunction under subsection (1) shall be issued against any person unless the Court has previously given notice to such person, and has afforded him an opportunity to show cause against the issue of the injunction.

(3) The Court may either on its own motion or on the application of any person aggrieved, rescind or alter any order made under subsection (1).

(4) Where such an application is received, the Court shall afford the applicant an early opportunity of appearing before it either in person or by pleader ; and if the Court rejects the application wholly or in part, it shall record in writing its reasons for so doing.

(5) Whoever knowing that an injunction has been issued against him under subsection (1) of this section disobeys such injunction shall be punished with imprisonment of either description for a term which may extend to three months, or with fine which may extend to one thousand rupees, or with both :

Provided that no woman shall be punishable with imprisonment.

Appendix IV

THE DISSOLUTION OF MUSLIM MARRIAGES ACT, 1939

ACT No. VIII OF 1939

Passed by the Indian Legislature

Received the assent of the Governor-General on the 17th March, 1939

(Published in the Gazette of India dated the 25th March, 1939)

An Act to consolidate and clarify the provisions of Muslim law relating to suits for dissolution of marriage by women married under Muslim law and to remove doubts as to the effect of the renunciation of Islam by a married Muslim woman on her married tie.

The Hanafi law is very favourable to women in many matters but in a few cases it involves great hardship to women. To overcome this difficulty, the Hanafi jurist have evolved the rule that in case of necessity a Hanafi case may be decided according to the law of another sect of the Sunnis. This important rule was not followed by the Anglo Indian Courts with the result that sometimes the Hanafi wives were put to great hardship. Thus a marriage cannot be dissolved when the husband is guilty of cruelty, desertion etc. The Ulema of pre-partition India felt the need for the reform of the enforcible law. At their instance the late Moulvi Muhammad Ahmad Kazmi, Advocate, M.L.A. and a member of the Working Committee of the Jamiat al-Ulama-i-Hind introduced a Bill in 1938 in the Legislative Assembly. It was passed with a few changes in 1939. It proved of immense help to the Muslim women and has been adopted by the Government of Pakistan. Certain charges have to be made in it to make it more useful.

Whereas it is expedient to consolidate and clarify the provisions of Muslim law relating to suits for dissolution of marriage by the women married under Muslim law and to remove doubts as to the effect of the renunciation of Islam by a married Muslim woman on her marriage tie. It is hereby enacted as follows :—

The Hanafi law is generally very favourable to women but in a few cases it involves great handing tö women. Thus there is no provision in it to dissolve a marriage when the husband treats his wife with cruelty, deserts her or does not maintain her. The Qadi can only admonish or imprison him but cannot dissolve the marriage. This and other similar matters resulted in great hardship to women. To overcome such difficulties the Hanafi jurists evolved the rule that in case of necessity a Hanafi Qadi could send a case to a Maliki, Shafi'i or Hanbali Qazi to be decided according to his own law which allows the dissolution of marriage or grant other relief in such cases. The British India Courts could not adopt this measure as there were no separate Courts for different Muslim sects nor did they themselves have recourse to this procedure. The result was that many Muslim women experienced great hardship. The Muslim Ulama realized this difficulty and at the instance of the Jamiat-al-Ulma-i-Hind, the late Mōhammad Ahmad Kazimi, a member of the Working Committee of the Jamiat and a member of the Legislative Assembly introduced a Bill in 1938 which after some modifications was passed in 1939. It has proved of immense help to Muslim women and is in force in India and Pakistan. The Pakistan Government has made a few changes in it to make it more useful.

1. Short title and extent. This Act may be called the Dissolution of Muslim Marriage Act, 1939.

2. It extends to all the provinces and the capital of the federation. A woman married under Muslim Law shall be entitled to obtain a decree for the dissolution of the marriage on any one or more of the following grounds, namely—of (1) that the whereabouts of the husband have not been known for a period of four years.

Under the Hanafi law a missing person could be presumed to be dead after a minimum period of sixty years from the time of his disappearance. The Indian Evidence Act, of 1872 prescribed the period of seven years when a person could be presumed to be dead. The Hanafi wives could take advantage of this provision of law. But this period of seven years was also found to be too long in view of the changed conditions of the times. Hence advantage was taken of the Hanafi rule to adopt the law of another Sunni sect in case of hardship.

This is the Maliki law and has been adopted in the Act to provide adequate relief to wives whose husbands are missing. This provision was suitable for ancient times when means of communication were difficult and a long time was necessary to trace a missing person. With the great facilities in communication now available, the period of four years is too long and may with advantage be reduced to two years.

(*ii*) That the husband has neglected or has failed to provide for her maintenance for a period of two years ;

(*ii-a*) That the husband has taken an additional wife in the contravention of the provisions of the Muslim Family Laws Ordinance, 1961 ;

(*iii*) That the husband has been sentenced to imprisonment for a period of seven years or upwards.

The period of seven years is too long. How can a young wife be deprived of the society of her husband for such a long time. For discussion of this aspect, see Ila and Zihar. It seems desirable to reduce the period of seven years to two years as in the case of Clause ii.

(*iv*) That the husband has failed to perform, without reasonable cause, his marital obligations for a period of three years ;

There seems to be no justification to fix the period at three years and the period of two years may be substituted for it. For discussion, see Chapter 23 "Other Grounds".

(*v*) That the husband was impotent at the time of marriage and continues to be so ;

(*vi*) That the husband has been insane for a period of two years or is suffering from leprosy or a virulent venereal disease.

Some Muslim jurists consider leucoderma also a ground for dissolution of marriage. It is obvious that if a wife does not want the dissolution of her marriage, she can continue the marital relation. But if she cannot bear this condition of her husband, she should not be made to live with him and lead a miserable life on that account.

(*vii*) That she, having been given in marriage by her father or other guardian before she attained the age of (sixteen)* years, repudiated the marriage before attaining the age of 18 years ;

Provided that the marriage has not been consummated ;

(*viii*) That the husband treats her with cruelty, that is to say,

(*a*) Habitually assaults her or makes her life miserable by cruelty of conduct even if such conduct does not amount to physical ill-treatment.

This provides relief not only when a husband inflicts physical cruelty on her but also when he is guilty of mental cruelty.

(*b*) associates with women of evil repute or leads an infamous life, or

(*c*) attempts to force her to lead an immoral life, or

(*d*) disposes of her property or prevents her exercising her legal rights over it.

Under Muslim law the wife is the absolute owner of her property and the husband has no control over it.. But in spite of this basic principle, of law the husbands did sometimes take forcible possession of their wives, property or prevented them from exercising their property rights over the same. This provision has clarified the position and provided a much needed relief to the wives.

(*e*) obstructs her in the observance of her religious profession or practice, or

(*f*) if he has more wives than one, does not treat her equitably in accordance with the injunctions of the Quran :

(*ix*) on any other ground which is recognised as valid for the dissolution of marriages under Muslim law :—

Provided that,—

(*a*) no decree shall be passed on ground (*iii*) until the sentence has become final ;

(*b*) a decree passed on ground (*i*) shall not take effect for a period of six months from date of such decree, and if the husband appears either in person or through an authorised agent within that period and satisfies the Court that he is prepared to perform his conjugal duties, the Court shall set aside the said decree ; and

(*c*) before passing a decree on ground (*v*) the Court shall, on application by the husband, make an order requiring the husband to satisfy the Court within a period of one year from the date of such order that he has ceased to be impotent, and if the husband so satisfies the Court within such period, no decree shall be passed on the said ground.

The Act does not cover all the provisions of Muslim law on the basis of which a wife can get a divorce. This sub-clause applies to such cases and relief can be given to a wife even when the Act has not provided for it.

Notice to be served on heirs of the husband when the husband's whereabouts are not known.—In a suit to which clause (*i*) of section 2 applies,

(*a*) the names and addresses of the persons who would have been the heirs of the husband under Muslim law if he had died on the date of the filling of the plaint shall be stated in the plaint ;

(*b*) notice of the suit shall be served on such persons ; and

(*c*) such persons shall have the right to be heard in the suit :

Provided that paternal uncle and brother of the husband, if any, shall be cited as a party even if he or they are not heirs.

Effect of Conversion to another faith.—The renunciation of Islam by a married Muslim woman on her conversion to a faith other than Islam shall not by itself operate to dissolve her marriage :

Provided that after such renunciation, or conversion the woman shall be entitled to obtain a decree for the dissolution of her marriage on any of the ground mentioned in section 2 :

Provided further that the provisions of this section shall not apply to a woman converted to Islam from some other faith who re-embraces her former faith.

Opinions differed about the effect of apostasy of the wife. The majority of Muslim jurists expressed that the marriage shall be dissolved on the wife's apostasy but some jurists held otherwise. This sub-clause has adopted the latter view.

Rights to Dower not to be affected.—Nothing contained in this Act shall affect any right which a married woman may have under Muslim law to her dower or any part thereof on the dissolution of marriage.

Repeal of section 5 *of Act XXVI of* 1937.– Section 5 of the Muslim Personal Law (Shariat) Application Act, 1937 is hereby repealed.

Appendix V

THE HINDU MARRIAGES ACT, 1955

(No. 25 of 1955)

1. *Short Title and Extent.* (1) This Act may be called the Hindu Marriage Act, 1955.

(2) It extends to the whole of India except the State of Jammu and Kashmir, and applies also to Hindus domiciled in the territories to which this Act extends who are outside the said territories.

2. (1) This Act applies—

(*a*) To any person who is a Hindu by religion in any of its forms or developments, including a Virashaiva, a Lingayat or a follower of the Brahmo, Prathana or Arya Samaj.

(*b*) To any person who is a Buddhist, Jaina, or Sikh by religion, and

(*c*) To any other person domiciled in the territories to which this Act extends who is not a Muslim, Christian, Parsi or Jew by religion, unless it is proved that any such person would not have been governed by the Hindu Law or by any custom or usage as part of that law in respect of any of the matters dealt with herein if this Act had not been passed.

Exception. The following persons are Hindus, Buddhists, Jainas or Sikhs by religion, as the case may be :—

(*a*) Any child legitimate, illegitimate, both of whose parents are Hindus, Buddhists, Jainas or Sikhs by religion,

(*b*) Any child, legitimate or illegitimate, one of whose parents is a Hindu, Buddhist, Jaina or Sikh by religion and who is brought up as a member of the tribe, community, group or family to which such parent belongs or belonged ; and

(*c*) any person who is a convert or re-convert to the Hindu, Buddhist, Jaina or Sikh religion.

(2) Notwithstanding anything contained in sub-section (1), nothing contained in this Act shall apply to the members of

any Scheduled Tribe within the meaning of clause (25) of article 366 of the Constitution unless the Central Government, by notification in the official Gazette, otherwise directs.

(3) The expression 'Hindu' in any portion of this Act shall be construed as if it included a person who, though not a Hindu by religion, is, nevertheless, a person to whom this Act applies by virtue of the provisions contained in this section.

At the time of Reforms a great difficulty was experienced in defining a Hindu with the result that the words 'Muslims' and non-Muslims were applied to the people in India. The present definition is not based on religious consideration but on cultural or political considerations. It includes persons who are monotheist or polytheist, vegetarians or otherwise.

3. *Definitions.* In this Act, unless the context otherwise requires,—(*a*) the expression "custom" and "usage" signify any rule which, having been continuously and uniformly observed for a long time, has obtained the force of law among Hindus in any local area, tribe, community, group or family :

Provided that the rule is certain and not unreasonable or opposed to public policy ; and

Provided further that in the case of a rule applicable only to a family it has not been discontinued by the family ;

(*b*) "district court" means, in any area for which there is a city civil court, that court, and in any other area the principal civil court of original jurisdiction, and includes any other civil court which may be specified by the State Government, by notification in the Official Gazette, as having jurisdiction in respect of the matters dealt with in this Act ;

(*c*) "full blood" and "half blood"—two persons are said to be related to each other by full blood when they are descended from a common ancestor by the same wife and by half blood when they are descended from a common ancestor but by different wives ;

(*d*) "uterine blood"—two persons are said to be related to each other by uterine blood when they are descended from a common ancestress but by different husbands ;

Explanation.—In clauses (*c*) and (*d*) "ancestor" includes the father and "ancestress" the mother ;

(*e*) "prescribed" means prescribed by rules made under this Act :

(*f*) (*i*) "sapinda relationship" with reference to any person extends as far as the third generation (inclusive) in the line of ascent through the mother, and the fifth (inclusive) in the line of ascent through the father, the line being traced upwards in each case from the person concerned, who is to be counted as the first generation ;

(*ii*) two persons are said to be *sapindas* of each other if one is a lineal ascendant of the other within the limits of *sapinda* relationship, or if they have a common lineal ascendant who is within the limits of *sapinda* relationship with reference to each of them ;

(*g*) "degrees of prohibited relationship"—two persons are said to be within the "degrees of prohibited relationship"

(*i*) if one is a lineal ascendant of the other ; or

(*ii*) if one was the wife or husband of a lineal ascendant or descendant of the other ; or

(*iii*) if one was the wife of the brother or of the father's or mother's brother or of the grandfather's or grandmother's brother of the other ; or

(*iv*) if the two are brother and sister, uncle and niece, aunt and nephew, or children of brother and sister or of two brothers or of two sisters ;

Explanation.—For the purposes of clauses (*f*) and (*g*) relationship includes—

(*i*) relationship by half or uterine as well as by full blood ;

(*ii*) illegitimate blood relationship as well as legitimate ;

(*iii*) relationship by adoption as well as by blood ; and all terms of relationship in those clauses shall be construed accordingly.

The degree and extent of prohibition provided in this section is more strict than in some other religions or laws. Thus the English Law now allows the marriage between a person and his brother's wife under certain conditions. But it cannot be denied that it is an improvement of the above-given Hindu Law.

4. *Overriding Effect of Act.* Save as otherwise expressly provided in this Act :—

(*a*) any text, rule or interpretation of Hindu law or any custom or usage as part of that law in force immediately before the commencement of this Act shall cease to have effect with respect to any matter for which provision is made in this Act.

(*b*) any other law in force immediately before the commencement of this Act shall cease to have effect in so far as it is inconsistent with any of the provisions contained in this Act.

5. *Conditions for a Hindu Marriage.*—A marriage may be solemnized between any two Hindus, if the following conditions are fulfilled, namely :

(*i*) neither party has a spouse living at the time of marriage ;

(*ii*) neither party is an idiot or a lunatic at the time of the marriage ;

(*iii*) the bridegroom has completed the age of eighteen years and the bride the age of fifteen years at the time of the marriage ;

(*iv*) the parties are not within the degrees of prohibited relationship, unless the custom or usage governing each of them permits of a marriage between the two:

(*v*) the parties are not *sapindas* of each other, unless the custom or usage governing each of them permits of a marriage between the two ;

(*vi*) where the bride has not completed the age of eighteen years, the consent of her guardian in marriage, if any, has been obtained for the marriage.

This section has introduced important changes and improvements in the Hindu Law of Marriage. It allows marriage between parties belonging to the same gotree and between such divergent clauses as Sikhs, Buddhists, and Jainas. The nature of marriage has been changed ; the rule of monogamy has been introduced and polygamy and polyandry have been prohibited. But in practice these forms of marriage still subsist to some extent and it may take more time before the Hindu society fully confirms to the new provisions of law.

6. *Guardianship in Marriage.*—(1) Whenever the consent of guardian in marriage is necesssary for a bride under this Act, the persons entitled to give such consent shall be the following in the order specified hereunder, namely :—

(*a*) the father ;

(*b*) the mother ;

(*c*) the paternal grandfather ;

(*d*) the paternal grandmother :

(*e*) the brother by full blood ; as between brothers the elder being preferred ;

(*f*) the brother by half blood ; as between brothers by half blood the elder being preferred ;

Provided that the bride is living with him and is being brought up by him ;

(*g*) the paternal uncle by full blood ; as between paternal uncles the elder being preferred ;

(*h*) the paternal uncle by half blood ; as between paternal uncles by half blood the elder being preferred ;

Provided that the bride is living with him and is being brought up by him ;

(*i*) the maternal grandfather ;

(*j*) the maternal grandmother ;

(*k*) the maternal uncle by full blood ; as between maternal uncles the elder being preferred ;

Provided that the bride is living with him and is being brought up by him.

(2) No person shall be entitled to act as a guardian in marriage under the provisions of this section unless such person has himself completed his or her twenty-first year.

(3) Where any person entitled to be the guardian in marriage under the foregoing provisions refuses, or is for any cause unable or unfit, to act as such, the person next in order shall be entitled to be the guardian.

(4) In the absence of any such person as is referred to in sub-section (1), the consent of a guardian shall not be necessary for a Marriage under this Act.

(5) Nothing in this Act shall affect the jurisdiction of a court to prohibit by injunction an intended marriage if in the interests of the bride for whose marriage consent is required, the court thinks it necessary to do so.

7. *Ceremonies for a Hindu Marriage.* (1) A Hindu marriage may be solemnized in accordance with the customary rites and ceremonies of either party thereto.

(2) Where such rites and ceremonies include the Saptapadi (that is, the taking of seven steps by the bridegroom and the bride jointly before the sacred fire), the marriage becomes complete and binding when the seventh step is taken.

8. *Registration of Hindu Marriages.* (1) For the purpose of facilitating the proof of Hindu marriages, the State Government may make rules providing that the parties to any such marriage may have the particulars relating to their marriage entered in such manner and subject to such conditions as may be prescribed in a Hindu Marriage Register kept for the purpose.

(2) Notwithstanding anything contained in sub-section (1), the State Government may, if it is of opinion that it is necessary or expedient so to do, provide that the entering of the particulars referred to in sub-section (1) shall be compulsory in the State or in any part thereof, whether in all cases or in such cases as may be specified, and where any such direction has been issued, any person contravening any rule made in this behalf shall be punishable with fine which may extend to twenty-five rupees.

(3) All rules made under this section shall be laid before the State Legislature, as soon as may be, after they are made.

(4) The Hindu Marriage Register shall at all reasonable times be open for inspection, and shall be admissible as evidence of the statements therein contained and certified extracts therefrom shall, on application, be given by the Registrar on payment to him of the prescribed fee.

(5) Notwithstanding anything contained in this section the validity of any Hindu marriage shall in no way be affected by the omission to make the entry.

9. *Restitution of Conjugal Rights.* (1) When either the husband or the wife has, without reasonable excuse, withdrawn from the society of the other, the aggrieved party may apply, by petition to the district court, for restitution of conjugal rights and the court, on being satisfied of the truth statements made in such petition and that there is no legal ground why the application should not be granted, may decree restitution of conjugal rights accordingly.

(2) Nothing shall be pleaded in answer to a petition for restitution of conjugal rights which shall not be a ground for judicial separation or for nullity of marriage or for divorce.

10. *Judicial Separation.* (1) Either party to a marriage, whether solemnized before or after the commecement of this Act, may present a petition to the district court praying for a decree for judicial separation on the ground that the other party :

(*a*) has deserted the petitioner for a continuous period of not less than two years immediately preceding the presentation of the petition ; or

(*b*) has treated the petitioner with such cruelty as to cause a reasonable apprehension in the mind of the petitioner that it will be harmful or injurious for the petitioner to live with the other party ; or

(*c*) has, for a period of not less than one year immediately preceding the presentation of the petition, been suffering from a virulent form of leprosy : or

(*d*) has, for a period of not less than three years immediately preceding the presentation of the petition, been suffering from venereal disease in a communicable form, the disease not having been contracted from the petitioner ; or

(*e*) has been continuously of unsound mind for a period of not less than two years immediately preceding the presentation of the petition ; or

(*f*) has, after the solemnization of the mariage, had

sexual intercourse with any person other than his or her spouse.

Explanation.—In this section, the expression "desertion", with its grammatical variations and cognate expressions, means the desertion of the petitioner by the other party to the marriage without reasonable cause and without the consent or against the wish of such party, and includes the wilful neglect of the petitioner by the other party to the marriage.

(2) Where a decree for judicial separation has been passed, it shall no longer be obligatory for the petitioner to cohabit with the respondent, but the court may, on the application by petition of either party and on being satisfied of the truth of the statements made in such petition, rescind the decree if it considers it just and reasonable to do so.

This Section provides a new relief. It was not available amongst the Hindus except in the State of Bombay. In judicial separation, the relationship of husband and wife continues but the aggrieved party is allowed to live apart from the other spouse. Muslim Law does not allow this form of relief. Human beings after all have to satisfy their natural passions and when it cannot be done in a legitimate manner, they will have recourse to other means. Islam greatly discourage all such conditions as may lead a person to fall into error. Adultery is a cardinal sin under Christianity, but the white races now no longer attach much importance to this matter. The Act has adopted this view of Western nations.

NULLITY OF MARRIAGE AND DIVORCE

11. *Void Marriages.* Any marriage solemnized after the commencement of this Act shall be null and void and may, on a petition presented by either party thereto, be, so declared by a decree of nullity if it contravenes any one of the conditions specified in clauses (*i*), (*iv*) and (*v*) of Section 5.

12. *Voidable Marriages.* Any marriage solemnized, whether before or after the commencement of this Act, shall be voidable and may be annulled by a decree of nullity on any

of the following grounds, namely :

(*a*) that the respondent was impotent at the time of the marriage and continued to be so until the institution of the proceeding ; or

(*b*) that the marriage is in contravention of the condition specified in clause (*ii*) of section 5 ; or

(*c*) that the consent of the petitioner, or where the consent of the guardian in marriage of the petitioner is required under section 5, the consent of such guardian was obtained by force or fraud ; or

(*d*) that the respondent was at the time of the marriage pregnant by some person other than the petitioner.

(2) Notwithstanding anything contained in sub-section (1), no petition for annulling a marriage —

(*a*) on the ground specified in clause (*c*) of subsection (1) shall be entertained —

(*i*) the petition is presented more than one year after the force had ceased to operate or, as the case may be, the fraud had been discovered ; or

(*ii*) the petitioner has, with his or her full consent, lived with the other party to the marriage as husband or wife after the force had ceased to operate or, as the case may be, the fraud had been discovered .

(*b*) on the ground specified in clause (*d*) of subsection (*l*) shall be entertained unless the court is satisfied—

(*i*) that the petitioner was at the time of the marriage ignorant of the facts alleged ;

(*ii*) that proceedings have been instituted in the case of a marriage solemnized before the commencement of this Act within one year of such commencement and in the case of marriages solemnized after such commencement within one year from the date of the marriage ; and

(*iii*) that marital intercourse with the consent of the petitioner has not taken place since the discovery by the petitioner of the existence of the grounds for a decree.

13. *Divorce.*—(1) Any marriage solemnized, whether before or after the commencement of this Act, may, on a petition presented by either the husband or the wife, be dissolved by a decree of divorce on the ground that the other party —

(*i*) is living in adultery ; or

(*ii*) has ceased to be a Hindu by conversion to another religion ; or

(*iii*) has been incurably of unsound mind for a continuous period of not less than three years immediately preceding the presentation of the petition ; or

(*iv*) has, for a period of not less than three years immediately preceding the presentation of the petition, been suffering from a virulent and incurable form of leprosy ; or

(*v*) has, for a period of not less than three years immediately preceding the presentation of the petition, been suffering from venereal disease in a communicable form ; or

(*vi*) has renounced the world by entering any religious order ; or

(*vii*) has not been heard of as being alive for a period of seven years or more by those persons who would naturally have heard of it, had that party been alive ; or

(*viii*) has not resumed cohabitation for a space of two years or upwards after the passing of a decree for judicial separation against that party ; or

(*ix*) has failed to comply with a decree for restitution of conjugal rights for a period of two years or upwards after the passing of the decree.

(2) A wife may also present a petition for the dissolution of her marriage by a decree of divorce on the ground,

(*i*) in the case of any marriage solemnized before the commencement of this Act, that the husband had married again before such commencement or that any other wife of the husband married before such com mencement was alive at the time of the solemnization of the marriage of the petitioner :

Provided that in either case the other wife if alive at the time of the presentation of the petition ; or

(*ii*) that the husband has, since the solemnization of the marriage, been, guilty of rape, sodomy or bestiality.

The Anglo Indian counts held in a number of cases that a Hindu marriage is a sacrament and so cannot be dissolved. The result of this notion was that Hindu women suffered great hardship in many cases. This section has set aside this notion so that both the husband and the wife can get their marriage dissolved under certain conditions.

This section has brought about a radical change and has provided a much needed relief.

14. *No petition for divorce to be presented within three years of marriage.*—(1) Notwithstanding anything contained in this Act, it shall not be competent for any court to entertain any petition for dissolution of a marriage by a decree of divorce, unless at the date of the presentation of the petition three years have elapsed since the date of the marriage :

Provided that the court may, upon application made to it in accordance with such rules as may be made by the High Court in that behalf, allow a petition to be presented before three years have elapsed since the date of the marriage on the ground that the case is one of exceptional hardship to the petitioner or of exceptional depravity on the part of the respondent, but, if it appears to the court at the hearing of the petition that the petitioner obtained leave to present the petition by any misrepresentation or concealment of the nature of the case, the court may, if it pronounces a decree, do so subject to the condition that the decree shall not have effect until after the expiry of three years from the date of the marriage or may dismiss the petition without prejudice to any petition which may be brought after the expiration of the said three years upon the same or substantially the same facts as those alleged in support of the petition so dismissed.

(2) In disposing of any application under this section for leave to present a petition for divorce before the expiration of three years from the date of the marriage, the court shall have regard to the interests of any children of the marriage and to the question whether there is a reasonable probability of a reconciliation between the parties before the expiration of the said three years.

15. *Divorced persons when may marry again.*—When a marriage has been dissolved by a decree of divorce and either there is no right of appeal against the decree or, if there is such a right of appeal, the time for appealing has expired without an appeal having been presented, or an appeal has been presented but has been dismissed, it shall be lawful for either party to the marriage to marry again :

Provided that it shall not be lawful for the respective parties to marry again unless at the date of such marriage at least one year has elapsed from the date of the decree in the court of the first instance.

16. *Legitimacy of children of void and voidable marriages.* Where a decree of nullity is granted in respect of any marriage under section 11 or section 12, any child begotten or conceived before the decree is made who would have been the legitimate child of the parties to the marriage if it had been dissolved instead of having been declared null and void or annulled by a decree of nullity shall be deemed to be their legitimate child notwithstanding the decree of nullity :

Provided that nothing contained in this section shall be construed as conferring upon any child of a marriage which is declared null and void or annulled by a decree of nullity any rights in or to the property of any person other than the parents in any case where, but for the passing of this Act, such child would have been incapable of possessing or acquiring any such rights by reason of his not being the legitimate child of his parents.

17. *Punishment of bigamy.*—Any marriage between two Hindus solemized after the commencement of this Act is void if at the date of such marriage either party had a husband or

wife living ; and the provisions of section 494 and 495 of the Indian Penal Code (Act XLV of 1860) shall apply accordingly.

18. *Punishment for contravention of certain other conditions for a Hindu marriage.*—Every person who procures a marriage of himself or herself to be solemnized under this Act in contravention of the conditions specified in clauses (*iii*), (*iv*), (*v*) and (*vi*) of section 5 shall be punishable.

(*a*) in the case of a contravention of the condition specified in clause (*iii*) of section 5, with a simple imprisonment which may extend to fifteen days, or with fine which may extend to one thousand rupees, or with both ;

(*b*) in the case of a contravention of the condition specified in clause (*iv*) or clause (*v*) of section 5, with simple imprisonment which may extend to one month, or with fine which may extend to one thousand rupees, or with both ; and

(*c*) in the case of a contravention of the condition specified in clause (*vi*) of section 5, with fine which may extend to one thousand rupees.

19. *Court to which petition should be made.*—Every petition under this Act shall be presented to the district court within the local limits of whose ordinary original civil jurisdiction the marriage was solemnized or the husband and wife reside or last resided together.

20. *Contents and verification of petitions.*—(1) Every petition presented under this Act shall state as distinctly as the nature of the case permits the facts on which the claim to relief is founded and shall also state that there is no collusion between the petitioner and the other party to the marriage.

(2) The statements contained in every petition under this Act shall be verified by the petitioner or some other competent person in the manner required by law for the verification of plaints, and may, at the hearing, be referred to as evidence.

21. *Application of Act V of* 1 08—Subject to the other provisions contained in this Act and to such rules as the High Court may make in this behalf, all proceedings under this Act shall be regulated, as far as may be, by the Code of Civil Procedure, 1908 (Act V of 1908).

22. *Proceedings may be in camera and may not be printed or published.*—(1) Proceeding under this Act shall be conducted in camera if either party so desires or if the court so thinks fit to do, and it shall not be lawful for any person to print or publish any matter in relation to any such proceeding except with the previous permission of the court.

(2) If any person prints or publishes any matter in contravention of the provisions contained in subsection (1), he shall be punishable with fine which may extend to one thousand rupees.

23. *Decree in proceedings.*—(1) In any proceeding under this Act, whether defended or not, if the court is satisfied that :—

(*a*) any of the grounds for granting relief exists and the petitioner is not in any way taking advantage of his or her own wrong or disability for the purpose of such relief, and

(*b*) where the ground of the petition is the ground specified in clause (*f*) of sub-section (1) of section 10, or in clause (*i*) of sub-section (1) of section 13, the petitioner has not in any manner been accessory to or connived at or condoned the act or acts complained of, or where the ground of the petition is cruelty the petitioner has not in any manner condoned the cruelty, and

(*c*) the petition is not presented or prosecuted in collusion with the respondent, and

(*d*) there has not been any unnecessary or improper delay in instituting the proceeding, and

(*e*) there is no other legal ground why relief should not be granted, then, and in such a case but not otherwise, the court shall decree such relief accordingly.

(2) Before proceeding to grant any relief under this Act, it shall be the duty of the Court in the first instance, in every case where it is possible so to do consistently with the nature and circumstances of the case, to make every endeavour to bring about a reconciliation between the parties.

Section 23 of the Act provides that a court shall decree the petition if it is satisfied that the petitioner, if relying on the ground given in clause (1) of sub-section (1) of section 10, has not been accessory to or committed the act or condoned the act or acts complained of. Adultery was not a ground for dissolution of marriage by a court under the Hindu Law. This idea has been adopted from the English Law. To take advantage of this provision it is necessary that the petitioner should not have been himself or herself guilty of adultery or should not have been accessory, to or connived at others adultery. It is also necessary that he or she should not have condoned the act.

24. *Maintenance pendente lite and expenses of proceedings.*—Where in any proceeding under this Act it appears to the Court that either the wife or the husband, as the case may be, has no independent income sufficient for her or his support and the necessary expenses of the Proceeding, it may, on the application of the wife or the husband, order the respondent to pay to the petitioner the expenses of the proceeding, and monthly during the proceeding such sum as, having regard to the petitioner's own income and the income of the respondent, it may seem to the court to be reasonable.

This section has been adopted from the English Law and did not find any place in the Hindu Law administered by the Anglo Indian Courts.

25. *Permanent alimony and maintenance.*—(1) Any court exercising jurisdiction under this Act may, at the time of passing any decree or at any time subsequent thereto, on application made to it for the purpose by either the wife or the husband, as the case may be, order that the respondent shall, while the applicant remains unmarried, pay to the applicant for her or his maintenance and support such gross sum or such monthly or periodical sum for a term not exceeding the life of the applicant as, having regard to the respondent's own income and other property, if any, the income and other property of the applicant and the conduct of the parties, it may seem to the court to be just, and any such payment may be secured, if necessary, by a charge on the immovable property of the respondent.

(2) If the court is satisfied that there is a change in the circumstances of either party at any time after it has made an order under subsection (1), it may, at the instance of either party, vary modify or rescind any such order in such manner as the court may deem just.

Neither the Hindu Law nor the Muslim Law makes it the wife's duty to maintain the husband even when he is destitute while she is wealthy. This idea has been taken from the English law. This is also the law in the U.S.A.

26. *Custody of children.*—In any proceeding under this Act, the court may, from time to time, pass such interim orders and make such provisions in the decree as it may deem just and proper with respect to the custody, maintenance and education of minor children, consistently with their wishes, wherever possible, and may, after the decree, upon application by petition for the purpose, make from time to time, all such orders and provisions with respect to the custody, maintenance and education of such children as might have been made by such decree or interim orders in case the proceeding for obtaining such decree were still pending, and the Court may also from time to time revoke, suspend or vary any such orders and provisions previously made.

27. *Disposal on property.*—In any proceeding under this Act, the Court may make such provisions in the decree as it deems just and proper with respect to any property presented, at or about the time of marriage, which may belong jointly to both the husband and the wife.

28. *Enforcement of, and appeal from decrees and orders.*—All decrees and orders made by the Court in any proceeding under this Act shall be enforced in like manner as the decrees and orders of the Court made in the exercise of its original civil jurisdiction are enforced, and may be appealed from under any law for the time being in force :

Provided that there shall be no appeal on the subject of costs only.

29. *Savings and repeals.* (1) A marriage solemnized between Hindus before the commencement of this Act, which

is otherwise valid, shall not be deemed to be invalid or ever to have been invalid by reason only of the fact that the parties thereto belonged to the same *gotra* or *pravara* or belonged to different castes or sub-divisions of the same caste.

(2) Nothing contained in this Act shall be deemed to affect any right recognized by custom or conferred by any special enactment to obtain the dissolution of a Hindu marriage, whether solemnized before or after the commencement of this Act.

(3) Nothing contained in this Act shall affect any proceeding under any law for the time being in force for declaring any marriage to be null and void or for annulling or dissolving any marriage or for judicial separation pending at the commencement of this Act, and any such proceeding may be continued and determined as if this Act had not been passed.

(4) Nothing contained in this Act shall be deemed to affect the provisions contained in the Special Marriage Act, 1954 (43 of 1954) with respect to marriages between Hindus solemnized under that Act, whether before or after the commencement of this Act.

30. *Repeals.*—The Hindu Marriage Disabilities Removal Act 1946 (XXVIII of 1946), the Hindu Marriages Validity Act, 1949 (XXI of 1949), the Bombay Prevention of Hindu Bigamous Marriages Act, 1946 (Bombay Act XXV of 1946), the Bombay Hindu Divorce Act, 1947 (Bombay Act XXII of 1947), the Madras Hindu (Bigamy Prevention and Divorce) Act, 1949 (Madras Act VI of 1949), the Saurashtra Prevention of Hindu Bigamous Marriages Act, 1950 (Saurashtra Act V of 1950) and the Saurashtra Hindu Divorce Act, 1952 (Saurashtra Act XXX of 1952) are hereby repealed.

Appendix VI

THE MUSLIM FAMILY LAWS ORDINANCE, 1961

The Dissolution of Muslim Marriages Act, 1939, had provided great relief to Muslim wives but there was a great demand that some more safeguards were necessary and that it was also necessary that the cases under the Act be decided speedily. The Pakistan Government set up a Law Commission to go into the matter. The Commission consisted of seven members one of whom represented the Ulama. It submitted its report on 1st June, 1956. Maulana Ehtishamul Haq submitted a separate dissenting report. The majority recommended that there should be compulsory registration of marriages and divorce and a standard Nikahnama be prescribed. It also stated that child-marriages should be prevented by law and that pronouncement of three divorces at a single sitting should be considered to amount to one divorce only. It also recommended that the judges trying matrimonial cases should try to bring about a reconciliation between the parties. The Commission also said that permission to take a second wife should not be given unless the applicant was in a position to support both wives and his children in the standard of living to which the family was accustomed and that the husband shall have to pay the Meher agreed upon however high it might be. In the absence of specification the whole dower shall be payable on demand. The Commission also recommended that the wife could claim maintenance for the past three years. The Commission also suggested the establishment of Matrimonial Courts which shall decide a case within three months. Maulana Sahib and other Ulama did not agree with most of the views of the Commission. Their objections may be summarised as under :

"There is no priest-hood in Islam so that no Nikah-khwans can be appointed by the Government. Registration of marriages is useful but even then it should not be made compulsory. It may result in inconvenience while the presence of witnesses and solemnization of marriage in public adequately serve the purpose.

Fixation of age at 18 years for the bridegroom and 15 years for the bride is uncalled for. Shariat has not fixed such ages and none need be fixed now. To discourage child-marriages we must educate people.

The pronouncement of three divorces at one time: The majority of Muslim jurists consider that the pronouncement of three divorces at one time amounts to three divorces. To remove the disadvantages following such practices, Muslims should he taught the proper method of divorce. Polygamy has been allowed by Islam and practised by the Prophet (Peace be on him) and his Companions. It is not necessary to obtain the permission of any authority for the second, third or fourth marriage of a man. It is also unnecessary.

The enactment about the payment of dower fixed how high it may be is unreasonable. The parties may have recourse to arbtration."

The report was not given effect to until 1961 when certain recommendations were given effect to. This is the background of the Ordinance of 1961.

THE MUSLIM FAMILY LAWS ORDINANCE BEING ORDINANCE VIII OF 1961

(Promulgated by the President on the 2nd March, 1961)

An Ordinance to give effect to certain recommendations of the Commission on Marriage and Family Laws.

Whereas it is expedient to give effect to certain recommendations of the Commission on Marriage and Family Laws:

Now therefore in pursuance of the Proclamation of the seventh day of October, 1958, and in exercise of all powers enabling him in that behalf, the President is pleased to make and promulgate the following Ordinance.

1. (1) *Short Title, Extent, Application and Commencement*: This Ordinance may be called the Muslim Family Laws Ordinance, 1961.

(2) It extends to the whole of Pakistan, and applies to all Muslim citizens of Pakistan, wherever they may be.

(3) It shall come into force on such date as the Central Government may, by notification in the official Gazette, appoint in this behalf.

2. *Definitions*: In this Ordinance, unless there is anything repugnant in the subject or context—

(*a*) "Arbitration Council" means a body consisting of the "Chairman" .... and a representative of each of the parties to a matter dealt with in this Ordinance :

Provided that where any party fails to nominate a representative within the prescribed time, the body formed without such representative shall be the Arbitration Council.

(*b*) "Chairman" means the Chairman of the Union Council or a person appointed by the Central or a Provincial Government, or by an officer authorised in that behalf by any such Government, to discharge the functions of Chairman under this Ordinance ;

Provided that where the Chairman of the Union Council is a non-Muslim, or he himself wishes to make an application to the Arbitration Council, or is, owing to illness or any other reason, unable to discharge the functions of Chairman, the Council shall elect one of its Muslim members as Chairman for the purposes of this Ordinance.

(*c*) "Prescribed" means prescribed by rules made under Section 11;

(*d*) "Union Council" means the Union Council or the Town or Union Committee constituted under the Basic Democracies Order, 1959 (P. O. No. 18 of 1959), and having in the matter jurisdiction as prescribed ;

By Gazette of Sind Extra-ordinary dated March, 1972, the Government of Sind are pleased to :

(1) Appoint all civil judges to perform within the respective jurisdiction the functions of the chairman of a Local Council.

Under the amendment the civil judge having jurisdiction of the area concerned will act as the Chairman of an Arbitration Council.

3. *Ordinance to Override other laws, etc*: (1) The provisions of this Ordinance shall have effect notwithstanding any law, custom or usage and the registration of Muslim marriages shall take place only in accordance with those provisions.

(2) For the removal of doubt, it is hereby declared that the provisions of the Arbitration Act, 1940 (X of 1940), the Code of Civil Procedure, 1908 (Act V of 1908), and any other law regulating the procedure of courts, shall not apply to any Arbitration Council.

4. *Succession*: In the event of the death of any son or daughter of the propositus before the opening of succession, the children of such son or daughter, if any, living at the time the succession opens, shall per stripes receive a share equivalent to the share which such son or daughter, as the case may be, would have received, if alive.

Under the Muslim Law if a person dies during the life-time of his father, his children could not inherit to their grand-father when he died. This sometimes caused great hardship to them particularly if their father did not leave any property for their support. Muslim women in Pakistan demanded necessary modification of the law. Under the provisions of the section the grand children shall be entitled to get the share of their father. Curiously enough, the women did not seek any relief for the widow though she too is put to great hardship sometimes.

5. *Registration of marriages.* (1) Every marriage solemnized under Muslim Law shall be registered in accordance with the provisions of this Ordinance.

(2) For the purpose of registration of marriages under this Ordinance, the Union Council shall grant licences to one

or more persons to be called Nikah Registrars, but in no case shall more than one Nikah Registrar be licensed for any one Ward.

(3) Every marriage not solemnized by the Nikah Registrar shall, for the purpose of registration under this Ordinance, be reported to him by the person who has solemnized such marriage.

(4) Whoever contravenes the provisions of subsection (3) shall be punishable with simple imprisonment for a term which may extend to three months, or with fine which may extend to one thousand rupees, or with both.

(5) The form of *nikah nama* the registers to be maintained by Nikah Registrars, the records to be preserved by Union Councils, the manner in which marriages shall be registered and copies of *nikah nama* shall be supplied to the parties, and the fees to be charged therefor, shall be such as may be prescribed.

(6) Any person may, on payment of the prescribed fee, if any, inspect at the office of the Union Council the record preserved under subsection (5), or obtain a copy of any entry therein.

6. *Polygamy.* (1) No man, during the subsistence of an existing marriage, shall, except with the previous permission in writing of the Arbitration Council, contract another marriage, nor shall any such marriage contracted without such permission be registered under this Ordinance.

(2) An application for permission under subsection (1) shall be submitted to the Chairman in the prescribed manner, together with the prescribed fee, and shall state the reasons for the proposed marriage, and whether the consent of the existing wive or wives has been obtained thereto.

(3) On receipt of the application under subsection (2), the Chairman shall ask the applicant and his existing wife or wives each to nominate a representative, and the Arbitration Council so constituted may, if satisfied that the proposed marriage is necessary and just, grant, subject to such conditions, if any, as may be deemed fit, the permission applied for.

(4) In deciding the application the Arbitration Council shall record its reasons for the decision. and any party may, in the prescribed manner, within the prescribed period, and on payment of the prescribed fee, prefer an application for revision, in the case of West Pakistan, to the Collector and, in the case of East Pakistan, to the Sub-Divisional Officer concerned and his decision shall be final and shall not be called in question in any court.

(5) Any man who contracts another marriage without the permission of the Arbitration Council shall

(*a*) pay immediately the entire amount of the dower, whether prompt or deferred, due to the existing wife or wives, which amount, if not so paid, shall be recoverable as arrears of land revenue; and

(*b*) on conviction upon complaint be punishable with simple imprisonment which may extend to one year, or with fine which may extend to five thousand rupees, or with both.

If a person contravenes the provisions of this section, we shall have to pay the entire amount of the dower of the former wife or wives even when in the ordinary circumstances the same be not payable as when it is deferred. He shall also be liable to simple imprisonment which may extend up to one year or such fine up to five thousand rupees as may be fixed or may be awarded both imprisonment and fine. A case shall commence against him only on the complaint of some one whoever he may be. It may be noted that the polygamous marriages without permission shall be perfectly lawful.

7. *Talaq*: (1) Any man who wishes to divorce his wife shall, as soon as may be after the pronouncement of *talaq* in any form whatsoever, give the Chairman notice in writing of his having done so, and shall supply a copy thereof to the wife.

(2) Whoever contravenes the provisions of subsection (1) shall be punishable with simple imprisonment for a term which may extend to one year or with fine which may extend to five thousand rupees or with both.

(3) Save as provided in subsection (5), a *talaq* unless revoked earlier, expressly or otherwise, shall not be effective until the expiration of ninety days from the day on which notice under subsection (1) is delivered to the Chairman.

(4) Within thirty days of the receipt of notice under subsection (1), the Chairman shall constitute an Arbitration Council for the purpose of bringing about a reconciliation between the parties, and the Arbitration Council shall take all steps necessary to bring about such reconciliation.

(5) If the wife be pregnant at the time *talaq* is pronounced, *talaq* shall not be effective until the period mentioned in subsection (3) or the pregnancy, whichever be later, ends.

(6) Nothing shall debar a wife whose marriage has been terminated by *talaq* effective under this section from re-marrying the same husband, without an intervening marriage with a third person, unless such termination is for the third time so effective.

This section has been rather carelessly drafted. Thus the expression "as soon as may be" is very uncertain and should not be used in any legal provision. Clause 3 constitutes an infringement of the injunction in this respect of the Quran. Under the Quranic injunction the period of ninety days commences from the time of the pronouncement of the divorce. This lacuna could have been very easily avoided.

8. *Dissolution of marriage otherwise than by talaq* : Where the right to divorce has been duly delegated to the wife and she wishes to exercise that right, or where any of the partiea to a marriage wishes to dissolve the marriage otherwise than by *talaq*, the provisions of section 7 shall, *mutatis mutandis* and so far as applicable, apply.

9. *Maintenance* : (1) If any husband fails to maintain his wife adequately, or where there are more wives than one, fails to maintain them equitably, the wife, or all or any of the wives, may in addition to seeking, any other legal remedy

available apply to the Chairman who shall constitute an Arbitration Council to determine the matter, and the Arbitration Council may issue a certificate specifying the amount which shall be paid as maintenance by the husband.

(2) A husband or wife may, in the prescribed manner, within the prescribed period, and on payment of the prescribed fee, prefer an application for revision of the certificate, in the case of West Pakistan, to the Collector and, in the case of East Pakistan, to the Sub-Divisional Officer concerned and his decision shall be final and shall not be called in question in any Court.

(3) Any amount payable under subsection (1) or (2), if not paid in due time, shall be recoverable as arrears of land revenue.

The wives who got decrees for maintenance against their husbands had to spend money which sometimes they could ill-afford to spend. Besides, the husband could prolong the proceedings to embarrass the wife. This section provided a speedy method of recovery.

10. *Dower*: Where no details about the mode of payment of dower are specified in the *nikah nama*, or the marriage contract, the entire amount of the dower shall be presumed to be payable on demand.

The general view of the Courts formerly was that in the absence of specification half the dower was considered to be prompt and the balance to be deferred. This section makes the whole unspecified dower to be prompt, this is, immediately payable.

11. *Power to make rules*: (1) The Provincial Government may make rules to carry into effect the purposes of this Ordinance.

(2) In making rules under this section, the Provincial Government may provide that a breach of any of the rules shall be punishable with simple imprisonment which may

extend to one month, or with fine which may extend to two hundred rupees, or with both.

(3) Rules made under this section shall be published in Official Gazette, and shall thereupon have effect as if enacted in this Ordinance.

12. *Amendment of Child Marriage Restraint Act,* 1929 *(XIX of* 1929): In the Child Marriage Restraint Act, 1929 (XIX of 1929),—

(1) in section 2,—

(*a*) in clause (*a*), for the word "fourteen" the word "sixteen" shall be substituted;

(*b*) in clause (*c*). the word "and" shall be omitted; and

(*c*) in clause (*d*), for the full-stop at the end a comma shall be substituted, and thereafter the following new clause (*e*) shall be added, namely:—

(*e*) "Union Council" means the Union Council or the Town or Union Committee constituted under the Basic Democracies Order, 1959 (P. O. No. 18 of 1959), within whose jurisdiction a child marriage is or is about to be solemnized.";

(2) section 3 shall be omitted;

(3) in section 4, for the words "twenty-one" the word "eighteen" shall be substituted;

(4) in section 9, after the words "under this Act", the words "except on a complaint made by the Union Council, or if there is no Union Council in the area, by such authority as the Provincial Government may in this behalf prescribe, and "such cognizance shall in no case be taken" shall be inserted; and

(5) section 11 shall be omitted.

13. *Amendment of the Dissolution of Muslim Marriages Act,* 1939 *(VIII of* 1939): In the Dissolution of Muslim Marriages Act, 1939 (VIII of 1939), in section 2—

(*a*) after clause (*ii*), the following new clause (*iia*) shall be inserted namely :—

"(*iia*) that the husband has taken an additional wife in contravention of the provisions of the Muslim Family Laws Ordinance, 1961" ; and

(*b*) in clause (*vii*), for the word "fifteen" the word "sixteen" shall be substituted.

Appendix VII

DIVORCE REFORM ACT, 1969

The Act came into force on 1st January, 1971. It has introduced radical changes in the English law of divorce. It has introduced divorce by mutual consent and even unilateral divorce with certain safeguards for the respondent. It is necessary for divorce by mutual consent that the parties should have lived apart for a minimum period of two years and the consent of a party should not have been obtained by misleading him or her. As regards unilateral divorce, it is necessary that (1) the parties should have lived apart for a period of five years 2(*e*) the dissolution of the marriage would not result in grave hardship, financial or otherwise, to the respondent. The Court will also take into consideration the interest of the children and other persons concerned. The respondent can also plead that it would in all circumstances be wrong to dissolve the marriage 4(2) (*b*). The court will also take into consideration the financial position of the respondent, 6(1) (*b*). It will also consider certain other matters specified in section 6(2).

Divorce Reform Act, 1969

An Act to amend the grounds for divorce and judicial separation; to facilitate reconciliation in matrimonial causes; and for purposes connected with the matters aforesaid.

(22nd October 1969).

BE IT ENACTED by the Queen's Most Excellent Majesty, by and with the advice and consent of the Lords Spiritual and Temporal, and Commons, in this present Parliament assembled, and by the authority of the same, as follows :—

1.—After the commencement of this Act the sole ground on which a petition for divorce may be presented to the court by either party to a marriage shall be that the marriage has broken down irretrievably.

Before the passing of the new Act, there were several grounds on which a divorce could be obtained. This Act prescribes only one ground on which a divorce can now be granted. But the section is so exhaustive that it includes every conceivable ground for separation ; the only condition being that it should have led to the irretrievable breaking up of the marriage. The next section describes the condition on the basis of which a marriage may be considered to have broken down.

2.—(1) The court hearing a petition for divorce shall not hold the marriage to have broken down irretrievably unless the petitioner satisfies the court of one or more of the following facts, that is to say—

(*a*) that the respondent has committed adultery and the petitioner finds it intolerable to live with the respondent ;

The mere fact that the other party has been guilty of adultery is not sufficient for divorce ; it is also necessary that the petitioner must establish that he or she finds it intolerable to live with the other party. As a general rule this fact will be substantiated only by the statement of the petitioner.

(*b*) that the respondent has behaved in such a way that the petitioner cannot reasonably be expected to live with the respondent ;

This clause is very exhaustive. It allows the court to judge whether the circumstances are such that it will not reasonably be possible for the petitioner to live with the respondent. The word "behaved" also gives the section extensive meaning. Circumstances and status of the parties will be material considerations in the decision of a case on this ground.

(*c*) that the respondent has deserted the petitioner for a continuous period of at least two years immediately preceding the presentation of the petition ;

The word "continuous" could sometimes lead to difficulty. Thus the deserting party may return to its duty and stop the desertion before the completion of the period of two years but after some time may again desert the other party. The court would have to judge in such a case of the cessation was genuine or merely illusory.

This difficulty has been removed by section 3(5). It provides that the continuation of the period of desertion shall not be deemed to have ceased if the parties resume living together provided that the period or periods during which they have lived together should not exceed six months. This period will be ignored and will not constitute desertion nor living together 3(5).

The period of two years will be deemed to be continue if the deserting party becomes incapable during the prescribed period of two years of forming an intention *e.g.* due to insanity. This is subject to the condition that evidence proves the fact that in the absence of the disability, the desertion would have continued.

Formerly the English law did not allow unilateral divorce or even divorce by mutual consent. It has now taken a realistic view of human affairs.

(*d*) that the parties to the marriage have lived apart for a continuous period of at least two years immediately preceding the presentation of the petition and the respondent consents to a decree being granted ;

This is a new ground for divorce. In spite of their best efforts, the parties do sometimes make a mistake in the selection of their partner and this makes life very unhappy and miserable. The English law, however, did not allow them any relief. This and the next sub-section have now removed this difficulty. It is akin to Mubarah (Khula) in Muslims law, and allows the dissolution of marriage by mutual consent. But the provision of this sub-section is subject to the condition that the parties should have lived apart for a continuous period of two years. The Muslim law does not make it a condition for separation that the parties should have lived apart for any period of time. The object of the provision seems to see if the rift between the parties is of a grave nature and of such a long standing as two years. The parties shall be deemed to live apart only when they do not live in the same house.

Section 5 provides that it shall be open to the respondent to plead that he or she was misled by the petitioner about some material fact which influences him or her to consent to the divorce. Section 6 provides further restrictions on the applicability of this sub-section.

(*e*) that the parties to the marriage have lived apart for a continuous period of at least five years immediately preceding the presentation of the petition.

This sub-section provides a new relief to the parties and allows a unilateral divorce. The English courts at one time considered *Talaq* to be very inequitable, opposed to natural justice, opposed to morals and opposed to public policy. It is expected that with the introduction of sub-sections '*d*' and '*e*', the English courts will change their view of *Talaq*. It differs from a *talaq* inasmuch as it makes it a condition that the parties should have lived apart, that is, not in the same house, for the last five years. This provision about living in different houses ignores the fact that it is not only quite possible but even probable that the parties must have been living a very unhappy and miserable life while living together in the same house. Muslim law does not consider it necessary that the parties should have lived apart for any length of time. Partners do not make up their minds on the spur of the moment and it is only when they have been living a very unhappy and even intolerable life that they take the decisive step to give up all relations and to live apart from each other.

The condition of living apart for five years will only add to their misery. Moreover the period of five years is too long. It is quite possible that even when unhappy with each other they might have been influenced to live together by such consideration as the interest of children. It is, therefore, desirable to reduce the waiting period of five years if not giving it up altogether. It cannot, however, be denied that the Act is quite liberal and is likely to prove of great help to English spouses. It is to be hoped that after some time the waiting periods of two and five years will be reduced to a reasonable extent.

(2) On a petition for divorce it shall be the duty of the court to inquire, so far as it reasonably can, into the facts

alleged by the petitioner and into any facts alleged by the respondent.

(3) If the court is satisfied on the evidence of any such fact as is mentioned is sub-section (1) of this section, then, unless it is satisfied on all the evidence that the marriage has not broken down irretrievably, it shall, subject to section 4 of this Act and section 5(5) of the Matrimonial Causes Act 1965, grant a decree nisi of divorce.

(4) For the purpose of sub-section (1)(*c*) of this section the court may treat a period of desertion as having continued at a time when the deserting party was incapable of continuing the necessary intention if the evidence before the court is such that, had that party not been so incapable, the court would have inferred that his desertion continued at that time.

If the deserting parts becomes unable for some reason or other to form an intention, the court will have to judge whether in the absence of the disability the desertion would have continued. It will arrive at its judgment on the evidence provided before it.

(5) For the purpose of this Act a husband and wife shall be treated as living apart unless they are living with each other in the same houshold.

This sub-section ignores the fact that living in the same house does not necessarily mean that they were not living unhappily. Thus it is possible that they not even on talking terms, do not share their meals, may be sleeping in different rooms. In such a case their living together serves no purpose.

(6) Provision shall be made by rules of court for the purpose of ensuring that where in pursuance of sub-section (1)(*d*) of this section the petitioner alleges that the respondent consents to a decree being granted the respondent has been given such information as will enable him to understand the consequences to him of his consenting to a decree being granted and the steps which he must take to indicate that he consents to the grant of a decree.

This sub-section is meant to ensure that the respondent had given his or her consent after fully understanding the consequences of his or her act. This safeguard is further strengthened by section 5.

3.—(1) Provision shall be made by rules f court for requiring the solicitor acting for a petitioner for divorce to certify whether he has discussed with the petitioner the possibility of a reconciliation and given him the names and addresses of persons qualified to help effect a reconciliation between parties to a marriage who have become estranged.

(2) If at any stage of proceedings for divorce it appears to the court that there is a reasonable possibility of a reconciliation between the parties to the marriage, the court may adjourn the proceedings for such period as it thinks fit to enable attempts to be made to effect such a reconciliation.

The power conferred by the foregoing provision is additional to any other power of the court to adjourn proceedings.

(3) Where the parties to the marriage have lived with each other for any period or periods after it became known to the petitioner that the respondent had, since the celebration of the marriage, committed adultery, then,

(*a*) if the length of that period or of those periods together was six months or less, their living with each other during that period or those periods shall be disregarded in determining for the purposes of section 2(1)(*a*) of this Act whether the petitioner finds it intolerable to live with the respondent ; but

(*b*) if the length of that period or of those periods together exceeded six months the petitioner shall not be entitled to rely on that adultery for the purposes of the said section 2(1)(*a*).

Sub-section 2(1)(*a*) provides that a divorce may be granted when the respondent has committed adultery and the petitioner finds it intolerable to live with the respondent. But the fact that the petitioner did live with the respondent would not lead to the result that the respondent can live with the petitioner provided that the period or periods during which thev lived together does not exceed six months.

(4) Where the petitioner alleges that the respondent has behaved in such a way that the petitioner cannot reasonably be expected to live with him, but the parties to the marriage have lived with each other for a period or periods after the date of the occurrence of the final incident relied on by the petitioner and held by the court to support his allegation, that fact shall be disregarded in determining for the purposes of section 2(1)(*b*) of this Act whether the petitioner cannot reasonably be expected to live with the respondent if the length of that period or of those periods together was six months or less.

The fact that the parties have lived together will not effect the petitioner's right under 2(1)(*b*) if the period or periods of such residence does not exceed six months.

(5) In considering for the purposes of section 2(1) of this Act whether the period for which the respondent has deserted the petitioner or the period for which the parties to a marriage have lived apart has been continuous, no account shall be taken of any one period (not exceeding six months) or of any two or more periods (not exceeding six months in all) during which the parties resumed living with each other, but no period during which the parties lived with each other shall count as part of the period of desertion or of the period for which the parties to the marriage lived apart, as the case may be.

Desertion is a ground for divorce, but desertion shall not be deemed to have ceased or its continuity is broken by the mere fact that the parties have lived together for a period or periods not exceeding six months.

(6) References in this section to the parties to a marriage living with each other shall be construed as references to their living with each other in the same household.

4.—(1) The respondent to a petition for divorce in which the petitioner alleges any such fact as is mentioned in paragraph (*e*) of section 2(1) of this Act may oppose the grant of a decree nisi on the ground that the dissolution of the marriage will result in grave financial or other hardship to him and that it would in all the circumstances be wrong to dissolve the marriage.

(2) Where the grant of a decree nisi is opposed by virtue of this section, then,

(*a*) if the court is satisfied that the only fact mentioned in the said section 2(1) on which the petitioner is entitled to rely in support of his petition is that mentioned in the said paragraph (*e*), and

(*b*) if apart from this section it would grant a decree nisi, the court shall consider all the circumstances, including the conduct of the parties to the marriage and the interests of those parties and of any children or other persons concerned, and if the court is of opinion that the dissolution of the marriage will result in grave financial or other hardship to the respondent and that it would in all the circumstance be wrong to dissolve the marriage it shall dismiss the petition.

(3) For the purposes of this section hardship shall include the loss of the chance of acquiring any benefit which the respondent might acquire if the marriage were not dissolved.

A party can claim a unilateral divorce under section 2(1)(*a*) if they have lived apart for the last five years. They will be considered to be living apart if they are not living or have lived together in the same house. This section restricts the petitioners claim. It will not be given a relief under section 2(1)(*e*) if the respondent proves that the dissolution of the marriage will result in grave financial or other hardship to him or her and that the dissolution of the marriage was not justifiable. The expression "other hardship" is very exhaustive and can mean a number of things or situation sub-clause (3) gives one instance of what is included in "hardship".

5.—Where the court on granting a decree of divorce held that the only fact mentioned in section 2(1) of this Act on which the petitioner was entitled to rely in support of his petition was that mentioned in paragraph (*d*), it may, on an application made by the respondent at any time before the decree is mahe absolute, rescind the decree if it is satisfied that the petitioner misled the respondent (whether intentionally or unintentionally) about any matter which the respondent took into account in deciding to consent to the grant of a decree.

6.—(1) The following provisions of this section shall have effect where—

(*a*) the respondent to a petition for divorce in which the petitioner alleged any such fact as is mentioned in paragraph (*d*) or (*e*) of section 2(1) of this Act has applied to the court under this section for it to consider for the purposes of sub-section (2) hereof the financial position of the respondent after the divorce ; and

(*b*) a decree nisi of divorce has been granted on the petition and the court has held that the only fact mentioned in the said section 2(1) on which the petitioner was entitled to rely in support of his petition was that mentioned in the said paragraph (*d*) or (*e*).

(2) The court hearing an application by the respondent under this section shall consider all the circumstances, including the age, health, conduct, earning capacity, financial resources and financial obligations of each of the parties, and the financial position of the respondent as, having regard to the divorce, it is likely to be after the death of the petitioner should the petitioner die first ; and notwithstanding anything in the foregoing provisions of this Act but subject to sub-section (3) of this section, the court shall not make absolute the decree of divorce unless it is satisfied—

(*a*) that the petitioner should not be required to make any financial provision for the respondent, or

(*b*) that the financial provision made by the petitioner for the respondent is reasonable and fair or the best that can be made in the circumstances.

(3) The court may if it thinks fit proceed without observing the requirements of sub-section (2) of this section if—

(*a*) it appears that there are circumstances making it desirable that the decree should be made absolute without delay, and

(*b*) the court has obtained a satisfactory undertaking from the petitioner that he will make such financial provision for the respondent as the court may approve.

This section provides further restrictions to the relief under section 2(1) (*a*, *e*). The respondent can oppose the petition for divorce before and even after a decree nisi has been passed. Sub-section (2) states the matter to be taken into consideration before passing a decree nisi or absolute. Sub-section (3) allows the court to proceed with the case without observing the requirement of sub-section (3) under the case mentioned in paragraph (*a*), (*b*), above,

7.—(1) Provision may be made by rules of court for enabling the parties to a marriage, or either of them, on application made either before or after the presentation of a petition for divorce, to refer to the court any agreement or arrangement made or proposed to be made between them, being an agreement or arrangement which relates to, arises out of, or is connected with, the proceedings for divorce which are contemplated or, as the case may be, have begun, and for enabling the court to express an opinion, should it think it desirable to do so, as to the reasonableness of the agreement or arrangement and to give such directions, if any, in the matter as it thinksf it.

(2) In section 3 of the Matrimonial Causes Act 1967 (consideration of agreements or arrangements by divorce county courts) after the word "1965" there shall be inserted the words "or of section 7 of the Divorce Reform Act 1969".

Section 3 of Matrimonial Causes Act reads as under : —

3.—(1) A person shall not be prevented from presenting a petition for divorce, or the court from granting a decree of divorce, by reason only that the petitioner has at any time, on the same facts or substantially the same facts as those proved in support of the petition, been granted a decree of judicial separation or an order under, or having effect as if made under the

Matrimonial Proceedings (Magistrates' Courts) Act 1960 or any corresponding enactments in force in Northern Ireland, the Isle of Man or any of the Channel Islands.

(2) On a petition for divorce in such a case as is mentioned in the foregoing sub-section, the court may treat the decree of judicial separation or the said order as sufficient proof of the adultery, desertion or other ground on which it was granted, but shall not grant a decree of divorce without receiving evidence from the petitioner.

(3) For the purposes of a petition for divorce in such a case, a period of desertion immediately preceding the institution of proceedings for a decree of judicial separation or for such an order as aforesaid having the effect of a decree of judicial separation shall, if the parties have not resumed co-habitation and the decree or order has been continuously in force since it was granted, be deemed immediately to precede the presentation of the petition.

8.—(1) After the commencement of this Act the existence of any such fact as is mentioned in section 2(1) of this Act shall be a ground on which either party to a marriage may present a petition for judicial separation ; and the ground of failure to comply with a decree for restitution of conjugal rights and any ground on which a decree of divorce a mensa et thoro might have been pronounced immediately before the commencement of the Matrimonial Causes Act 1857 shall cease to be a ground on which such a petition may be presented.

(2) Accordingly for sub-section (1) of section 12 of the Matrimonial Causes Act 1965 there shall be substituted the following sub-section :

> "(1) A petition for judicial separation may be presented to the court by either party to a marriage on the ground that any such fact as is mentioned in section (2)1 of the Divorce Reform Act 1969 exists, and sections 2(2), (4), (5) and (6), 3 and 7 of that Act and paragraph 2 of Schedule I to this Act shall, with the necessary modifications, apply in relation to such a petition as they apply in relation to a petition for divorce."

(3) The court hearing a petition for judicial separation shall not be concerned to consider whether the marriage has broken down irretrievably, and if it is satisfied on the evidence of any such fact as is mentioned in section 2(1) of this Act, it shall, subject to section 33 of the Matrimonial Causes Act 1965 (restrictions on decree for dissolution or separation affecting children) grant a decree for judicial separation.

Section 33 of the Matrimonial Causes Act 1965 is as under:—33.—(1) Notwithstanding anything in part I of this Act but subject to the following sub-section, the court shall not make absolute a decree of divorce or nullity of marriage in any proceedings begun after 31st December 1958, or make a decree of judicial separation in any such proceedings, unless it is satisfied as respects every relevant child who is under sixteen that—

(*a*) arrangements for his care and upbringing have been made and are satisfactory or are the best that can be devised in the circumstances ; or

(*b*) it is impracticable for the party or parties appearing before the court to make any such arrangements.

(2) The court may if it thinks fit proceed without observing the requirements of the foregoing sub-section if—

(*a*) it appears that there are circumstances making it desirable that the decree should be made absolute or should be made, as the case may be, without delay ; and

(*b*) the court has obtained a satisfactory undertaking from either or both of the parties to bring the question of the arrangements for the children before the court within a specified time.

9.—(1) The provisions of the Matrimonial Causes Act 1965 specified in Schedule I to this Act shall have effect subject to the amendments set out in that Schedule, being amendments consequential on the foregoing provisions of this Act.

(2) Each of the provisions of the Matrimonial Causes Act 1965 specified in column 1 of Schedule 2 to this Act is, to the

extent specified in relation to it in column 2 of that Schedule, hereby repealed.

(3) Without prejudice to any provision of this Act or of the Matrimonial Causes Act 1965, as amended by this Act, which empowers or requires the court to dismiss a petition for divorce or judicial separation or to dismiss an application for a decree nisi of divorce to be made absolute, nothing in section 32 of the Supreme Court of Judicature (Consolidation) Act 1925 (rules as to exercise of jurisdiction) or in any rule of law shall be taken as empowering or requiring the court to dismiss such a petition or application on the ground of collusion between the parties in connection with the presentation or prosecution of the petition or the obtaining of the decree nisi or on the ground of any conduct on the part of the petitioner.

10.—This Act (including the repeals and amendments made by it) shall not have effect in relation to any petition for divorce or judicial separation presented before the commencement of this Act.

11.—(1) This Act may be cited as the Divorce Reform Act 1969.

(2) This Act shall be construed as one with the Matrimonial Causes Act 1965.

(3) This Act shall come into operation on 1st January 1971.

(4) This Act does not extend to Scotland or Northerr Ireland.

DIVORCE REFORM ACT, 1969

SCHEDULE 1

CONSEQUENTIAL AMENDMENTS OF THE MATRIMONIAL CAUSES ACT 1965

1. In section 3(1) after the word "petitioner" there shall be inserted the words "or respondent".

2. In section 4(1) and (2) for the words "on the ground of adultery" there shall be substituted the words "in which adultery is alleged" and in section 4(1) for the words "on that ground" there shall be substituted the words "and alleging adultery".

3. In section 5(6) for the words from "opposes" to "desertion" there shall be substituted the words "alleges against the petitioner and proves any such fact as is mentioned in section 2(1) of the Divorce Reform Act 1969".

4. In section 15(*b*) for the words "on the ground of her husband's insanity" there shall be substituted the words and alleging any such fact as is mentioned in section 2(1)(*e*) of the Divorce Reform Act 1969 where the court is satisfied on proof of such facts as may be prescribed by rul es of court that her husband is insane"

5. In section 16(3) for the words from the beginning to "insanity" there shall be substituted the words "where on a petition for divorce presented by a wife the court granted her a decree and held that the only fact mentioned in section 2(1) of the Divorce Reform Act 1969 on which she was entitled to rely was that mentioned in paragraph (*e*), then if the court is satisfied on proof of such facts as may be prescribed by rules of court that the husband is insane".

6. In section 17(2) for the words from the beginning to "she" there shall be substituted the words "where on a petition for divorce presented by the husband he satisfies the court of any such fact as is mentioned in section 2(1)(*a*), (*b*) or (*c*) of

the Divorce Reform Act 1969 and the court grants him a decree of divorce, then if it appears to the court that the wife" and for the words "innocent party" there shall be substituted the word "husband".

7. In section 20(1) (*b*) for the words "on the ground of her husband's insanity" there shall be substituted the words "and the court held that the only fact mentioned in section 2(1) of the Divorce Reform Act 1969 on which she was entitled to rely was that mentioned in paragraph (*e*) and the court is satisfied on proof of such facts as may be prescribed by rules of court that the husband is insane".

8. In section 26(6), as amended by the Family Provision Act 1966, in the definition of "court", after the word "court", where first occurring there shall be inserted the words "means the High Court and".

9. In section 30(2)—

(*a*) in paragraph (*a*) for the words "on the ground of her husband's insanity" there shall be substituted the words "and the court is satisfied on proof of such facts as may be prescribed by rules of court that her husband is insane".

(*b*) in paragraph (*b*) the word "divorce" and the words "or judicial separation" shall be omitted ; and

(*c*) after paragraph (*a*) there shall be inserted the following paragraph :—

"(*aa*) a petition for divorce or judicial separation is presented by a husband and the court is satisfied on proof of such facts as may be prescribed by rules of court that his wife is insane ; or".

10. In section 34(3) for the words "on the ground of the husband's insanity" there shall be substituted the words "in favour of a wife where the court held that the only fact mentioned in section 2(1) of the Divorce Reform Act 1969 on which she was entitled to rely was that mentioned in paragraph

(*e*) and the court is satisfied on proof of such facts as may be prescribed by rules of court that the husband is insane".

11. In section 46(2) after the definition of "adopted" there shall be inserted the following definition:—

> " 'the court' (except in sections 26, 27, 28 and 28*a*) means the High Court or, where a country court has jurisdiction by virtue of the Matrimonial Causes Act 1967, a country court ; and".

12. In Schedule 1, in paragraph 2 after the word "Act" there shall be inserted the words "or of section 2(1)(*c*) of the Divorce Reform Act 1969".

SCHEDULE 2

REPEALS IN THE MATRIMONIAL CAUSES ACT 1965

Provision	*Extent of Repeal*
Section 1 ..	The whole section.
Section 5 ..	Sub-sections (1), (2), (3) and (4).
Section 6 ..	In sub-section (1), except as applied by section 10 or 14 of the said Act of 1965, paragraph (*c*).
Section 7 ..	In sub-section (1), except as applied by the said section 10 or 14, the words from "either" to "collusion or".
Section 30 ..	In sub-section (2)(*b*), the word "divorce" and the words "or judicial separation".
Section 42 ..	Sub-sections (1) and (3) so far as they apply in relation to proceedings for divorce or judicial separation. In sub-section (2), the words "this Act and".